THE GOOD
FOOD GUIDE
2009

Distributed by Littlehampton Book Services Ltd
Faraday Close, Durrington, Worthing, West Sussex BN13 3RB

Copyright © Which? Ltd 2008

Base mapping by Cosmographics
Data management and export by AMA DataSet Limited, Preston
Printed and bound by Scotprint

A catalogue record for this book is available from the British Library

ISBN: 978 1 84490 046 6

The Good Food Guide is a registered trade mark of Which? Ltd

Consultant Editor: Elizabeth Carter
Senior Project Editor: Caroline Blake

The Good Food Guide makes every effort to be as accurate and up-to-date as
possible. Some entries have already been printed in *The Good Food Guide
London*, but all details have been checked again. All *Good Food Guide* inspections
are anonymous but every main entry has been contacted separately for details.

As we are an annual Guide, we have strict guidelines for fact-checking
information ahead of going to press, so some restaurants were dropped if they
failed to provide the information we required. Readers should still check details
at the time of booking, particularly if they have any special requirements.

For a full list of Which? books, please call 01903 828557, access our website
at www.which.co.uk, or write to Littlehampton Book Services. For other
enquiries call 0800 252100.

Please send updates to: goodfoodguide@which.co.uk or 2 Marylebone Road,
London, NW1 4DF.

FSC
Mixed Sources
Product group from well-managed
forests and other controlled sources

Cert no. TF-COC-2217
www.fsc.org
© 1996 Forest Stewardship Council

"You can corrupt one man. You can't bribe an army."

Raymond Postgate, founder of
The Good Food Guide, 1951

CONTENTS

Introduction

The Good Food Guide is an annual report. Everything recorded in these pages has happened to someone in the last year. The list of reporters at the back of the book is testimony to that. It is the substance of all these experiences that makes up the recommendations. Restaurants that featured in the last edition have been re-nominated, and their entries assessed afresh. Each one must draw a clear recommendation in favour from readers and inspectors. Where there is doubt, the restaurant is left out.

Unfortunately, the gastronomic map is not always convenient. For all the publicity cooking now attracts, good food is still only found in isolated pockets. No amount of research alters the fact that Humberside is not the most fruitful area in which to look for places to eat out. As far as is practicable, the coverage aims to be relevant across the country and to every cuisine, but it is wise to travel with an open mind. While some of the restaurants are expensive and luxurious, others are more humble, the meals less ambitious. This is a guide to food that may not always be served on starched lined cloths by waiters in black. However, all serve good food. All offer value for money in their own way. In the end, good food is about variety and choice.

Although much has changed since Raymond Postgate first published *The Good Food Guide* in 1951, the ethos of the original book remains – it will always be the voice of the consumer. The Guide does not accept sponsorship, advertising or free meals and all reviewers conduct their inspections anonymously. This is why *The Good Food Guide* remains the UK's most trusted, best-selling, best-loved restaurant bible. In buying and using the Guide you are supporting its aim to improve standards of food and restaurateuring. This is a book to be used.

If you would like to contribute, please log on to: www.which.co.uk/gfgfeedback.

We collect, read and count every piece of feedback – and we may well use some of your recommendations in next year's edition.

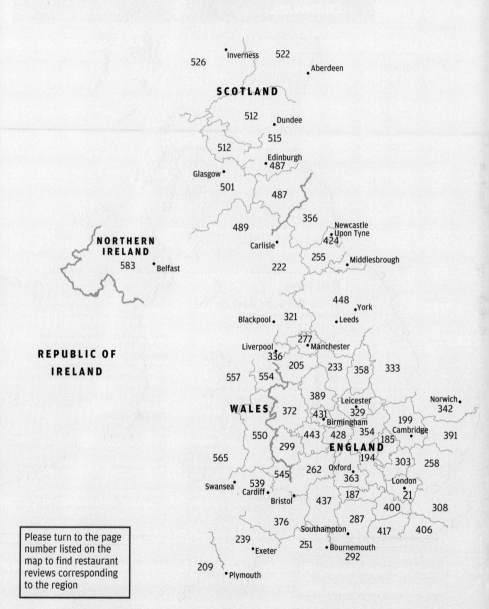

SCOTLAND

526
Inverness
522
Aberdeen

512
Dundee
515
Edinburgh
487

Glasgow
501
487

356
Newcastle
Upon Tyne
424

489
Carlisle
255
Middlesbrough
222

448
York
Blackpool
321
Leeds

277
Liverpool
Manchester
336

NORTHERN IRELAND
583
Belfast

REPUBLIC OF IRELAND

557
554
205
233
358
333

389
Leicester
Norwich
342

WALES
372
431
329
Birmingham
199
Cambridge
391

550
443
428
354
185

299
ENGLAND
194
303
258

565
262
Oxford
363
London
21

545
Swansea
539
Cardiff
437
187
400
308

Bristol
376
287
417
406

239
251
Southampton
Bournemouth
292

Exeter
209
Plymouth

Please turn to the page number listed on the map to find restaurant reviews corresponding to the region

FRANCE

How to use The Guide

The Guide is organised by county/region. Maps in each section work alongside the full-page maps at the back of the book

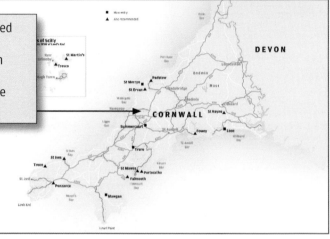

▪ St Ives

Little Harbour Restaurant
Modern cuisine by the harbour
1 The High Street, New Town, NT1 1AB
Tel no: 01234 567890
www.littleharbourrestaurant.co.uk
Modern European | £43
Cooking score: 3

 V

If you want to secure the much-desired view over the harbour from this former lifeboat house, ask for a table by the window on the upper floor. The décor throughout is light, bright and minimalist, with white-painted walls and white napery. Dinner starts with an amuse-bouche – maybe creamed cauliflower and Stilton soup served in a tiny tureen – and 'excellent' home-made granary and tomato bread. Fish is a strong suit, as in a creamy nage of black bream or mackerel tempura with a sesame and soy dipping sauce which 'was an absolute *tour de force*' at inspection. Or you could start with terrine of duck with fig chutney. Finish with a taster selection of chocolate, including a mould of dark chocolate and orange mousse, and banana and white chocolate ice cream. Plenty of wines are served by the glass from an international list. House Australian is £12.95.
Chef: Frederick Igor **Open:** all week 11.30 to 2, 5 to 10 (6 to 9.30 low season) **Closed:** 25 and 26 Dec
Meals: alc (main courses L £8–£15, D £14 to £20)
Service: not inc. **Extra details:** No parking. Vegetarian meals. Children's helpings.

ALSO RECOMMENDED

Jasper Jones
2 The Cresent, Old Town, OT1 1AB
Tel no: 01234 567890
Seaside café with a great position overlooking the beach and St Ives Bay. The lively menu offers simple stuff using the freshest seafood: crisp calamari or moules marinière (both £5.95) to start, followed by fish, chips and mushy peas in herb batter (£9.95) or whole local grilled lemon sole (£10.95). Breakfast and light lunches are also served (baguettes from £5.50). Wines from £10.95. Open all week, Apr to Oct.

Cuisine, price, score and symbols are quick to find

the content on these pages is sample text only

Features, articles and interviews are dropped in throughout the book

CORNWALL

The White Bar and Grill
Spectacular alfresco beach dining
10 The High Street, New Town, NT2 2BC
Tel no: 01234 567890
www.thewhitebarandgrill.co.uk
Global/Seafood | £46
Cooking score: 4
V

The position of this restaurant is rather special, with unbeatable views over the sea. It is closed over winter, so there's no opportunity to enjoy the view over the bay on the stormiest of days, but there's a large terrace for a truly Mediterranean experience in summer. Lunch can be a satisfying Cornish crab sandwich or crispy fried chilli squid with black spice, Thai salad and citrus white miso. In the evening, Jones pushes the boat out with scallop risotto with piquillo peppers, mascarpone and lemon vodka, followed by twice-cooked Barbary duck on braised salsify with seared foie gras and a gooseberry and Cointreau sauce. Finish with blood orange and Campari posset with a ginger glass biscuit.
Chef: Chris White **Open:** all week 12 to 3.45, 6 to 10 **Closed:** Nov to Mar **Meals:** alc (main courses L £7–£13, D £17 to £20) **Service:** not inc. **Extra details:** 70 seats outside. Vegetarian meals.

READERS RECOMMEND

Bistro Eleven
Modern British
Harbour Road, Old Town, OT2 2AB
Tel no: 01234 567890
'Fantastic fish in a harbourside setting'

Café Cod
Modern British
20 The High Street, New Town, NT1 1AB
Tel: 01234 567890
'Excellent food in a quirky, hippy style setting'

Barry the Fish
Fish
Harbour Road, Old Town, OT1 1AB
Tel no: 01234 567890
'Fast, slick and stylish dining'

Send your reviews to

Raymond Blanc Manoir aux Quat' Saisons

Why did you become a chef?
As a boy in Besançon, I saw the pleasure people had in eating in a restaurant and thought 'I want to give that pleasure to people myself'.

Do you have a favourite source for your ingredients?
Of course. Le Manoir's own garden.

Who would you invite to your ideal dinner party?
They have to be passionate about food. So: the composer Rossini, for whom so many dishes are named. He was an amusing conversationalist, too, and a good cook. Marcel Proust probably didn't know what the kitchen looked like – but he loved his food. Then some painters and other musicians, another writer or two, perhaps some genial chefs – and of course my family.

What's your guilty food pleasure?
None. I refuse to feel guilty about food.

What era of history would you most like to have eaten in? Actually there's no epoch in which mankind was capable of eating better than we can eat today.

'Readers Recommend' are supplied by readers, for readers. These entries are the local, up-and-coming places to watch and are the voice of our thousands of loyal followers

Scoring

We should begin by saying that a score of 1 is actually a significant achievement. We reject many restaurants during the compilation of the Guide. Obviously, there are always subjective aspects to rating systems, but our inspectors are equipped with extensive scoring guidelines, so that restaurant bench-marking around the UK is accurate. We also take into account the reader feedback that we receive for each restaurant, so that any given review is based on several meals.

1/10	Capable cooking, with simple food combinations and clear flavours, but some inconsistencies.
2/10	Decent cooking, displaying good basic technical skills and interesting combinations and flavours. Occasional inconsistencies.
3/10	Good cooking, showing sound technical skills and using quality ingredients.
4/10	Dedicated, focused approach to cooking; good classical skills and high-quality ingredients.
5/10	Exact cooking techniques and a degree of ambition; showing balance and depth of flavour in dishes, while using quality ingredients.
6/10	Exemplary cooking skills, innovative ideas, impeccable ingredients and an element of excitement.
7/10	High level of ambition and individuality, attention to the smallest detail, accurate and vibrant dishes.
8/10	A kitchen cooking close to or at the top of its game – highly individual, showing faultless technique and impressive artistry in dishes that are perfectly balanced for flavour, combination and texture. There is little room for disappointment here.
9/10	This mark is for cooking that has reached a pinnacle of achievement, making it a hugely memorable experience for the diner.
10/10	It is extremely rare that a restaurant can achieve perfect dishes on a consistent basis. We have awarded this mark for the first time in four years.

Symbols

Restaurants that may be given main entry status are contacted ahead of publication and asked to provide key information about their opening hours and facilities. They are also invited to participate in the £5 voucher scheme. The symbols on these entries are therefore based on this feedback from restaurants, and are intended for quick, at-a-glance identification. The wine bottle symbol, however, is an accolade assigned by the Guide's team, based on their judgement of the wine list available.

 Accommodation is available.

 It is possible to have three courses at the restaurant for less than £30.

V There are more than five vegetarian dishes available on the menu.

 The restaurant is participating in our £5 voucher scheme. (Please see the vouchers at the end of the book for terms and conditions.)

 The restaurant has a wine list that our inspector and wine expert have deemed to be exceptional.

£XX The pricing for each restaurant is aligned with our online feedback system: www.which.co.uk/gfgfeedback. The price indicated on each review represents the average price of a three-course dinner, excluding wine.

Good Food Guide
Restaurant of the Year
Winner
ramsons, Ramsbottom

Reader Awards

The Good Food Guide has always recognised excellence and good service at restaurants throughout the UK. *The Good Food Guide Restaurant of the Year* award is run annually between April and June, and presents readers with the opportunity to nominate their favourite local establishment. For this year's award, members of the public were invited to nominate establishments for ten different regions, with the criteria that restaurants should be independently owned and offer regional or local produce. Nominations were submitted via our online feedback form (www.which.co.uk/gfgfeedback), by sms text messaging, and by postal vote. We received thousands of nominations and *The Good Food Guide* team picked the overall winner from the list of regional winners.

The Readers' Restaurant of the Year (2009 edition)
ramsons, Ramsbottom

1. WALES - Fairyhill, Reynoldston

2. EAST ENGLAND - Great House, Lavenham

3. LONDON - Pied-à-Terre

4. MIDLANDS - Perkins, Plumtree

5. NORTHERN IRELAND - Bay Tree, Holywood

6. NORTH EAST - Weaver's Shed, Golcar

7. NORTH WEST - ramsons, Ramsbottom

8. SCOTLAND - Ee-Usk, Oban

9. SOUTH EAST - Hungry Monk, Jevington

10. SOUTH WEST - Allium, Fairford

Editors' Awards

Other awards in this Guide have been allocated by *The Good Food Guide* team and are as follows:

Restaurant newcomer of the year
Michael Wignall at the Latymer, Surrey

Pub newcomer of the year
The Yew Tree, Kent

Wine list of the year
Holbeck Ghyll, Cumbria

Best chef
Simon Rogan for L'Enclume and Rogan & Co, Cumbria

Up-and-coming chef
Marcus Eaves, L'Autre Pied, London

Best pub chef
Dominic Chapman, Royal Oak, Berkshire

Best fish restaurant
The Captain's Galley, Scotland

Best value for money
Côte, London

Best family restaurant
Gallery Café, Whitworth Art Gallery, Manchester

Best use of local produce
The Hardwick, Wales

Restaurants with a notable wine list

London

1 Lombard Street City
Almeida, Islington
Andrew Edmunds, Soho
Anglesea Arms, Shepherd's Bush
Aubergine, Chelsea
Bacchus, Shoreditch
Bentley's, Piccadilly
Bibendum, South Kensington
Bleeding Heart, Clerkenwell
Bonds, City
Bradleys, Swiss Cottage
Café du Jardin, Covent Garden
Cambio de Tercio, Earls Court
Chez Bruce, Balham
Clarke's, Notting Hill
Club Gascon, City
Enoteca Turi, Putney
Eyre Brothers, Shoreditch
Fifth Floor, Knightsbridge
Glasshouse, Kew
Gordon Ramsay, Chelsea
Gordon Ramsay at Claridge's, Mayfair
Greenhouse, Green Park
Greyhound, Battersea
Hakkasan, Fitzrovia
Kensington Place, Notting Hill
La Trompette, Chiswick

Le Cercle, Belgravia
Le Gavroche, Mayfair
Le Pont de la Tour, Bermondsey
L'Etranger, South Kensington
Locanda Locatelli, Marble Arch
Maze, Mayfair
Metrogusto, Islington
Nobu London, Mayfair
Odette's, Primrose Hill
Oxo Tower, South Bank
Pearl, Holborn
Pétrus, Belgravia
Pied-à-Terre, Fitzrovia
Quo Vadis, Soho
Ransome's Dock, Battersea
Rasoi Vineet Bhatia, Chelsea
Rex Whistler Restaurant at Tate Britain, Westminster
Rhodes W1 Restaurant, Marble Arch
Richard Corrigan at Lindsay House, Soho
Ristorante Semplice, Mayfair
Roussillon, Chelsea
RSJ, Southwark
The Capital, Knightsbridge
The Don, City
The Ledbury, Westbourne Park
The Square, Mayfair
Tom Aikens, Chelsea
Umu, Mayfair
Wolseley, Mayfair

Zaika, Kensington
Zuma, Knightsbridge

Rest of UK

36 On The Quay, Emsworth
60 Hope Street, Liverpool
A Touch of Novelli at the White Horse, Harpenden
Airds Hotel, Port Appin
Albannach, Lochinver
Aldens, Belfast
Alimentum, Cambridge
Angel Restaurant, Long Crendon
Anthony's Restaurant, Leeds
Ardeonaig Hotel, Ardeonaig
Arundel House, Arundel
Arundell Arms, Lifton
Auberge du Lac, Welwyn Garden City
Balmoral, Number One, Edinburgh
Bath Priory, Bath
Bell at Skenfrith, Skenfrith
Blue Lion, East Witton
Bodysgallen Hall, Llandudno
Box Tree, Ilkley
Braidwoods, Dalry
Brasserie Forty Four, Leeds
Brian Maule at Chardon d'Or, Glasgow

Callow Hall, Ashbourne
Carlton Riverside, Llanwrtyd Wells
Castle Hotel, Taunton
Castle House, Hereford
Castleman Hotel, Chettle
Cayenne, Belfast
Cellar, Anstruther
Champany, Inn Linlithgow
Cherwell Boathouse, Oxford
Clytha Arms, Clytha
Combe House, Gittisham
Congham Hall, Orangery, Grimston
Corse Lawn House, Corse Lawn
Crooked Billet, Newton Longville
Crown at Whitebrook, Whitebrook
Crown Hotel, Southwold
Culinaria, Bristol
Danesfield House, Oak Room, Marlow
Darroch Learg, Ballater
Devonshire Arms, Bolton Abbey
Dylanwad Da, Dolgellau
Fairyhill, Reynoldston
Firenze, Kibworth Beauchamp
Fischer's Baslow Hall, Baslow
Forth Floor, Edinburgh
Fourth Floor Café and Bar, Leeds
Fox & Hounds, Hunsdon

Foxhunter, Nant-y-derry
Fraiche, Oxton
Gidleigh Park, Chagford
Gilpin Lodge, Windermere
Gravetye Manor, East Grinstead
Greens' Dining Room, Bristol
Greyhound, Stockbridge
Haldanes, Edinburgh
Hambleton Hall, Hambleton
Hart's, Nottingham
Holbeck Ghyll, Windermere
Horn of Plenty, Gulworthy
Hoste Arms, Burnham Market
Hotel du Vin & Bistro, Winchester
Hotel du Vin & Bistro, Tunbridge Wells
Hotel du Vin & Bistro, Henley-on-Thames
Hotel du Vin & Bistro, Birmingham
Hotel du Vin & Bistro, Harrogate
JSW, Petersfield
Killiecrankie House, Killiecrankie
Kinloch House Hotel, Blairgowrie
Kitchin, Edinburgh
Knockinaam Lodge, Portpatrick
La Cachette, Elland
La Chouette, Dinton
La Luna, Godalming
Lake Country House, Llangammarch Wells
Le Champignon Sauvage, Cheltenham
Le Manoir aux Quat' Saisons, Great Milton
Le Poussin at Whitley Ridge, Brockenhurst
Le Vignoble, Aberystwyth
L'Enclume, Cartmel
Lewtrenchard Manor, Lewdown
Lime Tree, Manchester

Linen Room, Dumfries
Linthwaite House, Bowness-on-Windermere
Little Barwick House, Barwick
London Carriage Works, Liverpool
Longueville Manor, St Saviour, Jersey
Lords of the Manor, Upper Slaughter
Lucknam Park, Colerne
Lumière, Cheltenham
Maes-y-Neuadd, Harlech
Magpies, Horncastle
McCoy's at the Tontine, Staddlebridge
Melton's, York
Melton's Too, York
Midsummer House, Cambridge
Montagu Arms Terrace, Beaulieu
Morston Hall, Morston
Mr Underhill's, Ludlow
Nantyffin Cider Mill Inn, Crickhowell
New Angel, Dartmouth
No. 6, Padstow
Northcote Manor, Langho
Oakley and Harvey at Wallett's Court, St Margaret's-at-Cliffe
Old Bridge Hotel, Huntingdon
Old Vicarage, Ridgeway
Olive Branch, Clipsham
Olive Tree at The Queensberry Hotel, Bath
Orestone Manor, Maidencombe
Penmaenuchaf Hall, Penmaenpool
Pheasant, Keyston
Pintxo People, Brighton
Plas Bodegroes, Pwllheli
Rampsbeck Country House Hotel, Watermillock
ramsons, Ramsbottom
Read's, Faversham
Restaurant 22, Cambridge

Restaurant Martin Wishart, Edinburgh
Restaurant Nathan Outlaw, Fowey
Restaurant Sat Bains, Nottingham
riverstation, Bristol
Rothay Manor, Ambleside
Sangster's, Elie
Sasso, Harrogate
Seafood Restaurant, Padstow
Seafood Restaurant, St Andrews
Seafood Restaurant, St Monans
Seaham Hall, White Room, Seaham
Second Floor, Manchester
Sharpham Park, Charlton House Hotel, Shepton Mallet
Sharrow Bay, Ullswater
Simon Radley at the Chester Grosvenor, Chester
Simpsons, Birmingham
Sir Charles Napier, Chinnor
Sous le Nez en Ville, Leeds
Spire, Liverpool
St Tudno Hotel, Terrace Restaurant, Llandudno
Stagg Inn, Titley
Star Inn, Harome
Stravaigin, Glasgow
Summer Isles Hotel, Achiltibuie
Sycamore House, Little Shelford
Tan-y-Foel Country House, Capel Garmon
The Anchor Inn, Sutton
The Angel Inn, Hetton
The Boar's Head Hotel, Ripley
The Cross, Kingussie

The Crown, Newport
The Dower House, Royal Crescent, Bath
The Fat Duck, Bray
The Griffin Inn, Fletching
The Harrow at Little Bedwyn, Little Bedwyn
The Mirabelle at The Grand Hotel, Eastbourne
The Plough, Bolnhurst
The Vineyard at Stockcross, Newbury
The Yew Tree, Barfreston
Three Chimneys, Isle of Skye
Three Lions, Stuckton
Tyddyn Llan, Llandrillo
Ubiquitous Chip, Glasgow
Valvona & Crolla Caffè Bar, Edinburgh
Vintners Rooms, Edinburgh
Walnut Tree Inn, Llandewi Skirrid
Weavers Shed, Golcar
Webbe's at the Fish Café, Rye
Weezos Restaurant @ The Old Toll House, Clitheroe
Wellington Inn, Lund
West Stoke House, West Stoke
Westerly, Reigate
Whatley Manor, Easton Grey
White Moss House, Grasmere
Wildebeest Arms, Stoke Holy Cross
Winteringham Fields, Winteringham
Ye Olde Bulls Head, Beaumaris
Ynyshir Hall, Eglwysfach
Yorke Arms, Ramsgill
Ziba, Liverpool

Top 40 2009

It is four years since the Guide awarded a mark of 10 out of 10 to Gordon Ramsay, and nine years since Nico Ladenis won the mark, showing how great an achievement it is to score a perfect 10.

1. Fat Duck, Bray, Berkshire (10)
2. Gordon Ramsay, Royal Hospital Road, London (9)
3. Pétrus, London (8)
4. Le Manoir aux Quat'Saisons, Great Milton, Oxfordshire (8)
5. Square, London (8)
6. Le Champignon Sauvage, Cheltenham, Gloucestershire (8)
7. Le Gavroche, London (8)
8. Waterside Inn (8)
9. Vineyard at Stockcross, Newbury, Berkshire (8)
10. Pied-à-Terre, London (8)
11. Restaurant Nathan Outlaw, Fowey, Cornwall (8)
12. Tom Aikens, London (8)
13. L'Enclume, Cartmel, Cumbria (8)
14. Restaurant Martin Wishart, Edinburgh, Scotland (8)
15. Maze, London (7)
16. The Capital, London (7)
17. Bohemia, St Helier, Jersey (7)
18. Hibiscus, London (7)
19. Danesfield House, Marlow, Buckinghamshire (7)
20. Gidleigh Park, Chagford, Devon (7)
21. Restaurant Sat Bains, Nottingham (7)
22. Anthony's, Leeds, Yorkshire (7)
23. Andrew Fairlie at Gleneagles, Auchterarder, Scotland (7)
24. Holbeck Ghyll, Windermere, Cumbria (7)
25. Fischer's Baslow Hall, Baslow, Derbyshire (7)
26. Simon Radley at the Chester Grosvenor, Cheshire (7)
27. Michael Wignall at the Latymer, Pennyhill Park, Surrey (7)
28. Whatley Manor, Easton Grey, Wiltshire (7)
29. Hambleton Hall, Hambleton, Leicestershire and Rutland (7)
30. Tyddyn Llan, Llandrillo, Wales (7)
31. Harry's Place, Great Gonerby, Lincolnshire (7)
32. The Creel, St Margaret's Hope, Orkney, Scotland (7)
33. Mr Underhill, Ludlow, Shropshire (7)
34. Old Vicarage, Ridgeway, Derbyshire (7)
35. Castle Hotel, Taunton, Somerset (6)
36. The Greenhouse, London (6)
37. Club Gascon, London (6)
38. Kitchin, Edinburgh (6)
39. Simpsons, Edgbaston, Birmingham (6)
40. Crown at Whitebrook, Whitebrook, Wales (6)

Longest-serving restaurants

The Good Food Guide was founded in 1951. Here is a list of restaurants which have appeared consistently since their first entry into the Guide.

Connaught, London, 56 years
Gay Hussar, London, 52 years
Gravetye Manor, East Grinstead, 52 years
Porth Tocyn Hotel, Abersoch, 52 years
Sharrow Bay, Ullswater, 48 years
Rothay Manor, Ambleside, 40 years
Le Gavroche, London, 39 years
Summer Isles Hotel, Achiltibuie, 39 years
The Capital, London, 38 years
Ubiquitous Chip, Glasgow, 37 years
Druidstone, Broad Haven, 36 years
Plumber Manor, Sturminster Newton,
    36 years
Waterside Inn, Bray, 36 years
White Moss House, Grasmere, 36 years
Isle of Eriska, Eriska, 35 years
Airds Hotel, Port Appin, 33 years

Farlam Hall, Brampton, 32 years
Corse Lawn House, Corse Lawn, 31 years
Hambleton Hall, Hambleton, 30 years
Pier Hotel, Harbourside Restaurant, Harwich,
    30 years
Grafton Manor, Bromsgrove, 29 years
Magpie Cafè, Whitby, 29 years
RSJ, London SE1, 28 years
Seafood Restaurant, Padstow, 28 years
Sir Charles Napier, Chinnor, 28 years
The Dower House, Royal Crescent, Bath,
    28 years
Kalpna, Edinburgh, 27 years
Le Caprice, London, 27 years
Little Barwick House, Barwick, 27 years
Moss Nook, Manchester, 27 years
Ostler's Close, Cupar, 26 years

LONDON

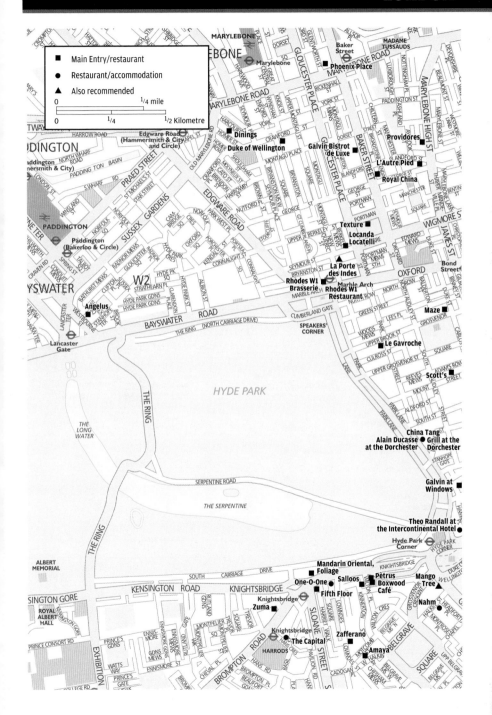

- ■ Main Entry/restaurant
- ● Restaurant/accommodation
- ▲ Also recommended

0 .... 1/4 mile

0 .... 1/4 .... 1/2 Kilometre

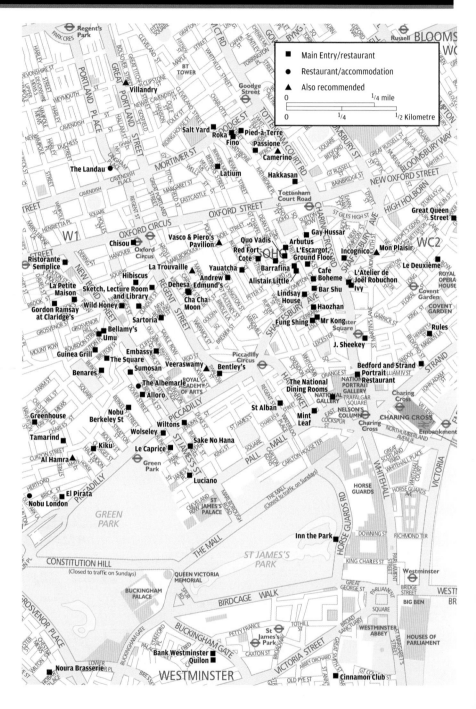

Main Entry/restaurant
Restaurant/accommodation
Also recommended

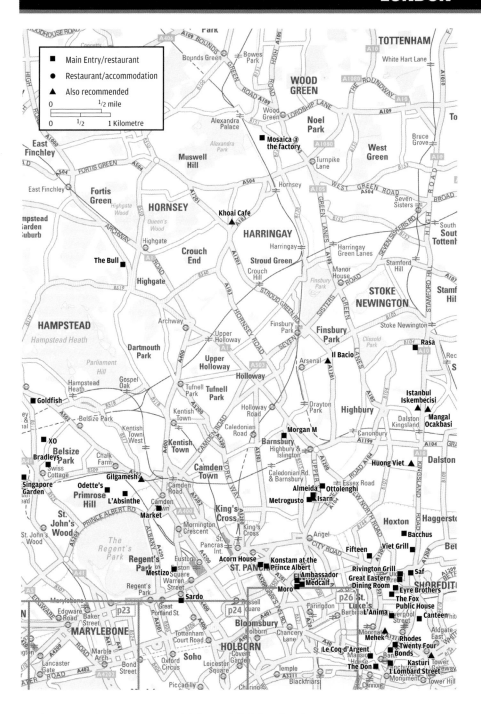

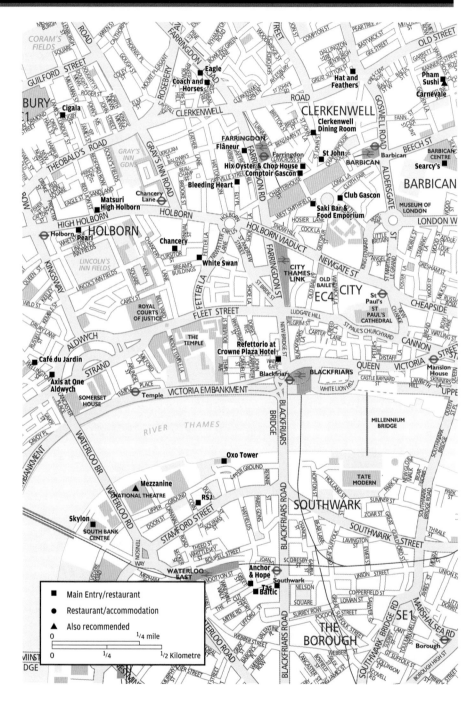

Eagle
Coach and Horses
Hat and Feathers
Pham Sushi
Carnevale
Cigala
CLERKENWELL
Clerkenwell Dining Room
FARRINGDON
Flâneur
Farringdon
St John
Barbican
BARBICAN CENTRE
Searcy's
Hix Oyster & Chop House
BARBICAN
Comptoir Gascon
Bleeding Heart
BARBICAN
Club Gascon
Matsuri
High Holborn
MUSEUM OF LONDON
Chancery Lane
Saki Bar & Food Emporium
LONDON W
Holborn
Pearl
Chancery
White Swan
CITY THAMES LINK
EC4 CITY
St Paul's
ST PAUL'S CATHEDRAL
CHEAPSIDE
ROYAL COURTS OF JUSTICE
Refettorio at Crowne Plaza Hotel
Café du Jardin
Axis at One Aldwych
Blackfriars
BLACKFRIARS
Mansion House
Temple
Oxo Tower
MILLENNIUM BRIDGE
Mezzanine
TATE MODERN
RSJ
SOUTHWARK
Skylon
SOUTHWARK STREET
Anchor & Hope
Southwark
Tas Baltic
SE1
THE BOROUGH
Borough

- ■ Main Entry/restaurant
- ● Restaurant/accommodation
- ▲ Also recommended

0   1/4 mile
0   1/4   1/2 Kilometre

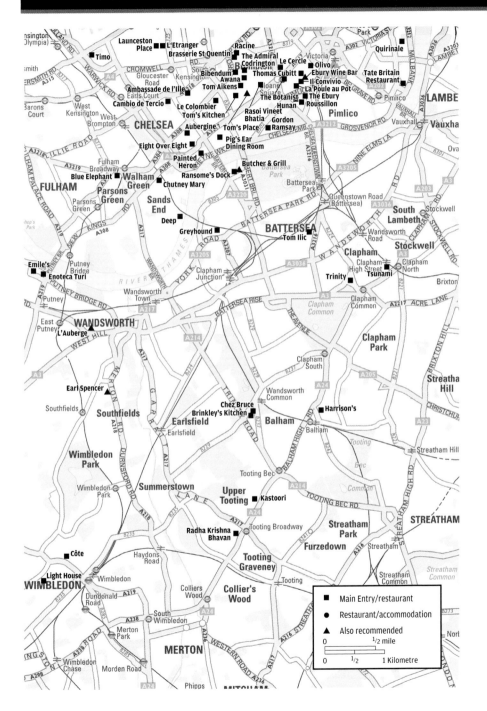

Legend:
- ■ Main Entry/restaurant
- ● Restaurant/accommodation
- ▲ Also recommended

0   ½ mile
0   ½   1 Kilometre

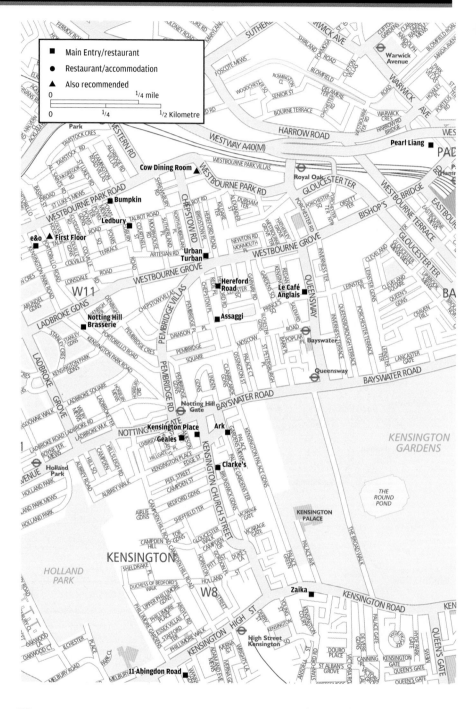

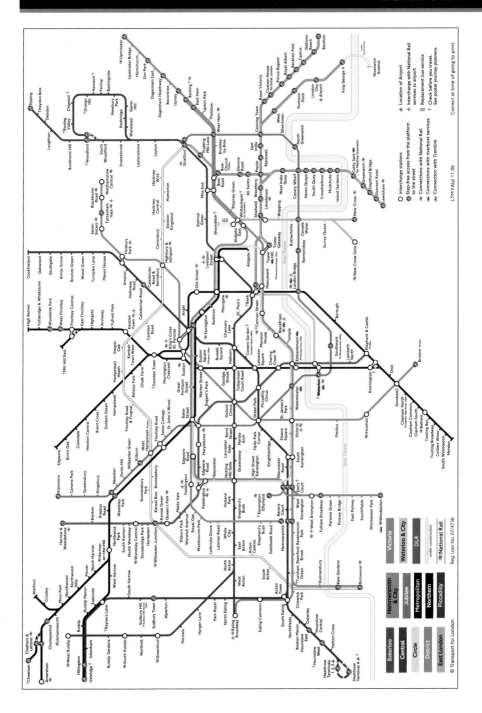

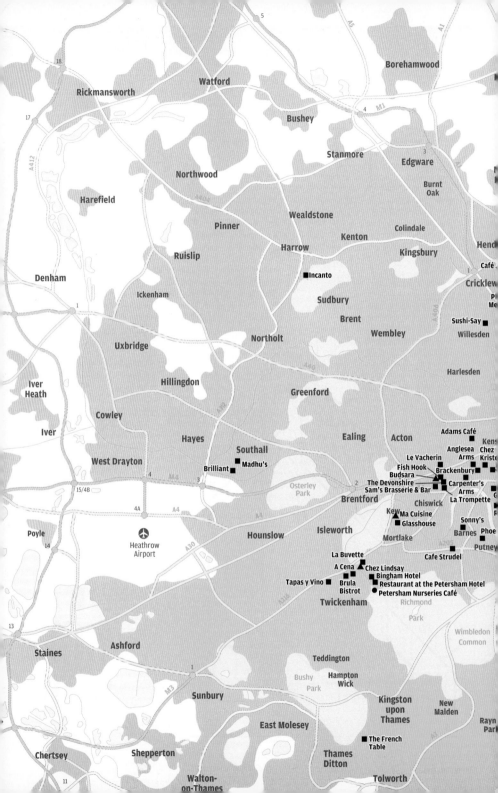

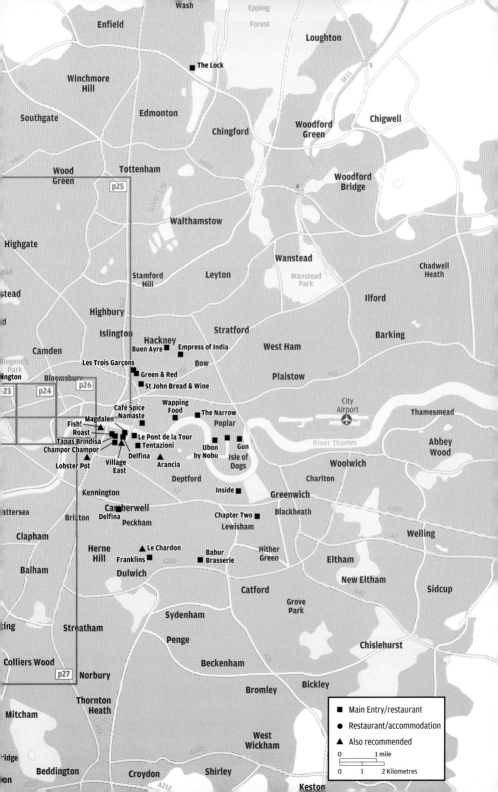

Belgravia

Le Cercle
Exquisite harmony and precision
1 Wilbraham Place, SW1X 9AE
Tel no: (020) 7901 9999
⊖ Sloane Square
French | £30
Cooking score: 5

£5 OFF ♦ **V**

An elegant, über-cool basement done out in neutral colours with marble floors, billowing white drapes and carefully positioned spotlights is the fashionable setting for this trendy destination near Sloane Square. Like its elder brother, Club Gascon (see entry), this kitchen deals in exquisite tapas-sized tasting dishes loosely rooted in the culinary traditions of southwest France. There are no conventional starters: instead the menu grazes its way from 'Végétal' through 'Terroirs' to 'Plaisirs' and 'Gourmandises': the result is a procession of precise, harmonious and daringly creative constructions. Regional specialities are eagerly taken on board, considered, then reinvented, whether it's persillade of snails, boudin noir and apples and a sweet pepper jelly or Pyrénean milk-fed lamb with a potato tian and coriander pesto. Elsewhere, the kitchen applies its verve and imagination to, say, vanilla-glazed black cod, swede cake and passion fruit, veal and squid 'plancha' with black aromatic polenta or strawberries 'tartare' with muesli and vintage balsamic. Each dish is flagged with a recommended wine (which helps to keep pace with the cavalcade of fast-moving flavours), and the full list is an all-French affair that explores the regions in depth – paying special attention to the rare wines of the sud-ouest . Prices start at £18 (£4.50 a glass).
Chef/s: Thierry Beyris. **Open:** Tue to Sat L 12 to 2, D 6 to 10.45. **Closed:** Sun, Mon and bank hols. **Meals:** alc (main courses £6 to £35). Set L £19.50 (4 courses). Set D 6 to 7 £21.50. Bar menu available. **Service:** 12.5% (optional). **Details:** Cards accepted. 60 seats. Air-con. Separate bar. Wheelchair access. Music. Children's portions.

Nahm
Seriously researched Thai food
Halkin Hotel, 5 Halkin Street, SW1X 7DJ
Tel no: (020) 7333 1234
www.nahm.como.bz
⊖ Hyde Park Corner
Thai | £55
Cooking score: 3

Secreted within the high-rolling Halkin Hotel, Nahm is the sleek brainchild of Aussie chef David Thompson and a showcase for his assiduously researched version of Thai cuisine in all its palate-thrilling diversity. Lunches feature noodles, rice combos and creative curries (minced sea bass with wild ginger and green peppercorns, for example) framed by a few neat starters and desserts. Dinner is an altogether different proposition, and you can opt for the multi-course Nahm Arharn menu or cherry-pick from the esoteric carte. Here you might encounter pork and clam salad with dried prawns and pomelo, curious soups involving ingredients like ivy gourd leaves, fascinating specialities based around pungent nam prik relish and centrepieces such as stir-fried Longhorn beef with chilli paste or squid with spring onions and orange chillies. Wine prices are pure upper-crust Belgravia (around £35 is the bottom line), but there is plenty of premium stuff on show – especially if German whites or New World reds are to your taste.
Chef/s: Matthew Albert. **Open:** Mon to Fri L 12 to 2, all week D 7 to 10.30. **Closed:** bank hols. **Meals:** alc (main courses £8.50 to £17). Set L £20 (2 courses) to £26. Set D £55. **Service:** 12.5% (optional). **Details:** Cards accepted. 76 seats. Air-con. Separate bar. Wheelchair access. Music. Children's portions.

Noura Brasserie

Stylish Lebanese venue
16 Hobart Place, SW1W 0HH
Tel no: (020) 7235 9444
www.noura.co.uk
⊖ Victoria
Lebanese | £36
Cooking score: 3

 V

The Belgravia branch of Noura was the
original, and remains a pace-setting, smart
venue in which to eat some well-wrought
Lebanese and Middle Eastern food. The
extensive menu comes equipped with a little
glossary, so you can tell your loubieh bel zeit
(green beans cooked in tomatoes and olive oil)
from your moutabbal (grilled aubergine purée
with sesame oil and lemon juice). Meat dishes
range from familiar chargrilled lamb skewers
to a brace of whole grilled quail, fish might be
red mullet with tahina sauce and fried bread,
and there are enough hot and cold meze to
provide variation over the course of several
visits. Finish with one of the Lebanese desserts
such as atayef (blinis filled with clotted cream
and served with syrup) or with home-made
ice creams such as orange blossom, rosewater
and lemon, or pistachio. Lebanese wines are
evident on an international list, which starts at
a stiffish £24.
Chef/s: Badih Asmar. **Open:** all week 11.30am to
11.30pm. **Meals:** alc (main courses £11.50 to
£22.50). Set L £18. Set L and D £30 to £40.
Service: not inc. **Details:** 120 seats. 15 seats
outside. Air-con. Separate bar. Wheelchair access.
Music. Children allowed.

Olivo

Echoes of Sardinia
21 Eccleston Street, SW1W 9LX
Tel no: (020) 7730 2505
www.olivorestaurants.com
⊖ Victoria
Italian | £35
New Chef

The original branch of Mauro Sanna's olive-
themed empire, Olivo scores a hit with its
cheery Med-inspired atmosphere and rustic
food. Crowds of commuters and Belgravia
locals sit at close-packed wooden tables amid
the boisterous hubbub and revel in the
conviviality of it all. Vernaccia (a chilled
Sardinian aperitif) signals the kitchen's island
loyalties, and the menu always features a few
native specialities – including the much-
vaunted bottarga (salted grey mullet roe) and
traditional malloreddus pasta. Elsewhere, the
Italian mainland contributes plenty of robust
ideas, ranging from black tagliatelle with
cuttlefish ragù to sautéed lamb's kidneys with
lentils and artichokes or braised duck with
chilli-flecked broccoli. Frozen yoghurt with
blueberry sauce is an Olivo trademark dessert,
or you might prefer to continue on the island
path with sebada (cheese fritters with honey).
Sardinian house wine is £15.50 (£3.75 a
glass), and there's Ichnusa Sardinian beer too.
Chef/s: Sandro Messa. **Open:** Mon to Fri L 12 to
2.30, all week D 7 to 11. **Closed:** bank hols.
Meals: alc (main courses £13 to £19). Set L £19.50 (2
courses) to £23. **Service:** not inc. **Details:** Cards
accepted. 45 seats. Air-con. No music. Wheelchair
access. Children allowed.

Pétrus

Among London's finest
The Berkeley, Wilton Place, SW1X 7RL
Tel no: (020) 7235 1200
www.marcuswareing.com
⊖ Knightsbridge
Modern French | £75
Cooking score: 8

🍷 V

'Dining here is always a positive, memorable experience,' comments a reporter clearly lucky enough to be something of a regular at this shining Knightsbridge star. You enter via the lobby of the Berkeley Hotel, and immediately step into another world. In a city where much contemporary dining takes place amid hard-edged, brightly-lit surroundings, Pétrus is a womb-like space, expansive but sultrily sepulchral at the same time. Dark wood panelling and chairs upholstered in an oxblood shade set a sober tone, which is reinforced by the tender ministrations of staff drilled in the old-school courtesies. The whole experience is a gloriously unreconstructed gesture to the way things used to be done. None of which can be said of Marcus Wareing's menus. True, there's Oscietra caviar for the high-rollers (or even for those who happen to like it), but it comes with tea-smoked mackerel and a duck egg tart. Vitello tonnato has been given a thorough makeover and appears as a starter, the veal poached and finely sliced, the tuna air-dried, and with an honour guard of smoked anchovies, capers, and a white onion and nutmeg mousse. The tastebuds thus challenged, mains proceed in a more stately vein, offering roast and glazed Angus fillet with pommes Anna, trompette mushrooms and Italian artichokes, but what is likely to stop you in your tracks is the sheer intensity and depth of flavour achieved in these dishes. Slow-cooking has been brought to a fine art, usefully applied to the poaching of sea bass or – gloriously – to Norfolk suckling pig, which has had one full revolution of the clock in the oven before emerging in the company of braised chicory and pommes mousseline. There is a comfort factor to the food here, notwithstanding all the breathless experimentation, that comes from not denaturing the principal ingredients too much. That, plus impeccable sourcing. At dessert, an assemblage of vanilla crème, spiced poached pears, chestnuts and pear sorbet shows what can be done with that often shy-flavoured fruit, while Valrhôna chocolate might go into a mousse alongside peanut parfait, salt caramel jelly and raspberry cream. What with all the incidentals (appetisers, pre-desserts, petits fours and so forth), you will leave Pétrus having got through a fair amount of food, and yet the lightness of touch is such that you aren't likely to feel outfaced. A desert-island wine list accompanies, and one that doesn't just stick to the hallowed regions of France, but strikes out fruitfully into North America, the Middle East and central Europe. Prices are naturally high, but a page of wines by-the-glass starts from £5 for a dry white Bordeaux. NB. Shortly before the Guide went to press it was announced that Gordon Ramsay Holdings' Pétrus contract with the Berkeley Hotel would end in September 2008 and Marcus Wareing would part company with GRH, but stay on at the Berkeley to continue running the fine dining operation. As we understand it, GRH plan to take the Pétrus name with them, so the restaurant will be renamed.

Chef/s: Marcus Wareing. **Open:** Mon to Fri L 12 to 2.30, Mon to Sat D 6 to 11. **Closed:** Christmas. **Meals:** Set L £30 to £80, Set D £65 to £80. **Service:** 12.5%. **Details:** Cards accepted. 70 seats. Air-con. Separate bar. No music. No mobile phones. Wheelchair access. Children's portions.

La Poule au Pot

Classic French bistro cooking
231 Ebury Street, SW1W 8UT
Tel no: (020) 7730 7763
⊖ Sloane Square
French | £38
Cooking score: 2

Unreconstructed French bistro food is getting increasingly hard to come by in the capital, but this place keeps the tricolor flying. The

atmosphere is all shady nooks lit by flickering candles, the service amiable to a fault, and the menu an untranslated listing of the dishes of eras gone by. A plate of ratatouille as a starter gives a flavour of the approach. There's usually a textbook fish soup, and then the main-course business offers tuna niçoise or skate in black butter to the fish crowd, duck breast with lime or venison grand veneur to the carnivores. Finish with chocolate mousse or fruit terrine. Wines are an entirely French affair, starting with house at £14.50 (or £30 a magnum!) and ascending to the glorious 1982 vintage of Ch. Ducru-Beaucaillou for £255.
Chef/s: Kris Goleblowski. **Open:** Mon to Sun L 12.30 to 2.30 (3 Sat, 3.30 Sun), Mon to Fri D 6.45 to 11.15. **Meals:** alc (main courses £15 to £24.50). Set L £19.75. **Service:** 12.5%. **Details:** Cards accepted. 70 seats. 30 seats outside. Air-con. No music. No mobile phones. Wheelchair access. Children's portions.

Thomas Cubitt
Dapper Belgravia gastropub
44 Elizabeth Street, SW1W 9PA
Tel no: 020 7730 6060
www.thethomascubitt.co.uk
⊖ Victoria
Gastropub | £35
Cooking score: 3

Victorian master builder Thomas Cubitt was responsible for the much of Belgravia's grand design, so it's fitting that he should be honoured in this dapper gastropub. At street level is the boisterous bar with roll-back windows opening out onto a sunny terrace: here, cask ales go splendidly with an all-day menu of open-minded pub grub (gammon terrine with piccalilli, ploughman's, steamed Shetland mussels). Upstairs is a handsome dining room where restrained colour schemes and intricate mantelpieces set the tone and the well-considered menu hikes its way around the land. Set off with rolled River Test smoked trout and Devon crab with lime and basil, move on to herb-crusted rack of Welsh lamb with butter beans or braised Norfolk pork

belly with parsnip mash, mustard creamed leeks and Granny Smith beignets, and call it a day with Yorkshire rhubarb and ginger trifle. A dozen wines by the carafe or glass top the knowledgeably chosen, worldwide list; bottle prices start at £18.
Chef/s: Phillip Wilson. **Closed:** Good Fri, 25 Dec. **Meals:** alc (main courses £16 to £22). Set D Mon to Fri £19.50 (2 courses) to £24.50. **Service:** 12.5%. **Details:** Cards accepted. 125 seats. 25 seats outside. Air-con. Separate bar. Music. Children allowed.

Zafferano
An Italian gem
15 Lowndes Street, SW1X 9EY
Tel no: (020) 7235 5800
www.zafferanorestaurant.com
⊖ Knightsbridge
Italian | £44.50
Cooking score: 6

V

The atmosphere remains relaxed and easy-going, with staff as 'attentive and friendly, as ever' at this unassuming Knightsbridge restaurant. The food is strongly rooted in traditional Italian cooking, with the focus firmly on quality raw materials. Copious praise continues to pour in from readers, whether singling out pre-meal 'nibbles' of a vol-au-vent filled with salt cod brandade, the excellent home-made bread or simply expressing delight in a simple plate of Parmesan, fine Italian ham and toast with sliced porcini and a salad of spring vegetables. Alongside the uncommon panache and consistency of the cooking, the kitchen has the confidence to send out three large langoustine cooked simply in their shells and served with nothing more than a dressed salad of rocket and cherry tomatoes (pronounced 'lovely') or 'perfect pasta' simply teamed with superb porcini (dry as well as fresh to add extra flavour), the seasoning 'just right' and the 'carta de musica' on the side 'a crunchy complement' – the bread wafer thin, seasoned with just a little salt to give flavour. There is a complete truffle menu in season, while desserts include a near-legendary tiramisu. The wine list is an Italian gem aimed at those with deep pockets. House wine is £22.

Chef/s: Andy Needham. **Open:** all week L 12 to 2.30 (3 Sat and Sun), D 7 to 11 (10.30 Sun). **Closed:** 25 Dec to 2 Jan. **Meals:** Set L £29.50 (2 courses) to £34.50, Set D £34.50 (2 courses) to £44.50. **Service:** 12.5%. **Details:** Cards accepted. 90 seats. Air-con. Separate bar. Wheelchair access. Music. Children allowed.

ALSO RECOMMENDED

▲ Ebury Wine Bar

139 Ebury Street, Belgravia, SW1W 9QU
Tel no: (020) 7730 5447
www.eburywinebar.co.uk
⊖ **Victoria**
Modern European

This bow-fronted Belgravia stalwart – open for more than 40 years – is an enduringly popular affair, its *trompe l'oeil* interior and enterprising wine list drawing a well-heeled crowd. The menu is an appealing mix of such dishes as home-cured gravad lax with dill mayonnaise (£7.50), while grilled halibut served with confit Mediterranean vegetables might head-up mains (£18.95) and the short grill section could feature calf's liver and bacon. Lime and lemon tart accompanied by a raspberry coulis (£5.50) might catch the eye at dessert. Wines come fashionably listed by style, with house from £13.50 and bags of choice by-the-glass. Closed Sun L.

▲ Mango Tree

46 Grosvenor Place, Belgravia, SW1X 7EQ
Tel no: (020) 7823 1888
www.mangotree.org.uk
⊖ **Victoria**
Thai

An auspicious Belgravia address and an upper-crust location behind Buckingham Palace set the scene for this swanky Thai restaurant. Inside, glittering minimalist design and no-expense-spared trappings provide the backdrop for intricate, beautifully presented food that mixes familiarity

with something more challenging. Dishes to look for include spiced grilled aubergine salad with crispy shallots (£6.80), yellow curry with monkfish and butterfish, and grilled lamb rack with sautéed mushrooms, kwo choi and nam jim sauce (£18.50). There are also interesting stir-fries, vegetables and noodle specialities, plus East-West desserts such as lychee and lime cheesecake with lychee jelly (£5.50). House wine is £19 (£5.25 a glass). Open all week. Related to Awana (see entry).

Bloomsbury

Cigala
Unbuttoned Spanish hangout
54 Lamb's Conduit Street, WC1N 3LW
Tel no: (020) 7405 1717
www.cigala.co.uk
⊖ **Holborn**
Spanish | £30
Cooking score: 1
V

There isn't a bullfighting poster or castanet in sight at this refreshingly unadorned Spanish hangout, but Cigala scores heavily with its spot-on Hispanic food. A menu of no-nonsense tapas is served in the boisterous downstairs bar, while the restaurant impresses with its more ambitious daily repertoire. Start with a plate of jamón de Teruel, grilled asparagus with Manchego cheese and truffle oil or Moorish aubergine salad (no doubt a throwback to Jakes Hodges' days at Moro). Two versions of paella are on show (try the peasant version with rabbit, chicken and black pudding); otherwise fill up with grilled leg of lamb, chickpeas and quince alioli or grilled sea bream with pea, broad bean and herb salad – but leave room for some traditional torrones. The fascinating list of all-Spanish wines and cracking sherries is well worth exploring; prices start at £15.25 (£3.95 a glass).

Chef/s: Jake Hodges. **Open:** Mon to Sat 12 to 10.45 (12.30 Sat), Sun 12.30 to 9.30. **Closed:** 24 to 26 Dec, 1 Jan, Easter Sun and Mon. **Meals:** alc (main courses £11 to £18). Set L £15 (2 courses) to £18. Tapas menu available. **Service:** 12.5% (optional).

Details: Cards accepted. 60 seats. 20 seats outside. Air-con. Separate bar. No music. Wheelchair access. Children's portions. Children allowed.

READERS RECOMMEND

Norfolk Arms
Gastropub
28 Leigh Street, Bloomsbury, WC1H 9EP
Tel no: 020 7388 3937
www.norfolkarms.co.uk
'Modern English food and tapas'

Patisserie Deux Amis
French
63 Judd Street, Bloomsbury, WC1H 9QT
Tel no: 020 7383 7029
'Wide range of delicious baked goods'

▮ Chinatown

Fung Shing
Quality Cantonese
15 Lisle Street, WC2H 7BE
Tel no: (020) 7437 1539
www.fungshing.co.uk
⊖ Leicester Square
Chinese | £31
Cooking score: 2

V

There may be no shortage of eating options in Chinatown, but Fung Shing has for many years represented a beacon of quality among the bargain basements and ten-minute noodle bars around it. In one sense, the menu may look formula Cantonese, but the standard of ingredients and the care taken in cooking and seasoning are what elevate it above the norm. Among favourite dishes are crispy prawns with chilli and garlic, sizzling chicken with ginger and spring onion, Singapore noodles and – naturally – sweet-and-sour pork, but the intrepid might investigate stir-fried pigeon, curried crab or stir-fried eel in a basket. Tables are smart, staff are helpful, and the lengthy wine list gives the lie to those who imagine that Chinese restaurants don't necessarily take wine that seriously. House wines are £15.
Chef/s: Frank Cheung. **Open:** all week, 12 to 11.30. **Closed:** Christmas. **Meals:** alc (main courses £8 to £30). Set L and D £18 to £36 (min 2 people). **Service:** 10%. **Details:** Cards accepted. 100 seats. Air-con. Music. Children allowed.

★NEW ENTRY★
Haozhan
New-wave Chinese raising the bar
8 Gerrard Street, W1D 5PJ
Tel no: (020) 7434 3838
www.haozhan.co.uk
⊖ Leicester Square
Chinese | £30
Cooking score: 3

The received opinion is that if you want interesting Chinese food in London, avoid Chinatown, especially Gerrard Street. So it's good to see a new-wave Chinese bucking the trend. The interior is clean and contemporary and the surprisingly short menu mostly Cantonese with styles borrowed from Japan, Malaysia and Vietnam (very good, delicately cooked Thai-style gai lan, say, and the odd Malaysaian curry). This is an interesting little restaurant in any language. Jasmine ribs are meaty and tender, deep-fried (but greaseless) curry soft-shell crab 'excellent' and unusual Marmite prawns have an 'edgy and subtle flavour'. Not all dishes are 'as good as the kitchen intended', but standouts have included Szechuan soup, a glorious crispy quail with chilli and salt, and a hotpot of braised aubergine and minced pork with silky, creamy home-made tofu. Skip dessert. Service is unsmiling, while wines are a mixed bunch, ranging from £11 to a short list of reserve vintages at overstated prices.
Chef/s: Chee Loong Cheong. **Open:** all week, 12 to 11.30 (12 Fri and Sat, 11 Sun). **Closed:** 24 and 25 Dec. **Meals:** alc (main courses from £8.50 to £19). **Service:** 10% (optional). **Details:** Cards accepted. 75 seats. Children allowed.

Mr Kong
Rising from the ashes
21 Lisle Street, WC2H 7BA
Tel no: (020) 7437 7341
⊖ Leicester Square
Chinese | £20
Cooking score: 3

£30

Fans of this long-standing Chinatown stalwart will be pleased to hear that, following refurbishment after a kitchen fire, it re-opened in January 2008 offering the same high-quality cooking from a mix of classic Cantonese and more unusual specials. Sweet and sour pork and crispy aromatic duck are there for those that want them, but clued-up diners head straight to the separate menu of specials. At inspection, 'sandstorm' prawns – a huge pile of prawns under an avalanche of golden fried garlic and tongue-prickingly hot chillies – and a deeply savoury dish of duck wrapped with yam both impressed. Readers single out for praise the crispy salt, pepper and chilli quail – 'possibly the best dish I've eaten in the last couple of years' – as well soft-shell crab followed by pork and garlic sprouts: 'wonderfully delicious and authentic'. It's not just the quality of cooking that separates Mr Kong from its nearby rivals: staff are notably friendly, especially the manager, who chats happily to regulars and takes time to play with customers' kids. House wine is £9.50.
Chef/s: K Kong. **Open:** all week 12 to 2.45am. **Closed:** 2 days Christmas. **Meals:** alc (main courses £6.90 to £28). Set menu £10 (2 courses) to £17.80 (4 courses). **Service:** 10%. **Details:** Cards accepted. 110 seats. Air-con. Music. Children allowed.

Readers recommend

A 'readers recommend' review is a genuine quote from a report sent in by one of our readers. We intend to follow up these suggestions throughout the year to come.

▌ Covent Garden
L'Atelier de Joël Robuchon
Showcase for a French superstar
13-15 West Street, WC2H 9NE
Tel no: (020) 7010 8600
www.joel-robuchon.com
⊖ Leicester Square
French | £80
Cooking score: 6

One of the first to lead the ongoing cross-Channel charge of superstar French chefs, Joël Robuchon (named 'chef of the century' in his home country) decided to set out his London stall in this three-tier Covent Garden pleasuredome. Those who fancy getting up close and personal with the movers and shakers should head for the ground-floor L'Atelier, which is laid out like a sushi bar with stools lined up along the counter, modish red and black colour schemes and a menu of exquisite, jewel-like 'tasters'. Robuchon's signature dish – a pair of miniature beef and foie gras burgers with caramelised bell peppers – never fails to wow, but it's closely challenged by the likes of sautéed squid with baby artichoke, chorizo and tomato water or single scallops cooked in their shells with seaweed butter. Indeed, the truffle mash is worth the trip alone. A more conventional carte is available in the first-floor dining room (La Cuisine), which offers similar dishes in a less animated, monochrome setting. Here you might also find red mullet 'en pissaladière' with citrus dressing or roast milk-fed rib of veal with ratte potatoes and olives, plus eye-popping desserts including the 'snow white' (black truffle ice cream, caramel and ginger cream and crisp butterscotch biscuits). Prices will take your breath away, although the set lunch and pre-theatre menus offer some monetary relief. The monumental wine list matches prestigious French names with contributions from the New World; expect to pay upwards of £20 a bottle.
Chef/s: Frederic Simonin. **Open:** all week L 12 to 2.30, D 5.30 to 11.30 (10 Sun). **Meals:** alc (main courses £12 to £45). Set L £19 (2 courses) to £25. Set

D 5.30 to 6.30 £27 (2 courses) to £35.
Service: 12.5%. **Details:** Cards accepted. 101 seats.
Air-con. Separate bar. Wheelchair access. Music.
Children allowed.

Axis at One Aldwych
Keep it British, keep it simple
Aldwych, WC2B 4BZ
Tel no: (020) 7300 0300
www.onealdwych.com
⊖ Covent Garden
Modern British | £35
Cooking score: 3

A spiral staircase sweeps down to the high-ceilinged dining room where a slick modern makeover delivers waves of sea green silk cascading down walls, a screen of slender metal tree trunks, and leather armchairs that qualify for the most comfortable in town. The modern British menu reads simply and enticingly, and delivers the flavours it promises with creditable panache, say a classic Cheddar Gorge cheese soufflé with Russet apple chutney, or a modish pairing of smoked eel with marinated beetroot and crispy pork. Main courses are equally straightforward, say rump and kidney of Herdwick lamb with roast salsify and sautéed mushrooms or wild garlic and leek risotto. If the pricey carte is beyond your budget, the set-price menu (lunchtime and pre/post theatre) is very good value considering the smart theatreland location, and level of cooking: white bean soup with smoked bacon, slow-cooked pork with Puy lentils and apple, then sticky toffee parfait, all for £17.50. Although wine prices are highish, there's a good selection by-the-glass from £4.50.
Chef/s: Tony Fleming. **Open:** Mon to Fri L 12 to 2.30,
D Mon to Sat D 5.45 to 10.45 (11.30 Sat). **Meals:** alc
(main courses £16 to £23) Set L and D £15.50 (2
courses) to £17.50. **Service:** not inc. **Details:** Cards
accepted. 110 seats. Air-con. Separate bar.
Wheelchair access. Music. Children allowed.

Café du Jardin
Theatreland stalwart
28 Wellington Street, WC2E 7BD
Tel no: (020) 7836 8769/8760
www.lecafedujardin.com
⊖ Covent Garden
Modern European | £28
Cooking score: 2

The two-storey corner site in the heart of Covent Garden's theatreland shows higher ambition than most nearby eating places and draws a mature clientele including many tourists. The street-level, conservatory-style area is the best spot, with big picture windows giving views of street action, and front-of-house is capable of getting you out in time for the show 'in a relaxed way'. The cooking style is all-embracing. A twice-baked soufflé of courgette is counterpointed with strong Blackstick Blue cheese. Monkfish, too, makes an impact, teamed with shrimp in a Thai green curry, while honey-glazed duck confit comes with turnips tossed in palm sugar and soy. To round things off there are classic confections such as lemon tart and crème brûlée. A thoroughly commendable wine list has been assembled which mixes and matches an international bunch, opening with a couple of vin du pays at £12.50.
Chef/s: Tony Howorth. **Open:** all week L 12 to 3, D
5.30 to 12 (12 to 11 Sun). **Closed:** 24 and 25 Dec.
Meals: alc (main courses £14 to £17). Set menu L
and pre/post theatre D £13.50 (2 courses) to £16.50.
Service: 15% (optional). **Details:** Cards accepted.
100 seats. 20 seats outside. Air-con. Wheelchair
access. Children allowed.

Le Deuxième

Buzzing brasserie
65A Long Acre, WC2E 9JH
Tel no: (020) 7379 0033
www.ledeuxieme.com
⊖ Covent Garden
Modern European | £30
Cooking score: 2

Smaller but just as bustling as nearby big brother Café du Jardin (see previous entry), this dependable brasserie feels like the pulse of Covent Garden, particularly on a Saturday night. In addition to a range of fixed-price deals, the menu offers a crowd-pleasing selection of modern European brasserie food such as warm salad of smoked bacon, black pudding and potato with soft-boiled egg, then perhaps rump of lamb with couscous, baba ganoush and high-octane chilli oil or côte de boeuf with pommes allumettes and béarnaise. Warm chocolate fondant with milk ice cream, and sticky toffee pudding find their place at dessert stage. Sound ingredients, unpretentious cooking and attentive, friendly service hit the mark, while the wine list is as fine a monument to good drinking at fair prices as at Café du Jardin. House selections start at £14.50. (The Forge at 14 Garrick Street, WC2 is from the same stable).
Chef/s: Simon Conboy. **Open:** Mon to Fri L 12 to 3, D 5 to 12, Sat 12 to 12, Sun 12 to 11. **Closed:** 24 and 25 Dec. **Meals:** Set L and pre/post theatre D £13.50 (2 courses) to £16.50 (served all day Sun). **Service:** 15% (optional). **Details:** Cards accepted. 60 seats. Air-con. Wheelchair access. Children allowed.

Great Queen Street

Short, punchy menus, great atmosphere
32 Great Queen Street, WC2B 5AA
Tel no: (020) 7242 0622
⊖ Covent Garden
British | £22
Cooking score: 4

Tom Norrington-Davies's brand of bare boards clattering, no-frills décor and scrupulously seasonal menus owes more than a nod to the pioneering work done by its older sibling the Anchor & Hope in Waterloo (see entry). Great Queen Street is more of a modern Brit brasserie than a pub, though, and bookings are taken – in fact they are a must – but it delivers a similarly clamorous atmosphere. Short menus change daily with crab on toast and Middle White terrine typical of the simple, big-on-flavour starters. At inspection, a venison pie for two was quite simply one of the most perfect examples one could wish for – meat falling apart in a deep, rich sauce with a moreish crust. One reader initially expressed disappointment at the size of the chocolate pot, only to go on to describe 'every spoonful' as 'a mini moment'. The wine list offers a dozen or so by the glass, several by the magnum and has majors in France and Italy; prices start at a very reasonable £12. However, more than one reporter has taken issue with wines under £20 being served in small tumblers instead of the proper wine glasses produced for the upper-level wines; comments on service are also mixed.
Chef/s: Tom Norrington-Davies. **Open:** Mon D 5 to 12, Tue to Sat 11am to 12 (midnight). **Closed:** Christmas, New Year, bank hols. **Meals:** alc (main courses £12 to £22). **Service:** not inc. **Details:** Cards accepted. 60 seats. 8 seats outside. Separate bar. Wheelchair access. Children allowed.

Average price

The average price listed in main-entry reviews denotes the price of a three-course meal, without wine.

Incognico

Dependable cooking in theatreland
117 Shaftesbury Avenue, WC2H 8AD
Tel no: (020) 7836 8866
www.incognico.com
⊖ Leicester Square
Modern European
Cooking score: 2

Incognico seems to have been whisked from a street corner in Paris or Florence. Inside, dark wood panelling, gold-tiled ceiling and vintage mirrors exude a relaxing, clubby ambience – you find yourself slipping into the reddish brown leather chairs to watch the commotion outside. With easy access to London's theatreland, the details appear right, but Incognico has, in recent time, become less a destination restaurant and more a venue that people visit if they are in the area. This may be due to the intense competition around and the high pricing policy here. The appealing brasserie menu keeps strictly to the basics: a tian of crab with avocado dressed with olive oil and lemon is a pleasant but undemanding start, and roast sea bass arrives with crushed potatoes, olives and pesto – an accurate but predictable combination. Service is efficient but impassive at times. Wines are arranged by grape variety, heavily European, with prices from £18.50 right up to £1,950 for a 1937 Chateau Yquem. Our questionnaire was not returned, so the following information may have changed.
Chef/s: Dafydd Watkin. **Open:** Mon to Sat L 12 to 3, D 5.30 to 11. **Meals:** alc (main courses £12.50 to £18.50). **Service:** 12.5%. **Details:** 85 seats.

Symbols

🛏 Accommodation is available.

£30 Three courses for less than £30.

V More than five vegetarian dishes.

£5 OFF £5-off voucher scheme.

🍾 Notable wine list.

The Ivy

Gold-dust theatreland ticket
1-5 West Street, WC2H 9NQ
Tel no: (020) 7836 4751
www.the-ivy.co.uk
⊖ Leicester Square
Modern British
Cooking score: 3

Though eclipsed in the celebrity stakes by sister restaurant Scott's , this theatreland classic continues to play to packed houses. Regulars keep coming back in their droves for the surefire mix of upbeat atmosphere, slick service and consistently well-prepared food. One reader commented, 'It's not as snooty as you'd think'. It's comfort food in the truest sense (eggs Benedict, corned beef hash, salmon fishcakes or shepherd's pie), and the menu changes infrequently, not because the kitchen is lazy but because dishes have been perfected with repetition. Bang-bang chicken and crispy duck and watercress salad are among the perennial starters, followed by menu mainstays such as pan-fried skate wing with soft roes and brown shrimps or roast Landes chicken with Madeira jus and dauphinois potatoes. Elsewhere are soups and pasta for lighter appetites, and the iconic Scandinavian iced berries with hot white chocolate sauce for pudding. Given the plum location just off Shaftesbury Avenue and the low-key glitz of the surroundings (stained glass, wood panelling, leather banquettes), prices are surprisingly reasonable – though a wine list with a preference for French classics is not somewhere to search for a bargain, with slim pickings under £30; a dozen are served by the glass.
Chef/s: Alan Bird and Gary Lee. **Open:** all week L 12 to 3 (3.30 Sun), D 5.30 to 12. **Closed:** 25 and 26 Dec, 1 Jan, Aug bank hol. **Meals:** alc (main courses £11.50 to £39.50). **Service:** not inc. **Details:** Cards accepted. 100 seats. Air-con. No music. No mobile phones. Wheelchair access. Children's portions.

J. Sheekey
Seafood restaurant of the old school
28-32 St Martin's Court, WC2N 4AL
Tel no: (020) 7240 2565
www.j-sheekey.co.uk
⊖ Leicester Square
Modern Seafood | £48
Cooking score: 4
V

Much about J. Sheekey's feels old-fashioned, but then there has been a restaurant on this central site since 1896. It maintains a congenial atmosphere in the series of intimate, clubby rooms and offers a menu reliant on a well-practiced repertoire, the gamut running from crab pâté via leek and smoked haddock tart to pan-fried skate wing with brown buter and capers, and Bramley apple and butterscotch crumble. Good raw materials are more often than not improved by the treatment they receive – pan-fried fillet of plaice with surf clams and shrimps, for example, or roasted mixed shellfish with sea purslane and garlic butter – but on the downside flavours don't always pack a punch. Service is friendly and well-drilled. There's good drinking on a wine list that favours France, though prices play a part in bumping up the final bill. House wines from £17.75.

Cooking score

A score of 1 is a significant achievement. The score in any review is based on several meals, incorporating feedback from both our readers and inspectors. As a rough guide, 1 denotes capable cooking with some inconsistencies, rising steadily through different levels of technical expertise, until the scores between 6 and 10 indicate exemplary skills, along with innovation, artistry and ambition. If there is a new chef, we don't score the restaurant for the first year of entry. For further details, please see the scoring section in the introduction to the Guide.

Chef/s: Martin Dickinson. **Open:** all week L 12 to 3, D 5.30 to 12 (6 to 11 Sun). **Closed:** 25 and 26 Dec, 1 Jan. **Meals:** alc (main courses £12.75 to £39.50). **Service:** 12.5%. **Details:** Cards accepted. 100 seats. Air-con. Separate bar. No music. No mobile phones. Children allowed.

Rules
Traditional British repertoire
35 Maiden Lane, WC2E 7LB
Tel no: (020) 7836 5314
www.rules.co.uk
⊖ Covent Garden
British | £43
Cooking score: 3
£5 OFF

Established by Thomas Rule in 1798, during the reign of George III, this old stager is the longest-running restaurant in the capital. Now embarked on its third century of feeding and watering the theatre-goers and habitués of Covent Garden, it caters to a pleasingly diverse clientele with little or nothing of the stuffiness the clubby décor might lead you to fear. Service can be a little disjointed during very busy sessions, but the food is as pleasingly patriotic as can be. Coronation chicken terrine, cold Hebridean salmon with potato salad and summer pudding with clotted cream could be one route through; dressed Dorset crab with lemon mayonnaise, steak, kidney and oyster pudding with runner beans and treacle sponge with custard another. The seasonal game in the autumn months remains a delight, the crème brûlée gets rave reviews and London tap water is urged upon you as an alternative to marked-up mineral water by the bottle. Wines are mostly French, with particular attention paid to rich Rhône reds, and start at £21 a bottle, £13.95 for a half-litre jug, or £6.95 for a large glass.
Chef/s: Richard Sawyer. **Open:** all week, 12 noon to midnight. **Closed:** Christmas. **Meals:** alc (main courses £17.95 to £24.50). **Service:** 12.5%. **Details:** Cards accepted. 98 seats. Air-con. Separate bar. No music. No mobile phones. Wheelchair access. Children's portions.

ALSO RECOMMENDED
▲ Bedford and Strand
1a Bedford Street, Covent Garden, WC2E 9HH
Tel no: (020) 7836 3033
www.bedford-strand.com
⊖ Covent Garden
Modern European

This artfully styled bar, wine room and bistro is a real one-off. Owned by a team of young wine enthusiasts, it has an inspiring drinks list and a nostalgic, straight-talking menu. Start with chicken liver pâté with sourdough toast and pickles (£5), English asparagus with a poached egg or steak tartare, then move on to omelette Arnold Bennett (£13.50), home-made pork and leek sausages with mashed potato and caramelised onion gravy or braised oxtail with horseradish mash and spring greens. There's also a deli counter offering cheeses and tapas-style small dishes. Wines start at £19.50 a bottle. Open all week.

▲ Mon Plaisir
21 Monmouth Street, Covent Garden, WC2H 9DD
Tel no: (020) 7836 7243
French

As indelibly French as restaurants get, Mon Plaisir remains a beacon of Gallic charm amid the bustle of the West End. A brasserie menu is now available in the afternoons, and the pre-theatre deal is handy too. Pâté en croûte made with venison and Armagnac (£8.95) is a typical starter, while mains offer roast cod with Parmesan velouté and basil gnocchi (£15.95) or duck magret with baby carrots and and spiced pear chutney. Veg are charged extra

Please send us your feedback

To register your opinion about any restaurant listed in the Guide, or a new restaurant that you wish to bring to our attention, please visit the web address at the bottom of the page. Your feedback informs the content of the book and will be used to compile next year's reviews.

and you might end, if you've time, with warm chocolate mousse served with passion fruit sorbet (£7.50). Wines start at £12.75.

READERS RECOMMEND
Christopher's
North American
18 Wellington Street, Covent Garden, WC2E 7DD
Tel no: (020) 7240 4222
www.christophersgrill.com
'American cuisine with a point to prove'

Clos Maggiore
Modern European
33 King Street, Covent Garden, WC2E 8JD
Tel no: 020 7379 9696
www.closmaggiore.com
'A touch of the mediterranean in Covent Garden'

▮ Fitzrovia
Fino
Tapas in style
33 Charlotte Street (entrance in Rathbone Street), W1T 1RR
Tel no: (020) 7813 8010
www.finorestaurant.com
⊖ Tottenham Court Road, Goodge Street
Spanish | £30
Cooking score: 2

Turn off Charlotte Street into Rathbone Street to find the discreet entrance to this stylish basement tapas bar. While the Hart brothers' Barrafina (see entry) captures the fast-paced buzz of a genuine tapas bar in Barcelona or Madrid, Fino has a more restrained feel, with less clatter and more formality from waiters as they deliver all manner of dishes to your table. Expect to graze your way through an extensive menu that ranges from crab croquetas via cod bilbaina and arroz negro (black rice), through crisp pork belly or morcilla and duck egg, to milk-fed lamb cutlets and a selection of tortillas (something of a signature at both Hart operations). In addition, foie gras with chilli jam and stuffed courgette flowers add an international flavour to the mainly classic Spanish choices. The all-Spanish wine list opens at £16. Our questionnaire was not returned, so some of the information below may have changed.

Chef/s: Nieves Barragan. **Open:** Mon to Sat L 12 to 2.30, D 6 to 10.30. **Closed:** Christmas, bank hols. **Meals:** alc (tapas £5.50 to £19.70). **Service:** 12.5% (optional). **Details:** Cards accepted. 90 seats. Air-con. No music. Wheelchair access. Children allowed.

Hakkasan
Chinese dining on a grand scale
8 Hanway Place, W1T 1HD
Tel no: (020) 7927 7000
⊖ **Tottenham Court Road**
Chinese | £50
Cooking score: 5
🍾

Hakkasan founder Alan Yau sold his share in the restaurant (and sister dim sum emporium Yauatcha) for £30 million in January 2008, but his ongoing presence as a consultant should ensure that standards remain high at this beacon of upmarket oriental dining. Comparisons with standard Chinese restaurants are facile; Hakkasan offers event dining on a grand scale, from the secretive location down an alley behind Tottenham Court Road to an entrance guarded by a bouncer, and the dining room itself, a moodily-lit basement divided by fretwork screens that, in the evening, can feel very much like eating in a nightclub (an effect enhanced by cocktail-swigging barflies and very high noise levels. Ingredients are top-drawer and the cooking style modern and creative. A meal might start with roasted mango duck with lemon sauce ahead of roasted silver cod with Champagne and Chinese honey or grilled lamb chop with sour plum sauce, with perhaps some stir-fried water chestnut with sugarsnap peas and cloud ear mushrooms on the side. Prices, unsurprisingly, are very high; for a much cheaper (and more relaxed) experience, come for lunchtime dim sum, when it's possible to escape for £20 a head if you stick to drinking

tea. At inspection, prawn har gau and pan-fried turnip cake were textbook versions of classic dishes, while baked Thai spring onion puffs, lamb cheung fun and baked venison puffs were successful twists on the dim sum repertoire. The global wine list is an eye-opening exploration of how Chinese food can be matched to wine, grouped under unusual headings such as 'biodynamics: spiritual wines' and 'curious vines: distinctive wines', with plenty of interest around the £30 mark; ten are available by-the-glass.

Chef/s: Tong Chee Hwee. **Open:** all week L 12 to 2.45 (4 Sat and Sun), D 6 to 12 (12.30 Sat and Sun). **Closed:** 24 and 25 Dec. **Meals:** Set menus £55 to £108. **Service:** 13% (optional). **Details:** Cards accepted. 230 seats. Air-con. Separate bar. Wheelchair access. Music. Children allowed.

Latium
Chic, creative Italian
21 Berners Street, W1T 3LP
Tel no: (020) 7323 9123
www.latiumrestaurant.com
⊖ **Goodge Street**
Italian | £30
Cooking score: 2
£5 OFF

The specialities of the Lazio region around Rome are the draw at Maurizio Morelli and Claudio Pulze's chic Italian restaurant in the area to the north of Oxford Street. A recent refurbishment has added a fresh, relaxing feel to the place, and there is now a chef's table for up to six people. Ravioli is a favourite medium and has its own menu of starters and mains, in which the little parcels may encase anything from mixed fish with sea bass bottarga to oxtail with celery sauce. Elsewhere there may be offerings such as stewed baby octopus with chickpeas and Savoy cabbage, followed by poached guinea fowl with black truffle, sprouting broccoli and baby vegetables. Ravioli also crop up at dessert stage, filled perhaps with apple, pine nuts and raisins, served on vanilla sauce. Gelati, sorbetti and tiramisu are all on hand for those who want to stay in more familiar territory. Apart from Champagnes, the wine list is all Italian, and usefully gathers up some fine growers. Prices open at £14.50.

Chef/s: Maurizio Morelli. **Open:** Mon to Fri L 12 to 3, Mon to Sat D 6.30 to 10.30 (11.30 Sat). **Meals:** Set L £19.50. Set D £28.50. **Service:** 12.5%. **Details:** Cards accepted. 50 seats. Air-con. Wheelchair access. Music. Children's portions.

Passione

Sassy southern-Italian food
10 Charlotte Street, W1T 2LT
Tel no: (020) 7636 2833
www.passione.co.uk
⊖ Goodge Street
Italian | £50
Cooking score: 4

Gennaro Contaldo's intimate but big-hearted restaurant aptly embraces the man's devotion to his native Italian food. The simple, modern regional cooking is rustic and flavour-driven, using seasonal and wild produce (sorrel, rocket, fungi), while bread and pasta are made daily. The surroundings – dark-wood floors, lightwood chairs and foodie photos – are clean-edged, upbeat and convivial. Expect tagliatelle with mushrooms and truffle, or perhaps grilled and pan-fried veal teamed with asparagus and celeriac in thyme. Elsewhere, there could be pan-fried fillet of halibut in a herb crust with Jerusalem artichoke purée and green beans. Desserts might feature a cold rhubarb mousse with rhubarb sauce, or maybe the signature gelato passione (limoncello and wild strawberry ice cream). Gennaro's suitably patriotic all-Italian wine list starts at £15.50, but there's little choice by-the-glass.

Chef/s: Gennaro Contaldo. **Open:** Mon to Fri L 12.30 to 2.15, Mon to Sat D 7 to 10.15. **Closed:** 23 Dec to 2 Jan. **Meals:** alc (main courses £21 to £26). **Service:** 12.5%. **Details:** Cards accepted. 40 seats. Separate bar. Children's portions.

★ READERS' RESTAURANT OF THE YEAR ★
LONDON

Pied-à-Terre

One of London's best
34 Charlotte Street, W1T 2NH
Tel no: (020) 7636 1178
www.pied-a-terre.co.uk
⊖ Goodge Street
French | £65
Cooking score: 8

'A small but precise restaurant' writes a reporter striving to characterise the beguiling interior of this artfully designed restaurant. Mirrors, careful lighting and a large skylight ease any feeling that this could be a cramped space. Enthusiasm for the food is universal: 'certainly one of London's best', observes more than one contributor. Shane Osborn's cooking is inventive yet simple, exciting yet carefully controlled for flavour and texture. Thinly sliced marinated raw scallop and wafers of crunchy Jerusalem artichoke, for example, are interspersed with slivers of black truffle and baby rocket and matched with a dollop of mellow brandade mousse. Steamed and roasted breast of pigeon comes with a robust sausage made of the leg meat and is teamed with chickpeas, chorizo and red pepper oil – it's a dish whose marriage of flavours takes in sweet, fatty, bitter, salt and fruity. Or witness a set lunch of fried smoked eel and haricots blancs in a 'lovely, foamy sauce', its counterpart a Jerusalem artichoke risotto with black truffle and slivers of seared foie gras, followed by roast partridge breast and confit leg – 'as good a meal as I have eaten in London – or anywhere'. Fine judgment is applied to desserts, which can achieve a simplicity that belies the effort that created them, viz. a pre-dessert of walnut soup and passion fruit mousse or a dessert proper of blood orange jelly with a fromage blanc mousse, topped with poached clementine and served with mint ice cream. 'Exquisite' canapés provide an auspicious start, and petits fours 'finish on a high note'. Care and attention to detail are second to none, and there is nothing complacent about the smooth-running operation; the wine service in particular is highly knowledgeable. This is just as well, as a treasure trove of a wine list is on hand. The main list hoves into view with pedigree selections from the French regions, but turns up interesting bottles from around the globe; prices start at £22, £6 by-the-glass.

Chef/s: Shane Osborn. **Open:** Mon to Fri L 12.15 to 2.30, Mon to Sat D 6.15 to 11. **Meals:** Menu du jour £24 (2 courses) to £30, Tasting menu £80. **Service:** 12.5% (optional). **Details:** Cards accepted. 40 seats. Air-con. Wheelchair access. Music.

Roka

Stylish Japanese food
37 Charlotte Street, W1T 1RR
Tel no: (020) 7580 6464
www.rokarestaurant.com
⊖ Goodge Street
Japanese | £25
Cooking score: 4

V

This bustling younger sibling of Zuma (see entry) occupies a corner site in the heart of London's media district. The interior is a study in stylish simplicity, and draws inspiration from the traditional Japanese izakaya, with chefs busily working on the spectacular robata charcoal grill. Their presence adds to the vibrancy and authenticity of the experience, as does the erudite, willing service. The menu includes sushi and sashimi, warm bites and salads, roka dishes and, of course, offerings from the grill. You could kick off with maki rolls, whose fillings range from simple cucumber or avocado to crispy prawn, avocado, chilli, chrysanthemum and dark sweet soy. Next, look to the grill for dishes such as scallop skewers with wasabi and shiso or black cod marinated in yusu miso and home-made hajikami. The 'warm bites and salads' selection runs from lobster and abalone dumplings to grilled vegetables and lemon miso dressing. For dessert, perhaps green apple and shochu sorbet with lemon yuzu jelly or banana and green tea steamed cream with tonka bean ice cream. Wines start at £21.

Chef/s: Hamish Brown. **Open:** all week L 12 to 3.30 (12.30 to 3.30 Sat and Sun), D 5.30 to 11.30 (10.30 Sun). **Closed:** 25 Dec, 1 Jan. **Meals:** Tasting menu £50 (12 dishes). **Service:** 12.5%. **Details:** Cards accepted. 88 seats. 20 seats outside. Air-con. Separate bar. Wheelchair access. Music.

Salt Yard

Classic tapas with a sophisticated edge
54 Goodge Street, W1T 4NA
Tel no: (020) 7637 0657
www.saltyard.co.uk
⊖ Goodge Street
Mediterranean | £35
Cooking score: 2

There's an appealing casual vibe to this modern tapas joint that seems true to the original Spanish ethos. Classic tapas gets a sophisticated and contemporary re-fashioning, so that roasted chorizo comes spiked with Moscatel vinegar, while croquettes are richly stuffed either with morcilla or Cornish crab and chilli. Elsewhere are dishes that are effectively miniature main courses – roasted organic chicken leg with potato gnocchi, new season garlic and fresh sorrel, say, while vegetable options include the best thing on the menu, the signature dish of courgette flowers stuffed with Monte Enebro cheese and drizzled with honey. Wine is an integral part of the experience, whether something interesting from Italy or one of eight sherries (all available by-the-glass). Occasionally Salt Yard's faults – prices for small plates that easily stack up, a charmless basement that lacks the verve of the ground floor, and staff eager to turn tables – are hard to swallow. The no-bookings Dehesa in Soho (see entry), is the latest venture.

Chef/s: Ben Tish. **Open:** Mon to Fri 12 to 11, Sat D 5 to 11. **Closed:** banks hols, Christmas. **Meals:** Set menu £25 to £30. **Service:** 12.5% (optional). **Details:** Cards accepted. 64 seats. 6 seats outside. Air-con. Separate bar. Wheelchair access. Music. Children allowed.

Sardo

Faithful family-run Sardinian
45 Grafton Way, W1T 5DQ
Tel no: (020) 7387 2521
www.sardo-restaurant.com
⊖ **Warren Street**
Italian | £30
Cooking score: 4

Londoners in the know have long been getting their fix of sunny Sardinia at Sardo, a faithful family-run outfit offering fresh flavours of the southern Med: from plump Italian olives and carta di musica (flatbread with olive oil and salt) to a dessert of sebadas (flaky puff pastry filled with sweet cheese and topped with honey) via several tasty courses in between. Grilled, tender baby squid stuffed with calamari and topped with a tasty tomato sauce kicks of a meal with a summery burst of flavours, though the pastas steal the show – say, spaghetti tossed with olive oil and red mullet roe, which emulsifies into a creamy, delicately fishy sauce. Simple but vibrant flavours and an emphasis on good-quality ingredients maintain the momentum in main courses such as seared tuna steak with rocket and cherry tomatoes on the vine, or salsiccia – a toothsome Sardinian sausage served with endive and potatoes. Warm surroundings are boosted by charming service and while it may not be cheap, it's certainly worth the taste of Sardinia without the airfare. A lovely Italian wine list, too, with prime Sardinian grapes headlining. House wines from £14.
Chef/s: Roberto Sardu. **Open:** Mon to Fri L 12 to 3, Mon to Sat D 6 to 11. **Meals:** alc (main courses £12 to £16.50). **Service:** 12.5% (optional). **Details:** Cards accepted. Air-con. Wheelchair access. Music.

Readers recommend

A 'readers recommend' review is a genuine quote from a report sent in by one of our readers. We intend to follow up these suggestions throughout the year to come.

ALSO RECOMMENDED
▲ Camerino

16 Percy Street, Fitzrovia, W1T 1DT
Tel no: (020) 7637 9900
www.camerinorestaurant.com
⊖ **Tottenham Court Road, Goodge Street**
Italian

A light, breezy Italian just off Tottenham Court Road combining quirky design (lots of fuchsia and softer pink tones, with swirling murals on the walls) with well-crafted Italian food. Minestrone soup (£6.50) or calf's liver with pancetta and crispy sage (£14.50) bring a taste of traditional Italy, though the menu also boasts more contemporary creations such as open ravioli with seafood and cannellini beans and a dessert of basil pannacotta (£4.50). Service tends to be charming, though can occasionally falter. There is a well-priced set lunch menu (£15.50 for two courses), and the wine list roams Italy, with a Sicilian house white at £16.50 a bottle. Closed Sat L and Sun.

▲ Villandry

170 Great Portland Street, Fitzrovia, W1W 5QB
Tel no: (020) 7631 3131
www.villandry.com
⊖ **Great Portland Street**
Modern European

These days Villandry is more a restaurant-cum-bar than the fully-fledged food emporium it used to be, with smart, white-clad tables spilling out on to the street in fine weather and a strong line in takeaway meals for picnics or home consumption. Casual all-day dining ranges from coffee and croissants to chicken Caesar salad, with the lively bar serving food at lunch and dinner. The large restaurant at the back is mainly influenced by France and Italy: crudités with hot anchovy dip, spaghettini au pistou (£9) say, followed by cassoulet of duck confit (£17.50) and chargrilled calf's liver with creamed polenta, crispy pancetta and sauce diable. Finish with lemon tart (£5.75). House wine is £16.50. Closed Sun D.

READERS RECOMMEND

Pescatori

Seafood
57 Charlotte Street, Fitzrovia, W1T 4PD
Tel no: (020) 7580 3289
'Classy, modern Mediterranean seafood'

▌ Green Park

Greenhouse

A world away from busy Mayfair
27a Hays Mews, W1J 5NY
Tel no: (020) 7499 3331
www.greenhouserestaurant.co.uk
⊖ Green Park
Modern European | £60
Cooking score: 6

🍷 **V**

Recent refurbishment has softened and simplified this light, spacious dining room, reached via a canopied walkway through a garden of extravagant greenery. Soft-toned creams and greens create an effect that is smart and tranquil, a world away from busy Mayfair. Antonin Bonnet remains at the stoves and his modern European repertoire fits in perfectly, underpinned by classical themes and well-sourced produce. Menus are liberally sprinkled with luxury items, and adventurous ideas are enhanced on the plate by skilful cooking, fine presentation and interesting variations of flavour. For example, an opener of apple jelly filled with apple and celery juice contrasts well with a crisp 'cigar' of carrot filled with coconut espuma, while the freshness of sea urchin and crab is pointed by an intense konbu jelly, bringing 'Japanese flavours to mind'. Another element at work is the comfort factor, which produces milk-fed rump of veal with bitter praline, parsnip Chantilly and fresh morels, and classics like Dover sole meunière with truffled celery and celeriac rémoulade. The cheese trolley, with its perfect-condition French cheeses, may prove hard to resist, although desserts include 'snix', a chocolate, salted caramel and peanut deconstruction of a Snickers bar. With a sky's-the-limit budget, the wine list is magnificent, but mere mortals should explore the lower reaches of the impressive by-the-glass selection. House wine is £22.
Chef/s: Antonin Bonnet. **Open:** Mon to Sat L 12 to 2.30, D 6.45 to 11. **Closed:** Sun, Christmas, bank hols. **Meals:** Set L £29 to £60, Set D £60 to £70. **Service:** 12.5%. **Details:** Cards accepted. 70 seats. Air-con. Separate bar. No music. Wheelchair access. Children's portions.

ALSO RECOMMENDED

▲ Al Hamra

31–33 Shepherd Market, Green Park, W1J 7PT
Tel no: (020) 7493 1954
⊖ Green Park/Hyde Park Corner
Middle Eastern

Al Hamra has been a familiar presence on Shepherd Market since 1984. The lengthy classical Lebanese menu offers a familiar selection of hot and cold meze – say hummus with tahini (£4.75), tabbouleh, smoked cod's roe with garlic and olive oil, grilled halloumi cheese or aromatic spiced lamb sausages. In addition, there are the usual kebabs (from £15), chargrilled lamb cutlets and fillets (both £18.50) and baked Dover sole and everyday Lebanese desserts to finish. House wine is £15.

▌ Holborn

Chancery

Chic bolthole in lawyerland
9 Cursitor Street, EC4A 1LL
Tel no: (020) 7831 4000
www.thechancery.co.uk
⊖ Chancery Lane
Modern European | £34
Cooking score: 4

£5
OFF

Legal eagles from the chambers of Chancery Lane and Holborn take time out to support this discreet restaurant housed in one of the neighbourhood's lofty stone-faced buildings. Inside, the mood of chic, urbane exclusivity is enhanced by mahogany parquet floors, arches and displays of abstract artwork on brown walls. Andrew Thompson's food is suitably confident, attuned to the seasons and free-roaming in its intentions. Barbecued quail with pickled cabbage and chilli mayonnaise might appear as a starter alongside a potage of monkfish and oysters with noodles and herb oil, while main courses could see roast saddle of lamb served with tagliatelle, sweet pea and mint emulsion or almond-crusted duck breast in company with a fricassee of vegetables and honey mustard sauce. Desserts such as strawberry shortcake with Devon clotted cream or chocolate mousse with fresh cherries and white chocolate sauce ensure that meals end with familiar reassurance rather than edgy challenges. The neatly balanced global wine list is as crisply set out as the menu, promising sound drinking from well-regarded sources. House recommendations start at £16 (£5.50 a glass).

Chef/s: Andrew Thompson. **Open:** Mon to Fri L 12 to 2.30, D 6 to 10.30. **Closed:** Sat, Sun, bank hols, Christmas, New Year. **Meals:** Set L and D £14.50 (2 courses) to £34. **Service:** 12.5% (optional). **Details:** Cards accepted. 55 seats. Air-con. Separate bar. Wheelchair access. Music. Children's portions.

Matsuri High Holborn
Traditional Japanese dining
71 High Holborn, WC1V 6EA
Tel no: (020) 7430 1970
www.matsuri-restaurant.com
⊖ Holborn
Japanese | £45
Cooking score: 3

V

Chic contemporary Japanese design contributes to the relaxed feeling at the Holborn outpost of Matsuri, as does the unfailingly courteous service. The place boasts one of the longest sushi counters in the country, as well as simply set varnished wood tables for a choice of eating modes. Traditional Japanese fare is offered via a series of set menus, teppanyaki, sushi and a carte. Expect chawanmushi, dobinmushi (a clear soup of shrimp and vegetables) and lightly roasted beef tataki, as well as the less familiar likes of

stewed ox tongue in wholegrain mustard sauce, grilled foie gras topped with miso paste or grilled sea bream on a bed of Japanese 'ratatouille'. Maki roll options include soft-shell spider crab, eel and cucumber, and the delectable salmon skin. Ice creams and sorbets are the approved way to finish. A high-end wine list reflects the location is offered, with Burgundies and clarets in the expected profusion. House Chilean is £16, but the selection of sakés and Japanese liqueurs is where the real interest lies.

Chef/s: Hiroshi Sudo. **Open:** Mon to Sat L 12 to 2.30, D 6 to 10. **Closed:** Sun, Christmas and bank hols. **Meals:** alc (main courses £17 to £35). Set menus £25 to £70. **Service:** 12.5%. **Details:** Cards accepted. 117 seats. Air-con. Separate bar. No mobile phones. Wheelchair access. Music. Children allowed.

Pearl
Sound flavours and a stunning setting
252 High Holborn, WC1V 7EN
Tel no: (020) 7829 7000
www.pearl-restaurant.com
⊖ Holborn
Modern French | £50
Cooking score: 5

The marble banking hall of the one-time Pearl Assurance building makes a stunning setting for Pearl, creating a dramatic light-strewn bar (best seen in the evening) and handsome dining room. Recent reports suggest that the restaurant is 'on top form', offering 'a well-balanced package of elegant surrounds, professional service and accomplished cooking'. Jun Tanaka's sparely described menus can surprise with combinations like oxtail tortellini with parsnip purée, crisp oysters and ginger vinaigrette, but there are understated dishes too: braised monkfish teamed with gratinated razor clam and a tomato, black olive and onion tart, is more classically orientated. Presentation is as minutely considered as the surrounds seem to demand, and if the odd dish suffers from over-elaboration there is no questioning the soundness of flavours and combinations. Classy desserts include a well-

made Brillat Savarin cheesecake with a terrine of citrus fruits or a harmoniously balanced assemblage of apricot Bakewell tart and almond ice cream. The wine list has been a star from the word go and expert advice is on hand to guide diners through the list, whether matching a series of glasses (from £5.50) to your meal or helping to navigate the realms of top-class Bordeaux and Burgundy. There are a few budget options and house wine is £22.
Chef/s: Jun Tanaka. **Open:** Mon to Fri L 12 to 2.30, Mon to Sat D 6 to 10. **Closed:** Sun. **Meals:** Set L £29, Set D £50. **Service:** 12.5%. **Details:** Cards accepted. 72 seats. Air-con. Separate bar. Wheelchair access. Music. Children allowed.

White Swan
Part of a gastropub group
108 Fetter Lane, EC4A 1ES
Tel no: (020) 7242 9696
www.thewhiteswanlondon.com
⊖ Chancery Lane
Gastropub | £34
New Chef

Brothers Tom and Ed Martin have established a whole group of thriving London gastropubs (see also, for example, the Gun). This one is comprised of a cleanly restored ground-floor pub, a mezzanine level and a handsome first-floor dining room done in wood tones, with crisply dressed tables and a mirrored ceiling. Andy Storer has taken charge of the cooking since last year's Guide, but maintains the style of upbeat brasserie food that has previously drawn in the crowds. Smoked black pudding salad is garnished with quails' eggs and given a tarragon mustard dressing, freshwater eel is fashioned into a tian and tricked out with new potato, walnuts and horseradish. For mains, there could be sea bass with clams and pancetta or a serving of Gloucester Old Spot belly pork with puréed celeriac, sauced with cider and Calvados. Vegetable sides are extra, and you might finish with sticky toffee pudding with Earl Grey ice cream. An ample wine list commendably includes three pages of wines by-the-glass from £3.70. Bottles start at £14.

Chef/s: Andy Storer. **Open:** Mon to Fri L 12 to 3, D 6 to 10. **Closed:** Sat, Sun, Christmas and bank hols. **Meals:** alc. Set L £29. **Service:** 12.5%. **Details:** Cards accepted. 50 seats. 8 seats outside. Air-con. Separate bar. Music. Children's portions.

READERS RECOMMEND
The Bountiful Cow
Gastropub
51 Eagle Street, Holborn, WC1R 4AP
Tel no: (020) 7404 0200
'A pub renowned for its steaks'

Vivat Bacchus
Global
47 Farringdon Street, Holborn, EC4A 4LL
Tel no: (020) 7353 2648
www.vivatbacchus.co.uk
'Fine dining for real wine enthusiasts'

▌Hyde Park

★NEW ENTRY★
Alain Ducasse at The Dorchester
Unashamedly aristocratic French cooking
The Dorchester Hotel, 53 Park Lane, W1K 1QA
Tel no: (020) 7629 8866
www.alainducasse-dorchester.com
⊖ Hyde Park Corner
French | £75
Cooking score: 6

Although not the first restaurant for Alain Ducasse in London, this is the only one deemed important enough to bear his name, so expectations are high. In the spacious, though muted, dining room you do get to marvel at the starry fibre-optic threads shrouding the private table, but like everything here, this privacy comes at a hefty price. After an inauspicious start, standards have improved. Ducasse has devised a menu so retro that it could be an homage to Escoffier (think beef Rossini, duck à l'orange), and the kitchen is clearly focused on quality ingredients, prepared with clockwork precision. First up, spicy crab served in two parts – hot with its brown meat and an emulsion of chilli pepper, and cold with avocado and a crab gelée – then loin of veal from Limousin, paired with seasonal vegetables and braised lettuce. Dessert was an exquisite arrangement, a biscuit base with grenache, subtly infused with rose, interwoven between layers of white chocolate and raspberries (each one painstakingly filled with a drop of coulis made from the fruit)l elsewhere, the boozy rum baba is 'every bit as good as the one in Monte Carlo'. Breads, amuse-bouche and petits fours are made with real care – though oddly macaroons and dark chocolates arrive as pre-desserts. Service too has settled into the groove, and although some linguistic problems remain, you are looked after with exceptional hospitality. The wine list, with France taking centre stage and other countries appearing as extras, features an impressive collection from Domaine de la Romanée-Conti, and a 1985 Le Pin for £5,700. If you are looking for affordability, then the experience can be enervating with no wines listed by-the-glass, and prices accelerating from £25 with limited choices until you reach three figures.

Chef/s: Jocelyn Herland. **Open:** Tue to Sat L 12 to 2, D 6.30 to 10. **Closed:** Sun, Mon 10 to 31 Aug, 26 to 30 Dec. **Meals:** alc (£55 for 2 courses) to £75. Set L £35 (3 courses). **Service:** 12.5% (optional). **Details:** Cards accepted. 82 seats. Air-con. Wheelchair access.

Symbols

 Accommodation is available.

 Three courses for less than £30.

 V More than five vegetarian dishes.

 £5-off voucher scheme.

Notable wine list.

★NEW ENTRY★
China Tang at The Dorchester
Glitzy jet-set dining
The Dorchester Hotel, 53 Park Lane, W1K 1QA
Tel no: (020) 7629 8888
www.thedorchester.com
⊖ Hyde Park Corner
Chinese | £40
Cooking score: 2

 V

If looks alone could make a restaurant, China Tang would have nothing to worry about. A brainchild of David Tang, owner of the fashion house Shanghai Tang, it has quickly established itself on the jet-set's itinerary. Easy to see why, given the salubrious location – a subterranean space at the Dorchester Hotel, with a glittery dining room designed to resemble a 1920s cruise liner, flushed with silk embroidery covers, elegant lattice screens and glorious antiques. Service, on the other hand, is somewhat somnolent and lacking in charm. The menu does not stray beyond Cantonese, although Peking duck (£48) has received much praise. Pleasures are flickering; fried bean curd with spicy salt and pepper was exemplary, but the spell was broken by ordinary crispy rice noodles with pork, before roast duck in glass noodles restored proceedings. Desserts steer well away from the Orient, despite mangosteen making a brief appearance in a meringue. Highly respectable dim sum is an economical option at lunchtime. The wine list, focusing on prestige labels can easily burn a hole in your pocket, with no bottles under £29.

Chef/s: Ringo Chow. **Open:** all week, L 11 to 3.30 D 5.30 to 12. **Meals:** alc (main courses from £10 to £150). Set L £15 (2 courses). **Service:** 12.5%. **Details:** Cards accepted. 150 seats.

Also recommended

An 'also recommended' entry is not a full entry, but is provisionally suggested as an alternative to main entries.

Beer for dining

Ask for the beer list in many restaurants and the sommelier will start to smile...

Restaurants are realising that the quality of independent breweries around the globe and the fact that the UK has such a strong

brewing tradition means that beer is no longer seen as the uncouth younger brother of wine. Indeed, several beers make the perfect partner for certain foods. If you've never tried an IPA with spicy food, then you are missing out.

Brayside's **The Drunken Duck Inn** has a brewery on the premises and consequently has a range of several distinctive and impressive ales on offer for diners to match with their foods.

Pearl restaurant in London have produced an entire tasting menu where the food is paired with gourmet beers rather than wines.

Manchester's **Market Restaurant** located in the Northern Quarter have had a beer menu running to nearly 30 different beers for several years and serve the exquisite Deus for £26 a bottle.

Despite the wine-heavy leanings suggested by its name, there is an excellent range of beers on offer at Brighton's **Hotel Du Vin**.

Ever the pioneer, in 2006 Michel Roux Jr from **Le Gavroche** announced he was introducing a beer list which sent other London restaurants into a panic to assemble their own offerings.

Diners in Leeds' **Anthony's** Restaurant can enjoy the beer list that has been put together, including some terrific beers from US micro-breweries.

The sensational **London Carriage Works** at the Hope Street Hotel in Liverpool serve a Peroni Gran Riserva and winner of the title the world's best fruit beer: Cains' Raisin.

Grill at the Dorchester

Reborn Park Lane veteran
The Dorchester Hotel, 53 Park Lane, W1A 2HJ
Tel no: (020) 7629 8888
www.thedorchester.com
⊖ Hyde Park Corner
Modern British | £55
Cooking score: 5

Once a staunch bastion of smoked salmon and roast beef, the Dorchester's outdated Grill Room has shed its old skin – although it still shows a tendency for tartan overkill and baronial excesses (just look at those gaudy murals of swaggering Highland clansmen). Chef Aiden Byrne is the driving force behind the transformation: he is one of British gastronomy's ambitious risk-takers, although all that intricacy and embellishment is founded on true classic principles. Plain-speaking menus often conceal more than they reveal, but it's not difficult to be seduced by the intriguing prospect of salt cod mousse with pork belly and shrimp chorizo, chilled beetroot gazpacho with avocado sorbet and vodka jelly or roast squab pigeon with a smoked peanut crust. The kitchen's allegiance to the British larder is obvious across the board, from Denham Castle lamb with fennel risotto to poached West Coast turbot with razor clams, spring vegetables and lemon thyme butter. Elsewhere, Dover sole with béarnaise sauce is a remembrance of things past, although the Grill Room's much-lauded Angus beef now appears in a very different suit of clothes (perhaps with braised Devon snails, parsley pearl barley, bone marrow and smoked bacon as accessories). To finish, a sharp intake of breath may be required before ordering chocolate and cep mousse with grapefruit and chocolate gnocchi or considering the sanguine subtleties of red pepper cannelloni with strawberry parfait and roast strawberries. The blue-blooded wine list pulls no punches and it's not for the financially faint-hearted, although the section headed '30 under 30'

should fit the bill if money is an issue. France steals the limelight, with other big players from the wine world lending serious support.
Chef/s: Aiden Byrne. **Open:** all week L 12 to 2.30 (12.30 to 3 Sun), D 6.30 to 11 (6 to 11 Sat, 7 to 10 Sun). **Meals:** alc (main courses £19.50 to £42). Set L £25 (2 courses) to £27.50. **Service:** 12.5% (optional). **Details:** Cards accepted. 75 seats. Air-con. Separate bar. No music. Wheelchair access. Children's portions.

Mandarin Oriental, Foliage

Haute grazing with superb park view
66 Knightsbridge, SW1X 7LA
Tel no: (020) 7201 3723
www.mandarinoriental.com/london
⊖ Knightsbridge
Modern European | £60
Cooking score: 5

There's no doubt the painterly Georges Seaurat-like vistas of Hyde Park are a great lure (it should be noted that the best views are from the first and more elegant elevated section of the Adam Tihany-designed dining room, rather than the corridor-like window area). But it's Chris Staines's flexible grazing menus that make eating at Foliage so enticing – delicately judged servings from an adventurous and often surprising choice of what are still termed starters, intermediates, mains, cheese and desserts, though should really be seen as 'haute tapas'. Successes at a recent lunch included 'exquisitely presented' tuna tartare with fabulous wasabi ice cream, pickled oyster and a modish crispy cluster of kateifi strands, and pressed lamb shoulder with a deeply savoury rissole, pea purée and earthy smoked tomato. Not every dish delivered on perfect intensity of flavour – both sweetbreads with glazed leeks, morels and crushed peanuts, and scallops with cauliflower, cep and sherry were bland. However a dessert of yoghurt mousse partnered with chopped Alfonso mango accentuated with grated coconut and cubes of hibiscus jelly was a playful finish. It's a shame the waiting staff can't lighten up, though –

'service was curiously joyless'. Dinner offers more choice in the same format or a tasting menu and the discerningly edited wine list highlights some more off-beat producers from France and beyond.

Chef/s: Chris Staines. **Open:** all week L 12 to 2.30, D 7 to 10.30. **Meals:** Set L £29 (£37 including 2 glasses wine). Set D £60. **Service:** 12.5%. **Details:** Cards accepted. 40 seats. Air-con. Separate bar. No music. Wheelchair access. Children's portions.

▌Knightsbridge

Amaya
Sleek, high-gloss Indian
15 Halkin Arcade, Motcomb Street, SW1X 8JT
Tel no: (020) 7823 1166
www.amaya.biz
⊖ Knightsbridge
Indian | £40
Cooking score: 3

V

Occupying a platinum-standard Belgravia site overlooking Halkin Arcade, this overtly ambitious, high-fashion Indian certainly knows how to show off its assets. The interior is a minor miracle of sleek gloss and extravagance, with vibrant murals and Indian statues providing the backdrop to a vast triangular dining area. Chefs go about their work in a stunning open kitchen, and dishes are based on three cooking styles: tandoori, sigri (charcoal grill) and tawa (iron skillet). The idea is to graze from an unconventional menu that might offer griddled wild sea bass with an almond and mustard crust, tamarind-glazed duck and 'ultra-soft' lamb dori kebabs ('unzipped' at the table). The kitchen also breaks with convention by offering mandarin and goats' cheese salad, flash-grilled rock oysters and stir-fried tofu with sea salt, pepper and chilli, and there's a bunch of unusual curries and biryanis (try the artichoke and herb version) for good measure. Vegetables are innovative, while desserts might include an Indian take on tiramisu involving mango. The carefully chosen wine list is a good match for the food, with Knightsbridge prices from £20.25.

Chef/s: Karunesh Khanna. **Open:** all week L 12.30 to 2.15 (12.45 to 2.45 Sun), D 6.30 to 9.30 (6 to 10.30 Sun). **Meals:** alc (main courses £10.50 to £31). Set L £16.50 to £25, Set D £37.50 to £60. **Service:** 12.5%. **Details:** Cards accepted. 100 seats. Air-con. Separate bar. Music. Children allowed.

Boxwood Café
New York comes to Knightsbridge
Berkeley Hotel, Wilton Place, SW1X 7RL
Tel no: (020) 7235 1010
www.gordonramsay.com
⊖ Knightsbridge
Modern British | £40
Cooking score: 3

⇌ **V**

Nestling in a discreet corner of the Berkeley Hotel, the Boxwood seems to tip its hat to New York's café society. The evocative, split-level room is an ample space complete with monochrome photographs of manicured box hedges and shimmering gold-effect walls. The prevailing mood of swish socialising is matched by a businesslike menu that keeps its finger firmly on the casual city food button. Tagliolini with langoustine and chilli is up there alongside potted salt-beef brisket and fried West Mersea oysters with fennel, while main courses explore the world of veal and foie gras burgers, Dornoch lamb with ratatouille and Scottish lobster risotto with violet artichokes. Warm sugared doughnuts with coffee milkshake play it for Uncle Sam, while warm heritage apple caramel tart is British to the core. Expect Knightsbridge prices on the eclectic wine list, but the bidding opens at £20 (£5 a glass).

Chef/s: Stuart Gillies. **Open:** all week L 12 to 3 (4 Sat and Sun), Mon to Sat D 6 to 11. **Meals:** alc (main courses £12.50 to £29). Set L £25, Set D £55.

Also recommended

An 'also recommended' entry is not a full entry, but is provisionally suggested as an alternative to main entries.

Service: 12.5%. **Details:** Cards accepted. 100 seats. Air-con. Separate bar. No mobile phones. Wheelchair access. Music. Children's portions.

The Capital
Finely-tuned French gastronomie
22-26 Basil Street, SW3 1AT
Tel no: (020) 75911202
www.capitalhotel.co.uk
⊖ Knightsbridge
Modern French | £58
Cooking score: 7

🍷 🛏

The Capital is a captivating small hotel, its elegant, welcoming wood-panelled dining room a haven of excellence. If it already feels French, then the menu seems to confirm that impression, with its assiette Landaise and fricassée of frogs' legs. But look a little more closely and Eric Chavot's wide-ranging inventiveness soon shows through: perhaps in a saddle of rabbit provençale with seared calamari and tomato risotto. Strong but well-balanced flavours are characteristic, typified by an appetiser of rich chicken parfait or a starter of langoustine served with dice of rich, slow-cooked pork belly and a dollop of truffle-scented potato 'espuma'. Assemblies are thoughtful – for one reporter pan-fried foie gras with pineapple and mango spring roll – timings are generally careful, and dishes have an inherent simplicity and coherence which gives them a timeless feel: a meaty piece of turbot, for example, served with delicate mushroom ravioli and gnocchi and a sticky but well-balanced sauce diable. French cheeses are painstakingly presented, and full marks for offering such a 'refreshingly light dessert' as Granny Smith and ginger carpaccio, though there's also coffee, chocolate and caramel melting pot with Baileys ice cream. Service, from a multitude of staff, has been impeccable. Modest budgets beware though: much sifting through top-class, top-price wines is needed to reveal anything in the £30 region on the wine list. For those with deep pockets, the detail is in the classic French regions, but other wine growing areas, old and new, offer fine alternatives. There's a selection of half-bottles, and a few by-the-glass from £6.
Chef/s: Eric Chavot. **Open:** Mon to Fri L 12 to 2.30, D 6.45 to 11. **Meals:** Set L £29.50 (3 courses), Set D £58 (3 courses), Tasting menu £70. **Service:** 12.5% (optional). **Details:** Cards accepted. 33 seats. Air-con. No mobile phones.

Fifth Floor
Chic brasserie
Harvey Nichols, 109-125 Knightsbridge, SW1X 7RJ
Tel no: (020) 7235 5250
www.harveynichols.com
⊖ Knightsbridge
Modern British | £32
Cooking score: 3

🍷 V

The Fifth Floor restaurant is the most serious of several dining options on Harvey Nichols' fifth floor – other choices include a bar, café and roof terrace. It's a striking, retro/futuristic room decked out in clinical quantities of white – throw in a Persian cat, and you'd have a Bond villain's space den. Food-wise, expect posh brasserie fare, perhaps cured 'gravad' beef with sweet mustard and chive dressing and watercress salad followed by pan-fried plaice with bacon lardons, button mushrooms and Jersey Royals, with fresh raspberry mille-feuille and raspberry Chantilly to finish. Jonas Karlsson's Swedish roots show on the set-price Swedish market menu, which might offer a trio of pickled herring with Absolut Vodka jelly followed by veal with summer vegetable ragoût. Another option is the tasting menu, where dishes have a more classical flavour. The 750-strong wine list kicks off with a manageable selection of recommended wines, starting at £18.
Chef/s: Jonas Karlsson. **Open:** all week L 12 to 3 (4 Fri and Sat, 5 Sun), Mon to Sat D 6 to 11. **Closed:** 25 and 26 Dec. **Meals:** alc (main courses £17.50 to £24), Set L and D £19.50 (2 courses) to £24.50. **Service:** 12.5%. **Details:** Cards accepted. 120 seats. Air-con. Separate bar. Wheelchair access. Music. Children's portions.

One-O-One
Creative, confident fish cookery
Sheraton Park Tower, 101 Knightsbridge,
SW1X 7RN
Tel no: (020) 7290 7101
www.oneoonerestaurant.com
⊖ Knightsbridge
Seafood | £55
Cooking score: 5

All is sleek designer chic at the restaurant at the base of the Sheraton Park Tower, a recent makeover finally pulling the operation together and allowing it to stand alone from the hotel. Closure allowed Pascal Proyart time to rework ideas – to stunning effect. His new menu is divided into four sections, two devoted to fish, two mixing meat and fish. The culinary idiom is essentially modern French with Asian undertones, but the USP here is the serving of small tasting dishes. The cooking is creative and confident, full of twists and turns and surprising technique, but with a strong sense of direction and purpose. Norwegian red king crab with sweet chilli, ginger and spiced cuttlefish tagliatelle certainly packed a punch; full of flavour, it slightly outshone a chilled version served with aïoli sauce. Similarly, a slow-poached Norwegian cod loin with chorizo carpaccio, squid à la plancha with olive oil, garlic and anchovies delivered layers of savoury complexity, while scallop with pork belly was succulent and subtle. Lunch is quite a bargain: pheasant with vine leaf and autumn truffle, endive and foie gras charlotte, chestnut mousse and wild cranberry sauce poivrade, and chocolate soufflé with a 'delicate, fresh' mint ice cream being the highlights of a £24 four-plate meal. Service is friendly and easy-going, yet polite and correct. Predominantly French wines aim for the upper end of the market; house wine is £22.
Chef/s: Pascal Proyart. **Open:** all week, L 12 to 2.30 (12.30 Sat and Sun), D 6 to 10. **Meals:** alc (main courses £8 to £17). Set L £15 (2 courses) to £35.

Service: not inc. **Details:** Cards accepted. 50 seats. Air-con. Separate bar. Wheelchair access. Music. Children's portions.

Racine
Dependable French cooking
239 Brompton Road, SW3 2EP
Tel no: (020) 7584 4477
⊖ Knightsbridge, South Kensington
French | £33
Cooking score: 4

Co-owner and chef Henry Harris left in late 2007, but the classic French cooking continues to enjoy faithful support among the denizens of Knightsbridge. The dining room is subdued, with little to distract beyond the brown leather banquettes and mirror-lined walls, but readers find it is 'always a pleasure to dine here', reserving particular praise for the attentive front-of-house team. Dependable perennials include steak tartare or crème caramel, and consistent highlights have included a starter of smoked eel served with pickled cucumber, quail's egg and horseradish. Fricassee of rabbit, paired with Savoy cabbage, mustard and sage, underlines the kitchen's intention of keeping things simple, while a classy ballottine of poulet noir with lentils, salsify and lardons 'is not a dish one expects to find on an inexpensive lunch menu'. Clafoutis with griottines and crème anglaise flambéed with a little Kirsch makes a comforting finale. Like the restaurant name, the wine list (starting from £16.50) is rooted in France.
Chef/s: Henrik Ritzen. **Open:** all week L 12 to 3 (3.30 Sat and Sun), D 6 to 10.30 (10 Sun). **Closed:** 25 Dec. **Meals:** alc (main courses £15 to £24). Set L and early D £17.50 (2 courses) to £19.50.
Service: 14.5 (optional). **Details:** Cards accepted. 67 seats. Air-con. Children's portions.

Salloos

Refined Pakistani family affair
62-64 Kinnerton Street, SW1X 8ER
Tel no: (020) 7235 4444
⊖ Knightsbridge
Pakistani | £40
Cooking score: 3

V

Muhammad Salahuddin (nicknamed Salloo) opened this well-heeled restaurant in a discreet Knightsbridge backwater in 1976 and it is still run as a family affair. Its avowed aim has always been to serve the kind of food that might be eaten in Pakistani homes, and many recipes are part of Salahuddin family folklore. The charcoal-fired tandoor is used to good effect for shish kebabs, chicken tikka, lamb chops and the like, while the remainder of the short menu promises a mixed bag of refined curry house standards (chicken jalfrezi, lamb biryani) plus some more intriguing specialities: look for nargisi kofta (Indian 'Scotch eggs'), gurdi masala (stir-fried kidneys with hot spices) and haleem akbari (shredded lamb with wheatgerm and lentils). The wine list opens with Corney & Barrow house selections at £15.50.
Chef/s: Abdul Aziz. **Open:** Mon to Sat L 12 to 3, D 7 to 11.30. **Closed:** Sun, 25 and 26 Dec. **Meals:** alc (main courses 14.50 to 17.50). **Service:** 12.5%. **Details:** Cards accepted. 65 seats. Air-con. Separate bar. No music.

▌Lancaster Gate

★NEW ENTRY★
Angelus

Fine dining with an edge
4 Bathurst Street, W2 2SD
Tel no: (020) 7402 0083
www.angelusrestaurant.co.uk
⊖ Lancaster Gate
French | £36
Cooking score: 4

Itching to break the bonds of fine dining, Thierry Tomasin, the free-thinking yet focused ex-head sommelier from Le Gavroche and former general manager of Aubergine, gives this former pub a rare edge. It's in an area of London that 'desperately needs a good-quality restaurant'. The space is rather cramped, but dark wood, mirrors, chandeliers, buttoned-back leather banquettes and 'oddly positioned' white-clad tables hit all the right Parisian brasserie notes. The carte has great appeal, taking in starters of 'very tasty' foie gras crème brûlée and a generous warm scallop salad with Charlotte potatoes and truffled vinaigrette, while lighter main courses could include John Dory with a viennoise crust, pak choi and vin jaune sauce with clams. Output is variable but, at its best, sound judgement is evident: in, for example, 'delicious and perfectly prepared' pigeon 'façon Bécasse' with buttered Savoy cabbage and marjoram. The wine list accords pride of place to the French regions, but there are a few from other wine-growing regions, including the southern hemisphere. House wine is £13.
Chef/s: Olivier Duret. **Open:** Tue to Sun 12 to 11. **Closed:** 23 Dec to 3 Jan. **Meals:** alc (main courses £16 to £20). **Service:** 12.5%. **Details:** Cards accepted. 35 seats. 12 seats outside.

▌Marble Arch
Locanda Locatelli

Top-end, ingredients-led cooking
8 Seymour Street, W1H 7JZ
Tel no: (020) 7935 9088
www.locandalocatelli.com
⊖ Marble Arch
Italian | £40
Cooking score: 6

🍾 **V**

As befits a photogenic chef at the top of his game, Giorgio Locatelli has imbued his stellar restaurant with lashings of Mayfair chic; it's become a home-from-home for London's smart set, who drool over the dazzling David Collins interior design. Locatelli has lost none of his instinct for straight-and-true regional 'cucina', and the kitchen delivers disarmingly simple, ingredients-led cooking (at a price) – whether it's a clever salad of deep-fried calf's foot with mustard fruits, an unshowy nettle risotto or roast breast of organic chicken with seasonal vegetables. Home-made pasta is one of the star turns (perhaps tagliatelle with kid ragù and chilli or red onion ravioli with Chianti sauce and salted ricotta) and fish is treated with proper respect: roast monkfish appears with walnut and caper sauce, while chargrilled mackerel is given a herb crust. To finish, the tart of the day is generally worth a punt; otherwise, consider a tiramisu pick-me-up, peach millefoglie with dark chocolate sorbet or the colour-coded combo of green tea mousse, pistachio sponge, green apple and Prosecco sorbet. The wine list is an oenophile's tour of the Italian regions, with extended stop-overs in Tuscany and Piedmont, a mind-boggling brigade of Barolos and other big names. Prices are worldy-wise, but there are a few bottles under £20 as well as a decent choice by-the-glass (from £3.50).

Chef/s: Giorgio Locatelli. **Open:** all week L 12 to 3, D 6.45 to 11. **Closed:** bank hols. **Meals:** alc (main courses £11 to £32.50). **Service:** not inc. **Details:** Cards accepted. 80 seats. Air-con. No music. No mobile phones. Wheelchair access. Children's portions.

Rhodes W1 Brasserie
Feel good food in a trendy setting
Cumberland Hotel, W1A 4RS
Tel no: (020) 7479 3838
www.garyrhodes.com
⊖ **Marble Arch**
Modern British | £40
Cooking score: 3

As the lavish furnishings and lively music would suggest, Rhodes W1 Brasserie is intent on serving up big, brash and emphatically British dishes to a yuppie crowd. True to Gary Rhodes' no-nonsense approach, contemporary reworkings of fish and chips and eggs Benedict are true crowd pleasers. An inspection starter of rich scrambled duck eggs on toasted brioche showed the right measure of continental *savoir faire*. Meanwhile, a main of pan-fried salmon with cabbage and bacon, new potatoes, Meaux mustard and butter

sauce proved an equally well judged combination on a menu pitched primarily at carnivores. Be warned however, prices do stretch beyond the boundaries of typical brasserie fare, and service can be somewhat intrusive. A generous wine list begins at £3.50 a glass.

Chef/s: Gary Rhodes. **Open:** all week L 12 to 2.30, D 6 to 10.30. **Meals:** alc (main courses £13 to £22). **Service:** 12.5%. **Details:** Cards accepted. 142 seats. Wheelchair access. Music. Children allowed.

★NEW ENTRY★
Rhodes W1 Restaurant
British cooking in a formal setting
Great Cumberland Place, W1A 4RF
Tel no: (020) 7479 3737
www.rhodesw1.com
⊖ **Marble Arch**
British | £80
Cooking score: 5

♪ V

Rhodes W1, with its expensive decorative trimmings, chandeliers, and well-spaced tables, suits the well-heeled customers, who stop at the Brasserie for comfort food (see entry), or continue on to the formal dining room if something more luxurious is called for. A bevy of staff helps to maintain a high degree of efficiency. The menu offers some luxurious ingredients and generally appealing taste combinations, such as well-timed fillet of halibut with crab tortellini, buttered leeks and shellfish bisque and the cooking is at its best when its stays in classical territory – a 'rich and enjoyable' fillet of beef with foie gras, artichokes and Madeira jus, for example. Technique is mostly sound, dishes are prettily presented and the kitchen clearly works hard, making bread and producing a whole succession of nibbles, the best on an inspection being a gazpacho with a spicy bite alongside fresh crab on toast. End on a high note with highly accomplished desserts such as expertly rendered passion fruit soufflé paired with an intense dark chocolate sorbet. The wine list begins at £8 a glass and ventures well beyond

France: there are even a couple of clever German wine choices, a region often ignored. Although mark-ups are not fierce by Mayfair standards, there is little under £40 on the list. **Chef/s:** Paul Welburn. **Open:** Tue to Fri L 12 to 2.30; Tue to Sat D 7 to 10.30. **Closed:** Sun, Mon, 10 days in Aug, Christmas, New Year. **Meals:** £65 for 3 courses, £55 for 2 courses. **Service:** 12.5%. **Details:** Cards accepted. 46 seats. Separate bar. Wheelchair access. Music. Children allowed.

★NEW ENTRY★
Texture
Striking culinary imagination
34 Portman Street, W1H 7BY
Tel no: (020) 7224 0028
www.texture-restaurant.co.uk
⊖ **Marble Arch**
Modern European | £45
Cooking score: 4
V

The cool, stylish, ornately plastered white room is divided by glass displays and contemporary art, while bare wood tables, cream leather chairs and modern lighting create a buzzy, high-volume look. The cooking essays a degree of experimentation, new Nordic cuisine with more than a hint of contemporary French fashion to it (Agnar Sverrisson was formerly head chef at Le Manoir aux Quat'Saisons, see entry) and technique is versatile enough to attempt, for example, chargrilled pigeon with sweetcorn, bacon popcorn and red wine essence. Best value is at lunch, when a range of ten starter-sized dishes, all priced at £8.50, is offered, otherwise there's a pair of tasting menus from £55 or a more conventional three-course à la carte. At inspection, a great piece of roast Icelandic lamb gained impact from a side bowl of rich lamb broth. On the downside, flavours don't always pack a punch: Mediterranean tuna, smoked, Asian flavours, arrived under a porcelain dome that, when lifted, released an aromatic puff of wood smoke, but failed to follow through with any definite taste. Service is well-drilled and co-founder Xavier

Rousset's classy wine list is particularly strong in France. Entry level is £18 with reasonable action under £30. **Chef/s:** Agnar Sverrisson. **Open:** Tue to Sat L 12 to 2.30, D 6.30 to 11. **Closed:** Sun, Mon, Christmas, New Year. **Meals:** Tasting Menu £55 to £59. **Service:** 12.5%. **Details:** Cards accepted. 60 seats. Air-con. Separate bar. Wheelchair access. Music.

ALSO RECOMMENDED
▲ **La Porte des Indes**
32 Bryanston Street, Marble Arch, W1H 7EG
Tel no: (020) 7224 0055
www.pilondon.net
Indian

The lush subcontinental ambience of this centrally-sited Indian restaurant incorporates tropical foliage, luxurious drapes and a waterfall. Amid such thorough-going elegance, you will eat well-executed dishes with more than a hint of Mughal opulence to them. Garlicky king scallops in saffron sauce (£10.50), salmon steaks rolled in mustard seed, fennel, chilli and aniseed (£14.50) and seafood thali (£23) are items from the carte, or there are fixed-price menus from £27. A wide assortment of breads and rice preparations accompanies. Wines offer an expansive choice, beginning with a by-the-glass range from £5. Closed Sat L.

■ Marylebone

★ BEST UP-AND-COMING CHEF ★
L'Autre Pied
Relaxed, good-value sibling of Pied-à-Terre
5–7 Blandford Street, W1U 3DB
Tel no: (020) 7486 9696
www.lautrepied.co.uk
⊖ **Bond Street**
Modern European | £35
Cooking score: 6

L'Autre Pied continues to impress, with the young Marcus Eaves displaying a cool, mature approach to some attractively understated cooking. There's an intelligent streak of novelty, perhaps in a well-wrought starter of crab with avocado purée, tzatziki mousse and a lime and coriander nage that delivered 'dazzling flavour', or a salad of smoked eel, marinated young vegetables, lardo di Colonnata and potato crisps. The kitchen stands by the quality of the output and a sense of balance characterises such dishes as a trio of lamb − tender, pink loin, slow-cooked breast and a tiny, meaty sausage − accompanying Jerusalem artichoke, 'superb' potato and Parmesan gnocchi and a restrained mint jus. At the same time the cooking has a sense of seasonality, expressed, for example, in pollock served with crushed Jersey Royals, spring vegetables and herb broth, a style that continues into dessert with blood orange mille-feuille with a rich lemon curd ice cream. Bread is another hit, and the occasional appearance of David Moore overseeing service reveals the level of care Pied-à-Terre puts into this, their second, more keenly priced opening. The wine list works its magic at all price levels, offering a good range by-the-glass and the majority of the strong worldwide selection under £40. House wine is £11.50.

Chef/s: Marcus Eaves. **Open:** all week L 12 to 2.45 D 6 to 10.45. **Closed:** Christmas. **Meals:** alc (main courses £16.95 to £21.50). Set L and pre-theatre D £16.50 (2 courses). **Service:** 12.5% (optional). **Details:** Cards accepted. 53 seats. Air-con. No music.

Dinings
Good-value Japanese cooking
22 Harcourt Street, W1H 4HH
Tel no: (020) 7723 0666
⊖ Marylebone
Japanese | £36
Cooking score: 3

While the tiny proportions of this 'izakaya'-style basement restaurant with its hard narrow benches and minimalist concrete interior can be uncomfortable, it's far better to dwell on Tomanari Chiba's good food and the kindly, attentive service. The regular menu of sushi and sashimi and the lunchtime 'donburi' (rice bowls) menu are always reliable, but the imaginative blackboard 'tapas' specials are where the fun is. Sea urchin tempura, yellowtail collar, pork shoulder teriyaki and kumamoto oysters with caviar have all impressed us this year. Desserts might be an appealing east-west fusion, for example matcha crème brûlée or black sesame crème caramel. Prices are remarkably low (with most mains hovering around a tenner) given that the quality of the produce is commensurate with pricier London restaurants. A short list of wines (£14.50) and sakés is well-suited to the cuisine. The six-seater ground floor sushi counter is perfect for single diners. Our questionniare was not returned, so some of the information below may have changed.

Chef/s: Tomanari Chiba. **Open:** Mon to Fri L 12 to 2.30, Mon to Sat D 6 to 10.30. **Closed:** Sun, 25 and 26 Dec. **Meals:** alc (main courses £4 to £16). **Service:** 10%. **Details:** Cards accepted. 32 seats. Music. Children allowed.

★NEW ENTRY★
Duke of Wellington
Neighbourhood pub with lots of promise
94a Crawford Street, W1H 2HQ
Tel no: (020) 7723 2790
⊖ Baker Street
Gastropub | £25
Cooking score: 1

£30

Occupying a corner site, this updated neighbourhood boozer has adopted the gastropub formula of dark timber flooring, funky lighting, leather banquettes, abstract artwork and bare tables. The cooking style focuses on using well-sourced, good-quality ingredients. Flavours are robust and clear and portions generous; witness a main course confit of duck leg with sarlardaise potatoes, pickled red cabbage and griottine cherry jus. Start with ham hock and parsley terrine with piccalilli, and finish with rum Baba with Chantilly cream. There's a small, smarter restaurant upstairs, but the menu remains pretty much the same. House wines start at £14.50.

Chef/s: Fred Smith. Open: all week L 12 to 3 (12:30 to 4.30 Sat and Sun), D 6.30 to 10. Closed: 25 to 26 Dec, 31 Dec. Meals: alc (main courses £11 to £16). Service: not inc. Details: Cards accepted. Air-con. Music. Children's portions.

Galvin Bistrot de Luxe

Sophisticated French food in an elegant setting
66 Baker Street, W1V 7DH
Tel no: (020) 7935 4007
www.galvinbistrotdeluxe.co.uk
⊖ Baker Street
French | £32
Cooking score: 5

Galvin offers a welcome retreat from the brashness of Baker Street. Inside, a masculine, clubby feel pervades thanks to the dark wood panelling and white-clad tables – perhaps more so now that a bar with lots of mahogany, leather chairs and banquette seating has opened in the basement. The appeal of the menu is not hard to find, delivering good renditions of dishes that soothe rather than challenge. The straightforwardness of the cooking is another confidence-booster, as the repertoire runs from ballottine of foie gras via steak tartare to duck breast and confit leg with Savoy cabbage and red wine jus. Well-sourced raw materials remain the foundation, evident in a 'delicious and beautifully cooked' confit pork belly and pig cheek ('slowly simmered to melting, flaking tenderness') and classics like steamed fillet of brill with mussels and chive beurre blanc. Oeuf à la neige has been praised, as has an intensely-flavoured soufflé of English raspberries. Service is generally well-drilled. The bias of the wine list is appropriately French, but New World countries and modern styles are well-represented. Bottles start at £13.95 and an excellent 17 or so come by-the-glass.
Chef/s: Chris Galvin, Jeff Galvin, Sian Rees. Open: Mon to Sat L 12 to 2.30, D 6 to 11, Sun 12 to 9.30. Closed: D 24 Dec, 25 to 26 Dec, 1 Jan. Meals: Set L £15.50, Set D £17.50 (6 to 7). Details: 105 seats. 12 seats outside. Air-con. Separate bar. Wheelchair access. Children's portions. Car parking.

Phoenix Palace

Chinese blockbuster
3-5 Glentworth Street, NW1 5PG
Tel no: (020) 7486 3515
⊖ Baker Street
Chinese | £25
Cooking score: 2

 £30

This sprawling, bustling Chinese restaurant beneath a vast apartment block just off Baker Street is one of central London's best venues for reliably good Chinese cooking. The large dining room is smarter and more elaborately decorated than most in Chinatown and its hefty 200-dish menu boasts a strong showing of seafood, hotpots and one-plate rice and noodle specialities. Dim sum has impressed (it's particularly popular at the weekend with families), as have chef's specials like ma po aubergine with minced beef, and winter melon, dry shrimp and vermicelli hot pot. Look out, too, for game dishes such as venison with celery, or sautéed hare fillet with shallot and bean sauce. House wine is £10. Our questionnaire was not returned, so some of the information below may have changed.
Chef/s: Mr Tan. Open: all week 12 to 11.30 (10.30 Sun). Meals: alc (main courses £6 to £28). Set D £15.50 (2 Courses) to £26.80. Service: 12.5%. Details: Cards accepted. 250 seats. Air-con. Music. Children allowed.

Providores

Marylebone's foremost Oceanic eatery
109 Marylebone High Street, W1U 4RX
Tel no: (020) 7935 6175
www.theprovidores.co.uk
⊖ Baker Street, Bond Street
Tapas | £45
Cooking score: 4

Peter Gordon's Marylebone village eatery offers an informal all-day Tapas Room (really a tapas-cum-wine-cum-breakfast bar) on the ground floor; you navigate the crowds to reach the more sedate Providores restaurant upstairs. The monochrome space (plain white walls, black leather banquettes with matching

Michel Roux Jnr. Le Gavroche

Why did you become a chef?
With a name like Roux and a family of chefs, what else?

What three ingredients could you not do without?
Salted butter from Brittany, chocolate, vanilla.

Who would you invite to your ideal dinner party?
Eric Cantona.

What's your guilty food pleasure?
No guilt in enjoyment!

What is the most unusual ingredient you've cooked or eaten?
Heron in Hong Kong.

What won't you tolerate in the kitchen?
Violence.

Do you always read reviews of your restaurant?
Yes.

What era of history would you most like to have eaten in?
Now.

black leather upholstered chairs and white-clothed tables) continues the 'unfussy, unbuttoned' feel and lets Gordon's fusion food stand out. His cooking is intricate and creative, displaying myriad ingredients from the global larder. Combinations are 'exciting and innovative' but well thought-through: say a main course of pan-fried sea bass served on a salad of palm heart, samphire, soba noodles and sesame, seaweed with yuzu tamari dressing and wasabi and bonito furikake, or perhaps a pomegranate pannacotta with blackberry jelly, summer berries and a manuka honey snap to finish. The almost exclusively New Zealand wine list is also something of an education, with prices starting at £21.50 and with a decent selection by-the-glass.

Chef/s: Peter Gordon. **Open:** all week L 12 to 2.30 (2.45 Sat and Sun), D 6 to 10.15 (10 Sun). **Closed:** 24 Dec to 3 Jan. **Meals:** alc (main courses £18 to £25). **Service:** 12.5%. **Details:** Cards accepted. 38 seats. Air-con. Separate bar. Music. Children allowed.

Royal China
First-rate dim sum
24–26 Baker Street, W1M 7AB
Tel no: (020) 7487 4688
www.royalchinagroup.co.uk
⊖ Baker Street
Chinese
New Chef

Step inside this branch of the Royal China group (also in Queensway, Docklands and Fulham) and the signature gold flying-geese on black lacquered walls will be instantly familiar. Less frenetic than the Queensway HQ, it can still get 'thunderous when full' with lunchtime queues a testament to the first-rate dim sum, but despite the intensity of covers service is smooth and efficient. Hong Kong-style crispy garlic-roasted pigeon is worth pre-ordering, while other highlights this year have been an appealing deep-fried whitebait with hot and spicy salt, a hot pot of silky Japanese bean curd with minced pork and dried scallops and 'chiu chow' – stir-fried chicken fillets with chilli sauce. Where there are niggles, they seem to focus on uniformity of flavours and oiliness, and one reporter feels that 'standards have settled into a groove', and Royal China is 'no longer a flag bearer for Cantonese cooking'. Wines start at £17.

Chef/s: Mr Man. **Open:** Mon to Tue 12 to 11, Fri to Sat 12 to 11.30, Sun 11 to 10. **Closed:** Christmas. **Meals:** alc (main courses £L £8 to £15, D £10 to £25). **Service:** 12.5% (optional). **Details:** Cards accepted. 160 seats. Air-con. Wheelchair access. Music. Children allowed.

READERS RECOMMEND

Kandoo
Persian
458 Edgware Road, Marylebone, W2 1EJ
Tel no: (020) 7724 2428
'Enchanting Persian food'

Le Relais de Venise
French
120 Marylebone Lane, Marylebone, W1U 2QG
Tel no: 020 7486 0878
www.relaisdevenise.com
'A one-dish restaurant that pulls in the crowds'

Original Tagines
Moroccan
7A Dorset Street, Marylebone, W1U 6QN
Tel no: (020) 7935 1545
'Great value food that rocks the kasbah'

▮ Mayfair

The Albemarle
Rejuvenated British stalwart
Brown's Hotel, 30 Albemarle Street, W1S 4BP
Tel no: (020) 7518 4060
www.roccofortehotels.com
⊖ Green Park
British | £49
Cooking score: 4

🖺 V

The dining room at Brown's is imperious in scale and stature with oak panelling and pillars, austerity kept partly in check by soft colours – although photographic exhibits by Herbetus von Hohenlohe would seem 'more at home in department stores'. The restaurant has seen various incarnations in recent years, now Mark Hix (ex-Ivy), alongside executive chef Lee Stretton, oversees a thoroughly British, produce-led menu featuring pies, hotpots, game and grills – even eggs get their own section. There is an earthier undertone to the cooking; cod chitterlings make an appearance, as does Brown Windsor soup, while roast meats from the carvery feature on the daily lunch menu, say a roast rib of beef 'thickly sliced, juicy and pink'. Inspection highlights were Dorset crab and bittercress followed by roasted scallops with hedgerow garlic. Desserts are British institutions: treacle tart, spotted dick or apple crumble. Covering 14 pages, the wine list starts from £23 (£7 a glass), and primarily focuses on the Old World, with France taking centre stage.

Chef/s: Lee Stretton. **Open:** all week L 12 to 3 (Sun 12.30 to 3) D 6 to 10.30 (Sun 7 to 10.30). **Meals:** alc (main courses £14.50 to £29.75). Set L £25 (2 courses) to £30. **Service:** 12.5%. **Details:** Cards accepted. 85 seats. Air-con. Separate bar. No mobile phones. Wheelchair access. Children allowed.

Alloro
Top spot for Italian business lunches
19-20 Dover Street, W1S 4LU
Tel no: (020) 7495 4768
www.alloro-restaurant.co.uk
⊖ Green Park
Italian | £35
Cooking score: 2

🍾 V

A blue awning picks out this outwardly unassuming but internally classy Mayfair restaurant, which combines a relaxed bar-dining area with a 'white-linen zoned restaurant'. Décor is smart, clean-lined and modern, with high-back banquettes and burgundy leather chairs. In the kitchen, the modern Italian cooking takes a confident, intelligently simple approach driven by quality ingredients and offered on a fixed-price carte (watch out for those supplements), bolstered by daily specials. Typical choices might be home-made pappardelle served with sautéed chicken livers and fresh goats' cheese, followed by veal cutlet milanese, while the classy, all-Italian wine list catches the eye too, with some eight by-the-glass and ten half-bottles. House wine is £18.

Chef/s: Daniele Camera. **Open:** Mon to Fri L 12 to 2.30, Mon to Sat D 7 to 10.30. **Closed:** Sun, 21 Dec to 4 Jan, Easter, bank hols. **Meals:** Set L £27 (2 courses) to £32, Set D £29.50 (2 courses) to £39 (4 courses). **Service:** 12.5%. **Details:** Cards accepted. 65 seats. Air-con. Separate bar. Children allowed.

Bellamy's
Classy French brasserie in Mayfair mews
18-18a Bruton Place, W1J 6LY
Tel no: (020) 7491 2727
⊖ **Green Park**
French | £45
Cooking score: 4

Entering this popular Mayfair dining room through the adjoining food shop and oyster bar only serves to whet the appetite for the classic French brasserie cooking. The carte divides into entrées, caviar, salads, fish, meat and side-order options, with the short, appropriately all-French wine list on the reverse. Here, there's a strong representation from Bordeaux, Burgundy and the Rhône, and prices start at £24 (£6.50 a glass). The cooking is assured, the emphasis on the simple execution of good-quality ingredients seen in dishes such as rillettes of duck, followed, perhaps, by a brochette of langoustine or veal sweetbreads meunière. There's also a good-value two- or three-course fixed-price option. The décor is a classy take on the classic French brasserie look: pastel yellow walls decorated with French posters, prints and mirrors, green leather chairs and matching banquette seating, white-clothed tables and polished-wood floors. Gallic service is relaxed but professional. (The oyster bar, open all-day during the week, offers a variety of shellfish and their famous open sandwiches.)

Chef/s: Stéphane Pacoud. **Open:** Mon to Fri L 12 to 3, Mon to Sat D 6 to 11. **Closed:** Sun, 24 Dec to 2 Jan. **Meals:** alc (main courses £18.50 to £27.50). Set L £24 (2 courses) to £28.50. **Service:** 12.5%. **Details:** Cards accepted. 74 seats. Air-con. Children's portions.

Benares
Eye-opening new-wave Indian
12A Berkeley Square, W1J 6BS
Tel no: (020) 7629 8886
www.benaresrestaurant.com
⊖ **Green Park**
Indian | £55
Cooking score: 3

Designed to impress the moneyed Mayfair set with its über-glamorous looks, Benares is a swanky new-breed Indian restaurant where the only echoes of curry house familiarity are tandoori chicken and Hyderabadi lamb biryani, and where diners are encouraged to order a glass of Krug Grand Cuvée with their karara kekda (crisp soft-shell crab and squid salad). Chef Atul Kotchhar isn't bound by borders or tradition, and he's happy to absorb ideas from all over for his eye-opening, intelligent take on Indian cuisine. To start, spice-crusted scallops are given a mint and grape dressing, while main courses might move into the realms of batter-fried John Dory with crushed peas and Gorkha tomato chutney, grilled roe deer fillet with pickled pumpkin risotto or sage-infused carrot and cauliflower dumplings in cashew sauce. Spice-friendly Rieslings and other aromatic whites are stand-out options on the serious wine list; prices start at £18 (£5 a glass).

Chef/s: Atul Kotchhar. **Open:** Mon to Fri L 12 to 2.30, all week D 5.30 to 10.30 (6 to 10 Sun). **Closed:** 25 Dec. **Meals:** alc (main courses £14.50 to £35). Set L and D £25 (2 courses) to £30. **Service:** 12.5%. **Details:** Cards accepted. 140 seats. Air-con. Separate bar. Wheelchair access. Music. Children's portions.

Average price

The average price listed in main-entry reviews denotes the price of a three-course meal, without wine.

Le Caprice

Infectiously upbeat atmosphere
Arlington House, Arlington Street, SW1A 1RJ
Tel no: (020) 7629 2239
www.le-caprice.co.uk
⊖ Green Park
Modern British | £47
Cooking score: 4

Like its sister restaurant the Ivy (see entry), first-time visitors to this celebrity haunt might wonder quite what all the fuss is about: the décor, while pleasant, has a dated look, from the 1980s-style slatted blinds and raffia-backed chairs to the black-and-white photos of half-forgotten stars. And visit at lunchtime and it's a sea of suits: Le Caprice is a favourite haunt of Mayfair hedge fund managers. Once seated, however, the slick service, overseen by the legendary Jesus Adorno, glides into action, and the infectiously upbeat atmosphere begins to work its considerable charm. Simple stuff done well could be the menu's mantra: dressed Dorset crab with celeriac rémoulade, followed by chicken milanese – succulent meat in a golden casing of breadcrumbs dripping with garlic and parsley butter – with perfect side orders of creamed spinach and rustling French fries deserving equal star billing. Puddings include a peach, Amaretto and elderflower trifle – retro without being old-fashioned. Europe (France especially) dominates the wine list, which opens at £18.50 but soon sails past the £30 mark. A stool at the bar remains one of the best places in London for solo diners, while Sunday brunch (12 to 5pm) is an ineffably glamorous way to spend a weekend afternoon.
Chef/s: Paul Brown. **Open:** all week L 12 to 3 (5 Sun), Mon to Sat D 5.30 to 12, Sun 6 to 11. **Closed:** 24 Dec D, 25 and 25 Dec, 1 Jan. **Meals:** alc (main courses £14.25 to £26). **Service:** 12.5%.
Details: Cards accepted. 74 seats. Air-con. Children's portions.

Chisou

A taste of Tokyo
4 Princes Street, W1B 2LE
Tel no: (020) 7629 3931
www.chisou.co.uk
⊖ Oxford Circus
Japanese | £25
Cooking score: 4

V

The spirit of Tokyo's gregarious eating houses is alive and well in this affluent but uncluttered restaurant in London's 'Little Japan' between Regent Street and Hanover Square. Regular contingents of Japanese businessmen and ex-pats testify to its enduring popularity, both as a lunchtime drop-in for noodles and rice bowls and as a full-on evening rendezvous. The kitchen shows off the full range of its capabilities with authentic specialities including grilled, lightly-salted capelins (similar to smelts), diced raw tuna with grated yam and wasabi sauce, and tofu with fiery kimchee, spring onion and sesame oil. Spanklingly fresh, visually dazzling sushi is also a good bet, and the regular menu covers most bases from tempura to teriyaki; it's also worth exploring the list of appetisers, sunomono and salads (try tiny cubes of octopus with wasabi served in a saké cup, beef tataki or pan-fried spicy burdock roots sprinkled with sesame seeds). To drink, check out the assortment of vintage and blended sakés or have a shot of plum wine on the rocks. Prices on the short, conventional wine list start at £13.80 (£3.80 a glass).
Chef/s: Kodi Aung. **Open:** Mon to Sat L 12 to 2.30, D 6 to 10.15. **Closed:** Sun, bank hols. **Meals:** alc (main courses £7 to £18.50). Set L £12.50 to £19.
Service: not inc. **Details:** Cards accepted. 55 seats. 8 seats outside. Air-con. Music. Children allowed.

Also recommended

An 'also recommended' entry is not a full entry, but is provisionally suggested as an alternative to main entries.

Which? Campaigns

To find out more about Which? food and drink campaigns, please visit:
www.which.co.uk

The Connaught

Watch this space...
16 Carlos Place, W1K 2AL
Tel no: (020) 7592 1222
www.the-connaught.co.uk
⊖ Bond Street, Green Park
Modern European
New Chef

After 56 unbroken years in the *The Good Food Guide*, our 'longest serving' restaurant closed in March 2007 for a £60m 'intensive restoration and (whisper it) renovation'. Then, with the expiration of Angela Hartnett's (and Gordon Ramsay Holdings) restaurant tenancy in September 2007, there was intense speculation as to who would step up to the plate – Hartnett being a tough act to follow. The announcement that the French chef Hélène Darroze will take over has created quite a buzz, for the highly talented Darroze's route into cooking was unconventional: as a graduate with a business degree she went to work in the offices of Alain Ducasse in Monte Carlo, who then spotted her culinary potential. Her eponymous restaurant on Paris's Left Bank, not far from the Boulevard St Germain, is highly acclaimed and Darroze will split her time equally between London and Paris. The restaurant, to be called Hélène Darroze at the Connaught, was due to open as we went to press. Phone for details.

El Pirata

Good-value tapas in Mayfair
5–6 Down Street, W1J 7AQ
Tel no: (020) 7491 3810
www.elpirata.co.uk
⊖ Hyde Park Corner
Spanish | £27
Cooking score: 1

£30

This good-value Mayfair restaurant is something of an institution among London's Spanish community. Rapid delivery of tapas is its stock in trade, but for the best atmosphere make sure you bag a table on the ground floor, where walls are covered with prints by Picasso

and Miró, tables are packed and the atmosphere is lively. The menu is divided between fish and meat: grilled or deep-fried squid, say, or sardines fritas, while meat comes in the form of kidneys in sherry, meatballs or chicken croquettes, and there's always excellent jamón Iberico pata negra. Plates are delivered in no particular order by fast-paced waiters who retain a good sense of humour even under pressure. For something more substantial, order paella, either valenciana and marinera. Flans and crema Catalana are typical desserts. The all-Spanish wine list opens at £13.95. The restaurant did not respond to our questionnaire, so some of the information below may have changed.
Chef/s: Ramon Castro. **Open:** Mon to Fri 12 to 11, Sat D 6 to 11.30. **Closed:** Sun, bank hols. **Meals:** alc (£4.25 to £17.50). Set L £9.95, Set D £14.95 to £19.50. **Service:** 10% (optional). **Details:** Cards accepted. 85 seats. 16 seats outside. Air-con. Separate bar. Children allowed.

Embassy

An ambassador for British seafood
29 Old Burlington Street, W1S 3AN
Tel no: (020) 7851 0956
www.embassylondon.com
⊖ Green Park, Piccadilly Circus
Modern European | £45
Cooking score: 4

Embassy is a lively place in the evening – the bar is a popular drinking spot for the downstairs nightclub – which adds much-needed atmosphere to the ground-floor dining room. The long, narrow, chandeliered room is formal, the monochromatic interior sounding a gently sombre note (though light floods in through full-length windows), the faintly pensive tone appears to have been picked up by certain members of the staff. However, the kitchen likes to assemble vibrant ideas on the plate and fish is a strong suit: scallops with roast chicory, orange and Merlot vinegar or cannelloni of cod brandade, alongside roast foie gras with caramelised mango. Main courses tend towards orthodox renditions of modern classics like slow-cooked belly pork with Bramley apple sauce, and wild sea bass with spaghetti of mussels and oysters. Desserts like chocolate tiramisu with espresso sorbet are capably handled. Things are quieter during the day and the al fresco pavement terrace is a good spot for lunch on a hot day. Given the Mayfair location, the short, global wine list has a surprising number of bottles under £30. House wine is £18.50.

Chef/s: Garry Hollihead. **Open:** Tue to Fri L 12 to 3, Tue to Sat D 6 to 11.30. **Closed:** Sun and Mon. **Meals:** alc (main courses £12 to £24). **Service:** 12.5%. **Details:** Cards accepted. 120 seats. 24 seats outside. Air-con. Separate bar. Music.

Galvin at Windows
Outstanding views of London
Hilton Hotel, 22 Park Lane, W1Y 4BE
Tel no: (020) 7208 4021
www.hilton.co.uk/londonparklane
⊖ Hyde Park Corner, Green Park
French | £58
Cooking score: 6

Located on the 28th floor of the Hilton Hotel, Galvin at Windows is aptly named – floor-to-ceiling windows give an unparalleled view over London, including a rare overhead sight of Buckingham Palace. The subdued contemporary design, with walnut and gold colours alongside pastel green leather chairs and yellow curtains, creates a bright and airy feel. When it comes to the food, Chris Galvin and André Garrett oversee a menu that is accessible and sophisticated, a showcase for fine raw materials. The food never missed a beat at inspection, opening with a delightfully light pea and mint purée and going on to a poached Scottish lobster salad cleverly offset by crunchy mango slices and herb fromage frais. For main course, pot-au-feu of poulet noir played nicely against a delicate court bouillon enhanced by the simplicity of perfectly cooked spring vegetables – there is no pretense to the cooking, every component makes its own distinct impression. For dessert, cold marinated pineapple with lime granita and some mint jelly garnished with fresh

coriander cress arrived with a tantalising variation of warm roasted pineapple 'made special' by a touch of Espelette pepper. As one reporter noted: 'there is creamy luxury about the experience wherever you turn, be it the cooking, service or views'. You cannot really expect low prices in Park Lane but set menus are good value. The Euro-centric wine list may begin at £18.50 (£5 for a glass) but it quickly moves north to £2,564 for a 1982 Château Mouton-Rothschild and choices are restricted below £30.

Chef/s: Chris Galvin and André Garrett. **Open:** Sun to Fri L 12 to 3 (4 Sun), Mon to Sat D 6 to 11. **Meals:** alc £58 (3 courses). Set L £29. Menu dégustation £75. **Service:** 12.5%. **Details:** Cards accepted. 108 seats. Air-con. Separate bar. No music. Wheelchair access.

Le Gavroche
Beacon of French gastronomy
43 Upper Brook Street, W1K 7QR
Tel no: (020) 7408 0881
www.le-gavroche.co.uk
⊖ Marble Arch
French | £70
Cooking score: 8

'If only we could afford to go more often', say fans of this beacon of French gastronomy in the heart of Mayfair. True, the à la carte can seem prohibitively expensive, but canny readers recommend the lunchtime set as offering 'some of the best value in London'. On the carte, icons such as soufflé Suissesse and omelette Rothschild are always there, sharing menu space not only with the expected classics of haute cuisine – lobster mousse with caviar and Champagne butter sauce or roast rib of French veal with creamed morel sauce and potato mousseline – but also more modern creations along the lines of a warm salad of roast vegetables and crispy breaded chicken, or red mullet with crushed potatoes, cockles and clams in an olive oil dressing. At inspection, the set lunch yielded a master class of culinary technique that delivered enjoyment on a grand scale: amuse bouche included a breadcrumbed tiger prawn on a bed of diced avocado ahead of a starter of gratinated oysters à l'alsacienne, the salty smoothness of the oysters forming an intriguing contrast with the astringency of its vinegary bed of cabbage. It made a light, pleasing prelude to a beguilingly rich main course of lamb neck with potato mousseline and braised turnips. Dessert could have been vanilla crème brûlée with almond sacristains, but the pungent whiff of one of London's best-kept cheeseboards proved irresistible. Unsurprisingly, Le Gavroche is not the place to come for cutting-edge décor: there's a formality to the furnishings in both the upstairs bar and basement dining room, underscored by a dress code that requires male diners wear a jacket. That said, the unfailing friendliness of staff ensures that there's nothing stuffy about the experience, and the atmosphere is one of the most upbeat in London. Upmarket French bottles make up the meat of the wine list, but unless your budget stretches that far it is more rewarding to scour other regions, where well-chosen and affordable bottles (starting at about £20) mingle with the stars. The restaurant has also introduced its own beer menu.

Chef/s: Michel Roux. **Open:** Mon to Fri L 12 to 2, Mon to Sat D 6.30 to 11. **Closed:** Sun, 25 Dec to 2 Jan. **Meals:** alc (main courses £26 to £48). Set L £48 (including wine). Tasting menu D £95. **Service:** 12.5%. **Details:** Cards accepted. 70 seats. Air-con. Separate bar. Children's portions.

Gordon Ramsay at Claridge's

Aristocrat à la mode
Brook Street, W1A 2JQ
Tel no: (020) 7499 0099
www.gordonramsay.com
⊖ Bond Street
Modern European | £65
Cooking score: 5

🍷 🍽 V

Claridge's is synonymous with stately, old-world opulence and it's worth soaking up some of its aristocratic Art Deco majesty as you saunter through the grand hotel foyer on your way to the restaurant. However, be warned that the clientele is an odd mixture of old-school Mayfair, tourists and footballer's wives. It's fair to say that the jury is still out on the design of the re-branded dining room with its orangey-pink walls, purple chairs and OTT three-tiered light fittings, but the cooking more than makes amends. Fixed-price menus with extras aplenty are the order of the day and just about everything is firmly grounded in classical technique: veloutés, purées and confits abound. Dorset blue lobster might find its way into ravioli with basil vinaigrette, rump of Cumbrian lamb appears with mousseline, confit garlic and thyme jus, while Casterbridge beef keeps company with a pot-au-feu of root vegetables and jasmine consommé. Occasionally the kitchen goes à la mode, serving fillet of black bream with smoked potato purée, maple and almond-glazed chicken wings and wilted greens, while desserts show GR-inspired finesse across the board (butter-poached William pear with walnut financier and coffee ice cream, for example). However, at inspection, waiting staff stood around chatting and didn't bring our desserts. After half-an-hour, we reminded them of our order, but a further 15-minute wait brought the wrong dishes entirely. The wine list is a heavyweight French thoroughbred with pages of rare vintages jetting into the financial stratosphere, plus an enviable selection from elsewhere and a mouthwatering choice of 'stickies'; prices start at around £20.

Chef/s: Steve Allen and Mark Sargeant. **Open:** all week L 12 to 2.45 (3 Sat and Sun), D 5.45 to 11. **Meals:** Set L £30, Set D £65. **Service:** 12.5%. **Details:** Cards accepted. 100 seats. Air-con. Separate bar. No music. No mobile phones. Wheelchair access. Children's portions.

Guinea Grill

Beefy true-Brit food
30 Bruton Place, W1J 6NL
Tel no: (020) 7409 1728
www.theguinea.co.uk
British | £55
Cooking score: 2

Never a dedicated follower of fashion, the Guinea Grill remains a bastion of Bulldog Britishness in the heart of Mayfair. Devotees pack the two low-key, low-ceilinged dining rooms at the back of an old-school pub for trencherman platefuls of steak and kidney pie and other flag-waving classics. Steaks from 28-day dry-aged Scotch beef are strong contenders, and the kitchen also turns its hand to a motley assortment of dishes including smoked trout terrine with jellied quails' eggs, veal cutlet with marsala sauce and chicken Caesar salad, not forgetting various patriotic puds. Hefty sandwiches are served in the bar for those who want a snack with their pint of Young's, and the French-biased wine list has a fair spread of sound names at W1 prices: expect to pay at least £15 a bottle (£5 a glass).
Chef/s: Mark Newbury. **Open:** Mon to Fri L 12.30 to 2.30, Mon to Sat D 6 to 10.30. **Closed:** Sun, Christmas and bank hols. **Meals:** alc (main courses £12.50 to £35). Bar menu available. **Service:** 12.5%. **Details:** Cards accepted. 46 seats. Air-con. Separate bar. No music.

Hibiscus

Dazzling French cuisine in an experimental vein
29 Maddox Street, W1S 2PA
Tel no: (020) 7629 2999
www.hibiscusrestaurant.co.uk
⊖ Oxford Circus
French | £60
Cooking score: 7

When Claude and Claire Bosi first moved into the West End of London from their established base in Ludlow, Shropshire in 2007, there were some who wondered whether the business was altogether at home here. Hibiscus now occupies a ground-floor room in an office building just off Regent Street, the décor understated but comfortable, and the clientele a mix of city slickers, well-to-do tourists and Bosi fans. If we had our doubts then, they are now comprehensively dispelled. Hibiscus has acclimatised well, and a spring inspection found much to praise wholeheartedly. The cooking is high-rolling French cuisine with the accent on experiment based on sound culinary understanding. A main course that combines roast blade of Herefordshire beef with a razor clam cooked in lardo di Colonnata was a triumph of texture and taste. Another of grilled Pyrénean kid offered well-rested meat with the gentleness of veal, upheld by sweet garlic purée, pickled turnip, and a side dish of cottage pie made with some of the organ meat – a superb peformance. It's the kind of cooking that can look rather fragmented on presentation, but which comes into its own as the various ingredients are combined while eating. That was the case with a first course of mackerel tartare, garnished with Gariguette strawberries, celery and a dressing of wasabi and honey. It's also what sustains faith in desserts that might partner more of those strawberries, gratinated in sweet olive oil, with Parmesan sorbet, alongside a serving of whipped egg white topped with 75-year-old balsamic, or match a high-octane chocolate tart with an ice cream of Indonesian basil. 'The food is creative,' a reporter points out, 'but not so intellectualised that you fail to enjoy eating there. In other words, fresh, quality

Symbols

 Accommodation is available.

 Three courses for less than £30.

V More than five vegetarian dishes.

 £5-off voucher scheme.

 Notable wine list.

ingredients get to shine and, considering the high technique of the cooking, it's a lot of fun to eat at Hibiscus'. An opulent wine list will provide the enjoyment of agonised debate for the seriously resourced. Wines by-the-glass from £5 are very well chosen, though, including an excellent Petaluma Riesling, and the sommelier's selections are worth a look.

Chef/s: Claude Bosi. **Open:** Mon to Fri L 12 to 2.30, D 6.30 to 10. **Closed:** Last 2 weeks Aug, Christmas and New Year. **Meals:** Set L £25, Set D £60. **Service:** 12.5%. **Details:** Cards accepted. 45 seats. Air-con. No music. Wheelchair access. Children's portions.

Kiku

Long-established Japanese achiever
17 Half Moon Street, W1J 7BE
Tel no: (020) 7499 4208/4209
www.kikurestaurant.co.uk
⊖ Green Park
Japanese | £31
Cooking score: 4

In smart premises just off Piccadilly, Kiku has been serving reliable, polished Japanese cooking to central London since way before it became fashionable. The décor is restful, in muted shades of brown, and those who don't intend to linger can station themselves comfortably at the bar instead of taking a table. A series of fixed-price menus offers the expected range of dishes at different tariffs, but it's the à la carte menu that will most likely catch the eye. Cold appetisers include grated yam with quail's egg yolk or wasabi-dressed octopus, while the hot ones offer the enticing devil's tongue plant topped with sweet miso. Sashimi are present and correct, and the perhaps unfamiliar casserole dishes, such as mackerel with white radish, are worth a look. Lighter options include a range of noodle variations and there are chazuke soup dishes with flaked salt salmon or pickled plums. Finish up with the likes of green tea ice cream or Champagne sorbet. A range of sakés, as well as Japanese beers, provides the ethnically-appropriate alternative to a serviceable list of Western wines.

Chef/s: H. Shiraishi and Y. Hattori. **Open:** Mon to Sat L 12 to 2.30, all week D 6 to 10.15 (Sun 5.35 to 9.45). **Closed:** 25 and 26 Dec and New Year. **Meals:** alc (main courses £8.20 to £26) Set L £18 Set D £46 to £65. **Service:** 12.5%. **Details:** 95 seats. Air-con. Separate bar. Wheelchair access. Music. Children allowed.

Luciano

Classy Italian food
72-73 St James's Street, SW1A 1PH
Tel no: (020) 7408 1440
www.lucianorestaurant.co.uk
⊖ Green Park
Italian | £53
Cooking score: 4

£5 OFF V

A joint venture between Marco Pierre White and Sir Rocco Forte, Luciano occupies the site of Madame Prunier's fish restaurant, a popular venue of the early 1900s. It sits well with its fashionable past, and with the moneyed refinement of St James's Street. Its interior is big on personality, from the retro, clubby bar to the old-style glamour of the dining area. The name of one particular personality – MPW – is emblazoned on everything from the sign to the menus. In the kitchen, Marco Corsica delivers classy, big-flavoured Italian cooking, starting with antipasti such as king scallops with pumpkin and bottarga or carpaccio of Aberdeen Angus with mustard dressing. Straightforward primi include home-made ravioli with buffalo ricotta and spinach, and spaghetti with clams, chilli and garlic. Fresh fish puts in a good showing, perhaps as wild sea bass with tomato, olives and potato, while meat options run from slow-cooked leg of rabbit with porcini mushrooms to beef fillet with foie gras and truffle. As you'd expect, the wine list is largely Italian, and while most options are £20 and above, it opens at a reasonable £15.95.

Chef/s: Marco Corsica. **Open:** all week L 12 to 3, D 6 to 11. **Closed:** 25 Dec, bank hols. **Meals:** alc (main courses £17.50 to £29.95), Set L and D £51.

Service: 12.5%. **Details:** Cards accepted. 130 seats. 40 seats outside. Air-con. Separate bar. No music. Wheelchair access. Music. Children's portions.

Maze
Compelling flavour juxtapositions
10-13 Grosvenor Square, W1K 6JP
Tel no: (020) 7107 0000
www.gordonramsay.com
⊖ **Bond Street**
French | £50
Cooking score: 7

🍷 V

Maze shares a square with the US Embassy and a discreet entrance with Maze Grill, a recent addition to Gordon Ramsay's portfolio (see entry). Nevertheless, passers-by not in the know would be surprised to find a restaurant of such gastronomic ambition among the square's imposing but rather austere buildings. Inside, it's all very informal in an expensively unadorned, monochrome way – tables are clothless, the staff well-briefed and relaxed. Jason Atherton's menu is based on small dishes – tapas-sized portions, the recommendation being for around five or six per head. Confident, pace-setting cooking and compelling flavour juxtapositions are what to expect. Slow-roasted prawns with pumpkin purée, rye croûtons and vanilla oil, a 'stunning' crab mayonnaise and avocado with sweetcorn sorbet and Oscietra caviar, as well as marinated beetroot with mild, creamy Sairass goats' cheese, pine nuts and Cabernet Sauvignon dressing were star turns at a meal where delivery was uniformly impressive and 'not a dish could be faulted'. If a succession of small dishes doesn't appeal, there is also a carte, where some of the same compositions reappear, allowing you to progress in a more familiar rhythm through three courses – perhaps slow-roast quail with walnut purée, pickled lemons and white bean and Madeira sauce through rare-breed pork 'head-to-toe' – an oily, sticky cheek, slow-cooked belly served with a slick of olive oil mash, parsnip and spiced lentils and little parcel of deep-fried trotter with an intense gribiche-style sauce –

before coming to land on a chocolate moelleux with pistachio sabayon and milk and honey ice cream. There is also a good-value four- or six-course set lunch. The wine list offers 'Wines by Flight', where three glasses follow a theme, either by grape variety, country or vintage. Champagne, port, sherry and premium sakés are well-represented, while Bordeaux, Burgundy and Italy are the main attractions in the Old World. Bottle prices start at £20.
Chef/s: Jason Atherton. **Open:** all week L 12 to 2.30, D 6 to 10.30. **Meals:** Set Lunch £28 (4 courses) to £42.50 (6 courses). **Service:** 12.5%. **Details:** Cards accepted. 120 seats. Air-con. Separate bar. Wheelchair access. Music. Children allowed.

★NEW ENTRY★
Maze Grill
Something to beef about
10-13 Grosvenor Square, W1K 6JP
Tel no: (020) 7495 2211
www.gordonramsay.com
⊖ **Bond Street**
North American | £40
Cooking score: 5

'Wow, this place is buzzing', exclaimed a reporter on the latest offering from Gordon Ramsay Holdings, and early reports indicate that Maze Grill is set to run and run. It shares an entrance with big brother Maze on Grosvenor Square (see preceding entry), and inside soft sage green, pale oak and brown are the colours du jour. Meat is the thing (from grain- and grass-fed Brits to 'eye-wateringly expensive' imported prime U.S.D.A. and Wagyu), the cooking of which is built on admirable principles, both in sourcing from specialists and in the execution. The simple, uncluttered presentation on wooden boards also highlights the care and precision of the cooking. Onglet, for example (the cheapest steak at £10), is full of flavour and is stiff competition for a more expensive cut such as Aberdeen Angus fillet, while separately priced sides of béarnaise or peppercorn sauce, fries and onion rings are 'faultless'. Elsewhere, there are good starters of imaginative salads, pâtés

Food suppliers online

Rococo Chocolates
www.rococochocolates.com
With flavours and packaging as elaborate and exquisite as the name suggests, this chocolate maker manages to combine the qualities of a small, premier business with a comprehensive and extensive online service.

Montezumas
www.montezumas.co.uk
For a modern twist to a traditional treat, no other chocolate seller compares to Montezumas which insists all its ingredients are 'fairly traded'. Piranha fish have never looked so enticing as when rendered in marbled chocolate.

Betty's
www.bettysbypost.com/home
The delicacies of the world famous Yorkshire teashop chain can now be indulged on demand. Betty's luxury teas, coffees, cakes and biscuits are all available, as well as fruit cakes, studded with glazed fruit and nuts and presented in a distinctive octagonal tin.

Pure Flavour
www.pureflavour.co.uk
Though set up to provide tea time treats to those with a sweet tooth but on a restricted diet, this should not put anyone off Pure Flavour. It offers brownies, muffins and an assortment of sponges alongside a range of ready meals. You can also sign up for the Cake Club to receive a mystery cake every month.

Well Hung Meat
www.wellhungmeat.com/
Once a family business, now Well Hung Meat delivers a wide range of organic meat and poultry from a small group of hand picked farms across the south west

of England. Monthly and BBQ delivery boxes are also available as well as a broad assortment of cuts of lamb and beef.

Donald Russell
www.donaldrussell.com
Gourmet Scottish butcher by appointment to the Queen, Donald Russell supplies beef and lamb from grass-fed herds as well as an assortment of wild game including venison, partridge and hare. Traditional pies such as steak and kidney and shepherd's are also available.

Graig Farm
www.graigfarm.co.uk
Though produce now comes from a range of sources Graig Farm was one of the first suppliers of organic meat. Now the company offers patés, cheeses and other deli items as well as sustainable fish and rarer meats such as wild boar, mutton and goat.

and small tapas-style plates as well as an impressive sweet onion soup with beignet of oysters, crispy bacon and mushroom purée, while a few fish dishes and the likes of Gloucester Old Spot chop offer alternatives to steak. Among desserts, cinnamon doughnuts with hot chocolate dipping sauce and café coupe has found favour. Service is spot-on and wines open at £20.

Chef/s: Jason Atherton. **Open:** all week L 12 to 2.30 (Sat and Sun 4), D 5.45 to 10. **Meals:** alc (main courses £10 to £28 and market price). Set L £15 (2 courses) to £18. **Service:** 12.5% (optional). **Details:** Cards accepted. 80 seats. Air-con. Separate bar. Wheelchair access. Music. Children's portions.

Nobu Berkeley St

Cool international brand
15 Berkeley Street, W1J 8DY
Tel no: (020) 7290 9222
www.noburestaurants.com
⊖ **Green Park**
Japanese | £70
Cooking score: 5

V

Nobu is a global brand, extending its influence across continents, as one glance at its website map will attest. A certain gigantism is reflected within each individual branch, witness the 200 diners who reliably pack out this particular venue, marvelling at (and perhaps subtly trying to outdo) the glamorous David Collins décor. The menu formula matches the Old Park Lane original (see entry), since both are in the capable executive hands of New Zealander Mark Edwards. Splash that cash for the opulent likes of lobster wasabi, wagyu beef sashimi or the exquisitely presented skewered kushiyaki dishes of scallops, salmon or shrimp. Fixed-price deals, based perhaps on chicken with wasabi pepper sauce, come with miso soup and rice in the prescribed manner, and the tempura-battered items, including pumpkin, sweet potato and Japanese eggplant, are unfailingly done to a brittle crisp. Interlopers such as lamb Anti-Cucho, Gloucester Old Spot pork with spicy miso,

and octopus carpaccio with bottarga add lustre. Drink one of the fine sakés, or take a deep breath and plunge into the wine list, perhaps via the glass selection, which opens at £5.50 for an entirely fitting New Zealand Sauvignon.

Chef/s: Mark Edwards. **Open:** Mon to Fri L 12 to 2.15, all week D 6 to 11 (12 Thur to Sat, 9.15 Sun). **Closed:** 24 to 26 Dec, 1 Jan. **Meals:** alc (main courses £9 to £29.50). Set L £25 to £40. Set D £60 to £80. **Service:** 15%. **Details:** 200 seats. Air-con. Separate bar. Wheelchair access. Music.

Nobu London

Innovative Japanese fusion
19 Old Park Lane, W1K 1LB
Tel no: (020) 7447 4747
www.noburestaurants.com
⊖ **Hyde Park Corner**
Japanese
Cooking score: 5

🍷 ╘ V

One first-time visitor, worried that Nobu would be a rather formal affair, was delighted to find the restaurant 'lively and laid back'. And while it may be looking a little dated these days, the food still wows. Nobu Matsuhisa's signature style combines Japanese cuisine with South American influences to stunning effect, and starters might feature ceviche, a simple collection of seafood and vegetables with a spicy citrus dressing 'that zings with freshness', or 'meltingly delicious' beef from the 'new style' sashimi menu. Courgette and sweet potato tempura is a revelation, and the much-imitated black cod with miso 'deserves its acclaimed reputation', the fish flaking beautifully from the caramelised sweet marinade. Only scallops with spicy garlic sauce disappointed, the flavour of accompanying mushrooms overwhelming the dish. The innovative dessert menu might include apple toban yaki – a combo of apple seared with sesame oil, soy sauce toffee, peanut crumble and gyokuro ice cream. The wine list helps push up the bill.

There are a few bottles hovering at around £23 but most rise north of £30 quickly; there's also an extensive saké list.

Chef/s: Mark Edwards. **Open:** all week L 12 to 2.15 (12.30 to 2.30 Sat and Sun), D 6 to 10.15 (11.15 Sat, 9.45 Sun). **Meals:** alc (main courses £18.50 to £29.50). Set L £26 to £50. Set D £70. **Service:** 15% (optional). **Details:** Cards accepted. 160 seats. Air-con. No music. Wheelchair access. Children allowed.

★NEW ENTRY★
La Petite Maison
A taste of Nice
54 Brook Mews, W1K 4EG
Tel no: (020) 7495 4774
www.lpmlondon.co.uk
⊖ **Bond Street**
French | £42
Cooking score: 3

La Petite Maison is, nutshell-wise, the London version of a long-standing restaurant in Nice, brought to us by the team behind those modern Japanese restaurants Roka and Zuma (see entries). The premise is simple: Niçoise dishes served in an attractive, light but noisy triangular-shaped room. Main courses are advertised for sharing, with a couple designed for solo diners – an 'impeccable' roast baby chicken marinated in lemon, for example – but 'ignore any attempt to persuade you that starters are sharing material'. Shared or not, a 'packed with flavour' plate of marinated sardines served with grapes, tomatoes and capers, or deep-fried courgette flowers with sage, anchovies and onions typify the style. An underwhelming whole sea bream baked 'en papillote' left one table gazing wistfully at those tucking into a whole roast black leg chicken with foie gras, undoubtedly the (pricey) star dish here – which must be ordered in advance. To keep the bill in check, one dessert, say a dark chocolate tart with orange cream, and several spoons will suffice. Expect to pay at least £23 for even the humblest offerings on the Francophile wine list.

Chef/s: Raphael Duntoye. **Open:** Mon to Fri L 12 to 2.30pm, Mon to Sat D 6 to 11pm. **Meals:** alc (main courses £9 to £70). **Service:** 12.5%. **Details:** Cards accepted. 85 seats. Air-con. Wheelchair access. Music. Children allowed.

Ristorante Semplice
Simple yet subtle cooking
10 Blenheim Street, W1S 1LJ
Tel no: (020) 7495 1509
www.ristorantesemplice.com
⊖ **Green Park**
Italian | £30
Cooking score: 5
🍸 **V**

Semplice translates as 'simplicity', which is hardly an accurate description given the restaurant's sleek interior of walnut panels, wavy gold-frescoed walls, handsome black and cream leather, and streaks of inventiveness in the cooking. The regional cuisine of Lombardy and Piedmont takes pride of place, with rarely seen carpaccio of Fassano beef, Alba-style, served alongside noteworthy pastas like a squid ink stracci perfectly married with cuttlefish, clams and a parsley sauce, or craftily rich yet subtle linguine with a ragù of rabbit and black olives. Main courses seldom miss a beat. Milk-fed veal sourced from Piedmont is wrapped in Parma ham before roasting and served with sautéed spelt, asparagus and earthy morels. Desserts represent a final creative flourish in the form of a rhubarb and strawberry strudel with Modena balsamic vinegar. Service stands out – 'exuding the sort of warmth more normally associated with small family restaurants in rural Italy than on the doorstep of New Bond Street'. The all-Italian wines are assembled with care and intelligence; moderately-priced too, from £14 right up to £1,200 for the highly revered 1985 Barbaresco Sori Tidin from superstar winemaker Gaja. In between these extremes, there are gems from every region.

Chef/s: Marco Torri. **Open:** Mon to Fri L 12 to 2.30, Mon to Sat D 7 to 11. **Closed:** Sun, Christmas, Easter, bank hols. **Meals:** alc (main courses £18 to £23.50).

Set L £16 (2 courses) to £19. **Service:** 12.5%. **Details:** Cards accepted. 55 seats. 10 seats outside. Air-con. Wheelchair access. Music. Children allowed.

★NEW ENTRY★
Sake No Hana
Alan Yau's homage to Japanese food
23 St James's Street, SW1A 1HA
Tel no: (020) 7925 8988
⊖ Green Park
Japanese | £60
Cooking score: 5

Alan Yau's latest temple of cool has produced a reader response unlike any other new London opening. While some hail it as 'pure and unadulterated joy . . .for people who understand and love Japanese food', others have taken issue with the tatami mat seating where you 'have to take your shoes off, and then lever yourself into a table sunken into a pit in the floor' (ordinary tables are available). The drinks list is also a puzzler since it offers no wine, but promises quality speciality sakés and Champagnes at a price. The menu structure is quite complex, too, with multi-course tasting options – there are no starters or mains, just an array of dishes 'some tiny, some large'. The trick is to order the right combination of individual small dishes and those large enough to share. As for what to drink, the saké sommelier has been described as a 'star' so take his advice. Among highlights have been a tiny appetizer of mountain yam, sliced finely 'rather like noodles', with salmon roe, a small piece of wasabi root and a dipping sauce of dashi; 'very good' sashimi; Chilean sea bass with sweet miso, ginkgo nuts and shimeji mushrooms; takiawase of 'extremely tender' pork rib, or poulet noir ni – a pot of 'deeply flavoured' black leg chicken with soya bean, carrot, sugarsnap and yuzu pepper – and 'excellent' eel rice. With so many options, execution is almost bound to be patchy, but when on song, dishes will amaze. As will the final bill.
Chef/s: Masakazu Kikuchihara, Noboru Ishii. **Open:** Mon to Sat L 12 to 3, D 6 to 11 (11.30 Fri and Sat). **Closed:** 24 and 25 Dec. **Meals:** alc (main courses

from £8 to £70). **Service:** not inc. **Details:** Cards accepted. 77 seats. Air-con. Separate bar. No music. Wheelchair access.

★NEW ENTRY★
Sartoria
Sharply cut Italian
20 Savile Row, W1S 3PR
Tel no: (020) 7534 7000
www.danddlondon.com
⊖ Oxford Circus, Piccadilly Circus
Italian | £45
Cooking score: 2

Mayfair isn't exactly short of Italian restaurants, but brand recognition helps Sartoria stand out from the crowd. It is owned by D&D London (formerly Conran Restaurants), which means that visitors can expect a familiar combination of slick service, well-prepared (if rather undemanding) cooking and stylish surroundings, here referencing the Savile Row location with subtly suit-themed décor that appeals to corporate diners on expense accounts. Dishes tend towards the simple and classic – beef carpaccio or braised artichokes with mint and basil might be followed by veal milanese with rocket and cherry tomatoes, or a pasta course such as tagliolini carbonara, in which smoked eel replaces the pancetta. Finish with pannacotta or tiramisu. Charming Italian waiters add brio to proceedings, as does an all-Italian wine list with decent choice under £30. There's also a very natty bar serving potent cocktails.
Chef/s: Alain Marchetti. **Open:** Mon to Fri L 12 to 3, D 5.30 to 11, Sat 3 to 11. **Closed:** Sun, 26 Dec, 1 Jan, bank hols. **Meals:** alc (main courses £17 to £30). Set L and D £20 (2 courses) to £25. **Service:** 12.5%. **Details:** Cards accepted. 150 seats. Air-con. Separate bar. Wheelchair access. Music. Children's portions.

Scott's

Peerless people-watching opportunities
20 Mount Street, W1K 2HE
Tel no: (020) 7495 7309
www.scotts-restaurant.com
⊖ **Green Park**
Seafood | £50
Cooking score: 4

The resurrection of this classic fish restaurant has been one of the most glamorous London openings of the last few years. A huge crustacean display, glittering with fresh ice and looking like a recumbent Barbara Hepworth sculpture, dominates the front half of the restaurant, where light floods in through tall windows; green leather banquettes edge the rest of an oak-panelled dining room that offers peerless people-watching opportunities. Menus mix classic British cookery with splashes of Med colour, from soused mackerel with samphire to scampi provençale with fennel pilaf. A few meat dishes – Glencoe venison, rump of Cornish lamb – are available too. At inspection, onion tart topped with a poached egg was gloriously rich; to follow, the white flesh of a pair of slip soles slid easily from the bone, their sweet flavour matched by the accompanying cockles and shrimps and gently cut by a chervil butter sauce. To finish, Queen of Puddings more than merited its name. Glossy staff deliver slick service, though their smooth charm can at times seem patronising; for one visitor, they also failed to deal with a bickering family who upset everybody within earshot. France dominates a wine list that moves with swift ease past the £30 mark; 25 are available-by-the-glass or carafe. Note that the pavement terrace is one of the most-prized al fresco spots in Mayfair come the summer.
Chef/s: Kevin Gratton. **Open:** all week 12 to 10.30. **Closed:** 1 Jan, 25 Aug. **Meals:** alc (main courses £16 to £39.50). **Service:** 12.5%. **Details:** Cards accepted. 105 seats. Air-con. Separate bar. No mobile phones. Wheelchair access. Children allowed.

Sketch, Lecture Room and Library

A sumptuous pleasure palace
9 Conduit Street, W1S 2XG
Tel no: (020) 7659 4500
www.sketch.uk.com
⊖ **Oxford Circus**
Modern European | £70
Cooking score: 6

V

When Sketch opened at the end of 2002, attention focused on the stratospheric pricing and extravagant décor of its Lecture Room and Library, the top-floor fine-dining segment of the restaurant-cum-gallery complex. With the resurgence of Mayfair's luxury restaurant scene, it means that prices, though still very steep, no longer raise eyebrows as high as they once did. The interior design remains utterly unique, a sumptuous pleasure palace of padded white leather walls, oversized armchairs and beautifully chosen tableware. Sketch's presiding creative genius is co-owner and consultant chef Pierre Gagnaire, whose protégé Pascal Sanchez is executive head chef, delivering a style of cooking that tends to favour one ingredient presented several ways. That might mean langoustine prepared as a tartare, a mousseline with cardamom, pan-fried in beurre noisette, as a langoustine jelly, and grilled. Likewise, fillet of Simmental beef appears alongside ravioli filled with beef jus, thin slices of Wagyu beef fillet, and a pancake with bone marrow. Robust appetites may be disappointed by portion sizes, and a lingering suspicion of pretentiousness is not helped by dishes with names such as 'France as Seen by Pierre Gagnaire'. On the other hand, theatricality is all part of the appeal of a restaurant that aims to offer event dining rather than everyday eating (though bargain hunters should note a good three-course set lunch for £35). A 99-page wine list combines both quality and quantity (from £18) and an excellent by-the-glass choice includes a fantastic line-up of fortified wine.

Chef/s: Pierre Gagnaire and Pascal Sanchez. **Open:** Tue to Fri L 12 to 4, Tue to Sat D 6.30 to 12. **Closed:** Sun, Mon, Christmas, 1 Jan, bank hols. **Meals:** alc (main courses £32 to £52). Set L £30 (2 courses) to £35, Tasting menu £90 (8 courses). **Service:** 12.5%. **Details:** Cards accepted. 50 seats. Air-con. Separate bar. No mobile phones. Wheelchair access. Music. Children's portions.

The Square

One of the capital's most famous dining rooms
6-10 Bruton Street, W1J 6PU
Tel no: (020) 7495 7100
www.squarerestaurant.com
⊖ Green Park
Modern French | £65
Cooking score: 8

♣

'A pleasant ambiance and very good value' says one reporter, 'lovely food in a quirky setting' adds another. The Square opened in 1991 in the teeth of a recession and, as fears grow once again for the state of the UK economy, it's safe to say that, whatever the fall-out from the credit crunch and the rising cost of living, The Square will not number among any casualties on the London restaurant scene. This is one of the capital's most famous dining rooms, but it's not for the hope of seeing a famous face or eating in super-cool surroundings that regulars – many of whom have stayed loyal since the early nineties – return; rather, it's for the cooking of co-owner Philip Howard, a chef who has shunned the limelight of TV and magazine columns to develop a total mastery of kitchen craft. Presentation is superb and evidently the result of serious time spent on each dish, yet the results never taste tricksy or overwrought and there's no sense of chef grandstanding; instead, the cooking is all about demonstrating an innate understanding of how ingredients should work together to deliver the most enjoyment to the person eating them. The menus have been keenly seasonal long before the term became fashionable. For spring, that might mean starting with steamed courgette flowers filled with a mousseline of chicken and goats' cheese

with girolles, pickled vegetables and hazelnut oil, ahead of slow-cooked Icelandic cod with crushed new potatoes, langoustine claws, parsley and lemon, with peach Melba soufflé to finish. The exemplary wine list excels in an exhaustive selection of classic French regions, but the rest of the world is by no means neglected; the collection of sweet wines is another highlight for oenophiles. Prices, of course, are steep, but the Square delivers a complete package, with attentive service from true professionals underscoring the impressive food and drink. There's a good-value set lunch menu; at the other end of the spectrum, the eight-course tasting menu is £90.

Chef/s: Philip Howard. **Open:** Mon to Fri L 12 to 2.45, all week D 6.30 to 10.45 (10 Sun). **Closed:** bank hols L, 25 Dec, 1 Jan. **Meals:** Set menu £65. **Service:** 12.5%. **Details:** Cards accepted. 75 seats. Air-con. Wheelchair access. Children allowed.

Sumosan

Modern Japanese for the in-crowd
26 Albemarle Street, W1S 4HY
Tel no: (020) 7495 5999
www.sumosan.com
⊖ Green Park
Japanese | £50
Cooking score: 4

V

Handy for the big hotels, designer shops, auction houses, galleries and hedge funds, Sumosan feeds on the crowds supplied by all of the above: wealthy A-listers unfussed by sumo-sized bills and bonsai portions. The room, in clean lines and soft colours, remains contemporary and comfortable, although perhaps beginning to look a little faded. The menu is a by now familiar Japanese-western fusion with an indulgent dose of luxury ingredients as befits the locale, though there's a reasonable bento lunch popular with business and single diners. If you're in a position to shell out, be assured the standard is high. There's no doubting the quality of the sushi and sashimi. The vast, 'slightly silly' array of sushi rolls ranges from the gimmicky T&T (a love-it-or-hate-it house special of tuna and truffle),

Peking duck or Philadelphia, to more classical choices such as cucumber and salmon skin. Rock shrimp tempura and Chilean sea bass proved good choices, the waiter-recommended lobster salad less so. The latter's presentation in a verdant dome at least elicited an 'ooh' and an 'aah'. And the bill? That elicited an 'oh.' Wines open at £18, with an extensive saké choice from £21.

Chef/s: Bubker Belkhit. **Open:** Mon to Fri, L 12 to 3, all week D 6 to 12 (11 Sun). **Closed:** Christmas, bank hols. **Meals:** Set menus £22.50 to £79. **Service:** 15%. **Details:** Cards accepted. 150 seats. Air-con. Separate bar. Music.

Tamarind

First-rate contemporary Indian cuisine
20 Queen Street, W1J 5PR
Tel no: (020) 7629 3561
www.tamarindrestaurant.com
⊖ Green Park
Modern Indian | £45
Cooking score: 4

It is a truth universally acknowledged that basement restaurants don't work. Yet Tamarind, in the heart of Mayfair, remains one of the few exceptions to the rule – it is a prime spot for first-rate Indian cuisine. The menu mixes the contemporary with the traditional, with the north-west Indian influence of cooking in the tandoor giving prominence to a range of 'kababs': from grilled paneer stuffed with spiced fig and raisins and marinated in yoghurt, spices and saffron, via suprême of chicken marinated with cream, cheese, coriander stem and cardamom, to 'seekh kabab' (ground lamb with garlic, green chilli, peppers, coriander and spices). Other main courses may include rich curries of slow-cooked lamb shanks or fillet of sea bass with cumin, turmeric and spinach, tossed in a tangy tomato sauce. Start, perhaps, with grilled shrimp, scallops and batter-fried baby squid in a lime-dressed salad of rocket with toasted cumin and chaat masala, and finish with gulab jamun – a

dumpling of unsweetened reduced milk, served with caramel sauce. House vin de pays d'Oc is £17.

Chef/s: Alfred Prasad. **Open:** all week L 12 to 2.45, D 6 to 11.15. **Closed:** Christmas, bank hols L. **Meals:** Set L £18.95, pre theatre £24, tasting menus £52 and £72. **Service:** 12.5%. **Details:** Cards accepted. 85 seats. Air-con. Music.

Theo Randall at the InterContinental

Approachable Italian cooking on Park Lane
InterContinental London Hotel, 1 Hamilton Place, W1J 7QY
Tel no: (020) 7318 8747
www.theorandall.com
⊖ Hyde Park Corner
Italian | £45
Cooking score: 6

⊟ V

Given chef Theo Randall's stellar River Café pedigree, it's a shame not to hear more buzz about his eponymous restaurant. As Park Lane's hotel dining rooms fill up with ever-fancier chefs and fancier food, it's a real pleasure to find such rustic, ingredient-driven Italian cooking as Randall's in a five-star hotel. Antipasti are wholesome and generous, plated unfussily: Parma ham with trevise, Parmesan and aged balsamic or fresh Devon crab salad with rocket, fennel and aïoli are classic examples. Pasta and risottos are exemplary and the wood-fired oven is put to good use for the likes of Cornish monkfish with Roseval potatoes, artichokes and pancetta. While there can be few complaints about quality of ingredients, cooking or consistency, lunch reminded one reporter why this excellent restaurant doesn't enjoy a higher profile. Only a handful of tables were taken in the spacious, though windowless, dining room (decked out in modish pistachio and brown) and polite, well-drilled, if rather stiff waiting staff were clearly underemployed. When full, it's lively and vibrant, but on a quiet service 'it feels a little corporate'. However, the set lunch remains one of London's better deals: bruschette, say, followed by a spikey puntarelle salad, a flawless trevise risotto, stuffed organic chicken breast, and a soft chocolate cake with mascarpone to finish. Fittingly, the wine list is predominantly Italian, though not exclusively so, with French and New World bottles making up the 160-strong list, which opens at £21.

Chef/s: Theo Randall. **Open:** Mon to Fri L 12 to 3, Mon to Sat D 5.45 to 11.15. **Closed:** Sat L and Sun. **Meals:** alc (main courses £24 to £30). Set L £21 (2 courses) to £25. **Service:** 12.5%. **Details:** Cards accepted. 124 seats. Air-con. Separate bar. Wheelchair access. Music. Children's portions. Car parking.

Umu

Gilt-edged Kyoto cuisine
14-16 Bruton Place, W1J 6LX
Tel no: (020) 7499 8881
www.umurestaurant.com
⊖ Green Park
Japanese | £55
Cooking score: 5

♨ V

London's first Kyoto restaurant is anonmyously hidden away down a Mayfair side-street. Use the palm-operated security pad to gain entrance, and marvel at the interior: here is a high-gloss world created by cutting-edge designer Tony Chi that spares nothing when it comes to lavish, sensory indulgence. You know immediately that this is not going to be cheap. Chef Ichiro Kubota has Kyoto in his blood and revels in the city's arcane gastronomic heritage. He explores the high-art world of refined kaiseki banquets in depth, and you can opt for the ultra-formal ritual or assemble your own feast from core component dishes on the carte. Among the appetisers, look for miso gratin with scallops, maitake and king oyster mushrooms or chu toro salad with quail's egg and Japanese pickles. Sashimi is a blend of ancient and modern (tsukuri of tuna with balsamic vinegar and sesame seeds, for example), while main courses naturally call upon gold-standard Wagyu beef; also note the Iberico

pork (marinated in three miso flavours) and grilled lobster with soy sauce velouté.

Soups venture well beyond the Japanese norm, while the creative impulse also shows in Kyoto sundaes (vanilla and black bean ice cream with green tea cake) and other crossover desserts. To drink, don't ignore the dazzling collection of around 70 premium sakés; otherwise brace yourself for eye-watering prices but supreme quality on the vast wine list, which spans the globe from France through majestic New World selections to Japanese Château Mercian. Expect to pay from £30 a bottle (£6 a glass).

Chef/s: Ichiro Kubota. **Open:** Mon to Sat L 12 to 2.30, D 6 to 11. **Closed:** Sun, Christmas and bank hols. **Meals:** alc (main courses £10 to £39). Set L £21 to £45, Set D £90 to £125 (inc wine). **Service:** 12.5% (optional). **Details:** Cards accepted. 56 seats. Air-con. No mobile phones. Wheelchair access. Music. Children allowed.

★NEW ENTRY★
Wild Honey

A balance of skill, imagination and value
12 St George Street, W1S 2FB
Tel no: (020) 7758 9160
www.wildhoneyrestaurant.co.uk
⊖ Bond Street
Modern British | £30
Cooking score: 6

With its Georgian front and clubby interior of oak panelling, polished boards and banquette seating, Wild Honey feels as if it has been operating from this Mayfair site for decades. This latest opening by Anthony Demetre and Will Smith extends the Arbutus formula (see entry) and is, in one reporter's opinion, 'a real treat'. The menu moves from day to day, and although in many ways it shows the inclinations of simple British cooking, its real loyalty is to be reassuringly cosmopolitan – for example starters include red mullet with vegetables à la grecque, and braised shoulder of hare with soft polenta and Parmesan. The results can be brilliant, full-blooded and sensual: glazed salsify and roast quince enriching a main course of wild duck or intensely flavoured roast Buccleuch beef perfectly partnered by baked onion and autumn vegetable purée. From the 'excellent value-for-money' £15.50 lunch, reporters have praised 'a deliciously meaty mouthful' of tête-de-veau (with sauce gribiche), 'unctious long-cooked' shortrib of beef, and an 'authentic floating island'. As at Arbutus, the wine list has been skilfully assembled and offers great value, starting at £12.50; most bottles are also available in 250ml carafes. **Chef/s:** Colin Kelly. **Open:** all week L 12 to 2.30, D 6 to 10.30 (9.30 Sun). **Closed:** 25 and 26 Dec, 1 Jan. **Meals:** alc (main courses £14.95 to £17.95). Set L £15.50, pre-theatre (6 to 7) £17.50. **Service:** 12.5% (optional). **Details:** Cards accepted. 65 seats. Air-con. Wheelchair access. Children's portions.

Wiltons

Old-school British aristocrat
55 Jermyn Street, SW1Y 6LX
Tel no: (020) 7629 9955
www.wiltons.co.uk
⊖ Green Park
British | £50
Cooking score: 4

V

Wiltons' reign in the heart of Mayfair started when it opened as a shellfish stall in 1742; since then it has established itself as a premier British restaurant and the epitome of 'old school', complete with a uniformed doorman to greet diners. Inside, it feels for all the world like a cosseted gentlemen's club, with print-festooned walls, impeccably groomed staff and an archaic 'jacket and tie' policy. The menu is old-school, too, an ultra-conservative mix of grills, roasts, crustacea and seasonal game: come here if you enjoy potted shrimps, beef consommé (served hot or cold), lobster Newburg and lamb cutlets. Occasionally the kitchen indulges in flights of fancy and the modern world intrudes, but it's back to the good old days for English savouries (mushrooms on toast) and domestic puds (sherry trifle, apple and fig crumble). Crowds of suited-and-booted regulars also congregate in the refurbished Oyster Bar for bivalves and bottles of Bollinger. Needless to say, the big,

beefy wine list list is stuffed with heavyweight clarets and Burgundies from some of the golden years – all at predictably rarefied prices. Expect to pay at least £32 a bottle (£7 a glass). **Chef/s:** Jerome Ponchelle. **Open:** Mon to Fri L 12 to 2.30, D 6 to 10.30. **Closed:** Sat, Sun, Christmas and bank hols. **Meals:** alc (main courses £18 to £50). Set D Fri £55. **Service:** 12.5%. **Details:** Cards accepted. 90 seats. Air-con. No music. No mobile phones. Wheelchair access. Jacket and tie required. Children allowed.

Wolseley

All-day dining haven
160 Piccadilly, W1J 9EB
Tel no: (020) 7499 6996
www.thewolseley.com
⊖ Green Park
Modern European | £40
Cooking score: 2

Built in the 1920s as a car showroom, this beautiful art deco building makes a stunning setting for Chris Corbin and Jeremy King's café-restaurant in the 'grand European tradition'. On the glitzy Ritz strip, it has a casual feel with waiters creating a draught as they rush past the closely packed tables delivering crowd pleasing dishes such as all-day sandwiches, salads, crustacea, hamburgers, steak tartare and weiner Holstein – service is remarkably good considering that up to one thousand customers pass through here each day. An excellent starter of chicken liver parfait might precede salt cod on parsley and garlic mash with black olive tapenade, but the food occasionally shows signs of strain: a chopped salad looked 'wilted and weary', while an otherwise good dessert of 'hearty and well-spiced' apple strudel 'seemed to have been left cut for some time'. However, afternoon tea is 'a treat'. Wines start at £18. **Chef/s:** Julian O'Neill. **Open:** Mon to Fri 7am to 12am, Sat 8am to 12am, Sun 8am to 11pm. **Closed:** Christmas and New Year, Aug bank hol.

Service: 12.5%. **Details:** Cards accepted. 150 seats. Air-con. Separate bar. No music. Wheelchair access. Children's portions.

READERS RECOMMEND

The Café at Sotheby's
British
34–35 New Bond Street, Mayfair, W1A 2AA
Tel no: (020) 7293 5077
www.sothebys.com
'An eclectic selection of food and wine'

Kai Mayfair
Chinese
65 South Audley Street, Mayfair, W1K 2QU
Tel no: (020) 7493 8988
www.kaimayfair.co.uk
'Chinese food with class'

Truc Vert
Modern European
42 North Audley Street, Mayfair, W1K 6ZR
Tel no: (020) 7491 9988
www.trucvert.co.uk
'Splendid value deli-cum-restaurant'

▌Oxford Circus

★NEW ENTRY★
Dehesa
Upscale Spanish dining in a chic corner site
25 Ganton Street, W1F 9BP
Tel no: (020) 74944170
www.dehesa.co.uk
⊖ Oxford Circus
Spanish/Italian | £20
Cooking score: 3

£30

Fans of Goodge Street Italo-Spanish tapas restaurant, Salt Yard, are a loyal bunch, but reports suggest they're finding it hard to resist the allure of its Soho sister, Dehesa. This second restaurant for Simon Mullins and Sanja Morris takes the ingredients-driven, modern style of Salt Yard's cooking and recontextualises it successfully in a well-located, chic corner site. Named after the woodland area and home to Iberico pigs in Spain, Dehesa puts a strong emphasis on charcuterie, with whole hams on display. Recommended tapas dishes include classic Spanish morcilla croquetas, stuffed courgette flowers and chargrilled baby squid with chickpea purée. The part-Italian, part-Spanish wine list (from £15) wins over sherry fans with rare finds from cult bodegas such as Fernando de Castilla. A casual feel pervades, with a no-reservations policy, bar stools and high narrow tables intended for quick pit-stops. The bay window tables are hot tickets.
Chef/s: Arturo Ortiz. **Open:** all week L 12 to 3 (11 to 3 Sat, 11 to 5 Sun), Mon to Sat D 5 to 11. **Closed:** last week in Dec. **Meals:** alc (tapas £4 to £7.50). **Service:** 12.5%. **Details:** Cards accepted. 38 seats. 18 seats outside. Air-con. Music. Children allowed.

★NEW ENTRY★
The Landau
Elegant hotel dining
Langham Hotel, 1 Portland Place, W1B 1JA
Tel no: (020) 7636 1000
www.thelandau.com
⊖ Oxford Circus
Modern European | £47
Cooking score: 4

Andrew Turner is a chef with a track record of good London hotel openings – at 1880 at the Bentley Kempinski, and prior to that at Brown's (see entry). Now he's starring at the Landau, the Langham Hotel's stylishly revamped restaurant. His food takes a broadly European perspective, with grazing menus a trademark (and representing a good way of sampling the range), and an à la carte that offers a well-balanced, simply dressed salad of truffles and artichokes with quails'eggs, or pumpkin soup with cep and more quails'egg as openers. Main dishes are mostly classics with a modern touch: Dover sole meunière with onions three ways, balsamic, parsley and purple potatoes, for example, or Gloucester Old Spot pork, honey-glazed parsnips,

pickled cabbage and star anise. Desserts such as Granny Smith apple mille-feuille and sherbet with chocolate oil are followed by good coffee and chocolates, and service is generally praised. The wine list is extensive without being intimidating, covering a wide range of countries and including good New World growers such as Ridge. Prices start from £22.
Chef/s: Andrew Turner. **Open:** all week, L 12.30 to 2.30, D 5.30 to 11 (10 Sun). **Meals:** alc (main courses £9.50 to £30). Set L £20 (2 courses) to £32.50, pre theatre £20 (2 courses) to £27.50. **Service:** 12.5% (optional). **Details:** Cards accepted. 100 seats.

Piccadilly

Bentley's
A seafood institution
11-15 Swallow Street, W1R 7HD
Tel no: (020) 7734 4756
www.bentleys.org
⊖ Piccadilly Circus
£43
Cooking score: 4

There is a lot to like about Bentley's, with its handsome ground floor bar and attractive dining area, and full-dressed dining room upstairs. The atmosphere is clubby, but in a friendly way. Richard Corrigan's appealing menu is straightforward with plenty to please, from a generous portion of very fresh crab with a good mayonnaise to nicely grilled tiger prawns with a chickpea purée laced with olive oil and well-judged chilli, and the likes of smoked haddock with crushed potatoes, a poached egg and a few greens as a base to follow. But there have been a few niggles, too: Belvelly smoked eel, for example, was 'rather a let-down', the eel lacking in taste, accompanying potato pancakes were pleasant, but crème fraîche 'was not the most imaginative accompaniment'. For dessert, a lemon posset, while pleasant, was overwhelmed by the thick layer of rhubarb and ginger on a crumble top. Chocolate and hazelnut meringue with buttermilk sorbet made a better finish. The Guide has not seen a copy of the wine list this year, nor was our questionnaire returned, so some of the information below may have changed.
Chef/s: Brendan Fyldes. **Open:** Sun to Fri L 12 to 2.45, all week D 6 to 11. **Meals:** alc (main courses £13.95 to £40). **Service:** 12.5%. **Details:** Cards accepted. 200 seats. Air-con. No music. Wheelchair access. Children's portions.

St Alban
Modern flair, cosmopolitan accent
Rex House, 4-12 Lower Regent Street, SW1Y 4PE
Tel no: (020) 7499 8558
www.stalban.net
⊖ Piccadilly Circus
Modern European | £31
Cooking score: 4

Chris Corbin and Jeremy King's 'energetic' dining room is thoroughly contemporary, sporting curvy banquettes, bright colours and linear images of household and domestic items on the frosted plate glass windows and walls. Industrious waiting staff ensure the whole set-up runs like clockwork, while the kitchen is able to satisfy, raiding the northern Mediterranean and Iberian countries with gusto. A shrimp salad with tonnato dressing has plenty of flavour and bite, a dish of deep-fried soft-shell crab with tarragon mayonnaise is 'great comfort food'. Among main courses confit duck leg with candied fruit and blood oranges is a fresh take on the classic duck à l'orange, while well-timed gilthead bream requires nothing more than a zingy citrus dressing. It is undoubtedly the quality of the raw materials that elevates these dishes above their inherent simplicity, an impression made again in the form of a Braeburn apple tart with vanilla ice cream. The wine list mirrors the food in its sweep. House wine from £15.75.

Chef/s: Dale Osborne. **Open:** all week L 12 to 3, D 5.30 to 12 (11 Sun). **Meals:** Set menu £15.50 (2 courses) to £19.75. **Service:** 12.5% (optional). **Details:** Cards accepted. 140 seats. Separate bar. Wheelchair access. Music. Children's portions.

ALSO RECOMMENDED
▲ Veeraswamy
99-101 Regent Street, Piccadilly, W1R 8RS
Tel no: (020) 7734 1401
www.veeraswamy.com
⊖ Piccadilly Circus
Indian

After its 80th-birthday remodelling in 2006, Veeraswamy – London's oldest Indian restaurant – has certainly regained its former 1920s glamour and added an eye-catching modern-day edge, too. It's a classy look with dramatic lighting from richly coloured glass shades and gleaming chandeliers, black granite flecked with gold, dark wood or floral carpets decorating floors, and silver jali screens offering a modicum of privacy. The cooking combines classical pan-Indian dishes with more modern themes, ranging from a home-style Lucknow chicken korma with saffron (£15.50) to a classic Hyderabad lamb biryani (£18). House wine kicks off at £18.50. Open all week. See also sister London restaurants Amaya and Chutney Mary.

█ Soho
Alastair Little
Durable Soho icon
49 Frith Street, W1D 4SG
Tel no: (020) 7734 5183
⊖ Tottenham Court Road
Modern European | £40
Cooking score: 2

Hailed as a trailblazer during London's gastronomic renaissance of the 1980s, this Soho landmark has stood the test of time, although Alastair Little moved on a while back. The spare minimalist dining room is much as it was in the early days, with rustic stripped pine floors, modern art and a calm, laid back feel. Juliet Peston has been the driving force here for a number of years and the food still has a sharp Mediterranean sting in its tail. Sizzling prawns with parsley, chilli and garlic is a perennial favourite, and the kitchen also pleases the faithful with carpaccio, risottos and fillet steak with Caesar salad. Elsewhere, expect eclectic adventures in the form of smoked eel with chorizo, beetroot and Pardina lentil vinaigrette, nettle and ricotta ravioli or sea bass with soba noodles, shrimps, seaweed and soy broth. The sunny theme continues with desserts such as 'beautiful Helen pear' with pistachio praline or affogato all caffè. Globetrotting wines fit the bill from £18.50 (£3.50 a glass). **Chef/s:** Juliet Peston. **Open:** Mon to Fri L 12 to 3, Mon to Sat D 5.30 to 11.30. **Closed:** Sun, bank hols, 25 and 26 Dec. **Meals:** Set L and D £35 (2 courses) to £40. Theatre menu £18 (2 courses) to £23. **Service:** not inc. **Details:** Cards accepted. 60 seats. 4 seats outside. Air-con. No music. Children's portions.

Andrew Edmunds
46 Lexington Street, W1F OLW
Tel no: (020) 7437 5708
⊖ Oxford Street, Piccadilly Circus
Modern European | £25
Cooking score: 2
 £30

There's a distinct touch of the Dickensian about the dark, candle-lit interior of this Soho stalwart. The décor is rustic, tables are crammed in tightly and elbow-to-elbow dining is somewhat inevitable, but while the basement dining room is a touch gloomy, upstairs offers prime viewing of the bustle in the street. The kitchen has been serving up a daily changing menu for over 30 years and it still delivers modern dishes with varying degrees of input from the British repertoire: roll-mop herrings with potato and apple salad at one end, rib-eye steak with a caper and anchovy butter at the other, with sticky toffee pudding a typical dessert. The kitchen's output, and hence reports, are mixed and service can sometimes be 'indifferent', yet the place has built up a loyal following possibly because Andrew Edmunds is a wine buff and his blackboard menu of wine specials often features unusual and boutique wines at good prices. House wines start at £14.50.

Chef/s: Rebecca St John-Cooper. **Open:** all week L 12.30 to 3 (1 to 3 Sat, 1 to 3.30 Sun), D 6 to 10.45 (10.30 Sun). **Closed:** Christmas and New Year, Easter, August bank hol. **Meals:** alc (main courses) £10 to £18. **Service:** 12.5%. **Details:** Cards accepted. 42 seats. 4 seats outside. Air-con. No music. No mobile phones. Wheelchair access. Children allowed.

Arbutus

Uncluttered seasonal menu
63-64 Frith Street, W1D 3JW
Tel no: (020) 7734 4545
www.arbutusrestaurant.co.uk
⊖ **Tottenham Court Road**
Modern European | £30
Cooking score: 6

Two years on, there's a lot to be said for Arbutus under its proprietors Anthony Demetre and Will Smith. All is neat, uncluttered and unshowy: functional modern design with plain wooden chairs and simply dressed tables is the backdrop to an equally uncluttered seasonal menu built around excellent raw materials from leading suppliers. The menu offers an intriguing array of dishes, from crisp warm ox tongue teamed with escarole salad and gribiche sauce, via braised pig's head with potato purée and caramelised onions, to 'impeccably fresh-tasting' squid and mackerel burger with parsley and razor clams. There's some fine and original cooking in main courses, too, with a proper appreciation of the importance of flavour: saddle of rabbit teamed with a cottage pie made of the shoulder in late summer, for example, or a well-judged piece of halibut served with potatoes lyonnaise and hispi cabbage in early spring. It is worth remembering the good value set-price menus. Lunch might consist of porchetta with Granny Smith apple purée and pecorino, followed by Elwy Valley lamb with aubergines and courgettes, then vanilla

cheesecake. Slight mis-timing on the part of service occasionally unsettles, but the performance is usually sound. Prices start at £12.50 on an appealing wine list, with many available in 250 ml carafes.

Chef/s: Anthony Demetre. **Open:** all week L 12 to 2.30 (Sun 3), D 5 to 11 (Sun 5.30 to 9.30). **Closed:** 25 and 26 Dec, 1 Jan. **Meals:** Set L £15.50, Pre theatre £17.50. **Service:** 12.5%. **Details:** Cards accepted. 75 seats. Air-con. No music. Wheelchair access. Children's portions.

Bar Shu

Fiercely authentic Szechuan cooking
28 Frith Street, W1D 5LF
Tel no: (020) 7287 8822
⊖ **Leicester Square**
Chinese | £35
Cooking score: 4

Bar Shu specialises in Szechuan cookery, renowned for its spiciness, yet dining takes place in a calm environment with dark wood furnishings, intricate wood carvings and lanterns. A moreish plate of shelled edamame beans, diced carrots, wood-ear fungus and a dash of sesame oil dressing is a gentle introduction before the full-on assault on the senses: baby cuttlefish with crunchy celery and baby pak choi, festooned with lip-tingling pickled red chillies; 'deliriously rich' red braised belly of pork, guaranteed to have you mopping up the sauce. A Szechuan favourite of dry-fried ya cai (preserved mustard green) with minced pork should not be missed. Presentation is dazzling. A whole deep-fried sea bass arrives like a piece of sculpture, made special by an excellent sweet-and-sour sauce. To finish, try deep-fried taro rolls. Service can appear glum but it is accommodating. Wines, an unlikely companion to all this firepower, start from £19.90.

Chef/s: Fu Wenhong. **Open:** all week 12 to 11.30. **Closed:** 25 and 26 Dec. **Meals:** alc (main courses £7 to £68). Set L £19.50 to £22.50, Set D £22.50 to £24.50 (all min 2). **Service:** 12.5%. **Details:** Cards accepted. 150 seats. Air-con. Wheelchair access. Music.

Barrafina

Real-deal tapas
54 Frith Street, W1D 4SL
Tel no: (020) 7813 8016
www.barrafina.co.uk
⊖ **Tottenham Court Road**
Spanish/Tapas | £28
Cooking score: 4

V

A tiny slice of Barcelona street life transported to Soho, Barrafina is the brainchild of brothers Sam and Eddie Hart, and comes out of the same stable as Fino (see entry). But this is a very different plate of tapas: it's a fast-turnover, no-bookings joint with just 23 high stools grouped around a marble counter and the frenetic open kitchen in full view. At peak times, be prepared to hang around for up to an hour with a drink and a nibble until a seat becomes free. Top-notch Spanish provisions form the bedrock of the short core menu, which is bolstered by daily seafood specials and much else besides: the results are as sharp as a matador's espada. Among the seriously good things on offer are ham croquetas, prime cured meats, octopus with capers and more red-blooded delights such as morcilla with piquillo peppers, grilled quail with alioli and pork chops with cauliflower purée. If thoughts turn to something sweet, try classic Santiago tart, strawberry salad or crema Catalana. Sherries are plentiful and the brief all-Spanish wine list starts at £15 (with everything available by-the-glass).

Chef/s: Nieves Barragan. **Open:** all week L 12 to 3, D 5 to 11. **Closed:** bank hols. **Meals:** alc (dishes £4.50 to £14.50). **Service:** 12.5%. **Details:** Cards accepted. 23 seats. 10 seats outside. Air-con. No music. Children's portions. Children allowed.

★NEW ENTRY★
Café Boheme

13-17 Old Compton Street, W1D 5GQ
Tel no: (020) 7734 0623
www.cafeboheme.co.uk
⊖ **Piccadilly, Leicester Square**
French | £30
Cooking score: 3

V

At last – a perfect brasserie in Soho. Café Boheme has always been owned by Nick Jones of Soho House, and has recently been refurbished to revamp its Bohemian charm. Henry Harris (ex-Racine) has composed a simple menu of classic dishes, catering for breakfast, brunch, lunch, dinner and even midnight dining. Staff are utterly charming, without being intrusive. The entrance is something of a thoroughfare, but once inside you're met with Parisian bistro chic – think deep red leather banquettes and fringed lampshades. A starter of pâté au campagne and pain polaine brought coarse, spiced meat in a delicate jelly, with capers and gherkins on the side. For mains, a huge slab of steak was perfectly cooked, medium-rare. Simple spring greens on the side were buttered and frites were fresh and crispy. For dessert, try the Coupe Boheme (espresso, Chantilly and vanilla ice cream), served in a tall glass on a silver platter with a doily. A chocolate mousse was served in a similar fashion and brought a light and velvety texture to the palate. It's fantastic to find solid bistro classics at reasonable prices in the heart of town.

Chef/s: Henry Harris and Andy Beddoes. **Open:** all week 8 to 2.30am (midnight Sun). **Closed:** 25 Dec. **Meals:** alc (main courses £10 to £19). **Service:** 12.5%. **Details:** Cards accepted. 75 seats. 30 seats outside. Air-con. Separate bar. Wheelchair access. Music. Children's portions.

SOHO

★ BEST VALUE RESTAURANT ★

Côte

Bustling bistro in the middle of town
124–126 Wardour Street, W1F 0TY
Tel no: (020) 7287 9280
www.cote-restaurants.co.uk
⊖ Tottenham Court Road
French | £22
Cooking score: 2

Bistros are like buses. You spend years waiting for decent, simple fare in Soho, and suddenly two land at once. Côte is closer to Oxford Street than Henry Harris's Cafe Boheme, and it's cheaper. Created by the Strada team (who brought us Côte in Wimbledon last year, see entry), it has a buzzy Soho vibe. The uncluttered interior channels the famous bistros of Paris and the food follows suit. Expect 'fantastic value and presentation' from dishes such as moules mariniere or a terrine of duck, chicken and pork liver with toasted sourdough and grape chutney followed by 'perfect' grilled chicken with home-made frites and Provençale sauce. Other choices include a substantial list of grills and steaks, and light mains such as a summer risotto with broad beans or scallops with ratatouille. Desserts range from 'average' ice cream to an 'excellent' creme caramel. House wines start at £13.95.
Chef/s: Mr Gazne. **Open:** Mon to Wed 8am to 11pm; Thu and Fri 8am to 12am; Sat 9am to 12am; Sun 9am to 10.30. **Meals:** (alc) mains £8.50 to £12.95. **Service:** 12.5%. **Details:** Cards accepted. 150 seats. Air-con. Wheelchair access. Music. Children allowed.

Gay Hussar

Time-honoured Hungarian legend
2 Greek Street, W1D 4NB
Tel no: (020) 7437 0973
www.gayhussar.co.uk
⊖ Tottenham Court Road
Hungarian | £25
Cooking score: 1

Born in 1953 (and now in its fifty-second year as a Guide entry), this redoubtable Soho legend hardly changes as the decades pass. The dark, narrow downstairs room, which has been likened to an antique railway carriage, remains an even-tempered bolthole for political high-rankers (their caricatures line the walls) as well as curious tourists. The resolutely traditional menu tempts famished devotees with a succession of Hungarian classics – bowls of goulash soup, slabs of fish terrine with beetroot sauce, sautéed calf's liver with paprika, smoked goose and gargantuan helpings of roast duck. It's all generous, girth-expanding stuff, but leave room for one of the time-honoured desserts – perhaps sweet cheese pancakes, poppy seed strudel or dobos torta (layered gateau with a caramel topping). Bull's Blood and Tokaji are the drinks of choice; otherwise, quaff the Hungarian house wine at £16.50 (£10.35 a carafe, £3.75 a glass).
Chef/s: Carlos Mendonca. **Open:** Mon to Sat L 12.15 to 2.30, D 5.30 to 10.45. **Closed:** Sun, bank hols. **Meals:** alc D (main courses 9.50 to £17). Set L £17 (2 courses) to £19.50. **Service:** 12.5% (optional). **Details:** Cards accepted. 72 seats. Air-con. Wheelchair access. Music. Children's portions.

L'Escargot, Ground Floor

Classic French at reasonable prices
48 Greek Street, W1D 4EF
Tel no: (020) 7439 7474
www.lescargotrestaurant.co.uk
⊖ **Tottenham Court Road, Leicester Square**
French | £32
Cooking score: 3

An old Soho player from the boho days, L'Escargot ventured into the heartland of French cuisine when the idea of eating snails might provoke a shudder of distaste among Brits. The groundfloor dining room is all pastel tones, comfy banquettes and mirrored walls, and offers a menu of fashionable French stuff interpreted with a light touch. Seared tuna comes in a salad with a radish and sesame seed dressing, while the snails themselves are served in red wine à la bordelaise. Fine raw materials inform the main-course choice, which runs from black bass with Swiss chard and salsa verde to Elwy Valley lamb with pommes boulangère and sautéed curly kale. A fashion-conscious way to finish might be bitter chocolate and walnut brownie with poached pineapple and toffee cream. The menu du jour offers exemplary central London value. Wines from western Europe and the New World include plenty of halves, and start with house French at £16.
Chef/s: Joseph Croan. **Open:** Mon to Fri L 12 to 2.30, Mon to Sat D 6 to 11.30. **Closed:** Sun, 25 and 26 Dec, 1 Jan. **Meals:** alc (main courses £12.95 to £14.95). Set L and D (before 7) £18. **Service:** 15%. **Details:** Cards accepted. 80 seats. Air-con. Music. Children allowed.

Symbols

 Accommodation is available.

 Three courses for less than £30.

 V More than five vegetarian dishes.

 £5-off voucher scheme.

 Notable wine list.

Quo Vadis

Reviving the classic hotel grill
26-29 Dean Street, W1D 3LL
Tel no: (020) 7437 9585
www.quovadissoho.co.uk
⊖ **Tottenham Court Road**
British | £46
Cooking score: no score

It's all change at Quo Vadis, though the glamorous, exceptionally light dining room with its stained glass windows, antique mirrored panels and well-spaced leather banquette tables remains little changed, bar a different roster of notable contemporary art on the walls. New owners Sam and Eddie Hart are setting out to establish the dining room as a viable alternative to The Ivy (see entry) with a resolutely modern British brasserie comfort menu, and a report within a few days of opening has been favourable – though it's too early for the Guide to give a score. Head chef Jean-Philippe Petruno is ex Fino (see entry), but the Spanish influence is barely discernible, limited to the inclusion of grilled razor clams among the crustacea on an extremely likeable and flexible menu. Highlights have included a huge pile of piquant, pimento and tomato-rich brown shrimps on toast, a large bowl of late-spring morels with cream, parsley and garlic, 'a wholly decadent' macaroni with bone marrow, and 'luscious' turbot with sea asparagus. Only nursery puds disappoint: the bread to fruit ratio of summer pudding 'is all wrong', treacle tart is similarly stodgy. The keenly priced wine list offers plenty of contemporary classics, is particularly strong on France and has a good choice of magnums too.
Chef/s: Jean-Philippe Petruno. **Open:** Mon to Fri L 12 to 3, Mon to Sat D 5.30 to 11. **Closed:** Sun. **Service:** 12.5%. **Details:** Cards accepted. 85 seats. Air-con. Separate bar. Wheelchair access. Children's portions.

Red Fort

Indian new-wave veteran
77 Dean Street, W1D 3SH
Tel no: (020) 7437 2525/2115
www.redfort.co.uk
⊖ Tottenham Court Road
Indian | £45
Cooking score: 3

V

Amin Ali was one of the standard-bearers for new wave Indian cuisine during the '80s, and the Red Fort remains one of his enduring success stories. It has seen several incarnations over the years, and currently looks the business with its overtly plush decor and smartly attired staff. The kitchen deals in so-called 'Mughal court cooking' from Lucknow and Hyderabad, although it has a penchant for Britain's native ingredients: classic rogan josh makes use of Herdwick lamb, while Scottish hare is cooked with mustard, turmeric, red chilli and pickles. Elsewhere, there is plenty to tantalise the eye and the palate, witness hara kebabs (spinach patties with orange rind, sun-dried tomato, cashews and raisins), kandhari champ (lamb chops jazzed up with star anise and pomegranate jus) and baby aubergines with whole chillies in peanut, tamarind and sesame sauce. Below stairs is Akbar, a funked-up, high-gloss evening rendezvous for drinks and snacks. Wines are far from cheap, but there is some serious drinking on offer: expect to pay at least £25 (£7 a glass).
Open: Mon to Fri L 12 to 2.15, all week D 5.45 to 11.15. **Meals:** alc (main courses £15 to £33). Set L £12. Set D £16. **Service:** 12.5% (optional). **Details:** Cards accepted. 77 seats. Air-con. Separate bar. No mobile phones. Wheelchair access. Music. Children allowed.

Richard Corrigan at Lindsay House

Still pulling out all the stops
21 Romilly Street, W1D 5AF
Tel no: (020) 7439 0450
www.lindsayhouse.co.uk
⊖ Leicester Square
Modern British | £56
Cooking score: 6

£5 OFF ▮ **V**

Ring the doorbell to gain entrance to Richard Corrigan's restaurant in a modest Soho terrace. Once inside, it exudes an understated, grown-up feel with the country-in-the-city style of the dining rooms (spread over two floors) contributing to a relaxed tone. An attractive menu positions the cooking style squarely within the modern European ambit, and dishes are put together with a high degree of refinement from classic French techniques and a focus on textural contrast. A supremely successful first course brought Corrigan's Irish background to the fore with crubeens teamed with beetroot and horseradish rémoulade and a salad of dandelions and Jabugo ham, while poached lobster is kitted out with a risotto of shellfish and tarragon (and a surcharge), and proved to be highly satisfying. Game is well handled generally, as is evidenced by a gutsy main course of partridge with chorizo, black pudding and confit lemon. Spot-on cooking, too, in a dish of butter-poached monkfish with Baby Gems, clams and grilled langoustine. Classy desserts include a well-made cherry chocolate cake with sour cherry ice cream, and 'a sublimely delicate and tangy lime soufflé served with a lime sorbet'. Our inspector described the wine list as notable with a good selection by-the-glass, but very high mark-ups. The list contains over 350 references from small specialist growers through to well-known producers. Bottles from £22.
Chef/s: Chris McGowan. **Open:** Mon to Fri L 12 to 4, Mon to Sat D 6 to 11. **Closed:** Sun. **Meals:** Set menus £56 and £68, Pre-theatre £27. **Service:** 12.5% (optional). **Details:** Cards accepted. 50 seats. Air-con. Children's portions.

Yauatcha

Glamour in spades
15-17 Broadwick Street, W1F ODL
Tel no: (020) 7494 8888
www.yauatcha.com
⊖ Tottenham Court Road
Chinese | £25
Cooking score: 4

V

A neat combination of experimentation and familiarity distinguishes Alan Yau's tea house, pastry shop, all-day dim sum restaurant and glamorous evening venue. During the day, tables in the stylish ground floor restaurant-cum-tea room are at a premium. The moody, low-lit basement is seen at its best in the evening. Char siu buns are reliably superb, as is prawn chueng fun and beancurd roll with enoki and cloud ear mushrooms, while meltingly delicate Chilean sea bass mooli rolls have been a triumph. Venison puffs are something of a signature, while at the upper end of the menu you'll find larger plates, say Szechuan tea-smoked duck (with pancakes and Thai cucumber, kumquat and plum sauce), and luxury ingredients like Wagyu beef. Western desserts may seem at odds with what comes before, but maintain the creative pace with exquisite cakes. The global wines lean sensibly towards white to aid food matching (starting at £24), but smoothies, cocktails, and a lengthy, largely Chinese tea list also demand attention.

Chef/s: Soon Wah Cheong. **Open:** all week 11 to 11.15 (11.30 Fri and Sat, 10.30 Sun). **Closed:** 24 and 25 Dec. **Meals:** alc (dim sum £4 to £38). **Service:** 12.5%. **Details:** Cards accepted. 180 seats. Air-con. Wheelchair access. Music.

ALSO RECOMMENDED

▲ Cha Cha Moon
15-21 Ganton Street, Soho, W1F 9BN
Tel no: (020) 7297 9800
⊖ Oxford Circus
Chinese

Behind the trendy neon-lit exterior, Cha Cha Moon sees Alan Yau returning to the core components of canteen cooking that brought him success with Wagamama. A utilitarian ethos prevails; expect long queues while fellow customers are herded on and off the benches. Inside, it's easy to see why Cha Cha Moon is so popular: the kitchen hastily serves up generous portions of Hong Kong stalwarts, all priced at a remarkable £3.50. Chilli prawn lao mian and roast duck noodle soup proved particularly impressive on inspection. But with the scale of the operation, some of the cooking inevitably suffers; a portion of beef ho fun was disappointing. The wine list is cursory, the real stars of the show being the cocktails, all priced at £5. Open all week from 12 to 11.30pm.

▲ La Trouvaille
12A Newburgh Street, Soho, W1F 7RR
Tel no: (020) 7287 8488
⊖ Oxford Circus
French

Unconventional French cooking with regional overtones is the deal at this re-invented bistro just off Carnaby Street. 'Slightly cured' salmon with sea salt and Lapsang Suchong tea, Jerusalem artichoke coulis and sorrel mousse sets the tone, mains might include Herdwick mutton with seared scallops, braised lettuce, cauliflower mash and cardamom sauce, while desserts could feature banana bavarois with guava coulis and tamarillo. Two-course lunch £16.50, dinner £29.50. Deli platters and simpler dishes are served in the wine bar below stairs. The fascinating Gallic wine list includes some prime pickings from Southern France and Corsica. Vin de pays d'Oc £14.50. Closed Sun.

▲ Vasco & Piero's Pavilion

15 Poland Street, Soho, W1F 8QE
Tel no: (020) 7437 8774
www.vascosfood.com
⊖ Oxford Circus
Italian

A veteran of the Soho scene, this vintage family-run Italian remains a favourite with celebs and ordinary folk. Menus change each session and the kitchen has its heart in Umbria, with many specialities imported direct from the region. Handmade pasta is a star turn (try aubergine tortellini or meat-filled agnolotti with rosemary), but the choice extends to crostino of chicken livers with marinated mushrooms, herb-crusted cod with cannellini beans and desserts such as pear and Amaretto mousse. Lunch is a carte (main courses from £14.50), dinner is fixed-price (2 courses £24.50); also note the great-value early-evening menu (served 5.30 to 7.30). Regional Italian wines from £15.50. Closed Sat L and all Sun.

READERS RECOMMEND

Randall & Aubin

Seafood
14-16 Brewer Street, Soho, W1R 3FS
Tel no: (020) 7287 4447
www.randallandaubin.com
'Oysters and champagne in the heart of town'

▌St James's Park

Inn the Park

British food and park views
St James's Park, SW1A 2BJ
Tel no: (020) 7451 9999
www.innthepark.com
⊖ St James's Park
British | £28
Cooking score: 2

£30

Another successful Oliver Peyton venture, this unique restaurant occupies an architect-designed, wooden building by the lake in St James's Park. The turfed roof terrace is the place to sit on fine days, but an expansive floor-to-ceiling glass wall makes the most of the setting in any weather. Whether you opt for self-service snacks or a sit-down meal, all offerings celebrate British food, with ingredients drawn from specialist suppliers, artisan producers and rare breed farmers. You could start with nettle soup with wild mushrooms and smoked bacon or Cornish Yarg with wild herbs, cauliflower and walnut salad. After that, Wellington of wild mushrooms with white Stilton, spinach and organic spelt or beer-battered haddock with chips and tartare sauce keep the flag flying. Desserts sing from the same song sheet: Eton mess or gooseberry and elderflower fool with ginger nut biscuits are typical. Wines from £14.50.

Chef/s: Oliver Smith. **Open:** Mon to Fri 8am to 10.45pm. Sat and Sun 9 am to 10.45pm. **Meals:** alc (main courses £12.50 to £21.50), Set L and D weekends only £25.50 (2 courses), £39 (3 courses). **Service:** 12.5%. **Details:** Cards accepted. 80 seats. 110 seats outside. No music. Wheelchair access. Children's portions.

▌Trafalgar Square

Mint Leaf
Sleek subterranean Indian cooking
Suffolk Place, SW1Y 4HX
Tel no: (020) 7930 9020
www.mintleafrestaurant.com
⊖ Charing Cross
Modern Indian | £55
Cooking score: 2

V

Diverting contemporary design creates a
sleek, sexily lit ambience at this underground
Indian eatery towards the bottom end of
Haymarket. A series of set menus, including a
vegetarian one, offer a variety of ways of
experiencing the cooking, which updates
many traditional dishes, alongside some
inspired new ones. Paneer braised with chilli
and coconut tempered with asafoetida,
chicken in tomato, onion and garlic with
crushed red chillies, and cauliflower cooked in
tomato and coriander with green chilli all
crop up among the main dishes on the £40
menu. Aim higher and you could find yourself
setting about a whole clove-spiced rack of
lamb cooked in the tandoor, served with
cumin-roasted beetroot and snow pea salad.
Finish with lemongrass and ginger crème
brûlée or tandoori-smoked pineapple. An
extensive wine list, as well as inventive
cockails, provide for stimulating drinking.
Wines start at £20.
Chef/s: Ajay Chopra. **Open:** all week, 12 noon to
midnight. **Closed:** 25 and 26 Dec, 1 Jan. **Meals:** alc
(main courses £6 to £23). Set L and D £35 to £75.
Service: 12.5%. **Details:** Cards accepted. 144 seats.
Air-con. Separate bar. Wheelchair access. Music.
Children's portions.

The National Dining Rooms
Wide range of British food
The Sainsbury Wing, The National Gallery,
WC2N 5DN
Tel no: (020) 7747 2525
www.thenationaldiningrooms.co.uk
⊖ Leicester Square
British | £30
New Chef

There are grand views of Trafalgar Square
from these stylish, high-ceilinged rooms in
the National Gallery's Sainsbury Wing. The
menu offers something for everyone, from
cakes through pies, tarts and wonderful
British cheeses to full three-course meals.
Linking it all is Oliver Peyton's love of British
food. The snacky bakery menu doles out big
scoops of nostalgia (split pea and ham soup,
shepherd's pie and banana split all make a
showing) while the main menu offers a more
modern take on the British theme, with
regional ingredients at its heart. You might
kick off with chilled cucumber and ginger
soup with Dorset crab followed by braised ox
cheek with cauliflower purée or smoked
haddock fishcakes with creamed sorrel. Finish
on a resoundingly traditional note with Eton
mess or warm treacle tart and clotted cream.
There is a decent children's menu, and
afternoon visitors could try the epic afternoon
tea. Wines start at £18.
Chef/s: Jozef Kontek. **Open:** all week 10 to 5 (8.30
on Wed). **Closed:** 25 Dec. **Meals:** Set D £24.50 (2
courses) to £33.50. **Service:** 12.5%. **Details:** Cards
accepted. 80 seats. Air-con. Wheelchair access.
Music. Children's portions.

National Portrait Gallery, Portrait Restaurant

A feast for the eyes
Orange Street, WC2H OHE
Tel no: (020) 7312 2490
www.searcys.co.uk
⊖ Leicester Square, Charing Cross
Modern British | £32
Cooking score: 2

V

The view's the thing at this dizzily located restaurant atop the new wing of the National Portrait Gallery – so procure a window seat if you want to enjoy the panoramic cityscapes. It's a buzzy, minimalist space that allows the exteriors to speak for themselves and doesn't try to compete with the visual delights on show downstairs. Menus are tailored to the crowds, with breakfast, weekend brunch and afternoon tea provided in addition to lunch and dinner. The kitchen sends out a raft of lively modern dishes that appeal to true-Brit traditionalists and those with more eclectic tastes: expect to see wild leek and Stilton tart, salmon fishcakes and rump of Welsh lamb with colcannon alongside broad bean, lemon and mint risotto or slow-roast pork belly with apricots, lentils and sherry jus. To finish, try strawberry crème brûlée with strawberry sorbet or chocolate and praline 'lava' cake with Frangelico (hazelnut liqueur) ice cream and hazelnut brittle. House wine is £15.30.

Chef/s: Katarina Todosijevic. **Open:** all week L 11.45 to 2.45 (11.30 to 3 Sat and Sun), Thur and Fri D 5.30 to 10. **Closed:** 25 and 26 Dec. **Meals:** alc (main courses £14 to £22). Brunch £19.95 (2 courses) to £24.95. Pre-theatre menu £14.95 (2 courses) to £17.95. **Service:** 12.5% (optional). **Details:** Cards accepted. 90 seats. Air-con. No music. Wheelchair access. Children's portions.

▌Westminster

Bank Westminster

Contemporary brasserie and bar
45 Buckingham Gate, SW1E 6BS
Tel no: (020) 7630 6644
www.bankrestaurants.com
⊖ St James's Park
Modern British | £30
New Chef

£5 OFF

This crisply stylish bar and brasserie is situated at the rear of the Crowne Plaza Hotel. The super-sized Zander bar gives way to a light and lovely conservatory dining room, whose floor-to-ceiling windows overlook a romantic Victorian courtyard complete with fountain and flowers. The modern elegance of the interior is mirrored by the menu, which sits traditional dishes alongside cosmopolitan creations. Snacky options include meze, an Asian sharing platter, salads and lunchtime sandwiches. If you want a full meal, plunge in with starters such as chilli squid with Thai noodle salad or fresh asparagus with a lightly poached egg and hollandaise sauce. Main courses travel from fish and chips or calf's liver with bacon to Thai green curry, via marinated chicken breast with Malayan spices, sweet potato, coconut and lime. The wine list is as wide-ranging as the menu, and opens at £14.50.
Chef/s: Gavin Maguire. **Open:** Mon to Fri 12 to 11, Sat 5 to 11. **Closed:** Bank Hols. **Meals:** alc (main courses £10.50 to £19.95). **Service:** 12.5%. **Details:** Cards accepted. 120 seats. 20 seats outside. Air-con. Separate bar. Wheelchair access. Children's portions.

Symbols

 Accommodation is available.

 Three courses for less than £30.

V More than five vegetarian dishes.

 £5-off voucher scheme.

 Notable wine list.

Cinnamon Club

Intelligent modern Indian cooking
Old Westminster Library, Great Smith Street,
SW1P 3BU
Tel no: (020) 7222 2555
www.cinnamonclub.com
⊖ Westminster
Modern Indian | £40
Cooking score: 4

V

Housed in the former Westminster Library, this erudite-looking restaurant retains the bookcases and parquet flooring from its previous life. Outsized antique lights peer down from above, but these days white-clad tables take the place of reading desks. This cultured setting is a perfect backdrop for Vivek Singh's creative take on Indian cuisine. The menu offers a cornucopia of dishes, full of unexpected twists – there is nothing ordinary about this food. Such innovation doesn't come cheap, but the political patrons from the nearby Houses of Parliament seem undeterred. The set pieces are commendable: a gently spiced warm potato fritter with tomato chutney and yoghurt eases you into a typical dinner, perhaps followed by carpaccio of cured organic salmon paired with onion seeds and green pea relish. Main courses push the bar upwards – a roast saddle of Oisin red deer embellished with pickling spices impressed one reporter, as did the delicate spicing that elevated a mushroom and spinach stir-fry. Marinated berries in pomegranate jelly with Champagne granita form a fitting end, and the cogs are oiled throughout by fleet-footed service that is both cordial and knowledgeable. The well-researched wine list is a fine match for the food, offering a commendable diversity of styles and regions. Bottle prices start from £19, while an enterprising selection of glasses begins at £4.
Chef/s: Vivek Singh. **Open:** Mon to Sat L 12 to 2.45, D 6 to 10.45. **Closed:** Sun, some bank hols.
Meals: alc (main courses £14 to £29), Set L and early evening D £18 (2 courses) to £22.
Service: 12.5%. **Details:** Cards accepted. 220 seats. Air-con. Separate bar. Children allowed.

★NEW ENTRY★

Quilon

Bombay bling meets Keralan cooking
Crowne Plaza London St James, 41 Buckingham Gate, SW1E 6AF
Tel no: (020) 7821 1899
www.thequilon.co.uk
⊖ Victoria
Modern British | £50
Cooking score: 2

Bombay bling meets Keralan cooking at this smart, upscale hotel dining room in the Crown Plaza hotel. Quilon's cuisine is a refined, if slightly sanitised, take on South Indian food – not a knobbly cocum pod in sight – but while it doesn't attempt to scale the searing flavour peaks of Keralan street food, this is a good, gentle introduction to a fascinating palette of flavours. A fair number of meat dishes are offered but the focus is on seafood and vegetarian dishes. An inspection dinner kicked off with a pappad and pickles, washed down with tap water – served, for once, with a smile! The stand-out dish was a sculpted slab of crisp-fried squid paired with a sweet, sticky and richly spiced prawn and spinach relish. Avial – a medley of snake gourd, yam, longbeans and carrots simmered in coconut, green chilli, cumin and yoghurt – lacked punch and crunch, but the parathas, pachadi and appam passed muster. Bibinca, a traditional Goan dessert, rounded the meal off richly. It's good to see a choice of fine teas offered alongside the coffees and brandies – and mango lassi on the wine list, which runs from carafes of quaffable Indian Sauvignon Blanc at £12 all the way to Premier Cru territory.

Chef/s: Sriram Aylur. **Open:** Mon to Fri L 12 to 2.30, Mon to Fri D 6 to 11, Sun L 12.30 to 3.30, D 6 to 10.30. **Closed:** Sat. **Meals:** Set menus L £17, D £40. **Service:** 12.5%. **Details:** Cards accepted. 19 seats. Air-con. Separate bar. Wheelchair access. Music. Children allowed.

★NEW ENTRY★
Quirinale
Italian fit for parliamentary power lunches
1 Great Peter Street, SW1P 3LL
Tel no: (020) 7222 7080
www.quirinale.co.uk
⊖ Westminster
Italian | £35
Cooking score: 3

Named after Rome's presidential palace, this discreet Italian sits just round the corner from the Houses of Parliament. Its understated frontage fits the ministerial Westminster postcode, while the David Collins-designed interior ticks all the right modern style boxes. Limestone-clad stairs lead down to an intimate basement dining room, a light vision in pastel tones, with bevelled mirrors, white linen, cream leather and limed oak. Chef Stefano Savio, who hails from Brescia in northern Italy, cooks with flair and passion, delivering simple, attractively presented dishes built around tip-top seasonal produce, much imported directly from Italy. Flavour is everything in dishes such as tagliolini with fresh crab, chilli and tomato, or herb-crusted loin of venison teamed with soft polenta and sautéed wild mushrooms, while a warm chocolate budino, served with vanilla ice cream, is well worth the advertised 15-minute wait. The extensive wine list is predominantly Italian and kicks off at £17.

Chef/s: Stefano Savio. **Open:** Mon to Fri L 12 to 3, D 6 to 10.30. **Closed:** Sat and Sun, 17 Dec to 31 Dec, 1st week Jan, Aug. **Meals:** alc (main courses £9.75 to £19.50). **Service:** 12.5%. **Details:** Cards accepted. 50 seats. Air-con. Music. Children's portions.

Rex Whistler Restaurant at Tate Britain
British food against a unique backdrop
Millbank, SW1P 4RG
Tel no: (020) 7887 8825
www.tate.org.uk
⊖ Pimlico
Modern British | £29
Cooking score: 2

Head for the basement of Tate Britain to find this handsome restaurant, where stylishly simple furnishings play a wise second-fiddle to Rex Whistler's spectacular mural. Richard Oxley's contemporary British cooking showcases some of the country's best ingredients – perhaps steamed Cornish cockles with wild garlic or potted smoked ham with piccalilli to start, followed by pan-fried Rhug Estate pork loin with smoked black pudding and Braeburn relish or wild sea trout with crushed sweet peas and spinach. Desserts deliver a similar mix of tradition and modernity: sticky toffee pudding with Jersey double cream or Coteaux du Layon-poached pear with pear jelly and ginger cake are typical of the scope. Wines are taken very seriously here, thanks to the efforts of head sommelier Hamish Anderson, whose extensive, expertly annotated list opens at a very reasonable £15 a bottle.

Chef/s: Richard Oxley. **Open:** all week L only 11.30 to 3. **Closed:** 24 to 26 Dec. **Meals:** alc (main courses £15.50). **Service:** 12.5%. **Details:** Cards accepted. 90 seats. 20 seats outside. Air-con. No music. Wheelchair access. Children's portions.

■ Belsize Park

XO
Sleek pan-Asian hangout
29 Belsize Lane, NW3 5AS
Tel no: (020) 7433 0888
www.rickerrestaurants.com
⊖ Belsize Park
Fusion/Pan-Asian | £25
Cooking score: 2

🍷 V £30

The fourth member of Will Ricker's glamorous pan-Asian stable has been given the full high-gloss treatment, with stark monochrome décor and mirrors providing the backdrop to fashionable grazing and stars-in-their-eyes socialising. True to the Ricker principle, scaled-down taster dishes are the order of the day, and the menu is a style-led compendium of dim sum, salads, futo maki rolls and more, drawn from across the Far East. Pick and share as many items as you fancy from a list that might include crispy pork belly with soy and black vinegar alongside duck, coconut and betel leaf red curry or mixed tempura of butternut squash, aubergine and baby corn. Specials ring the changes with, perhaps, sea bass and green tea soba noodles, while desserts tend to be westernised stand-bys such as chocolate pudding or vanilla pannacotta. The ultra-modern wine list has plenty of in-vogue stuff from the New World; prices start at £15. **Chef/s:** Jon Higgonson. **Open:** all week L 12 to 3 (4 Sat and Sun), D 6.30 to 11 (6.30 to 11 Sat, 6 to 10 Sun). **Closed:** Christmas. **Meals:** alc (dishes £6 to £12.50). **Service:** 12.5%. **Details:** Cards accepted. 92 seats. Air-con. Separate bar. Wheelchair access. Music. Children's portions.

Readers recommend

A 'readers recommend' review is a genuine quote from a report sent in by one of our readers. We intend to follow up these suggestions throughout the year to come.

■ Camden

★NEW ENTRY★
Market
43 Parkway, NW1 7PN
Tel no: (020) 7267 9700
⊖ Camden Town
British | £25
Cooking score: 1

£30

The overriding decorative impression is of rough-and-ready functionality, but locals have quickly adopted Market as their ideal neighbourhood eatery. Perhaps not surprisingly, as there is little competition in the area. Dan Spence's time at Medcalf (see entry, Clerkenwell) shows in the no-frills British dishes, and while at times the cooking can be hit-and-miss, there are good things to be had on the constantly changing menu. Cauliflower cheese soup, then Welsh Black pork belly with lentils and apple sauce, or grilled slip sole with new potatoes and caper butter and a pear and ginger crumble to finish, represent good value. Cottage pie or sea bass, mash peas and mint may turn up on the bargain set lunch. House wine is £13.50. **Chef/s:** Dan Spence. **Open:** Mon to Sat L 12 to 2.30, D 6 to 10.30, Sun L 1 to 3.30. **Closed:** bank hols. **Meals:** alc (main courses £8.50 to £13). Set L Mon to Fri £10 (2 courses). **Service:** 12.5% (optional). **Details:** Cards accepted. 38 seats. Music. Children's portions.

ALSO RECOMMENDED
▲ Gilgamesh
The Stables, Chalk Farm Road, Camden, NW1 8AH
Tel no: (020) 7482 5757
www.gilgameshbar.com
⊖ Chalk Farm
Global

Named after an ancient Mesopotamian hero, Gilgamesh is a vast and lavishly decorated restaurant in the heart of Camden. The interior replicates that of a palace built in Babylonian times, combining the history with contemporary and modern art, so the hand-carved Indian furnishings, Middle Eastern bas reliefs and ambient Arabesque music are impressively over the top. Ian Pengelly's menu trawls through Thailand, Hong Kong and Japan for inspiration, so expect dim sum, a team of sushi chefs preparing sashimi (£4 to £14) and nagiri dishes (£3.60 to £6.20), tempura dishes such as lemon sole with ponzu (£16), and speciality main courses like beef rending (£14). Wines from £18. Open all week, 11 to late.

▮ Crouch End

ALSO RECOMMENDED
▲ Khoai Café

6 Topsfield Parade, Crouch End, N8 8PR
Tel no: (020) 8341 2120
⊖ Finsbury Park
Vietnamese

This is a reliable, small, friendly local restaurant and a good place to introduce yourself to Vietnamese food. The dining room has been furnished by someone with an addiction to pine and although basic, it is very clean. The starters are the standard fare: spring rolls, satay etc with the summer rolls always being fresh and fragrant. The pho (noodle soup) is outstanding and excellent value at around £7. It is more than enough for a light meal or lunch (starter-size portions are also available). Main courses are the usual choice of beef, chicken, prawn and tofu in various sauces (tamarind is of particular note) along with a variety of noodle dishes. The fish dishes are well-executed. It is best to stick to the Vietnamese beers but the restaurant does also have a reasonable wine list. Open all week.

Readers recommend

A 'readers recommend' review is a genuine quote from a report sent in by one of our readers. We intend to follow up these suggestions throughout the year to come.

▮ Dalston

ALSO RECOMMENDED
▲ Huong Viet

An-Viet House, 12-14 Englefield Road, Dalston, N1 4LS
Tel no: (020) 7249 0877
www.huongviet.co.uk
⊖ Angel, Liverpool Street
Vietnamese

Islington's Vietnamese Community Centre is the unlikely backdrop for for this bustling canteen. The decor is disctinctly shabby, but bargain-basement prices are the attraction. The all-purpose menu works its way through traditional pho soups (from £3.50), salads, noodles and 'wood charcoal' BBQ specialities such as kingfish wrapped in a banana leaf (£6.50). However, at inspection, soups were insipid and salads were wilted, but locals still seem to flock here in their droves. House wine is £8.90; otherwise drink Vietnamese beer. Closed Sun.

▲ Mangal Ocakbasi

4 Stoke Newington Road, Dalston, N16 8BH
Tel no: (020) 7254 7888
www.mangal2.com
Turkish

Stumble down an unprepossessing side street to find this rough-and-ready ocakbasi. The menu is in the window to peruse as you queue outside. The clientele is a bizarre mix of local Turkish folk and well-heeled theatre-goers grabbing a bite before a show at the Arcola. Hot and cold starters range from £2 to £4, and could include patlican salata (lightly grilled aubergine with chopped peppers) or lahmacun (a Turkish pizza). Mains are priced between £5 and £11, with pirzola (seasoned, tender lamb chops) and bildricin (grilled quails) being of particular note. All dishes are served with salad and bread. Open all week.

Euston
Mestizo

A breath of Mexican fire
103 Hampstead Road, NW1 3EL
Tel no: (020) 7387 4064
www.mestizomx.com
⊖ Warren Street/ Euston
Mexican | £30
Cooking score: 2

Sexy design and sultry lighting make a fitting backdrop for the authentically fiery Mexican cooking on offer at Mestizo, which also has a branch in Madrid. Graze on tacos and antojitos (appetising bites such as tortillas loaded with melted cheese, chorizo or mushrooms), or choose from the main menu. This deals in the likes of mole dishes with pork or chicken, stuffed poblano peppers or shredded beef in onions and pepper, with garlicky sweet chillies, beans and rice. Salads or soups open the proceedings, and there are head-turning desserts such as the cheese and coconut cake topped with mango coulis. Prices are gentle enough that you will feel sorely tempted to bang up the bill with shots from the extensive tequila and mescal list, a cocktail or two, or one of the serviceable handful of Latin American wines. House Chilean is £12.50.
Chef/s: Dulce Aguillera and Miguel Benett. **Open:** all week, noon to midnight. **Closed:** Christmas and Easter. **Meals:** alc (main courses £9.50 to £18.50). **Service:** not inc. **Details:** 75 seats. Air-con. Separate bar. Wheelchair access. Music. Children's portions.

Golders Green
Café Japan

Superb sushi in suburbia
626 Finchley Road, NW11 7RR
Tel no: (020) 8455 6854
⊖ Golders Green
Japanese | £23
Cooking score: 3

Sparklingly fresh sushi has drawn the crowds to this basic Japanese eatery in the heart of Golders Green for many years. Ever-friendly staff provide a warm welcome, calling 'irashaimasei' (Japanese for 'welcome') in unison when you walk in the door, but it's the food that steals the show. There are set meals on hand for the indecisive, providing a mix of soup, salad and sushi or cooked dishes, though it is the à la carte that throws up the real gems. A salmon salad sees seared slices of fish arranged around leaves and topped with a tangy ginger dressing, while tender butterfish teriyaki or black cod in miso are highlights from the small selection of cooked items. Then there's the sushi: as-fresh-as-they-come slices of tuna, turbot, scallop or sea urchin (among several options) served on solid wooden blocks either as sashimi or nigiri. Sushi rolls come packed with the likes of prawn tempura and asparagus or crispy-fried yellow tail with spicy sauce. It is all expertly rendered, fairly priced and served with a smile. Drinks include green tea, beer and wines starting from £12 a bottle, or £3 a glass. Cash only at lunchtime.
Chef/s: Koichi Konnai. **Open:** Sat and Sun L 12 to 2, Wed to Sun D 6 to 10 (9.30 Sun). **Closed:** Mon, Tue, 3 weeks Aug. **Meals:** alc (main courses £4.50 to £20). Set L £8.50 (2 courses), Set D £12 (2 courses) to £18. **Service:** not incl. **Details:** Cards accepted. 39 seats. Air-con. Music.

Average price

The average price listed in main-entry reviews denotes the price of a three-course meal, without wine.

Philpott's Mezzaluna

Amiable, flexible and generous
424 Finchley Road, NW2 2HY
Tel no: (020) 7794 0455
www.philpotts-mezzaluna.com
Italian | £28
Cooking score: 4

The shop-front restaurant with floor-to-ceiling windows is an amiable place, a smart, relaxed and friendly neighbourhood venue with strong Italian influences in both menu and wine list. Flexibility and generosity are watchwords – menus for lunch are priced at one to four courses, dinner at two, three or four courses, and portions are more than ample. Starters like scallops with fennel and orange salad, an intermediate pasta of spaghetti with lobster, then mains of calf's liver with shallots, balsamic and polenta, or herb-crusted plaice with Jersey Royal potatoes, cucumber and mustard, exemplify the robust approach. Desserts are excellent and might include chocolate fondant with gelato or vanilla pannacotta with strawberries. It's all very good value for money. House wine is £14.
Chef/s: David Philpott. **Open:** Tue to Sun L 12 to 3, D 7 to 11. **Closed:** Mon, 25 and 26 Dec, 1 Jan.
Meals: Set L £12 (1 course) to £25 (4 courses), Set D £23 (2 courses) to £33 (4 courses). **Service:** not inc.
Details: Cards accepted. 60 seats. 9 seats outside. Air-con. Wheelchair access. Music. Children's portions.

▌Hampstead

★ NEW ENTRY ★

Goldfish

Modern Chinese in the village of Keats
82 Hampsted High Street, NW3
Tel no: (020) 7794 6666
⊖ Hampstead
Chinese | £42
Cooking score: 2

 V

This new arrival on Hampstead's high street promotes itself as a modern Chinese restaurant. Dining takes place in snug rooms with low ceilings, each room decorated in different and eclectic styles – think waterfalls, murals of goldfishes and dark wood panelling. The menu, devised by Kevin Chow, (ex Cocoon), covers many of the popular staples but isn't run-of-the-mill, note strawberry chilli chicken or mocha pork ribs in chocolate and coffee sauce. Steamed dim sum platter revealed a deft hand, but bright green deep-fried prawns covered with wasabi cream may not be to everyone's taste, and over-reliance on cornflour for sauces can result in uniformity of flavour and texture. Far better was tender and smoky pan-fried ostrich served with wild mushrooms, asparagus and black pepper sauce, and Fortune tofu – deep-fried bean curd with bamboo piths and oyster sauce, topped with bonito flakes. Service is friendly but easily diverted. Wines start from £12.50.
Chef/s: Kevin Chow. **Open:** all week L 12 to 3, D 6 to 10.30 (11 Fri & Sat, 10 Sun). **Meals:** alc (main courses £8.50 to £40). Set L £25 (2 courses).
Service: 10%. **Details:** Cards accepted. 30 seats. Air-con. Music.

Symbols

 Accommodation is available.

 Three courses for less than £30.

V More than five vegetarian dishes.

 £5-off voucher scheme.

 Notable wine list.

Readers recommend

A 'readers recommend' review is a genuine quote from a report sent in by one of our readers. We intend to follow up these suggestions throughout the year to come.

Highbury

ALSO RECOMMENDED
▲ Il Bacio

178–184 Blackstock Road, Highbury, N5 1HA
Tel no: (020) 7226 3339
www.ilbaciohighbury.co.uk
⊖ Highbury and Islington
Italian

Families and Italian football fans gather at this informal venue for seriously huge pizzas (from £6), trattoria staples and a range of authentic Sardinian specialities. Try goats' cheese with asparagus and stewed pears in red wine (£6.95) or a mighty bowl of minestrone before spaghetti bottarga e vongole (with pressed dried grey mullet roe and clams). The place oozes genuine 'dolce vita' thanks to effusively friendly staff. Fascinating wines from Sardinia and mainland Italy start at £10.95 (£2.95 a glass). Closed Mon to Fri L. There are two branches on Stoke Newington Church Street, N16, as well as a new, more rustic sister eatery, La Sardegna, a few doors down on the Blackstock Road.

Highgate
The Bull

Relaxed, stylish pub dining
13 North Hill, N6 4AB
Tel no: (0845) 4565 033
www.inthebull.biz
⊖ Highgate
Modern European | £25
New Chef

 £30

This popular Highgate pub blends pubby informality with relaxed sophistication. White napery and clear Perspex chairs segue into more conventional pub furnishings. The menu performs a similar trick, switching between the traditional comforts of fish and chips, a mixed grill or a steak sandwich, and more modern offerings such as rare-grilled tuna steak with spinach and potato aloo or spiced yoghurt and mint-marinated lamb chops with roasted new potatoes and grilled aubergine. Starters are in the same vein – chicken Caesar salad or dressed Dorset crab with wholemeal ciabatta, rocket, aïoli and lemon are typical options. Finish with pure comfort food – perhaps bread-and-butter pudding with custard or treacle tart with vanilla ice cream. A respectable and interesting list of wines includes a fair bit of bubbly and a few half-bottles, plus a fair selection by-the-glass.

Chef/s: Ian Aungier. **Open:** Tue to Sun L 12 to 2.30, all week D 6 to 10.30. **Meals:** alc (main courses £11.95 to £16.50), Set L £10 (one course), £15 (2 courses). **Service:** 12.5%. **Details:** Cards accepted. 120 seats. 70 seats outside. Air-con. Separate bar. Wheelchair access. Music. Children's portions. Car parking.

Islington
Almeida

30 Almeida Street, N1 1AD
Tel no: (020) 7354 4777
www.danddlondon.com
⊖ Angel, Highbury & Islington
French
Cooking score: 4

Refurbished in February 2008, this wine bar and restaurant has a slick but elegant new look and an impressive new chef in the form of Alan Jones (ex Lucknam Park). 'Undoubtedly a change for the better' is the general consensus. Still popular with the theatre crowd (the Almeida theatre is opposite and Sadler's Wells is nearby), it has menus to fit around the performances. The dining room flaunts a sophisticated Gallic edge, with cushioned bistro chairs and striking modern art on the walls. The food follows suit, offering a modern take on French classics. An inspection meal opened with white asparagus with balsamic and oil, and a charcuterie platter including outstanding chicken foie gras. Satisfying main courses included roast duck with spring greens and bacon, gratin dauphinoise and the warmth of green peppercorns, and rump of lamb with a slightly dry pea terrine and sweet garlic morels. A selection of 'practically perfect' sorbets (quenelles of raspberry, passionfruit and lemon) provided a happy ending, as did cheeses including an first-class Roquefort. A vegetarian set menu is also available. Service is good-humoured and unobtrusive; house wines start at a very reasonable £15.

Chef/s: Alan Jones. **Open:** Mon to Sat L 12 to 2.30, D 5.30 to 10.45, Sun 1 to 9. **Closed:** Christmas, Easter Mon. **Meals:** alc (main courses £12.50 to £25). Bar tapas menu available. **Service:** 12.5% (optional). **Details:** Cards accepted. 100 seats. Air-con. Separate bar. No music. Wheelchair access.

Metrogusto

Up-to-the minute Italian cooking
13 Theberton Street, N1 0QY
Tel no: (020) 72269400
www.metrogusto.co.uk
⊖ Angel
Italian | £28
Cooking score: 3

£5 OFF 🍷 £30

Metrogusto appeals for its unaffected, down-to-earth style. There's plenty of light in both main and rear dining rooms, where plain wooden furniture contrasts agreeably with interesting works of art and a genuine attempt is made to create an Italian atmosphere. In the kitchen, materials are sound as a bell, treated with simplicity and resulting dishes perfectly attuned to the times. There may be grilled green asparagus served with Parmesan sauce, or grilled, stuffed squid with a piquant tomato sauce. Grilled sea bass makes a fine main course, served with black olive tapenade sauce, or there could be baked rack of lamb with honey and rosemary. Desserts continue the quality Italian route, soaking citrus sorbet with limoncello liqueur or serving a great affogato – warm espresso coffee and vanilla ice cream. The all-Italian wine list concentrates on good producers and starts at £16.50.

Chef/s: Antonio di Silvo. **Open:** Fri to Sun L 12 to 2.30, Mon to Sat D 6.30 to 10.30 (11 Fri and Sat). **Closed:** Christmas, Easter. **Meals:** alc (£12.50 to £19.50). Set menu £18.50. **Service:** 12.5%.

Details: Cards accepted. 60 seats. 10 seats outside. Air-con. Wheelchair access. Music. Children's portions.

Morgan M

Stylish venue for serious dining
489 Liverpool Road, N7 8NS
Tel no: (020) 7609 3560
www.morganm.com
⊖ Highbury & Islington
French | £40
Cooking score: 6

V

The corner site is painted a chic baize-green, which gives some clue to the elegant dining room within. It's an object lesson in how to transform a simple space into a civilized venue for serious dining. Well-spaced and beautifully set tables, warm yet fresh colours and windows with frosted panels eclipsing the street life outside conjure the private gastronomic world of Morgan Meunier. Morgan comes from Champagne and his cooking is firmly anchored in a very sure classical technique. From this base he gives his imagination loose rein, but with enough control to ensure an ideal balance of tastes and textures: more particularly, he gives a nod to the foams and mousses of molecular cuisine, yet his real orginality is in transforming classics of the French repertoire with daring but disciplined pairings – like the ever-praised amuse bouche of beetroot soup with Roquefort foam, or a new variant, the chilled cream of broad bean with a foam of horseradish. His classic Landais foie gras is brilliantly enhanced by the accompaniments of an almond coulis and an Amaretto gelée; seared fillet of veal is paired with cannelloni of sweetbread, while steamed asparagus comes with 'a heavenly' morel and vin jaune sauce. Dark chocolate moelleux (70 per cent Valrhona Guanaja) shows that desserts maintain the highest standards. The focus of the good wine list is still very French, especially classed-growth claret, but there are now some fine bottles from Italy, too.

Chef/s: Morgan Meunier. **Open:** Wed to Fri and Sun L 12 to 2, Tue to Sat D 7 to 10. **Closed:** Sun D, Mon, 23 to 30 Dec. **Meals:** £36 to £45 (tasting menu). **Service:** 12.5%. **Details:** Cards accepted. 48 seats. Air-con. Wheelchair access.

Ottolenghi

Ultra-hip deli diner
287 Upper Street, N1 2TZ
Tel no: (020) 7288 1454
www.ottolenghi.co.uk
⊖ Angel, Highbury & Islington
Mediterranean | £30
Cooking score: 2

V

A hip combination of deli, takeaway and casual diner, Ottolenghi hit the ground running when it opened and has never looked back. Check out the goodies on the deli counter and find a seat at one of the long refectory tables. Lunch is gregariously informal and dinner is an array of starter-sized dishes. The kitchen seeks bold inspiration from the Med, North Africa and beyond: pistachio-crusted tuna with papaya and cucumber salsa, terrine of polenta, courgettes and wild mushrooms with watercress pesto, and lemon sole with beetroot carpaccio and skordalia sauce are typical. At inspection, service was brusque – we were told we had to vacate the table in half-an-hour, and then received slack service. Italy, Spain and Portugal dominate the brief wine list; prices start at £15.50 (£4.50 a glass). There are outlets in Notting Hill, Kensington and Belgravia (visit website for details).
Chef/s: Yottam Ottolenghi and Sami Tamimi. **Open:** Mon to Sat 8 to 10, Sun 9 to 7. **Closed:** 25 and 26 Dec, 1 Jan. **Meals:** alc D (main courses £9 to £13). Set L£9.50 to £14.50. **Service:** not inc. **Details:** Cards accepted. 45 seats. 6 seats outside. Air-con. Wheelchair access. Music. Children's portions.

ALSO RECOMMENDED

▲ Isarn

119 Upper Street, Islington, N1 1QP
Tel no: (020) 7424 5153
⊖ Highbury & Islington
Thai/Indonesian/Malaysian

This long narrow room has built up a loyal following amongst discerning Islingtonites, so it's no surprise to find that the restaurant is owned by Tina Juengsoongneum, sister of Alan Yau (pioneering founder of Busaba, Hakkasan and Yauatcha). Tables are cramped, so ask to be seated in the rear dining area, which is bright, airy and modern. Hot red duck curry (£8.90) was perfect comfort food, accompanied by delicate jasmine rice (served in an ornate silver pot). Baby pak choi (£6.50) was served in a lip-smacking garlic broth. At inspection, a chocolate pudding with vanilla ice cream and a peanut crisp (£4.50) had a delicate texture on the outside and warm goo inside. Open 12 to 3 and 6 to 11 all week.

READERS RECOMMEND

Duke of Cambridge

Gastropub
30 St Peter's Street, Islington, N1 8JT
Tel no: (020) 7359 3066
www.dukeorganic.co.uk
'A pioneering organic operation'

Rooburoo

Indian/Pakistani/Bangladeshi
21 Chapel Market, Islington, N1 9EZ
Tel no: (020) 7278 8100
www.rooburoo.com
'Fresh, clean flavours in a modern setting'

Average price

The average price listed in main-entry reviews denotes the price of a three-course meal, without wine.

King's Cross

Acorn House
Clear
69 Swinton Street, WC1X 9NT
Tel no: 020 7812 1842
www.acornhouserestaurant.com
⊖ Kings Cross
Modern British | £35
Cooking score: 2

With the new Eurostar terminal at St. Pancras it seems that King's Cross is starting to discover its inner Gallic spirit, and a year on, eco-friendly Acorn House is beginning to find its feet in tempering British produce with continental style cooking. While the daytime mood of brisk functionality might deter some – with salads and sandwiches on offer to the lunching lawyers of Farringdon – the canteen setting takes on a new life in the evenings, once the lights are dimmed and the austerity of the environs become less apparent. An inspection found Mediterranean dominance on the menu – true to head chef Arthur Potts Dawson's training at The River Café and Fifteen (see entries) – with dishes boasting three different varieties of olive oil. Pan-fried sea trout with courgettes and lemon characterised the kitchen's summer inclination towards fish, with beetroot cured salmon with spring leaf a superior starter. A modest wine list starts at £13 a bottle.
Chef/s: Arthur Potts Dawson. **Open:** Mon to Sat L 12 to 3, D 8 to 10. **Closed:** bank hols. **Meals:** alc (main courses £12 to £22). **Service:** 12.5%. **Details:** Cards accepted. 50 seats. Wheelchair access. Music. Children allowed.

Konstam at the Prince Albert
Local sourcing in central London
2 Acton Street, WC1X 9NA
Tel no: (020) 7833 5040
www.konstam.co.uk
⊖ King's Cross
Modern British | £27
Cooking score: 3
 £30

Local sourcing is an approach that doesn't have to be confined to the leafy shires. It can work in London too, where arguably the need for it is all the greater. Oliver Rowe, star of the BBC2 series *The Urban Chef*, has brought this philosophy to King's Cross. Ingredients come mainly from the area covered by the Tube map, while cooking methods are derived from further afield. Start, perhaps, with a tart of goats' cheese, broad beans and onion, or a pâté of duck liver and bacon with a runner bean chutney and toast. The café idiom ensures there's no artful pretension, just well-executed culinary favourites. Mains might include chargrilled sea bass with sprouting broccoli and almond sauce, or nicely rendered roast pork belly with puréed parsnip, braised red cabbage and cider sauce. It can't get much more local than the London porter that goes into an ice cream with currants, served alongside blackberry and lavender raspberry versions, or there may be a boozy trifle of sloe gin, sherry and brambles. Wines from Surrey, Sussex and Kent form the backbone of a tiny list, starting with French varietals at £15.50 per bottle, £4.25 a glass.
Chef/s: Oliver Rowe. **Open:** Mon to Fri L 12.30 to 3, Mon to Sat D 6.30 to 10.30. **Closed:** Sun, Christmas and New Year. **Meals:** alc (main courses £12.50 to £16.50). Set L and D £30. **Service:** not inc.
Details: 70 seats. Air-con. Wheelchair access. Music. Children's portions.

READERS RECOMMEND

Camino
Spanish
3 Varnishers Yard, King's Cross, N1 9FD
Tel no: (020) 7841 7331
www.barcamino.com
'Sunny Spanish vigour in King's Cross'

▌Primrose Hill

★NEW ENTRY★
L'Absinthe
Lively neighbourhood bistro
40 Chalcot Road, NW1 8LS
Tel no: (020) 7483 4848
⊖ Chalk Farm
French | £25
Cooking score: 3

 £30

In plush Primrose Hill, a stone's throw from Regent's Park, L'Absinthe occupies a prime corner on a predominantly residential street. It is steadily building a loyal local following, with visitors drawn by the warmth of the service, the robust flavours on offer and the excellent value for money. Traditional French bistro dishes dominate the menu, ham hock terrine, say, or goats' cheese on toast to start, with duck confit or steak with pommes frites to follow, and daily specials announced on a blackboard. Desserts are mostly classics such as pot au chocolate and poached pear with ice cream and chocolate sauce, though absinthe crème brûlée appears to be something of a favourite. The all-French wine list is well-considered and, as a wine shop is run from the same premises, the restaurant only adds corkage to the shop price (a nice touch).
Chef/s: Christophe Favre. **Open:** Tue to Sun L 12 to 2.30 (4 Sat and sun), D 6 to 10.30 (9.30 Sun). **Closed:** Mon. **Meals:** alc (main course £9 to £17) Set L £8 (2 courses). **Service:** 12.5% (optional). **Details:** Cards accepted. 65 seats. Air-con. Children allowed.

Odette's
New-look Primrose Hill veteran
130 Regents Park Road, NW1 8XL
Tel no: (020) 7586 8569
⊖ Chalk Farm
Modern European | £40
Cooking score: 5

🍾 V

Revitalised, rejuvenated and bullish in its new incarnation, Odette's now sports an eye-blinkingly brash new look involving jewelled lampshades, gaudy yellow chairs, leaf-motif wallpaper and swagged curtains. Welsh chef Bryn Williams rules in the kitchen and his virtuoso cooking has added a new dimension to this trusty Primrose Hill veteran. He famously won the fish course for the Queen's 80th-birthday banquet, and high-end seafood cookery is undoubtedly his forte. Organically-farmed and sustainable species are top of his list: he pairs seared wild sea trout with fresh peas, horseradish and pea shoots, matches pan-fried halibut with carrots and offers roast pollock with chickpeas, chorizo, confit tomato and confit lemon. Elsewhere, he applies his impressive skills to roast rump of Elwy lamb with crispy sweetbread, asparagus, broad beans and mint, and sends out saddle of rabbit with Bayonne ham, baby artichokes and Parmesan. Seasonal themes also point up desserts such as rhubarb and mint parfait with poached rhubarb and rhubarb jelly. The wine list is a treasure trove for fans of big-name French tipples, although there's also plenty of top stuff from Italy, Australia and elsewhere. House selections open the bidding at £22 (£6 a glass).
Chef/s: Bryn Williams. **Open:** Tue to Fri L 12 to 2.30 (3.30 Sun), Tue to Sat D 6.30 to 10.30. **Closed:** Mon. **Meals:** Set L £14.95 (2 courses) to £18.95. Set D £35 (2 courses) to £40. **Service:** 12.5% (optional). **Details:** Cards accepted. 65 seats. 12 seats outside. Air-con. Separate bar. No mobile phones. Wheelchair access. Music. Children's portions.

Stoke Newington
Rasa

Currying favour with veggies
55 Stoke Newington Church Street, N16 0AR
Tel no: (020) 7249 0344
www.rasarestaurants.com
⊖ Finsbury Park
Indian vegetarian | £24
Cooking score: 2

V

The original Rasa – and to many still the best in a growing chain with branches in Bond Street, Fitzrovia, Euston, King's Cross, Northwood and Newcastle – is dedicated to the vegetarian cuisine of Kerala. An informative menu describing the background of the dishes and how they are normally served in their homeland is helpful to those unfamiliar with anything more exotic than chicken tikka. Starters are typically snacky things such as vadai (deep-fried patties of mixed lentil batter laced with spices), while main courses focus on dosas – rice pancakes with various fillings – or curries such as beet cheera pachadi (beetroot and spinach blended with yoghurt, roasted coconut, mustard seeds and curry leaves). Desserts include kesari, a Brahmin recipe of semolina, mango, cashew nuts and raisins. Our questionnaire was not returned, so some of the information below may have changed.
Chef/s: Rajan Karattil. **Open:** Sat and Sun L 12 to 3, all week D 6 to 10.45 (11.45 Fri and Sat). **Closed:** 24 to 26 Dec, 1 Jan. **Meals:** alc (main courses £3.50 to £5.95). Set L and D £16. **Service:** 12.5% (optional). **Details:** Cards accepted. 64 seats. Air-con. Wheelchair access. Music.

Please send us your feedback

To register your opinion about any restaurant listed in the Guide, or a new restaurant that you wish to bring to our attention, please visit the web address at the bottom of the page. Your feedback informs the content of the book and will be used to compile next year's reviews.

ALSO RECOMMENDED
▲ Istanbul Iskembecisi
9 Stoke Newington Road, Stoke Newington, N16 8BH
Tel no: (020) 7254 7291
www.istanbuliskembecisi.co.uk
Turkish

A popular family-run restaurant producing great-value Turkish food without frills until the wee small hours. The signature 'iskembe' is tripe soup (£3) to which you add vinegar, lemon juice, salt and pepper; otherwise choose from a fistful of meze ranging from tarama and kisir (cracked wheat salad) to enginar (artichokes, broad beans and other vegetables cooked in olive oil). Main courses (from £7.50) are mostly protein-laden kebabs and grills plus Albanian-style liver, stuffed vine leaves and 'kuzu firm' (oven-baked lamb with tomato sauce). Plentiful vegetarian options, too. House wine is £10 (£2.75 a glass). Open all week until 5 in the morning.

Swiss Cottage
Bradleys

Admirable neighbourhood restaurant
25 Winchester Road, NW3 3NR
Tel no: (020) 7722 3457
www.bradleysnw3.co.uk
⊖ Swiss Cottage
Anglo-French | £32
Cooking score: 3

£5 OFF ♦ V

Tucked away behind Swiss Cottage tube station and handily placed for the Hampstead Theatre, Simon and Jolanta Bradley's self-named restaurant serves its neighbourhood admirably. Inside, it is easy on the eye – thanks to pretty flowers, pastel colours and paintings by local artists. The kitchen casts its net wide for ingredients, pulling in Rossmore oysters, Dorset crab and Orkney lamb as well as fish from the Looe day-boats. To start, an assiette of wild rabbit with mustard sauce might keep company with hot and cold foie gras with onion confit and potato galette.

Classic Anglo-French themes also point up main courses of brill with braised lettuce and pea fricassee or grilled rump steak with Montpelier butter and hand-cut chips, while desserts broaden the horizons with, perhaps, Alfonso mango, lime leaf cream and passionfruit sorbet. The wine list is a mightily impressive French-led selection that keeps its prices in check and provides invigorating drinking from all quarters. Vin de pays is £13.95 (£3.75 a glass).
Chef/s: Simon Bradley. **Open:** all week L 12 to 3, Mon to Sat D 6 to 11. **Meals:** alc (main courses £13.50 to £17). Set L Tue to Sat £12.50 (2 courses) to £16.50, Sun £18 (2 courses). Set D £23.
Service: 12.5% (optional). **Details:** Cards accepted. 60 seats. Air-con. Wheelchair access. Music. Children's portions.

Singapore Garden
Vibrant south-east Asian cooking
83-83A Fairfax Road, NW6 4DY
Tel no: (020) 7328 5314
⊖ **Swiss Cottage**
South-east Asian | £30
Cooking score: 2
V

Star-spotting is one of the diversions at this stylish, fast-paced Asian restaurant, which has been serving sharply presented renditions of Singaporean, Malaysian and Chinese food to Swiss Cottage since 1984. The lengthy menu is something of an Aladdin's Cave, in that, if you search patiently enough, you will find most things you might reasonably hanker for in the circumstances. Beef rendang, otak otak fishcakes with lime leaf and chilli, and sambal prawns in the shell are all present and correct, and so are some more unusual specialities, like chiew yim soft-shell crab with garlic and chillies, yin-yang Dover sole with asparagus, or chilli lobster with a piquant sauce and noodles. Fresh fruit platters are a palate-cleansing way to finish. Wines start at £15 a bottle, £4 a glass.
Chef/s: Kok Sum Toh. **Open:** all week, L 12 to 3, D 6 to 11 (11.30 Fri and Sat). **Closed:** 4 days at Christmas. **Meals:** alc (main courses £7.20 to £29).

Set L and D £25 to £38.50. **Service:** 12.5%. **Details:** 85 seats. 12 seats outside. Air-con. Wheelchair access. Music. Children allowed.

▌Willesden
Sushi-Say
Local sushi favourite
33B Walm Lane, NW2 5SH
Tel no: (020) 8459 2971
⊖ **Willesden Green**
Japanese | £32
Cooking score: 4

Advance bookings are advisable at this sushi stalwart, where crowds flock daily for its top-notch raw fish. A two-year-old refurbishment still looks smart, with a neutral colour scheme and a swish sushi bar at its entrance, from which arrive the restaurant's trump card – some of the finest, top-grade sushi found in north London. Whether it is familiar options of salmon and mackerel or the more adventurous abalone and toro (beautifully marbled slices of fatty tuna), it all comes thickly sliced, pert and full of fresh sea flavour. For those who prefer their food cooked, there are hot dishes aplenty including gyoza (Japanese dumplings filled with minced pork and vegetables), chicken yakitori skewers, grilled horse mackerel with salt, and king prawn tempura wrapped in gossamer-light batter. Bandana-clad staff work the narrow room with efficiency and, while bills can add up if you go à la carte, sushi sets (starting at £13) keep prices down, with more substantial evening set meals from £21. Plum wine and saké feature on the drinks list, with wines starting at £12.50 a bottle or £3.10 a glass.
Chef/s: Katsuharu Shimizu. **Open:** Tue to Sun L 12 to 2 (1 to 3 Sat and Sun), D 6.30 to 10.30 (6 to 11 Sat, 6 to 10 Sun). **Closed:** Mon, 25 and 26 Dec, 1 Jan. **Meals:** alc (main courses £7.50 to £20.50). Set L £9.80 to £15.80, Set D £21 to £35. **Service:** not inc. **Details:** Cards accepted. 40 seats. Air-con. No music. Wheelchair access. Children allowed.

Barbican

Searcy's

Ideally placed for arts lovers
Level 2, Barbican Centre, Silk Street, EC2Y 8DS
Tel no: (020) 7588 3008
www.barbican.org.uk
⊖ Barbican, Moorgate
British | £29
New Chef

£30

Perfectly placed for pre- or post-show dining, this restaurant occupies the second level of the Barbican centre and has impressive city views. The recently refurbished interior is themed around warm wood and metals, while the menu is a stylish British affair with native produce at its heart. Kick off with a Brixham crab cake with sorrel mayonnaise or English asparagus tart with poached duck egg and Parmesan. Main courses follow the same patriotic trend, offering Middle White pork belly with spring vegetables and pancetta, croquette of Montgomery Cheddar with English cauliflower and Jersey Royals or roast spring chicken with seasonal salad. Finish with carrot cake, ice chocolate parfait with lemon peel and Chantilly cream or spiced pineapple carpaccio with elderflower sorbet. The wine list crams a lot into two pages. It's an accessible international selection, efficiently annotated and divided by style, with plenty by-the-glass. Bottles are priced from £18.50. **Chef/s:** Quentin Fitch. **Open:** Mon to Fri 12 to 10.30, Sat 5 to 10.30. **Closed:** Sun, bank hols. **Meals:** Set L and D £24.50 (2 courses) to £28.50. **Service:** 12.5%. **Details:** Cards accepted. 120 seats. Air-con. Separate bar. Wheelchair access. Music. Children allowed. Car parking.

ALSO RECOMMENDED

▲ Carnevale

135 Whitecross Street, Barbican, EC1 8JL
Tel no: (020) 7250 3452
www.carnevalerestaurant.co.uk
Vegetarian

Duck down the back streets of the City to find this vegetarian haven. The atmosphere is a bit worthy, which is somewhat inevitable given the ultra-healthy-crowd that this place inevitably attracts. The front of the restaurant operates as a deli by day, but by night the locals book early to get the seats in the tiny garden. Starters include grilled halloumi with oven-roasted tomatoes and spinach, or quinoa with wild mushroom, spinach, apricot and ginger chutney. Mains are simple and incredibly flavoursome, but seem pricey for what they are (a stuffed red pepper is £11.50). Puddings were simple but superb, though an apple and pear crumble was served close to cold. There is a short list of organic wines and house wines start at £12.50, or £4.95 by the glass.

▲ Pham Sushi

159 Whitecross Street, Barbican, EC1Y 8JL
Tel no: (020) 7251 6336
www.phamsushi.co.uk
⊖ Old Street, Barbican
Japanese

Take a swift turn down this Barbican back street to find this rough-and-ready sushi bar in the midst of a parade of run-down shops. A simple canteen feel dominates, with piped music, elbow-to-elbow tables and high seats at the bar beside the chef. Service is nothing to write home about but gets the job done. At inspection, dishes of particular note included chicken teriyaki (£4.80) and a sea bass sashimi (£9), beautifully served with lemon and coriander. Vegetable tempura (£6) was slightly undercooked, but still clean and fresh. Open for lunch and dinner from Mon to Fri and for Dinner only on Saturday.

READERS RECOMMEND

Kipferl

Delicatessen
70 Long Lane, Barbican, EC1A 9EJ
Tel no: 020 7796 2229
www.kipferl.co.uk
'Austrian fare with an emphasis on cakes'

▌Bethnal Green

Green & Red

A taste of real Mexico
51 Bethnal Green Road, E1 6LA
Tel no: (020) 7749 9670
www.greenred.co.uk
⊖ Liverpool Street
Mexican | £25
Cooking score: 3

V

At the forefront of a movement introducing real Mexican food to London, Green & Red in Shoreditch focuses on the home-style cooking of Jalisco, Mexico's tequila territory. The menu is organised into 'small dishes', mains, and sides, and sharing is encouraged by the team of young, friendly staff. Fresh and lively octopus ceviche, a salad of broad beans, or guacamole and tortilla chips lend themselves to sharing tapas-style, before the largely meat-based main courses, evidently of good provenance, all served with refried beans and home-made tortillas. The menu changes only rarely. The tequila offer is the best in London, designed for the connoisseur, not the 'slamming' masses. Quality tequilas including aged and rare examples are available in bottles, 50ml shots or flights – presumably for novice drinkers. Mexican beers, good cocktails and an all-Latin American wine list complete the picture.
Chef/s: Eric Medina. **Open:** all week D 5.30 to 12 (1 Sat, 10.30 Sun). **Closed:** Christmas. **Meals:** Set menu £25. **Service:** not inc. **Details:** Cards accepted. 55 seats. 10 seats outside. Air-con. Separate bar. Wheelchair access. Music. Children's portions.

Les Trois Garçons

Lewis-Carroll-style brasserie
56 Redchurch Street, E2 7DP
Tel no: (020) 7613 1924
www.lestroisgarcons.com
⊖ Liverpool Street
French | £45
Cooking score: 3

Les Trois Garçons themselves are three antique dealers (commemorated in a painting hanging above diners' heads) who have filled this East End pub conversion with all manner of vintage finds, from stuffed animals bedecked with costume jewellery to a stunning collection of glass chandeliers; the look is French brasserie re-imagined by Lewis Carroll. Proximity to City expense accounts, the uniqueness of the setting and the restaurant's ongoing popularity with the East London fashion crowd dictate some stiff pricing that, at inspection, was not merited by amateurish service and unwelcome close tables, but the quality of cooking is sound and, given the surroundings, surprisingly subtle. Med-accented modern French dishes might include tomato salad with an escabèche of sardines in tomato aspic, followed, perhaps, by seared noisette and rack of lamb with braised artichokes, aubergines and Jersey Royal potatoes. Puddings offer the same mix of tweaked classics, say tian of lemon curd with blueberries or poached rhubarb served with milk ice cream. Table-turning can operate; if you find yourself with an early slot, finish the evening over some very well-mixed cocktails at sister bar Loungelover round the back (booking recommended).
Chef/s: Jérôme Henri. **Open:** Mon to Sat D 7 to 12. **Closed:** Sun, Christmas, New Year, bank hols. **Meals:** Set menu (Mon to Wed) £25 (2 courses) to £29. **Service:** 12.5%. **Details:** Cards accepted. 70 seats. Air-con. Wheelchair access. Music.

Also recommended

An 'also recommended' entry is not a full entry, but is provisionally suggested as an alternative to main entries.

Canary Wharf

Gun

Popular Thames-side gastropub
27 Coldharbour, E14 9NS
Tel no: (020) 7515 5222
www.thegundocklands.com
Gastropub | £30
Cooking score: 3

Steeped in history, with a notable Lord Nelson/Emma Hamilton connection, the Gun forms part of the Martin Brothers' ever-expanding gastropub empire. Predictably, given its location in the shadow of Canary Wharf, there's a strong business contingent during the week, though with an enviable riverside terrace (and spectacular views of the O2 Arena), custom is brisk at weekends too. The bar-dining room has been sympathetically and tastefully restored, service is friendly, helpful and charming and the kitchen clearly shows ambition. A simply described starter of Dorset crab and toast was a delicate sidestep from the expected, while pressed ham terrine, with an inventive pineapple chutney, showed a gutsier side to the kitchen. Fish is a strong suit, sourced daily from nearby Billingsgate. This clearly paid dividends at inspection, with sea bass (served with a fricassee of carrots, morels, pearl onions, Baby Gem and Noilly Prat velouté) pronounced the standout dish. Passion-fruit tart is a good way to end. The wine list is firmly footed in the Old World, with classic Burgundy and a fashionable leaning towards Italy, Austria and Spain.

Chef/s: Jake Tuttil. **Open:** all week L 12 to 3 (11.30 to 4 Sat and Sun), D 6 to 10.30 (9.30 Sun). **Closed:** Christmas. **Meals:** alc (main courses £13 to £19). **Service:** 12.5%. **Details:** Cards accepted. 42 seats. 35 seats outside. Wheelchair access. Music. Children's portions.

Which? Campaigns

To find out more about Which? food and drink campaigns, please visit:
www.which.co.uk

Ubon by Nobu

Modish Japanese glamour
34 Westferry Circus, E14 8RR
Tel no: (020) 7719 7800
www.noburestaurants.com
⊖ Canary Wharf
Japanese | £50
Cooking score: 5

V

A trip to Ubon begins with a meandering odyssey through the labyrinthine grounds and landscaped gardens of the Four Seasons Hotel: finally, a lift whisks visitors up to the fourth floor where the dining room opens out with bewitching river views. Like its close relations Nobu at Hyde Park Corner and Nobu Berkeley Street (see entries), this is a restaurant that lives and breathes celebrity glamour. It also tackles contemporary Japanese cuisine head-on and makes much of its sexy allure: executive chef Mark Edwards claims dominion over all three kitchens, so it's not surprising that there is common ground between the menus. Rock shrimp tempura with ponzu, yellowtail sashimi with jalapeño dressing, toro tartar with caviar and – of course – the relentlessly plagiarised black cod with sticky sweet miso all find a place here. The full repertoire fuses high-art tradition with high-impact modernism; F1 grade wagyu beef is served in 75gram nuggets and desserts veer into sensory overkill with outrageous asemblages including rice pudding with toban yaki, yuzu zest, almond crumble and mint and cinnamon ice cream. Wine prices are not for those of a nervous disposition, but if you're happy to spend upwards of £30 there's no shortage of top-quality names.

Chef/s: Mark Edwards. **Open:** Mon to Fri L 12 to 2, Mon to Sat D 6 to 10. **Closed:** Sun, bank hols. **Meals:** alc (main courses £12 to £32.50). **Service:** 15% (optional). **Details:** Cards accepted. 120 seats. Air-con. Wheelchair access. Music. Children's portions. Car parking.

▋City

★NEW ENTRY★
1 Lombard Street
Sophisticated French cooking in the City
1 Lombard Street, EC3V 9AA
Tel no: (020) 7929 6611
www.1lombardstreet.com
⊖ Bank
Modern European | £57
Cooking score: 6
🍾

A former banking hall, One Lombard Street is divided into a brasserie and more formal restaurant – a somewhat sombre room, with a high ceiling, contemporary furnishings and Titian's *The Rape of Europa* as the focal point. Herbert Berger has been at the helm for a decade and his food is beautifully conceived and presented. Recent standout dishes have included a 'sparkling' salad of crab with a chilled tomato and cucumber gelée and brown crabmeat embellished with horseradish, a mignon of veal served with a delicate amalgam of green pea compote à la française, truffles, girolles and Chablis velouté. Rhubarb compote jelly with vanilla yoghurt Chartreuse and rhubarb sabayon, accompanied by elderflower sorbet and shortbread also won praise. Similarly, a scattering of surprises throughout the meal – a silky asparagus and foie gras cappuccino at the start, and a mixed fruit and star anise granita prior to the main dessert – were equally accomplished. However service is inconsistent, with managers demonstrating 'commendable attitude', but junior staff 'impassive'. The wine list, starting at £21, is geographically varied, though the emphasis is on France. It features many distinguished labels (with particularly strong representation from Domaine Leflaive) but it is not without mercy as mark-ups are pleasingly low.
Chef/s: Herbert Berger. **Open:** Mon to Fri L 12 to 2.30, D 6 to 10. **Closed:** Sat, Sun, 24 Dec, bank hols. **Meals:** alc (main courses £14.50 to £34.50). Set L £38 (2 courses) to £44, Tasting Menu £32 (5

courses) to £45 (9 courses). **Service:** 12.5%. **Details:** Cards accepted. 40 seats. Air-con. Separate bar. Wheelchair access.

★NEW ENTRY★
L'Anima
Slick in the City, with pasta a highlight
1 Snowden Street, EC2A 2DQ
Tel no: (020) 74227000
www.lanima.co.uk
⊖ Liverpool Street
Italian | £37
Cooking score: no score

Chef-proprietor Francesco Mazzei, ex of St Alban (see entry), has named his new restaurant after the Italian for soul. At first glance you would wonder if it has any: the City location is sterile and the low white chairs and simple décor rather cold-looking, with rationed glances of a semi-open kitchen blocked off by pillars. But get the smart, competent staff to crack a smile and everyone is laughing. Start with subtly smoky wood-roast aubergine topped with strips of burrata mozzarella, then try a luscious, tomato-based seafood stew with fregola – the Sardinan cross between tiny pasta and couscous. Pasta, though, is the surefire star, with tortelli stuffed with ricotta and herbs an exemplary version, and tagliolini with wild mushroom and summer truffle not far behind. Dessert might be the iced chocolate truffle, wrapped in waxed paper to impressive effect, or the house sorbets. Wines, kept in a vast glass-walled cave, highlight the Italian regions at resolutely reasonable prices: glasses are £5 and up. L'Anima was still new when the Guide went to press (hence no score), and it is not too wild a hope that inconsistencies, like an occasionally heavy hand with the salt, will vanish given time, just as the opening hours may extend.
Chef/s: Francesco Mazzei. **Open:** Mon to Fri L 12 to 2.30, D 5.30 to 12. **Closed:** Sat and Sun. **Meals:** alc (main courses £8.50 to £25.50). **Service:** 12.5% (optional). **Details:** Cards accepted. 80 seats. Air-con. Separate bar. No mobile phones. Wheelchair access. Music. Children allowed.

Bonds

Well-oiled and well-established feel
Threadneedle Hotel, 5 Threadneedle Street,
EC2R 8AY
Tel no: (020) 7657 8088
www.theetoncollection.com
⊖ Bank
Modern French | £37
Cooking score: 6
£5 OFF 🍷 🛏

There's no doubting the splendour of the
Threadneedle Hotel – just take a look at the
lobby – and the high-vaulted, walnut-
panelled elegance of Bonds has a well-oiled
and well-established feel. The customers are a
loyal bunch, drawn back time and time again
by Barry Tonks's modern French, with a
European bias, cooking. The menus may read
quite plainly, but the emphasis is on the
ingredients, and the kitchen brings off
successive dishes with convincing panache.
Start, maybe, with steak tartare with celeriac
rémoulade for a forthright introductory salvo.
Pasta is always well-considered, as when
ravioli of native blue lobster are served with a
lobster and Armagnac bisque, while main
course fish might deliver a stunningly fresh
wild halibut with Jerusalem artichoke, cep,
celeriac purée and chicken jus. Meats favour
slow cooking, as in pork belly with a 'risotto'
of pearl barley and chorizo served with
caramelised onions and pork cider sauce, or
perhaps rump of beef with honey-roast
carrots, beetroot marmalade and potato
gratin. After that, crème brûlée with cassis
sorbet is flawlessly executed, as is the chocolate
fondant with almond milk chocolate. As to
the wine list, it's a heavyweight tour of the
world's major growing areas, with a strong
selection of Champagnes, Bordeaux and
Burgundies underlining Bonds' city-dining
credentials. Elsewhere, a page of house
selections (from £5.75 a glass, £16.50 a bottle)
should keep those without bonuses happy.
Chef/s: Barry Tonks. **Open:** Mon to Fri L 12 to 2.30,
D 6 to 10. **Closed:** Sat and Sun, Christmas, bank
hols. **Meals:** alc (main courses £12.95 to £23). Set
menu £19.50 (2 courses) to £24.50. **Service:** 12.5%.

Details: Cards accepted. 80 seats. Air-con.
Separate bar. Wheelchair access. Music. Children's
portions.

Club Gascon

Passion, innovation and foie gras
57 West Smithfield, EC1A 9DS
Tel no: (020) 7796 0600
www.clubgascon.com
⊖ Barbican, Farringdon
French | £55
Cooking score: 6
£5 OFF 🍷

For more than a decade Pascal Aussignac
has devoted his time to exploring and
celebrating the idiomatic regional cuisine of
southwest France. He abandoned
conventional courses long before the fashion
for grazing took hold in the capital and his
menus are built around collections of little
dishes with headings like 'la route de sel' and
'les paturages'. The result is a labour of love,
passion and diligence, played out in a jewel-
like, marble-walled room hard by Smithfield
Market. At the heart of things is foie gras: it
appears in at least six different guises, perhaps
with sherry and cherries or served in a flan
with port sauce and 'soldiers'. Elsewhere,
Aussignac's boundlessly fertile imagination
and taste for carefully considered innovation
might yield asparagus coulis with eucalyptus
jelly and baby lobster or glazed squab pigeon
with crunchy grapes, verjuice and muesli.
Many ingredients are sourced direct from
France and the kitchen also applies its skills to
dishes from the orthodox world of haute
cuisine (duck carpaccio with spring truffle and
crispy artichoke or roast turbot with garden
pea purée, verbena and belly pork, for
example). To conclude, who could resist the
blissful prospect of fresh summer cheese with
lavender honey and confit rhubarb or a white
chocolate 'boule' with lime and pineapple?
The huge wine list is also a celebration and the
perfect opportunity to sample rarities from
Gaillac, Irouléguy and other southerly
backwaters – although big boys from

Bordeaux also get in on the act. 'Vins au verre' start at £5.50 a glass, with bottle prices from £24.

Chef/s: Pascal Aussignac. **Open:** Mon to Fri L 12 to 2, Mon to Sat D 7 to 10.30. **Closed:** Sun, bank hols. **Meals:** alc (main courses £9.50 to £22). Set L £28. Set D £42. **Service:** 12.5% (optional). **Details:** Cards accepted. 45 seats. Air-con. Separate bar. Wheelchair access. Music. Children allowed.

Le Coq d'Argent
Rooftop dining 'par excellence'
No. 1 Poultry, EC2R 8EJ
Tel no: (020) 7395 5000
www.coqdargent.co.uk
⊖ Bank
French | £33
Cooking score: 1

Renowned for its top-of-the-world terrace and eye-popping views of the London skyline, this illustrious rooftop restaurant is a magnet for City suits. An express lift sends customers up to the foliage-filled bar and airy dining room. The kitchen deals in bourgeois food with some regional add-ons, augmenting its core output with caviar and crustacea. Escargots and frogs' legs figure among the starters, alongside roast squab pigeon and baby artichoke salad with shiitake mushrooms. Mains amble all the way from coq au vin and tournedos Rossini to grilled yellow fin tuna atop sweet-and-sour aubergine compote. Desserts also cover a lot of ground, from pear 'Belle Hélène' to frozen brown sugar and ginger parfait with roasted plums. Top-end French vintages and everyday tipples share the honours on the colossal wine list; prices start at £17.

Chef/s: Mickael Weiss. **Open:** Mon to Fri L 11.30 to 3, Mon to Sat D 6 to 10 (6.30 Sat), Sun 12 to 3. **Closed:** Christmas, bank hols. **Meals:** alc (main courses £16 to £25). Set L and D £24 (2 courses) to £28.50. **Service:** 12.5% (optional). **Details:** Cards accepted. 150 seats. 180 seats outside. Air-con. Separate bar. Wheelchair access. Music. Children's portions.

Jean Christoph Novelli

Why did you become a chef?
To share my passion, expression, vision and creativity with others. I channelled my whole being into cooking.

What three ingredients could you not do without?
Vanilla pods, star anise and lemongrass.

What's the most unusual ingredient you've cooked or eaten?
A one-legged frog. It was the only one I could catch - his mates hopped off and I was left with the one who just went around and around in circles.

What's your guilty food pleasure?
Chocolate pancakes from Findus.

What era of history would you most like to have eaten in?
The early 16th century. I could have hosted banquets for Henry VIII at my house (Crouchmore Farm, near Luton) as he used to stay here on the way to visit Anne Boleyn's family. It would probably have received Royal approval and been voted the best Inn of the Year instead of one of the best cookery schools in the world!

The Don

Modern cooking in an historic venue
The Courtyard, 20 St Swithin's Lane, EC4N 8AD
Tel no: (020) 7626 2606
www.thedonrestaurant.co.uk
⊖ Bank
Modern European | £32
Cooking score: 2

Like its sibling Bleeding Heart (see entry), the Don offers ultra-modern versatile dining to a knowledgeable City crowd. The premises were once the preserve of Scottish wine merchant George Sandeman, who set up shop here at the end of the eighteenth century. What he would have made of a menu that takes in grilled tiger prawns on tabbouleh with pomegranate dressing or monkfish gasconne with haricots and chorizo, is anybody's guess. There is a core of traditionalism too, though, that produces duck confit with red cabbage and pommes purée, as well as rib-eye steak au poivre, with bread-and-butter pudding for afters. The port wine on which the place once thrived might turn up as the poaching medium for a pear stuffed with pistachio paste, or else on its own in a glass to round off a meal. And thereby hangs a tale, for the wine list is a beauty, strongest in classic French reds but also finding a range of exciting New World bottles, and even a Chinese blend of Chardonnay, Riesling and Muscat made by Austrian specialist Lenz Möser in Shandong province.

Vins du patron start at £16.45, or £4.45 a glass, for a Cabernet Franc rosé from New Zealand.
Chef/s: Matthew Burns. **Open:** Mon to Fri L 12 to 2.30, D 6 to 10. **Closed:** Sat, Sun bank hols. **Meals:** alc (main courses £12.95 to £24.50). **Service:** 12.5%. **Details:** 80 seats. Air-con. Separate bar. No music. Wheelchair access.

The Fox Public House

A local with a real dining experience
28 Paul Street, EC2A 4LB
Tel no: (020) 7729 5708
www.thefoxpublichouse.com
⊖ Old Street, Liverpool Street
Gastropub | £23
Cooking score: 3

This unpretentious pub admirably combines the role of traditional local (with a boisterous ground floor bar) with a proper restaurant experience – in the first-floor dining room. Here, in a darkly Gothic set of wax-splattered candelabra, chandeliers, Victorian mirrors and old chairs and dining tables, the fortnightly-changing menu is short, seasonal and no-nonsense, with tersely described dishes relying on first-rate raw materials to make their point. There is little adornment: chicken liver parfait is teamed with red onion relish, or there could be spinach soup with Greek yoghurt to start. Crab, chips and mayonnaise makes a satisfying main course, as does rib-eye steak with béarnaise. Finish with chocolate St Emilion, or fig tart with lemon ice cream. House wine is £13.25.
Chef/s: Amanda Pritchett. **Open:** Mon to Fri L 12 to 3, D 6 to 10, Sat D 6 to 11, Sun L 12 to 5. **Closed:** Christmas, bank hols. **Meals:** alc (main courses £9.50 to £15). **Service:** 12.5%. **Details:** Cards accepted. 35 seats. Separate bar. Music. Children's portions.

Symbols

🛏 Accommodation is available.

£30 Three courses for less than £30.

V More than five vegetarian dishes.

£5 OFF £5-off voucher scheme.

🍾 Notable wine list.

Refettorio at The Crowne Plaza Hotel

An Italian yardstick for the City
19 New Bridge Street, EC4V 6DB
Tel no: (020) 7438 8052
www.refettorio.com
⊖ Blackfriars
Italian | £35
Cooking score: 2

As clean-lined, smart and up-to-date as its contemporary hotel setting, this City Italian presses all the right style and quality buttons. At lunchtimes it positively buzzes with suits, though evenings are generally quieter. The menu is unashamedly Italian, and, with Giorgio Locatelli (of Locanda Locatelli fame, see entry) as consultant, this is a class act, albeit at City prices. But with star turns like great breads and home-made pasta, plus the 'convivium' with its cracking selection of regional cheeses and cold meats designed for sharing, there are no complaints. The kitchen certainly knows its stuff, delivering clean-cut dishes based on high-quality ingredients – linguine with lobster, slow-cooked roast saddle of lamb served with grilled vegetables, and a classic tiramisu with coffee ice cream for dessert. The décor's impressive too, with its long bar of polished wood, brown leather seating and low-slung light shades. The well-chosen, user-friendly, all-Italian wine list steps out with house Salento at £16.
Chef/s: Mattia Camorani. **Open:** Mon to Fri L 12 to 2.30, Mon to Thu D 6 to 10.30 (10 Fri and Sat). **Closed:** Sun, Christmas and bank hols. **Meals:** alc (main courses £8.50 to £22.50). **Service:** 12.5%. **Details:** Cards accepted. 80 seats. Air-con. Separate bar. Wheelchair access. Music. Children allowed.

Rhodes Twenty Four

Exemplary ingredients and stunning views
Tower 42, 25 Old Broad Street, EC2N 1HQ
Tel no: (020) 7877 7703
www.rhodes24.co.uk
⊖ Liverpool Street
Modern British | £55
Cooking score: 5

After negotiating the airport-like security checks, lifts whisk you directly to the restaurant on the 24th floor, where sweeping windows provide unobstructed views of the city skyline. The muted colour scheme does not detract from the stunning outlook, while space between tables is 'perfect for private deal-making'. Indeed, there are few discordant notes: service is discreet and considerate and the kitchen uses exemplary ingredients and keeps a tight rein on flavours. At inspection excellent breads were followed by 'superb' smoked eel, lightly coated with brioche and deep-fried, accompanied by a trio of sauces with an unusual beetroot crème fraîche taking centre stage. But the 'knockout dish' was a roasted partridge served medium-rare 'with a gamey undertone' alongside 'outstanding' buttered bacon and cabbage, and caramelised turnips. Desserts are more traditional, with bread-and-butter pudding or hot Russet and Bramley apple pie with blackberry ice cream and good old custard. The wine list is enterprising and diverse. Although it opens at £25, prices, especially in the mid-range, reflect its lofty position. Interestingly, premiums at the upper reaches are rather more reasonable, such as a 1983 Château Margaux at £400.

Chef/s: Adam Gray. Open: Mon to Fri L 12 to 2.15, D 6 to 8.30. Closed: Sat and Sun, bank hols. Meals: alc (main courses £16.50 to £27). Service: 12.5%. Details: Cards accepted. 75 seats. Air-con. Separate bar. Wheelchair access. Music. Children's portions.

Saki Bar and Food Emporium

Modern Japanese cooking
4 West Smithfield, EC1A 9JX
Tel no: (020) 7489 7033
www.saki-food.com
⊖ Farringdon
Japanese | £33
Cooking score: 3

V

Bypass the mini food store on the ground floor and head downstairs to the smart, minimalist restaurant in the basement. Here deep red walls, black leather and dark wood combine to create a dramatic look – everything, including the food, makes a full-on visual impact. Iconic dishes from the modern Japanese repertoire such as miso-marinated grilled black cod predictably find their way on to the menu. Elsewhere, there's high-quality sushi and sashimi, duck and foie gras teriyaki, and slow-grilled Iberico pork with sea salt and black peppers, as well as soups and udon noodles. Green tea tiramisu is worth trying for dessert. The good-value lunch menu is a great introduction, and variously-priced set menus help with choice at dinner. Cocktails, beers and saké are alternatives to the impressive wine list, which kicks off at £15.50.

Chef/s: Yoshitaka Onozaki. Open: Mon to Fri L 12 to 2.30, Mon to Sat D 6 to 10.30. Closed: Sun, bank hols. Meals: Set L £17.50 to £35, set D £23, £35, £55 and £65. Service: 12.5%. Details: Cards accepted. 80 seats. Air-con. Separate bar. Wheelchair access. Music. Children allowed.

ALSO RECOMMENDED

▲ Mehek

45 London Wall, City, EC2M 5TE
Tel no: (020) 75885043
www.mehek.co.uk
Indian

A pan-Indian restaurant in the City, Mehek (the name means 'fragrance') is enthusiastically supported for its friendly approach, light, eye-catching décor and the reliability of its cooking. A range of set menus supplements the main carte, which deals in vibrantly spiced dishes such as the starter of battered spicy whitebait (£3.90) and a range of favourite main courses like chicken dopiaza, lamb pasanda (both £7.90) and king prawn jalfrezi (£12.20). Specials include Hyderabadi duck, marinated in sesame seeds, coconut, peanuts and spices (£9.90). Finish with one of the Indian ice cream desserts (around £3.50). Wines from £13.50. Open Mon to Fri.

■ Clerkenwell

Ambassador

Streetwise all-day winner
55 Exmouth Market, EC1R 4QL
Tel no: (020) 7837 0009
www.theambassadorcafe.co.uk
⊖ Farringdon
Modern British | £25
New Chef

V

The brainchild of London restaurant veteran and wine aficionado Clive Greenhalgh, the Ambassador seems to be doing everything right. It confidently bridges the gap between gastro-café and no-frills neighbourhood restaurant, pulling in the crowds with its pared-down décor, engaging service and pavement tables overlooking Exmouth Market. Lunchtime callers get satisfaction from bowls of shellfish bisque, BLTs and fillets of plaice with samphire, while evening visitors can expect a fleshed-out menu that embraces ballottine of foie gras with pistachios and marinated cherries or a 'grand aïoli' for two, involving fillet of salt cod with spring vegetables. For afters, try peach mousse or strawberry soufflé. The wine list is a labour of love that bypasses big-name clichés in favour of fascinating rarities: expect lively drinking from £9.50 a carafe (£3.50 a glass). **Chef/s:** Dan Doherty. **Open:** all week L 12 to 2.30 (11 to 3.30 Sat, 11 to 4 Sun), Mon to Sat D 6 to 10.15). **Closed:** 1 week Christmas to New Year. **Meals:** alc (main courses from £9.50 to £17). Set L and pre-theatre £12.50 (2 courses). **Service:** not inc. **Details:** Cards accepted. 70 seats. 20 seats outside. Separate bar. Wheelchair access. Music. Children's portions.

Bleeding Heart
Romantic venue for fine French dining
The Cellars, Bleeding Heart Yard, Greville Street, EC1N 8SJ
Tel no: (020) 7242 8238
www.bleedingheart.co.uk
⊖ Farringdon
French | £34
Cooking score: 2
♦ V

On a summer's evening, heading into the courtyard that fronts the Bleeding Heart's collection of informal bistro, tavern and restaurant, you could convince yourself you were somewhere continental, not just off Farringdon Road. The cellar restaurant is equally charming, with exposed bricks, wooden beams and flickering candles. Starters might include 'deliciously savoury' snails in a single raviolo, or a simple classic such as potted shrimps, while main courses might include suckling pig served three ways – roasted, confit and as a boudin blanc – or pot-roast new season's lamb with spring vegetables. Particularly impressive is the vast selection of immaculately kept cheeses. Oenophiles will be drawn to the 450-bottle selection from all over the world, including the restaurant's own vineyard in Hawkes Bay, New Zealand. Wines start at £14.25.
Chef/s: Peter Reffell. **Open:** Mon to Fri L 12 to 2.30, D 6 to 10.30. **Closed:** Sat, Sun, Christmas to New Year, bank hols. **Meals:** alc (main courses £12.95 to

£26.50). **Service:** 12.5% (optional). **Details:** Cards accepted. 140 seats. 15 seats outside. Air-con. Separate bar. No music. Children allowed.

Clerkenwell Dining Room
69-73 St John Street, EC1M 4AN
Tel no: (020) 7253 9000
www.theclerkenwell.com
⊖ Farringdon
Modern British | £32
Cooking score: 3

Like its stablemate the Chancery (see entry), this Clerkenwell restaurant is valued for its reliable modern cooking – 'an eclectic mix of traditional European dishes with a twist'. It's a regular place for corporate entertainment, according to one reporter, who praised the warm crusty bread, and a red pepper salad with ricotta, spinach, pine nuts, Parmesan and baby artichokes. Tagliatelli of razor, cockles and poularde clams served with chilli, parsley and garlic has proved a hit too, as has a top-drawer halibut with pork belly, sweet pea purée and apple and walnut salsa. Visitors to the simply decorated ground-floor restaurant can also expect oxtail ravioli with lemon and rosemary dressing, and lamb rump with Provençale vegetables, samosa and balsamic jus, followed by strawberry shortcake with mascarpone and white chocolate ice cream. Wines are a well considered global selection, and prices start at £16. Our questionniare was not returned, so the information following may have changed.
Chef/s: Andrew Thompson and Daniel Groom. **Open:** Mon to Fri L 12 to 3, Mon to Sat D 6 (7 Sat) to 11. **Closed:** 25 Dec, bank hols. **Meals:** alc (main courses from £15). **Service:** 12.5% (optional). **Details:** Cards accepted. 110 seats. Air-con. Wheelchair access. Children's portions.

Scores on the Doors

To find out more about the Scores on the Doors campaign, please visit the Food Standard's Agency website: www.food.gov.uk or www.which.co.uk.

Coach and Horses

Easy-going, unfussy gastropub
26-28 Ray Street, EC1R 3DJ
Tel no: (020) 7278 8990
www.thecoachandhorses.com
⊖ Farringdon
Gastropub | £25
Cooking score: 2

A tongue-in-cheek sign depicting four mice and a pumpkin marks out this reborn Clerkenwell boozer (circa 1855), which now ticks along happily as a grown-up gastropub with all the right credentials. Service is friendly, there are real ales on handpump and the daily-changing, ingredients-led menu reads well. You can nibble on crab toasts, duck rillettes and Scotch eggs in the bar, enjoy a couple of 'small plates' at lunchtime (feta and spinach spring rolls, rollmops with saffron potato) or go for the full works in the evening. Salt-beef terrine, free-range duck leg with cherry and dandelion salad, and strawberries with cream and lemon shortbread show patriotic conviction, although Europe also steps up to the mark with plates of charcuterie and roast skate with San Manzano tomatoes and black olives followed by banana tarte Tatin. The short, appetising wine list opens with a dozen house selections from £13 (£3.70 a glass).
Chef/s: Nick Leonard. Open: Mon to Fri and Sun L 12 to 3, Mon to Sat D 6 to 10. Closed: bank hols, Christmas, New Year. Meals: alc (main courses £11.50 to £13.50). Bar menu available.
Service: 12.5%. Details: Cards accepted. 80 seats. 25 seats outside. Wheelchair access. Music. Children's portions.

Comptoir Gascon

Rustic French deli-bistro
61-63 Charterhouse Street, EC1M 6HJ
Tel no: (020) 7608 0851
www.clubgascon.com
⊖ Farringdon, Barbican
French | £22
Cooking score: 4

If you long for the honest, gutsy charm of traditional French cooking, this deli-cum-bistro could be the answer. Specialising in the wine and food of south-western France, it offers everything from foie gras to chocolates to take away, and a bistro menu with cassoulet, omelettes and cheeses at its heart, served in evocative, rough-walled surroundings. Starters to share include potted duck rillettes, fresh oysters with grilled chipolatas, and mackerel with fondant potato on toast. Main courses are divided into 'mer', 'vegetal' and 'terre'. From the sea, expect roast pollock with spicy chorizo and mushrooms, while vegetable offerings include salads and mini cheese raviolis with celery and fennel. Earthy animal dishes might be beef onglet (a particularly flavoursome cut) with sauce bordelaise or braised pork belly with celeriac mash. Other specialities include all things duck, from foie gras to confit with potato gratin. A short, French wine list starts at £18.
Chef/s: Julien Carlon. Open: Tue to Sat L 12 to 2, D 7 to 10. Closed: Sun, Mon, 25 Dec, 1 Jan. Meals: alc (main courses £8.50 to £14). Service: 12.5%. Details: Cards accepted. 30 seats. 8 seats outside. Air-con. No mobile phones. Music.

Eagle

The godfather of gastropubs
159 Farringdon Road, EC1R 3AL
Tel no: (020) 7837 1353
⊖ **Farringdon**
Modern European | £25
Cooking score: 2

Farringdon's genre-defining gastropub is cherished for its laid back vibes and full-blooded victuals. People still adore the quirky, bare-boarded room, where the chairs are hard, nothing fits and the style is deliberately deconstructed. Even so, the Eagle's fiercely egalitarian stance suits everyone: drink wherever you like, eat wherever you like from a blackboard menu hung above the bar. It's an ever-changing seasonal slate, with Spanish and Italian influences and a few nods to old England along the way. 'Bifeana' (the Eagle's iconic steak sandwich) has been a fixture for as long as anyone can remember, but the choice could extend to Romney Marsh lamb chops with grilled artichokes and olives, osso buco, and grilled asparagus salad with pecorino, mint and broad beans. A few tapas dishes are also on show, beer drinkers are well-served and there are some gutsy wines, too (prices from £11.50, £3 a glass).
Chef/s: Ed Mottershaw. **Open:** all week L 12 to 3.30 (12.30 to 3 Sat and Sun) Mon to Sat D 6.30 to 10.30.
Closed: 1 week Christmas, bank hols (exc Good Fri D). **Meals:** alc (main courses £8.50 to £15.50).
Service: not inc. **Details:** Cards accepted. 60 seats. 24 seats outside. Wheelchair access. Music. Children's portions.

Flâneur

A great place to hang about
41 Farringdon Road, EC1M 3JB
Tel no: (020) 7404 4422
www.flaneur.com
⊖ **Farringdon**
Modern European | £29
Cooking score: 2

With a name like Flâneur (translation: to hang about) you'd expect this deli-restaurant to be relaxed and easy. And it is – to a point. Flâneur's lean warehouse aesthetic is panoramic – from the billboard-high shelves stuffed with goodies to the fat wood-barrelled lampshades and oversized wooden chairs – while tables stuffed every which way among the food displays create a great ambience. Calendar-correct dishes of English asparagus (from Seven Score Farm in Kent) with fried Italian egg and Parmesan or goats' cheese salad with rocket, pistachio, honey and rose syrup dressing vie for attention on the daily-changing menu with plates of charcuterie, Craig Farm's breast of organic chicken (served with courgette pappardelle, Gorgonzola and cream), or chargrilled Herdwick lamb chop (with spinach, aubergine imam, lemon and dukkah). An international wine list is grouped by price, starting with the most expensive at £41 (red) £34 (white) and descending to £16.
Chef/s: Simon Phelan. **Open:** Mon to Fri 8am to 11pm, Sat 10am to 11pm. **Closed:** Sun, Christmas, bank hols. **Meals:** Set menu £21 (2 courses) to £26.
Service: 12.5%. **Details:** Cards accepted. 70 seats. Air-con. No music. Wheelchair access. Children allowed.

★NEW ENTRY★
Hat and Feathers

Period dining room, contemporary food
2 Clerkenwell Road, EC1M 5PQ
Tel no: (020) 7490 2244
www.hatandfeathers.com
⊖ Old Street
Gastropub | £28
Cooking score: 1
V

This bar and restaurant occupies a former hat factory, built in 1860 by two theatre designers. Its period dining rooms play up the building's old time glamour, while the partially covered wine terrace strikes a modern note with decking, heating and Panton chairs. The menu aims to match the formality of interior, so expect simple but classy dishes with a European flavour. Starters could include pan-fried scallops or beetroot risotto with basil foam and a Parmesan wafer, followed by pork belly with Savoy cabbage, Parma ham and apple purée or baked halibut with braised chicory, grapefruit and nicely al dente wilted greens. You could finish with apple tart or chocolate fondant. As we went to press there was 50% off the a la carte on Monday evenings, and a 25% discount at all times to EC1 residents. Drink options include wines, beers and cocktails.

Chef/s: Mr Perry Butler. **Open:** Mon to Fri L 12 to 2.30, Mon to Sat D 6 to 10.30. **Closed:** 25 and 26 Dec, 1 Jan, bank hols. **Meals:** alc (main courses £13.95 to £18.95). Express L £14.50. **Service:** 12.5%. **Details:** Cards accepted. 84 seats. 150 seats outside. Air-con. Separate bar. Wheelchair access. Music. Children's portions. Children allowed. Car parking.

★NEW ENTRY★
Hix Oyster & Chop House

British ingredients resplendently unadorned
35-37 Greenhill Rents, Cowcross Street, EC1M 6BF
Tel no: (020) 7017 1930
⊖ Farringdon
British | £33
Cooking score: no score

'It's like an episode of the *Krypton Factor* trying to find this place' noted one visitor of Mark Hix's latest venture. Truly a neighbourhood secret, this traditional chop house is all white linen and black and white tiles inside. You can perch at the bar for Champagne and oysters or settle on 'not-too-comfy bistro chairs' for more substantial offerings. Impeccable, seasonal and British ingredients are resplendently unadorned: soft-boiled duck egg comes with asparagus soldiers or salted ox cheek is served with a simple green bean salad. Mains include mutton chop curry, whole grilled John Dory and a range of prime steaks (at prime prices); side orders such as greens or chips are extra. An inspection meal, taken soon after opening (hence no score), kicked off with an 'extremely cold' goats' cheese, pickled walnut salad and beetroot, went on to a 'hefty' beef flank and oyster pie and closed with an 'exquisite' drop scone with English honey and honeycomb ice-cream. Service was 'inept' – has it improved? Reports please. House wine £14.

Chef/s: Stuart Tattershall. **Open:** Sun to Fri L 12 to 3, Mon to Sat D 6 to 11. **Meals:** alc (main courses £10.75 to £34.50). **Service:** 12.5% (optional). **Details:** Cards accepted. 52 seats. Air-con. No music. Children allowed.

Medcalf

Lively bistro cooking in Exmouth Market
40 Exmouth Market, EC1R 4QE
Tel no: (020) 7833 3533
www.medcalfbar.co.uk
⊖ **Farringdon**
Modern European | £30
Cooking score: 4

One Albert Medcalf opened up his butcher's shop on these premises before the First World War, and the blue frontage and sign retain a feeling of those bygone days. Step inside, though, and you're in a firmly twentyfirst-century world where the bar is equipped with sofas for lolling and the restaurant serves up modern bistro cooking of a high order. Potted shrimps on toast or leek and potato soup might be homely ways to start, or you could venture forth into the more speculative waters of sautéed duck livers with pancetta. Nicely balanced main-course choices include proper Irish stew with pearl barley, as well as roast monkfish with a stew of chickpeas and chorizo. Confidently stepping up a gear, there's roast confit guinea fowl with a potato cake seasoned with anchovy and rosemary. Comforting desserts include ginger cake with poached pear and clotted cream or chocolate and pistachio brownie with raspberry ice cream. The wine list confines itself to France, Spain and Italy, with selections that won't frighten the horses. Glass prices open at £3.55, bottles £13.75.
Chef/s: Brent Taylor. **Open:** all week L 12 to 3 (4 Sat and Sun), D 6 to 10 (10.30 sat and Sun). **Closed:** 24 Dec to 2 Jan, bank hols. **Meals:** alc (main courses £10.50 to £14.50). **Service:** 12.5%. **Details:** 50 seats. 20 seats outside. Air-con. Separate bar. Wheelchair access. Music. Children allowed.

Average price

The average price listed in main-entry reviews denotes the price of a three-course meal, without wine.

Moro

Vibrant Clerkenwell favourite
34-36 Exmouth Market, EC1R 4QE
Tel no: (020) 7833 8336
www.moro.co.uk
⊖ **Farringdon**
Spanish/North African | £32
Cooking score: 4

Moro's charms are many. Seemingly the more formal and fashion-conscious London's dining scene becomes, the more loud, vibrant, friendly Moro cocks a snook at it all and just goes about its business. The reward for that confidence is full tables every night of the week. Menus, which change weekly, include 'interesting Spanish food with a twist' plus some influences from Turkey, the Middle East and North Africa. The execution tends towards the simple, with wood-roasting, chargrilling and slow-cooking making the most of ingredients that are more seasonal than luxurious. Labneh (a yoghurt-like cheese) with salted anchovies and fresh chilli, and a beautifully flavoured beetroot soup with black cumin and yoghurt were appetite-whetting first courses. Then came butch main dishes such as chicken with calçots (a Catalan onion), and mackerel fillet with flatbread, cabbage salad and walnuts. A minor complaint at inspection was the repetition of a few too many garnishes (peppers, radishes, yoghurt etc.) across dishes. Puddings usually offer a delicious home-made ice cream (perhaps with a slug of Pedro Ximenez), cheese with membrillo, and tarts – be warned, popular choices such as yoghurt cake with gazientep pistachios and chocolate tart run low quickly. The Spanish wine list, a fitting partner to the food, is deemed 'unusual' and 'good value', opening at £12.50.
Chef/s: Samuel and Samantha Clark. **Open:** Mon to Sat L 12.30 to 2.30, D 7 to 10.30. Tapas 12.30 to 10.30. **Closed:** Sun, Christmas and bank hols. **Service:** not inc. **Details:** Cards accepted. 85 seats. 12 seats outside. Air-con. Separate bar. Wheelchair access. Children allowed.

St John

Simple, quality nose-to-tail dining
26 St John Street, EC1M 4AY
Tel no: (020) 7251 0848
www.stjohnrestaurant.com
⊖ Farringdon
British | £35
Cooking score: 6

Superior simplicity – that's Fergus Henderson's approach to running his no-frills British restaurant. Sure, tables in the sparse, hard-edged dining room are too close together and the scuffed white floorboards, wooden tables and schoolroom chairs add to the high noise level during busy periods, but the simplicity and quality of the food on offer is unparalleled. (NB. As the Guide went to press the restaurant told us they would be refurbishing over the summer of 2008). The open kitchen shows the chefs at work as they prepare a menu that changes twice daily – demonstrating a healthy obsession with careful sourcing and a desire to show English produce at its dazzling best. The popular langoustine with mayonnaise and the oft-reported (sometimes with mixed feelings) signature dish of roast bone marrow on toast with parsley salad are menu staples, but Henderson is a famous champion of offal and mains usually feature at least one or two examples, say chitterlings and chips or tripe, peas and bacon. More traditional tastes are satisfied by smoked haddock with mustard and mash or roast duck breast and radishes (served perhaps with sides of spring greens and Jersey Royal potatoes). Seasonal treats like peach jelly and Jersey cream or chocolate pot and cherries are satisfying desserts. The all-French wine list opens with vins de pays at £17. NB. As the Guide went to press, the restaurant told us they would be refurbishing over the summer of 2008.
Chef/s: Fergus Henderson. **Open:** Mon to Fri L 12 to 3, Mon to Sat D 6 to 11. **Closed:** Sun, Christmas, New Year, bank hols. **Service:** not inc. **Details:** Cards accepted. 110 seats. Air-con. Separate bar. Children allowed.

Limehouse

The Narrow

Riverside gastropub
44 Narrow Street, E14 8DP
Tel no: (020) 7592 7950
www.gordonramsay.com
⊖ Limehouse
British | £25
Cooking score: 3

 £30

Gordon Ramsay's venture into the gastropub format got off to a flying start, seducing even those who had expected to find, in the words of one reporter, 'a triumph of style over substance'. An awning now means diners can enjoy the riverside setting whatever the weather, while they tuck into dishes from the heartening menu. Starters such as potted salmon and granary toast or prawn cocktail, are followed by fortifying, feel-good mains like lamb stew, fishcake with tartare sauce, hake and chips with mushy peas, beef and red wine pie with mash – everything is designed to press the requisite buttons, and presentation is exemplary. To finish, there's apple and pie and custard, sticky toffee pudding, or lemon and vanilla cheesecake with rhubarb. The range of cask-conditioned ales and quality bottled beers and ciders is cheering enough, but there is also an intelligently composed short wine list, with 11 options by-the-glass from £3.50.
Chef/s: Mark Sargeant. **Open:** all week, Mon to Fri L 11.30 to 3, Sat and Sun L 12 to 4, Mon to Fri D 6 to 11, Sat and Sun D 5 to 11 (10.30 Sun). **Meals:** alc (main courses £7.50 to £14). **Service:** 12.5%. **Details:** 34 seats. 42 seats outside. Separate bar. Wheelchair access. Music. Children's portions. Car parking.

READERS RECOMMEND

The Grapes

Seafood
76 Narrow Street, Limehouse, E14 8BP
Tel no: 020 7987 4396
'Fresh fish in a Dickensian setting'

▍Shoreditch

Bacchus

Style and substance in edgy Hoxton
177 Hoxton Street, N1 6PJ
Tel no: (020) 7613 0477
www.bacchus-restaurant.co.uk
⊖ Old Street
Global | £45
Cooking score: 6

£5 OFF 🍷 V

Cynics wondered about this über-cool Hoxton pub conversion, questioning the wisdom of sitting an ambitious molecular gastronomy 'gastropub' in a rather shady spot of East London. But Bacchus has matured in the last year, morphing successfully into that rare thing, a destination neighbourhood restaurant. Pub origins are clear, but tablecloths, candles, Riedel glasses and comfortable chairs have elevated the ambience. The vibe is youthful and casual like most – though by no means all – of its customers. It's a fitting setting for Nuno Mendes, often visible at the pass or even serving tables, to showcase his talent 'with verve on a level with Heston Blumenthal'. It is all tasting menus now (exhibiting better balance and bolder flavour combinations than previously), and trendwatchers will note the fashionable molecular touches, in 'nitro macarons', or 'oysters and onions old but new', and a dish rather preciously subtitled 'memories of San Sebastian'. Ingredients and references garnered from Asia and Europe make Mendes' cooking hard to classify; far easier to focus on the trendy techniques – spherification, sous vide, jellies and the like. Some cringe at the chutzpah, others delight at the 'accessible' and 'affordable' ambitious cooking and 'new ideas'. Wines start at £19, with the bulk in the £20 to 40 bracket and include a much-improved selection by-the-glass. Jugs of tap water flavoured with herbs are a pleasant touch.

Chef/s: Nuno Mendes. **Open:** Mon to Sat D 6 to 12. **Closed:** Sun, Christmas. **Meals:** Set D £45 (5 courses) to £60 (7 courses). **Service:** 12.5%. **Details:** Cards accepted. 45 seats. Air-con. Wheelchair access. Music. Children allowed.

Eyre Brothers

Full-dress Iberian rendezvous
70 Leonard Street, EC2A 4QX
Tel no: (020) 7613 5346
www.eyrebrothers.co.uk
⊖ Old Street
Spanish/Portuguese | £35
Cooking score: 2

🍷

David and Richard Eyre's stylish Shoreditch set up takes the gastropub principle and transmutes it into into a full-on, grown-up restaurant complete with floor-to-ceiling windows, gleaming white walls and black leather banquettes. This is one of the few London venues where genuine Iberian cuisine forms the backbone of the menu, and ingredients are spot-on – from jamón Ibérico Bellota and free-range Pata Negra pork to piquillo peppers and bacalhau (salt cod). The result is a mix of diehards such as Cádiz-style fried fish with lemon, chilli and parsley salad or pollo al ajillo alongside home-cured yellowfin tuna escabèche, monkfish with morcilla, butter beans and saffron, and aged T-bone steak with salt-cured pork back-fat and warm Roseval potato salad. Tapas nibbles are served in the bar. The imaginative wine list is a great-value selection of modern names with an emphatic Iberian slant (right down to the sherries and ports). A star-studded international cast provides impressive support and there are cracking house selections from £15 (£3.90 a glass).

Chef/s: David Eyre and João Cleto. **Open:** Mon to Fri L 12 to 3, Mon to Sat D 6 to 11 (6.30 Sat). **Closed:** Sun, bank hols, Christmas, New Year. **Meals:** alc (main courses £14 to £25). Bar menu available. **Service:** 12.5% (optional). **Details:** Cards accepted. 70 seats. Air-con. Separate bar. Wheelchair access. Music. Children allowed.

Fifteen

Trendy modern Italian
15 Westland Place, N1 7LP
Tel no: (0871) 330 1515
www.fifteenrestaurant.com
⊖ Old Street
Italian | £40
Cooking score: 2

Jamie Oliver's famous social enterprise Fifteen hasn't lost any of its pulling power, not even now he's turned his attention to new high street chain Jamie's Italian. Both the downstairs dining room and groundfloor trattoria are heaving at lunch and dinner, with weekend dinner reservations remaining elusive. The cuisine, modern Italian based on quality Italian and British ingredients, is crowd-pleasing stuff, though who's still impressed by such Jamie-isms as 'funky leaf salad' or 'wicked Sicilian fisherman's stew'? The cooking, shored up by strong produce rather than dazzling skill in the kitchen, fares fine without such gimmickry, though assemblies of Buccleuch beef with beetroot and horseradish crème fraîche or mozzeralla salad with blood oranges and mint can't go wrong. At inspection, the kitchen came unstuck with simple linguine carbonara, which was undercooked, not authentically al dente, and overpowered by too much fresh marjoram. With prices (from £9 for starters, £20 for mains) just a few pounds below London's better Italians, Fifteen is no bargain.
Chef/s: Drew Parkinson. **Open:** All week, L 12 to 3, D 6 to 10. **Closed:** Christmas and New Year. **Meals:** Set menus, £22 (2 courses), £25 (3 courses), Tasting menu £60. **Service:** 12.5% optional. **Details:** Cards accepted. 68 seats. Air-con. Wheelchair access. Music. Children allowed.

Great Eastern Dining Room

Grazing in the City
54-56 Great Eastern Street, EC2A 3QR
Tel no: (020) 7613 4545
www.rickerrestaurants.com
⊖ Old Street
Fusion/Pan-Asian | £35
Cooking score: 3

£5 OFF **V**

An old fabric warehouse in desirable Shoreditch is the setting for this high-fashion pan-Asian hangout. Like other members of Will Ricker's stable, it's an energetic, glitz-strewn playground that attracts a young, affluent crowd with money to spend and glamorous encounters in mind. The bar pulsates with serious chatter – likewise the über-hip dining room, with its bold black and red colour schemes. A menu of little dishes for grazing and sharing suits the socialising perfectly: there are no conventional starters or mains – instead, the kitchen pumps out trendy dumplings, tempura, grills and more, all based on genuine ingredients (check the glossary on the back of the menu if the names are baffling). Work your way through creative dim sum (miso-roasted pumpkin gyoza dumplings with black vinegar dip), salads (duck with watermelon and cashews), curries and specials such as 'eight treasures' tofu. To finish, East meets West in the shape of, say, lemongrass brûlée with ginger biscuit. The wine list is suitably modish, with elite names and exciting drinking from £14.50 (£3.40 a glass).
Chef/s: Andy Lau. **Open:** Mon to Fri L 12 to 3, Mon to Sat D 6 to 11. **Closed:** Sun, bank hols and Christmas. **Meals:** alc (main courses £8 to £20). Set L & D £25 to £45. Bar menu available. **Service:** 12.5% (optional). **Details:** Cards accepted. 60 seats. Air-con. Separate bar. No mobile phones. Music. Children allowed.

Rivington Grill
No-frills, nostalgic Brit food
28-30 Rivington Street, EC2A 3DZ
Tel no: (020) 7729 7053
www.rivingtongrill.co.uk
⊖ Old Street
British | £28
Cooking score: 2

How apt – Brit food in the heart of the heart of the Brit Art district. This light, loft-style restaurant takes some of Britain's best regional food and serves it up with a hefty sprinkling of nostalgia: fish fingers and chips with mushy peas, roast Lancashire suckling pig with greens and apple sauce and Devon Red free-range chicken with sage and onion stuffing and roast potatoes are typical samples from the no-frills menu. If this sounds predictable, look to starters such as black-headed gull's eggs with mustard cress and celery salt or smoked eel with Jersey Royals, Old Spot bacon and horseradish. A delightful 'on toast' selection includes Welsh rarebit, potted Morecambe Bay shrimps and soft herring roes with capers and parsley. The comfort factor is cranked up for dessert: offerings include chocolate mousse, lemon posset and rhubarb crumble with custard. A classy selection of wines starts at £15 but most bottles are over £20. Part of Caprice Holdings, this restaurant has a twin in Greenwich.
Chef/s: Simon Wadham. **Open:** all week L12 to 3, D 6 to 11 (10.30 Sun). **Closed:** 25 and 26 Dec. **Meals:** alc (main courses £9.75 to £23.50), Sunday set L £22.50. **Service:** 12.5%. **Details:** Cards accepted. Air-con. Wheelchair access. Music. Children's portions.

Please send us your feedback

To register your opinion about any restaurant listed in the Guide, or a new restaurant that you wish to bring to our attention, please visit the web address at the bottom of the page. Your feedback informs the content of the book and will be used to compile next year's reviews.

★NEW ENTRY★
Saf
Inventive vegan and raw-food specialist
152 Curtain Road, EC2A 3AT
Tel no: (020) 7613 0007
ww.safrestaurant.co.uk
⊖ Old Street
Vegetarian | £25
Cooking score: 3

V

For a vegan raw-food specialist, this Shoreditch newcomer is surprisingly stylish, with clean-lined design, modern furnishings, a large bar area and a semi open-plan kitchen in the centre of the room. The food is far more inventive than might be expected from such a restaurant, delivering clever ingredient combinations, attractive presentation and a range of faux dairy products made from nut milk. Chive caviar and soured cream sitting atop crispy sweet potato latkes provides an impressive start to a meal. To follow, a more wholesome wild mushroom croquette served with a swirl of truffle alfredo sauce and accompanied by a salad of micro-leaves and edible flowers balances earthy and floral flavours to great effect. Meals round off nicely with a rich dark chocolate ganache tart with drunken cherry sorbet. A mean selection of cocktails are mixed at the bar, (made using organic spirits and juices where possible) and the wine list is long, carefully selected and also demonstrates a commitment to organic, sustainable and bio-dynamic producers. Bottles start at £17 (£4 a glass). An interesting newcomer that should appeal to vegans and non-vegans alike.
Chef/s: David Bailey. **Open:** Mon to Fri L 12 to 3.30, Mon to Sat D 6.30 to 11. **Closed:** 25 and 26 Dec, bank hols. **Meals:** alc (main courses L £5 to £9, D £8.50 to £11.50). Bar menu available.
Service: 12.5% (optional). **Details:** Cards accepted. 70 seats. 25 seats outside. Air-con. Wheelchair access. Music. Children's portions.

★NEW ENTRY★
Viet Grill

Astonishing value
58 Kingsland Road, E2 8DP
Tel no: (020) 7739 6686
www.vietgrill.co.uk
⊖ Old Street
Vietnamese | £15
Cooking score: 2

V

Before we begin, this restaurant is not situated in the most salubrious part of town (think more urban grime, less Hoxton glamour), but it is certainly worth the expedition. A sleek, bright room defies all the canteen stereotypes often associated with Vietnamese dining. Decadent birdcages hang in draped windows and dark wood is offset with patterned wallpapers. At inspection a mango, chilli and calamari salad was absolutely outstanding. Summer rolls were fresh and fragrant – it's hard to believe that you're eating £3 plates at this level. Dishes with names such as 'feudal roasted beef' and 'stuffed swimming crabs' entice and delight in equal measure. Other successful mains included a duck curry with lemongrass and coconut milk, the gloriously tender meat falling off the bone. On a pedantic note, red wine is served in comedy half-bottle glasses (rectified with a standard white wine glass upon request). The service is offhand but efficient. Mind you, it's easy to forgive them for having bunked off charm school at these prices.
Chef/s: Vinh Vu. **Open:** Mon to Sat L 12 to 3, D 5.30 to 11 (11.30 Sat). Sun 12 to 10.30. **Closed:** Christmas. **Meals:** alc (main courses £4 to £12). **Service:** 10%. **Details:** Cards accepted. 80 seats.

▌Spitalfields

Canteen

Spitalfields success story
2 Crispin Place, E1 6DW
Tel no: (0845) 6861 122
www.canteen.co.uk
Modern British | £25
Cooking score: 3

V

Peddling British food of years gone by with bags of twenty-first century attitude, Canteen is a thrilling success story deep in the bowels of Spitalfields Market. The plate-glass frontage, communal bench tables and marble booths may suggest a '30s American diner, but the menu tells a different story: devilled kidneys on toast, macaroni cheese, gammon with parsley sauce, stews and rice pudding invoke all our yesterdays, and the kitchen never shirks from its flag-waving responsibilities. All-day breakfasts, roasts with the trimmings and 'fast service' one-dish lunches are part of the package, and a recently introduced snack menu offers anything from Scotch eggs to fish finger sandwiches. The wallet-friendly global wine list includes a lively selection of appetising stuff from £12.50 (£3.25 a glass); also check out the seasonal Brit-inspired cocktail list and the 20-strong contingent of exclusively British beers and ciders. Canteen has a branch in the Royal Festival Hall complex on the South Bank, and a further outlet is scheduled to open at 55 Baker Street, W1 around October 2008.

Symbols	
🛏	Accommodation is available.
£30	Three courses for less than £30.
V	More than five vegetarian dishes.
£5 OFF	£5-off voucher scheme.
🍾	Notable wine list.

Chef/s: Cass Titcombe. Open: all week 8am to midnight. Meals: alc (main courses £7.50 to £13.50). Service: 12.5% (optional). Details: Cards accepted. 75 seats. 80 seats outside. Air-con. Separate bar. No music. No mobile phones. Wheelchair access. Children's portions.

St John Bread & Wine
The upper-crust of City brasseries
94-96 Commercial Street, E1 6LZ
Tel no: (020) 7251 0848
www.stjohnbreadandwine.com
⊖ Liverpool Street
Modern British | £25
Cooking score: 3

Tucked away behind Spitalfields market, this Fergus Henderson spin-off is even more relaxed and unbuttoned than its elder sibling (St Johns see entry). A take-out bakery and wine shop as well as a restaurant, it's open all day from breakfast through lunch and dinner. With an open kitchen, plain white walls (save for the rows of coat pegs), simple wood furniture and parquet floor, it's as endearingly unpretentious as its signature British food. Quality seasonal ingredients and humble, less-common cuts reign supreme on tersely scripted daily-changing menus driven by simplicity and flavour. Take smoked eel and horseradish, perhaps pigeon and hispi cabbage, or a cracking Eccles cake served up with Lancashire cheese. Service is on-the-ball and there's no pressure to follow three-course convention, while the Francophile wine list comes in user-friendly ascending-price-order mode, starting with vins de pays at £17 (£4.35 a glass). Chef/s: James Lowe. Open: all week L 12 to 6 (4 Sat and Sun), D 6 to 10.30 (9 Sun). Closed: Christmas to New Year, bank hols. Meals: alc (main courses £11 to £13). Service: not inc. Details: Cards accepted. 54 seats. Air-con. Children allowed.

■ Tower Hill

Café Spice Namaste
Vibrant colours and Asian flavours
16 Prescot Street, E1 8AZ
Tel no: (020) 7488 9242
⊖ Tower Hill
Indian/Pan Asian | £35
Cooking score: 2

 V

Famous for its vivid décor as well as its distinctive take on Indian cuisine, Cyrus Todiwala's flagship restaurant has clocked up more than a decade in Whitechapel. The interior exudes spicy exotic warmth with its saffron, blue and cinnamon colours, and there's plenty to catch the eye on the menu. Influences come from across the Sub-continent, although the kitchen also champions British ingredients – from Loch Fyne scallops and Cornish lamb to Heritage potatoes. Starters like flash-grilled squid, 'dynamite' with potent Goan spices, or Cheltenham beetroot and coconut samosas might precede ostrich bhuna or monkfish chettinad cooked in a palate-tingling 'devilled' sauce. Todiwala is a proud Parsee, so it's no surprise that his dhansaks are authentic and elaborately iconic. Beyond the numerous tandooris and curries, the kitchen also conjures up some pan-Asian flavours, as in bamboo shoot, enoki mushroom and chickpea xacutti. In summer, the Ginger Garden is a peaceful outdoor oasis, complete with Parsee murals, a mosaic bar and a tandoor. Wines start at £15.50 (£4.25 a glass). Chef/s: Cyrus Todiwala and Angelo Collaco. Open: Mon to Fri L 12 to 3, Mon to Sat D 6.15 to 10.30 (6.30 to 10.30 Sat). Closed: Sun, bank hols. Meals: alc (main courses £12.50 to £16.50). Service: 12.5% (optional). Details: Cards accepted. 140 seats. 40 seats outside. Air-con. Wheelchair access. Music. Children's portions.

▌Wapping

Wapping Food

Industrial-chic food arena
Wapping Hydraulic Power Station, E1W 3ST
Tel no: (020) 7680 2080
www.thewappingproject.com
⊖ Wapping/Shadwell
Modern European | £30
Cooking score: 3

£5
OFF

A riot of arty post-modernism and industrial chic, Wapping Food occupies the shell of a disused hydraulic power station: it's a huge arena that also includes multi-media events, installations, shows and exhibitions amid the ironwork and mechanical relics. Enjoy a lavender Martini before checking out the day's menu, which reads like a foodie shopping list: there might be smoked marlin with golden beetroot or whole fried quail with kimchee, chill and peanuts to start, ahead of confit duck with pickled baby spring vegetables and onion jam or chargrilled sardines with artichokes, samphire and salsa verde. To finish, gin and tonic sorbet should hit the spot. Brunch is the thing at weekends; the owners have also launched a new bar menu, plus a line-up of cocktails based on local ingredients and herbs from their garden. Fans of Aussie wine will have a field day: everything on the fashionable wine list (apart from a few Champagnes) is from Down Under, with bags of quaffable stuff from £16.75 (£4.50 a glass).
Chef/s: Cameron Emirali. **Open:** all week 12 to 11 (10 to 11 Sat, 10 to 5.30 Sun). **Closed:** bank hols, 24 Dec to 3 Jan. **Meals:** alc (main courses £12.50 to £22). Set L and D £45. Bar menu available.
Service: 12.5% (optional). **Details:** Cards accepted. 150 seats. 45 seats outside. Separate bar. Wheelchair access. Music. Children's portions. Car parking.

▌Whitechapel

ALSO RECOMMENDED
▲ Kasturi

57 Aldgate High Street, Whitechapel, EC3N 1AL
Tel no: (020) 7480 7402 / 7481 0048
www.kasturi-restaurant.co.uk
⊖ Aldgate
Indian

'Far superior to other run-of the-mill Indian restaurants in the East End' is the verdict of one regular at this popular Whitechapel venue. The cooking of the Northwest Frontier is the focus, from the kebab-ke-karishma selection for two (£12.95) as a shared starter, to chicken afghani lababdar (£8.95), with tomato, pepper and onions, or Patiala shahi gosht (£8.95), a sumptuous lamb dish. More familiar Indian dishes, such as dhansak and madras curries, or biryani variations, are available and vegetarians are well-served with a broad selection of dishes including full vegetable thali with tandoori naan and pilau rice (£9.95). Wines from £14.95. Open all week.

▌Balham

★NEW ENTRY★
Brinkley's Kitchen
Modern European dining in leafy suburb
35 Bellevue Road, SW17 7EF
Tel no: (020) 8672 5888
www.brinkleys.com
⊖ Tooting Bec
Modern European | £25
Cooking score: 1

Popular Wandsworth eatery Amici has been replaced with the latest outpost of the Brinkley group, the restaurant and bar providing a convivial atmosphere for its well-heeled diners. Much of the sleek décor remains, but some may find the open-plan kitchen an unwelcome distraction. The menu offers dishes such as chargrilled calamari with fresh red chilli and rocket, homemade ravioli with roasted pumpkin and seared tuna niçoise with anchovies. The wild card, a dish of pepper and citrus-crusted tuna tataki was under par, but the kitchen returned to form with an indulgent warm chocolate fondant tart and lemon sorbet served with vodka. House wine is £12.50.

Chef/s: Paolo Zanca. **Open:** Mon to Fri L 12 to 4, D 6 to 11. Weekend brunch 11 to 4. **Meals:** alc (main courses £8.50 to £20). Set D (for parties of 10 people) £24 to £30. **Service:** 12.5% (optional). **Details:** Cards accepted. 110 seats. Air-con. Separate bar. No music. Children allowed.

Please send us your feedback

To register your opinion about any restaurant listed in the Guide, or a new restaurant that you wish to bring to our attention, please visit the web address at the bottom of the page. Your feedback informs the content of the book and will be used to compile next year's reviews.

Chez Bruce
A neighbourhood star
2 Bellevue Road, SW17 7EG
Tel no: (020) 8672 0114
www.chezbruce.co.uk
⊖ Balham
Modern European | £40
Cooking score: 6

Oh, fortunate Wandsworth Common residents to have such a restaurant on their doorstep – remarkably down-to-earth and much praised by reporters for its lack of pretension and the friendliness of its staff. There are slightly more tables fitted into the room than is comfortable, with precious little space for the staff, or for extravagant gestures by the customers. However, the demand is such that the slight discomfort is tolerated with a smile and an atmosphere of camaraderie; the prices, after all, are extraordinarily reasonable. Bruce Poole's cooking makes use of the best seasonal ingredients for his own style of unfussy modern British cooking with a veneer of Mediterranean influence. A classic, unimpeachable foie gras and chicken liver parfait may appear alongside a beautiful, delicately flavoured chilled consommé of langoustine and mayonnaise, or a witty, robust schnitzel of rabbit with anchovy and capers. Mains include a very fine côte de boeuf with béarnaise and real chips (for two), as well as lighter dishes such as grilled sea bream with piquillo peppers and asparagus. Puddings are worth saving space for: lemon curd ice cream, warm chocolate tart with cherries or iced banana parfait with rice pudding. The cheeseboard on its own is a reason to visit. The young sommelier Terry Threlfall has injected new colour and energy into the already awesome wine list – the addition of wines from his native Canada make interesting reading and tasting. With 16 wines by-the-glass, starting at less than £5, and many hundreds of bottles, he's got plenty to choose from.

Chef/s: Bruce Poole and James Lawrence. **Open:** all week L 12 to 2 (3 Sat and Sun), D 6.30 to 10.30 (9.30 Sun). **Closed:** 24 to 26 Dec, 1 Jan. **Meals:** Set L Mon to Fri £25.50, Set L Sat £32.50, Set D £40 to £50 (4 courses). **Service:** 12.5%. **Details:** Cards accepted. 70 seats. Air-con. No mobile phones.

★NEW ENTRY★
Harrison's
Brasserie cooking with promise
15-19 Bedford Hill, SW12 9EX
Tel no: (020) 8675 6900
www.harrisonsbalham.co.uk
⊖ Balham
Modern European | £24
Cooking score: 1

The latest venture by Sam Harrison, of Sam's Brasserie and Bar (see entry) in Chiswick, is located at the heart of South London's 'nappy valley'. The menu is clearly in sync with local palates, offering solid, if unchallenging, brasserie dishes. The kitchen shows some promise with Dan Edwards (formerly of Launceston Place) at the helm, delivering the likes of lentil, pancetta and bay leaf soup and a 'generous' main course of tender lamb shank ragù. To finish try the passionfruit crème brûlée. The cellar boasts a mix of Old and New World wines, with plenty offered by-the-glass (from £3.75). Bottles start at £13.50. **Chef/s:** Dan Edwards. **Open:** all week L 12 to 3 (9 to 4 Sat and Sun), D 6 to 10.30 (6.30 to 10.30 Sat, 10 Sun). **Meals:** alc (main courses £9.50 to £13.50). Set L Mon to Fri £11.50 (2 courses) to £15, set D Mon to Fri, £14 (2 courses) to £17. **Service:** 12.5% (optional). **Details:** Cards accepted. 90 seats. 12 seats outside. Separate bar. No music. Children's portions.

READERS RECOMMEND
Lamberts
Modern British
2 Station Parade, Balham, SW12 9AZ
Tel no: (020) 8675 2233
www.lambertsrestaurant.com
'Legendary Sunday roasts and kid-friendly too'

▌Battersea
Greyhound
Restaurant masquerading as a gastropub
136 Battersea High Street, SW11 3JR
Tel no: (020) 7978 7021
www.thegreyhoundatbattersea.co.uk
Gastropub | £28
Cooking score: 4

The comfortable, traditional front bar with its big brown leather sofas is at odds with the restaurant tucked away at the back. Here linen-clad tables are carefully laid, and neutral tones and old French posters pull the awkwardly shaped room into a cohesive whole. The nook-and-crannyishness works in its favour – at quiet times the few diners do not feel deserted, while the odd corners and high ceilings allow for private conversations when the place is packed. The menu has an Italian flavour, but relies on British ingredients – salted Galloway in carpaccio of beef with Montgomery cheddar in place of Parmesan – and the kitchen knows no bounds in its enthusiasm. Butter and ricotta are home-made, they smoke their own salmon and they even make their own bottarga. Whether these extra efforts make a demonstrable difference it's hard to say, but the cooking is well up to scratch, the portions generous and staff knowledgeable and proud of what they produce. The wine list is exceptional: interesting, enormous, plenty by-the-glass and kindly priced, from its £13 bottom to its £1,100 1966 Château Latour top. **Chef/s:** Diego Sales. **Open:** Tue to Sun L 1 to 3, Tue to Sat D 7 to 10. **Closed:** Mon. **Meals:** Set L £16 (2 courses) to £20. **Service:** 12.5%. **Details:** Cards accepted. 46 seats. 20 seats outside. Separate bar. Wheelchair access. Music.

Ransome's Dock

A good, reliable place for family and friends
35-37 Parkgate Road, SW11 4NP
Tel no: (020) 7223 1611
www.ransomesdock.co.uk
Modern European | £33
Cooking score: 3

£5 OFF

Ransome's Dock has been a feature of this Battersea back road for years and is a pleasant place to while away a few of hours, especially in good weather when the lovely terrace overlooking the moored barge is open. There's nothing newfangled about Martin Lam's cooking, either. His palette of tastes and textures is strictly of the Elizabeth David school. A starter of warm smoked eel, for example, served with deep purple beetroot, is given extra oomph with a dollop of horseradish cream, while main courses, including Mrs David's lamb and aubergine casserole, and calf's liver with garlic mash and cabbage, are for the hearty of appetite. But though dishes are perfectly well executed, they are not the reason that people make the trek here. The real draw is, and always has been, the wine list. Lam has a passion for wine and his list, as he says, is one for sharing with friends rather than for looking impressive – there's plenty on the long list in the low- to mid-price bracket to give customers food for thought and tempt them to try something different, with house wines ranging from £15.50 to £22.50.

Chef/s: Martin and Vanessa Lam. **Open:** Mon to Sat 12 to 11, Sun L 12 to 3.30. **Closed:** Christmas. **Meals:** alc (main courses £9.50 to 22.50). Set menu £15.50 (2 courses). **Service:** 12.5% (optional). **Details:** Cards accepted. 54 seats. 20 seats outside. Separate bar. Wheelchair access. Music. Children's portions.

Also recommended

An 'also recommended' entry is not a full entry, but is provisionally suggested as an alternative to main entries.

★NEW ENTRY★

Tom Ilic

Imaginative, gutsy, big-on-flavour cooking
123 Queenstown Road, SW8 3RH
Tel no: (020) 7622 0555
www.tomilic.com
Modern British | £25
Cooking score: 4

£30

There's no doubt that Tom Ilic's eponymous restaurant looks and feels more like a neighbourhood bistro than a serious restaurant. The plain double dining room with its bare tables and homely pot plants would not necessarily lead one to expect this standard of cooking, but in bringing together the best ingredients from the daily market and combining them on a menu that is short, imaginative and very reasonably priced, serious intent is apparent. Tom Ilic is now in familiar territory (he was a chef here a decade ago, when the premises were known as the Stepping Stone) and is happily turning out his brand of imaginative, gutsy, big-on-flavour cooking. He flaunts his passion for meat cookery with starters such as braised pig's cheeks and chorizo with garlic and parsley mash and mains of slow-cooked beef with roasted bone marrow, caramelised root vegetables and garlic bread. But equally well-considered have been fish dishes like the hand-picked crab tortellini with shellfish nage and seared mackerel with horseradish soufflé that opened a good-value Sunday lunch in early January. That meal went on to deliver 'with deceptive and effortless flair' rump of lamb with 'perfect' mash and spinach, a 'belting' squab pithiviers with Savoy cabbage and lentil cream, and ended with a quite outstanding sticky toffee pudding, 'the best I have ever had'. The manageable wine list is helpfully categorised by style. Prices start at £13.

Chef/s: Tom Ilic. **Open:** Wed to Fri and Sun L 12 to 2.30 (3.30 Sun), D Tue to Sat 6 to 10.30. **Closed:** Mon, 25 to 29 Dec. **Meals:** alc (main courses £9.75 to £13.50). Set L £12.50 (2 courses). Set Sun L £14.50 (2 courses). **Service:** not inc. **Details:** Cards accepted. 55 seats.

ALSO RECOMMENDED
▲ Butcher and Grill

39–41 Parkgate Road, Battersea, SW11 4NP
Tel no: (020) 7924 3999
www.thebutcherandgrill.com
⊖ Battersea Park
Modern European

Though non-meat eaters are catered for, it's
not the ideal choice for those of a sensitive
disposition – the restaurant area is beyond a
fully-stocked butcher's counter. But for true
carnivores this is a no-holds-barred treat. The
meat is of impeccable standard, well-hung and
properly butchered, and the cooking is as
simple as can be – steaks (from £15.50), calf's
liver (£14.50) and burgers (£9.50) thrown on
to a grill and cooked as requested, served with
classic sauces and a pleasing array of sides –
buttered spinach (£3), gratin dauphinoise
(£3.25) and salads (£2.75) are all there to
tempt. The wine list, understandably heavy on
the reds, starts at £14.50. Closed Sun D.

█ Bermondsey
Le Pont de la Tour

Stunning river views
36d Shad Thames, SE1 2YE
Tel no: (020) 7403 8403
www.danddlondon.com
⊖ Tower Hill, London Bridge
Modern European | £50
Cooking score: 3

Soak in that glorious view of Tower Bridge –
you're paying for it, after all. A meal at this
crowd-pleasing venue comes at a price, but the
restaurant, opened in 1991, still impresses its
core audience of couples, out-of-towners and
business folk. Strong on classics such as veal
Rossini, steak tartare and fruits de mer, the
menu offers more modern elegant dishes like
salmon with beetroot, potato and dandelion
or strawberries and Champagne with
madeleines. For something simpler don't
overlook the grill, where there are decent
burgers and B.L.Ts. The restaurant is rightly

well-known for wine. In a bulky tome, strong
on Champagne, Burgundy and Italy, you'll
find rare and not-overpriced treats including
German reds, Slovenian wines, magnums etc.
House is £19. If you're lucky you'll get a hot
'keep-it-to-yourself' tip.
Chef/s: Lee Bennett. **Open:** all week L 12 to 3 (4
Sun), D 6 to 11 (10 Sun). **Meals:** alc (main courses
£16.50 to £35). Set L and D £20 (2 courses) to £25,
Set Sun L £21.50 (2 courses) to £26. **Service:** 12.5%.
Details: Cards accepted. 92 seats. 71 seats outside.
Separate bar. Wheelchair access. Music. Children's
portions.

Tentazioni

New-wave Italian near Tower Bridge
Lloyds Wharf, 2 Mill Street, SE1 2BD
Tel no: (020) 7237 1100
www.tentazioni.co.uk
⊖ London Bridge
Italian | £38
Cooking score: 3
£5 OFF **V**

A vibrant red colour scheme makes a bold,
confident impression at this new-wave Italian
eatery on one of the redeveloped wharves not
far from Tower Bridge. There is an
encouraging freshness and vivacity to both the
service approach and Riccardo Giacomini's
cooking. A five-course tasting menu, with the
option of pre-selected Italian wines, indicates
the level of ambition, and vegetarians have
their own menu to choose from – something
of a novelty in the Italian context. From the
main menu, home-made pasta stands out,
perhaps pappardelle with rabbit and black
olives or green ravioli filled with ham, peas
and lettuce, garnished with Parma ham and
zucchini. Mains embrace the high-flier's
option of a grilled half-lobster and beef fillet
with béarnaise on the same plate, or the likes
of spiced pheasant breast sauced with orange
and served with asparagus risotto and quails'
eggs. Finish with a selection of creamy gelati
and tangy sorbetti, or a cooked cheese dish
such as fried provolone with rocket and
balsamic. The mostly Italian wine list has a few

Grand old greats

Sometimes only the best will do. Special occasions are all the more memorable for being held in glittering surroundings with great food that will live long in the memory.

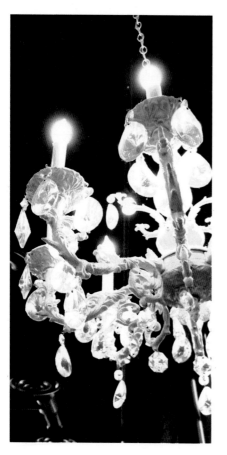

Connaught Hotel, London
The Good Food Guide's longest-serving establishment has made a graceful entry into the gastronomic modern age, but the tone of dignified Edwardian stolidity endures.

Inverlochy Castle, Fort William
Baronial splendour just outside the historic lochside town. Vast public rooms and a dining-room that overlooks a trout lake where you might catch your own dinner.

Sharrow Bay, Ullswater
Long before Lakeland became a culinary beacon, Sharrow Bay set the pace. High-rolling, supremely accomplished Anglo-French haute cuisine in relaxed civility.

Bodysgallen Hall, Llandudno
A seventeenth-century manor house in 200 acres of sumptuous parkland, Bodysgallen is a world of old-fashioned courtesy and comfort, and gently inventive cooking.

Waterside Inn, Bray
Veteran Michel Roux has passed on the reins to son Alain, but the air of Gallic ultra-refinement is sustained, and the riverside setting is a summer idyll worth travelling for.

Dower House, Royal Crescent, Bath
Set amid the grand sweep of one of England's grandest crescent buildings, the Dower House offers an assured mix of Georgian splendour and contemporary grande luxe.

Number One, Balmoral, Edinburgh
Arrive in the Scottish capital by train, and you'll have a two-minute walk to the Balmoral. This magnificent old railway hotel is unashamedly classical French in approach.

foreign interlopers (including a Slovenian Sauvignon Blanc at £62!), and opens with Abruzzo varietals at £15, or £5 a glass.
Chef/s: Riccardo Giacomini. **Open:** Tue to Fri 12 to 2.45, Mon to Sat D 6.30 to 10.45. **Closed:** Sun, Christmas. **Meals:** alc (main courses £15 to £22.50). Set L £14.95 to £40. Set D £40. **Service:** 12.5%. **Details:** 50 seats. Music. Children's portions.

ALSO RECOMMENDED
▲ Arancia
52 Southwark Park Road, Bermondsey, SE16 3RS
Tel no: (020) 7394 1751
www.arancia-uk.co.uk
⊖ Bermondsey/Elephant & Castle
Italian

With bright décor, a lively atmosphere and a short Italian menu offering big, bold flavours, it's no wonder locals love this place. Expect gutsy regional dishes in the shape of fresh sardines grilled with chilli and served with grilled aubergine and sun-dried tomato salad (£6), or Gloucester Old Spot pork stew finished with gremolada and served on soft polenta. The short, all-Italian wine list opens at £12.95. Closed Sun and Mon.

▌Blackheath
Chapter Two
Rock-solid reliability and brilliant value
43-45 Montpelier Vale, SE3 0TJ
Tel no: (020) 8333 2666
www.chaptersrestaurants.co.uk
Modern European | £25
Cooking score: 4

£30

Sitting comfortably in suburban Blackheath, Chapter Two gets on with serving 'reliably excellent food' at prices that would seem almost unbelievable in the central London. Like its elder brother Chapter One (see entry, Locksbottom, Kent), it wins friends with a combination of finely tuned unpretentious cooking and relaxed cosmopolitan surroundings – in this case two floors linked by a spiral staircase with pale

wood, steel and contemporary canvases in plentiful supply. Identical set menus do duty for lunch and dinner (although prices are higher in the evening), and a seasonal undercurrent runs through proceedings. Starters of braised pig's cheek with confit onion and potato purée or grilled red mullet with pickled vegetables and chive crème fraîche could give way to roast loin of venison with braised leeks and port jus or sea trout with a trout tortellino, celeriac and ginger velouté. To finish, try hot chocolate fondant with blood orange granita and cardamom ice cream, or lemon posset with apple and vanilla compote. The 'brilliantly chosen and fantastically reasonable' wine list also wins praise: prices start at £13.95 (£4.15 a glass).
Chef/s: Trevor Tobin. **Open:** all week L 12 to 2.30 (3 Sun), D 6.30 to 10.30 (9 Sun). **Closed:** first few days Jan. **Meals:** Set L £15.95 (2 courses) to £19.95, Set D £18.45 (£2 courses) to £23.95. **Service:** 12.5% (optional). **Details:** Cards accepted. 75 seats. Air-con. Wheelchair access. Music. Children's portions.

▌Clapham
Trinity Restaurant
A proper restaurant, perfect for entertaining
4 The Polygon, Clapham Old Town, SW4 0JG
Tel no: (020) 7622 1199
www.trinityrestaurant.co.uk
⊖ Clapham Common
Modern European | £40
Cooking score: 3

Trinity is the triumphant re-establishment in Clapham of chef/proprietor Adam Byatt of the much-lamented Thyme, and locals have welcomed him back like the prodigal son. He is certainly a talented cook, but his style may not be to everyone's taste – he combines great earthy flavours and textures to create rather complicated, slightly surprising dishes: 'oyster – cucumber – scallop' turns out to be (very good) ravioli with a champagne velouté; 'foie gras – peach – duck' find themselves uncomfortably juxtaposed in a terrine, the accompanying peach and vanilla chutney adding further sweetness. Elsewhere, the 'very good value' lunch has delivered well-reported duck hearts and duck egg followed by slow-cooked beef. There's a decent wine list that copes with special occasions as well as more humble day-to-day dining, with ten wines by-the-glass/carafe starting at under £4.

Chef/s: Adam Byatt. **Open:** Tue to Sat L 12.30 to 2.30, Sun L 12 to 3, Mon to Sat D 6.30 to 10.30. **Closed:** Christmas. **Meals:** alc (main courses £17 to £21). Set L £15 (2 courses) to £20. **Service:** 12.5%. **Details:** Cards accepted. 60 seats. Air-con. Wheelchair access. Children allowed.

Tsunami

Good Westernised Japanese food
5-7 Voltaire Road, SW4 6DQ
Tel no: (020) 7978 1610
www.tsunamirestaurant.co.uk
⊖ Clapham North
Japanese | £34
Cooking score: 2

The décor – mock python banquettes, black rubber floor, a chandelier of the rising sun – which may have been avant-garde five years ago now begins to look a little tired, but trendy 30-something locals flock to this unfortunately named Clapham restaurant, knowing they're on to a good thing. Here is Japanese food westernised in the style of Nobu, but without the ritual and at a fraction of the cost. Raw fish enthusiasts will be pleased by the sushi and sashimi, others are happy to see seared tuna and salmon sashimi, feather-light tempura and a black cod to challenge Nobu's. Customers wishing to go off the beaten track will find some gems: agedashi tofu (tofu tempura served in dashi with daikon & bonito flakes) or hira unagi (grilled marinated eel with rice & pickle), but there are precious few steps into the unfamiliar. Though there are a selection of sakes on the slightly dull wine list, nearly everyone sticks to wine which, starting at £3.95 per glass, is also pretty good value.

Chef/s: Ken Sam. **Open:** Mon to Fri D 6 to 11, Sat 12.30 to 11, Sun 1 to 9. **Closed:** 3 days Christmas, 31 Dec, 1 Jan. **Service:** optional. **Details:** 60 seats. Air-con. Separate bar. Wheelchair access. Children allowed.

▌East Dulwich

Franklins

No-nonsense British food
157 Lordship Lane, SE22 8HX
Tel no: (020) 8299 9598
www.franklinsrestaurant.com
Modern British | £25
Cooking score: 2

 £5 OFF £30

A happy-go-lucky amalgam of boisterous neighbourhood bar and bustling brasserie, Franklins goes about its business with friendliness and confidence. Make your way past the throngs of drinkers to reach the ever-so-casual dining room with its functional furnishings, paper-clothed tables and exposed brickwork hung with mirrors. The kitchen works to a menu of tersely described, seasonal dishes with a strong retro-British slant: gull's egg, pork belly and piccalilli, lamb stew with mash, and rhubarb tart typify the no-nonsense approach. A few European interlopers show up from time to time (say, chicken hearts with frisée and olives, artichokes gribiche and caramel pannacotta), but savouries such as black pudding on toast bring it all back home. Saturday brunch pleases the locals and the succinct wine list shows a liking for France. Prices start at £13.50 (£3.50 a glass). A second branch is now open at 205-209 Kennington Lane, SE11 5QS, tel: (020) 7793 8313.

Chef/s: Ralf Wittig and Asher Wyborn. **Open:** all week 11 to 11 (11 to 12 Thur and Fri, 10 to 12 Sat, 12 to 11 Sun). **Closed:** 25 and 26 Dec, 1 Jan. **Meals:** alc (main courses £11.50 to £19). Set L Mon to Fri £12 (2 courses) to £15. **Service:** not inc. **Details:** Cards accepted. 42 seats. 16 seats outside. Air-con. Separate bar. No mobile phones. Wheelchair access. Music. Children's portions.

ALSO RECOMMENDED

▲ Le Chardon

65 Lordship Lane, East Dulwich, SE22 8EP
Tel no: (020) 8299 1921
www.lechardon.co.uk
French

Unmistakeably a French bistro, Le Chardon has just notched up ten years in this striking listed Victorian building. Almost as long-running, the menu offers plenty of choice, opening for hearty breakfasts and going on to the likes of fish soup (£4.75), properly tricked out with rouille, croûtons and grated Swiss cheese, or a dozen escargots in garlic butter (£8.50). Mains range from entrecôte with soft green peppercorn sauce (£11.45) to whole roast sea bass with garlic confit and mixed herbs provençale (£12.75). A global wine list opens at £11.95. Open daily. A second branch has opened at 32 Abbeville Road, Clapham, tel (020) 8673 9300.

▌Elephant and Castle

ALSO RECOMMENDED

▲ Lobster Pot

3 Kennington Lane, Elephant and Castle, SE11 4RG
Tel no: (020) 7582 5556
www.lobsterpotrestaurant.co.uk
⊖ **Kennington**
Seafood

Hervé Régent waits to welcome seafood-lovers with an array of nautical *objets* and a backdrop of seagulls crying over gently susurrating waves. Thus acclimatised, you can proceed to the main business, which centres on fresh lobsters cooked to order, but you might also ponder the likes of grouper fillet in Cajun spices (£18.50) as the menu gestures towards distant shores. Otherwise, the accent is firmly French. Prawns and scallops in a sauce of wild mushrooms and garlic £11.50) is one way to start. Meat-eaters might opt for duck-leg stew with flageolet beans (£18.50). A short French wine list opens at £14.50, or £3.50 a glass. Closed Sun and Mon.

▌Greenwich

Inside

Good-natured Greenwich bistro
19 Greenwich South Street, SE10 8NW
Tel no: (020) 8265 5060
www.insiderestaurant.co.uk
Modern European | £28
Cooking score: 1

A godsend for Greenwich, this good-natured restaurant does the neighbourhood proud with its jolly atmosphere, attractively priced menus and enjoyable bistro-style food. The open-plan kitchen sends out well-wrought dishes along the lines of seared fillet of Irish beef with red cabbage, horseradish mash, beetroot and thyme jus or halibut with steamed leeks, broad beans and chive velouté. To start, there might be pressed foie gras terrine with shallot chutney and toasted brioche or Cornish mussels with lemongrass, chilli and coconut milk. Desserts have included dark chocolate, hazelnut and white chocolate chip brownie or treacle tart with lemon and ginger ice cream. The compact wine list keeps its prices in check, with vins de pays at £12.95 (£3.50 a glass). **Chef/s:** Gut Awford and Brian Sargeant. **Open:** Tue to Sun L 12 to 2.30 (3 Sat and Sun), Tue to Sat D 6.30 to 11. **Closed:** Mon, Christmas. **Meals:** alc (main courses £13 to £18). Set L £11.95 (2 courses) to £15.95 (£17.95 to £21.95 Sat and Sun). Set D £16.95 (2 courses) to £20.95. **Service:** not inc. **Details:** Cards accepted. 38 seats. Air-con. Wheelchair access. Music. Children's portions.

Putney

Emile's

An enduring favourite
96-98 Felsham Road, SW15 1DQ
Tel no: (020) 8789 3323
www.emilesrestaurant.co.uk
⊖ Putney Bridge
Modern British | £34
Cooking score: 1

On the food front, the menu at this well-established neighbourhood restaurant near Putney High Street follows a broadly European path, although there are occasional influences from further afield in, say, grilled fillet of red mullet in miso with cashew nuts and Japanese-style salad with sesame and soy dressing. Otherwise, expect starters such as pressed pork knuckle terrine, or modern-sounding sauté of chicken livers with red wine and shallot jus on toasted brioche, topped with a soft-poached egg. To follow, you might go for the ever-popular baked fillet of beef Wellington or perhaps fillet of pork stuffed with golden raisins and couscous and served with a Moroccan-style vegetable tagine. Finish with classic treacle tart or vanilla pannacotta. Our questionnaire was not returned, so the information following may have changed.
Chef/s: Andrew Sherlock and Matthew Johnson. **Open:** Mon to Sat D only 7.30 to 11. **Closed:** 24 to 30 Dec, 2 Jan, Easter Sat, banks hols. **Meals:** Set D £12.50 (2 courses) to £23.50. **Service:** not inc. **Details:** Cards accepted. 100 seats. Wheelchair access. Music. Children allowed.

Enoteca Turi

Long-standing Putney crowd-pleaser
28 Putney High Street, SW15 1SQ
Tel no: (020) 8785 4449
www.enotecaturi.com
⊖ Putney Bridge
Italian | £35
Cooking score: 3

Putney High Street is such a mishmash of signs and neons that it's easy to miss this comparatively discreet corner restaurant. Inside it's a standard of modern elegance, with polished wood underfoot, a rich deep red on the walls and acres of white linen on the tables. Giuseppe Turi is passionate about food and wine. Each dish on the menu has a by-the-glass recommendation from the 300-strong entirely Italian wine list, which opens at £14. If you choose to go off-piste, the list itself makes fascinating reading – each bin is carefully annotated with helpful information, encouraging customers to explore and experiment. But that's not to knock the food into second place. The shortish menu offers an agreeable selection of Italian country cooking – vegetable antipasti with a superb fava bean purée is a perennial favourite, as is pasta with crab and chilli. Mains might include a perfectly cooked veal chop, roast rabbit Sicilian-style or pan-fried halibut. It's all well prepared and presented and it pleases the Putney crowd, who continue to make a bee-line for it above all other Italians, modern or classical, in the area.
Chef/s: Giuseppe Turi. **Open:** Mon to Sat L 12 to 2.30, D 7 to 11. **Closed:** 25 and 26 Dec, 1 Jan, L bank hols. **Meals:** alc (main courses £18.50 to £21.50). Set L £14.50 (2 courses) to £17.50. **Service:** 12.5 %. **Details:** Cards accepted. 80 seats. Air-con. Wheelchair access. Music. Children's portions.

Phoenix

Friendly neighbourhood restaurant
162-164 Lower Richmond Road, SW15 1LY
Tel no: (020) 8780 3131
www.sonnys.co.uk/phoenix.htm
⊖ Putney Bridge
Modern European | £27
Cooking score: 4

The Phoenix is set well back from Lower
Richmond Road with its entrance in a side
road. Once found, it proves to be a
comfortable and friendly neighbourhood
restaurant with generous tables, high ceilings
and on-the-ball waiting staff. The Anglo-
Italian menu opens with veal tongue teamed
with borlotti beans and salsa verde, or octopus
salad served alongside dill, paprika, red onion
and caperberries. A couple of pasta dishes, say
vincisgrassi maceratesi – a kind of lasagne –
come as starters or main courses, with main
courses proper running to the likes of
swordfish with peperonata, rocket salad and
tapenade or rump of lamb with marinated
aubergines and spring onions. Portions are
generous. Puddings are plentiful, among them
yoghurt cheesecake with rhubarb, maybe, or
chocolate espresso cake with latte cream. A
wide-ranging modern wine list favours Italy
and keeps prices within reason, opening
at £12.50.
Chef/s: Maciej Glowniak. **Open:** all week L 12 to
2.30 (Sun L 12.30 to 3), D 7 to 11 (11.30 Fri and Sat,
10 Sun). **Closed:** bank hols. **Meals:** Set L £13.50 (2
courses) to £15.50, set D £15.50 (2 courses) to

£17.50. **Service:** 12.5%. **Details:** Cards accepted. 80
seats. 40 seats outside. Air-con. Separate bar.
Wheelchair access. Music. Children's portions.

ALSO RECOMMENDED
▲ L'Auberge
22 Upper Richmond Road, Putney, SW15 2RX
Tel no: (020) 8874 3593
www.ardillys.com
⊖ East Putney
French

A white-fronted neighbourhood restaurant in
the old style, Pascal Ardilly's L'Auberge serves
unreconstructed French bistro fare to a
grateful Putney crowd. Grilled honeyed goats'
cheese salad with toasted almonds and
raspberry dressing (£5.75) is a typical hors
d'oeuvre. Mains offer guinea-fowl sauced with
pastis, or fillet of sea bass with tomato confit
and pesto (£15.50). Spoil yourself with
chocolate and praline mousse with salted
butter caramel sauce to finish (£6.95).
Midweek fixed-price menus are good value at
£17 for three courses. The short French wine
list starts at £13.50. Open Tue to Sat D only.

▍ South Bank
Anchor & Hope
No-frills food served with trademark gusto
36 The Cut, SE1 8LP
Tel no: (020) 7928 9898
⊖ Waterloo, Southwark
Modern British | £25
Cooking score: 4

The Anchor and Hope remains a highly
accessible eating and drinking place with a
big, buzzy bar, a laid back attitude (no
bookings), and a daily menu that makes a
virtue of flexibility. The cooking is simple,
precise, and – like the pub itself – unfussy; it
certainly draws a loyal following. The kitchen
is a busy one, delivering tasty potted shrimps
or smoked herrings and lentils, while main
courses range from braised veal breast with
flageolet beans and cream via roast rabbit with

mustard, spring onions, butter beans and aïoli, to pumpkin and ricotta rotollo with salsify and Parmesan. Puddings bring on coffee and walnut cake with vanilla ice cream and pistachio meringue with whipped cream and rhubarb. The global wine list crowds one side of an A4 page and opens with French vin de pays at £12.

Chef/s: Jonathan Jones. **Open:** Tue to Sun L 12 to 2.30 (2 Sun), Mon to Sat D 6 to 10.30. **Closed:** bank hols, Christmas. **Meals:** alc (main courses £11 to £27). Set Sun L £30. **Service:** not inc. **Details:** Cards accepted. 50 seats. 12 seats outside. Air-con. Separate bar. Wheelchair access. Music. Children allowed.

Oxo Tower

Iconic riverside restaurant
Oxo Tower Wharf, Barge House Street, SE1 9PH
Tel no: (020) 7803 3888
http://www.harveynichols.com
⊖ Blackfriars, Waterloo
Modern British | £50
Cooking score: 2

🍸 V

Perched on the eighth floor of the Oxo Tower, this Harvey Nichols-owned restaurant occupies some of the finest restaurant real estate in London. Its broad terrace overlooking the Thames is one of the most agreeable places to lunch on a fine summer's day; the spacious dining room with floor-to-ceiling glass windows means an evening meal is accompanied by a dramatic view of the twinkling city below (providing you have a well-positioned table). It's a shame then, that on inspection, food didn't quite achieve the same wow-factor as its high-altitude location, although the prices could certainly give you vertigo. The modern European menu takes in several cuisines – spiced crab spring rolls, mango chutney and daikon salad, or sea trout ballottine with Armenian bread. Sunday lunch mains included a rather fussily dressed – but flavoursome – roast halibut steak with red wine and Jerusalem artichokes, and a roast beef and Yorkshire pudding that arrived wearing a strange wig of salad. However,

some readers have pointed out the cheaper Oxo Tower Brasserie (also situated on the eighth floor, next to the main restaurant) is 'bustling and vibrant' with 'equally stunning views over London.' Wines at the main restaurant start at £25.

Chef/s: Jeremy Bloor. **Open:** all week L 12 – 2.30 (4 Sun), D 6 to 11 (6.30 to 10 Sun). **Meals:** alc (main courses £20 to £26). **Service:** 12.5% optional. **Details:** Cards accepted. 150 seats. 80 seats outside. Air-con. Separate bar. No mobile phones. Music. Children allowed.

Skylon

Capturing the spirit of the Festival of Britain
Belvedere Road, SE1 8XX
Tel no: (020) 7654 7800
www.danddlondon.com/restaurants/skylon
⊖ Waterloo
Modern British | £39
Cooking score: 2

The reworking of the interior of this restaurant on Level 3 of the Royal Festival Hall is 'a brilliant job', the vast space houses a bar, grill and dining room with floor-to-ceiling windows providing a panoramic river and cityscape. In the kitchen, Helen Puolakka keeps an eye on London fashion, the broad British brush strokes augmented by contemporary combinations like carpaccio of scallops with liquorice vinaigrette and dried cranberries. Bold combinations are favoured at main course – caramelised pork belly and butter poached lobster, say, or braised ox cheek served with truffled pommes purée – but when tried at an inspection lunch, both dishes were found to require more attention to detail. Indeed, disappointments have been reported elsewhere, and prices are high for one and all. The smartly assembled wine list spans various styles and budgets, and starts at £15. A section devoted to rare wines from the 1950s is, unsurprisingly, at prices as elevated as this restaurant.

Chef/s: Helena Puolakka. **Open:** all week L 12 to 2.30, D 5.30 to 10.45. **Meals:** Set L £19.50 (2 courses) to £24.50. Set L & D £29.50 (2 courses) to

£34.50. Pre & post theatre £24.50 (2 courses) to £29.50. **Service:** 12.5%. **Details:** Cards accepted. 92 seats. Air-con. Separate bar. Wheelchair access.

ALSO RECOMMENDED
▲ Mezzanine
National Theatre, South Bank, SE1 9PX
Tel no: (020) 7452 3600
British

The restaurant of the National Theatre is near the Olivier auditorium and boasts great views of the river. A two-course pre-theatre menu is on offer at £19.95. Those with more time to relax might go for cocotte of wild mushrooms with Westcombe Cheddar, spinach and mustard (£6.75), followed by perhaps guinea fowl with buttered cabbage and parsnip crisps (£13.95) or cod with peas, baby Gem lettuce and pancetta (£12.95). Dishes for two to share are a new feature, and desserts include blood orange trifle (£3.95). Wines start at £13.25. Open Mon to Sat D, with L on Saturdays and matinée days.

▌Southwark
Baltic
East European chic
74 Blackfriars Road, SE1 8HA
Tel no: (020) 7928 1111
www.balticrestaurant.co.uk
⊖ Southwark
Eastern European | £27
Cooking score: 3

A sleek, minimalist venue that pays homage to the earthy world of East European cuisine and the head-rocking pleasures of vodka, Baltic occupies an eighteenth-century coachbuilder's workshop not far from the Tate Modern. The place shows off its cool chic with a long bar and a white-walled dining room compete with trussed ceilings, galleries and skylights. The restaurant's name gives a clue to the food's geographical pivot: ideas from the Baltic and Adriatic keep company with Scandinavian emigrés, and the kitchen

majors in cockle-warming, cold-weather nourishment. There are tongue-twisters aplenty on the menu, but English descriptions solve any linguistic embarrassment. You might begin with a bowl of krupnik (pearl barley and sour rye soup) or kaszanka (Polish black sausage with red cabbage and pear purée) before rabbit braised in cider, roast goose leg or something with a faraway flavour such as rump of lamb with smoked aubergine salad. Pierogi and blinis every which way please the old guard, while desserts might include Hungarian chocolate and hazelnut torta. Around 30 vodkas keep the youngbloods fuelled up, and the wine list has oodles of quaffable stuff from £14.50.
Chef/s: Piotr Repinski. **Open:** all week L 12 to 3, D 6 to 11.15. **Closed:** Christmas. **Meals:** alc (main courses £9.50 to £18.50). Set L and pre-theatre D £14.50 (2 courses) to £17.50. **Service:** 12.5% (optional). **Details:** Cards accepted. 100 seats. Air-con. Separate bar. Wheelchair access. Music. Children's portions.

Champor-Champor
Off-the-wall Asian razzamatazz
62-64 Weston Street, SE1 3QJ
Tel no: (020) 7403 4600
www.champor-champor.com
⊖ London Bridge
Malaysian /Pan Asian | £30
Cooking score: 3

Riotous décor sets the tone in this quirkily off-the-wall restaurant, whose name translates roughly as 'mix and match'. Inside, it looks more like a parody of the Pitt Rivers Museum than a restaurant, with its bizarre ethnic curios, tribal masks and carvings. The kitchen mixes and matches with equal abandon, fusing traditional Malay village cuisine with influences from Thailand, China and elsewhere. Dinner is built around a concise menu that might open with steamed boneless chicken with sweet mango and chilli salsa or baby squid in South Indian rasam soup with melinjau crackers. Next comes a Western-style 'inter-course' (perhaps pear purée with orange blossom ice) before

Balinese baked sea bream in a banana leaf with fennel som tam or satay lamb fillet with perchik sauce, sweet potato and Szechuan pepper mash. Desserts are shot through with wacky ideas like steamed green tea cake and smoked banana ice cream. Cocktails and 'mocktails', Asia-Pacific beers and saké are alternatives to the compact global wine list; prices start at £14.50 (£4.95 a glass). **Chef/s:** Adu Amran. **Open:** Thur and Fri L 12 to 2, Mon to Sat D 6 to 10.15. **Closed:** Sun, Easter and Christmas. **Meals:** Set D £24.50 (2 courses) to £42.50. **Service:** 15% (optional). **Details:** Cards accepted. 46 seats. Air-con. Wheelchair access. Music. Children allowed.

Delfina

Where art and food come together
50 Bermondsey Street, SE1 3UD
Tel no: (020) 73570244
www.delfina.org.uk
⊖ London Bridge
Global | £32
Cooking score: 4

£5
OFF

This former chocolate factory has been converted into an expansive white space where art and food come together. A large gallery displays contemporary exhibits and provides an unparalleled background for a daylight-filled, buzzing lunch venue. The kitchen works in tandem with small producers from around the country – salads from Secretts Farm in Surrey, pork from Suffolk, veal from Kent – as well as sourcing sustainable fish, but inspiration comes from near and far. Fusion is to the fore in starters such as salmon ballottine with green papaya, mooli salad and nam jim dressing, or chorizo and butternut squash ravioli with broccoli purée and sumac-dusted bok choi. However straightforward mains such as pan-fried coley with mustard mash, saffron, olive oil and tomato have their place as much as chargrilled marinated leg of lamb served with rosemary-salted kumara (a form of yam) potato chips and baba ganoush. Peach

tarte Tatin with lavender ice cream is a typical dessert. A good, global wine list offers French red and white at £16.50.
Chef/s: Richard Simpson. **Open:** Mon to Fri L 12 to 3, Fri D 7 to 10. **Meals:** alc (main courses £12.95 to £15.25). **Service:** 12.5%. **Details:** Cards accepted. 90 seats. Wheelchair access. Music. Children allowed.

Magdalen

English classics with vim and vigour
152 Tooley Street, SE1 2TU
Tel no: (020) 7403 1342
www.magdalenrestaurant.co.uk
⊖ London Bridge
Modern British | £33
Cooking score: 3

In a smart double-decker restaurant of deep aubergine walls, chocolate-dark wood and crisp white linen, gently attentive staff serve simply described, simply presented dishes from a daily-changing British menu. Excellent ingredients include neglected cuts of meat (ox cheek, lamb's tongue), and the results are terrific. Starters on a warm spring evening included a poached egg on English asparagus with crisp wafers of bacon, and a duo of quail and snails (on toast). A main of roast hake, chorizo and grilled peppers was exceptionally well judged; on offer to share were roast Hereford wing rib or, as a one-off to tie in with London's Greek food week, slow-cooked suckling kid with tomatoes, fennel and olives. The latter's liver was served as a special and cooked to silky perfection. Magdalen does have the odd shortcoming: some find the ambience a little subdued, and portions aren't huge (though not necessarily a bad thing given the high-calorific desserts of chocolate and hazelnut truffle cake or custard tart with prunes and Armagnac). The mainly European wine list opens at £16 with a clutch available by the glass or carafe.
Chef/s: James Faulks. **Open:** L 12 to 3.30, D 6.30 to 10.30. **Closed:** Sat L, Sun, all public hols. **Meals:** Set menu £15.50 (2courses) £18.50 (3 courses). **Service:** Not inc. **Details:** Cards accepted. 90 seats. Air-con. Separate bar. Wheelchair access. Music. Children allowed.

Roast

Best of British in an old London market
Floral Hall, Borough Market, Stoney Street,
SE1 1TL
Tel no: (020) 7940 1300
www.roast-restaurant.com
⊖ London Bridge
Modern British | £38
Cooking score: 4

You may be sitting amid the bustling London environs of Britain's oldest food market, but the supplies come from far and wide. Lamb from Snowdonia, fish from Dorset, garlic from the Isle of Wight and haggis from Orkney are among the temptations, and the menu notes gratefully that 'our foragers brave all sorts of conditions to collect wild leaves and vegetables for us'. Feel privileged, then, as you scan the appetising market menus, which take in Neal's Yard curd goat cheese with pickled beetroot and port, crab and avocado salad with pea shoots, and main courses such as grilled mackerel with rhubarb, chilli and mint. A vegetarian main course might be baked celeriac with wild mushrooms and a poached egg. The eponymous roasts are always a lure, not least the slow-cooked pork belly with Bramley apple sauce and mash. It might be surprising to find a tasting menu in such surroundings, but £75 buys you a right royal spread, from a glass of Chapel Down fizz through to custard tart, and then Tunworth soft cheese from Hampshire. The fine list gives English wines a fair shake of the stick, before introducing a parade of varietals, organics and biodynamics, as well as a handsome range by the glass from £4.50 for a Languedoc Viognier. Prices are on the heavy side, alas.
Chef/s: Lawrence Keogh. **Open:** Mon to Fri 7am to 11pm, Sat 8am to 11pm, Sun 12 to 4. **Meals:** alc (main courses £14.50 to £22). Set L or D £75. **Service:** 12.5%. **Details:** 110 seats. Air-con. Separate bar. No music. Wheelchair access. Children's portions.

RSJ

Well-supported South Bank restaurant
33 Coin Street, SE1 9NR
Tel no: (020) 7928 4554
www.rsj.uk.com
⊖ Waterloo, Southwark
Modern British | £30
Cooking score: 3

£5 OFF 🍷 **V**

The Wilkinsons set up shop on this corner site at the end of converted Victorian terrace 30 years ago, and have witnessed quite a few changes to the neighbourhood. RSJ's long-standing appeal is the list of wonderful Loire wines and a sensibly modern menu that for many years fused French and British styles, but is now incorporating Italian dishes – 'following a visit by the chef to Italy' according to one surprised regular. Now mozzarella and vine tomato gallette with pesto, rabbit ravioli, and wild mushroom tagliatelle appear alongside foie gras and organic chicken terrine, roast halibut with sauce vierge and grilled rib-eye steak with truffle dressing. The good-value fixed-price menu continues to be singled out for its consistent dishes, say a well-reported loin and confit of rabbit or roast gammon with pilaf rice, nectarine and cress salad. Enterprising desserts such as fresh fig, orange and raspberry salad with liquorice ice cream round things off in style. The unique and much-lauded wine list, which concentrates almost entirely on the Loire, demonstrates just how good these grapes can be when handled by great winemakers. House wines start at £15.75.
Chef/s: Ian Stabler and Alex Lovett. **Open:** Mon to Fri L 12 to 2, Mon to Sat D 5.30 to 11. **Closed:** Sun, Christmas. **Meals:** alc (main courses £10.95 to £18.95). Set menu £15.95 (2 courses) to £18.95. **Service:** 12.5%. **Details:** Cards accepted. 90 seats. 12 seats outside. Air-con. No music. Children's portions.

Tapas Brindisa

Bustling Spanish tapas bar – one of the best
18-20 Southwark Street, SE1 1TJ
Tel no: (020) 7357 8880
www.brindisa.com
⊖ Borough
Spanish | £20
Cooking score: 3

 £30

A concrete floor, mirrored walls scrawled with in-house promotions, and placemats that double as menus help crank up the volume and lend an informal air to proceedings at this bustling, cheery Spanish tapas bar. Tightly packed tables and all-day opening add to the authenticity, and there are plenty of interesting Spanish specialities, ranging from first-rate Iberian hams, regional charcuterie and perfect-condition cheeses to hot tapas (served at lunch and dinner) like classics of spinach with pine nuts and raisins, chorizo with piquillo pepper and patatas bravas, or larger plates of rare fillet steak, caramelised onion and torta de barros cheese, or lamb cutlets with aïoli and mint salad. Desserts include the ubiquitous crema catalana, but the turrón mousse with PX vinegar and macerated raisins is worth exploring. The patriotic, concise wine list includes a good selection of sherries. House wines from £15.75.
Chef/s: José Manuel Pizarro. **Open:** Mon to Sat 11 to 11 (from 9 Fri and Sat). **Closed:** Sun, Christmas and New year. **Meals:** alc (tapas from £3 to £20). **Service:** 12.5%. **Details:** Cards accepted. 45 seats. 9 seats outside. Air-con. Separate bar. Wheelchair access. Music. Children allowed.

ALSO RECOMMENDED

▲ fish!

Cathedral Street, Southwark, SE1 9AL
Tel no: (020) 7407 3803
www.fishdiner.co.uk
⊖ London Bridge
Modern Seafood

Hard by Southwark Cathedral and the foodie delights of Borough Market, this swanky glass and steel pavilion deals in fish, the whole fish and nothing but the fish. Pick your species (perhaps organic salmon, Icelandic cod, John Dory or skate), tick the menu box, decide whether you want it steamed or grilled and select a sauce (hollandaise, salsa verde etc). Expect to pay around £14 for most main items; add on a starter – say smoked haddock rarebit (£6.95) or devilled whitebait – and try bread-and-butter pudding (£5.25) for afters. Fish-friendly wines from £14.95 (£3.75 a glass). Open all week.

▲ Village East

171-173 Bermondsey Street, Southwark, SE1 3UW
Tel no: (020) 73576082
www.villageeast.co.uk
⊖ London Bridge
Modern European

Brasserie dining in a warehouse-sized conversion not far from London Bridge station is the name of the game here, with seasonal menus that deal in the common currency of big-city eating. A pairing of seared scallops with pork belly (£7.80) is a fashionable way to start. Mains run the gamut from whole sea bream with smoked paprika, fennel and preserved lemon (£14.80) to roast rack of lamb with a red onion and olive tart and glazed turnip (£17.80). Scottish beef is available in various cuts and with various sauces, sides are mostly £3, and to finish there's chocolate fondant with pistachio ice cream (£6). Wines from £14.50. Open all week.

READERS RECOMMEND

The Table

Modern European
83 Southwark Street, Southwark, SE1 0HX
Tel no: 020 7401 2760
www.thetablecafe.com
'Friendly canteen at an architects' practice'

Also recommended

An 'also recommended' entry is not a full entry, but is provisionally suggested as an alternative to main entries.

Tooting

Kastoori

Gujarati food with a personal stamp
188 Upper Tooting Road, SW17 7EJ
Tel no: (020) 8767 7027
www.kastoorirestaurant.com
⊖ Tooting Broadway
Gujarati Vegetarian | £21
Cooking score: 3

V

Sunny colours and statuettes of Hindu temple dancers add a touch of exoticism to Manoj and Dinesh Thanki's long-running vegetarian venue. Since opening in 1987, Kastoori has become one of the most distinctive Gujarati restaurants in the capital and the food has an instantly-recognisable thumbprint. The kitchen takes its cue from the owners' native Katia Wahd (a temperate region famed for its tomatoes), and fills its larder with a harvest festival of indigenous fruit and vegetables. Among the starters are pani puri, masala kachori ('the sweet and spicy one'), samosas and mogo (cassava) bhajias, while big dishes centre on curries (including an iconic tomato version). The Thankis spent many years in Uganda, and their menus also include some African ingredients and dishes: look for 'family specials' such as matoki (green banana curry) and kasodi (sweetcorn cooked in coconut milk with peanut sauce). Finish in traditional style with gulab jamun or khir (aromatic rice pudding 'like granny never made it'). House wine is £10.95 (£2.50 a glass).
Chef/s: Manoj Thanki. **Open:** Wed to Sun L 12 to 2.30, all week D 6 to 10.30. **Closed:** 25 and 26 Dec. **Meals:** alc (main courses £4.75 to £6.25). **Service:** not inc. **Details:** Cards accepted. 82 seats. Air-con. Wheelchair access. Music. Children's portions. Car parking.

Radha Krishna Bhavan

The spirit of Kerala in the heart of Tooting
86 Tooting High Street, SW17 0RN
Tel no: (020) 8682 0969
⊖ Tooting Broadway
South Indian | £20
Cooking score: 1

The Haridas family's colourfully bedecked restaurant evokes the beaches of Kerala in the heart of Tooting. While the menu has its share of dhansaks, masalas and other curry house staples, top billing goes to the sizeable contingent of South Indian snacks and starters, including several kinds of dhosa and vada (fried lentil-flour doughnuts with ginger, onions and green chillies). Dishes such as sweet mango and yam cooked with fresh coconut, yoghurt, cumin and green chillies liven up the choice of vegetables. However, the kitchen also focuses on Cochin specialities, say chicken poori – puffed bread sandwiches – or kappa meen masala (boiled and spiced tapioca served with fish curry). Drink lassi, juice or beer or workaday wines from £9.95.
Chef/s: Terab Ali. **Open:** all week L 12 to 3, D 6 to 11 (12 Fri and Sat). **Closed:** 25 and 26 Dec. **Meals:** alc (main courses £4.95 to £7.95). **Service:** 10%. **Details:** Cards accepted. 50 seats. Air-con. Wheelchair access. Music. Children's portions.

Wimbledon

★NEW ENTRY★
Côte

Elegant bistro in a village setting
8 High Street, Wimbledon Village, SW19 5DX
Tel no: (020) 8947 7100
www.cote-restaurants.co.uk
⊖ Wimbledon
French | £20
Cooking score: 2

Wimbledon has been crying out for a place like Côte – a restaurant with all the elegance, informality and buzz of a classic Parisian bistro. The menu veers towards Provençale cooking, with specialities including pissaladière, a traditional flatbread from Nice, served with caramelised onions and anchovies, while Bayonne ham with a celeriac rémoulade, steak (served blue as requested), crisp duck confit with 'absolutely exquisite' mash and an intense chocolate pot served in a tiny espresso cup, are typical choices. The cheese platter may have been similarly minute – three thumb-size pieces – but was served at the right temperature. Service is slightly erratic, but charming all the same. For a more casual dining experience, ask to sit in the booths towards the front of the restaurant, but for group/occasion dining, head for the more formal tables towards the rear. House wines start at £12.95. A new branch of Côte has recently opened in Soho (see entry).

Open: Mon to Fri 12 to 11, Sat 9.30 to 11, Sun 9.30 to 10.30. **Closed:** Christmas Day. **Meals:** Set menu £9.95 (two courses) to £11.95. **Service:** 12.5%. **Details:** Cards accepted. 90 seats. 8 seats outside.

Light House Restaurant
A Wimbledon beacon
75-77 Ridgway, SW19 4ST
Tel no: (020) 8944 6338
www.lighthousewimbledon.com
⊖ Wimbledon
Modern European | £28
Cooking score: 3

 £5 OFF £30

The name says it all in this bright and breezy contemporary-styled restaurant. Light floods in through big windows and the clattery wooden floors and walls hung with modern art add to the cheerful ambience, while reports highlight the neighbourhood feel of the place. The menu delivers an interesting selection of brasserie-style dishes, say slow-roasted belly pork with Bramley apple and prune terrine and caper berries to start, or seared chicken livers with celeriac rémoulade and crispy ham. Main courses range from a simple wild mushroom risotto with grated fresh truffle to roast lamb rump with herb-roasted root vegetables and sweet-and-sour button onions.

To finish, warm ginger cake with vanilla ice cream has proved successful, as have pear and buttermilk sorbets. Staff are 'very helpful'. House wine from £13.50.

Chef/s: Chris Casey. **Open:** all week L 12 to 2.30, D 6 to 10.30. **Closed:** Christmas and Easter Mon. **Meals:** Set L £14.50 (2 courses) to £17, Set Sun L £18 (2 courses) to £23, early evening set D (Mon to Thur) £14.50 (2 courses) to £18.50. **Service:** 12.5% (optional). **Details:** Cards accepted. 80 seats. 15 seats outside. Air-con. Wheelchair access. Music. Children's portions.

ALSO RECOMMENDED
▲ Earl Spencer
260-262 Merton Road, Wimbledon, SW18 5JL
Tel no: (020) 8870 9244
www.theearlspencer.co.uk
⊖ Southfields
Gastropub

Once an imposing Edwardian drinking hall, the Earl Spencer has moved with the times. Food now grabs much of the limelight, although the place still flaunts its pub virtues with real ales and open fireplaces. Order and pay at the bar from a daily menu of robust gastropub dishes. Start with octopus, chorizo and tomato stew (£6.50) or chicken liver pâté with spiced crabapples; move on to slow-roast neck end of pork with greens and mustard sauce (£11.50) or salmon and dill fishcake with purple sprouting broccoli, and finish with apple crumble or buttermilk pudding (£5). House wine is £11 (£2.80 a glass). Open all week.

▮Chelsea

Admiral Codrington

Fish-friendly Chelsea watering hole
17 Mossop Street, SW3 2LY
Tel no: (020) 7581 0005
www.theadmiralcodrington.com
⊖ South Kensington
Gastropub | £30
New Chef

Known locally as 'The Cod', this Victorian pub in a residential backwater may look like just another Chelsea drinkers' den, but it has a few tricks up its sleeve. Out front is a rollicking, Sloaned-up bar with real ales on tap and a short menu of upmarket pub grub running from eggs Benedict to smoked haddock fishcakes. Elbow your way through the scrum and you will eventually reach the long dining room with its sliding glass roof and piscatorial prints. Seafood fans are well-served with the likes of fish pie or pan-roasted sea bream with braised chicory, baby fennel and citrus fruits, while others should find comfort in Caesar salad with a soft-poached egg, veal Holstein or slow-roast rump of spring lamb with 'seasonal pods' and marjoram jus. Puddings such as rhubarb crème brûlée provide a satisfying finish, and the workmanlike wine list offers sound drinking from £13.50 (£3.60 a glass).
Chef/s: Simon Levy. **Open:** all week L 12 to 2.30 (4.30 Sun), D 6.30 to 10.30 (9.30 Sun). **Closed:** 24 to 27 Dec. **Meals:** alc (main courses £8 to £18). Bar menu available. **Service:** 12.5% (optional).
Details: Cards accepted. 50 seats. 20 seats outside. Separate bar. Music. Children allowed.

Aubergine

Polished and understated French cooking
11 Park Walk, SW10 0AJ
Tel no: (020) 7352 3449
www.auberginerestaurant.co.uk
⊖ South Kensington
Modern French | £68
Cooking score: 5

 V

In an area better known for its casual all-day food, Aubergine can seem a little out of place. The dining room, with its muted shades and calm atmosphere, is very grown up. William Drabble has been at the helm for a decade and concentrates on technique and understated flavours rather than fashionable trends. There is a good-value lunch, but the carte is priced high at £68, especially during these credit-crunch times. However there are luxurious ingredients bolstered by amuse-bouche, pre-desserts and the like. Successful starters have included a 'vibrant and sassy' carpaccio of wild salmon, marinated in treacle and brandy, and cleverly paired with a beetroot and apple fondue. Flavours are clear and concise. A warm salad of rabbit with peas and grain mustard vinaigrette, featuring the saddle, loin and kidneys sandwiched between potato galettes showed sound technique, although the impact was 'a tad old school'. Pastry work is commendable: an assiette of banana in the form of tarte Tatin, poached meringue, banoffi pie and parfait was well-reported. The wine list is expansive, with a strong line-up from France and minor contributions from the New World. There are verticals from leading Burgundy producer Domaine de la Romanée-Conti as well as Châteaux Latour and Margaux from the Médoc. Prices start high (£27); the budget-conscious will need to restrict themselves to the lesser-known French regions.
Chef/s: William Drabble. **Open:** Mon to Fri L 12 to 2.15, Mon to Sat D 7 to 11. **Closed:** Sun, bank hols. **Meals:** alc £68 (3 courses). Set L £29, Gourmand menu £77. **Service:** 12.5%. **Details:** Cards accepted. 50 seats. Air-con. No music.

Symbols

 Accommodation is available.

 Three courses for less than £30.

V More than five vegetarian dishes.

 £5-off voucher scheme.

 Notable wine list.

Awana

Suave Malaysian high-flyer
85 Sloane Avenue, SW3 3DX
Tel no: (020) 7584 8880
www.awana.co.uk
Malaysian | £35
Cooking score: 1
V

Swathes of teak and glass, plush leather seating, batik fabrics and upholstered wall panels make the point that Awana is no down-home Malaysian 'hawker' hangout. What it offers is a suave, Sloane-friendly take on native cuisine, with authentic flavours, top-drawer ingredients and some flashy dishes for those who want to indulge. Journey though honey-roast duck soup with mustard greens and sour plums, pomelo and green mango salad, curried lamb shank with pumpkin and sweet potato, and chargrilled butterfish wrapped in a banana leaf. Also, don't miss the ikan roti (Malaysian flatbread) and achar pickle. For something more casual, try the dedicated satay bar at the back, which has an all-day menu of Penang street food. 'Awana' translates as 'in the clouds' – a reminder, perhaps, of its far-from-earthbound prices as well as its lofty aspirations. There are some high-flying names on the wine list, with bottles jetting skywards from £19.
Chef/s: Lee Chin Soon. **Open:** all week 12 to 3, 6 to 11 (11.30 Thur to Sat). **Closed:** 25 and 26 Dec, 1 Jan. **Meals:** alc (main courses 9.50 to £21). Set D £36. Bar menu available. **Service:** 12.5%. **Details:** Cards accepted. 80 seats. Air-con. Separate bar. Music. Children's portions.

Please send us your feedback

To register your opinion about any restaurant listed in the Guide, or a new restaurant that you wish to bring to our attention, please visit the web address at the bottom of the page. Your feedback informs the content of the book and will be used to compile next year's reviews.

Le Colombier

French through and through
145 Dovehouse Street, SW3 6LB
Tel no: (020) 7351 1155
www.lecolombier.co.uk
⊖ South Kensington
French | £33
Cooking score: 2

Didier Garnier's restaurant is French through and through, from the blue awning over the front terrace (closely packed with tables and chairs) to the crisp, white-clothed tables and buzzing atmosphere inside. Escargots encased in garlic cream and puff pastry, and goose rillettes are the kind of French comfort food everyone likes to eat, while main courses can be as simple as lamb cutlets with sauce paloise or fillet of pork with sauce diable, but there's also duck confit and a good Scottish rib of beef for two with béarnaise sauce. Crêpes suzette and tarte au citron are typical puddings. The wine list is French, too, with a good range of half-bottles and some reasonably priced Bordeaux and Burgundies. House wine is £14.90.
Chef/s: Philippe Tamet. **Open:** all week L 12 to 3, D 6.30 to 10.30. **Meals:** alc (main courses £15 to £21). Set weekday menu £17.50, Set Sun menu £19. **Service:** 12.5%. **Details:** 35 seats. 25 seats outside. No music. No mobile phones. Wheelchair access.

The Ebury

Stylish sophistication
11 Pimlico Road, SW1W 8NA
Tel no: (020) 7730 6784
www.theebury.co.uk
⊖ Sloane Square
Modern European | £25
New Chef
£30

The ground floor of this handsome corner building houses a stylish seafood bar, brasserie and lounge. The air of moneyed cool extends upstairs, where the large dining room pits flirtatious red chandeliers against understated furniture, bare floors and white walls. The menu here is a modern, metropolitan take on

classic French and European themes, so expect starters such as foie gras parfait with sweet pickles and brioche, ricotta and herb gnocchi with wild mushrooms, asparagus and Parmesan cappuccino or salad of soused octopus. Main courses continue in the same vein, offering niçoise salad with cured tuna and Parmesan dressing, slow-cooked pork belly with pea and Parmesan polenta, caramelised apple, smoked bacon and sage, or sea bass with saffron crushed potatoes and bouillabaisse sauce. Side-orders run from rocket and Parmesan salad or sautéed broccoli with brown butter and almonds to hand-cut chips. Finish with hot chocolate fondant with kumquat ice cream or a sautéed cherry pancake with basil honey. The first floor is also the place to hear the Ebury's resident jazz trio, who play every Thursday, Friday and Saturday. The simply presented wine list has plenty from France, and offers fair coverage of the rest of the world. Bottles are priced from £14.50.
Chef/s: Daniel Hillier. **Open:** all week 12 to 11.30. **Closed:** 25 Dec. **Meals:** alc (main courses £14.50 to £16.50). Set L £19.50 (3 courses), D £29.95 (3 courses). **Service:** 12.5%. **Details:** Cards accepted. 60 seats. Air-con. Separate bar. Wheelchair access. Music. Children's portions.

Eight Over Eight
Glitz, glamour and grazing
392 King's Road, SW3 5UZ
Tel no: (020) 7349 9934
www.rickerrestaurants.com
⊖ Sloane Square
Fusion/Pan-Asian | £27
Cooking score: 2

V

Named after the Chinese lucky number eight, this quasi-oriental outpost of Will Ricker's fusion empire is housed in a converted theatre pub right on the King's Road main drag. Chelsea's glitterati come here in their droves for serious gossip and star-watching, with the prospect of some pretty food on the side. The menu plunders the Far East in esoteric detail, then conveniently carves everything up into sushi, salads, curries and the like. Pick and

graze at will from an assortment of little dishes that might include black cod sui mai dumplings, agedashi tofu tempura and barbecued beef sirloin with yuzu koshu (check the glossary at the back if youi're baffled by the names). Fanciful desserts might include exotic brûlées (sesame, ginger and green tea) plus cookies and cream mochi. Cocktails and healthy drinks provide endless fun, and the exciting global wine list promises fashion-conscious drinking from £16.
Chef/s: Grant Brunsden. **Open:** Mon to Sat L 12 to 3, all week D 6 to 11. **Closed:** 25 and 26 Dec. **Meals:** alc (main courses £8 to £19.50). Set L £15. **Service:** 12.5% (optional). **Details:** Cards accepted. 95 seats. Air-con. Separate bar. Wheelchair access. Music. Children's portions.

Gordon Ramsay
As haute as cuisine comes
68-69 Royal Hospital Road, SW3 4HP
Tel no: (020) 7352 4441
www.gordonramsay.com
⊖ Sloane Square
French | £85
Cooking score: 9

🍾 V

The name appears beside the otherwise discreet canopied entrance and requires no introduction. Yet with Gordon Ramsay seemingly bent on world domination, it's good to know that his London flagship is in good hands. The marvelous Jean-Claude Breton continues to direct the perfectly orchestrated service, ensuring that there are no distractions from the serious business of enjoying the food. And serious business it is. Under the guidance of Mark Askew, Clare Smyth is interpreting Ramsay's very French, very refined cooking with intelligence. It's as haute as cuisine comes and you won't have your senses jarred by oddball pairings here. Instead, she adopts a relatively hands-off approach to main ingredients and has an eye for seasonality within the confines of a slowly evolving repertoire. Thus an April lunch saw milk-fed belly of pork braised to a delicate soft fusion of meat and fat and served with polenta,

purple sprouting broccoli and madeira jus. Elsewhere, perfectly timed scallops, partnered to great effect by a fine mille-feuille of potato, Parmesan velouté and truffle 'smarties', were considered the highlight of one reporter's meal, the dish seeing off stiff competition from Barbary duck, pink and well-flavoured, served with creamed Savoy cabbage, chestnuts, beetroot, turnips, black trumpet mushrooms and nicely judged Madeira jus. Amid all the sighs of satisfaction, however, there is the odd report of less happy proceedings: some mis-timing, especially of fish, for example. Yet it would be wrong to lay too much emphasis on these doubts. The overwhelming response is one of ringing endorsement. The reporter who declared 'I would rather eat here rarely than have a multitude of cheaper meals in undistinguished restaurants' speaks for many. Flawless simplicity distinguishes desserts, say a refreshing pineapple and coconut soup with chilli syrup ahead of a well-made tarte Tatin with vanilla ice cream, or a textbook rum Baba with caramelised blood oranges and vanilla cream. Extras are stunning, especially the balls of strawberry ice cream in white chocolate served in a bowl 'steaming with dry ice'. When it comes to the wine list, the sommelier is notably helpful, offering assured guidance through the 37 pages. It's a showcase for the world's finest, from a detailed coverage of France to an imaginative global selection with prices to match, but turns up credible options in minor appellations, such as benchmark Minervois from Château d'Oupia for £24, or £5 by-the-glass.
Chef/s: Gordon Ramsay, Mark Askew and Clare Smyth. **Open:** Mon to Fri L 12 to 2.30, D 6.30 to 11. **Closed:** Sat and Sun. **Meals:** Set L £40, Set D £85, Prestige menu £110. **Service:** 12.5%. **Details:** Cards accepted. 50 seats. Air-con. Separate bar. No music. No mobile phones. Wheelchair access. Children's portions.

Also recommended

An 'also recommended' entry is not a full entry, but is provisionally suggested as an alternative to main entries.

Hunan
Rustic home-cooked Chinese food
51 Pimlico Road, SW1W 8NE
Tel no: (020) 7730 5712
www.hunanlondon.com
⊖ Sloane Square
Chinese | £39
Cooking score: 3

It may be set among eye-wateringly priced antique shops, but there's a distinctly modest air to Michael Peng's restaurant. Indeed, this is no ordinary Chinese restaurant. The aim of the kitchen is to serve rustic home-cooked dishes and the idea is to forget any notions of a conventional menu. Instead, the preferred mode of eating here is the leave-it-to-us menu, in which a long succession of small dishes is brought to the table one after the other – reporters are much taken with 'the variety of flavours' and the fact that there is 'minimal rice and noodles'. A typical menu could open with shark fin soup, take in steamed duck and angelica root and stir-fried spicy frogs' legs with Chinese leaves, go on to steamed prawn and spinach dumplings, pig's ear and tongue salad, and stir-fried fillet of lamb with baby Chinese celery, with the chef's special slow-braised pork hock with 'gai lan' vegetables something of a show-stopper. Dessert could be sweet red bean pancake with almond jelly. House wine is £14.
Chef/s: Michael Peng. **Open:** Mon to Sat L 12 to 2, D 6.30 to 11. **Closed:** Sun, Christmas, bank hols. **Meals:** Set menus £38.80 to £42.80. **Service:** 12.5% (optional). **Details:** Cards accepted. 44 seats. Air-con. Music. Children's portions.

Readers recommend

A 'readers recommend' review is a genuine quote from a report sent in by one of our readers. We intend to follow up these suggestions throughout the year to come.

Il Convivio

Charming Italian conviviality
143 Ebury Street, SW1W 9QN
Tel no: (020) 7730 4099
www.etruscarestaurants.com
⊖ Victoria, Sloane Square
Italian | £38
Cooking score: 2
 V

Occupying a neatly converted terraced house in one of Belgravia's most plutocratic enclaves, this suave Italian is indeed a convivial rendezvous. Quotes from Dante are inscribed on the deep-red walls of the dining room, although most punters make a beeline for the conservatory, where the retractable roof offers weatherproof dining. The bi-lingual menu shows the kitchen's eagerness
to add new vigour to mainstream dishes: a salad of mozzarella and tomatoes is drizzled with pistachio oil, Parma ham is accompanied by home-made sweet-pickled vegetables, while confit of pork belly is perked up with cherries marinated in Cabernet Sauvignon. You might also find a dish of spaghetti with cured pig's cheek and a risotto involving wild pollock carpaccio with fig and anchovy pesto. To finish, try semolina vin Santo cake with fresh pear or sample the slate of organic Italian cheeses. Italy rules on the wine list, with prices starting at £13.50 (£3.95 a glass). **Chef/s:** Lukas Pfaff. **Open:** Mon to Sat L 12 to 3, D 6.45 to 11. **Closed:** Sun, bank hols. **Meals:** alc (main courses £9 to £22).Set L £17.50 (2 courses) to £21.50. **Service:** 12.5% (optional). **Details:** Cards accepted. 65 seats. Air-con. Separate bar. Music. Children allowed.

Painted Heron

Breaking the mould of Indian cooking
112 Cheyne Walk, SW10 0DJ
Tel no: (020) 7351 5232
www.thepaintedheron.com
⊖ Sloane Square
Modern Indian | £28
Cooking score: 3

When it opened in 2002, the Painted Heron was hailed as an Indian restaurant for the twenty-first century. It continues to follow a steady upward trajectory, building on a foundation of unshowy but accomplished modern Indian cooking that eschews most Indian names (aside from the occasional use of the word 'tandoori' or 'tikka') in favour of plain English (freshwater giant king prawns, tandoor-roasted with pickled lime extract). The menu is mainly a blend of the modern and the classic: venison is served in a biryani with curry and cucumber raita, while sea bass fillets appear in coriander and green chilli marinade with masala mash and curry. Fried Indian rice pudding with chocolate mousse adds to the unpredictability of it all. A modern global wine list opens at £15. Our questionnaire was not returned, so some of the information below may have changed.
Chef/s: Yogesh Datta. **Open:** Sun to Fri L 12 to 2.30, all week D 6.30 to 10.30. **Closed:** 25 and 26 Dec, 1 Jan. **Meals:** alc (main courses £11 to £18). **Service:** 12.5% (optional). **Details:** Cards accepted. 75 seats. 20 seats outside. Air-con. Music.

Pig's Ear Dining Room

Lively Chelsea gastropub
35 Old Church Street, SW3 5BS
Tel no: (020) 7352 2908
www.thepigsear.co.uk
⊖ Sloane Square
Gastropub | £30
Cooking score: 2

This corner-site gastropub with its chocolate-brown frontage is a few yards from the King's Road. Big windows ensure the place is filled with daylight, and there is an infectious breeziness about Chris Sharpe's cooking. A daily-changing menu might deal in the likes of chicken and fig boudin with Puy lentils, celeriac and bacon, or baked crottin de Chavignol goats' cheese with hazelnuts, red wine pear and a salad of watercress and dandelion for starters. Mains are a cut above even the gastropub norm, industriously wrapping rabbit loin in pancetta and partnering it with black pudding, wild mushrooms and salsify, or baking halibut 'en papillote' and serving it with spring greens, shoots of monk's beard and a buttery blood orange sauce. Finish with poached baby pineapple with vanilla cream cheese and an almond tuile or pistachio ice cream and shortbread. A concise, upmarket wine list kicks off with house vins de pays at £15, and there are ten wines by-the-glass from £3.50. **Chef/s:** Chris Sharpe. **Open:** all week L 12 to 3.30 (Sun 4.30), Mon to Sat D 7 to 10.30. **Closed:** 25 and 31 Dec. **Meals:** alc (main courses £11.50 to £17.50). **Service:** 12.5%. **Details:** 60 seats. Separate bar. Wheelchair access. Music. Children allowed.

Rasoi Vineet Bhatia

A Chelsea town house, Indian-style
10 Lincoln Street, SW3 2TS
Tel no: (020) 7225 1881
rasoirestaurant.co.uk
⊖ **Sloane Square**
Indian | £55
Cooking score: 5

It would be unfair to reveal too much about the Rasoi Vineet Bhatia experience to the uninitiated, as part of this high-end Indian restaurant's charm is the journey it takes you on, from upper class Chelsea side-street to an exotic world of incense, rich silks, fragrant spices and quirky objets d'art. One gains admittance only by ringing the doorbell. If some find that a little intimidating, it's more than made up for by the warm welcome within. Though Vineet Bhatia's cuisine is variously described as evolved, modern or posh, the simple things often stand out. A small cup of mango lassi is a perfect amuse on a

hot day; mini poppadoms with sweet mango chutney make this curry house cliché something special. At its best it is exciting stuff, as seen in more luxurious dishes such as grilled chilli and ginger lobster, seafood biryani or the signature chocolate samosas. Nothing comes cheap, though the tasting menu at £75 with its array of exotic tastes probably offers better value than the cheaper menus, which can play a little safe. A mélange of grilled vegetables with Indian pesto from the set lunch menu was as dated as it sounds – although the vegetables were individually cooked and spiced to perfection – and a fresh coconut pannacotta, though in itself 'marvellous', came with too-soft white chocolate and cardamom ice cream on a triangular glass plate, and looked equally passé. The wine list is as strong as ever, with lots of tempting half-bottles, some great spice-friendly selections from Alsace and Germany and classy choices from Bordeaux, Australia and California. Prices are as expected of SW3 – let that be a warning. Those on a lower budget should try Bhatia's new, more casual restaurant Urban Turban in Notting Hill (see entry).
Chef/s: Vineet Bhatia. **Open:** Mon to Fri L 12 to 3, Mon to Sat D 6 to 11. **Closed:** bank hols. **Meals:** Set L £21 (2 courses) to £26. **Service:** 12.5%. **Details:** 54 seats. Air-con. No music. No mobile phones. Children's portions. Car parking.

Roussillon

French gem goes from strength to strength
16 St Barnabas Street, SW1W 8PE
Tel no: (020) 7730 5550
www.roussillon.co.uk
⊖ **Sloane Square**
French | £55
Cooking score: 6

If Roussillon appears a touch unassuming from outside, once through the front door all becomes clear. Two intimate dining rooms are decorated in fashionable neutral tones (creams and browns) with artwork providing splashes of colour. Here, Alex Gauthier celebrates classical French cooking (alongside the wines of South-West France), with an adventurous menu – including options like dégustation, vegetarian or umami – all driven by prime seasonal British produce. It's fine-tuned cooking, highly accomplished and imaginative. On a spring menu there might be Welsh spring lamb three ways (roasted leg, grilled cutlet and braised shoulder) served with baby leeks and a thyme and Parmesan gratin, or maybe coriander-marinated pink daurade teamed with clams, shallots and parsley, courgettes, asparagus and a lemon aromatic jus. Service is slick and professional, while the wine list is a corker of some 400 bins – from the famous and classic to the lesser-known. France is obviously the first love, with the namesake Roussillon plus Languedoc, Provence and the South West sharing a starring role. There are 18 or so by-the-glass, with bottles starting at £18. And don't miss the lunch deal, which includes a half-bottle of wine, water and coffee – it is great value.

Chef/s: Alexis Gauthier. **Open:** Mon to Fri L 12 to 2.30, Mon to Sat D 6.30 to 10.30. **Closed:** Sun, Dec 25 and 26, Jan 1. **Meals:** set L £35 (includes half bottle of wine), set D £55. **Service:** 12.5%. **Details:** Cards accepted. 50 seats. Air-con. Children's portions.

★NEW ENTRY★
The Botanist
Terrific British pub/brasserie
Sloane Square, SW1W 8EE
Tel no: (020) 7730 0077
www.thebotanistsloanesquare.com
⊖ Sloane Square
Gastropub | £32
Cooking score: 3

With a trio of gastropubs across London (White Swan, The Gun, the Empress of India), this is Tom and Ed Martin's first foray into West London. The brothers have chosen an enviable location – a generous corner plot spreading out onto Sloane Square. The interior is appealing, too: art-deco ceiling lamps, cream leather, Victorian illustrations of botanical specimens. Open all day (from breakfast, via afternoon tea to dinner) and bursting at the seams with self-assured Chelsea residents (which guarantees a certain booming ambience) the Botanist has certainly hit the ground running. In such circumstances food can sometimes be secondary, but not here. The menu is straightforward, focusing on popular modern British dishes and it gets the basics right. Start with crayfish linguine – it hit the right spot at inspection – then first-rate roast chicken, perhaps served with bread sauce, and finish with exemplary rhubarb and apple crumble with 'proper custard'. Add to it agreeable service, fair prices, plus a pleasing wine list (from £15), and you have all the hallmarks of a whopping success.

Chef/s: Shannon Wilson. **Open:** Mon to Fri 8am to 11.30pm, Sat and Sun 9am to 11.30pm. **Meals:** alc (main courses £11.50 to £19). **Service:** 12.5%. **Details:** Cards accepted. 65 seats. Air-con. Separate bar. Wheelchair access. Music. Children allowed.

Tom Aikens
The epicentre of modern French cooking
43 Elystan Street, SW3 3NT
Tel no: (020) 7584 2003
www.tomaikens.co.uk
⊖ South Kensington
French | £65
Cooking score: 8

🍷 V

'Continues to improve with time' was one reporter's verdict on Tom Aikens's cooking this year, declaring 'the kitchen is at the top of its game'. Dining takes place in a sleek monochromatic interior and ordering is straightforward – chose from the carte, tasting menu or a classical version featuring Aitkens's signature dishes. The lunch menu is a bargain. Underpinning it all are notably fresh and well-sourced materials. There appears to be a new-found confidence in the kitchen. The extravagant combinations that occasionally marred previous visits have been recalibrated and there are now fewer components on the plate – foams, for example, are kept sensibly in check, only appearing when they truly add dimension – and flavours are more assured:

viz. an appetiser of salmon confit served with cucumber, cauliflower cream and cucumber foam, punctuated with some dill, has been a stunning introduction. Lobster and rabbit may appear as an 'exceptional pairing', the rabbit fillet subtly enhanced with vanilla and a cannelloni of the leg meat, and an 'expressive and impressive' dish of roasted salt marsh lamb with shallot mashed potato works well in tandem with goats' cheese gnocchi, lamb's sweetbread, potato crisps and garlic flower. At dessert stage, lemon jelly, lemon foam and vanilla crème anglaise arrives in a small beer bottle (with a straw), then the primary dessert, a 'brilliant' trio of rhubarb: poached, parfait and meringue with vanilla mousse. From the copious selection of 'superb' breads through to a dazzling array of petits fours, presentation is 'a thing of beauty'. The wine list features a catalogue of bottles, with prices opening at £22 but rapidly moving north. There are fine wines from France to please the classicists and the New World for the modernists, including California's cult estate of Screaming Eagle from the 1997 vintage at £4,000.

Chef/s: Tom Aikens. **Open:** Mon to Fri L 12 to 2.30, Mon to Fri D 6.45 to 11. **Closed:** 15 to 31 Aug, 24 Dec to 4 Jan. **Meals:** alc £65 (3 courses). Set L 29, Tasting £80, Classic £100. **Service:** 12.5%. **Details:** Cards accepted. 60 seats. Air-con. Separate bar. No music.

Tom's Kitchen
Chunky, vibrant brasserie food
27 Cale Street, SW3 3QP
Tel no: (020) 7349 0202
www.tomskitchen.co.uk
⊖ Sloane Square, South Kensington
Modern British | £34
Cooking score: 4

The second Chelsea front that Tom Aikens opened, not all that far from his main, eponymous centre of operations (see entry), has been an unqualified success. On the first floor is a relaxing bar, where you can slouch about on sofas under ceiling fans, feeding on snacks, brunch or a full meal, while your laptop feeds off the Wi-fi signal. Downstairs is a more restaurant space, although it's still pretty laid back here, to the extent perhaps of table-sharing, refectory-style. A typically intelligent, carefully constructed brasserie menu offers a range of chunky, vibrant dishes that are high on flavour, and built from conscientiously sourced ingredients. Choice is as wide as the brasserie format mandates, with starters running from sautéed foie gras with a duck egg, bacon and balsamic jus, to squid cooked in lime and paprika with aïoli. Mains include simple burgers with 'big chips' or roast pumpkin pasta, but are also prepared to go for it. Two of you might feast on braised lamb shoulder cooked for seven hours, dressed in onions and balsamic, or there could be Middle White pork, roasted almost as slowly, and served with lentils and grain mustard mash. Megrim sole is a fish possibility, classically sauced with lemon, caper and raisin butter. Crowd-pleasing desserts take in chocolate fondant with pecan ice cream or mango pannacotta with berry mousse and passionfruit sauce. Service is good and snappy, as is the wine list, which has a nice mix of well-selected brasserie choices backed up by the kinds of fine wines SW3 is used to. Bottles start at £14, glasses at £4.

Chef/s: Guy Bossom. **Open:** all week L 12 to 3 (10 to 3 Sat and Sun) D 6 to 11. **Meals:** alc (main courses £12.50 to £42). **Service:** 12.5%. **Details:** 76 seats. Air-con. Separate bar. Wheelchair access. Music. Children allowed.

ALSO RECOMMENDED
▲ Tom's Place
1 Cale Street, Chelsea, SW3 3QT
Tel no: (020) 7351 1806
www.tomsplace.org.uk
⊖ Sloane Square, South Kensington
Seafood

Tom Aikens's cheery, workmanlike take on the English chippy (takeaway downstairs, a dozen or so tables upstairs) offers a lot more than fish and chips. The culinary magnum opus embraces mainly Cornish-landed fish in all its sustainable forms, served battered, pan-fried, grilled or in a bowl – in other words, gurnard, chips and tartare sauce (£12.50), moules marinère (£14), and grilled butterfly mackerel with beetroot, potato and fresh herb salad (£12.50). Dover sole with spinach and champagne sauce (£18.50) could be a daily special. Drink English wines (from £16) and beer and finish with ice cream. No bookings. Open all day, every day.

▮ Earls Court

Cambio de Tercio

Clearly proud of its Spanish accent
163 Old Brompton Road, SW5 0LJ
Tel no: (020) 7244 8970
www.cambiodetercio.co.uk
⊖ **Gloucester Road**
Spanish | £35
Cooking score: 2

 🍷 V

This Brompton Road locale is a real find, with its lively, vibrant atmosphere as upbeat as its dramatic décor and modern Spanish cooking. Bold-painted walls are hung with striking paintings, the black-slate floor matched by black leather banquettes and round-back chairs, while white-clothed close-packed tables don black undercloths too. It's fun, sexy, even romantic, with a resolute Spanish accent that's picked up by the patriotic wine list (headed up by an impressive range of sherries), bustling service and atmosphere. You can follow three-course convention, or, with every dish offered tapas-style, go the grazing route instead − perfect for sharing. Expect quality ingredients, stunning presentation and some gutsy flavours, perhaps fried Andalusian baby squid with lime, or maybe chargrilled lamb chops served with aubergine purée, manzanilla green olives and glazed potato. House wine is £17. Sister restaurants Tendido Cero (directly opposite) and the new Tendido Cuatro (108-110 New King's Road, SW6, tel: 020 7371 5147), both offer a more casual tapas experience.

Chef/s: Alberto Criado. **Open:** all week L 12 to 2.30, D 7 to 11.30 (11 Sun). **Closed:** 21 Dec to 2 Jan. **Meals:** alc (main courses £16 to £19.75. **Service:** not inc. **Details:** Cards accepted. 40 seats. Air-con. Wheelchair access. Music. Children allowed.

▮ Fulham

Blue Elephant

Extravagant Thai fantasies
3-6 Fulham Broadway, SW6 1AA
Tel no: (020) 7385 6595
www.blueelephant.com
⊖ **Fulham Broadway**
Thai | £35
Cooking score: 1

V

The capital's most opulent Thai restaurant is awesome in scale: blink and you might almost imagine you had been beamed up to some fantasy version of the land of a thousand temples. It's a seductive, headily perfumed show that comes complete with exotic foliage, cascading waterfalls and carp ponds, not to mention a gilt-edged bar resembling a royal barge. The menu is an equally showy assortment of floridly described mainstream dishes, bolstered by crossovers and special inventions. Seared foie gras with tamarind sauce is one of the eyebrow-raisers, alongside a version of 'larb' (usually a meat salad) made with salmon tartare, sea bass grilled in a bamboo case and rack of English lamb 'napped in krapraow sauce.' Elsewhere satays, curries and stir-fries please the traditionalists. Sunday brunch is a sumptuous family spread, and the lengthy global wine list is a keen match for the food; prices start at £19 (£5.50 a glass).
Chef/s: Sompong Sae-Jew. **Open:** Mon to Fri L 12 to 2.30 (3 Sun), all week D 7 to 11 (6.30 to 11 Fri, 6 to 11 Sat, 7 to 10.30 Sun). **Closed:** 25 and 26 Dec. **Meals:** alc (main courses £11 to £17). Set L Sun £25. Set D £35 to £100. **Service:** 12.5%. **Details:** Cards accepted. 300 seats. Air-con. Separate bar. Wheelchair access. Music. Children allowed.

Chutney Mary

Seductive modern Indian
535 King's Road, SW10 0SZ
Tel no: (020) 7351 3113
www.realindianfood.com
⊖ Fulham Broadway
Indian | £45
Cooking score: 3

V

Divided between a bright plant-filled conservatory and an inviting area with elegant silk wall hangings, this subterranean dining room has always been memorable. So it's good to note that Siddharth Krishna's cooking has moved up a notch or two. A startlingly fresh scallop malabar, quickly pan-seared and accompanied with a 'velvety and vibrant-coloured' coconut, ginger, saffron sauce, saw one reporter tempted to lick every drop off the plate. To follow, a subtle chicken achari korma was tempered by yoghurt, and scented with roasted cumin and sun-dried fenugreek leaves. 'Purple clouds' proved to be an exemplary variation of delicately spiced stir-fried aubergine with tomato relish. Alphonso mango with mango pannacotta, acutely East-West in conception, was 'a happy end' to that meal. 'Charismatic service' treats diners with genuine care and the wine list is intelligently compiled to complement the spicy food. Prices start from £19.25 (£4.75 a glass), with many bottles between £20 to £35.
Chef/s: Siddharth Krishna. **Open:** Fri to Sun L 12.30 to 2.30 (3 Sun), all week D 6.30 to 11.30 (10.30 Sun). **Meals:** alc (main courses £13.50 to £29.50). Set L Sat and Sun £22, set D £45. **Service:** 12.5%. **Details:** Cards accepted. 100 seats. Air-con. Music.

Deep

Fish by the river
The Boulevard, Imperial Wharf, SW6 2UB
Tel no: (020) 7736 3337
www.deeplondon.co.uk
⊖ Fulham Broadway
Seafood | £30
Cooking score: 4

Deep may be hard to find (in part of a waterside development between Fulham and Chelsea) but once inside it boasts a sleek, contemporary interior and an attractive terrace that overlooks the Thames. The kitchen takes a fashion-conscious view of things: menus are inventive and seasonally aware, the mostly-fish repertoire built around the owner's policy of not using endangered species. Combinations are well-considered and perfectly balanced, with shellfish and smoked fish permeating starters, whether ballottine of gravad lax, a selection of herrings or native lobster served with lemon and mayonnaise. Main courses revolve around the likes of steamed halibut with eggs, prawns and horseradish in warm butter or grilled Dover sole with summer greens. If you're in the mood for meat, there could be braised shoulder and roast leg of lamb provençale or braised pork belly. End with Neal's Yard cheeses or raspberry financier with white chocolate ice cream. The international wine list is organized by style and the base price is £16.
Chef/s: Fredrik Bolin. **Open:** Tue to Fri and Sun L 12 to 3, Tue to Sat D 7 to 11. **Closed:** Mon, Christmas, Easter, bank hols. **Meals:** alc (main courses £11.50 to £24). **Details:** Cards accepted. 60 seats. 30 seats outside. Air-con. Wheelchair access. Music. Children's portions. Car parking.

Hammersmith

★NEW ENTRY★
Carpenter's Arms
Great local with good food
91 Black Lion Lane, W6 9BG
Tel no: (020) 8741 8386
⊖ Stamford Brook
Gastropub | £25
Cooking score: 2

This corner-sited pub may look traditional from the outside, but the uncomplicated single bar room with its plain wood floor and junk shop tables and chairs bears the hallmarks of a modern-day gastropub. The menu changes daily, delivering refreshingly robust and uncomplicated creations, classic British dishes with the odd nod towards France and Italy. Potted shrimps and roast bone marrow share the stage with a whole roast poussin or roast halibut served with pig's trotter, carrots and grain mustard, and the roll-call of dishes reporters recommend include gutsy peppered venison Barnsley chop (served with roast swede and steeped raisins) and oxtail, pearl onion and parsnip pie. The style of cooking is light and its simplicity and clear flavours reflect prime materials treated confidently. Desserts range from poire belle Hélène to pumpkin Bakewell with candied sage, Valrhona chocolate and mascarpone. The food represents good value for money – and so do the wines, which start at £13.50.
Chef/s: Paul Adams. **Open:** all week L 12 to 3 (12.30 to 4 Sun), D 7 to 10 (7.30 to 9 Sun). **Meals:** alc (main courses from £10.25 to £16.50). **Service:** 12.5% (optional). **Details:** Cards accepted. 35 seats. 20 seats outside.

Chez Kristof
Flag-waving French food
111 Hammersmith Grove, W6 0NQ
Tel no: (020) 8741 1177
www.chezkristof.co.uk
⊖ Goldhawk Road/Hammersmith
French | £30
New Chef

V

Famed for his forays into populist Polish food and East European chic, Jan Woroniecki is now promoting the earthy virtues of French regional cuisine in this corner site on Hammersmith Grove. Like his other ventures, Chez Kristof buzzes. The menu is as recognisably Gallic as the 'Marseillaise' with its bagna cauda, boudin noir, moules and poule au pot. There are bowls of onion soup if you need comforting, plus salads (walnuts, dandelion and blue cheese) and heartwarming platefuls of grilled belly pork with braised cabbage and apple sauce, duck confit or hake with black olives, anchovies and capers. Desserts are much-loved patisserie cornerstones including tarte Tatin, profiteroles and tarte au citron. The wine list doesn't shirk its patriotic duties, offering an all-French line-up from well-respected regions: prices start at £14 (£10 a carafe, £4 a glass).
Chef/s: Slawek Stawicki. **Open:** all week L 12 to 3, D 6 to 11.15. **Meals:** alc (main courses £12 to £16.50). Set L and pre-theatre D £14.50 (2 courses) to £17.50. **Service:** 12.5%. **Details:** Cards accepted. 90 seats. 30 seats outside. Air-con. Separate bar. No music. Wheelchair access. Children's portions.

Gate

Vibrant, global vegetarian cooking
51 Queen Caroline Street, W6 9QL
Tel no: (020) 8748 6932
www.thegate.tv
⊖ Hammersmith
Vegetarian | £24
Cooking score: 2

The sparse, contemporary interior of this former church might conjure memories of college days, but the food is a far cry from canteen grub. The globe-trotting vegetarian menu has its roots in the childhood memories of owners Adrian and Michael Daniel, whose Indo-Iraqi Jewish grandmother ignited Adrian's love of vegetarian cooking. Typical starters are broad bean falafel, onion tart and Indo-Iraqi potato cakes. Move on to a risotto of butternut squash, dolcelatte and thyme, a pan-fried corn and polenta cake with roasted baby artichokes and fennel, grilled red pepper with courgettes and salsa rossa, or shiitake won-ton and pumpkin laksa. To finish, perhaps pressed chocolate and chestnut torte or rhubarb, pear and ginger crumble. Amid such a vibrant array of dishes, it's comforting to know that there are meze options for the undecided. The short but respectable wine list starts at £14.

Chef/s: Mariusz Wegrodski. **Open:** Mon to Fri L 12 to 3, Mon to Sat D 6 to 11. **Meals:** alc (main courses £12 to £13.75). **Service:** 12.5%. **Details:** Cards accepted. 60 seats. 30 seats outside. Air-con. No music. No mobile phones. Children's portions.

River Café

Thames Wharf, Rainville Road, W6 9HA
Tel no: (020) 7386 4200
www.rivercafe.co.uk
⊖ Hammersmith
Modern Italian | £65
Cooking score: 6

It's been a tough year for Rose Gray, Ruth Rogers and the team at River Café. A fire in the kitchen did significant damage to the kitchen and saw the Thameside restaurant closed from April until August 2008. Judging by a pre-fire inspection, the kitchen is as reliable and calendar-conscious as ever. You could set your clock by the arrival of seasonal favourites on the River Café's daily-changing menus. White truffles from Alba, wild salmon, grouse (or 'gallo cedrone' in River Café parlance) and the best asparagus are what makes these hard-to-get tables catnip to foodies. Portions are large, unmanageably so for those who like to do the 'full' Italian meal from antipasti to dolci via primi (the pasta is renowned) and secondi. It's all classical, simply plated, arguably too simply cooked food – fans of more 'gastronomic' Italian cooking should look elsewhere. The all Italian wine list covers the length and breadth of Italy with the power regions of Piemont and Tuscany being particularly well represented. The charming, always fashionably clad staff, who aren't half as flakey as they look, are dab hands at picking at something interesting from the list at prices from £12.50. First-time visitors are urged to try for a summery weekend when the riverside terrace really comes into its own.

Chef/s: Rose Gray, Ruth Rogers. **Open:** Mon to Fri L 12.30 to 2.15 (Sat 2.30) Sun L 12 to 3. Mon to Thu D 7 to 11, Fri and Sat D 7 to 11.30. **Closed:** Christmas, bank hols

READERS RECOMMEND

Tosa

Japanese
332 King Street, Hammersmith, W6 0RR
Tel no: (020) 8748 0002
'Authentic taste at a reasonable price'

▌Kensal Rise

READERS RECOMMEND
Salusbury

Gastropub
50-52 Salusbury Road, Kensal Rise, NW6 6NN
Tel no: (020) 7328 3286
'This old-school gastropub shows real class'

Samson Miro

75 Chamberlayne Road, Kensal Rise, NW10 3ND
Tel no: (020) 8962 0275
'Fantastic wine shop, with tapas on small tables by night'

▋Kensington

11 Abingdon Road

Pefectlypitched neighbourhood restaurant
11-13 Abingdon Road, W8 6AH
Tel no: (020) 7937 0120
⊖ High Street Kensington
Modern European | £25
New Chef

Owner Rebecca Mascarenhas is well-known as the driving force behind Sonny's and the Phoenix (see entries), and has scored another hit with this bright and breezy restaurant just off the Kensington main drag. It's a big, airy venue with a skylight letting in the sunbeams, trendy artwork on pastel walls and a concise menu that seems perfectly pitched for the neighbourhood. The kitchen delivers busy contemporary dishes with strong Mediterranean leanings, as in roast rabbit leg with tarragon, pancetta and sweet potato mash or grilled fillet of sea bass with crispy chorizo, courgettes and purple potatoes. Start with beef carpaccio or salmon cured with grappa and conclude proceedings with poached peach in wine and Amaretto, or pannacotta with caramelised oranges. Artisan cheeses are served with quince paste, and the carefully assembled global wine list promises lively drinking from £13.75 (£3.75 a glass).
Chef/s: Mikele Pais. **Open:** all week L 12.30 to 2.30 (3 Sun), D 6.30 to 11 (10 Sun). **Closed:** bank hols. **Meals:** alc (main courses £14 to £18.50), Set L and D £17.50 (2 courses). **Service:** 12.5% (optional). **Details:** Cards accepted. 80 seats. Air-con. Separate bar. No music. Wheelchair access. Children's portions.

Popeseye

Steak and chips and nothing more
108 Blythe Road, W14 0HD
Tel no: (020) 7610 4578
www.popeseye.com
⊖ Olympia
Steaks | £25
Cooking score: 1

The formula hasn't changed for a couple of decades – and why should it? This is the place for honest-to-goodness steak and chips and nothing more. The straightforward neighbourhood restaurant takes its name from the Scottish word for rump steak, although sirloin and fillet are also from grass-fed Aberdeen Angus, which is hung for a minimum of two weeks and delivered daily from Scotland. Chips are good and there is a variety of mustards, ketchup and béarnaise too. With weights ranging from six to thirty ounces, starters are clearly redundant, but for anyone wanting more there is salad, while home-made desserts, ice cream or farmhouse cheeses bring up the rear. House wine is £11.50. A second branch can be found at 277 Upper Richmond Road, SW15, tel (020) 8788 7733.
Chef/s: Ian Hutchinson. **Open:** Mon to Sat D only 6.45 to 10.15. **Closed:** Sun, bank hols. **Meals:** alc (steaks £9.95 to £45.50). **Service:** 12.5%. **Details:** Cash only. 34 seats. Air-con. Wheelchair access. Children's portions.

Timo

Italian creativity
343 Kensington High Street, W8 6NW
Tel no: (020) 7603 3888
www.timorestaurant.net
⊖ High Street Kensington
Italian | £36
Cooking score: 2

 V

The sea-green frontage is as vivid as Franco Gatto's cooking at this agreeable Italian restaurant that's a world away from the old-style trattoria. A pastoral mural and crisply dressed tables are the backdrop for dishes such as octopus salad with celery, French beans and new potatoes in a lemony dressing, while pasta options might take in tagliolini with prawns, radicchio and saffron. Veal scallopini turn up dressed in lemon and parsley, with asparagus, new carrots and sprouting broccoli, to make an enlivening spring main course. A fish alternative could be grilled monkfish with borlotti beans in a balsamic reduction. Italian cheeses with mustard fruits are a savoury way to end things, or you might opt for strawberry bavarese with pistachio cream. No fewer than four exclamation marks draw our attention to the tiramisu. With the exception of Champagne, wines are patriotically Italian, and would represent a good chance to explore some flavours we see all too rarely in retail outlets, but for the stiffness of the mark-ups. Prices start at £17.

Chef/s: Franco Gatto. **Open:** Mon to Sat L 12 to 2.30, D 7 to 11. **Closed:** Sun, Christmas, Easter and bank hols. **Meals:** alc (main courses £16.90 to £22.50). Set L £17.90. **Service:** 12.5%. **Details:** 58 seats. 2 seats outside. Air-con. Separate bar. No mobile phones. Wheelchair access. Music. Children's portions.

Zaika

Contemporary Indian cuisine
1 Kensington High Street, W8 5NP
Tel no: (020) 7795 6533
www.zaika-restaurant.co.uk
⊖ High Street Kensington
Modern Indian | £30
Cooking score: 3
🍾 V

Zaika's name translates as 'sophisticated flavours' and its aim is to deliver a classy, innovative take on Indian cuisine, with dishes ranging from classic favourites to original fusions of East and West. Grandly housed in a former bank, the restaurant is decked out in a sumptuous mix of spicy colours. Modern furnishings and large windows create a light, contemporary setting. Starters include an appealing list of platters, each themed round one ingredient. The cheese option, for

example, comprises tandoori paneer, crispy paneer and Stilton 'pakoras', goats' cheese and smoked cashew nut samosa with pear and clove chutney. Main courses run from classic rogan josh made with Herdwick lamb to creative East-West dishes such as tandoori monkfish with curry leaf risotto. Other options include tandoori kingfish marinated in Goan spices and served with coconut milk infused with coriander leaves, shallots, green chillies, ginger and aubergine chutney. The wine list is chosen with spices in mind, and opens at £17.

Chef/s: Sanjay Dwivedi. **Open:** Mon to Sun 12 to 2.45, D 6 to 10.45 (Sun 9.45). **Meals:** alc (main courses £15 to £21). Set D £39 to £58, Set L £19.50. **Service:** 12.5%. **Details:** Cards accepted. 80 seats. Air-con. Separate bar. Music. Children's portions.

▪ Knightsbridge

Zuma
Super-cool, modern and dynamic
5 Raphael Street, SW7 1DL
Tel no: (020) 7584 1010
www.zumarestaurant.com
⊖ Knightsbridge
Modern Japanese | £52
Cooking score: 5
🍾 V

Fashionable restaurants are notoriously short-lived, but Zuma continues to succeed. The dining room mixes 'hardcore and Zen': exposed ventilation, concrete and steel alongside swathes of warm wood and stone. Calmer by day, the action starts at the bar when night falls, tranquillity is brushed aside and the service brigade steps up to mark, keen to help the sophisticated clientele through the edgy menu. All the bases are covered, with top-notch sashimi, inventive sushi and delicate tempura among robata grills and more contemporary ideas. You don't have to be minted to eat here, as entry-level dishes such as grilled chicken wings and vegetarian options are consistently good. The cooking features lively ingredients: sea bream with wasabi, apple and ponzu showing off sharp citrusy flavours, a 'vibrantly seasoned' carpaccio of

beef, marinated with nori vinaigrette and dry miso, or a 'spicy and flavoursome' red miso quail. West-facing desserts, say lemon croquettes with rhubarb compote and almond ice cream, make a refreshing way to end. Beginning with noble sakés, the wine list, diverse and enterprising, is rife with imaginative choices. Prices reflect the Knightsbridge location, ranging from £22 to £1,976 for a 1961 Cheval Blanc.
Chef/s: Ross Shonhan. **Open:** all week L 12 to 2.30 (from 12.30 Sat and Sun), D 7 to 11. **Closed:** 24 and 25 Dec, 1 Jan. **Meals:** alc (main courses £3.80 to £90). Set D £96 (min 2). **Service:** 13%. **Details:** Cards accepted. 127 seats. Air-con. Separate bar. Wheelchair access. Music. Children allowed.

Maida Vale

★NEW ENTRY★
The Warrington
Upmarket gastropub food in stylish setting
93 Warrington Crescent, W9 1EH
Tel no: (020) 7592 7960
www.gordonramsay.com/thewarrington
⊖ Maida Vale, Warwick Avenue
Gastropub | £32
Cooking score: 2

Gordon Ramsay has done well in securing this grand pub with its opulent Art Nouveau friezes and marble pillars. The ground floor bar is everything you would want in a local: a wide selection of beers and a succinct menu featuring the likes of pork pie and piccalilli. Upstairs, the cream and beige restaurant is more understated and offers a simple menu that might, in May, include Dorset snails, crab and carrot soup or perfectly-cooked asparagus, 'although the accompanying soft-boiled duck egg was not the yolky volcano it should have been'. Mains range from roasted chicken with Gem and morels to an upmarket take on pie and mash with guinea fowl topped with pastry. Desserts are pub favourites such as a sweet treacle tart. Wines starts at £13.50 and rise to £130, with a wide range by-the-glass.

Chef/s: Daniel Kent. **Open:** all week L 12 to 2.30 (12 to 4 Sat and Sun), Tue to Sun D 6 to 10 (Fri and Sat 10.30). **Meals:** alc (main courses £11.50 to £19.50). **Service:** 12.5% (optional). **Details:** Cards accepted. 82 seats. Air-con. Separate bar. No music. Children's portions.

Notting Hill
Ark
Inviting neighbourhood Italian
122 Palace Gardens Terrace, W8 4RT
Tel no: (020) 7229 4024
www.ark-restaurant.com
⊖ Notting Hill Gate
Italian | £32
Cooking score: 2
V

A front terrace ablaze with flowers marks out this ever-popular neighbourhood Italian restaurant close to Notting Hill Gate tube. Inside it's equally inviting, with more floral embellishments, painted panelling and Roman blinds setting the tone in the long, narrow dining room. The kitchen makes its own breads and pasta (try black lobster ravioli with clam and saffron bisque) and there's a special menu devoted to truffles during the autumn season. Otherwise, expect straightforward antipasti such as Parma ham with a warm chickpea pancake and grilled baby artichokes, plus 'secondi piatti' ranging from roast organic salmon with mussels and purple sprouting broccoli to osso buco or confit of duck with braised endive and Seville orange sauce. Desserts usher in tiramisù, pears poached in grappa and hot chocolate fondant with cinnamon ice cream. A map showing Italy's main regions points up the geographical allegiances of the wine list. Prices start at £15 (£4 a glass).

Chef/s: Alberto Comai. **Open:** Tue to Sat L 12 to 3, Mon to Sat D 6.30 to 11. **Closed:** Sun, bank hols. **Meals:** alc (main courses £13 to £19.50). **Service:** 12.5%. **Details:** Cards accepted. 65 seats. 12 seats outside. Air-con. Separate bar. Wheelchair access. Music. Children allowed.

Assaggi

Satisfying, rustic Italian food
The Chepstow, 39 Chepstow Place, W2 4TS
Tel no: (020) 7792 5501
⊖ Notting Hill Gate
Italian | £40
Cooking score: 4

Camped above a pub in a row of terraced houses, this laid back Notting Hill Italian sets out its stall with tall windows, chunky furniture and bold abstract canvases on bright orange walls. The set up is deceptively simple, and it belies the carefully wrought dishes that emerge from Nino Sassu's kitchen. Robustly satisfying, rustic food with a strong Southern Italian accent is the order of the day and menus are resolutely written in their native language (although staff are happy to translate). Sardinian 'carta da musica' breads open the show and everything is moulded around judiciously sourced ingredients, many of which are imported direct from Italy. Among the antipasti you might find a salad of pears, broad beans and pecorino, stuffed squid or grilled vegetables marinated in olive oil and herbs, while pasta could include 'lasagna bianca', gnocchi and the like. Mains bring equally direct ideas, ranging from lamb chops with caponata and grilled sea bass to authentic fritto misto with all manner of piscine delights. Desserts aim for classic simplicity (bavarois doused with espresso, ricotta cheesecake) and the concise all-Italian wine list opens with Sardinian Argiolas at £21.95 (£5 a glass).
Chef/s: Nino Sassu. **Open:** Mon to Sat L 12.30 to 2.30, D 7.30 to 11. **Closed:** Sun, bank hols and 2 weeks Christmas. **Meals:** alc (main courses £13 to £25). **Service:** not inc. **Details:** Cards accepted. 35 seats. Air-con. No music. Children's portions.

Bumpkin

Fun-loving Notting Hillbilly
209 Westbourne Park Road, W11 1EA
Tel no: (020) 7243 9818
www.bumpkinuk.com
⊖ Westbourne Park, Ladbroke Grove
British | £35
Cooking score: 2

The name conjures up sepia-tinted images of country life, but this Bumpkin is from well-bred city stock – even though it's kitted out in ersatz rustic garb. There's no doubting the restaurant's easy-going nature, but it can boom like a well-heeled rave at peak times. Choose the ground-floor brasserie if you can stand the din, or venture upstairs to the slightly more sedate restaurant: either way, the kitchen feeds the Notting Hill hordes with beefed-up British grub from creditable sources. Cooked-to-order pies and 'deep pots' (macaroni cheese, say) are staples, the rotisserie starts turning in the evening and the menu jogs its way through devilled chicken livers on toast, fishcakes with brown crab mayonnaise, and pork belly with apple sauce and spring greens before reaching nursery puds. Real ales and organic ciders please the fans, and the live-wire wine list has some splendid possibilities from £14 (£3.50 a glass). A second branch is due to open in September 2008 at 102 Old Brompton Road, SW7 3RD, tel: (020) 7373 2403.
Chef/s: Steven Rangiwahia. **Open:** all week L 12 to 3 (11 to 4 Sat, 12 to 4 Sun), D 6 to 12 (11 Sun). **Meals:** alc (main courses £9.50 to £17.50). Set L Sun £24 (2 courses). **Service:** 12.5%. **Details:** Cards accepted. 100 seats. Air-con. Wheelchair access. Music. Children's portions.

Clarke's

Full-on healthy flavours
124 Kensington Church Street, W8 4BH
Tel no: (020) 7221 9225
www.sallyclarke.com
⊖ Notting Hill Gate, High Street Kensington
Modern British | £43
Cooking score: 4

Hailed as a trailblazer when she opened her iconic restaurant in the '80s, Sally Clarke has ridden the waves of fashion and never strayed far from her original concept. It all started in California and was driven by a healthy respect for seasonal ingredients. Since then, Clarke's has earned its reputation with disarmingly simple food and full-on flavours that go straight to the senses: Sally's touchstones have always been char-grilled meat and fish, colourful salad leaves and bread (which has made her a foodie household name). Diners are now offered a choice at lunch *and* dinner (Sally relented in 2006), but the kitchen has not been troubled by the changes. More sun-drenched Mediterranean themes have been added to the mix of late: Trentino speck with blood oranges, bitter leaves and pomegranate dressing, calf's liver with potato and cavolo nero 'champ', sage and red wine glaze or fillet of Cornish brill with green olive and spring onion relish, spinach and 'parchment-baked' potato, for example. Meals always end with a pair of Neals Yard cheeses and a rare accompaniment (homemade fig 'salami'), plus pure-and-simple desserts like yoghurt pannacotta with new season's rhubarb. The hand-picked wine list pays homage to Sally's beloved California with a glorious selection of obscure, esoteric West Coast bottles, ably supported by top names and treasures from France, Italy and elsewhere. Prices start at £15 (£4 a glass).
Chef/s: Sally Clarke and Raffaele Colturi. **Open:** Mon to Sat L 12.30 to 2 (12 to 2 Sat), D 7 to 10. **Closed:** Sun, Christmas and Easter. **Meals:** alc L (main courses £16). Set D £43.25 (3 courses) to

£49.50. **Details:** Cards accepted. 80 seats. Air-con. No mobile phones. Wheelchair access. Children allowed.

e&o

Style-dining for the Notting Hill set
14 Blenheim Crescent, W11 1NN
Tel no: (020) 7229 5454
www.rickerrestaurants.com
⊖ Ladbroke Grove
Fusion/Pan-Asian | £25
Cooking score: 3

A pulsating honeypot for media celebs, glitterati and star-watchers, this voguish Notting Hill hangout packs 'em in. The booming bar and sparse dining room provide a chic backdrop to serious socialising and glamorous encounters, all played out to the gastronomic accompaniment of tiny dishes designed for sharing and grazing. 'Eastern and oriental' is the theme (hence the lower-case moniker) and – like other restaurants in Will Ricker's stable – the menu (with its glossary for the uninitiated) is sliced up into soups, tempura, maki rolls and the like. Dim sum (duck and shiitake gyozas) and salads (warm aubergine and coriander) sit alongside curries ('green' chicken and lychee) and BBQs (Korean lamb cutlets with kim chee). Specials such as steamed sea bream with tamarind add even more variety, and desserts yo-yo between East and West (crispy bananas with coconut sorbet or cookies and cream mochi, for example). Sexy cocktails are much in demand and the globetrotting wine list struts its stuff with prices from £9.50 a carafe (£3.50 a glass).
Chef/s: Simon Treadway. **Open:** all week L 12 to 3 (12 to 4 Sat, 12.30 to 4 Sun), D 6 to 11 (10.30 Sun). **Closed:** 25 and 26 Dec, Aug bank hol. **Meals:** alc (main courses £6.50 to £21.50). **Service:** 12.5% (optional). **Details:** Cards accepted. 84 seats. 20 seats outside. Air-con. Separate bar. Wheelchair access. Music. Children's portions.

The Good Food Guide 2009

Geales

Posh fish and chips
2 Farmer Street, W8 7SN
Tel no: (020) 7727 7528
www.geales.com
⊖ Notting Hill
Modern Seafood | £30
Cooking score: 1

This legendary fish and chip shop (established in 1939) was given a major revamp by new owners Mark Fuller and Garry Hollihead in 2007. With pristine, if rather close-packed, cloth-clad tables and smart leather chairs, there's obviously more on offer than fish and chips. Loch Fyne oysters and potted brown shrimps, even dressed crabs and roasted native lobster appear on the menu, alongside salmon and leek fishcakes and a token sirloin steak with béarnaise sauce. Otherwise there's battered cod, haddock, sole and breaded scampi to be had, with chips, mushy peas, tartare sauce and the like, all charged extra. Finish with treacle tart or Eton mess. Wines start at £12.95. Our questionnaire was not returned, so some of the information below may have changed.
Chef/s: Garry Hollihead. **Open:** Tue to Sat L 12 to 2.30, D 6 to 11, Sun D 6 to 10.30. **Meals:** alc (main courses £10 to £17). **Service:** optional.
Details: Cards accepted. 60 seats. 16 seats outside. Air-con. Wheelchair access. Children allowed.

★NEW ENTRY★
Hereford Road

A showcase for great British produce
3 Hereford Road, W2 4AB
Tel no: (020) 7727 1144
www.herefordroad.org
⊖ Bayswater
British | £30
Cooking score: 4

It's no surprise that diners at this former butcher's shop will find the same robust, simple British food as that pioneered by Fergus Henderson at St John (see entry). Tom Pemberton has worked in both St John restaurants and is simply doing what he does best in this, his own venture. The focus is on innovation rather than complexity, with a menu full of common sense. Here is a kitchen prepared to produce the perfect lamb broth; and it's not afraid to offer a whole crab on its daily menu and it shows no qualms at serving things like ox liver and heart. The ingredients are, of course, first-class, which means dishes such as fresh grilled anchovies, braised duck leg with turnip, or onglet, chips and aïoli speak for themselves. The kitchen is also faithful to some old-fashioned dishes such as devilled kidneys or braised beef and carrots. Desserts continue the traditional tone with rice pudding and sticky date pudding. The value is good, the décor is simple. House wine is £13.
Chef/s: Tom Pemberton. **Open:** all week L 12 to 3, D 6 to 10.30 (10 Sun). **Meals:** alc (main courses from £9 to £15). **Service:** not inc. **Details:** Cards accepted. 70 seats.

Kensington Place

Dependable and energetic brasserie
201-209 Kensington Church Street, W8 7LX
Tel no: (020) 7727 3184
www.egami.co.uk
⊖ Notting Hill Gate, Kensington High Street
Modern British | £39
Cooking score: 4

🍷 V

Now in its 21st year and post Rowley Leigh, Kensington Place is coming of age nicely. The showroom-sized restaurant, notoriously challenging when it comes to the acoustics, continues to sizzle. Service, too, is adaptable and perky even when pushed to the limit. The menu, which has been updated, no longer relies on the old favourites – it is still appealing, but not particularly distinctive. Cornish crab lasagna served with salsify, piment d'Espelette and an almond and onion crust ensures a good start, but the standout at inspection was a credible French classic, bouillabaisse. Desserts lean heavily towards France, and apple tart fine with beurre noisette ice cream is well worth the 15-minute wait. The reality is that the cooking at this pioneer of the modern day brasserie continues to be reliable, but is no longer the flag-bearer it once was. Extending over 12 pages, the wine list has always been notable, international in its outlook and rampant with exciting bottles. Prices start low from £16.50, aided by numerous choices by-the-glass, half-bottles and temperate premiums to encourage experimentation. **Chef/s:** Henry Vigar. **Open:** all week L 12 to 3 (3.30 Sat and Sun) D 6.30 to 10.30 (11 Fri and Sat; 10 Sun). **Closed:** 24 to 26 Dec, 1 to 3 Jan. **Meals:** alc (main courses from £14.50 to £19) Set L £24.50, Set D 16.95 to £24.50. **Service:** 12.5%. **Details:** Cards accepted. 120 seats. Air-con. Separate bar. Children allowed.

★NEW ENTRY★

Le Café Anglais

Inspired by a famous Parisian brasserie
8 Porchester Gardens, W2 4DB
Tel no: (020) 7221 1415
www.lecafeanglais.co.uk
⊖ Bayswater
French | £40
Cooking score: 5

Swagger and cool on the second floor of Whiteley's Shopping Centre, where Rowley Leigh has opened his 140-seater homage to a Parisian brasserie. The room is handsome; huge windows with latticed panes give plenty of light, there are big tarnished mirrors, vast light fittings and comfortable banquettes. The atmosphere crackles. Polished service takes an interest. On view in the open kitchen is a huge rotisserie turning chickens (offered whole, half, breast, or leg), game, lamb and rib of beef (served for two with bone marrow, shallots and red wine). The menu offers some very good things to eat indeed; on one table there may be fish pie, at another oeuf en gelée, while hors d'oeuvres of Parmesan custard with anchovy toasts and a first-course pike boudin with fines herbes and beurre blanc have been described as 'sublime'. A lunch special of confit of duck with bubble and squeak and spiced clementines was 'a nice old favourite well done'. Desserts such as a 'deeply comforting'

Queen of Puddings and bitter chocolate soufflé with pistachio ice cream are followed by good coffee. Prices start at £15 on the mainly French wine list and climb quickly, but there are plenty of options by-the-glass or 250ml carafe.
Chef/s: Rowley Leigh, Colin Westall. **Open:** all week L 12 to 3.30, D 6.30 to 11 (10 Sun). **Meals:** alc (main courses £11 to £18). Set L (Mon to Fri) £16.50 (2 courses). **Service:** 12.5% (optional)

Notting Hill Brasserie

A balance of elegance and informality
92 Kensington Park Road, W11 2PN
Tel no: (020) 7229 4481
www.nottinghillbrasserie.com
⊖ Notting Hill Gate
Modern European | £45
Cooking score: 4

With a jazz quartet in the elegant front bar and a warmly decorated interior made up of a series of small, enticingly lit dining rooms with comfortable chairs, this is not a brasserie in the conventional sense. There's skill in the kitchen, too, with food well-timed and attractively presented. The menu reads simply and enticingly and delivers the flavours it promises with creditable panache. Textural combinations are well-conceived, too, and while some dishes are jazzed up with a few voguish flourishes like tart of crottin de Chavignol and beetroot with balsamic dressing, the repertoire is on the whole a promising mix of classic recipes, ranging from chicken liver and foie gras parfait with Seville orange marmalade to fillet of sole with potato purée, leeks and chive velouté. Meat main courses might take in duck magret with squash purée, spinach and baby carrots, while desserts include an intriguing celery and lime parfait with raspberry sorbet, lychee and tequila soup. France dominates the wine list, with prices starting at £15 for a Chardonnay or vin de pays.
Chef/s: Karl Burdock. **Open:** Wed to Sun L 12 to 3, all week D 7 to 11 (10.30 Sun). **Closed:** bank hols. **Meals:** Set L £17.50 (2 courses) to £22.50.

Service: 12.5%. **Details:** Cards accepted. 90 seats. Air-con. Separate bar. Wheelchair access. Music. Children allowed.

ALSO RECOMMENDED
▲ First Floor
186 Portobello Road, Notting Hill, W11 1LA
Tel no: (020) 7243 0072
www.firstfloorportobello.co.uk
⊖ Notting Hill Gate
Modern European

A famous Portobello Road destination with a pervading mood of faded bohemian elegance. A crystal chandelier, tall windows and dried flowers set the tone in the first-floor restaurant, which serves on-the-money modern European food with splashes of Mediterranean colour. Truffle Burrata cheese with violet artichokes (£8.50) could lead on to herb-crusted sea bass on fennel confit with cherry tomato caponata (£16.95), while desserts (£6.50) have included amaretti-shaped gnocchi with caramelised peaches and pecan ice cream. The ground-floor bar is a busy daytime pit-stop and late-night clubbing venue, while private rooms on the top floor are pure Gothic fairytale. House wine is £13. Restaurant closed Mon.

▌Paddington
Pearl Liang
Dim sum takes the prize here
8 Sheldon Square, W2 6EZ
Tel no: (020) 7289 7000
www.pearlliang.co.uk
⊖ Paddington
Chinese | £30
Cooking score: 2

£5 OFF **V**

'Ask for directions if you are coming here for the first time' advises a reporter, referring to Pearl Liang's out-of-the-way setting in the 'amphitheatre' of Paddington Basin. Outward appearances aren't arresting, but once inside, the moodily lit bar, friendly waitresses and fuchsia upholstery bid a warm welcome.

Finely prepared Cantonese dim sum is an attractive lunch proposition with a weekday set deal that leaves change from a tenner. Recent highlights have been chicken feet in black bean sauce, ox tripe with ginger and spring onions ('for the adventurous'), or the shredded taro crispy prawn roll. The à la carte offers gutsy five-spice beef shin or pork trotter slices alongside fashionably light lobster sashimi. The 'uneven wine list, punctuated by pricey clarets' starts at £13.80.
Chef/s: Paul Ngo. **Open:** all week 12 to 11. **Closed:** Christmas. **Meals:** Set menus £23, £38 and £68. **Service:** 12.5%. **Details:** Cards accepted. 160 seats. Air-con. Separate bar. Wheelchair access. Music. Children's portions.

▌Shepherd's Bush
Adams Café
Genuine ethnic bargains
77 Askew Road, W12 9AH
Tel no: (020) 8743 0572
⊖ Ravenscourt Park
North African/ Mediterranean | £17
Cooking score: 3

£5 OFF **V**

Over the years, this amazingly unpretentious, jam-packed venue has become one of the benchmarks for genuine North African cooking in the capital. In a colourful setting of Moroccan posters and ethnic artefacts, it offers boldly aromatic dishes with a touch of refinement – all at bargain-basement prices. Seven versions of couscous are the main event, closely challenged by earthy tagines and long-cooked stews (try the version with lamb, prunes, almonds and sultanas); there are also grills and kebabs for those who like their first-class protein in hefty chunks. Start the ball rolling with brik ('fans' of crisp filo pastry with various fillings), grilled merguez sausages or a bowl of harira (Moroccan lentil soup), and finish with sticky sweetmeats or Moroccan-style pancakes doused in honey sauce. The short wine list features some gluggable North African and Middle Eastern stuff, plus a smattering from France. Prices start at £10 (£3 a glass), or you can BYO (£3 corkage).

Chef/s: Sofiene Chahed. **Open:** Mon to Sat D only 7 to 11. **Closed:** Sun, bank hols, Christmas to New Year. **Meals:** Set D £11.50 (1 course) to £16.95. **Service:** 12.5%. **Details:** Cards accepted. 60 seats. Wheelchair access. Music. Children allowed.

Anglesea Arms

Top-notch gastropub
35 Wingate Road, W6 0UR
Tel no: (020) 8749 1291
⊖ Ravenscourt Park
Gastropub | £25
Cooking score: 2

They say don't judge a book by its cover; the unsuspecting would never guess the culinary know-how going on behind the doors of this innocuous-looking gastropub. One reporter, arriving early in the evening, found the tables in the bright exposed brick dining room already occupied with eager customers patiently waiting for the kitchen to open – the result of the no-booking policy. A nod from front-of-house to the open-plan kitchen signalled the start of service and the chefs swung into action, firing out dishes from the blackboard menu. A starter of ham hock terrine and celeriac rémoulade punched flavour. Mains of lamb shank with chorizo, butter bean, kale and cherry tomatoes, and chicken breast, rösti potato, Savoy cabbage and crushed celeriac were both intensely tasty, but slightly overwhelmed by a rich, cloying stock. Dessert was a sinfully rich St Emilion chocolate served with crème fraîche. Prices are on the high side for gastropub food, but friendly, personal service and a comprehensive list boasting over 140 wines to suit all budgets make this a firm local favourite.

Chef/s: Matthew Cranston. **Open:** all week L 12.30 to 3 (Sun 3.30), D 6.30 to 10.30 (Sun and Mon 10). **Meals:** alc (mains £13.50 to £14.95). **Service:** not inc. **Details:** Cards accepted. 40 seats. 18 seats outside. Air-con. Separate bar. No music. Wheelchair access. Children allowed.

Brackenbury

The ideal casual neighbourhood restaurant
129-131 Brackenbury Road, W6 0BQ
Tel no: (020) 8748 0107
www.thebrackenbury.co.uk
⊖ Goldhawk Road
Modern European | £30
Cooking score: 4

A quiet residential street is an unlikely setting for this little gem of a neighbourhood restaurant, which succeeds year after year by delivering simple, seasonal food at fair prices. The split-level dining room is cosy, its casual theme emphasised by polished dark-wood tables, high-backed chairs and cushioned banquettes. The menu changes daily, technical execution is good, and prices are kept down partly through avoiding luxury ingredients. So expect dishes such as smoked eel with cucumber salad and horseradish cream, or a well-timed fillet of brill on a bed of tender Puy lentils with spring onions and a little parsley caper butter. For dessert, lemon and vanilla cheesecake has delivered a pleasingly crumbly biscuit base and a 'tasty filling with firm texture'. The wine list is sensibly organised by style and spans a wide range of countries with fair mark-ups. House wine is £13, or £3.50 a glass.

Open: Sun to Fri L 12.30 to 2.45 (Sun 3.30), Mon to Sat D 7 to 10.45. **Closed:** 1 to 13 Jan. **Service:** 12.5%. **Details:** Cards accepted. 60 seats. 16 seats outside. No music. Children's portions.

Snows on the Green

Fully-grown neighbourhood restaurant
166 Shepherd's Bush Road, W6 7PB
Tel no: (020) 7603 2142
www.snowsonthegreen.co.uk
⊖ Goldhawk Road, Shepherd's Bush
Modern European | £28
Cooking score: 4

A Brook Green favourite since 1990, Sebastian Snow's aptly named restaurant wins friends with its grown-up feel, soft lights and cleverly crafted food. Sebastian clearly knows his stuff and he confidently eschews highfalutin ingredients and fashion-led gestures in favour of big-hearted dishes with a French and Mediterranean slant. His signature starter of foie gras with fried egg and balsamic vinegar seems set to stay, but other ideas come and go. You might see a cassoulette of duck and 'pork bits' alongside eggs 'en meurette', while main courses pump up the generosity and comforting earthiness with, say, seven-hour pot-roast knuckle of lamb with anchovies, wet polenta and pistou or sea bream with saffron mash, blood oranges and spinach. Pasta and risottos are added to the mix, and the choice of puddings could run to caramelised lemon curd tart or chocolate fondant pudding with basil ice cream; also take note of the unpasteurised Italian cheeses served with toasted walnut bread and pickled grapes. The well-chosen wine list has a broad global sweep, with prices starting at £13.50 (£3.75 a glass).

Chef/s: Sebastian Snow. **Open:** Mon to Fri L 12 to 3, Mon to Sat D 6 to 11. **Closed:** Sun, bank hol Mon, 4 days Christmas. **Meals:** alc (main courses £12.50 to £17). Set L and D £13.50 (2 courses) to £16.50. **Service:** 12.5% (optional). **Details:** Cards accepted. 70 seats. 10 seats outside. Air-con. Wheelchair access. Music. Children's portions.

■ South Kensington

★NEW ENTRY★
Ambassade de l'Ile
Bold cooking from an exceptional talent
117-119 Old Brompton Road, SW7 3RN
Tel no: (020) 7373 7774
www.jc-aa.com
⊖ South Kensington
French | £65
Cooking score: no score

This last year has seen a number of leading French chefs (Alain Ducasse, Hélène Darroze) hot footing it to London. The latest to arrive is Jean-Christophe Ansanay-Alex of l'Auberge de l'Ile (l'Ile Barbe, Lyon), though setting up in the ex-Lundum's site in South Kensington instead of Mayfair may seem an odd choice until you realise that this part of London is now the French quarter. The design of the monochromatic dining room is offbeat: thick black carpets, walls padded with white leather, plus flat-screen televisions showing the kitchen at work. An early report of a meal taken during the soft opening – hence no score – was full of praise. Crayfish jelly, partnered with white peach and almond milk saw 'razor sharp' balance and flavour. 'Nearly as brilliant' was l'omble chevalier (a freshwater lake fish from Haut-Savoie – 'a rare treat in London'), perfectly timed with its skin separately deep fried and served with earthy mousseron mushrooms. Lyonnais classics are also given a refreshing spin with plump French quail, painstakingly stuffed with pigeon heart and, for additional magic, a blast of sweet and sour from a varnish of honey and cider vinegar. Not everything worked perfectly as intended, but there is no denying that this is a chef with immense talent and one not afraid to take risks. For dessert, peach soufflé was flawless, petits fours, especially the coffee sablé and hazelnut macaroons, outstanding, and breads, canapés and amuse bouche are first class. The wine list is spread over 38 pages with France holding centre court, but there's good support from the rest of Europe. Prices start high (£25), with many over three figures, but there are some fabulous labels including a page devoted to Domaine de la Romanée Conti.

Chef/s: Jean-Christophe Ansanay-Alex. **Open:** Mon to Sat L 12 to 2, D 7 to 10. **Closed:** Sun. **Meals:** Set menus L £30, D £65 to £90 (5 courses). **Service:** 12.5%. **Details:** Cards accepted. 42 seats. Air-con. Separate bar. Wheelchair access. Children allowed.

Tom Aikens

Why did you become a chef?
My father is a wine dealer so I spent much of my childhood visiting vineyards.

What is the most unusual cookery book you've come across in your life?
'An English Physician'. It was written in 1825 by an English physician who lived on the continent for many years. It's on French domestic cookery, combining economy with elegance - it was the first and only edition.

Do you always read reviews of your restaurant?
Yes, thoroughly - feedback is crucial to a team. If they are not good, we work on it. When they are good, we celebrate!

What era of history would you most like to have eaten in?
I would have liked to have dined with Henry VIII at one of his banquets.

For which recipe will you take the secret to the grave?
My mother's apple crumble - it is truly unique.

Bibendum

Enthralling South Ken icon
Michelin House, 81 Fulham Road, SW3 6RD
Tel no: (020) 7581 5817
www.bibendum.co.uk
⊖ South Kensington
Anglo-French | £44
Cooking score: 4

🍾 V

Since opening its doors as a restaurant during the late '80s, the old Michelin HQ has established its place as one of the most atmospheric and enthralling places to eat in the capital. Visitors can't fail to notice the mosaic-tiled floors and the iconic stained glass windows portraying the M-man in all his inflated glory – not to mention the cityscape views from the first-floor dining room. Unfussy renditions of modern British and French dishes are the kitchen's stock-in-trade, and there's much to enjoy. Middle White brawn with eggs 'au verte' vies for attention with escabèche of mackerel or omelette Arnold Bennett, while main courses offer haddock and chips alongside calf's tongue and boudin noir with braised cabbage and grain mustard. Two can share poulet Bresse with tarragon or roast best end of lamb with Jerusalem artichoke purée and fried garlic, while desserts cover everything from crème brûlée and apple 'tarte fine' to chocolate and peanut parfait. The ground-floor Oyster Bar is ideal for drinks, casual eating and a spot of Sloaney celeb-spotting. Legions of grand French vintages dominate the colossal wine list and there's a generous choice of half-bottles – although the real everyday treasures are the house selections, which offer fine drinking from £17.95 (£4.75 a glass).
Chef/s: Matthew Harris. **Open:** all week L 12 to 2.30 (3 Sat and Sun), D 7 to 11 (10.30 Sun). **Closed:** 24 Dec (D only), 25 and 26 Dec. **Meals:** alc (main courses £17 to £29) Set L £25 (2 courses) to £29.50. Set D Sun £29.50 (3 courses). **Service:** 12.5% (optional). **Details:** Cards accepted. 85 seats. Air-con. Separate bar. No music. No mobile phones. Wheelchair access. Children's portions.

Brasserie St Quentin
Long-running brasserie
243 Brompton Road, SW3 2EP
Tel no: (020) 7589 8005
www.brasseriestquentin.co.uk
⊖ Knightsbridge, South Kensington
French | £27
Cooking score: 3

This well-established Knightsbridge restaurant has the air of an authentic French brasserie, from its Francophile wine list to the classically based menu. Traditionalists can enjoy a starters such as fish soup or sautéed scallops with garlic butter followed by steak, fries and sauce béarnaise or new season Elwy Valley lamb on minted pea purée, perhaps with dauphinoise potatoes and French beans. Other dishes have a more modern edge, possibly thanks to the young kitchen team. A Mediterranean influence informs a starter of linguine with crab, chilli and coriander, while good-value lunchtime options might include spatchcock quail with couscous, rocket and Madeira dressing. Puddings typically include chocolate fondant with burnt orange ice cream, and pineapple carpaccio with banana and passionfruit sorbet. The wine list covers France in loving detail, and includes a few finds from further afield. Bottles start at £14.50.
Chef/s: Gary Durrant. **Open:** all week L 12 to 3, D 6 to 10.30 (10 Sun). **Closed:** 22 to 29 Dec. **Meals:** Set L £18 to £26, alc (main courses L £12.55 to £20.50). **Service:** 12.5%. **Details:** Cards accepted. 55 seats. Air-con. Children allowed.

L'Etranger
France with a difference
36 Gloucester Road, SW7 4QT
Tel no: (020) 7584 1118
www.circagroupltd.co.uk
⊖ Gloucester Road
Modern European | £45
Cooking score: 4

A little enclave of France with a difference, where chefs Jerome Tauvron and Kingshuk Dey's take on grand-mère's classics with Vietnamese and Japanese touches is exciting, successful and certainly superior to much formulaic fusion cooking. Theirs is more East meets West, celebrating at least two of the world's great cuisines. The restaurant is aptly avant garde and sophisticated, the interiors decorated in subtle lilac and grey. The tuna spring rolls are a great starter, but alternatives like Charolais beef tartare, kadafi rolled scallops with ponzu sauce or asparagus and avocado maki make for a delightfully dithery exercise in choice. The shoulder of lamb with ginger-spiced aubergine, the lemongrass-crusted halibut fillet with garlic spinach and the miso-roasted duck breast with coriander butter can all be vouched for as excellent mains. After these riches, desserts are beautifully light: try the white peach soufflé or the blood orange terrine with hazelnut. Service by charming girls and a very knowledgeable young sommelier is immaculate. The list is one of the best in London: many of the top-end premium wines have been bought at auction and gently priced with mark-ups well below West End rates. The collection of vintage and prestige cuvée Champagnes is probably the best in the capital, with a string of fine years from Dom Perignon and Salon in particular.
Chef/s: Jerome Tauvron. **Open:** Mon to Fri and Sun L 12 to 3, all week D 6 to 11 (Sun 6 to 10). **Closed:** Christmas. **Meals:** Set L and early bird £16.50 (2 courses) to £19.50. Brunch £18.50 (2 courses) to £22.50. **Service:** 12.5%. **Details:** Cards accepted. 75 seats. Air-con. Wheelchair access. Music. Children's portions.

Launceston Place

Reborn Kensington stalwart
1A Launceston Place, W8 5RL
Tel no: (020) 7937 6912
www.egami.co.uk
⊖ Gloucester Road
Modern British | £38
Cooking score: 4

Tucked away in an exclusive residential backwater, Launceston Place is 'quintessentially Kensington'. Now part of the D&D group, its once-quirky interior has been homogenised – with neutral caramels, creams and dark grey the various rooms 'have lost of some of their character', but improved comfort levels are compensation. Tristan Welch has been recruited from Pétrus to add a fine-dining edge to the cooking, and his menu of luxury ingredients – foie gras, Oscietra caviar, rose veal – as well as amuse-bouche and pre-desserts, means expectations are great. Highlights of a June meal included an amuse of tomato consommé with a cucumber foam, and a starter of roast duck foie gras with rhubarb compote and elderflower soup, but much of the cooking lacked cohesion. Cornish mackerel on toast with green tomatoes and Cambridge sauce, for example, 'lacked flavour', a comment that has featured in other reports. On the plus side, the set lunch menu is good value, delivering well-reported free-range chicken with broccoli and Jersey Royals and caramel parfait with blood orange mousse. The diverse wine list, kicking off from £16.50, is both interesting and affordable.
Chef/s: Tristan Welch. **Open:** Tue to Sun L 12 to 2.30 (3 Sun), D 6.30 to 10.30. **Closed:** Mon. **Meals:** Set L £19 (2 courses) to £24, Set D £37.50, Tasting menu £48. **Service:** 12.5%. **Details:** Cards accepted. 60 seats. Separate bar. Wheelchair access. Children's portions.

▌Westbourne Park
The Ledbury

Innovative ideas and sound techniques
127 Ledbury Road, W11 2AQ
Tel no: (020) 7792 9090
www.theledbury.com
⊖ Westbourne Park
Modern European | £50
Cooking score: 6
🍷 V

The Ledbury's airy dining room with a small terrace outside (ideal for summer evenings) is as well turned out as its chic clientele. The modern European repertoire fits in perfectly, underpinned by classical themes and well-sourced produce. Adventurous ideas are enhanced on the plate by skilful cooking, fine presentations and interesting variations of flavour and texture. For example, a Douglas Fir infusion adds a modish twist to a delicate loin of roe deer and sweet potato, and fillet of John Dory is steamed with ras el hanout, the north African spice blend lifting the distinctive flavour of the fish without overpowering it, and a garnish of crab and pine nuts adds a welcome crisp texture contrast. The occasional slip (some mis-timing at inspection), slightly lets the side down, but is mercifully rare; in general, the kitchen delivers 'fantastic food'. Cheeses are carefully sourced and in ripe condition, and desserts are a strong suit, offering the likes of frozen yoghurt parfait topped with excellent and ultra-seasonal Alphonso mangoes (only available for about a month around May). Service has been praised this year, but at times it can seem a little over-intrusive. The wine list is extensive and well thought out, with excellent growers from both Old and New World, at acceptable mark-ups.
Chef/s: Brett Graham. **Open:** Mon to Sat L 12 to 2.30, D 6.30 to 10.30; Sun L 12 to 2.45, D 6.30 to 10. **Closed:** Christmas, Boxing Day, New Year and Notting Hill Carnival. **Service:** 12.5% optional. **Details:** 60 seats. 30 seats outside. Air-con. No music. Wheelchair access. Children allowed.

★NEW ENTRY★

Urban Turban

Mumbai street food, tapas-style
98 Westbourne Grove, W2 5RU
Tel no: (020) 7243 4200
⊖ Royal Oak, Bayswater, Queensway
Indian | £25
Cooking score: 2

 £30

Urban Turban is Vineet Bhatia's prototype for a chain of street food eateries, the corner site delivering huge windows and a spacious interior of banquettes and mirrors, dominated by a huge central bar. Bhatia's cooking style (see Rasoi Vineet Bhatia, Chelsea) has always shown great respect for his roots in traditional Indian regional cooking. The result here is a menu that kicks off with collection of tapas-style dishes inspired by Mumbai street food, including such highlights as 'gun powder' prawns and home-smoked honey and mustard tandoori salmon with cucumber dill raita. 'Classic helpings' are more substantial dishes – spicy prawn masala with coriander and lemon, say, or lamb biryani. Breads are delicious and desserts include crispy samosas filled with coconut, almonds and raisins alongside a stunning star anise ice cream. House wines from £16.

Chef/s: Satish Shenow. **Open:** Sat to Sun L 12.30 to 3.30, all week D 6 to 11. **Meals:** alc (tapas £6, main courses £6 to £12). **Service:** 12.5% (optional). **Details:** Cards accepted. 120 seats. Air-con. Separate bar. Wheelchair access. Music. Children's portions.

ALSO RECOMMENDED

▲ Cow Dining Room

89 Westbourne Park Road, Westbourne Park, W2 5QH
Tel no: (020) 7221 0021
www.thecowlondon.co.uk
⊖ Royal Oak
British

Re-invented London pub meets neighbourhood bistro in Tom Conran's zippy conversion of a Bayswater boozer. The ground-floor 'saloon bar' is a one of the best spots in town for plates of oysters and pints of Guinness, but things take a serious turn in the upstairs dining room. Evening menus keep the punters happy with interesting food that doesn't try to be flash: expect 'fruits de mer' and starters such as jellied pork and piccalilli (£8) followed by pasta and, say, sea trout with brown shrimps and samphire (£21). Strawberry crème brûlée (£6) is a typical sweet. Wines from £13.75. The dining room is open Sat and Sun L and all week D.

READERS RECOMMEND

Lucky 7

American
127 Westbourne Park Road, Westbourne Park, W2 5QL
Tel no: (020) 7727 6771
www.lucky7london.co.uk
'Tip-top burgers and shakes'

Barnes

Sonny's

Well-run neighbourhood restaurant
94 Church Road, SW13 0DQ
Tel no: (020) 8748 0393
www.sonnys.co.uk
⊖ Hammersmith
Modern European | £25
Cooking score: 3

Sonny's bears all the hallmarks of a well-run neighbourhood restaurant. Over the past years there's been a reasonably high turnover of chefs and management, but the changes seem not to affect the standards of service and food and the very local, regular clientele keep on coming. They're particularly comfortable with the current chef, Owen Kenworthy, because he's worked here for some time, stepping up from the role of sous chef. His seasonal menu offers good, classic cooking with an emphasis on Britishness. This is a place to eat English asparagus in season, or Shetland mussels with cream and white wine, followed by poached spring chicken with petit pois or gilthead bream with cockle consommé, and Colston Bassett Stilton with poached pear to finish. For a well-to-do restaurant in a smart neighbourhood, the à la carte menu is kindly priced; the tempting set menus and a well-thought out wine list starting at £3.50 a glass make it even more so. NB As we went to print, a major refurb was due for September 2008.
Chef/s: Owen Kenworthy. **Open:** all week L 12 to 4, Mon to Sat D 7 to 11. **Closed:** bank hols. **Meals:** Set L £13.50 (2 courses) to £15.50, Set D £17 (2 courses) to £21. **Service:** 12.5%. **Details:** Cards accepted. 100 seats. Air-con. Children's portions.

Chiswick

Fish Hook

A fine catch in Chiswick
6-8 Elliott Road, W4 1PE
Tel no: (020) 8742 0766
www.fishhook.co.uk
⊖ Turnham Green
Seafood | £29
Cooking score: 2

The unambiguous name should leave you in doubt that seafood is the kitchen's passion in this uncluttered Chiswick restaurant. Chef/proprietor Michael Nadra casts his net far and wide, and the result is a bonanza of ideas that could run from steamed Shetland mussels with cream, Pernod and smoked ham hock to glazed smoked eel with a potato and shallot pancake. He is also tuned to the market and the seasons, so the haul might include crisp sea bass with buttered courgettes and crab ravioli, monkfish with spätzli and roasted Jerusalem artichokes plus a cassoulet of octopus, pollack and slow-roast belly pork. A couple of extras are added to assuage those who don't fancy fish (perhaps goats' cheese salad or fillet steak with shiitake mushrooms and mash), while desserts such as tarte Tatin with cinnamon and Calvados ice cream provide a sweet-toothed finale. Appropriate whites claim pole position on the well-spread wine list; expect prices from £14.75 (£3.75 a glass).
Chef/s: Michael Nadra. **Open:** all week L 12 to 2.30 (3.30 Sat and Sun), D 6 to 10.30 (10 Sun). **Closed:** Christmas. **Meals:** alc (main courses £16). Set L £12.50 (2 courses) to £15. **Service:** 12.5%. **Details:** Cards accepted. 54 seats. Air-con. Wheelchair access. Music. Children's portions.

Sam's Brasserie and Bar

All-singing, all-dancing favourite
11 Barley Mow Passage, W4 4PH
Tel no: (020) 8987 0555
www.samsbrasserie.co.uk
⊖ Chiswick Park, Turnham Green
Modern European | £26
Cooking score: 3

V

Sam Harrison is the Sam in question, one-time general manager of Rick Stein's Padstow empire. He opened this buzzy, relaxed, young-at-heart brasserie in a former paper factory in 2005 – it's been divided into a dining area with smaller mezzanine level, an open-to-view kitchen and a big bar area. Large oval lampshades, banquette seating or chairs and plain lightwood tables fill the dining area and soften those hard industrial edges. Majoring in affordability and flexibility, it's an open all-day, every-day from breakfast operation. The crowd-pleasing menu changes twice daily for lunch and dinner, delivering straightforward modern European dishes along the lines of line-caught red mullet served with risotto Nero and chive butter or sirloin steak with chips and béarnaise sauce. Desserts include the likes of lemongrass pannacotta with a mango and lime compote. There's a good-value fixed-price lunch offering too, while wines are an equally pleasing fashionable concern, with plenty by-the-glass and 500ml carafe. Bottles start from £13.50. (See entry for sister brasserie Harrison's in Balham).

Chef/s: Ian Leckie. **Open:** all week L 12 to 3 (4 Sat and Sun), D 6.30 to 10.30 (10 Sun). **Closed:** 24 Dec to 26 Dec. **Meals:** alc (main courses £9 to £17.50). Set L £12 (2 courses) to £15, set D £14 (2 courses) to £17. **Service:** 12.5%. **Details:** Cards accepted. 100 seats. Air-con. Separate bar. Music. Children's portions.

★NEW ENTRY★
The Devonshire

Ramsay's pub formula rolls on
126 Devonshire Road, W4 2JJ
Tel no: (020) 7592 7962
www.gordonramsay.com
⊖ Turnham Green
Gastropub | £26
Cooking score: 2

The good folk of Chiswick seem to have been spoiled of late, with a host of new openings along the High Street. This time, the Ramsay roadshow rolls into the backstreets of town in the form of another gastropub to add to his ever-burgeoning stable. A dark wood, traditional pub has been given a cosmetic overhaul to create a standard bar area with comfy chairs, and an austere dining room. The menu is formulaic, echoing Ramsay's first gastropub outing with the Narrow and his latest offering the Warrington in Maida Vale (see entries). At inspection, starters included potted Morecambe Bay shrimps with granary toast (the bread being decidedly ordinary) and a home-made pork pie with piccalilli. Stone bass with Savoy cabbage, bacon and pickled cockles was well-executed, but very plain. The Hereford beef in ale pie with mash was altogether more succesful, with melt-in-the-mouth pastry and a deep, heart-warming sauce. Desserts are a traditional affair, with the likes of bread-and-butter pudding with custard making an appearance. Prices reflect the simplicity of the menu and the low-key setting. House wines start at £13.50, rising to £75 for a Château Grand Puy Lacoste.

Chef/s: Mark Sergeant. **Open:** all week L 11.30 to 3 (12 to 4 Sat and Sun), D 6 to 11 (5 to 10.30 Sat and Sun). **Meals:** alc (main courses from £12 to £16). **Service:** 12.5%. **Details:** Cards accepted. 42 seats. 20 seats outside. Separate bar. Music. Children's portions.

Child-friendly dining

At long last, parents are finding it easier to bring their little ones along to try decent restaurants.

Evesham Hotel, Evesham
This Georgian hotel has been in the same family since 1975, and the owners have a wonderfully relaxed attitude to children. There's a bespoke junior à la carte, penned in a determined hand by several Jenkinson grandchildren, offering good things like chicken and pasta served with fresh vegetables. And (a good idea, this) prices vary with the size of portion/age of the kids.

Gallery Café, Manchester
This lunch spot has revitalised the Whitworth Gallery's atmosphere. Peter Booth cooks from a tiny kitchen facing onto a sunny yellow room hung with a changing selection of artwork. The menu is simple, cheerful and exactly what's required.

There's an emphasis on seasonal, local produce, with a chart on the wall indicating what's in season, and kids get a fresh, appealing menu and a gallery resource kit for £5. No cards, but cheques are accepted.

Hanson at the Chelsea Restaurant, Swansea
Tucked down a side street in the heart of Swansea's wining and dining district, this smart little restaurant has a tranquil, personal feel far removed from the bustle of the city centre. Children are given an excellent welcome and their own menu offering appealing homemade dishes such as soup of the day, toad-in-the-hole with gravy and mash, or fresh cod in batter with hand cut chips.

Inn the Park, London
Overlooking the lake in St James's Park and open all day, from breakfast and elevenses through to lunch, afternoon tea and dinner, there can be few finer places to eat on a summer's day. An ideal place for kids to let off steam in the park before tucking into their very own menu of organic salmon and smoked haddock fishcakes with spinach or roast chicken breast with carrots, followed by ice cream or Victoria sponge sandwich with strawberry sauce.

J Baker's Bistro Moderne, York
Jeff Baker came to York with a red-hot CV and in two years his Bistro Moderne has become a red-hot ticket. The atmosphere is laid-back, relaxed and fun, perfect for making kids feel welcome, so it's good that he's mindful of the needs of families and delivers an intelligent children's menu (think cheese omelette, or bangers and mash and knickerbocker glory).

La Trompette

Neighbourhood gem with stellar food
5-7 Devonshire Road, W4 2EU
Tel no: (020) 8747 1836
www.latrompette.co.uk
⊖ Turnham Green
French | £38
Cooking score: 6

For Chiswick devotees, La Trompette is a neighbourhood bolthole 'par excellence': it's forever packed (with crowds often spilling out onto the pavement tables on fine evenings), but service always seems to run along steadily. For others, it is a hotly sought-after destination restaurant that oozes cordial understated luxury and delivers top-end food with a pronounced southern French accent. The kitchen's take on tuna niçoise is a dazzler involving green bean and caper vinaigrette, tapenade, sauce vierge and quails' eggs, but there are also other full-blooded seasonal treats to start the ball rolling (boudin blanc with spinach, Madeira sauce and pistachios, for example). A seam of seasonality teases its way through the menu, witness fillet of turbot with white asparagus, crushed charlotte potatoes, surf clams and chive oil or slow-cooked shoulder of lamb which needs nothing more elaborate than some creamed spuds and glazed spring vegetables. The sheer accuracy of James Bennington's cooking is remarkable and his spot-on flavours seldom fail to impress: as one reader noted 'there was no salt and pepper on the tables and no need for it either.' Puddings are headed by 'the most amazing tarte Tatin', although it's also worth considering the palate-cleansing possibilities of iced lime parfait with mango sorbet and passion fruit. Cheese 'from the board' fully merits its modest £5 supplement and superb home-baked breads deserve a special mention. La Trompette's glorious 600-bin wine list is a real thriller – an Aladdin's cave of fabulous bottles drawn from France's elite regional vineyards, plus all manner of gems cherry-picked from unlikely corners of the globe (Slovenia and Uruguay included). Prices start at £18 (£4.50 a glass).
Chef/s: James Bennington. **Open:** all week L 12 to 2.30, D 6.30 to 10.30. **Closed:** 25 and 26 Dec, 1 Jan. **Meals:** Set L £23.50. Set D £37.50. **Service:** 12.5% (optional). **Details:** Cards accepted. 70 seats. 16 seats outside. Air-con. Separate bar. No music. Wheelchair access. Children's portions.

Le Vacherin

A little bit of Paris in Chiswick
76-77 South Parade, W4 5LF
Tel no: (020) 8742 2121
www.levacherin.co.uk
⊖ Turnham Green
French | £35
Cooking score: 4

Few places in London feel as though they could have been transplanted directly from Paris, but Le Vacherin, looking out on to a quiet, leafy road in Chiswick, 'makes you feel like you are in an old Parisian bistro'. The menu itself has branched out a bit though. Wild sea trout with crushed peas and mint, or pappardelle with courgette flowers, broad beans, aged Parmesan and lemon hardly sound traditional, but there are still escargots de bourgongne, rock oysters with shallot vinegar and duck confit with endive tarte Tatin. The food, pronounced 'simple but excellent, the portions are just right' by one reporter, has seen both 28-day aged châteaubriand with roast bone marrow and côte de boeuf with sauce béarnaise praised this year. Good side dishes include crisp, salty frites and creamed spinach. The signature dish (although available only in its season – November to February), is the soft mountain cheese after which the place is named. Finish with île flottante or a tarte fine of figs. Service is friendly and attentive. The all-French wine list offers good value with house wines from the south-west at £15.50.
Chef/s: Malcolm John. **Open:** Tue to Sun L 12 to 3, (4 Sun), all week D 6 to 10 (10.30 Fri and Sat). **Closed:** bank hols. **Meals:** alc (main courses £12 to £18.95).

Set menus £23 to £35. **Service:** 12.5%.
Details: Cards accepted. 70 seats. Air-con.
Wheelchair access. Music.

ALSO RECOMMENDED
▲ Budsara
99 Chiswick High Road, Chiswick, W4 2ED
Tel no: (020) 8995 5774
Thai

Owned by a family that used to run a local
Thai supermarket, this friendly Chiswick
newcomer (on the site of the Thai Bistro)
offers a simple menu of authentic staples
in tasteful modern surroundings. Standout
dishes from the familiar repertoire have
included classic tom yum goong soup (£5.95),
boldly-spiced nam tok goong salad (£5.95)
and sea bass with punchy red curry paste
(£9.95). Incidentals such as pad Thai noodles
are also up to the mark. House wine is £12.50
a bottle, although Singha Thai beer is probably
a better bet. Open all week.

▌Croydon

★NEW ENTRY★
Le Cassoulet
Great new local in the suburbs
18 Upper Selsdon Road, CR2 6PA
Tel no: (020) 8633 1818
www.lecassoulet.co.uk
French | £35
Cooking score: 3

Le Cassoulet is the epitome of what the
English think a local French bistro should be –
well-upholstered seats with plenty of dark red
and gold, sweet but efficient Anglo/French
service and a roll-call of France's greatest hits
for a menu: frogs' legs, moules marinière, foie
gras, oysters and snails all get a look-in, while
mains include chateaubriand, blanquette de
veau and the house speciality, cassoulet. It's a
familiar, nostalgic type of cuisine, but happily
the kitchen knows what it's doing – this is the
second restaurant of chef Malcolm John, who
has proved in his Chiswick restaurant Le

Vacherin (see entry) that he can cook to please
a well-to-do local clientele (who seem to have
taken it upon themselves to discover the
place). Portions are on the generous side,
rendering the classic, rather dull puddings
redundant, but the impressive cheeseboard is
hard to ignore. Wines are, of course, French,
with a commendable number served by-the-
glass and 500ml pichet. Starting at £3.60 a
glass, with plenty under £20, there's also
enough scope at the top end for locals on a big
night out.
Chef/s: Philip Amponsa. **Open:** all week L 12 to 3, D
6 to 10.30 (Fri and Sat 11). **Closed:** 25 and 26 Dec, 1
Jan. **Meals:** alc (main courses £12.50 to £20). Set L
£16.50, set Sun L £19.50. **Service:** 12.5%.
Details: Cards accepted. 60 seats. Air-con.
Wheelchair access. Music. Children allowed.

▌Forest Hill
Babur
Ethnic art meets Indian innovation
119 Brockley Rise, SE23 1JP
Tel no: (020) 8291 2400
www.babur.info
Indian | £25
Cooking score: 2

'Art is integral to Babur,' say the owners, who
have dropped the word 'brasserie' from
their restaurant name following an eye-
catching refit. Visitors can now marvel at
striking hand-woven 'kantha' table runners,
'kalamkari' dyed fabrics and antique print
blocks before perusing the menu. The kitchen
has a deep affection for the traditions of Indian
regional cooking, but it isn't afraid to bring on
board unexpected ingredients such as
ostrich in its search for innovation. Clove-
smoked cutlets of Yorkshire deer are seasoned
with rock salt and fennel seeds, spicy rounds
of paneer tikka are filled with papaya and
pumpkin chutney, while black cod is served
with mustard mash. Elsewhere, Kerala
provides dry-fried lamb with tomato rice,
tandoori-roasted beef ribs are simmered with
Goan spices, and pickle-spiced baby
aubergines are accompanied by masala upma

(Indian couscous). Light lunches are good value, while Sunday heralds a leisurely family buffet that runs well into the afternoon. The wine list has been thoughtfully tailored to suit the food; prices start at £13.50.

Chef/s: Jiwan Lal and Enam Rahman. **Open:** all week L 12 to 2.30 (4 Sun), D 6 to 11.30. **Closed:** 26 Dec. **Meals:** alc (main courses £9 to £13.50). Sun buffet L £10.95. **Service:** not inc. **Details:** Cards accepted. 72 seats. Air-con. Wheelchair access. Music. Children allowed.

▌Hackney

Empress of India

Useful all-day operation
130 Lauriston Road, E9 7LH
Tel no: (020) 8533 5123
www.theempressofindia.com
Gastropub | £30
Cooking score: 3

Located in a handsome former florist's shop, the Empress of India is a useful all-day operation, open for breakfast, afternoon tea, brunch or a full three-course dinner. Part of Tom and Ed Martin's gastropub empire, it resembles a Parisian brasserie with its unusual mussel shell chandeliers, tiled floor and bright red banquettes. The dinner menus are pitched somewhere between bistro and fine-dining: grilled seabass fillet with pommes purée, braised kale and crayfish butter, or fricassee of rabbit and tarragon with creamed leeks and brown rice. Produce is good, though sometimes one too many flavours sneaks on to the plate. Rotisserie dishes like chicken or Hereford steak have the edge by virtue of their simplicity. The varietally-organised wine list starts at £13, and there's a good selection of draught beers. Our questionnaire was not returned, so some of the information below may have changed.

Chef/s: Tim Wilson. **Open:** Mon to Fri L 12 to 2.30 (Sat 12 to 10), D 7 to 10. **Closed:** 25 and 26 Dec. **Meals:** alc (main caourses £9./50 to £15.50). **Details:** Cards accepted. 60 seats. 35 seats outside. Air-con. Wheelchair access. Music. Children's portions.

ALSO RECOMMENDED

▲ Buen Ayre

Broadway Market, Hackney, E8 4QJ
Tel no: (020) 7275 9900
www.buenayre.co.uk
Argentinian

At the heart of Broadway Market (the new Borough, don't you know), lies this rustic and austere Argentinian steak house. Revolutionary posters line the walls of a small room filled with tiny wooden tables and chairs. Old-fashioned trombone and piano music adds to the traditional vibe. You will be met with brusque service, with a huge bias towards the Argentinian meat on the menu. (We dare you to try to order the French veal and escape without reproach.) However, the attitude is simply a result of their huge pride in Argentinian produce, and the atmosphere is actually low-key and friendly. Start with empanadas to (£4.50) and move on to succulent steaks (£15 to £18.50), all served with a side salad of roast peppers, leaves and toasted seeds. To finish, the flan casero is perfect comfort food (£4). House wines start at £11.80, or £3.30 a glass.

READERS RECOMMEND

Namo

Vietnamese
178 Victoria Park Road, Hackney, E9 7HD
Tel no: (020) 8533 0639
www.namo.co.uk
'Canteen cooking with a contemporary feel'

Symbols	
🛏	Accommodation is available.
£30	Three courses for less than £30.
V	More than five vegetarian dishes.
£5 OFF	£5-off voucher scheme.
🍾	Notable wine list.

▮ Harrow-on-the-Hill

★NEW ENTRY★

Incanto

High-brow dining on the hill
41 High Street, HA1 3HT
Tel no: (020) 8426 6767
www.incanto.co.uk
⊖ Harrow-on-the-Hill
Italian | £30
Cooking score: 2

Harrow-on-the-Hill has always attracted a well-heeled set by virtue of the close proximity of Harrow School. The sleek, modern restaurant is housed in a Grade II listed building that has been lovingly restored, and there's a deli section at the front. On the food front, much is imported from Italy, but in season the kitchen uses herbs and salads from its own garden. Dishes are well executed and while portions have been found to be small, and prices relatively high for the area, this does not seem to have deterred the locals – Incanto is packed most weekends. At inspection, service was 'arch and verging on pretentious', with waiters serving salt and checking on the table to the point of irritation. However, a rack of lamb served with Jersey Royal potatoes and beetroot purée was both hearty and delicate at one and the same time. Desserts were a mixed bag, with a trio of apples – in a tartlet, as pie ice cream and in a crumble roll with pistachio – arriving slightly overdone and in tiny portions, more appealing was bread-and-butter pannetone. The wine list is predominantly Italian with house wine starting at £13.90.

Chef/s: Franco Montone. **Open:** Tue to Sat L 12 to 2.30, D 6.30 to 10.30, Sun 12.30 to 4. **Closed:** Mon. **Meals:** alc (mains £13.75 to £17). **Service:** 10%. **Details:** Cards accepted. 60 seats. Air-con. Wheelchair access. Music. Children's portions.

▮ Kew

Glasshouse

A great all rounder
14 Station Parade, TW9 3PZ
Tel no: (020) 8940 6777
www.glasshouserestaurant.co.uk
⊖ Kew Gardens
British | £38
Cooking score: 5

Destination quality restaurants on the South West perimeter of London are few and far between. As part of the Nigel Platts-Martin/Bruce Poole group of restaurants, Glasshouse gets everything so right, seemingly so effortlessly, that one wonders why so many other restaurants get it so wrong. In keeping with the name, the outside glass walls of the triangular room let sunlight flood the room during the day; in the evening, clever lighting and well-placed frosting allow for intimacy and privacy. Anthony Boyd's cooking is not flash or clever, just very good. The menu, which follows a set-price formula, is tweaked daily and quality is a constant: a duck salad with balsamic dressing, for example, is given extra dimension with the addition of a deep-fried truffled egg, while grilled halibut with brandade and aïoli and provençale vegetables is a combination of flavour and texture that evokes summer. Beautiful versions of old-fashioned puddings like lemon posset with blueberry compote, and vanilla yoghurt with poached rhubarb are almost enough to divert customers away from the superb cheeseboard. Sommelier Emmanuel Hardonnière presides over the 500-strong list and he delights in leading customers to the right choice for the occasion. Starting at £15 per bottle, and with over 30 wines by-the-glass, those on a budget needn't fear.

Chef/s: Anthony Boyd. **Open:** all week L 12 to 2.30 (Sun 3), D 6.30 to 10.30, (Sun 7). **Closed:** 24 to 26 Dec, 1 Jan. **Meals:** Set L £23 (Mon to Fri), £25 (Sat) £29.50 (Sun), Set D £37.50. **Service:** 12.5% (optional). **Details:** Cards accepted. 65 seats. Air-con. Children's portions.

ALSO RECOMMENDED

▲ Ma Cuisine

9 Station Approach, Kew, TW9 3QB
Tel no: (020) 83321923
www.macuisinekew.co.uk
⊖ Kew
French

Decent French country cuisine is served at this staunchly Gallic restaurant run by John McClements. With checked cloths on close-packed tables, black and white chequered floor and Toulouse Lautrec posters on pale yellow walls, it conjures up a traditional view of the French bistro, as does a menu which features skate rillette (£4.50) or assiette charcuterie (£5) to start, and mains of confit rabbit leg (£12.50) and steak tartare (£17.50). Equally traditional are desserts of crème brûlée (£4.50) and crêpes suzette (£4.95). The good-value French wine list starts at £12.50. Open all week. A branch of Ma Cuisine is at 6 Whitton Road, Twickenham.

▐ Richmond

★NEW ENTRY★
Bingham Hotel

Romantic river views and seriously good food
61-63 Petersham Road, TW10 6UT
Tel no: (020) 8940 0902
www.binghamhotel.co.uk
Modern British | £35
Cooking score: 5

This boutique hotel makes the most of a couple of Georgian townhouses, giving the old grand entertaining spaces over to a very attractive bar and restaurant. The outside terraces looking over the well-kept garden to the river beyond are immensely popular in summer, but the new look of the rich gold and straw colours of the interior, with chic chairs and sofas makes a beguiling backdrop to dinner when the weather is less clement. In charge of the kitchen is Shay Cooper – a man with ambition and the culinary ability to back

it up. A starter of artichoke salad, cep marmalade, baby leaves and truffle hollandaise was a stunning combination, unadvertised shavings of summer truffle taking it to a higher plain of extravagance, while the disparate flavours of lemon sole, spiced lentils and seared scallop were brought together with an orange juice-laced vinaigrette. A main course dish of rack of lamb with spiced aubergine arrived with its own pot of sweet, long-braised lamb shoulder; a dish of saddleback pork, offering a selection of porcine cuts, was given a quirkiness with the addition of smoked potato. Puddings are as showy as the savoury courses: lemon parfait with shortbread and gin and tonic sorbet, cheesecake with fig ripple ice cream and Earl Grey jelly. This being a dining room that sees itself going places, the wine list is long and impressive, but there are a fair number of wines by-the-glass (starting at £4.50) and carafe as well as one or two bottles under £20.
Chef/s: Shay Cooper. **Open:** all week L 12 to 2.30 (4 Sun), Mon to Sat D 7 to 10. **Meals:** alc (main courses £14 to £21). Set L £19.50 (2 courses) to £23. **Service:** 12.5%. **Details:** Cards accepted. 38 seats. 10 seats outside. Air-con. Separate bar. Wheelchair access. Children's portions. Car parking.

La Buvette

French bistro drawing the crowds
6 Church Walk, TW9 1SN
Tel no: (020) 8940 6264
www.brula.co.uk
French | £27
Cooking score: 3

£30

On the face of it, this is a strange place to have a reasonably smart French bistro – attached to a municipal church hall with with no parking, no vehicular access and precious little signage, it looks more like an olde worlde tea-room. There are plenty of outdoor tables, but the interior lacks charm and is badly lit. But such is the reputation of owners Lawrence Hartley and Bruce Duckett, (who also run Brula Bistrot in St Margaret's, Twickenham, see entry), that Richmond locals flocked to it when it opened four years ago and a steady stream have been coming back ever since. They come partly for the familiarity of the menu – a rustic fish soup with rouille and Gruyère, and ballottine of foie gras with Armagnac jelly always feature among first courses, onglet with garlic butter, chips and salad on the mains – and partly because the pricing is gentle, the cooking dependable, and the service charming and friendly. With less than 50 wines, the all-French list still has plenty of well-known names and finds plenty of scope for unusual gems; at around £3 for house wine it's very kindly priced.

Chef/s: Bruce Duckett and Buck Carter. **Open:** all week L 12 to 3, D 6 to 10.30. **Closed:** 25 and 26 Dec, 1 Jan, Good Fri. **Meals:** alc exc Sun L (main courses £10 to £18.75). **Service:** 12.5% (optional). **Details:** Cards accepted. 50 seats. 30 seats outside. No music. Wheelchair access. Children's portions.

★NEW ENTRY★
Café Strudel
Authentic Viennese cuisine in East Sheen
Upper Richmond Road, SW14 7PJ
Tel no: (020) 8487 9800
www.caféstrudel.co.uk
⊖ Richmond
Viennese | £35
Cooking score: 3

It's often said that you can judge a restaurant by the quality of its bread – and the dense, wondrously complex sourdough served at this unassuming Viennese restaurant-cum-coffee-house in East Sheen speaks volumes. The coffee is outstanding, too, and the cakes are to die for. The ambience is welcoming and informal – don't hesitate to drop in for a *kleiner brauner* and a slice of *sachertorte* on your way back from the supermarket – but the quality of the dishes on the dinner menu, and the calibre of the suppliers printed proudly alongside them, point to a serious approach in the kitchen. To start, perhaps, a gratinated globe artichoke stuffed with mushroom duxelles and a mound of fresh salad, or chilled cucumber soup spiked with vodka, served with a stridently flavoured tomato sorbet and

topped with lacy fronds of chervil. Main-course dishes breathe new life into authentic Viennese classics – to wit, a textbook rendition of *Wiener schnitzel* with lamb's lettuce and buttery mashed potato, and a gutsy, rich goulash featured meltingly tender chunks of well-flavoured beef, a crisp parsnip rösti and an impressively crafted stuffed potato dumpling. One of the best Austrian wine lists in Britain runs the gamut of native grape varietals (including such rarities as dry Furmint) and name-checks interesting producers like Jamek and Heidi Schrock. Prices are fair, but start at a relatively steep £17 a bottle.

Chef/s: Yacine Benghazal. **Open:** Tue to Sat 10 to 12, Sun 10 to 4. **Closed:** Mon. **Service:** Not inc. **Details:** Cards accepted. 40 seats. 10 seats outside. Wheelchair access. Music. Children allowed.

Petersham Nurseries Café
Wonderful food in a magical setting
Church Lane, off Petersham Road, TW10 7AG
Tel no: (020) 8605 3627
www.petershamnurseries.com
⊖ Richmond
Modern British | £45
Cooking score: 4

Ten minutes by taxi from the nearest train station, five on foot from the bus stop, no parking to speak of – the idea that this 'café' tucked into the back of a large greenhouse down the end of a no-through lane should enjoy any success at all is theoretically impossible. But such is the beguiling combination of the shabby-chic setting and Skye Gyngell's cooking that tables are hard to come by, even in the winter months. Gyngell is a great champion of fresh, local food and many of her salads and herbs are grown in the surrounding nursery. The short, daily-changing menu has less choice as lunchtime progresses, but typical in spring months are globe artichokes with speck, buffalo mozzarella and marjoram salmoriglio, with monkfish, clams, with roasted almonds, rosemary and aïoli to follow – beautifully presented, generously portioned and steeply

priced. The wine list has improved over the years and now offers a decent if short selection, but most of the ladies who lunch here stick to the likes of elderflower cordial. Service, though amazingly sweet and good-natured, should be better.
Chef/s: Skye Gyngell. **Open:** Tue to Sun L 12 to 3. **Meals:** alc (main courses £16 to £25). **Service:** 12.5% (optional). **Details:** Cards accepted. 80 seats. Wheelchair access. Children allowed.

Restaurant at the Petersham Hotel
Classic, well-executed cooking
Nightingale Lane, TW10 6UZ
Tel no: (020) 8940 7471
www.petershamhotel.co.uk
Modern British | £38
Cooking score: 4

The restaurant in this grown-up hotel has one of the finest rural vistas in Greater London, overlooking the legally protected view of grazing cows in Petersham Meadow, the river and its boats meandering beyond. It gives the restaurant a timeless peacefulness that makes it difficult to believe that it is only five minutes from the centre of Richmond. Alex Bentley's cooking has softened over his four-year tenure – gone are the showy sauces and finishes, replaced by good-quality ingredients, served the way the clientele want it rather than the way the chef necessarily would choose. But it's not all smoked salmon and fillet steak with béarnaise sauce: a terrine of foie gras is given a savoury gaminess with the addition of hare and smoked bacon, Jabugo ham lends a meatiness to a dish of grilled monkfish wittily finished with a scattering of crispy spinach. Puddings are familiar fare (crème brûlée, marble chocolate cheesecake) and there are some intriguing dessert wines to match – the Austrian Trockenbeerenauslese seems remarkable value at £8.50 a glass and £29.50 per 375cl bottle. Otherwise the Bordeaux-heavy list delivers a good selection of half-bottles from house wine standard (£9.50) to 1996 Chateau Kirwan 3eme cru (£34.00).

Chef/s: Alex Bentley. **Open:** all week L 12.15 to 2 (12.30 to 2.45 Sun), D 7 to 9.30 (8.30 Sun). **Meals:** Set L £18.50 (2 courses) to £25, Sun L £31.50. **Service:** 10%. **Details:** Cards accepted. 80 seats. Air-con. Separate bar. Children's portions. Car parking.

ALSO RECOMMENDED
▲ Chez Lindsay
11 Hill Rise, Richmond, TW10 6UQ
Tel no: (020) 8948 7473
www.chezlindsay.co.uk
French

A great local with a laid back attitude, the sunniness of the bright yellow room helps one overlook the scruffiness of the furnishings and at the back there's an excellent view of Richmond Bridge and the Thames. The menu reflects chef proprietor Lindsay Wotton's passion for all things Breton, from seafood and galettes (from £3.50) to cream and cider – here served traditionally in earthenware cups. The seafood platter (from £15.75) is one of the best-value in London. Follow with old-fashioned chicken breast with Calvados cream sauce (£12.95). Set menus at lunch (£9.75) and evening (£16.50) help keep the cost down and the restaurant full. House wine is £14.95. Open all week.

▮ Southall
Brilliant
Southall's royal favourite
72-76 Western Road, UB2 5DZ
Tel no: (020) 8574 1928
www.brilliantrestaurant.com
⊖ Southall
Indian | £23
Cooking score: 3

The Anand brothers' seminal Southall evergreen has no truck with the fashion-led fusion flaunted by some 'new wave' Indian restaurants in the capital. Opened as a 36-seater, it continues to evolve and now boasts all mod cons from karaoke to plasma screens

showing Bollywood films. The menu doesn't change a great deal (why tamper with a good thing?) although it does tip its hat to 'healthy options'. The kitchen delivers North Indian and Punjabi cooking with a degree of consistency seldom found elsewhere, thanks to impeccable ingredients, fine-tuned spicing and a respect for family tradition. Butter chicken still reigns supreme as the signature starter after all these years; otherwise kick off with fish pakora or papri chaat. Curries are mostly old faithfuls like masala lamb, keema peas and karahi prawns: they may sound familiar, but the flavours dazzle. A supporting cast of gold-standard vegetables, rice and breads (including standout romali roti) plays its part, and there's benchmark pistachio kulfi to finish. Drink lassi, beer or the house wine (£9).
Chef/s: Jasvinderjit Singh and Gulu Anand. **Open:** Tue to Fri L 12 to 2.30, Tue to Sun D 6 to 11.30. **Closed:** Mon. **Meals:** alc (main courses £4.50 to £13). Set L and D £17.50 (groups of 10+). **Service:** 10%. **Details:** Cards accepted. 225 seats. Air-con. Separate bar. Wheelchair access. Music. Children allowed. Car parking.

Madhu's

Chic, high-gloss Indian
39 South Road, UB1 1SW
Tel no: (020) 8574 1897
www.madhusonline.com
Indian | £22
Cooking score: 3

Sister to the Brilliant restaurant in nearby Western Road (see entry above), Madhu's is reaping the benefits of a high-gloss makeover. The mood is chic, service is impeccable and the food reaches parts that few other provincial curry houses can dream of – thanks to expert spicing and spot-on timing. A goodly number of new specialities (flagged with the 'M' logo) now feature on the menu, including a few with their roots in East African cuisine: look for nyamah choma (a Masai warrior dish of marinated lamb ribs) and mogo jeera (fried cassava with roasted

cumin seeds). The remainder of the repertoire is taken up with tandooris (including salmon), butter chicken, karahi gosht, keema mutter (minced lamb with peas) and other Southall favourites. Many dishes are offered in big, family-sized 'matungi' bowls for sharing, and back-up comes from wondrous breads, rice and vegetable dishes. Beer and lassi suit the chilli-fuelled food, although the carefully chosen wine list is also worth exploring; prices start at £9 (£3 a glass).
Chef/s: J. P. Singh. **Open:** Wed to Mon L 12.30 to 3, D 6 to 11.30. **Closed:** Tue. **Meals:** alc (main courses £9 to £12). Set L and D £17.50 to £20. **Service:** not inc. **Details:** Cards accepted. 105 seats. Air-con. Wheelchair access. Music. Children's portions.

▌Tottenham Hale

The Lock

Cool canalside eatery
Heron House, Hale Wharf, Ferry Lane, N17 9NF
Tel no: (020) 8885 2829
www.thelockrestaurant.com
⊖ Tottenham Hale
Modern British | £26
Cooking score: 5

Here is an example of forward thinking if ever there was. Fabrizio Russo and chef Adebola Adeshina hit the ground running when they opened in one of the more unlikely quarters of North London at the start of 2006. Since then, the place has been gently repositioned from 'Dining Bar' to 'Restaurant', but the same laid back, bright city feel pervades it still, and the location – by the Lea Valley reservoir and the canal system – is quite a draw. 'I dine here often as I work nearby,' explains a reporter, 'and so far I have never failed to have lovely food'. 'Friendly, jovial and knowledgeable staff' do their bit too. What they will bring you is cool, mix-and-match cooking of the modern British stamp, from 'soup in a cup' to hot chocolate fondant with cinnamon ice cream. Ideas are innovative; this isn't just a roll-call of contemporary classics. Crispy lamb with a polenta fritter and pea purée is the kind of starter you're unlikely to find anywhere else, while mains might incorporate monkfish tail roasted on its single bone, with borlotti beans, truffle butter and a roast red pepper sauce, or two servings of rabbit – the saddle stuffed, the leg confit – with chicken cannelloni and roasting juices. It all pleases and satiates in equal measure, although the desserts are worth a punt if you've room: mixed berry custard tart with cider sorbet is but one possibility. The tasting menu is a good introduction to what The Lock is about, but there must be at least four of you to take it. An up-to-date wine list jumbles nationalities together, with prices from £14.95, and there is a tempting cocktail menu too.

Chef/s: Adebola Adeshina. **Open:** Tue to Fri L 12 to 2, Sun L 12 to 4, Tue to Sat D 6 to 10. **Meals:** alc (main courses £10.95 to £24.95). Set L £11.95. **Service:** 10%. **Details:** 56 seats. 28 seats outside. Separate bar. Wheelchair access. Music. Children's portions. Car parking.

▌Twickenham

A Cena
Well-regarded neighbourhood Italian
418 Richmond Road, TW1 2EB
Tel no: (020) 82880108
www.acena.co.uk
Italian | £28
Cooking score: 2

Lunchtimes suggest a sleepiness in this elegant Italian, but come evening the joint is jumping with the denizens of this affluent neighbourhood out for supper. The room itself is nothing much to speak of – white walls contrast with dark wood and a big bar used more for dispensing drinks than for drinking dominates the centre of the space – but there's plenty of colour and atmosphere provided by customers and friendly, efficient staff. Cooking is based on fresh seasonal ingredients simply cooked, and though it's not always perfect, it's pretty good – Parmesan and rosemary fritelli was a bit heavy with the advertised lemon, but roast duck with saffron

risotto to follow was excellent. The all-Italian wine list has plenty under £20, starting at £16 a bottle, £4 a glass.

Chef/s: Nicola Parsons. **Open:** Tue to Sun L 12 to 2, Mon to Sat D 7 to 10. **Closed:** bank hols. **Meals:** alc (main courses £15 to £22). Set Sun L £25. **Service:** not inc. **Details:** Cards accepted. Air-con. Separate bar. Wheelchair access. Music. Children's portions.

Brula Bistrot
Gallic neighbourhood gem
43 Crown Road, St Margaret's, TW1 3EJ
Tel no: (020) 8892 0602
www.brula.co.uk
French | £29
Cooking score: 4

V

Readers reckon that this happy neighbourhood bistro is 'a perfect local', serving thoughtful, no-frills food to a select, unsnobbish clientele. The mood is relaxed, prices are fine and there's no intrusive background music to spoil the show. Brula is also a diamond venue for private functions and celebratory bashes. Menus change weekly, and the kitchen has its heart in the French bourgeois world of duck confit, beef bourguignon, bouillabaisse and roast lamb with pissaladière. Elsewhere it summons up a few more contemporary themes, as in scallops with Jerusalem artichoke purée, trompettes de mort and Bayonne ham or grilled sea bass with salt cod beignet, fennel purée and tapenade, but it's back to the old world for crème brûlée, profiteroles or apple 'tarte fine' with cinnamon ice cream. Affordable set lunches and early-evening dinners bring in throngs of Twickenham locals, who also take full advantage of the very attractive Gallic wine list (prices from £13). Owners Bruce Duckett and Lawrence Hartley also run La Buvette in Richmond (see entry).

Chef/s: Toby Williams and Jamie Russel. **Open:** all week L 12 to 3, D 6 to 10.30. **Closed:** last 2 weeks Aug, 1 week Christmas. **Meals:** alc (main courses L £10, D £15.75). Set L £15 (2 courses) to £20, Set D

£22.50 (2 courses) to £29. **Service:** 12.5% (optional). **Details:** Cards accepted. 46 seats. 10 seats outside. No music. Wheelchair access. Children's portions.

Tapas Y Vino
Modern and traditional tapas
111 London Road, TW1 1EE
Tel no: (020) 88925417
www.elvinotapas.co.uk
⊖ Twickenham
Spanish | £20
Cooking score: 2

V

John McClements seems to be taking over this corner of Twickenham, but this recent string to his bow takes his cooking out of the grand French tradition and into tapas. He hasn't splashed out on the interior: tables and chairs are basic and the looped Gypsy Kings on the sound system might grate, but the food is fun and relatively cheap. A generous plate of Jabugo ham is unmissable, but there is plenty else on offer: from clams with chickpeas and chorizo, or perfect deep-fried squid with a properly pungent aïoli, to hare royal, here served as a slice of deep, rich pâté. Portions are small, so multiple ordering is de rigueur, but at £4.50 or less per portion there is little chance of a massive bill at the end. Fill up on the savouries: desserts are not a strong point and nor, despite the name, is the wine list. Note: no children under 10 after 9pm.
Chef/s: Michael Jackson. **Open:** Mon to Sun, L 12 to 3, D 7 to 10.30. **Closed:** Sun. **Meals:** alc (main courses £12 to 15). **Service:** 10% (optional). **Details:** Cards accepted. 45 seats. Children allowed.

▌Wood Green
Mosaica @ The Factory
Funky populist dining room
Chocolate Factory, Clarendon Road, N22 6XJ
Tel no: (020) 88892400
www.mosaicarestaurants.com
⊖ Wood Green
Modern European | £25
Cooking score: 3

£5 OFF £30

A defunct factory on an industrial estate not far from Wood Green Shopping Centre is the bizarre setting for this funky, laid back dining room. The wood-floored interior bypasses post-modernist chic in favour of a mishmash of furniture and trendy art – plus an open-to-view kitchen for those who like a bit of theatre with their food. Bold flavours and colourful ideas keep punters on their toes, and menus are pared down to the bare essentials: try ordering 'asparagus with grastrix and parmy'. Elsewhere, starters of grilled sardines with gremolata or smoked haddock risotto give way to sea bass with vanilla 'pots' and samphire or lamb rump with sweet potato mash and spinach. For pudding, consider Greek yoghurt with honey pannacotta or mixed berry cheesescake with a brandy-snap 'cigar'. The no-frills wine list kicks off affordably at £13.50 (£3 a glass).
Chef/s: Johnnie Mountain. **Open:** Tue to Fri and Sun L 12 to 2.30, Tue to Sat D 6.30 to 9.30. **Closed:** Mon, bank hols, 25 Dec. **Meals:** alc (main courses £12 to £16). **Service:** 10% (optional). **Details:** Cards accepted. 80 seats. 15 seats outside. Air-con. Wheelchair access. Music. Children's portions. Car parking.

ENGLAND

Bedfordshire, Berkshire,
Buckinghamshire, Cambridgeshire,
Cheshire, Cornwall, Cumbria, Derbyshire,
Devon, Dorset, Durham, Essex,
Gloucestershire & Bristol,
Greater Manchester,
Hampshire (inc. Isle of Wight),
Herefordshire, Hertfordshire, Kent,
Lancashire, Leicestershire and Rutland,
Lincolnshire, Merseyside, Norfolk,
Northamptonshire, Northumberland,
Nottinghamshire, Oxfordshire, Shropshire,
Somerset, Staffordshire, Suffolk, Surrey,
Sussex - East, Sussex - West, Tyne & Wear,
Warwickshire, West Midlands, Wiltshire,
Worcestershire, Yorkshire

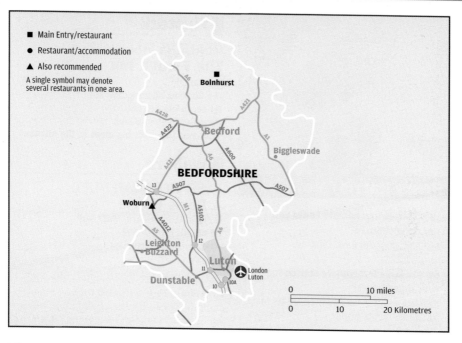

- ■ Main Entry/restaurant
- ● Restaurant/accommodation
- ▲ Also recommended

A single symbol may denote several restaurants in one area.

▌Bolnhurst

The Plough

Top-of-the-range gastropub
Kimbolton Road, Bolnhurst, MK44 2EX
Tel no: (01234) 376274
www.bolnhurst.com
Gastropub | £30
Cooking score: 5

The Plough is simply a great place to be. The interior is welcoming, the cask beer is beautifully kept, the wine list 'fabulous' and the food is good – there's clearly some talent at the stoves. This, coupled with Martin Lee's diligent sourcing of raw materials (local where possible) and strict seasonality, produces some great results. French onion soup, or maybe chargrilled Cornish scallops with spinach and fennel, black olive and rosemary, set the standard for the eight or so starters. Next up could be an exemplary côte de boeuf for two to share, with frites and béarnaise sauce, or brill teamed with monk's beard, tomato and a confit of garlic, or free-range chicken from the local village of Cardington served with Puy lentils, cabbage and red onion marmalade. Puddings are simple, but none the worse for it. Baked rice pudding with raspberry jam is suck-your-thumb nursery food at its best, and the hot chocolate tart and blood orange compote is an interesting take on this evergreen combination. Much of the globe is well represented on the thoughtfully selected wine list. House red and white are £13.95.

Chef/s: Martin Lee. **Open:** Tue to Sun L 12 to 2, Tue to Sat D 6.30 to 9.30. **Closed:** Sun D and Mon. **Meals:** alc (main courses £12.95 to £24.95). Set L £13 (2 courses) to £17. **Service:** not inc. **Details:** Cards accepted. 80 seats. 25 seats outside. Wheelchair access. Children's portions.

Readers recommend

A 'readers recommend' review is a genuine quote from a report sent in by one of our readers. We intend to follow up these suggestions throughout the year to come.

Henry Harris Café Boheme

What three ingredients could you not do without?
Sea salt, good lemons, tabasco.

Do you have a favourite source for your ingredients?
Richard Vaughan of Pedigree Meats for his Middle White pork.

What's the most unusual ingredient you've cooked or eaten?
Puffin which was quite dreadful. Jelly fish for the crunch.

What's your guilty food pleasure?
M&S taramasalata.

If you have a lazy morning at home, what's your favourite brunch dish?
Kippers.

What era of history would you most like to have eaten in?
19th century.

What's your least favourite ingredient and why?
White pepper - it's harsh, unforgiving and overpowering.

▌Finstock

READERS RECOMMEND
The Plough Inn
Gastropub
The Bottom, Finstock, OX7 3BY
Tel no: 01993 868333
www.theplough-inn.co.uk
'Thatched pub with big ideas in the kitchen'

▌Woburn

ALSO RECOMMENDED
▲ Paris House
Woburn Park, Woburn, MK17 9QP
Tel no: (01525) 290692
www.parishouse.co.uk
French

Paris House stands imposingly in the grounds of Woburn Park, a striking timbered house built in 1878 for the Paris Exhibition. It was transplanted to these shores bit by bit, and has made an apt setting for Peter Chandler's classic French cooking for nigh on 25 years. His dinner menu, at £57 (the three-course weekday lunch is £30, £35 at weekends), might start with scallop and mushroom gratin with white wine sauce, followed by fillet of beef with red wine and shallot sauce, or delice of salmon in champagne sauce. Hot raspberry soufflé is a good way to finish. France dominates the wine list, which opens at £18.50.

READERS RECOMMEND
Inn at Woburn
British
George Street, Woburn, MK17 9PX
Tel no: (01525) 290441
www.theinnatwoburn.com
'Decadence in an 18th-century coaching inn'

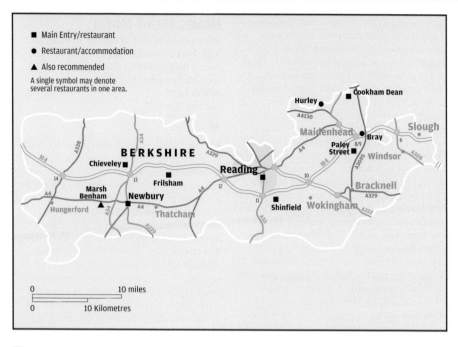

- ■ Main Entry/restaurant
- ● Restaurant/accommodation
- ▲ Also recommended

A single symbol may denote
several restaurants in one area.

▌Bray

The Fat Duck

Consummate excitement and achievement
1 High Street, Bray, SL6 2AQ
Tel no: (01628) 580333
www.fatduck.co.uk
Modern British | £95
Cooking score: 10

🍾 **V**

Unless you have spent the last several years
obstinately not reading the papers or watching
TV, you will know that the Fat Duck is now
the most famous restaurant in the UK. Its
presiding intelligence, Heston Blumenthal
OBE, has taken the place to new levels of
achievement with each successive year of
operations, and the place is still notoriously
difficult to get into. In journalistic shorthand,
what is going on within the modest walls of a
converted cottage in the well-heeled village of
Bray is 'molecular gastronomy'. The term is
now shopsoiled through excessive handling,
and is anyway disowned by Blumenthal and

his team. In the sense that it denoted the
appliance of science to the culinary arts, it
retains a grain of truth but, as devotees will tell
you, the food at the Fat Duck is about so much
more than that. What do we want a restaurant
to do? Feed us well, memorably, courteously,
perhaps, and offer value for money at what it
does. This place does all that – and more. It's
the 'more' that is the first thing to excite. 'This
is the restaurant as theatre,' as our inspector
notes, 'with waiters as performers.' Nearby
tables disappear momentarily amid the clouds
of billowing liquid nitrogen in which many of
the dishes are presented. A star-turn called
'Sound of the Sea' sees diners putting on iPods
to listen to crashing waves and seagulls, while
ingesting an edible 'sand' of ground tapioca
and dried eels ('they don't tell you what it is
until you've eaten it'), with four kinds of
seaweed, two kinds of clam and an oyster.
Certain dishes have held on to their menu
places over the years, but with modifications
and refinements. Others evoke the 200-year-
old maxim of Brillat-Savarin: 'The discovery
of a new dish does more for human happiness

than the discovery of a new star'. Ballottine of Anjou pigeon, cooked pink, comes with spiced demi-glace, pickling brine and black pudding, a work of tremendous depth. Roast foie gras benzaldehyde with almond fluid gel, cherry and chamomile ('one of the best dishes on the menu') is a dazzlingly successful combination of richness with intense sweet and sour notes. Nor is everything about surrealist juxtapositions. Pot-roast loin and braised belly of pork with green cabbage and a stunningly rich truffled macaroni gratin is another resounding triumph. Not the least heartening aspect of the whole business is that kids love it too. It's all great fun of course, but is also craftily educational, making both them and their elders think about flavours, analyse what's going on in their mouths, to a degree that hyper-refined haute cuisine of the old school tends not to. And then there's ice cream that tastes of breakfast to finish, as well as chocolate délice with matching sorbet and cumin caramel, or the long-running mango and lychee bavarois with mango and Douglas fir purée, green peppercorn jelly and a preternaturally concentrated blackcurrant sorbet. It all adds up to an experience of the most wondrous enchantment, even at £125 a head for the tasting menu, and is why we award the first maximum score to appear in the Guide since 2005. If there are mutters of regret in readers' reports, they concern the wine mark-ups, which are on the energetic side, to say the least. It is a superb list, one of the best in the country, but when red wines by-the-glass start at £9 for a Dão Reserva and whites at £12 for a Sancerre, it's clear that nobody is going to be done any favours. This is a pity.

Chef/s: Heston Blumenthal. **Open:** Tue to Sun L 12 to 1.45, Tue to Sat D 7 to 9.45. **Closed:** 2 weeks at Christmas. **Meals:** Set L and D £95 to £125. **Service:** 12.5%. **Details:** Cards accepted. 40 seats. Air-con. No music. Children allowed.

Hinds Head Hotel

The traditional side of Heston Blumenthal
High Street, Bray, SL6 2AB
Tel no: (01628) 626151
www.hindsheadhotel.co.uk
British | £28
Cooking score: 4

This late seventeenth-century inn is owned by Heston Blumenthal and stands across the road from the Fat Duck (see entry), but it is not an extension of the restaurant. It was always the intention to run the Hinds Head as the village pub and the traditional character of the building has not changed a bit. The place is, however, more food focused, but the food is as traditional as the surroundings. Little has changed since Clive Dixon took over the kitchen. Among starters, potted shrimps has made a favourable impression, not least for managing to be both 'gutsy and delicate', while dandelion salad with bacon and quails' eggs (a successful combination) is equally well judged. For main course there might be Lancashire hotpot with an oyster slipped into the middle and pickled red cabbage cutting the rich fattiness of the meat and potatoes, a perfect steak with bone marrow sauce and triple-cooked chips, or the legendary oxtail and kidney pudding. Desserts, meanwhile, run from quaking pudding – a spicy baked egg confection made to an early English recipe derived from research at Hampton Court kitchens – to treacle tart with milk ice cream. Service is brisk but friendly, and house wine starts at £13.25

Chef/s: Heston Blumenthal and Clive Dixon. **Open:** all week L 12 to 2.30, Mon to Sat D 6.30 to 9.30. **Closed:** Sun D. **Meals:** alc (main courses £13.95 to £19.50). **Service:** 12.5%. **Details:** Cards accepted. 90 seats. Air-con. Children's portions.

Waterside Inn
Epitome of refined French cuisine
Ferry Road, Bray, SL6 2AT
Tel no: (01628) 620691
www.waterside-inn.co.uk
French | £125
Cooking score: 8

By an old ferry crossing on the upper reaches of the Thames, the Waterside Inn is enviably positioned. Indeed, it isn't too fanciful to say that proprietor Michel Roux invented Bray as a destination all those years ago. The old place has weathered culinary fashions since the 1970s, gliding unruffled through the fads and fancies being explored elsewhere, committed to an indelibly French way of doing things, from menu-writing to the discussion of wine choices. A major refurbishment is programmed for the period immediately after Christmas 2008, so it would be a waste of space to describe the present décor. It would be extremely strange, however, if the new interior were to be anything other than entirely calm and restful. Service is from an immaculate French team, who are ever-watchful without appearing in the least intrusive, with trays of citrus slices presented for plopping into the water, or sugar for the coffee. A reporter who ate from the carte noted that everything from the get-go to the final morsel was 'beautifully prepared and presented, with great attention to detail, but always remaining real food,' not forgetting the 'divine classic raspberry soufflé'. There is both artistry and complexity in Alain Roux's approach, with dishes being built up in deceptively simple layers. Seafood is always sensitively handled. A smooth risotto of Cornish crab is partnered by squid stuffed with Vénéré black rice and clams, while scallops are filled with a mousse of their corals and set on a bed of thinly-sliced artichoke in a lemon fumet. Main courses given the thumbs-up this year have included grilled fillets of rabbit on celeriac fondant with an Armagnac sauce and glazed chestnuts, and breasts of the famous Anjou pigeon teamed with quail in a jus spiked with lime. There are occasional tales of flavours coming out a little pallidly in the context of the premium asked but, when the kitchen is on song, there are those who think this is as good as classic French cuisine gets in the British Isles. Well-kept French and English cheeses might precede a dessert such as crème brûlée infused with tropical fruits served with coconut and nutmeg ice-cream or the refreshing lemon croquant with sweet basil sorbet. Wines appear in a faintly intimidating leather binder, and if the sheer profusion doesn't bemuse, the prices certainly will. There is plenty to titillate the wealthy, but the sommelier is also on hand to recommend more modest bottles.

Chef/s: Alain Roux. **Open:** Wed to Sun L 12 to 2, D 7 to 10 also Tue D 1 Jun to 31 Aug. **Meals:** alc (main courses £38.50 to £55). Set L £44 to £93.50, Set L Sun £57.50 to £93.50, Set D £93.50. **Service:** 12.5%. **Details:** Cards accepted. 70 seats. Air-con. Separate bar. No music. No mobile phones. Wheelchair access. Children allowed. Car parking.

▌Chieveley
The Crab at Chieveley
The crab with the golden view
Wantage Road, Chieveley, RG20 8UE
Tel no: (01635) 247550
www.crabatchieveley.com
Seafood | £45
Cooking score: 3

The Crab is a picture-perfect inn on a quiet country road near M4 junction 13, its reputation being founded on a dedicated seafood menu. Inside, the décor is decidedly nautical with fishing nets, cork floats and shells hanging from the ceiling in the restaurant, and fish is delivered daily from Cornwall. Starters could be anything from seafood risotto with chorizo and tarragon oil to crab salad with lemon mayo, red pepper and tomato dressing. Continue with haddock florentine, served with spinach and mustard grain cream or skate wing with tagliatelle nero, crispy fennel salad and salsa verde. Meaty choices include crispy ham hock terrine with seared foie gras to start, followed by spring lamb rump with Provençale vegetable tian, fondant potato and basil jus. Finish with lemongrass crème brûlée with strawberry soup, or chocolate fondant with White Russian shooter and vanilla ice cream. The wine list – arranged by style – covers most bases quite affordably, with prices from £18.50.

Chef/s: Jamie Hodson. **Open:** all week L 12 to 2.30, D 6 to 9.30. **Meals:** alc (main courses £18.50 to £38.50). Set menu £15.95 (2 courses) to £19.95. Set Sun L £22.50. **Service:** 10%. **Details:** Cards accepted. 80 seats. 50 seats outside. Separate bar. Wheelchair access. Music. Children's portions. Car parking.

Cookham Dean
Inn on the Green
Boutique hotel meets country pub
The Old Cricket Common, Cookham Dean, SL6 9NZ
Tel no: (01628) 482638
www.theinnonthegreen.com
Modern Anglo-French | £45
Cooking score: 4

£5 OFF

Tucked away beside Cookham Dean's expansive village green, this inn has a deceptively traditional appearance. You can stop by for a pint in time-honoured style, but the interior is more boutique hotel than country pub. There are velvet sofas, rich touches of gold on the ceilings and large areas of rustic wood panelling that should look out of place, but somehow add to the quirky charm. This is the rural partner to the Embassy in London (see entry), and shares some common themes – links with the music industry, via one of the owners, (indicated by gold and platinum discs on the wall) and a menu overseen by executive chef Gary Hollihead. The food is weighted towards traditional and classical themes, but presented with modern economy and style. You could start with pan-fried scallops with French black pudding and Granny Smith apple purée, followed by roast rump of lamb with

boulangère potatoes, baby spinach and wild mushrooms or cod in batter with fat chips and tartare sauce. Desserts are in the same homely but modern vein: perhaps pear and blackberry crumble tart with cinnamon and honey ice cream, or tarte Tatin with Calvados crème fraîche. The international wine list opens at £15.50 a bottle and includes a respectable selection by-the-glass.

Chef/s: Gary Hollihead. **Open:** Tue to Sat 7 to 10, Sun 12 to 5. **Closed:** Sun pm, Mon. **Meals:** alc (main courses £11 to £17), Set L and D £17.95 (2 courses), £21.95 (3 courses). **Service:** 12.5%. **Details:** Cards accepted. 40 seats. 30 seats outside. Air-con. Separate bar. No mobile phones. Wheelchair access. Music. Children's portions. Car parking.

Frilsham
Pot Kiln
Rooted in the countryside
Frilsham, RG18 0XX
Tel no: (01635) 201366
www.potkiln.co.uk
Gastropub | £30
Cooking score: 1

£5 OFF

It seems everyone falls in love with the 'fantastic position' of Mike Robinson's truly rural, down-to-earth little pub, which is 'surrounded by woods and meadows with lovely walks'. Local ingredients get top billing, too (say, Yattendon partridge with local bacon or deer shot by the landlord himself), and bread and pasta are made on the premises. That said, reporters this year have failed to be as impressed by the food or the service. When it is on form the kitchen can deliver good earthy dishes such as veal sweetbreads on toast with winter chanterelles and parsely and caper butter or slow-braised rabbit with lemon, rosemary and garlic. House vins du pays is £12.95. Reports please.

Chef/s: Mike Robinson. **Open:** all week L 12 to 3, D 6 to 11. **Closed:** 25 Dec. **Meals:** alc (main courses £13 to £18.50). **Service:** 10%. **Details:** Cards accepted. 45 seats. 100 seats outside. Separate bar. Wheelchair access. Children's portions. Car parking.

Hurley

Black Boys Inn

Cuisine bourgeoise with flair
Henley Road, Hurley, SL6 5NQ
Tel no: (01628) 824212
www.blackboysinn.co.uk
Modern British | £30
Cooking score: 5

The village of Hurley was on the winning side in the Civil War, and the name of the Inn refers to a soubriquet once awarded to the future Charles II, although the logo creatively now features a pair of chimney sweeps. Among the former coaching inns of England, it has been given a brisk makeover, and this enhances the attractions of Simon Bonwick's decidedly accomplished cooking. His style is cuisine bourgeoise, although it comes with a distinctly higher gloss than that humble designation might imply. True, duck rillettes with toasted pain de campagne and sauce gribiche fits the bill precisely, but dressing a tartare of bluefin tuna in liquorice and saffron – a longstanding and effective starter – shows the kitchen is able to work in a dimension beyond the simple domestic classics. A rendition of cassoulet might be the accompaniment to a fish main course that pairs monkfish and scallops in sherry vinegar, or there could be pot-roast squab pigeon with rowanberry sauce. A reader who hailed the cooking as generally superb was left a little browbeaten when her request for meat to be cooked well-done was peremptorily refused, and there are still niggles about the service at times. Harmony is restored, perhaps, with the appealing dessert choice, which extends from date and pecan sticky toffee pudding to an apricot and marzipan fritter with apricot smoothie. An extensive wine list furnishes plenty of options, not least for the generous selection by-the-glass, from £4.45. Bottle prices start at £17.95.
Chef/s: Simon Bonwick. **Open:** Tue to Sun L 12 to 2, Tue to Sat D 7 to 8.45. **Closed:** 25 Dec to 7 Jan. **Meals:** alc (main courses £14.50 to £18.50).

Service: not inc. **Details:** Cards accepted. 52 seats. 30 seats outside. Wheelchair access. Music. Children allowed. Car parking.

Marsh Benham

ALSO RECOMMENDED
▲ Red House
Marsh Benham, RG20 8LY
Tel no: (01635) 582017
www.redhousemarshbenham.co.uk
Gastropub

This prettily thatched gastropub offers a simple menu of comfort food and classics. Its traditional and gently stylish interior includes a large bar and a book-lined dining room that overlooks water meadows. Oak-smoked salmon with herb blinis, cream cheese and chives (£7.25) is a typical starter, while main courses might include pavé of halibut with braised fennel, grilled baby vegetables and celeriac purée (£17.95) or cannon of local lamb with Parma ham and mille-feuille of aubergine (£17.50). Finish with tiramisù or apple and blackberry crumble (both £5.50). An international wine list starts at £14. Open all week.

Newbury

The Vineyard at Stockcross
Striking cooking in stunning surroundings
Newbury, RG20 8JU
Tel no: (01635) 528770
www.the-vineyard.co.uk
Modern European | £42
Cooking score: 8

First impressions count, and this modern hotel's fire and water feature beside the entrance is quite a head-turner for first timers. Regulars, however, know this is just the prelude to John Campbell's striking cooking and dazzling wine list. Moreover, the eye-catching steel grapevine balustrade that wends its way round the classy split-level dining room further endorses the serious interplay between fine wine and food. This spacious, well-lit, elegant area comes decked out in soothing creams and beiges, with comfortable armchair-style seating and works from proprietor Sir Peter Michael's modern art collection on the walls. Service is a class act too, slick, professional and knowledgeable, but with a genuine friendly and unstuffy approach that is perfectly attuned to the kitchen's contemporary cuisine. Campbell's cooking is thoughtful, innovative and highly engineered, utilising bags of modern technique and technology, but stopping short of the cutting-edge gastronomy practised elsewhere. So while foams and jellies make an appearance, they have a purpose and in each dish clarity of flavour never wavers. Well-considered combinations and components play with texture and colour, while the tersely scripted menus often bring an element of surprise – a main course of turbot cleverly teamed with pork belly, langoustine and lemongrass, for example, or perhaps a signature dessert of cucumber, lime, mango and yoghurt. The wine list is quite a tome, some 2,000 bins showcasing a renowned collection from California backed by an Old World selection that is impressive in its own right. There is plenty of sommelier guidance and interest by-the-glass for those with a tighter budget. House wines are £20 to £25. **Chef/s:** John Campbell and Peter Eaton. **Open:** all week L 12 to 1.45, D 7 to 9.30. **Meals:** alc (main courses £28 to £35). Set L £19 (2 courses) to £24, Set D £35 (2 courses) to £42, Tasting menu £88. **Service:** not inc. **Details:** Cards accepted. 85 seats. 35 seats outside. Air-con. Separate bar. Wheelchair access. Music. Children's portions. Car parking.

Symbols

 Accommodation is available.

 Three courses for less than £30.

V More than five vegetarian dishes.

 £5-off voucher scheme.

 Notable wine list.

▮ Paley Street

★ BEST PUB CHEF ★

Royal Oak
Upper tier pub food
Paley Street, SL6 3JS
Tel no: (01628) 620541
Gastropub | £24
Cooking score: 5

This classy, although still rustic, dining pub is owned by Michael Parkinson and his son Nick. The bar has that relaxed and informal feel lent by beams, an open fire and leather sofas, while the smarter dining room has small but reasonably well-spaced tables. Dominic Chapman's cooking follows the purist's credo of keeping things simple to accentuate the quality of the raw materials, and the flavours hit home. Start, perhaps, with eloquently flavoured smoked eel with beetroot and horseradish, then move on to salt-beef stovey paired with a fried egg and mustard sauce, or a 'perfect' Lancashire hotpot. What inspires most confidence is the intimation that dishes have been properly road-tested from kitchen to arrival on the plate, an impression reinforced by desserts such as a properly indulgent rhubarb trifle with the lightest of lemon sponge as its base. A fine collection of Bordeaux is at the heart of the wine list. Otherwise it's a pick and mix of good and prestigious bottles with brief contributions from all over. House wine is £15. **Chef/s:** Dominic Chapman. **Open:** Mon to Sat L 12 to 2.30, D 6.30 to 9.30 (10 Fri and Sat). Sun L 12 to 3.30. **Closed:** 26 Dec, 1 and 2 Jan. **Meals:** alc (main courses £9.50 to £25). **Details:** Cards accepted. 46 seats. 40 seats outside. Air-con. Separate bar. No mobile phones. Wheelchair access. Music. Children's portions. Car parking.

Which? Campaigns

To find out more about Which? food and drink campaigns, please visit:
www.which.co.uk

Reading

London Street Brasserie

Bright and airy riverside brasserie
2-4 London Street, Reading, RG1 4SE
Tel no: (01189) 505036
www.londonstbrasserie.co.uk
Modern European | £35
Cooking score: 3

£5 OFF **V**

Invariably crowded, bustling and cheery, this bright and airy brasserie overlooking the River Kennet can be counted on to produce food that is good value for money. There are plenty of interesting choices on the Mediterranean-inspired menu: a board of Italian charcuterie, for example, or fish soup with red mullet, and partridge breast with sweetcorn pancakes, spinach and port jus all make a good start. Main courses try out new juxtapositions, as when venison fillet is teamed with haggis and figs and sauced with port, redcurrant and juniper, or roast cod with smoked paprika, basil fritters and warm chorizo salad. Desserts are variations on popular themes: perhaps dark chocolate tart and sorbet. Service has been described as 'friendly and laid back' and house wine is £14.
Chef/s: Paul Brotherton. **Open:** all week 12 to 11.
Meals: alc (main courses £13.50 to £20). Set menu £13.50 (2 courses). **Service:** not inc. **Details:** Cards accepted. 70 seats. 20 seats outside. Separate bar. Wheelchair access. Music. Children's portions. Car parking.

Shinfield

L'Ortolan

A Berkshire institution
Church Lane, Shinfield, RG2 9BY
Tel no: (0118) 9888500
www.lortolan.com
Modern French | £60
Cooking score: 6

V

Alan Murchison waves the flag for fine food in the depths of moneyed Berkshire, his classically designed former vicarage a haven of fine dining. Service is from a well-drilled team – 'not too formal' – and the cooking is very much in the modern French mould, with some artful combinations of ingredients wedded to deft technique. Visitors are struck by the intensity of flavours right from the word go: for example, in a starter of hot smoked salmon served with juniper and gin-pickled rhubarb and baby sorrel, or a twice-baked goats' cheese soufflé given earthy flavour and texture from beetroot terrine and watercress salad. Accurate timing can be taken as read, producing lightly-seared fillet of sea bass and sweet roasted scallops with artichoke and tomato salad and well-judged liquorice jus, or stuffed saddle of rabbit served alongside with carrots, peas and lettuce ravioli. Meals are invariably well-balanced, ending perhaps with a text book crispy bitter chocolate mousse that is perfectly positioned on the bittersweet continuum and given a lift by spiced cherries and vanilla ice cream. France is the main concern of the wine list, with Burgundy and Bordeaux enthusiastically launching into three-figure prices. Knowledgeable dabbling around the rest of the world satisfies all palates, but with limited choice below £30. House wine is £18 and there's a selection by-the-glass from £5. A sister restaurant, La Bécasse, is in Ludlow, Shropshire (see entry).
Chef/s: Alan Murchison. **Open:** Tue to Sat L 12 to 2, D 7 to 9. **Closed:** Sun and Mon. **Meals:** Set L £22 (2 courses) to £26, alc £54 (2 courses) to £60. Menu gourmand £65. **Service:** 12.5%. **Details:** Cards accepted. 60 seats. Separate bar. Wheelchair access. Children's portions. Car parking.

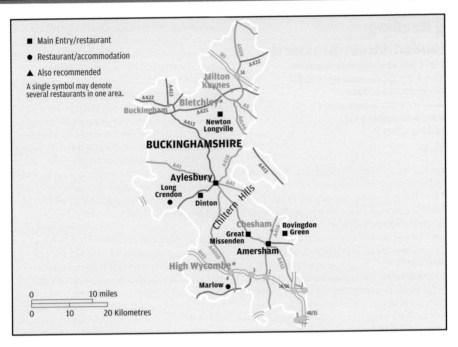

- ■ Main Entry/restaurant
- ● Restaurant/accommodation
- ▲ Also recommended

A single symbol may denote
several restaurants in one area.

▌Amersham

Artichoke

Intricate food in a listed building
9 Market Square, Amersham, HP7 0DF
Tel no: (01494) 726611
www.theartichokerestaurant.co.uk
Modern European | £38
Cooking score: 4

Flanked by posh shops and tailor-made for the
Home Counties affluence of Old Amersham,
this swanky conversion of a sixteenth-century
listed building now trades as a
serene contemporary restaurant. Ancient
beams and a mighty open fireplace add
character to the pint-sized dining room,
which provides an intimate backdrop to
Laurie Gear's ambitious modern food. There
are plenty of intricate ideas on show here: the
eponymous globe artichoke might appear in a
terrine alongside organic salmon, pickled
oyster, cucumber jelly and liquorice foam,
while the Jerusalem tuber could be turned
into purée to go with a dish of wild New

Forest venison, glazed fig, roast butternut
squash gnocchi and sauce grand veneur. Much
of the repertoire is driven by the seasons,
whether it's salsify and girolles with John
Dory or kohlrabi, black truffles and pickled
walnuts or fillet of Aberdeen Angus beef.
Desserts maintain the elaboration with, say,
ravioli of coconut tapioca with pineapple,
passion fruit, banana sorbet and lime sabayon.
Classy French bottles catch the eye on the
auspicious wine list, although you will be
hard-pressed to find much choice below £20;
alternatively, drink by-the-glass
(from £6.50).
Chef/s: Laurie Gear. **Open:** Tue to Sat L 12 to 3, D
6.30 to 11. **Closed:** Sun, Mon, 1 week from May bank
hol, 2 weeks late Aug, 1 week Christmas. **Meals:** alc
L (main courses £14 to £20). Set L £18.50 (2
courses) to £22.50, Set D £38 (3 courses) to £47.50.
Service: 12.5% (optional). **Details:** Cards accepted.
24 seats. 4 seats outside. Wheelchair access. Music.
Children's portions.

Aylesbury
Hartwell House
Country-house splendour in the Chilterns
Oxford Road, Aylesbury, HP17 8NR
Tel no: (01296) 747444
www.hartwell-house.com
Modern European | £40
Cooking score: 4

£5 OFF 🛏️

Hartwell is a slice of heritage England owned by the Historic House Hotels group, who also have Bodysgallen Hall, Llandudno, and Middlethorpe Hall, York (see entries). It is a handsome country-house in the Chilterns with all the accoutrements of a modern hotel, from spa treatments to 90 acres of sumptuous landscaped parkland in which to wander. The tone is as formal as it gets (no trainers please, gentlemen, at dinner), which is all in keeping with the majestically wide-ranging menus Daniel Richardson offers. A no-choice, three-course dinner deal supplements the carte, and there is also, of course, a tasting menu that runs to six courses. The cooking is in the highfalutin idiom, accompanying scallops with a purée of roasted celeriac, pea shoots and coconut foam in a first course, which may be followed by the option of a palate-cleansing sorbet of clementine anointed with champagne. Wrappings of one sort or another are a familiar main-course technique, whether it be the bandaging of monkfish in Parma ham, with creamed corn and ratatouille galette and aubergine caviar, or the application of a pastry jacket to venison loin, which is further garnished with an Agen prune mousse, Savoy cabbage, potato rösti, and a juniper-scented sauce. Fine British cheeses come with raisin bread and home-made bsicuits, or you could go the whole hog with one of the show-stopping desserts – perhaps raspberry-studded apple bavarois, with green apple sorbet and raspberry jelly. A list of Cellarman's Choices, all available by-the-glass from £5.75, opens the substantial, French-led wine list. House wines are £17.50.

Chef/s: Daniel Richardson. Open: all week L 12.30 to 1.45, D 7.30 to 9.45. Meals: alc (main courses £21 to £28.50). Set L £19.50 to £29.95. Set L Sun £32.95. Set D £39 to £65. Service: not inc. Details: Cards accepted. 60 seats. Separate bar. No music. No mobile phones. Wheelchair access. Car parking.

Bovingdon Green
ALSO RECOMMENDED
▲ Royal Oak
Frieth Road, Bovingdon Green, SL7 2JF
Tel no: (01628) 488611
www.royaloakmarlow.co.uk
Gastropub

A cosy whitewashed country pub with a child-friendly attitude, sprawling gardens and a flexible menu of robust gastropub food. 'Small plates' such as beetroot-cured salmon with preserved lemons and caperberries (£6.75) head up a regularly-changing menu that goes local with Marlow venison sausage 'toad' (£11.50) and looks east for Indian-spiced mackerel on sautéed new potato and okra salad. To finish, plum and blackberry cobbler with honeycomb ice cream (£5.25) strikes a seasonal note. Local beers, and around 30 all-European wines from £12 (£3.10 a glass). Open all week.

Dinton
La Chouette
English country pub with a Belgian accent
Westlington Green, Dinton, HP17 8UW
Tel no: (01296) 747422
Modern European | £34
Cooking score: 4

🍾

It would be slightly over-egging the pudding to say that Frédéric Desmette has created a little corner of the Home Counties that is forever Belgium – a village green and an old beamed pub couldn't really be anywhere other than rural England – but the proprietor's homeland certainly informs some of the culinary traditions, and supplies some of the ingredients, on offer here. A slug of fine

Belgian beer, Duvel, goes into the sauce for an enterprising starter serving of brill, while bière blanche finds its way into a main course that features Scottish salmon. Fish is much in evidence, with skate, scallops and crayfish among the first courses. Meat-eaters may be regaled with duck breast in green peppercorns, or flavourful rump steak in classic béarnaise. It is all served with gusto and care, in the form maybe of fixed-price menus that end with a surprise dessert, in which one may well find quality Belgian chocolate given star billing. Perhaps unexpectedly in the modest country surroundings, a heroic wine list – itself worth the journey – is offered. It is a document of true Francophilia, with arrays of Alsace grands crus, gorgeous clarets and Burgundies, and a choice of no fewer than three Savennières, a monumental, little-seen Chenin from the Loire. Prices are not giveaway, but the quality is outstanding. Don't forget to check the bin-ends. Vins maisons are £14.50, but are hardly the point.

Chef/s: Frédéric Desmette. **Open:** Mon to Fri L 12 to 2, Mon to Sat D 7 to 9. **Meals:** alc (main courses £14 to £17.50). Set L £14.50 to £39.50. Set D £30 to £39.50. **Service:** 12.5%. **Details:** Cards accepted. 30 seats. Separate bar. Music. Children's portions. Car parking.

Great Missenden
La Petite Auberge
Indelibly French
107 High Street, Great Missenden, HP16 0BB
Tel no: (01494) 865370
French | £35
Cooking score: 3

£5
OFF

Hubert Martel's welcoming French bistro continues to delight a loyal band of regulars with its unreconstructed cuisine bourgeoise. An artichoke heart is just the right receptacle for a clump of forest mushrooms, and scallops gain from being briefly seared and then dressed in saffron vinaigrette. Rich sauces add value to mains such as turbot in mustard butter, or pink-cooked Gressingham duck breast in port, while Calvados and pine nuts

are the preferred medium for veal sweetbreads. The desserts are simple and unimpeachably French – à la crème brûlée or nougatine glacée, sauce chocolat – and so is the wine list, which confines itself to the principal regions, from £15.50 for Muscadet up to Château Talbot 2000 at £109.

Chef/s: Hubert Martel. **Open:** Mon to Sat D 7.30 to 10. **Closed:** 2 weeks Christmas, 2 weeks Easter, bank hols. **Meals:** alc (main courses £16.80 to £18.90). **Service:** not inc. **Details:** Cards accepted. 30 seats. No music. Wheelchair access. Children's portions.

Long Crendon
Angel Restaurant
Fish-loving country restaurant
47 Bicester Road, Long Crendon, HP18 9EE
Tel no: (01844) 208268
www.angelrestaurant.co.uk
Modern British | £25
Cooking score: 1

£5
OFF

Originally a village pub (although the tag 'inn' was dropped some years ago), this sixteenth-century listed building now serves admirably as a country restaurant-with-rooms. Its first duty is still as a provider of hospitality, with several distinctive dining areas and a cheerfully decorated conservatory. A specials board above the bar gives prominence to daily deliveries of fish: grilled lemon sole with cockle butter, plum tomato and shallot salad, for example. Otherwise the kitchen sends out a broad swathe of dishes taking in roast quail wrapped in pancetta on black pudding with grain mustard dressing and herb-crusted English lamb with ratatouille and rosemary sauce. As a finale, consider plum crème brûlée or apple and blackberry crumble. The wine list is an immensely informative tome featuring classy names and trendy grape varieties from France and 'down under'; prices start at £15.25 (£4.75 a glass). In addition, the choice of 500ml pichets (from £11.50) has been expanded to over 60 by popular demand.

Chef/s: Trevor Bosch. Open: all week L 12 to 2.30, Mon to Sat D 7 to 9.30. Meals: alc (main courses £15.50 to £27.50). Set L £15 (2 courses) to £19.95. Service: not inc. Details: Cards accepted. 75 seats. 30 seats outside. Air-con. Separate bar. Wheelchair access. Music. Children's portions. Car parking.

▌Marlow

Danesfield House, Oak Room
Innovative, edgy cooking in a Gothic pile
Henley Road, Marlow, SL7 2EY
Tel no: (01628) 891010
www.danesfieldhouse.co.uk
French | £55
Cooking score: 7

🍾 🍽

Magnificent grounds and views over the River Thames are part of the attraction of this Victorian Gothic pile, but no such views are forthcoming from the somewhat regal limed-panelled dining room. However it does focus your attention on what's on the plate. Adam Simmonds relishes 'taking you on a revelatory journey'. His 'creativity and modernity' begins with a lime and lager jelly with lime granita – a witty take on shandy – then, as a clever contrast, follows with a watercress soup and poached quail's egg. The first proper course 'showed elements of pure genius': confit chicken oysters with mizuna, dandelion and spring truffle, enhanced by an undertone of mustard, its centerpiece a quivering, barely-cooked hen's egg – 'a brilliant marriage of flavours'. Indeed, flavours and textures are subtle, finely balanced and beautifully judged, and while tastes are not intense, they are true. Roasted loin and rack of rabbit, for example, partnered with white asparagus purée, pineapple jelly and spring white truffle, were given an extra dimension by a perfumed consommé. Carefully managed pre-desserts, an exotic fruit soup with banana sorbet followed by fruit jellies (blackcurrant, apricot, pineapple), and a dozen cheeses, mostly French, arrive with home-made apricot bread and digestives. These are inspirationally rounded off by apple and celery sorbets, epitomising a kitchen on top form. Desserts

are equally gentle-tasting, as in a lime parfait, lime leaf-infused tapioca topped with a sensational ginger foam. The impressive wine list extends over 33 pages, with several strengths, not least a run of Champagnes. Prices from £16.95 are moderate for the quality and include 20 wines by-the-glass from £6.

Chef/s: Adam Simmonds. Open: Wed to Sat L 12 to 2, Tue to Sat D 7 to 10. Closed: Sun and Mon, bank hols. Meals: Set L £25 (2 courses), Set D £55 (3 courses) to £75 (tasting menu). Service: 12.5%. Details: Cards accepted. 30 seats. Air-con. Separate bar. Wheelchair access. Music. Car parking.

Hand & Flowers
Confident cooking
126 West Street, Marlow, SL7 2BP
Tel no: (01628) 482277
www.thehandandflowers.co.uk
Modern British | £35
Cooking score: 6

'Almost good enough to tempt me to move to Marlow so that this would be my local,' enthused one happy visitor to the Kerridges' pleasant whitewashed pub. The atmosphere is relaxed and informal, and the wooden beams and cosy nooks and crannies of the pub-restaurant make it a real delight, but you won't find anything remotely 'trad pubby' on the menu (oh, except the superb fish and chips served in the bar). Judiciously sourced seasonal produce, natural flavours and an avoidance of gimmickry are the watchwords of Tom Kerridge, as in starters of potted crab with brown bread and cucumber and dill chutney, or home-cured sardines with tomato. Combinations of flavours can be imaginative: fillet of sea bream with lobster, seaweed and smoked aubergine, or squab pigeon and foie gras en croûte, and, at dessert stage, passion-fruit parfait with compressed pineapple and white chocolate ice cream. Elsewhere, pork belly with braised white beans, followed by a chocolate torte, were highlights of a meal that came 'without the stuffiness you can sometimes find at that level of cooking', and service has been particularly singled out for praise this year. The wine list offers a fair selection of reasonably priced bottles, starting at £15.50.

Chef/s: Tom Kerridge and Chris Mackett. **Open:** all week L 12 to 2.30 (Sun 3), D 6.30 to 9.30. **Closed:** 24 to 26 Dec. **Meals:** alc (main courses £15.50 to £19). **Service:** not inc. **Details:** Cards accepted. 55 seats. 20 seats outside. Music. Children's portions. Car parking.

Vanilla Pod
Skilled cooking in comfortable surroundings
31 West Street, Marlow, SL7 2LS
Tel no: (01628) 898101
www.thevanillapod.co.uk
Modern British | £40
Cooking score: 5

£5 OFF V

A refurbishment at Vanilla Pod has seen air-conditioning installed, a brighter, more contemporary feel introduced and a switch to more sociable round tables. But while the surroundings have changed, Michael Macdonald's skilled, enlivening cooking continues. Lunch menus change weekly, the carte and tasting menus monthly, and there are highly accomplished dishes – created with mainly local produce – throughout. Lemon risotto with garden peas and ricotta was a light, appropriate thing to find on a spring menu, as was a main course of roasted halibut with asparagus and clams. Not surprisingly, given the restaurant's name, vanilla is used often, perhaps in a starter of seared scallops with vanilla-poached pear purée, red wine shallots and a vanilla dressing, or more familiarly in a dessert of crème brûlée with strawberry soup. French technique is brought to bear on meat dishes such as fillet of lamb with crisp garlic potatoes and madeira jus, or poached duck breast with celeriac purée, pommes Anna and baby onions. The wine list makes a good fist of most regions, and there is a wide choice below £25. House wines are nearly all £18, or £4 for a small glass.
Chef/s: Michael Macdonald. **Open:** Tue to Sat L 12 to 2, D 7 to 10. **Closed:** Christmas, New Year and bank hols. **Meals:** Set L £19.50. Set D £40 to £50.

Service: not inc. **Details:** Cards accepted. 36 seats. 8 seats outside. Air-con. Separate bar. No music. Children's portions.

■ Newton Longville
Crooked Billet
Pub full of surprises
2 Westbrook End, Newton Longville, MK17 0DF
Tel no: (01908) 373936
www.thebillet.co.uk
Modern British | £25
Cooking score: 2

£5 OFF ♦ V £30

In a quiet Buckinghamshire village not far from Milton Keynes, the Crooked Billet is the very image of lovingly nurtured local hostelry, complete with a thatched roof. But a quick glance at the menu and wine list tells a different story. There's a confident creative spirit at work in the kitchen: crispy squid confit receives a chorizo and feta stuffing, while pressed duck and smoked duck terrine comes with purple fig chutney. Elsewhere, 'la marmite dieppoise' should please fish fans, while meat-lovers might be taken by crispy pork belly with Puy lentils, tarragon and Savoy cabbage. Desserts aim high, with fashionable combos such as vanilla pannacotta with sweet tomato jam and a basil wafer. Lunches are served in the bar, although this is much more than pub grub: expect sandwiches, brasserie dishes (smoked haddock fishcake) and several items lifted from the evening restaurant menu. Finally, there's the wine list: a real dazzler that opens up a fascinating world of drinking possibilites, with an amazing number available by-the-glass. Bottle prices start at £14.
Chef/s: Emma Gilchrist. **Open:** Tue to Sun L 12 to 2 (3 Sun), Mon to Sat D 7 to 9.30. **Closed:** 25 Dec. **Meals:** alc (main courses L £8 to £16, D £12 to £23). Bar menu available. **Service:** not inc. **Details:** Cards accepted. 50 seats. 50 seats outside. Separate bar. Music. Children's portions. Car parking.

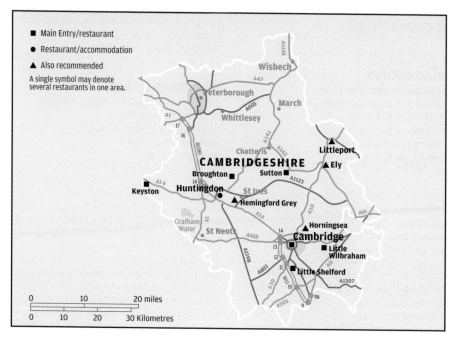

■ Broughton

The Crown Inn

Relaxed gastropub with seasonal offerings
Bridge Road, Broughton, PE28 3AY
Tel no: (01487) 824428
www.thecrownbroughton.co.uk
Gastropub | £25
Cooking score: 2

In a village north of Huntingdon, Simon Cadge's hostelry is well worth seeking out. Upbeat and modishly rustic, it's a welcoming place much loved by locals and visitors alike. Cadge's modern menu showcases local produce, reveals realistic ambition, and the resulting clear focus is much appreciated. Chargrilled squid with fresh red chilli, rocket and lemon, followed by marinated chump of lamb served with mash, spinach, English asparagus (of course), baby onions, smoked bacon and red wine sauce typify the style. Elsewhere lemon sole is paired with fresh linguine and given zing with lemon zest, red onions, capers, white wine and salmoriglio (a sauce of lemon, olive oil and garlic), and pub credentials are maintained with classics such as sausage and mash and rib-eye steak and chips. Finish with vanilla pannacotta with poached rhubarb and milk foam. House wine is £12.50. More reports please.
Chef/s: Simon Cadge. **Open:** Wed to Sun 12 to 2 (3 Sun), D 6.30 to 9. **Closed:** Mon and Tue. **Meals:** alc (main courses £10.50 to £17.50). Set menu £11 (2 courses) to £14.50. **Service:** not inc. **Details:** Cards accepted. 60 seats. 72 seats outside. Separate bar. Wheelchair access. Music. Children's portions. Car parking.

Readers recommend

A 'readers recommend' review is a genuine quote from a report sent in by one of our readers. We intend to follow up these suggestions throughout the year to come.

Send your reviews to: www.which.co.uk/gfgfeedback

Cambridge

★NEW ENTRY★

Alimentum

Dedicated to first-class food
152-154 Hills Road, Cambridge, CB2 8BP
Tel no: (01223) 902089
www.restaurantalimentum.co.uk
Modern European | £30
Cooking score: 5

Close to the station, this Cambridge newcomer was the first restaurant in Britain to serve 'ethical' foie gras (made seasonally in Spain), and responsible sourcing in general is a prime consideration – even the air conditioning units are 'programmed to save the planet'. But the supreme reason for Alimentum's fast-won popularity is the flair of the cooking, the motivated service and the warm appeal of a room that manages to be both uncluttered yet plush, the focal point a rich burgundy silken wall panel. Chef David Williams's fixed price lunch/dinner menus are a good, gently-priced intro to his cuisine, revealing a love of sunny flavours in eye-catching choices like confit of chicken with ratatouille, or cod penne with sorrel and peas. The à la carte is a definite notch up: 'pure, fresh and simple' pea soup with little ovals of pea mascarpone, served with first-rate breads, then roast lamb – pink, thick, juicy meat edged with the crispest fat for extra flavour – served with a timbale of succulent lamb's neck on a bed of finely-diced Mediterranean vegetables. The chef is no slouch at desserts, either: don't miss the 'intense, rich but beautifully light' Tainori Valrhona chocolate tart with chocolate ice cream. Wines are approached with the same passion as the food. A really good feature is that a number from the main fine list are available in little quarter carafes. A real find.
Chef/s: David Williams. **Open:** Mon to Sun L 12 to 2.30, Mon to Sat D 6 to 9.30. **Closed:** 24 to 30 Dec, 1 Jan. **Meals:** alc (main courses £14.95 to £19.95, Set L £12.50 (2 courses) to £15.50, set D £14.50 (2 courses) to £17.50. **Service:** 12.5%. **Details:** Cards accepted. 62 seats. Air-con. Separate bar. Wheelchair access. Music. Children's portions.

Midsummer House

Midsummer Common, Cambridge, CB4 1HA
Tel no: (01223) 369299
www.midsummerhouse.co.uk
Modern French | £60
Cooking score: 6

What to make of Midsummer House? While some reporters heap praise on Daniel Clifford's 'absolutely amazing' cooking and 'exceptional ingredients', other diners have left puzzled or alienated. Service has been described as 'knowledgeable and friendly' but also as 'snooty'. The restaurant occupies a detached riverside house on the common, with watery views from the bar upstairs and a garden vista from the conservatory dining room. It's a tranquil setting, and one where the food is the star. Daniel Clifford certainly has outstanding technical expertise, and his playful dishes show these to the full – gratuitously or thrillingly so, depending on your outlook. Recent high points have included a starter of a beetroot crisp tube with goats' cheese, served with a subtle horseradish ice cream, while hand-dived scallops with tiny batons of apple were 'excellent quality' but slightly undercooked. Clifford's madcap streak showed in a tilting cup of potato and black truffle atop a white china pyramid. It wasn't clear whether the contents were meant to spill on to the chicken dish below, but spill they did. On the bright side, he maintained a steady stream of invention throughout the meal, which was interspersed with successful curios such as cauliflower velouté with tiger prawn, cucumber and lettuce or a pre-dessert of ginger, lemon and chamomile foam, jelly, cream and ice cream. Not surprisingly, test tubes put in a showing, perhaps filled with foam and Granny Smith granita as an accompaniment to an over-spiced tarte Tatin. The effort is maintained to the end, when there are hand-made chocolates to savour and you leave believing that the relatively high prices have paid for much sweat and experimentation in the kitchen. The real – but occasional – problem here is not so much Clifford's audacious invention as the fact that simpler aspects of taste are sometimes overlooked in the quest for originality (garlic cream with tarte Tatin, anyone?). The wine list is pricey and convoluted, making it hard to find much under £50.

Chef/s: Daniel Clifford. **Open:** Wed to Sat L 12 to 1.30, Tue to Sat D 7 to 9.30. **Closed:** Sun and Mon. **Meals:** alc D £60, L £30. **Service:** 12.5% (optional). **Details:** Cards accepted. 44 seats. Separate bar. No music. Children allowed.

Restaurant 22
Intimate home-from-home dining
22 Chesterton Road, Cambridge, CB4 3AX
Tel no: (01223) 351880
www.restaurant22.co.uk
Modern European | £28
Cooking score: 2

Cherished for its personal charm, intimacy and cosy atmosphere, this terraced Victorian house is a favourite destination, just a stroll from Cambridge city centre. New owners have taken over since the last edition of the Guide, but the kitchen brigade remains and – apart from a few licks of fresh paint – little else has changed. The food has lots of contemporary accents, although there is always enough familiarity to keep the old guard satisfied. To begin, crab and salmon ceviche with avocado purée might appear alongside three-cheese torte, while main courses could embrace everything from best end of lamb with confit shoulder, capers and anchovies to grilled sea bass, Swiss chard and sorrel beurre blanc. An extra fish course is available for a supplement (smoked haddock fishcake with soft-boiled quail's egg, for example) and desserts have included dark chocolate and amaretti cheesecake with kumquats. The

revamped wine list offers a broad selection of well chosen bottles dominated by France. House wines start at £14.25 (£4.25 a glass). **Chef/s:** Martin Cullum and Seb Mansfield. **Open:** Tue to Sat D 7 to 9.45. **Closed:** Sun and Mon. **Meals:** Set D £27.50 (3 courses). **Service:** not inc. **Details:** Cards accepted. 38 seats. Air-con. No mobile phones. Music. Children allowed. Car parking.

ALSO RECOMMENDED
▲ Cotto
183 East Road, Cambridge, CB1 1BG
Tel no: (01223) 302010
Modern European

This restaurant, café and bakery has changed hands, but new chef-patron Hans Schweitzer has preserved the produce-driven approach that has become its hallmark. The no-choice menu offers up to six courses, all based around regional British ingredients: perhaps new season Heirloom and cherry tomatoes with garlic and basil sourdough flatbread from the applewood-fired stone oven, or slow-roasted organic Longhorn beef cheeks in Pinot Noir and wild garlic jus with tiny Suffolk potatoes. According to one reporter, this is 'some of the best food in Cambridge.' Three courses £30. Wines from £12. Open all week.

■ Ely

ALSO RECOMMENDED
▲ Boathouse
5-5a Annesdale, Ely, CB7 4BN
Tel no: (01353) 664388
www.cambscuisine.com
British

On a summer's day outdoor seating by the Great Ouse is a draw at this converted boathouse. The food is a good mix of traditional English and modern European ideas, so expect poached pear, Yorkshire Blue and roasted pecan nut salad (£6) or baked duck parcel with sweet and sour cucumber to start (£7), then steamed mutton and onion suet pudding with buttered carrots and spring greens (£12), or the house speciality – a selection of sausages, sauces and mash (£10). Cookies and cream with maple pecan fudge ice cream makes a good finale. House wine is £13. Open all week.

Hemingford Grey
ALSO RECOMMENDED
▲ The Cock
47 High Street, Hemingford Grey, PE28 9BJ
Tel no: (01480) 463609
www.cambscuisine.com
Gastropub

Doubling as affluent village boozer and chic country restaurant, the rejuvenated Cock now sports trendy pale colours, stripped wood floors and food that lives happily in both camps. Fish specials are chalked up on one blackboard, home-made sausages with a choice of mash on another. The rest of the menu is sound populist stuff, ranging from duck parcels with sweet-and-sour cucumber (£7) and slow-cooked pork belly with seared foie gras, rhubarb and red wine sauce (£14) to wholesome desserts such as carrot cake or fruit crumble (£5). Around 40 well-chosen wines from £12 (£2.90 a glass). Open all week.

Horningsea
ALSO RECOMMENDED
▲ The Crown & Punchbowl
High Street, Horningsea, CB5 9JG
Tel no: (01223) 860643
www.thecrownandpunchbowl.co.uk
Gastropub

Once a local watering hole, now a contemporary bar/restaurant-with-rooms, this seventeenth-century village hostelry pulls in crowds from Cambridge and the Milton Business Park. Food is the attraction and the place delivers on all counts. One blackboard spells out the day's fish specials, another lists assorted sausages with a choice of mash and sauces. Elsewhere, the printed menu advertises seared pigeon breast with lentil salad, beetroot

and Camembert tian (£5.95), chargrilled venison steak with celeriac mash, cherry and marsala sauce (£15.95) and desserts such as orange crème brûlée with lavender shortbread (£4.95). The nifty wine list kicks off at £12.50 (£3.50 a glass). Closed Sun D.

Huntingdon
Old Bridge Hotel
Crowd-pleasing modern menu
1 High Street, Huntingdon, PE29 3TQ
Tel no: (01480) 424300
www.huntsbridge.com
Modern British | £28
New Chef
🍷 ╍ 🛏£30

This handsome eighteenth-century building overlooking the River Ouse had a change of gear in 2007, when John Hoskins sold off the other properties in his Huntsbridge group. But the formula of serving modern food in an informal manner, backed up by first-class, good-value wines remains. The arrival of Alex Tyndall came to our attention as the Guide went to press – he was senior sous chef at Chapter Two and worked at Chapter One before that (see entries). The cooking seems likely to continue on similar lines, a blend of traditional favourites with modern bistro dishes: starters of Caesar salad or home-smoked duck breast with pear chutney and chicory, apple and walnut salad, alongside main courses of bouillabaisse, poached breast of corn-fed chicken with wild mushroom and potato cake, leeks and a morel and cream sauce, and chargrilled Aberdeenshire steak with béarnaise sauce. Reasonable mark-ups for the more expensive wines, plus around 15 or so wines by-the-glass from £3.65, highlight the owners' aim to encourage adventurous drinking. House wines start at £13.95.
Chef/s: Alex Tyndall. **Open:** all week L 12 to 2, D 6.30 to 9.30. **Meals:** alc (main courses £11 to £25). Set L £14.75 (2 courses). **Service:** not inc.
Details: Cards accepted. 80 seats. 30 seats outside. Air-con. Separate bar. No music. Wheelchair access. Children's portions. Car parking.

Keyston

Pheasant

Foodie thatched pub
Loop Road, Keyston, PE28 0RE
Tel no: (01832) 710241
www.thepheasant-keyston.co.uk
Modern European | £25
Cooking score: 2

£5 OFF   £30

In a well-heeled Cambridgeshire village, this whitewashed pub has a thatched roof and beams on display as a testament to its age. Food is in the ascendancy here – with various dining rooms to choose from – and plus-points are flexibility (just have a light meal of dressed crab with capers and anchovy) and the fact that there's always something interesting on offer, whether it be sautéed lamb's sweetbreads with pea and mint velouté and pea shoots to start, or port and blackcurrent jelly with madeleines and Jersey clotted cream to finish. In between, Jay Scrimshaw delivers a wealth of modern European ideas: roast rabbit with chargrilled polenta, roast tomato, basil, rocket and dandelion, or new season's rump of lamb with beetroot tart, feta cheese and tsatsiki. The interesting wine list starts at £13.75.
Chef/s: Jay Scrimshaw. **Open:** Tue to Sun L 12 to 2.30, D 6 to 9.30. **Closed:** Mon except bank hols. **Service:** not inc. **Details:** Cards accepted. 80 seats. 40 seats outside. Separate bar. Wheelchair access. Children's portions. Car parking.

Little Shelford

Sycamore House

Simple yet imaginative
1 Church Street, Little Shelford, CB2 5HG
Tel no: (01223) 843396
Modern British | £25
Cooking score: 2

£5 OFF   £30

Two simple, white-walled dining rooms provide a modest backdrop to Michael Sharp's uncomplicated yet imaginative style of cooking. The ever-changing menus offer four choices at each course, providing the freedom to focus firmly on quality, freshness and seasonality. Sample starters include a black pudding crêpe with horseradish cream, roasted onion and herb soup with a herb dumpling, and crab cakes with curry oil. Main courses continue in the same vein: crispy duck with soy sauce and spring onion gravy, spiced beef and chestnut pie with potato pastry, and blackened sea trout with citrus vinaigrette are typical of the style. Desserts have more homely leanings, and might take in sticky toffee pudding with butterscotch sauce or Bramley apple and mincemeat crumble. The wine list is simply annotated, and reasonably priced. Bottles start at £13.
Chef/s: Michael Sharp. **Open:** Wed to Sat D 7.30 to 9. **Meals:** Set D £25 (3 courses). **Service:** not inc. **Details:** Cards accepted. 24 seats. No music. No mobile phones.

Little Wilbraham

Hole in the Wall

Accomplished seasonal cooking
2 High Street, Little Wilbraham, CB1 5JY
Tel no: (01223) 812282
Modern British | £24
Cooking score: 4

£30

Christopher Leeton and Jenny Chapman's welcoming, traditional looking country dining pub does the local community proud. As one reporter remarked, it is a place serving 'good English food, well cooked and presented, without any of the hype of a gastropub.' Menus deliver plenty of choice with crowd-pleasing, modern focused dishes backed up by good flavours from well-sourced local ingredients. Appealing ideas among starters might include Bottisham smoked mackerel, potato and bacon pâté with crayfish tails and crème fraîche, for example, and twice-baked Cropwell Bishop Stilton and sprouting broccoli soufflé with roasted walnut sauce. Twelve-hour Dingley Dell pork belly served with home-made baked beans, peppered leeks and smoked paprika sauce has been praised, as has warm baked egg custard tart with poached rhubarb for dessert. Locally brewed ales confirm pub credentials, but four dozen wines span the globe and offer reasonable prices from £13.25.

Chef/s: Christopher Leeton. **Open:** Tue to Sun L 12 to 2, Tue to Sat D 7 to 9. **Closed:** 2 weeks Jan. **Meals:** alc (main courses £10.75 to £16.50). Set Sun L £21.60. **Service:** not inc. **Details:** Cards accepted. 60 seats. 20 seats outside. Separate bar. Wheelchair access. Children's portions. Car parking.

▌Littleport

ALSO RECOMMENDED
▲ Fen House
2 Lynn Road, Littleport, CB6 1QG
Tel no: (01353) 860645
French

Established in 1987 and still a treasured Fenland oasis, David Warne's exclusive Georgian residence is well worth a trip – even though it is only open two evenings a week. David looks to France for culinary inspiration and his fixed-price menus (£37.75 plus a complimentary cheese course) swim safely in the mainstream. A tartlet of chicken livers with garlic cream sauce might precede saddle of lamb or poached medallions of monkfish with ginger butter sauce, while desserts could

Cooking score

A score of 1 is a significant achievement. The score in any review is based on several meals, incorporating feedback from both our readers and inspectors. As a rough guide, 1 denotes capable cooking with some inconsistencies, rising steadily through different levels of technical expertise, until the scores between 6 and 10 indicate exemplary skills, along with innovation, artistry and ambition. If there is a new chef, we don't score the restaurant for the first year of entry. For further details, please see the scoring section in the introduction to the Guide.

feature apple sorbet in a biscuit cornet with Calvados custard. Around 50 wines from £15. Open Fri and Sat D only.

▌Sutton
The Anchor Inn
Warm welcome and relaxed feel
Sutton Gault, Sutton, CB6 2BD
Tel no: (01353) 778537
www.anchorsuttongault.co.uk
Modern British | £25
Cooking score: 2
£5 OFF ▐ V £30

The location may be 'slightly out of the way' in the wide-open expanses of Fens by the New Bedford River, but the unpretentious Anchor Inn draws customers from near and far (booking is advised). It welcomes with an open fire at the door and the relaxed feel in the three dining rooms is very much in keeping with the unpretentious cooking. The approach is relatively simple and well-received dishes have included Denham Estate venison loin steak with Parmesan dauphinoise and a port and redcurrant gravy, and smoked fillet of mackerel served on a fennel and orange salad with sautéed new potatoes and a warm citrus vinaigrette. To finish, the kitchen may dream up a trio of chocolate: tart, ice cream and white chocolate and hazelnut mousse. A nice, reasonably priced wine list gathers some 60 bottles from around the world, starting with French vin de pays at £13.65.

Chef/s: Adam Pickup. **Open:** all week L 12 to 2, D 7 to 9. **Closed:** D 25 and 26 Dec. **Meals:** Set L £13.65 (2 courses) to £13.65. **Service:** not inc. **Details:** Cards accepted. 55 seats. 40 seats outside. Wheelchair access. Children's portions. Car parking.

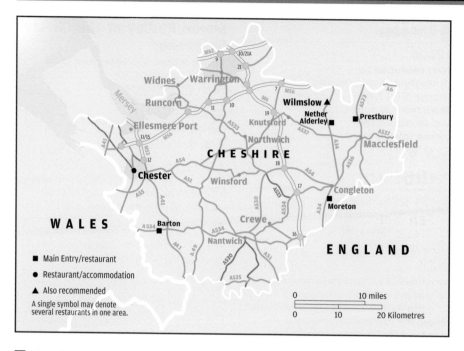

■ Barton

★NEW ENTRY★
Cock O Barton
Extensively refurbished gastropub
Barton Road, Barton, SY14 7HU
Tel no: (01829) 782277
www.thecockobarton.co.uk
Gastropub | £27
Cooking score: 2

No prizes for guessing that this extensively
refurbished gastropub is to be found in the
Cheshire village of Barton, but a bonus point
for knowing that it's the operation of former
Le Mont, Manchester, chef Robert Kisby. The
menu observes a degree of Gallic influence, as
in a starter of classic vichyssoise. However,
Kisby has rooted the Cock O Barton firmly in
Cheshire and the North West and the kitchen's
assured cooking uses much local produce,
including lamb from Wirswall and the
seemingly ubiquitous Goosnargh duck. The
platter menu provides an interesting option
for those wishing to try various dishes. A fish
platter consists of several pots of seafood,
including a potato salad enlivened with
smoked eel, potted shrimp and seared Loch
Fyne scallops. Sadly, any merits in the kitchen
are undone by a disorganised and seemingly
disinterested front-of-house team, whose
inattentive service makes 'the higher than
average cost seem too high a price to pay'.
House wine is £16.50.
Chef/s: Robert Kisby. **Open:** all week L 12 to 6, D 6
to 10. **Meals:** Set L and early D £13.75 (2 courses).
Service: not inc. **Details:** Cards accepted. 40 seats.
30 seats outside. Air-con. Wheelchair access. Music.
Children's portions. Car parking.

Scores on the Doors

To find out more about the Scores on the
Doors campaign, please visit the Food
Standard's Agency website:
www.food.gov.uk or www.which.co.uk.

Chester

Locus

Jazzy evening venue
111 Boughton, Chester, CH3 5BH
Tel no: (01244) 311112
www.locustheplace.co.uk
Modern British | £28
Cooking score: 1

A pair of dining rooms done out in today's muted colours, with a mixture of slate and wood floors sets the tone at this lively city dinner venue, which also offers live jazz on Sunday evenings. Andrew Smyth offers a take on today's brasserie style, with main dishes such as red mullet and noodles in shellfish cream sauce, or venison Diane with honey-roast vegetables. Vegetarian dishes have included red pepper and artichoke strudel with rocket and watercress. You might kick things off with curried parsnip soup, and end in fine style with pineapple poached in passion-fruit liqueur with mango sauce, or a choice from the English and Irish cheeses. House wines and cellar selections provide good drinking to suit all budgets, with prices starting at £11.95, or £4.95 for a large glass.
Chef/s: Andrew Smyth. **Open:** Tue to Sat D 6.30 to 10, Sun D 5.30 to 9. **Closed:** 24 to 26 Dec, 1 Jan. **Meals:** alc (main courses £12.50 to £21.45). Set D (Tue to Thur) £11.95 (2 courses). Set D Sun £15.95. **Service:** not inc. **Details:** Cards accepted. 42 seats. Separate bar. Wheelchair access. Music. Children allowed. Car parking.

Symbols

 Accommodation is available.

 Three courses for less than £30.

 More than five vegetarian dishes.

 £5-off voucher scheme.

🍷 Notable wine list.

Simon Radley at the Chester Grosvenor

Reliably refined, with added imagination
Eastgate, Chester, CH1 1LT
Tel no: (01244) 324024
www.chestergrosvenor.com
Modern European | £65
Cooking score: 7

🍷 ⊨ V

After 20 years, off and on, at the Chester Grosvenor, chef Simon Radley deserves to have his name in lights. As the Guide went to press this was about to happen, with the Arkle restaurant due to emerge from refurbishment as Simon Radley at the Chester Grosvenor. The hushed Library Bar, also refitted, becomes the Arkle Bar. What's unlikely to change is Radley's assured, imaginative style or playful outlook. Customers looking for luxury might enjoy a first course called 'lobster and langoustine', a fat, light seafood raviolo dusted with Parmesan and served on a sweet pumpkin purée. Those prepared to slum it could try ham hock with a Dover sole fillet and cauliflower cream. Main courses might include Herdwick mutton with a little pastilla-style parcel of the flaked meat, or beef fillet cooked at 53 degrees precisely and served with intense mushrooms, shaved truffles, and a tiny, perfect quenelle of clotted cream. Dessert might be a delicious but impractical trio of chocolate 'croustades', pastry cups that runneth over with saucy chocolate paired with curry or fruit essences. If refurbishment meant the retirement of the cheese trolley, laden with well-kept continental and English choices, there would be a riot in the hotel hallways. With assistance it's possible to find a bottle for around £35, but the extensive, French-led list is happy hunting territory for those with deeper pockets.
Chef/s: Simon Radley. **Open:** Tue to Sat 7 to 10. **Closed:** Sun and Mon, 24 to 27 Dec. **Meals:** Set D £59 to £70. **Service:** 12.5%. **Details:** Cards accepted. 45 seats. Air-con. Separate bar. No music. No mobile phones. Wheelchair access. Children's portions. Car parking.

The Good Food Guide 2009

ALSO RECOMMENDED

▲ Brasserie 10/16

Brookdale Place, Chester, CH1 3DY
Tel no: (01244) 322288
www.brasserie1016.com
Modern European

'The parking in Chester in dearer than the food,' quipped one reporter about this buzzy cosmopolitan brasserie. Prices here are 'unbelievable' – especially at lunchtime, when £6.95 will buy you smoked trout with cucumber salad followed by chicken with black pudding and grain mustard mash. The full menu deals in generous eclectic food along the lines of steamed mussels with saffron cream, steaks, and braised oxtail bourguignon with parsnip purée (£12.95), with passion-fruit cheesecake (£4.95) for dessert. The wine list promises bargains aplenty from £10.95 (£2.75 a glass). Open all week (all day Sun).

■ Congleton

READERS RECOMMEND
L'Endroit

70/72 Lawton Street, Congleton, CW12 1RS
Tel no: 01260 299548
www.lendroit.co.uk
'Small restaurant priding itself on traditional French cooking'

■ Moreton

★NEW ENTRY★
Pecks

After eight...
Newcastle Road, Moreton, CW12 4SB
Tel no: (01260) 275161
www.pecksrest.co.uk
Modern British | £22
Cooking score: 3

When they took over Pecks in late 2007, Andrew and Sue Pear retained the 'dinner at eight' concept. It means that everyone starts at the same time and your multi-course meal is synchronised with the other 100 or so customers in the restaurant. What could be a gimmicky approach is actually very sensible and hugely enjoyable. Head chef Michael Brooke has been here for 21 years and his menus change monthly to utilise the very freshest seasonal produce. The style is ultimately modern British, but Brooke isn't afraid to display some global influences. Over seven courses the menu can take in French onion soup, tuna sashimi and leg of lamb with an individual hotpot, while the seemingly never-ending desserts include the 'best cheesecakes in Cheshire'. A full and reasonable wine list is available (from £13.50), but every Tuesday to Thursday guests have the chance to BYO with no corkage charge.
Chef/s: Michael Brooke. **Open:** Tue to Sun L 12 to 2, Tue to Sat D at 8 (1 sitting). **Closed:** Sun D, Mon. **Meals:** Set L £16.25, Set D £ 29.95 (Tue to Thu), £38.95 (Fri and Sat). **Service:** not inc. **Details:** Cards accepted. 110 seats. Air-con. Wheelchair access. Music. Children's portions. Car parking.

■ Nether Alderley

The Wizard

A magic place
Macclesfield Road, Nether Alderley, SK10 4UB
Tel no: (01625) 584000
Modern British | £30
Cooking score: 2

The magical Wizard restaurant has been impressing visitors for the last 11 years, its quiet rural location inspiring a peaceful and considered atmosphere in which to enjoy Paul Beattie's modern British cooking. He takes a straightforward approach to good quality produce, with starters such as gravad lax with a firm and fresh new potato salad 'full of vital citrus and earthy flavours', and a 'delicious' goats' cheese and Cheddar pâté served on hot toasted walnut bread typically illustrating his style. Mains again reflect a sensible choice of produce, teaming perfectly ripe roast cherry tomatoes with penne and homemade pesto, and showing an appreciation for crowd-pleasing flavours in dishes such as rack of lamb with bubble and squeak and a rosemary jus. House wine is £14.50.

Chef/s: Paul Beattie. **Open:** Tue to Sun L 12 to 2, Tue to Sat D 7 to 9.30. **Meals:** Set Sun L £18.95 (2 courses) to £22.95. **Service:** 10%. **Details:** Cards accepted. 80 seats. 20 seats outside. Children's portions. Car parking.

▌Prestbury

White House

Classy neighbourhood venue
The Village, Prestbury, SK10 4DG
Tel no: (01625) 829336
www.thewhitehouseinprestbury.com
Modern British | £32
Cooking score: 3

£5
OFF

Head Chef James Roberts has gradually asserted his own personality over this Prestbury venue, constructing an impressive take on a modern British menu. With influences drawn from all corners – starters include king prawn dim sum, and scallops with Parma ham and sweet potato – there is much to be applauded. Mains tend towards a thorough investigation of quality duck, beef and pork dishes, with the addition of some fish, but a finale of a cappuccino of vanilla crème and home-made biscuits makes an enjoyable point about the good quality food on offer. The affluence of the area – your neighbouring tables are likely to be taken by premiership footballers – is noted in the ten or so Champagnes and sparkling wines on offer (starting at £24.25 for a notable Prosecco). The rest of the wine list – which runs to over 100 labels – largely favours some safe choice French wines with the occasional New World surprise.

Chef/s: James Roberts. **Open:** Tue to Sun L 12 to 2, D 6 to 9 (Sat 7 to 10). **Closed:** 25 Dec, 1 Jan. **Meals:** alc (main courses £9 to £22). Set D £18 to £22 (3 courses). **Service:** not inc. **Details:** Cards accepted. 72 seats. 32 seats outside. Air-con. Separate bar. No mobile phones. Wheelchair access. Music. Children's portions. Car parking.

▌Rainow

READERS RECOMMEND
The Highwayman Inn
Gastropub
Macclesfield Road, Rainow, SK10 5UU
Tel no: 01625 573245
'A gastropub that stands and delivers'

▌Wilmslow

ALSO RECOMMENDED
▲ Heddy's
100-102 Water Lane, Wilmslow, SK9 5BB
Tel no: (01625) 526855
www.heddys.com
Middle Eastern

A magnet for devotees of affordable Middle Eastern and Mediterranean food, Heddy Ghazizadeh's popular Wilmslow restaurant delivers the goods with impressive consistency and genuine gusto. Mixed meze platters (£16 for two) promise a cornucopia of dishes; otherwise the menu offers hot and cold starters ranging from falafel, tabbouleh and mutabal to lahma bil-ajeen (pancakes topped with minced lamb and vegetables). High-protein kebabs and couscous (from £11.50) are main course favourites, with baklava (£3.95), halva and homemade ice creams bringing up the rear. House French is £13.50 (£3.75 a glass), but it's worth checking out the beefy Lebanese bottles. Takeaways. Closed L Mon and Sat.

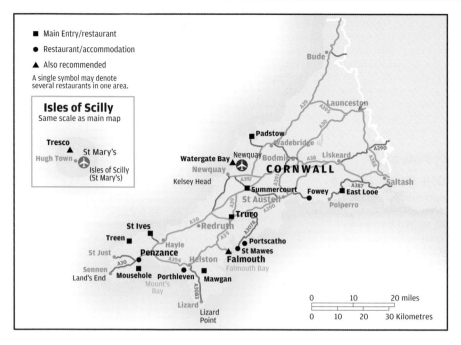

Main Entry/restaurant

Restaurant/accommodation

▲ Also recommended

A single symbol may denote
several restaurants in one area.

Isles of Scilly
Same scale as main map

East Looe
Trawlers on the Quay
Sea-fresh fish
The Quay, East Looe, East Looe, PL13 1AH
Tel no: (01503) 263593
www.trawlersrestaurant.co.uk
Seafood | £30
Cooking score: 3

£5
OFF

Situated right on the East Looe quay, Trawlers
is naturally about spanking-fresh seafood. A
reporter appreciates the quality of the raw
materials, pointing out that when they are this
fresh, the simpler preparations are often the
best. Begin with a bowl of seafood soup, if you
will, or try a timbale combining prawns, crab
and avocado with crème fraîche and a chive
dressing. Mains explore different herby
seasonings, perhaps coriander with ginger and
lime for John Dory, or thyme and lemon with
a trio of fish. A tomato and basil salsa makes a
fitting accompaniment to crisp-skinned sea
bass on herbed mash. One meat and one

vegetarian option are usually available, the
former possibly roast duck breast sauced with
brandy and green peppercorns. Finish with
dark chocolate and orange terrine, or apple
and Calvados pancakes with clotted cream ice
cream. Wines start at £13.95, or £3.75 a glass.
Chef/s: Mark Napper. **Open:** Tue to Sat D 6.30 to
10.30. **Meals:** alc (main courses £14.95 to £18.95).
Service: not inc. **Details:** Cards accepted. 36 seats.
12 seats outside. Wheelchair access. Music.
Children's portions.

Falmouth

ALSO RECOMMENDED
▲ Three Mackerel
Swanpool Beach, Falmouth, TR11 5BG
Tel no: (01326) 311886
www.thethreemackerel.com
Modern British

Vibrant cooking with a Mediterranean slant is
the deal in this bright, buzzy café and terrace
overlooking Swanpool Beach. It is clearly on
good form judging by recent reports. Fish is a

strength, say risotto of scallops and chorizo (£9.95) or local seafood poached in crab bisque (£14.95). Lunch brings beef stroganoff (£11.95) and a few tapas dishes, while dinner can include fillet of beef with hand-cut chips (£17.95), or duck breast with gratin dauphinoise (£15.95). To finish, orange tart with lemon sorbet is recommended. Open all week.

■ Fowey

Old Quay House
Waterside restaurant
28 Fore Street, Fowey, PL23 1AQ
Tel no: (01726) 833302
www.theoldquayhouse.com
Modern British | £35
Cooking score: 2

This smart modern restaurant enjoys a spectacular waterfront location, with uninterrupted views across the Fowey Estuary. From the terrace you could almost dip your toes in the water. The menu takes its cue from the surroundings and offers a good number of fish and seafood options: starters such as moules marinière or confit grilled sardines could be followed by grilled lemon sole with crayfish butter and roast carrots or roast haddock with bubble and squeak, poached duck egg and mustard hollandaise. Alternatives might be roast beetroot and fromage blanc with walnut dressing or a charcuterie plate for two to start, and then a cassoulet of local duck or butternut squash risotto with walnut and rocket. Finish with chocolate fondant, plum tart with caramel ice cream and liquorice syrup, or tarte Tatin for two with Calvados crème fraîche. The wine list is helpfully divided by style, and covers everywhere from France to New Zealand. Bottles from £15.50.
Chef/s: Jane Carson. **Open:** all week D 7 to 9, summer L 12.30 to 2.30. **Meals:** alc L (main courses £12 to £16). Set D £27.50 (2 courses) to £35. **Service:** not inc. **Details:** Cards accepted. 38 seats. 38 seats outside. Separate bar. Wheelchair access. Music.

Restaurant Nathan Outlaw
Making waves in Cornwall
Marina Villa Hotel, Esplanade, Fowey, PL23 1HY
Tel no: (01726) 833315
www.themarinahotel.co.uk
Modern British | £45
Cooking score: 8

Since he opened in the Marina Villa Hotel in 2007, Nathan Outlaw has been making discreet but powerful waves. The stylish, contemporary dining room offers a stunning view of the Fowey Estuary, but contains no extraneous décor to distract from the classy cooking; even napery has been banished to ensure a relaxed ambience. Outlaw's food is naturally centred on impeccable local and regional produce, meats, seafood and locally-grown vegetables, all of which come together in dishes that speak boldly and eloquently for themselves. Reports this year have been full of praise, as much for the 'unique experience' as for the 'incredible food'. As one who tried the eight-course tasting menu noted: 'some of the dishes, like the black bream with pickled chicory tart, pistachio and grapefruit, I have consigned to my memory bank as amongst the best I have ever eaten'. Elsewhere, cured salmon with marinated beetroot risotto, the flavours pointed by horseradish and dill, might open a meal. For others, it could be pork belly with curry and apple, fried eggs and cress. Variations on a theme may well appear among main courses, for example lamb teamed with salsify and garlic and sweetbreads with balsamic, as well as 'hugely satisfying' pairings of ling with ham, razor clams and shallot, sweet basil with bacon. Otherwise, dishes such as the benchmark rose veal with cauliflower, sage, onions and mushrooms impress in all the right ways – tender, flavourful meat, perfect accompaniments delivering resonant depths of flavour. The British cheeses are in flawless nick, and clear flavours distinguish desserts such as spiced red wine-poached pear with vanilla rice pudding and ice cream, and blood orange mousse with toasted almond ice cream. Appetisers, pre-

desserts and petits fours are all in tune with the rest of the meal, and service receives plaudits again this year for its ease, charm and general professionalism. The user-friendly wine list is grouped by style and prices start at £25.
Chef/s: Nathan Outlaw. **Open:** Sat L 12 to 1.30, Tue to Sun D 7 to 9 (open Mon in season). **Meals:** Set D £32.50. **Service:** not inc. **Details:** Cards accepted. 36 seats. Separate bar. Music. Car parking.

▌Mawgan

New Yard
A kitchen feeding off its location
Trelowarren, Mawgan, TR12 6AF
Tel no: (01326) 221595
www.trelowarren.com
Modern British | £24
Cooking score: 2

The clean and spare look of this former coach house on the Trelowarren Estate can make it a 'noisy, echoey room' when busy, but much effort goes into the cooking and there's a resolute focus on value on the plate. The kitchen literally feeds off its location; one glance at the menu tells you that Greg Laskey is proud of his Cornish produce. Monkfish is wrapped in Cornish Coppa ham and served with an open ravioli of local mushrooms and artichokes, while sirloin steak from the Lanarth Estate comes with hazelnuts, bacon and creamed potatoes, and the list extends to wild garlic soup, Falmouth Bay crab, and 'very good' venison. With generous portions, one can be outfaced at dessert stage. If not, try the home-made ice cream, or the walnut and sultana bread-and-butter pudding. Wines are a decent spread of contemporary styles from £14.50.
Chef/s: Greg Laskey. **Open:** all week L 12 to 2 (2.30 Sun), D 7 to 9.30. **Closed:** Mon mid Sept to Whitsun. **Meals:** Set L £14.95, set D £22. **Service:** not inc. **Details:** Cards accepted. 45 seats. 20 seats outside. Wheelchair access. Music. Children's portions. Car parking.

▌Mousehole

2 Fore Street
An honest bistro with harbour views
2 Fore Street, Mousehole, TR19 6QU
Tel no: (01736) 731164
www.2forestreet.co.uk
Modern British | £24
Cooking score: 2

From the large shop front windows giving views over the picturesque harbour to the distressed wooden tables and white walls with nautical artwork, this bistro presents an honest openness. First-class and generally local raw materials underpin the operation and Joe Wardell's simple, compact menu is an expectedly – though not exclusively – fishy affair. Think sardines with marinated beetroot, or a well-reported lobster platter with a selection of home-made bread, followed by fried skate wing with capers, croûtons and red chard or 'perfect' rib-eye steak with chunky chips. Lunch has delivered 'superb' blue cheese and broccoli soup and 'excellent' crab and spinach bake, while straightforward desserts – like lemon curd pannacotta with vanilla shortbread – continue the theme. Nothing is too much trouble for the keen, friendly staff. The short, well-chosen wine list starts at £13.50. Must book dinner.
Chef/s: Joe Wardell. **Open:** all week 10 to 5, D 6 to 9.30. **Closed:** all Jan. **Meals:** alc (main courses £10.50 to £14.75). **Service:** not inc. **Details:** Cards accepted. 36 seats. 20 seats outside. Wheelchair access. Music. Children's portions.

▌Padstow

★NEW ENTRY★
Custard

An English diner to warm the heart
1st Floor, 1a The Strand, Padstow, PL28 8BS
Tel no: (0870) 1700740
www.custarddiner.com
British | £25
Cooking score: 3

Snug in the crowded heart of Padstow, this modern-retro restaurant has décor and dishes to arouse rose-tinted nostalgia. Billed as 'an English diner', its stylish but homely first floor rooms have the feel of a re-imagined tearoom, complete with touches of chintz. To match this, old school favourites might include prawn cocktail or mature Scottish beef with Cornish potatoes. However, much of the menu has a more sophisticated edge: witness starters of wood pigeon with a soft hen's egg and black pudding or chicken and duck liver parfait with red onion jam from a winter lunch menu, or spring dinnertime mains such as pork fillet with parsnips, white pudding hash and red wine or Cornish pollock with white beans, mussels and wild garlic. Desserts are a reunion of old friends: hot cross bun pudding, baked egg custard with Garibaldi biscuits and meringue with raspberries and lemon curd ice cream are typical offerings. The interesting, expertly-annotated wine list starts at £16.50.
Chef/s: Dan Gedge. **Open:** Mon, Wed to Sun L 12 to 2.30, D 7 to 9.30. **Closed:** Tue, 25 Dec, 1 May.
Meals: alc (main courses £9.50 to £16.50).
Service: not inc. **Details:** Cards accepted. 65 seats. Air-con. Music. Children's portions.

Average price

The average price listed in main-entry reviews denotes the price of a three-course meal, without wine.

No. 6

Refined, ambitious, accomplished
6 Middle Street, Padstow, PL28 8AP
Tel no: (01841) 532093
www.number6inpadstow.co.uk
Modern European | £45
Cooking score: 6

In a town not short of fine-dining options (relative to its Lilliputian size), this is Padstow's current trailblazer. Plumb in the centre, and hard to miss, it feels both smart and relaxed, the tables dressed in their crispest whites, with minimal floral adornments contributing to the keen, modern design tone. Paul Ainsworth writes his menus in the modern style too, with each headline protein – prawn, veal, pollock – subtitled with its respective elaborations. Of these there may well be quite an accumulation. Pork might consist of glazed cheek, belly and trotter, with pickled pears and béarnaise, and that's just as a starter. Contemporary combinations familiar from other go-to kitchens might feature, as in scallops with black pudding, salmon with beetroot and horseradish, or venison with red cabbage and chocolate, but the degree of refinement in the cooking here is such that dishes never feel like clichés. Indeed, they gain from the patient construction of flavours, with something like sea bream from Newlyn day-boats ably supported by smoked eel, green beans and onions stewed in red wine. Saddle of local lamb is attended by a fricassee of its offals, along with artichokes, lemon and thyme, to constitute solid yet graceful impact. This is one place where the tasting menu (a seven-course affair, with or without wines) is a definite temptation and represents fine value. Today's preference for raiding childhood memories at dessert stage crops up in a serving of almond trifle with marzipan pannacotta, raspberries, and gingerbread and battenburg ice cream, but there might equally be a cheesecake of white chocolate and blueberry served with dark chocolate and sesame sorbet. Service is commended as top-drawer, and there is a fabulous wine list to ponder. The

Eat with the seasons

These days, you'll be hard-pressed to find an establishment or chef that doesn't profess an interest in seasonal food.

Gordon Ramsay has recently attracted praise and criticism in equal measure for suggesting that chefs should be fined for serving food out of season. Here are some restaurants that avoid the wrath of Ramsay.

The success of the **Three Chimneys** on the Isle of Skye is at least partly down to its adherence to the finest Highland produce such as venison and crab, all accessed at the peak of its season.

Urmston's **Isinglass Restaurant** sources local quality foods, with hand-gathered nettles and burdock appearing on the menu.

It's often a question of food yards rather than food miles for Southwold's **Sutherland House** which prints food miles on the menu.

Martin Burge at **Whatley Manor** in Wiltshire sources much of the food on his menu from surrounding farms and fishermen.

Sourcing 90 per cent of his ingredients from local Cornish suppliers, **New Yard's** Greg Laskey creates delicious wild garlic soup and serves Cornish cheeses.

Goods Shed in Kent is based in a daily farmer's market and takes its produce from only local suppliers emphasising the superior taste of fresh, seasonal foods.

By keeping the menu pared down, the **Petersham Nurseries Café** in Surrey can focus on sourcing the perfect ingredients from the walled gardens of Petersham House itself.

Native Welsh ingredients are prominent at **Ye Olde Bulls Head** in Beaumaris and diners can enjoy seasonal, local skate and beef.

With a frequently changing menu, London's **The River Café** can claim to have been at the forefront of the current obsession with seasonality.

Local seafoods and meats are the speciality at **Monachyle Mhor** in Scotland and their new fish venture Mhorfish has been hailed as the best fish and chip shop in Britain.

wines of an Oregon grower, Cristom Vineyards, receive star billing, and are followed by Champagne cocktails and a handsome range by-the-glass (from £4.75). If you looked no further, you would have been well served, but the list then takes off on a VIP tour of the global vineyard, with many sumptuous growers and ripe vintages.

Chef/s: Paul Ainsworth. **Open:** Tue to Sat D 7 to 10. **Meals:** Set D £45 to £55. **Service:** 10%. **Details:** Cards accepted. 50 seats. Wheelchair access. Music. Children's portions.

Rick Stein's Café
Good-value bistro food
10 Middle Street, Padstow, PL28 8BQ
Tel no: (01841) 532700
www.rickstein.com
Seafood | £22
Cooking score: 2
 £30

A family-friendly attitude is one of the virtues of Rick Stein's cheerful, functional café set in a former fisherman's cottage in the centre of Padstow. It's a popular place, there's lots of animated chatter and close-packed tables are constantly in demand. And it's not surprising when the kitchen delivers value for money and generous helpings of straightforward bistro food (especially fish). Salt-and-pepper prawns or hot-smoked salmon with beetroot and horseradish dressing are typical, along with mains of whole lemon sole with roasted red pepper, garlic and oregano, and goujons of plaice with tartare sauce and chips. Desserts range from lemon posset to Bakewell tart. Breakfast is served between 8am and 10am (try the smoked haddock with poached egg or the hot bacon sandwich). The short wine list opens at £16.50.

Chef/s: Luke Taylor. **Open:** all week L 12 to 2, D 7 to 9.30. **Closed:** 24 Dec D to 27 Dec, L 1 May. **Meals:** alc (main courses £9.50 to £16.95). Set D £21.95. **Service:** not inc. **Details:** Cards accepted. 40 seats. 121 seats outside. Music. Children's portions.

St Petroc's Bistro
Long-standing fixture of the Rick Stein Empire
4 New Street, Padstow, PL28 8EA
Tel no: (01841) 532700
www.rickstein.com
Seafood | £29
Cooking score: 2

This long-standing fixture of the Rick Stein empire is a light, bright and breezy white-painted hotel just above the harbour and the crowds. The bistro has Stein's trademark combination of white walls, wood floors and large contemporary canvases, and places the emphasis on fish. Generally the kitchen succeeds in its efforts. Relatively unfussy dishes included curried crab mayonnaise, with main courses offering whole grilled lemon sole with anchovy butter or salmon with sorrel sauce, but there's also rib-eye steak with béarnaise and calf's liver with balsamic caramelised onions and crisp pancetta. Desserts run to raspberry pithiviers with crème anglaise and crème brûlée. House wines from £16.50.

Chef/s: Robert Brinham. **Open:** all week L 12 to 2, D 7 to 10. **Closed:** 24 Dec D to 27 Dec L, 1 May. **Meals:** alc (main courses £10.50 to £18.95). Set menu £15 (Nov to March). **Service:** not inc. **Details:** Cards accepted. 75 seats. 20 seats outside. Separate bar. Wheelchair access. Children's portions.

Seafood Restaurant
Rick Stein's expensively revamped flagship
Riverside, Padstow, PL28 8BY
Tel no: (01841) 532700
www.rickstein.com
Seafood | £50
Cooking score: 5

A £2.5m refit has given Rick Stein's flagship restaurant a fresh new look, and brought a seafood bar to its heart. Here you can order anything from the menu without booking, and watch the preparation of seafood platters, sushi and sashimi. Although Rick Stein is no longer in the kitchen he is still an effective ambassador for his restaurants. This, his first, opened in 1975 and continues to reflect his passion for fish brought straight to the kitchen from the boats that tie up within sight of the restaurant. As Stein puts it, this is not supposed to be a temple of gastronomy, it's a relaxed environment in which to enjoy exhilaratingly fresh fish. The general thrust of the cooking is towards simplicity, but this does not mean predictability; flavours come from all over the world, so alongside classics like oysters, 'fruits de mer' or fish and shellfish soup with rouille and Parmesan, starters could include crab, ginger and coriander broth or Chinese-style steamed scallops. Main courses reflect a similar scope: fish and chips, monkfish vindaloo, Singapore chilli crab, and chargrilled whole Dover sole with sea salt and lime are typical players. Despite the changes to the interior there is a comforting sense of continuity; the same paintings are back on the walls and a buzzy, unbuttoned atmosphere prevails. To help things along, the wine list provides a lengthy, nicely annotated selection from around the world, with a good number available by-the-glass. Bottles are priced from £17.

Chef/s: David Sharland and Stephanie Delourme. **Open:** L 12 to 2, D 7 to 10. **Closed:** 25, 26 Dec, 1 May. **Meals:** alc (main courses £17.50 to £48). **Service:** not inc. **Details:** Cards accepted. 120 seats. Air-con. Wheelchair access. Children's portions.

▎Penzance

Abbey Restaurant
There's a new kid on the block
Abbey Street, Penzance, TR18 4AR
Tel no: (01736) 330680
www.theabbeyonline.com
Modern European | £40
Cooking score: 6

Abbey Street leads down to the harbour; to get your bearings, look out for the brilliant blue exterior of the Abbey Hotel, which is next door to this striking modern restaurant. There are two contrasting areas: a cavern-shaped bar/ lounge, 'ceilings, the lot' painted a deep red

(with a plasma screen view of the kitchen at work), and a light, art-strewn first floor dining room with windows looking out to Mount's Bay. Since last year's Guide, Michael Riemenschneider has taken over from Ben Tunnicliffe and his creative and confident cooking has made quite a splash locally. Sourcing and timing of materials are both admirable and combinations are well-considered, be they pigeon with foie gras and spinach and an 'intense' ragoût made from the leg meat, the more adventurous langoustine 'cooked in a meaty veal stock' with pearl barley, broad beans and asparagus (the standout dish at inspection) or halibut with jellies of pickle and cucumber. That same sense of balance runs through desserts: citrus assiette, for example, delivers a lemony charlotte, sorbet and 'unusual but very good' pumpernickel pudding. The wine list displays evidence of imagination throughout, there's plenty of choice by-the-glass and bottles start at £16.

Chef/s: Michael Riemenschneider. **Open:** Tue to Sat L 12 to 2.30, D 6.30 to 9.30. **Closed:** bank hols. **Meals:** Set L £24.95. Menu surprise £85. Tasting menu £89. **Service:** not inc. **Details:** Cards accepted. 24 seats. Air-con. Separate bar. Music.

Bay Restaurant
A breath of fresh sea air
Hotel Penzance, Britons Hill, Penzance, TR18 3AE
Tel no: (01736) 366890
www.bay-penzance.co.uk
Modern European | £30
Cooking score: 3

Famed for its dreamy views of Penzance harbour and Mount's Bay, this contemporary restaurant in the Hotel Penzance (formerly Mount Prospect) is also known for its eye-popping art exhibitions. On the food front, bistro-style lunches of Tregagles rib-eye steak or hake fillet with salsa verde give way to evening meals with a more ambitious outlook. The kitchen takes a broad, open-minded approach to things culinary, serving South Coast scallops with chervil, avocado and pink grapefruit salad, and pairing smoked paprika-dusted medallions of monkfish with Nanterrow goats' cheese pesto. Seasonal West Country produce also turns up in fillet of Cornish beef with caramelised red onions, Savoy cabbage and beetroot jus or breast of red-leg partridge and pigeon with buttered winter greens, chestnuts and juniper jus. Artisan Cornish cheeses are alternatives to sweet-toothed offerings such as elderflower and ginger baba with honey-roasted fig and cardamom anglaise. A special 'local food heroes' dinner is served on the third Sunday of each month. The well-spread wine list opens with house selections at £13.75 (£4 a glass).

Chef/s: Ben Reeves and Katie Semmens. **Open:** Mon to Fri L 12 to 2, all week D 6 to 9.30. **Meals:** Set L £11 (2 courses) to £14. Set D £22 (2 courses) to £47.50 (9 courses). **Service:** not inc. **Details:** Cards accepted. 50 seats. 10 seats outside. Air-con. Separate bar. No mobile phones. Wheelchair access. Music. Children's portions. Car parking.

Harris's
Cornish produce in a cosy bistro
46 New Street, Penzance, TR18 2LZ
Tel no: (01736) 364408
www.harrissrestaurant.co.uk
Modern European | £32
Cooking score: 2

£5
OFF

'This little restaurant doesn't get the recognition it deserves because of its side street location', notes a reporter who has been visiting Harris's for more than ten years. Indeed, the owners have been here for nearly four decades (so someone should able to point you in the right direction), serving their brand of uncomplicated food that allows fresh local Cornish produce to take centre stage. Fish plays a leading role, with supplies from Newlyn's fish market just three miles away; perhaps steamed John Dory served with a saffron sauce, while meat-lovers might prefer the roast Cornish spring lamb with red wine and rosemary sauce. There's a good-value light lunch and generous enough carte, while the

wine list spans the globe in country order, offers reasonable mark-ups and house selections from £13.50.
Chef/s: Roger Harris. **Open:** Tue to Sat, L 12 to 2, D 7 to 9.30 (open Mon June to Sept). **Closed:** Christmas. **Meals:** alc (main courses L £10.50 to £14.95, D £16.95 to £27.50). **Service:** 10%. **Details:** Cards accepted. 40 seats. Wheelchair access. Children allowed.

Summer House
Echoes of the sunny Med
Cornwall Terrace, Penzance, TR18 4HL
Tel no: (01736) 363744
www.summerhouse-cornwall.com
Mediterranean | £32
Cooking score: 2

Ciro and Linda Zaino's self-styled 'boutique B&B'-cum-Mediterranean restaurant is a strange-looking hexagonal Regency house hidden away in a mews just a hop from the sea. The dining room is suffused with sunny colour, and guests can also eat al fresco in the seductive Italianate courtyard with its palm trees and terracotta pots. Ciro's food is true to his native roots and he cooks with verve. He buys fish from the Penzance boats and deals with it in straightforward fashion: lemon sole is seared and served with ginger and saffron sauce, while sea bass might be spiked with Pernod. Italy contributes pappardelle with black olives and aubergine caviar, while France is the inspiration for fillet of pork with prunes and Armagnac. Spiced figs with mascarpone gelato or Normandy apple tart with Calvados highlight the same influences when it comes to desserts. Meanwhile, the 40-bin list puts all of its money on Italy; prices start at £14 (£4 a glass).
Chef/s: Ciro Zaino. **Open:** Thur to Sun D only 7.30 to 9.30. **Closed:** Nov to Feb. **Meals:** Set D £31.50. **Service:** 10%. **Details:** Cards accepted. 22 seats. 22 seats outside. Separate bar. No mobile phones. Music. Car parking.

Porthleven

★NEW ENTRY★
Kota
Personable family-run restaurant
Harbour Head, Porthleven, TR13 9JA
Tel no: (01326) 562407
www.kotarestaurant.co.uk
Modern European | £25
Cooking score: 2

Kota is a cheery place with an informal, rustic interior of beamed ceilings and plain wood tables and is lifted right out of its harbourside restaurant niche by 'striking' paintings on walls, and cooking that tends to impress. It may not be particularly polished or refined, but the manner in which good raw materials are combined demonstrates real skill. Even when dishes are as simple as oxtail stew with gremolada and a spring root vegetable, or lamb rump with butternut squash, caponata and herb-garlic oil, they have a straightforwardness about them that is appealing. Soy mirin dressing with rare sesame-crusted tuna, and wasabi tartare alongside tempura battered cod reflect Jude Kereama's Maori, Chinese and Malaysian roots. These are good ideas, well executed and backed up by honest-tasting desserts such as spiced apple and ginger pudding with rhubarb ice cream. House wine is £12.50.
Chef/s: Jude Kereama. **Open:** Fri to Sat L 12 to 2, Tue to Sat D 6 to 9 (winter), Fri to Mon L 12 to 2, all week D 6 to 9 (summer). **Closed:** Jan, first week Feb. **Meals:** alc (main courses £10.95 to £17.95). **Service:** not inc. **Details:** Cards accepted. 35 seats. Separate bar. Music. Children's portions.

Scores on the Doors

To find out more about the Scores on the Doors campaign, please visit the Food Standard's Agency website: www.food.gov.uk or www.which.co.uk.

Portscatho
Driftwood
Seascapes and seasonal food
Rosevine, Portscatho, TR2 5EW
Tel no: (01872) 580644
www.driftwoodhotel.co.uk
Modern European | £43
Cooking score: 5

Paul and Fiona Robinson's elegant Cornish hotel enjoys some of the finest panoramic views you could wish for, thanks to its glorious position perched high above the sea at Rosevine. Huge plate-glass windows make the most of the vistas, while sunny yellow and blue seaside colours point up the 'driftwood' theme – as well as adding to the holiday feel in the pretty, wood-floored dining room. Fresh-from-the-boats Cornish seafood naturally makes a big impact on Chris Eden's seasonal dinner menus; he serves filleted skate with aubergine caviar, crab, fennel and red peppers, and might match halibut with mushroom duxelles, squid and kohlrabi carpaccio and gremolada oil. His fondness for locally-garnered produce also shows in other dishes such as a terrine and parfait of Terras Farm duck with pickled apple purée, loin of venison with prune and juniper purée, or free-range Penvose Farm chicken with farfalle pasta, romaine lettuce, celery and tarragon. To conclude, guests should be suitably impressed by Bocaddon cheesecake with rhubarb and cardamom or vanilla crème brûlée with butterscotch, caramelised pears and Calvados ice cream. The carefully-chosen, 60-bin wine list is particularly strong on bottles from the New World. Prices start at £15 (£3.75 a glass).
Chef/s: Chris Eden. **Open:** all week D only 7 to 9.30. **Closed:** 8 Dec to 5 Feb. **Meals:** Set D £40. **Service:** not inc. **Details:** Cards accepted. 34 seats. Separate bar. No mobile phones. Music. Car parking.

St Ives

Alba
Good food by the harbour
Old Lifeboat House, Wharf Road, St Ives, TR26 1LF
Tel no: (01736) 797222
www.thealbarestaurant.com
Modern European | £30
Cooking score: 3

V

Alba has found its niche in this strikingly updated lifeboat house overlooking the harbour, which now ticks over as a relaxed, well-supported restaurant. The freshness of ingredients has impressed (local produce is taken seriously here), and dishes are shot through with big flavours, contrasts, colour and touches of finesse, as in a warm salad of scallops with slow-cooked vegetables and orange. Overall, the food treads a modern European path, taking in anything from fillet of Barbary duck breast with roasted red onions, sun-dried tomatoes, crispy polenta and balsamic jus to roasted monkfish with braised oxtail, roasted vegetable Parmentier and deep-fried leeks. To finish, expect desserts like pannacotta with caramelised orange and saffron. The wine list covers a lot of ground, with house selections from £12.95.
Chef/s: Grant Nethercott. **Open:** all week L 11.30 to 2, D 5 to 9.45 (6 to 9 low season). **Closed:** 25 & 26 Dec. **Meals:** alc (main courses £14.95 to £19.95). Set menu £13.50 (2 courses) to £16.50. **Service:** not inc. **Details:** Cards accepted. 65 seats. Air-con. Wheelchair access. Children's portions.

Porthminster Beach Café
Fresh seafood in fabulous beachside location
Porthminster Beach, St Ives, TR26 2EB
Tel no: (01736) 795352
www.porthminstercafe.co.uk
Seafood | £35
Cooking score: 4

As locations go, this one would be hard to beat. Porthminster Point looks over the sands and the bay towards the Godrevy lighthouse. Some readers have been reminded of

Australia, which may been what attracted Mick Smith, himself Australian-born, to St Ives in the first place. Add to that 'deliciously fresh seafood and wonderful service,' and, as another reporter comments 'what's not to love?' Fowey mussels crop up reliably, perhaps in a starter with chorizo and a buttery dressing of saffron, coriander and basil, or as an accompaniment to a main-course dish of paprika-baked hake, with parsnip fondant, tomato velouté and olive purée. Dishes are quite robust, but retain both balance and excitement, as when sea bass caught right on the doorstep (or in the bay, rather) is teamed with a gyoza dumpling of crab and langoustine, and a dressing of chilli tamarind jam. Meat dishes have included pink-roasted duck with salsify, peppered spinach and a sauce of pink gooseberries and Cointreau. Wines from £11.95 complete the picture. Porthgwidden Beach Café (open Apr to Oct) is under the same ownership.
Chef/s: Isaac Anderson and Mick Smith. **Open:** all week. L 12 to 4, D 6.30 to 10. **Closed:** Mon in winter. **Meals:** alc (main courses £10.50 to £21.50). **Service:** not inc. **Details:** Cards accepted. 57 seats. 70 seats outside. No mobile phones. Music. Children's portions.

St Andrews Street Bistro
Boho-chic bistro
16 St Andrews Street, St Ives, TR26 1AH
Tel no: (01736) 797074
Modern European | £22
Cooking score: 1

Tucked away down a narrow street behind the harbour, this boho-chic bistro – chandeliers, candelabras, low lighting, Persian rugs, funky artwork – has a relaxed and unpretentious feel. Menus of a sensible length keep things simple but maintain interest, focusing on showing off good raw materials. The cooking is a robust mix of English domestic and broadly Mediterranean ways, with game terrine and apple chutney cropping up among the likes of stuffed baby squid with ricotta, marjoram, chilli and anchovies, or thyme and

feta lamb chops with baked courgette, potato and tomato. Elsewhere, morcilla (black pudding) with apples, watercress and cider, and trout stuffed with chestnut mushrooms, garlic and bacon have been praised. However, service has been described as 'atrocious', with customers walking out after long waits for a table. The wine list opens at £11.95.
Chef/s: Stuart Knight. **Open:** all week 6 to 10pm. **Meals:** alc (main courses £11 to £15). **Service:** not inc. **Details:** Cards accepted. 60 seats. Wheelchair access. Music. Children's portions.

ALSO RECOMMENDED

▲ Blas Burgerworks
The Warren, St Ives, TR26 2EA
Tel no: (01736) 797272
www.blasburgerworks.co.uk
Modern British

Blas Burgerworks is an eco-friendly eatery offering utilitarian, modern design, furniture made from reclaimed or sustainably sourced timber and, where possible, fresh, seasonal local produce. Burgers are made from Cornish meat, whether 100% local beef (bacon cheeseburger £8.50), or free-range chicken (from £7.95). Vegetarian options include a sunflower burger using tofu, ginger, coriander, tahini sauce, sweet roast peppers and fresh salad sprouts (£7.95), and there's chargrilled local fish in all its sustainable forms. Chips are good, house wine is £13. Dinner only. No credit cards.

▌St Mawes

Hotel Tresanton
Fashionable Cornish retreat
27 Lower Castle Road, St Mawes, TR2 5DR
Tel no: (01326) 270055
www.tresanton.com
Modern European | £40
Cooking score: 4

🛏 V

A swanky Olga Polizzi makeover transformed this one-time Cornish yachtsmen's club and seaside bolthole into a fashionable destination

for the weekend and holiday crowd. Much depends on the weather, when the glorious terrace comes into its own and the sea views are at their best. Otherwise, seek solace in the dining room, which has been suitably decked out in seaside shades of blue and yellow – with mosaic floors lending a Mediterranean feel to it all. Sunny threads also weave their way through a culinary repertoire that puts most of the emphasis on local ingredients – especially from nearby waters: porbeagle shark with ratatouille, scallops with baby fennel and asparagus, or John Dory with peas, pea shoots and pancetta are typical. For those of a red-blooded persuasion, the kitchen also serves pigeon breast with oxtail and butter beans followed by sirloin of Calenick beef with broccoli, green beans and baby onions. To conclude, weigh up the fruity merits of, say, cherry and almond tart or raspberry and chocolate mille-feuille with raspberry sorbet. Italy and France share most of the honours on the modern 100-bin wine list, although there is plenty of interesting drinking across the range. Prices start at around £20 (£5 a glass).
Chef/s: Paul Wadham. **Open:** all week L 12 to 2.30, D 7 to 9.30. **Meals:** Set L £23 (2 courses) to £30. Set D £42. **Service:** not inc. **Details:** Cards accepted. 50 seats. 60 seats outside. Separate bar. No music. No mobile phones. Wheelchair access. Children's portions. Car parking.

▌Summercourt

Viners Bar and Restaurant
Casual Cornish dining
Carvynick, Summercourt, TR8 5AF
Tel no: (01872) 510544
www.vinersrestaurant.co.uk
Modern European | £30
Cooking score: 4

Kevin and Jane Viner set out to please all-comers at their cleverly converted pub among the holiday cottages of Carvynick. The whole set up now occupies two floors and has exposed beams, farmhouse furniture and varnished wood floors. Casual dining is emphatically the message. Culinary excesses have been stripped away and the kitchen

delivers a succession of well-wrought dishes without affectation – whether you are eating slow-braised beef ribs in the bar or a medley of lamb with port and thyme jus in the restaurant. Kevin Viner is a long-serving champion of Cornish produce and he builds his menus around what is seasonal. Mussels might be steamed in coconut milk with lemongrass and chilli, saffron-infused fillets of red mullet are served on a warm salad of poached fennel and orange, while grilled duck breast comes with roasted apple, celeriac and beetroot. Twice-baked West Country cheese soufflé is an ever-present starter, and Viner's emblematic bread-and-butter pudding is never off the menu; otherwise finish with apple strudel doused in cinnamon syrup or layered raspberry shortbread with Grand Marnier ice cream. House wines are £15.95 (£4.25 a glass).
Chef/s: Kevin Viner. **Open:** Sun L 12.30 to 2.30, Tue to Sun D 5.30 to 9. **Closed:** Sun D in winter. **Meals:** alc (main courses £13 to £21). Set L £15.95 (2 courses) to £18.95. Bar menu available. **Service:** not inc. **Details:** Cards accepted. 90 seats. 10 seats outside. Wheelchair access. Music. Children's portions. Car parking.

Treen
Gurnard's Head
Gastropub on Cornwall's culinary map
Treen, TR26 3DE
Tel no: (01736) 796928
www.gurnardshead.co.uk
Gastropub | £22
Cooking score: 3

Overlooking the rocky promontory of Gurnard's Head and surrounded by rugged moorland, this rambling old inn stands on the windswept coastal road between St Ives and Penzance. It has been placed firmly on Cornwall's culinary map by Charles and Edmund Inkin, who also created the Felin Fach Griffin (see entry, Wales), and makes a welcome pit-stop for coast path walkers and foodies. They come for the welcoming, laid back atmosphere, the short daily menus and

the honest, unfussy cooking of top-notch local and seasonal ingredients. 'Simple is best' appears to be the kitchen's philosophy, so follow jellied pork and herb terrine or cauliflower soup with Parmesan toast, with perfectly cooked roast hake with mash and sprouting broccoli, or a well-executed confit pork belly served with haricot beans, sea beet and thyme. To finish, try the Cornish cheeses or, perhaps, poppyseed cheesecake and poached pear. Expect a good global selection of wines, starting at £13.75, with 11 choices by-the-glass from £3.20.
Chef/s: Robert Wright. **Open:** all week L 12 to 2.30, D 6.30 to 9.30. **Closed:** 24 and 25 Dec. **Meals:** alc (main courses £11 to £12.50). **Service:** not inc. **Details:** Cards accepted. 50 seats. Separate bar. Wheelchair access. Music. Children's portions.

Tresco
ALSO RECOMMENDED
▲ Island Hotel
Tresco, TR24 OPU
Tel no: (01720) 422883
www.tresco.co.uk
Modern British

The many luxuries of this smart hotel include manicured grounds and a private beach. You can eat on the terrace looking towards Blockhouse or in the dining room with its panoramic sea views. 'Fresh, seasonal and local' is the mantra behind the £38 set menu, but flavours are wide-ranging – perhaps seared monkfish with chicory, lime and orange salad and aïoli dressing, followed by peppered duck breast with butternut squash purée, cocotte potatoes, bok choi and orange sauce. Other options include the unchallenging 'simple and plain' menu and a terrace bar menu of light bites and snappy modern dishes. A substantial wine list starts at £16. Open all week.

Also recommended

An 'also recommended' entry is not a full entry, but is provisionally suggested as an alternative to main entries.

Truro

Saffron
Eclectic eating house
5 Quay Street, Truro, TR1 2HB
Tel no: (01872) 263771
www.saffronrestauranttruro.co.uk
British | £30
Cooking score: 2

Nic and Traci Tinney's café fulfils its function as a contemporary eating house with a bright, eclectic feel and flexible, keenly-priced menus, which include sensible choices for children. But the set up seems to have lost some of its edge: offhand service and a lack of atention to detail have been cited, although the kitchen still puts its faith in local ingredients. The weekly-changing menus advertise grilled monkfish and wok-fried greens with noodles and red pepper picada alongside Moroccan-spiced chicken with lemon and olive couscous. Start with grilled squid with petit salad and mango salsa and finish with lemon citrus curd tart with syllabub cream. An enterprising and fairly-priced wine list from around the world opens at £11.70.
Chef/s: Nik Tinney. Open: Tue to Sat, 10 to 10 (Jan to May) Mon to Sat, 10 to 10 (June to Dec). Closed: 25 & 26 Dec, bank hols, Mon D Jan to May. Meals: Set L £12.50, Early supper £9.95 (2 courses) to £12.95, Set D £19.50. Service: not inc. Details: Cards accepted. 42 seats. Wheelchair access. Music. Children's portions.

Tabb's
New home for a Cornish favourite
85 Kenwyn Street, Truro, TR1 3BZ
Tel no: (01872) 262110
www.tabbs.co.uk
Modern British | £30
Cooking score: 4

The denizens of Truro have taken Nigel and Melanie Tabb to their hearts since the couple opened their stylishly intimate restaurant in the centre of town. Soothing lilac walls, fresh flowers and slate floors set the tone and the food continues to make an impact. Fresh home-baked breads are a must-try accompaniment to unusual soups (chilled tomato with beetroot sorbet and pepper oil) or starters such as duck and smoked haddock paella or scallops with chorizo, snow peas and black tagliatelle. Main courses make exemplary use of seasonal Cornish produce and key suppliers are given a name check on the menu: loin of wild venison comes with lentil hash and green chilli oil, while braised leg of Terras Farm duck is stuffed with gizzards and served with seared liver and tarragon reduction. Fish from the coast is also given its due (John Dory with Jerusalem artichokes, toasted pumpkin seeds and dill butter sauce, for example), and Nigel Tabb's desserts should not be missed – likewise his home-made chocolates. The reasonably-priced, 40-bin wine list opens with house recommendations from £12.95 (£3.50 a glass).
Chef/s: Nigel Tabb. Open: Tue to Sat L 12 to 2, D 6.30 to 9. Closed: Sun, Mon. Meals: alc (main courses £14 to £21.50). Service: not inc. Details: Cards accepted. 30 seats. Separate bar. No mobile phones. Wheelchair access. Music. Children's portions.

Watergate Bay

ALSO RECOMMENDED
▲ Fifteen Cornwall
On the beach, Watergate Bay, TR8 4AA
Tel no: (01637) 861000
Italian

Jamie Oliver's Fifteen Foundation comes to Cornwall with this exciting venture overlooking one of the West Country's grooviest surfing destinations. The location is as hip as they come, the views are stunning and the place delivers all-day food from breakfast onwards. Lunch is a mixed bag of rustic Italian dishes straight out of the 'pukka' mould: pappardelle of Higher Laity lamb ragù with orange and rosemary gremolada (£11), 'wicked fish stew' (£19) and apple and thyme cake with pear sauce (£6), for example. Dinner is a six-course tasting menu at £50 a head. Global wines from £19 (£5 a glass). Open all week.

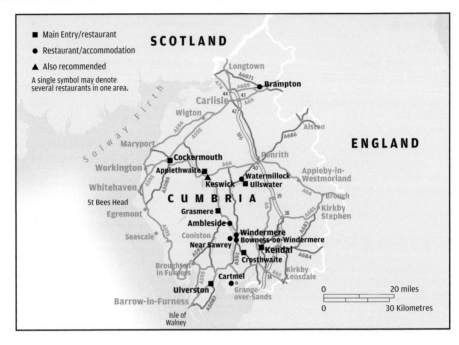

Map legend:
- ■ Main Entry/restaurant
- ● Restaurant/accommodation
- ▲ Also recommended

A single symbol may denote several restaurants in one area.

■ Ambleside

Drunken Duck Inn

Handsome Lakeland all-rounder
Barngates, Ambleside, LA22 0NG
Tel no: (015394) 36347
www.drunkenduckinn.co.uk
Gastropub | £38
Cooking score: 3

⊨ V

The sort of Lakeland pub that walkers hope to stumble across but so rarely do, the Drunken Duck, at a crossroads of winding lanes in the countryside above Ambleside, is not the easiest place to find. Beams and a crackling fire in the narrow bar set the welcoming tone. Here, sandwiches might include Cumberland sausage and onion marmalade, washed down, perhaps, with a pint from the Duck's Barngates Brewery. Things take a fancier turn in the dining room next door, from the surroundings (smart, if cramped) and the wine list to the ambition of the cooking, which tends towards the heartily rich: duck rillettes with liver parfait and toasted brioche followed by fillet of Cumbrian beef with Whinow blue cheese rarebit, fondant potato and sauce forestière, then sticky toffee pudding to finish. High prices (around £10 for a starter and double that for a main), however, raise eyebrows, with portion sizes deemed 'mean' and cooking standards slipping notably around public holidays. There are bedrooms available at the inn itself and in an annexe round the corner, overlooking a garden and a tarn for fly-fishing.

Chef/s: Neil McCue. **Open:** all week L 12 to 2 (2.30 Sat and Sun), D 6 to 9. **Service:** not inc.
Details: Cards accepted. 58 seats. 8 seats outside. Separate bar. No music. No mobile phones. Wheelchair access. Children's portions. Car parking.

Which? Campaigns

To find out more about Which? food and drink campaigns, please visit:
www.which.co.uk

Lucy's on a Plate

Bustling, informal eatery
Church Street, Ambleside, LA22 0BU
Tel no: (01539) 431191
www.lucysofambleside.co.uk
Modern British | £25
Cooking score: 2

From a specialist deli-cum-grocery store opened in 1989, Lucy Nicholson's Ambleside food empire has expanded to include a wine bar and bistro, a cookery school and mail order foods. Key to the whole operation is Lucy's on a Plate, a bustling, informal eatery located down a quiet side street. Expect bare boards, scrubbed pine tables, chapel chairs, open fires and a walled courtyard for alfresco meals. A lively café by day, serving everything from coffee and cake to home-made quiche and salad, Lucy's transforms into an atmospheric restaurant at night, with twinkling lights and candles everywhere. Using top-notch Cumbrian produce, notably Herdwick lamb and local game, the menu takes in scallops with a creamy lemon and watercress sauce and roast pork loin with apple and cider cream. Desserts are justifiably famous, the mind-boggling choice of over 30 ranging from sticky toffee pudding to nutty raspberry pavlova. House wine is £11.50.
Chef/s: Michael McMullen. **Open:** all week 10 to 9. **Closed:** 25 and 26 Dec. **Meals:** alc (main courses £10.50 to £25). Set Sun L £12 (2 courses). **Service:** not inc. **Details:** Cards accepted. 65 seats. 20 seats outside. Separate bar. Wheelchair access. Music. Children's portions.

Rothay Manor

Traditional Lakeland country house
Rothay Bridge, Ambleside, LA22 0EH
Tel no: (015394) 33605
www.rothaymanor.co.uk
British | £40
Cooking score: 1

The Regency-style building on the Coniston road is handy for Ambleside, yet well protected from its bustle by beautiful, secluded grounds. In typical country-house style, comfortable lounges have deep armchairs and sofas, open fires and lush garden views, yet the atmosphere is relaxed and informal. The setting of polished mahogany tables and soft candlelight is thoroughly traditional and both the cooking and service are in keeping. Anything from two to five courses can be ordered at dinner, with six choices at the main stage. Dishes typically run from game terrine with Cumberland sauce or sautéed kidneys in madeira sauce to seared salmon with prawn, asparagus and coriander risotto or beef fillet with red wine and thyme sauce. Nostalgic desserts might include a classic sticky toffee pudding or champagne and raspberry jelly with vanilla ice cream. House wine is £16.
Chef/s: Jane Binns. **Open:** all week L 12.30 to 1.45, D 7.15 to 9. **Closed:** 3 weeks from 2 Jan. **Meals:** Set L £19.50, Set D £34 (2 courses) to £38. **Service:** not inc. **Details:** Cards accepted. 60 seats. Wheelchair access. Children's portions. Car parking.

ALSO RECOMMENDED
▲ Chesters Café
Skelwith Bridge, Ambleside, LA22 9NN
Tel no: (015394) 32553
www.chesters-cafebytheriver.co.uk
Café

This stylishly refurbished all-day café – squishy sofas, winter fires and a warm, tasteful décor – is in a glorious location beside the River Brathay. There's a mind-boggling array of home-made cakes, perhaps banana and walnut loaf (£1.95) or lemon cream pie

(£3.25), as well as light lunch dishes such as ham hock and pea pie (£8.50) or roast squash, goats' cheese and pine-nut quiche (£7.95). In fine weather, the beautiful riverside terrace is a great draw. Under the same ownership as the Drunken Duck, Ambleside and the Punch Bowl Inn at Crosthwaite (see entries). Open all week.

█ Applethwaite

Underscar Manor
Italianate villa in a lovely setting
Applethwaite, CA12 4PH
Tel no: (01768) 775000
www.keswickrestaurant.co.uk
Modern British | £38
Cooking score: 5

The Italianate villa is in 'a lovely hillside setting' at the foot of Skiddaw and on a good day has 'majestic views' across Derwentwater and Cat Bells. Take aperitifs in the lounge before going into the conservatory-style dining room, which affords a verdant view. Robert Thornton's cooking aims for the kind of ornate refinement often expected in such surroundings. Main courses might be typified by a trio of Kendal-bred lamb cuts (cutlet, noisette, chump) presented with lentils, carrots, celeriac, fine beans, gratin dauphinoise and – just for good measure – mint and port sauce. Much of it works well, with starters ranging from the kitchen's variations on its signature savoury cheese soufflé to breast of quail served with a spring roll of the leg, leek, mushroom and pine kernel cannelloni with a sweet-and-sour sauce. Finish with a trio of rhubarb: poached, sorbet and in a crumble ice cream. The cooking is rich, and can be 'very filling', but reporters have left content with both food ('excellent'), and service ('efficient, understated but precise'). The wine list, strong in France, opens at £21.

Chef/s: Robert Thornton. **Open:** all week L 12 to 1, D 7 to 8.30. **Closed:** 2 to 3 days beginning of Jan. **Meals:** Set L £28, Set D £38. **Service:** not inc. **Details:** Cards accepted. 50 seats. No mobile phones. Car parking.

█ Bowness-on-Windermere

Linthwaite House
A constantly evolving hotel and kitchen
Crook Road, Bowness-on-Windermere, LA23 3JA
Tel no: (015394) 88600
www.linthwaite.com
Modern British | £50
Cooking score: 5

£5 OFF 🍷 🛏 V

Set in 14 acres of wooded gardens on a hillside overlooking Lake Windermere, this well-proportioned country house 'has magical views, especially at sunset'. Aperitifs can be enjoyed on the terrace or in the modern conservatory, and the stylish lounges have a lived-in atmosphere. At inspection, a state-of-the-art kitchen was being built, and the two interconnected dining rooms have already been smartly refurbished to give the place an uplifting modern feel. Couple this with a new chef, and it is easy to see that Linthwaite House has moved up a gear. Paul Peters places a strong emphasis on local produce and suppliers are often named on the menus. His set-price dinner offers a choice of around six dishes for each course, and there is a separate vegetarian menu. Start perhaps with pressed terrine of Cumbrian ham, fruit chutney and toasted brioche, or a signature seared scallops with caramelised cauliflower florets, hazelnut dressing and sherry vinegar. A main course loin of lamb, Lancashire style, comes with confit shoulder to emphasise different textures, plus hotpot vegetables and lamb jus, while fillet of bream is served with shrimp couscous, shellfish cream and baby spring vegetables. Finish with a 'wobbly' vanilla pannacotta with lovely roasted figs and a light lemon sorbet. The French-accented wine list is arranged according to style, and starts at £19.50.

Chef/s: Paul Peters. **Open:** all week L 12.30 to 2, D 7 to 9. **Meals:** Set L Mon to Sat £15.95 (2 courses) to £18.95, Set D £50 (4 courses). **Service:** not inc. **Details:** Cards accepted. 50 seats. 20 seats outside. Separate bar. No mobile phones. Wheelchair access. Music. Children's portions. Car parking.

▇ Brampton
Farlam Hall
Family-run country house hotel
Brampton, CA8 2NG
Tel no: (016977) 46234
www.farlamhall.co.uk
Modern British | £40
Cooking score: 3

Looking every inch the old-fashioned country house hotel, Farlam Hall is a well-managed operation (run by the same family for 32 years) and offers just the sort of hospitality that both travellers and locals appreciate. Nothing is posh or grand, indeed the scale is personable, with an abundance of chintz and highly-polished furniture. Barry Quinion's daily four-course, short choice menu follows the English country house tradition of a single sitting for dinner. The cooking is based on sound technique and an abundance of regional materials, delivering terrine of pheasant, herb and pistachio ahead of tenderloin of local pork teamed with its slow-cooked shoulder and served with parsnip and apple purée, crisp west Cumbrian pancetta and some good seasonal vegetables. Service, free of pretence or affectation, is perfectly judged. A commendable short wine list looks around the world for inspiration; prices open at £20.

Chef/s: Barry Quinion. **Open:** all week D only 8 to 8.30. **Closed:** Christmas. **Meals:** Set D £40 (4 courses). **Service:** not inc. **Details:** Cards accepted. 40 seats. Wheelchair access. Car parking.

▇ Cartmel
★ BEST CHEF ★

L'Enclume
To the edge of gastronomic possibilities
Cavendish Street, Cartmel, LA11 6PZ
Tel no: (015395) 36362
www.lenclume.co.uk
Modern European | £50
Cooking score: 8

With last year's proposed move to Henley shelved, there have been a few changes at L'Enclume. The most obvious is in the restaurant itself: the tables are now bare – dark wood with black corduroy place mats – and there are new chairs to match the tables. With rustic walls and slate floor it is a stark look, but the former smithy does have a more spacious air. In addition, midweek lunches have stopped, the à la carte is no more and a second outlet, Rogan & Company (see following entry), has opened in Cartmel serving more traditional food. Menus have been repositioned (a conventional three-course set dinner, a 10-course introduction and 15-course tour), to facilitate Simon Rogan's drive to push to the edge of gastronomic possibilities. He has moved from his original pledged allegiance to Marc Veyrat, and the locally-foraged herbs that were such a feature of early menus, delivering instead, in rapid succession, dishes that have left reporters mightily impressed not only by the tastes, textures and often bizarre combinations, but also by the extraordinary level of innovation and technical skill. Some explanation may be required as descriptions are so determined to intrigue: 're-hydration, de-hydration' is a Caribbean cocktail tuile and a soda syphon squirt of dried fig essence in a shot glass; 'hot pot' sees the Lancashire classic broken down into flavour components of meat, potato and red cabbage; and 'garlic and truffle' is a play on texture and temperature with frozen truffle pearls and garlic crisp. Other ideas and flavours are easier to grasp, 'monk cheeks, squid ink, saffron, passion fruit', say, or the

'Middle East on the plate' that was 'the triumph' of one reporter's meal – slow-cooked confit lamb lightly crumbed to give the hint of a crunch, topped with date foam and served with 'the lightest' hummus and tomato confit. Desserts hit the experimental button again with 'surrealists nitro slammer', a stunning tequila poached in nitrogen, or 'stiffy tacky pudding', a witty take on Cartmel's very own best seller. Staff are superb, knowledgeable and understanding. The wine list is strong in high-quality labels from France and beyond, with good drinking to suit all pockets. House wines from £28 to £41.

Chef/s: Simon Rogan. **Open:** Sat and Sun L 12 to 1.30, Tue to Sun D 6.45 to 9.30. **Closed:** Mon, bank hols. **Meals:** Set menus £39, £50 (10 courses), £70 (15 courses). **Service:** not inc. **Details:** Cards accepted. 40 seats. Wheelchair access. Music. Children allowed. Car parking.

★NEW ENTRY★
Rogan & Company
Perfect laid back brasserie
Bridge House, Devonshire Square, Cartmel, LA11 6QD
Tel no: (015395) 35917
www.roganandcompany.co.uk
Modern European | £26
Cooking score: 4

Rogan & Company represents a branching out for Simon Rogan, although the intention has not been to extend his brand of scientific gastronomy here, but to offer good, modern European brasserie cooking. And good it is, too. Just round the corner from L'Enclume (see entry), the former antique shop looks the part (its restrained mix of fine original features and contemporary style points feels positively city-slick), and the imaginative décor extends to a sleek ground-floor lounge bar and casual eating area (lunchtime sandwiches, fish and chips) plus three open-plan dining rooms and a smaller bar on the first floor. Simon Rogan and Richard Broughton run a vibrant, thoroughly contemporary kitchen, with

plenty to fire the imagination. Velouté of shellfish with tarragon and shrimp tortellini is rich and full of flavour, and has preceded a main course of well-timed halibut topped with a soft herb crust and accompanied by a crisp, plump anchovy fritter, asparagus and delicate herb risotto. Main course meat might be organic chicken fricassee with macaroni cheese and buttered chard, or that brasserie staple, prime rib steak, béarnaise sauce and thick-cut chips. The inventive impulse continues through to desserts such as apricot sablé with star anise mousse and Sauternes-poached apricots. Staff are helpful and efficient and wines start at £18.

Chef/s: Simon Rogan and Richard Broughton. **Open:** all week L 12 to 2.30, D 6.30 to 9.30. **Meals:** alc (main courses £12 to £18.50). **Service:** 12.5%. **Details:** Cards accepted. 75 seats. Air-con. Separate bar. Wheelchair access. Music. Children's portions.

▌Cockermouth
Quince & Medlar
Smart Lakeland vegetarian
11-13 Castlegate, Cockermouth, CA13 9EU
Tel no: (01900) 823579
Vegetarian | £26
Cooking score: 4

A pink, three-storey building next to Cockermouth Castle (and not far from Wordsworth's house, if you're exploring the area for the first time), the Quince & Medlar provides a homely, candlelit setting for fine vegetarian dining. If you've time to linger over aperitifs or coffee, so much the better, as the sofas and armchairs in the vermilion-hued lounge area look seriously inviting. Colin Le Voi draws inspiration from around the world to fashion his seasonally-inspired menus. Begin, perhaps, with a tart of Allerdale goats' cheese and caramelised red onion, before going on to Lebanese coconut milk pancake filled with chilli-spiced aubergine and served on a sauce of lime and coriander. Interesting ideas include transporting a gingered poached pear from its normal home on the dessert menu, and filling it with mung beans, capers and olives, alongside a sesame-dressed salad of pickled walnuts. Actual puddings might take in the likes of iced fruit and nut coffee meringue with toffee sauce, or white chocolate cheesecake with raspberry sauce. Service has been known to be a little sluggish, but overall the picture is one of serene contentment. A meticulously chosen list of vegetarian and vegan wines (all of them organic) starts at £11.60 for house French.

Chef/s: Colin Le Voi. **Open:** Tue to Sat D 7 to close. **Meals:** alc (main courses £13.95). **Service:** not inc. **Details:** Cards accepted. 26 seats. No mobile phones. Music. Children allowed.

▮ Crosthwaite
Punch Bowl Inn
Stylish country pub with good food
Lyth Valley, Crosthwaite, LA8 8HR
Tel no: (015395) 68237
www.the-punchbowl.co.uk
Gastropub | £35
Cooking score: 3

£5 OFF ⊨ V

The Punch Bowl comfortably straddles the divide between pub and restaurant, living up to its reputation as a free house, dispensing real ales and pub hospitality, but elsewhere it puts on a visibly stylish show for customers in search of food. There's another new chef in the kitchen, but despite an early wobble the consensus view is that things have settled down. Given chicken liver parfait with fig chutney and slow-cooked belly pork with confit root vegetables and apple jus, this is not aiming to be cutting edge food, but it is well-sourced, properly cooked and attractively presented, even if prices 'are on the high side'. Elsewhere, there could be steamed mussels in white wine and garlic served with home-made bread, sirloin steak with chips and béarnaise, or spring pea and mint risotto. Meals finish strongly with a rhubarb and custard tart with gingerbread ice cream. House wine is £16.95.

Chef/s: Jonathan Watson. **Open:** all week L 12 to 6, D 6 to 9.30. **Meals:** alc (main courses £11.95 to £18.95). Bar menu available. **Service:** not inc. **Details:** Cards accepted. 65 seats. 54 seats outside. Separate bar. Wheelchair access. Music. Children's portions. Car parking.

▮ Grasmere
Jumble Room
Eclectic jamboree
Langdale Road, Grasmere, LA22 9SU
Tel no: (015394) 35188
www.thejumbleroom.co.uk
Global | £38
Cooking score: 2

£5 OFF V

A thoroughly welcoming, stone-built restaurant and shop in one of Lakeland's favourite towns, the Jumble Room is a hugely popular venue. Its loyal band of regulars returns enthusiastically for cooking that draws inspiration from all over the globe, with east Asian notes particularly accented. Thai-spiced tiger prawn choo chee curry makes an enlivening main course, after su dong po, a starter of stickily-glazed belly pork with pink grapefruit and pak choi. Those tacking to the west will go for smoked haddock and spinach soufflé, perhaps, before chump of organic Mansergh Hall lamb on caponata, with pesto-dressed gnocchi and a jus incorporating olives and rosemary. Desserts to conjure with might include raspberry and white chocolate cheesecake or pannacotta with baked plums. A concise cosmopolitan list opens with house wines at £11.99.

Chef/s: Chrissy Hill and David and Trudy Clay. **Open:** Wed to Sun L 12 to 3.30, D 6 to 10. **Meals:** alc (main courses £13.50 to £21.50). **Service:** not inc. **Details:** 50 seats. 10 seats outside. Wheelchair access. Music. Children's portions.

White Moss House
Traditional food and hospitality
Rydal Water, Grasmere, LA22 9SE
Tel no: (015394) 35295
www.whitemoss.com
British | £40
Cooking score: 5

This beautiful old house dates from 1730 and was bought in 1827 by William Wordsworth for his son. It remained in the poet's family for 100 years, and now stands in the heart of 'Wordsworth country'. Peter and Susan Dixon have lived here since 1981, and in their hands the house has flourished as an unstuffy hotel with a reputation for its food. The interior offers full-on traditional charm, from the oak-panelled hall with its grandfather clock to the cottagey dining room. A log fire warms the lounge on colder days, while the flower-bedecked terrace is an ideal place to start a summer evening. Peter's cooking is as traditional as the surroundings. His five-course dinner menu offers no choices until dessert, allowing him to lavish time and attention on every aspect of each dish. After an opening soup and a starter of line-caught sea bass poached in the Aga with champagne, sorrel and saffron sauce, you could move on to roast fillet of Cumbrian air-dried Galloway beef marinated in Coniston real ale, served with woodland mushroom sauce, beetroot with redcurrant and mint, leeks stir-fried with Pernod and steamed baby carrots. For dessert, perhaps bread-and-butter pudding or pineapple and strawberries steeped in dessert wine with mango sorbet. Next comes a British cheese plate, typically followed by coffee with chocolate-covered Kendal mint cake. The engrossing wine list starts with Bordeaux and Burgundy then roams the world with a discerning eye. Bottles from £13.95.
Chef/s: Peter Dixon. **Open:** Thur to Sat D 7.30 for 8. **Closed:** Dec, Jan, Feb. **Meals:** Set D £39.50 (5 courses inc coffee). **Service:** not inc. **Details:** Cards accepted. 18 seats. Separate bar. No music. No mobile phones. Wheelchair access. Children's portions. Car parking.

■ Kendal
Bridge Street Restaurant
Popular Lake District restaurant
1 Bridge Street, Kendal, LA9 7DD
Tel no: (01539) 738855
www.one-bridgestreet.co.uk
Modern British | £25
Cooking score: 3

Julian and Elizabeth Ankers have settled in quickly at their spacious, elegant stone-built restaurant. With its undressed tables, palette of creams and browns and comfortable high-backed chairs it feels just right. The kitchen's cooking follows suit, playing to the gallery with a broad modern bistro repertoire that includes some standards like warm shallot and red onion tartlet, or Peter Gott's speck ham with Thornby Moor Crofton cheese (alongside roasted beetroot, watercress and pear salad), and hot chocolate fondant with praline ice cream and warm chocolate sauce. In between might be caramelised duck breast and crispy leg accompanied by a savoury apple and quince crumble, or monkfish wrapped in pancetta and served with a tomato and chorizo casserole. There's a strong seasonal feel to regularly-changing menus, which are based on quality produce from local suppliers where possible. Service is attentive and friendly and the global wine list is cannily chosen and good value. House wine is £11.95.
Chef/s: Julian Ankers. **Open:** Tue to Sat L 12 to 2, 6.30 to 9. **Closed:** Sun and Mon, 25 Dec to 26 Dec. **Meals:** Set L £10.95 (2 courses) to £12.95, Set D £21.99 (2 courses) to £24.99. **Service:** not inc. **Details:** Cards accepted. 36 seats. 10 seats outside. Air-con. Separate bar. Music. Children's portions.

Keswick

ALSO RECOMMENDED
▲ Swinside Lodge
Grange Road, Newlands, Keswick, CA12 5UE
Tel no: (017687) 72948
www.swinsidelodge.com
Modern British

This Georgian hotel occupies a tranquil spot at the foot of Cat Bells, with views over Derwentwater. The £40 four-course dinner menu sits comfortably with the country-house setting. A meal might open with lemon peppered trout fillet with potato and chive salad and mild horseradish dressing, followed by cream of celeriac and Blengdale Blue cheese soup with fresh home-made bread. A typical main course is roast breast of Swinside pheasant wrapped in cured ham with a corn fritter, seasonal vegetables, kumquat and rosemary chutney and red wine jus. For dessert, perhaps rhubarb mousse with orange and blueberry salad. Wines from £15.25. Open all week D only.

Near Sawrey

Ees Wyke
Beatrix Potter bolt-hole
Near Sawrey, LA22 0JZ
Tel no: (015394) 36393
www.eeswyke.co.uk
Modern British | £32
Cooking score: 2

Visitors to Ees Wyke can expect a full measure of dewy-eyed nostalgia: this is Beatrix Potter country and the hotel is right on the tourist trail to that good lady's home village. There are also dreamy views to be admired, with the still waters of Esthwaite close by and dramatic sheep-grazed fells as a backdrop. Hosts Richard and Margaret Lee look after their guests well, mingling in the lounge as aperitifs are sipped. Then it's time for dinner in true Lakeland style: five courses served in a plush dining room, with a plate of North Country cheeses to round things off. The

evening's menu might begin with broccoli and walnut soup with goats' cheese, ahead of smoked haddock and mushroom pancake. Main courses herald noisettes of local lamb with wine jus, mint and garlic, or grilled lemon sole, while desserts offer, say, chocolate truffle pear with raspberry coulis. The workmanlike wine list opens with six house selections from £16 (£4 a glass).
Chef/s: Richard Lee. **Open:** all week D only 7.30 (1 sitting). **Meals:** Set D £32. **Service:** not inc. **Details:** Cards accepted. 16 seats. Separate bar. No music. No mobile phones. Car parking.

Ullswater

Sharrow Bay
Pure class in glorious isolation
Ullswater, CA10 2LZ
Tel no: (01768) 486301
www.sharrowbay.co.uk
British | £60
Cooking score: 6

There are many beautifully sited hotels in the Lake District, but Sharrow Bay must have the loveliest location of them all. It is squirreled away in glorious isolation down a winding lane, with views straight down the length of Ullswater. This was the first place in England to adopt the tag of a country-house hotel and it still lives up to most people's idea of what that should involve: well-maintained gardens; plushly upholstered sitting rooms and thickly carpeted dining rooms that would seem stiffly formal were it not for the friendliness of the staff. Menus showcase top-quality ingredients, classically prepared, simply cooked and dressed in light sauces to allow flavours to shine through. At inspection, Suissesse soufflé of Stilton, spinach and onion combined feather-light texture with punchy flavour. To follow, fried fillet of turbot with shrimp risotto, ravioli of lobster and crayfish sauce was quite simply sublime, its complementary flavours melding in perfect harmony. Sticky toffee pudding was invented here in the 1970s and remains the benchmark for this happiest marriage of sponge and sauce.

Burgundy and Bordeaux lead a blockbuster wine list specialising in classic French regions, but there is room within the 50 pages for all the major areas of both the Old and New Worlds, with something to suit all pockets. Prices, in fact, are reasonable overall.

Chef/s: Colin Akrigg. **Open:** all week L 12.30 for 1, D 7.30 for 8 (1 sitting). **Meals:** Set L £43 (4 courses), Set D £60 (5 courses). **Service:** not inc. **Details:** Cards accepted. 60 seats. Air-con. Wheelchair access. Music. Car parking.

Ulverston

Bay Horse
Great views over Morecambe Bay
Canal Foot, Ulverston, LA12 9EL
Tel no: (01229) 583972
www.thebayhorsehotel.co.uk
British | £35
Cooking score: 3

V

Great views over Morecambe Bay are a feature that this eighteenth-century hotel and restaurant makes much of, and the food is also worth more than a passing glance thanks to first-rate raw materials. The kitchen deals in modern European treatments, with multiple flavours generally handled with assurance in dishes such as honey-roasted rack of salt marsh lamb with lemon and crushed coriander, or sea bass fillets poached in a Noilly Prat and chive cream sauce. Toasted goats' cheese with fresh figs and Parma ham is one way to start, and if you fancy a plain steak, the aged Aberdeen Angus sirloins or fillets come highly recommended, although reporters have been equally content with hot sandwiches of roast belly pork with fresh sage and apple sauce from the very good value 'light bite' menu. An up-to-date wine list embraces a broad spectrum of modest and reasonably-priced bottles. House wine is £16.50.

Chef/s: Robert Lyons and Kris Hogan. **Open:** Tue to Sun L 12 to 2, all week D 7.30 for 8 (1 sitting). **Closed:** few days early Jan. **Meals:** alc (main courses £18.50 to £25.50). **Service:** not inc.

Details: Cards accepted. 50 seats. 20 seats outside. Separate bar. Wheelchair access. Music. Car parking.

Watermillock

Rampsbeck Country House Hotel
Glorious views and appealing ideas
Watermillock, CA11 0LP
Tel no: (017684) 86442
www.rampsbeck.fsnet.co.uk
Anglo-French | £43
Cooking score: 3

The view over Ullswater is arresting by any standards, but this eighteenth-century hotel is also gloriously sited amid 18 acres of majestic grounds. Some welcome refurbishment of the dining room has taken place this year. Andrew McGeorge still heads the kitchen, relying on first-class materials to underpin the operation while perking up interest on his four-course dinner menus with some appealing ideas. An inventive streak runs through the cooking, bringing on John Dory with shrimp risotto and lemongrass foam to start, followed by roasted halibut with confit beetroot, braised onions and a red wine fumet. Meat dishes might include a neat pairing of fillet of beef with veal sweetbreads wrapped in air-dried Cumbrian ham and served alongside shallot confit, celeriac fondant and a madeira wine sauce. A simpler Sunday lunch has included well-reported carrot and cumin soup and roast sirloin of beef with Yorkshire pudding and a dollop of horseradish sauce. Finish in style with hot plum soufflé and nutmeg ice cream. Wines are sorted into detailed style categories – light and crisp, medium-bodied, for example – and there are useful tasting notes. House wines from £11.25.

Chef/s: Andrew McGeorge. **Open:** all week L 12 to 1.15, D 7 to 8.30. **Closed:** early Jan to mid Feb. **Meals:** Set L £23 (2 courses) to £29, Set D £43 to £49.50. **Service:** not inc. **Details:** Cards accepted. 40 seats. Separate bar. No music. No mobile phones. Wheelchair access. Car parking.

Windermere

Gilpin Lodge

Serene Lakeland retreat
Crook Road, Windermere, LA23 3NE
Tel no: (015394) 88818
www.gilpinlodge.co.uk
Modern British | £47
Cooking score: 6

£5 OFF 🍷 🍽 V

A couple of miles from Lake Windermere and blessed with 20 acres of country gardens and woodland for a setting, Gilpin is every inch the serene Lakeland retreat. Decorated to a high standard, the four dining-rooms are civilised spaces, with fresh flowers on the tables, gleaming glasses and silverware, and a tranquil, muzak-free ambience. When Chris Meredith describes his cooking style as 'imaginative without being silly', many a seasoned eater-out will know just what he means. Local produce is enthusiastically hauled in, and may be sampled via a number of menus, from the frequently changing carte, a vegetarian and vegan listing, and of course the bells-and-whistles tasting menu. Mixing and melding of culinary styles produces first courses such as veal sweetbreads glazed in sherry vinegar with crisp potatoes and carrot purée or lobster ravioli with pak choi and a lemongrass and lobster cream. Cumbrian air-dried ham is the garnish for a main course of pot-roasted chicken with pasta and wild mushrooms, while braised pig's head makes a fashionable option, garnished with pickled ginger, glazed roots and mash. The signature Chocolate Indulgence dessert will exert a powerful pull for many, while lighter appetites might go for immaculately-risen prune and Armagnac soufflé with matching ice cream. It is all served with keenness and charm. The wine list is a labour of love, having been carefully compiled and furnished with informative, unpretentious notes. Wines by-the-glass start at £5.25, there are plenty of halves, and a notably good set of dessert wines from £14.25 for a half-bottle of sweet Bordeaux.

Chef/s: Chris Meredith. **Open:** all week, L 12 to 2, D 6.45 to 9.15. **Meals:** Set L £25. Set D £47 to £100 (7 courses with wines). **Service:** not inc. **Details:** Cards accepted. 65 seats. 20 seats outside. Separate bar. No music. No mobile phones. Children allowed. Car parking.

★ WINE LIST OF THE YEAR ★

Holbeck Ghyll

High standards maintained in the kitchen
Holbeck Lane, Windermere, LA23 1LU
Tel no: (015394) 32375
www.holbeckghyll.com
Modern British | £53
Cooking score: 7

£5 OFF 🍷 🍽 V

Holbeck Ghyll is an early nineteenth-century mansion with glorious views over Lake Windermere and beyond. Traditional country-house elegance is the prevailing style, from the oak-panelled entrance hall with its inglenook fireplace to the two well-appointed dining rooms. Add to this the polished yet cheerful service, and the stage is set for David McLaughlin's confident and innovative cooking. He offers an attractive range of dishes from set-price menus, and his approach is uniformly straightforward. As with most modern menus, there is more on the plate than in the descriptions, but compositions make sense; witness hand-dived scallops from the West Coast which came on a celeriac purée with balsamic and slivers of truffle, or veal sweetbreads in a 'ravishing ravioli' with asparagus and morels and a rich foamy sauce. Main course options follow a similar vein: roast loin of Lakeland venison was accompanied by an expertly-made herb spätzli in a rich reduced sauce, while turbot was teamed with crisp boneless oxtail in a beetroot foam. Desserts maintain the momentum: crème brûlée was a revelation for one reporter, topped by an apple sorbet decorated with apple crisps and served with a cider sauce, or there is the cheese menu on which 14 British and French goodies are described in detail. The dazzling wine list 'is a pleasure to browse', clearly a labour of love and choice is impeccable. From a strong base in France the list turns up interesting bottles from many other regions – for something unusual go to the 'Fantastic Finds' section – and there's a good line-up of half bottles. House wines start at £20 a bottle.

Chef/s: David McLaughlin. **Open:** all week 12 to 2, 7 to 9.30. **Meals:** Set L £29.50, Set D £52.50. **Service:** not inc. **Details:** Cards accepted. 50 seats. 35 seats outside. Separate bar. No music. No mobile phones. Wheelchair access. Car parking.

Jerichos at the Waverley

New home for old favourite
College Road, Windermere, LA23 1BX
Tel no: (015394) 42522
www.jerichos.co.uk
Modern British | £35
Cooking score: 5

After ten years running their stand-alone restaurant in Windermere town centre, Chris and Jo Blaydes recently relocated to the Waverley Hotel, an imposing Victorian residence at the end of a quiet terrace. Original features including a tiled foyer and a large pitch-pine staircase are in stark contrast to the dining room's thoroughly contemporary look. Nothing seems to have changed on the food front, and Chris continues to head up a small kitchen team that works to a concise dinner menu of confidently-executed dishes with a European slant. You might begin with confit of corn-fed Gressingham duck on coarse-grain mustard mash with port reduction, ahead of poached fillet of wild sea bass with buttered new potatoes, glazed greens, roasted scallop and hot emulsion vinaigrette or slow-roast Gloucester Old Spot pork belly with chorizo-glazed carrots, celeriac and apple purée and red wine sauce. To conclude, there are finely-crafted desserts ranging from semolina and olive oil galette with chocolate almond ganache to aniseed-tinged pannacotta with poached pink rhubarb and balsamic reduction. A couple of personal wine recommendations appear on

the menu and the full list also has food in mind, with helpful matching suggestions throughout. Prices start at £13.50.

Chef/s: Chris Blaydes. **Open:** Fri to Wed D only 7 to 9.30. **Closed:** Thur, Christmas. **Meals:** alc (main courses £14.50 to £20.50). **Service:** not inc. **Details:** Cards accepted. 36 seats. No music. Car parking.

Samling

Luxurious country-house dining
Ambleside Road, Windermere, LA23 1LR
Tel no: (015394) 31922
www.thesamling.com
Modern British | £55
Cooking score: 4

This luxurious country-house stands a few hundred feet above Windermere in 67 acres of its own land. Against such majestic surroundings the small, perfectly formed building takes on the appearance of a dolls' house. Its interior has been lavishly furnished in classic country style. Starters such as red mullet with crushed ratte potatoes, minestrone and basil or mosaic of free-range chicken with leek, prune and spiced lentils point the way. These might be followed by loin of Herdwick mutton with braised shoulder, langoustine and Jerusalem artichoke or roast duck breast with confit duck gizzard, wild garlic and foie gras. In keeping with the other courses, desserts typically include local specialities – rhubarb, for example, or apples from the Samling garden. Choices such as coffee cappuccino with warm orange doughnuts or saffron-poached pear with upside-down pudding and olive oil ice cream end the meal on a playful, decadent note. The ever-growing wine list is weighted towards the higher end of the market; entry level is £32.

Chef/s: Nigel Mendham. **Open:** all week L 12 to 2.30, D 7 to 9.30. **Meals:** Set D £55, Tasting menu £67. **Service:** not inc. **Details:** Cards accepted. 22 seats. Separate bar. No mobile phones. Music. Car parking.

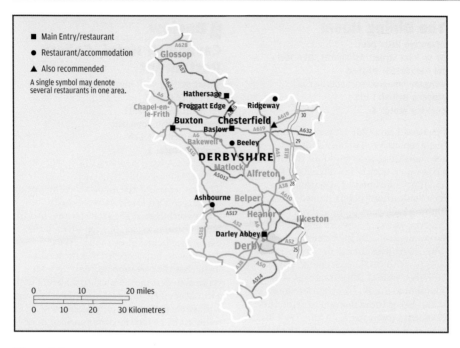

- ■ Main Entry/restaurant
- ● Restaurant/accommodation
- ▲ Also recommended

A single symbol may denote several restaurants in one area.

■ Ashbourne

Callow Hall

Family-run Victorian country-house hotel
Mappleton Road, Ashbourne, DE6 2AA
Tel no: (01335) 300900
www.callowhall.co.uk
Modern British | £38
Cooking score: 3

£5 OFF 🍷 🛏️

There's a true sense of dedication about this family-run Victorian country-house hotel in a lovely rural setting. It is a very personal operation, with attentive service and a four-course dinner menu that appeals for well-executed straightforwardness: cream of celeriac soup, followed by fish or sorbet, then, say, fillet of beef en croûte with mushroom duxelles. Even more exotic and imaginative dishes, like starters of slow-roasted belly pork with seared king scallops, steamed pak choi and teriyaki sauce, or mains of breast of guinea fowl with Thai-style crushed sweet potato and confit duck tian, are similarly sure-footed. To finish there may be chilled dark chocolate soufflé with chocolate fudge sauce, or hot bread and almond pudding with crème anglaise and almond and Amaretto ice cream. France is the first love on the wine list, but the rest of the world maintains high standards, with plenty of halves and a list of fine wines completing the picture. Bottles start at £13.50.

Chef/s: Anthony Spencer and David Spencer. **Open:** Sun L 12.30 to 1.30, Mon to Sat D 7.30 to 9.30. **Closed:** 25 and 26 Dec. **Meals:** Set L £28.50, Set D £42 (5 courses). **Service:** not inc. **Details:** Cards accepted. 80 seats. Separate bar. Wheelchair access. Children's portions. Car parking.

The Dining Room

Inventive little gem

33 St John Street, Ashbourne, DE6 1GP
Tel no: (01335) 300666
www.thediningroomashbourne.co.uk
Modern British | £37
Cooking score: 4

Peter and Laura Dale are justly proud of their
'little restaurant' – a cosily domestic
seventeenth-century building on Ashbourne's
main street, with beams, an old cooking range
and limestone lintels. The setting may
seem endearingly old-fashioned, but there's
nothing backward-looking about Peter's food.
An ever-growing network of local
producers keeps the kitchen topped up
with ingredients for a daringly short menu
(just two choices for each course, plus a
'refresher' sorbet). What impresses is the
attention to detail – from the five kinds of
home-baked bread that appear with three
flavoured butters to the biscuits, spelt loaf and
green tomato chutney offered with the
dazzling British cheeseboard. Even something
as simple as home-smoked salmon takes on a
new life as part of a jaw-dropping mélange
with local asparagus 'several ways', grains of
paradise, pink grapefruit, pea biscuit and wild
rice 'krispies'. After that, consider a beefy
assemblage involving 12-hour ox cheek, fried
'mock' onion, bacon, spring cabbage and
horseradish mash. Finally, catch your breath
before taking on a wildly elaborate dessert
such as dark chocolate brownie with banana
ice cream, home-made marshmallow, lime
jelly, espresso and cocoa nibs. Fifteen-course
tasting menus are even more challenging,
while the compact wine list promises sound
drinking at eminently fair prices from £16
(£4.50 a glass).
Chef/s: Peter Dale. **Open:** Tue to Sat L 12 to 1.30, D
7 to 8.30. **Closed:** Sun, Mon, 1 week over Shrove
Tue, 1 week autumn, 2 weeks after Christmas.
Meals: alc (main courses £20). Set D £37 to D £45
(15 courses). **Service:** not inc. **Details:** Cards
accepted. 16 seats. No mobile phones. Wheelchair
access. Music. Children's portions.

▌Baslow

Cavendish Hotel, Gallery Restaurant

Smart setting with lovely views

Baslow, DE45 1SP
Tel no: (01246) 582311
www.cavendish-hotel.net
Modern British | £39
Cooking score: 3

This 'rather grand' restaurant sports fine art on
its walls and has lovely views of the
Chatsworth Estate. The atmosphere is formal
but not stuffy; in fact, one reporter felt the
experience lacked 'gloss' in the service
department, but conceded that the food was
'first-class'. Expect modern cooking with
classical undertones. A meal could begin with
a trio of smoked, potted and tempura salmon
with sweet pepper and teriyaki dressing,
followed by an intermediate course of honey-
roasted figs with dolcelatte, rocket and a
Parmesan tuile. A commitment to local,
seasonal produce is evident in main courses
such as braised shoulder of Castlegate lamb
Wellington with roasted root vegetables,
buttered spring greens, thyme and madeira
sauce, while lighter options might include
seabass on a warm salad of fennel and orange
with spiced crayfish and squid. Finish with
orange crème brûlée with hazelnut biscuits or
excellent British cheeses. A substantial and
intelligent wine list opens at £15.95.
Chef/s: Chris Allison. **Open:** L 12 to 2.30, D 6.30 to
10. **Closed:** 25 Dec (exc. residents). **Meals:** Set D
£29.50 (2 courses) to £51.50 (5 courses).
Details: Cards accepted. 50 seats. Separate bar.
Wheelchair access. Music. Children's portions. Car
parking.

Readers recommend

A 'readers recommend' review is a
genuine quote from a report sent in by
one of our readers. We intend to follow
up these suggestions throughout the year
to come.

Fischer's Baslow Hall

Small, friendly country-house hotel
Calver Road, Baslow, DE45 1RR
Tel no: (01246) 583259
www.fischers-baslowhall.co.uk
Modern European | £68
Cooking score: 7

This solid Edwardian country house fronted by lawns and mature trees has an interior that is agreeable and happily relaxed. There's a 'lovely'drawing room with an open fire 'for relaxing before and after the meal', and everyone is agreed that service is 'unfussy and friendly'. Rupert Rowley's cooking stands out from the crowd not least because he starts with high-quality raw materials, takes seasonality and local ingredients seriously and his dishes aim to entice rather than baffle, with fine renditions of wood pigeon with watercress and apple salad, a 'very good main dish' of red mullet, or pheasant with pickled red cabbage. At another well-reported meal, a main course that combined slow-cooked rib and braised oxtail of Derbyshire beef with pommes Anna and red wine sauce impressed for its perfectly matured and precisely seasoned meat. Other ingredients come from far and wide and are treated with inventive personal touches without seeming overworked. A starter of oriental marinated salmon might be teamed with pickled shoots, Scottish langoustine and wasabi dressing, or John Dory partnered with seared beef fillet and vegetable tagliatelle. Ring the changes at dessert stage with poached banana, peanut cream and yoghurt and banana sorbet, or light out for the wilder shores of coconut soufflé with coconut and Malibu sorbet. France, primarily Bordeaux and Burgundy, is the mainstay of the quality-focused wine list, while Italy, Spain and the New World turn in brief but well-chosen alternatives. House bottles start at £21.
Chef/s: Rupert Rowley. **Open:** Tue to Sun L 12 to 1.30, Mon to Sat D 7 to 9. **Closed:** 25 and 26 Dec. **Meals:** Set L £27 to £38, Set D £38 to £68.

Service: not inc. **Details:** Cards accepted. 50 seats. Separate bar. No mobile phones. Wheelchair access. Car parking.

Rowley's

Exuberant Baslow brasserie
Church Lane, Baslow, DE45 1RY
Tel no: (01246) 583880
www.rowleysrestaurant.co.uk
Modern European | £29
Cooking score: 3

The Fischers and chef Rupert Rowley from nearby Baslow Hall (see entry) are the brains behind this exuberant brasserie in the centre of town. With its all-day bar, al fresco terrace, cool purple colour schemes and striking contemporary artwork it is a world away from country-house decorum – although the kitchen is equally committed to local produce. Astute sourcing ensures regular supplies of traditionally-reared Peak District beef (for chargrilled steaks) and the menu also features home-made lamb shank sausages served with butter bean casserole. Fish fans can rely on benchmark bouillabaisse, smoked haddock brandade fishcakes or fillet of cod with artichoke, courgette and potato salad, while desserts keep it safe and simple with sticky toffee pudding, crème brûlée or raspberry and white chocolate parfait. The wine list was being updated as the Guide went to press, but expect a good international spread from around £14 a bottle.
Chef/s: James Grant. **Open:** all week L 12 to 2.30, Mon to Sat D 6 to 9 (10 Fri and Sat). **Meals:** alc (main courses L £7 to £14, D £12 to £16). Set L Sun £19.50 (2 courses) to £23.50. **Service:** not inc. **Details:** Cards accepted. 60 seats. 16 seats outside. Separate bar. No mobile phones. Wheelchair access. Music. Children's portions. Car parking.

Average price

The average price listed in main-entry reviews denotes the price of a three-course meal, without wine.

▮ Beeley

Devonshire Arms

Well-to-do country inn
Devonshire Square, Beeley, DE4 2NR
Tel no: (01629) 733259
www.thedevonshirearms.co.uk
Gastropub | £25
Cooking score: 3

The revitalised Devonshire Arms, on the edge of the Chatsworth Estate, belongs to the new breed of well-to-do country inns, combining beams, open fires and stone floors with bold contemporary touches and offering ambitious food based around judicious sourcing of ingredients. The kitchen subjects sound British ingredients to modern European treatments, as in fried duck egg with mixed beans, pancetta, chorizo, mustard mayonnaise and sun-blushed tomatoes, or beef fillet with crispy bacon, horseradish, sticky lentils and Parmentier potatoes. Fish is also well represented by, say, halibut with fennel mash, peas, broad beans, wholegrain mustard and caviar. Elsewhere, a Devonshire Classics menu maintains pub credentials with bangers and mash or cod and chips. Praline brûlée with gingerbread ice cream is one option for afters; otherwise expect anything from vanilla cheesecake to coconut pannacotta with pineapple and passion-fruit compote. House wine is £14.
Chef/s: Alan Hill. **Open:** all week 12 to 9.30.
Meals: alc (main courses £10.95 to £17.95).
Service: not inc. **Details:** Cards accepted. 60 seats. 30 seats outside. Wheelchair access. Music. Children's portions. Car parking.

Please send us your feedback

To register your opinion about any restaurant listed in the Guide, or a new restaurant that you wish to bring to our attention, please visit the web address at the bottom of the page. Your feedback informs the content of the book and will be used to compile next year's reviews.

▮ Buxton

Columbine

Generous food for culture vultures
7 Hall Bank, Buxton, SK17 6EW
Tel no: (01298) 78752
www.buxtononline.net/columbine
Modern British | £22
Cooking score: 2

V

Handily located just down the hill from Buxton's renowned opera house and theatre, Kim and Steve McNally's self-styled 'restaurant with cellars' is a boon to the local scene. As the description suggests, their two-floored Georgian house has the bonus of overspill seating in the subterranean vaults of the building. The mood is leisurely, prices are very fair and the food aims for generous, all-round satisfaction. Begin with a salad of duck breast with honey and mustard seed dressing or a bowl of Cullen skink, ahead of a local plateful loaded with High Peak lamb's liver, black pudding and smoked bacon with red wine gravy or halibut dusted in oatmeal with lemon and ginger butter sauce. Vegetarians have their own menu, while homely desserts such as summer pudding or treacle tart could close the show. The reasonably-priced wine list opens with house Duboeuf at £9.95 (£2.65 a glass).
Chef/s: Steve McNally. **Open:** Mon to Sat D only 7 to 9.30. **Closed:** Sun, 24 Dec to first Sat in Jan.
Meals: alc (main courses £11 to £14). **Service:** not inc. **Details:** Cards accepted. 40 seats. No mobile phones. Music. Children's portions.

▮ Chesterfield

ALSO RECOMMENDED
▲ Old Post

43 Holywell Street, Chesterfield, S41 7SH
Tel no: (01246) 279479
www.theoldpostrestaurant.co.uk
Modern British

A fine old Elizabethan building – and one-time post office – is the setting for Hugh and Mary Cocker's pint-sized local restaurant (booking essential). Ambitious modern cooking is the name of the game: begin with seared scallops, creamed celeriac, sauce nantaise and chorizo (£7.50), proceed to medallions of Derbyshire beef on corned beef hash with bordelaise sauce (£21.95), and conclude with treacle and lemon tart with nutmeg ice cream (£6.35). Set lunches are great value (2 courses £12.25) and things really buzz on Sundays. House wine is £12.95. Closed Mon, Tue and Sat L and Sun D.

▌Darley Abbey

Darleys
Modern food in a terrific setting
Darley Abbey Mills, Haslams Lane, Darley Abbey, DE22 1DZ
Tel no: (01332) 364987
www.darleys.com
Modern British | £35
Cooking score: 4

V

A converted cotton mill (complete with an old toll bridge) by the fast-flowing River Derwent sounds like a dream ticket for nostalgia-fuelled tourists, and this enterprising venue certainly pulls out all the stops. Once inside, however, you leave the past behind and enter a contemporary, design-led world. There's nothing quaint or archaic about the food either: lunch menus keep it simple (seared tuna with salsa verde, rump of beef with horseradish potato gratin), while dinner finds the kitchen in more ambitious mood. Chorizo risotto with crispy razor clams and bouillabaisse dressing or honey-glazed pork belly with apple purée, lavender crème fraîche and sesame crackling show serious intent, and mains picks up the baton with, perhaps, fillet of brill, ox-cheek ravioli, wild mushrooms and leek foam or Gressinhgam duck breast with crab and ginger spring roll and spiced plum reduction. For afters, 'tutti fruity' parfait with cherry soufflé and caramel wafer sounds fun, or you might go for a toffee and banana cone with white rum ice cream. The wine list is a broad international slate bolstered by some classic vintages; 15 house recommendations set the ball rolling from £14 (£3.50 a glass).
Chef/s: Jonathan Hobson. **Open:** all week L 12 to 2, D 7 to 9. **Closed:** bank hols, 2 weeks after Christmas. **Meals:** alc D (main courses £19 to £21.50). Set L £15.95 (2 courses) to £17.95. **Service:** not inc. **Details:** Cards accepted. 60 seats. 16 seats outside. Air-con. Separate bar. Wheelchair access. Music. Children's portions. Car parking.

▌Froggatt Edge

ALSO RECOMMENDED
▲ Chequers Inn
Froggatt Edge, S32 3ZJ
Tel no: (01433) 630231
www.chequers-froggatt.om
Gastropub

A favourite with Peak District walkers, this lovely old coaching inn is still more pub than 'gastro', but has an appealing menu: goats' cheese with polenta chips, poached egg and hollandaise (£6), followed by homity pie with Henderson's relish (£8), or fillet of local beef with garlic mash and roast shallots (£18). Among desserts might be Bakewell pudding and custard (£5). There's plenty of good drinking under £20 on a wine list that opens at £13. Accommodation. Open all week.

▌Hathersage

George Hotel
Simple, fresh food
Main Road, Hathersage, S32 1BB
Tel no: (01433) 650436
www.george-hotel.net
Modern British | £33
Cooking score: 4

This characterful 500 year-old building was once an inn. These days it is a smart, modern hotel with the kitchen very much at the heart of the operation. Helen Heywood has been head chef since 2006, initially with the restaurant's previous head chef, Ben Handley, as executive chef. Now firmly at the helm in her own right, she remains true to the restaurant's long-standing commitment to straightforward cooking using the freshest ingredients. Everything is home-made, from breads to relishes and petits fours, and while there is a pleasing lack of fuss, the food is not without invention. Typical of the style are starters such as confit mackerel and brown shrimp rillettes with peppered crème fraîche and herb salad or tarte fine of marinated beetroot and goats' cheese with shallot crisps and toasted hazelnut dressing. Main courses continue in the same modern British vein, so you might encounter chargrilled Castlegate fillet steak with braised shin and onion pie, butternut squash fondant, roasted shallots and red wine sauce or poached salmon and herb noisettes with Scottish langoustine, croquette potatoes and fennel and ginger cream. Desserts range from homely rhubarb crumble with clotted cream to pineapple and passion-fruit mille-feuille with coconut ice cream. A substantial wine list, arranged by style, opens at £15.50.

Chef/s: Helen Heywood. **Open:** L 12 to 2.30, D 7 to 10. **Meals:** Set D £26.50 (2 courses) to £33 (3 courses). **Service:** not inc. **Details:** Cards accepted. 50 seats. Separate bar. Wheelchair access. Children's portions. Car parking.

▌Ridgeway
Old Vicarage
Inventive but elegant cuisine that thrills at every turn
Ridgeway Moor, Ridgeway, S12 3XW
Tel no: (0114) 2475814
www.theoldvicarage.co.uk
Modern British | £40
Cooking score: 7
£5 OFF ♠ ⊟

Though she achieved fame as a presenter, you wouldn't describe Tessa Bramley as a TV chef nowadays. To eat at the Old Vicarage is to realise that this is both unjust, and exactly as it should be. Unjust, because, from the moment Bramley starts helping you order, she plays the part of host with consummate ease – and the food is superb. So while it might seem folly

not to have her on the box more often, this would surely deprive diners of her reassuring presence and culinary expertise. Reports attest to this geniality, one stating that 'hospitality was clearly at the forefront of its agenda' and another highlighting the 'gentle service' and 'unstuffy joviality' of staff. Still, Bramley's masterful balance of professional courtesy and warmth can make the younger staff appear a little clunky in comparison. Despite this cosiness, the menu hardly plays safe – one reports on dishes that 'sounded a little alarming on paper but all worked perfectly', another describes the food as 'a revelation of irresistible flavours'. As the vast majority of ingredients are gathered from the restaurant's own garden in season, the menu changes often in accordance with what's best. So you might find sage-roasted saddle of Ridgeway hare with spiced pears and beetroot, or sweet woodruff ice cream with an old English raspberry sherry trifle. There is a strong sense that Bramley eschews tradition and follows her instincts too – hence dishes such as lime and ginger-roasted guinea fowl. Holding it all together is Bramley's impressive ability to present the unusual and surprising without ever once seeming brash or too bold. A subtle balancing act that leaves you wowed. The wine list is another gem, a powerful draw in itself with southern hemisphere stars measuring up to the best from Europe. Prices start at £22.

Chef/s: Tessa Bramley, Nathan Smith and Anthony Parkin. **Open:** Tue to Fri L 12.30 to 2, D 7 to 9.30, Sat D 6.30 to 9.45. **Closed:** Sun and Mon, bank hol Mon and Tue, 25 Dec to 4 Jan, 2 weeks Aug. **Meals:** Set L £30 (2 courses) to £40, Set D £60 to £65. **Service:** not inc. **Details:** Cards accepted. 46 seats. 16 seats outside. No mobile phones. Wheelchair access. Children's portions. Car parking.

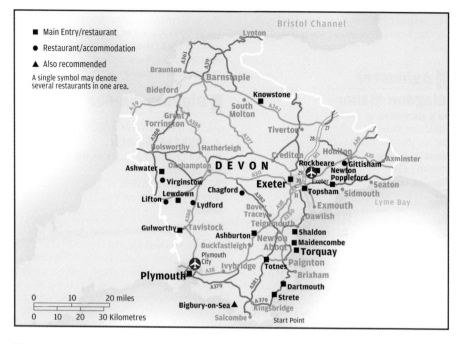

Main Entry/restaurant
Restaurant/accommodation
Also recommended

A single symbol may denote several restaurants in one area.

Ashburton

Agaric

Real food in a convivial setting
30 North Street, Ashburton, TQ13 7QD
Tel no: (01364) 654478
www.agaricrestaurant.co.uk
Modern British | £33
Cooking score: 4

There's a sense of true dedication about this shop-fronted restaurant in the middle of town. It is a very personal operation, with Nick Coiley's classical-based modern cooking appealing for well-executed straightforwardness with everything made on the premises, from the 'very good' bread to ice cream. Local produce is the mainstay of the menu, seen in starters such as twice-baked Hill Farm cheese and thyme soufflé, or a warm salad of pigeon breast and smoked bacon teamed with beetroot and raspberry vinegar, followed, perhaps, by lightly-spiced crispy duck leg with spinach and spiced plum sauce,

or monkfish au poivre with brandy, port and cream. Other reference points have included a main course vegetarian option of a meze plate of warm hummus, falafel, tsatsiki and cheesy filo cigars, and indulgences such as hot chocolate soufflé, or a powerfully-flavoured Seville orange crème brûlée. Sophie Coiley runs front-of-house with unpretentious hospitality and the short, to-the-point wine list offers good drinking at ungreedy prices from £14.95.
Chef/s: Nick Coiley. **Open:** Wed to Sun L 10 to 2, D 7 to 9. **Closed:** Mon and Tue. **Meals:** alc (main courses £13.95 to £16.95). Set L £12.95. **Service:** not

Scores on the Doors

To find out more about the Scores on the Doors campaign, please visit the Food Standard's Agency website: www.food.gov.uk or www.which.co.uk.

inc. **Details:** Cards accepted. 28 seats. 12 seats outside. Separate bar. Wheelchair access. Children's portions.

Ashwater

Blagdon Manor

In a glorious rural setting
Ashwater, EX21 5DF
Tel no: (01409) 211224
www.blagdon.com
British | £35
Cooking score: 2

Steve and Liz Morey's comfortable, seventeenth-century country-house hotel in a glorious rural setting is a classic partnership: she is an affable and calm hostess offering genuine hospitality, while he cooks with intelligence and an unerring feeling for local and home-grown produce. Scallops teamed with beetroot and vegetable consommé make an enjoyable starter at dinner, or you might pick red mullet with caramelised plum tomatoes and black olive sorbet. Main courses might turn up braised beef and oxtail with horseradish mash, wild mushroom and dumplings, or cod with lyonnaise potatoes, pan-fried groats pudding and madeira-braised turnips. Lemon and honey sponge pudding teamed with honey ice cream and a compote of dates, figs and satsumas has made an enjoyable dessert, but the selection of West Country cheeses with home-made bread is strongly recommended too. There's a shorter, good-value lunch menu, and the 40-bin, wide-ranging wine list opens with house recommendations from £13.50.

Chef/s: Steve Morey. **Open:** Wed to Sun L 12 to 2, Tue to Sat D 7 to 9. **Closed:** residents only Sun D, Mon and Tue L. **Meals:** Set L £20, Set D £35. **Service:** not inc. **Details:** Cards accepted. 28 seats. Separate bar. Wheelchair access. Car parking.

Bigbury-on-Sea

ALSO RECOMMENDED
▲ Oyster Shack

Milburn Orchard Farm, Stakes Hill, Bigbury-on-Sea, TQ7 4BE
Tel no: (01548) 810876
www.oystershack.co.uk
Seafood

A laid-back summertime hot-spot for fans of fresh Devon seafood, the Oyster Shack delivers exactly what it promises. Oysters from the Avon estuary are served every which way (from £1.65 each), lobsters and crabs are 'cracked at the Shack', and the kitchen also has its own way with all sorts of locally-landed fish: expect anything from grilled sardines with tapenade (£5.50) to baked hake with sweet-and-sour pepper chutney, Parma ham and aïoli (£16.95). House wine is £12.50. Open all week. A second branch is now open at Hannaford's Landing, 11-13 Island Street, Salcombe; tel (01548) 843596.

Chagford

Gidleigh Park

Silky country-house experience
Chagford, TQ13 8HH
Tel no: (01647) 432367
www.gidleigh.com
Modern European | £41
Cooking score: 7

£5 OFF 🍷 ⊨ V

Gidleigh Park celebrates its 80th birthday during 2008, an occasion that will be marked by the opening of its newly created, walled kitchen garden – as well as numerous other celebratory junketings. The hotel itself – a dashingly handsome, half-timbered Edwardian edifice – is surrounded by glorious grounds, with 40 acres of Devon woodland as a backdrop. At its best it provides a silkily-orchestrated, country-house experience that begins in the capacious lounges overlooking Gidleigh's lauded vistas. Following the 2006 refit, there are now three interconnecting dining rooms, where some reporters have felt a touch uneasy, noting the hushed tones and an atmosphere of 'all-pervading dreariness not helped by the dark panelled walls.' Michael Caines MBE is still emphatically in charge of the kitchen and his cooking is a high-art take on contemporary French cuisine (with all the elaboration that suggests). He is also a crusading champion of West Country produce: Dartmoor lamb, Hatherleigh venison and Brixham scallops regularly appear in season (the latter might be gilded with black truffles and served with caramelised cauliflower purée, sweet raisin vinaigrette and cauliflower velouté). This is a kitchen which can fashion a simple warm salad of pigeon with apples and hazelnuts as well as applying eclectic skills to slow-poached Cornish sea bass with Thai purée, stir-fried shiitake mushrooms, fresh noodles and lemongrass foam. Meals are interspersed with the obligatory 'fine dining' extras, culminating in dazzling desserts such as a brilliantly original pistachio soufflé or a beignet of coconut rice pudding with spiced poached pineapple and mango sorbet. Some have found the food underwhelming, but there are no such quibbles about the superbly professional, amiable service or the magisterial 650-bin wine list (which is trumpeted by a seriously clued-up young sommelier). Wine drinkers are offered an encyclopaedic choice of fabulous stuff, ranging from awe-inspiring pedigree French vintages to California's dreamiest tipples. Top names and savvy choices abound, although quaffers shouldn't be intimidated – especially as there is plenty of fine drinking by-the-glass. Bottle prices start at £28. Interested guests can take a guided tour of the purpose-built cellar, which holds around 7,000 bottles.

Chef/s: Michael Caines. **Open:** all week L 12 to 1.45, D 7 to 9.30. **Meals:** Set L Mon to Thu £27 (2 courses) to £35, Set D £85 and tasting menu £95.

Service: not inc. **Details:** Cards accepted. 52 seats. Separate bar. No music. Wheelchair access. Children's portions. Car parking.

▌ Dartmouth

New Angel

Continues to thrive

2 South Embankment, Dartmouth, TQ6 9BH
Tel no: (01803) 839425
www.thenewangel.co.uk
Modern Anglo-French | £35
Cooking score: 3

Once a place to make a foodie pilgrimage for Joyce Molyneux's superlative cooking (when it was the Carved Angel), this harbourside restaurant is now a vehicle for celebrity chef John Burton-Race, who can often be observed at close quarters in the noisy open kitchen (when he's not on television or generally grabbing the headlines). Local sourcing is clearly taken very seriously here, with Dartmouth crab, Crediton duck and Blackawton lamb all making an appearance on the menu, which sticks to classic French with a modern British slant. Starters of chicken and duck liver parfait with spiced pear and toasted brioche or hand-dived scallops with pea purée, pea shoots and tarragon vinaigrette may be followed by grilled fillet of brill, cauliflower purée, Parmentier potatoes, wild mushrooms and red wine sauce or grilled rib of South Devon beef with big chips, bordelaise beans and red wine sauce. House wines start at £22. Readers should note that we have had some complaints about the booking policy at this restaurant, whereby a credit card reference is taken at time of booking, and is charged with a deposit fee if there are any subsequent cancellations.

Chef/s: John Burton-Race and Robert Spencer. **Open:** all week L 12 to 2.30, D 6.30 to 9.30. **Closed:** 25 and 26 Dec D, Jan. **Meals:** Set L £19.50 (2 courses) to £24.50, Set D £35. **Service:** not inc. **Details:** Cards accepted. 70 seats. Air-con. Separate bar. Music. Children's portions.

★NEW ENTRY★

Seahorse Restaurant

An ambassador of all things piscine
5 South Embankment, Dartmouth, TQ6 9BH
Tel no: (01803) 835147
www.seahorserestaurant.co.uk
Seafood | £35
Cooking score: 4

The Seahorse is the first solo venture for Mitch Tonks, the founder of the popular FishWorks chain of seafood restaurants and fishmongers. Occupying a prime spot on the marina at Dartmouth, it has a timeless, Harry's Bar quality to it, with lofty ceilings, highly polished walnut tables, Art Deco lamps and comfortable button-back leather banquettes. An open kitchen allows diners to watch Tonks and chef Mat Prowse at close quarters, with a wood-burning oven being a main focal point. As an ambassador of all things piscine, it comes as no surprise to find a menu packed with great fish, much of it coming from Brixham a few miles away, but that doesn't mean that grilled meat and poultry is handled with any less precision. At inspection, a starter of light-as-a-feather gnocchi arrived with a rich, deeply-flavoured sauce of veal shin, beef and porcini, while Dover sole meunière was expertly cooked. The wine list majors on Italy, with sections dedicated to named small producers and families; five different bottles of various vintages and styles are opened each day to be sold by-the-glass.

Chef/s: Mitch Tonks and Mat Prowse. **Open:** Thur to Sun L 12 to 3 (Sun 4), Wed to Sat D 6 to 10.30. **Meals:** alc (main courses £12 to £21). **Service:** not inc. **Details:** Cards accepted. 40 seats. Air-con. Music. Children's portions.

▌Exeter

Michael Caines at ABode Exeter

Vibrant venue with cathedral views
Royal Clarence Hotel, Cathedral Yard, Exeter, EX1 1HD
Tel no: (01392) 223638
www.michaelcaines.com
French | £40
New Chef
£5 OFF ▐

The Royal Clarence Hotel makes a vibrant venue for Michael Caines's ABode group. A spacious Champagne Bar sets the opulent tone, while the chic, uncluttered restaurant has polished boards, big mirrors and bold canvases inspired by the cathedral (visible through the front windows). Judging by reports, continuity remains in the kitchen, with Tom Williams-Hawkes now in charge of a modern repertoire with the accent on fine West Country produce. Start with Brixham scallops teamed with crispy belly pork, pea purée, shallot and bacon velouté, or try terrine of foie gras with rhubarb compote and mushrooms à la grecque. Fine raw materials might include Pipers Farm loin of lamb served with a confit of the shoulder, boulangère potatoes, fennel purée and tapenade jus, or roast sea bass with roasted vegetables and gazpacho sauce. Sophisticated desserts have included raspberry and lime soufflé with vanilla bourbon ice cream and mille-feuille of pistachio and apricot parfait with dark chocolate fondant and almond foam. House wines start at £19.25.

Chef/s: Tom Williams-Hawkes. **Open:** Mon to Sat L 12 to 2.30, D 7 to 9.30. **Closed:** Sun. **Meals:** alc (main courses £23.50 to £25). Set L £14.50 (2 courses) to £19.50, Tasting menu £58. **Service:** 10% (optional). **Details:** Cards accepted. 60 seats. Air-con. Separate bar. Wheelchair access.

Gittisham

Combe House

Ambitious food in impressive surroundings
Gittisham, EX14 3AD
Tel no: (01404) 540400
www.thishotel.com
Modern British | £42
Cooking score: 4

The impressive mile-long drive through the 3,500 acre estate and the grandeur of the Grade 1-listed Elizabethan mansion may overawe, but rest assured, Combe House is no snooty, mind-the-Louis-XV-furniture kind of place. Dining here 'is like visiting a rich, elderly (and very well-fed) aunt in the country'. The service is friendly and warmly attentive, the surroundings grand but − comfortingly − a little frayed round the edges. Hadleigh Barrett displays sound cooking skills, but he has a little honing to do. He creates stylish and imaginative dishes − think scallops with spiced cauliflower purée and ginger velouté in early summer, or slow-roast fillet of beef with horseradish pommes purée and braised oxtail dumpling in winter − with flavours that are big and in combinations which strike a good balance between traditional and innovative. Praise must also go to the first-class ingredients used; many are sourced locally (the menu lists suppliers), or own-grown, and the kitchen makes its own charcuterie, smoked salmon and trout, all of which feature on the menu. Happily, the wine list keeps up the standards, with plenty of decent offerings available by-the-glass and for around £20 a bottle, plus choices for those with deeper pockets.

Chef/s: Hadleigh Barrett and Stuart Brown. **Open:** all week L 12pm to 2pm, D 7pm to 9.30pm. **Closed:** last 2 weeks Jan. **Meals:** Set L £22 (2 courses) to £28, Set D £42. **Service:** not inc. **Details:** Cards accepted. 100 seats. 125 seats outside. Separate bar. Music. Children's portions. Car parking.

Gulworthy

Horn of Plenty

Soul-soothing surroundings, meticulous food
Gulworthy, PL19 8JD
Tel no: (01822) 832528
www.thehornofplenty.co.uk
Modern British | £45
Cooking score: 6

A 'grandstand vista of the leafy unspoilt Tamar Valley' is one reason why readers adore this enchantingly tranquil 200-year-old country house set in five acres of gardens and orchards. The scenery may be breathtaking, but there's much more to enjoy at the Horn of Plenty: even a one-night sleepover can be 'total perfection', thanks largely to the exquisite food created by 'super league' chef Peter Gorton and his team. Visitors can look forward to confident displays of high-end gastro-wizardry, with no shortage of invention, creativity or meticulous application across the board. A starter of sautéed scallops and king prawns wrapped in prosciutto sitting on coriander lentils with an oriental dressing sets the standard for things to come. Mains show what the kitchen can do with top-drawer ingredients gleaned from Devon's larder and beyond: lightly spiced venison is classically paired with celeriac purée, red wine shallots and Cassis sauce, while roast fillet of beef is embellished with truffle gnocchi. Vegetarians are treated to a grande assiette, while desserts could be as straight and true as individual apple cheesecake with apple sorbet; otherwise, wait 20 minutes for a dazzling trio of chocolate that brings together a dark pithiviers, mint-tinged white chocolate ice cream and a milky mousse. France leads the way on the finely-constructed wine list, which boasts an excellent choice of vintages from the classic regions, plus serious back-up from Italy and beyond. Eleven enticing house selections start at £15 (£4.25 a glass).

Chef/s: Peter Gorton. **Open:** all week L 12 to 4, D 7 to 11.30. **Closed:** 24 to 26 Dec. **Meals:** Set L £26.50. Set D £45. **Service:** not inc. **Details:** Cards accepted.

60 seats. 15 seats outside. Air-con. No mobile phones. Wheelchair access. Music. Children's portions. Car parking.

▌Knowstone
Mason's Arms
Impeccably crafted modern food
Knowstone, EX36 4RY
Tel no: (01398) 341231
www.masonsarmsdevon.co.uk
Modern British | £34
Cooking score: 6

The setting is a picture-perfect thatched thirteenth-century pub in a rural backwater on the edge of Exmoor: it sounds like a rose-tinted bucolic prospect, yet the Mason's Arms is a world away from ploughman's and pints. To be sure, you can still sup Devon ales by the massive fireplace in the bar, but the real action takes place in the cosy green-walled dining room at the back of the pub. Mark Dodson is a veteran of big country-house kitchens including the Waterside Inn, Bray (see entry), but he has scaled down and fine-tuned his food to suit his new surroundings. Accuracy, clear flavours and a sure touch typify his impeccably crafted modern dishes, whether it's a salad of wood pigeon with pine nuts and blackcurrant sauce or a duo of chicken liver parfait and ham hock terrine with vegetables à la grecque and brioche toast. Main courses point up the locality: suprême of Devonshire Red corn-fed chicken is served with roasted garlic, chanterelles and smoked bacon potato rösti, while West Country seafood gets a decent outing in the shape of, perhaps, fillet of halibut cleverly fashioned with a potato crust and cider cream sauce. Cheeses from Devon and Somerset bring up the rear, alongside high-end, definitely-not-pubby desserts such as pineapple and ginger sablé with rum sauce or lemon and mascarpone mousse with passion fruit syrup. The wine list is a neat, unfussy selection of sound bottles, mostly from France and the New World. House selections start admirably at £11.75 (£4 a glass).

Chef/s: Mark Dodson. **Open:** Tue to Sun L 12 to 2, Tue to Sat D 7 to 9. **Closed:** Mon, first 2 weeks Jan. **Meals:** alc (main courses £14 to £18.50). Set L Sun £31.50. **Service:** not inc. **Details:** Cards accepted. 28 seats. 16 seats outside. Separate bar. Wheelchair access. Music. Children's portions. Car parking.

▌Lewdown
Lewtrenchard Manor
Modern food in country-house setting
Lewdown, EX20 4PN
Tel no: (01566) 783222
www.lewtrenchard.co.uk
Modern British
Cooking score: 6
£5 OFF 🍷 🛏

Hidden in its own secret valley on the edge of Dartmoor, this Jacobean manor is a rich feast of period features, from ornate plasterwork to oak panelling and antique furniture. Its granite-framed windows look out on immaculate grounds designed by Walter Sorel, where streams, ponds and woodland allow for tranquil postprandial walks. While the gardens and the house alone are enough to attract visitors, chef/patron Jason Hornbuckle has also made this a dining destination. His cooking places a welcome emphasis on seasonal, local and home-grown produce; and contrary to what the historic setting might suggest, his 'superb dishes' strike a vibrantly modern note. Expect technical precision and clarity of flavour from starters such as ballottine of foie gras with confit chicken ravioli and hazelnut foam, and main courses of pan-fried turbot with shiitake mushroom duxelles, watercress purée and chicken jus or fennel-infused poached loin of rare breed pork with celeriac, beetroot and red onion marmalade. Desserts range from crème brûlée to strawberry jelly with a green peppercorn tuile and elderflower sorbet. Praised for its 'value for money', the restaurant offers three courses for £19 at lunchtime. For diners seeking a more detailed insight into Hornbuckle's art, the 'purple carrot' dining experience offers dinner in a private room watching the kitchen action on flat-screen TV. The impressive, French-dominated wine list opens at £20.

Chef/s: Jason Hornbuckle. **Open:** Tue to Sun L 12 to 2, all week D 7 to 9. **Closed:** 25 Dec, 1 Jan. **Meals:** Set L £15 (2 courses) to £19 (3 courses). Set D £45 (3 courses). **Service:** not inc. **Details:** Cards accepted. 40 seats. Separate bar. Wheelchair access. Music. Children's portions. Car parking.

▌Lifton

Arundell Arms

Personal charm in a seductive setting
Lifton, PL16 0AA
Tel no: (01566) 784666
www.arundellarms.com
Modern British | £40
Cooking score: 5
£5 OFF 🍷 🛏 V

Anne Voss-Bark's civilized inn with 20 miles of private fishing along the Tamar eschews voguish minimalism and favours the enduring virtues of personable hospitality and good food. It operates on several levels: as a pub offering good bar food, a comfortable hotel and an ambitious restaurant. Steven Pidgeon's cooking is highly polished and unpretentious; the focus, as it always has been, is on excellent raw materials from local or regional suppliers. Sensible-length menus keep things uncluttered and centred on the main ingredients, perhaps in the form of boned and stuffed quail with shallots, garlic and herbs, or Falmouth Bay scallops with a poached oyster, parsley and white wine. At main course, fish comes in for meaty treatments in the modern style, thus a fillet of black bream may be paired with haricot beans, tomato and wild garlic, but meats themselves are more mainstream. Mignon of Devon beef, for example, comes with roasted artichokes, Savoy cabbage and a peppercorn sauce. Desserts can deliver majestic flavours, as did a hot chocolate fondant that came with clotted cream and treacle toffee ice cream. We were not sent the wine list this year, so are unable to comment, but house wines open at £15.

Chef/s: Steven Pidgeon. **Open:** all week L 12.30 to 2, D 7.30 to 9.30. **Closed:** Christmas. **Meals:** Set L £24, Set D £40. **Service:** not inc. **Details:** Cards accepted. 70 seats. 20 seats outside. Separate bar. No mobile phones. Wheelchair access. Music. Children's portions. Car parking.

▌Lydford

Dartmoor Inn

West Country food hero
Moorside, Lydford, EX20 4AY
Tel no: (01822) 820221
www.dartmoorinn.com
Modern British | £25
Cooking score: 3
£5 OFF 🛏 £30

Famed for its unswerving dedication to West Country produce and all things local, this happy Dartmoor pub is a labour of love for Philip and Karen Burgess. The interior comprises a matrix of tiny rooms done out in the best country style, with garlands of dried flowers and rustic colour schemes and the owners are forever making improvements: how many inns can boast a fashion boutique? That said, food remains top of the agenda and everything has an instantly recognisable thumbprint. The kitchen goes about its work with flair and dexterity, whether it is serving ham hock terrine with baby carrots and mustard dressing or crab salad with radishes and sorrel. Mains are also deceptively simple: fillet of red mullet with roasted spices and red pepper rouille or marjoram-crusted rump of lamb with shallot purée, for example. A few 'easy dining' options are available in the bar (lamb's liver and bacon, chargrilled fish salad), cheeses fly the flag and desserts are familiar creations such as English apple cake. Prices on the appetising global wine list start at £13 (£3.40 a glass).

Chef/s: Andrew Honey and Philip Burgess. **Open:** Tue to Sun L 12 to 2.30, Mon to Sat D 6.30 to 10. **Meals:** alc (main courses £14 to £22). Set L and D £13.75 (2 courses) to £17.50. **Service:** not inc. **Details:** Cards accepted. 65 seats. 15 seats outside. Separate bar. No mobile phones. Wheelchair access. Music. Children's portions. Car parking.

▌Maidencombe

Orestone Manor

Classy country-house dining
Rockhouse Lane, Maidencombe, TQ1 4SX
Tel no: (01803) 328098
www.orestonemanor.com
Modern British | £38
Cooking score: 2

This comfortable and welcoming nineteenth-century house has no pretensions or grandeur, since it is a well-run family enterprise. Meals might begin with a drink on the terrace in fine weather, taking in the fabulous sea view. In the kitchen, Chris May does a good job of managing the demands of traditionalists and modernists, serving (at lunch) bowls of crab bisque and beef bourguignon alongside mackerel en croûte with a tomato and shallot salad. It is all underpinned by the wholesome feeling of good ingredients. Evening choices have included Start Bay crab and loin of hare in a pearl barley broth, with mains of Suffolk shepherd's pie with pommes purée and spiced pickled red cabbage, or fillets of red mullet with saffron vinaigrette, potato and herb salad. West country cheeses are a fine alternative to desserts such as zabaglione with vanilla biscotti. A good selection of house wines opens at £14.95.
Chef/s: Chris May. **Open:** all week L 12 to 2, D 7 to 9. **Closed:** 2 to 26 Jan. **Meals:** Set L £15 (2 courses) to £17.95, Set D £31 (2 courses) to £38. **Service:** not inc. **Details:** Cards accepted. 30 seats. Air-con. Separate bar. Wheelchair access. Music. Children's portions. Car parking.

▌Newton Poppleford

Moores'

Lovely coastal setting
6 Greenbank, High Street, Newton Poppleford, EX10 0EB
Tel no: (01395) 568100
www.mooresrestaurant.co.uk
Modern British | £25
Cooking score: 1

Many have found Moores' a convenient stop-off on the long haul from London to Cornwall, and certainly this stretch of the east Devon coastline – only six miles outside Exeter – looks a tasty proposition. The same could be said of Jonathan Moore's cooking, which offers a bold rendition of the modern British mode. Start with a salad of local seafood marinated in lime, coconut and ginger, and proceed to roast monkfish on wild and red rice with champagne vanilla cream, or rack of spring lamb with sautéed Savoy cabbage, herbed fondant potato and a jus enriched with vintage port. Awaiting you at meal's end will be something like apricot-glazed bread-and-butter pudding with Devonshire clotted cream. A short international list opens with Spanish house wines at £12.95 a bottle (£3.50 a glass).
Chef/s: Jonathan Moore. **Open:** Tue to Sun L 12 to 1.30, Tue to Sat D 7 to 9.30. **Closed:** Christmas, first 2 weeks of Jan. **Meals:** Set L £18.45, Set L Sun £17.45, Set D £24.50. **Service:** not inc. **Details:** Cards accepted. 32 seats. 12 seats outside. No mobile phones. Wheelchair access. Music. Children's portions.

▌Plymouth

Tanners

Lively cooking from brothers in whites
Prysten House, Finewell Street, Plymouth,
PL1 2AE
Tel no: (01752) 252001
www.tannersrestaurant.com
Modern British | £30
Cooking score: 3
V

Christopher and James Tanner are now
household names on the TV chef circuit,
although they have never neglected their
culinary duties in Plymouth. Their
buzzy restaurant occupies a
venerable fifteenth-century merchant's house
that ranks as one of the oldest buildings in the
town. History looms large, with tapestries
on rough-stone walls, but there's nothing
archaic about the food. West Country fish
makes a big impact: seared John Dory comes
with a cassoulet of shellfish, while fillet
of halibut is accompanied by champ, spinach
and braised clams. Elsewhere, carpaccio of
venison is served with celeriac rémoulade and
pickled wild mushrooms, roast cannon and
confit shoulder of lamb are jazzed up with
sweet pepper and black olive jus, and
clever desserts might feature iced Granny
Smith mousse with chilled rhubarb soup and
mascarpone sorbet. Simpler dishes appear at
lunchtime (navarin of lamb, seafood stew) and
the carefully annotated wine list provides
sound drinking from serious growers. Prices
start at £13.95 and there's a decent choice by-
the-glass – thanks to a 'verre du vin'
preservation system.
Chef/s: Christopher and James Tanner, Jay Barker
Jones. **Open:** Tue to Sat L 12 to 2.30, D 7 to 9.30.
Closed: Sun, Mon, 24 to 26 Dec. **Meals:** Set L £14.50
(2 courses) to £18.50. Set D £27 (2 courses) to £34.
Service: not inc. **Details:** Cards accepted. 50 seats.
30 seats outside. Separate bar. No mobile phones.
Wheelchair access. Music. Children's portions.

▌Rockbeare

Jack in the Green

Devon food champion
Rockbeare, EX5 2EE
Tel no: (01404) 822240
www.jackinthegreen.uk.com
Modern British | £28
Cooking score: 3
V

An amalgam of unpretentious roadside
hostelry and sophisticated contemporary
restaurant, this white-painted pub by the A30
comprises a rabbit warren of print-festooned
rooms plus a four-acre expanse of garden for al
fresco meals. The commendably short
restaurant menu is true to the region and
customers can put together their own 'totally
Devon meal experience' by pinpointing
selected dishes. To start, ham hock terrine with
pickled vegetables and grain mustard vies with
Dartmouth smoked salmon, while mains
might range from grilled sea bass with
lemongrass, lime and coconut to organic
Creedy Carver duck breast with fondant
potato, apples and Calvados. Finish with
rhubarb brûlée or Devon cheeses. Simpler
dishes are available in the bar, where you can
feast on faggots while quaffing pints of
locally-brewed Otter Ale and other premium
West Country brews. The ambitious 100-bin
wine list spreads its net wide, but keeps prices
in check. Most house selections are £14.50
(£3.60 a glass).
Chef/s: Matt Mason and Craig Sampson. **Open:** Mon
to Sat 12 to 2 (2.30 Fri and Sat), 6 to 9.30 (10 Fri
and Sat). Sun 12 to 9.30. **Closed:** 25 Dec to 5 Jan.
Meals: alc (main courses £17.50 to £23.50). Set L
and D Mon to Sat £25 (3 courses). Set L Sun £18.95
(2 courses) to £24.45. Bar menu available.
Service: not inc. **Details:** Cards accepted. 140 seats.
30 seats outside. Air-con. Separate bar. Wheelchair
access. Music. Children's portions. Car parking.

█ Shaldon

★NEW ENTRY★
Ode
Showcasing local produce
21 Fore Street, Shaldon, TQ14 ODE
Tel no: (0871) 9606037
www.odetruefood.co.uk
Modern British | £35
Cooking score: 2

A passion for organic and local produce forms the backbone of Tim Bouget's family-run restaurant in the picturesque Devon coastal village of Shaldon. This means exceptional raw ingredients, whether it's line-caught local fish or organic fruit and vegetables. The mantra of sustainability extends to the intimate 24-cover dining room in this Georgian townhouse, which has been refurbished by local craftsmen using reclaimed woods, recycled glass and environmentally friendly materials. Once you have secured one of the highly-prized tables, enjoy Paignton brown crab blini with poached Hafod Farm egg and hollandaise sauce, followed by fillet of local mackerel with Rowswell Farm beets, horseradish and pink fir potatoes. Wines are sourced from organic estates, with bottles starting at £16.50 and struggling to get above £45.
Chef/s: Tim Bouget. **Open:** Thur to Fri L 12 to 1.30, Wed to Sat D 7 to 9.30, Sun brunch 11 to 1.30. **Closed:** first 2 weeks Oct, bank hols, 25 to 26 Dec. **Meals:** alc (main courses £16 to £22). Set L £15.95 (2 courses) to £19.95. **Service:** not inc. **Details:** Cards accepted. 24 seats. No mobile phones. Music.

█ Strete
Kings Arms
Pretty pub serving seafood
Dartmouth Road, Strete, TQ6 ORW
Tel no: (01803) 770377
www.kingsarms-dartmouth.co.uk
Seafood | £26
Cooking score: 2
£5 OFF £30

This eighteenth-century pub is quite a looker, thanks to the elaborate cast iron balcony running along the front of the building. It's not the only selling point: a new section of the South West Coast path runs past its front door, and there are views of Start Bay from the patio, garden and dining room. While it remains a real pub inside, the main feature is the seafood. You might begin with Bigbury Bay oysters on ice with red wine shallot vinegar or fish soup with saffron and rouille. Main courses range from fillet of sea bass and fresh soya beans with an orange-soy glaze to fillet of turbot with local asparagus and hollandaise sauce. For meat-eaters, there might be West Country rib-eye steak with grilled tomato, salsa verde and chips. Afterwards, perhaps summer fruit champagne jellies with vanilla-seed ice cream. A decent selection of wines opens at £15.
Chef/s: Rob Dawson. **Open:** Mon to Sun L 11.30 to 3, Mon to Sat D 6 to 11. **Closed:** Mon in winter, last 3 weeks of Jan. **Meals:** alc (main courses D £14 to £22). **Service:** not inc. **Details:** Cards accepted. 36 seats. 40 seats outside. Separate bar. No mobile phones. Children's portions. Car parking.

Topsham

La Petite Maison
Well-rendered French style
35 Fore Street, Topsham, EX3 0HR
Tel no: (01392) 873660
www.lapetitemaison.co.uk
Anglo-French | £34
Cooking score: 4
£5
OFF

The Pestells' small restaurant on a bend in Fore Street retains the feeling of a private home inside, although the food brought to the table is a cut above the domestic. Despite the unfailingly welcoming, informal tone, there is no doubt about the level of ambition here. This is a serious operation in a county where the competition is pretty fierce. Consistency is the watchword of the kitchen, and a loyal regular reports that many of the renditions of classic French dishes, such as confit of duck with gratin dauphinoise, cabbage, bacon and a madeira sauce, are 'as good as any restaurant in France, and have not been messed around with'. That straightforward approach doesn't at all preclude creativity; witness a first-course ensemble consisting of a crab galette, crab cappuccino bisque and a roll of smoked salmon filled with crab in ginger and coriander mayonnaise. Main courses deliver some neat spins on intuitive combinations, as in herb-crusted pork medallions with slow-roast belly, black pudding, creamy leeks and caramelised apple, or a pairing of sea bass and monkfish with a potato cake, vegetable 'spaghetti', spinach and a chive beurre blanc. Gallic influence is tangible in desserts such as apricot and almond tart with Amaretto mascarpone, or profiteroles with dark chocolate ice-cream. Proceedings might commence with an aperitif of sparkling wine with a drop of fruit liqueur in it, before choosing from the France-weighted wine list, which begins at £15.

Chef/s: Douglas Pestell and Sara Bright. **Open:** Tue to Sat D 7 to closing. **Meals:** Set D £33.95. **Service:** not inc. **Details:** Cards accepted. 30 seats. Music. Children allowed.

Torquay

Elephant
English Riviera hot-spot
3-4 Beacon Terrace, Torquay, TQ1 2BH
Tel no: (01803) 200044
www.elephantrestaurant.co.uk
Modern British | £40
Cooking score: 6
£5
OFF

Forget Basil Fawlty and his rantings, Simon Hulstone's Elephant is now making the headlines and trumpeting its presence in Torquay. Glorious views of the 'English Riviera', big mirrors and walls draped with menus from prestigious international restaurants set the tone in the handsome first-floor Room. This is now the fine-dining arm of the set-up, and it's a showcase for Simon Hulstone's ambitious, ingredients-led cooking. West Country seafood and meat from Devon farms are the cornerstones of his fixed-price dinner menus, and the results show enviable freshness as well as eye-catching pizazz. Scallops (courtesy of a local diver called Don) are paired with foie gras and served atop butternut squash and date chutney, while rope-grown Brixham mussels are done simply in white wine and Pernod cream. Fashionable 'low temperature' cooking is applied to Haford Farm eggs (served disarmingly with peas à la française) and aged fillet of Ruby Red beef on the bone (dressed with a countryside combo of snail and wild garlic butter). Intricate technique also shows in fillet of rose veal osso buco, which is poached before being roasted. Desserts are equal to the task: gingerbread tansy pudding is matched with pumpkin and vanilla ice cream, while blackcurrant mousse comes with liquorice jelly and crème fraîche sorbet. Our rating (and details) refer to the Room, but the Elephant's revamped ground-floor brasserie is also well worth noting. Its informal setting is matched by a flexible, all-comers' menu that sees Thai fishcakes, chicken Caesar salad and venison sausages alongside Dover sole with pickled lemon and vegetable tempura or slow-cooked belly pork with braised Puy lentils. The concise, cosmopolitan wine list is a well-spread affair, with prices from £14.50 (£3.50 a glass).

Chef/s: Simon Hulstone. **Open:** Tue to Sat D only 7 to 9.30. **Closed:** Sun, Mon. **Meals:** Set D £32.95 (2 courses) to £39.50. **Service:** not inc. **Details:** Cards accepted. 24 seats. Air-con. Separate bar. No mobile phones. Wheelchair access. Music. Children's portions.

▌Totnes

Effings

Good food in offbeat Totnes
50 Fore Street, Totnes, TQ9 5RP
Tel no: (01803) 863435
Modern European | £20
Cooking score: 2

A Totnes fixture for some years now, Effings is an 'intimate' deli/café offering a daytime menu based on decent local ingredients. Take your pick from a fashionably modern medley, perhaps assemblages of plates of own-made pâtés and terrines, or Italian-style antipasto of air-cured ham, salami, cheese and marinated vegetables. Among the few hot dishes on offer there could be the popular tartlet of local crab or a rich cassoulet, while dessert might bring raspberry crème brûlée with 'lovely' home-made blueberry ice cream. Though results can occasionally prove inconsistent, service is good and the wine list of about a dozen bottles opens at £13.75.

Chef/s: Karl Rasmussen. **Open:** Mon to Sat 9 to 5. **Closed:** Sun, bank hols. **Meals:** alc (main courses £6.50 to £13.95). **Service:** not inc. **Details:** Cash only. 14 seats. Air-con. No music. No mobile phones. Wheelchair access. Children's portions.

▌Virginstow

Percy's

Casual, restorative and uncompromising
Coombeshead Estate, Virginstow, EX21 5EA
Tel no: (01409) 211236
www.percys.co.uk
Modern British | £40
Cooking score: 4

£5 OFF ▭

This country-house hotel in a 'marvellous location' is the kind of place you dream about escaping to: casual, restorative and uncompromising in pursuit of quality. The kitchen runs on ecologically sound principles, ensuring that most of its organic raw materials don't have to travel too far to reach it. The Bricknell-Webbs' surrounding 130-acre organic estate supplies pork and lamb, seasonal game, eggs, vegetables, herbs and salad leaves; what exceptions there are, such as fish from Cornwall, clearly earn their place. Simplicity seems to be the key to the operation, with Tina Bricknell-Webb cooking four-course dinners with a refreshing lack of fuss. Her repertoire ranges from seared squid and scallops on a bed of mixed leaves to roast loin of lamb with rosemary jus. Goats' cheese teamed with grilled aubergine, courgette and red pepper might precede monkfish in a spring onion and coriander batter with tomato salsa. Fine local cheeses precede mainstream desserts such as lemon tart or apple, oatmeal and ginger crumble with custard. Service, however, has been reported hit-and-miss this year. The short, to-the-point wine list opens at £16.

Chef/s: Tina Bricknell-Webb. **Open:** all week D only 6.30pm. **Meals:** Set D £40. **Service:** not inc. **Details:** Cards accepted. 20 seats. Separate bar. Wheelchair access. Car parking.

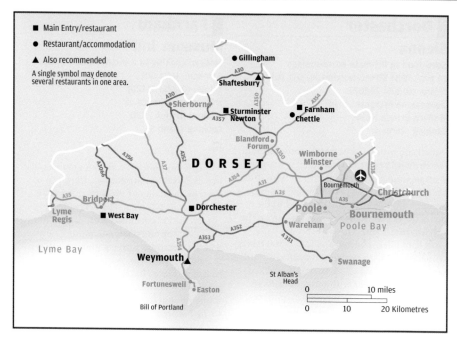

▌Chettle

Castleman Hotel
Family-owned former dower house
Chettle, DT11 8DB
Tel no: (01258) 830096
www.castlemanhotel.co.uk
Modern British | £23
Cooking score: 2

£5 OFF 🍷 🛏 £30

The entire village of Chettle has been owned by the Bourke family for more than 150 years, and the hotel is housed in what was the dower house – a tranquil and idiosyncratic building overlooking Cranborne Chase. Lovely period features abound in the galleried hall, Regency drawing room and relaxed restaurant, where owner Edward Bourke is master of all he surveys. His partner Barbara Garnsworthy holds sway in the kitchen and she is happy to deploy local ingredients for a Euro-repertoire that could range from a warm salad of pheasant and bacon with cranberry and juniper dressing to chocolate and brandy pot

with shortbread. In between, expect classic roast duck breast with bigarade sauce and grilled fillet of sea bass with roasted peppers and romesco sauce. The wine list has been put together with knowledge and enthusiasm: producers are among the best, prices are eminently fair and half-bottles show up well. House wines are £12 (£3 a glass).
Chef/s: Barbara Garnsworthy and Richard Morris.
Open: Sun L 12.30 to 2, all week D 7 to 9.30. **Closed:** 25, 26 and 31 Dec, Feb. **Meals:** alc (main courses £9 to £16.50). Set L Sun £21. **Service:** not inc.
Details: Cards accepted. 45 seats. Separate bar. No music. Wheelchair access. Children's portions. Car parking.

Readers recommend

A 'readers recommend' review is a genuine quote from a report sent in by one of our readers. We intend to follow up these suggestions throughout the year to come.

Dorchester

Sienna
Good food in intimate surroundings
36 High West Street, Dorchester, DT1 1UP
Tel no: (01305) 250022
www.siennarestaurant.co.uk
Modern British | £36
Cooking score: 4

'Small and intimate but fresh' neatly sums up
the Browns' bright shop-fronted restaurant
with its simple modern interior. It wins, too,
for Russell Brown's good cooking. His menus
are appealing, flavours are clear and well-
defined and presentation are as spot-on as the
service from Elena Brown. Start, perhaps,
with ham hock, chicken and foie gras terrine,
which comes with tarragon mayonnaise and
pea-shoot salad. Moving on, twice-cooked
pork belly is teamed with morcilla sausage,
caramelised apple and cider sauce, or there
could be roast fillet of pollack with Savoy
cabbage, bacon and red wine jus. Raw
ingredients are good quality and a winter
report on the six-course tasting menu was
particularly taken by the 'good selection of in-
season dishes' that included roast breast of
partridge with fondant potato, wild
mushrooms and Jerusalem artichoke velouté,
as well as pleasing canapés and petits fours.
Among desserts, iced mandarin parfait with
cranberry and raisin compote and ginger foam
has pleased. The well-constructed wine list
opens at £14.75.
Chef/s: Russell Brown. **Open:** Tue to Sat L 12 to 2, D
7 to 9. **Closed:** Sun and Mon, 2 weeks spring and
autumn. **Meals:** Set L £18.50 (2 courses) to £21.50,
Set D £29.50 (2 courses) to £36.50. **Service:** not inc.
Details: Cards accepted. 15 seats. Air-con. Music.

Farnham

Museum Inn
Modern cooking in a picture-book village
Farnham, DT11 8DE
Tel no: (01725) 516261
www.museuminn.co.uk
Modern British | £30
Cooking score: 5

The museum reference denotes the fact that
this exquisite seventeenth-century inn was
built by the father of modern archaeology,
Augustus Pitt-Rivers. The period feel is
conscientiously retained with flagged floors,
an inglenook and plenty of antique furniture,
and the inn sits in a pretty village with quaint
thatched cottages to complete the picture.
Matthew Davey has taken up the kitchen reins
since last year's Guide, but maintains the high
standard of polished modern British cooking
set by his predecessors. Lamb sweetbreads,
fried crisp, come with pancetta and peas as one
possible starter; chicken and leek terrine with
tarragon dressing is another. The absence of
anything fish-based among first courses is a
surprise, but is made up for by mains such as
grilled whole plaice with confit red peppers,
seasoned with garlic and oregano. Other
options might include local lamb with
provençale vegetables, spinach and new
potatoes roasted in balsamic, all sauced with a
syrupy jus of red onion, tomato and basil.
Finish with dark chocolate fondant, served
with chocolate ice cream and fruit kebabs or
the signature raspberry Eton mess. Wines are a
worldwide tour of famous names, with a run
of vintages of Mouton-Rothschild for the
lottery-winners, and house wines from
£14.50 for the rest of us.
Chef/s: Matthew Davey. **Open:** all week, L 12 to 3, D
Mon to Sat 6 to 11, Sun 7 to 10.30. **Meals:** alc (main
courses £14 to £18.50). **Service:** not inc.
Details: Cards accepted. 100 seats. 36 seats
outside. No music. Wheelchair access. Children
allowed. Car parking.

▌Gillingham
Stock Hill
Austrian flavours in a Dorset domicile
Stock Hill, Gillingham, SP8 5NR
Tel no: (01747) 823626
www.stockhillhouse.co.uk
Modern European | £39
Cooking score: 5

🛏 V

Peter and Nita Hauser recently clocked up 22 years as caring hosts at this delightfully tranquil Victorian mansion approached via a meandering beech-lined drive. Inside, Stock Hill looks unshowily affluent, with chintzy colour schemes, William Morris wallpaper and curios adding to the personality of the place. Peter Hauser's refined, flavour-driven cooking regularly earns praise and he is proud of his Austrian roots: note the red and white flags printed alongside native specialities on his daily-changing menus. Viennese paprika beef goulash 'Fiaker style' is served authentically with fried egg, pickled gherkin and spätzli, while pork tenderloin is filled with red onion confit, shallow-fried in egg and breadcrumbs and paired with baby leeks perfumed with ginger. Starters tend to be mainstream European – witness paupiettes of local smoked salmon stuffed with mackerel mousse or poached mushroom ravioli in clear chicken broth – while desserts offer anything from mini Viennese cheesecake with mango sorbet to sticky toffee pudding with pecan sauce. Everyone has a good word for the genuine welcome ('as if you were visiting friends') and the 'comfortable', attentive service. The comprehensive wine list covers most major producing countries across the globe, with a page of Austrian gems adding a patriotic note. House recommendations start at £17.10 (£4.95 a glass).
Chef/s: Peter Hauser and Lorna Connor. **Open:** Tue to Fri and Sun L 12.15 to 1.45, all week D 7.15 to 8.45. **Meals:** Set L £27, Set D £39. **Service:** not inc. **Details:** Cards accepted. 30 seats. 8 seats outside. No music. No mobile phones. Children's portions. Car parking.

▌Poole
READERS RECOMMEND
Hardy's
14 High Street, Poole, BH15 1BP
Tel no: 01202 660864
'Superior seafood that draws in the madding crowd.'

▌Shaftesbury
ALSO RECOMMENDED
▲ La Fleur de Lys
Bleke Street, Shaftesbury, SP7 8AW
Tel no: (01747) 853717
www.lafleurdelys.co.uk
Modern British

The comfortably appointed restaurant in this small hotel in the centre of Shaftesbury provides 'immaculate service and attention to detail'. Asparagus soup with soft-boiled quail's egg and rosemary dumplings (£7) and saddle of Seka venison with blueberries, pears and shallots in a rich red wine sauce (£23) show that the cooking has a firm English accent, although alongside these are mix-and-match dishes like seared scallops with creamed lentils, crispy pancetta and lime dressing (£8.50) and baked fillet of brill with coriander, garlic and mustard seed wrapped in filo pastry and served with a garlic sauce (£23). House wine is £15. Closed Sun D, and Mon and Tue.

▌Sturminster Newton
Plumber Manor
Country-house dynasty
Sturminster Newton, DT10 2AF
Tel no: (01258) 472507
www.plumbermanor.com
Anglo-French | £30
Cooking score: 2

🛏

The lovely, peacefully located Plumber Manor has been home to generations of the Prideaux-Brune dynasty since the 1600s, and Brian

Prideaux-Brune has been at the stoves ever since it became a country-house hotel. It is thus a very personal operation, with attention to detail ensuring first-class service and consistent, appealing food. The cooking is simple Anglo-French, say smoked salmon paupiettes with smoked trout mousse or chicken liver parfait with red onion marmalade as starters. Among main courses, loin of pork with apples and sage jus, and lemon sole with grapes and white wine reveal good raw materials treated with respect. Even the more exotic offerings, of crab mousse with crevettes and a light curry sauce or confit and suprême of Aylsbury duck with mango coulis are as deftly handled. The same could be said of the competitively-priced wine list, with good-value basics from £15, a strong selection of French classics and sound New World choices.
Chef/s: Brian Prideaux-Brune. **Open:** Sun L 12 to 1.30, all week D 7 to 9. **Meals:** Set D £30. **Service:** not inc. **Details:** Cards accepted. 65 seats. Separate bar. Wheelchair access. Children's portions. Car parking.

West Bay
Riverside Restaurant
Consistently good seafood restaurant
West Bay, DT6 4EZ
Tel no: (01308) 422011
www.thefishrestaurant-westbay.co.uk
Seafood | £32
Cooking score: 3

Reached via a walkway over the river, this 'stylish, relaxed' restaurant has water seemingly on every side. Run by the Watson family since 1964, its ongoing success is down to a simple philosophy: take the freshest local fish and don't fiddle around with it. An attractive prospect in any weather, it has a chalet-style dining room and a sun-trap terrace. The menu starts as it means to go on: classics like Devon rock oysters or West Country fresh mussels marinière are typical of the unfussy style. Fish main courses come with simple embellishments – spinach and sorrel sauce with brill, for example, or just sea salt

and lemon with grilled fillets of lemon sole. Other options are lobsters, seafood platters and a short list of meat and vegetarian choices. The popular home-made puddings might include mocha crème brûlée with chocolate cookies. A nicely-annotated wine list opens at £12.50 a bottle.
Chef/s: George Marsh, Tony Shaw. **Open:** all week L 11.30 to 2.30 Tue to Sat D 6.30 to 9. **Closed:** 30 Nov to 12 Feb. **Meals:** alc (main courses £12.25 to £35.50), Set L Tue to Fri £21.50 (3 courses), £16.50 (2 courses). **Service:** not inc. **Details:** Cards accepted. 90 seats. 30 seats outside. No music. No mobile phones. Wheelchair access. Children's portions.

Weymouth

ALSO RECOMMENDED
▲ Crab House Café
Fleet Oyster Farm, Ferryman's Way, Weymouth, DT4 9YU
Tel no: (01305) 788867
Seafood

More of a shack than a 'house', this seaside café is a real charmer that scores with its engaging atmosphere, glorious Chesil Beach location and fish from the Weymouth boats. Menus depend on the haul, and the choice extends far beyond 'Crab House crabs'. Scallops with garlic and spring onion (£8.50) is a zingy starter, while mains could be anything from cod fillet with curried mixed beans (£15.50) to whole whiting with feta and olives. Lively desserts (£4.95) range from chocolate bourbon tart to mango pannacotta. Around 40 gluggable wines from £13.90 (£3.80 a glass). Closed Tue, also Mon in winter.

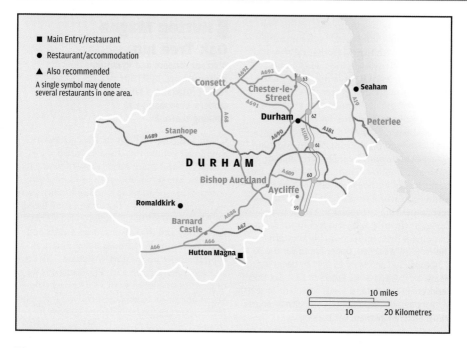

- ■ Main Entry/restaurant
- ● Restaurant/accommodation
- ▲ Also recommended

A single symbol may denote several restaurants in one area.

▌Durham

Bistro 21

Country-style bistro
Aykley Heads House, Aykley Heads, Durham, DH1 5TS
Tel no: (0191) 3844354
Modern European | £35
Cooking score: 2

The feel is relaxed and unpretentious, the welcome friendly and menus of a sensible length keep things simple at Terry Laybourne's country-style bistro set in a restored seventeenth-century building. The focus is on showing off good raw materials, so a late spring menu could bring local asparagus with melted butter, and a partnering of best end of spring lamb with ratatouille, or lightly-smoked sea trout with warm potato and leek salad with honey-roasted red onion. English summer pudding or Pimms jelly with spearmint ice cream make a nice, seasonal finish. Wines are a decent selection at fair mark-ups opening with house Georges

Duboeuf at £14.80. Our questionnaire was not returned, so some of the information below may have changed.
Open: all week L 12 to 2 (4 Sun), Mon to Sat D 7 to 10.15. **Meals:** alc (main courses £14.50 to £22).
Service: 10%. **Details:** Cards accepted. 24 seats. Separate bar. No music. No mobile phones. Children's portions. Car parking.

★NEW ENTRY★

Gourmet Spot

A sense of adventure in sparkly surroundings
The Avenue, Durham, DH1 4DX
Tel no: (0191) 3846655
www.gourmet-spot.co.uk
Modern British | £37
Cooking score: 2

A made-over restaurant attached to a hotel, G-Spot, as one might prefer not to call it, offers ambitious cooking by Sean Wilkinson. The dining room is small, dark and modern, with

the odd daub of bright, sparkly paint. The menu is heavily influenced by fashionable techniques, with foams, froths and savoury jellies applied to most plates. Highlights include a starter of light, zingy king prawn tempura with pickled ginger, fennel and grapefruit foam and a main course of slow-cooked belly pork with a dark, vanilla-inflected sauce. Some dishes, such as guinea fowl with wild mushroom risotto, look and taste more conventional. Desserts include 'tea and toast', a hollow balloon of Earl Grey ice cream served with teatime adjuncts like a jammy coulis and shortbread biscuit. If you have something particular in mind, wines by-the-glass (from £3.25) can feel limited: the main list is brief but reasonably thought-out.
Chef/s: Sean Wilkinson. **Open:** Tue to Sat D 6.30 to 12. **Closed:** Sun and Mon, 25 and 26 Dec, 1 Jan. **Meals:** alc (main courses £14.95 to £23). Set D £55. **Service:** not inc. **Details:** Cards accepted. 24 seats. 14 seats outside. Separate bar. Wheelchair access. Music. Children allowed. Car parking.

ALSO RECOMMENDED

▲ Almshouses Café Restaurant

Palace Green, Durham, DH1 3RL
Tel no: (0191) 3861054
www.the-almshouses.co.uk
Café

Next to the cathedral, this long-established café/restaurant (here for 25 years) offers honest home cooking and baking with a few global influences thrown in. Red pepper and chorizo soup (£3.95) might start, while chicken, leek and tarragon terrine with salad (£6) makes a good light lunch dish. Otherwise there's tagine of lamb and chickpeas with preserved lemon couscous (£6.65) or smoked haddock and prawn pie with buttered spinach (£6.80). Gooseberries poached in white wine and elderflowers (£3.20) is a good way to finish. Wines are priced from around £11.50. Open all week until 5pm in winter, 8pm in July and August.

■ Hutton Magna

Oak Tree Inn
Discreet dinners and invention
Hutton Magna, DL11 7HH
Tel no: (01833) 627371
Modern European | £30
Cooking score: 2

Claire and Alastair Ross are the enthusiastic double act behind this discreet North Country pub/restaurant in a row of terraced cottages. She serves and pulls pints while he cooks. Time spent in top London kitchens was well spent, judging by the upbeat food listed on Alastair's blackboard menus. He follows the market and the seasons, buys locally and looks to Europe for culinary inspiration. A typical dinner might start with ham, chicken and vegetable terrine with Puy lentil dressing or rillettes of salmon with a soft-poached egg, ahead of cumin-roasted best end of lamb with provençale vegetables or lemon sole with steamed Shetland mussels, leek risotto and curry butter sauce. To conclude, a mixed bag of desserts could embrace peanut butter parfait and coffee semifreddo as well as sticky toffee pudding. The concise global wine list is notable for its ungreedy mark-ups: prices start at £11.95 (£3.10 a glass). Also check out the intriguing selection of bottled world beers.
Chef/s: Alastair Ross. **Open:** Tue to Sat D only 6 to 11, Sun 5.30 to 10.30. **Closed:** Mon, 25 and 26 Dec, 1 Jan. **Meals:** alc (main courses £16.50 to £18.50). **Service:** not inc. **Details:** Cards accepted. 25 seats. Separate bar. Music. Car parking.

Please send us your feedback

To register your opinion about any restaurant listed in the Guide, or a new restaurant that you wish to bring to our attention, please visit the web address at the bottom of the page. Your feedback informs the content of the book and will be used to compile next year's reviews.

▮ Romaldkirk
Rose and Crown
Lovely country inn, in picture postcard village
Romaldkirk, DL12 9EB
Tel no: (01833) 650213
www.rose-and-crown.co.uk
British | £30
Cooking score: 3

£5
OFF

A gem in a jewel box of a village, the Rose and Crown stands squarely on the village green complete with ancient oaks and village pump. Sit outside on sunny afternoons, or in winter warm your cockles in the snug bar, feasting on smoked haddock kedgeree or belly pork and pease pudding. The dining room – evenings only – fairly sparkles with glowing candles, burnished silver, thickly-varnished panelling, and a four-course menu that offers good value. A delicate goats' cheese soufflé in a chive cream sauce, perhaps, ahead of a mid-course of celery, apple and blue cheese soup that achieved a fine balance of flavours alongside their own-baked bread rolls, while the sea bream fillets with shredded fennel and a fresh tomato sauce impressed. So, too, did a bold Amaretto ice cream and a warm lemon tart with vanilla ice cream. Add a decent, straightforward wine list (from £14.50) and attentive service and you have a thoroughly well-honed operation.
Chef/s: Christopher Davy and Andrew Lee. **Open:** Sun L 12 to 1.30, all week D 7.30 to 9. **Closed:** Christmas. **Meals:** Set menu £30 (4 courses). **Service:** not inc. **Details:** Cards accepted. 24 seats. 24 seats outside. Separate bar. No mobile phones. Car parking.

▮ Seaham
Seaham Hall, White Room
Refined by the seaside
Lord Byron's Walk, Seaham, SR7 7AG
Tel no: (0191) 5161400
www.seaham-hall.com
Modern European | £50
New Chef

Though the seaside hotel building remains grand and the ante-room's proportions still impress, Seaham Hall is looking a little unloved these days, inside and out. It is to be hoped that with the appointment of Kenny Atkinson (formerly head chef at the Tean Restaurant, St Martin's on the Isle), some refurbishment is on the cards, too. Atkinson was due to take over just as the Guide went to press, so no menus were forthcoming, but first-class ingredients, imaginative presentation and sound cooking skills are to be expected. The wine list is a time-consuming but interesting read, with excellent choices by-the-glass from £5 alongside some big hitters; you don't need to spend more than £25 for something worthwhile.
Chef/s: Kenny Atkinson. **Open:** all week L 12 to 3, D 7 to 11. **Meals:** Set L £19.50, Set D £50 to £65. **Service:** not inc. **Details:** Cards accepted. 40 seats. Air-con. Separate bar. No mobile phones. Wheelchair access. Music. Children's portions. Car parking.

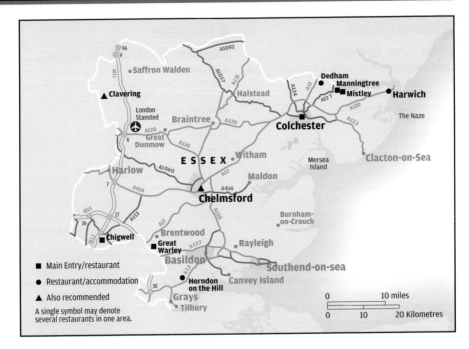

Legend:
- ■ Main Entry/restaurant
- ● Restaurant/accommodation
- ▲ Also recommended

A single symbol may denote several restaurants in one area.

0 — 10 miles
0 — 10 — 20 Kilometres

■ Chelmsford

ALSO RECOMMENDED
▲ Barda

30-32 Broomfield Road, Chelmsford, CM1 1SW
Tel no: (01245) 357799
www.barda-restaurant.com
Modern European

A bright spark lighting up the Chelmsford scene, Barda strikes a contemporary note with its walnut floors, cool lighting and confident brasserie-style food. Light lunches and fixed-price menus (two courses £14) give way to a more ambitious carte that straddles everything from 'paella de carne' (£7) to cherry clafoutis with sweet biscuits (£6). In between, expect mains including sea bass 'en papillote' with king prawns, chilli and lemongrass (£17) and seared duck breast with pak choi and roasted red pepper jus. House wine is £13.50. Closed Sat L, Sun D and Mon.

■ Chigwell

Bluebell

Vibrant modern cooking
117 High Road, Chigwell, IG7 6QQ
Tel no: (020) 85006282
www.thebluebellrestaurant.co.uk
Modern European | £35
New Chef

Greg Molen's neighbourhood restaurant is housed in a whitewashed cottage and brings a splash of colour to this old Chigwell village. A new chef has taken over but the formula remains the same – vibrant modern cooking and bags of choice. The good-value set-price lunch menu offers tea-smoked duck breast with noodle salad and oriental dressing, and whole grilled sea bass with fennel braised in tomato, chilli and garlic, while the evening carte delivers warm fillets of smoked eel with potato salad and horseradish cream, and slow-cooked pork belly with caramelised parsnips and pears, roasted carrots and creamed potatoes. Desserts include banoffee trifle with whipped mascarpone, crème anglaise and home-made boudoir biscuits. House wine is £13.95. More reports please.

Chef/s: Russell Ford. **Open:** Tue to Fri L 12 to 3.45, D 6.45 to 12.30. Sat D 6.45 to 1am, Sun L 12 to 6.30. **Closed:** Sat L and Mon. **Meals:** Set L £14.95 (2 courses) to £18.95, Set D £24.95, Sun L £22.95. **Service:** not inc. **Details:** Cards accepted. 95 seats. Air-con. Music. Children's portions.

▮ Clavering

ALSO RECOMMENDED
▲ Cricketers

Clavering, CB11 4QT
Tel no: (01799) 550442
www.thecricketers.co.uk
Gastropub

The Oliver family pub has been given a facelift of late, but the cooking remains loyal to local produce and Mediterranean influences. It certainly draws the crowds, but while you're unlikely to run into Jamie O, you can buy one of his cookbooks. Dinner in the restaurant (£27.50 for three courses) could include king prawn and avocado pear tian with lime mascarpone and dill oil, followed by half a roast duckling with an orange and star anise jus and quince compote. Food in the bar offers the same menu with everything priced individually for more flexibility of choice. Worldwide wine list with prices from £12.30. Accommodation. Open all week.

▮ Colchester

The Lemon Tree

Easy-going local favourite
48 St Johns Street, Colchester, CO2 7AD
Tel no: (01206) 767337
www.the-lemon-tree.com
Modern European | £20
Cooking score: 2

£5 OFF ⓥ £30

Jolly Mediterranean vibes emanate from this bright and breezy town-centre restaurant, especially when crowds spill out onto the plant-filled terrace and listen to occasional

sessions of summertime jazz. A chunk of Cochester's Roman city wall forms part of the private 'cavern' at the back of the main dining room, which has been upgraded with leather chairs and tiled floors. The easy-going menu is topped up with daily specials, and visitors can look forward a mix of home-grown and eclectic dishes, taking in smoked gammon and baby leek terrine with piccalilli, seared tuna with sea-spiced aubergine and crispy rice noodles, and a duo of local pork on butter bean mash with rosemary-scented butter. After that, consider white chocolate and raspberry truffle or mango and coconut crème brûlée with shortbread. 'Quick-stop' lunches and set menus suit daytime crowds in a hurry. House vin de pays is £2.55.

Chef/s: Paul Wassan. **Open:** Mon to Sat L 12 to 5, D 5 to 9.30 (10 Fri and Sat). **Closed:** Sun, bank hols, 25 Dec, 31 Dec and 1 Jan. **Meals:** alc (main courses £13 to £19). Set L £12.50 (2 courses) to £16.50. **Service:** not inc. **Details:** Cards accepted. 90 seats. 45 seats outside. Air-con. No mobile phones. Wheelchair access. Music. Children's portions.

▮ Dedham

Sun Inn

Ancient inn, Italian influence
High Street, Dedham, CO7 6DF
Tel no: (01206) 323351
www.thesuninndedham.com
Gastropub | £25
Cooking score: 3

 🛏 £30

Gastropub is definitely the word for Piers Baker's informal fifteenth-century coaching inn-cum-dining room, where the menu gravitates towards Italy and the kitchen demonstrates a degree of skill and imagination. Celeriac, chickpea and cavolo nero soup, and agnolotti stuffed with veal, pigeon and pancetta are a million miles from the old-school trattoria repertoire. Main courses return in part to the more familiar and home-grown, with evidence of well-sourced ingredients: 'delicately fresh and sweet' sea bream, 'meltingly tasty' salt marsh lamb, or first-class farmyard chicken served with roast potatoes, anchovy and spring garlic. For dessert, panna cotta with grappa and caramelised blood oranges has been well reported. Four real ales are on tap, along with an adventurous wine list that majors in Italy and offers very fair prices. Bottles start at £12.50, 500ml carafes from £8.50.

Chef/s: Ugo Simonelli and Piers Baker. **Open:** Mon to Sun 11 to 11. **Closed:** 25 and 26 Dec. **Meals:** Set menu Mon to Thu £13.50 (3 courses). **Service:** not inc. **Details:** Cards accepted. 60 seats. 100 seats outside. Separate bar. Music. Children's portions. Car parking.

■ Great Warley

The Headley
Prettily situated pub-restaurant
Headley Common, Great Warley, CM13 3HS
Tel no: (01277) 216104
www.theheadley.co.uk
Gastropub | £24
Cooking score: 3

£30

The setting is a great plus, as the Headley is by the village green close to the M25 (J28 and 29). There may be a traditional look to the outside, but the sprawling, open-plan interior (spread over two floors) is thoroughly modern, with big leather sofas and chunky wooden tables. This is the first pub venture for Daniel Clifford (of Midsummer House, Cambridge, see entry), which gives notice that food is in the ascendancy. The carefully selected dishes are a cut above for a country pub, say terrine of pork fillet with black pudding, apple and grain mustard, or a risotto of spring peas and mint. Main courses can be as traditional as steak and kidney pie, but there's also fillet of sea bream with home-made pasta and shellfish velouté. Leave room if you can for desserts, which include sticky toffee pudding with fig ice cream and a dark chocolate Black Forest gâteau with boozy Kirsch cherries. House wine is £16.

Chef/s: Daniel Clifford. **Open:** Tue to Sat L 12 to 3, D 6 to 9.30. Sun 12 to 5. **Closed:** Sun D and Mon. **Meals:** Set Sun L £18 (2 courses) to £22.

Service: not inc. **Details:** Cards accepted. 160 seats. 80 seats outside. Air-con. Separate bar. Wheelchair access. Music. Children's portions. Car parking.

■ Harwich

Pier Hotel, Harbourside Restaurant
Fresh seafood and harbour views
The Quay, Harwich, CO12 3HH
Tel no: (01255) 241212
www.milsomhotels.com
Seafood | £30
Cooking score: 2

£5 OFF ⊨ V

The name gives the game away, and points up the enduring appeal of this cheery hotel on Harwich quay. Seafood is the main business in the first-floor restaurant overlooking the Stour Estuary, and the kitchen bags the pick of the day's catch. Expect to find smoked haddock fishcakes and Dover sole with nut brown butter alongside modish seared tuna on rhubarb pickle. Meat fans might prefer ham hock and pistachio terrine followed by rack of lamb on a sage potato cake, while desserts hop from apple and date pudding to mango pannacotta. The wide-ranging wine list has more reds than you might expect in a dedicated seafood restaurant; prices start at £14. The ground-floor Ha'penny Pier bistro is an altogether simpler affair, with prices to match.

Chef/s: Chris Oakley. **Open:** all week L12 to 2, D 6 to 9.30. **Closed:** D 25 Dec. **Meals:** alc (main courses £9 to £32). Set L £18.50 (2 courses) to £24.
Service: 10%. **Details:** Cards accepted. 70 seats. 30 seats outside. Air-con. Separate bar. Wheelchair access. Music. Children's portions. Car parking.

Horndon on the Hill

Bell Inn
Multi-talented medieval pub
High Road, Horndon on the Hill, SS17 8LD
Tel no: (01375) 642463
www.bell-inn.co.uk
Modern European | £27
Cooking score: 2

Once a stopover for pilgrims and merchants waiting to cross the Thames at Higham's Causeway, this medieval inn now offers sustenance and hospitality for M25 refugees and others. An old-time atmosphere still permeates the traditional bar, while the main dining room aims for something calmer. The food shows ambition and ingenuity: sea bass on confit tomato with chorizo and spring onion dressing is an exciting way to start, or you might prefer to plump for potted wild rabbit. As for main courses, pan-fried brill with mussel and clam chowder or roast duck breast with roasted red onion, wild garlic and blackberry jus should fit the bill, while cleverly crafted desserts such as Bramley apple and toffee crème brûlée with apple sorbet round things off. The reasonably-priced wine list starts at £11.25 (£3.75 a glass).
Chef/s: Stuart Fay. **Open:** all week L 12 to 1.45 (2.15 Sun), D 6.30 to 9.45 (from 7 Sun). **Closed:** bank hol Mon. **Meals:** alc (main courses £10.50 to £16.50). **Service:** not inc. **Details:** Cards accepted. 80 seats. 36 seats outside. Separate bar. No music. No mobile phones. Wheelchair access. Children's portions. Car parking.

Manningtree

ALSO RECOMMENDED
▲ Lucca
39-43 High Street, Manningtree, CO11 1AH
Tel no: (01206) 390044
www.luccafoods.co.uk
Italian

This new venture from Sherri Singleton (of the Mistley Thorn, Mistley, see entry) sees a 100-seater pizzeria opening in the heart of Manningtree. Pizzas from the wood-fired oven could be classics such as margherita (£5.85), quattro formaggi (£6.95), or perhaps salsiccia, with home-made fennel sausage, tomatoes, red onion and fiore de latte mozzarella (£7.95). Daily specials might be lamb stracotto or crispy duck agrodolce (both £8.95) and there are pasta and salad dishes too. Finish with ricotta cheesecake with orange and pine nuts (£4.95). House wine is £12.95. Open all week.

Mistley

Mistley Thorn
A local favourite
High Street, Mistley, CO11 1HE
Tel no: (01206) 392821
www.mistleythorn.com
Gastropub | £22
Cooking score: 2

There's a contemporary feel to this eighteenth-century inn overlooking the Stour Estuary. Straightforward pub cooking at reasonable prices (especially at lunch) is the forte, with a flexible attitude, a leaning towards local produce and a kitchen that generally succeeds in its efforts. As befits a place close to the source, seafood appears in the form of Mersea Island rock oysters, day-boat calamari with chilli, garlic and coriander or beer-battered local fish with tartare sauce, minted mushy peas and hand-cut fries. Meat dishes display a fondness for chargrilling, whether rib-eye steak with tempura onion rings or leg of lamb with mint vinaigrette and garlic mash, while desserts tend to be homely, although elderberry jelly with Chantilly cream sounds intriguingly different. On the wine front, prices start at £11.95 and you can drink very well for under £20.
Chef/s: Sherri Singleton and Chris Pritchard. **Open:** Mon to Fri L 12 to 2.30, D 6.30 to 9.30, Sat and Sun 12 to 9.30. **Closed:** 25 Dec. **Meals:** Set L £11.95 (2 courses) to £13.95. **Service:** not inc. **Details:** Cards accepted. 75 seats. 15 seats outside. Separate bar. Wheelchair access. Children's portions. Car parking.

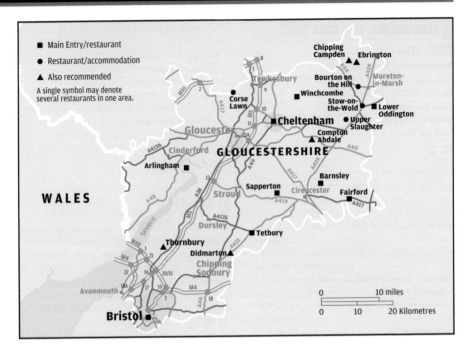

Arlingham

★NEW ENTRY★

Old Passage Inn

Idyllic riverside seafood dining
Passage Road, Arlingham, GL2 7JR
Tel no: (01452) 740547
www.fishattheoldpassageinn.co.uk
Seafood | £35
Cooking score: 3

The beauty of this isolated riverside location is a hard act to follow, but the Old Passage Inn succeeds admirably. The dining room is light and bright, with wide doors opening onto a terrace and with unrivalled views across the river to the village of Newnham. Despite classical pretentions (Corinthian columns support the ceiling), the interior feels modern and informal. The menu is almost entirely seafood, but with a few meat and vegetable options. Oysters and lobsters are from the kitchen's seawater tanks, the latter perhaps served 'amoricaine' (baked in a spicy sauce with Gruyère) which proved subtle enough to allow the sweet lobster meat its own voice. Also satisfying was a starter of potted brown shrimps, while Fowey mussels marinière were plentiful and perfectly tender – home-made bread rolls proved an ideal partner for the remaining liquor. The only dish that failed to excite at inspection was a slightly bland Cornish fish stew, but the kitchen hit its stride again with desserts of baked lemon tart with raspberry sorbet and tarte Tatin with cinnamon sauce and vanilla ice cream. The wine list covers France particularly well, and opens at £14.80. More reports please.
Chef/s: Raoul Moore. **Open:** Tue to Sun L 12 to 2, Tue to Sat D 7 to 9. **Meals:** alc (main courses £14 to £21). **Service:** not inc. **Details:** Cards accepted. 65 seats. 22 seats outside. Air-con. Wheelchair access. Music. Children's portions. Car parking.

▌Barnsley

Barnsley House

Grand setting for Italian-influenced cooking
Barnsley, GL7 5EE
Tel no: (01285) 740000
www.barnsleyhouse.com
Modern European | £43
Cooking score: 4

Built at the end of the seventeenth century, Barnsley House sits in gorgeously appointed gardens designed by the late Rosemary Verey – whose home this once was. It is easy to find on the main street, and from the entrance through a stone-flagged hall, it is clear that the place is going to be grand (with plenty of up-to-the-minute amenities). The centre of culinary gravity is Italian, with risottos, ingredients such as prosciutto and salt cod, and a house speciality rendition of eastern Italy's vincigrassi – an eighteenth-century baked pasta dish containing Parma ham, porcini and truffles. Red mullet with potato purée, vine tomatoes, marinated courgettes and crisp squid, and praline and amaretti parfait with agrum salad and lemon yoghurt sorbet have been praised, but reports of an 'indifferently' cooked leg of lamb 'badly paired' with a rich goats' cheese show that some combinations don't always convince. Wines start at £18.
Chef/s: Graham Grafton. **Open:** all week L 12 to 2.30 (3 Sat and Sun), D 7 to 9.30 (10 Fri and Sat). **Service:** 12.5%. **Details:** Cards accepted. 55 seats. 20 seats outside. Separate bar. Children's portions. Car parking.

▌Bourton on the Hill

Horse and Groom

A proper pub with all-round virtues
Bourton on the Hill, GL56 9AQ
Tel no: (01386) 700413
www.horseandgroom.info
Modern British | £25
Cooking score: 2

Set high on a hill not far from the busy A44, the honey-stone Horse and Groom enjoys spectacular views across the Cotswolds. Brothers Will and Tom Greenstock have done a grand job restoring and rejuvenating the pub without losing sight of its entrenched virtues as a watering hole. That said, great-value food is now the big draw. A network of trusted local suppliers provides much of the produce for daily-changing blackboard menus, and influences come from far and wide: Dexter beef pasties with onion gravy now sit shoulder-to-shoulder with Old Farm lamb and apricot tagine with lemon and spring onion couscous. Fish comes up from the West Country (grilled Cornish sardines with radicchio and salsa verde, for example) and desserts span everything from plum jam steamed pudding to lemon tart with mascarpone cream. Keenly-priced house selections (from £11.75, £2.75 a glass) top the well-spread wine list.
Chef/s: Will Greenstock. **Open:** Tue to Sat L 11 to 3, Sun 12 to 3, Mon to Sat D 6 to 11. **Closed:** 25 Dec. **Meals:** alc (main courses £10 to £16). **Service:** not inc. **Details:** Cards accepted. 75 seats. 54 seats outside. Separate bar. No music. Children's portions. Car parking.

Bristol

The Albion

Gastropub with a rustic, nose-to-tail approach
Boyces Avenue, Clifton Village, Bristol, BS8 4AA
Tel no: (0117) 9733522
www.thealbionclifton.co.uk
Gastropub | £30
Cooking score: 3

Until three years ago the Albion was a sticky-carpeted boozer for students, but since its smart renovation this dining pub has become a firm favourite with Bristol foodies. Jake Platt concentrates on bold and gutsy West Country cooking, with many suppliers and growers getting name checks on his interesting menus, which change twice a day. A rustic, nose-to-tail approach is best illustrated by dishes such as fried pig's cheek, pig's ear and parsley salad, duck hearts on bone marrow toast and confit of suckling lamb with fried sweetbreads and Roman gnocchi. Not that seafood is handled any less expertly – Dorset crab with celeriac and brown bread or wild mussels with cider and cream being two favourite starters. Desserts can have Mediterranean influences, with the pistachio and polenta cake with roast figs and crème fraîche working particularly well. Eight house wines are available by-the-glass from £3.90, and bottles start at £14.50.
Chef/s: Jake Platt. **Open:** Tue to Sun 12 to 3, Tue to Sat 7 to 10. **Closed:** 25 and 25 Dec. **Meals:** Set menu £25 (2 courses) to £30. **Service:** not inc.
Details: Cards accepted. 80 seats. 40 seats outside. Separate bar. Wheelchair access. Music.

Bell's Diner

Inventive, ambitious cooking
1-3 York Road, Montpelier, Bristol, BS6 5QB
Tel no: (0117) 9240357
www.bellsdiner.com
Modern European | £30
Cooking score: 5

A former grocer's shop in a Bohemian quarter of Bristol, Bell's Diner may have a modest frontage, but step inside and the place has a sophisticated and refined look that matches Christopher Wicks's highly polished modern cooking. His imaginative dishes are backed up by solid techniques and there are plenty of flavour sensations conjured from high-quality produce, much of it local and intelligently sourced. Although combinations here may occasionally surprise and amuse, they are often based on classic flavour marriages and rarely done just for effect. A two-hour poached hen's egg served with Iberico ham, pepper confetti and buttered soldiers may raise a smile for its inventiveness, but a starter of smoked fish soup packed with haddock, mussels, oysters, dill, chives and chervil demonstrates the solid grasp of the classics. Main courses strike a similar balance between innovation and tradition, with a relatively straightforward dish of brill with artichoke, mint oil, peas, broad beans and pea shoots rubbing shoulders with a more outlandish suckling pig matched with cauliflower purée, raisins, spinach, apple and coffee jus. Desserts play to the gallery, with the signature dish of vindaloo ice cream cone with mango, pineapple, kiwi and passion fruit being joined by the likes of a lemon 'fantasy' featuring a mini tart, soufflé, sorbet, mousse and sherbet air. The modern, interesting wine list is sensibly priced, with house wines starting at £14.
Chef/s: Christopher Wicks. **Open:** Tue to Fri L 12 to 2.30, Mon to Sat D 7 to 10. **Closed:** 24 to 26 Dec. **Meals:** alc (main courses £14.50 to £21). Tasting menu L and D £45. **Service:** 10%. **Details:** Cards accepted. 50 seats. Wheelchair access. Music. Children's portions.

Bordeaux Quay

Eco-friendly dining
V-Shed, Canons Way, Bristol, BS1 5UH
Tel no: (0117) 9431200
www.bordeaux-quay.co.uk
Modern European | £28
Cooking score: 2

£30

Since it opened in September 2006, Barny Haughton's eco-friendly fine dining restaurant, brasserie, bar, deli and cookery school has become a Bristol landmark and

gained national recognition for its commitment to sustainability and sourcing organic and local produce. The upstairs restaurant, with splendid views of the harbour and beyond, offers an à la carte and set menu with seasonal Mediterranean-influenced dishes such as duck, beetroot, walnut and tarragon salad followed by Pimm's sabayon and Somerset strawberries. The bustling brasserie below may suffer from inconsistencies in the service – long waits for food are not uncommon – but dishes are honest and rustic, with mussels steamed with chilli, fennel, lemon and parsley and braised rabbit leg with tarragon, wholegrain mustard and cabbage. The clever and keenly-priced wine list combines New and Old world names and an intelligent choice of grapes. Every wine is available by-the-glass and prices start at £15.
Chef/s: Barney Haughton and Liz Payne. **Open:** Mon to Sat 8 to 11.30, Sun 9 to 5. **Closed:** 25 and 26 Dec. **Meals:** Set menus £15, £19.50 and £23. **Service:** 10%. **Details:** Cards accepted. 240 seats. 70 seats outside. Separate bar. Wheelchair access. Music. Children's portions.

Café Maitreya

Tantalising, vibrant vegetarian food
89 St Mark's Road, Easton, Bristol, BS5 6HY
Tel no: (0117) 9510100
www.cafemaitreya.co.uk
Vegetarian | £22
Cooking score: 4

After the drab, monochrome vegetarian cafés and restaurants of yesteryear, Café Maitreya is like an explosion of technicolor. Bright, contemporary and vibrant, this is a place that genuinely puts a smile on your face. Mark Evans conjures up tantalising flavours from his well-sourced ingredients, many of them local, organic and wild. He pushes each dish to its limit, adding fruit or something sweet, perhaps, to give an unexpected twist – braising shallots with liquorice, or adding nougatine to a feta and pecan tortellini. The menu is short – four starters and five main

courses – but it makes up for its brevity by the amount of work that goes into each dish. These are technically accomplished, with a lot of things going on and several flavours vying for attention. A starter of Double Worcester and sweet basil soufflé with a red chilli croûte and hot, caramelised mandarin segments could be followed by roast butternut squash and chestnut tarte Tatin or a pot-au-feu made with parsnip and Welsh Harlech cheese. A trifle consisting of rosehip, champagne, raspberry, honeycomb and honey lavender ice cream or a steamed orange, cranberry and stem ginger pudding served with orange crème anglaise and cranberry compote are among the show-stopping desserts. The organic wine list starts at £13.25 and stays within Europe to avoid unnecessary transportation. A nice touch.
Chef/s: Mark Evans. **Open:** Tue to Sat D 6.30 to 9.45. **Closed:** Sun and Mon, Christmas and New Year. **Meals:** Set D £18.50 (2 courses) to £21.95. **Service:** not inc. **Details:** Cards accepted. 50 seats. Wheelchair access. Music. Children's portions.

Casamia

Ambitious young chefs aiming high
38 High Street, Westbury on Trym, Bristol, BS9 3DZ
Tel no: (0117) 9592884
www.casamiarestaurant.co.uk
Italian | £35
Cooking score: 5

Paco and Susan Sanchez-Iglesias took an enormous leap of faith when they decided to transform their traditional Italian neighbourhood restaurant into something altogether more cutting-edge. Their unflagging support of sons Peter and Jonray has paid off, for Casamia is now one of the most exciting restaurants in the region. These passionate, hard-working young chefs create innovative and contemporary Italian cuisine based on adventurous re-workings of classic dishes. From the concise, seasonal menu, starters might include a velvety ravioli of Jersey Royals with wild mushrooms and white truffle oil or rare-roasted local wood

pigeon breast served with assorted textures and essences of coffee, caramelised almonds and Amaretto. Mains also display inventiveness and unusual flavour combinations, with a thick piece of meltingly tender slow-cooked Gloucester Old Spot suckling pig served with sautéed Jerusalem artichokes, a purée of the same vegetable spiked with ras el hanout and small cubes of chocolate jelly. This could be followed by a pannacotta flavoured with pine nuts and served with a tart Bramley apple purée and zesty lemon sorbet. Paco and Susan run front-of-house as if welcoming people into their own home, although the restaurant now attracts as many travelling gastronomes as it does regulars. The Italian-heavy wine list kicks off at £13.50 for a bottle of house red and there are some real finds under £20. At £15 for two courses lunch is exceptional value for the cooking and skill involved.
Chef/s: Jonray and Peter Sanchez-Iglesias. **Open:** Wed to Sat L 12.30 to 2.30, Tue to Sat D 6 to 10.30. **Closed:** 25 Dec, 1 week Sept. **Meals:** alc (main courses £19.95 to £25.50). Set L £15 (2 courses) to £20. **Service:** not inc. **Details:** Cards accepted. 40 seats. 10 seats outside. Separate bar. No mobile phones. Wheelchair access. Music. Children's portions.

Culinaria
Talented chef keeping things simple
1 Chandos Road, Bristol, BS6 6PG
Tel no: (0117) 9737999
www.culinariabristol.co.uk
Modern European | £30
Cooking score: 4

Stephen and Judy Markwick have ruled the Bristol restaurant scene for almost 30 years and show no sign of abdicating. But then why would they? Their latest venture has been their most successful and the reason for their enduring appeal is because they have always ignored the fashions and fads around them and just got on with the job. These are restaurateurs who clearly love what they do, which is serving the very best seasonal ingredients in

an informal and convivial setting. Stephen's experience in the kitchen brings with it the confidence to keep things simple, to the extent that he is not afraid of sending out a plate of asparagus with a jug of melted butter if that asparagus is from a local grower and at the peak of freshness. Stephen's deep understanding of flavour combinations and sound techniques is underpinned by a simple love of Elizabeth David and Jane Grigson, and their works can be spotted on the bulging bookcases in the airy dining room. The weekly-changing menu includes signature dishes of Provençal fish soup with aïoli and sauce rouille and ham hock terrine with celeriac rémoulade. Mains include breast of duck, peas, bacon and Sauternes sauce or poached fillet of brill, prawns, asparagus and cream. Desserts stick to old favourites, with blueberry sherry trifle and egg custard tart with nutmeg ice cream. The concise wine list is similarly well-constructed, with prices beginning at £14.
Chef/s: Stephen Markwick. **Open:** Thur to Sat L 12 to 2, D 6.30 to 9.30. **Closed:** Christmas, New Year, 4 other weeks. **Meals:** Set L £15.50 (2 courses) to £20. **Service:** not inc. **Details:** Cards accepted. 30 seats. 8 seats outside. No mobile phones. Wheelchair access. Children's portions.

Greens' Dining Room
Unfussy British and Mediterranean dishes
25 Zetland Road, Bristol, BS6 7AH
Tel no: (0117) 9246437
www.greensdiningroom.com
Modern European | £28
Cooking score: 3

The understated and welcoming interior of Simon and Andrew Green's neighbourhood bistro is mirrored by the food, which pays homage to the brothers' main influences – Elizabeth David, Claudia Roden and Jane Grigson. Simon and Andrew are very different chefs – one is more rustic – but the common ground is in simple, unfussy British and Mediterranean dishes, with occasional influences from further afield. There is a

degree of confidence in the cooking and they are not afraid of keeping things simple – Lebanese meatballs with cucumber, yoghurt and mint to start, perhaps, followed by braised leg of rabbit, button mushrooms, baby onions and bacon, or grilled ox tongue with carrots, beetroot relish and horseradish cream. Desserts are just as uncomplicated, with, for example, crema Catalana. Service is attentive and knowledgeable and there is a reasonably-priced wine list with 18 by-the-glass. A bottle of house wine starts at £11.95.
Chef/s: Andrew and Simon Green. **Open:** Tue to Sun L 12.30 to 3, Tue to Sat D 6.30 to 10.30. **Closed:** 10 days Christmas. **Meals:** Set L £10 (2 courses), Set D £21.50 (2 courses) to £27.50. **Service:** not inc. **Details:** Cards accepted. 38 seats. 16 seats outside. Music. Children's portions.

The Kensington Arms
Laid-back gastropub
35-37 Stanley Road, Redland, Bristol, BS6 6NP
Tel no: (0117) 9446444
www.thekensingtonarms.co.uk
Gastropub | £25
Cooking score: 2
V

Can a pub with a kitchen attached ever really remain a proper pub? The 'Kenny' certainly seems to have seamlessly blended both – as a place to grab a pint and a bar snack, or to try out the solid British cooking. Fresh flowers on the bar, petrol blue walls, gleaming glasses and linen napkins mark this out as a stylish operation but, with the exception of the formal dining area upstairs, it has a laid back air – though service could be tightened up on busy nights. Reassuringly, the concise and simply-executed menu is reprinted daily and is on-the-button in incorporating seasonal produce, say chargrilled British asparagus with Parmesan and lemon oil. Mains are similarly straightforward, with fish and chips making an appearance, albeit with Yorkshire 'caviar' in tow, or shank of the locally-sourced Mendip lamb, slow-braised with mash.

Treacle tart or a board of West Country cheese and chutney round up a simple but well-cooked meal. The wine list starts at £13.50.
Chef/s: Jules Nicholls. **Open:** Mon to Fri L 12 to 3, Mon to Sat D 6 to 10, Sat L 11 to 3, Sun L 12 to 4. **Service:** not inc. **Details:** Cards accepted. 65 seats. 30 seats outside. Air-con. Separate bar. Wheelchair access. Children's portions.

★NEW ENTRY★
Primrose Cafe & Bistro
Bustling café by day, charming bistro by night
1 Clifton Arcade, Boyces Avenue, Clifton, Bristol, BS8 4AA
Tel no: (0117) 9466577
www.primrosecafe.co.uk
Modern British | £25
Cooking score: 2

Hidden away in an elegant Victorian shopping arcade in a Clifton backwater, the Primrose is a bustling café by day. At night, out come the candles and the place is transformed into a charming and intimate bistro with a different kitchen team headed by Tara Hoffman. A chef who includes River Café and Chez Panisse on her CV – as well as Bristol's Quartier Vert – Hoffman's cooking is governed by seasonal and local produce, but has a bias towards rustic French and Italian. You suspect that her bookshelves are lined with the works of Elizabeth David and Alice Waters. Such inspiration shows in a simple but effective starter of English asparagus with soft-boiled egg and tarragon dressing and a main course of Cornish hake with tomato, mussel and saffron stew, which arrives with garlicky aïoli. A dessert of rosewater and cardamom ice cream with pistachio biscotti adds a Middle Eastern flavour, particularly if enjoyed in the continental-style al fresco dining area. An interesting wine list majors in France, Spain and Italy and starts at £13.
Chef/s: Tara Hoffman. **Open:** Mon to Sat D 7 to 9.30. **Closed:** Christmas and New Year, bank hols. **Meals:** alc (main courses £11.50 to £16.50). Set

menu £14.95 (2 courses) to £17.95. **Service:** not inc.
Details: Cards accepted. 65 seats. 30 seats outside.
Music. Children allowed.

riverstation

Veteran of Bristol's harbourside scene
The Grove, Bristol, BS1 4RB
Tel no: (0117) 9144434
www.riverstation.co.uk
Modern European | £28
Cooking score: 3

Now into its tenth year, this modernist eatery
is a veritable veteran of Bristol's ever-
expanding harbourside restaurant scene. It
remains one of the city's most consistent places
and the daily-changing menu rarely misses a
beat when it comes to sound cooking
techniques and sticking rigidly to the seasons.
Ambitious dishes such as 'cassoulet' of roast
monkfish wrapped in lardo served with crisp
smoked pork and spinach, rub shoulders with
simple but well-executed brasserie classics like
deep-fried lamb sweetbreads in a herb crust
with sauce gribiche and a well-dressed
watercress salad. Finish with American baked
cheesecake with passion-fruit sauce or
Amaretto bavarois with morello cherries.
Light lunches and 'early bird' suppers are good
value, as is the menu in the lower-level bar
with its pleasant al fresco area slap bang on the
water's edge. The international wine list is
affordable and interesting, with ten house
wines available by-the-glass (from £3.50) and
bottle (£13.50).
Chef/s: Tom Green and Peter Taylor. **Open:** all week
L 12 to 2.30 (Sun 3), Mon to Thur D 6 to 10.30, Fri
and Sat 6 to 11, Sun 6 to 9. **Closed:** 25, 26 Dec, 1
Jan. **Meals:** alc (main courses £13 to £19). Set L
£12.50 (2 courses) to £14.75. **Service:** not inc.
Details: Cards accepted. 128 seats. 22 seats outside.
Separate bar. No music. Children's portions.

ALSO RECOMMENDED

▲ Hotel du Vin & Bistro

The Sugar House, Narrow Lewins Mead, Bristol,
BS1 2NU
Tel no: (0117) 9255577
www.hotelduvin.com
Modern European

One of the original outlets for this ever-
expanding group occupies a stunning
eighteenth-century sugar warehouse. The
French brasserie-inspired dining room,
complete with wood panelling, flickering
candles and shelves of dusty old wine bottles,
offers simple Anglo-French cooking with the
occasional Med flourishes. Starters of devilled
lambs' kidneys (£6.75) and smoked duck
breast with beetroot and horseradish cream
(£7.95), for example, then roast rump of lamb
with Puy lentils and creamed leeks (£16.50),
or chargrilled rib-eye steak with béarnaise
sauce and frites (£18.95). To finish, there
might be pear and cherry trifle (£6.75). An
impressive and extensive wine list focuses on
regional France. Bottles start at £14.50. Open
all week.

■ Cheltenham

Le Champignon Sauvage

Cheltenham dining landmark
24-26 Suffolk Road, Cheltenham, GL50 2AQ
Tel no: (01242) 573449
www.lechampignonsauvage.co.uk
French | £48
Cooking score: 8

The Everitt-Matthaises have clocked up more
than 20 years at their very personally-run
restaurant in Cheltenham. While the
unassuming frontage gives nothing away, the
consensus — that this remains one of Britain's
finest restaurants — is amply testified by a
succession of recommendations. David
Everitt-Matthias continues to cook creatively
and confidently. Sourcing is admirable, the
cooking led by local produce and materials are
generally impeccably handled. The pairing of

unusual flavours and textures is clearly a passion and has seen the combination of 'superb' roasted native lobster, confit of duck hearts and pumpkin with nougat velouté work well together, while a main course of well-timed fillet of zander was matched with caramelised cauliflower, smooth cauliflower purée and a few girolles, and drizzled with a red wine and hibiscus sauce that added 'a slightly sweet, floral hint'. Elsewhere, the food combines a few earthy touches, such as 'beautifully pink' Goosnargh duck on a bed of 'excellent' walnut mash, served with chicory that had been caramelised in maple syrup and a good reduction of cooking juices. Novel touches at dessert stage have included a cylinder of passion-fruit cream served with a slice of caramelised mango, a smooth coconut sorbet and little cubes of fresh mango, and a warm prune cake paired with pressed apple and a well-made wild cherry stone ice cream. The wine list is 15 pages long, mostly French but with a reasonable selection from the more established New World locations. It is very fairly priced, with house wine at just £14. **Chef/s:** David Everitt-Matthias. **Open:** Tue to Sat L 12.30 to 1.15, D 7.30 to 8.30. **Closed:** Sun, Mon, 10 days Christmas and New Year, 3 weeks June. **Meals:** Set L and D £28, set D £48. **Service:** not inc. **Details:** Cards accepted. 40 seats. Air-con. Separate bar.

Hackett's at the Malvern View Hotel

Charming restaurant-with-rooms
Cleeve Hill, Cheltenham, GL52 3PR
Tel no: (01242) 672017
www.malvern-viewhotel.co.uk
Modern British | £40
Cooking score: 3

£5 OFF 🛏

There is a cheerful, feel-good atmosphere at Paul and Anna Hackett's smart restaurant-with-rooms on the outskirts of Cheltenham, fuelled by their sheer enthusiasm for what they do. Generous, well-spaced tables look on to the leafy garden – though the Malvern view is seasonal (when the leaves have

dropped). Food is clearly taken seriously, with prominence given to fine raw materials. Start with mussels in white wine, ginger, smoked garlic and chilli, before continuing with something like expressively-flavoured, gutsy roast chump of Herdwick lamb with dauphinoise potatoes, spicy couscous and minted cream, or turbot served with a sun-dried tomato and courgette risotto with lobster cappuccino. Desserts aim to indulge, with a hot cinnamon and apple soufflé served with apple ice cream. House wine is £14.75. **Chef/s:** Paul Hackett. **Open:** Tue to Sun L 12 to 3, Tue to Sat D 7 to 10. **Closed:** 3 weeks Jan. **Meals:** alc (main courses £8.25 to £18.95). **Service:** not inc. **Details:** Cards accepted. 40 seats. 16 seats outside. Wheelchair access. Music. Children's portions. Car parking.

Lumière

Consistent, contemporary restaurant
Clarence Parade, Cheltenham, GL50 3PA
Tel no: (01242) 222200
www.lumiere.cc
Modern European | £38
Cooking score: 5

 ☆

There's a relaxed feel to this 'bright but welcoming' modern restaurant just off Cheltenham's main shopping street, where courteous, informed service from Lin Chapman enhances the enjoyment of her husband Geoff's hugely accomplished cooking. Fresh materials lay a secure foundation, perhaps in the form of a small bowl of chunky mushroom and chorizo soup with a warming garlic and spice taste. Clear flavours and attractive presentation are part of the deal, evident in a starter of first-class scallops with well-judged celeriac purée and a pot of lemongrass courgettes. Among main courses, chargrilled venison has been tender and well-timed, served with excellent Pink Fir Apple potatoes and a good port sauce, while baked monkfish medallions with a caper-herb butter have been spot-on. Desserts are properly indulgent, with bitter chocolate torte served with salty caramel ice cream, and

white chocolate rum and raisin cheesecake presented with a little chocolate ice cream. The wine list is arranged by style and draws heavily on the New World: Eagle Vale Merlot 2004, for example at £30, or an excellent Rustenburg Chardonnay 2005 from South Africa at £33. House wine is £18.50.
Chef/s: Geoff Chapman. **Open:** Wed to Sat D 7 to 8.30. **Closed:** 2 weeks Jan, 2 weeks summer. **Meals:** Midweek set menu £32 (2 courses) to £38. **Service:** not inc. **Details:** Cards accepted. 30 seats. Air-con. No music. No mobile phones.

ALSO RECOMMENDED
▲ Brosh
8 Suffolk Parade, Cheltenham, GL50 2AB
Tel no: (01242) 227277
www.broshrestaurant.co.uk
Middle Eastern

A local favourite with readers, who love its chilled-out, unstuffy atmosphere and 'very different' food. Ever-helpful staff certainly know their way around the unusual menu, which draws merrily from the Mediterranean, North Africa and Middle East (especially the owners' native Israel). Kaleidoscopic meze are a big hit on Wednesdays and Thursdays, and the organically-biased repertoire works its way through crab brik with harissa (£8.50), Forest of Dean lamb kefte with spinach, red onion, lemon peel and prune sauce (£14.95), and authentic desserts like mamoul (rosewater pastry filled with date purée, £3). Two dozen global wines from £12.95 (£4.50 a glass). Open Wed to Sat D only.

▌Chipping Campden

ALSO RECOMMENDED
▲ Eight Bells
Church Street, Chipping Campden, GL55 6JG
Tel no: (01386) 840371
www.eightbellsinn.co.uk
Gastropub

Built in 1380 to house stonemasons working on the nearby church (and once used to store the bells), this antique Cotswold inn still looks the business with its flagstone floors, mighty stone walls and a priest hole in the country-style beamed dining room. Beyond the history there is modern food to be sampled: a warm salad of black pudding, chorizo, peppers and bacon (£6.85) is typical, although the kitchen also turns out toad-in-the-hole (£11), beef Stroganoff and fillet of salmon wrapped in Parma ham. Desserts are standards (sticky toffee pudding, chocolate crème brûlée) and good-value wines start at £13.75 (£3.55 a glass). Accommodation available. Open all week.

▌Compton Abdale

ALSO RECOMMENDED
▲ Puesdown Inn
Compton Abdale, GL54 4DN
Tel no: (01451) 860262
www.puesdown.cotswoldinns.com
Gastropub

John and Maggie Armstrong have cleverly rejuvenated this one-time local boozer set back from the A40, transforming it into a forward-looking gastropub/restaurant with a liking for seasonal produce. Lunch is a no-frills affair but the kitchen aims higher in the evening. Puesdown nettle soup or seared scallops with celeriac purée and pea foam (£8.50) might precede loin of venison with blackberry and red wine jus (£13.50), steamed mutton pudding or wild sea bass with saffron mash and sauce vierge. Desserts (£6.25) offer homely nourishment in the shape of glazed rice pudding or apple charlotte. Well-chosen wines from £11.95. Regular cookery demonstrations and accommodation. Open all week.

▌Corse Lawn

Corse Lawn House

Dedicated to food lovers and oenophiles
Corse Lawn, GL19 4LZ
Tel no: (01452) 780771
www.corselawn.com
Modern European | £32
Cooking score: 3

🍷 ⊏ V

Today's newly refurbished incarnation of the Hine family's comfortably appointed Queen Anne residence remains an affable hotel and restaurant. Andrew Poole heads a sound kitchen that mixes old favourites with more modern ideas, emphasising quality produce. The same compositions appear, whether you eat in the bistro or dining room: tried-and-tested ideas like wild mushroom vol-au-vent, and fillet of gurnard with shellfish and saffron broth are mixed in with baked queen scallops with provençale stuffing and mains of whole roast quail with gremolada, mushroom and herb risotto. Finish with a lemon posset with blueberry compote or hot passion-fruit soufflé with passion-fruit sorbet. The wine list remains as impressive as ever, delving deep into France, but with a quality supporting cast from the rest of the world, particularly Australia, New Zealand and South Africa. House wines from Spain and France are £15.70.
Chef/s: Andrew Poole and Martin Kinahan. **Open:** all week 12 to 2, 7 to 9.30. **Closed:** 3 days Christmas. **Meals:** Set bistro L £15.50 (2 courses) to £18.50, Set bistro D £18.50 (2 courses) to £21.50. Set restaurant L £21.50 (2 courses) to £24.50, Set restaurant D £31.50. **Details:** Cards accepted. 70 seats. 40 seats outside. Separate bar. Wheelchair access. Children's portions. Car parking.

Average price

The average price listed in main-entry reviews denotes the price of a three-course meal, without wine.

▌Didmarton

ALSO RECOMMENDED
▲ Kings Arms

The Street, Didmarton, GL9 1DT
Tel no: (01454) 238245
Gastropub

Built in the seventeenth-century as a coach-stop, the Kings Arms is a welcoming, atmospheric inn with smart guest rooms. A Mediterranean touch to the cooking brings things up to date, with starters such as crayfish cocktail and tomato salsa (£5.95) and a balanced range of main dishes from chicken breast wrapped in Parma ham with watercress cream (£10.75) to fillet steak béarnaise on champ (£16.95). Look to the board for fish specials, and round things off with a pudding such as apple and rhubarb crumble (£5.50). Fine cask ales are supplemented by a short, fairly-priced wine list that starts at £13.75. Open all week.

▌Ebrington

ALSO RECOMMENDED
▲ Ebrington Arms

Ebrington, GL55 6NH
Tel no: (01386) 593223
www.theebringtonarms.co.uk
Gastropub

In lush countryside two miles from Chipping Campden and Hidcote Gardens, this seventeenth-century Cotswold inn is currently on good form. New chef James Dixon pulls in the crowds (full houses at weekends) with his up-to-speed gastropub food, which reflects the richly productive local area. Roast rump of Lighthorne lamb with parsnip, thyme and Dijon mustard purée is a winner (£14.50), but the kitchen also works its way through pan-fried pigeon breasts with braised lentils and red wine jus (£5.50), beer-battered pollock and puds such as treacle tart with custard (£4.75). House wine is £12.50 (£3.10 a glass). Accommodation available. Closed Mon.

Fairford

★ READERS' RESTAURANT OF THE YEAR ★
SOUTH WEST

Allium

A country restaurant of some class
1 London Street, Fairford, GL7 4AH
Tel no: (01285) 712200
www.allium.uk.net
Modern European | £39
Cooking score: 6

On the main street of this pretty village, Allium is a calm, relaxing place. A palette of creams and browns with splashes of colour provided by contemporary paintings gives the bar and spacious restaurant a classy, modern feel. Erica Graham's dependable hand on the tiller is appreciated, while husband James is a chef with an eye for detail, as is handsomely evidenced by excellent, labour-intensive appetisers and a pre-dessert of muscovado jelly, which impressed at inspection. He is something of a food crusader, too, championing high-quality local produce on regularly-changing, seasonal menus and delivering some fine and original cooking with a proper appreciation of the importance of flavour. This is evident in starters such as wood pigeon with foie gras and meaty slices of mushroom, and in main courses, where the combination of an apricot and braised mutton shoulder pie went perfectly with flavourful slices of loin of mutton; pollock teamed with braised spelt, confit chicken wings, carrot purée and crayfish and red wine sauce also made a satisfying, gutsy dish. Fine British cheeses, or orange and Grand Marnier soufflé with stem ginger ice cream, round things off. From a strong base in France, the wine list turns up interesting bottles from all corners of the world (including England) and attends well to both under-£25 and the-sky's-the-limit budgets. House wines open at £17.50.
Chef/s: James Graham. **Open:** Wed to Sun L 12 to 3, Wed to Sat D 7 to 12. **Closed:** Christmas. **Meals:** Set menus £19.50 to £38.50, Tasting menu £50.

Service: not inc. **Details:** Cards accepted. 34 seats. Separate bar. Wheelchair access. Music. Children's portions.

Lower Oddington

Fox Inn

Civlised Cotswold pub
Lower Oddington, GL56 0UR
Tel no: (01451) 870555
www.foxinn.net
Gastropub | £25
Cooking score: 1

V

'Prosperous and stylish' just about sums up this pretty, mellow stone pub in an archetypal Cotswold hamlet. The rambling interior is all natural colours and exposed stone, with pine tables, polished stone floors, fresh flowers and evening candles. Chef Ray Pearce has been here for ten years now, which means that his menus evolve gently, yet remain comfortingly familiar and he makes good use of local produce. Hot baked red pepper pesto and mozzarella tart might start things off, followed by whole baked lemon sole with lemon and herb butter, or slow-cooked lamb shank with red wine, rosemary and roasted garlic. Classic crème brûlée makes a good finish. House wine is £12.95.
Chef/s: Ray Pearce. **Open:** all week L 12 to 3 (3.30 Sun), Mon to Sat D 6.30 to 12, Sun D 7 to 10.30. **Closed:** 25 Dec. **Meals:** alc (main courses £10.95 to £15.50). **Service:** not inc. **Details:** Cards accepted. 80 seats. 80 seats outside. Separate bar. Wheelchair access. Children's portions. Car parking.

Please send us your feedback

To register your opinion about any restaurant listed in the Guide, or a new restaurant that you wish to bring to our attention, please visit the web address at the bottom of the page. Your feedback informs the content of the book and will be used to compile next year's reviews.

■ Sapperton

Bell at Sapperton

Local produce and Cotswold gentility
Sapperton, GL7 6LE
Tel no: (01285) 760298
www.foodatthebell.co.uk
Modern European | £30
Cooking score: 4

One glance at this impeccably maintained Costwold pub will tell you that it oozes prosperity and affluence at every turn. The owners have renovated the interior with good taste and a genuine feel for the building's character: the result is genteel, but also gentrified. In the kitchen, there's unswerving allegiance to the local food of the region – notably Copsegrove Farm's naturally-reared beef, which might be potted, turned into corned beef or given more conventional treatment. Elsewhere, rabbit is braised in Ashton Press cider, shank of Lighthorne lamb is slow-cooked with tomatoes and fresh sage, while braised Old Spot pig's cheeks could be sent out with parsnip mash, ginger and lime sauce. Wild salmon is from the River Severn, other fish comes up from the West Country: John Dory and River Fowey mussels with home-made pappardelle and coriander, for example. To conclude, there are carefully wrought desserts such as rich bitter chocolate tart with poached pear, plus exemplary regional cheeses. 'Classic pub classics' and lighter dishes are the main contenders at lunchtime, and the pub fervently supports the efforts of independent Cotswold breweries. The wine list is a well-considered collection with some particularly tasty Italians on show. Prices start at £14.95 for French house selections, and around 16 are available by-the-glass (from £4).
Chef/s: Ivan Reid. **Open:** all week L 12 to 2, D 7 to 9.30. **Closed:** 25 Dec. **Meals:** alc (main courses £13 to £18). **Service:** not inc. **Details:** Cards accepted. 70 seats. 50 seats outside. No music. Wheelchair access. Children's portions. Car parking.

■ Stow-on-the-Wold

Old Butcher's

Quality ingredients and cooking impress
7 Park Street, Stow-on-the-Wold, GL54 1AQ
Tel no: (01451) 831700
www.theoldbutchers.com
Modern British | £24
Cooking score: 3

As the name suggests, this was once a butcher's shop, but today's stylish-looking brasserie gives no clue to its past incarnation. A contemporary glass frontage and terraced, street-side tables offer an appealing cosmopolitan look somewhat out of step with the rest of this traditional Cotswold market town. Inside there's a smart bar and banquette seating or high-back chairs teamed with un-clothed tables. Service is suitably unbuttoned; it's a 'friendly, buzzy, relaxed place'. Peter Robinson's equally modern cooking – driven by local and seasonal produce – delivers clean-cut, well-presented dishes with a nod to the Mediterranean and beyond. Breaded veal served with prosciutto and Parmesan, perhaps a spinach and Taleggio risotto, or calf's liver, bacon and onions are typical, while a pistachio pavlova teamed with rhubarb and vanilla ice cream might head up desserts. The short, fashionable wine list (displayed on the reverse of the daily menus) fits the bill, offering a clutch of house wines from £13 (£3.50 by-the-glass).
Chef/s: Peter Robinson. **Open:** all week L 12 to 2.30, D 6 to 9.30. **Meals:** alc (main courses £10.50 to £16). **Details:** Cards accepted. 45 seats. 12 seats outside. Air-con. Separate bar. Wheelchair access. Music. Children's portions.

Unicorn Hotel

Sturdy Cotswold hotel
Sheep Street, Stow-on-the-Wold, GL54 1HQ
Tel no: (01451) 830257
www.birchhotels.co.uk
Modern European | £27
New Chef

An ever-so-English setting betwixt the ancient Fosse Way and the local parish church creates just the right first impression for visitors to this hardy stone-built hotel. Jacobean furniture and log fires reinforce the mood, and the kitchen taps into a network of local Cotswold producers – although dishes in Shepherd's Restaurant often have an Anglo-European edge. Goats' cheese and roast beetroot terrine with cranberry relish is an intriguing starter, or you might plump for a warm salad of black pudding and mustard new potatoes. Main courses could deliver medallions of pork with sage and Stilton creamed potatoes or fillet of cod with prawn, pea and chorizo risotto, while desserts have featured citrus tart with crème fraîche or bitter chocolate fondant with banana ice cream. Three dozen wines offer dependable drinking from £14 (£3.50 a glass).
Chef/s: Stuart Wiggins. **Open:** all week L 12 to 2, D 7 to 9. **Meals:** alc (main courses £12 to £16). Bar menu available. **Service:** not inc. **Details:** Cards accepted. 40 seats. Separate bar. Wheelchair access. Music. Children's portions. Car parking.

Tetbury

Calcot Manor

Light, airy conservatory dining
Tetbury, GL8 8YJ
Tel no: (01666) 890391
www.calcotmanor.co.uk
Modern British | £39
Cooking score: 3

Calcot may once have been a humble farmhouse, but it sits in 220 acres of prime Gloucestershire countryside, and has been deftly renovated into a luxury hotel with modern accoutrements and appealingly light décor. The Conservatory restaurant, with its pitched glass roof, is where the best of Michael Croft's cooking is to be had, in a menu of modern British dishes, buttressed by some neat touches of traditionalism. Seared Orkney scallops are served with an up-to-the-minute dressing of curried pumpkin and lemon, while baby onions braised in madeira and a sweetcorn pancake are the lustrous accompaniments to foie gras. Mains might give fish a North African spin, as in sea bass with spiced aubergine and lemon and herb tabbouleh, or else partner Duchy organic beef rump with a beef and onion pie, all sauced in red wine. Traditional lardy cake is teamed with contemporary cinnamon-roasted apple and vanilla ice cream, or you might finish with white chocolate mousse, garnished with lychee jelly and mango, or a plate of British farmhouse cheeses. A classical, French-led list opens with wines by-the-glass from £4.50 (or £3 for a smaller 'tasting measure', a nice idea). As well as the Conservatory, there is a venue for more informal eating in the shape of the Gumstool Inn.
Chef/s: Michael Croft. **Open:** all week, L 12 to 2, D 7 to 9.30 (9 Sun). **Meals:** alc (main courses £17.50 to £19). Set L £23. **Service:** not inc. **Details:** 100 seats. 12 seats outside. Air-con. Separate bar. No mobile phones. Wheelchair access. Music. Car parking.

★NEW ENTRY★
The Chef's Table

Classy town-centre deli-bistro
49 Long Street, Tetbury, GL8 1AA
Tel no: (01666) 504466
Modern European | £25
Cooking score: 4

Michael Bedford last appeared in the Guide in 2007 when he ran the Trouble House (see entry). He's now moved a few miles into Tetbury and opened this town-centre deli-cum-bistro, which he runs with bags of good humour and evidence of serious domestic

enterprise on every shelf. The result is genuine, unaffected natural cooking, whether in the deli itself, or upstairs in the simple, bare-boards bistro with its theatre-style kitchen. It is open for breakfast (croissant, pain au chocolat) and good value lunches of, say, braised pork belly with creamy Savoy cabbage, meat juices and herb breadcrumbs (a dish typical of the unadorned approach), or a meaty piece of turbot served with mussels, cockles, clams and ratte potatoes that is all about great flavours, immediacy and subtlety. No bookings are taken, so it is worth knowing that everything listed on the regularly changing blackboard is available to take away – be it truffled macaroni cheese or organic chicken Kiev with olive oil mash and Café de Paris butter. House wine is £15.75.
Chef/s: Michael Bedford. **Open:** Mon to Sat 9.30 to 3.30. **Closed:** Sun, 25 to 26 Dec, 1 Jan. **Meals:** alc (main courses £6.95 to £14). **Service:** not inc. **Details:** Cards accepted. Children's portions.

■ Thornbury

ALSO RECOMMENDED
▲ Ronnies
11 St Mary Street, Thornbury, BS35 2AB
Tel no: (01454) 411137
www.ronnies-restaurant.co.uk
Modern British

Located in the town's shopping precinct, Ronnies may sound like a dodgy nightclub, but it has fast become the eatery of choice for the locals. The Ronnie in question is Ron Faulkner, whose CV includes stints with Anton Mosimann and Ed Baines, as well as Quaglino's. A coffee lounge in the morning, things move up a gear at lunch, with a well-priced 'market' menu at £13.75 for two courses. The à la carte dinner menu might start with Lyme Bay diver-caught scallops with Italian bacon, garlic purée and sage butter (£7.50) and follow with roasted Gressingham duck breast with confit duck hash, cabbage and bacon and thyme jus (£14.75). An intelligent wine list starts at £13.75 with ten by-the-glass. Closed Sun.

■ Upper Slaughter
Lords of the Manor
Likeable new chef in a stylish setting
Upper Slaughter, GL54 2JD
Tel no: (01451) 820243
www.lordsofthemanor.com
Modern European | £49
Cooking score: 6

There have been changes here since the last edition of the Guide. A major refurbishment has updated this secluded seventeenth-century former rectory, ditching the traditional country-house look for a vibrant style that has seen some antiques and oil paintings retained, but mixed in with 'trendy' wall coverings, contemporary armchairs, and 'splashes of bright colour'. 'It really works', especially in the dining room, where huge paintings inject bold colour. A new chef has taken over the kitchen, too. Matt Weedon made a name for himself at Glenapp Castle (see entry) and he appears to be living up to these new surroundings with deceptive effortlessness. Early reports are full of praise. A starter of Cornish crab is served three ways – as a beignet, white meat with mayonnaise, and a delicate parfait with coriander and lime – the subtle flavours and contrasting textures finding favour at inspection. A main course of red mullet is accompanied by palourde clams and cockles and served with a risotto of mussels and an 'intense' bouillabaisse sauce. Fillet of beef comes with oxtail ballottine and bone marrow, and loin of lamb, accompanied by its braised shoulder and caramelised sweetbreads, is teamed with wild garlic and a slick of rosemary jus. Dessert could well be passion-fruit soufflé with coconut sorbet and a little jug of piña colada sauce. Cheeses are also very fine. An extensive and impressive 634-bin wine list has pricey peaks but starts at £19.50.
Chef/s: Matt Weedon. **Open:** all week L 12 to 2.30, D 7 to 9.45. **Meals:** Set price alc £49, tasting menu £65. **Service:** 10% optional. **Details:** Cards accepted. 50 seats. 30 seats outside. Separate bar. Car parking.

▮ Winchcombe

5 North Street

Intricate, contemporary cuisine
5 North Street, Winchcombe, GL54 5LH
Tel no: (01242) 604566
Modern European | £33
Cooking score: 6

V

Squeezed into a centuries-old, bow-fronted, timber-framed building just off the town's main street, the Ashenford's pint-sized restaurant proves that 'good things do come in small packages'. Two cosily rustic, intimate rooms with old timbers and beams are filled with polished-wood tables. Deep red walls and high-backed brown-leather chairs add a more contemporary note, but, like everything here, in an 'unpretentious' way. Service follows suit – very friendly, unstuffy but highly professional, with Kate Ashenford a charming front-of-house. Fixed-price menus ('London food at country prices') for lunch and dinner display Marcus Ashenford's pedigree and assured, confident, modern style. At dinner there are three menus with price options to suit all pockets, plus a seven-course tasting menu surprise (and vegetarians are not forgotten, either). The fine-tuned cooking takes a modern European approach, delivering emphatic flavours and some bold thinking in dishes such as roasted scallop paired with Old Spot belly pork, sweet onion, creamed artichoke and sesame dressing, or roasted sea bass teamed with a Salcombe crab mousse, braised lettuce, carrot purée and a lightly-spiced sauce. Rare-breed sirloin of beef comes with horseradish mash, slow-cooked beef and root vegetables with braising jus. Dessert could offer pear cream with pear and cinnamon crumble and blackcurrant sorbet. Canapés, freshly baked breads (mini loaves), amuse bouche and petits fours excel too, helping make 'every visit a special experience'. The short, sharp, well-selected wine list offers plenty of interest, starting with Argentinean house wine at £17 (£4.50 glass).

Chef/s: Marcus Ashenford. **Open:** Wed to Sun L 12.30 to 1.30, Tue to Sat D 7 to 9. **Meals:** Set L £24.50, Set D £33 to £55. **Service:** optional. **Details:** Cards accepted. 26 seats. No mobile phones. Wheelchair access. Music. Children's portions.

Wesley House

Modern British food in a half-timbered gem
High Street, Winchcombe, GL54 5LJ
Tel no: (01242) 602366
www.wesleyhouse.co.uk
Modern British | £38
Cooking score: 3

The endearingly rickety-looking old building with its ancient timbering and mullioned windows once accommodated John Wesley, founder of Methodism. Today, it houses a comfortably furnished restaurant-with-rooms, where Martin Dunn cooks an accomplished modern British menu that attracts a loyal band of regulars. Roast pigeon makes a robust starter, and comes with beetroot and walnut salad dressed in aged Spanish vinegar, while mains run from gently-treated sea bream (grilled, with asparagus risotto and caper butter), to a pair of cuts of three-week-hung Scottish beef with wild mushrooms, mash and a sauce of madeira. Finish in style with coconut rice pudding cakes and mango sorbet or banana Tatin with praline ice cream. Wines are well-chosen, including lots of vibrant New World flavours, and open with nine house selections from £16.50 (£4.50 a glass). A subsidiary venture, the Wesley House Bar and Grill, is next door.

Chef/s: Martin Dunn. **Open:** all week L 12 to 2, Mon to Sat D 7 to 9 (Sat 9.30). **Meals:** Set L £24.50, Set D £38. **Service:** not inc. **Details:** 60 seats. Air-con. Separate bar. Music. Children's portions.

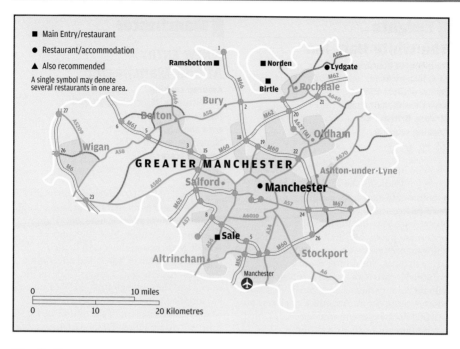

- ■ Main Entry/restaurant
- ● Restaurant/accommodation
- ▲ Also recommended

A single symbol may denote several restaurants in one area.

■ Birtle

The Waggon at Birtle

Good Lancashire fare in a former pub
131 Bury and Rochdale Old Road, Birtle, BL9 6UE
Tel no: (01706) 622955
www.thewaggonatbirtle.co.uk
Modern British | £25
Cooking score: 3

 £5 OFF £30

The whitewashed building may look like a former pub from the outside, but inside it is airy and light with lots of pale wood and simple table settings. 'Consistently excellent food from a frequently-changed menu in a relaxed atmosphere' was how one reporter succinctly summed up the Waggon's appeal. David Watson runs two menus in tandem, one a fixed-price market menu of simpler fare, the other a carte that tries out a few more elaborate options, yet still without going all fancy-pants on us. You might start with a tart of sweet potato, beetroot and red onion glazed in Lancashire cheese, or tempura-battered black

pudding from its spiritual home in nearby Bury, with apple, bacon, Lancashire cheese and a mustard vinaigrette. See the blackboard for today's fish specials, or go for boiled brisket or a roast duck leg for meat mains. Lemon cheesecake mousse on a ginger biscuit base is an appealing way to finish. Detailed tasting notes make the business of choosing wine easier, and there is a list of half-a-dozen house wines at £12.95 a bottle (£3.25 a glass).
Chef/s: David Watson. **Open:** Wed to Sat 6pm to 10, Sun 12.30 to 7.45. **Meals:** alc (main courses £8.50 to £18.50). Set D Wed to Fri £15.50. **Service:** not inc. **Details:** Cards accepted. 60 seats. Separate bar. Wheelchair access. Music. Children's portions. Car parking.

Scores on the Doors

To find out more about the Scores on the Doors campaign, please visit the Food Standard's Agency website:
www.food.gov.uk or www.which.co.uk.

Lydgate
The White Hart Inn
Re-invented country inn
51 Stockport Road, Lydgate, OL4 4JJ
Tel no: (01457) 872566
www.thewhitehart.co.uk
Modern British | £29
Cooking score: 4

£5 OFF V £30

High up in Pennines, overlooking the urban
sprawl of Oldham, the White Hart is
a traditional Lancashire coaching inn
tastefully re-invented for the twenty-first
century. It's a fascinating hybrid of serious
restaurant, pubby bar/brasserie
and contemporary stopover that manages to
cover all bases. The dining room puts on a
fashionable face with stylish furnishings,
vibrant colour schemes and a menu that isn't
short on innovation. An 'amuse' of olives and
oriental duck brochette could precede seared
lamb fillets with sweetbreads and
'petit niçoise' or carpaccio of beetroot with
Cheshire goats' cheese fritters. Next, there
might be roast rump of lamb with rosemary
and nettle gnocchi or fillet of line-caught
Anglesey sea bass with confit fennel, red
wine and caper dressing. Order a plate of 'four
counties' cheeses as a savoury alternative to
chilled strawberry soup with rice pudding
parfait or vanilla-roasted pineapple with pink
grapefruit sorbet. The White Hart also houses
the 'Pub at Lydgate' – a rustic red-walled bar
with real ales and a brasserie-style menu
ranging from bespoke Saddleworth sausages
to coq au vin. The wine list is a sharp
international slate that garners rich pickings
from reputable sources; house selections
provide a 'quick taste' of what's on offer, from
£15 (£3 a glass).
Chef/s: John Rudden. **Open:** Mon to Sat L 12 to 2.30,
D 6 to 9.30. Sun 1 to 7.30. **Meals:** alc (main courses
£12 to £22). Set L Sun £19.75 (2 courses) to £23.50.
Bar menu available. **Service:** not inc. **Details:** Cards
accepted. 50 seats. 30 seats outside. Air-con.
Separate bar. No mobile phones. Wheelchair
access. Music. Children's portions. Car parking.

Manchester

★NEW ENTRY★
ABode Manchester
Assured cooking
107 Piccadilly, Manchester, M1 2DB
Tel no: (0161) 2477744
www.abodehotels.co.uk
Modern European | £35
Cooking score: 4

You wonder whether launching top quality
restaurants and hotels has become something
of a breeze for Michael Caines and Andrew
Brownsword, who in May 2008 opened
ABode Manchester, the fourth in their
popular UK chain of hotels and fine-dining
ventures. Although it's Caines's name on the
restaurant, the Gidleigh Park chef (see entry)
has installed long-time collaborator Ian
Matfin in the kitchens of the refurbished
former Rossetti Hotel. Despite a rather
gloomy feel to the basement room – an
assortment of low-key browns and blacks, not
helped by the absence of natural light – the
talents on display 'are bright enough to
illuminate the room'. The three menus –
grazing, tasting and à la carte – offer ample
choice to sample these skills. From the carte,
'truly succulent' pan-fried scallops are supercharged with a cumin velouté, and a terrine of
foie gras comes with a measured whizz of
rhubarb foam and some cubes of lilac-
flavoured jelly that take the dish to another
level. At main course stage, a beautifully pink
piece of Goosnargh duckling is judiciously
flavoured with Chinese five-spice. Desserts
include a delicious glazed lemon tart and an
'absurdly good' chocolate orange confit
mousse with orange sorbet. House wine
is £18.50.
Chef/s: Ian Matfin. **Open:** Mon to Sat L 12 to 2.30, D
6 to 10. **Closed:** Sun. **Meals:** alc (main courses £18
to £22). Set L £9.95. **Service:** 10% (optional).
Details: Cards accepted. 61 seats. Air-con. Separate
bar. Wheelchair access. Music. Children's portions.
Car parking.

Chaophraya

High-quality Thai food
Chapel Walk, Manchester, M2 1HN
Tel no: (0161) 8328342
www.chaophraya.co.uk
Thai | £20
Cooking score: 4

V

Chaophraya's seemingly effortless arrival on to the Manchester restaurant scene has set a high standard for future openings in the North West. Not only has the consistently high quality of the Thai food been a revelation, but also the 'excellent, efficient, friendly and knowledgeable' service has shown that the relatively poor service hampering other establishments should not be tolerated. Chaophraya is actually three operations in one – a bar and tapas-style eatery downstairs, and a 150-seat à la carte restaurant upstairs. With a menu that easily lists more than 100 dishes – curries, stir fries, soups, seafood, meat and noodles (before you even come to the separate vegetarian menu) – there is likely to be something for everyone. Relatively plain dishes such as 'spankingly fresh' chargrilled sea bass, or chicken and peppers with onion on a sizzler dish show that quality produce does not need to hide behind spices. House wine is £11.75

Chef/s: Satit Jansanga. **Open:** all week L 12 to 4.30, D 5 to 10.30. **Closed:** 25 Dec, 1 Jan. **Meals:** alc (main courses £8 to £26). Set menu £17 (2 courses) to £25. **Service:** not inc. **Details:** Cards accepted. 150 seats. Air-con. Separate bar. Music. Children's portions.

★ BEST FAMILY RESTAURANT ★

Gallery Café

Modest café with lots to offer
Whitworth Art Gallery, Oxford Road, Manchester, M15 6ER
Tel no: (0161) 2757497
www.themoderncaterer.co.uk/the-gallery-cafe
Modern British | £15
Cooking score: 2

This lunch spot has revitalised the Whitworth Gallery's atmosphere and brightened breaks for the university and hospital staff who work nearby. Peter Booth cooks from a tiny kitchen facing on to a sunny yellow room hung with a changing selection of artwork. The menu is simple, cheerful and exactly what's required. Breakfast dishes include boiled egg and soldiers. For lunch, soup might be green lentil with vegetable, and there's always a simple hot dish like pasta with new season's courgettes, sweet peas, Parmesan and lemon zest. Sandwiches might include a house club or a wrap of smoked mackerel and salad leaves, and desserts are brownies or towering, homespun sandwich cakes. There's an emphasis on local produce, with a chart on the wall indicating what's in season. Kids get a fresh, appealing menu and a gallery resource kit for £5. Fairtrade wine is £3 a glass, or try the organic cider or lager from Liverpool. No cards, but cheques are accepted.

Chef/s: Peter Booth. **Open:** Mon to Sat 10 to 4.30, Sun 12 to 4. **Closed:** Good Friday, 24 Dec to 1 Jan. **Meals:** alc (main courses £3.25 to £6.95). **Service:** optional. **Details:** Cash only. 45 seats. 16 seats outside. No music. Wheelchair access. Children's portions. Car parking.

Greens

Vintage Manchester veggie
43 Lapwing Lane, West Didsbury, Manchester,
M20 2NT
Tel no: (0161) 4344259
www.greensrestaurant.net
Vegetarian | £22
Cooking score: 2

One of Manchester's veteran veggie campaigners, Greens is no doubt feeding off main man Simon Rimmer's rising profile as a TV celeb chef and pundit. He certainly has bags of flair, talent and creativity when it comes to creating meatless dishes, and crowds continue to pack his pint-sized Didsbury dining room. The world is Rimmer's larder and his menus are designed to keep customers' taste buds on red alert – although some dishes are fixtures (deep-fried oyster mushrooms with Chinese pancakes and plum sauce is still king of the hill). Elsewhere, expect kaleidoscopic global flavours, vibrant colours and hefty portions: goats' cheese and almond fondant with balsamic beetroot and pesto is a visual treat, Malaysian 'kurry-me' noodles come with deep-fried tofu, more oyster mushrooms and asparagus, while familiar 'afters' might see bread-and-butter pudding or apple and blueberry crumble jostling for the limelight. House wines start at £12 (£3.25 a glass).

Chef/s: Simon Rimmer. **Open:** Tue to Fri and Sun L 12 to 2 (12.30 to 3.30 Sun), all week D 5.30 to 10.30. **Meals:** alc (main courses £9 to £11). Set L Sun and D Sun to Fri 5.30 to 7 £13.95 (2 courses). **Service:** not inc. **Details:** Cards accepted. 48 seats. 8 seats outside. Wheelchair access. Music. Children's portions.

Lime Tree

Long-running neighbourhood restaurant
8 Lapwing Lane, West Didsbury, Manchester,
M20 2WS
Tel no: (0161) 4451217
www.thelimetreerestaurant.co.uk
Global | £27
Cooking score: 3

'Never a poor meal' reports one regular of this long-running neighbourhood restaurant. The menu started out with a strong classical French influence, but has evolved over twenty-odd years to include dishes with a more modern edge. The décor, too, is up-to-date, without feeling formal or pretentious. Starters such as tempura prawns with a warm rice noodle salad and chicken liver and mushroom parfait with chutney, pickles and toast are typical of the menu's scope. Move on to roast loin of Shropshire lamb moussaka and minted yoghurt, cannelloni of crab, scallops and prawns with wilted spinach and seafood sauce, or seared halibut steak with crushed new potatoes, asparagus and Morecambe Bay shrimp butter sauce. An appealing choice of side orders might include deep-fried courgettes with basil and Parmesan or sautéed baby spinach with garlic butter. The carefully-compiled wine list is full of interest and includes an impressive selection by-the-glass. Bottles start at £13.

Chef/s: Jason Parker and Jason Dickinson. **Open:** Tue to Fri L 12 to 2, all week D 5.30 to 10. **Closed:** 25 and 26 Dec. **Meals:** alc (main courses £10.95 to £21.50), Set D early eve £15.95 (3 courses), Set Sun L £16.95. **Service:** not inc. **Details:** Cards accepted. 75 seats. 15 seats outside. Music. Children's portions.

Little Yang Sing

Crowd-pleasing Cantonese stalwart
17 George Street, Manchester, M1 4HE
Tel no: (0161) 2287722
www.littleyangsing.co.uk
Chinese | £20
Cooking score: 1

V

Not so 'little' these days, this 200-seater L-shaped basement remains one of the most popular destinations for authentic Cantonese food in central Manchester. Daytime dim sum attract a host of regular devotees, who come in for spicy meat and nut dumplings, Shanghai mini buns, shredded duck rolls and curiosities like curried minced beef samosas. The full menu focuses on hardy perennials such as steamed sea bass with black bean sauce, aromatic crispy duck and sizzling fillet steak with ginger and spring onion, plus a contingent of earthy casseroles, one-plate rice and noodle dishes and a few chilli-spiked interlopers from Szechuan. Drink tea, saké or house wine from £12.95 (£3.60 a glass).
Chef/s: Warren Yeung. **Open:** all week 12 to 11.30 (till 12 Fri, 12.30 Sat, 10.45 Sun). **Closed:** 25 Dec. **Meals:** alc (main courses £9 to £14). Set L £9.95 (2 courses) to £11.95. Set D £19.50 to £28.95. **Service:** not inc. **Details:** Cards accepted. 200 seats. Air-con. Wheelchair access. Music. Children allowed.

Moss Nook

Defying passing fashion in style
Ringway Road, Manchester, M22 5WD
Tel no: (0161) 4374778
www.mossnookrestaurant.co.uk
Anglo-French | £42
Cooking score: 4

£5
OFF

A vision of rustic contentment, and yet a mere mile from Manchester airport, Moss Nook is an old stager that has benefited from the long experience of Kevin Lofthouse, at the stoves here for 25 years now. The place is run with an eye to soft-focus comfort, with none of the

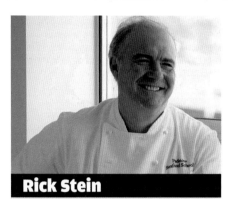

Rick Stein

What makes you what you are today?
Cornish fish.

Where do you like to eat out?
J Sheekey, Café Anglais in London, Ripley's in St Merryn, La Coupol in Paris and La Tupina in Bordeaux.

What is the most unusual cookery book you've come across in your life?
Alan Davidson's 'Fish Cookery of Laos'.

What is your guilty food pleasure?
A portion of Stein's fish and chips.

What dish is your first food memory?
My mum used to make lovely blackcurrant fool.

What is the most unusual food item you've eaten?
Black Water beetles fried with five spice and soy sauce in Guangzhou, China. I only discovered how to pull the entrails out after consuming a plateful of them.

What is your least favourite food item and why?
Mexican chocolate moles. I just don't think chocolate, chilli and chicken works, sorry!

angular contours of modern restaurant design, just plenty of flowers, chiller buckets for the wine and the option of terrace dining. What more could the weary air passenger require? Apart, that is, from Lofthouse's assured Anglo-French cooking. There is melon still among the starters, and no compunction about calling the midday meal 'luncheon', but quality on the plate continues to hold up. Start with a mousse of turbot, accompanied by scallops and sauced with tomato and basil, before going on to best end of local lamb with pommes Anna and mushrooms or veal escalope with beetroot salad and Café de Paris sauce. Take a glass of Beaumes-de-Venise to accompany a dessert such as raspberries and cream layered between cinnamon wafers. A French-led wine list makes room for some New World interlopers, and there is a good choice of halves. The sommelier's selection starts at £16.50 for a bottle of Mâcon Chardonnay (£4.50 for a glass).
Chef/s: Kevin Lofthouse. **Open:** Tue to Fri L 12 to 1.30, Tue to Sat D 7 to 9.30. **Closed:** 2 weeks at Christmas. **Meals:** alc (main courses £15 to £23). Set L £19.50. Set D £37. **Service:** not inc. **Details:** Cards accepted. 65 seats. 20 seats outside. Air-con. No music. No mobile phones. Children allowed. Car parking.

Second Floor
Fine dining with outstanding views
Harvey Nichols, Exchange Square, Manchester, M1 1AD
Tel no: (0161) 8288898
www.harveynichols.com
Modern British | £36
Cooking score: 5

🍶 V

Alison Seagrave's tenure at Harvey Nichols' Second Floor continues, with this smart city centre restaurant continuing to come up with interesting and engaging ideas. Despite glowing reports for the food, some readers feel the room is 'slightly sterile' The large windows give excellent views of the Manchester skyline, but the light from them also casts the room into a very stark relief, leading some to

prefer the more relaxed surroundings of the brasserie. However, it is in the restaurant where Seagrave is 'cooking up a storm' with her confident modern European repertoire. A recent meal featured rabbit with hot apple jelly and foie gras foam, and an 'incredible' dish of roasted wild mushrooms, served simply with a doughy brioche and a perfectly-cooked egg. For mains, turbot with pan-fried watermelon, fondue of celery and ginger velouté achieved a good balance between satisfaction and experimentation, while a dessert of fine, bitter chocolate terrine, served with a sharp blood orange jelly and a milk ice cream made a great finish. House wines start at £14.50.
Chef/s: Alison Seagrave. **Open:** Mon 12 to 6, Tue to Sat 12 to 10.30, Sun 12 to 5. **Closed:** Easter bank hol. **Meals:** alc (main courses £14 to £22). **Service:** not inc. **Details:** Cards accepted. 50 seats. Air-con. Separate bar. Wheelchair access. Music. Children's portions.

The French at the Midland Hotel
Old-fashioned service in splendid surroundings
16 Peter Street, Manchester, M60 2DS
Tel no: (0161) 2363333
www.qhotels.co.uk
Modern European | £46
Cooking score: 3

🛏 V

Diners at this long-standing hotel restaurant may be able to glimpse the lobby, but The French is essentially an opulent bubble. The décor is Belle Epoque, the tone set by long-standing maitre'd Bruno Lucchi. The elegant silverware and remnants of guéridon service (where food is presented, cooked or finished in front of the diner) make it unique in the city, a novelty to be relished, but the cooking is not always as refined as the setting. Dishes that take account of the outside world – a starter of spiced carpaccio of beef with Asian noodle salad, say, or a main course of cumin-marinated lamb with feta – do not succeed as clearly as those with a narrower, more classical scope, such as twice-baked blue cheese soufflé with hazelnut and watercress salad or a hefty pork chop with a smooth cauliflower cheese purée. Dessert, which might feature hot chocolate fondant with pistachio ice cream, is a high point. The wine list, which is quality, predominantly French and classified by style, runs to only four pages from £23.50. Wine by-the-glass comes from the hotel list, starting at £4.30.

Chef/s: Paul Beckley. **Open:** Tue to Thur D 7 to 10.30, Fri and Sat D 7 to 11. **Meals:** alc (main courses £21.95 to £29.95). Set D Tue to Thur £29 (2 courses) to £45 (4 courses). **Service:** not inc. **Details:** Cards accepted. 50 seats. Air-con. Separate bar. No mobile phones. Wheelchair access. Music. Children allowed.

★NEW ENTRY★
Vermilion
Top-end Manchester opulence
Lord North Street, Miles Platting, Manchester, M40 8AD
Tel no: (0161) 2020055
Fusion/Pan-Asian | £35
Cooking score: 2

Located on the edge of an industrial estate, a trip to Vermilion begins by questioning the accuracy of your sat nav. However, the disappointing view of the by-pass is quickly forgotten when you walk through glass doors and into what is arguably Manchester's most opulent restaurant. Black laquered furniture, multi-coloured Buddha-head lamps arranged on a floor-to-ceiling central column and gigantic seedpod seating areas in the upstairs bar make for a stunning venue. Almost inevitably, the Asian fusion food – overseen by Chumpol Jangprai – comes second to the décor. The à la carte focuses largely on fish dishes: starters of soft-shelled crab with lemongrass and mango or fresh water prawns with mango salad, and mains of red snapper, barramundi and rock lobster. There are meat dishes, too, and an entirely separate menu for vegetarians including breaded mixed vegetables dressed with chilli and pineapple sauce. The cooking is assured without being

exciting, but if the food can ever match the showmanship of the decoration then Vermilion will be one to watch. House wine is £15.

Chef/s: Chumpol Jangprai. **Open:** Sun to Fri L 12 to 3, all week D 6 to 10.30. **Closed:** 25 Dec and 1 Jan. **Meals:** alc (main courses £12.50 to £18.50). Set L £15, Set D £25. **Service:** 10%. **Details:** Cards accepted. 140 seats. Air-con. Separate bar. Wheelchair access. Music. Children's portions. Car parking.

Yang Sing
Legendary Manchester restaurant
34 Princess Street, Manchester, M1 4JY
Tel no: (0161) 2362200
www.yang-sing.com
Chinese | £30
Cooking score: 2
V

This legendary Manchester restaurant has been offering Cantonese dining via various banquet menus for over three decades. Unlike many Chinese restaurants that stick with crowd-pleasing dishes, the Yang Sing investigates more unusual flavours with occasionally startling results, such as an incredible suckling pig with soy-flavoured jellyfish, and it has built a strong reputation for dim sum, say steamed beef dumplings with ginger and spring onion, or tempura chilli stuffed with prawn. However the vast 600-seater in the heart of Manchester's Chinatown is the central operation in Gerry and Harry Yeung's growing empire, and with a recent deal to expand into the hotel business (with the adjacent Yang Sing Oriental), there are fears that standards have dropped, with several reporters noting that the establishment seems 'tired'. Perhaps a firmer hand needs to be kept on the founding operation of the Yeungs' empire. House wine is £14.50.

Chef/s: Harry Yeung. **Open:** all week 12 to 10.45. **Closed:** 25 Dec. **Meals:** Set menu £22. **Service:** not inc. **Details:** Cards accepted. 220 seats. Air-con. Wheelchair access. Music. Children's portions.

ALSO RECOMMENDED

▲ EastzEast

Princess Street, Manchester, M1 7DL
Tel no: (0161) 2445353
www.eastzeast.com
Indian

A larger, brasher sister restaurant is now open by the river Irwell, but the original EastzEast is favoured for its dark, shiny interior, efficient service and doorman in full regalia. A menu dominated by Punjabi dishes keeps diners in the city rather than peeling off to the famous curry mile of Rusholme. Poppadoms and the extensive pickle tray are the best way to start, perhaps followed by chargrilled, marinated chicken boti (£3.95) and an excellent lamb sukha bhuna (£8.95) served on the bone for maximum flavour. The coloured lighting, which moves through the spectrum, may prove a distraction too far for some. Dinner only.

▲ Grado

New York Street, Piccadilly, Manchester, M1 4BD
Tel no: (0161) 2389790
www.heathcotes.co.uk
Spanish

Paul Heathcote looks to Spain for his newest venture, a clean, carefully-styled restaurant off busy Piccadilly Gardens. You might eat tapas like charred, salted pimientos de padron (£3) at the bar or take a seat for a starter such as gambas with alioli (£7.95) or chicory, blue cheese and walnut salad. To follow, try a gooey pan of baked bomba rice with chicken and jamón (£14) or one of the daily-changing roasts such as suckling pig with potatoes and morcilla (£12.95). Inconsistencies like a burnt Santiago tart (£6) and an erratic hand with the salt make the pricing seem a little high, but the sherries (from £3.15) and an excellent sommelier numb the pain.

▲ Luso

63 Bridge Street, Manchester, M3 3BQ
Tel no: (0161) 8395550
Portuguese

Personable service and a bright, airy dining room set Luso apart from its mid-market competitors in Manchester. The food is Portuguese in the broadest possible sense, encompassing the styles and ingredients that explorers introduced to far-off provinces. Dishes from the tapas-style lunchtime menu might include salt cod fritters (£4) and for the main event the traditional domed cataplana cooking pot could make an appearance, with a cargo of fish, tomatoes and rice (£16). An occasional lack of refinement might show itself, for example in a pork vindaloo (£15.50) struggling under too much sauce. The wine list is entirely Portuguese, with two of each colour by-the-glass from £5.50.

▲ Market Restaurant

104 High Street, Manchester, M4 1HQ
Tel no: (0161) 8343743
www.market-restaurant.com
Modern European

A long-standing fixture in Manchester's Northern Quarter, this 'intimate, relaxed' restaurant has always marched to the beat of its own drum. Along with a warm welcome, expect the likes of pea and crème fraîche tart (£6.25) to start, then sweetcorn and chilli risotto (£13.95), or roast duck breast and confit leg with black cherry sauce and creamy mash (£17.95). Desserts could be chocolate pavlova with white chocolate sauce or summer pudding (both £6.25). Good wines from £15.95 and a fine selection of bottled beers. Closed Sun and Mon.

▲ That Café

1031 Stockport Road, Levenshulme, Manchester, M19 2TB
Tel no: (0161) 4324672
www.thatcafe.co.uk
Global

Over the years, Alison Eason and her team have done a grand job at this tireless neighbourhood beacon, which is famed for its animated vibes, monthly jazz sessions and colourful food. A globetrotting menu keeps the customers interested with eclectic starters such as seared scallops on Bombay vegetables with coconut curry sauce (£7.75) or a savoury brûlée of blush tomatoes, feta and chives, ahead of Cajun-blackened hake on saffron chowder (£15.75) or fillet of beef with crisp polenta and marinated artichoke hearts. Finish, perhaps, with cranberry parfait and port syrup (£4.95). House wine is £10.50. Open Sun L and Tue to Sat D.

READERS RECOMMEND

City Cafe (at the City Inn Hotel)
Modern European
1 Auburn Street, Manchester, M1 3DG
Tel no: (0161) 242 1000
www.cityinn.com
'Attentive service and interesting twists'

Stock
Italian
4 Norfolk Street, Manchester, M2 1DW
Tel no: (0161) 839 6644
'Superior Italian housed in the former stock exchange'

▌Norden

Nutters
Friendly outfit with loyal fan club
Edenfield Road, Norden, OL12 7TT
Tel no: (01706) 650167
www.nuttersrestaurant.co.uk
Modern British | £32
Cooking score: 3

V

Don't be put off by the name (it's eponymous). Nutters is an impressive eighteenth-century manor house with six acres of groomed grounds overlooking Ashworth Moor. It's a grand venue for sure, with Gothic arches and ornate woodwork, a cosy bar and several interconnecting dining rooms – two in conservatory extensions – plus a large terrace for al fresco meals with views. Though it may be a lavish setting, there's always a welcome (it is a family concern) and the place has an ardent loyal following, probably drawn by the attentive but unobtrusive service that allows you 'to feel special'. Andrew Nutter's kitchen turns out ambitious food that celebrates the best of local produce, say medallions of Parkington pork with its own belly confit delivered with creamy cabbage and a madeira and chive sauce. A six-course surprise gourmet menu takes all the stress out of making a decision yourself. House wine is £13.90.

Chef/s: Andrew Nutter. **Open:** Tue to Sun L 12 to 2 (4 Sun), D 6.30 to 9.30. **Closed:** Mon. **Meals:** alc (main courses £16.50 to 19.25). Set L £15.95 (3 courses), Sun L £22. **Service:** not inc. **Details:** Cards accepted. 150 seats. Separate bar. No mobile phones. Wheelchair access. Music. Children's portions. Car parking.

Ramsbottom

ramsons

Civilised restaurant with Italian perspective
18 Market Place, Ramsbottom, BL0 9HT
Tel no: (01706) 825070
www.ramsons-restaurant.com
Anglo-Italian | £35
Cooking score: 5

£5 OFF V

Chris Johnson's civilised restaurant has plenty of enthusiastic supporters. The stylish chocolate, mushroom and pale blue interior exudes the right air of informality, and the food, with its stress on local produce, is contemporary without being too fashionable. Its clearly-focused Italian perspective is evident in well reported starters of brown shrimp ravioli with lobster bisque and tagliatelle with rabbit, nutmeg and tomato sauce. Dishes are frequently complex but never fussy, flavours are fine-tuned so that they balance rather than compete with each other, although one reporter thought the oxtail pudding accompanying a seared loin of locally-reared veal should be a stand-alone dish as 'it is gorgeous'. Praise, too, for venison with poached pear, pumpkin purée and redcurrant sauce, and roast fillet of pork with sage and parsley, tarte Tatin and rosemary and Calvados sauce. Desserts might include custard pot with raspberries. Service comes in for praise. ramsons is also a paradise for vinophiles: Johnson's personally-selected all-Italian wine list a triumph, giving a spirited account of all regions with a mix of bargains, classics and modish bottles jumbled up together. Downstairs is a simple hideaway bar where the price of a bottle of wine decides the menu.
Chef/s: Abdulla Naseem. **Open:** Wed to Sat L 12 to 2.30, D 7 to 9.30. Sun L 1 to 3.30. **Meals:** Set menus £16.50 to £60. **Service:** not inc. **Details:** Cards accepted. 34 seats. Air-con. Separate bar. Music. Children allowed.

Sale

Hanni's

Handsome-value ethnic food
4 Brooklands Road, Sale, M33 3SQ
Tel no: (0161) 9736606
Eastern Mediterranean | £23
Cooking score: 2

£5 OFF V £30

A gastronomic landmark in a converted shop by Brooklands Metrolink station, Hanni's is famed for its distinctive ethnic food and outstanding value for money. The kitchen looks to the Eastern Mediterranean and the Middle East for a repertoire of dishes with strikingly exotic flavours and bold contrasts. In the meze department you can expect to find palate-sharpening morsels ranging from familiar cold dips to hot falafel, arayes (toasted pitta bread filled with minced lamb) and turlu (aubergines, potatoes and peppers in a rich tomato sauce). Protein-laden kebabs dominate the list of main courses, along with house specialities such as lamb kleftiko with okra, mezalica (chicken and mushrooms in brandy and cream sauce) and five takes on couscous. Finish with sticky baklava, preserved figs with yoghurt or something savoury such as fried halloumi in filo pastry. The brief international wine list opens with house Chilean at £12.95 (£3 a glass).
Chef/s: Hovanan Hoonanian and Mehmet Eken.
Open: Tue to Sat D only 5.30 to 10 (6 to 10.30 Sat).
Closed: Sun, Mon. **Meals:** alc (main courses £12 to £18). **Service:** not inc. **Details:** Cards accepted. 40 seats. Air-con. Wheelchair access. Music. Children's portions.

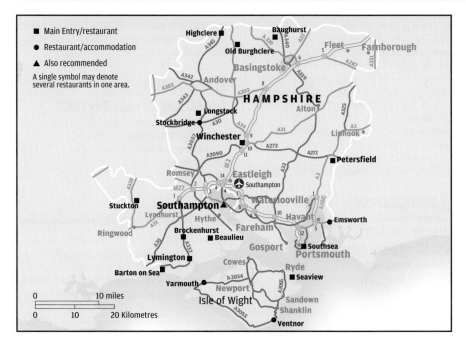

- ■ Main Entry/restaurant
- ● Restaurant/accommodation
- ▲ Also recommended

A single symbol may denote
several restaurants in one area.

Alresford

READERS RECOMMEND
Caracoli
Modern British
15 Broad Street, Alresford, SO24 9AR
Tel no: (01962) 738 730
www.caracoli.co.uk
'Relaxed, quality coffee house, eatery and
foodstore'

Alton

READERS RECOMMEND
The Anchor Inn
Modern British
Lower Froyle, Alton, GU34 4NA
Tel no: 01420 23261
www.anchorinnatlowerfroyle.co.uk
'A country gem that prides itself on patriotic
grub'

Barton on Sea
Pebble Beach
Contemporary seaside dining
Marine Drive, Barton on Sea, BH25 7DZ
Tel no: (01425) 627777
www.pebblebeach-uk.com
contemporary | £30
Cooking score: 3

This 'friendly' modern café/brasserie has
'wonderful' views across Christchurch Bay to
the Needles and the Isle of Wight. Make the
most of it by sitting on the terrace in fine
weather. Luckily the food is no afterthought.
Fish makes a strong showing, from starters of
scallop risotto or crab spring roll to shellfish
platters and main courses such as blackened
cod, which is marinated in soy sauce, saké and
sugar, and comes with stir-fried pak choi,
shiitake mushrooms and rice noodles. The
menu happily flits between classics and
international dishes, so other mains run from
spring lamb navarin to stir-fried duck fillet

with red pepper, pak choi, oyster mushroom and spring onions served with sweet plum purée and duck reduction. For dessert, perhaps hot chocolate fondant or banana and peanut shortbread tart. The wine list opens at £14.95. **Chef/s:** Pierre Chevillard. **Open:** L 12 to 2, D 6.30 to 9.30, all day Sun. **Closed:** Evening 25 Dec, Evening 1 Jan. **Meals:** alc (main courses £11 to £40). **Service:** not inc. **Details:** Cards accepted. 70 seats. 40 seats outside. Air-con. Separate bar. No mobile phones. Wheelchair access. Music. Children's portions. Children allowed. Car parking.

Baughurst

★NEW ENTRY★
Wellington Arms
Country dining pub
Baughurst Road, Baughurst, RG26 5LP
Tel no: (0118) 9820110
thewellingtonarms.com
Gastropub | £25
Cooking score: 3

£30

This former hunting lodge, found down country lanes between Basingstoke and Newbury, is attracting a lot of local attention. Jason King's daily chalkboard menus ooze interest and imagination, while Simon Page runs front-of-house in an amiable manner – together they have worked wonders, refurbishing the building with style, developing a kitchen garden and setting up a network of local suppliers. Chargrilled local asparagus with poached egg (free-range from their own chickens) and goats' cheese, then roast Woods Farm pork belly with sticky red cabbage and damson plums or seared turbot on marsh samphire sautéed in butter and garlic are typical choices. Finish with home-grown rhubarb and raspberry jelly. The simpler, fixed-price lunch menu is a bargain, and with only eight tables in the bar-cum-dining room, booking is essential. House wine is £14.50.
Chef/s: Jason King. **Open:** Wed to Sun L 12 to 2.30, Tue to Sat D 6.30 to 9.30. **Meals:** Set L £15 (2 courses) to £18. **Service:** 10% (optional).

Details: Cards accepted. 32 seats. 35 seats outside. Wheelchair access. Music. Children's portions. Car parking.

Beaulieu

Montagu Arms, Terrace
Palace Lane, Beaulieu, SO42 7ZL
Tel no: (01590) 612324
www.montaguarmshotel.co.uk
Modern British | £45
New Chef

As we went to press we learnt that Matthew Tomkinson, who had been heading the team at the Goose at Britwell Salome, was to take over the kitchens here. Shaun Hill will remain in his advisory role as director of cooking, but the day-to-day running of the kitchen will be in Tomkinson's hands – so impressive gastro-credentials all round. At the Goose, Tomkinson's menus followed modern lines, dishes avoided over-elaboration and allowed quality seasonal ingredients to shine and his cooking looks set to continue in that vein. Expect robust combinations – something like croustade of local game topped with sautéed foie gras and served with confit shallots and garlic, followed by saddle of venison with a grand veneur sauce or honey-roast breast of wild duck with a combination of crispy leg-meat samosa, caramelised baby onion, cabbage and creamed potato. The wine list opens at £17.
Chef/s: Matthew Tomkinson. **Open:** all week L 12 to 2.30, D 7 to 9.30. **Service:** not inc. **Details:** Cards accepted. 60 seats. 25 seats outside. Separate bar. Wheelchair access. Music. Car parking.

Brighton

READERS RECOMMEND
The Chimney House
Gastropub
28 Upper Hamilton Road, Brighton, BN1 5DF
Tel no: 01273 556 708
www.chimneyhouse.co.uk
'Unfussy neighbourhood Gastropub.'

Brockenhurst
Le Poussin at Whitley Ridge
Innovative, complex food
Beaulieu Road, Brockenhurst, SO42 7QL
Tel no: (01590) 622354
www.lepoussin.co.uk
Modern British | £45
Cooking score: 6

Alex Aitkens' protracted sojourn in the Whitley Lodge Hotel continues, as he waits for work on the original Poussin at Parkhill to reach completion. For the time being, it is business as usual at this one-time royal hunting lodge in the heart of the New Forest. Visitors make a beeline for the place in anticipation of strikingly innovative, complex food that takes its cue from the native produce of the region – especially game, fungi and fish. A spring salad of marinated butternut squash, wild mushrooms and baby vegetables with truffle dressing is as simple as it gets; elsewhere, ingredients often come in clusters (loin of rabbit filled with its own liver wrapped in prosciutto with cutlets, rillette, Puy lentils and yet more wild mushrooms, for example). Seafood from the Hampshire boats could yield fillets of sea bass with crab risotto, pea shoots and fennel embellished with cappuccino of crab, while desserts are marvels of panache and elaboration: consider chocolate fondant with a baby banana split and chocolate milk plus a rice crispie cake with praline cream. The wine list is a stunning worldwide collection that has remarkable strength in depth, from old-school pedigree classics to some of the New World's most desirable vintages. Pricing is fair and drinker-friendly, with modest bottles weighing in at around £15 (£3.95 a glass).
Chef/s: Alex Aitken. **Open:** all week L 12 to 2 (12.30 to 2.30 Sun), D 6.30 to 9.30 (7 to 9 Sun). **Meals:** Set L Mon to Sat £15 (2 courses) to £20. Set L Sun £27.50 (3 courses). Set D £45. **Service:** 12.5% (optional). **Details:** Cards accepted. 50 seats. 50 seats outside. Separate bar. Wheelchair access. Children's portions. Car parking.

Simply Poussin
Sound cooking and good value
The Courtyard, Brookley Road, Brockenhurst, SO42 7RB
Tel no: (01590) 623063
www.simplypoussin.co.uk
Modern British | £20
Cooking score: 3

There's good eating to be had at Alex Aitken's 'small, informal and intimate' sibling of Le Poussin (see entry above). Found in the centre of Brockenhurst, it is a welcoming place where good service, sound cooking and good value go hand-in-hand – part of the appeal is the set-price two-course menu, and the excellent comfort food found on the carte. Cooking follows unfussy brasserie lines, deploying good raw ingredients in starters such as twice-baked creamy cheese soufflé, or smoked salmon cannelloni. Simplicity seems to be the key to the operation, with main courses offering quail pie or whole roasted poussin, and hot passion-fruit soufflé or chocolate fondant for dessert. House wine is £15. NB: Simply Poussin was being refurbished as the Guide went to press.
Chef/s: Alex Aitken. **Open:** Tue to Sat L 12 to 2, D 6.30 to 9.30. **Meals:** Set L £10.50 (2 courses), Set D (Tue to Thur) £10.50 (2 courses). **Service:** 10%. **Details:** Cards accepted. 32 seats. 10 seats outside. Wheelchair access. Music. Children's portions. Car parking.

Emsworth
Fat Olives
Highly polished but homey
30 South Street, Emsworth, PO10 7EH
Tel no: (01243) 377914
www.fatolives.co.uk
Modern British | £25
Cooking score: 3

A grey-painted converted fisherman's cottage near the Emsworth quayside is home to the Murphys' appealingly homey restaurant. The

Set menus

If you want to try some of the best restaurants in Britain, without incurring huge costs, try the set menu.

Here are some of the best offers from our top 40 restaurants:

Londoners might like to investigate the **Tom Aikens** set menu which at £29 for three courses offers incredible value for money.

Simpsons in Birmingham not only does a set lunch menu for £25 for three courses but also a set dinner menu for just five pounds more.

The refined surroundings of North Lincolnshire's **Winteringham Fields** offers an extensive, rather than an expensive set lunch menu, with a variety of choices over three courses for £39.

Berkshire's **Vineyard** restaurant offers an excellent seasonal menu from as little as £19 for two courses.

They're renowned for knowing a good deal when they see one in Scotland and Edinburgh's **Restaurant Martin Wishart** offers a three-course lunch menu for £22.50.

Anthony's Restaurant in Leeds gives diners the chance to sample a two-course lunch set menu for just £19.95 or a three-course menu for £23.95.

Tyddyn Llan is one of the leading restaurants in Wales, but they still offer good value for money with a set lunch menu for £21.50 for two courses (Fridays and Saturdays only, or by arrangement) and the popular Sunday lunch is £25 for three courses.

Another option for financially-astute diners in Scotland is **The Kitchin** which offers three courses for just £21.50 to enjoy the work of this incredible chef.

Finally, **Bohemia** in Jersey does a three-course menu for £19.50, or a two-course menu for £16.50. Fantastic value in a beautiful setting.

front-of-house is run with commendable warmth, welcoming unbooked last-minuters as readily as anyone else, and a regular praises the 'beautifully presented, locally sourced fish and meat'. That translates as brill in a black olive crust with red pepper risotto or squab pigeon with swede, cabbage and crème fraîche from a menu choice that's expansive and inspiring. Begin, perhaps, with a chunky terrine of duck, pheasant, foie gras and prunes or trendy seared scallops with pea velouté and pancetta. 'Puddings are really innovative,' comments a reader, casting an eye perhaps over the more show-off creations, such as chocolate délice with praline ice-cream and Frangelico foam. The wine list offers a brisk global sweep, with house Chardonnay and Cabernet from Chile at £12.95.

Chef/s: Lawrence Murphy. **Open:** Tue to Sat L 12 to 1.45, D 7 to 9.15. **Closed:** 2 weeks at Christmas, 2 weeks in Jun-Jul. **Meals:** alc (main courses £14.50 to £21.95). Set L £17.95. **Service:** net prices. **Details:** Cards accepted. 28 seats. 10 seats outside. Wheelchair access. Music. Children allowed.

36 On The Quay
A dream ticket for South Coast visitors
47 South Street, Emsworth, PO10 7EG
Tel no: (01243) 375592
www.36onthequay.co.uk
Modern European | £35
Cooking score: 6

Ramon and Karen Farthing bagged a prime spot on Emsworth's cobbled quayside when they settled into this endearing seventeenth-century cottage more than ten years ago. Now they have four spicily-named letting rooms (plus a self-contained cottage in the village) in addition to their high-ranking restaurant. It's a near-perfect package for south coast visitors who want to pitch camp between Chichester and Portsmouth. Ramon's cooking is assured, intricate and boldly adventurous when it needs to be: a starter of seared scallops with pea shoot, crisp apple and Serrano ham dust, offset by a passion-fruit dressing and beetroot syrup shows something of the style. Main

courses also rely on lots of cohesively arranged components; witness a medallion of beef fillet on Jerusalem artichoke velouté with a ravioli of mushrooms and veal sweetbreads accompanied by spinach and morel sauce. The speciality dessert is a five-part extravaganza exploring just one fruit (perhaps banana or mango or lime); otherwise set your sights on hot Bramley apple and honey soufflé with cinnamon ice cream and baked apple pastry. Meals are fashionably interspersed with appetisers, mid-course extras and 'refreshers', but the show never descends into effete pomposity – thanks partly to the unselfconscious mood created by Karen Farthing and her team out front. France is the wine list's natural home and it is stuffed with top-drawer bottles from the classic regions – although it pays to head south for the best value. Elsewhere there are some particularly tasty offerings from Italy and California, while seasonal selections offer a fine assortment of appetising names from £15 (£4.75 a glass).

Chef/s: Ramon Farthing. **Open:** L 12 to 1.45, D 6.45 to 9.45. **Closed:** 3 weeks Jan, last week May, last week Oct. **Meals:** Set L £19.95 (2 courses to £24.95). Set D £46.95 (3 courses). **Service:** not inc. **Details:** Cards accepted. 50 seats. Separate bar. No music. No mobile phones. Wheelchair access. Children's portions.

▮ Highclere
Marco Pierre White's Yew Tree
Smart country inn
Hollington Cross, Andover Road, Highclere, RG20 9SE
Tel no: (01635) 253360
Anglo-French | £40
Cooking score: 5

Trust MPW to fashion what may be very close to the perfect roadside inn. A seventeenth-century building of whitewashed brick, it is not far from the castle and boasts all the interior detail one could wish for: old beams and brickwork and an inglenook fireplace, but also tables dressed smartly enough to get into the Ritz, a wealth of food-inspired art and a menu that allows Neil Thornley scope to interpret the Marco style with his own panache. Heritage dishes abound, but are brought off with real culinary élan, including kedgeree with smoked haddock, braised oxtail and kidney pudding, and rib-eye steaks with various dressings. There are favourites from further afield too, long since absorbed into the English repertoire – starters such as Baltic-style herrings with beetroot salad, duck rillettes with green peppercorns, even foie gras parfait in truffle jelly. Desserts line up sherry trifle, rice pudding and Eton mess, but also cherry clafoutis or a show-stopping blackberry soufflé with hot blackberry sauce. Drinking extends from a selection of pedigree cask-conditioned English ales and Weston's ciders to a sophisticated wine list that mixes some affordable New Worlders in among the glamorous French stuff. The bidding opens at £15.50 (£4 a glass) for Chilean Sauvignon or Merlot.

Chef/s: Neil Thornley. **Open:** all week, L 12 to 2.30 (3 Sun), D 6 to 9.30 (9 Sun). **Closed:** 25 and 26 Dec D, 1 Jan D. **Meals:** alc (main courses £12.50 to £19.50). Set L Mon to Sat £18.50. Set D Sun £15.50. **Service:** not inc. **Details:** Cards accepted. 75 seats. 28 seats outside. Separate bar. Wheelchair access. Children's portions. Car parking.

▌Isle of Wight

The George Hotel
Modern dining with superb sea views
Quay Street, Yarmouth, Isle of Wight, PO41 0PE
Tel no: (01983) 760331
www.thegeorge.co.uk
Modern European | £37
Cooking score: 3

⌷ V

It's all change at the classy seventeenth-century George, with a smart new conservatory-style brasserie driving its dining scene. The hotel is set in a cracking position on the water's edge, and the brasserie at the rear certainly laps up the Solent views. Sleek and

coolly modern, it offers plain tables and limed floorboards teamed with Philippe Starck lampshades, contemporary artwork and a zinc-topped bar; there's a stylish covered terrace, plus tables on the waterfront patio, too. The modern brasserie food comes with a sunny European accent, with chef Jose Graziosi – who hails from Italy's Abruzzo region – using quality organic and local produce (asparagus, say, or locally-farmed duck), with fish a speciality. Expect clear-flavoured well-presented dishes like a fillet of Isle of Wight sea bass served with a potato rösti and a vanilla and orange vinaigrette. The fashionable, compact, global wine list offers a 14-strong house selection at £15.75, £4.45 by-the-glass.

Chef/s: Jose Graziosi. **Open:** all week L 12 to 3, D 7 to 10. **Meals:** alc (main courses £16.50 to £27.50). **Service:** optional. **Details:** Cards accepted. 65 seats. 120 seats outside. Air-con. Separate bar. No mobile phones. Wheelchair access. Music. Children's portions.

Hambrough Hotel
Stunning views of Ventnor Bay
Hambrough Road, Ventnor, Isle of Wight, PO38 1SQ
Tel no: (01983) 856333
www.thehambrough.com
Modern British | £39
Cooking score: 4

£5 OFF ⌷

The setting is a great plus, as this stylish boutique hotel on the Isle of Wight's southern fringe has stunning views of Ventnor Bay. The dining room is a light, minimalist space, all bare boards, neutral colours and white-clothed tables, throwing the emphasis on the great view outside and on the sharply observed modern cooking. Craig Atchinson's kitchen deals in ambitious food, turning out, for example, Bembridge crab with fennel salad, sushi nori, a beignet of brown meat and mango and curry oil. Ingredients are first-rate and, despite their intricacy, dishes are well balanced; witness a fat tronçon of turbot with white and green asparagus, morels, beans and spring cabbage with morel essence, or a trio of lamb – roasted loin, braised shoulder and sweetbreads – with crushed peas, broad beans, fennel and rosemary jus. Desserts tend to be variations on themes with kalamansi (a citrus fruit) parfait with blood orange sorbet and chilled blood orange soup a typical example. House wine is £14.

Chef/s: Craig Atchinson. **Open:** all week L 12 to 2.30, D 6 to 9.30. **Meals:** Set D £30 to £38.50. **Service:** not inc. **Details:** Cards accepted. 26 seats. 15 seats outside. Air-con. Separate bar. Wheelchair access. Music. Children's portions.

Seaview Hotel

Modern seaside dining
High Street, Seaview, Isle of Wight, PO34 5EX
Tel no: (01983) 612711
www.seaviewhotel.co.uk
Modern European | £27
Cooking score: 2

 V £30

As the name suggests, there are sea views from the front terrace and bedrooms of this Victorian hotel – now a thoroughly modern boutique retreat – but don't expect the same from its two dining rooms. However, they more than compensate with their nautical blue-and-white theming, while the aptly-named Sunshine restaurant has a modern conservatory that is 'ablaze with light' during the day. There's a modern accent to the kitchen's brasserie-style output, too. Line-caught sea bass seems to fit with the location, perhaps served with baby onions, sautéed Little Gem, pancetta and a red wine sauce, or opt for island rib-eye steak with cottage pie, celeriac purée and beef sauce. A compact wine list offers a decent selection of organic options, half-bottles, by-the-glass and Chilean house from £14.95.

Chef/s: Andrew Morgan. **Open:** all week L 12 to 2, D 7 to 9.30. **Meals:** Set L and D £26.95. **Service:** not inc. **Details:** Cards accepted. 85 seats. 35 seats outside. Air-con. Separate bar. No music. Wheelchair access. Music. Children's portions.

■ Longstock
Peat Spade Inn

Atmospheric dining in fly-fishing heaven
Village Street, Longstock, SO20 6DR
Tel no: (01264) 810612
www.peatspadeinn.co.uk
British | £28
Cooking score: 2

Andrew Clark and Lucy Townsend have created an upbeat country retreat brimming with charm and character at this 'gem of a Test Valley dining-pub' in the heart of fly-fishing country. The interior has been fetchingly remodelled with polished floorboards and scrubbed-wood tables matched by vibrant red walls and ceiling (the rear Rod Room is resplendent in green); tall candlesticks, an endearing medley of chairs, old photographs and thoughtful curios complete the picture. Service is friendly and attentive. Andrew Clark's simple, classic English dishes rely on prime seasonal produce, much of it local: confit duck leg served with herb new potatoes and a white bean dressing, perhaps, while desserts like rhubarb and custard with shortbread wink at comfort. The well-chosen wine list is French-dominated with house bottles kicking in at £13.50.

Chef/s: Andrew Clark. **Open:** all week L 12pm to 2pm, D 7pm to 9.30pm. **Meals:** alc (main courses £10 to £17). Set £30. **Service:** optional. **Details:** Cards accepted. 55 seats. 40 seats outside. Wheelchair access. Music. Children's portions. Car parking.

▌Lymington

Egan's

Easy-going local favourite
Gosport Street, Lymington, SO41 9BE
Tel no: (01590) 676165
Modern British | £28
Cooking score: 2

V

A reliable fixture of the Lymington scene, John and Deborah Egan's relaxed bistro-style restaurant scores with its easy-going attitude and skilfully crafted food. John Egan keeps faith with the local larder and fish is the standout attraction. Halibut is given a soft herb crust and served with crayfish thermidor and smoked haddock champ, while sea bream might be paired with tiger prawns, pesto mash and champagne sauce. Elsewhere, the kitchen looks to the New Forest for seasonal dishes of many parts, including saddle of venison with griottine cherry sauce, wild mushroom risotto and venison pie. Vegetarians have their own menu. Those looking for a sweet-toothed finale might go for chocolate torte with lemon posset or choux buns filled with mascarpone and espresso mousse. Wines are a good-value bunch, with house recommendations opening at £13.95 (£3.95 a glass).
Chef/s: John Egan. **Open:** Tue to Sat L 12 to 2, D 6.30 to 10. **Closed:** Sun, Mon and 25 Dec to 8 Jan. **Meals:** alc D (main courses £15 to £19). Set L £12.50 (2 courses) to £14.50. **Service:** not inc. **Details:** Cards accepted. 50 seats. 20 seats outside. Separate bar. No mobile phones. Wheelchair access. Music. Children's portions.

▌Old Burghclere

Dew Pond

Glorious country views and modern cooking
Old Burghclere, RG20 9LH
Tel no: (01635) 278408
www.dewpond.co.uk
Anglo-French | £32
Cooking score: 3

There really is a dew pond at Keith and Julie Marshall's sixteenth-century country-house restaurant, and lovely views over rural Hampshire to enjoy. Inside, the country feel (and views) continue in a couple of interconnecting dining rooms and a pair of cosy lounges where original oak beams, colourful artwork (for sale), black leather-upholstered chairs and best white linen add to the relaxed and unstuffy feel of the place (although staff come formally clad). The cooking follows a modern course, with local produce a feature on the fixed-price three-course dinner menu. There's plenty of choice and an uncomplicated light touch in dishes such as herb-crusted best end and rump of spring lamb teamed with provençale vegetables and a red wine and rosemary stock reduction, or in hot chocolate rum-and-raisin fondant served with vanilla ice cream to finish. Wines start out at £12.50, with plenty of choice by-the-glass.
Chef/s: Keith Marshall. **Open:** all week D only 7 to 9.30. **Closed:** 2 weeks Christmas and New year. **Meals:** Set D £32. **Service:** not inc. **Details:** Cards accepted. 48 seats. No music. No mobile phones. Wheelchair access. Children's portions. Car parking.

Petersfield

JSW

Classy, modern professional operation
20 Dragon Street, Petersfield, GU31 4JJ
Tel no: (0871) 4265950
Modern Anglo-French | £35
Cooking score: 6
V

JSW is to be found just off the centre of this pleasant market town in a converted seventeenth-century coaching inn, the updated monochrome interior translating into an attractive, stylish modern restaurant-with-rooms. The cooking makes a virtue out of simplicity and economy – Jake Watkins has a modern outlook, with local and seasonal materials helping to give his food its particular identity. 'Wonderfully cooked' fish (from day-boats on the Solent) is a strong suit: say fricassee of Dover sole with cep and asparagus to start, or a main course of wild sea bass with sauce vierge and shellfish velouté, while a salad of home-smoked duck with pickled pears and duck confit, followed by loin of lamb with shallot purée and slow-cooked tomatoes typify meat offerings. Much of it works well, as was attested by the reporter who singled out a 'sublime' caramelised onion tart with goats' cheese from an eight-course tasting lunch, and declared a cep risotto and the salted caramel mousse for dessert to be 'bursting with flavour.' Fine home-made rolls open the proceedings and excellent English cheeses make an alternative to dessert. And then there is the wine list. It's a well-rounded global collection that matches European classics (including an exceptional range from Alsace and Germany) with interesting New World bottles. House wines are £18.

Chef/s: Jake Watkins. **Open:** Tue to Sat L 12 to 1.30, D 7 to 9.30. **Closed:** 2 weeks summer, New Year. **Meals:** Set L £19.50 (2 courses), set D £36.50 (2 courses). **Service:** not inc. **Details:** Cards accepted. 44 seats. 28 seats outside. Wheelchair access. Children allowed. Car parking.

Southampton

ALSO RECOMMENDED

▲ The White Star Tavern

28 Oxford Street, Southampton, SO14 3DJ
Tel no: (023) 80821990
www.whitestartavern.co.uk
Gastropub

The former hotel for ocean-going passengers has morphed nicely into a contemporary pubby bistro. It's a hive of activity as the bar is integrated with the dining area and the vibe is informal, perhaps too informal as this year diners have complained about the music being too loud in the bar. Output from the cosmopolitan kitchen can range from chicken liver parfait with fig jam (£6.50) and home-made Scotch egg with curried mayo (£4.25) via various salads and pasta dishes to such crowd-pleasers as prime fillet burger (£11) or calf's liver with bacon and mulled shallots (£13.50). House wine is £14.25. Open all week. More reports please.

Southsea

Montparnasse

Modern thinking and astute technique
103 Palmerston Road, Southsea, PO5 3PS
Tel no: (023) 92816754
www.bistromontparnasse.co.uk
Modern European | £32
Cooking score: 4

Montparnasse has gone from strength to culinary strength over recent years. There is consummate attention to detail from first to last, and the acclamation of the cooking that crops up in reports – 'never ever had a bad meal here' – indicates that customers appreciate what Kevin Bingham is trying to do. Materials are sourced with the greatest of care, reaching the plate in the form, perhaps, of a seared breast of pigeon with tarragon gnocchi and smoky bacon or smoked salmon and brown shrimp butter terrine with saffron mayonnaise. An apple charlotte points up the flavours of a chargrilled duck breast, while a good sense of flavouring is apparent in perfectly timed Dover sole teamed with prawns and scallops, coconut rice and coconut and ginger velouté. Novel touches at dessert stage have included a trio of white chocolate and raspberry pannacotta, raspberry jelly and white chocolate ice cream. The sensibly-brief wine list offers a surprisingly wide choice; starting at £12.95 there is a smattering of halves, but no desire to impress with too many posh bottles.

Chef/s: Kevin Bingham. **Open:** Tue to Sat L 12 to 1.45, D 7 to 9.30. **Closed:** Sun and Mon, 25 and 26 Dec, 1 Jan. **Meals:** Set menu £26.50 (2 courses) to £31.50. **Service:** not inc. **Details:** Cards accepted. 30 seats. Music. Children allowed. Car parking.

READERS RECOMMEND
Eight Kings Road
French
8 Kings Road, Southsea, PO5 3AH
Tel no: (08451) 303234
'Modern French fare in a stylish setting'

■ Stockbridge
Greyhound
Elegant inn in famous fishing country
31 High Street, Stockbridge, SO20 6EY
Tel no: (01264) 810833
Modern British | £30
Cooking score: 4

🍷 ⊨

The angling mementoes and paraphernalia that deck out the bar are a reminder that this elegant inn by the River Test is in famous fishing country. With winter fires and summer drinking by the river it has the seasons covered, but food is centre stage. Jon Howe's cooking takes its cue from Britain's regional larder. Ingredients are subjected to forthright modern treatments, say steamed mussels with tomato, chilli and basil, or twice-baked goats' cheese soufflé with beetroot and horseradish purée, but the signature fishcakes with poached egg and chive beurre blanc still feature as a starter. Roast loin of free-range pork teamed with black pudding hash cake,

sauerkraut and apple makes a gutsy main course, and for pudding you might consider baked Grand Marnier cheesecake with clementine syrup and lemon curd, or fine British and Irish cheeses. Good drinking is to be had, whether real ale or a glass of something from the well-priced wine list, which offers house wines from £15.50 to £19.50.

Chef/s: Jon Howe. **Open:** all week L 12 to 2 (Fri to Sun 2.30), Mon to Sat D 7 to 9 (Fri and Sat 9.30). **Closed:** Sun D, Christmas and 1 week end of Dec, beginning of Jan. **Meals:** alc (main courses £17.50 to £19.75). Set L £18.25 (2 courses) to £23.50. **Service:** not inc. **Details:** Cards accepted. 50 seats. Children's portions. Car parking.

■ Stuckton
Three Lions
An auberge in Hampshire
Stuckton, SP6 2HF
Tel no: (01425) 652489
www.thethreelionsrestaurant.co.uk
Anglo-French | £40
Cooking score: 5

£5 OFF 🍷 ⊨

Mike and Jayne Womersley run a self-styled 'English auberge' on the edge of the New Forest, newly redecorated throughout since last year's Guide. Comfy sofas in the bar and a floral, farmstead ambience in the dining-room make the place thoroughly welcoming, as does the proprietors' approach. So welcoming, indeed, that previous guests have included Madonna, the late Sir Edward Heath, Murray Walker and Status Quo, though not, we trust, all at once. Mike Womersley has always favoured a fascinatingly terse style of menu writing, and isn't about to change. Thus you will be apprised of the principal couple of components, but told next to nothing of the cooking style or any other elements. Start with roast quail and honey bacon, or asparagus and wild mushrooms, and go on to either sea bass and tarragon sauce or local venison and roast shallots. The understatement succeeds because, while refreshingly free of long-winded menu-ese, it also ensures surprise and delight when the plate itself arrives.

Presentations are kept simple and clean-looking, the kind of approach you might tell yourself (optimistically) you could replicate at home, and the quality of raw materials thus shines all the more lustrously, from the Poole and Brixham fish to the free-range pork and dry-cut Scottish beef. Desserts might be something as familiar as caramelised apple tart, or as surprising as basil bananas and brûlée cream. An enthusiast's wine list is annotated as unfloridly as the menu. Choices are sound throughout, with a plethora of properly mature reds, plenty of half-bottles, and a house slate that kicks off with blended French country wines at £14.75 (£3.25 a glass).

Chef/s: Mike Womersley. **Open:** Tue to Sun L 12 to 2, Tue to Sat D 7 to 9. **Meals:** alc (main courses £17.75 to £23.50). Set L midweek £19.75. **Service:** not inc. **Details:** Cards accepted. 60 seats. 20 seats outside. Separate bar. No mobile phones. Wheelchair access. Music. Children's portions. Car parking.

▌Trotton

READERS RECOMMEND
The Keepers Arms
Gastropub
Terwick Lane, Trotton, GU31 5ER
Tel no: (01730) 813724
www.keepersarms.co.uk
'Friendly local pub serving modern classics'

▌Winchester

Chesil Rectory
Much-loved historic setting
1 Chesil Street, Winchester, SO23 0HU
Tel no: (01962) 851555
www.chesilrectory.co.uk
Modern French | £49
Cooking score: 5

£5
OFF

A chesil is a shingly beach or riverbank, denoting that this lovely old beamed building, the oldest in Winchester, once stood right by the river. Time has worn away the town's topography, but the house itself defies the passing centuries and, under Carl Reeve's tutelage, has long been a destination restaurant. As our readers testify, the surroundings are almost enough of a lure in themselves, so it is all the more to the credit of Robert Quéhan that his cooking manages to shine out too. The style is a gentle rendition of modern French modes, with dishes achieving a multi-layered but not jarring complexity. Start perhaps with lobster ravioli, served alongside seared scallops and vegetable julienne in a coriander and lobster bisque. A little mango, lobster's new best friend, also finds its way into the dish. Fish is grandly treated in main courses too, for example Solent sea bass served with puréed parsnip, braised fennel and artichoke in an oyster and vanilla sauce. The good things of France turn up reliably in meat dishes that might add truffle and foie gras to Hampshire beef fillet with shallot marmalade and mash. Lamb from the Pyrenees and duck from Challans are handled with equal panache. A witty spin on the petits fours of yore informs a dessert called After Eight, an iced chocolate and mint parfait layered with crunchy chocolate and served with mint ice cream, or there might be a trio of crèmes brûlées, in the form of vanilla, coffee and whisky variations. The principal regions of France head up the carefully-compiled wine list. Prices start at £17 for a South African Chenin Blanc or, in the red corner, £19.50 for a peppery Négrette from the Frontonnais in southwest France.

Chef/s: Robert Quéhan. **Open:** Wed to Sat L 12 to 1.30, Tue to Sat D 7 to 9.30. **Meals:** Set L £23, Set D £49. **Service:** not inc. **Details:** Cards accepted. 45 seats. Music. Children's portions.

Readers recommend

A 'readers recommend' review is a genuine quote from a report sent in by one of our readers. We intend to follow up these suggestions throughout the year to come.

Hotel du Vin & Bistro

Stylish town house hotel with popular bistro
Southgate Street, Winchester, SO23 9EF
Tel no: (01962) 841414
www.hotelduvin.com
Modern European | £35
Cooking score: 3

The original Hotel du Vin is found in a Georgian town house in the heart of Winchester, its elegant lines and hallmark green livery catching the eye from the street. Inside, the French-style bistro comes awash with wine-themed prints and colourful posters teamed with bare floorboards, polished-wood tables and black leather-upholstered chairs – it's noted for its lively, informal bonhomie. There's a bijou champagne bar, too, and pretty walled gardens (one with a novel cigar shack for smokers). The crowd-pleasing menu has a modern European edge, the kitchen focusing on good produce simply cooked, say a fillet of halibut paired with buttered spinach and a forestière sauce or perhaps honey-roast pork belly with shallots and caramelised apples. The super wine list is predictably 'a highlight' with house bottles from £14.50 and a bevy by-the-glass alongside starry names and vintages. **Chef/s:** Matthew Sussex. **Open:** all week L 12 to 2, D 7 to 10.30. **Closed:** L Dec 31. **Meals:** alc (man courses £15 to £19). **Service:** 10%. **Details:** Cards accepted. 60 seats. Separate bar. Wheelchair access. Children's portions. Car parking.

Wykeham Arms

Landmark Winchester hostelry
75 Kingsgate Street, Winchester, SO23 9PE
Tel no: (01962) 853834
Modern British | £25
Cooking score: 3

'The Wyk' is arguably as much of a Winchester landmark as the nearby college and cathedral. Hidden away among the cobbled streets in the oldest part of the city, the 250-year-old building certainly knows how to flaunt its heritage: legions of tourists point their cameras at its ancient exterior before packing into the maze of atmospheric little rooms stuffed with curios and memorabilia of every description. Lunch is a mix of sandwiches and upmarket pub grub (smoked salmon and broad bean risotto, Greek salad with balsamic syrup), while dinner moves up a couple of notches for, say, steamed fillets of sea bass with smoked aubergine, sun-blush tomato and anchovy caviar and saffron potatoes ahead of chocolate nemesis with honeycomb and praline anglaise. Real ale buffs are well-served, while the serious-minded wine list bulges with heavyweight Burgundies and younger stuff from around the globe. House selections start at £12.50. **Chef/s:** William Spencer. **Open:** all week L 12 to 2.30 (12 to 1.45 Sun), Mon to Sat D 6.30 to 8.45. **Closed:** 25 Dec. **Meals:** alc (main courses L £6 to £10, D £11 to £17). **Service:** not inc. **Details:** Cards accepted. 71 seats. 52 seats outside. Separate bar. No music. Wheelchair access.

READERS RECOMMEND

The Black Rat

Modern British
88 Chesil Street, Winchester, SO23 0HX
Tel no: 01962 844465
www.theblackrat.co.uk
'Quirky menu that's pulling in the crowds'

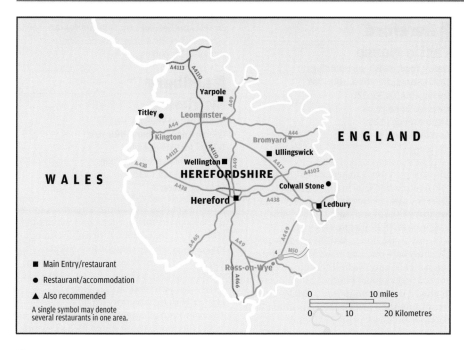

■ Colwall Stone

Colwall Park

Appealing mock-Tudor retreat
Walwyn Road, Colwall Stone, WR13 6QG
Tel no: (01684) 540000
www.colwall.com
Modern British | £32
Cooking score: 3

£5 OFF ▬

Dewy-eyed views of the glorious Malvern Hills are a feature of this smartly turned out mock-Tudor hotel, which stands amid landscaped gardens in the heart of Elgar country. Inside, pride of place goes to the impressive, oak-panelled Seasons Restaurant which comes complete with wrought-iron chandeliers dangling from its vaulted ceiling. Chef James Garth garners raw materials from near and far for an accessible menu of contemporary dishes with a few individual touches. Goosnargh duck appears as a pressed terrine with truffle dressing, herb-crusted loin of Longdon Marsh lamb comes with thyme potatoes and Mediterranean vegetables, while chargrilled Scotch beef fillet arrives on the plate with fondant potato, roast shallot, garlic and flageolet beans. Fish is also given the full treatment (seared fillet of halibut with buttered spinach, saffron potatoes and asparagus, for example) while desserts could involve rice pudding with peach and orange compote or lime and ginger crème brûlée. French bottles (from £14.95) take up the lion's share of the wine list.

Chef/s: James Garth. **Open:** all week L 12 to 2, D 7 to 9.30. **Closed:** 25 Dec D. **Meals:** alc (main courses £18 to £21.50). Set L £16.95 (2 courses) to £19.95. Bar menu available. **Service:** not inc. **Details:** Cards accepted. 40 seats. Air-con. Separate bar. No mobile phones. Wheelchair access. Music. Children's portions. Car parking.

Hereford

Castle House

Classy food, swish surroundings
Castle Street, Hereford, HR1 2NW
Tel no: (01432) 356321
www.castlehse.co.uk
Anglo-French | £35
Cooking score: 5

£5 OFF 🍷 🛏

Close to Hereford's ancient and modern tourist attractions, including its world-famous cathedral and the trendy Left Bank Village (a hip mix of shops and eating places), this Regency town house plies its trade as a seriously swish hotel. At its heart is the elegantly laid-out restaurant, where visitors can sample Claire Nicholls' exciting contemporary food. Fine local ingredients are deployed with dexterity and a feel for current trends – witness grilled smoked salmon with beetroot and black pepper jelly and horseradish bread wafers or lemon and thyme-roasted free-range chicken breast with broad beans, chorizo and sweet potato chips. Elsewhere, Hampton Bishop asparagus is partnered with langoustine, new potato and quail's egg salad, while fillet of Herefordshire beef sits comfortably with spring onion rösti, crushed peas and carrot purée. For sheer indulgence and dramatic impact, don't miss out on dessert: the kitchen conjures up temptations aplenty, from white chocolate and marshmallow parfait with dark chocolate truffle sauce to crème brûlée with a fruity combo of marinated strawberries, raspberry ice and a strawberry jam croque-monsieur. The informative international wine list cuts a broad swathe, from classic big-name Burgundies and Bordeaux to eye-popping goodies from Italy, Australia and South Africa – all at fair prices. House selections start at £14 (£3.50 a glass).
Chef/s: Claire Nicholls. **Open:** all week L 12.30 to 2, D 7 to 10. **Meals:** alc (main courses (£11 to £19). Set L Sun £24 (3 courses). Set D £49 (7 courses). **Service:** not inc. **Details:** Cards accepted. 35 seats.

35 seats outside. Air-con. Separate bar. No mobile phones. Wheelchair access. Music. Children's portions. Car parking.

Ledbury

Malthouse

Idyllic out-of-the-way setting
Church Lane, Ledbury, HR8 1DW
Tel no: (01531) 634443
www.malthouse-ledbury.co.uk
Modern British | £30
Cooking score: 3

Down a cobbled lane a little way off Ledbury's market square, this creeper-clad restaurant looks a treat in summer. A first-floor lounge makes an agreeable spot for aperitifs, the walled courtyard even more so. Ken Wilson cooks an ambitious menu that has more than a touch of country-house grandeur to it, especially in the lengthily detailed descriptions. You might start with curried John Dory tempura on spiced red lentils, pea shoots and cucumber, as a build-up to lamb chump accompanied by potato tart, Savoy cabbage, roasted roots and a rosemary-scented red wine sauce. If you're in the market for classical haute cuisine, though, there is also beef fillet glazed in blue cheese, with mushrooms, garlicky mash, spinach and a wine-rich sauce. A range of dessert wines is on offer to go with something like tonka bean pannacotta with roasted rhubarb and strawberry sorbet. Wines are a nice balance of Old and New Worlds, starting with Chilean house selections at £12.50.
Chef/s: Ken Wilson. **Open:** Sat L 12 to 1.30, Tue to Sat D 7 to 9. **Closed:** 25 Dec, 1st week of Jan. **Meals:** alc (main courses £15.75 to £19.50). Set D Tue to Thur £24.50. **Service:** not inc. **Details:** Cards accepted. 30 seats. 16 seats outside. No mobile phones. Wheelchair access. Music. Children's portions.

▌Titley

Stagg Inn
Country pub that's a cut above
Titley, HR5 3RL
Tel no: (01544) 230221
www.thestagg.co.uk
Modern British | £27
Cooking score: 5

🍾 ⊨ £30

Steve and Nicola Reynolds run a highly polished operation at the Stagg, a handsome whitewashed country inn set amid Herefordshire's rolling acres. Blow the cobwebs away with an energising hike along one of the numerous public footpaths in the locale, and work up an appetite for Steve's accomplished cooking. Expert local sourcing, particularly of meats, is the foundation of the menus, which are served with calm assurance in an atmosphere of unforced warmth. The cooking aims for deep flavours, which are brought off with aplomb, as in devilled lambs' kidneys or smoked haddock risotto to begin. A warm salad of beetroot, Perroche goats' cheese, smoked salmon and walnuts prepares the palate for the main courses, which may sound substantial but are generally well-judged. Saddle of venison with horseradish gnocchi and braised fennel provides an interesting juxtaposition of flavours, while the local beef might appear more classically with celeriac purée, dauphinoise potatoes and a red wine sauce. Fish might be carefully cooked cod in a herb jacket, with roast tomatoes and mash. Desserts are of the kind that will tempt, even if you didn't think you needed one: apricot and almond tart with local clotted cream, rhubarb jelly with ginger ice cream or a trio of crème brûlée variants that marshals vanilla, coffee and cardamom. As though all that weren't enough, there's an imaginative and fairly-priced wine list to go at. It gathers in bottles from all the major producing countries, and manages to encompass a broad spread of grape varieties. Prices open at £12.90 for a scented Torrontés from Argentina.

Chef/s: Steve Reynolds. **Open:** Tue to Sun L 12 to 2, Tue to Sat D 6.30 to 9. **Closed:** 25 and 26 Dec, 1 week in Nov, 1 week in Feb. **Meals:** alc (main courses £13.90 to £16.90). Set L Sun £15.75. **Service:** not inc. **Details:** Cards accepted. 70 seats. 20 seats outside. Separate bar. No music. No mobile phones. Children's portions. Car parking.

▌Ullingswick

Three Crowns
Modern food in the middle of nowhere
Ullingswick, HR1 3JQ
Tel no: (01432) 820279
www.threecrownsinn.com
Modern British | £26
Cooking score: 4

£5 OFF £30

In this small half-timbered and red-brick country pub set back from the single-track lane that leads from the tiny village of Ullingswick to Bleak Acre, Brent Castle cooks some surprisingly ultra-modern pub food. He may limit choice to five per course, but he scores some palpable hits with the likes of Little Hereford cheese soufflé or fried squid with butter bean salad, lemon and black pepper oil. Dishes are based on first-class raw materials, and the strength of the cooking lies in the fact that everything is freshly made from fine local and regional materials. At main course stage, slow-roasted belly of organic pork is teamed with home-made black pudding and Pommery mustard mash, while roast breast and confit leg of duck (with Hereford cider brandy and apples and peppercorns), puts the emphasis on sound technical skills and flavour. To finish, an English cheeseboard is an appealing alternative to desserts such as lemon tart with rhubarb and strawberry compote or warm chocolate fondant with Black Forest ice cream. House wine is £14.50.

Chef/s: Brent Castle. **Open:** Tue to Sun L 12 to 3, D 7 to 10. **Closed:** Mon, 25 and 26 Dec. **Meals:** Set L (not Sun) £12.95 (2 courses) to £14.95, D £26.45. **Details:** Cards accepted. 75 seats. 30 seats outside. Wheelchair access. Children's portions. Car parking.

■ Wellington

★NEW ENTRY★

The Wellington

Wellington, HR4 8AT
Tel no: (01432) 830367
www.wellingtonpub.co.uk
Gastropub | £25
Cooking score: 2

Looks can be deceiving. The austere, unprepossessing red-brick façade of the 'Welly' hides a real gem, a lively bar serving local ales and a comfortable rustic dining room where chef-patron Ross Williams delivers inventive daily menus that name check first-class ingredients sourced within ten miles of the pub. Pork comes from co-chef Chris Potts's smallholding in the village, Hereford beef and Welsh lamb from Broadfield Farm in Kinnersley and fruit and vegetables from Court Farm in nearby Tillington. Mushroom soup with tarragon pesto or chicken liver parfait with red onion marmalade make good starts, ahead of main courses such as mallard with red wine, braised Puy lentils and parsnip crisps or stuffed pork loin with sage and apple mash. Desserts include champagne rhubarb and cardamom crème brûlée or lemon tart with Dairy House clotted cream. House wine £12.50.
Chef/s: Ross Williams. **Open:** all week L 12 to 3, Tue to Sat 6 to 11 (open Sun in summer). **Closed:** Mon D, 25 Dec. **Meals:** alc (main courses £11.50 to £17). **Service:** not inc. **Details:** Cards accepted. 75 seats. 25 seats outside. Separate bar. Music. Children's portions. Car parking.

■ Yarpole

Bell Inn

Untarnished country hostelry
Green Lane, Yarpole, HR6 0BD
Tel no: (01568) 780359
www.thebellinnyarpole.co.uk
Modern British | £25
Cooking score: 2

While Claude Bosi is making waves at Hibiscus in Mayfair (see entry), his brother Cedric holds the reins at this archetypal hostelry in the Herefordshire countryside. The Bell is a pub that has stayed true to its roots, with roaring fires and real ales in the drinkers' bar, plus an old cider press in the dining room. The kitchen works to a seasonal menu with earthy bistro overtones and a liking for local produce; the Anglo-French connection shows in a fricassee of Hereford snails with garlic and parsley, Cornish hake fillet with piperade, and sirloin steak with rösti, Hampton Bishop asparagus and dijonnaise sauce. There's also some down-home pub grub in the shape of fish pie or gammon steak with parsley sauce, while desserts cement the cross-Channel partnership with everything from lemon posset to cherry clafoutis. The tidy wine list promises sound drinking from £13 (£3.15 a glass).
Chef/s: Mark Jones. **Open:** Tue to Sun L 12 to 2.30, D 6.30 to 9.30. **Closed:** Mon (exc. bank hols). **Meals:** alc (main courses £9 to £16). **Service:** not inc. **Details:** Cards accepted. 75 seats. 60 seats outside. Separate bar. No music. No mobile phones. Wheelchair access. Children's portions. Car parking.

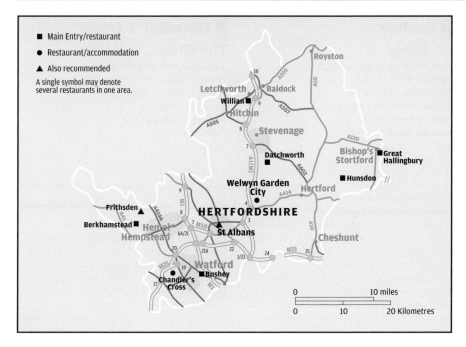

▌ **Berkhamsted**

★NEW ENTRY★
Eat Fish
Good neighbourhood fish restaurant
163-165 High Street, Berkhamsted, HP4 3HB
Tel no: (01442) 879988
www.eatfish.co.uk
Seafood | £25
Cooking score: 1

With the exception of two meat dishes, Eat
Fish heartily plunders the rivers and seas for its
menu. The increasingly popular small/large
plate option operates on many dishes here.
Expect to see hand-dived scallops with black
pudding and crispy bacon or monkfish scampi
with mixed leaves and a genuine tartare sauce,
while mains of fillet of pollock with parsnip
champ and tomato and cider chutney or fish
and chips with mushy peas are simply
conceived plates of food. Lemon posset with
orange shortbread may be a suitable way to

end the meal. Don't expect culinary fireworks
and you won't be disappointed, but full marks
for the unerring freshness of the fish and for
the extremely jolly service. House red and
white are £14 and £13 respectively.
Chef/s: Paul Sim. **Open:** all week L 12 to 3 (Sun
from 12.30), D 6 to 10 (Sun 9). **Closed:** 25 and 26
Dec, 1 Jan. **Meals:** alc (main courses £11 to £18). Set
L £9.95 (2 courses). **Service:** not inc. **Details:** Cards
accepted. 75 seats. 30 seats outside. Air-con.
Separate bar. Wheelchair access. Music. Children's
portions.

Symbols

🛏 Accommodation is available.

£30 Three courses for less than £30.

V More than five vegetarian dishes.

£5 OFF £5-off voucher scheme.

🍾 Notable wine list.

▌Bushey

St James

Contemporary neighbourhood restaurant
30 High Street, Bushey, WD2 3DN
Tel no: (020) 89502480
www.stjamesrestaurant.co.uk
Modern British | £28
Cooking score: 1

A fresh, contemporary setting with stripped floorboards, exposed brick walls and bold sections of red and white paintwork, St James is 'small enough to be intimate but large enough not to feel intimidated'. Reporters are quick to praise the knowledgeable waiting staff, while the cooking is described as 'consistently good' and 'excellent value'. Fish and seafood make a good showing, for example grilled tiger prawns with leek and asparagus risotto and prawn bisque followed by an open seared-salmon coulibiac with spinach butter sauce. Other choices range from a starter of Moroccan lamb and feta in filo pastry with spicy tomato relish to classic rack of lamb with a herb crust, boulangère potatoes, sautéed greens and a red wine and shallot jus. Finish with a fresh fruit platter and sorbet or sinful Toblerone cheesecake. Wines from £9.95.

Chef/s: Simon Trussell. **Open:** all week L 12.30 to 2.30, D 6.30 to 9.30. **Closed:** bank hols. **Meals:** alc (main courses £16.05 to £25.95), Set L £14.95, Set D £16.95 (2 courses). **Details:** Cards accepted. Air-con. Separate bar. No mobile phones. Wheelchair access. Music. Car parking.

▌Chandler's Cross

The Grove, Colette's

Ambitious, extravagant cooking
Chandler's Cross, WD3 4TG
Tel no: (01923) 296015
www.thegrove.co.uk
Modern European | £54
Cooking score: 3

The Grade II–listed mansion, formerly the country seat of the Earls of Clarendon, has extensive grounds and facilities include a golf course, spa and several restaurants. Collette's is the chandeliered and softly coloured gastronomic flagship. Christopher Warrick heads the kitchen and his menu showcases a series of intricate and complex dishes. While technical capacity is clear – best end of Lighthorne lamb paired with sweetbreads and a light ragoût of broad beans is robust but not overpowering – and breads, amuse-bouche and petits fours are commendable, this ambitious kitchen tries too hard to impress and does not always know which flavour to omit. At inspection, scallops arrived with boudin noir, fried pain perdu, buttered Hispi cabbage and Lisbon onions, all finished off with a sweet and sour jus. The sheer quantity of flavours overwhelmed the shellfish. Service, however, is assured and charming and the wine list an adequate partner to the food, with quality representation from the Old World and helpful tasting notes. Prices start from £24.

Chef/s: Christopher Warrick. **Open:** Tue to Sat D 7 to 9.30 (and Sun D on bank hols). **Closed:** Sun (except bank hols), Mon. **Meals:** alc (£49 for 2 courses, £54 for 3 courses). **Service:** 12.5%. **Details:** Cards accepted. 45 seats. Air-con. Separate bar. Wheelchair access. Car parking.

▮ Datchworth

The Tilbury

A convivial oasis
Watton Road, Datchworth, SG3 6TB
Tel no: (01438) 815550
www.thetilbury.co.uk
Gastropub | £27
Cooking score: 4

£5 OFF £30

'Quite simply – good honest food' states Paul Bloxham's menu, emphasising a commitment to local produce that has earned the TV chef a loyal following at this relaxed pub in the heart of a rural Hertfordshire village. Refurbishment of the Tilbury has been sympathetic, blending old wood, rough brick walls and open fires with contemporary touches. Drinkers are not neglected and it makes a convivial oasis. In the kitchen seasonality is all. Dishes tend to be refreshingly straightforward with clean, clear flavours that speak of themselves: local wild mushrooms on toast with béarnaise, say, and mains of pancetta-wrapped rabbit pie teamed with carrots and wholegrain mustard, or chargrilled rib-eye with chips and Café de Paris butter that's all about a hunk of beefy, grass-fed meat. Desserts, too, garner praise – vanilla pannacotta with red wine-poached rhubarb and shortbread or a pear and almond tarte fine with raspberry jam. House wine is £14.50.
Chef/s: Paul Bloxham and Ben Crick. **Open:** Tue to Sun L 12 to 3, Tue to Sat D 6 to 9. **Closed:** 25 and 26 Dec, 1 Jan. **Meals:** Set L £12.95 (2 courses) to £15.95. **Service:** not inc. **Details:** Cards accepted. 70 seats. 40 seats outside. Wheelchair access. Music. Children's portions. Car parking.

Readers recommend

A 'readers recommend' review is a genuine quote from a report sent in by one of our readers. We intend to follow up these suggestions throughout the year to come.

▮ Frithsden

ALSO RECOMMENDED

▲ Alford Arms

Frithsden, HP1 3DD
Tel no: (01442) 864480
www.alfordarmsfrithsden.co.uk
Gastropub

A buzzing honeypot hostelry in the depths of Ashridge Estate (National Trust), this on-the-money Chiltern gastropub scores with its generous food. The place is upping its green credentials, and seasonal menus now tick most of the local and organic boxes. 'Small plates' such as potted ham with maple pears (£6) might precede braised Chiltern lamb hotpot (£11.75) or sea bass Kiev on confit vine tomatoes with cauliflower and watercress purée. To finish, treacle tart with lemongrass crème fraîche sounds enticing. Around 30 all-European wines, plus a smattering from English vineyards; prices from £14.50 (£3.75 a glass). Open all week.

▮ Great Hallingbury

Anton's Restaurant

Exceptional value
Great Hallingbury Manor, Great Hallingbury, CM22 7TJ
Tel no: (01279) 506475
www.greathallingburymanor.com
Modern British | £40
Cooking score: 4

Anton Edelman brings his name and executive chef skills to Great Hallingbury Manor. He chose well – handy for Stansted Airport yet in an idyllic lakeside setting, the sleek bar eliding into a contemporary garden restaurant where you can watch the chefs at work through a strip window. Top-quality fish and meat, locally sourced, are elegantly handled, and flexibility and value for money are the name of the game – choose just one course or a full meal from the weekly-changing, gently-priced menus. Pea soup with garlic and smoked bacon froth is an inventive

variation of an old staple, while the special starter of the day might be tender, super-fresh razor clam with garlic, finely diced breadcrumbs and tomato. The 'Hatfield Heath' stuffed saddle of rabbit, with its ragoût and fresh tagliatelle, makes a great dinner dish, while trencherman appetites will be sated by rib-eye of beef with home-made chips and béarnaise sauce. On a hot day in June, one reporter found the gazpacho of summer fruits with mint sorbet to be a perfect finale. Service is 'warm and responsive', and wines are fairly priced with 14 good choices by-the-glass.
Chef/s: Anton Edelman and Martin Nesbit. **Open:** Sun to Fri L 12 to 3, Mon to Sat D 7 to 9.30. **Closed:** Sat L and Sun D. **Meals:** alc (main courses £9.50 to £18.50). Set menu £14.50 (2 courses) to £17.50. **Service:** 10% (optional). **Details:** Cards accepted. 70 seats. Air-con. Wheelchair access. Music. Children allowed. Car parking.

Hunsdon

Fox & Hounds
Born-again local pub
2 High Street, Hunsdon, SG12 8NH
Tel no: (01279) 843999
www.foxandhounds-hunsdon.co.uk
Gastropub | £25
Cooking score: 2
£5 OFF | £30

Revamped in the best possible taste, this one-time local boozer hasn't strayed far from its original purpose as a busy watering hole, but it now also wins friends as a country pub restaurant of the best sort. Chef/landlord James Rix learned his trade in trendy London addresses including the Cow Dining Room (see entry), and he brings a sure touch to business in the kitchen. Lunch and dinner menus change daily, ideas come thick and fast and there's no stinting on the generosity. Starters of sautéed duck hearts with peas and broad beans or a salad of Berkswell cheese, radishes and organic leaves set the tone, before grilled swordfish with cockle and mussel minestrone or roast loin of Essex Pig Co. Old Spot with warm lentil, spinach and mustard salad. Desserts are palate-pleasing standards

like treacle tart with clotted cream, and the easy-going wine list has plenty of decent drinking from £16.25 (£3.95 a glass).
Chef/s: James Rix. **Open:** Tue to Sun L 12 to 2.45, D Tue to Sat 6.30 to 9.30. **Closed:** Mon, 26 Dec, 1 Jan and Tue after bank hols. **Meals:** alc (main courses £12 to £17.50). Set L £12.50, Set D £13.50. **Service:** 10% (optional). **Details:** Cards accepted. 80 seats. 40 seats outside. Separate bar. Wheelchair access. Music. Children's portions. Car parking.

St Albans

ALSO RECOMMENDED
▲ Darcys
2 Hatfield Road, St Albans, AL1 3RP
Tel no: (01727) 730777
www.darcysrestaurant.co.uk
Modern European

Visitors love the 'relaxed and intimate' atmosphere at this smart contemporary restaurant close to the centre of St Albans. There's a 'real fusion of flavours', ranging from hoisin duck pancakes (£14 for 2) and salt-and-pepper squid, to grilled kangaroo with game chips and Moroccan-style lamb cutlets (£16). Banoffee and chocolate cookie sandwich (£5.50) or unusual cocktail desserts make a good finish. House wine is £13.50. Open all week.

Welwyn Garden City

Auberge du Lac
Grand country showpiece
Brocket Hall, Welwyn Garden City, AL8 7XG
Tel no: (01707) 368888
www.brocket-hall.co.uk
Modern French | £55
Cooking score: 5

Set amid the lavish grounds of Brocket Hall estate, Auberge du Lac is certainly not intimidated by its surroundings. The building itself – a former hunting lodge – now puts on a grand show as a hospitality venue for all seasons, complete with splendid waterside views over an ornamental lake. Phil Thompson continues to fine-tune his culinary style, creating dishes that are complex, overtly modern French and emphatically seasonal. A spring meal might begin with a risotto of creamed garlic, madeira-braised snails, wild garlic leaf and parsley foam or seared yellow fin tuna with pomelo grapefruit and radish salad with an exotic 'Siam vinaigrette'. Young nettles from the estate could show up as a garnish for fillet of line-caught sea bass with 'fork-rolled' gnocchi and mustard-glazed ham, while beetroot and horseradish offer bold support to slow-roast sirloin of British Excellence beef and salt-beef croustillant. Desserts might wow the senses with high-impact visual wizardry (chocolate liqueur parfait with pistachio cream, golden raisins and nougatine) or provide cleansing citrus refreshment (Muscat jelly with orange compote and fresh orange foam). Seek counsel from the sommelier if you want to navigate your way through the gold-standard 700-bin wine list: Champagnes and premium French vintages loom large, but there is plenty to suit all palates and pockets. Prices start at around £25, with light relief in the shape of plentiful selections by-the-glass (from £5.50).

Chef/s: Phil Thompson. **Open:** Tue to Sun L 12 to 3, Tue to Sat D 7 to 10.30. **Closed:** Mon. **Meals:** Set L £29.50 to £37.50, Set D £55 (3 courses) to £75 (7 courses). **Service:** 10% (optional). **Details:** Cards accepted. 70 seats. 50 seats outside. Air-con. Separate bar. No mobile phones. Wheelchair access. Music. Children's portions. Car parking.

Willian

The Fox

Surefire cooking in a stylish hamlet pub
Willian, SG6 2AE
Tel no: (01462) 480233
www.foxatwillian.co.uk
Gastropub | £25
Cooking score: 2

V

Affable service and consistent output from the kitchen is what the Fox is all about. Situated in the micro-village of Willian, the pub is an oasis in an area bereft of decent places to eat and the zeal Cliff Nye and his team lavish on the place is tangible. It's popular, too, so booking is advisable. Start with grilled sardines paired with a punchy caper and tomato salsa, or half a dozen spanking fresh Brancaster oysters, harvested from the beds near sister eatery the White Horse at Brancaster Staithe (see entry, Norfolk). Mains, bolstered by a handful of chef's specials, may offer a rose-pink herb-crusted rack of lamb with polenta and ratatouille, or perhaps roasted belly of pork with apple purée and roasted parsnips. To finish, home-made doughnuts with rhubarb compote and vanilla pastry cream or a cherry and Amaretto cheesecake are more than adequate. The wine list offers a decent spread of global names and the house red and white pitch in at £10.80.

Chef/s: Hari Kodagoda. **Open:** all week L 12 to 2 (3 Sun). Mon to Fri D 6.45 to 9.15, Sat D 6.30 to 9.30. **Meals:** alc (main courses £9 to £16.50). **Service:** No inc. **Details:** Cards accepted. 65 seats. 16 seats outside. Air-con. Separate bar. No mobile phones. Wheelchair access. Children's portions. Car parking.

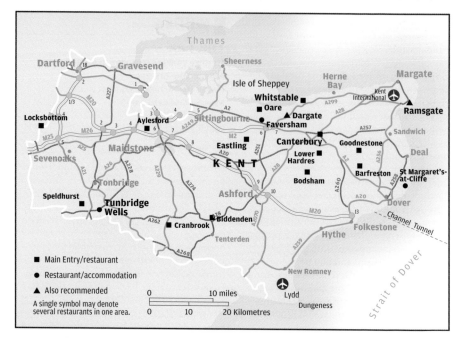

▋Aylesford

Hengist

Ancient setting, modern French cooking
7-9 High Street, Aylesford, ME20 7AX
Tel no: (01622) 719273
www.hengistrestaurant.co.uk
Modern French | £30
Cooking score: 3

Aylsford is reputed to be one of the oldest villages in England, but as far as Hengist is concerned Ye Olde Englande stops at the door. Owned by the team behind Thackeray's in Tunbridge Wells (see entry), with chef Jean-Marc Zanetti at the stove, expect a modern French menu in pared-back surroundings with lots of contemporary touches. Local and regional materials play a role, say buttered Kentish asparagus served with grilled Capricorn goats' cheese and aged balsamic dressing or rump of new season's Romney Marsh lamb teamed with summer vegetable ratatouille, caramelised red onions and lamb mint sauce. An assiette of chocolate – fondant, white chocolate ice cream, milk chocolate and praline tart – is an indulgent way to finish. There has been praise for the good-value lunch deal and for the 'unflappable' staff. Plenty of good drinking under £25 is to be had on the French-dominated wine list, opening with house Australian at £13.95 and a baker's dozen by-the-glass.

Chef/s: Jean-Marc Zanetti. **Open:** Tue to Sun L 12 to 2.30, Tue to Sat D 6.30 to 10.30. **Closed:** Sun D, Mon. **Meals:** Set L £10.95 to £12.95. set D £15.95 to £19.95. **Service:** 10%. **Details:** Cards accepted. 70 seats. 10 seats outside. Air-con. Separate bar. Wheelchair access. Music. Children's portions. Car parking.

Barfreston

The Yew Tree
Food and wine top of the agenda
Barfreston, CT15 7JH
Tel no: (01304) 831000
www.yewtree.info
Gastropub | £25
Cooking score: 4

 £30

Here's a place to test the mettle of your Sat Nav. Found down narrow Kentish lanes, just seven miles from Dover, this pretty country pub now puts food and wine top of the agenda. A table-filled terrace leads into an intimate bar – serving local real ales – while an up-to-date style of wooden floorboards and undressed tables typifies the look in the light dining room. Ben Williams used to be head pastry chef at The Square in London (see entry) and while his cooking here is less intricate (and prices commensurately lower), a certain level of high-gloss proficiency is not lacking. His menus keep things within sensible bounds, however, and are built around carefully considered combinations such as a textbook onion tarte Tatin or a soft-boiled duck egg with smoked eel 'soldiers'. Asparagus, broad beans and peas make congenial partners for a main course of new season's Kentish lamb, sauced with red wine, or there may be roasted sea bream with crushed new potatoes, Thai-spiced shellfish and vegetable spaghetti. Finish with vanilla rice pudding and poached rhubarb. Service is friendly and efficient. The wide-ranging wine list, compiled by business partner and wine merchant Ben Bevan, concentrates on quality without showiness or fanfares. Bottles are picked with total assurance and an eye for value at every level. Prices start at £12.50.
Chef/s: Ben Williams. **Open:** all week L 12 to 3 (Sun 4), Mon to Sat D 7 to 9. **Meals:** alc (main courses £10 to £16). Set L Mon to Fri £9.95 (2 courses).
Service: not inc. **Details:** Cards accepted. 38 seats. 32 seats outside. Separate bar. Wheelchair access. Children's portions. Car parking.

Biddenden

West House
28 High Street, Biddenden, TN27 8AH
Tel no: (01580) 291341
www.thewesthouserestaurant.co.uk
Modern European | £30
Cooking score: 5

A heavily beamed, sixteenth-century former weaver's cottage in the centre of a Weald village, the West House mixes stylishly-restrained décor with some assured cooking. Graham Garrett's regularly changing menus are appealing and concise. An allegiance to local produce ensures seasonality, while foraged foods often pepper the menu; look out for chickweed, wild sorrel, wild garlic and hogweed. The contemporary cooking is big on clear, clean flavours and textures: nettle soup with spiced langoustine, say, or ham hock terrine with pea cream and slow-cooked hen's egg. Then, maybe, 'a brilliant pairing' of Old Spot pork belly with roast scallop and coconut, or baked shoulder and breast of Romney Marsh lamb with ewes'-milk cheese, potato purée and broad beans. High standards extend to desserts such as coffee pannacotta paired with liquorice ice cream and tiramisù foam. Breads and a smooth-textured chicken liver parfait appetiser have also been praised, while the Francophile wine list is several cuts above the average; mark-ups are fair and start with £14.95 vin de pays. Do note that booking is essential at this very personally run restaurant. Casual visitors have reported finding it inexplicably closed, or being turned away at the door ('and it wasn't even late, or full').
Chef/s: Graham Garrett. **Open:** Tue to Fri L 12 to 1.45, Tue to Sat D 7 to 9 (10 Fri and Sat), Sun L 12 to 2.30. **Closed:** Christmas, New Year, 2 weeks summer. **Meals:** Set L £21 (2 courses) to £24, set D £29.50. **Service:** 12.5 % (optional). **Details:** Cards accepted. 32 seats. Separate bar. Wheelchair access. Children's portions. Car parking.

Chris Lee Bildeston Crown

Why did you become a chef?
I started as a kitchen porter, was fascinated in what the chefs were cooking and asked if I could become a chef.

What three ingredients could you not do without?
Lobster, mirepoix, truffles.

What is the most unusual cookery book you've come across in your life?
El Bulli 1998-2002.

What's the most unusual ingredient you've cooked or eaten?
Chicken comb and testicals.

What's your guilty food pleasure?
KFC.

What won't you tolerate in the kitchen?
Whistling. It's a kitchen, not a building site.

What did it mean to be awarded the up-and-coming chef award in The Good Food Guide 2008?
It was fantastic! Not only for me, but also the hotel and restaurant.

Bodsham
Froggies at the Timber Batts
Traditional pub, classic French food
School Lane, Bodsham, TN25 5JQ
Tel no: (01233) 750237
www.thetimberbatts.co.uk
Gastropub | £30
Cooking score: 1

France meets Kent at this off-the-beaten track pub on the North Downs where beams and open fires are matched by food that wears a striped jersey and a beret. The cooking may not be innovative but ingredients are fresh and locally sourced. All the usual suspects such as French onion soup, duck leg confit and beef bourguignon are present and correct, but there are also good things like stuffed mussels and roasted rack of Romney Marsh lamb. Locally shot game gets a good showing, and there's simpler pub food such as first-class egg and chips served alongside croque-monsieur in the bar. An (almost) all-French wine list opens with house wines at £15, produced by the owner's cousin in the Loire Valley. Good real ales, too.
Chef/s: Joel Gross. **Open:** all week L 12 to 2.30, Mon to Sat D 7 to 9.30. **Closed:** 1 week Christmas.
Meals: Set Sun L £23. **Service:** not inc.
Details: Cards accepted. 50 seats. 40 seats outside. Separate bar. Children's portions. Car parking.

Canterbury
ABode Canterbury
Modern boutique hotel dining
High Street, Canterbury, CT1 2RX
Tel no: (01227) 766266
www.abodehotels.co.uk
Modern European | £40
Cooking score: 4

🛏 V

Part of Michael Caines' growing chain of boutique hotels, ABode Canterbury occupies what was once the city's County Hotel. Restorations have made a feature of the old beams, but the overall look is one of please-all modernity; think calming neutral shades, unobtrusive modern art and capacious sofas. The Michael Caines restaurant is one of several dining options at the hotel. With Mark Rossi in the kitchen, it turns out gently modish cooking along modern European lines. Good but modestly proportioned dishes from the lunch menu have included leek soup with smoked eel, guinea fowl with ham hock beignet and broad beans, and mango and pineapple brochette on lemongrass skewers with passion-fruit ice cream. An evening meal might take in pan-fried foie gras with lamb's lettuce, orange, candied walnuts and spiced Matusalem rum jus followed by hake and lobster with mangetout, shiitake mushrooms, saffron onion purée and lobster hollandaise sauce. Impressive trimmings could include canapés, 'fantastic' breads and a taster of mushroom and hazelnut broth. While Rossi's skill is indisputable, the front-of-house team can appear 'poorly trained', and one visitor found it hard to tell who was in command. On the plus side, there is a substantial wine list comprising 188 bins divided by grape type. Bottles start at £17.50.

Chef/s: Mark Rossi. **Open:** all week L 12 to 2.30, Mon to Sat D 7 to 10. **Meals:** alc D (main courses £21.50 to £26.95), Set L £15 (2 courses) to £19.50 (3 courses). **Service:** 10%. **Details:** Cards accepted. 74 seats. Air-con. Separate bar. No music. No mobile phones. Wheelchair access. Children's portions. Car parking.

Goods Shed
Championing fresh local supplies
Station Road West, Canterbury, CT2 8AN
Tel no: (01227) 459153
Modern British | £32
Cooking score: 1

The Goods Shed should be one of the benchmarks by which other places in this diminutive cathedral city are judged. It has a great location, a quirky atmosphere and it laudably champions local produce. However its performance is erratic. In the no-frills, simple raised section overlooking the permanent farmer's market, big windows give views of trains pulling into Canterbury West

station. Fresh local supplies (many bought from the market) energise the menu from day to day. Blackboards are scrawled with calendar-correct offerings. In early June, for example, there could be gazpacho soup, crab, Armagnac and saffron tart, or rabbit and pork terrine to start, followed by lamb shank with chickpeas and aïoli, while hake can appear teamed with brown shrimp and either sea spinach or wood sorrel. Our questionnaire was not returned, so some of the information below may have changed.

Chef/s: Rafael Lopez. **Open:** Tue to Sun L 12 to 2.30 (3 Sat and Sun), Tue to Sat D 6 to 9.30. **Closed:** 25 and 26 Dec, 1 Jan. **Meals:** alc (man courses £10 to £18). **Service:** not inc. **Details:** Cards accepted. 80 seats. Children's portions. Car parking.

Cranbrook

Apicius
Modest restaurant, big statement cooking
23 Stone Street, Cranbrook, TN17 3HE
Tel no: (01580) 714666
www.restaurant-apicius.co.uk
Modern European | £30
Cooking score: 6

On the main street running through Cranbrook this intimate restaurant is a prime destination, attracting faithful regulars through its high standards, professionalism and warmth. Tim Johnson showcases fine raw materials, many of them local, on his short, set-priced menus and a high degree of technical competence suffuses everything. Roast scallops (in a smoked-bacon brochette) are timed to a nicety, their juicy sweetness pointed by the bacon and a slick of light vanilla cream, while a main course brill with roasted artichokes, garlic, tomatoes and white onion purée is 'really meaty and devastatingly fresh', the timing and technique effortlessly passing muster. Robustness characterises other dishes: a starter of 'three lovely lamb faggots' with pea purée and tomato jus, or a main course of 'perfect, tender' roast squab pigeon on Puy lentils with pommes mousseline and a little jug of foie gras sauce. Similarly, desserts are not afraid to mobilise challenging juxtapositions, as in a well thought-out roasted banana and liquorice caramel pannacotta with a 'stunning' lavender granita, or three ways with apple – the sweetness of the Tatin and cider cream anchored by a sharp-tasting green apple sorbet. A carefully considered wine list offers good value. Prices start at £17.

Chef/s: Tim Johnson. **Open:** Wed to Fri and Sun L 12 to 2, Tue to Sat D 7 to 9. **Closed:** 2 weeks at Christmas, Easter, summer. **Meals:** L £22 (2 courses) to £26, D £25 (2 courses) to £29.50. **Service:** 12.5% (optional). **Details:** Cards accepted. Wheelchair access.

▎Dargate

ALSO RECOMMENDED
▲ Dove

Plum Pudding Lane, Dargate, ME13 9HB
Tel no: (01227) 751360
Gastropub

The address suggests picture-postcard Olde England, as befits the old village pub, but the posh-plated, smart restaurant-style cooking is at odds with the scuffed floorboards, simple wooden tables and very casual service. Corn-fed chicken and foie gras terrine with Armagnac prunes (£6.25) and fillet of sea bass with brown shrimp and confit of red peppers (£16.95) are well-prepared, if pricey, à la carte offerings. Go for lunch and look to the blackboard for confit duck and bavette of beef (both £10) or generously filled baguettes. House wine £14. Closed Sun D and all Mon. Reports please.

▎Eastling

★NEW ENTRY★
Carpenter's Arms

Quality ingredients and cooking impress
The Street, Eastling, ME13 0AZ
Tel no: (01795) 890234
Gastropub | £22
Cooking score: 4

The Carpenter's Arms stands well off the beaten track down narrow Kentish lanes, portraying its age with beams, low ceilings, exposed timbers and inglenooks. It's comfortable, cosy and soothing, the setting for food that stretches well beyond the usual pub standard. Simon Wills's cooking deals in often simple, straightforward ideas, yet with an intelligent streak – as in deep-fried pig's cheek with tartare sauce, or sea trout served on a wild garlic bubble and squeak with aïoli. Much of the food runs along familiar lines, taking in potted crab and a gutsy beef shin, bacon and claret pie, its everyman appeal also striking a balance between the richness of a text book cassoulet (homage to time spent in Parisian brasseries) and the comfort of a smoked haddock pie with a potato and cheese crust. Excellent bread has made a similar positive impression, while classy desserts have featured a blood orange jelly with burnt cream. House wine is £11.

Chef/s: Simon Wills. **Open:** Tue to Sun L 12 to 2, Tue to Sat D 7 to 9. **Closed:** 1 week Jan. **Meals:** alc (main courses £11 to £12.50). **Service:** not inc.
Details: Cards accepted. 30 seats. 20 seats outside. Separate bar. No music. Children's portions. Car parking.

▌Faversham

Dining Room at the Railway Hotel

Sharply focused modern cooking
Preston Street, Faversham, ME13 8PE
Tel no: (01795) 533173
www.railwayhotelfaversham.co.uk
Modern British | £34
Cooking score: 4

At first sight this solid red brick building opposite Faversham station looks like a 'grotty mid nineteenth-century station pub'. On closer examination, all the old features have been well restored and the old-fashioned bar is worth a look. The separate dining room makes a comfortable and pleasantly decorated setting for Anthony North and Jonny Butterfield's sharply focused modern cooking, which is powered by a prodigious talent for sourcing prime raw materials, mostly locally sourced or foraged. Thus dishes on the short-choice, monthly-changing menu are seasonally aware, with an early spring dinner featuring Bluey's scallops in a salad with prawns, foraged leaves and blood orange and chilli, and Hollowshore huss with foraged pesto, purées of onion and squash and beetroot dressing. At its best, the food is boldly innovative without being disconnected or outlandish, and while some combinations may raise eyebrows (seared grey mullet with grilled sweet potatoes, spicy teriyaki and coconut foam), ideas really do work on the plate. However, not everything is quite so eccentric – note rib-eye of beef with cheese and onion mash and roast garlic mushrooms. Bread and accompanying vegetables are well-reported, desserts can include an unusual carrot cake with carrot crisps and carrot and caramel purée, and staff are 'knowledgeable and thoughtful'. The pub is part of Shepherd Neame, and the brewery-supplied wine list opens at £12.50.
Chef/s: Anthony North and Jonny Butterfield. **Open:** Wed to Sun L 12.30 to 2.30 (Sun 3), Wed to Sat D 7 to 9. **Closed:** Mon and Tue. **Meals:** alc (main courses £13 to £16.50). Set L £18 (2 courses) to £20. **Service:** not inc. **Details:** Cards accepted. 40 seats. Separate bar. Children's portions. Car parking.

Read's

Pedigree country restaurant
Macknade Manor, Canterbury Road, Faversham, ME13 8XE
Tel no: (01795) 535344
www.reads.com
Modern British | £52
Cooking score: 6
£5 OFF ♦ 🛏

Before crossing the threshold of this 'lovely building' one can tell this restaurant-with-rooms is a place of serious intent and high standards, for the gardens are beautifully kept. They also contribute some of the kitchen's fine vegetables – ingredients are the defining element here – and the menu, too, is appealing, with presentation as spot-on as the youthful service. David Pitchford's technical skills are impressive; he likes to keep things simple, using careful balance and pretty much faultless composition to make an impact. And make an impact he does. Witness a lunch that began with the simplicity of sautéed soft herring roes on toast and rich chicken liver parfait. Flavours were then built up robustly in main courses, partnering crispy pork belly with black cabbage, honey-roasted turnips and apple purée, and thornback ray with rocket, gherkins and caperberry dressing. Dinner has brought praise for Mongomery Cheddar soufflé on smoked haddock in a creamed sauce, and pan-fried red mullet with leaf spinach, pan-roasted potatoes and a Seville orange and thyme sauce. Attentive effort pays off in fine desserts, too, such as a dark chocolate tart with its crisp pastry and prune and Armagnac ice cream. The impressive, extensive wine list is high on quality and generously inclusive outside France, which remains, however, its main port of call. 'Best Buys' offer a useful, edited version for those on a budget. House wines are £16.

Tap water

It's often the simplest things that cause us consternation, and water is a common bugbear. Current concerns surround three themes: tap, taste and cost.

'Tap' is simple enough. In responding to a request for tap water an establishment is meeting a legal requirement and should do so gracefully. Scowling, 'forgetting' or illegally refusing are signs of poor service, which is totally unacceptable.

Taste is more complex. While the majority of mineral waters are largely indistinguishable from their filtered counterparts, some spa waters listed on much-mocked 'water menus' do have a unique taste. However, as these flavours can be unusual and are positively disliked by many, these products are often better enjoyed on their own rather than with food.

Cost is the greatest bugbear. All liquids served in restaurants incur a massive mark up. But the industry suffers from notoriously precarious margins and these sales shore-up the finances. Restaurants have to pay their way and we do too. Insisting on cheaper water could lead to higher-priced starters or the unwelcome return of the cover charge. One way or another, there's always a price to be paid for fine dining.

A price not worth paying is that of the environmental consequences of the packaged water industry. Bottled water is the gas guzzler of the dining room. Shifting a heavy product in heavy packaging from increasingly remote places is unsustainable. So, ultimately, it's the cost to the planet not to the pocket that should make us think twice when responding to the waiter's refrain 'still or sparkling?'.

Chef/s: David Pitchford and Ricky Martin. **Open:** Tue to Sat L 12 to 2, D 7 to 9.30. **Closed:** 25 and 26 Dec. **Meals:** Set L £24, set D £52. **Service:** not inc. **Details:** Cards accepted. 40 seats. 12 seats outside. No music. Wheelchair access. Children's portions. Car parking.

▌Goodnestone
Fitzwalter Arms
The hub of village life
The Street, Goodnestone, CT3 1PJ
Tel no: (01304) 840303
Gastropub | £23
Cooking score: 2

 £5 OFF £30

The Fitzwalter Arms is the hub of village life, attracting both locals and tourists visiting the gardens of neighbouring Godmersham Park, while its no-nonsense simplicity extends to a rustic daily menu that seldom misses a beat. With around five dishes per course, each usually a demonstration of loyalty to fresh local produce, the food is rough round the edges – nothing fey – but cooked with intelligence and care. Brawn with parsley, red onion and caper salad, for example, then black bream fillet with squid and gremolada, are appealing choices, or there could be a richly flavoured, traditional coq au vin, locally reared pork or seasonal game. Treacle tart and raw Jersey cream makes a good finish. House wine is £11.95.
Chef/s: David Hart and Dominic O'Sullivan. **Open:** Mon & Wed to Sun L 12 to 2 (Sun 2.30), Mon & Wed to Sat D 7 to 9. **Closed:** 25 Dec, 1 Jan. **Meals:** alc (main courses £10.50 to £18.50). **Service:** not inc. **Details:** Cards accepted. 24 seats. 20 seats outside. Separate bar. Music. Children's portions.

Readers recommend

A 'readers recommend' review is a genuine quote from a report sent in by one of our readers. We intend to follow up these suggestions throughout the year to come.

▌Locksbottom
Chapter One
Refined food at unbeatable prices
Farnborough Common, Locksbottom, BR6 8NF
Tel no: (01689) 854848
www.chaptersrestaurants.co.uk
Modern European | £30
Cooking score: 5

Housed in a striking mock-Tudor building that has become a landmark for local foodies, Chapter One is now sitting pretty after an extensive refurbishment. Visitors will notice a new bar fashioned from German alabaster and volcanic rock, cream and chocolate colours with splashes of dark red in the dining room, plus bespoke photographs on the walls. The setting may be suburban Kent, but Andrew McLeish's food should strike a chord with City commuters (or others) used to the gastronomic ways of the metropolis: expect high levels of accomplishment, married with a penchant for in-vogue ingredients and sophisticated gestures. Escabèche of red mullet with warm ratte potato salad, pomelo and parsley water might set the tone, before halibut poached at 50°C with cockle and winkle provençale or rump of Kentish lamb with braised navarin, purple artichokes, tomato jus and bagna cauda. Dishes often come with neat embellishments (cranberries, mushrooms, truffle mayonnaise and roasted apples with a pressed rabbit and foie gras terrine), and meals peak with dazzling desserts such as organic lemon tart with crème fraîche sorbet and passion-fruit mille-feuille. As readers are keen to point out, all of this comes at prices that are refreshingly modest given the quality on offer. France leads the pack on the pedigree wine list, although elite names from elsewhere also feature prominently. Prices start at £14.50 (£3.75).
Chef/s: Andrew McLeish. **Open:** all week L 12 to 2.30 (3 Sun), D 6.30 to 10.30 (9 Sun). **Closed:** first few days Jan. **Meals:** Set L Mon to Sat £18 (3 courses), Set D £29.50. **Service:** 12.5% (optional). **Details:** Cards accepted. 110 seats. 20 seats outside. Air-con. Separate bar. Wheelchair access. Music. Children's portions. Car parking.

Lower Hardres

Granville

Country pub with a laid back ambience
Street End, Lower Hardres, CT4 7AL
Tel no: (01227) 700402
Gastropub | £27
Cooking score: 4

Spacious and comfortable with a laid back
ambience, this solid country pub is well
matched by a thoughtful blackboard menu
that eschews culinary somersaults in favour of
a bedrock of well-executed modern British
ideas. The kitchen relies on a network of local
suppliers, but the repertoire is wider in scope,
with prosciutto and artichokes rubbing
shoulders with a never-off-the-menu crispy
duck, smoked chilli salsa and sour cream.
Descriptions are refreshingly to-the-point,
producing on one dreary winter's day hearty
garlic and thyme-roasted mushrooms on
tapenade toast, then braised pork belly with
crackling and apple sauce. Fish may be
handled quite robustly, too, as when a whole
gilthead bream is stuffed with garlic and
rosemary and served with purple sprouting
broccoli and roast potatoes. There's also a good
home-made foccacia and desserts such as a
'perfect' flourless chocolate cake. Drinkers
have their own bar and there's a blackboard
wine list with reasonable choice. House wines
start at £11.50. Related to the Sportsman at
Seasalter, Whitstable, (see entry).
Chef/s: Jim Shave, Ezra Gaynor and Tony Rosier.
Open: Tue to Sun L 12 to 2, Tue to Sat D 7 to 9.
Closed: 25 and 26 Dec. **Meals:** alc (main courses
£11.95 to £18.95). **Service:** not inc. **Details:** Cards
accepted. 55 seats. 40 seats outside. Separate bar.
Music. Children's portions. Car parking.

Average price

The average price listed in main-entry
reviews denotes the price of a three-
course meal, without wine.

Oare

★NEW ENTRY★
Three Mariners

Fuss-free approach to British food
2 Church Road, Oare, ME13 0QA
Tel no: (01795) 533633
www.thethreemarinersoare.co.uk
Gastropub | £20
Cooking score: 3

Set in a village of creeks and boats, this down-
to-earth seventeenth-century pub is in tip-
top condition at the moment. It still lives up to
its title, dispensing Shepheard Neame ales and
pub hospitality, but it also takes a fuss-free
approach to British food. The comfort food
menu is short, a focal point for the best of local
produce, and execution is generally on-the-
money: leek and celeriac soup, say, or soft
herring roes on toast. Fish from local day-
boats could produce skate cheeks on rocket
purée with wild garlic salad, while a main
course of roasted duck breast is served with a
rich potato gratin and spring cabbage mixed
with shredded duck confit. Home-made
bread is good, and sticky toffee pudding,
rhubarb crumble and lemon cheesecake have
all had the thumbs up, as has the sheer value
for money. Staff, too, are a delight. House
wine is £12.
Chef/s: John O'Riordan. **Open:** Wed to Sun L 12 to 3
(Sun 4), D 6 to 9.30. **Closed:** Mon and Tue.
Meals: alc (main courses £10 to £14). Set L (Wed to
Fri) £10. **Service:** not inc. **Details:** Cards accepted.
50 seats. 25 seats outside. Separate bar. Music.
Children's portions. Car parking.

Orpington

READERS RECOMMEND
Vero

Italian
332 High Street, Orpington, BR6 0NQ
Tel no: 01689 821561
http://www.vero-restaurant.co.uk
'Good-value neighbourhood Italian'

Ramsgate

ALSO RECOMMENDED
▲ Surin
30 Harbour Street, Ramsgate, CT11 8HA
Tel no: (01843) 592001
www.surinrestaurant.co.uk
Thai

Named after chef/owner Damrong Garbutt's home town in Thailand, this cosy restaurant down by Ramsgate harbour remains a firm local favourite. Seafood from local day-boats gets special treatment in dishes such as whole sea bass steamed in soya, ginger and spring onion (£12.95); elsewhere the kitchen absorbs ideas from Cambodia and Laos for glass noodle salad with minced pork and prawns (£7.50), dry pork curry with coconut cream and stir-fried beef with garlic and pepper. Drink locally brewed Surin beer or house wine (£8.95). Closed all Sun and Mon L.

St Margaret's-at-Cliffe
Oakley and Harvey at Wallett's Court
Refreshing country-house hotel
Westcliffe, St Margaret's-at-Cliffe, CT15 6EW
Tel no: (01304) 852424
www.wallettscourt.com
Modern British | £40
Cooking score: 3

£5 OFF 🍴 🛏

It may seem like Gavin Oakley's family hotel has been around forever, but that's not to say it's dated. The seventeenth-century farmhouse may have a certain historical gravitas (the estate figures in the Domesday Book), but it is run as a modern country-house set up. Steve Harvey's food is modern, too, but not aggressively so, its backbone of fairly conservative dishes enlivened by a few surprise elements, such as pomegranate molasses and ras el hanout with chargrilled quail. Timings and seasoning do not please all reporters, but successes have included venison loin with juniper, blackberry, port jus and bitter

chocolate, and herb-crusted salmon with a julienne of leeks and carrots and champagne velouté sauce. Finish, perhaps, with hot chocolate brownie and peanut butter ice cream. An individual and instructive wine list brings fine growers to the table. Bottles start from £15.95.
Chef/s: Steve Harvey. **Open:** Sun L 12 to 2, Mon to Sun D 7 to 9. **Closed:** 24 to 26 Dec. **Meals:** Set L Sun £25, Set D £40. **Service:** 10% (optional).
Details: Cards accepted. 70 seats. No mobile phones. Wheelchair access. Music. Car parking.

Speldhurst
George & Dragon
Local food in an ancient pub
Speldhurst, TN3 0NN
Tel no: (01892) 863125
www.speldhurst.com
Modern British | £22
New Chef

V

'Food from a farm, not a factory' is the slogan behind this revitalised medieval pub, which ranks as one of the most ancient hostelries in the region. Antiquity oozes from the timber-framed exterior, mighty beams and huge inglenook, although the kitchen creates dishes that are in touch with today's trends. The menu reflects the seasons, ingredients are local (look for the biodynamically-grown vegetables) and there's no shortage of sharp modern ideas. New chef Brett Mather serves hare ragù with pappardelle and Parmesan and sends out rump of Ashdown venison with thyme jus and game chips. Elsewhere, Groombridge asparagus is put to good use and Kentish lamb chops appear with rosemary and cannellini beans, while fish might be represented by fillet of wild sea bass with parsley and clam broth. Locally foraged fruit with burnt cream could feature among the list of desserts, and the astutely chosen global wine list provides sound drinking from £13.80 (£3.50 a glass).

Chef/s: Brett Mather. **Closed:** 25 Dec and 1 Jan. **Meals:** alc (main courses £8 to £18). **Service:** 12.5% (optional). **Details:** Cards accepted. 100 seats. 140 seats outside. Separate bar. Wheelchair access. Music. Children's portions. Car parking.

▌Tunbridge Wells

Hotel du Vin & Bistro

Lively brasserie cooking in Georgian splendour
Crescent Road, Tunbridge Wells, TN1 2LY
Tel no: (01892) 526455
www.hotelduvin.com
Modern European | £30
New Chef

🍾 🛏️

The Tunbridge Wells outpost of this successful bistro, wine bar and hotel chain, which extends in a graceful arc from Brighton to Glasgow, is a rather grand sandstone Georgian mansion. It runs to the same level of brisk effectiveness as the other branches, and the menu offers the group style of modern brasserie cooking, rendered by Paul Nixon with some flair. A salad of black pudding and bacon with a boiled egg makes a nice late breakfast at any time of day, or you might opt for Thai fishcakes with chilli butter. A list of simple classics such as fish pie or chargrilled rib-eye steak with garlic butter and chips buttresses the more elaborate main-course offerings, such as pan-roasted grey mullet with caramelised swede purée and pancetta. Vegetarians might choose artichoke and pesto gnocchi, while the naughty-but-nice dessert approach makes comprehensive use of chocolate and toffee. Wines are as extensive and alluring as they are throughout the chain. The average price might feel high, but there is actually plenty below £25. House French at £14.50 kicks things off, but there is so much else to explore that it would seem unadventurous to stick there.
Chef/s: Paul Nixon. **Open:** all week, L 12 to 1.45 (Sun 2.30), D 7 to 10 (10.30 Fri and Sat). **Meals:** alc (main courses £12 to £18.75). Set L and D £17.50. Set Sun L and D £24.95. **Service:** 10%. **Details:** 85 seats. 20 seats outside. Separate bar. No music. Wheelchair access. Children's portions. Car parking.

Thackeray's

Elegant French polish
85 London Road, Tunbridge Wells, TN1 1EA
Tel no: (01892) 511921
www.thackerays-restaurant.co.uk
Modern French | £38
Cooking score: 6

Novelist William Makepeace Thackeray once lived in this listed Georgian house on Tunbridge Wells common – and there's a blue plaque to prove it. The building has done duty as a top-class restaurant for many years, and current chef/co-proprietor Richard Phillips is not about to let its reputation slip. The interior has a cool, elegant feel, with ancient low ceilings and shiny floorboards blending with subtle colours and more up-to-the-minute design flourishes; outside is a seductive Japanese terrace garden for tranquil al fresco meals. Highly polished modern French food is the order of the day, whether you pick from the carte or the midweek 'menu du jour'. Fish from the South Coast ports is generally a good bet. The possibilities might range from an assiette of hand-dived scallops with creamed corn, cauliflower purée and chive beurre blanc to medallions of monkfish with butternut and sage risotto and spiced red wine dressing. Fillet of Sussex Breed beef is there for local meat aficionados, while Old Black Spot pork with creamed cabbage, apple compote, ginger and clove jus points up the kitchen's loyalties to traditional breeds. A sharing plate of desserts brings all manner of sweet delights for two to drool over – otherwise apricot soufflé with milk chocolate and Grand Marnier ice cream might tempt. Thackeray's Selection provides a choice of two dozen eclectic wines from £13.95 (£4.50 a glass), and the full list balances French regional classics with some lively stuff from other countries.
Chef/s: Richard Phillips and Christopher Bower. **Open:** Tue to Sun L 12 to 2.30, Tue to Sat D 6.30 to 10.30. **Closed:** Mon. **Meals:** alc (main courses £21.50 to £26.50). Set L £15.95 (2 courses) to £16.95. Set D £26.50 (2 courses) to £28.50. **Service:** 12.5%.

Details: Cards accepted. 60 seats. 30 seats outside. Air-con. Separate bar. Wheelchair access. Music. Children's portions. Car parking.

▌Whitstable

JoJo's

Appealing, friendly and value for money
209 Tankerton Road, Whitstable, CT5 2AT
Tel no: (01227) 274591
Modern European | £20
Cooking score: 4

There's no change at Nikki Billington and Paul Watson's cheerful, informal, tapas-style restaurant. With its contemporary low-key décor, matching chunky wood tables clustered around an open-plan kitchen (with bar stool seating for the full theatre effect) and attractively understated cooking, it remains one of the hardest to book restaurants in the area. Billington is no purist when it comes to tapas, scouring the Mediterranean for ideas: alongside platters of chorizo and Serrano ham there could be thinly-sliced lamb cannon with tzatziki and Italian charcuterie such as lonzino or fiocco di spalla, while dolmades and hummus are alternatives to patatas bravas. Look to the specials board for new ideas; sourcing from local producers is a strength, so local lamb may be turned into koftas with feta, and fish from local day-boats (a strong suit) can be as simple as Dover sole grilled with lemon butter or roasted sardines with lemon and black pepper. Service is warm and welcoming. Note that the restaurant is unlicensed, so BYO and expect to pay £2 corkage (£3 if your wine comes from the local Tesco).
Chef/s: Nikki Billington and Joe Billington. **Open:** Wed to Sun L 12.45 to 2.30, Wed to Sat D 6.30 to 10. **Closed:** Sun D, Mon and Tue. **Meals:** alc (tapas £3.50 to £7.95). **Service:** not inc. **Details:** Cash only. 34 seats. 12 seats outside. Wheelchair access. Music. Children allowed.

Sportsman

Sophisticated cooking in a no-frills pub
Faversham Road, Seasalter, Whitstable, CT5 4BP
Tel no: (01227) 273370
www.thesportsmanseasalter.co.uk
Modern British | £30
Cooking score: 5

There's a lot to admire about Steve Harris's cooking. He has developed his own style which is a sophisticated form of the new no-frills British cooking – curing his own hams, churning his own butter, even making his own sea salt – while working with local farms to produce first-rate pork, lamb and chicken. The pub, too, has its own style: tucked away in marsh and farm land a couple of miles from touristy Whitstable, it's a large, shabby building, full of light and big plain wooden tables. But with the kitchen rising a good couple of notches both in scope and quality of cooking, the Sportsman must now be treated as a serious restaurant, albeit one where ordering at the bar is de rigueur and napkins remain resolutely paper. The short blackboard menu offers an intriguing array of dishes, from smoked mackerel on Bramley apple jelly with soda bread, or perfect pork terrine to some fine and original cooking in main courses, with proper appreciation of the importance of flavour: the combination of a smoked herring roe sauce with a perfectly timed fillet of brill 'was inspired', and reporters continue to endorse the never-off-the menu crispy duck with chilli salsa, sour cream and 'excellent roast potatoes'. Desserts, no less inventive, include rhubarb sorbet served with burnt cream or a strawberry ice lolly with cake milk and elderflower foam. Service is laid back; house wines are £11.95.
Chef/s: Stephen Harris. **Open:** Tue to Sun L 12 to 2, Tue to Sat D 7 to 9. **Closed:** Sun D and Mon. **Meals:** alc (main courses £12.95 to £21.95). **Service:** not inc. **Details:** Cards accepted. 50 seats. Children's portions. Car parking.

Wheelers Oyster Bar

Inventive seafood cooking
8 High Street, Whitstable, CT5 1BQ
Tel no: (01227) 273311
Seafood | £30
Cooking score: 2

The quaint-looking blue and pink shop stands out on Whitstable's cluttered High Street. 'Established 1856' reads the legend outside, and the tiny Victorian seafood bar with just four stools and a 'rather sombre' and cramped 16-seater parlour are just as old-fashioned. But, reassuringly, Mark Stubbs is known for his up-to-date cooking of very fresh fish. Local and seasonal ingredients are the mainstay of the menus and fresh, clear flavours shine through in starters such as skate cheeks deep-fried in five-spice tempura and served with Arabic salad, followed by roast zander with summer bean salad, wild garlic, crisp bacon and cucumber vinaigrette. To finish, there may be raspberry and hazelnut soufflé. Booking is essential and the restaurant is unlicensed, so BYO.
Chef/s: Mark Stubbs. **Open:** Thur to Tue 1 to 7.30. **Closed:** Wed, 7 to 25 Jan. **Meals:** alc (main courses £16.50 to £19.50). **Service:** not inc. **Details:** Cash only. 16 seats. Air-con. Wheelchair access. Children's portions.

Williams & Brown Tapas

A taste of Spain
48 Harbour Street, Whitstable, CT5 1AQ
Tel no: (01227) 273373
Spanish | £24
Cooking score: 2
£30

With its light and bright corner site, simple décor, open-to-view kitchen and tightly packed tables, Williams & Brown can be counted on to produce convincing modern tapas. It's all the more pleasing for eschewing cheesy Spanish theming. A blackboard is scrawled with the day's offerings, and there is plenty of choice, including baked chorizo in cider, morcilla with chickpeas, garlic, sultanas and pine nuts, and chicken livers with garlic.

The food has authenticity, with vibrant flavours gracing dishes like paella Granada – a vegetarian version, with spinach, pine nuts and saffron rice. Seafood comes in the form of seared scallops with samphire and asparagus or pan-fried prawns with sherry. Service is suitably friendly and house wine is £14.50.
Chef/s: Christopher Williams and Matt Sibley. **Open:** all week L 12 to 2 (12.30 to 2.30 Sat and Sun), D 6 to 9 (9.30 Sat). **Closed:** 25 to 27 Dec , 2 to 3 Jan. **Meals:** alc (tapas from £4.50 to £9.95). **Service:** not inc. **Details:** Cards accepted. 32 seats. 8 seats outside. Air-con. No mobile phones. Children allowed.

ALSO RECOMMENDED
▲ Whitstable Oyster Fishery Co.

Royal Native Oyster Stores, Horsebridge Road, Whitstable, CT5 1BU
Tel no: (01227) 276856
www.oysterfishery.co.uk
Seafood

The rough edged, wood-floored Victorian oyster store is right on the beach, so naturally seafood is the draw. Shellfish is piled on ice in the bar, while in the restaurant tables are covered with checked cloths and the blackboard menu delivers grilled rock oyster with spinach and cheese (£7.50), potted shrimps, well-reported local huss or whole roast local wild sea bass with rosemary and garlic (£22). White chocolate cheesecake with raspberry coulis (£5.95) is a typical dessert. Service has been praised this year. Wine starts at £14.50. Closed Mon.

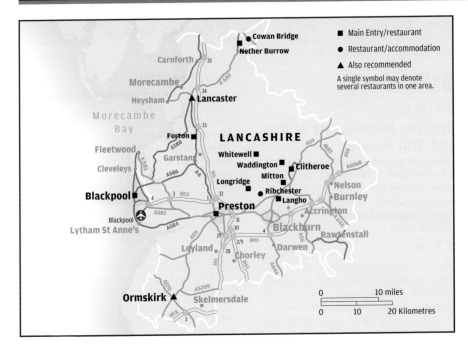

■ Blackpool

Kwizeen

Quirky take on local produce
47-49 King Street, Blackpool, FY1 3EJ
Tel no: (01253) 290045
www.kwizeenrestaurant.co.uk
Modern British | £24
Cooking score: 2

£5 OFF   £30

Don't be put off by the eccentric name, because this Blackpool firecracker wows just about everyone with its cheeky take on modern British cuisine. Main man Marco Callé-Calatayud is currently promoting Kwizeen as a 'local produce restaurant' and has introduced new Lancashire-inspired menus based on ingredients sourced within a 30-mile radius. Holidaymakers, party conference delegates and others can can now tuck in to Garstang Blue cheese and ham ravioli, Bowland beef 'lobby' with thyme suet dumpling, Pugh's suckling pig with chicken tournedos and fondant potatoes, and even locally-farmed Weatheroak ostrich fillets with chilli and chocolate sauce. Warm garlic Morecambe Bay shrimps accompany salmon soufflé, while the chunky chips served with sirloin of veal are made from potatoes grown in the locality. To finish, choose blueberry and apple pie or something more exotic such as rum and pineapple tarte Tatin with mango sorbet. House wine is £10.
Chef/s: Marco Callé-Calatayud. **Open:** Mon to Fri L 12 to 1.30, Mon to Sat D 6 to 9. **Closed:** Sun. **Meals:** alc (main courses £13 to £16). Set L £8.50 (2

Please send us your feedback

To register your opinion about any restaurant listed in the Guide, or a new restaurant that you wish to bring to our attention, please visit the web address at the bottom of the page. Your feedback informs the content of the book and will be used to compile next year's reviews.

courses). Set D 6 to 7 £15.95. **Service:** not inc. **Details:** Cards accepted. 40 seats. No mobile phones. Music. Children's portions.

Clitheroe

★NEW ENTRY★
Weezos Restaurant @ The Old Toll House
Local food against an exotic background
1-5 Parson Lane, Clitheroe, BB7 2JP
Tel no: (01200) 424478
www.weezos.co.uk
Modern European | £26
Cooking score: 1

There's a subtle African vibe in this cheerful restaurant at the bottom of a steep street in Clitheroe – Kathy Smith and Stosie Madie also own eateries in the Gambia. Wooden masks hang on brightly coloured walls and the background music is Ali Farka Touré, but the 'imaginative and creative' food draws its inspiration from much closer to home. Bowland meat, vegetables from the next village and fish from Fleetwood are used to good effect in dishes such as grilled mackerel salad with new potato, beetroot and crispy pancetta salad, and local asparagus with Parmesan and poached egg. Mains might include 'rich and dense' Cumbrian fell-bred heather-fed lamb shank, or rare-breed pork belly braised in soy sauce and served with local sausages, spring cabbage, pak choi and egg noodles. For dessert, Yorkshire rhubarb is sharp and earthy in a crumble with crème anglaise. The short but interesting wine list opens at £15 (£3.75 a glass).
Chef/s: Stosie Madie. **Open:** Thur to Sat D 7 to 9. **Meals:** alc (main courses £13 to £17). **Service:** not inc. **Details:** Cards accepted. Wheelchair access. Music. Children allowed.

Cowan Bridge

★NEW ENTRY★
Hipping Hall
First-rate food in a sophisticated setting
Cowan Bridge, LA6 2JJ
Tel no: (01524) 271187
www.hippinghall.com
Modern British | £49.50
Cooking score: 6

Hipping Hall is a seventeenth-century house of manageable proportions that has been impeccably renovated so that it is both full of character and extremely stylish and comfortable. There is a naturalness about the place, which helps to make it homely and relaxing, and sophisticated and charming young staff help too. Owner Andrew Wildsmith is ever-present, taking orders and managing front-of-house efficiently. The dining hall, with its high-beamed ceiling, grand fireplace and minstrels' gallery makes a dramatic setting for Jason Birkbeck's impressive cooking – he honed his talents at such places as the Gleneagles Hotel, Northcote Manor and the Samling Hotel (see entries). Owner and chef have tracked down the best local suppliers, including Stewart Lambert of Kitridding Farm who supplies them with beef, pork and lamb, and many of their vegetables and herbs come from the Hall's own walled garden. Starters teaming mackerel with refogado (a spicy Portuguese tomato sauce) in a carefully composed mille-feuille, with tapenade and basil oil, and confit belly of Gloucester Old Spot with roast langoustine, Sevruga caviar and cauliflower purée in pork jus, both exhibit stunning technique. Loin of lamb with confit neck, well-timed vegetables, a shallot purée and lamb jus was impressive, adding up to a fine main course. High standards are maintained through to desserts, as when roasted black figs are accompanied by a brittle brandy-snap filled with mascarpone cream and served with red wine syrup. Wines are intelligently listed by style; house bottles start at £17, and prices remain reasonable throughout.

Chef/s: Jason Birkbeck. **Open:** all week D 7 to 9.30, Sun L 12 to 1.30. **Closed:** Jan 1 to 18. **Meals:** Set Sun L £29.50, Set D £49.50. **Service:** not inc.
Details: Cards accepted. 28 seats. Separate bar. No mobile phones. Wheelchair access. Music. Car parking.

Forton
Bay Horse Inn
Unpretentious and consistently good
Bay Horse Lane, Forton, LA2 0HR
Tel no: (01524) 791204
www.bayhorseinn.com
Modern British | £28
Cooking score: 3

V

Still resolutely a pub, complete with drinkers' bar and roaring fire in winter, this rurally located inn (yet just minutes from the M6) is also a popular venue for some 'unpretentious but innovative and delicious' cooking. Craig Wilkinson responds to the seasons and sourcing is a strength, much of it 'seriously promoted' local produce. The team, both in the kitchen and front-of-house are enthusiastic and industrious. One who expressed delight at a meal that opened with Morecambe Bay potted shrimps and went on to 'delicious' halibut served with fresh asparagus, a 'lovely tomato-flavoured dressing' and baby new potatoes, declared it 'perfect for late April'. Equally enthusiastic reports have praised a Sunday lunch of 'perfectly cooked' roast sirloin of aged Cumbrian Galloway beef with duck fat roast potatoes, Yorkshire pudding and red wine gravy, and Herdwick mutton hotpot with pickled red cabbage. Sticky toffee pudding is a good way to finish. House wine from £12.95.

Chef/s: Craig Wilkinson. **Open:** Tue to Sun L 12 to 3, D 6.30 to 11. **Closed:** Mon except bank hols, Tue after bank hols, 25 and 26 Dec, 1 Jan. **Meals:** alc (main courses £11.50 to £16.95). Set Sun L £15.95 (2 courses) to £19.95. **Service:** not inc. **Details:** Cards

accepted. 50 seats. 24 seats outside. Separate bar. Wheelchair access. Music. Children's portions. Car parking.

Lancaster
ALSO RECOMMENDED
▲ Quite Simply French
27A St Georges Quay, Lancaster, LA1 1RD
Tel no: (01524) 843199
www.quitesimplyfrench.co.uk
French

There are no prizes for guessing the prevailing theme at this converted quayside warehouse overlooking the River Lune. Gallic bistro-style food served in relaxed cavernous surroundings is the order of the day, and it attracts regular crowds of locals and tourists. Lobsters from the tank are a speciality, but the daily menu also promises shallot tarte Tatin with Dijon mustard chantilly (£5.20), slow-braised lamb casserole and seared wild halibut with wild mushroom and garlic cream (£16.75). Almond crème brûlée (£3.95) is a typical dessert. House French is £12.75 (£2.95 a glass). Open Sun L and all week D.

Langho
Northcote Manor
Ever-evolving regional cuisine
Northcote Road, Langho, BB6 8BE
Tel no: (01254) 240555
www.northcotemanor.com
Modern British | £41.50
Cooking score: 6

🍷 🍴 V

Chef Nigel Haworth is probably better known to a wider audience since his appearance on BBC2's *Great British Menu* in the spring of 2008, though he's been a regional food hero in the North West for years, regarded as a culinary heavyweight whose modern approach to cooking is rooted in the quality ingredients of his home region. Northcote's own organic kitchen garden grows salad leaves, vegetables, soft fruits and herbs, and menus reflect the best of each season. Haworth's style is based on sound classical technique, and his ever-evolving repertoire delivers a 'stack of appealing menu options' that can make choosing tough. Fillet of local Ribble Valley beef teamed with smoked marrowbone, forest mushrooms, watercress and parsley mash is one option, roast halibut served with a Shorrocks cheese fondue and tempura of cauliflower and bacon is another. A melting ginger pudding might catch the eye at dessert, served with Simpson's iced double cream and caramel custard. Then there's the selection of Lancashire cheeses, perfect if you want to continue exploring the encyclopaedic corker of a wine list, which offers plenty of half-bottles and house wine from £17.

Chef/s: Nigel Haworth. **Open:** all week, L 12 to 1.30 (2 Sun), D 7 (6.30 Sat) to 9.30 (10 Sat, 9 Sun). **Meals:** alc (main courses £22.50 to £25). Set L £24.50, D £50 to £85. **Service:** optional. **Details:** Cards accepted. 80 seats. Separate bar. No mobile phones. Wheelchair access. Music. Children's portions. Car parking.

▌Longridge

Longridge Restaurant
North Country food renaissance
104-106 Higher Road, Longridge, PR3 3SY
Tel no: (01772) 784969
www.heathcotes.co.uk
Modern British | £38
Cooking score: 5

V

The flagship of Paul Heathcote's north country restaurant empire has launched itself into a new era with bags of confidence: the interior has a fresh contemporary look (all muted colours, suede seating and clever illumination), chef James Holah is fully revved-up in the kitchen, and there's a re-awakened seasonal impetus to the menus. As before, the emphasis is on re-invented modern British food with serious regional and local input, but no rose-tinted spectacles: this is up-front, full-blooded stuff for the twenty-first century, not a nostalgic peepshow. Heathcote's home-made black pudding remains one of the

stars (especially when it crops up as part of an English salad with beetroot, egg, anchovy, radishes and hash browns), honey-glazed Goosnargh duck with spiced apples and green peppercorns tops the main courses, while the main man's signature bread-and-butter pudding with apricot coulis and clotted cream rounds things off impressively. Dig deeper in springtime and you might find ravioli of Cornish cock crab and basil, pork cheeks braised in apple juice, and poached rump of lamb with young vegetables and a ragoût of borlotti beans. If anyone doubted Heathcote's commitment to all things British, the array of cheeses accompanied by pear and saffron chutney, artisan biscuits and Hawes fruit cake should seal the case. The wine list is as classless and unstuffy as everything else here, but the quality shines through. The Longridge selection includes a dozen options from £3.85 a glass, while bottle prices start at £14.95 each for a pair of Italians.

Chef/s: Paul Heathcote and James Holah. **Open:** Tue to Fri and Sun L 12 to 2.30, Tue to Sun D 7 to 9.30. **Closed:** Mon. **Meals:** alc (main courses £20). Set L £22.50 to £25. Set D £45. **Service:** not inc. **Details:** Cards accepted. 60 seats. Separate bar. No mobile phones. Music. Children's portions. Car parking.

Thyme
Great-value local pitstop
1-3 Inglewhite Road, Longridge, PR3 3JR
Tel no: (01772) 786888
Modern European | £26
Cooking score: 2

Two knocked-through terraced cottages provide the setting for this modern brasserie and café bar in the centre of Longridge. Alex Coward is an 'excellent host', who also dictates goings-on in the kitchen. A lunchtime set menu provides unbeatable value, or you can call in for just a plate of sandwiches or a bowl of Bantry Bay mussels. Evening meals up the tempo, with eclectic ideas and well-sourced Lancashire produce: Reggie Johnson's corn-fed chicken livers with a sweetcorn pancake and a lightly-poached egg could precede slow-cooked Goosnargh duckling or Bowland lamb shank with sweet potato, orange and mint mash. Fish often receives exotic treatment, as in fillet of coriander-crusted sea bass with scallop tempura and oriental noodle salad, while desserts sing a familiar song (treacle tart with custard sauce, marmalade bread-and-butter pudding); also ask to see the Lancastrian cheese menu. Recommendations on the compact wine list start at £13.95 (£3.50 a glass).

Chef/s: Alex Coward. **Open:** Tue to Sat L 12 to 2, D 6 to 9.30, Sun 12 to 8. **Closed:** Mon. **Meals:** alc (main courses £14 to £19). Set L £8.95 (2 courses) to £10.95. Set D 6 to 7.30 £9.95 (2 courses) to £11.95. **Service:** not inc. **Details:** Cards accepted. 40 seats. Air-con. No mobile phones. Wheelchair access. Music. Children's portions.

▌Mitton

Three Fishes

Celebrating Lancashire's larder
Mitton Road, Mitton, BB7 9PQ
Tel no: (01254) 826888
www.thethreefishes.com
Modern British | £20
Cooking score: 5

V

Dreamed up by crusading North Country chef Nigel Haworth (see entry for Northcote Manor), the Three Fishes puts reborn regional food back in its natural home, the country pub. This whitewashed stone inn has scored a resounding hit since opening in 2004 and it regularly plays to full houses – even though it only accepts bookings for big parties. The mantra is 'real beer, real food, real people,' and it's followed to the letter: the menu name checks its local 'food heroes' in loving detail and every dish is a celebration of Lancashire's larder. Here you will find proper fish pies, heather-reared Bowland lamb hotpot with pickled red cabbage, slow-cooked shoulder of mutton with herb dumplings and all manner of old-fashioned home-cured meats – plus elm wood platters piled high with cheeses, pickles, smoked fish and other

Nathan Outlaw

At what age did you cook your first meal for other people?
I started helping to cook for paying customers when I was eight, cooking eggs and bacon and doing the toast.

What three ingredients could you not do without?
Salt, milk and marmite.

What's your guilty food pleasure?
Cake in all forms.

What won't you tolerate in the kitchen?
People with no smiles on their faces.

Do you always read reviews of your restaurant?
Yes of course, and like most chefs I dread a bad one.

What era of history would you most like to have eaten in?
I would have loved to have tried out some of the food in the late '80s and early '90s. Nico Ladenis at Ninety Park Lane, Harvey's with Marco Pierre White and Pierre Koffman at Tante Claire.

provisions. This is pub grub of the best sort, and it's all rounded off with fruit crumbles, curd tarts and sponge puddings. Kids have their own 'young person's' menu and milkshakes to drink. Co-owner Craig Bancroft has put together an intriguing 60-bin wine list that is well above the typical pub norm in its range and quality: prices start at £12.50 (£3.15 a glass). The Three Fishes was always intended to be the first in a family of pubs: the Highwayman at Nether Burrow is already doing great things (see entry) and a third outlet, the Clog and Billycock at Pleasington, was due to open as the Guide went to press.

Chef/s: Richard Upton. **Open:** Mon to Sat L 12 to 2, D 6 to 9, Sat 5.30 to 9, Sun 12 to 8. **Closed:** 25 Dec. **Meals:** alc (main courses £7.50 to £17). **Service:** not inc. **Details:** Cards accepted. 140 seats. 40 seats outside. Separate bar. No music. Wheelchair access. Children's portions. Car parking.

Nether Burrow

The Highwayman
A true local for the twenty-first century
Nether Burrow, LA6 2RJ
Tel no: (01524) 273338
Modern British | £20
Cooking score: 3

V

Out of the same stable as the Three Fishes, Mitton (see entry), this extravagantly refurbished Victorian inn stands in the North Country borderlands where Lancashire meets Cumbria and Yorkshire. Photos of Lancashire's 'food heroes' line the walls of the bar, and there's a roll-call of their names on the menu to emphasise the flag-waving commitment to regional produce: meet Andrew Holt, the black pudding man and all the rest. Like its big brother, the Highwayman is deliberately billed as a twenty-first century 'local' rather than a contrived 'gastropub' and the food is the kind of stuff that makes drinkers (and even children) drool. Feast your eyes on plates of locally-cured meats, warm Flookburgh shrimps with toasted muffins, Lancashire cheese and onion pie, Herdwick

mutton pudding with 'forager's mash' and black peas, curd tarts and more besides. Kids can drink milkshakes, grown-ups can dip into the 60-bin wine list, which has been astutely assembled by co-owner Craig Bancroft. House wine is £12.50 (£3.15 a glass). No bookings, apart from large parties.

Chef/s: Michael Ward. **Open:** Mon to Sat L 12 to 2, Mon to Fri D 6 to 9, Sat 5.30 to 9, Sun 12 to 8. **Closed:** 25 Dec. **Meals:** alc (main courses £7.50 to £17). **Service:** not inc. **Details:** Cards accepted. 120 seats. 60 seats outside. Separate bar. No music. Wheelchair access. Children's portions. Car parking.

Ormskirk

ALSO RECOMMENDED
▲ Eagle & Child
Malt Kiln Lane, Bispham Green, Ormskirk, L40 3SG
Tel no: (01257) 462297
www.ainscoughs.co.uk
British

Combining the virtues of local drinkers' pub, casual country restaurant and farm shop, this eighteenth-century inn stands in a wedge of rustic Lancashire a few miles from the M6. A reliable team conjures up unshowy food with a seasonal accent and plenty of local connections – witness grilled black pudding, white pudding and chorizo salad (£6.50), pork, tomato and basil sausages with mash (£10) and pigeon wrapped in pancetta with madeira sauce. Finish with raspberry and chocolate cheesecake (£4.50) or one of Mrs Dowsons luxury ice creams. Impressive real ales and quaffable wines from £12.60 (£2.25 a glass). Open all week.

Readers recommend

A 'readers recommend' review is a genuine quote from a report sent in by one of our readers. We intend to follow up these suggestions throughout the year to come.

▌Preston

Winckley Square Chop House

British brasserie
23 Winckley Square, Preston, PR1 3JJ
Tel no: (01772) 252732
www.heathcotes.co.uk
British | £26
Cooking score: 3

V

One of Paul Heathcote's collection of restaurants, this brasserie is a showcase for British food. It sports a stylish jumble of decorative styles and is furnished with a mixture of antique and modern furniture. The atmosphere is relaxed and unbuttoned, but the food is taken seriously. The kitchen's focus is on 'Lancashire favourites and British classics', which translates (sometimes a little loosely) as anything from Whitby cod in beer batter with hand-cut chips, mushy peas and tartare sauce to roast chump of lamb with broad bean and herb couscous, home-dried tomatoes and parsley or risotto of charred sweetcorn, tarragon, leeks and crème fraîche. British favourites are charmingly deployed – a grilled rump steak might come with Marmite butter, for instance, while an appetiser of hand-cut potato crisps comes with thyme and Maldon salt. Desserts are more imaginative than you might expect; glazed apple tart with goats' cheese and lemon thyme ice cream is one example. A respectable wine list starts at £14.95

Chef/s: Phil Harkins. **Open:** Mon to Sat L 12 to 2.30, D 6 to 10. Sun 12 to 9. **Closed:** 25 Dec. **Meals:** alc (main courses £11 to £19.95), Set D Mon only £15 (3 courses). **Service:** not inc. **Details:** Cards accepted. 90 seats. Air-con. Separate bar. Wheelchair access. Music. Children's portions.

Scores on the Doors

To find out more about the Scores on the Doors campaign, please visit the Food Standard's Agency website: www.food.gov.uk or www.which.co.uk.

ALSO RECOMMENDED
▲ Bangla Fusion

Liverpool Old Road, Much Hoole, Preston, PR4 5JQ
Tel no: (01772) 610800
www.banglafusion.co.uk
Indian

Readers are raving about this sumptuous Subcontinental fusion restaurant south of Preston. Plush surroundings, 'fun' staff and a menu that breaks the curry house mould are just a few of its attributes. Baltis and biryanis (from £8.95) are eclipsed by the likes of cremeguru steak marinated in fennel with almond sauce (£16.45) and sizzling stir-fried duck with tortillas. Sunday lunch is a family buffet (from £9.95), early doors 'teatime menus' are served 5 to 7 Mon to Thur, and 'naasta tapas' is available in the wine bar at weekends. House wine is £12.25. Closed Mon to Fri L. There's a branch on Edenfield Road, Norden, near Rochdale – the premises once occupied by Nutters (see main entry).

▌Ribchester
White Bull

Reborn village local
Church Street, Ribchester, PR3 3XP
Tel no: (01254) 878303
whitebullrib.co.uk
Gastropub | £20
Cooking score: 3

Chris and Kath Bell have done a grand job transforming what was a sturdy old hostelry into a top-drawer pub with a strong reputation for food and drink. There are no 'gastro' frills here: the White Bull is defiantly a proper local complete with a games room, pool table and regularly-changing North Country real ales on handpump. Local influences loom large in the kitchen, as you might expect from a chef who used to man the stoves at Paul Heathcote's flagship restaurant in Longridge (see entry). Chris keeps things simple and likes big, bold, punchy flavours. He serves Bury black pudding with potato purée, fried egg and English mustard butter, dishes up grilled Cumberland sausages and isn't afraid to offer fish and chips with mushy peas. Elsewhere, his cheffing background shows in smoked chicken, truffle and green bean salad with celeriac crisps or rump of lamb with spiced aubergine, grilled courgettes and lentil vinaigrette. For afters, consider roast plums with vanilla ice cream or whisky and orange syllabub. Thirty affordable wines from £13 (£3.50 a glass).

Chef/s: Chris Bell. **Open:** Tue to Sun L 12 to 2.30, D 6 to 9. **Closed:** Mon. **Meals:** alc (main courses £8 to £12.50). Set L Sun £13.50 (2 courses) to £17. **Service:** not inc. **Details:** Cards accepted. 70 seats. 30 seats outside. Separate bar. Wheelchair access. Music. Children's portions. Car parking.

▌Waddington

★NEW ENTRY★
Waddington Arms
Handsome old pub in idyllic village location
Waddington, BB7 3HP
Tel no: (01200) 423262
www.waddingtonarms.co.uk
Modern British | £20
Cooking score: 1

The approach to this handsome old pub is about as pretty as it gets: a narrow stream runs through the centre of the classic Bowland village, flanked by immaculately kept flower beds. Then the Waddington Arms hoves into view, all mellow stone with window boxes bursting with colour. Inside, magnificent flagged floors, a huge inglenook fireplace with a wood stove, chunky mirrors and mis-matched furniture create a welcoming feel. The watchword here is comfort. There's no pretension in the kitchen either, with good hotpots, roast rump of lamb with dauphinoise potatoes, steak and ale pie all getting the thumbs-up. Look to the specials board for modern touches such as prawn tempura with dipping sauce, or blue cheese and pea risotto.

House wine is £10.50 and there are local ales on tap, including Copper Dragon and Moorhouses.

Open: Mon to Fri L 12-2.30, D 6 to 9.30; Sat 12 to 9.30, Sun 12 to 9. **Meals:** alc (main courses 8.50 to 12.95). **Service:** not inc. **Details:** Cards accepted. Wheelchair access. Music. Children's portions. Car parking.

▌Whitewell
The Inn at Whitewell
Upper-tier pub food
Whitewell, BB7 3AT
Tel no: (01200) 448222
www.innatwhitewell.com
Modern British | £29
Cooking score: 3

This handsome, rambling Bowland inn has superb views over the River Hodder towards the Trough of Bowland. It adheres to the old-fashioned values of inn-keeping, offering warmth, comfort, real ales and good food. Choose between any of the bars or more formal restaurant (there's a terrace taking in those views, too), and while the décor may be olde-worlde, the cooking takes a modern approach with a nod to the Mediterranean and reliance on first-rate produce, much of it local. Seared king scallops, avocado purée, crispy smoked bacon, anchovy salad and a savoury dressing makes a good start, while loin of Bowland lamb served with a cassoulet of beans and root vegetables, potato purée and slow-roast tomatoes, or brochette of pork loin marinated with lemon and thyme with hotpot-style potatoes and Bramley apple compote are typical main course choices. British and Irish cheeses are an alternative to homely puddings. The wine list, a comprehensive global affair with a strong showing in France, offers a dozen halves and opens at £12.50.

Chef/s: Jamie Cadman. **Open:** all week D 7.30 to 9.30. **Meals:** alc (main courses £15.50 to £25). **Service:** not inc. **Details:** Cards accepted. 60 seats. Separate bar. No music. No mobile phones. Children's portions. Car parking.

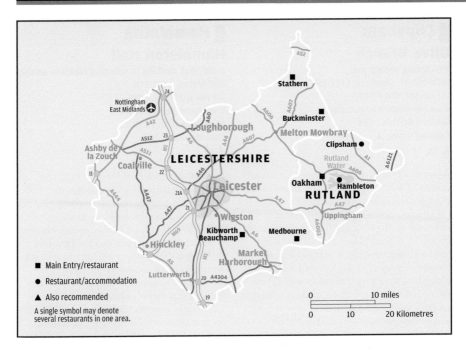

Main Entry/restaurant
● Restaurant/accommodation
▲ Also recommended
A single symbol may denote
several restaurants in one area.

0   10 miles
0   10   20 Kilometres

■ Buckminster

Tollemache Arms

Good address for seasonal game
48 Main Street, Buckminster, NG33 5SA
Tel no: (01476) 860007
www.thetollemachearms.com
Modern British | £32
Cooking score: 4

🛏 V

A Victorian country inn with a fresh. modern
feel inside, the Tollemache is handy for the old
market towns of Oakham and Melton
Mowbray as well as the Buckminster Estate,
which provides game through the winter
months. Mark Gough's radar is clearly attuned
to the contemporary British idiom, offering
Buckminster pigeon breast on toast with
onion marmalade as one way to start, or
perhaps peppered loin of hare with grilled
goats' cheese. Fish dishes are not quite as
plentifully in evidence as they might be –
turbot with oyster mushrooms is a notable
exception – but then you are in an
undoubtedly landlocked part of England.
Meat dishes come up to snuff, though, in the
form of venison with glazed pumpkin and red
cabbage, or chicken breast with creamed leeks
and madeira sauce. A milkshake made with
champagne and vodka, flavoured with red
fruits, is something of a signature dessert, or
you might opt for a cheese-based finisher such
as soft Chaource served warm with figs or
apple and Stilton tart. An interesting wine list
opens with Loire house selections, a
Sauvignon and a Pinot Noir, at £13.75.
Chef/s: Mark Gough. **Open:** Tue to Sun L 12 to 3, Tue
to Sat D 6 to 11.30. **Meals:** alc (main courses £10 to
£23.50). Set L £15.50. Set D (Tue to Thu) £15.50. Set
L Sun £18.50. **Service:** not inc. **Details:** Cards
accepted. 50 seats. 20 seats outside. Separate bar.
Wheelchair access. Music. Children's portions. Car
parking.

Which? Campaigns

To find out more about Which? food and
drink campaigns, please visit:
www.which.co.uk

Clipsham

Olive Branch

Welcoming village pub
Main Street, Clipsham, LE15 7SH
Tel no: (01780) 410355
www.theolivebranchpub.com
Modern British | £24
Cooking score: 3

A couple of miles off the A1 in the pint-sized county of Rutland, Clipsham is an appealing village whose chief boast is the Olive Branch. Old books piled on shelves and a roaring fire in winter set the tone and form a comforting backdrop to Sean Hope's mix-and-match modern cooking style. A party of January lunchers emerged highly satisfied from a repast that took in parsnip soup with thyme crème fraîche, Lincolnshire sausages with red cabbage and best mash, and top-notch pork and Stilton pie with piccalilli and apple chutney. In the evenings it all moves up a gear, and on come baked lemon sole stuffed with scallop mousse on artichoke rösti, and duck breast with beetroot gratin and stir-fried spring onions. Treat yourself to a finale of mascarpone pannacotta with rhubarb compote or vibrant sorbet variations such as mandarin, blackberry and pineapple. Wines are sorted by style and are notable for their imaginative range and great value. Prices start at £14 (or £3.75 a glass) for southern French house tipples.

Chef/s: Sean Hope. Open: Mon to Fri L 12 to 3, D 6 to 11. Sat 12 to 11, Sun 12 to 10.30. Closed: 25 and 26 Dec, 1 Jan. Meals: alc (main courses £12.75 to £22.50). Set L Sun £19.50. Service: not inc. Details: Cards accepted. 44 seats. 24 seats outside. Separate bar. Wheelchair access. Music. Children's portions. Car parking.

Also recommended

An 'also recommended' entry is not a full entry, but is provisionally suggested as an alternative to main entries.

Hambleton

Hambleton Hall

Ambitious cooking in splendid lakeside setting
Hambleton, LE15 8TH
Tel no: (01572) 756991
www.hambletonhall.com
Modern British | £70
Cooking score: 7

Built in the 1880s for a brewery magnate, Hambleton is a solidly imposing edifice with a majestically pitched roof, sumptuous gardens and a restful lakeside location. In the era of the Bright Young Things, Noël Coward was one of its habitués. The gorgeous interiors now form the backdrop for a well-run hotel with a dining room of serious intent. In an atmosphere where all could be suffocatingly grand, a reporter is gratified to note that the welcome is 'friendly but professional', and the focus is firmly on Aaron Patterson's vibrant modern British cooking. Influences are drawn from the European heartlands as well as the domestic larder, so langoustine might be teamed in a first course with tortellini of confit pork belly and rhubarb, while mains might take in sea bream with tartare-flavoured mash, clams and hazelnuts, or roast venison loin with caramelised endive, spiced pineapple and cocoa. The cooking may be tried via any number of set-menu formulas, including the tasting option of five courses, built around a sesame-roast scallop with pak choi, lemongrass and ginger, followed by breast of Goosnargh duck with white raisins. Desserts tack to a more traditional line in passion-fruit soufflé or pear Tatin, but don't stint at chocolate and olive oil truffle with salted caramel, pistachios and baked banana for those with the will to branch out. 'The aim of this (wine) list is to surprise you,' declares proprietor Tim Hart, and surprise it does, with a cosmopolitan listing of 'Wines of the Moment', ranging from Spanish Cariñena to New Zealand Riesling, but also with an unfashionable spread of Germans and

Austrians, and a generous array of dessert wines, amid the more expected roll-call of French treasures. Prices open at £16.
Chef/s: Aaron Patterson. **Open:** all week L 12 to 1.30, D 7 to 9.30. **Meals:** alc (main courses £36 to £39). Set L £27, Set L Sun £45. Set D £40 to £65. **Service:** 12.5%. **Details:** 64 seats. 20 seats outside. Separate bar. No music. No mobile phones. Wheelchair access. Children's portions. Car parking.

▌Kibworth Beauchamp

Firenze

Relaxed atmosphere, simple Italian food
9 Station Street, Kibworth Beauchamp, LE8 0LN
Tel no: (0116) 2796260
www.firenze.co.uk
Modern Italian | £40
Cooking score: 3
£5 OFF ▮ V

This bright and contemporarily decorated restaurant stands by a roundabout in the heart of Kibworth Beauchamp and eager reporters testify to its ongoing popularity. The name of the game is to combine good-quality ingredients with uncomplicated modern Italian cooking to produce a menu with broad appeal. Lino Poli has a sureness of touch with richer dishes that coaxes astonishing depth of flavour out of rigatoni with oxtail ragoût or a griddled breast of pigeon with polenta cooked with lardo, spinach and beans. Classics come in the form of bollito misto or breaded stuffed escalopes of pork, while risotto may be teamed with orange and mackerel. Hot chocolate pudding with caramel has proved a good choice among desserts. The relaxed atmosphere is a plus, Sarah Poli is impressive front-of-house, and the polished, appealingly partriotic all-Italian wine list opens at £13.50.
Chef/s: Lino Poli and Stuart Batey. **Open:** Mon to Sat L 12 to 3, D 7 to 11. **Closed:** Sun, bank hols, 1 week Christmas. **Meals:** Set L £12, set D £15 to £25. **Service:** not inc. **Details:** Cards accepted. 60 seats. Wheelchair access. Music. Children's portions.

▌Medbourne

Horse & Trumpet

Modern cooking in a rural setting
Medbourne, LE16 8DX
Tel no: (01858) 565000
www.horseandtrumpet.com
Modern British | £34
Cooking score: 5

The former village pub is a 'stunning building' that has been converted to give several small dining rooms. While the setting is decidedly country-restaurant, the food is unmistakably modern and Gary Magnani's menus continue to develop along contemporary lines, with terse descriptions belying food of great technical complexity and dramatic impact. The nine-course tasting menu is one way to order, but there are interesting choices on the carte (with some cross-over dishes) that could deliver scallops teamed with squid ink pasta, bacon and coconut or a delicate crab salad spiked with fennel biscuit and served with avocado cream. Meat cookery is of the highest order too, with loin and braised shoulder of East Langton boar well matched by liquorice purée and bok choi at main course stage, and saddle of lamb complemented by minted rösti, aubergines and peppers. Interesting dessert combinations could take in white chocolate sorbet with apricot jelly and yoghurt crisp. This year, however, reporters have found the service to be a quite a few steps behind the cooking. The modern wine list is exactly right for the job – unfussy, with a dozen offered by-the-glass from £3.45. Bottles prices start at £19.
Chef/s: Gary Magnani. **Open:** Tue to Sun L 12 to 1.45 (2.30 Sun), Tue to Sat D 7 to 9.30. **Closed:** Mon, 2 weeks Jan. **Meals:** Set L £20, Set D £34, tasting menu £48.50 (9 courses). **Service:** not inc. **Details:** Cards accepted. 48 seats. 20 seats outside. Wheelchair access. Music.

▌Oakham

Lord Nelson's House Hotel, Nick's Restaurant

Modern food in an old-fashioned setting
11 Market Place, Oakham, LE15 6DT
Tel no: (01572) 723199
www.nelsons-house.com
French | £42
Cooking score: 3

£5 OFF

The hotel address may sound grand enough, but this turns out to be an endearing little place tucked into one corner of Oakham's market square. The dining room is done in warm tones, with swagged drapes and dark wood tables. The kitchen produces a well-wrought version of modern European cooking, partnering a smoked salmon terrine with anchovy and basil butter and beetroot sorbet, or scallops with truffled cauliflower purée as first courses. Mains bring on essays in flavour contrast, such as cannon of lamb with baby carrot tart, puréed carrots, tortellini of foie gras, fennel marmalade and a red wine jus. The liquidiser must be getting some stick, as purées cropped up in every main course of the menu we were sent, sometimes even two in one dish. Finish with lemon tart and raspberry sorbet or sticky toffee pudding with banana and date ice cream. The short wine list opens with New World varietals at £15.95 a bottle (£4.50 a glass).
Chef/s: Dameon Clarke. **Open:** Tue to Sun L 12 to 2.30. Tue to Sat D 6 to 10. **Meals:** alc (main courses £19.50 to £23.95). Set L £20. Set D £27.95. **Service:** not inc. **Details:** Cards accepted. 50 seats. No mobile phones. Wheelchair access. Music. Children's portions. Car parking.

▌Stathern

Red Lion Inn

Authentic country pub
2 Red Lion Street, Stathern, LE14 4HS
Tel no: (01949) 860868
www.theredlioninn.co.uk
Modern British | £25
Cooking score: 2

£30

It's a credit to the sympathetic refurbishment of this country pub that one visitor told us it 'hasn't been prettied up,' praising its 'log fires and pub atmosphere'. From its garden to the flag-floored bar with its selection of real ales, the Red Lion still feels like the real thing. The cooking takes its cue from the surroundings, offering a relaxed style of eating with a sense of tradition. Fish and chips, sausages and mash and apple crumble are typical choices, but so are more sophisticated creations such as chicken liver parfait with home-made brioche, followed by local partridge with chestnut cabbage, caramelised pear and bread sauce. The kitchen has an excellent relationship with nearby suppliers, so expect game from Belvoir Castle, sausages from the village butcher and vegetables from local farms. If the ales and speciality beers don't tempt you, the wine list is well above your average pub offering. Prices from £12.50.
Chef/s: Edward Leslie. **Open:** Food served Tue to Sun L 12 to 2, Tue to Sat D 7 to 9.30. **Closed:** Jan 1. **Meals:** alc (main courses £10.95 to £16.50), set L £13 (2 courses). **Service:** not inc. **Details:** Cards accepted. Separate bar. Wheelchair access. Music. Children's portions. Car parking.

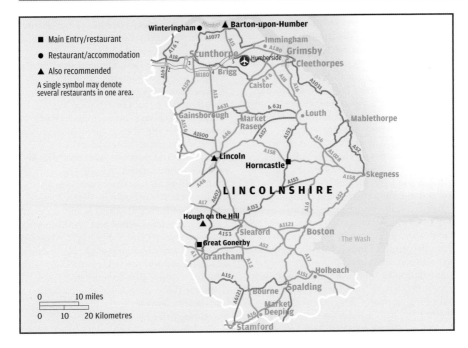

Map legend:
- ■ Main Entry/restaurant
- ● Restaurant/accommodation
- ▲ Also recommended

A single symbol may denote several restaurants in one area.

0 ——— 10 miles
0   10   20 Kilometres

Winteringham ● ▲ Barton-upon-Humber, Immingham, Grimsby, Scunthorpe, Humberside, Cleethorpes, Brigg, Caistor, Gainsborough, Market Rasen, Louth, Mablethorpe, ▲ Lincoln, Horncastle ■, Skegness, LINCOLNSHIRE, Hough on the Hill ▲, Sleaford, Boston, The Wash, ■ Great Gonerby, Grantham, Bourne, Spalding, Holbeach, Market Deeping, Stamford

■ Barton-upon-Humber

ALSO RECOMMENDED
▲ Elio's

11 Market Place, Barton-upon-Humber, DN18 5DA
Tel no: (01652) 635147
Italian

Elio Grossi's family-run trattoria has been a Humberside favourite since 1983 and now has the bonus of a covered conservatory/courtyard as well as a revamped dining room with new-look leather chairs. Seafood specials are the stars of the show, and the line-up might include anything from monkfish with fennel sauce (£18.75) to seared tuna with a balsamic and olive oil reduction. Elio's fish soup (£6.25) is legendary, pizzas and pasta show up well and desserts (£5.75) run from cassata to chocolate trifle. Genuine Italian service and an inviting regional wine list; house selections £12.95 a litre (£2.95 a glass). Accommodation available. Open Mon to Sat D only.

■ Great Gonerby

Harry's Place

Remarkable Lincolnshire treasure
17 High Street, Great Gonerby, NG31 8JS
Tel no: (01476) 561780
Modern French | £56
Cooking score: 7

£5 OFF

It's a testament to Harry and Caroline Hallam's self-belief, tenacity and sheer dedication that they have continued to thrive in this Lincolnshire backwater for more than two decades. This is a truly remarkable, one-off set up: the Hallams do business in a pretty Georgian house with a cosy dining room that comprises three immaculately-laid tables plus vases of fresh flowers, a few antiques and family photos on the walls. Caroline is the perfect greeter and orchestrator out front, while Harry keeps things tight in the kitchen, matching the domestic mood with a brief dinner menu of just two choices at each stage. Sourcing ingredients is a personal passion and everything here is as precise and polished as can be, right down to the last, time-consuming detail. The evening begins with finely wrought canapés, before a soup (locally grown celeriac) or something more intricate such as a salad of Filey lobster with avocado, truffle oil dressing and a vivid relish of mango, lime, ginger and basil. Main courses are equally forthright – perhaps seared Scottish monkfish with a sauce of red wine, sage, thyme and crispy lardons or fillet of pure Aberdeen Angus beef sauced with madeira and tarragon plus horseradish hollandaise. Desserts are deceptively simple (caramel mousse brûlée served with raspberries and strawberries, for example) and there's also a fabulous array of prime cheeses from Britain and Europe. Like the menu, the wine list is a single handwritten sheet: on it you will find around two dozen bins gleaned almost exclusively from France, Spain and Italy. Prices start at £20 (£4.50 a glass).

Chef/s: Harry Hallam. **Open:** Tue to Sat L 12.30 to 2, D 7 to 8.30. **Closed:** Sun, Mon, bank hols, 1 week Christmas. **Meals:** alc (main courses £35). **Service:** not inc. **Details:** Cards accepted. 10 seats. No music. No mobile phones. Wheelchair access. Children's portions. Car parking.

▐ Horncastle

Magpies

A personally run Wolds favourite
73 East Street, Horncastle, LN9 6AA
Tel no: (01507) 527004
www.eatatthemagpies.co.uk
Modern European | £32
Cooking score: 5

A row of terraced houses in a modest Lincolnshire Wolds town is the setting for this very model of a personally run provincial restaurant. Andrew Gilbert and partner Caroline Ignall run the show with a small team of helpers and the whole place has a delightfully appealing feel with its mellow yellow and red colour schemes. Andrew Gilbert honed his skills with Tessa Bramley at the Old Vicarage, Ridgeway (see entry) –

and it shows in his creative use of ingredients and clear-flavoured dishes. Partridge breast marinated in tamarind and orange with oriental-style noodles and caramelised pecans brings a touch of fusion to Lincolnshire, although loin of pork stuffed with apricots and almonds on traditional red cabbage is rooted much closer to home. Lincoln Red beef makes regular appearances (perhaps served on a celeriac and potato rösti with wild mushrooms and madeira sauce) and Grimsby provides seafood in the shape of, say, baked halibut on crab risotto with vanilla bisque. Desserts are elaborate without over-gilding the lily: warm vanilla waffles are given a makeover with poached pear, vanilla parfait and maple syrup sauce, for example. Magpies' wine list is a real treat: top-flight names from Bordeaux and Burgundy keep company with some excellent, wallet-friendly stuff from elsewhere (Italy scores heavily, in particular). Half-bottles show up well and 18 house recommendations begin with Corney & Barrow French at £13.40.

Chef/s: Andrew Gilbert. **Open:** Wed to Fri and Sun L 12 to 2.30, Wed to Sun D 7 to 9.30. **Closed:** Mon, Tue. **Meals:** Set L £21 (2 courses) to £25, Set D £32. **Service:** not inc. **Details:** Cards accepted. 34 seats. 10 seats outside. Air-con. Separate bar. No mobile phones. Wheelchair access. Music. Children's portions.

▐ Hough on the Hill

ALSO RECOMMENDED
▲ The Brownlow Arms

Grantham Road, Hough on the Hill, NG32 2AZ
Tel no: (01400) 250234
www.thebrownlowarms.com
Modern European

Once the home of Lord Brownlow, this handsome seventeenth-century stone inn is now a congenial upmarket inn-with-rooms. An intimate country-house atmosphere prevails and the food follows the seasons. Warm terrine of salmon, prawns and scallops (£6.95) might precede slow-cooked shoulder of lamb with winter roots and Rioja jus (£14.95), while desserts have featured coffee and Amaretto crème brûlée with coffee ice cream. Eat by the log fire in winter; relax on the terrace in summer. House wine £14.95. Open Tue to Sat dinner and Sun lunch. No children in restaurant.

▊ Lincoln

ALSO RECOMMENDED
▲ Wig & Mitre

30–32 Steep Hill, Lincoln, LN2 1LU
Tel no: (01522) 535190
www.wigandmitre.com
Modern British

Found close to Lincoln's cathedral and castle, part of the appeal of this ancient pub – which dates in part from the fourteenth century – is its warm and homely interior and beamed ceilings. Open all day, extensive menus range from breakfast (full English £10.25), through sandwiches and light meals (minute fillet steak au poivre with salad, £9.95) to dinner, perhaps salt-roast hake with herb mash (£13.25) or rump of lamb with steamed kidney pudding (£15.95). Try chocolate torte with lime jelly for dessert (£5.25). Good value wines from £12.95. Open all week. The proprietors also own Caunton Beck in Caunton, Nottinghamshire (see entry).

▊ Winteringham

Winteringham Fields

Winteringham, DN15 9PF
Tel no: (01724) 733096
www.winteringhamfields.com
Anglo-French | £75
Cooking score: 6

♦ 🍴

It has been a turbulent year at Winteringham Fields: Robert Thompson departed, his replacement came and went, and chef/patron Colin McGurran donned his whites to work in the kitchen alongside current chef Andrew Foster. Amid such a merry-go-round, it must have taken nerves of steel to launch an ambitious new makeover, adding a kitchen, a lounge and a gaudy-glamorous 50-seater

dining room to the existing complex of restaurant-with-rooms. A test meal in May confirmed the growing, perhaps inevitable, feeling that it will be a long, hard haul to reproduce the perfectionist brilliance of its years under the ownership of Germain Schwab. It can still touch the heights – an amuse of tomato gazpacho, a starter of foie gras and suckling pig ballottine with a spiced apple chutney, and the inspired pairing of halibut with a faggot of softly-braised beef cheek and tender seasonal asparagus were highlights at inspection. But then consistency wavered. A main course of calf's liver that was nicely caramelised on one side was mushy and uncooked on the other. At dessert, the flavours of vanilla and star anise accompanying a roasted peach with lychee sorbet were overpowered by port; better was a silky smooth chocolate tartlet with crisp pastry and a garnish of gold leaf. So, too, was a subtle lavender ice cream, but presentation generally did not have the artistry or the wow factor of previous visits. And the service, historically so scholarly and precise, occasionally creaked. This remains high calibre dining. It is still comfortably the best for miles around, but if it aspires to once more become one of the elite restaurants worth crossing the country for, it is work in progress.

Chef/s: Colin McGurran and Andrew Foster. **Open:** Tue to Sat L 12 to 2, D 7 to 9. **Closed:** Sun and Mon, from Christmas to 1st week Jan. **Meals:** alc (main courses £18 to £29). Set L £39.95, menu surprise £79. **Service:** optional. **Details:** Cards accepted. 50 seats.

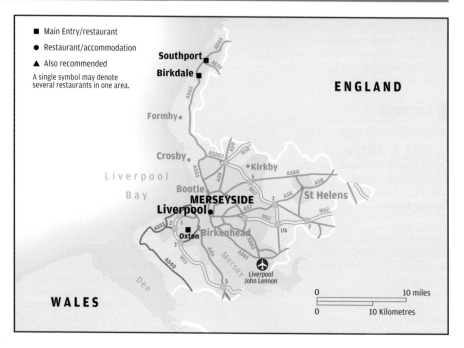

- ■ Main Entry/restaurant
- ● Restaurant/accommodation
- ▲ Also recommended

A single symbol may denote several restaurants in one area.

▌Birkdale

Michael's

Cosy neighbourhood restaurant
47 Liverpool Road, Birkdale Village, Birkdale,
PR8 48G
Tel no: (01704) 550886
www.michaelsbirkdale.co.uk
Modern European | £25
Cooking score: 2

£30

Set in pretty Birkdale village, 'this fabulous little neighbourhood restaurant' is an unpretentious, 'cosy' place that has developed a strong following for affordable menus of 'well-crafted dishes', often using local ingredients. Michael Wichmann's ambition (and Francophile leanings) comes across clearly in combinations like Goosnargh chicken breast stuffed with asparagus and tarragon mousse, but the thrust of the menu is posh comfort food: smoked salmon with potato pancake, fennel and beetroot salad, for instance, or roasted rump of Forest of Bowland lamb with potato-leek gratin and mashed minted broad beans, and a good range of steaks. Desserts include a 'decadent' dark and white chocolate mousse. A short wine list starts with house Spanish at £12.

Chef/s: Michael Wichmann. **Open:** Tue to Sat D 6 to 8.45 (9.30 Fri and Sat). **Closed:** 1 Jan. **Meals:** alc (main courses £10.50 to £21). Set D 6 to 7.30 £13.95 (2 courses) to £16.95. **Service:** not inc.
Details: Cards accepted. 34 seats. Air-con. Music. Children's portions.

Please send us your feedback

To register your opinion about any restaurant listed in the Guide, or a new restaurant that you wish to bring to our attention, please visit the web address at the bottom of the page. Your feedback informs the content of the book and will be used to compile next year's reviews.

The Good Food Guide 2009

▌Liverpool

★NEW ENTRY★
Blake's
Situated in the Beatles-themed hotel
Hard Day's Night Hotel, Central Buildings, 41
North John Street, Liverpool, L2 6RR
Tel no: (0151) 2432121
www.harddaysnighthotel.com
British | £30
Cooking score: 4

While a Beatles-themed hotel sounds like
shorthand for tacky, the reality is something
quite different and Beatlemania entered a
whole new phase when this multi-million
pound luxury hotel opened in February 2008.
Its restaurant, Blakes, is named after Sir Peter
Blake, who designed the cover of *Sgt Pepper's
Lonely Hearts Club Band*. The walls are
punctuated by black and white portraits of the
sixty historical figures that featured on the
cover, while four oversized white lampshades
dominate the elegant modern dining room,
with its soaring ceiling and muted colours.
The simple menu is packed with
uncomplicated British classics, delivered by a
bevy of perky young staff. On inspection a
creamy fish pie brimmed with chunky seafood
hidden under a neat quenelle of smooth mash.
Starters include smoked trout and cream
cheese on oatcakes served with a Liverpool
speciality, Baltic wafers. Other mains include
English lamb with Bury black pudding and
whole grilled Dover sole. Wine-lovers can
choose from a good assortment, priced
between £13 and £30.
Chef/s: Richard Moore. **Open:** all week L 12 to 3, D
6 to 10.30. **Meals:** alc (main courses £12 to £20).
Service: not inc. **Details:** Cards accepted. 75 seats.
Air-con. Separate bar. Wheelchair access. Music.
Children's portions. Children allowed. Car parking.

London Carriage Works
Happening hotel dining in the heart of the city
Hope Street Hotel, 40 Hope Street, Liverpool,
L1 9DA
Tel no: (0151) 7052222
www.tlcw.co.uk
Modern British | £32
Cooking score: 5

The building once housed a manufacturer of
coaches and carriages, one whose pretensions
to grandeur were sufficient for the place to be
fashioned in the style of a Venetian palazzo. It
may be a long way from the Grand Canal to
Hope Street, but Liverpool – European
Capital of Culture in 2008 – has always
thrived on ebullient self-confidence. This is
the ambitious restaurant arm of what is now a
pace-setting hotel in a trendy part of the city,
with Paul Askew heading up the kitchen.
Much north-western produce finds its way
into dishes such as a starter of slow-roast north
Welsh belly pork with braised red cabbage and
apple, or rump of Bowland beef with
portobello mushrooms, caramelised onions,
spinach and Roma tomatoes for main. The
cooking makes ingenious use of a variety of
techniques without leaving culinary logic
behind, trying out an east Asian mode for
seared chilli squid with bok choi, spring
onions and ginger, or going the Italian route
with a risotto of smoked haddock that
incorporates baby tomatoes, leeks,
mascarpone and Parmesan. Crème brûlée is
subject to daily-changing flavour additions,
there's hot chocolate fondant with caramelised
almonds and white chocolate ice-cream, and
the British and French cheeses are described
and served with all the solicitude aficionados
hope to see. So too the wines, which begin
with a generous selection by-the-glass (from
£3.75), and then take off on a briskly efficient
world tour. Mark-ups are a little forbidding,
but there is enough choice below £25 for the
budget-conscious not to feel neglected.
Bottles start at £13.95.

LIVERPOOL

Chef/s: Paul Askew. **Open:** all week L 12 to 3, D 5 to 10. **Meals:** alc (main courses £14.50 to £24). Set L £25. **Service:** not inc. **Details:** Cards accepted. 90 seats. Air-con. Separate bar. Wheelchair access. Music. Children's portions.

The Side Door
Relaxed venue in theatreland
29a Hope Street, Liverpool, L1 9BQ
Tel no: (0151) 7077888
www.thesidedoor.co.uk
Modern European | £25
Cooking score: 2

Handy for Liverpool's theatreland, here is yet another good eating option on Hope Street. Done in cream and pillar-box red, it's a nicely relaxed venue, offering up-to-date brasserie dining that uses some of the best of the North West, from the asparagus of Formby to cod from Fleetwood and Goosnargh duck. Start with peppered salmon and caponata, or perhaps marinated quail in pistachio dressing, before a main course such as calf's liver and pancetta with olive oil mash and onions cooked in sweet sherry, or that cod served grilled, with ink risotto and a red pepper dressing. One party thoroughly enjoyed a Sri Lankan-style prawn starter from the specials, even if the mustard mash that came with a lamb main course was on the eye-watering side of strong. Desserts might be rhubarb and custard tart, or strawberry crème brûlée. Spanish house wines, a Viura and a Tempranillo, are £13.
Chef/s: Sean Millar, Alex Navarro and Jay Brown. **Open:** Mon to Sat L 10 to 2.30, D 5.30 to 10. **Closed:** Sun, Christmas and bank hols. **Meals:** alc (main courses £10.95 to £14.95). Set D £17.95. **Service:** not inc. **Details:** Cards accepted. 55 seats. Air-con. Separate bar. Music. Children's portions.

60 Hope Street
Merseyside minimalist with in-vogue food
60 Hope Street, Liverpool, L1 9BZ
Tel no: (0151) 7076060
www.60hopestreet.com
Modern European | £37
Cooking score: 4

In Liverpool's metropolitan heartland, not far from the Philharmonic Hall, 60 Hope Street is an elegant slice of Georgian architecture that has become equally popular with culture vultures and fashionable foodies. It is also a place of two halves, comprising a basement café/bistro and an animated ground-floor dining room with stripped floorboards and big mirrors. The kitchen delivers what one reporter called 'classy, elegant and fabulous food,' full of confident gestures and up-to-the-minute themes. Seared scallops get a 'pea whack fritter' (this is Liverpool, after all), while fillet of monkfish is paired with king prawn tortellini, prawn bisque and crispy kale. North Country meat and game are given more earthy treatment, as in roast rump of winter Swaledale lamb with hotpot, braised red cabbage or loin of Cumbrian venison with roast beetroot, parsnip purée and juniper jus. To conclude, the kitchen dons its party gear for smiley offerings like deep-fried jam sandwich and Carnation milk ice cream or rhubarb and custard trifle with 'popping candy'. By contrast, the wine list puts on a serious face, although prices are far from intimidating. France leads the way, but choice across the board is spot-on, with classy names and vintages to tempt all palates and pockets. House wines kick off at £13.95 (£4.75 a glass).
Chef/s: Sara Kershaw. **Open:** Mon to Fri L 12 to 2.30, Mon to Sat D 5 to 10.30. **Closed:** Sun and bank hols. **Meals:** alc (main courses £17 to £27). Set L £14.95 (2 courses) to £17.95. **Service:** not inc. **Details:** Cards accepted. 90 seats. 12 seats outside. Air-con. Separate bar. Music. Children's portions.

Spire

Classy modern cooking
1 Church Road, Liverpool, L15 9EA
Tel no: (0151) 7345040
www.spirerestaurant.co.uk
Modern European | £25
Cooking score: 4

£5 OFF ▲ £30

Bare bricks, modern artwork and simple furnishings set a crisply modern tone in this popular and welcoming restaurant. The cooking reflects the air of unfussy, up-to-date class. Everything is made on site and produce is carefully sourced from around Britain: Scottish beef, Whitby cod and Shetland salmon are typical players. Staff are charming, efficient and really understand what's on the menu. At lunch this includes simple, internationally inspired starters such as confit of duck leg with shredded noodle salad and Moroccan dressing followed by comfort food (steak and chips, 'posh' chicken and mushroom pie) or lighter options such as fresh sautéed fettuccini with Mediterranean vegetables and mozzarella. In the evening, try home-smoked duck with avocado and baby Gem salad and a mango crème fraîche dressing or roasted home-made black pudding infused with apple and pancetta with sautéed spinach, poached free-range egg and red wine sauce for starters. Grilled fillet of Shetland salmon with sautéed spinach and sweetcorn sauce or three flavours of belly pork with Savoy cabbage, vegetables and red wine sauce are typical mains. Desserts range from steamed syrup sponge pudding at lunch to caramelised banana samosa with vanilla ice cream and butterscotch sauce in the evening. The wine list offers interesting choices from around the world, starting at £11.95 a bottle.
Chef/s: Matt Locke. **Open:** Tue to Fri L 12 to 2.30, Mon to Sat D 6 to 9.30. **Closed:** bank hols.
Meals: alc D (main courses £14.50 to £16.50), Set L £11.95 (2 courses), £14.95 (3 courses). **Service:** not inc. **Details:** Cards accepted. 68 seats. Air-con. Music. Children's portions.

Ziba

Bullish Merseyside glamour
Hargreaves Buildings, 5 Chapel Street, Liverpool, L3 9AG
Tel no: (0151) 2366676
www.racquetclub.org.uk
Modern British | £30
New Chef

£5 OFF ▲ 🛏

Housed amid the Victorian opulence of the revitalised Racquet Club, opposite the iconic Liver Building, Ziba is a big-name venue that embraces a swanky bar and a glamorous dining room lit by chandeliers. New chef James Morgan is continuing in the same vein as his predecessor with creative menus inspired by judiciously sourced British produce. Claremont Farm asparagus with cured beef and fried duck egg is a typically plain-speaking starter, or you might prefer a bowl of Swaledale lamb broth. To follow, corn-fed Goosnargh chicken is given the tandoori treatment with curried potato, spinach and dhal jus, Orkney rib-eye steaks are served with chips, and roast cod comes with smoked salmon, capers and cauliflower purée. Desserts stay close to home with steamed lemon sponge, sticky toffee pudding or nutmeg and apple brûlée with doughnut fingers. The wine list is a serious contender, comprising a smart choice from the Old and New Worlds neatly organised by style. House Australian is £16.50 (£4 a glass).
Chef/s: James Morgan. **Open:** Mon to Sat L 12 to 2.30, D 6.30 to 10. **Closed:** Sun, bank hols and Christmas. **Meals:** alc (main courses £11 to £18). Set L £19 (3 courses). Bar menu available. **Service:** not inc. **Details:** Cards accepted. 100 seats. Air-con. Separate bar. Music. Children's portions.

Which? Campaigns

To find out more about Which? food and drink campaigns, please visit:
www.which.co.uk

Galton Blackiston Morston Hall

Why did you become a chef?
Because my cricketing career didn't take off and I always enjoyed cooking as a young boy.

Who makes you what you are today?
The staff around me, both in the kitchen and out front, and of course my wife.

What three ingredients could you not do without?
Salt, pepper and butter.

What's the most unusual ingredient you've cooked?
Pig's ear and pig's head.

What's your guilty food pleasure?
McDonalds' McFlurry.

Do you always read reviews of your restaurant?
Of course, you always learn something from reviews.

What era of history would you most like to have eaten in?
I'm pretty happy with the era I am in now. We are starting to eat more healthily.

Oxton

Fraiche

Shining star of the Wirral
11 Rose Mount, Oxton, CH43 5SG
Tel no: (0151) 6522914
www.restaurantfraiche.com
Modern French | £45
Cooking score: 6

The Wirral peninsula may not be top of anyone's list as a gastronomic destination, as witness our fairly blank map. It only takes one outstanding establishment, though, to break the mould, and here, beyond a shadow of a doubt, it is. That it only caters 20 covers at a time raises the ante. Look smart, book ahead and prepare to abandon your culinary preconceptions. Exactly what branch of modern gastronomy Marc Wilkinson's cooking occupies is a question we can leave to one side for the time being, other than that it clearly owes a lot to the avant-gardism of contemporary France. Within the small, light but enveloping ambience of the relaxing dining room, there is quite a culinary firework display going on. Three fixed-price deals are on offer. In ascending order of price, these are the Elements and Signature menus, and then a Bespoke option, effectively a *menu surprise* in which you get to ask the chef to incorporate a few of your favourite things. Think of it as a kind of 'Challenge Marc'. This year's crop of extraordinary dishes has included veal loin cooked rosé, with butternut squash done fashionably slowly, on cep extract ('extracts' are a favoured means of achieving intensity), halibut with wild rice and aubergine yoghurt, and rib-eye of Dexter beef with celery heart and puréed butternut. Starters set the ball rolling, and tongues wagging, with the likes of asparagus velouté with cured ham and Parmesan ice cream, or fennel confit with beetroot and extract of elderflower. The descriptions are sufficiently terse to arouse the keenest anticipation, and what turns up at the table scarcely disappoints. An exploration of a single flavour is another technique brought off with great aplomb, whether it be as a 'Taste of Tomato' first course, or a trio of 'Chocolate Textures' to finish. As to what the pre-dessert of 'lemongrass with pistachio soil' will consist of, there is only one way to find out. However, some readers have commented that service is somewhat lacking, wanting more explanations of the dishes on the set menu, rather than having dishes placed before them without announcement. Adding to the dazzle of the cooking is a fantastic wine selection that, as well as featuring interesting ranges from single growers (in the Alto-Aidge or Coonawarra, for example), rummages productively through the world's cellars to find enlivening and purposeful flavours. The arrangement is by style. The bidding opens at £17, and there are glasses from £4.50.

Chef/s: Marc Wilkinson. **Open:** Fri and Sat L 12.15 to 1.30, Wed to Sat D 7 to 9. **Meals:** Set L £22 to £37. Set D £35 to £55. **Service:** not inc. **Details:** Cards accepted. 20 seats. 10 seats outside. Separate bar. No mobile phones. Wheelchair access. Music. Children allowed.

▌Southport

Warehouse Brasserie

Glitz, glitterati and bubbles
30 West Street, Southport, PR8 1QN
Tel no: (01704) 544662
www.warehousebrasserie.co.uk
Global | £27
Cooking score: 3

V

Fashioned out of an old clothes warehouse, this is Southport's answer to metropolitan glitz and glamour, complete with noisy crowds of well-heeled trendy young things. The whole place spreads itself over two floors of unashamed luxury, with mirrored panelling, prints, warm colours and flashes of Art Deco. Global flavours are sprinkled liberally over the upbeat menu, which divides up casually into small and large dishes of every description. Here you will find satay-spiced squid with Asian peanut salad, sesame-glazed duck breast with gingered oriental greens and crispy noodles, rack of lamb with pistachios and caramelised apricots – even 'East West'

chips. Cheeseburgers, chargrilled chicken Caesar salad and fillet steak with béarnaise sauce bring it all back home, while the choice of desserts plays safe with sticky toffee pudding, chocolate brownie and pannacotta with champagne rhubarb. The frivolously described wine list (all 'bubbles', 'blonds' and 'red heads') offers a lively choice for all pockets; house selections start at £13.95.

Chef/s: Marc Verité. **Open:** Mon to Sat L 12 to 2, D 5.30 to 10.30. **Closed:** Sun, Christmas. **Meals:** alc (main courses £8 to £22). Set L £13.95 (2 courses) to £16.95. Set D £14.95 (2 courses) to £17.95. **Service:** not inc. **Details:** Cards accepted. 90 seats. Air-con. Separate bar. No mobile phones. Wheelchair access. Music. Children's portions.

ALSO RECOMMENDED

▲ Tyndall's

23 Hoghton Street, Southport, PR9 0NS
Tel no: (01704) 500002
Anglo-French

Right in the town centre, opposite the Little Theatre, this informal brick and bay-windowed town house offers some promising Anglo-French cooking. Two-course mid-week deals are good value from £10.95 (before 7pm) to £12.95, while 'Gourmet' dishes include black pudding with marmalade sauce (£5.50), crab and seafood salad (£12.95) and fillet of beef with red wine and mushroom sauce (£17.95). Around two dozen quaffable wines start at £13.95. Closed Sun and Mon.

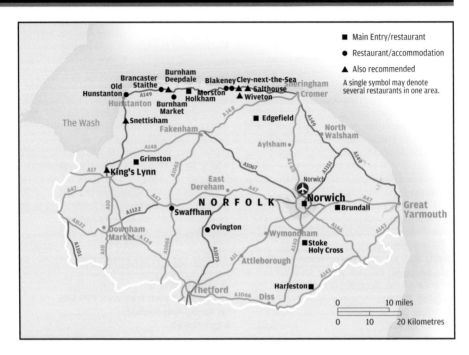

Main Entry/restaurant

● Restaurant/accommodation

▲ Also recommended

A single symbol may denote several restaurants in one area.

▌Blakeney

White Horse Hotel

Local food and hospitality
4 High Street, Blakeney, NR25 7AL
Tel no: (01263) 740574
www.blakeneywhitehorse.co.uk
Modern British | £23
Cooking score: 1

£5 OFF 🍴 £30

Up the hill from Blakeney quay, this long-serving hostelry remains an oasis for bird-watchers, sailing people and North Norfolk revellers. One menu is now served throughout the place: order at the bar if you are in the pub, enjoy table service in the conservatory and expect full paraphernalia in the sunny yellow-walled Stables Restaurant. The kitchen maintains reliable supply lines, buying wisely from local producers and fishermen for a daily-changing repertoire with seasonal shifts. Jonny Webster's Morston mussels are a great favourite, but you might also see charred sardines with chickpea, preserved lemon and chilli relish before rack of lamb with roast beetroot or black bream with parsnip purée, oyster mushrooms and Alsace lardons. Finish with the Blakeney 'Black Forest gâteau' or white chocolate rice pudding with port-soaked figs. The 60-strong Adnams wine list is priced from £11.95 (£3 a glass).
Chef/s: Duncan Philp. **Open:** all week 12 to 2.15, D 6 to 9. **Closed:** 25 Dec. **Meals:** alc (main courses £10.50 to £17.50). **Service:** not inc. **Details:** Cards accepted. 110 seats. 30 seats outside. Separate bar. No music. No mobile phones. Children's portions. Car parking.

Please send us your feedback

To register your opinion about any restaurant listed in the Guide, or a new restaurant that you wish to bring to our attention, please visit the web address at the bottom of the page. Your feedback informs the content of the book and will be used to compile next year's reviews.

▌Brancaster Staithe
The White Horse
Coastal pub with a view
Brancaster Staithe, PE31 8BY
Tel no: (01485) 210262
www.whitehorsebrancaster.co.uk
Modern British | £25
Cooking score: 3

On a clear day you can gaze across the tidal marshes to Scolt Head Island from the conservatory restaurant and sun-deck terrace of this revitalised North Norfolk pub; alternatively, take advantage of the new sunken landscaped garden for lounging and al fresco snacking. Seasonal seafood is a big player on the monthly menu and specials list: oysters are harvested from 'beds' at the bottom of the garden, and there are plentiful supplies of cockles and mussels too. Beyond bivalves, the kitchen serves up plates of locally-smoked salmon, sea bass on warm potato salad and grilled black bream with pea and shrimp risotto. Red meat fans can order steak and chips or marinated rump of lamb with rösti, olive, tomato and rosemary jus, while everyone should be tempted by lemon tart or sticky date and hazelnut pudding for afters. Real ales are on handpump and the well-spread wine list provides sound drinking from £12 (£3 a glass).

Chef/s: Nicholas Parker. Open: all week L 12 to 2, D 6.30 to 9. Meals: alc (main courses L £6 to £12, D £10 to £18). Bar menu available. Service: not inc. Details: Cards accepted. 90 seats. 90 seats outside. Separate bar. No mobile phones. Wheelchair access. Music. Children's portions. Car parking.

▌Brundall
Lavender House
Energetically run country restaurant
39 The Street, Brundall, NR13 5AA
Tel no: (01603) 712215
www.thelavenderhouse.co.uk
Modern British | £38
Cooking score: 2

V

There's no doubting Richard Hughes' energy or enthusiasm: he writes recipe books and runs a thriving cookery school as well as holding sway at Lavender House. Set in a village a few miles to the east of Norwich, this country restaurant occupies a seriously pretty sixteenth-century thatched building. It is a relaxed setting for fixed-price dinners peppered with fashionable 'inter-courses'. Norfolk producers are given a name check on the menu, which opens with canapés and a complimentary appetiser. Starters might range from spiced belly of Shropham pork with cucumber, ginger and sesame to Cromer crab ravioli with tomato fondue, before crispy sea bream with peas, lettuce and Brancaster mussels or fillet and shin of Barnard's beef with smoked potato purée and port sauce. 'A theme of lemon' (posset, meringue, sorbet and drizzle cake) is a suitably showy dessert. Lavender House now boasts a special 'theatre table' overlooking the kitchen: named the Opitz Room, it honours legendary Austrian wine maker Will Opitz – whose wines naturally appear on the carefully assembled international list.

Chef/s: Richard Hughes and Richard Knights. Open: Tue to Sat D only 7 to 9. Closed: Sun, Mon. Meals: Set D £38.50. Service: not inc. Details: Cards accepted. 50 seats. Separate bar. No music. Wheelchair access. Jacket and tie required. Children's portions.

Best of organic

Some chefs have been following an organic ethos for years; others have recently realised the appeal of using produce grown according to strict standards.

Opinions differ on whether it's best to prioritise organic food or to embrace wider eco-principles by insisting on low food miles too. These restaurants combine the two, often bolstering their offers with organic or bio-dynamic wine.

The Walnut Club, Hathersage
Carefully-presented modern European dishes in a clean, contemporary setting, with the glories of the Peak District on the doorstep.

Bordeaux Quay, Bristol
Barney Haughton's restaurant and brasserie (not to mention the bar, deli, bakery and cookery school) use a mixture of Soil Association-approved and locally grown ingredients.

Daylesford Organic Farm Shop Café, Kingham
The Gloucestershire base and London café outposts specialise in carefully packaged, high-class organics for daytime consumption.

The Duke of Cambridge, Islington
The first officially certified organic pub looks to the Med as well as the UK for flavoursome, rustic dishes to populate a menu that changes twice daily.

Mill Race, Leeds
An old hand at organics, and admirably transparent about sourcing and suppliers. Modern British dishes follow the seasons, and there's a wine shop and box scheme too – organic, of course.

Charlton House, Shepton Mallet
Owner Roger Saul's Sharpham Park farm provides organic rare breed meat and spelt for chef Elisha Carter to incorporate into a sprightly, seasonal menu.

Iglu, Edinburgh
An 'ethical eaterie' in the city with a committed approach to organics and inventive, colourful food.

Acorn House, King's Cross
This eco-friendly restaurant isn't exclusively organic (sustainability, seasonality and shipping issues play a part) but you're unlikely to swallow many chemicals in its Italian-slanted dishes.

Lasswade Country House, Llanwrtyd Wells
The menu changes frequently at this country house hotel where local, organic produce is put firmly to the fore by chef-proprietor Roger Stevens.

▮ Burnham Deepdale

ALSO RECOMMENDED
▲ Deepdale Café

Main Road, Burnham Deepdale, PE31 8DD
Tel no: (01485) 211055
www.deepdalecafe.co.uk
Café

A popular local meeting-place, the café sits on an attractive bit of the North Norfolk coast, prime walking territory in which to work up an appetite for the honest-to-goodness home-style cooking. Smoked salmon and scrambled eggs on wholemeal toast (£6.95), all-day brunch or chunky sandwiches such as Camembert, rocket and plum chutney (£4.95) are what draw the crowds in. Fine local mussels turn up in the form of a large bowl of marinière (£8.75). Early birds can get a fortifying breakfast from 7.30am. Home-made desserts are chalked up on the board, along with the day's specials. Unlicensed but BYO. Open all week.

▮ Burnham Market

Fishes

Local fish, global flavours
Market Place, Burnham Market, PE31 8HE
Tel no: (01328) 738588
www.fishesrestaurant.co.uk
Seafood | £34
Cooking score: 4

🛏

Having consolidated their reputation as one of the top seafood restaurants on the North Norfolk coast, Matthew and Caroline Owsley-Brown have added a further string to their bow in the shape of three delightful guest rooms. Fishes occupies a fine-looking building with big bay windows overlooking Burnham Market's picture-perfect village green. Inside, all is relaxed as can be. Seafood is, of course, the kitchen's business (Matthew learned his trade with Rick Stein in Padstow) and the owners have fostered a fruitful relationship with many of the local fishermen, shellfish 'growers' and curers. The

result is vivid, forthright food with a fashionably global outlook. Brancaster oysters might be served with tingling yuzu juice, octopus is deep-fried in beetroot tempura batter, while Burnham Overy Staithe mussels are steamed 'mouclade style'. Bigger fish and bigger dishes also show the same imaginative intent: whole sea bream is marinated with oregano and Moroccan five-spices, roasted in a clay oven and served with hummus, tzatziki and harissa. To finish there are English cheeses plus desserts ranging from warm rhubarb and custard tart to dark chocolate crème brûlée with banana, prune, oat samosas and tonka bean sabayon. Whites naturally dominate the carefully chosen wine list, although playful, and serious reds are not neglected. Prices start at £18.50 (£5 a glass).
Chef/s: Matthew Owsley-Brown. Open: Tue to Sun L 12 to 2.15, D 6.45 to 9.30. Closed: Mon (exc bank hols), 4 days Christmas. Meals: Set L £19 (2 courses) to £22. Set D £33 (2 courses) to £38. Service: not inc. Details: Cards accepted. 42 seats. Separate bar. No music. No mobile phones. Car parking.

Hoste Arms

Versatile pub/hotel enterprise
The Green, Burnham Market, PE31 8HD
Tel no: (01328) 738777
www.hostearms.co.uk
Modern British | £29
Cooking score: 2

🍾 🛏 V £30

There may be no shortage of converted seventeenth-century coaching inns around the country, but this one piles on the style, catering ambidextrously to locals stopping by for a pint as much as well-heeled out-of-towners on weekend breaks. Rory Whelan cooks an appealing brasserie-style menu that takes in Brancaster oysters in the season, perhaps served with orange and rice wine vinegar. An east Asian bent is favoured for a few dishes, perhaps partnering salmon with bok choi, won ton and red pepper in a dressing of chilli, ginger and coriander. Mains might dive into the sea for a combination of

Bryan Webb Tyddyn Llan

Why did you become a chef?
I thought it would be easier than working down the coal mine.

What three ingredients could you not do without?
Veal bones to make stock. Good butter and salt.

What's the most unusual ingredient you've cooked or eaten?
Spinal cords as part of a plate of offal at Checchino dal 1887 in Rome.

Do you always read reviews of your restaurant?
Yes.

If you could only keep one kitchen implement, what would it be?
My palate knife.

What era of history would you most like to have eaten in?
The seventies, when the masters of nouvelle cuisine in France were mastering their craft.

What's coming up next for you?
My first cookery book.

monkfish, halibut and tiger prawns served with brown shrimp risotto, or raid the English larder for steak and kidney pudding with honey-glazed parsnips and carrots. Pair a glass of dessert wine with something like dark chocolate fondant served with toffee and almond ice cream and crushed honeycomb. The wine list is rather flash, incorporating a run of Chablis from Jean Durup, as well representatives of all five of the Bordeaux first-growth clarets, including Mouton '82 at £870.50. Thankfully, a wide selection by-the-glass is available, opening at £3.25 for southern French house wines.

Chef/s: Rory Whelan. **Open:** all week L 12 to 2, D 7 to 9. **Meals:** alc (main courses £10.75 to £24.25). **Service:** not inc. **Details:** Cards accepted. 140 seats. 100 seats outside. Air-con. Separate bar. Wheelchair access. Music. Children's portions. Car parking.

▮ Cley-next-the-sea

ALSO RECOMMENDED
▲ Cley Windmill
Cley-next-the-sea, NR25 7RP
Tel no: (01263) 740209
Modern British

Cley Windmill is a familiar landmark on the never-ending skyline of the North Norfolk coast, well-known for its quirky B&B in the round tower, but less known for its food. Interesting set-price, three-course dinners (£25) are built around the top-quality produce for which this area is known. Thus Cley-smoked fish salad with balsamic dressing might be followed by chicken breast on a bed of chorizo and chickpeas with sweet pepper sauce, while chocolate torte with raspberry coulis is a winner for dessert. House wine £11.25. Open all week.

▌Edgefield

The Pigs

Gutsy food in a proper pub
Norwich Road, Edgefield, NR24 2RL
Tel no: (01263) 587634
www.thepigs.org.uk
Gastropub | £25
Cooking score: 1

 £30

The Pigs is a proper pub, with billiards, darts, a quiz night, local real ales and good old-fashioned food. The brains behind Byfords (a deli in Holt) and the Lavender House in Brundall, Norfolk (see entry) are 'committed to providing honest food, locally sourced, reasonably priced' and it seems they are right on the button, with game from Edgefield shoots and vegetables often brought in by locals from their allotments. There is a relaxed, easy vibe in the dining room, and the cheerful staff are well-informed. A 'plate of piggy pieces' is one of several 'delicious' ways with pork, 'Iffits' are very good-value tapas, or there could be beef dripping toast with sea salt, or a bread roll of salt brisket with pickled red cabbage, horseradish cream and parsnip crisps. Puddings are along the lines of 'my nan's tipsy trifle' and double cream tapioca. The wine list is short but functional, with a quaffable Pinot Grigio at £14.
Chef/s: Tim Abbott. **Open:** Tue to Sun L 12 to 2.30 (3 Sun), Tue to Sat D 6 to 9. **Closed:** Mon except bank hols. **Meals:** alc (main courses £9.95 to £14.95). **Service:** not inc. **Details:** Cards accepted. 100 seats. 90 seats outside. Wheelchair access. Music. Children's portions. Car parking.

▌Grimston

Congham Hall, Orangery

Country-house dining in rural Norfolk
Lynn Road, Grimston, PE32 1AH
Tel no: (01485) 600250
www.conghamhallhotel.co.uk
Modern British | £46
Cooking score: 3

Every inch the country-house hotel, Congham Hall is a Georgian manor of impeccable proportions set in serene grounds. Its restaurant in the orangery is a light space adorned with chandeliers which looks out over oak-dotted meadows. Service is polite and formal. Given all this, Jamie Murch's menus are surprisingly modern. Starters can be elaborate – witness carpaccio of roe deer, artichoke and green bean salad, Parmesan and creamed horseradish, where the flavours of the tender venison struggled to compete. Much better was a main of sea bass with roast new potatoes, broad beans, fennel and dill fish velouté, the fillet cooked to split-second perfection. Breast and ballottined leg of guinea fowl in a thyme jus might figure among à la carte main courses. Puddings are a high spot, with even the set lunch including such delights as a trio of lemon desserts. The wine list is extensive. Bottles start at £19.50 for a modest Chilean Sauvignon.
Chef/s: Jamie Murch. **Open:** all week L 12 to 1.45, D 7 to 9.15. **Meals:** Set L £19.50, Set D £46. **Service:** not inc. **Details:** Cards accepted. 50 seats. 20 seats outside. Separate bar. Wheelchair access. Car parking.

▌Great Yarmouth

READERS RECOMMEND

Seafood Restaurant

Seafood
85 North Quay, Great Yarmouth, NR30 1JF
Tel no: (01493) 856009
'Long standing neighbourhood stalwart'

Readers recommend

A 'readers recommend' review is a genuine quote from a report sent in by one of our readers. We intend to follow up these suggestions throughout the year to come.

▌Harleston

Momiji Japanese Restaurant

Simple Japanese dining
3 Redenhall Road, Harleston, IP20 9EN
Tel no: (01379) 852243
www.momiji-japanese-restaurant.co.uk
Japanese | £22
Cooking score: 2

The décor might be described as Anglo-Japanese, in that this endearing timbered building looks like an old tea-shop from the street, but inside there are subtle touches of east Asia in the form of silk wall-hangings, paper lanterns and bamboo. The menu is helpfully explanatory for the uninitiated, and the format is izakaya dining (think lots of little dishes for all to share). The expected standards are all here, from tempura tiger prawns to teriyaki dishes, pork gyoza dumplings with dipping sauce to an kaké sea bass (a kind of sweet-and-sour dish with stir-fried vegetables). One or two items might look less Japanese, such as a side-order of buttery sautéed potatoes with bacon and onion, and you can finish in Stateside fashion if you like with warm pecan pie, served with vanilla ice-cream and maple syrup. To drink, there are Japanese beers and sakés, as well as shochu, a spirit made from sweet potato or barley. Grape wines start at £11.50.
Chef/s: Taka Nakamoto. **Open:** Fri to Sat L 12 to 2, Tue to Sat D 6.30 to 11. **Closed:** 25 and 26 Dec, 1 and 2 Jan. **Meals:** alc (main courses £7.45 to £13.50). Set L and D £19.50 to £19.95. **Service:** not inc. **Details:** Cards accepted. 45 seats. Wheelchair access. Music. Children allowed.

Please send us your feedback

To register your opinion about any restaurant listed in the Guide, or a new restaurant that you wish to bring to our attention, please visit the web address at the bottom of the page. Your feedback informs the content of the book and will be used to compile next year's reviews.

▌Holkham

Victoria at Holkham

Idiosyncratic colonial hotel
Park Road, Holkham, NR23 1RG
Tel no: (01328) 711008
www.victoriaatholkham.co.uk
Modern British | £30
New Chef

Standing proud at the gates of Holkham Hall (a lavish Victorian pile and ancestral seat of the Earls of Leicester), the brick-and-flint 'Vic' does duty as an idiosyncratic hotel, bar and restaurant decorated in high colonial fashion. The interior might suggest the Last Days of the Raj, but the food is much closer to home: carpaccio of Holkham venison with a salad of pickled walnuts, winter berries and rocket typifies the kitchen's devotion to all things local and seasonal. Elsewhere twice-baked Norfolk Dapple cheese soufflé appears with pear purée and braised baby fennel, while tempura of Thornham oysters makes a fitting companion for medallions of local beef with champ and Guinness cream. To finish, there's a roll-call of puddings spanning everything from sticky toffee apple sponge with bay leaf custard to iced zabaglione parfait with amaretti biscuits. House wines start at £13.50.
Chef/s: Ricardo Juanico. **Open:** all week L 12 to 2.30, D 7 to 9. **Meals:** alc (main courses £12 to £18). Set L and D £25 (2 courses) to £30. Bar menu available. **Service:** not inc. **Details:** Cards accepted. 70 seats. 100 seats outside. Wheelchair access. Music. Children allowed. Car parking.

▌Kings Lynn

ALSO RECOMMENDED
▲ Titchwell Manor

Titchwell, Kings Lynn, PE31 8BB
Tel no: (01485) 210221
www.titchwellmanor.com
Modern European

Elegantly restyled former farmhouse in a stunning coastal location overlooking salt marshes and sea. The excellent-value set lunch menu, bar menu and the evening carte focus on locally sourced ingredients, be it oysters (£9) and roast sea bass, served with crab ravioli, crab and ginger bisque and sautéed asparagus (£18), both landed at nearby Brancaster quay, or rare-breed meats and venison (with confit cabbage and thyme jus, £19) from nearby Houghton Estate. Or there could be beef onglet (a particularly flavourful cut of meat) with caramelised baby vegetables, short rib compote and beef jus (£14). House wine £14.50. Open all week.

Morston

Morston Hall
Unpretentious North Norfolk hotel
Morston, NR25 7AA
Tel no: (01263) 741041
www.morstonhall.com
Modern European | £50
Cooking score: 5

It may look grand, set behind high walls in secluded grounds, but this seventeenth-century flint-and-brick house close to Morston's tidal quay is comfortable, relaxed and unpretentious. Start with drinks and nibbles by the fire in the stone-flagged hall, or in one of two conservatories; the second is where a set, no-choice dinner of four courses is served. Menus change daily, the limited number of dishes allowing the kitchen to focus on local and seasonal ingredients. A recent inspection meal opened with a rich and perfectly constructed terrine of confit guinea fowl and foie gras, served with braised endive and an intense black pudding sauce, then chargrilled local asparagus wrapped in Parma ham with a smooth hollandaise sauce. A main course of sea bream was teamed with fennel, baby carrots and 'a delicately flavoured' crab bisque. Portions are just right, allowing room for properly kept cheeses and dessert, the latter taking in a warm Rothschild soufflé with white chocolate ice cream. Dishes are well-balanced and timing mostly spot-on, while service has been described as 'very slick': 'nothing is too much trouble for the young,

professional staff'. Of course, you could just come here for the wine – the pin-sharp global list has plenty to entice with good drinking to be had for under £30.
Chef/s: Galton Blackiston. **Open:** Sun L 12.30 for 1 (1 sitting), all week D 7.30 for 8 (1 sitting). **Closed:** 2 days Christmas, 1 month Jan. **Meals:** Set Sun L £32, Set D £50 (4 courses). **Service:** not inc.
Details: Cards accepted. 50 seats. No music. Wheelchair access. Children's portions. Car parking.

Norwich

Mad Moose Arms, 1Up Restaurant
Pub/brasserie on the up
2 Warwick Street, Norwich, NR2 3LD
Tel no: (01603) 627687
Modern British | £28
Cooking score: 2

£5 OFF   £30

In Norwich's fashionable 'golden triangle' close to the University of East Anglia, the Mad Moose Arms is an upwardly mobile pub that has come on by leaps and bounds of late. The ground-floor bar gets overrun with drinkers and pool players, but head upstairs to the high-ceilinged 1Up restaurant if you are looking for colourful modern brasserie food. Charred smoked salmon with fine green beans, candied hazelnuts and vanilla infusion sets the eclectic tone, ahead of roast Norfolk pheasant breast with herb gnocchi, confit salsify and red wine sauce or pan-fried black bream with fennel, chorizo and saffron butter sauce. Round things off with a fruity combo of 'free-standing' crème brûlée with poached rhubarb, glazed fig, pomegranate and rhubarb sorbet. The good-value, 40-bin wine list starts at £12.95 (£3.50 a glass). Related to the Wildebeest Arms, Stoke Holy Cross and Mackintosh's Canteen in Norwich itself (see entries).
Chef/s: Eden Derreck. **Open:** Sun L 12 to 3, Mon to Sat D 7 to 10. **Closed:** 25 Dec. **Meals:** alc (main courses £10 to £18). Set D Mon to Thur £15 (2 courses) to £20. Bar menu available. **Service:** not

inc. **Details:** Cards accepted. 45 seats. 60 seats outside. Separate bar. Wheelchair access. Music. Children's portions.

Tatlers

International cooking
21 Tombland, Norwich, NR3 1RF
Tel no: (01603) 766670
www.tatlers.com
Modern British | £22
New Chef

 £30

This characterful restaurant occupies a period house in the historical Tombland area of Norwich. The dining rooms are of the scrubbed-floorboard, heritage-hued variety. Food-wise, expect an exuberantly international affair. Starters range from classic chicken liver parfait with pear chutney, caper berries and hot toast to Thai-style tom yam soup. In a similar vein, mains run from chargrilled pigeon breast and black pudding with vine tomatoes and new potatoes to fresh grilled fillet of mackerel on spicy lentil dhal with Blakeney spinach and Greek yoghurt. On Monday to Thursday evenings (and Monday to Saturday lunch) a good-value set menu offers three courses for £18. These choices have a more restrained, familiar feel – perhaps smoked salmon and free-range eggs on toast followed by Aberdeen Angus minute steak with hand-cut chips. A decent wine list starts at £15 a bottle and includes plenty by-the-glass.
Open: Mon to Sat L 12 to 2.30, D 6 to 9.15.
Meals: alc (main courses £11.95 to £16.95). Set L and D £14 (2 courses), £18 (3 courses). **Service:** not inc. **Details:** Cards accepted. 36 seats. Separate bar. Children's portions.

Average price

The average price listed in main-entry reviews denotes the price of a three-course meal, without wine.

ALSO RECOMMENDED
▲ Mackintosh's Canteen
Unit 410, Chapelfield Plain, Norwich, NR2 1SZ
Tel no: (01603) 305280
www.mackintoshscanteen.co.uk
Modern British

There is a faint hint of the roadside caff about the logo on this redbrick building that is part of the local Animal Inns group. There the similarities end, as quality dining is offered on two floors, with the upstairs featuring the special menu. This might range from smoked haddock fishcake with smoked salmon and celeriac rémoulade (£6.50), via grilled sea bass with king prawn risotto in tomato, ginger and coriander coulis (£16.95) or Gressingham duck breast with dauphinoise potatoes (£17.95), to a properly boozy version of tiramisù (£5.50). Norfolk cheeses (£6.95) will tempt those with a savoury tooth. Wines from £13.95. Open all week.

▮ Old Hunstanton

★NEW ENTRY★
Neptune Inn & Restaurant
Cosy but classy operation
85 Old Hunstanton Road, Old Hunstanton, PE36 6HZ
Tel no: (01485) 532122
www.theneptune.co.uk
Modern British | £35
Cooking score: 5

Kevin Mangeolles and Jacki Everest refurbished this eighteenth-century roadside inn during 2007, after moving from the George Hotel on the Isle of Wight (see entry). It is a small, cosy but classy operation with wooden flooring, white walls, an adjacent bar area, neatly dressed diners and a jazz soundtrack. The menu is ever-changing, innovative and highly elaborate. It is questionable whether a glass of parsley soup added anything to an otherwise terrific starter of ham terrine topped with a perfect runny deep-fried egg, itself coated with a delicate onion-seed crust. Baked leek custard with mature cheddar sauce might have offered simpler flavours. Nevertheless, the technical expertise, presentation and quality of (often local) ingredients here is of the highest order. A main course fillet of grey mullet, fennel confit, sweet potato gnocchi and orange sauce might seem an ingredient too far, but was a masterpiece of composition: the subtle sauce perfectly matching the succulent seared fish. Confit and loin of organic pork was a popular choice at a neighbouring table. Desserts can be as simple as sticky toffee pudding, but it is a shame not to test the chef's mettle by sampling intricate constructions such as the trio of chocolate desserts: chocolate tart of the utmost fragility, with white chocolate and thyme ice cream and Manjari chocolate soup. The wine list too deserves merit, including seven house wines (£14.95) available by the glass. Service (from Jacki) is chatty, informal yet effortlessly professional.

Chef/s: Kevin Mangeolles. **Open:** all week D 7 to 9.30 (Lunch by appointment). **Closed:** 26 Dec, last 3 weeks Jan. **Meals:** alc (main courses £17 to £19.50). **Service:** not inc. **Details:** Cards accepted. 30 seats. Separate bar. No mobile phones. Music.

▌ Ovington
Café at Brovey Lair
Intimate, personally run restaurant
Carbrooke Road, Ovington, IP25 6SD
Tel no: (01953) 882706
www.broveylair.com
Pacific Rim fish and seafood | £47.50
Cooking score: 6

£5 OFF 🍴

Tina Pemberton still pretty much has the market cornered in this part of East Anglia with her innovative pan-Asian cooking. The personally run restaurant-with-rooms combines kitchen and dining room in one elegant, modern space where fish and seafood are cooked in front of you on a teppan grill. Intimate, with just one sitting and a no-choice four-course menu (discussed on booking), 'it's like a dinner party and doesn't feel like

Norfolk at all'. The cooking blends accomplished sophistication with skilled simplicity. Balance and flavours are spot-on, as evidenced by sesame-coated Chinese five-spice scallops served on a watercress and rocket salad with a zingy lime, ginger and spring onion vinaigrette, and a spinach and sweet potato soup with cumin, lemon and toasted pumpkin seeds. A main-course tagine of baked halibut is partnered with pickled lemons, cherry tomatoes, olives, tiger prawns and a Medjool date couscous, while the theme is continued with a Moroccan almond and orange cake served with plums roasted in rum and orange (one of two options for dessert). Mike Pemberton oversees the tables with 'effortless communication, which is what good service is all about'. Wines start at £17.50. If you are planning to stay, the house take on breakfast is as interesting as dinner. Booking is essential.

Chef/s: Tina Pemberton. **Open:** all week D only 7.45 (1 sitting). **Closed:** 25 Dec. **Meals:** Set D £47.50 (4 courses). **Service:** 10%. **Details:** Cards accepted. 24 seats. 20 seats outside. Air-con. Wheelchair access. Music. Car parking.

▌ Ringstead
READERS RECOMMEND
Gin Trap
British
6 High Street, Ringstead, PE36 5JU
Tel no: 01485 525264
www.gintrapinn.co.uk
'Traditional fare on the Norfolk coast'

▌ Salthouse
ALSO RECOMMENDED
▲ Cookies Crab Shop
The Green, Salthouse, NR25 7AJ
Tel no: (01263) 740352
www.cookies.shopkeepers.co.uk
Seafood

The tiny brick-and-cobbled cottage overlooks the village green and acres of salt marsh, an idyllic spot for such a thriving business. For 50 years three generations of the McKnespiey family have been selling the best crab, smoked fish and shellfish for miles, either to eat in – at table in the shop, in the garden shed or under a gazebo in the garden – or to take away. The menu is simple and incredibly good value: soups, sandwiches (including crab and hot roast salmon), their famed crab salad (£4.90) or the special lobster salad (£8.50). Order tea or BYO (there's no corkage charge). Open daily.

■ Snettisham

ALSO RECOMMENDED
▲ Rose and Crown

Old Church Road, Snettisham, PE31 7LX
Tel no: (01485) 541382
www.roseandcrownsnettisham.co.uk
Gastropub

All rambling rooms, low ceilings and open fires, this fourteenth-century gem has moved with the times when it comes to food. A new chef is at the helm, but the kitchen still puts its faith in seasonal Norfolk produce and daily deliveries of North Sea fish. 'Classics' such as Holkham bangers and sorrel mash share the billing with in-vogue sashimi tuna carpaccio (£5.95), rack of lamb with hot mint jam (£15.50) and monkfish with squid ink tagliatelle and king prawn tempura. Desserts (£5.20) put lemon and almond pudding alongside vanilla fudge parfait with coffee mille-feuille. Real ales plus three dozen wines from £12.50 (£3.50 a glass). Open all week.

■ Stoke Holy Cross
Wildebeest Arms

Fashionable pub/restaurant
82-86 Norwich Road, Stoke Holy Cross, NR14 8QJ
Tel no: (01508) 492497
www.thewildebeest.co.uk
Modern European | £26
Cooking score: 2

Close to the by-pass four miles south of Norwich, this fashionable pub/restaurant is popular with travellers and city escapees looking for a cosmopolitan retreat. As the name suggests, there's a touch of Afro-exoticism about the open-plan interior with its wicker chairs, greenery and tribal artefacts. The kitchen delivers well-tuned modern food with a European accent: salt cod fishcake with tomato fondue and celeriac rémoulade or beetroot-cured gravad lax with an oyster beignet might give way to fillet of sea bass with leeks, courgettes and lemon butter sauce or braised shin of beef with oxtail ravioli and truffle mash. For dessert, consider frozen almond and Amaretto parfait or chilled white chocolate rice pudding with caramelised banana and caramel sauce. The wine list is an inspired selection of bottles from across the globe, with France and Australia as the main attractions; notes are informative and prices are fair. House wines start at £14.95 (£3.95 a glass); also look for the new 'premium selections'.

Chef/s: Daniel Smith. **Open:** all week L 12 to 2, D 7 to 9. **Closed:** 25 and 26 Dec. **Meals:** alc (main courses £12 to £18). Set L £13.95 (2 courses) to £16.95, Set D £15 (2 courses) to £18.50. **Service:** not inc. **Details:** Cards accepted. 60 seats. 54 seats outside. Air-con. Separate bar. Music. Children's portions. Car parking.

Symbols

 Accommodation is available.

 Three courses for less than £30.

V More than five vegetarian dishes.

£5 OFF £5-off voucher scheme.

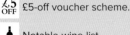 Notable wine list.

Which? Campaigns

To find out more about Which? food and drink campaigns, please visit:
www.which.co.uk

Swaffham

Strattons
Eco-friendly Palladian townhouse
4 Ash Close, Swaffham, PE37 7NH
Tel no: (01760) 723845
www.strattonshotel.com
Modern British | £40
Cooking score: 3

⊏ V

The Scott family run this fascinating Palladian townhouse villa as an 'art boutique hotel' and restaurant with a big eco-heart. Recycling, food miles, regionality, local supplies and foraging define much of what they do, and the whole enterprise is refreshingly relaxed. The restaurant has been given a facelift of late, with stripped floorboards, rich colours, bespoke seating and artwork inspired by silver birches (iconic trees of the nearby 'Brecks'). The Scotts have built up a network of Norfolk suppliers over the years and are developing their own kitchen garden to bring produce even closer to home. Dinner is a four-course affair that might open in summer with Cromer crab, Bloody Mary jelly, steamed samphire and chilli mayonnaise. To follow, there could be a parcel of Papworth pork or baked Narborough trout served with vegetarian haggis and spring onion mash, before a taster-course of three Norfolk cheeses. The evening comes to a close with treacle pud and custard or a trio of sorbets and ices. Organic wines naturally feature prominently on the well-chosen list; prices start at £14.

Chef/s: Vanessa Scott and Maggie Cooper. **Open:** Mon to Sat D only 7 to 9 (residents only Sun D). **Closed:** Sun, Christmas. **Meals:** Set D £40 (4 courses). **Service:** not inc. **Details:** Cards accepted. 25 seats. 10 seats outside. Separate bar. No mobile phones. Music. Children's portions. Car parking.

Wiveton

ALSO RECOMMENDED
▲ Wiveton Bell
Blakeney Road, Wiveton, NR25 7TL
Tel no: (01263) 740101
www.wivetonbell.co.uk
Gastropub

The Bell overlooks the village green and church in sleepy Wiveton, a mile from glorious, bird-rich saltmarshes. The bucolic setting lures pub-goers from the coast for Nick Anderson's inventive seasonal menus, served in a rustic-chic setting of oak-planked floors, stripped beams and bold artwork on Farrow and Ball-painted walls. Typical offerings take in whole plaice with cockle and parsley butter (£15.95), rib-eye steak with all the trimmings and béarnaise sauce (£16.95), and lemon posset (£5.95). House wine £12.50. Accommodation. Open all week.

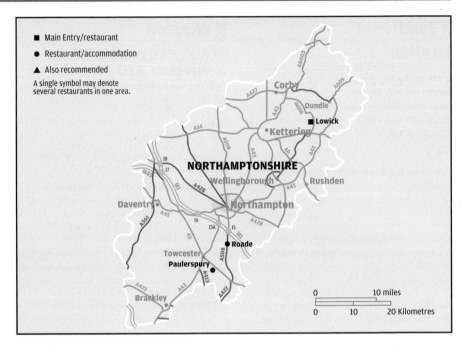

Lowick

Snooty Fox
Steaks win the day
16 Main Street, Lowick, NN14 3BH
Tel no: (01832) 733434
www.snootyinns.com
Modern British | £25
Cooking score: 3

A good-looking sixteenth-century manor house complete with gables and other historic appendages is the setting for this middle-England village pub-cum-restaurant. Inside, it has the expected beamed ceilings, exposed stone walls and original features, although these days it is better known for its full-blooded food. Main man Clive Dixon has moved to the Hinds Head Hotel, Bray (see entry, Berkshire), but the thrust and impetus of the menu remains unchanged: a rotisserie/grill holds centre stage and it is fed with supplies of dry-aged, butchered-to-order Aberdeenshire steaks from the display counter.

The kitchen also tackles breast of wood pigeon with beetroot risotto, pot-roast chicken with woodland mushroom tartlet, fish from Brixham and desserts such as lemon thyme brûlée with raspberry soup. 'Tapas and nibbles' are available in the bar. Real ale buffs have a great choice of brews from near and far; wine drinkers can peruse the wide-ranging list, which opens with house recommendations from £12.95 (£3 a glass).
Chef/s: James Nicholls. **Open:** all week L 12 to 2.30, D 6.30 to 9.30. **Closed:** 1 Jan. **Meals:** alc (main courses £10 to £22). Set L £9.95 (2 courses) to £12.50. Set D Mon £10 (2 courses). Bar menu available. **Service:** not inc. **Details:** Cards accepted.

Average price

The average price listed in main-entry reviews denotes the price of a three-course meal, without wine.

120 seats. 96 seats outside. Separate bar. Wheelchair access. Music. Children's portions. Children allowed. Car parking.

Paulerspury

Vine House
Beguiling home-from-home
100 High Street, Paulerspury, NN12 7NA
Tel no: (01327) 811267
www.vinehousehotel.com
Modern British | £30
Cooking score: 3

£5 OFF

Julie and Marcus Springett's enchanting restaurant-with-rooms is a very personal set up: she is ever-present out front, he takes charge of the kitchen. They have been resident at this rambling 300-year-old stone cottage since 1991 and rarely stray from their successful formula. Ingredients reflect the seasons, and menus (the same for lunch and dinner) are kept short: there are just three choices at each stage, plus the option of a 'slate' of unpasteurised British cheeses. A starter of Cornish red mullet drizzled with basil oil or jokey treacle-baked beans with home-cured pancetta could be followed by local venison with red wine sauce and triple-cooked chips or wild sea bass with warm gazpacho sauce. Desserts mix homeliness (hot apricot bread-and-butter pudding) with a touch of rustic class (organic Bramley apple mousse with cracked black pepper and Stilton biscuits). France provides the backbone for the 70-bin wine list, which has a fondness for classic old-school names. A quartet of house selections starts things off at £15.95.
Chef/s: Marcus Springett. **Open:** Tue to Sat L 12 to 2.30, all week D 7 to 10. **Closed:** 1 week Christmas. **Meals:** Set L and D £29.95. **Service:** 12.5%. **Details:** Cards accepted. 33 seats. 10 seats outside. Separate bar. No music. No mobile phones. Wheelchair access. Children allowed. Car parking.

Roade

Roade House
Well-tuned modern food
16 High Street, Roade, NN7 2NW
Tel no: (01604) 863372
www.roadehousehotel.co.uk
Modern British | £31
Cooking score: 4

Originally built as a roadside inn, the Roade House has blossomed under the direction of Chris and Sue Kewley: two decades down the line it is a favourite pitstop and peaceful retreat within easy reach of the M1 and the supercharged world of Silverstone. Over the years, Chris has honed his culinary style and he continues to offer well-tuned modern food with plenty of interesting touches. Carpaccio of tuna comes with guacamole and citrus fruits, while fillet of pollock is 'blackened' and served with a sunny warm salad of Mediterranean vegetables and new potatoes. A strong classical vein also runs through the menu in the shape of roast guinea fowl with apple and Calvados sauce (albeit with goats' cheese beignets) or calf's liver with pancetta, onion confit and red wine butter. Desserts often have an exotic fruity slant – warm peppered pineapple or ice nougat parfait with kumquats and kumquat sorbet, for example. The wine list is stylistically focused, with attention paid to quality as well as variety. Prices, from £14 (£4 a glass), are very comfortable.
Chef/s: Chris Kewley. **Open:** Mon to Fri L 12 to 1.45, Sun 12 to 2, Mon to Sat D 7 to 9.30. **Closed:** bank hol Mon. **Meals:** Set L £20 (2 courses) to £23. Set D £26 (2 courses) to £31. **Service:** not inc. **Details:** Cards accepted. 45 seats. Air-con. Separate bar. No music. No mobile phones. Wheelchair access. Children's portions. Car parking.

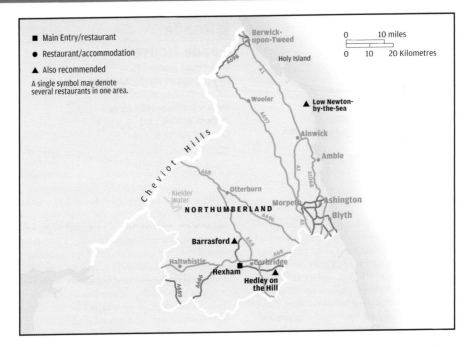

Barrasford

ALSO RECOMMENDED
▲ Barrasford Arms

Barrasford, NE48 4AA
Tel no: (01434) 681237
www.barrasfordarms.co.uk
Gastropub

Whether you're walking along Hadrian's Wall or tootling by in the motor, make time to find this handsome old stone pub – Tony Binks's reputation in these parts is worth the effort. His approach is simple: good, local ingredients prepared and presented without fuss. The menu is short and to the point, twice-baked cheddar cheese soufflé (£6), say, or North Tyne sea trout gravad lax. A classic braised rump of Northumbrian beef in Newcastle Brown ale with baby onions and Richard Woodall's air-dried ham (£13.50) is faultless, or go for roast butternut squash and sage risotto (£8). Leave room for good puddings (£5), which might include sticky pistachio meringue with vanilla and orange

mascarpone, Brockbushes strawberries and passion fruit. House wine starts at £12.50. No food Sun D and Mon L.

Hedley on the Hill

ALSO RECOMMENDED
▲ Feathers Inn

Hedley on the Hill, NE43 7SW
Tel no: (01661) 843607
www.thefeathers.net
Gastropub

It may be difficult to locate, but it really is worth taking the trouble to find this solid, no-nonsense pub. Real ales, decent wines, log fires, a cosy, intimate atmosphere and wholesome, locally sourced food should be enough to draw you. Home-made black pudding, free-range egg and devilled gravy (£5.50), or potted North Sea shrimps, toast and watercress salad with lemon (£6) may start the meal well. Move on to wild local sea trout, new potatoes, samphire and butter sauce (£13), or slow-cooked Currock Hill lamb in real ale with dauphinoise potatoes and buttered greens (£10). Finish with burnt Northumbrian cream (£5). House wines start at £11.50. No food Sun D or Mon.

▍Hexham

★NEW ENTRY★

Bouchon Bistrot

Appealing bistro in a pretty market town
4-6 Gilesgate, Hexham, NE46 3NJ
Tel no: (01434) 609943
www.bouchonbistrot.co.uk
French | £23
Cooking score: 4

 £30

A reminder that simplicity takes skill, Gregory Bureau's first restaurant is a gem in this country town. The décor is elegant but not stiff; the ground floor, with its fire, is welcoming for lunch and the purple-hued first floor more suited to dinner. The menu cleaves to Bureau's French upbringing, offering seldom-seen dishes like leeks vinaigrette. First courses might be garlic sausage with dressed Puy lentils or a show-stopping courgette, mushroom and thyme soup. To follow, Northumberland meat could be showcased in a daube of venison, or there could be a neat, pretty fish dish like seared red mullet with fennel and tarragon buerre blanc. Dessert, perhaps pear belle Hélène or crème caramel with langue-de-chat biscuits, is perfectly good but perhaps lacking a little luxury. Keen prices and friendly, impeccable service ensure local support and, as a sop to the rosbifs, Sunday heralds a roast with huge, bronzed Yorkshire puddings alongside the French classics. House wines are cuvée Duboeuf, from £3.10 a glass (also available by the carafe).
Chef/s: Nicholas Dunhill. **Open:** Tue to Sat L 12 to 2 and D 6 to 9.30, Sun L 12 to 3. **Closed:** Mon, 25 and 26 Dec, 1 Jan. **Meals:** alc (main courses £11.95 to £16.95). Set L £9.95 to £12.95, Set L Sun £13.50 to £15.50, Set D (6pm to 7pm) £12.95 to £14.95.

Service: not inc. **Details:** Cards accepted. 80 seats. Air-con. Wheelchair access. Music. Children's portions.

▍Logframlington

READERS RECOMMEND

The Anglers Arms

Gastropub
Weldon Bridge, Logframlington, NE65 8AX
Tel no: 01665 570271
www.anglersarms.fsnet.co.uk
'Tempting bait for tired ramblers'

▍Low Newton-by-the-Sea

ALSO RECOMMENDED

▲ Ship Inn

The Square, Low Newton-by-the-Sea, NE66 3EL
Tel no: (01665) 576262
www.shipinnnewton.co.uk
Gastropub

It is nigh on a decade since Christine Forsyth and her daughter bravely took on this old whitewashed pub tucked into a corner of a hidden square in this tiny village. Together they have created a cosy, convivial space, with live music, good food and beer brewed on the premises. Tuck into kipper pâté with oatcakes (£3.75), then Turnbull's lamb cutlets with mint sauce, mashed potatoes and roasted veg (£9.50) or fresh local crab with herb salad and crusty bread (£11.50). Apple crumble and cream (£3.75) is a good, traditional finish. Drink Ship Hot Ale, Dolly Daydream or Sandcastles at Dawn. House wine starts at £12.50. Open all week. No cards taken.

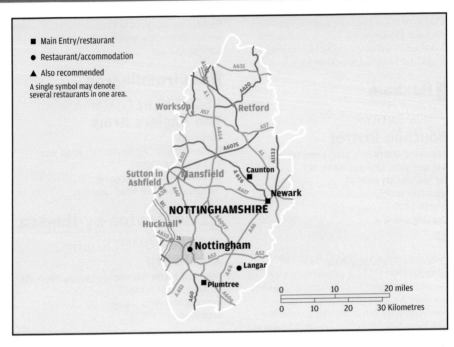

Caunton

Caunton Beck

Handsome pub in quiet, leafy location
Main Street, Caunton, NG23 6AB
Tel no: (01636) 636793
Modern European | £26
Cooking score: 2

How many pubs try to be all things to all people and invariably fall short? Well, not Caunton Beck. If you turn up at 8am you can have breakfast, food is served all day, every day, either in the delightfully lush garden (weather permitting), at a plain oak table in the stone-flagged, beamed bar, or in the slightly more formal restaurant. The food is well-prepared from quality ingredients and offers good value: charcuterie for two is a substantial plateful, with Parma ham piled high above home-made celeriac rémoulade and fat Italian olives. The batter on haddock tempura 'shatters satisfyingly', while crab and coriander risotto is an innovative and delicious idea. Mains might include Red House Hill roast pork with apple and cider compote and crackling, or grilled halibut with slow-roast vine tomatoes and basil pesto. Wine suggestions are helpfully printed under each menu choice, with bottles starting at £16.

Chef/s: Valérie Hope. **Open:** all week 8am to 11pm. **Meals:** alc (main courses £12.50 to £16.50). Set menu £11 (2 courses) to £13.95. **Service:** not inc. **Details:** Cards accepted. 90 seats. 40 seats outside. Separate bar. No music. Wheelchair access. Children's portions. Car parking.

Please send us your feedback

To register your opinion about any restaurant listed in the Guide, or a new restaurant that you wish to bring to our attention, please visit the web address at the bottom of the page. Your feedback informs the content of the book and will be used to compile next year's reviews.

▌Langar

Langar Hall
Grand family home in a peaceful setting
Langar, NG13 9HG
Tel no: (01949) 860559
www.langarhall.com
Modern British | £34
Cooking score: 4

 £5 OFF

The peaceful idyll begins as visitors head up the long drive, past the croquet lawns, medieval ponds and ancient trees, towards this very distinctive early-Victorian mansion. Owner Imogen Skirving has imbued the place with her own personality and it still feels like a rather grand family home – complete with crystal chandeliers, statues and marble pillars. Pickings from the hotel's kitchen garden find their way into the larder, along with game from nearby Belvoir Estate and a bountiful harvest provided by local producers. Home-cured peppered fillet of beef with celeriac rémoulade might sit alongside creamed goats' cheese with roast tomatoes, tomato jelly and basil oil, while Langar lamb is a favourite main course (roast cutlet and leg with chargrilled vegetables, for example). Despite the landlocked location, fish also figures prominently: witness seared scallops with pea and pancetta risotto or steamed turbot with asparagus and sorrel sauce. A fulsome selection of desserts might include English strawberry tartlet with pistachio ice cream or lime soufflé with coconut ice cream. France and the New World dominate the sound wine list; prices start at £14.75. Marcus Welford, co-founder of the Olive Branch, Clipsham (see entry), has been taken on as restaurant manager and plans are afoot to simplify the food and menus.
Chef/s: Garry Booth. **Open:** all week L 12 to 2, D 7 to 10. **Meals:** alc (main courses £12.50 to £21). Set L £14.50 (2 courses) to £20. Set D £20 (2 courses) to £25. Light menu available. **Service:** 10% (optional). **Details:** Cards accepted. 30 seats. 20 seats outside. Separate bar. No music. No mobile phones. Wheelchair access. Music. Children's portions. Car parking.

▌Newark

Café Bleu
Vibrant local bistro
14 Castle Gate, Newark, NG24 1BG
Tel no: (01636) 610141
www.cafebleu.co.uk
Modern European | £28
Cooking score: 1

 £5 OFF £30

A bright fixture of the Newark scene for more than a decade, this strikingly designed Trentside bistro makes much of its multi-coloured murals on distressed walls and sustains the bonhomie with regular live music sessions. The kitchen's no-nonsense approach could produce starters of seared swordfish with salsa verde or poached chicken breast with herb and asparagus mousse, while main courses bring on fillet of cod with shellfish butter and citrus fruit salad or braised collar of pork with pancetta and apple 'hash', seared scallop and creamed leeks. There's no stinting when it comes to calorific desserts such as baked almond tart with poached blackcurrants and clotted cream. Lunch menus put the emphasis on casual one-dish meals in a similar vein, and the 40-bin wine list has plenty of good-value drinking from £12.95 (£3.45 a glass).
Chef/s: Mark Cheseldine. **Open:** all week L 12 to 2.30 (2 Sat, 3 Sun), D Mon to Sat 7 to 9.30 (6.30 to 10 Sat). **Meals:** alc (main courses £11 to £16). **Service:** not inc. **Details:** Cards accepted. 80 seats. 60 seats outside. No mobile phones. Wheelchair access. Music. Children's portions.

Please send us your feedback

To register your opinion about any restaurant listed in the Guide, or a new restaurant that you wish to bring to our attention, please visit the web address at the bottom of the page. Your feedback informs the content of the book and will be used to compile next year's reviews.

Nottingham

French Living

Enduring old-world brasserie
27 King Street, Nottingham, NG1 2AY
Tel no: (0115) 9585885
www.frenchliving.co.uk
French | £20
Cooking score: 1

Fashions come and go, but the charm of French Living endures, evoking the spirit of olde-worlde French brasseries. The kitchen revels in the earthy glories of gratinée à l'oignon, cassoulet and casserole of wild boar, but it also cooks fillet of venison with soft red wine and blueberry sauce, and salmon with oyster mushrooms, sweet potato mash and watercress sauce. There are no surprises when it comes to desserts such as crème brûlée, and it's worth exploring the patriotically Gallic cheeses. House French is £9.50. Enter via the French Living deli and café.
Chef/s: Jeremy Tourne. **Open:** Tue to Sat L 12 to 2, D 6 to 10. **Closed:** Sun and Mon, Christmas. **Meals:** Set L £7.90, pre theatre £9.50, Set L and D £16.50 to £21.50. **Service:** not inc. **Details:** Cards accepted. 44 seats. Air-con. Music. Children's portions.

Hart's

Nottingham culinary landmark
1 Standard Court, Park Row, Nottingham, NG1 6GN
Tel no: (0115) 9110666
www.hartsnottingham.co.uk
Modern British | £35
Cooking score: 5

It may seem like Tim Hart's contemporary restaurant occupying part of the former Nottingham General Hospital has been around forever, but that's not to say Hart's is dated. The light, spacious dining room has a wooden floor and a lively array of contemporary art, and seriousness of intent is apparent from the well-proportioned tables and good linen. Mark Osborne's food is

modern, but not aggressively so. Its backbone of fairly conservative brasserie dishes is enlivened by a few surprise elements, such as goats' cheese and basil ice cream with chilled gazpacho, and tomato jelly wth ballottine of sea trout. Those with simpler tastes might go for English asparagus with goats' cheese, poached free-range egg and hot mayonnaise. Main courses are no less inventive, taking in a well-timed fillet of brill with a fricassee of crayfish and artichokes with scallop tortellini, or roast chump of lamb with white onion purée, wild garlic leaves and pommes Anna. To finish, serious temptation is offered in the shape of a stunning lavender pannacotta with raspberry compote and a ('rather superfluous') side of marshmallow, or an 'appealing' apple crumble soufflé. Service is hard to fault. Wines, from £16.50 are an intriguing bunch, arranged by style to make navigation and choice easier.
Chef/s: Mark Osborne. **Open:** all week L 12 to 2, D 7 to 10 (Sun 9). **Closed:** 26 Dec and 1 Jan. **Meals:** Set L £15.95, Set D (Mon to Thu) £22.50, Set Sun L £20. **Service:** 12%. **Details:** Cards accepted. 80 seats. 12 seats outside. Separate bar. Wheelchair access. Children's portions. Car parking.

★NEW ENTRY★
Larwood & Voce

Cricketing foodie pub that's a winner
Fox Road, West Bridgford, Nottingham, NG2 6AJ
Tel no: (0115) 9819960
Gastropub | £23
Cooking score: 3

Right beside Trent Bridge cricket ground and named after the two English cricketers who bowled out the Australians to win the 1932-33 Ashes series, this lively city pub is an unlikely setting to find cracking pub food. But it's a real winner, balancing an ability to hit the mark as a true community pub – think large plasma screens and oodles of drinking space – with foodie ambitions (an open-to-view kitchen and blackboards listing home-made bar nibbles give an indication that food is important here). The frequently changing modern British menu underlines the fact, with seasonal foods from named local suppliers: Brickfield Farm asparagus with hollandaise or devilled lambs' kidneys on toast, crisp Beechmast Farm pork belly with baked red onion and apple sauce or salt-baked sea bass with braised lettuce and Jersey royals. Desserts do not disappoint – try the fruit-packed pomegranate and elderflower jelly with vanilla ice cream. A classic bar lunch menu, decent ales and a raft of wines from £13.50 complete the picture.

Chef/s: John Molnar. **Open:** Mon to Fri 12 to 10, Sat 9am to 10pm, Sun 9 to 9. **Meals:** alc (main courses £9.50 to £19). Set L £6.95 (2 courses) to £8.95. **Details:** Cards accepted. 65 seats. 35 seats outside. Separate bar. Wheelchair access. Music. Children's portions.

Restaurant Sat Bains

Confident cooking with a sense of direction
Old Lenton Lane, Nottingham, NG7 2SA
Tel no: (0115) 9866566
www.restaurantsatbains.net
Modern European | £49
Cooking score: 7

The former farmhouse down a narrow lane on the very outskirts of Nottingham has been turned into a smart restaurant-with-rooms. A stone-flagged, leather-seated bar leads to a double dining room – one part a conservatory looking over a walled garden – where a neutral palette of stone, brick, and brown adds up to a tasteful combination of rustic and contemporary. Sat Bains's cooking is confident with a sense of direction and purpose, and has made quite a splash in Nottingham and beyond. Presentation is a strong point, an opening riff on flavours of the Mediterranean – cod brandade, confit tomato, fennel juice with lemongrass (to be swigged out of a mini bottle), squid, its ink, pasta and mango served in a tin – admirably setting the scene for a tasting menu in May. Sourcing and timing of materials are admirable, with only the occasional stumble,

and combinations are well-considered, be they scallop served with pig's head carpaccio, apple, chicory and fennel, or a piece of organic salmon atop scrambled cucumber jelly, the flavour pointed by a sharp hit of grapefruit. Elsewhere, an occasional Asian twist sees, for example, cumin teamed with Goosnargh duck, butternut purée and an intense foie gras cream. And that delight in the spicy/sour end of the taste spectrum runs through desserts, too: figs with a restrained pine nut ice cream and shavings of aged Parmesan; a pre-dessert of coconut mousse and powerful passion-fruit jelly; then a small chunk of pure chocolate with an intense liquorice mousse and slick of tangy lime. And just when you're thinking of something sweet, along comes a simple dish of Gariguette strawberries. The wine list is expensive (from £26), arranged by style, but offers serious, food-friendly wines guaranteed to set off the kitchen's artistry.

Chef/s: Sat Bains. **Open:** Tue to Sat D 7 to 9. **Closed:** Sun and Mon, 2 weeks Jan, 2 weeks Aug. **Meals:** Set D £49, tasting menu (7 courses) £67. **Service:** 12.5%. **Details:** Cards accepted. 30 seats. Air-con. Separate bar. Wheelchair access. Children allowed. Car parking.

World Service

Seamless fusion of the old and new
Newdigate House, Castle Gate, Nottingham, NG1 6AF
Tel no: (0115) 8475587
www.worldservicerestaurant.com
Global | £35
Cooking score: 4

£5 OFF **V**

World Service is a seamless fusion of the old and new, housed in a modern extension to seventeenth-century Newdigate House. A 'rather elegant terrace' leads into the bar, and the 'cool, calm' dining area is filled with patterned fabrics, ornate mirrors, oriental artefacts and plain wooden tables. The international fusion of the past few years has given way to a menu that is more modern European in style. Starters of grilled wild sea bass with pressed provençale vegetables, or salt cod croquette with soused tomato and cockle salad might be followed by sea trout with warm potato salad and salsa verde, or slow-roasted suckling pig teamed with onion marmalade, rösti potato, cider and vanilla sauce. Exceptional desserts include a baked rhubarb and vanilla Alaska tart. Service is of the good, friendly variety. A short-choice light lunch is good value, and the wine list starts at £14.

Chef/s: Preston Walker and Chris Elson. **Open:** all week L 12 to 2 (Sun 2.30), 7 to 10 (Sun 9). **Closed:** 1 to 7 Jan. **Meals:** alc (main courses £13 to £21). Set L £12 (2 courses) to £16.50. **Service:** 10% (optional). **Details:** Cards accepted. 80 seats. 40 seats outside. Separate bar. Music.

ALSO RECOMMENDED
▲ Delilah
15 Middle Pavement, Nottingham, NG1 7DX
Tel no: (0115) 9484461
www.delilahfinefoods.co.uk
Deli/Café

It is worth supporting this well-stocked independent deli in the centre of Nottingham. Drop in for coffee, sandwiches (hot roast lamb with mint jelly £3.95), platters of French cheeses and the likes of rare-breed burger with Gorgonzola and red onion marmalade (£7.95), all served to just nine bar stools at a counter at the back of the shop. Wines by-the-glass £4.50; bottles are what's on sale in the deli, priced at retail plus £5. Open all week.

▲ Iberico World Tapas
Shire Hall, High Pavement, Nottingham, NG1 1HN
Tel no: (0115) 9410410
Spanish/Pan Asian

There's a buzz to this low-vaulted basement tapas bar beneath the Galleries of Justice. It's a casual branching out for the owners of the city's World Service (see entry) with menus mixing Spanish classics (maybe chorizo in cider, or crispy fried squid with alioli £5) with modish international flavours (black cod in spicy miso £7.50, beef skewers with truffle sauce £5.50). Good quality ingredients,

simple décor and cheerful service draw the after-work crowd, but the simpler lunch menu is popular too. House wine £15. Closed Sun and Mon.

■ Plumtree

Perkins
Railway station turned restaurant
Station House, Station Road, Plumtree, NG12 5NA
Tel no: (0115) 9373695
www.perkinsrestaurant.co.uk
Modern European | £28
Cooking score: 2

 £30

Now run by the founder's sons, with chef Sarah Newham in the kitchen, this sweet redbrick railway station-turned-restaurant pleases a well-heeled local crowd with some smart French-influenced cooking. At inspection, a signature Anglo-Indian mulligatawny soup impressed, as did pollock with chickpea and chorizo cassoulet. Puddings are more of-the-moment, say toffee apple crème brûlée with iced apple pressé. There's an old-fashioned air to proceedings, most notable in the 1970s cordon bleu-style side dishes of broccoli hollandaise, ratatouille and carrots with caraway. The waiting staff look the part too in their classic black and whites, but we found the rather stiff, 'trained' side misjudged in such an otherwise likeable country restaurant. Entry level options are the weekly-changing prix-fixe lunch and dinner menus. A 50-strong New and Old World wine list opens at £12.95.

Chef/s: Sarah Newham. **Open:** Mon to Sat L 12 to 2, D 6.30 to 9.45, Sun L 12 to 3.30. **Meals:** Set L £11.25 (2 courses), Set D £24.50 (Mon to Thurs only). **Service:** not inc. **Details:** Cards accepted. 76 seats. 20 seats outside. Separate bar. Wheelchair access. Music. Children allowed. Car parking.

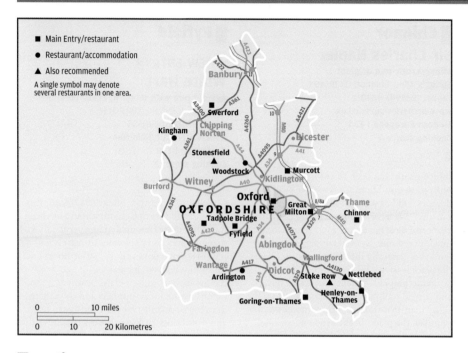

- ■ Main Entry/restaurant
- ● Restaurant/accommodation
- ▲ Also recommended

A single symbol may denote
several restaurants in one area.

▌Ardington

Boar's Head

In-tune country pub food
Church Street, Ardington, OX12 8QA
Tel no: (01235) 833254
www.boarsheadardington.co.uk
Gastropub | £35
Cooking score: 3

Looking every inch the well-groomed
Oxfordshire country pub, with its pristine
black and white exterior, rustic porches and
the village church in the background, the
Boar's Head has been dispensing hospitality
and sustenance for more than 150 years. Under
the stewardship of Bruce Buchan and co it is
now a serious contender in the local food
stakes, with a reputation for sourcing the very
best from the region's farms and producers.
Fillet of venison from nearby Lockinge Estate
could appear with trompettes and fondant
potato, while an assiette of suckling pig might
be accompanied by squid chips. Fish has to
travel up from the West Country, but the
results are worth the journey: Cornish turbot
is cooked with mussels in Chardonnay, while
feuilleté of red mullet could be served with
girolles and tomato butter sauce. Rounding
off the concise menu are desserts such as hot
Grand Marnier soufflé with iced chocolate
cream. The wine list veers towards France,
with prices from £15.50.

Chef/s: Bruce Buchan. **Open:** all week L 12 to 2, D 7
to 9.30. **Closed:** 25 and 26 Dec, 1 Jan. **Meals:** alc
(main courses £17.50 to £19.50) Set L Sun £22.50 (3
courses). Bar menu available. **Service:** not inc.
Details: Cards accepted. 40 seats. 30 seats outside.
Separate bar. No mobile phones. Wheelchair
access. Music. Children's portions. Car parking.

Readers recommend

A 'readers recommend' review is a
genuine quote from a report sent in by
one of our readers. We intend to follow
up these suggestions throughout the year
to come.

Chinnor
Sir Charles Napier
Idiosyncratic and original
Sprigg's Alley, Chinnor, OX39 4BX
Tel no: (01494) 483011
www.sircharlesnapier.co.uk
Modern European | £34
Cooking score: 4

Julie Griffiths has been running the Napier with great good humour for more than four decades and has won countless friends along the way: 'We have only been going there for 22 years and have never had a less than excellent meal,' noted one devoted couple. At its best (and that generally means hot summer days) the place is irresistibly seductive with its gorgeous gardens, foliage-entwined terrace and surreal sculptures: don't be put off by the shiny inanimate gorillas and other beasts that populate the place. In the kitchen, seasonal ingredients are treated with due respect, whether it is game, foraged fungi or wild garlic from the nearby Chiltern woods. Winter might see roast partridge with confit carrots, sarladaise potatoes and morel velouté, while summer brings wild turbot with garlic and lemon thyme or lamb cutlets with confit shoulder, crushed peas and paloise sauce. Regulars are quick to praise the cheeseboard and also the choice of puddings – perhaps gooseberry fool with citrus madeleine or rhubarb and vanilla crumble tart.

The global wine list is a knowledgeable, impeccably chosen slate with plenty of half-bottles and adventurous house recommendations from £15.95 (£4 a glass). **Chef/s:** Sam Hughes. **Open:** Tue to Sun L 12 to 3 (3.30 Sun), Tue to Sat D 6 to 10. **Closed:** Mon, 3 days Christmas. **Meals:** alc (main courses £16.50 to £24.50). Set L Tue to Fri £14.50 (2 courses), Set D Tue to Fri £16.50 (2 courses). **Service:** 12.5% (optional). **Details:** Cards accepted. 70 seats. 70 seats outside. Air-con. Separate bar. Wheelchair access. Music. Children's portions. Car parking.

Fyfield
★NEW ENTRY★
White Hart
Age-old pub with modern, seasonal menus
Main Road, Fyfield, OX13 5LW
Tel no: (01865) 390585
www.whitehart-fyfield.com
Gastropub | £28
Cooking score: 2

Owned by St John's College in Oxford, this 500-year-old former chantry house has been a pub since 1580. Dominated by a great hall with soaring eaves and a splendid minstrels' gallery, plus original oak beams, flagstone floors and mullion windows, it creaks with age. Seasonal menus are bang up-to-date, however, with menus listing local suppliers and the kitchen drawing on mainly modern European ideas and delivering cooking that is a cut above the pub average. A meal may open with chicken liver parfait with spiced apricot chutney or an antipasti board laden with meats, mozzarella and marinated peppers (ideal for sharing), then roast belly of Kelmscott pork with celeriac purée and cider jus or whole plaice with brown shrimp and caper butter. Finish with prune and Armagnac tart with vanilla bean ice cream. Wines from £15.50. **Chef/s:** Mark Chandler. **Open:** Tue to Sat L 12 to 2.30, D 7 to 9.30, Sun L 12 to 4. **Closed:** Mon. **Meals:** alc (main courses £12.50 to £18.50). Set L £15 (2 courses) to £18. **Service:** not inc. **Details:** Cards accepted. 60 seats. 50 seats outside. Separate bar. No mobile phones. Music. Children's portions. Car parking.

Please send us your feedback

To register your opinion about any restaurant listed in the Guide, or a new restaurant that you wish to bring to our attention, please visit the web address at the bottom of the page. Your feedback informs the content of the book and will be used to compile next year's reviews.

▋ Goring-on-Thames

Leatherne Bottel

Delightful waterside dining
The Bridleway, Goring-on-Thames, RG8 0HS
Tel no: (01491) 872667
www.leathernebottel.co.uk
Modern European | £40
Cooking score: 3

£5
OFF

Snug beside the Thames, this is a 'delightful setting' for al fresco dining. Inside the cottagey building, a log fire and vibrant paintings add colour and warmth. The cooking reflects chef Julia Storey's years in New Zealand, so occasional Pacific Rim influences sit cheek-by-jowl with updated European classics. Starters from the à la carte dinner menu run from sesame-crusted carpaccio of yellow fin tuna with crispy shisou leaf salad and wasabi crème fraîche to seared scallops with parsley purée, girolles, cauliflower cream and crisp pancetta. You could follow with roast saddle of venison with lemon thyme fondant potato, creamed leeks, ratatouille, juniper and red wine sauce or roast fillet of brill with crab and pea risotto and sweet chilli jam. Finish with dark chocolate and pistachio truffle mousse with pistachio anglaise. Service is 'good and friendly' and the wine list – clearly a labour of love – offers an impressive selection from France, and plenty of half-bottles.

Chef/s: Julia Storey and John Abbey. **Open:** Tue to Sun L 12 to 2.30, D 7 to 9. **Closed:** Oct, Nov, Jan to Mar. **Meals:** alc D (main courses £21 to £24.50), Set L £19.50 (2 courses) to £24.50 (3 courses). **Service:** 10%. **Details:** Cards accepted. 42 seats. 50 seats outside. Separate bar. No music. Wheelchair access. Children allowed. Car parking.

▋ Great Milton

Le Manoir aux Quat' Saisons

The good life
Church Road, Great Milton, OX44 7PD
Tel no: (01844) 278881
www.manoir.com
French | £100
Cooking score: 8

🍷 🛏 V

Raymond Blanc's mellow stone manor house has its own intrinsic splendour. Inside, rooms are comfortably furnished and decorated in soothing tones that lend a distinctly English country-house air and are more than matched by exquisite gardens where much of the kitchen's fresh produce is grown organically to precise requirements. It's worth choosing a sunny day when drinks are served on the terrace, there may well be croquet on the lawn and the chance to enjoy a stroll around the gardens. Of the various dining rooms the conservatory is the best place to be, especially when the garden is in full bloom. The focus, as it always has been, is on excellent raw materials delivered to you via formidable technical skill. Picturesque delivery has always been a hallmark of the Blanc style, although this is never at the expense of flavour composition. Indeed, highlights of a late-May lunch of Manoir classics ('created by us over the years') included an irreproachable risotto of spring vegetables topped with Sicilian tomatoes and mascarpone cream, which was in turn succeeded by a serving of roasted Icelandic halibut with citrus fregola and confit of fennel, a dish marked by astonishing clarity of flavours. All this does not come cheap, and quality can vary at a single meal. At that same May lunch, fillet of beef served with morels, white asparagus, a few spears of green beans and red wine jus was, despite 'superb beef', 'nothing extraordinary'. Occasional niggles have surfaced elsewhere – predictable (and rather meanly portioned) canapés and petits fours, for example, which sometimes diminish the value of the encounter for their reporters – but many more write to say that food and service are impossible to fault. Benchmark cheeses are kept in pristine condition, bread is as good as it comes, and nobody picks holes in desserts such as rhubarb and Gariguette strawberry crumble with a cream cheese crème glacée. Service can be slow, but staff are often smooth and charming and, at their best, manage to balance super-efficiency with relaxed friendliness. A thick wine list of 41 pages offers impeccably sourced wines firmly centred on France, but with acknowledgement of the rest of the wine-producing world – some are organically or biodynamically grown. There's a page of wines by-the-glass from £6, and bottle prices start at £26.

Chef/s: Raymond Blanc and Gary Jones. **Open:** all week L 12.15 to 2.15, D 7.15 to 9.45. **Meals:** Set mid-week L £45, Set menus L and D £95 to £116. **Service:** not inc. **Details:** Cards accepted. 90 seats. Air-con. Separate bar. Wheelchair access. Children's portions. Car parking.

▊ Henley-on-Thames
Hotel du Vin & Bistro
Buzzing atmosphere
New Street, Henley-on-Thames, RG9 2BP
Tel no: (01491) 848400
www.hotelduvin.com
Modern European | £30
New Chef
£5 OFF 🍷 ☕

The former Brakspear brewery has made a stylish transition from grain to grape, with the huge bistro kitted out in the hotel group's trademark chic style, with lots of wine bottles and colourful copies of famous paintings to the fore. There's a new chef in the kitchen but the bistro menu is as before, contemporary without being too fashionable. Its clearly focused Mediterranean perspective is evident in the likes of cured bresaola or rabbit rillette. Confit duck leg as a main course may be teamed with spinach, gnocchi, beetroot purée and aromatic honey, while wild sea bass could be accompanied by saffron-braised fennel and sauce vierge. Crème brûlée and vanilla pannacotta are typical desserts. Wine,

inevitably (given the name), is another important cog in the machine. Prices start at £14.50, but value for money is variable.
Chef/s: Neil Falzon. **Open:** all week L 12 to 2, D 6 to 10. **Meals:** Set menus from £10.95. **Service:** 10%. **Details:** Cards accepted. 90 seats. 50 seats outside. Air-con. Separate bar. Wheelchair access. Children's portions. Car parking.

▊ Kingham
★NEW ENTRY★
Kingham Plough
A country pub of some class
Kingham, OX7 6YD
Tel no: (01608) 658327
www.thekinghamplough.co.uk
Gastropub | £26
Cooking score: 5
🛏

The honey-stone inn that stands opposite Kingham's pretty green was rescued from obscurity, and certain closure, in August 2007 by Adam Dorrien-Smith and Emily Watkins, a former sous-chef at the Fat Duck. It is fast making a name for itself – the large bar and vaulted dining room showing plenty of character with modern colours, antique trestle tables, big candles and bold paintings – with Emily producing a short, truly local menu which makes good use of artisan suppliers from within a 10-mile radius. Crisp duck egg served on chunky, full-flavoured pancetta and an intense watercress sauce has been a well-flavoured starter, followed by rich, gamey slow-cooked wood pigeon with artichoke purée and wilted spinach. Alternatively, try Hereford beef fillet with triple-cooked chips, or a simple cod pie with mash and spring greens. Rhubarb baked Alaska has been pronounced 'stunning'. Great bar snacks include hand-raised pork pies, potted rabbit and 'scotched' quail's eggs. The succinct, quite classic European wine list favours France and opens at £10, with fine wines ranging from £22 to £60.

Chef/s: Emily Watkins. **Open:** all week L 12 to 2, D 7 to 8.45. **Meals:** alc (main courses £10 to £18). **Service:** not inc. **Details:** Cards accepted. 70 seats. 25 seats outside. Separate bar. Wheelchair access. Music. Children's portions. Car parking.

▌Murcott

Nut Tree Inn

Idyllic whitewashed and thatched pub
Main Street, Murcott, OX5 2RE
Tel no: (01865) 331253
Gastropub | £30
Cooking score: 4

£5
OFF

The whitewashed and thatched Nut Tree is a new venture for Michael North, who is wowing local foodies with his impressive modern European cooking. Locals propping up the bar add to the relaxed and informal atmosphere in the tiny bar-cum-dining room with its low beams, deep sofas and linen-clothed tables by the inglenook. The compact, seasonal menu is built around excellent raw materials from leading local suppliers: Charolais beef reared near Abingdon, for example, which is hung for 28 days and served with triple-cooked chips. Deft handling and skilled cooking results in clear, well-defined flavours, as seen in a carefully judged roast pork belly with perfect crackling and potato purée, a light apple gravy cutting through the richness of the pork. Start, perhaps, with a rich, silky smooth chicken liver parfait with fruit chutney, then finish with a featherlight passion-fruit soufflé, served with its own tangy sorbet and creamy brûlée. Own-baked bread, a compact yet imaginative wine list (from £12.50) and friendly and efficient service complete the promising picture.
Chef/s: Michael North and Gary Farrell. **Open:** all week L 12 to 2, D 7 to 9 (6 to 8 Sun). **Closed:** Sun D in winter. **Meals:** alc (main courses £14 to £22). Set L (Mon to Fri) and D (Mon to Thu) £15 (2 courses) to £18. **Service:** not inc. **Details:** Cards accepted. 60 seats. 100 seats outside. Music. Children's portions. Car parking.

Raymond Blanc Manoir aux Quat' Saisons

Why did you become a chef?
As a boy in Besançon, I saw the pleasure people had in eating in a restaurant and thought 'I want to give that pleasure to people myself'.

Do you have a favourite source for your ingredients?
Of course. Le Manoir's own garden.

Who would you invite to your ideal dinner party?
They have to be passionate about food. So: the composer Rossini, for whom so many dishes are named. He was an amusing conversationalist, too, and a good cook. Marcel Proust probably didn't know what the kitchen looked like - but he loved his food. Then some painters and other musicians, another writer or two, perhaps some genial chefs - and of course my family.

What's your guilty food pleasure?
None. I refuse to feel guilty about food.

What era of history would you most like to have eaten in? Actually there's no epoch in which mankind was capable of eating better than we can eat today.

█ Nettlebed

ALSO RECOMMENDED
▲ White Hart
28-30 High Street, Nettlebed, RG9 5DD
Tel no: (01491) 641245
www.whitehartnettlebed.com
Gastropub

New management has taken over this centuries-old, brick-and-flint pub in the centre of an affluent village. There's a stronger pub atmosphere than before, and the food delivers familiar modern British classics with a twist, from starters like sweet potato and Gruyère tartlet (£5.50) or potato, spinach and chickpea samosa with tsatsiki to main courses of sea bass with fennel and olive salad and parsley mash (£13.95) or rump of lamb with shallot and thyme purée (£14.50). At dessert, lemon and thyme pannacotta (£5.50) could be teamed with red wine-poached pear. House wine is £12.95. More reports please.

█ Oxford

Branca
Crowd-pleasing livewire Italian
111 Walton Street, Oxford, OX2 6AJ
Tel no: (01865) 556111
www.branca-restaurants.com
Italian | £22
Cooking score: 1

V £30

A sure-fire hit with the under-30s and the university crowd, this populist Italian brasserie also pleases everyone with its all-day opening, flexible menus, special deals and boisterous buzz. Punters pack into the high-ceilinged dining room to pick from a menu that covers a lot of ground, from salads, pasta, risottos and stone-baked pizzas to restaurant-style dishes such as duck breast with cannellini beans and salsa verde. Set the ball rolling with king prawn bruschetta or roast Piedmontese pepper with buffalo mozzarella, and finish off with lemon tart or coffee and praline semifreddo. A new deli, café and garden were

due to open as the Guide went to press. Prices on the short, sharp Italian wine list start at £12.95 (£3.30 a glass).
Chef/s: Michael MacQuire. **Open:** all week 12 to 11. **Closed:** Set L Mon to Fri £6.45 (1 course). Set L and D Mon to Fri £10.45 (2 courses). **Meals:** alc (main courses £9 to £15). **Service:** not inc. **Details:** Cards accepted. 110 seats. Air-con. Separate bar. Wheelchair access. Music. Children's portions.

Cherwell Boathouse
Enchantment down by the riverside
50 Bardwell Road, Oxford, OX2 6ST
Tel no: (01865) 552746
www.cherwellboathouse.co.uk
Modern British/French | £25
Cooking score: 1

£5 OFF   ♦   V   £30

Punts can be hired from the Boathouse at the Verdin family's long-running Oxford institution, although the place is best known for its enchanting riverside location and gold-standard wine cellar. Serious relaxation beckons. English and French accents dominate the food, although the kitchen isn't averse to changing course and serving curried Cornish crab with green tea jelly or rounding off proceedings with piña colada trifle and roasted pineapple ice cream. Elsewhere the prevailing mood is summed up by dishes such as potted pig's head with caramelised onion, loin of local rabbit with its offal, braised leg, wild mushrooms and purple carrots, and iced damson parfait with greengage compote. Anthony Verdin's thoughtful wine list has blossomed over the years, although its heart still lies in the classic French regions – despite lots of new arrivals from elsewhere. Around 20 'favourite' recommendations are priced from £12.50 (£3.30 a glass).
Chef/s: Carson Hill and Clive Rogers. **Open:** all week L 12 to 2 (2.30 Sat and Sun), D 6 to 9.45. **Closed:** 25 to 30 Dec. **Meals:** alc (main courses £15.50 to £18). Set L Mon to Fri £12.50 (2 courses) to £22.50. Set D £24.50. **Service:** not inc. **Details:** Cards accepted. 65 seats. 40 seats outside. Separate bar. No music. Wheelchair access. Children's portions. Car parking.

Chiang Mai Kitchen

Hidden Thai
130a High Street, Oxford, OX1 4DH
Tel no: (01865) 202233
www.chiangmaikitchen.co.uk
Thai
Cooking score: 1

V

Hidden down a tiny alleyway off the High Street, this rickety seventeenth-century timber-framed building doesn't look much from the outside. Inside, it's a lovely old place with age warped floors and out-of-kilter doorways with Thai wood carvings and other artefacts giving a clue to its current identity. The place is popular and the food largely authentic with a few westernized crowd pleasers. Ingredients are bona fide, though, and the lengthy menu covers most bases (including a separate list of vegetarian dishes), with decent versions of spicy tom yam poh tak packed with seafood, gai pad phet (stir-fried chicken with curry paste, thai herbs and lime leaves) and mu pad prik king (pork cooked in coconut milk with long beans, Thai herbs and chilli). Our questionnaire was not returned, so some of the information below may have changed.
Open: all week L 12 to 2.30, D 6 to 10.30. **Closed:** Christmas, New Year, Easter. **Meals:** alc (main courses £7.50 to £12.50). **Service:** not inc. **Details:** Cards accepted. 65 seats. Air-con. Music.

Gee's

Dramatic Oxford landmark
61 Banbury Road, Oxford, OX2 6PE
Tel no: (01865) 553540
www.gees-restaurant.co.uk
Modern European | £35
New Chef

V

The Gee family built this capacious, light-filled conservatory as a floristry business during Victorian times, but for many years it has served Oxford admirably as a restaurant with a contemporary outlook. It is a style-conscious venue, and the food has a suitably upbeat feel. Scottish steaks and Jersey seafood show up strongly on the seasonal menus, which might work their way from pan-fried chicken livers with beetroot, through sea bass with chicory, broad beans and sauce vierge to summer pudding or chocolate nemesis with white chocolate and vanilla crème fraîche. Pre-theatre menus cut the mustard during the week and live jazz brings in local fans on Sunday evenings. The concise, no-frills wine list promises lively worldwide drinking from £16.50 (£11.50 a pichet, £4 a glass).
Chef/s: Nick Seckington. **Open:** Mon to Fri L 12 to 2.30, D 6 to 10.30, Sat and Sun 11 to 10.30. **Meals:** alc (main courses L £12 to £24, D £14.50 to £26.50). Set L (exc Sun) and pre-theatre £12.95 (2 courses) to £15.95. Set D £35. **Service:** not inc. **Details:** Cards accepted. 85 seats. 40 seats outside. Air-con. Separate bar. Wheelchair access. Music. Children's portions.

ALSO RECOMMENDED

▲ Al-Shami

25 Walton Crescent, Oxford, OX1 2JG
Tel no: (01865) 310066
www.al-shami.co.uk
Middle Eastern

Colourfully decorated Oxford haunt offering an extensive range of Lebanese food with hot and cold meze the main attraction. Baked cod fillet with hot sesame sauce (£12) and okra fried in olive oil, garlic and tomatoes (£6.40), have been recommended, along with dishes from the chargrill such as tender cubes of lamb with onions and tomatoes and chicken marinated in garlic, lemon juice and olive oil (£6.25). Finish with Arabic ice cream (£3). The short wine list offers a selection of Lebanese wines from £11.99. Open daily, takeaway service.

▲ Edamame

15 Holywell Street, Oxford, OX1 3SA
Tel no: (01865) 246916
www.edamame.co.uk
Japanese

An ultra-cheap Japanese joint feeding
students, tourists and locals with non-
formulaic Japanese home cooking. Lunch
brings a healthy assortment of dishes ranging
from eponymous edamame (£1.50) to bowls
of ramen noodles (from £6) and deep-fried
chicken teishoku with rice and miso soup.
Suppers extend the repertoire, although prices
rarely exceed £7: try takoyaki (octopus in
pancake balls with dried fish flakes and
seaweed powder), pork tonkatsu and kinpira
gobo (stir-fried burdock root with sesame and
sweetened soy). Sushi Thursday evening.
Drink cold oolong tea, yoghurt-based
calpis, or house wine (£10 a bottle, £2.50 a
glass). Cash-only at lunchtimes; no bookings.
Open Wed to Sun L, Thur to Sat D.

▮ Stoke Row

ALSO RECOMMENDED
▲ Crooked Billet

Newlands Lane, Stoke Row, RG9 5PU
Tel no: (01491) 681048
www.thecrookedbillet.co.uk
Gastropub

A star of film and TV in its own right – Patriot
Games and Land Girls are amongst its screen
credits – this out-in-the-sticks gem of a
country pub packs 'em in with its unique
celebrity atmosphere, live music events and
fine food. The kitchen works to an
eclectic handwritten menu that fizzes with
ideas and ingredients from all over. Partridge
and ham hock terrine with Oxford sauce and
toasted rye bread (£7) could be followed by
fillet of sea bass with sautéed garlic shrimps,
roast Mediterranean vegetables and salsa verde
(£17). For dessert, consider something
homespun like baked egg custard tart with
nutmeg ice cream (£5.50) Around 70 global
wines from £16.50 (£4.65 a glass). Open all
week.

▮ Stonesfield

ALSO RECOMMENDED
▲ White Horse

The Ridings, Stonesfield, OX29 8EA
Tel no: (01993) 891063
www.thewhitehorse.uk.com
Gastropub

Boarded up for years, this unprepossessing
village local has been rescued and revitalised
and now draws visitors for its seasonally
inspired cooking. Settle in the quirky, bare-
floored bar with open fire and battered sofa, or
head for the contemporary low-beamed
dining room, with its scrubbed tables,
informal atmosphere, and modern art on
terracotta walls, for dishes such as wild
mushroom risotto with rocket and Parmesan
(£10.95), steak and kidney pudding (£9.95),
or a hearty lamb shank with garlic butter bean
stew. Leave room for lemon tart with vanilla
mascarpone (£4.95). Closed Mon.

▮ Swerford

★NEW ENTRY★

Masons Arms

Charming country pub
Banbury Road, Swerford, OX7 4AP
Tel no: (01608) 683212
www.masons-arms.com
Gastropub | £25
Cooking score: 2

Set in three acres overlooking the Swere
Valley, this 300-year-old stone pub has been
stylishly redesigned – rugs on stripped
wooden floors, colourwashed walls, old pine
tables and chunky candles. Although it
remains a village pub where locals pop in for a
pint, Bill Leadbeater's interesting modern
food attracts diners too. His monthly-
changing menus and blackboard specials
champion locally sourced meats, be it Oxford
Down lamb, Old Spot pork, or Cotswold-
reared Shorthorn beef. Chargrilled 21-day
hung rib-eye steak with beetroot relish and

hand-cut chips, or confit lamb shoulder with mixed bean stew and rosemary jus make hearty mains, while chicken liver terrine with apple and ale chutney or smoked haddock with leek and potato soup are typical starters. Finish with almond and polenta cake with raspberry compote. The short wine list is accessible and varied, with house wines from £13.95.

Chef/s: Bill Leadbeater. **Open:** all week L 12 to 2 (4 Sun), Mon to Sat D 7 to 9. **Closed:** 25 and 26 Dec. **Meals:** alc (main courses £13.95 to £17.95). Set L £13.95 (2 courses) to £15.95. **Service:** not inc. **Details:** Cards accepted. 80 seats. 8 seats outside. Wheelchair access. Music. Children's portions. Car parking.

▌Tadpole Bridge
Trout at Tadpole Bridge
Great riverside setting
Tadpole Bridge, SN7 8RF
Tel no: (01367) 870382
www.troutinn.co.uk
Gastropub | £27
Cooking score: 1

There's much to like about this seventeenth-century pub, not least its setting on the banks of the Thames. Often crowded, the service throughout the various dining areas remains cheerful and hard-working. The kitchen provides simple, modern cooking that doesn't test diners but seems to satisfy. Start with Cornish mussels with garlic and cream or sautéed crevettes. Main courses are hearty, with calf's liver, braised red cabbage, mustard mash and red wine sauce offered alongside herb-crusted breast of chicken with champ potato, mushroom and thyme gravy. Traditional desserts include rice pudding with poached plums. House wines from £13.50.

Chef/s: Robert Skuse. **Open:** all week L 12 to 2, D 7 to 9. **Closed:** 25 Dec. **Meals:** alc (main courses £10.95 to £17.95). **Service:** not inc. **Details:** Cards accepted. 70 seats. 40 seats outside. Wheelchair access. Children's portions. Car parking.

▌Woodstock

★NEW ENTRY★
Feathers Hotel
Grand cuisine by a new young chef
Market Street, Woodstock, OX20 1SX
Tel no: (01993) 812291
www.feathers.co.uk
Modern British | £46
Cooking score: 4

A highly traditional restaurant (plus bistro), the Feathers is a venerable inn at the centre of this handsome market town. Inside, the dining area is a series of rooms: the first study-like and sober; the next brighter, with yellow wallpaper and background classical music. Service is formal. Russell Bateman has already worked in the kitchens of Pétrus and Midsummer House (see entries), but here he cooks for 'tweedy gents and distinguished visitors', and his daily menus seem tempered accordingly. At an evening inspection, an exemplary amuse bouche of chilled leek soup was followed by a starter of cod cheeks rested on Bayonne ham, the dish made memorable by a mound of cauliflower 'couscous' steeped in their juices. Then medium-rare breasts of squab pigeon, the juices matched by the bitter notes of chicory braised in red wine and rich, sweet griottine cherries, while a flawless pigeon 'samosa' of intense flavour and admirable delicacy lifted the dish (the accompanying truffle mash puréed to glueyness sounded the only duff note). The meal concluded brightly with chilled strawberry soup, English rhubarb, strawberries and vanilla ice-cream. Wine from the compendious list (including 19 'sommelier's choices' by-the-glass) starts at £19.

Chef/s: Russell Bateman. **Open:** Tue to Sun L 12 to 2, Mon to Sat D 7 to 9.15. **Closed:** Sun, bank hols D. **Meals:** Set L £19 (2 courses) to £24.50, set D £46. **Service:** 10% (optional). **Details:** Cards accepted. 40 seats. 60 seats outside. Separate bar. Wheelchair access. Music. Children's portions.

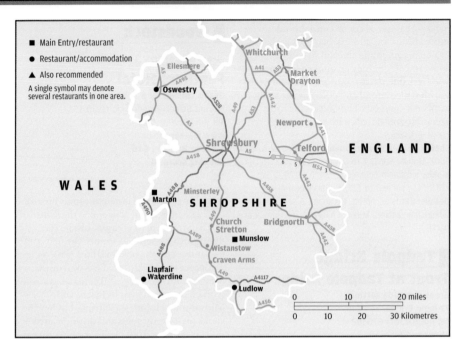

- ■ Main Entry/restaurant
- ● Restaurant/accommodation
- ▲ Also recommended

A single symbol may denote several restaurants in one area.

Church Stretton

Berry's Coffee House

17 High Street, Church Stretton, SY6 6BU
Tel no: 01694 724 452
www.berryscoffeehouse.co.uk
'Home-cooked food with local origins'

Llanfair Waterdine

Waterdine

Seasonal modern British cooking
Llanfair Waterdine, LD7 1TU
Tel no: (01547) 528214
www.waterdine.com
Modern British | £33
Cooking score: 4

£5
OFF

Ken and Isabel Adams' old drovers' inn offers terrific modern British cooking. A Welsh long house by design, it was built in the mid-seventeenth century and is set right on the border of Wales and England. Ken's short, imaginative menu offers a seasonal selection of some of the best the area has to offer, featuring home-grown local or organic produce, while fish is delivered fresh off Cornish day-boats. You might find smooth chicken liver pâté with pickled damsons alongside pork tenderloin stuffed with goats' cheese and served with orange and green pepper sauce. Desserts include rum pannacotta with poached plums and warm white chocolate sauce. This is a serious restaurant in pub clothing, so expect superb food. Remember, too, to book – unlike more informal venues, the Waterdine isn't equipped to deal with diners expecting a table at short notice. This is especially so at lunch, when casual callers without a reservation may find the place closed. House wines start at £15.50.
Chef/s: Ken Adams. **Open:** Wed to Sun L 12 to 3, Tue to Sat D 7 to 11. **Closed:** Mon. **Meals:** Set D £32.50, Set Sun L £22.50. **Service:** not inc. **Details:** Cards accepted. 22 seats. Separate bar. No music. Wheelchair access. Car parking.

▌Ludlow

★NEW ENTRY★

La Bécasse

Fine dining to knock your socks off
17 Corve Street, Ludlow, SY8 1DA
Tel no: (01584) 872325
www.labecasse.co.uk
Modern British | £49
Cooking score: 5

As Hibiscus closed its doors and decamped to London, the lament went up that Ludlow was dying. It proved to be premature. The old gourmet haven has landed on its feet with the restaurant's transformation into La Bécasse, a creation of Alan Murchison and sibling to his L'Ortolan venue in Shinfield, Berkshire (see entry). Up in Shropshire, within the restaurant's ancient stone and panelled walls, young chef Will Holland is in charge and already proving a winner, with fine dining to knock your socks off. Clearly swooning over the cornucopia of local produce, he puts together confident dishes that keep robust flavours working in perfect harmony. A tartare of mackerel with marinated beetroot and cauliflower, horseradish ice cream and dill dressing sounds pretty butch as a starter but is a well-balanced success, displaying the same mastery as a main course of rare-breed local pork loin with boulangère potatoes, apple and sage jelly with a perfectly crisp strip of crackling across the top. Desserts – so often a restaurant's weak spot – keep the flag flying, whether it's chocolate tart with ginger ice cream or creamy espresso parfait. While the kitchen is clearly in top gear, credit must also go to great service. The maître d'hôtel here is a shining beacon of friendly efficiency.
Chef/s: William Holland. **Open:** Wed to Sun L 12 to 2, Tue to Sat D 7 to 9 (Sat 9.30). **Meals:** Set L £20 (2 courses) to £24, set L and D £41 (2 courses) to £49, tasting menu (7 courses) £55. **Service:** not inc. **Details:** Cards accepted. 44 seats.

Mr Underhill's

Seductive hideaway, exquisite food
Dinham Weir, Ludlow, SY8 1EH
Tel no: (01584) 874431
www.mr-underhills.co.uk
Modern European | £48
Cooking score: 7

🍷 🛏

'A total joy,' sums up reporters' unbridled enthusiasm for this acclaimed restaurant-with-rooms, which nestles idyllically beside the tumbling waters of Dinham Weir. Chris and Judy Bradley have transformed the whole place into a seductive hideaway beneath the ramparts of Ludlow Castle: few can resist its serene charms or the prospect of sipping aperitifs in the fragrant courtyard on balmy evenings. Conviviality defines the mood in the delightful dining room, where Judy's presence ensures that the whole operation runs effortlessly (although the whole team 'excels'). Regulars know the score: dinner is a 'perfectly balanced', seven-course affair that can be tailored to the needs of individual guests, who may even find their names on the menu. Everything is done with consummate care, thoughtfulness and attention to detail, and the 'sheer flavour of the food' dazzles. A canapé 'cone' always opens proceedings (perhaps marinated salmon, spiced avocado or artichoke and caramelised hummus) ahead of a seasonal soup (almond velouté with crispy chorizo in late winter) and, say, duck liver custard '08' with quince confit and five-spice glaze. Fish comes next – it could be scallops and smoked haddock with herb pasta and garden sorrel – while the centrepiece is true to the region: perhaps Marches beef or slow-roast fillet of Mortimer Forest venison with red wine and elderberries accompanied by butternut squash risotto and creamed Savoy cabbage. Dinner reaches its climax with a veritable galaxy of desserts: Yorkshire rhubarb crumble with clove ice cream, Highland parfait with flapjack wafer, hot fondant apricot tart with apricot ice cream – it's all triumphantly seasonal. Finally, it's time for speciality cheeses from Britain and France, which are vividly offset by unusual marmalades (black cherry and liquorice, for example). The auspicious, lovingly assembled wine list is a joy to read, with fascinating names spread across the range: Italy, California and Alsace are particularly enticing. Eight house selections start at £16 (£4.50 a glass).

Chef/s: Chris Bradley. **Open:** Wed to Sun D only 7.15 to 8.30. **Closed:** Mon, Tue, 1 week June, 1 week Nov. **Meals:** Set D £45. **Service:** not inc. **Details:** Cards accepted. 30 seats. 30 seats outside. No music. No mobile phones. Children's portions. Car parking.

ALSO RECOMMENDED
▲ The Clive

Bromfield, Ludlow, SY8 2JR
Tel no: (01584) 856565
www.theclive.co.uk
Modern British

Once home to Clive of India, this restored brick farmhouse now enjoys new life as a contemporary bar and restaurant-with-rooms beside the A49. A meal in the family-friendly dining room might open with Wenlock Edge air-dried ham with roast pear, crumbled Gorgonzola and pine nuts (£6.25) before dry-aged rib of Bridgnorth beef with oyster mushrooms and pink peppercorn sauce (£16.95). To finish, perhaps try blueberry fudge and Jack Daniels parfait with praline wafers (£5.50) or one of the organic ice creams. The short, sharp wine list kicks off with house recommendations from £13.75 (£3.15 a glass). Open all week.

▌Marton
Sun Inn

Family-run country inn
Marton, SY21 8JP
Tel no: (01938) 561211
www.suninn.biz
Modern British | £25
New Chef
£5 OFF £30

The Gartells bring long experience of restaurateuring to the established Sun Inn, a greystone country inn not far from the Welsh border. A new, more speculative note has been brought to the menus with their arrival, ushering in Cornish crab with pineapple salsa and crispy rice noodles, perhaps followed by roast duckling sauced with honey, figs and cinnamon or, alternatively, black bream garnished with cherry tomatoes and olives. Meals end happily with sticky toffee pudding or white chocolate and raspberry parfait. A lively international wine list keeps prices in check, and opens with ten house wines from £11.90, or £3.10 a glass.

Chef/s: Peter Gartell. **Open:** Wed to Sun L 12 to 2, Tue to Sat D 7 to 11. **Meals:** alc (main courses £9.95 to £15.95). Set L Sun £15.95. **Service:** not inc. **Details:** Cards accepted. 60 seats. 40 seats outside. Separate bar. Wheelchair access. Music. Children's portions. Car parking.

▌Munslow
The Crown

Well-preserved Tudor inn
Munslow, SY7 9ET
Tel no: (01584) 841205
www.crowncountryinn.co.uk
Modern British | £25
Cooking score: 3
£5 OFF £30

Once a Shropshire 'Hundred House' where local justice was dispensed, the Crown nestles tidily below the undulating hills of Wenlock Edge. It's a good-looking, well-preserved place, with many fine features dating back to Tudor times – notably its inglenook fireplace

and rough-hewn oak beams. Food is served in the formal upstairs restaurant as well as the ground-floor bar, and the kitchen garners Wenlock Edge Farm dry-cured bacon, Muckleton Old Spot pork, Bishop's Castle venison and more for menus with a cross-Channel flavour. Free-range chicken is cooked two ways with roasted vegetables, crispy prosciutto, Catalonian pimento and nut salsa, while the day's fish might appear with a fricassee of red Camargue rice and crayfish tails. Grilled scallops with home-mushed peas and straw potatoes is a new take on an old favourite, British farmhouse cheeses are given due respect and the choice of desserts could extend to iced rhubarb and vanilla custard parfait. House wine is £13.95 (£3.95 a glass).
Chef/s: Richard Arnold. **Open:** Tue to Sun L 12 to 1.45, Tue to Sat D 6.45 to 8.45. **Closed:** Mon, 25 Dec. **Meals:** alc (main courses L £9 to £12, D £12 to £16.50). **Service:** not inc. **Details:** Cards accepted. 60 seats. 30 seats outside. Separate bar. Wheelchair access. Music. Children's portions. Car parking.

and a dessert of almond clafoutis with dark cherry griottines and Kirsch ice cream. The Menu du Marche (unavailable on Saturdays) is excellent value and the wine list favours France but gives the rest of the world fair coverage too. Prices from £15.95 a bottle.
Chef/s: Richard Jones and Mark Sebastian Fisher. **Open:** Tue to Sat D 6.30 to 9.30. **Closed:** 24 to 26 Dec, 1 Jan. **Meals:** Set D £19.95 (3 courses), £35 (4 courses). **Service:** not inc. **Details:** Cards accepted. Separate bar. No mobile phones. Wheelchair access. Music. Children's portions. Car parking.

▌Oswestry

Sebastians

Homely French restaurant
45 Willow Street, Oswestry, SY11 1AQ
Tel no: (01691) 655444
www.sebastians-hotel.co.uk
French | £27
Cooking score: 3

This little slice of France occupies a sixteenth-century hotel of the same name. It's a homely environment, with a terrace for summer drinks and a lounge warmed by a log fire in winter. The dining room has a relaxed, almost rustic look, with exposed beams and simple country-style furniture prettied up with white napery. The menu offers classics with a modern edge: perhaps a soup (curried parsnip velouté) followed by red mullet on spicy couscous with red pepper coulis. After a sorbet, you could try roast lamb with fondant potato, glazed shallots and a black olive and tomato sauce,

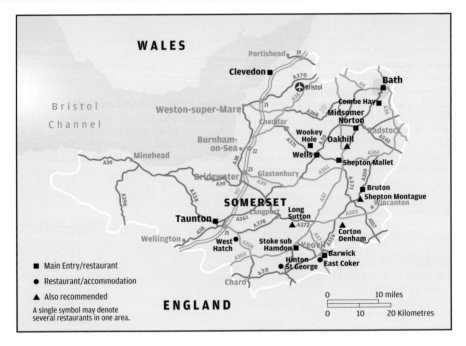

WALES

Portishead

Clevedon

Bristol

Bath

Bristol Channel

Weston-super-Mare

Combe Hay

Midsomer Norton

Cheddar

Radstock

Wookey Hole

Oakhill

Burnham-on-Sea

Wells

Shepton Mallet

Minehead

Bridgwater

Glastonbury

SOMERSET

Bruton

Shepton Montague

Wincanton

Langport

Long Sutton

Taunton

Corton Denham

Wellington

West Hatch

Stoke sub Hamdon

Yeovil

Barwick

Hinton St George

East Coker

Chard

ENGLAND

■ Main Entry/restaurant

● Restaurant/accommodation

▲ Also recommended

A single symbol may denote several restaurants in one area.

0   10 miles

0   10   20 Kilometres

▋Barwick

Little Barwick House

Seductive restaurant-with-rooms
Barwick, BA22 9TD
Tel no: (01935) 423902
www.littlebarwickhouse.co.uk
Modern British | £38
Cooking score: 6

In a tranquil village backwater to the south of Yeovil, Tim and Emma Ford's captivating Georgian dower house seduces visitors with its personable atmosphere, delightfully expansive gardens and unfaltering food. The quintessentially English dining room has been freshened up of late with a new hessian carpet spread over the floorboards and some extra paintings on the walls. Otherwise, it's business as usual in a kitchen that is praised for its rock-solid consistency across the board. Tim changes his menus each day depending on the markets and his local supply network. Fish from the West Country ports is always a

strong suit and it is treated with precision: grilled fillet of red mullet is served with carrot and orange escabèche and lemon chilli syrup, while sea bass might be teamed up with sun-dried tomato risotto, white wine and chive sauce. Somerset's farms contribute top-notch meat – perhaps tenderloin of pork with Savoy cabbage, fondant potato, mustard and tarragon sauce – and there's local game in season (saddle of roe deer with braised red cabbage, beetroot purée and rösti, for example). Desserts are impressively crafted creations such as balsamic strawberry tartlet served with a light strawberry mousse and a sorbet; otherwise sample the West Country cheeses with raisin bread and quince paste. The fabulous wine list dazzles at every turn, from high-end French and Californian vintages to keenly chosen everyday tipples with affordable price tags. Half-bottles are many and varied, while house recommendations start at £17.95 (£5 a glass).

Chef/s: Tim Ford. **Open:** Wed to Sun L 12 to 2, Tue to Sat D 7 to 9. **Closed:** Mon, 3 weeks after Christmas, 1 week Aug. **Meals:** Set L Wed to Sat £20.95 (2

courses) to £24.95, Set L Sun £27.95, Set D £37.95.
Service: not inc. **Details:** Cards accepted. 40 seats.
Air-con. No music. No mobile phones. Children
allowed. Car parking.

■ Bath

Bath Priory

Contemporary cooking in classic manor house
Weston Road, Bath, BA1 2XT
Tel no: (01225) 331922
www.thebathpriory.co.uk
Modern British | £55
Cooking score: 5

🍷 ⇋ V

Bath Priory is located a mile from the city
centre, a handsome honey-hued stone manor
house set in four acres of lush gardens. The
main action is in the well-upholstered dining
room where Chris Horridge delivers
unmistakably contemporary food, full of
twists and turns, froths and foams, not to
mention airs and ices. Novel combinations
include curing pigeon breast with citrus fruits
and birch, or pairing pork belly with papaya,
pain d'épices and rhubarb, but a tendency to
combine too many elements in a dish risks
taking the edge off it, as when a mixed
summer vegetable 'paillette' shares a plate with
olive ice cream, tomato fizz and nettle
tempura. When dishes pull together, the
results work well enough, as was the case with
an inspection main course of dab served with
pea and cucumber nicely acidulated with lime
pastille and teamed with a shot glass of
crayfish with passion fruit and coco nib.
Desserts can be confections of many parts –
perhaps Cox's apple wafers with soft liquorice,
five-spice ice and fennel seed and apple atoms.
Service lagged a few steps behind the cooking.
The broad and generous compass of the wine
list makes for fine worldwide drinking, taking
in a wide range of half-bottles and a good
selection of wines by-the-glass. House
selections start at £17.50.

Chef/s: Chris Horridge. **Open:** all week L 12 to 1.45,
D 7 to 9.30. **Meals:** Set L £20 (2 courses) to £25, Set
D £55. **Service:** not inc. **Details:** Cards accepted. 64
seats. 35 seats outside. Wheelchair access. Car
parking.

Cavendish Restaurant, Dukes Hotel

Elegant Georgian splendour
Great Pulteney Street, Bath, BA2 4DN
Tel no: (01225) 787963
www.dukesbath.co.uk
Modern British | £40
Cooking score: 3

⇋

Located on a splendid boulevard just a few
minutes from the city centre, this Grade I-
listed town house typifies the elegance and
Georgian splendour of Bath. The hotel's
Cavendish restaurant occupies the basement
and overlooks a secluded walled patio garden,
the main feature of which is a sparkling
fountain. The neatly appointed dining room is
a suitably refined setting for the ambitious,
well-presented cooking, which majors on
seasonality and local suppliers, many of whom
are listed on the menu. Starters of hand-dived
scallops with cauliflower tempura, cauliflower
purée and truffle honey demonstrate the
kitchen's contemporary style. Main courses
such as loin of Mendip venison, celeriac and
pear bake and spiced red cabbage follow in a
similar vein. Desserts are equally inventive
and include a well-judged hot chocolate
fondant with white chocolate mousse and
malted milk ice cream. The balanced wine list
kicks off at £16 and there are five by-the-
glass.

Chef/s: Fran Snell. **Open:** Tue to Sun L 12 to 2.30, all
week D 6.30 to 10. **Meals:** alc (main courses £19.95
to £23.95). Set L £12.95 (2 courses) to £15.95.
Service: not inc. **Details:** Cards accepted. 40 seats.
40 seats outside. Separate bar. Music. Children's
portions.

The Dower House, Royal Crescent

Cooking in an elegant setting
16 Royal Crescent, Bath, BA1 2LS
Tel no: (01225) 823333
www.royalcrescent.co.uk
Modern British | £40
Cooking score: 4

The Georgian elegance of the Royal Crescent Hotel opens onto beautifully landscaped gardens at the rear, a lovely setting for the Dower House. There's a subtle opulence to the décor, with mink-coloured silk and leafy shades of green linking perfectly with the colours of the garden (where summer tables are popular). Young chefs Gordon Jones and Mark Brega produce a modern, mainly British menu with local, seasonal foods backed up by good technical skills and immaculate, not over-elaborate presentation. Witness an early May meal that opened with rich and velvety morel velouté and perfectly poached pheasant egg, prettily topped with a chiffonade of parsley. Next, a tender, slow-braised pairing of sweet-glazed pork belly and ox tongue with slivers of beetroot and fresh baby leaves. A 'deeply rich' warm chocolate tart with a refreshing raspberry sorbet made a satisfying finish. The impressive wine list is predictably pricey, but it starts at £20 so there's a choice at all levels. There is also a reasonable selection of wines by-the-glass from £5.50 to £10.
Chef/s: Gordon Jones and Mark Brega. **Open:** all week L 12.30 to 2, D 7 to 10. **Meals:** Set L £25, alc L £37.50, alc D £55. **Service:** not inc. **Details:** Cards accepted. 70 seats. 45 seats outside. Separate bar. Music.

Average price

The average price listed in main-entry reviews denotes the price of a three-course meal, without wine.

The Garrick's Head

Bold, no-frills dishes
7-8 St Johns Place, Bath, BA1 1ET
Tel no: (01225) 318368
Gastropub | £28
Cooking score: 2
£5 OFF £30

The Garrick's Head occupies an historic site next to the city's famous theatre, but despite its location, the food is far from showy. Seasonality and local sourcing are the key elements here and the daily-changing menu is full of bold, no-frills food with classic British dishes benefiting from occasional rustic French influences. A typical starter of seared Cornish scallops with bacon and lovage salad could be followed by braised shin of beef with new potatoes and broccoli dressed with a soft-boiled egg, anchovy and capers. Desserts tend to be simple and not always as well-executed as the preceding courses. On inspection, lemon tart suffered from thick, uneven pastry and a bland, 'not very lemony' filling. The French and Italian-heavy wine list contains a number of bargains and with 18 served by-the-glass and house wines starting at £12.50, there is something for every pocket.
Chef/s: Hugh Dennis-Jones. **Open:** all week L 12 to 3, Mon to Sat D 6 to 10. **Closed:** 25 and 26 Dec, 1 Jan. **Meals:** alc (main courses £13 to £16.50). Set L £14 (2 courses) to £16. **Service:** 10%. **Details:** Cards accepted. 30 seats. 24 seats outside. Separate bar. Music. Children's portions. Children allowed.

King William

Local produce takes centre stage
36 Thomas Street, Bath, BA1 5NN
Tel no: (01225) 428096
www.kingwilliampub.com
Gastropub | £29
Cooking score: 3
£5 OFF £30

This diminutive pub may be a short walk from Bath's city centre, but that hasn't prevented tourists and locals from seeking it out. The elegant upstairs restaurant occupies two floors of this narrow building, while the two-room bar is the place to rub shoulders with the locals and tuck into the solid bar menu, which might include braised oxtail with fried lamb's heart and horseradish mash. Charlie Digney's love of nose-to-tail eating is stamped all over the menus, with prime local produce taking centre stage. Well-defined flavours can be found in a starter of pig's trotter salad with green lentils and truffle oil and a main course of fish stew with new potatoes and aïoli. Puddings can occasionally lack polish, although the hot chocolate pot with Ivy Farm cream is a tried and tested favourite. The French-heavy wine list opens at £12.

Chef/s: Adi Ware. **Open:** all week L 12 to 3, Mon to Sat 6 to 10. **Closed:** 25 and 26 Dec. **Meals:** set D £24 (2 courses) to £29. **Service:** not inc. **Details:** Cards accepted. 60 seats. Separate bar. Music. Children's portions.

Olive Tree at The Queensberry Hotel
Re-fashioned Bath town house
4-7 Russel Street, Bath, BA1 2QF
Tel no: (01225) 447928
www.thequeensberry.co.uk
Modern British | £41
Cooking score: 3
£5 OFF

Built in 1771 for the Marquis of Queensberry, this stately Bath townhouse is reaping the benefits of a serious makeover that has transformed it from a bastion of gentrified Englishness into one of the city's first boutique hotels. The Olive Tree restaurant is housed in the basement and – like the rest of the hotel – it sports a brand new look. The kitchen keeps faith with the seasons and makes the most of carefully sourced ingredients in their prime, whether it's juniper-cured sea trout with fennel and citrus fruits or baked vanilla cheesecake with roasted rhubarb. In between, expect meat and fish in equal measure, from slow-cooked Springleaze pork belly with mashed celeriac, caramelised apple and sherry vinegar to Cornish sea bass with Portland crab and butternut squash risotto. The heavyweight wine list reads like a Who's

Who of contemporary winemaking and its scope is awesome. Bottles are grouped by flavour and style, with mouthwatering descriptions to match; prices start at £15 and 30 are available by-the-glass (from £3.75).

Chef/s: Marc Salmon. **Open:** Tue to Sun L 12 to 2, all week D 7 to 10. **Meals:** alc (main courses £15.75 to £22.50). Set L £16 (2 courses) to £18. **Service:** not inc. **Details:** Cards accepted. 60 seats. Air-con. Separate bar. No mobile phones. Music. Children's portions.

White Hart Inn
One of Bath's oldest pubs
Widcombe Hill, Widcombe, Bath, BA2 6AA
Tel no: (01225) 338053
www.whitehartbath.co.uk
Gastropub | £25
Cooking score: 2
 £30

A mere two-minute walk from Bath's railway station, in sought-after Widcombe, the White Hart claims to be one of Bath's oldest pubs – but it is also unique in that it doubles up as a youth hostel. Popular with rugby fans, who fill the bar on match days, this busy place punches well above its weight when it comes to food. Rupert Pitt's simple European dishes are confident and refreshingly uncomplicated, his menu concise, seasonal and sensibly priced. In early summer, starters of broad bean and bacon soup or pigeon breast, bacon and black pudding salad could be followed by lamb steak with Moroccan couscous or grilled fillets of mackerel with cucumber and lemon salad. On a sunny day, grab a table in the delightful walled courtyard garden, which wouldn't look out of place in Tuscany. House wines start at £13.

Chef/s: Rupert Pitt, Jason Horn, Rachel Milsom and Luke Gibson. **Open:** all week L 12 to 2, Mon to Sat D 6 to 10. **Closed:** 25 Dec, bank hols. **Meals:** alc (main courses £10.80 to £13.90). **Service:** not inc. **Details:** Cards accepted. 50 seats. 50 seats outside. Wheelchair access. Music. Children allowed.

Adam Simmonds Oak Room

Why did you become a chef?
Because it involves being creative.

Who makes you what you are today?
Parents.

Who would you invite to your ideal dinner party?
Angelina Jolie, Lee Evans, Pelé.

What's your guilty food pleasure?
Chocolate.

What won't you tolerate in the kitchen?
Messy people.

Do you always read reviews of your restaurant?
Yes.

What dish is your first food memory?
Mum's over-cooked Sunday lunch.

What era of history would you most like to have eaten in?
The 1960s.

What's coming up next for you?
Making the Oak Room successful.

ALSO RECOMMENDED

▲ Yak Yeti Yak

12 Pierrepont Street, Bath, BA1 1LA
Tel no: (01225) 442299
www.yakyetiyak.co.uk
Nepalese

The move from Argyll Street to Pierrepont Street means that Yak Yeti Yak has swapped a small basement for a larger one. Nothing else has changed. The name still raises a smile, and it gives a clue to the food. Nepalese home-cooking is the deal, and the kitchen takes its food very seriously. Start with crispy fried cheese balls served with a sweet tomato and chilli dipping sauce (£3.90) or cauliflower pakora, then go on to chicken on the bone, stir-fried with a blend of spices, or beef marinated in spices and stir-fried with onions, sweet pepper and tomato (£7.90). There's a good selection of vegetarian dishes and set menus for a minimum of six people start at £11.50. House wine is £12.50. Open all week.

■ Bruton

Bruton House

Impressive and enterprising cooking
2-4 High Street, Bruton, BA10 0AA
Tel no: (01749) 813395
www.brutonhouse.co.uk
Modern British | £39
Cooking score: 6

🍽 V

In a quiet Somerset town best known for its highly-rated schools, the prominent blue frontage of Bruton House is difficult to miss, although the one-way system outside may mean you have to curb your appetite for a few more minutes until you find a parking space. Inside this restaurant-with-rooms, the décor is light and airy with plenty of buttermilk and white, as well as the occasional beam acting as a reminder of the building's vintage. The cooking is impressive and enterprising, with a solid grasp of sound culinary techniques as well as a passion for seasonality and sourcing exemplary ingredients, many of them local and wild. Starters have included chicken, foie gras and mushroom terrine with celeriac rémoulade and Dorset crab lasagne with foaming bisque. For main course you might find rabbit – served as a loin, rack and ravioli – with wild rabbit consommé or a tip-top piece of John Dory with a wild garlic and clam risotto. The well-honed desserts might include white and dark chocolate mousse with orange sorbet or poached pear pain perdu with pear sorbet, all served by friendly and cheery front-of-house staff who show an interest and knowledge about the dishes emerging from the kitchen. A good-value lunchtime menu and a well-considered vegetarian menu make this a venue that offers good food for all tastes and pockets. 'Fantastic' service, too. The wine list is full of bargains, and bottles kick in at £14, with some 15 by-the-glass.

Chef/s: Scott Eggleton. **Open:** Tue to Sat L 12 to 2, D 7 to 9.30. **Closed:** Sun and Mon. **Meals:** Set L £16.50 (2 courses) to £22, Set D £31 (2 courses) to £46.50. **Service:** not inc. **Details:** Cards accepted. 30 seats. Separate bar. Wheelchair access. Music. Children's portions.

▌Clevedon

★NEW ENTRY★
Murrays
Quality cooking on a fiercely seasonal menu
87-93 Hill Road, Clevedon, BS21 7PN
Tel no: (01275) 341555
www.murraysofclevedon.co.uk
Italian | £25
Cooking score: 4

£30

Located in an elegant sweep of Victorian shops a short walk from the town's majestic pier, Murrays used to be called the Olive Garden, but the owners decided that its name suggested purely Mediterranean influences when a lot of the produce was actually from Somerset. But whether it is direct from the markets of Milan or from the local area, the Murray family's prime concern is quality, and it shows on the fiercely seasonal menu – and in the produce sold in their delicatessen next

door. You could start with a simple plate of home-cured bresaola made from Somerset beef topside and served simply with capers, lemon and olive oil. Main courses take in well-made pasta dishes and pizzas, but the kitchen really excels with meat and fish – osso bucco made with Devon rose veal, say, or grilled fillet of wild Cornish sea bass with a fennel and almond crust, served with sautéed greens and topped with a silver-skinned anchovy. From an interesting, entirely Italian wine list, house wines start at £14 and there are a dozen by-the-glass.

Chef/s: Alex Murray and Reuben Murray. **Open:** Tue to Sat L 12 to 1.45, D 6 to 9.30. **Closed:** Sun and Mon, 25 Dec to 2 Jan. **Meals:** alc (main courses £16 to £19.50). **Service:** not inc. **Details:** Cards accepted. 70 seats. Air-con. Separate bar. Wheelchair access. Music. Children's portions.

▌Combe Hay
The Wheatsheaf
A destination dining venue
Combe Hay, BA2 7EG
Tel no: (01225) 833504
www.wheatsheafcombehay.com
Modern British | £25
Cooking score: 5

This impressive sixteenth-century pub has been stripped back to its original stone walls and flagstone floors, but enhanced by more contemporary furnishings – it's all solid oak tables, comfortable sofas and Lloyd Loom chairs. When the weather allows, tables in the terraced gardens are highly prized. Still a pub where locals can pop in for a pint of Butcombe bitter and a warm beef and horseradish sandwich, it is also very much a destination dining venue thanks to new chef Lee Evans, who has stamped his identity on the attractive and concise menu. Evans displays solid, precise techniques and imagination in his dishes, using an abundance of local produce including some from the pub's own garden. A starter of slow-roasted belly pork arrives with a perfectly seared diver-caught scallop and a pencil-thin strip of crackling, while a delectable fillet of pan-fried hake is twinned with duck confit wrapped in wild garlic picked at the bottom of the garden. Blood orange cheesecake with jelly and sorbet has been a hit at dessert. The 150-strong wine list is entirely European and prices rise steeply, but there are plenty of bargains to be found under £20. Glasses start at £3.90.

Chef/s: Lee Evans. **Open:** Tue to Sun L 12 to 2.30, D 6 to 9.30 (Fri to Sat 10). **Closed:** Mon. **Meals:** alc (main courses £15.50 to £22). Set L £18 (2 courses). **Service:** 10% for tables of 6 or more. **Details:** Cards accepted. 50 seats. 60 seats outside. Music. Children's portions. Children allowed. Car parking.

Corton Denham

ALSO RECOMMENDED
▲ Queens Arms
Corton Denham, DT9 4LR
Tel no: (01963) 220317
www.thequeensarms.com
Gastropub

Stylish, uncluttered yet still traditional, the Queens Arms has not forsaken its pub roots – so expect a real fire in winter and garden drinks on sunny days. Beautiful countryside rolls out on every side. Eat in the bar or the adjoining dining room; lunch brings everything from sandwiches to hearty options such as steak, kidney and Chimay Red pie with mash, crispy Old Spot bacon and local vegetables (£9.50). In the evening try seared scallops with Barkham Blue dressing, fennel, radicchio and hazelnuts (£6.20), then wild mushroom-stuffed quail on a nut and seed risotto with curly kale (£11.50). Wines start at £11.90. Open all week.

East Coker
Helyar Arms
'Real food' and traditional virtues
Moor Lane, East Coker, BA22 9JR
Tel no: (01935) 862332
www.helyar-arms.co.uk
Gastropub | £22
Cooking score: 1

£5 OFF ⌨ V £30

A 'real food inn' through and through, this fifteenth-century local is driven along by its dedication to traditional virtues. There are no TV screens, fruit machines or pub food clichés here; instead, log fires burn, a skittle alley provides distraction and the menu takes its cue from local, seasonal ingredients – some even brought in by the customers themselves. Expect a mix of pub classics such as salmon fishcakes or liver and bacon alongside slow-braised pork belly with black pudding, cider and sage jus or fillet of beef served with the unlikely combination of vanilla parsnip purée and blue cheese and walnut ice cream. Some 'lighter bites' and sandwiches are served at lunchtime, while puddings are mix of nursery comfort (steamed treacle and orange sponge) and fashionable chic (bay leaf crème brûlée with Earl Grey ice cream). House Argentinian is £12.50 (£2.30 a glass).

Chef/s: Mathieu Eke. **Open:** all week L 12 to 2.30, D 6.30 to 9.30 (9 Sun). **Closed:** 25 Dec. **Meals:** alc (main courses £8 to £17). Bar menu available. **Service:** not inc. **Details:** Cards accepted. 80 seats. 40 seats outside. Separate bar. Wheelchair access. Music. Children's portions. Car parking.

Hinton St George

Lord Poulett Arms

Elegantly restored seventeenth-century inn
High Street, Hinton St George, TA17 8SE
Tel no: (01460) 73149
www.lordpoulettarms.com
Gastropub | £23
Cooking score: 3

Twisting lanes lead you to a tiny village of Ham stone and thatched cottages with an elegantly restored seventeenth-century inn at its heart. Rug-strewn flagged floors, roaring log fires and a relaxed atmosphere are what to expect. In keeping with the rural-chic décor, the cooking successfully combines traditional pub dishes with more contemporary ideas. Gary Coughlan is a keen advocate of local ingredients, sourcing seasonal vegetables from a smallholding up the road and game from nearby shoots. Simple, confident cooking allows clean, clear flavours of the main ingredient to shine through. Dorset scallops with warm bacon salad, steamed neck of Somerset lamb and kidney suet pudding, and turbot with summer vegetable and blackeye bean broth, confirm the strong seasonal bias of the kitchen. Desserts may take in a classic steamed treacle sponge or the unusual – say forced rhubarb and Luscombe organic ginger beer soup with lemon sorbet. Lunchtime bar meals are equally imaginative. House wines from £11.
Chef/s: Gary Coughlan. **Open:** all week L 12 to 3, D 6.30 to 11. **Closed:** 26 Dec, 1 Jan. **Meals:** alc (main courses £9 to £14). **Service:** not inc. **Details:** Cards accepted. 75 seats. 70 seats outside. Separate bar. Wheelchair access. Children's portions. Car parking.

Scores on the Doors

To find out more about the Scores on the Doors campaign, please visit the Food Standard's Agency website: www.food.gov.uk or www.which.co.uk.

Long Sutton

ALSO RECOMMENDED
▲ Devonshire Arms

Long Sutton, TA10 9LP
Tel no: (01458) 241271
www.thedevonshirearms.com
Gastropub

The setting is rural Somerset at its prettiest, and the Devonshire Arms is a handsome, stylishly converted dining pub. The food is modern, with the lunchtime bar menu taking on reliable bistro favourites, say home-smoked chicken salad (£6.95) or bangers and mustard mash with red onion gravy. Dinner in the restaurant is more ambitious, broad-based modern cooking with strong local leanings that could start with crab crème brûlée (£5.95) followed perhaps by wood pigeon with caramelised shallots, Savoy cabbage and mash (£13.50), or fillet of West Country beef with red onion potato cake (£22.95). Wines from £11.75. Open all week. Accommodation. More reports please.

Midsomer Norton

Moody Goose at the Old Priory

Assured modern cooking in a medieval priory
17-19 Church Square, Midsomer Norton, BA3 2HX
Tel no: (01761) 416784
www.theoldpriory.co.uk
Modern European | £40
Cooking score: 4

A twelfth-century priory in a place called Midsomer Norton sounds like something Inspector Barnaby might be investigating in *Midsomer Murders*, but the savvy Somerset crowd know it as home to Stephen Shore's hotel and restaurant. Lovingly restored, the priory is a delightful labyrinth of a place, all tiny rooms, inglenooks, flagstones and old beams, and the dining room's simple décor is sympathetic to the building's character. The cooking aims high, an innovative modern approach underpinned by a classical theme and driven by quality local and seasonal ingredients – fish delivered daily from Brixham, for example, and produce from the Priory's kitchen garden. Presentation is classy, technique assured and flavours clear in dishes such as pink-roasted lamb rump served with flageolet purée and boulangère potatoes in a redcurrant and rosemary sauce, while a glazed lemon and lime tart could be teamed with a raspberry and vanilla milkshake. The well-chosen global wine list kicks off with a nine-strong house offering by-the-glass (£4) and bottle (£15).

Chef/s: Stephen Shore. **Open:** Tue to Sat, L 12 to 1.30, D 7 to 9. **Closed:** Sun and Mon, Christmas and bank hols. **Meals:** alc (main courses £15 to £22). Set L £16 (2 courses) to£20 (3 courses). Set D £25 (3 courses). **Details:** Cards accepted. 34 seats. Wheelchair access. Music. Children's portions. Car parking.

Milverton

READERS RECOMMEND
Globe

Fore Street, Milverton, TA4 1JX
Tel no: (01823) 400534
www.theglobemilverton.co.uk
'Old coaching inn refurbished in contemporary style'

Oakhill

ALSO RECOMMENDED
▲ Oakhill Inn

Fosse Road, Oakhill, BA3 5HU
Tel no: (01749) 840442
www.theoakhillinn.com
Gastropub

After the success of their Bath pubs the King William and Garrick's Head (see entries), Charlie and Amanda Digney spotted the potential of this old coaching inn, a short drive from Shepton Mallet and Wells. Dating from the early 1800s, the original parquet floors and real fireplaces are just some of the features that remain. A seasonal menu majors on

comforting pub classics: ham hock terrine with celeriac coleslaw (£6), braised lamb shoulder, cabbage and bacon, mash and gravy (£12), and jam roly poly with custard (£4.50). A keenly-priced wine list (from £12) is supplemented by a good choice of local beers and there are plans to open a microbrewery on site. Closed Sun D.

Shepton Mallet
Sharpham Park, Charlton House Hotel

A trailblazer for local produce
Shepton Mallet, BA4 4PR
Tel no: (01749) 342008
www.charltonhouse.com
Modern British | £52
Cooking score: 5

£5 OFF ♠ ⊨

The setting is a grand country house built at the beginning of the seventeenth century, bought by Mulberry founder and Somerset farmer Roger Saul 13 years ago and decorated in a nonchalantly idiosyncratic style, with a smart conservatory dining room. It's a relaxing place and the food is a joy. Elisha Carter's menus draw heavily on seasonal ingredients – head-to-tail, field-to-fork dining is very much to Carter's taste – bringing modern touches to what is essentially classical technique. Provenances are proudly stated, too, with starters taking in Jerusalem artichoke soup with braised Sharpham Park hogget, or Summerleaze Farm duck served three ways with turnip rémoulade, aubergine chutney, pear purée and air-dried spelt bread (a real strength is the selection of breads, all made on the premises). For main course loin of veal might be voguishly teamed with braised belly and served with polenta, terrine of leek and sage and shallot confit sauce, or brilliantly timed plaice wrapped in venison ham and served with parsley shrimp and caper sauce. Desserts are along the lines of delice of white chocolate parfait with griottine cherries, chocolate sorbet and lime syrup. House wine is £24.

Chef/s: Elisha Carter. **Open:** all week L 12 to 2.30, D 7 to 9.30. **Meals:** Set D £52.50. **Service:** not inc. **Details:** Cards accepted. 40 seats. 20 seats outside. Air-con. Separate bar. Wheelchair access. Music. Children's portions. Car parking.

ALSO RECOMMENDED
▲ Blostin's

29-33 Waterloo Road, Shepton Mallet, BA4 5HH
Tel no: (01749) 343648
www.blostins.co.uk
French

Nick and Lynne Reed's modest neighbourhood restaurant has been ticking over happily for years and it is not about to change. Regulars come here for the cosy, personable atmosphere and Nick's sympathetic French-inspired cooking. The fixed-price dinner menu (£16.95 /£18.95) might open with fish soup, rouille and croûtons before rump of lamb with parsnip chips and rosemary jus or salmon baked in filo pastry. Vegetarians have their own menu, and desserts might run to iced ginger meringue with cappuccino cream. House wine is £12.95. Open Tue to Sat D only.

▌Shepton Montague

ALSO RECOMMENDED
▲ Montague Inn

Shepton Montague, BA9 8JW
Tel no: (01749) 813213
Gastropub

This may not be the easiest pub to find, but the wide-reaching rural views and the food are a big draw. The ex-Royal Marine landlord is clearly in charge of the bar, while the kitchen is noted for its sourcing of local produce. Lunch brings a casserole of the week (£8.95), or a ploughman's of homemade pâté and local Cheddar, with fish pie every Friday. At dinner start with butternut squash and artichoke soup (£5.50), then go on to slow-cooked belly of pork (£13.95), with pear and Bing cherry

crumble tart (£5.50) for dessert. Blackboard specials extend choice, and house wine is £13.50. Closed Sun D and all Mon.

▌Stoke-sub-Hamdon
Priory House Restaurant

Personally run country restaurant
1 High Street, Stoke-sub-Hamdon, TA14 6PP
Tel no: (01935) 822826
www.theprioryhouserestaurant.co.uk
Modern British | £31
Cooking score: 5

£5
OFF

Built of warm ochre-coloured Ham stone, this used to be the local clergyman's home and it stands just a stroll from Stoke-sub-Hamdon's fourteenth-century priory (now owned by the National Trust). These days it houses Peter and Sonia Brooks' relaxed country restaurant, a pretty place that they have decorated in dark blue and beige, with framed botanical prints on the walls. Peter's cooking ploughs a fruitful furrow, without veering into uncharted territory; he sources as much as possible from top suppliers and growers in the county, as well as making everything from gravad lax to the beetroot chutney served with a starter of confit duckling and foie gras terrine. Mains looks to the land and sea for Bridport codling fillet with brown shrimp, mushrooms, tomato and lemon butter, loin of wild venison or fillet of local lamb with aubergine purée, redcurrant and rosemary sauce. Desserts are a high point, with a host of tarts showcasing the kitchen's pastry skills (the apricot and almond version comes with a luscious trio of Amaretto ice cream, clotted cream and crème anglaise). The concise, businesslike wine list offers a fine spread, with prices from £16 (£4 a glass); also, don't miss the selection of vintage Somerset Royal cider brandies.
Chef/s: Peter Brooks. **Open:** Sat L 12.30 to 2, Tue to Sat D 7 to 10. **Closed:** Sun, Mon and bank hols. **Meals:** alc (main courses £19.50 to £20.50). **Service:** not inc. **Details:** Cards accepted. 20 seats. Wheelchair access. Music. Children allowed.

Taunton

Castle Hotel

A Somerset favourite
Castle Green, Taunton, TA1 1NF
Tel no: (01823) 272671
www.the-castle-hotel.com
Modern British | £47
Cooking score: 6

🍷 🍴

Kit Chapman is a hotelier born and bred, with a knack for finding and nurturing chefs of real talent (TV's Gary Rhodes and Phil Vickery both made their names here). Richard Guest has been at the stoves for almost a decade and appears to be less fond of the studio lights, preferring to develop his craft. He takes the time to find the best suppliers and develop constructive relationships with them; 'time very well spent' according to one satisfied customer, who noted vegetables, in particular, 'tasted like your best memories of them'. A starter of scrambled duck egg with spiced oil covered in finely sliced smoked eel was delicious, as was Brixham crab and marinated vegetables. A trio of lamb – steamed neck pudding, with hotpot and roast rump – ranged from 'meltingly tender' to 'rich but very satisfying', while perfectly timed steamed sea bass was teamed simply with spring vegetables and wild garlic. 'In Somerset, there is no excuse for a poor cheese board; here we got a very good one' is one endorsement of the excellent selection, while rhubarb vacherin and marinated pineapple with crème fraîche sorbet are typical desserts. Not all reporters have gone away happy, complaining that dishes have lacked sparkle considering 'the rather high prices charged', and while service is friendly, it is not always competent; 'some staff did not speak English well enough to be able to understand nuance'. As for the wine list, there are 'some excellent wines at reasonable mark-ups' (from £17). Bottles have a bias to the classical appellations, but all the world is well-represented.
Chef/s: Richard Guest. **Open:** all week L 12.30 to 2, Mon to Sat D 7 to 9.30. **Meals:** alc £38 (2 courses) to £47. Fixed tariff £15.50 (1 course) to £30.

Service: 12.5%. **Details:** Cards accepted. 70 seats. 20 seats outside. Separate bar. No music. No mobile phones. Wheelchair access. Children's portions. Car parking.

Willow Tree

Up-to-date food in quaint surroundings
3 Tower Lane, Taunton, TA1 4AR
Tel no: (01823) 352835
Modern European | £30
Cooking score: 6

Look for the tall gabled building down an alley off Tower Street if you want to locate this little gem of a restaurant. Inside, it puts on a snug, cottagey face with exposed beams, an inglenook fireplace and a few modern paintings adding a splash of colour to the walls. The setting (and the name) might seem a touch twee, but the menu is a world away from the cosy clichés of teashop cooking: Darren Sherlock spent a decade in various Roux brothers' kitchens and it shows. His menus are sharply focused and imaginative without running riot, and style never seems to get in the way of substance. Tortellini of Quantock venison with warm apple purée and red wine jus or Montgomery's Cheddar soufflé with a walnut and celery cream sauce immediately put down a strong local marker that defines what is to follow. Slow-cooked Somerset lamb with spring vegetables has an earthy seasonal clarity that contrasts with the sunny Mediterranean colours of roast monkfish with pancetta, red onion confit, pepper and pine-nut salsa or sea bass with marinated baby squid, warm potato, olive and caper salad. To conclude, the kitchen makes a feature of multi-part fruity assiettes (perhaps banana or rhubarb) and also challenges the palate by serving beetroot ice cream with bitter chocolate tart. The well-travelled wine list is a suitably unshowy affair, with the emphasis firmly on quality and value for money: prices start at £14.95 (£3.95 a glass).
Chef/s: Darren Sherlock. **Open:** Tue to Sat D only 6.30 to 10. **Closed:** Sun, Mon, Jan and Aug. **Meals:** Set D Tue and Wed £27.50, Thur to Sat £32.50. **Service:** not inc. **Details:** Cards accepted.

30 seats. 10 seats outside. Separate bar. No mobile phones. Wheelchair access. Music. Children allowed.

▌Wells

Goodfellows

Accomplished seafood cookery
5 Sadler Street, Wells, BA5 2RR
Tel no: (01749) 673866
www.goodfellowswells.co.uk
Modern European | £35
Cooking score: 5

An unassuming shop in the heart of Wells hides a mix of culinary activities masterminded by chef Adam Fellows. Step into the newly refurbished patisserie-cum-café for coffee, 'delicious' cakes and light snacks. Press further on into the restaurant, set around a state-of-the-art open kitchen that delivers accomplished and versatile cooking of fresh seafood (sourced from day-boats off the Cornish and Devon coasts). The style is light and simple, with imaginative, distinctly Mediterranean influences. Flavour combinations are forthright, as seen in a starter of seared tuna carpaccio with mustard and herbs and tapenade dressing or a main course of sea bream with grilled Mediterranean vegetables and an aubergine and sesame purée. Meat dishes, say duck confit with parsnip purée, braised red cabbage and cep cream sauce, are equally accomplished. Skills extend to the excellent desserts, perhaps poached rhubarb with crumble biscuit and white chocolate sorbet, mouthwatering fruit tarts and a selection of British farmhouse cheeses, served with plum chutney and organic spelt and walnut bread. Light snacks and a good-value, fixed-price menu at lunch cater for shoppers and local businesses. The global wine list kicks off at £13.95.
Chef/s: Adam Fellows. **Open:** Tue to Sat L 12 to 2, D 6.30 to 9.30. **Closed:** Sun and Mon, 25 to 27 Dec. **Meals:** Set L £14.50 to £17 (3 courses). Set D £33 (3 courses). **Service:** not inc. **Details:** Cards accepted. 40 seats. Air-con. No mobile phones. Music. Children's portions.

Old Spot

Agreeable bistro-style restaurant
12 Sadler Street, Wells, BA5 3TT
Tel no: (01749) 689099
British | £26
Cooking score: 4

'This is an agreeable bistro-style restaurant' observes a reporter, 'and if you're fortunate enough to get one of the tables on the dais at the rear, you may see the west front of the cathedral'. Ian Bates' welcoming bistro in the heart of Wells continues to draw the crowds. The feel is relaxed and unpretentious ('good lighting, stylish bare oak tables and comfortable chairs'), and menus of a sensible length keep things simple but maintain interest, focusing on good, locally sourced raw materials. A March meal produced deep-fried lambs' sweetbreads with good tartare sauce and a successful partnership of braised shin of beef with pearl barley, bacon and thyme. That meal finished in style with rhubarb fool and shortbread, though others have endorsed boiled orange cake with citrus fruit and mascarpone. Service is spot-on. All in all it is very good value, a theme the lengthy wine list picks up with its notable selection at fair mark-ups. Prices start at £13.95 and there's a baker's dozen by-the-glass.
Chef/s: Ian Bates. **Open:** Wed to Sun L 12.30 to 2.30, Tue to Sat D 6.30 to 10.30. **Closed:** Mon, I week Christmas. **Meals:** Set L £15 (2 courses) to £17.50, Set D £21.50 (2 courses) to £26.50, Sun L £21.50. **Service:** not inc. **Details:** Cards accepted. 50 seats. Wheelchair access. Children's portions.

West Hatch

★NEW ENTRY★

Farmer's Inn

Eat the view
West Hatch, TA3 5RS
Tel no: (01823) 480480
www.farmersinnwesthatch.co.uk
Gastropub | £20
Cooking score: 2

Lost down winding lanes, a world away from Taunton just over the hill, this sixteenth-century inn looks out across the expanse of the Somerset Levels. Come for the view, the smartly refurbished interior – polished wood floors, squashy leather sofas and wood-burning fires – the flower-decked terrace, local ales and ciders, and the competent, modern British cooking. Daily menus make good use of local seasonal ingredients, say butternut squash and root ginger soup served with home-made soda bread to start, followed by braised ham hock with parsley mash, Calvados reduction and apple compote or whole sea bass stuffed with rosemary, capers and lemon. To finish, there may be apple and cinnamon strudel with clotted cream or coconut risotto with fresh mango and vanilla oil. Lunchtime extras include home-baked ham with free-range egg and chips, and foccacia sandwiches or baguettes. House wines start at £12, with ten by-the-glass.
Chef/s: Rodney Scott. **Open:** Mon to Fri L 12 to 2, D 7 to 9, Sat and Sun 12 to 9.30. **Closed:** 26 Dec.
Meals: alc (main courses £10.50 to £14.50). Set L £11 (2 courses) to £14. **Service:** not inc.
Details: Cards accepted. 60 seats. 25 seats outside. Separate bar. Wheelchair access. Music. Children's portions. Car parking.

Wookey Hole

★NEW ENTRY★

Wookey Hole Inn

Quirky village pub
Wookey Hole, BA5 1BP
Tel no: (01749) 676677
www.wookeyholeinn.com
Gastropub | £30
Cooking score: 1

Expect the unexpected at this highly individual early Victorian village pub located opposite Somerset's most popular tourist attraction – Wookey Hole Caves. The quirky interior comes as a surprise, as does the offbeat, eclectic menu, which trawls the globe for inspiration. Cooking and presentation are bold and ambitious – a plate of black tiger prawns in crispy Cajun tempura, say, served with teriyaki and chilli pesto dips, or chunky chicken liver pâté with orange compote. To follow, there could be roast lamb rump with sloe berry and red onion jam or pollack with smoked salmon, prawn and spinach cream sauce. Finish with date and pecan pudding with sticky toffee sauce. The simpler lunchtime choice offers burgers, salads, sandwiches and fishcakes.
Chef/s: Ashley Rainbow. **Open:** all week L 12 to 2.30, Mon to Sat D 7 to 9.30. **Closed:** 25 and 26 Dec.
Meals: alc (main courses £13.25 to £23).
Service: not inc. **Details:** Cards accepted. 60 seats. 100 seats outside. Separate bar. Wheelchair access. Music. Children's portions.

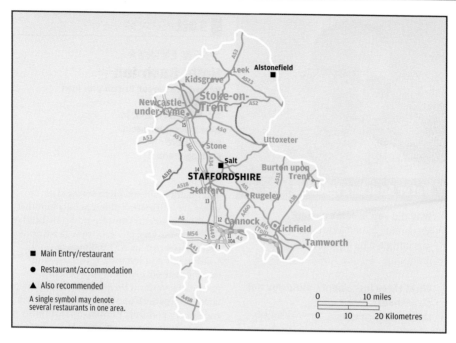

- ■ Main Entry/restaurant
- ● Restaurant/accommodation
- ▲ Also recommended

A single symbol may denote
several restaurants in one area.

0   10 miles

0   10   20 Kilometres

■ Alstonefield

★NEW ENTRY★
George
Idyllic village pub
Alstonefield, DE6 2FX
Tel no: (01335) 310205
Gastropub | £23
Cooking score: 2

Once the local tax collection centre, this 400-
year-old building is now a typical Dales pub,
its edge of the village green location and
comfortable down-to-earth informality
proving a pleasing draw. Good-value food
plays an important part too, and recent
successes have included a 'pleasing' carrot soup,
and a game pie filled with chunks of venison,
rabbit and duck. Good sandwiches, lemon and
dill-battered cod and chips, and local sausages
and mash keep walkers and visitors happy at
lunchtime, while dinner brings pork fillet
with Pink Lady apple jelly, black pudding and
rocket salad, then roast poussin with bacon,
fresh peas and carrots. Desserts include a well-
reported lemon posset with chocolate
shortbread and rhubarb crumble with a
'wonderful marble-coated tutti-frutti-style
ice cream'.
Chef/s: Wade Raithby. **Open:** all week L 12 to 2.30,
Mon to Sat D 7 to 9, Sun D 6.30 to 8. **Closed:** 25
Dec. **Meals:** alc (main courses £9 to £16).
Service: not inc. **Details:** Cards accepted. 30 seats.
50 seats outside. Separate bar. Children's portions.

Symbols

⊨	Accommodation is available.
£30	Three courses for less than £30.
V	More than five vegetarian dishes.
£5 OFF	£5-off voucher scheme.
★	Notable wine list.

Peter Sanchez Iglesias Casa Mia

Why did you become a chef?
My parents owned a restaurant, and I was intrigued by what the chefs were producing.

What three ingredients could you not do without?
Maldon salt, chocolate, virgin olive oil.

What is the most unusual cookery book you've come across in your life?
El Bulli, 1998-2002.

What won't you tolerate in the kitchen?
Chefs burping.

Do you always read reviews of your restaurant?
Whenever I know a review has been written, I wake up first thing in the morning and collect the paper.

What era of history would you most like to have eaten in?
Victorian era.

What did it mean to be awarded the up-and-coming chef award in The Good Food Guide 2008?
It felt amazing. First step onto the culinary map.

Salt

★NEW ENTRY★
Holly Bush Inn
No-nonsense great British pub food
Salt, ST18 0BX
Tel no: (01889) 508234
www.hollybushinn.co.uk
British | £20
Cooking score: 2

£30

The quaint, thatched premises lay claim to being one of Britain's oldest pubs, a hint that the food on offer is from the traditional end of the spectrum. But it is done in such a warm-hearted, competent way and in such comfortable and welcoming surroundings that it knocks many more experimental gastropubs for six. Old favourites include farmhouse pâté on toast, prawn cocktail, steak and kidney pudding, mustard-glazed pork chops and a hearty mixed grill. However, a meltingly-good venison casserole showed the kitchen does have a few surprises up its sleeve. The wine list is functional but extremely reasonable, with several bottles under £13, including the house wines for just £9.95. There is also a wonderful selection of real ales, which complement the food well. All in all this is no-nonsense, great British pub food. **Chef/s:** Paul Hillman. **Open:** Mon to Sat 12 to 9.30, Sun 12 to 9. **Closed:** 25 Dec. **Meals:** alc (main courses £8.50 to £16.50). **Service:** not inc. **Details:** Cards accepted. 64 seats. 150 seats outside. Wheelchair access. Children's portions. Car parking.

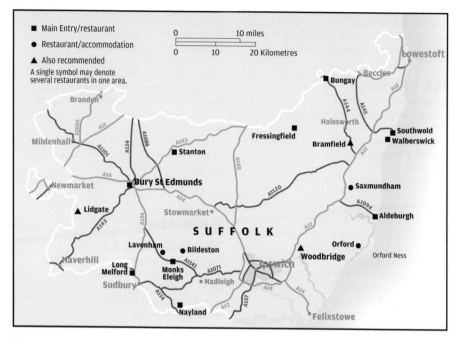

▌Aldeburgh

The Lighthouse Restaurant
Reliable neighbourhood restaurant
77 High Street, Aldeburgh, IP15 5AU
Tel no: (01728) 453377
www.lighthouserestaurant.co.uk
Modern British | £25
Cooking score: 2

 £30

The Lighthouse is a thorough-going
neighbourhood restaurant, timing menus
around the Snape Maltings performances in
the season, offering breakfasts to those up-
and-about early, and happily tailoring service
around local cinema screenings, whether
before or after. Between them, co-proprietor
Sara Fox and Guy Welsh have developed a style
of cooking that suits Aldeburgh down to the
ground, with modern bistro dishes such as
Cromer crab gratin or sautéed foie gras and
mushroom bruschetta to start, followed,
perhaps, by sausages and herbed mash with
gravy, sea bass with roasted red pepper, Puy

lentils and bacon or good fresh cod fillet with
white wine and thyme risotto. The fillet steak
comes with 'round chips'. Leave room for
creamy cardamom rice pudding to finish, and
all is well. A page of wines by-the-glass (from
£3.75 for 175ml) opens a well-written and
well-chosen list.
Chef/s: Guy Welsh and Sara Fox. **Open:** all week, L
12 to 2 (2.30 Sat and Sun), D 6.30 to 10. **Meals:** alc
(main courses £8.75 to £15.75). **Service:** not inc.

Symbols

🛏 Accommodation is available.

£30 Three courses for less than £30.

V More than five vegetarian dishes.

£5 OFF £5-off voucher scheme.

🍾 Notable wine list.

Details: Cards accepted. 100 seats. 15 seats outside. Air-con. No music. No mobile phones. Wheelchair access. Children's portions.

152 Aldeburgh
Colourful coastal location
152 High Street, Aldeburgh, IP15 5AQ
Tel no: (01728) 454594
www.152aldeburgh.co.uk
Modern European | £26
New Chef

 £5 OFF £30

Occupying a corner site on a road that leads down to the beach, 152 is a bright, well-appointed place that has proved a magnet for festival-goers and locals alike. Fish and seafood are a strong focus, perhaps in the form of a starter that pairs tiger prawns and scallops fried in garlic, or main courses such as skate with black butter and Savoy cabbage or superior cod and chips with tartare sauce. Meat-eaters needn't feel left out, however, as pot-roast lamb shank with olive oil mash and roasted roots heartily attests. The British farmhouse cheeses are a sophisticated way of rounding things off or there may be lemon tart with pistachio ice cream for a sweet alternative. The compact wine list offers a surprising preponderance of reds. Bottles start at £13.95, glasses at £3.95.
Chef/s: Mark Clements. **Open:** all week. L 12 to 3, D 6 to closing. **Meals:** alc (main courses £9.50 to £19.95). **Service:** not inc. **Details:** Cards accepted. 52 seats. 20 seats outside. No mobile phones. Wheelchair access. Music. Children's portions.

ALSO RECOMMENDED

▲ Regatta Restaurant and Wine Bar
171-173 The High Street, Aldeburgh, IP15 5AN
Tel no: (01728) 452011
www.regattaaldeburgh.com
Modern British

A recent refurbishment has lent a more grown-up, sophisticated look to this long-running favourite in the heart of Aldeburgh.

The menu remains weighted towards seafood; Mediterranean fish soup with rouille and croûtons (£5) and hand-cured gravad lax with dill mustard sauce (£11 as a main) are typical offerings. Other options include smokehouse specialities (perhaps cooked smoked salmon with crème fraîche, chilli chutney and lime and an eclectic selection of internationally inspired dishes such as Parmesan-glazed lasagne with ricotta, wild mushrooms, sweet potato and side salad (£10). Desserts include baked lemon cheesecake (£5.50). Wines from £11. Open all week.

▌Bildeston

The Bildeston Crown
Contemporary in attitude and operation
High Street, Bildeston, IP7 7EB
Tel no: (01449) 740510
www.thebildestoncrown.com
Modern British | £28
Cooking score: 5

 £30

This smartly-revamped inn on Bildeston's main street certainly delivers a 'wow factor on entering the building'. There's a cool, slightly offbeat look to the bar, lounge and restaurant. The exuberance of the décor is matched by a kitchen that is contemporary in attitude and operation, though some might quarrel with the complexity of the cooking. An intensely flavoured and soft-centred artichoke fondant, for example, was well-partnered with finely chopped pickled walnuts but was in danger of being eclipsed by an overly-rich Roquefort ice cream and an unadvertised pile of sliced artichoke steeped in truffle oil. More cohesive was salt cod served as a brandade and seared fillet with cockle chowder. Mains can be even more complex – note head-to-toe pork and its eight different cuts in miniature, including belly, loin, trotter and cheek – but the effort doesn't always pay off: an inspector's turbot was rather too well-cooked and its accompanying braised oxtail perhaps over-inventive. The combination of Crown classics – fish and chips, shepherd's pie – with the more adventurous choices for both lunch and dinner is worthy of note and certainly gives the kitchen a lot to do. House wine from £16. **Chef/s:** Christopher Lee. **Open:** all week L 12 to 3, D 7 to 10. **Closed:** D 25 Dec, D 1 Jan. **Meals:** Set menu £16 (2 courses) to £20. **Service:** not inc. **Details:** Cards accepted. 100 seats. 40 seats outside. Separate bar. Car parking.

▌Bramfield

ALSO RECOMMENDED
▲ Queen's Head

The Street, Bramfield, IP19 9HT
Tel no: (01986) 784214
www.queensheadbramfield.co.uk
Gastropub

Renowned for its use of organic produce, the Queens Head publishes a detailed list of its suppliers, many of them local farms. Despite its dining focus it retains the feel of a traditional pub, from its inglenook fireplace to the attractive garden. Expect wholesome home-made meals along the lines of local beef fillet carpaccio with mustard dressing (£7.50) followed by suprême of chicken wrapped in pancetta and stuffed with pesto, ricotta and pine nuts, served with salad and organic potatoes roasted in olive oil (£13.95). Finish with warm almond frangipane tart (£4.35). The wine list opens at £13.45 and includes several organic options. Open all week.

▌Bungay

Earsham Street Café

There should be one in every town
11-13 Earsham Street, Bungay, NR35 1AE
Tel no: (01986) 893103
Modern British | £20
Cooking score: 2

The warmth and chatter of the smart dining room at Earsham Street Café is familiar to many loyal patrons, both locals and visitors. The café's consistency over the years has been praised, as has its flexible attitude – open all day, you can pop in for a cake, light snack or full-blown meal. Menus follow the familiar modern British cookery route with fine local materials featuring prominently. Sticky pork belly with mango, cherry tomato and spring onion salad makes a good start, before continuing with something like gutsy baked smoked haddock with mustard mash, curly kale and prawn and caper butter or crisp confit of duck with herby mash, wild mushrooms and baby leeks. Brancaster mussels in white wine and cream or rare seared tuna with Niçoise-style salad make good light lunch dishes. Desserts range from vanilla crème brûlée with sloe gin and damson ice cream to Black Forest fondant with wild cherry ice cream. A well-rounded global collection of wines opens at £12.50.
Chef/s: Christopher Rice. **Open:** Mon to Sat 9.30 to 4.30 Sun L 12 to 2.30. **Closed:** bank hols, Christmas. **Meals:** alc (main courses £9.95 to £12). **Service:** not inc. **Details:** Cards accepted. 50 seats. 25 seats outside. Wheelchair access. Music. Children's portions.

▌Bury St Edmunds

Maison Bleue

Consistent French seafood restaurant
30-31 Churchgate Street, Bury St Edmunds, IP33 1RG
Tel no: (01284) 760623
www.maisonbleue.co.uk
French | £26
Cooking score: 2

This popular French seafood restaurant has a new look – cool contemporary colours teamed with stylish banquettes and chairs, artwork and lighting. The atmosphere remains warm and lively, with 'pleasant, helpful service' from a young French team. At lunchtimes, the *plat du jour* is a steal, as are the other flexible, affordable daily fixed-price options. Whichever route you take, expect intelligent, simple, 'well-flavoured' seafood dishes, perhaps poached brill fillet with winter vegetable brunoise and white wine sauce, and there are always a couple of meat offerings, like roasted English rack of lamb served with a

garlic sauce, if you're not in the mood for fish. France is understandably the focus of a well-selected wine list, with house offerings by-the-glass, carafe and by bottle from £11.95.
Chef/s: Pascal Canevet. **Open:** Tue to Sat, L 12 to 2.30, D 7 to 9.30 (10 Fri and Sat). **Closed:** Sun and Mon. **Meals:** alc (main courses) £14.15 to £21.95. Set L £13.95 (2 courses) to £16.95, Set D £25.95. **Service:** optional. **Details:** Cards accepted. 65 seats. Wheelchair access. Music. Children allowed. Car parking.

▌Fressingfield

The Fox and Goose Inn
Tudor trappings and intricate flavours
Church Road, Fressingfield, IP21 5PB
Tel no: (01379) 586247
www.foxandgoose.net
Modern British | £25
Cooking score: 1

Five centuries of history and a picture-perfect English village location add to the allure of this timber-framed Tudor guildhall hard by Fressingfield's medieval church. But all is not exactly as it seems. The atmospheric beamed dining room has been enlivened with brightly coloured contemporary artwork and the menu promises thoroughly modern food. Intricate flavours and daring marriages define Paul Yaxley's cooking – especially in the evening: this is a kitchen that dusts fillet of salmon with Lapsang Suchong and orange before serving it with basil crème fraîche, linguine and pickled salsify. To start, duck confit comes with ginger mousse, carrot and cardamom purée and a marmalade vinaigrette. Desserts could involve poached rhubarb with star anise, chilled rice pudding and pineapple sorbet. Around 50 wines offer serious drinking from top producers. House selections start at £12.95 (£3.50 a glass).
Chef/s: Paul Yaxley and Mat Wyatt. **Open:** Tue to Sun L 12 to 2, Tue to Sat D 7 to 9 (Sun 6.30 to 8.15). **Closed:** Mon, 27 to 30 Dec, last 2 weeks Jan. **Meals:** alc (main courses £12 to £18). Set L £12.95 (2 courses) to £15.50. Set D £38 (7 courses).

Service: not inc. **Details:** Cards accepted. 48 seats. 16 seats outside. Wheelchair access. Music. Children's portions. Car parking.

▌Lavenham

★ **READERS' RESTAURANT OF THE YEAR** ★
EAST

Great House
Peerless reputation for French food
Market Place, Lavenham, CO10 9QZ
Tel no: (01787) 247431
www.greathouse.co.uk
French | £27
Cooking score: 4

On the corner of the old market square, just yards from the magnificent timber-framed Guildhall, is Remy and Martine Crepy's smart restaurant-with-rooms. Refurbished since the last edition of the Guide, the new look has a sophisticated modern edge with wooden floors, white-clad tables and subdued colours all creating a distinctive yet relaxed atmosphere. Flavour combinations tend towards the classic, yet techniques often add a new twist, as in a starter of warm, lightly-smoked salmon with red beetroot coulis and dill jus. In a more classic vein, rich duck foie gras terrine may come with onion chutney and grilled brioche, while a delicate tartare of wild sea bass is accompanied by marinated cucumber, dill and mint cream. Meats, too, are of good quality, as in a main-course beef fillet skilfully cooked and served with red wine sauce and marrowbone. Desserts might include a classic crème brûlée. Service is friendly and accommodating, and the wine list is imaginatively put together – with an understandable French bias – at ungrasping prices. House wine is £11.50. A sister venue to Maison Bleue in Bury St Edmunds (see entry).
Chef/s: Regis Crépy. **Open:** Wed to Sun L 12 to 2.30, D Tue to Sat 7 to 9.30. **Meals:** Set L £16.95, Set D £26.95. **Service:** not inc. **Details:** Cards accepted. 50 seats. 24 seats outside. Wheelchair access. Music. Children's portions.

▌Levington

READERS RECOMMEND
Ship Inn
Gastropub
Church Lane, Levington, IP10 0LQ
Tel no: (01473) 659573
'The food is consistently good'

▌Lidgate

ALSO RECOMMENDED
▲ Star Inn
The Street, Lidgate, CB8 9PP
Tel no: (01638) 500275
Mediterranean

The setting is a quintessentially English, five centuries-old country pub with beams, chunky wooden furniture, open fires and real ales. But influences from the Catalan owner's homeland are evident on the lengthy blackboard menu, incorporating fish dishes such as monkfish marinera and paella (£15.95). The style also takes in wider Mediterranean and English modes, producing carpaccio of salmon (£5.90), lasagne and sirloin steak with Stilton (£16.95). Wines are mostly Spanish and start at £14.50. Closed Sun D.

▌Long Melford
Scutchers
Pretty village restaurant
Westgate Street, Long Melford, CO10 9DP
Tel no: (01787) 310200
www.scutchers.com
Modern British | £30
Cooking score: 2
£5
OFF

Easy to spot with its bright yellow exterior and red-painted sign, Scutchers occupies one of Long Melford's pretty village residences – parts of which date back to the fifteenth century. Old beams still lend the dining room a touch of rural simplicity, although readers confirm that the new open-plan look is rather elegant after recent renovations. Nick Barrett's food is rooted in the classic Euro-bistro world of lobster bisque, fillet steak with green peppercorn sauce and calf's liver with bacon and mash. He also ventures forth for sautéed foie gras on a rösti with black pudding and Puy lentil gravy and might serve fillet of wild halibut on crab noodles with lime butter sauce. Puddings are straight-and-true offerings such as crème brûlée with raspberry coulis or iced berries with hot white chocolate sauce. The carefully chosen wine list kicks off with 15 special selections from £15 (£3 a glass).
Chef/s: Nick Barrett and Guy Alabaster. Open: Tue to Sat L 12 to 2, D 7 to 9.30. Closed: Sun, Mon and Christmas. Meals: alc (main courses £12 to £22). Set L and D £15 (2 courses) to £20. Service: not inc. Details: Cards accepted. 60 seats. 40 seats outside. Air-con. Wheelchair access. Music. Children's portions. Car parking.

▌Monks Eleigh
Swan Inn
Imaginative cooking of local produce
The Street, Monks Eleigh, IP7 7AU
Tel no: (01449) 741391
www.monkseleigh.com
Gastropub | £28
Cooking score: 3
£30

The Ramsbottoms have always taken hospitality seriously, their 'personal service' commended by more than one contributor. The thatched, timber-framed pub in the middle of Monks Eleigh, with its light interior, pale walls and wooden tables, functions as a centre for eating, meeting and drinking and has an appropriately informal atmosphere. The blackboard menu reflects something of the region, championing the use of the freshest of foods, say game from local shoots or Cromer crabs. Start with grilled pigeon breast with crispy smoked bacon and walnut salad, or their own home-cured gravad lax with a dill and mustard mayonnaise. Follow that with braised lamb knuckle with a Puy lentil sauce or whole roast sea bass with ginger and coriander butter, and finish with creamy rice pudding. Real ales are on draught and wines are a decent selection from £12. **Chef/s:** Nigel Ramsbottom. **Open:** Wed to Sun L 12 to 2, Wed to Sat D 7 to 9. **Meals:** Set menu £13.50 to £17.50. **Service:** not inc. **Details:** Cards accepted. 40 seats. 16 seats outside. Separate bar. No music. Children's portions. Car parking.

▌Nayland
The White Hart Inn
Venerable country inn
11 High Street, Nayland, CO6 4JF
Tel no: (01206) 263382
www.whitehart-nayland.co.uk
Modern European | £28
New Chef

This whitewashed country inn is older than most, dating back as it does to the fifteenth century, as its overhanging beams and open fireplace attest. What has made it the hub of this pleasing Suffolk backwater is a skilled and presentation-conscious approach to food, which has traditionally been in the hands of a French chef. Didier Piot now takes up the reins to offer crab tian with cucumber sorbet and coriander dressing, organic salmon with a casserole of wild mushrooms and bacon and a warm salad of potato and capers, or pork tenderloin bound in herbed mousse and Parma ham, served with mustard mash and two sauces, apple and sage and a reduction of Cabernet Sauvignon vinegar. Vegetables are ordered separately. Dessert-lovers will light on something like champagne mousse with marinated raisins and toasted hazelnuts to round it all off. A short list opens with house wines at £15, or £3.95 a glass.
Chef/s: Didier Piot. **Open:** all week L 12 to 2, D 7 to 9. **Meals:** alc (main courses £10.95 to £20.95). Set L £17.90, Set L Sun £24.50. **Service:** net prices. **Details:** Cards accepted. 50 seats. 50 seats outside. Separate bar. No music. Children allowed. Car parking.

▌Orford
The Trinity, Crown and Castle
Going from strength to strength
Orford, IP12 2LJ
Tel no: (01394) 450205
www.crownandcastle.co.uk
Modern British | £28
Cooking score: 4

Ruth and David Watson's idiosyncratic Victorian hotel opposite Orford Castle's Norman keep goes from strength to strength. The simple, tasteful bar and restaurant provide a congenial backdrop for the main business here, which is food. While the cooking takes its cue from Suffolk's larder, ingredients are subjected to a forthright Mediterranean treatment: locally caught cod comes with saffron, sweet-roast garlic and red pepper risotto, lambs' kidneys with a creamy redcurrant and mustard sauce, while scallops with mango, pomegranate and dandelion leaf salad hint of the Middle East. The two-course midweek lunch is good value, offering a couple of choices at main and dessert stage, perhaps Suffolk lamb burger with celeriac rémoulade and sweet courgette pickles then vanilla pannacotta with rhubarb. An international line-up of wines at fair prices hits just the right note, with some 16 available by-the-glass and bottles from £14.95.
Chef/s: Ruth Watson and Max Dougal. **Open:** all week L 12 to 2.15, D 6.45 to 9.15. **Meals:** alc (main courses £14.95 to £19.50). Set L £14.95. **Service:** not inc. **Details:** Cards accepted. 46 seats. Separate bar. Wheelchair access. Car parking.

ALSO RECOMMENDED
▲ Butley-Orford Oysterage
Market Hill, Orford, IP12 2LH
Tel no: (01394) 450277
www.butleyorfordoysterage.co.uk
Seafood

Famed for its locally-bred Butley
Creek oysters and incomparable oak-smoked
fish, the Pinney family's idiosyncratic seafood
café has been doing its stuff since the mid-60s.
The oysters appear 'au naturel', in a soup
(£4.90) and as 'angels on horseback'.
Simplicity is the name of the game, whether it
is smoked cod's roe on toast (£6.80) or a
special such as cod with parsley sauce (£11.50).
Smoked chicken salad is a good bet if fish isn't
your bag, and there's treacle tart (£4.50) for
afters. Expect crowds and queues in summer –
especially during the Aldeburgh Festival.
Fish-friendly wines from £12.75. Open all
week; restricted evening hours Nov to Apr.

▋ Saxmundham
The Bell Hotel
Soothing East Suffolk bolthole
31 High Street, Saxmundham, IP17 1AF
Tel no: (01728) 602331
www.bellhotel-saxmundham.co.uk
Anglo-French | £26
Cooking score: 2

Andrew and Catherine Blackburn have turned
this seventeenth-century coaching house into
a pleasantly soothing retreat close to
Aldeburgh and the fashionable East Suffolk
coast. He cooks while she plays host in the
relaxed, uncluttered dining room. Andrew
works to a short menu with strong Gallic
accents: he pairs scallops and frogs' legs with
celeriac purée and parsley cream, presents roast
partridge on a rösti with braised red cabbage
and juniper sauce, and puts an oxtail faggot
alongside pan-fried fillet of beef. The same
serious intent typifies desserts such as hazelnut
torte with boozy macerated figs or roasted
pineapple with pineapple and coconut ice

cream drizzled with vanilla syrup. Drinkers
can seek solace in the reliable, 70-bin wine list
from Lay & Wheeler, which has a strong bias
towards French regional vineyards; prices start
at £12.75 for vins de pays.
Chef/s: Andrew Blackburn. **Open:** Tue to Sat L 12 to
2, D 6.30 to 9. **Closed:** Sun, Mon, 26 Dec, 1 Jan,
spring and autumn half-term. **Meals:** alc (main
courses £14 to £16.50). Set L £12.50 (2 courses) to
£15.50. Set D £18.50. **Service:** not inc.
Details: Cards accepted. 26 seats. 15 seats outside.
Separate bar. No mobile phones. Wheelchair
access. Music. Children allowed.

▋ Southwold
Crown Hotel
London by the seaside
90 High Street, Southwold, IP18 6DP
Tel no: (01502) 722186
www.adnams.co.uk
Modern British | £30
Cooking score: 2

The flagship of Southwold's fabled wine
merchant and brewing supremo, the Crown
has become a honeypot for the weekend
crowd since re-opening as a hip seaside venue
in the late '80s. Much of the action centres on
the pulsating brasserie-style bar, which can
seem like a free-for-all at peak times as punters
jostle for seats; for something less frenetic
book a table in the coolly decorated dining
room. Either way, the kitchen sends out big-
city food tailor-made for the swarms of
incomers. Local ingredients and global
flavours define the menus and fish is a front
runner: line-caught cod might appear with
tagliatelle and red pepper salsa verde, while
roast black bream could be perked up with a
chilli and grapefruit dressing. Southwold salt
marsh 'hogget' finds its way into a
tagine, Dingley Dell belly pork is cooked two
ways, and seasonal puds could run to lavender
pannacotta with passion fruit and mint salsa.
Adnams' wine list is an idiosyncratic, endlessly
diverting gem, and the 20-strong special
selection provides a mouthwatering taster of
what's on offer from £15 (£3.75 a glass).

Chef/s: Robert Mace. **Open:** all week L 12 to 2, D 6 to 9.30. **Meals:** alc (main courses £13 to £17.50). **Service:** not inc. **Details:** Cards accepted. 86 seats. 34 seats outside. Air-con. Separate bar. No music. No mobile phones. Wheelchair access. Children's portions. Car parking.

Sutherland House
Characterful showcase for local produce
56 High Street, Southwold, IP18 6DN
Tel no: (01502) 724544
www.sutherlandhouse.co.uk
British | £24
New Chef

This lovely old building was once a faded restaurant-with-rooms, but in the hands of Peter and Anna Banks it has been transformed. These days, the interior combines modern artwork, rich natural colours and funky light fittings with original beams and fireplaces. Alan Paton has moved on, but new man Daniel Burns continues to make excellent use of local produce – the menu even lists the distance the main ingredients have travelled. 'Excellent' tapas-style starters include potato, parsley and onion dumplings with pear and cardamon ketchup (1 mile) and pressed ox tongue (24 miles). Follow with Blythburgh free-range pork and black pudding sausages with kale, mash and golden sultana relish (4 miles) or steamed chicken breast with braised leeks, confit celeriac and sage and lentil risotto (36 miles). For dessert, perhaps rhubarb crumble tart with ginger cream or bread-and-butter pudding with vintage marmalade ice cream. Wines start at £12.90, but there is also an impressive local beer and cider menu. Reports please.
Chef/s: Daniel Burns. **Open:** all week L 12 to 12.30, D 7 to 9.30. **Closed:** 6 to 20 Jan, Mon and Tue Jan to May except bank hols, 25 Dec. **Meals:** alc (main courses £10.50 to £23.30). **Service:** not inc. **Details:** Cards accepted. 50 seats. 30 seats outside. Wheelchair access. Music. Children's portions.

▌Stanton
Leaping Hare
English vineyard restaurant
Wyken Vineyards, Stanton, IP31 2DW
Tel no: (01359) 250287
www.wykenvineyards.co.uk
Modern British | £26
Cooking score: 2

Ancient woodland and an Elizabethan manor house are among the attractions of the Carlisles' estate, and the working vineyard naturally provides its own further lures. Within the timbered barn are housed a café and restaurant, the latter showcasing some appealing Mediterranean-influenced cooking, courtesy of Jon Ellis. Spiced aubergine with minted yoghurt, hummus and pitta makes a good appetiser for main courses such as seared halibut with leeks, capers and crushed new potatoes, or local organic veal fillet with polenta and sprouting broccoli. Local sourcing of meats is heartening, while much of the fresh produce comes from the restaurant's own kitchen garden. Home-made ice creams and sorbets are a refreshing way to finish, or there may be dark chocolate torte with kumquats and Jersey cream. A short international wine list does the job, and of course features the estate's own wines, all of which may be tried by-the-glass, from £3.50.
Chef/s: Jon Ellis. **Open:** all week 10am to 6pm, D Fri and Sat 7 to 9.30. **Closed:** 25 Dec to 4 Jan. **Meals:** alc (main courses £12.95 to £17.95). Set L £22.95. **Service:** not inc. **Details:** Cards accepted. 70 seats. 20 seats outside. No music. No mobile phones. Wheelchair access. Children's portions. Car parking.

Readers recommend

A 'readers recommend' review is a genuine quote from a report sent in by one of our readers. We intend to follow up these suggestions throughout the year to come.

■ Walberswick

The Anchor

Good food, wine and beer
The Street, Walberswick, IP18 6UA
Tel no: (01502) 722112
www.anchoratwalberswick.com
Modern British | £25
Cooking score: 2

'Brilliant and very accommodating service, great food, local produce, the list could go on' enthuses an admirer of the Dorbers' Art and Crafts pub, which has been refurbished with 'good taste'. In the kitchen Sophie Dorber has set out her stall with a short, contemporary and appealing modern menu based on fresh, seasonal (occasionally own-grown) produce. Simplicity is a keynote, evident in smoked mackerel terrine with horseradish cream, and seared scallops with pancetta and Jerusalem artichoke purée. If the food appears to play safe, however, it is certainly not lacking in character. Ginger, greens and roast parsnips make perfect partners for five-spice belly pork, and a cardamom rice pudding with quince syrup constituted 'a perfect marriage' for one visitor. Mark Dorber is something of a beer guru, so check out the pumps and range of bottles, and there's plenty of good drinking to be had on the wine list, which starts at £12.50

Chef/s: Sophie Dorber. **Open:** all week L 12 to 3, D 6 to 9. **Closed:** 25 Dec. **Meals:** alc (main courses £10.75 to £14.75). **Service:** not inc. **Details:** Cards accepted. 100 seats. 120 seats outside. Separate bar. Wheelchair access. Children's portions. Car parking.

Please send us your feedback

To register your opinion about any restaurant listed in the Guide, or a new restaurant that you wish to bring to our attention, please visit the web address at the bottom of the page. Your feedback informs the content of the book and will be used to compile next year's reviews.

■ Woodbridge

ALSO RECOMMENDED
▲ Riverside

Quayside, Woodbridge, IP12 1BH
Tel no: (01394) 382587
www.theriverside.co.uk
Modern British

'The food and service have been consistently good for 20 years,' says one regular of this theatre-restaurant combo. A meal might open with home-made breads or Colchester oysters, followed by a starter of mackerel and potato terrine with caper dressing (£6). After that, perhaps chorizo and garlic steamed mussels with fries (£12) or roast Gressingham duck breast with dauphinoise potatoes and red wine sauce (£16). 'Excellent desserts' might include bread-and-butter pudding or chocolate tart (£6). For a complete night out, try the £30 dinner and film package. A similar, tapas-based deal is £18 at lunchtime. Wines from £14. Closed Sun D.

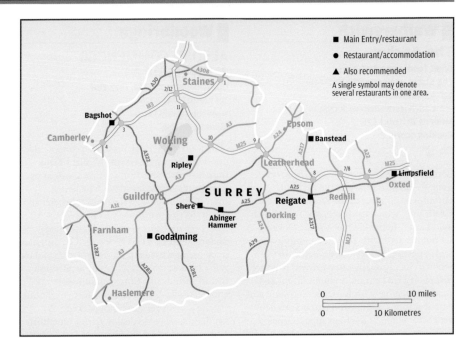

Abinger Hammer
Drakes on the Pond
High-class village restaurant
Dorking Road, Abinger Hammer, RH5 6SA
Tel no: (01306) 731174
www.drakesonthepond.com
Modern European | £44
Cooking score: 5

Standing by a village pond of rather grand proportions, Drakes is tucked away in a Surrey backwater with windows overlooking a rural stretch of the M25. From the outside it might be mistaken for a farmhouse, and the trim dining room now has a warm, fresh look, with chocolate-brown and terracotta walls and chocolate-toned furnishings. Proprietor John Morris remains in charge of the kitchen and he continues to deliver exciting food with lots of thought-provoking, palate-challenging possibilities. Starters tend to involve racy ideas and contrasts – spiced pineapple purée and chorizo with seared duck foie gras, or parsley and peanut purée plus a pork beignet with confit strips of squid, for example. Main courses move into the more conventional, classically trained world of fillet of halibut à la française (with broad beans, bacon and peas) or roast Gressingham duck breast, which is sent out with thyme sarladaise potatoes, baby vegetables and beetroot marmalade. The list of desserts makes familiar, comforting reading – sticky toffee pudding, warm chocolate brownie with raspberry sorbet, lemon posset, poached pear in mulled wine (albeit with a chocolate brûlée). The varied, carefully chosen wine list kicks off with ten house selections from £17.50 (£3.85) and there's a useful choice of half-bottles.
Chef/s: John Morris. **Open:** Tue to Fri L 12 to 1.30, Tue to Sat D 6.45 to 9.30. **Closed:** Sun, Mon.
Meals: alc (main courses £24 to £29). Set L £19.50 (2 courses) to £23.50. **Service:** not inc.
Details: Cards accepted. 30 seats. Air-con. No music. Wheelchair access. Children allowed. Car parking.

Bagshot

Michael Wignall At The Latymer

Innovative, inspired cooking in a luxury retreat
Pennyhill Park Hotel, London Road, Bagshot,
GU19 5EU
Tel no: (01276) 471774
www.pennyhillpark.co.uk
Modern European | £58
Cooking score: 7

Approach the Pennyhill Park hotel/spa/country-club complex via a long driveway through 125 acres of lush parkland. Luxury and comfort are watchwords and its main restaurant, the Latymer, certainly has everything going for it. It now bears the name of its new chef, Michael Wignall (ex-Devonshire Arms Country House Hotel in Bolton Abbey, Yorkshire, see entry) and has been completely refurbished. Remodelling has retained a sense of the period style of the original manor house while introducing a lighter, more contemporary touch to an intimate space. Leaded windows, a stone fireplace and dark beams, timbers and carved panelling blend with white linen, olive green banquettes and high-backed armchairs, while small etched-glass panels add a touch of privacy between tables. Michael Wignall is clearly inspired by his new surroundings and at inspection was found to be on top form. His complex and highly technical modern approach, underpinned by a classical theme, delivers elegantly light dishes of clear, intense flavours. The appealing fixed-price repertoire includes a ten-course tasting option – lunch is eight courses, alongside lunch and dinner cartes – that really shows off the style. Food is 'dressed to thrill', delivering consistently on the palate – demonstrated by royal Anjou pigeon with calf's sweetbreads, black olive gnocchi and lettuce farci, and a peanut parfait with sesame tuile, eucalyptus ice cream and bergamot negus to close. Cheeses, a stunning medley of some dozen petits fours and inspired canapés are equally fine-tuned and service is appropriately professional and knowledgeable, 'but with a genuine friendly touch too'. An extensive, carefully selected, global wine list offers almost everything by-the-glass as well as bottle (from £17), but most are in the £30-plus-and-rising range.
Chef/s: Michael Wignall. **Open:** Tue to Fri L 12 to 2, Tue to Sun D 7 to 9.30 (10 Fri to Sun). **Closed:** 25 Dec D to 31 Dec L. **Meals:** Set L £32, Gourmet menu £58, Set D £58 to £78. **Details:** Cards accepted. 52 seats. Air-con. Separate bar. Wheelchair access. Children's portions. Car parking.

Banstead

Post

Tony Tobin puts his stamp on Post
28 High Street, Banstead, SM7 2LQ
Tel no: (01737) 373839
www.postrestaurant.co.uk
Modern British | £29
Cooking score: 1

V

In 2006 TV chef Tony Tobin took over this old village post office, creating a delicatessen and brasserie on the ground floor and a formal dining room above, with comfortable leather chairs, crisp white tablecloths and faux orchids. Service is friendly and professional and menus are imaginative and sensibly priced. At inspection a seared sea bream fillet with sweet chilli couscous and wok-fried vegetables ticked all the right boxes with high-quality ingredients and precision timing, and a strawberry and lemon tipsy trifle laced with limoncello also received high praise. There were a few inconsistencies, such as bread rolls that could have been fresher and music 'that is a matter of taste', but overall Post's star appears to be in the ascendancy. Don't miss out on coffee 'because the petits fours are delicious'. An extensive wine list starts at £18.
Chef/s: Lewes Evans. **Open:** Tue to Fri L 12 to 2 Sun L 12 to 4, Tue to Sat D 6 to 10. **Closed:** Mon, 1 Jan. **Meals:** Set L £19.50, Set alc £28.50 (2 courses),

Tasting menu £42. **Service:** 12.5%. **Details:** Cards accepted. 45 seats. Air-con. Separate bar. Wheelchair access. Music.

Bishops Hall, Kingston-upon-Thames

READERS RECOMMEND
Frére Jacques

French
10–12 Riverside Walk, Bishops Hall, Kingston-upon-Thames, KT1 1QN
Tel no: 020 8546 1332
www.frerejacques.co.uk
'Authentic french food with great alfresco dining'

Godalming

La Luna

Living la dolce vita
10-14 Wharf Street, Godalming, GU7 1NN
Tel no: (01483) 414155
www.lalunarestaurant.co.uk
Italian | £32
Cooking score: 4

In the centre of town (Wharf Street can take some finding), La Luna's monochrome, spare décor is cool and understated but not cold, and service has been praised for its broadly-smiling, friendly approach. The modern Italian menu is straightforward and easy to digest. Ribollita (a traditional Tuscan bean soup) and courgette, saffron and Parmesan risotto might start, while pasta options include home-made black-ink tagliolini with cuttlefish string or potato gnocchi with kid-goat ragù. It's all appetite-whetting stuff. Simple main courses might be braised rabbit leg with crushed rosemary potatoes and stuffed artichoke or a roasted gilthead bream with olive pesto and steamed courgettes marinated in white balsamic, with sautéed spinach on the side. Finish with a traditional Neapolitan tart made with ricotta and spelt and served with orange blossom crème pâtissière, or proper home-made tiramisù. The wine list, broken up by regions, is Italian from beginning to end (apart from a handful of Champagnes), and opens with a page of sound choices from £14.
Chef/s: Valentino Gentile. **Open:** Tue to Sat L 12 to 2, D 7 to 10. **Closed:** Sun and Mon. **Meals:** alc (main courses £16.95 to £19.95). Set menu £14.95.
Service: not inc. **Details:** Cards accepted. 55 seats. Air-con. Wheelchair access. Music. Children's portions.

Limpsfield

Alexander's at Limpsfield

Delightful ambiance and good food
The Old Lodge, High Street, Limpsfield, RH8 0DR
Tel no: (01883) 714365
www.alexanders-limpsfield.co.uk
Anglo-French | £35
Cooking score: 1

V

When Alexander's opened in the winter of 2006 ambitions were high, but now, following a change of chef, a metamorphosis has taken place and dishes are 'less Heston Blumenthal, more Mrs Bridges'. Menus now offer ravioli filled with prawn mousse to start, then guinea fowl on a bed of lentils. Sunday lunches include traditional roast joints (somewhat spoilt by vegetables being pre-plated), and a separate vegetarian menu provides good choice, while a well-made, tangy lemon tart makes a good finish. On certain evenings a six-course tasting menu priced at just £25 represents great value for money. Staff are particularly friendly and there is a good selection of wines starting at £18.
Chef/s: Richard Drummond. **Open:** Wed to Sun L 12 to 2, D 7 to 9.30. **Closed:** Mon and Tue. **Meals:** Set menu £33 (2 courses) to £40, Midweek menu £27 (2 courses) to £34.50, Tasting menu £25 (6 courses).
Service: not inc. **Details:** Cards accepted. 60 seats. Separate bar. Wheelchair access. Music. Children's portions. Car parking.

▌Reigate

Dining Room

Interesting food in an oasis of calm
59A High Street, Reigate, RH2 9AE
Tel no: (01737) 226650
www.tonytobinrestaurants.co.uk
Modern British | £36
Cooking score: 2

TV chef Tony Tobin's Dining Room is a tranquil place, located on the first floor above the hubbub on the High Street. The ambiance is cool with mirrored and ivory painted walls bedecked with abstracts; lighting is subdued, soft music played and even the window boxes are planted with rosemary. In the background, black-clad waiting staff hover discreetly. Keenly-priced weekday meals offer the likes of roasted figs and Parma ham salad or wild mushroom and red onion tart with 'perfectly executed' pastry. Main dishes (mostly) cut the mustard, say chicken suprême with tomato and basil sauce, although roast lamb chump 'could have been more tender'. From the carte come seared sea scallops with a port wine reduction, guinea fowl or slow-roast duck with mushroom risotto. Desserts range from a fairly 'basic' summer berries pudding to a diet-defying chocolate marquise. The wine list opens at £15.95 .

Chef/s: Tony Tobin. **Open:** Mon to Fri and Sun L 12 to 2.30, Mon to Sat 7 to 10. **Closed:** Christmas to New Year. **Meals:** Set menu (not Sat) £19.50. **Service:** 12.5%. **Details:** Cards accepted. 70 seats. Air-con. Music. Children's portions.

Westerly

Unpretentious bistro de luxe
2-4 London Road, Reigate, RH2 9AN
Tel no: (01737) 222733
www.thewesterly.co.uk
Modern European | £27
Cooking score: 4
£5 OFF   £30

'Every town should have a Westerly', comments a reporter on Jon Coomb's relaxed and likeable bistro that delivers a touch of genuine, unpretentious class to Surrey's commuter belt. The décor fits the bill perfectly, an understated, unbuttoned, white-linen-free modern space dotted with contemporary artwork and decked out with light-wood floors, red high-backed banquettes and brown leather chairs. Coomb's Mediterranean-inspired cooking is refreshingly accessible and in tune with the current trend for high quality with affordability, driven by seasonal, first-class locally sourced produce (suppliers are admirably listed on the menu). The deceptively skilful, simple approach ticks all the right boxes. Expect braised Limousin veal served with porcini, gremolada and Parmesan, the not-to-be-missed signature bourride, perhaps featuring monkfish, bream, red mullet, mussels, prawns and clams, and finish with an almond cake teamed with Pedro Ximenez and raisin ice cream. Wines follow suit with an interesting list noted for reasonable mark-ups and a 13-strong selection by-the-glass, 375ml or 500ml pot Lyonnaise and bottle.

Chef/s: Jon Coomb. **Open:** L Wed to Fri 12.30 to 3, D Tue to Sat 7 to 10. **Closed:** Sun, Mon. **Meals:** alc (main course £16 to £17.50). Set L £17.50 (two courses) to £19.50 (three courses). **Service:** optional. **Details:** Cards accepted. 45 seats. Air-con. No music. Wheelchair access. Children's portions.

▌Ripley

Drake's Restaurant

Exquisite artisan food
The Clock House, High Street, Ripley, GU23 6AQ
Tel no: (01483) 224777
www.drakesrestaurant.co.uk
French | £46
Cooking score: 6

£5 OFF

An impressive illuminated clock crowns the pillared entrance to this fine-looking, three-storey Queen Anne town house. Inside, the dining room breathes understated elegance with its shades of green and local artwork on the walls; there's also a lovely

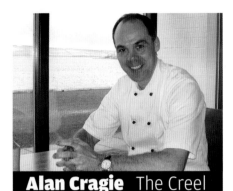

Alan Cragie The Creel

Why did you become a chef?
When I was a kid, an old family friend said to me; 'If you go into catering, you'll never be out of a job, you'll never go hungry and you can work anywhere in the world'.

Do you have a favourite source for your ingredients?
I buy almost everything from Orkney and the waters around it.

Do you always read reviews of your restaurant?
Yes. I don't seek them out. But if someone sends me one I'll read it.

If you have a lazy morning at home, what's your favourite brunch dish?
Smoked salmon and scrambled eggs, with bere bannocks on the side.

What era of history would you most like to have eaten in?
The time of the ancient Romans. Lots of feasting and gluttony!

What's coming up next for you?
We're thinking about a guesthouse with dinner somewhere on mainland Scotland.

walled garden for al fresco drinks. Steve Drake is keen to describe his endeavours as 'artisan cooking', although the results suggest a great deal more in the way of invention, technical prowess and finesse. A one-time Roux scholar, he creates luxurious, elaborate, time-consuming dishes of many parts; the accent is French and dishes set out to dazzle. Ingredients and flavours often appear in unlikely combinations, with surprising results: a starter of roasted cep, braised chicken wing, almond pannacotta and mushroom biscuit is a brilliant exercise in texture and contrast, likewise grilled red mullet with pumpkin mousse and pickled girolles. Fungi also find their way into equally artful main courses – braised sea bass with morels, parsley root purée, potato terrine and vanilla-scented velouté – while roast venison with orange and chestnut burger, Jerusalem artichokes and Szechuan pepper sauce shows a more eclectic spirit at work. 'Crème reversée' (France's answer to pannacotta) is Drake's signature dessert, served with Granny Smith sorbet and dried apple tuile; otherwise, try chocolate and olive oil ganache with lime and jasmine sorbet, lime jelly and milk foam. Steve's wife Serina is an affable, friendly presence out front, and the wine list does its job admirably. The choice is predominantly French, but there is also much to enjoy from elsewhere; prices start at £16, with plenty available by-the-glass (from £4).

Chef/s: Steve Drake. **Open:** Tue to Fri L 12 to 1.30, Tue to Sat D 7 to 9.30. **Closed:** Sun, Mon, 2 weeks Jan, 2 weeks Aug. **Meals:** Set L £21 (2 courses) to £26, Set D £38.50 (2 courses) to £46. **Service:** not inc. **Details:** Cards accepted. 42 seats. No music. No mobile phones. Children allowed.

Scores on the Doors

To find out more about the Scores on the Doors campaign, please visit the Food Standard's Agency website: www.food.gov.uk or www.which.co.uk.

▌Shere
Kinghams

Warm welcome at a popular village restaurant
Gomshall Lane, Shere, GU5 9HE
Tel no: (01483) 202168
www.kinghams-restaurant.co.uk
Modern British | £32
Cooking score: 3

 V

The red-brick, seventeenth-century building
looks endearingly weathered from the
outside, and sits in a sleepy Surrey village a
little to the east of Guildford. Paul Baker has
succeeded in establishing the kind of ambience
that has locals coming back for more, the
warmth of the front-of-house approach
enhanced by fireside dining on chilly nights.
His cooking is more up-to-date than the
surroundings might lead you to expect, with
king scallops in tomato, fennel and Pernod
broth kicking off a meal that might go on to
pork fillet in bacon and chorizo on a coriander
pancake with pineapple and chilli salsa.
Combinations work well, but there is also
room for the more traditional, as in duck
breast on braised baby leeks with a wild
mushroom and grain mustard sauce.
Ingenuity continues into desserts such as hot
rice pudding with roasted figs and strawberry
shortbread, but there could well be
blackcurrant and almond tart with vanilla ice
cream too. House wines are £14.95.
Chef/s: Paul Baker. **Open:** Tue to Sun L 12 to 2.30, D
7 to 10. **Closed:** 25 Dec to 6 Jan. **Meals:** alc (main
courses £13.95 to £18.95). Set L £16.50 (2 courses).
Service: not inc. **Details:** Cards accepted. 45 seats.
20 seats outside. Wheelchair access. Music.
Children's portions. Car parking.

▌Surbiton
The French Table

Relaxed, good value with ambition
85 Maple Road, Surbiton, KT6 4AW
Tel no: (020) 8399 2365
www.thefrenchtable.co.uk
French | £29
Cooking score: 3

This small neighbourhood restaurant set in a
leafy suburban parade is smart and stylish.
Glass-fronted – there's a small atrium roof at
the back to increase the sense of space – it is a
light, split-level room decked out in soothing
pastel tones with white linen-clad tables and
modern artwork on the walls. Chef-patron
Eric Guignard's cooking is French at heart
with a Mediterranean nod, his appealing
menu driven by quality produce, delicate
flavours and creative presentation. His
flamboyant, 'somewhat fussy approach' might
see the odd delay, but be patient, 'the food is
well worth the wait'. So expect cod meunière,
perhaps served with a clam, squid and herb
risotto and caper tapenade croûton, while a
coconut soufflé with chocolate milkshake
might catch the eye at dessert. The wine list is a
fashionable, globetrotting affair helpfully laid
out by style with plenty by-the-glass, a decent
selection of halves and bottles from £13.95.
Chef/s: Eric Guignard. **Open:** L 12 to 2.30 Tue to
Sun, D Tue to Sat 7 to 10.30. **Closed:** Mon except 25
and 26 Dec, 1 and 2 Jan. **Meals:** alc (main courses)
£10.80 to £16.50. Set L Tue to Fri £15.50 (2 courses)
to £18.50. Set L Sat and Sun £19.50 (3 courses).
Service: 12.5%. **Details:** Cards accepted. 48 seats.
Air-con. Wheelchair access. Music. Children's
portions.

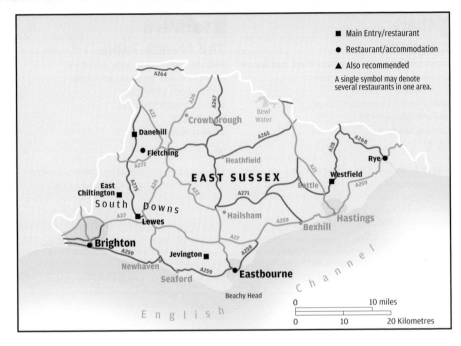

■ Brighton

Bill's Produce Store

Great food-market vibe
The Depot, 100 North Road, Brighton, BN1 1YE
Tel no: (01273) 692894
www.billsproducestore.co.uk
Modern British | £23
Cooking score: 3

Bill Collison's converted bus depot repeats the successful formula of his Lewes original: a fresh produce store and deli stuffed with organic and speciality ingredients and wines, with an eating area attached. Daytime choice is flexible and simple, along the lines of eggs Benedict, say, or the famed fish finger sandwiches, an Iberico charcuterie board and a selection of salads with home-made foccacia. In the evening, cooking follows unfussy brasserie lines and anyone in search of comfort food will not go away disappointed: the roll-call includes cauliflower macaroni cheese, roast lamb neck fillet with ratatouille, chorizo,

black olives, roast garlic and baby potatoes, and roast chicken and ham hock pie teamed with sweet potato, leek and mustard mash and buttered cabbage. A list of half-a-dozen or so wines complements the food. Expect to pay £14.95 for an Australian Chardonnay or Italian Merlot.
Chef/s: Andy Pellegrino. **Open:** Mon to Sat 8am to 10pm, Sun 10am to 4pm. **Closed:** 25 to 26 Dec, 1 Jan. **Meals:** Set L £12, Set D £18 (2 courses). **Service:** not inc. **Details:** Cards accepted. 96 seats. Air-con. Wheelchair access. Music. Children's portions.

Due South

Imaginative local food with a view of the sea
139 Kings Road Arches, Brighton, BN1 2FN
Tel no: (01273) 821218
www.duesouth.co.uk
Modern British | £30
Cooking score: 2

Geography drives this seafront restaurant. Food is sourced from a radius of 30 miles from Brighton beach and there is an emphasis on seasonality. On a sunny evening sit outside and watch Brighton walk by or, in inclement weather, get a grandstand view from the mezzanine level tucked under the arch (under Brighton promenade), which overlooks the sea. A larger dining area further back in the arch is suspended over the open-to-view kitchen. Dishes display imaginative combinations such as asparagus three ways, comprising rich bisque, a panacotta and some well-poached spears. A carefully grilled fillet of turbot with blackened skin and flaking flesh served with poached rock oysters and new potatoes, and a stew of rabbit flavoured with mustard and prunes show boldness in flavouring. To follow, a smoothly sweet pannacotta (a favourite here) was flavoured less firmly with hops from Hepworth's brewery. Bottled beer from Hepworth's, a small brewery near Horsham, is on the drinks list alongside an interesting selection of dessert wines. House wine is £13.50.

Chef/s: Michael Bremner. **Open:** all week L 12 to 3, D 6 to 10. **Closed:** 25 and 26 Dec. **Meals:** Set D £27.50 (2 courses) to £32.50. **Service:** 12.5%. **Details:** Cards accepted. 50 seats. 40 seats outside. Air-con. No mobile phones. Music. Children's portions.

★NEW ENTRY★
The Forager
Gastropub with locally foraged food
3 Stirling Place, Brighton, BN3 3YU
Tel no: (01273) 733134
www.theforagerspub.co.uk
Gastropub | £24
Cooking score: 2

 £30

Bek Misich and Paul Hutchinson have turned the former Stirling Arms into a gastropub offering foraged foods along with local game, seafood and organic Sunday roasts of Sussex beef. Dishes include asparagus-filled tortellini with hogweed seed, asparagus cream and wilted rocket, and slow-braised rabbit with truffle mash, wilted wild spinach and water celery; pennywort and wild garlic also pop up

occasionally. Sticky tof
bourbon toffee sauce i
food is honest, hearty a
It's definitely a pub: there's art
walls, local Harveys beer at the bar, an
according to the blackboard, a locally source
DJ. The wine list is a not-too-complicated affair that extends to Sussex wines, including Limney Sussex sparkling, which is both biodynamic and organic. Service is jeans and T-shirt friendly. House wine is £11.50.

Chef/s: Bek Misich. **Open:** all week L 12 to 3 (Sat and Sun 4), Mon to Sat D 6.30 to 10. **Closed:** 25 and 26 Dec, 1 Jan. **Meals:** alc (main courses £9.50 to £17.50). **Service:** not inc. **Details:** Cards accepted. 70 seats. 70 seats outside. Separate bar. Wheelchair access. Music. Children's portions.

Ginger Pig
Gastropub cooking that's a cut above
3 Hove Street, Hove, Brighton, BN3 2TR
Tel no: (01273) 736123
www.gingermanrestaurants.com
Gastropub | £30
Cooking score: 3

Just off the Hove seafront, the Ginger Pig was local boy Ben McKellar's first foray into gastropub territory (see also the Ginger Fox, Albourne). It doesn't look much like a pub, but the menu majors in dishes of the upmarket pub sort. Chargrilled pork chop with creamed cabbage, buttered mash and a Calvados sauce or smoked haddock with spinach, buttered mash, a poached egg and beurre blanc are brought off with some flair, and look pleasingly neater around the edges than most pub catering. Bookend those with truffle-oiled cauliflower soup and treacle sponge and custard, and all's right with the world – or with Hove, anyway. By the time the Guide appears, there should be rooms to let on the two floors above. Drinking proceeds by way of a short wine list that offers many options by-the-glass from £3. Note: no bookings.

Chef/s: Ben McKellar and Jos Holland Forrester. **Open:** Mon to Fri L 12 to 2, D 6.30 to 10. Sat and Sun L 12.30 to 4, D 6.30 to 10. **Closed:** 25 Dec.

...ls: alc (main courses £9.50 to £15.50).
...rvice: not inc. Details: Cards accepted. 60 seats.
40 seats outside. Air-con. Separate bar. Wheelchair access. Music. Children's portions.

Gingerman

Popular town-centre venue
21A Norfolk Square, Brighton, BN1 2PD
Tel no: (01273) 326688
www.gingermanrestaurants.com
Modern European | £32
Cooking score: 2

The original incarnation of Ben McKellar's burgeoning Brighton empire still draws in the crowds. In the bubbly ambience of a former tea room – ever-so-slightly cramped but recently refurbished – an intelligent menu of modern British fare is offered. Gilthead bream makes a handsome starter, accompanied by celeriac rémoulade and pink grapefruit vinaigrette, while main courses run the gamut from irresistible rib-eye steak with dripping chips and truffle butter to rabbit pie with honey-glazed Chantenay carrots and mash. Finish with white chocolate and lemon mousse with orange jelly or peaches poached in marsala with Amaretto ice-cream. It is all served with appreciable vigour and cheer. Wines start at £13.50.
Chef/s: David Keates. **Open:** Tue to Sun L 12.30 to 1.30, D 7 to 9.30. **Meals:** Set L £18, Set D £30. **Service:** not inc. **Details:** Cards accepted. 32 seats. Air-con. Wheelchair access. Music. Children allowed.

Gingerman at Drakes

Sophisticated high-end cooking
44 Marine Parade, Brighton, BN2 1PE
Tel no: (01273) 696934
www.gingermanrestaurants.com
Modern British | £35
Cooking score: 6

Ben and Pamela McKellar strode boldly into new territory when they opened this chic offshoot of Gingerman (see previous entry) in a bow-fronted hotel by Brighton's seafront. The original Georgian town house has been stylishly catapulted into the boutique world of the twenty-first century, and the basement dining room shows off its understated refinement with discreet lighting, pale colours and hushed tones. The cultured mood is matched by sophisticated high-end cooking that provides fine value without compromise. Langoustine ravioli with orange, chicory and langoustine foam is a suitably elegant starter; otherwise, consider the earthier temptations of roast wood pigeon breast with fried potato terrine. To follow, the kitchen might put together a 'trio of pork' involving braised shoulder with cauliflower purée, confit belly with celeriac purée and pancetta-wrapped fillet with cavello negro, which is a fine showcase for McKellar's talents. Seafood could be represented by basil-crusted halibut with violet artichokes and barigoule dressing and there's always a daily special from the local boats. To finish, choose savoury or sweet – perhaps Welsh rarebit with oysters or pineapple cream with hazelnut meringue and pineapple sabayon. Gingerman at Drakes is no longer open for lunch, but evening visitors can now enjoy the enticing prospect of a five-course tasting menu with wines to match. The list itself is concise but impeccably chosen, with classy names throughout and house selections from £13.50 (£3.65 a glass).
Chef/s: Ben McKellar and Andrew McKenzie. **Open:** all week D only 7 to 10. **Closed:** 25 Dec. **Meals:** alc (main courses £15 to £23). **Service:** not inc. **Details:** Cards accepted. 40 seats. Air-con. Separate bar. No mobile phones. Music. Children's portions.

Symbols	
🛏	Accommodation is available.
£30	Three courses for less than £30.
V	More than five vegetarian dishes.
£5 OFF	£5-off voucher scheme.
🍾	Notable wine list.

La Marinade

Good neighbourhood restaurant
77 St Georges Road, Kemp Town, Brighton,
BN2 1EN
Tel no: (01273) 600992
www.lamarinade.co.uk
Modern European | £28
Cooking score: 1

£5 OFF £30

Nick Lang runs the kitchen at his Kemp Town restaurant very much as a one-man band and jolly busy he must be too, judging by the ample and varied choice La Marinade always offers. There isn't quite the global reach in evidence of years gone by, which may be no bad thing. However it's still possible to go from seared scallops with morcilla in balsamic to either salmon on parsley mash with spinach and béarnaise or an accurate rendition of cassoulet, before lighting on a lemon and lime posset to send you away happy. An inspiring international jumble of wines opens with Chile's Norte Chico varietals at £12.25 (or £3.95 a glass).
Chef/s: Nick Lang. **Open:** Thur to Sat L 12 to 3, Tue to Sat D 6 to 11. **Meals:** alc (main courses £12.50 to £15.95). Set L and D £15. **Service:** not inc.
Details: Cards accepted. 40 seats. Air-con. Wheelchair access. Music. Children's portions.

Pintxo People

Little dishes, big flavours
95-99 Western Road, Brighton, BN1 2LB
Tel no: (01273) 732323
www.pintxopeople.co.uk
Spanish/Tapas | £30
Cooking score: 4

🍾 V

Barcelona comes to Brighton in the shape of this big-hitting venue, which oozes the kind of eclectic chic you might expect from such a gastronomically vibrant town. The whole set up operates on two levels, with the ground floor taken up by an all-day café bar-cum-deli dealing in mainstream pintxos (the Basque version of tapas). Things take a more experimental turn upstairs, and Miguel Jessen's restaurant menu pretty daring ideas alo... peppers and patatas bravas. ... assortment of little dishes that mig... include scallops with vanilla oil and ma... purée, grilled 'hanger' steak (a partcularly flavourful cut) with passion-fruit vinaigrette, or chickpea stew with paprika-marinated tofu and goats' cheese. Desserts are extravagantly complex (hot chocolate coulant with white chocolate and Earl Grey 'hearts' served atop a bed of dried bananas), and it is worth exploring the slate of artisan cheeses with apple sorbet and thick, rich quince. Tantalising Spanish regional wines and glorious sherries share the listings with bottles from other lands; prices start at £13.50. A second branch called Pinchito Tapas is at 32 Featherstone Street, Shoreditch, London EC1.
Chef/s: Miguel Jessen. **Open:** Tue to Fri D 6 to 12, Sat L 12 to 4, D 6 to 12, Sun L 12 to 4. **Closed:** Mon. **Meals:** alc (dishes £3 to £11). Set D £25 and £30. Bar menu available. **Service:** 12.5%. **Details:** Cards accepted. 110 seats. Air-con. Separate bar. Wheelchair access. Music. Children's portions.

Real Eating Company

Laid back all-day format
86-87 Western Road, Brighton, BN3 1JB
Tel no: (01273) 221444
www.real-eating.co.uk
Modern European | £30
Cooking score: 2

The Real Eating format has caught on in Sussex (there are branches in Lewes and Horsham too). It's all-day dining on most days of the week, starting with breakfasts of eggs royale and fresh fruit with Greek yoghurt, going through lunches where you might follow onion and cider soup with fishcakes and mayonnaise, all the way to a good-value fixed-price dinner menu, which deals in the likes of chargrilled squid salad and seared tuna with green beans, fennel and lemon. Indeed, if you brought your laptop, you might get installed here for a whole day. À la carte dining in the evening becomes a little more elaborate, perhaps offering rack of lamb with fondant

Jonray Sanchez Igelsias Casa Mia

Who makes you what you are today?
My family, failure and good supplies.

What's the most unusual ingredient you've cooked or eaten?
Electric Micro Cress.

Who would you invite to your ideal dinner party?
Heston Blumenthal, Ricky Gervais, Ben Stiller.

What's your guilty food pleasure?
HP sauce. Heinz Baked Beans.

What's your least favourite ingredient and why?
Coriander. Just can't stand it when put into salads, very odd.

What dish is your first food memory?
Mussels in white wine cooked by dad when I was around eight years old on holiday in Cornwall.

If you have a lazy morning at home, what's your favourite brunch dish?
Crumpets with cheese; fried egg and ketchup.

---

potato, spring greens, onion confit and seared vine tomatoes. House Italian is £14, and there is an inspired choice by-the-glass between £4 and £6.
Chef/s: Sharon Pengelley. **Open:** Tue to Sat 8am to 11pm, Sun and Mon 9 to 5. **Closed:** 25 and 26 Dec, 1 Jan. **Meals:** alc (main courses £12 to £15). Set D Tue to Thur £18. **Service:** 10% at D. **Details:** Cards accepted. 38 seats. 12 seats outside. Air-con. Wheelchair access. Music. Children's portions.

Sevendials
Unshowy Brightonian favourite
1 Buckingham Place, Brighton, BN1 3TD
Tel no: (01273) 885555
www.sevendialsrestaurant.co.uk
Modern European | £27
Cooking score: 3

Taking its name from the multi-pronged Seven Dials intersection (a short stroll from Brighton seafront), Sam Metcalfe's seminal brasserie is housed in a former bank and still retains its original red brick and stone fascia. Inside, high ceilings, big windows and polished floorboards set the tone, while flowers and family photos add a personal note. The menu changes every few weeks and it is packed with instantly appealing, boldly flavoured dishes in the modern mould: here you can feast on maple-glazed pork belly with black pudding, apple and grain mustard sauce, spiced roast fillet of sea trout with sweet potato fondant and herbed courgettes or grilled rump of lamb with Provençal green bean and new potato salad. Desserts are equally fuss-free offerings such as lemon crème brûlée or strawberry and almond tartlet. The well-spread wine list opens with a clutch of gluggable selections from £14 (£4 a glass). Sam Metcalfe also runs Sam's of Brighton at 1 Paston Place, tel: (01273) 676222. Reports, please.
Chef/s: Sam Metcalfe. **Open:** all week L 12 to 3 (12.30 to 4 Sun), Mon to Sat D 6 to 10.30 (6.30 Sat). **Meals:** alc (main courses £10.50 to £18.50). Set L

and D £12.50 (2 courses) to £15. **Service:** not inc. **Details:** Cards accepted. 60 seats. 50 seats outside. Wheelchair access. Music. Children's portions.

Terre à Terre
Tirelessly inventive vegetarian food
71 East Street, Brighton, BN1 1HQ
Tel no: (01273) 729051
www.terreaterre.co.uk
Vegetarian | £29
Cooking score: 3

 £5 OFF **V** £30

A short hop from the seafront takes you to one of the country's more singularly diverting vegetarian restaurants. In a big wide space, with a few tables outside at the back, Terre à Terre has shaken up the often worthy and fusty ambience of meat-free eating, and made it such fun that a broadly based clientele gives the place plenty of enthusiastic support. Nothing on the menu will sound familiar, so plunge on ahead with Yum Umplum sushi rice tempura, followed by Bengal babs (clue: they come on skewers and involve tandoori-spiced halloumi). Or perhaps mushroom cappuccino with Parmesan doughnuts, then 'Rösti Revisited', in which the fried potato is topped with garlic and nutmeg spinach, a poached egg, and tomato slathered with smoked tapenade. A side of smoky scrunch chips with bang bang salt maintains the hectic pace, and for afters, there is (what else?) a quince dosa served with sloe cider and agave coconut sorbet. A compact, well-chosen list of organic wines accompanies, from £17.15 for a Monastrell red from Spain's Yecla region. **Chef/s:** Glen Lester. **Open:** Tue to Sun 12 to 10.30 (11 Sat). **Closed:** Mon, Christmas. **Meals:** alc (main courses £13.75 to £14.45). Set L £16 (2 courses). Set D £31. **Service:** not inc. **Details:** Cards accepted. 100 seats. 12 seats outside. Air-con. Wheelchair access. Music. Children's portions.

ALSO RECOMMENDED
▲ Hotel du Vin & Bistro
2-6 Ship Street, Brighton, BN1 1AD
Tel no: (01273) 718588
www.hotelduvin.com
Modern European

The Brighton Hotel du Vin occupies an eccentric set of Gothic revival and mock Tudor buildings in the Lanes conservation area, a pebble's throw from Brighton beach. Heavily carved staircases and gargoyles add to the quirky charm. The menus are a trademark selection of modern bistro classics: breaded plaice goujons with tartare sauce (£6.75) and chicken liver and foie gras parfait with onion marmalade and toasted brioche (£6.75) followed by the likes of Provençale tomato, black olive and rocket risotto (£13.50) or confit duck leg with braised endive and red wine jus (£15). Wines from £14.50. Open all week.

▲ Love's Fish Restaurant
40 St James Street, Brighton, BN2 1RG
Tel no: (01273) 693251
www.lovesrestaurant.co.uk
Seafood

Having been through the wringer of a Gordon Ramsay makeover on *Kitchen Nightmares*, Allan Love's Kemp Town fish restaurant has emerged streamlined and smart. It's a long, narrow room with an infectious buzz, and a simple mix-and-match menu offering a run of poached, grilled or fried fish (£8.25) with sauces and veg charged separately, supplemented by blackboard specials. Strip fillets of salmon are gently cooked, plaice is served whole, but skate turns up as only half the wing. Grilled tiger prawns with chorizo in garlic and thyme butter (£6) is a good light starter. Finish with chocolate brownie and vanilla ice cream (£5.15). A short wine list offers everything by-the-glass. Open all week.

Cooksbridge

READERS RECOMMEND

Rainbow Inn

Gastropub
Resting Oak Hill, Cooksbridge, BN8 4PS
Tel no: 01273 400334
www.rainbowsussex.com
'Superior gastropub off the beaten track'

Danehill

Coach & Horses

Pastoral downland pub
School Lane, Danehill, RH17 7JF
Tel no: (01825) 740369
Modern British | £23
Cooking score: 2

Dreamy views of the South Downs add to the pastoral feel of this enchanting Victorian country pub, and there's a pretty garden out front for those who want to watch the sheep grazing in the fields. Drinkers congregate and play darts in the bar, although most people are now drawn to the converted stables where upbeat food is served in a rustic setting of stone walls and hop-garlanded beams. New chef Lee Cobb is continuing in the same vein as his predecessor and his menus are peppered with European ideas, whether it is Basque squid stew or goats' cheese and walnut risotto. He serves grilled sardines with saffron aïoli, pairs pan-fried pollack with crispy pancetta and black pudding, and offers grilled Toulouse sausages on braised butter beans. Open sandwiches are also available at lunchtime and the concise global wine list kicks off with vins de pays at £12.95 (£3.50 a glass).
Chef/s: Lee Cobb. Open: all week L 12 to 2 (2.30 Sat and Sun), Mon to Sat D 7 to 9 (9.30 Fri and Sat). Closed: 26 Dec. Meals: alc (main courses £11 to £16.50). Service: not inc. Details: Cards accepted. 60 seats. 100 seats outside. Separate bar. Wheelchair access. Music. Children's portions. Children allowed. Car parking.

East Chiltington

Jolly Sportsman

Updated country pub noted for quality cooking
Chapel Lane, East Chiltington, BN7 3BA
Tel no: (01273) 890400
www.thejollysportsman.com
Gastropub | £28
Cooking score: 3

V

The clapboard-and-tiled Jolly Sportsman looks every inch the part of an English country pub. Inside it achieves a generous blend of old and new in which the minimal (large contemporary art, chunky oak tables) co-exists with the traditional (real ales, real fire, blackboards). The kitchen buys carefully, setting great store by the provenance of raw materials and the results on the plate have pleased most reporters. Typically you might find roast quail with pomegranate and salsify salad alongside asparagus puff with chanterelles and hollandaise sauce, while main courses extend to grilled gurnard fillet with chorizo, roast tomato, spinach, beans and olive dressing, or roast pork belly with spring vegetables and thyme and hotpot potato. Desserts encompass steamed orange pudding with fresh custard or pannacotta with poached rhubarb. Service has been praised this year, and the international line-up of wines at fair prices (with France at its heart) opens at £14 and hits just the right note.
Chef/s: Bruce Wass. Open: Tue to Sun L 12 to 2.30 (Sun 4), Tue to Sat D 6 to 11. Closed: Mon except bank hols. Meals: alc (main courses £13.85 to £21.50). Set L £15.75. Service: not inc. Details: Cards accepted. 80 seats. 40 seats outside. Air-con. Separate bar. Wheelchair access. Children's portions. Car parking.

Eastbourne

The Mirabelle at The Grand Hotel

Creative cooking amid old-school splendour
King Edwards Parade, Eastbourne, BN21 4EQ
Tel no: (01323) 412345
www.grandeastbourne.com
Modern European | £37
Cooking score: 5

£5 OFF 🍷 🛏

The Mirabelle restaurant has always been a relaxing place to dine, with the full panoply of swagged drapes, crisp table linen and impeccably well-drilled staff on hand to reinforce the tone of elegant, but unstuffy, civility. While the setting may be delightfully old-school, there is nothing passé about Gerald Röser's cooking, which offers 'a modern approach to flavours and textures'. Röser is an old Sussex hand and knows his clientele well, so the menus don't make sudden lunges into unfamiliar territory, but nonetheless retain a feeling of freshness and inventiveness. Broad bean soup with ventrêche bacon, followed by curried mackerel kebab with tomatoes, onions and coriander might be one way to proceed, or there might be a long-standing classic such as roast duck magret with prune and bacon mash in a sauce of Banyuls. It's the kind of coking that understates itself, so that what turns up on the plate is generally more elaborate than the menu description would have it. A high-flier's wine list accompanies proceedings. France is as handsomely served as though Europeans had never reached the New World, but no sooner has it been gloriously ransacked, from Champagne to the Coteaux du Verdon, than Californians and Australians march past in serried ranks. It's all headed-up by a generous selection by-the-glass, from £5.50.
Chef/s: Gerald Röser. **Open:** Tue to Sat L 12.30 to 2, D 7 to 10. **Meals:** Set L £21, Set D £36.50 to £60. **Service:** inclusive. **Details:** Cards accepted. 50 seats. Air-con. Separate bar. Wheelchair access. Music. Children allowed. Car parking.

Fletching

The Griffin Inn

Cosy country inn with serious wine list
Fletching, TN22 3SS
Tel no: (01825) 722890
www.thegriffininn.co.uk
Modern European | £30
Cooking score: 1

£5 OFF 🍷 🛏

A sixteenth-century inn in a peaceable Sussex village, the Griffin overlooks the Ouse valley, and is all dark brickwork and ceiling beams within. Fine-weather dining gives Andrew Billings the chance to fire up the wood-burning oven and roast some Romney Marsh lamb or even Rye Bay lobster in it. Main menu items essay a tour of modern Britain, from seared scallops with pumpkin purée and lemon oil to loin of local venison with potato gratin, braised cabbage, and quince and parsnip chutney. Homely puddings such as plum frangipane tart with crème fraîche raise three cheers. And the loudest cheers of all may well be for the wine list, which is a testament to true passion. Here you can sample the white wine of Cassis in Provence, stirring Sicilian reds, Chilean Syrah and much else besides. Bottles start at £13.50 for house vins de pays, and there are nearly 20 by-the-glass.
Chef/s: Andrew Billings and Nick Peterson. **Open:** all week, L 12 to 2.30 (3 Sat and Sun), Mon to Sat D 7 to 9.30. **Closed:** 25 Dec. **Meals:** alc (main courses £11 to £22.50). Set L Sun £30. **Service:** not inc. **Details:** Cards accepted. 60 seats. 30 seats outside. Separate bar. No music. No mobile phones. Wheelchair access. Children's portions. Car parking.

Readers recommend

A 'readers recommend' review is a genuine quote from a report sent in by one of our readers. We intend to follow up these suggestions throughout the year to come.

Jevington

Hungry Monk
Popular Sussex stalwart
Jevington, BN26 5QF
Tel no: (01323) 482178
www.hungrymonk.co.uk
Anglo-French | £34
Cooking score: 2

£5
OFF

'Pretty well unchangeable' is one regular's fond verdict on this enduring stalwart of the Sussex dining scene. Indeed, the whole ambience of this restaurant is 'simply wonderful', with private sitting rooms where you can enjoy a pre-dinner drink, and a dining room that has a small and intimate feel. Nigel and Sue Mackenzie are not about to rock an exceedingly steady ship, and in the kitchen Gary Fisher prepares food that remains true to the spirit of generosity, wholesome flavour and comfort. Sound raw materials are the bedrock of his menus and dinner might begin with seared beef carpaccio with roasted vegetable salsa. Next comes calf's liver with toasted polenta, bacon and baby onion sauce or poached halibut fillet with pea purée and hollandaise. Aside from the famous banoffi pie, there's chilled almond soufflé and poached apricots for dessert. House wine is £16.
Chef/s: Gary Fisher and Matt Comben. **Open:** Tue to Fri and Sun 12 to 2, all week D 6.45 to 9.30. **Closed:** bank hols. **Meals:** Set L £16.95 (2 courses) to £20.50, Set D £33.95. **Service:** not inc.
Details: Cards accepted. 38 seats. Air-con. Separate bar. Wheelchair access. Music. Children's portions. Car parking.

Lewes

★NEW ENTRY★
Real Eating Company
Deli-brasserie combo for good food
18 Cliffe High Street, Lewes, BN3 1JB
Tel no: (01273) 221444
www.real-eating.co.uk
British | £25
Cooking score: 2

£30

This all day deli/brasserie with its cheese counter, aroma of saffron and neat rows of tables offers a short menu with imaginative choice. Some dishes may have southern European influences, others draw on ingredients from the delicatessen, but the cooking has an underlying simplicity that works well. A dish of crabmeat, for example, the dark and white meat separated carefully, was enhanced with fresh herbs such as tarragon, while the timing of fish (a fillet of sea bream, say) is immaculate. A late May menu was an exemplar of what seasonal English cooking should be: asparagus soup, tender guinea fowl resting on a bed of finely cooked asparagus and broad beans, and a delicate rhubarb fool. Decent wines and service – this can be stretched with a full house – sums up a place that displays genuine enthusiasm and knowledge as well as respect for fine food. The original is in Brighton (see entry).
Chef/s: Stephen Beadle. **Open:** all week L 12 to 3, D 6.30 to 9.30. **Closed:** 25 Dec, 1 Jan. **Meals:** alc (main courses £9 to £15). **Service:** 10% (D only).
Details: Cards accepted. 60 seats. 70 seats outside. Air-con. Wheelchair access. Music. Children's portions.

Pailin

Thai
20 Station Street, Lewes, BN7 2DB
Tel no: (01273) 473906
'Authentic Thai dishes refined by generations of families'

Pelham House

Modern European
St Andrew's Lane, Lewes, BN7 1UW
Tel no: 01273 488600
www.pelhamhouse.com
'Cosmopolitan cuisine in a historic dining room'

█ Rye

The George in Rye

Revitalised old coaching inn
98 High Street, Rye, TN31 7JT
Tel no: (01797) 222114
www.thegeorgeinrye.com
Modern British | £28
Cooking score: 1

Four centuries of history and a prominent location on Rye's attractive High Street make this Tudor coaching inn a highly attractive prospect. A bold refurbishment has bought the building up to date, but the interior still has a sense of deep-rooted antiquity. The cooking is thoroughly up-to-the-minute and daily menus have a seasonal ring. Roast butternut squash soup and guinea fowl with winter tabbouleh and pistachio sauce followed by plum and apple crumble made up one February dinner taken in the modern-looking restaurant. Elsewhere there's an atmospheric pubby bar with a blazing winter fire, real ales and a good bar menu, plus a pleasant, sheltered courtyard for when the weather is fine. House wine is £14.
Chef/s: Rod Grossman. **Open:** all week L 12 to 3, D 6.30 to 10. **Meals:** alc (main courses £13.25 to £16.50). **Service:** not inc. **Details:** Cards accepted. 30 seats. 38 seats outside. Separate bar. Wheelchair access. Music. Children's portions.

Landgate Bistro

Local ingredients in cosy surroundings
5-6 Landgate, Rye, TN31 7LH
Tel no: (01797) 222829
www.landgatebistro.co.uk
Modern British | £23
Cooking score: 3

V

Enthusiastically exploited local supply lines form the mainstay of proceedings at this small, beamed restaurant which feels fully in keeping with the largely unreconstructed coastal town in which it lies. Fish and seafood from Rye Bay, as well as local meats, game and dairy products from nearby farms, are what it is all about. They may turn up in the shape of sautéed scallops with caramelised walnuts or alternatively with bacon and shallots in sherry and mains such as Romney Marsh lamb with potato gratin and green beans. A pair of regulars who can't keep away heartily endorse the rabbit terrine, as well as the accurately timed turbot with duchesse potatoes and vegetable julienne. Pistachio ice cream with Calvados is a flash way to finish, while other boozy desserts might include chocolate cake with black cherries in Kirsch. The friendliness with which it is all served adds hugely to the occasion. A properly concise bistro wine list starts at £11.20 for French house wines (£3 a glass).
Chef/s: Martin Peacock. **Open:** Sat and Sun L 12 to 3, Wed to Sat D 7 to 9. **Meals:** alc (main courses £13.50 to £15.50). Set D Tue to Thur £17.50.
Service: 10%. **Details:** Cards accepted. 34 seats. Separate bar. No mobile phones. Music. Children's portions.

Webbe's at the Fish Café

Enterprising seafood venture
17 Tower Street, Rye, TN31 7AT
Tel no: (01797) 222226
www.thefishcafe.com
Seafood | £25
Cooking score: 4
£5 OFF | £30

Famous as the UK's first fireproof building (circa 1907), this unusual four-storey brick edifice now houses Paul Webbe's Fish Café – an exciting new venture that offers the denizens of Rye and beyond a taste of modern seafood cookery. Head upstairs to the classy contemporary surroundings of Webbe's restaurant for innovative evening meals based on piscine supplies from near and far. Wide-ranging influences point up dishes such as sesame-crusted tuna with oriental salad, chargrilled lobster with hand-cut chips and roast fillet of wild sea bass with mussels, clams, black noodles and basil sauce. There are also plenty of alternatives for meat eaters (rump of lamb with Mediterranean vegetables and garlic confit, for example) plus a raft of desserts ranging from raspberry crème brûlée with Drambuie ice cream to steamed chocolate sponge with marmalade ice cream. On the ground floor is a bright minimalist café with an open kitchen that feeds the punters with shellfish platters and brasserie dishes such as blackened Cajun-spiced salmon. Well-chosen wines from Europe and the New World feature on the reasonably priced list; house selections start at £14 (£3.50 a glass). The same team also runs the Wild Mushroom at Westfield (see entry).
Chef/s: Matthew Drinkwater and Paul Webbe.
Open: Tue to Sat D only 6 to 9. Closed: Sun, Mon.
Meals: alc (main courses £11 to £23). Service: not inc. Details: Cards accepted. 52 seats. Air-con. Wheelchair access. Music. Children's portions.

Westfield

Wild Mushroom

Traditional setting, contemporary food
Woodgate House, Westfield Lane, Westfield,
TN35 4SB
Tel no: (01424) 751137
www.wildmushroom.co.uk
Modern European | £26
Cooking score: 2
£5 OFF | £30

An out-of-the-way Victorian farmhouse down a country lane is the setting for Paul and Rebecca Webbe's pleasing local restaurant. Against a genteel bourgeois backdrop of starched linen and high-back chairs, visitors can look forward to food that eschews nostalgia in favour of contemporary ideas, local ingredients and global flavours. Fillet of Wickham Manor Farm lamb might appear with niçoise vegetables and tapenade, roast pork belly is partnered by Rye Bay scallops and celeriac and Bramley apple purée, while a mussel and Indian spice sauce adds zing to sea bass with salsify and Jerusalem artichokes. Desserts also pick up the modern theme, offering the likes of glazed lime mousse with pomegranate sorbet, passion fruit syrup and praline water. The wine list covers a lot of ground, from Mexican reds to whites from the nearby Carr Taylor vineyard. Prices start at £14.95 (£3.50 a glass) for Chilean house selections.
Chef/s: Paul Webbe. Open: Tue to Fri L 12 to 2 (Sun 2.30), D 7 to 9.30 (Sat 10). Closed: Mon, first 2 weeks Jan. Meals: alc D (main courses £12.50 to £19.95). Set L £15.95 (2 courses) to £18.95.
Service: not inc. Details: Cards accepted. 44 seats. Separate bar. No mobile phones. Wheelchair access. Music. Children's portions. Car parking.

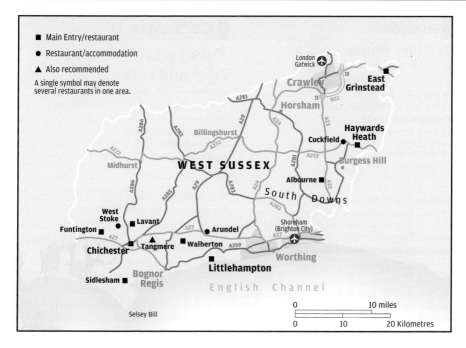

■ Albourne

Ginger Fox

A great spot for hungry walkers
Henfield Road, Albourne, BN6 9EA
Tel no: (01273) 857888
www.gingermanrestaurants.com/ginger_fox
Gastropub | £25
Cooking score: 4

V

This Ginger Fox has all the benefits of a country pub – views over the South Downs, al fresco seating, somewhere for kids to play and ample parking – but with all the culinary prowess of its Brighton-based big brothers: the Gingerman restaurants in Norfolk Square and Drakes Hotel, and the Ginger Pig pub in Hove (see entries). There's drinking room in the bar area and, unlike the Ginger Pig, the Fox takes bookings. Food is locally sourced and unfussy, with simple Brit dishes such as globe artichoke and asparagus salad with pickled quail's egg, and rib-eye steak with good chips served alongside more eclectic influences like wasabi-marinated salmon with crispy seaweed. Vegetarians and off-duty meat eaters will enjoy dishes like sweet potato and chickpea curry with jasmine rice, while snackers can opt for the three-cheese ploughmans with home-made pickled beets and coleslaw. Service is efficient and staff know their stuff. Ridgeview Sparkling Bloomsbury and its sparkling blush relative Fitzrovia, from nearby Ditchling, are available by-the-glass, while prices on the 50-bin wine list kick off at £13.50 a bottle (with most available in 350ml carafes).

Chef/s: David Keates. **Open:** Mon to Fri L 12 to 2 (Sat, Sun and bank hols 12.30 to 4), Mon to Sat D 6 to 10 (from 6.30 Fri and Sat). **Closed:** 25 Dec. **Meals:** alc (main courses £8.50 to £16.50). **Service:** not inc. **Details:** Cards accepted. 64 seats. 64 seats outside. Separate bar. Wheelchair access. Music. Children's portions.

■ Arundel

Arundel House
Amenable restaurant-with-rooms
11 High Street, Arundel, BN18 9AD
Tel no: (01903) 882136
www.arundelhouseonline.co.uk
Modern British | £28
Cooking score: 2

£5 OFF 🍷 🛏 £30

Standing in the shadow of Arundel's historic castle, this bow-windowed restaurant-with-rooms makes an ideal base camp for anyone visiting Goodwood and the local tourist hot spots. A congenial atmosphere prevails in the boldly decorated dining room, where guests can enjoy skilfully crafted dishes with a broadly European outlook. Lunch is straightforward (calf's liver and bacon, tagliatelle carbonara, marjoram-roasted guinea fowl) but evening menus show more than a touch of ambition. Begin with twice-baked Cornish crab and ginger soufflé with sweet red pepper coulis, before confit of Sussex pork belly with champ and braised Little Gems or saddle of local venison with wilted spinach and a red wine reduction flavoured with chocolate. To finish, rhubarb cheesecake with rhubarb-and-custard ice cream is another local treat, or you might prefer classic crème caramel with kumquat syrup. The wine list is a thoroughly impressive 150-bin slate, with fine personal selections, informative notes and a catholic global range. Prices start at £18 (£4 a glass).
Chef/s: Luke Hackman. **Open:** Mon to Sat L 12 to 2, D 7 to 12. **Closed:** Sun, Christmas and bank hols. **Meals:** alc (main courses L £10, D £16). **Service:** not inc. **Details:** Cards accepted. 32 seats. No mobile phones. Music. Children allowed.

Average price

The average price listed in main-entry reviews denotes the price of a three-course meal, without wine.

■ Chichester

★NEW ENTRY★
Field and Fork
Assured modern cooking
5 Baffins Court, Baffins Lane, Chichester, PO19 1UA
Tel no: (01243) 784888
Modern British | £24
Cooking score: 4

 £30

Sam Mahoney, ex-head chef of Kensington Place (see entry, London), decamped early in 2008 to open a tiny, smartly designed restaurant in a quiet courtyard in this fine Georgian town centre. It's a café by day and a restaurant in the evening, when Sam – with two chefs from Kensington Place – goes in for an imaginative modern British menu. At 6.30 candles are lit, flowers are placed on the table and out come 'sublime' salmon consommé with buckwheat noodles and dill salmon dumplings, or a 'superb' rack of lamb with a masterstroke of haricot beans with mint and spinach. Other mains go down the local Sussex route: stuffed loin of pork with parsley mash and red mullet with caramelised fennel tart and ratatouille vinaigrette. For dessert, a tart won praise for its thin yet dense high-sided pasty case crammed with the finest dark chocolate. Light lunches could produce asparagus risotto and jellied ham hock terrine as starters or main courses, home-made breads, petits fours and desserts are also available in the sister delicatessen across the courtyard. Janet Mahoney provides exemplary service; the wines, from a small wine list, are equally impressive. Prices start at £12.95.
Chef/s: Sam Mahoney. **Open:** Tue to Sat 8am to 9pm. **Closed:** Sun, Mon, bank hols. **Meals:** Set D £19.95 (2 courses) to £23.95. **Service:** not inc. **Details:** Cards accepted. 25 seats. 16 seats outside. Wheelchair access. Children's portions.

Cuckfield

Ockenden Manor

Classy country manor oozing history
Ockenden Lane, Cuckfield, RH17 5LD
Tel no: (01444) 416111
www.hshotels.co.uk
Modern French | £40
Cooking score: 6

£5 OFF

This entrancing sixteenth-century manor down a tiny lane rests calmly in nine acres of grounds complete with a walled garden. Inside, it is filled with gilt-framed paintings, oak panelling and stone fireplaces, with heraldic stained glass windows and an ornate painted ceiling adding to the historical trappings in the main dining room (for something less formal try the spacious conservatory terrace). Stephen Crane's cooking displays panache and serious intent in spades. He is obviously at home within the entrenched country-house world of pressed foie gras terrine and apple jelly, roast guinea fowl breast with buttered Savoy cabbage, and escalope of turbot with hollandaise sauce. However other dishes suggest a strong creative spirit at work – witness crispy calf's sweetbread with pickled mushrooms and pea-shoot salad, caper and raisin purée or grilled fillet of sea bass with truffled celeriac purée and red wine sauce. To conclude, the kitchen applies its abundant skills to oat crème brûlée with whisky ice cream and orange salad or warm chocolate tart with coconut sorbet and lychee foam; alternatively, explore the cheese trolley. A seven-course tasting menu is also available, along with a short menu for vegetarians. The comprehensive wine list is exactly what you might expect from an historic country-house hotel: Bordeaux and other classic French regions provide an abundance of serious bottles at serious prices, but the net is spread wide for fine drinking from beyond Europe. Ten house selections open the bidding at £19.50 a bottle (£5 a glass).

Chef/s: Stephen Crane. **Open:** all week L 12 to 2, D 7 to 9. **Meals:** Set D £47.50 (3 courses) to £65. **Service:** not inc. **Details:** Cards accepted. 40 seats. 15 seats outside. Separate bar. Wheelchair access. Music. Children's portions. Car parking.

East Grinstead

Gravetye Manor

Country-house grandeur with a light touch
Vowels Lane, East Grinstead, RH19 4LJ
Tel no: (01342) 810567
www.gravetyemanor.co.uk
Modern British | £49
Cooking score: 5

Built in Shakespeare's day, Gravetye is a vision of English stolidity, an imposing greystone manor house with grand interiors panelled in dark oak. Garden connoisseurs should allow time for a trip round the grounds, the landscaping of which was done by the great William Robinson, who lived here until his death in 1935. Despite the magnificence of the surroundings, Gravetye has always managed a light touch in its approach, forgoing a lot of the extraneous formality involved in country-house dining. A series of seasonally changing, as well as year-round, fixed-price menus represents a customer-friendly philosophy, and Mark Raffan is an inspired chef. A summer spread could take you from tian of Cornish crab with marinated tomatoes and avocado through Angus fillet with aubergine caviar, provençal veg and jus niçoise, to a poached white peach with strawberry granita and peaches-and-cream sauce. For year-rounders, the progression might be from chicken liver and foie gras parfait with spiced orange reduction to sea bass with saffron risotto, confit tomato and bouillabaisse, and then crème brûlée with shortbread and a compote of berries – all at the lower fixed price. Wines are a treasure trove of fine bottles, with all the principal regions given a fair shake. Lovers of Bordeaux and Burgundy will feel well looked after, but there are half-bottles in profusion, and good South African and Spanish stuff for the less Francocentrically minded. Prices open at £17 for whites and £22 for reds.

Chef/s: Mark Raffan. **Open:** all week, L 12 to 2, D 7 to 9.30. **Closed:** 25 Dec D. **Meals:** Set L £23. Set D £33 to £50. **Service:** 12.5%. **Details:** Cards accepted. 45 seats. Separate bar. No music. No mobile phones. Wheelchair access. Jacket and tie required. Children's portions. Car parking.

Funtington
Hallidays
Solid commitment to local produce
Watery Lane, Funtington, PO18 9LF
Tel no: (01243) 575331
www.halidays.com
Modern European | £34
Cooking score: 2

£5
OFF

Andy and Julia Stephenson are the proud owners of this country restaurant, complete with thatched roof, at the foot of the South Downs a few miles outside Chichester. An impressive commitment to regionalism involves not just sourcing fish from local boats and meat from nearby farmland, but also making use of the wild larder in the form of mushrooms, garlic, elderflowers, nettles and so forth. The drill is fixed-price menus of real allure, in which guinea fowl breast may be glazed in honey and served with some of those wild mushrooms, or brill might be teamed with roasted artichokes and a lemony beurre blanc. Bookending these, there could be salmon smoked in-house and served in the Russian fashion with blinis, sour cream and chives, and a pistachio meringue dessert with rhubarb and blood orange. The wine list essays a brisk global spin, opening with house selections at £3.30 for a small glass.

Chef/s: Andy Stephenson. **Open:** Wed to Sun L 12 to 1.30, D 7 to 9.15. **Closed:** Mon, tue, 1 week in Aug, 2 weeks in Mar. **Meals:** Set L £20.50, Set D £33.50. **Details:** Cards accepted. 26 seats. Separate bar. No music. Wheelchair access. Car parking.

Haywards Heath
Jeremy's
Good food in a splendid garden setting
Borde Hill, Balcombe Road, Haywards Heath, RH16 1XP
Tel no: (01444) 441102
www.jeremysrestaurant.com
Modern European | £31
Cooking score: 4

£5
OFF

Set amid the Borde Hill Estate and its splendid gardens, Jeremy's benefits greatly from its location. The main room is wide, bright and hung with local art, while the terrace for outdoor dining proves a strong lure in summer. Everything adds up to a feeling of rural peace and calm. Jeremy Ashpool is an experienced hand at the modern European repertoire, accompanying pigeon breast with Puy lentils and marsala for one no-holds-barred starter dish, or fashioning smoked haddock into a Parmesan-dressed risotto. Preparations may sound fairly rich, but the touch is light and assured, as when brill turns up with linguine, salsify and purple sprouting broccoli in a sauce of prawn bisque. Loin of local venison gets an outing with red cabbage, roasted parsnips and juniper, or there might be slow-roast pork belly with bubble and squeak in a cider-based apple sauce. Lemon posset with a compote of berries, or banana parfait with hot chocolate sauce, are the kinds of desserts to expect. A concise listing of western European and New World wines starts at £15 for southern French white and £15.50 for Veneto red.

Chef/s: Jeremy Ashpool. **Open:** Tue to Sun L 12.30 to 2.30, Tue to Sat D 7.30 to 10. **Meals:** alc (main courses £15.50 to £21). Set L and D £25 to £32.50. Set L Sun £26. **Service:** not inc. **Details:** Cards accepted. 55 seats. 35 seats outside. Separate bar. Wheelchair access. Music. Children allowed. Car parking.

Lavant

★NEW ENTRY★

Earl of March

Inspirational view
Lavant, PO18 OBQ
Tel no: (01243) 533993
www.earlofmarch.co.uk
Modern British | £30
Cooking score: 4

Taken over in 2007 by ex-Ritz executive head chef Giles Thompson, this now-stylish pub is a delight in two parts. In one area the feel of a pub is retained, complete with fireplace and comfy seating and menu to suit – mussels in cider, say, or ham, egg and chips, and hot roast beef with Sussex rough (a local bread). The restaurant is 'more like the Ritz's highly approachable country cousin' and overlooks the Downs and Goodwood racecourse (William Blake was inspired to write Jerusalem here). The very-British menu takes a resolutely local route, with diver-caught scallops with minted pea purée, a tartlet of vine tomatoes with olives and pesto, or partridge with dauphinoise potatoes and roast rack and confit shoulder of Southdown lamb with potato hotpot. Solent fish is sourced too: well-timed wild halibut combined with shellfish cream, a sharing plate of fried gurnard and mackerel with a chorizo and root vegetable salad are 'triumphant' menu additions. Pannacotta with stewed plums or the most sticky of toffee puddings may finish the meal. Service has been described as 'friendly and knowledgeable'. Good selection of wines by-the-glass and draught beers.
Chef/s: Giles Thompson. **Open:** Mon to Sat L 12 to 2.30, D 6 to 9.30, Sun L 12 to 4. **Meals:** alc (main courses £9.95 to £15.95). **Service:** not inc.
Details: Cards accepted. 50 seats. 60 seats outside. Separate bar. Wheelchair access. Music. Children allowed. Car parking.

Matt Tebbutt Foxhunter

Why did you become a chef?
For the sociable hours and great pay!

Who makes you what you are today?
My wife and children.

What three ingredients could you not do without?
Garlic, bay leaves and thyme.

Do you have a favourite source for your ingredients?
My forager Raoul.

If you could only keep one kitchen implement, what would it be?
Serrated knife.

What won't you tolerate in the kitchen?
Bullying or intimidation.

Do you always read reviews of your restaurant?
Yes.

What era of history would you most like to have eaten in?
Now. We have the most exciting restaurants.

Littlehampton

★NEW ENTRY★
East Beach Cafe
Stunning beach café
Littlehampton, BN17 5NZ
Tel no: (01903) 731903
www.eastbeachcafe.co.uk
Café | £22
Cooking score: 3

 £30

Formerly a homely seafront kiosk, the East Beach Cafe is now a stunning, cutting-edge building, where dining has been described as 'like eating inside a piece of modern art'. Architect Thomas Hetherwick's award-winning design was inspired by driftwood washed up on Littlehampton's pebbly beach. Inside, the single-storey steel shell resembles a curvy whitewashed iceberg, with floor-to-ceiling glass doors (open on sunny days) and black slatted wood panelling adding smart overtones. The seasonal menu, offering everything from a full English to Champagne, homes in on local fish lifted from the Solent, beer-battered fish and chips, ham hock with lentils, and East Beach burger. Inspection delivered 'sensational' deep-fried salt-and-pepper squid with chilli, partnered with strong radishes and spring onion which were tempered by cos lettuce and roasted garlic, as well as an impressive slab of sea bream with tomato salsa. Ice cream sundae or rhubarb orange trifle make a good finish. Service in this justifiably popular café is by accomplished jean-wearing, blue-aproned staff. The short but impressive wine list is from £12.95.
Chef/s: David Whiteside. **Open:** Tue to Sun L 12 to 3 (from 12.30 Sun), Tue to Sat D 6.30 to 9. **Meals:** alc (main courses £8.50 to £15.50). **Service:** not inc. **Details:** Cards accepted. 60 seats. 25 seats outside. Wheelchair access. Music. Children's portions. Car parking.

Sidlesham

★NEW ENTRY★
Crab and Lobster
Bang-up-to-date menus
Mill Lane, Sidlesham, PO20 7NB
Tel no: (01243) 641233
Gastropub | £33
Cooking score: 3

This 350-year-old pub hard by the banks of Pagham Harbour Nature Reserve has earned its spurs in times past, but current ownership by Sam Bakose has lifted the place to a higher level of food, service and atmosphere. Chef Antony Phillips devotes time and energy to sourcing local produce. The bang-up-to-date menu is crammed with Sussex beef, lamb, fish and crab, the latter coming in two guises, devilled with a herb crust and pea leaves or fashioned into parcel with crayfish then wrapped in smoked salmon with pickled cucumber. Similarly, local asparagus is teamed with poached organic egg and tarragon crème fraîche, a Barbary duck salad with mango, pumpkin seeds and pomegranate molasses dressing, while a seafood fish stew with added cinnamon and star anise was the highlight for one reporter. Finish with superlative crème brûlée or impeccably sourced Sussex cheeses.
Chef/s: Anthony Phillips. **Open:** all week L 12 to 2.30, D 6 to 9.30 (Sun 9). **Meals:** alc (main courses £12.50 to £18.50). **Service:** not inc. **Details:** Cards accepted. 50 seats. 40 seats outside. Wheelchair access. Music. Children's portions. Car parking.

Tangmere

ALSO RECOMMENDED
▲ Cassons
Arundel Road, Tangmere, PO18 0DU
Tel no: (01243) 773294
www.cassonsrestaurant.co.uk
Modern European

Expect a warm family welcome from 'Cass' and the rest of the team at this highly popular country restaurant a couple of miles from Chichester. Visitors are also keen to praise its delightful cottage atmosphere, great value for money and Vivian Casson's appealing food. Her menus are packed with seasonal ideas, whether it's butternut squash ravioli with chestnuts (£6.95), slow-roast spiced pork belly with cider and honey sauce (£17.95) or a 'tower' of chocolate mousse and rhubarb compote (£7.95). Monthly gourmet evenings are an 'absolute delight.' The 100-bin wine list opens with house selections from £15.50. Closed all Mon, Tue L and Sun D.

▮ Walberton

Oaks Restaurant

Robust food with the personal touch
Yapton Lane, Walberton, BN18 0LS
Tel no: (01243) 552865
www.kencancook.co.uk
Modern British | £28
Cooking score: 2

Ken Brown is well known in these parts as the man behind the Kencancook catering brand, but he is also making his presence felt at this enthusiastically run restaurant-with-rooms. The setting – a one-time pub – has been engagingly transformed with lots of polished wood, leather sofas and subdued lights: it feels classy in a relaxed, understated way. Full-on flavours typify the food, which might be as straightforward as smoked mackerel Caesar salad or as intricate as confit and smoked loin of rabbit with crispy pork belly, caper sauce and steamed rice. For afters choose between 'sweet' (steamed syrup sponge, hazelnut praline crème brûlée) and 'savoury' (Welsh rarebit). Weekday lunches offer something simpler (Petworth venison casserole with mash), while Sunday finds Ken slicing up roast joints on his antique mahogany carving trolley. Prices on the carefully chosen wine list start at £13.75.
Chef/s: Ken Brown. **Open:** Tue to Sun L 12 to 2.30, Tue to Sat D 7 to 10. **Closed:** Mon. **Meals:** alc (main courses £12.50 to £20). Set L £13 (2 courses) to £16.50. **Service:** not inc. **Details:** Cards accepted. 67 seats. 24 seats outside. Separate bar. Wheelchair access. Music. Children's portions. Car parking.

▮ West Stoke

West Stoke House

Georgian gem with a modern twist
Downs Road, West Stoke, PO18 9BN
Tel no: (01243) 575226
www.weststokehouse.co.uk
Anglo-French | £45
Cooking score: 6

West Stoke House is a 'Georgian gem' in the beautiful Sussex countryside. Yet step inside this 'impressive yet accessible' restaurant-with-rooms and find an unstuffy modern setting. Red leather sofas vye for attention with colourful abstract paintings and there are polished wooden floors and fireplaces with candelabra. The dining room is uncluttered. Darren Brown's light, lively contemporary cooking shows imagination and accomplishment. He loves themes and variations, but though dishes are complex, the concept is spot-on and the many parts coalesce into a convincing whole. Take an assiette of onion, including a velouté and tarte Tatin, that is 'a stunning homage to the bulb' to illustrate the style, or an impressive, classically executed roast breast of quail teamed with quail Kiev, confit leg, truffled potatoes and morel sauce. Roasted squab pigeon with crushed peas and pea shoots, cep purée, a tranche of caramelised foie gras and soft-fried quail's egg was the highlight at inspection. There is no stinting with desserts either: lemon chiboust with a perfect, brittle honeycomb biscuit and lemon posset, for example. It is all good value, too, and the smallish wine list reveals an equally ungreedy stance: a lush Vacqueras from the Gironde is a steal at £36, as is a steely, smoky Pouilly Fumé at £29. There are other less pricey choices, from £13.50.
Chef/s: Darren Brown. **Open:** all week L 12 to 2, Wed to Sat D 7 to 9. **Closed:** 25 and 26 Dec. **Meals:** Set L £19.50 (2 courses) to £24.50, Set Sun L £32.50, Set D £45 (4 courses). **Service:** not inc. **Details:** Cards accepted. 40 seats. 16 seats outside. Separate bar. Wheelchair access. Music. Children allowed. Car parking.

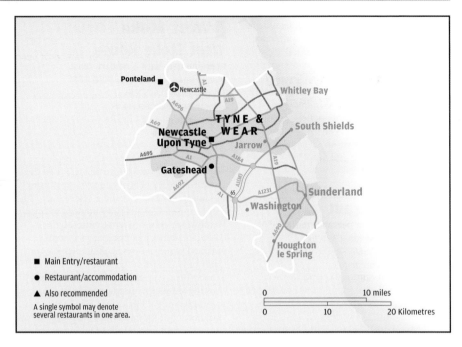

■ Main Entry/restaurant

● Restaurant/accommodation

▲ Also recommended

A single symbol may denote several restaurants in one area.

0		10 miles
0	10	20 Kilometres

▌Gateshead

Eslington Villa

Victorian retreat, modern food
8 Station Road, Gateshead, NE9 6DR
Tel no: (0191) 4876017
www.eslingtonvillaltd.co.uk
Modern European | £25
Cooking score: 3

Built around 1880, Eslington is a rather grand-looking Victorian villa secreted in two acres of leafy grounds with lovely views, a world away from the urban sprawl of Gateshead. The kitchen sets out its stall with a raft of skilfully crafted dishes from the broad international repertoire. Here you will find starters of crab ravioli with avocado pesto and sauce vierge alongside mushrooms on toast, followed by mains such as spiced duck confit with oriental rice or roast monkfish with spiced mussel and vegetable broth. Proceedings come to a pleasing conclusion with apple pithiviers and cinnamon crème anglaise, walnut tart or

the lush delights of caramelised rice pudding crème brûlée with Horlicks ice cream. Some 60 affordable wines from around the globe kick off with half a dozen house selections from £12.50 (£3.35 a glass).
Chef/s: Andy Moore. **Open:** Sun to Fri L 12 to 2, Mon to Sat D 7 to 10. **Closed:** bank hols. **Meals:** alc exc Sun L (main courses £16.50 to £19.50). Set L Mon to Fri £14 (2 courses) to £16. Set D Mon to Fri £16 (2 courses) to £20. **Service:** not inc. **Details:** Cards

Symbols

🛏 Accommodation is available.

£30 Three courses for less than £30.

V More than five vegetarian dishes.

£5 OFF £5-off voucher scheme.

🍷 Notable wine list.

accepted. 80 seats. 20 seats outside. Separate bar. Wheelchair access. Music. Children's portions. Car parking.

▌Newcastle upon Tyne

Blackfriars Restaurant
Modern food in an ancient setting
Friars Street, Newcastle upon Tyne, NE1 4XN
Tel no: (0191) 2615945
www.blackfriarsrestaurant.co.uk
Modern British | £30
New Chef
 V

Originally used as a refectory by medieval Dominican 'blackfriars', this adjunct to the friary (circa 1239) lays claim to being the oldest surviving dining room in the UK. The place revels in its antiquity, with medieval banquets staged in the stone-walled restaurant and picnics available for those who want to eat al fresco in the grassy courtyard. New chef David Mitchell is moving the food away from its global niche, with more emphasis on locally sourced ingredients including Northumbrian beef, North Sea fish and lamb from a farm in Morpeth. To start, there might be local black pudding beignet with apple compote or crab timbale with chilled cucumber soup, before braised belly pork with roast tenderloin, stewed prunes and glazed parsnips or roast venison with thyme mash. Desserts might include pannacotta with Chain Bridge honey and baked figs or lemon and lime posset. The short, eclectic wine list kicks off with house Duboeuf at £13 (£3.60 a glass).
Chef/s: David Miitchell. **Open:** all week L 12 to 2.30 (4 Sun), Mon to Sat D 6 to 10. **Closed:** bank hols. **Meals:** alc (main courses £11.50 to £20), Set L £11.50 (2 courses) to £14.50, Set D £16. **Service:** 10%. **Details:** Cards accepted. 70 seats. 40 seats outside. Air-con. Separate bar. Wheelchair access. Music. Children's portions.

Brasserie Black Door
Awash with the taste of the Med
Biscuit Factory, Stoddart Street, Newcastle upon Tyne, NE2 1AN
Tel no: (0191) 2605411
www.blackdoorrestaurant.co.uk
Modern European | £30
Cooking score: 4

Found on the ground floor of a refurbished biscuit factory – now Newcastle upon Tyne's most accessible art emporium – Brasserie Black Door is spacious and neatly modern, the atmosphere busy, convivial and unreservedly good-natured. The cooking, like the hospitality, is honest, generous and unfussy, its robust flavours awash with the taste of the Mediterranean, with the odd nod to the Far East. Lemon, crayfish and rosemary risotto is a good start, or there could be soft-shell crab with spiced crab mayonnaise, avocado purée and lime dressing. For mains, take a big-flavoured dish of black bream teamed with chorizo sausage and served with sautéed potatoes and curry vinaigrette or that popular brasserie standby, chargrilled rump of beef with hand-cut chips and béarnaise sauce. Save room for the likes of vanilla pannacotta with red wine prunes, and indulge in the surprisingly wide span of the sensibly brief wine list. Prices start at £14.
Chef/s: Nick Kleist. **Open:** all week L 12 to 2.30, Mon to Sat D 7 to 10. **Closed:** Sun D, 25 and 26 Dec, 1 Jan. **Meals:** alc (main courses £12.50 to £18.50). Set L £15 (2 courses) to £16.50. **Service:** not inc. **Details:** Cards accepted. 80 seats. Air-con. Separate bar. Wheelchair access. Music. Children's portions. Car parking.

Café 21

A new home for Quayside favourite
Trinity Gardens, Quayside, Newcastle upon Tyne,
NE1 3UG
Tel no: (0191) 2220755
www.cafetwentyone.co.uk
Modern European | £33
Cooking score: 3

Terry Laybourne's well-patronised brasserie
has moved a few more steps away from the
Tyne to spacious new premises in the midst of
the rebuilt riverside. The large, elegant room
has been done in peaceful dark grey with
splashes of lime green, giving it the air of a
contemporary hotel lobby. What hasn't
changed is the chef, Chris Dobson, or the style
of cooking, broadly brasserie, with the odd
trip to Spain or Italy. Unusually, the menu is
both long and appetising. Tried-and-true
combinations might include a Northumbrian
venison terrine with cornichons and radishes
or creamy celeriac and black truffle soup to
start, followed by something simple with a
flourish, like rump of lamb with garden pea,
bacon stew and a potato and wild garlic fritter.
Desserts go big on sundaes and sorbets, such as
pure, clear apricot. An occasional lack of focus
extends to the service, which is capable but can
be brusque. House wine is from a very
accessible £13 – the remaining selection is not
extensive, but well-edited.
Chef/s: Chris Dobson. **Open:** Mon to Sat L 12 to 2.30
(Sun 12.30 to 3), Mon to Sat D 5.30 to 10.30 (Sun
6.30 to 10). **Closed:** 25 and 26 Dec, 1 Jan. **Meals:** alc
(main courses £14.50 to £23). Set L £14 to £16.50
(Sun £16 to £18.50), Set D £14 to £16 (5.30 to 7).
Service: 10%. **Details:** Cards accepted. 82 seats.
Air-con. Separate bar. Wheelchair access. Music.
Children's portions.

Fisherman's Lodge

Confident cooking and smooth service
Jesmond Dene, Jesmond, Newcastle upon Tyne,
NE7 7BQ
Tel no: (0191) 2813281
www.fishermanslodge.co.uk
Modern Seafood | £50
Cooking score: 6

The Victorian lodge found down a single-
track road in a wooded park by a stream may
feel remote, but is 'but minutes from town'.
Ashley Paynton has taken over the stoves, but
reports confirm that the focus remains on
excellent raw materials delivered via sound
cooking skills. Seafood continues to be a
strong suit. The kitchen shows off its prowess
with confidence: meaty scallops from the Isle
of Skye are teamed with celeriac and truffle
purée, apple jelly and cumin foam, perfectly
timed black bream is partnered by tempura
oyster and caviar cream, while soft, supple
Gressingham duck breast comes with an
unusual combination of butternut squash
purée, chestnuts and cherries. Meals finish
strongly with a caramel torte served with
butterscotch ice cream, crisp nougatine and
caramel mousse or poached pear with a
wobbly almond pannacotta and pear granita.
Staff are 'ever so helpful without being
intrusive', and a well-conceived wine list
pours some good value options into an
international selection that has France at its
heart. Bottles start at £17.
Chef/s: Ashley Paynton. **Open:** Tue to Sat L 12 to 2,
D 7 to 10. **Closed:** Sun, Mon, 25 and 26 Dec.
Meals: Set L £17.50, early D menu £16.50 (2
courses) to £19, alc D £40 (2 courses) to £50.
Service: not inc. **Details:** Cards accepted. 60 seats.
20 seats outside. Air-con. Separate bar. Wheelchair
access. Music. Children's portions. Car parking.

Jesmond Dene House

Grandeur and contemporary style
Jesmond Dene Road, Newcastle upon Tyne,
NE2 2EY
Tel no: (0191) 2123000
www.jesmonddenehouse.co.uk
Modern British | £40
New Chef

⇌ V

Tyneside restaurant legend Terry Laybourne is
famed for big-city venues such as Café 21 (see
entry), but this venture finds him dipping his
toes into the luxury-laden world of country-
house hotels.The setting is a grandiose gothic
mansion overlooking the woody expanses of
Jesmond Dene, a short drive from the centre of
Newcastle. Following a lavish conversion,
it sports contemporary fabics and design
flourishes cheek-by-jowl with Arts and Crafts
features. Diners can choose to eat in the sedate
one-time music room or lighten up in the
leafy conservatory. Laybourne's trademark
sourcing of high-quality local produce is at
the heart of the kitchen's efforts, whether it's
oysters from Holy Island or organic Tyne
Valley beef. The result is a procession of
assured dishes, now under the direction of chef
Pierre Rigothier. Starters might include duck
foie gras and smoked eel terrine with tamarind
and ginger jelly, while mains could stretch to
roast halibut with glazed pak choi, girolles,
shiitake mushroom and soy sauce or organic
hill lamb with celeriac and almond couscous.
Desserts promise, say, iced nougat parfait with
morello cherry mousse and cherry croquant.
The mighty wine list travels the globe in
search of interesting drinking, from pedigree
French classics to innovative New World
tempters. House selections start at £16 (£4 a
glass).
Chef/s: Pierre Rigothier. **Open:** all week L 12 to
2.30, D 7 to 10. **Meals:** alc (main courses £20.50 to
£35). Set L £24 (3 courses). Bar menu available.
Service: 10%. **Details:** Cards accepted. 70 seats. 25
seats outside. Separate bar. Wheelchair access.
Music. Children's portions. Car parking.

▌Ponteland

Café Lowrey

Deceptively simple bistro cooking
33-35 The Broadway, Darras Hall, Ponteland,
NE20 9PW
Tel no: (01661) 820357
www.cafelowrey.co.uk
Modern British | £20
Cooking score: 4

This is a delightfully unfussy restaurant, from
the décor to the food. It's a bistro-style set up,
with friendly, capable staff and a menu
burgeoning with excellent local produce,
cooked with simplicity and flair. Crab and
pickled ginger risotto, Cheddar cheese and
spinach soufflé and marinated king prawn
spring rolls with sweet chilli sauce are typical
of the internationally inspired starters. The
mains have more of a British/European
flavour; examples include smoked haddock
fishcakes with spinach, a soft-poached egg and
herb cream, seared calf's liver with mash,
bacon, crispy onions, thyme and rosemary jus,
and confit of duck with Lyonnaise potatoes,
fine beans, rosemary and thyme jus. In a
similar vein, desserts might take in crème
brûlée, bread-and-butter pudding and lemon
polenta cake with honey-baked peaches and
mascarpone. A relatively short, global list of
wines starts at £13.50.
Chef/s: Ian Lowrey. **Open:** Tue to Fri 5.30 to 10, Sat
6 to 10, Sun 12 to 3. **Meals:** alc (main courses £9.50
to £19.50). Early evening set D £15.50, Set Sun L
£16.50. **Service:** not inc. **Details:** Cards accepted.
70 seats. Air-con. Wheelchair access. Music.
Children's portions. Car parking.

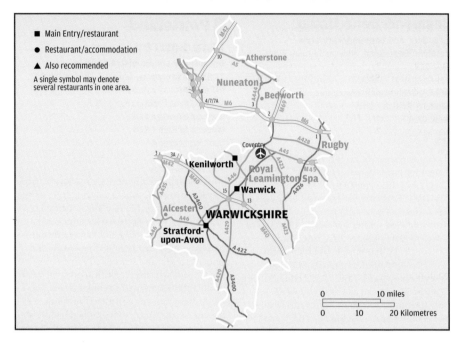

- ■ Main Entry/restaurant
- ● Restaurant/accommodation
- ▲ Also recommended

A single symbol may denote
several restaurants in one area.

▌Kenilworth

Restaurant Bosquet

Popular Gallic charmer
97A Warwick Road, Kenilworth, CV8 1HP
Tel no: (01926) 852463
www.restaurantbosquet.co.uk
French | £38
Cooking score: 4

An easy-to-miss terraced house on the main
road through Kenilworth, Bernard and Jane
Lignier's charmer of a restaurant has been
drawing appreciative crowds since opening
way back in 1981. Reporters approve of the
owners' 'resolutely French' approach to things,
and the dining room creates a mood of affluent
domesticity with its leather chairs, silk drapes
and and dark wood floors. Bernard hails from
southwest France and his cooking is imbued
with the richness and bold, earthy flavours of
the region. A slab of hot foie gras might be
served with beetroot chutney, confit of
suckling pig, black pudding and apple is
topped with celeriac purée, while three-week

aged fillet of beef comes with red wine sauce
and chips cooked in goose fat. There's
generally a fish dish of the day, while desserts
promise anything from lemon tart with
passion-fruit sorbet to raspberries and
strawberries served with a Muscat sabayon.
The all-French regional wine list naturally
favours the southwest, with emblematic
names such as Jurançon, Madiran and Cahors
on show. House wine is £15.50.

Chef/s: Bernard Lignier. **Open:** Tue to Sat D only 7
to 9.15. **Closed:** Sun, Mon and 1 week Christmas.
Meals: alc (main courses £19.50 to £20.50). Set Mon
to Fri £31. **Service:** not inc. **Details:** Cards accepted.
26 seats. No music. Children's portions.

Scores on the Doors

To find out more about the Scores on the
Doors campaign, please visit the Food
Standard's Agency website:
www.food.gov.uk or www.which.co.uk.

▍Stratford-upon-Avon

Malbec

A beacon of hope in Stratford
6 Union Street, Stratford-upon-Avon, CV37 6QT
Tel no: (01789) 269106
www.malbecrestaurant.co.uk
Modern European | £26
Cooking score: 2

Considering the tonnage of international tourism Stratford supports throughout the year, it is astonishing that quality dining is still such a rarity. Malbec remains the beacon of hope, and we can only suggest that you get your booking in good and early if you're going to hit town in anything like high season. You will be rewarded with Simon Malin's alluring, thoughtful cooking, which is built around inventive dishes of the likes of Cornish black bream with braised cabbage, mussels, orange and tarragon, or slow-cooked belly and roast tenderloin of Suffolk pork with creamed cauliflower and pickled cabbage. Simple starters include potted shrimps with cucumber, shallots and granary toast, while desserts aim for a light touch, as in blood orange jelly with toasted almond ice cream. Wines start at £15.
Chef/s: Simon Malin. **Open:** Tue to Sun L 12 to 2 (2.30 Sun), Mon to Sat D 7 to 9.30. **Closed:** 1 week Oct, 1 week Dec. **Meals:** alc (main courses £13.50 to £17.50). Set L Tue to Sat £15. **Service:** not inc. **Details:** Cards accepted. 40 seats. No mobile phones. Music. Children's portions.

▍Tanworth in Arden

READERS RECOMMEND
The Bell

Gastropub
The Green, Tanworth in Arden, B94 5AL
Tel no: (01564) 742212
www.thebellattanworthinarden.co.uk
'Interesting menu and a cosy fire in winter'

▍Warwick

Findons

Artistic local favourite
7 Old Square, Warwick, CV34 4RA
Tel no: (01926) 411755
www.findons-restaurant.co.uk
Modern European | £27
Cooking score: 2

Michael Findon's original paintings add a splash of contemporary colour to this reputable restaurant on the ground floor of an eighteenth-century town house. Chandeliers and gilt-framed mirrors lend a touch of elegance to the dining room, where Rosemary Findon ensures that proceedings run smoothly. Michael shows off his culinary skills with a catalogue of well-wrought mainstream dishes mostly inspired by the Mediterranean: expect calf's liver on wilted spinach with balsamic onions and pancetta or noisettes of Lighthorne lamb with basil and tomato sauce among the choice of main courses. Open the show with seared scallops, chive mash and lobster jus or suprême of wood pigeon with home-pickled beetroot and black pudding; conclude with cinnamon pannacotta and espresso freddo or 'profiterol bianchi' with bitter chocolate sauce. The

Cooking score

A score of 1 is a significant achievement. The score in any review is based on several meals, incorporating feedback from both our readers and inspectors. As a rough guide, 1 denotes capable cooking with some inconsistencies, rising steadily through different levels of technical expertise, until the scores between 6 and 10 indicate exemplary skills, along with innovation, artistry and ambition. If there is a new chef, we don't score the restaurant for the first year of entry. For further details, please see the scoring section in the introduction to the Guide.

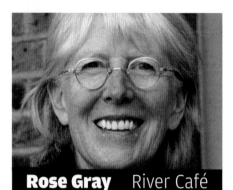

Rose Gray River Café

straightforward 40-bin wine list gets started with Italian house selections at £15.95 (£3.75 a glass).
Chef/s: Michael Findon. **Open:** Tue to Sat D only 6 to 9.30. **Closed:** Sun and Mon. **Meals:** alc (main courses £11 to £18). Set D £15.95 (2 courses). **Service:** 10%. **Details:** Cards accepted. 30 seats. 20 seats outside. Wheelchair access. Music.

ALSO RECOMMENDED

▲ Rose and Crown

30 Market Place, Warwick, CV34 4SH
Tel no: (01926) 411117
www.roseandcrownwarwick.co.uk
French

This popular pub buzzes with life all the day, thanks to its Market Square location and the quality of its food. Ingredients are sourced with an eye for freshness and ethics. Snacky options from the deli board include cheeses, antipasti and cured meats, while full meals have an international flavour. You could try crispy aromatic duck with hoi sin sauce and pancakes (£6) followed by crab and clam linguine with lemon and chilli dressing (£12.50), but there are also pub classics such as bangers and mash (£9) or fish and chips with mushy peas (£11.50). Wines start at £12.50. Open all week.

At what age did you cook your first meal for other people?
I was about ten. I started making meringues and rice pudding.

What three ingredients could you not do without?
Salted anchovies, pasta, extra virgin olive oil.

What's your guilty food pleasure?
Beluga caviar and white truffles.

What is the most unusual cookery book you've come across in your life?
'More food for pleasure' by Ruth Lowinsky.

If you have a lazy morning at home, what's your favourite brunch dish?
Anchovies on toast.

What era of history would you most like to have eaten in?
1950s and '60s, France and Italy.

What's coming up next for you?
An extension of River Café.

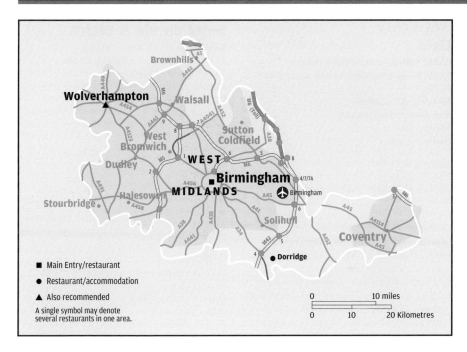

- ■ Main Entry/restaurant
- ● Restaurant/accommodation
- ▲ Also recommended

A single symbol may denote
several restaurants in one area.

| 0 | | 10 miles |
| 0 | 10 | 20 Kilometres |

■ Birmingham

Bank

Rock-solid second-city brasserie
4 Brindleyplace, Birmingham, B1 2JB
Tel no: (0121) 6334466
www.bankrestaurants.com
Modern European | £27
Cooking score: 2

 V

One of the most dependable fixtures of
Birmingham's rejuvenated restaurant scene,
Bank is everything you might expect from a
full-on big-city brasserie. It's set squarely in
the trendy urban playground known as
Brindley Place (overlooking the canal basin),
and spreads itself capaciously across a long bar
and a seriously designed, open-plan dining
area – with al fresco possibilities, too. The
style is brasserie through and through, with
breakfasts, express lunches, kids' menus and
theatre deals (Symphony Hall is just a stroll
away) bolstering the kitchen's regular output.
Expect a professional approach and a
cosmopolitan choice: this is the world of salt-
and-pepper squid, smoked haddock and leek
risotto and Malaysian-style marinated chicken
with sweet potato, as well as burgers and Old
Spot bangers 'n' mash. To finish, choose
between glazed lemon tart and warm
chocolate fondant. The wine list is an
invigorating, global slate with bags of variety
and sharp house selections from £14.75
(£3.85 a glass).
Chef/s: Stephen Woods. **Open:** all week L 11 to 4, D
4.30 to 10.30 (9.30 Sun). **Closed:** 26 Dec and 1 Jan.
Meals: alc (main courses £10.50 to £20), Set L and
D £12.50 (2 courses) to £15. **Service:** 12.5%
(optional). **Details:** Cards accepted. 160 seats. 60
seats outside. Air-con. Separate bar. Wheelchair
access. Music. Children's portions.

Average price

The average price listed in main-entry
reviews denotes the price of a three-
course meal, without wine.

★NEW ENTRY★
cielo

Italian with a contemporary twist
6 Oozells Square, Brindleyplace, Birmingham,
B1 2JB
Tel no: (0121) 6326882
www.cielobirmingham.com
Italian | £30
Cooking score: 1

The appointment of local favourite Andy Waters as executive chef has helped bring in the crowds at cielo and his advisory role continues, even with the opening of his own restaurant next door in June 2008 (too late for the Guide to inspect). In cielo's airy and contemporary space overlooking smart Oozells Square he has helped create a solid, appealing menu of 'Italian with a contemporary twist' – which here seems to be a rather upmarket version of the cuisine. Start, perhaps, with a neat cheesy tart of good pastry topped with asparagus and pancetta, and move on to saddle of monkfish with big, juicy prawns laced with lobster sauce. Vegetarian dishes can be very good and may include such treats as home-made open ravioli with wild mushrooms in a rich, buttery and garlicky sauce. It's all competently done but service can seem rather brusque and quick-off-the-mark. House wine is £14.95.

Chef/s: Gareth Ward. **Open:** Mon to Thur L 12 to 3, D 5.30 to 11, Fri and Sat 12 to 11, Sun 12 to 10. **Meals:** alc (main course £10.95 to £23.95). Set L and D (until 7) £11.95 (2 courses) to £14.95. **Service:** 10%. **Details:** Cards accepted. 104 seats. Air-con. Wheelchair access. Music. Children's portions.

Hotel du Vin & Bistro

Familiar food in a bistro setting
25 Church Street, Birmingham, B3 2NR
Tel no: (0121) 2000600
www.hotelduvin.com
Modern European | £30
Cooking score: 3

🍷 ⊟ V

The Victorian grandeur of the former Birmingham Eye Hospital has translated beautifully into boutique hotel romance. Original features include granite pillars, a sweeping staircase and a central courtyard. In true Hotel du Vin style, the bistro has a self-consciously Gallic charm. Don't expect to be challenged by the menu – the emphasis here is on pleasing all-comers, and they include couples, businessmen and families. At the heart is a list of 'simple classics' – perhaps chicken liver and foie gras parfait with red onion jam and home-made brioche followed by slow-braised blade of beef with pommes mousseline and bourguignon garnish. Other choices might include fresh baked gambas in a spicy tomato sauce followed by slow-roast pork belly with braised sticky red cabbage and port jus. Side-orders include roasted red onions with balsamic vinegar and hand-cut goose fat chips. As you'd expect from Hotel du Vin, wines are a high point. Bottles start at £14.50.

Chef/s: Nick Turner. **Open:** all week L 12 to 2, D 6 to 11. **Meals:** alc (main courses £12.95 to £17.95), Set menus from £10.95. **Service:** not inc. **Details:** Cards accepted. 100 seats. 40 seats outside. Separate bar. Wheelchair access. Music. Children's portions. Car parking.

Metro Bar & Grill

Cool big-city customer
73 Cornwall Street, Birmingham, B3 2DF
Tel no: (0121) 2001911
www.metrobarandgrill.co.uk
Modern European | £30
New Chef

The flagship branch of a burgeoning mini-chain, Birmingham's Metro is the very definition of a contemporary restaurant space. Beneath a dramatic atrium roof is a light-filled expanse full of big-city bustle and artworks that make bold, brash statements. Bold statements come from the menus too, which deal in the kinds of commodities – chargrilled chicken and bacon Caesar salad, beer-battered haddock with pea purée, tartare and chips, and lamb shank on couscous – that today's urban sophisticates expect to see. Chilli-fried squid with lemon mayo or halibut with prawn and coriander butter and Cajun potato wedges help to add variety. It all ends as you hope it will, with dark chocolate fondant and cherry ice cream, or Bailey's and ginger cheesecake. Vibrant New Worlders are the most eye-catching wines on a list that starts at £13.95 (£4.75 a glass) for Chilean Sauvignon and Cabernet.
Chef/s: Chris Kelly. **Open:** Mon to Fri 10am to 11pm, Sat D 6 to 11. **Closed:** bank hols. **Meals:** alc (main courses £9.95 to £19.95). **Details:** Cards accepted. 90 seats. 12 seats outside. Air-con. Separate bar. Music. Children allowed.

Opus

Bullish Brummie championing British produce
54 Cornwall Street, Birmingham, B3 2DE
Tel no: (0121) 2002323
www.opusrestaurant.co.uk
Modern British | £28
Cooking score: 2

'Helping Birmingham get with the programme,' enthused one of the many fans saying good things about this bold, bullish brasserie in the city's commercial district. A massive sign etched in concrete marks the spot and the building is defined by its floor-to-ceiling windows, skylights and cool cosmopolitan vibes. This is where the business crowd hangs out for leisurely lunches and others call in for intimate evening get-togethers. The kitchen champions British produce, buys wisely and takes full advantage of Birmingham's excellent wholesale market: here you will find Carlingford Loch oysters, Blythburgh free-range pork, Lyme Bay scallops, dry-aged Aberdeenshire beef and more besides. Starters such as Ragstone goats' cheese and beetroot salad might be followed by John Dory with wild mushroom and rocket risotto or Cornish lamb with brinjal potatoes, baby spinach and mint yoghurt, while desserts could run to iced lemon and pine-nut parfait. The no-nonsense, catholic wine list offers a decent choice, with prices from £13.75 (£3.75 a glass).
Chef/s: David Colcombe. **Open:** Mon to Fri L 12 to 2.30, Mon to Sat 6 to 9.30 (Sat 7 to 9.30). **Closed:** Sun, bank hols, 25 Dec to 1 Jan. **Meals:** alc (main courses £13 to £22). Set L and D Mon to Fri £15.50 (2 courses to £17.50. **Service:** 12.5%. **Details:** Cards accepted. 85 seats. Air-con. Separate bar. No music. Wheelchair access. Children's portions.

★NEW ENTRY★
Purnell's

Brummie fusion
55 Cornwall Street, Birmingham, B3 2DH
Tel no: (0121) 2129799
www.purnellsrestaurant.com
Modern European | £39
Cooking score: 4

'Brummie fusion' is how Glynn Purnell describes the food at his stylishly urban restaurant in Birmingham's commercial sector. But don't let the jokey mateyness fool you – and banish any thoughts of curry pies on the Blues' terraces. This is serious and upmarket stuff from a chef who likes to be slightly on the fun, maverick side, but who produces some of the most labour-intensive food in the city. A starter of salmon gets a coriander seed and orange cure and is then joined on the plate by an artistic gathering of wasabi, enoki mushrooms, borage leaves and an orange glaze. Main courses may feature unusual cuts such as Jacob's ladder of beef (the bones and meat above a rib roast), slow-cooked and served with courgette and basil purée, confit tomato and red wine syrup. There are all the fine-dining extras such as canapés, amuse-bouche and pre-desserts, but portions are generally dainty throughout, making the excellent desserts (perhaps hot cinnamon ravioli or a gloriously creamy lemon and honey parfait) especially welcome. And for those worried that his TV glory (on the BBC's *Great British Menu*) may make him neglect his duties, a note on the menu promises: 'Please be aware that our chef Glynn Purnell will attend and cook every lunch and evening service.' House wine is £19.95.

Chef/s: Glynn Purnell. **Open:** Tue to Fri L 12 to 1.45, Tue to Sat D 7 to 9.30. **Meals:** Set L £15.95 (2 courses) to £18.95, Set L and D £38.95. **Details:** Cards accepted. 45 seats. Separate bar. Wheelchair access. Music.

Simpsons

Civilised Birmingham high-flyer
20 Highfield Road, Edgbaston, Birmingham,
B15 3DU
Tel no: (0121) 4543434
www.simpsonsrestaurant.co.uk
Modern French | £50
Cooking score: 6

♦ 🛏

Andreas Antona's elegantly civilised restaurant-with-rooms stands head and shoulders above just about everything else in Birmingham. Set in the leafy Edgbaston suburbs, this classically proportioned Georgian mansion feels almost like a country retreat in the city, with its riot of rhododendrons and a gorgeous conservatory. Antona has trained up a class-act kitchen team who are capable of delivering refined modern French of a high order, with the added bonus of some challenging and exotic mixed marriages on the plate. Top-drawer ingredients, accomplished technique and

invention are the hallmarks of sophisticated dishes such as roast turbot fillet with crab ravioli, pak choi, lemongrass and ginger sauce or roast Cornish lamb with smoked aubergine, dhal, curry oil, coconut and cumin jus. Starters of, say, caramelised veal sweetbreads with king prawns, pistachios and shellfish cream suggest the kitchen is comfortable swimming in the mainstream, while desserts show what the prodigiously talented pastry chef can do (try the layered 'opera' gateau of coffee and Valrhona Guanaja chocolate with salted caramel ice cream or praline bavarois with lemon sponge and citrus butter). Alternatively, finish with something savoury such as pickled beetroot and goats' cheese with red wine vinaigrette and pine kernels. Fixed-price lunch and dinner menus offer outstanding value for the quality on offer. The magisterial wine list delves into the French regions for mouthwatering five-star names and also seeks out other gems (including some to-die-for Super Tuscans and Aussie reds), while those watching the pennies should be more than satisfied with the generous possibilities under £30.

Chef/s: Andreas Antona, Luke Tipping and Adam Bennett. **Open:** all week L 12 to 2, Mon to Sat D 7 to 9.30. **Closed:** bank hols. **Meals:** alc (main courses £21 to £27). Set L £20 (2 courses) to £25, Set D £30. **Service:** 12.5% (optional). **Details:** Cards accepted. 75 seats. 30 seats outside. Air-con. No music. Wheelchair access. Children's portions. Car parking.

ALSO RECOMMENDED

▲ Café Ikon

1 Oozells Square, Brindleyplace, Birmingham,
B1 2HS
Tel no: (0121) 2483226
www.ikon-gallery.co.uk
Spanish

Things remain resolutely bohemian in Café Ikon despite Broad Street and its tottering, half-dressed hordes being just a short stagger away. The café is part of the trendy Ikon Art Gallery and shares the same minimalist decor. It's a bijou, relaxed place (service can be variable, to put it politely), good for a casual

Best for business

When it comes to entertaining a client, these smart choices will help to seal the deal.

Le Gallois, Cardiff

The all-day dining set-up at this smart city restaurant makes it a good choice for breakfast meetings. Come for a 'full Welsh' of scallops, black pudding, crispy cockles and seaweed relish.

Ubon by Nobu, London

Sibling of Nobu Hyde Park Corner and Nobu Berkeley St, Canary Wharf's Ubon impresses with its beautifully presented sushi creations. Go for the speciality sake.

Restaurant Martin Wishart, Edinburgh

Scotland's top chef dazzles on Leith's reinvigorated waterfront. The serious wine list, which features rare Bordeaux vintages, will impress business associates.

Second Floor at Harvey Nichols, Manchester

Floor-to-ceiling windows frame views across Exchange Square from this central restaurant. Alison Seagrave is cooking at the top of her game.

Bonds, London

This high-ceilinged old banking hall is the former HQ of Citibank. The setting provides suitable gravitas for Barry Tonks' highly competent modern European cooking.

Anthony's Restaurant, Leeds

Anthony Flinn's provocative cooking provides a memorable talking point at this central city establishment.

Number One, Edinburgh

Serious French restaurant within the stellar surrounds of the five-star Balmoral hotel. Its chandeliered Palm Court serves afternoon tea, or you could chink Champagne flutes in the Bollinger Bar.

Simpsons, Birmingham

Executive chef Luke Tipping cooks classical French cuisine with a modern Black Country accent. The smart en-suite bedrooms are ideal for overnight business trips.

Restaurant Sat Bains, Nottingham

This outstanding restaurant is also a boutique hotel and is just minutes from the city centre, making it ideal for business diners. Sat Bains' extraordinary flavour combinations are matched by a fantastic fine wine list, so impressing your clients shouldn't be a problem.

catch-up with friends or a quick bite on your own. Plenty of tapas (from £3.65) and paellas (from £12.50) are on offer. Some dishes succeed more than others and they tend to be the simpler ones – nicely-cooked asparagus spears wrapped in melted Manchego cheese, for instance, or lovely, smoky padron peppers simply slicked with decent oil and grilled. House wines from £10.95. Open all week.

▮ Dorridge
The Forest
Revamped railway hotel
25 Station Approach, Dorridge, B93 8JA
Tel no: (01564) 772120
www.forest-hotel.com
Modern European | £26
Cooking score: 2
£5 OFF ⊏ V £30

Situated across the road from Dorridge BR station, the Forest was built in 1870 as a railway hotel serving the needs of local travellers. These days, it is within striking distance of the NEC and Birmingham International airport and attracts a different kind of commuter. Old and new blend seamlessly in the revamped interior, which encompasses a fashionable bar, conference facilities and a contemporary dining room with laminate floors and big mirrors. The brasserie look is matched by food with a plenty of palate-jingling ideas. Start the ball rolling with ravioli of goats' cheese with beetroot and walnuts, move on to scallops with risotto nero and Jerusalem artichokes or Cornish lamb 'in two styles', and close with rhubarb crumble soufflé or cured pineapple with ginger shortbread and rum sabayon. Some 'casual dining' options are also available (smoked haddock with poached egg and hollandaise) and the sprightly 60-bin wine list does the trick. Prices start at £12.95 (£3.60).
Chef/s: Dean Grubb. **Open:** all week L 12 to 2.30 (3 Sun), Mon to Sat D 6.30 to 10. **Closed:** 25 Dec. **Meals:** alc (main courses £11.50 to £21). Set L and D Mon to Fri £12.50 (2 courses) to £15.50, Set L Sun £14.50 (2 courses) to £17.50. **Service:** 10%

(optional). **Details:** Cards accepted. 70 seats. 60 seats outside. Air-con. Separate bar. Wheelchair access. Music. Children's portions. Car parking.

▮ Wolverhampton
ALSO RECOMMENDED
▲ Bilash
2 Cheapside, Wolverhampton, WV1 1TU
Tel no: (01902) 427762
www.thebilash.co.uk
Indian

You'll find this well-presented Bangladeshi restaurant in the heart of Wolverhampton opposite the Civic Centre. It enjoys local renown for its authentic, and sometimes innovative, freshly cooked food. Start with maacher shami kebab (a fishcake served with tamarind sauce or aloo tikka (£5.90) followed by home-made paneer shahlik (paneer marinated in yoghurt, ginger, garlic and spices then roasted in the tandoor, Goan prawn masala or Bilash's own distinctive chicken tikka masala (£12.90). There is a good-value lunch menu (£11.95 for 2 courses), and a pre-theatre menu is available. Wines from £18. Open all week.

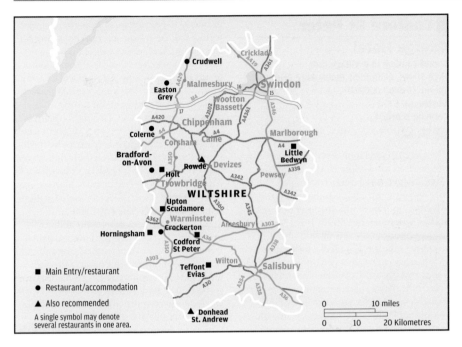

- ■ Main Entry/restaurant
- ● Restaurant/accommodation
- ▲ Also recommended

A single symbol may denote several restaurants in one area.

0   10 miles

0   10   20 Kilometres

■ Bradford on Avon

Swan Hotel

Impressive sixteenth-century coaching inn
1 Church Street, Bradford on Avon, BA15 1LN
Tel no: (01225) 868686
www.theswan-hotel.com
British | £26
Cooking score: 2

A neutral palette and a welcome lack of clutter give a modern look to this impressive stone-built sixteenth-century coaching inn. Original features such as the enormous fireplace in the dining room add character, and it has become a destination for people who care about food. Tom Bridgeman continues at the stoves, producing a style of food that is classic British gastro-pub with a few modern twists and turns. The short, good-value dinner menu, for example, could offer mussels, leek and saffron tart, then slow-roast belly pork with spring greens and clapshot (a Scottish dish of potatoes and turnips) with hot ginger pudding and vanilla ice cream for afters. Lunch brings a simpler choice and there are always daily specials. Reports have praised Cornish fish pie (for two to share), smoked haddock fishcakes, 'the best chicken (free-range) I've ever eaten', and rib-eye steak with 'absolutely delicious' hand-cut chips. Staff are friendly and efficient and the wine list continues the value-for-money policy, with prices starting at £13.50.

Chef/s: Tom Bridgeman. **Open:** all week L 12 to 2.30 (Sun 3), D 6.30 to 9.30. **Meals:** alc (main courses £8.50 to £19.50). Set L £10.50 (2 courses) to £14. **Service:** not inc. **Details:** Cards accepted. 50 seats. 25 seats outside. Separate bar. Music. Children's portions. Car parking.

Scores on the Doors

To find out more about the Scores on the Doors campaign, please visit the Food Standard's Agency website: www.food.gov.uk or www.which.co.uk.

Codford St Peter
George Hotel

Sound cooking in a village pub
High Street, Codford St Peter, BA12 0NG
Tel no: (01985) 850270
Gastropub | £24
Cooking score: 4

£5 OFF 🍴 £30

The George Hotel looks every inch the village pub with its solid white façade, simple but tastefully decorated interior and open fire. Its easy-going approach is just the ticket, too, allowing options of just drinking or snacking and full-on restaurant meals. Boyd McIntosh's food responds to the seasons and sourcing is a strength – the kitchen takes a lively approach to whatever comes its way. This could include a starter of dressed Cornish crab with lemon and truffle mayonnaise, or main courses of Wiltshire pork belly with black pudding, roasted apple and seed mustard cream, and garlic-roasted rump of lamb teamed with dauphinoise potatoes and thyme jus. Desserts have included caramelised peach and plum tart with raspberry ripple ice cream and sticky toffee banana pudding with caramel and chocolate sauce. House wine is £13.95.
Chef/s: Boyd McIntosh and James King Cole. **Open:** Wed to Mon L 12 to 3, Mon and Wed to Sat D 6.30 to 11. **Closed:** Tue. **Meals:** alc (main courses £9.50 to £14.95). **Service:** not inc. **Details:** Cards accepted. 55 seats. 60 seats outside. Children's portions. Car parking.

Colerne
Lucknam Park

Immaculate fine dining in a luxurious setting
Colerne, SN14 8AZ
Tel no: (01225) 742777
www.lucknampark.co.uk
Modern European | £60
Cooking score: 6

£5 OFF 🍷 🍴 V

The moment you step through the door of this eighteenth-century Palladian mansion you are immersed in an atmosphere of pure

indulgence. The ornate, crystal-chandeliered former ballroom is an appropriate setting for fine dining, with elaborate gold silk drapes framing views over manicured lawns and grand avenues of trees. An immaculate army of smiling waiters bringing plates of perfectly presented food with spot-on timing complements the scene. This lavish theme is picked up in chef Hywel Jones' elegant menus. Meals begin with aperitifs (perhaps by the log fire in the library) with irresistibly light Parma ham-twisted pastry appetisers, or teardrops of pâté de foie gras on fine biscuits. Starters may include superb Scottish diver-caught scallops, salted grapes and white asparagus in a delicately sweet-sour white port and verjus butter, or a warm spiced pork terrine paired with roast langoustine, crushed peas and a spiced jus. At inspection a main course of gilthead sea bream served on crushed potatoes and crabmeat with a subtle sauce of wild garlic and lemongrass revealed accomplished flashes of interesting flavours. To finish, try a refreshing 'lasagna' of exotic fruits offset with coconut sorbet and white chocolate foam, or maybe local cheeses with pickled pears and honey. The wine list is predominantly classic French, widely priced from £20 to four figures, but with choices by-the-glass from £5.
Chef/s: Hywel Jones. **Open:** all week L 12.30 to 2.30, D 7 to 10.30. **Meals:** Set L £25, Set D £65, Set Sun L £35. **Service:** not inc. **Details:** Cards accepted. 64 seats. No mobile phones. Wheelchair access. Children's portions. Car parking.

Crockerton
Bath Arms Crockerton

Proper pub, proper food
Clay Street, Crockerton, BA12 8AJ
Tel no: (01985) 212262
www.batharmscrockerton.co.uk
Gastropub | £23
Cooking score: 3

🍴 V £30

This much-favoured whitewashed pub on the Longleat Estate goes from strength to strength. It's a rambling old building oozing a cosy old English atmosphere and the unpretentious informality makes it a popular destination. The menu evolves gently, yet remains comfortingly familiar, with Dean Carr's cooking a nice mix of unchanging English classics and Mediterranean ways – baked mushroom Welsh rarebit crops up among the likes of roast scallops with carrot and spicy sultanas. The place's identity as an inn is expressed in simply prepared main courses like shepherd's pie or Cumberland sausage and champ, but there are more obvious restaurant dishes too, like poached duck breast with asparagus and balsamic onions or wild sea bass with rocket pesto and blue cheese fritters. Desserts such as sticky toffee pudding are supplemented by excellent home-made ice creams. The list of around 37 wines starts at £12.95 and maintains a no-fuss approach.

Chef/s: Dean Carr and Mark Payne. **Open:** all week L 12 to 2, D 6.30 to 9.30. **Meals:** alc (main courses £10.50 to £14.95). **Service:** not inc. **Details:** Cards accepted. 64 seats. 100 seats outside. Separate bar. Wheelchair access. Music. Children's portions. Car parking.

▮ Crudwell

Rectory Hotel
Local produce and serene surroundings
Crudwell, SN16 9EP
Tel no: (01666) 577194
www.therectoryhotel.co.uk
Modern British | £30
Cooking score: 3

£5
OFF 🛏

There's something timelessly serene about this delightful hotel set in three acres of formal walled gardens hard-by the local village church. The owners are keen advocates of local produce and procure just about everything (with the exception of fish) from within a 30-mile radius; their larder is also topped up with pickings from the vegetable patch across the road at the Potting Shed pub (see following entry). Seasonal flavours define the dinner menu, which might open with a warm brûlée of goats' cheese with sweet pepper chutney or

seared scallops and roasted squid with cauliflower purée. After that, expect seared chump of lamb with spring peas and rosemary jus, roast tenderloin of Gloucester Old Spot pork or monkfish with crab risotto and saffron sauce. Finally, peruse the cheese list or go for something exotically refreshing such as passion-fruit jelly with mango sorbet. Lunch is a simpler fixed-price affair, and the wine list offers respectable drinking at fair prices from £13.50 (£4.75 a glass).

Chef/s: Peter Fairclough. **Open:** all week L 12 to 2, D 7 to 9. **Meals:** alc (main courses £14.50 to £18). Set L £14.50 (2 courses) to £18.50. **Service:** not inc. **Details:** Cards accepted. 28 seats. Separate bar. Wheelchair access. Music. Children allowed.

ALSO RECOMMENDED
▲ The Potting Shed
Crudwell, SN16 9EW
Tel no: (01666) 577833
www.therectoryhotel.co.uk
Gastropub

Quirky modern touches among the requisite beams, exposed stone and open fire mean this re-energised village pub ticks all the right style boxes. No-frills British food is the focus of the menu and the repertoire is built around local and seasonal produce. At lunch, top billing goes to popular pub classics – cottage pie, fillet burger, fish and chips – while dinner impresses with mussels, bacon, apple and cider (£5.25) and pot-roasted chicken (£18 for two). Finish with a zingy lemon tart (£4.50). Owned by the nearby Rectory Hotel (see preceding entry). Open daily. Reports please.

▮ Donhead St Andrew
ALSO RECOMMENDED
▲ Forester Inn
Lower Street, Donhead St Andrew, SP7 9EE
Tel no: (01747) 828038
Gastropub

The setting of this smartly thatched and impeccably turned-out sixteenth-century inn on the Wiltshire/Dorset border may be olde-worlde, but the cooking is bang on-the-money, The menu plunders land and sea for a raft of vibrant dishes including Cornish squid with chorizo, cannelloni beans and chilli (£6.95), roast Gressingham duck breast with cavolo nero and fig jus (£14.95) and grilled fillets of mackerel with horseradish mash and beetroot. Finish, perhaps, with glazed lemon tart and blackcurrant sorbet (£5.50). France dominates the wine list, which includes house selections from around £13 (£3.30 a glass). Two guest rooms. Closed Sun D.

Easton Grey
Whatley Manor
Looking and cooking better than ever
Easton Grey, SN16 ORB
Tel no: (01666) 822888
www.whatleymanor.com
Modern European | £65
Cooking score: 7

£5 OFF   🍷 🛏 V

The Dining Room at opulently restored Whatley Manor has had a makeover since last year's Guide. Regulars will breathe a sigh of relief that the room looks better than ever, with buttermilk walls, a pale wood floor and colour provided by the fabric on the comfortable padded chairs. It is a modern look, but one that carries an air of quiet dignity. Quality table settings and knowledgeable, self-assured staff help too. Once settled at your table you are quite likely to be handed something like a glass of potato and rosemary foam alongside deep-fried goats' cheese and an intense essence of truffle to set the ball rolling. Martin Burge likes to keep you on your toes. Then sweet, juicy langoustines are paired with caramelised, full-of-flavour bacon and offset with a pumpkin purée and cumin oil. Impressively, this adds up to a fine opening course, not least because each element individually does its bit. Dishes are elaborately worked and yet emerge from the kitchen with a deceptive feeling of effortlessness about them. A case in point might be the 'sublime and delicate' goats' cheese ravioli that came dressed with hazelnut

sherbet, crisp apple and young leeks. Main courses teaming John Dory with Sauternes gel and a light truffle velouté, and Cornish lamb roasted in spices and served with slow-braised breast and pumpkin purée both exhibit stunning technique and a sound understanding of what works with what, and why. High standards are maintained through to desserts which dazzle with fruity fireworks, as when roasted black figs are accompanied by pistachio and yoghurt ice cream, mandarin sorbet and red wine reduction. A formidable wine list has been assembled. It opens in France before heading off into the wider world in search of interesting flavours. Not everything costs an arm and a leg either. If you wish to start modestly before working up a head of steam, a glass of Californian Merlot for £5.50 should do the trick.
Chef/s: Martin Burge. **Open:** Wed to Sun only D 7 to 9. **Closed:** Mon and Tue. **Meals:** Set D £65, Tasting menu £80. **Service:** 10%. **Details:** Cards accepted. 40 seats. Separate bar. Music. Car parking.

Holt
The Tollgate Inn
Endearing English country inn
Ham Green, Holt, BA14 6PX
Tel no: (01225) 782326
www.tollgateholt.co.uk
Gastropub | £27
Cooking score: 3

£5 OFF   🛏 £30

Part honey-coloured stone, part whitewash, the Tollgate presents a dual face to the world, and a vision of comfortable period Englishness within. Holt is only seven miles from Bath, but has enough charm of its own to keep you lingering, mainly in the form of Alexander Venables' cooking. He buys diligently from a network of excellent local suppliers and transforms the haul into a bright, vibrant, modern British menu. Chestnut mushroom soup with truffle oil or game risotto with a poached egg make interesting first courses. Beef from a local farm turns up in the form of classic Wellington, three-week-hung rump or rib-eye steak, and there may well also be grilled plaice with herb and lemon butter or rabbit ragoût cooked in mustard and cream. Finish in homely style with apple and pear crumble and proper custard. Wines are served in quantities to suit all occasions, from standard and large glasses to half-litre carafes and bottles (the last from £12.75). The range of cask-conditioned ales from micro-breweries is also exemplary.

Chef/s: Alexander Venables. **Open:** Tue to Sun L 11.30 to 3, Tue to Sat D 5.30 to 11. **Meals:** alc (main courses £13.50 to £18.80). Set L £14.95. **Service:** not inc. **Details:** Cards accepted. 60 seats. 40 seats outside. Separate bar. Wheelchair access. Music. Children's portions. Car parking.

■ Horningsham

Bath Arms
At the gates of Longleat House
Longleat Estate, Horningsham, BA12 7LY
Tel no: (01985) 844308
www.batharms.co.uk
Gastropub | £30
Cooking score: 2
£5
OFF

This seventeenth-century coaching inn stands beside the gates to Longleat House, fronted by 200-year-old pollarded lime trees. The smartly refurbished interior blends the traditional with the contemporary – bare boards in the bar and quirky Indian furnishings and artefacts elsewhere. The cooking is honest and unfussy, with concise set-dinner menus changing daily and making sound use of local seasonal ingredients. Longleat venison with rösti potato and wild mushrooms and Stourhead Estate rib-eye steak with cep, salsa verde and glazed carrots are typical mains, topped and tailed by plump and juicy scallops served with home-reared bacon and black pudding, and a rich chocolate tart with raspberry coulis. Excellent bar meals, too, and the set-lunch menu is great value for money. A well-balanced global wine list kicks off at £12.50.

Chef/s: Frank Bailey. **Open:** all week L 12 to 2.30, D 7 to 9 (Fri and Sat 9.30). **Meals:** alc L (main courses £10 to £15). Set D £29.50. **Service:** not inc.

Details: Cards accepted. 44 seats. 44 seats outside. Separate bar. Wheelchair access. Music. Children's portions. Car parking.

■ Little Bedwyn

The Harrow at Little Bedwyn
Fine dining with wines to match
Little Bedwyn, SN8 3JP
Tel no: (01672) 870871
www.theharrowatlittlebedwyn.co.uk
British | £40
Cooking score: 5
£5
OFF ♦ V

Roger and Sue Jones have just entered their second decade at the helm of this welcoming country restaurant near Marlborough. It's a supremely accomplished operation. Produce is A1 throughout, with Brixham fish, Welsh beef, free-range Gloucestershire pork and even local truffles in the autumn all playing their part. You might start enterprisingly with sautéed lamb's fries, served with a ragoût of morels, or perhaps a modern-classic partnering of seared scallops with chorizo and pea purée. Reader feedback has flowed thick and fast this year, praising the consistency of cooking and the high level of technical ability. Cornish turbot with wild mushrooms has been flawlessly timed, sea bass with Thai-accented squid and sweet chilli jam, and a serving of Welsh black beef on horseradish-spiked potato cake have all come in for plaudits. A pre-dessert of jelly and cream is one way of shamelessly indulging customers before the main business to come, which might well be rhubarb compote with ginger crumb, vanilla ice cream and sauce anglaise. The wine list is a treasure-trove of modern and classic bottles. Loire wines from Didier Dagueneau, Trimbach in Alsace, Hamilton Russell South African Chardonnay, a killer listing of pedigree Australians, together with a great selection by-the-glass from £6 – it hardly gets any better than this.

Chef/s: Roger Jones. **Open:** Wed to Sun L 12 to 2, Wed to Sat D 7 to 9. **Closed:** Mon, Tue, 2 weeks at Christmas, 2 weeks in Aug. **Meals:** alc (main courses £24). Set L £30. Set D £40 to £120.

Service: not inc. **Details:** Cards accepted. 32 seats. 28 seats outside. Wheelchair access. Music. Children's portions.

▌Rowde

ALSO RECOMMENDED
▲ George & Dragon

High Street, Rowde, SN10 2PN
Tel no: (01380) 723053
www.thegeorgeanddragonrowde.co.uk
Gastropub

A sixteenth-century coaching inn complete with original beams, open fireplaces and wooden floors. Fish and seafood, delivered daily from Cornwall is usually the star of the show. Look to the blackboard menus for moules marinière, whole crabs, lobster, John Dory and suchlike. Otherwise, you could start with beef carpaccio with rocket and mustard dressing (£7.50), and go on to lamb and cider stew with creamy mash (£14.50), or chargrilled rib-eye steak with shallots. Meals conclude with desserts such as chocolate and orange bread-and-butter pudding (£6). Wines from £14. Open all week exc Sun D.

▌Teffont Evias

Howard's House

Modern British food under a Swiss roof
Teffont Evias, SP3 5RJ
Tel no: (01722) 716392
www.howardshousehotel.co.uk
Modern British | £45
Cooking score: 3

£5 OFF ▭

Howard's House has been in the same family since the end of the seventeenth century. A hotel since 1990, the place has been tastefully renovated and is run with care and dedication by Bill and Noele Thompson. The modern British fare on offer shows plenty of creative flair, in meals that might start with watercress and nutmeg risotto with a blue cheese beignet, before halibut fillet with goats' cheese potato purée, asparagus and beetroot chutney or loin of locally reared pork garnished with Parma

ham and black pudding and a mustard-spiked potato cake. Variations on a theme at dessert stage might see passion fruit arriving in the forms of soufflé, pannacotta and sorbet. House wines from £15.75, £4.50 a glass.
Chef/s: Nick Wentworth. **Open:** all week, L 12.30 to 2, D 7 to 9. **Closed:** Christmas. **Meals:** Set L and D £27.95 to £45. **Service:** not inc. **Details:** Cards accepted. 40 seats. 16 seats outside. Separate bar. Wheelchair access. Music. Children's portions. Car parking.

▌Upton Scudamore

Angel Inn

Appealing, well-run dining pub
Upton Scudamore, BA12 0AG
Tel no: (01985) 213225
www.theangelinn.co.uk
Gastropub | £25
Cooking score: 3
▭ £30

This sixteenth-century coaching inn on the fringes of Salisbury Plain is whitewashed and inviting, boasting a walled garden and terrace, a civilised high-ceilinged bar and welcoming dining area with reasonably well-spaced tables. Blackboard specials and fresh fish from Brixham feature, and the kitchen takes care with ingredients. Warm salad of fresh asparagus wrapped in smoked salmon and served with roasted red pepper and Parmesan mayonnaise is one way to start, or there could be sautéed tiger prawns in a sweet chilli, spinach and garlic cream sauce, served as a starter or main course. Elsewhere look for rack of new-season lamb or pork tenderloin alongside mustard Puy lentils and Calvados jus. End with raspberry and chocolate brownie with clotted cream ice cream. Service has been described as 'excellent and friendly'. House wines from £13.25.
Chef/s: Nick Cooper. **Open:** all week L 12 to 3, D 6 to 11. **Closed:** 25 and 26 Dec, 1 Jan. **Meals:** alc (main courses £12.95 to £17.95). **Service:** not inc. **Details:** Cards accepted. 60 seats. 40 seats outside. Wheelchair access. Music. Children's portions. Car parking.

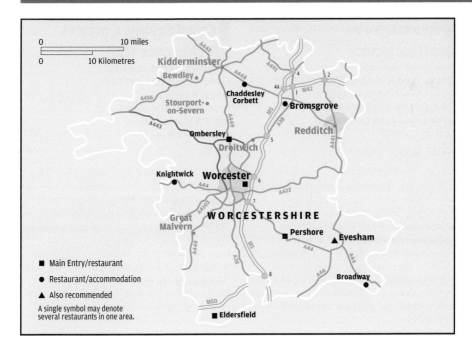

0 | 10 miles
0 | 10 Kilometres

Kidderminster
Bewdley
Stourport-on-Severn
Chaddesley Corbett
Bromsgrove
Redditch
Ombersley
Droitwich
Knightwick
Worcester
WORCESTERSHIRE
Great Malvern
Pershore
Evesham
Broadway
Eldersfield

■ Main Entry/restaurant

● Restaurant/accommodation

▲ Also recommended

A single symbol may denote several restaurants in one area.

■ Broadway

Russell's

Boutique brasserie with panache
20 High Street, Broadway, WR12 7DT
Tel no: (01386) 853555
www.russellsofbroadway.co.uk
Modern British | £35
Cooking score: 4

Once the HQ of world-renowned furniture designer George Russell (hence the name), this honey-coloured Georgian building has been painstakingly restored and transformed into a 'boutique restaurant-with-rooms'. The stylish bar and L-shaped dining room occupy the ground floor, with glass doors opening out onto a quiet courtyard that is highly prized for al fresco meals. Modern brasserie cooking is the kitchen's business and the menu spans everything from tapas plates, Caesar salad and an individual take on prawn cocktail to iced coffee parfait, citrus mousse with mint syrup and chocolate brownie with clotted cream ice

cream. In between, expect a globally inspired choice of well-executed dishes ranging from grilled fillet of sea bream with braised pak choi, fennel and nori salad to spiced lamb meatballs with chorizo, coriander and pappardelle or Scotch 'beef' liver with grain mustard mash, roasted beetroot, red onion and sage gravy. Devotees of traditional roasts shouldn't miss the restaurant's lavish 'Sunday Spreads' – garrulous family bonanzas centred around joints carved at the table. The concise list features wines from around the world and opens with 11 house selections from £15.95 (£4.50 a glass).

Chef/s: Matt Laughton. **Open:** all week L 12 to 2.30, Mon to Sat D 6 to 9.30. **Meals:** alc (main courses £11 to £27). Set L £12 (2 courses) to £15. Set D £15.95 (2 courses) to £22.95. **Service:** not inc. **Details:** Cards accepted. 60 seats. 30 seats outside. Air-con. Separate bar. Wheelchair access. Music. Children's portions. Car parking.

▮ Bromsgrove

Grafton Manor

Euro-Indian mélange
Grafton Lane, Bromsgrove, B61 7HA
Tel no: (01527) 579007
www.graftonmanorhotel.co.uk
Modern Indian/European | £29
Cooking score: 3

Built in Shakespeare's infancy for the Earl of
Shrewsbury, the Manor is an imposing pile
whose inhabitants have variously got
themselves mixed up in some of the more
colourful episodes of England's history, from
the Gunpowder Plot to the Glorious
Revolution. Not only is it a comfortable and
civilised place, but its kitchen partnership
offers a menu that takes the cooking of India as
its unexpected base. You might start with red
lentil sambar and dhal dumplings or
Maharashtrian prawns with carrot crisps,
before trying a vegetarian main course such as
baked aubergine and apple with paneer and
Indian vegetables. If the subcontinental mood
doesn't quite take you, you can make a safe
landing back in Europe via ham hock terrine
with pea and mint foam, followed by confit
duck leg with Jerusalem artichoke risotto and
sautéed leeks, and then a jelly and bavarois of
rhubarb with elderflower sorbet. The
international wine list makes an appreciable
effort to keep prices within the reach of most
budgets, and has a well-chosen range of eight
house wines from £11.65.
Chef/s: Tim Waldren and Adam Harrison. **Open:** all
week, L 12.30 to 2.30, D 7 to 9.30. **Closed:** 1st week
of Jan, bank hols. **Meals:** Set L and D £27.85 to
£29.95. Set L Sun £18.50. **Service:** net prices.
Details: Cards accepted. 60 seats. Separate bar. No
music. No mobile phones. Wheelchair access.
Children's portions. Car parking.

▮ Chaddesley Corbett

Brockencote Hall

A country hotel of some class
Chaddesley Corbett, DY10 4PY
Tel no: (01562) 777876
www.brockencotehall.com
Modern French | £35
Cooking score: 4

The setting is a great plus, as this Victorian
mansion stands beside an ornamental lake in
70 acres of parkland. Inside, the traditional
country house is comfortable with 'very
willing' staff creating a relaxed atmosphere.
Didier Philipot's cooking plies a modern
French line, drawing on nearby suppliers as
well as further afield, and aspirations are high.
Among starters, classic ideas such as dodine of
Périgord duck foie gras are bought up to date
with accompaniments of Armagnac and salt
flower and truffle salad. Main courses range
from fillet of John Dory teamed with
Morecambe Bay shrimps, ratte potato
brandade and smoked olive oil jus to noisette
of wild venison with forestière potato,
creamed Jerusalem artichoke and old
balsamico jus. Desserts might include Tahitian
vanilla crème brûlée, or brioche bread-and-
butter pudding with chocolate drops and
vanilla ice cream. With a French chef and a
French owner – Jospeh Petitjean – it is no
surprise to find the wine list dominated by
France, but the rest of the world is not
neglected and there's a global selection of
house wines from £16.
Chef/s: Didier Philipot. **Open:** Sun to Fri L 12 to
1.30, all week D £7 to 9.30. **Meals:** Set L £15 (2
courses) to £19, Set D £19 and £34.50.
Service: 10%. **Details:** Cards accepted. 70 seats.
Separate bar. Wheelchair access. Music. Children's
portions. Car parking.

Eldersfield

★NEW ENTRY★
Butchers Arms
Unpretentious village pub
Lime Street, Eldersfield, GL19 4NX
Tel no: (01452) 840381
Gastropub | £35
Cooking score: 4

James and Elizabeth Winter took over this tucked-away village inn on the border of Gloucestershire and Worcestershire in 2007 and even though they have relied almost entirely on word-of-mouth recommendations, tables are highly prized. A red-bricked pub with a small bar and an even smaller dining room, there is something undeniably homely about the place. With barely 18 covers and James solo in the kitchen, it feels like you have been invited to an intimate dinner party. This simple, hands-on approach stems from two of James' mentors – Alastair Little and Bristol chef Stephen Markwick (see Culinaria, Bristol). The food here is fiercely seasonal and locally sourced and shows respect for really good ingredients. A typical starter of pan-fried squab pigeon breast with wild mushroom salad could be followed by a main of wild Welsh sea trout with samphire and new potatoes, with comforting desserts including a top-notch marmalade pudding with Drambuie custard. A short, European-dominated wine list from £13.95 is complemented by a fine selection of local real ales and ciders.
Chef/s: James Winter. **Open:** Wed to Sun L 12 to 1, Tue to Sat D 7 to 8.45. **Closed:** Mon, 1 week early Jan. **Meals:** alc (main courses £14.95 to £17.50). **Service:** not inc. **Details:** Cards accepted. 18 seats. Children's portions. Car parking.

Evesham
ALSO RECOMMENDED
▲ Evesham Hotel
Cooper's Lane, Evesham, WR11 1DA
Tel no: (01386) 765566
www.eveshamhotel.com
Modern British

The third head chef in 30 years has joined this family-run Georgian hotel, but otherwise nothing else has changed. The vitality of the place derives largely from John Jenkinson's spirited approach, and daily-changing menus continue to offer the likes of marinated pigeon on creamed white cabbage (£8.75) ahead of venison with buttered celeriac dauphinoise (£15.50) or sea bream with sweet potato purée and pesto dressing. The drinks department is where all the stops are pulled out, the wine list being a hugely exhaustive collection that casts its net wide (but excludes France and Germany). Chilean house wine is £14.50. Open all week.

Knightwick
The Talbot
Teme Valley cuisine
Knightwick, WR6 5PH
Tel no: (01886) 821235
www.the-talbot.co.uk
British | £32
Cooking score: 1

Following the exasperations of the summer flooding in 2007, the Talbot was extensively refurbished. As one would expect from a place that has been catering for travellers since the fifteenth century, it has risen professionally from calamity and sailed on. Annie Clift sees her cooking as being very much rooted in the surrounding Teme Valley, while producing many ingredients (such as black pudding) herself. The results might come in the form of duck and mutton oak-smoked in-house, served with pickled nasturtium seeds and a balsamic reduction, black bream with pepper and onion couscous and wild garlic pesto or a

wine-rich oxtail stew ('cooked slowly all afternoon') with horseradish dumplings. Look to the bar menu for simpler fare, and don't miss the homely puddings such as bread-and-butter or orange and treacle tart. Eleven wines by-the-glass in two sizes (from £2.20 and £4.20) lead the vinous charge.
Chef/s: Annie Clift. **Open:** all week, L 12 to 2, D 6.30 to 9. **Closed:** 25 Dec D. **Meals:** Set L Sun £27, Set D £32. **Details:** Cards accepted. 60 seats. 60 seats outside. Separate bar. No music. No mobile phones. Wheelchair access. Children's portions. Car parking.

▌Ombersley

Venture In
Anglo-French cooking amid period charm
Ombersley, WR9 OEW
Tel no: (01905) 620552
Anglo/French | £35
Cooking score: 3

The venerable beamed building dates from the first half of the fifteenth century, and is the oldest house in this charming village near Droitwich. Period interiors include a huge inglenook fireplace, and the invitation to cross the threshold enshrined in the name is enhanced by the lure of Toby Fletcher's considered, smart-looking food. Fish-based starters might embrace a terrine of salmon, potato and leek, served with asparagus in saffron vinaigrette, or seared scallops with spring onion risotto in a butter dressing of lemon, garlic and parsley. A modern approach brings foaming sauces, perhaps of cep with beef fillet, as well as offals (best end of lamb with its braised heart, alongside creamed pumpkin), on to the main-course choice. The ubiquitous chocolate brownie dessert is here served with chocolate sauce and vanilla ice cream. A cosmopolitan spread of wines is priced in round figures, beginning with Chilean Sauvignon and a Côtes du Rhône red at £15.
Chef/s: Toby Fletcher. **Open:** Tue to Sun L 12 to 2, Tue to Sat D 7 to 9.45. **Closed:** 1 week at Christmas, 2 weeks in Feb, 2 weeks in Aug. **Meals:** Set L £25,

Set D £35. **Service:** not inc. **Details:** Cards accepted. 34 seats. Air-con. Separate bar. Wheelchair access. Music. Car parking.

▌Pershore

Belle House
Pleasingly simple yet elegant restaurant
5 Bridge Street, Pershore, WR10 1AJ
Tel no: (01386) 555055
www.belle-house.co.uk
Modern French | £26
Cooking score: 3

Steve Waite's restaurant scores with a pleasingly simple yet elegant décor and capable service, and it is also prepared to invest in decent ingredients. Short, set-priced menus have much of interest, and the broadly European style turns up anything from carpaccio of beef with warm new potato salad, Parmesan and balsamic dressing to roast venison with prune and orange sauce and walnut mashed potato, although fish dishes have included an unusual partnership of fillet of baked gurnard with noodle soup and tempura of scallops. The good-value lunch menu continues to be well reported, delivering food 'of a high standard', namely open ravioli of wild mushrooms and 'beautifully presented' braised pork with a cassoulet of beans, celeriac purée and a 'tasty' sauce. At dessert stage, warm hazelnut and chocolate brownie tart with coffee ice cream has been greatly appreciated. Wines are a fresh-faced global mix and priced from £13.95.
Chef/s: Steve Waite. **Open:** Tue to Sat L 12 to 2.30, D 7 to 9.30. **Closed:** Christmas and 2 weeks Jan, 1 week Aug. **Meals:** Set L £21, Set D £26. **Service:** not inc. **Details:** Cards accepted. 72 seats. Air-con. Separate bar. Wheelchair access. Music. Children's portions.

Also recommended

An 'also recommended' entry is not a full entry, but is provisionally suggested as an alternative to main entries.

■ Worcester

Brown's

Riverside restaurant that's hitting its stride
24 Quay Street, South Quay, Worcester, WR1 2JJ
Tel no: (01905) 26263
www.brownsrestaurant.co.uk
Modern European | £30
Cooking score: 3

£5 OFF V

The disastrous floods of summer 2007 which closed Browns for six months seem to have made it more determined to recapture the high ground as one of Worcester's premier dining venues. With a refurbishment (including some serious anti-flood measures) and a new executive chef (Martin Lovell), the riverside restaurant has hit its stride. There's a friendly buzz within the cream walls of the old cornmill and both the à la carte and fixed menus sparkle with good ingredients (local smoked salmon, Herefordshire perry) treated wisely. Get a table by the windows if you can for swan-filled vistas to accompany some excellent food enhanced by careful presentation – the little jar of home-made beetroot chutney and bijou rye loaf which accompany a perfect mini goats' cheese soufflé, for example. Everything hits the spot, whether a generous chunk of simply grilled, properly aged beef fillet or a fragrant chanterelle and pearl barley risotto with roast salsify. Desserts are top notch too.
Chef/s: Martin Lovell and Ian Courage. **Open:** Tue to Sat L 12 to 2.30, D 6.30 to 9.30, Sun L 12 to 3. **Closed:** Mon. **Meals:** Set menu £31.95 to £39.95 (4 courses). **Service:** not inc. **Details:** Cards accepted. Separate bar. Wheelchair access. Music. Children allowed.

The Glasshouse

Cool metropolitan all-rounder
Danesbury House, 55 Sidbury, Worcester, WR1 2HU
Tel no: (01905) 611120
www.theglasshouse.co.uk
Modern European | £32
Cooking score: 3

£5 OFF V

Spread over three floors of a custom-built venue close to the cathedral, the Glasshouse is the real deal – a bullish metropolitan brasserie with cool, informal vibes and an easy-going outlook. Co-founder Shaun Hill continues as executive chef – although much of his time is now spent in Wales at the reborn Walnut Tree Inn, Llandewi Skirrid (see entry, Gwent). His unmistakable thumbprint is all over the menu, and signature dishes from the old Ludlow days regularly put in an appearance: veal sweetbreads with potato and olive cake could precede shallot and cep tarte Tatin, cod with white bean cassoulet or pork loin with braised trotter, while desserts might include spice cake with iced apple parfait or a plate of rhubarb puddings. Factor in Sunday brunch, afternoon tea, a proper kids' menu, cocktails and beers and it is easy to see the all-round appeal of the place. Everything on the sharp global wine list is available by-the-glass or 250ml carafe, with bottle prices starting at £16.
Chef/s: Shaun Hill and Tom Duffill. **Open:** all week L 12 to 2.15, Mon to Sat D 5.30 to 9.30. **Closed:** bank hols, 25 and 26 Dec. **Meals:** alc (main courses £13 to £18). Set D £15 (2 courses) to £20. **Service:** not inc. **Details:** Cards accepted. 106 seats. 20 seats outside. Air-con. Separate bar. Wheelchair access. Music. Children's portions.

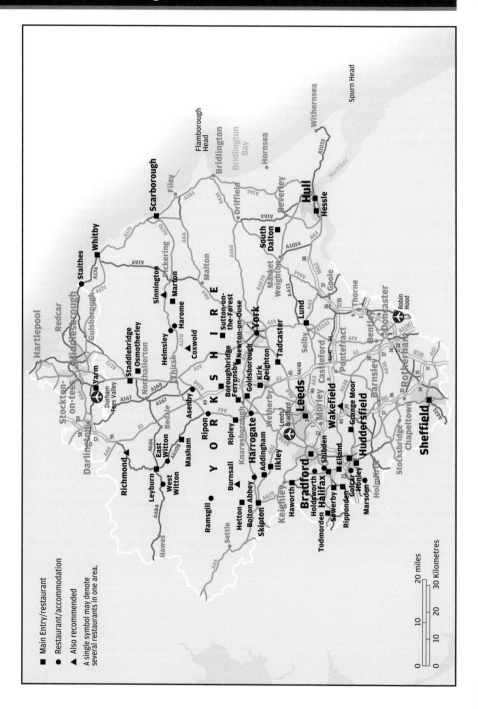

Spurn Head

Flamborough
Head

Bridlington
Bay

Bridlington

Hornsea

Withernsea

Humber

Hull

Hessle

Beverley

A165

A1079

A63

A164

Driffield

South
Dalton

Market
Weighton

A1034

Goole

Thorne

Robin
Hood

Doncaster

Bentley

Rotherham

Sheffield

Scarborough

Filey

A165

Whitby

Staithes

Guisborough

Redcar

Hartlepool

Middlesbrough

Stockton-
on-tees

Darlington

Richmond

Leyburn

West
Witton

East
Witton

Masham

Ripon

Ripley

Burnsall

Bolton Abbey

Skipton

Hetton

Settle

Ramsgill

Hawes

Harome

Coxwold

Helmsley

Sinnington

Pickering

Marton

Thirsk

Staddlebridge

Osmotherley

Northallerton

Bedale

Asenby

Knaresborough

Addingham

Ilkley

Keighley

Haworth

Todmorden

Holdsworth

Halifax

Sowerby

Ripponden

Marsden

Golcar

Honley

Holmfirth

Huddersfield

Elland

Shibden

Bradford

Leeds/
Bradford

Grange Moor

Wakefield

Morley

Castleford

Pontefract

Barnsley

Stocksbridge

Chapeltown

Leeds

Wetherby

Goldsborough

Kirk
Deighton

Boroughbridge

Ferrensby

Newton-on-Ouse

Sutton-on-
the-Forest

York

Tadcaster

Selby

Lund

Malton

Varm

Durham
Tees Valley

20 miles

30 Kilometres

20

10

0

▌ Addingham

Fleece

Dyed-in-the-wool Yorkshire champion
154 Main Street, Addingham, LS29 0LY
Tel no: (01943) 830491
Modern British | £25
Cooking score: 3

Still a proper Yorkshire watering hole complete with real ales, traditional games and blazing fires, the Fleece manages to pack 'em in with its cracking atmosphere and all-round food. Blackboards list an assortment of dyed-in-the-wool pub grub and more adventurous restaurant-style dishes, all founded on shrewdly sourced North Country produce. The kitchen proudly dishes up roast beef sandwiches with dripping and home-made pickled onions as well as ploughman's, trencherman meat and potato pies and toad-in-the-hole. But it isn't all cloth-capped nostalgia and warm-hearted Yorkshire generosity: punters also come here for an ever-changing array of daily specials that might run to a warm salad of chorizo and pears, roast Wigglesworth mallard with ginger and mandarins, or sautéed and steamed monkfish with tomato, garlic and herb vinaigrette. The carefully assembled wine list covers a lot of ground but keeps its prices on a tight rein: a dozen house selections start at £13.95 (£3.65). **Chef/s:** Andrew Cressy. **Open:** Mon to Sat L 12 to 2.15, D 6 to 9.15, Sun 12 to 8. **Meals:** alc (main courses £9 to £19.50). **Service:** not inc. **Details:** Cards accepted. 70 seats. 60 seats outside. Air-con. Separate bar. No music. Wheelchair access. Children's portions. Car parking.

▌ Asenby

Crab & Lobster

Eccectric, piscatorially inclined pub
Dishforth Road, Asenby, YO7 3QL
Tel no: (01845) 577286
www.crabandlobster.com
Seafood | £30
Cooking score: 3

Effigies of crabs and lobsters stranded on the roof should tell you that this is no ordinary thatched Yorkshire inn. Inside it is a riot of bric-à-brac, quirky curios and bohemian ephemera that give the bar and Edwardian-style 'dining pavilion' a mood of chic eccentricity. True to the pub's crustacean moniker, the food here is dominated by the harvest of the sea – even the lunchtime club sandwiches are filled with fish. Lobsters might be roasted with Thai spices, crab is used as a crust for Scottish salmon, and local halibut is given the Kiev treatment (with fennel and sweetcorn chowder as an accompaniment). Meat fans also do well, with Chinese-spiced spare ribs, peppered loin of venison and confit of Yorkshire lamb with hotpot potatoes and pickled red cabbage. Leave room for one of the hearty desserts – perhaps sticky date pudding. The up-tempo wine list casts off with a dozen house selections from £17 (£2.80 a glass). Luxury accommodation is available at the nearby Crab Manor Hotel. **Chef/s:** Mr S. G. Dean. **Open:** all week L 12 to 2.30, D 7 to 9.30 (6.30 to 9.30 Sat). **Meals:** alc (main courses £15 to £39). Set L £14.50, Set D £35. **Service:** not inc. **Details:** Cards accepted. 110 seats. 50 seats outside. Air-con. Separate bar. No mobile phones. Wheelchair access. Music. Children's portions. Car parking.

Bolton Abbey
Devonshire Arms

Sophisticated dining in country-house setting
Bolton Abbey, BD23 6AJ
Tel no: (01756) 710441
www.devonshirehotels.co.uk
Modern French | £58
Cooking score: 5

🍷 💺 V

After five years at the helm, Michael Wignall
has moved to the Latymer at Pennyhill Park in
Surrey (see entry), while Steve Smith comes
from Seaham Hall (see entry) to take the top
job at the Devonshire Arms' Burlington
restaurant. It has been a smooth transition. The
fishing rods are still at the door, the sofas are as
deep, the curtains are as rich, Sotheby's
catalogues are still casually arranged and
service is immaculate. Smith has a more
simple style than Wignall – but only slightly.
Early highlights have been a miniature plate of
sea bass ceviche from the market menu dotted
with cumin-flavoured aubergine purée and
avocado ice cream – a triumph of intense
flavours and sea-fresh fish. Veal sweetbreads,
incorporating morsels of chicken boudin and
peeled langoustine on puréed peas, morels and
madeira detonated another starburst of
exquisite tastes. Less successful was a cloyingly
sweet shot glass of rocket, lemon and
fermented ginger. More sweetness disturbed
an otherwise excellent foie gras with Yorkshire
rhubarb, hazelnut and watercress. And with a
pre-dessert of apricot, saffron and cream
cheese, followed by vanilla pannacotta,
orange and liquorice and a 'surprise' course of
chocolate ice lolly and sweet hot chocolate,
one reporter felt 'in danger of a sugar rush'. The
sensational wine list remains an encyclopaedic
volume the size of an old parish bible.
Famously, it is a rich connoisseur's delight –
some bottles wave goodbye to four figures –
but there are many bargains to be found below
£25 and some 20 wines-by-the-glass.

Chef/s: Steve Smith. **Open:** Sun L 12.30 to 2, Tue to
Sun D 7 to 9.30. **Closed:** Mon. **Meals:** Set menu £58
and £68. **Service:** 12.5%. **Details:** Cards accepted.
70 seats. Separate bar. No mobile phones.
Wheelchair access. Children's portions. Car parking.

Boroughbridge
Dining Room

Simple but classy cooking in a domestic setting
20 St James Square, Boroughbridge, YO51 9AR
Tel no: (01423) 326426
www.thediningroomonline.co.uk
Modern British | £27
Cooking score: 4

The green-fronted Queen Anne building is
home to the Astleys' enterprising small
restaurant, to which they have now added a
terrace for fine-weather dining. Reporters
note the very fair value for some polished
cooking based on locally sourced seasonal
ingredients. It is the kind of place where the
chef may well emerge at the evening's end to
check that all are departing satisfied. That they
usually do is testament to the flair that informs
the expansive fixed-price menus. Dishes are
not hampered by over-complication, but rely
on a repertoire of bright, familiar preparations
that work well. Rocket and goats' cheese tart
with pesto, followed by smoked haddock with
crushed potatoes, spinach and a creamy
mustard sauce, are the kinds of things to
expect. Sea bass has been dressed in a coconut
curry sauce as a starter, while black pudding
and Bramley apple have been the medium for
slow-cooked duck confit. Finish with white
chocolate and Cointreau parfait or a
frangipane tart of pear and cinnamon served
with Yorkshire clotted cream. Nine wines by-
the-glass from £3.95 head-up a list that zips
about briskly and finds room for a couple of
Gaston Hochar's Lebanese offerings. Chilean
house wines are £13.95.
Chef/s: Christopher Astley. **Open:** Tue to Sat D 7 to
9.15. Sun L 12 to 2. **Closed:** Mon, bank hols.
Meals: Set L Sun £24.50. Set D £26.50. **Service:** not

inc. **Details:** Cards accepted. 30 seats. 22 seats outside. Separate bar. No mobile phones. Music. Children's portions.

▌Bradford

Mumtaz

Kashmiri blockbuster
386-400 Great Horton Road, Bradford, BD7 3HS
Tel no: (01274) 571861
www.mumtaz.co.uk
Indian | £20
Cooking score: 2

V

This vast, ultra-modern conversion of a stone terrace not far from the city centre can feed 400 in a glass and granite bling-fest, but finding Mumtaz on Bradford's outer ring road can be tricky – look for neon signs and the large car park. The menu is essentially Kashmiri – with many karahi dishes, like cod in a pleasant spicy sauce of tomatoes, ginger and lime juice, or lamb cooked with fresh bitter gourd. Start with chargrilled lamb chops marinated in spices, shish kebab, or keema paratha (a chappati filled with spicy minced lamb and coriander) and finish with gulab jaman or kheer – a rice pudding with pistachio and saffron. Alcohol is not allowed on the premises, but the lassi is very good and makes a perfect accompaniment to the spicy food.
Open: all week 11am to midnight, (1 Fri and Sat). **Meals:** alc (main courses £8.95 to £15.50). **Service:** not inc. **Details:** Cards accepted. 400 seats. Air-con. Wheelchair access. Music. Children's portions. Car parking.

Please send us your feedback

To register your opinion about any restaurant listed in the Guide, or a new restaurant that you wish to bring to our attention, please visit the web address at the bottom of the page. Your feedback informs the content of the book and will be used to compile next year's reviews.

Prashad

Everyday vegetarian dishes of Gujarat
86 Horton Grange Road, Bradford, BD7 2DW
Tel no: (01274) 575893
www.prashad.co.uk
Indian | £12
Cooking score: 2

£5 OFF **V** £30

The décor is basic at this vegetarian chaat house, with a tiled floor, metal tables and plastic chairs, but a mirrored wall gives a sense of space and light. Prashad has been around as a takeaway since 1986 – the restaurant opened in 2004 – serving Kaushy Patel's everyday vegetarian dishes of her native Gujarat. Poppadoms with home-made pickles and chutneys open proceedings, paving the way for impressive street snack-style starters such as pea kachori – deep-fried spiced ground pea and garlic balls. Simpler main courses might be chunky potatoes cooked in a rich, tangy sauce or chickpeas in an onion and tomato sauce, and there are specialities including pancakes filled with lightly-spiced potato and onion and served with a spicy lentil soup and coconut and yoghurt chutney. Dessert might be carrot halva with ice cream. Alcohol is not served, so drink lassi or faluda.
Chef/s: Kaushy Patel and Minal Patel. **Open:** Tue to Fri L 11 to 3, D 6 to 9.30, Sat and Sun 11 to 10.30. **Closed:** Mon. **Service:** not inc. **Details:** Cards accepted. 25 seats. Music. Children's portions.

▌Burnsall

ALSO RECOMMENDED
▲ Devonshire Fell

Burnsall, BD23 6BT
Tel no: (01756) 729000
www.devonshirehotels.co.uk
Modern British

It was a breath of fresh air in 1997 when this fusty Victorian hotel was transformed by the Devonshire estate into a colourful brasserie bursting with vibrant artwork, modern fabrics and lilac walls, but the years have left it a little jaded. The arrival of a new general

Anthony Flinn Anthony's

Why did you become a chef?
I was about 7 when I found out that combining average ingredients together can result in something fantastic. I started mixing random ingredients to see what else can be made. I am still doing that today.

What three ingredients could you not do without?
Nuts, salt, coffee

What's the most unusual ingredient you've cooked or eaten?
Boiled suckling pig eyes. Don't ask.

What won't you tolerate in the kitchen?
Lying.

What's your least favourite ingredient and why?
Black pepper, massively over used and people use it as a seasoning when it is a spice. Salt is a flavour enhancer, pepper isn't.

What era of history would you most like to have eaten in?
Nouvelle cuisine, or the opening night of Marco's first flagship restaurant.

manager from the flagship Devonshire Arms signals changes at the Fell with the promise that the basic brasserie fare of burger and chips (£12), moules marinière and twice-baked cheese soufflé (£7) will be transformed to a more sophisticated 'restaurant-with-rooms'. The changes were not in place at the time of our inspection, but the timeless views over Wharfedale remain resolutely intact.

▌Coxwold

ALSO RECOMMENDED
▲ Abbey Inn
Byland Abbey, Coxwold, YO61 4BD
Tel no: **(01347) 868204**
www.bylandabbeyinn.com
Gastropub

Standing opposite the celebrated ruins of Byland Abbey, this equally renowned, ivy-clad inn is now owned by English Heritage and has all the expected touristy trappings. Traditional 'Mouseman' furniture is a showcase feature of the rustic dining rooms, and the menu flies the flag with regional dishes including savoury 'fat rascal' with poached egg (£4.95), braised lamb shank shepherd's pie with parsnip purée (£12.95), venison T-bone with chips and desserts such as Yorkshire parkin with Wensleydale cheese (£5.95). House wine is £13.95 Glorious patio gardens and delightful accommodation. Closed Mon, Tue and Sun D.

▌East Witton

Blue Lion
Gastropub that's hot on game
East Witton, DL8 4SN
Tel no: **(01969) 624273**
www.thebluelion.co.uk
Modern British | £29
Cooking score: 4

🍸 🛏 £30

East Witton is about as pretty and dainty as you get in the Dales and the clientele is definitely more shooter than shepherd, but there's nothing here to deter either. Steeped in woodsmoke from the big open fire and with old chairs and oak settles to sink into after a bracing walk, the Blue Lion is a delight. The adjacent moors naturally provide a spine to the menu: grouse, pheasant and partridge are regularly chalked up on the blackboard, often with the guns themselves tucking into something warm and hearty. Outside the shooting season expect full-bodied dishes like ham hock, parsley and foie gras served with yellow split pea purée or slow-braised mutton with cumin sweet potato. Chef John Dalby, who has maintained a solid level of gastropub quality for twelve years now, is equally deft with puddings: try soft-baked meringue with hazelnut ice cream or a sumptuous iced liquorice terrine. There's a compact wine list starting at £14.50, and hand-pulled beers star Masham's Black Sheep from the brewery down the road.

Chef/s: John Dalby. **Open:** all week L 12 to 2, D 7 to 9. **Meals:** alc (main courses £10.50 to £21.50). **Service:** not inc. **Details:** Cards accepted. 60 seats. 20 seats outside. Separate bar. Wheelchair access. Children's portions. Car parking.

▌Elland

La Cachette

Happy-go-lucky bistro
31 Huddersfield Road, Elland, HX5 9AW
Tel no: (01422) 378833
www.lacachette-elland.com
Modern European | £24
Cooking score: 3

Despite the name, La Cachette is definitely not in the business of hiding its light under a bushel: it went public from day one and succeeds admirably as a revved-up bistro-cum-wine bar. There have been some personnel changes of late, and chef Jonathan Nichols is now co-owner of the whole show. That said, the place still pleases all-comers with its light-hearted buzz and attractively priced modern food. Candlelit alcoves and big booths for party gatherings reinforce the congenial mood, and the kitchen is equally at home with light

lunches (wild mushroom linguine) and full-on evening meals. Standards such as moules marinière and grilled calf's liver keep company with more eclectic ideas including warm confit duck salad and hoisin drssing, rump of lamb with Moroccan chickpea fritter and buttered breast of chicken with creamed polenta. To close, go for sticky toffee pudding. The cracking value for money extends to the comprehensive wine list, which divides most of its attention between France and the New World. House selections start at £12.50 (£2.50 a glass).

Chef/s: Jonathan Nichols. **Open:** Mon to Sat L 12 to 2.30, D 6 to 9.30 (10 Fri and Sat). **Closed:** Sun, 2 weeks Jan, Aug, bank hols (exc Christmas). **Meals:** alc (main courses £11 to £20). Set L £11.95 (2 courses). Set D £18.95. **Service:** not inc. **Details:** Cards accepted. 90 seats. Air-con. Separate bar. Wheelchair access. Music. Children's portions. Car parking.

▌Ferrensby

General Tarleton

Relaxed coaching inn handy for the A1
Boroughbridge Road, Ferrensby, HG5 0PZ
Tel no: (01423) 340284
www.generaltarleton.co.uk
Gastropub | £28
Cooking score: 4

It may be only a few minutes' drive from the A1, but this relaxed coaching inn in open countryside offers a respite to travellers with its cosy bar, restaurant and lovely courtyard area. John Topham makes admirable use of local produce. Seasonality and freshness are to the fore and all sorts of influences show up among starters: chilli-salt spiced squid and crisp belly pork with sweet pepper salad and coriander and lime dressing alongside roast vine tomato filo tartlet with grilled Lowna Dairy goats' cheese, tapenade and pesto. Main courses take in crisped slow-braised shoulder of lamb with Puy lentils, bacon lardoons, roast shallots and garden thyme or roast breast of Goosnargh duckling with a spring roll and Asian-marinated red cabbage. Finish with something straightforward like brandy-snap basket with pistachio ice cream and hot chocolate sauce, or lemon posset. The wine list is well-chosen and reasonably priced, starting at £15.05.

Chef/s: John Topham. **Open:** all week L 12 to 2, D 6 to 9.15. **Meals:** alc (main courses £13.95 to £17.95). Set Sun L £22.95. **Service:** not inc. **Details:** Cards accepted. 140 seats. 80 seats outside. Children's portions. Car parking.

Golcar

★ READERS' RESTAURANT OF THE YEAR ★
NORTH EAST

Weavers Shed
From garden to kitchen
86-88 Knowl Road, Golcar, HD7 4AN
Tel no: (01484) 654284
www.weaversshed.co.uk
Modern British | £40
Cooking score: 5

£5 OFF 🍷 🛏️

Industrious domestic enterprise and a healthy dose of self-sufficiency define proceedings at Stephen and Tracy Jackson's stylishly rustic eighteenth-century cloth mill in the hills overlooking Huddersfield. On the food front, much depends on seasonal pickings from the kitchen garden, 'wild' plot and orchard, and a floral logo highlights dishes that make use of home-grown produce. After a little appetiser, you could begin with a risotto of wild and cultivated mushrooms with truffle and cep caramel and pickled fungi, while main courses might involve Goosnargh duck or twice-cooked saddle of rare-breed pork with grain mustard mash, choucroute and meaty juices. Another logo on the menu signals that fish is from sustainable stocks – thus you might find roast fillet of farmed sea bass served with roast salsify, spinach, mushroom sauce and crushed potatoes scented with chervil. To finish, try an Eccles cake served hot from the oven with a wedge of Mrs Kirkham's Lancashire cheese or something modish such as pineapple tarte Tatin with toasted coconut ice cream and spiced rum syrup. Some reporters feel that

simple set lunches (eggs Benedict, chargrilled Limousin sirloin, Queen of Puddings) don't live up to the restaurant's auspicious reputation, although the results are perfectly acceptable. The wine list, however, makes amends with its 'intelligent' choice of enthusiastically chosen bottles at restrained prices. Working with several top merchants, the Jacksons eschew famous names in favour of small elite producers and have a particularly soft spot for southern France and California. House recommendations are £15.50 (£4 a glass).

Chef/s: Stephen Jackson, Ian McGuinnigle and Cath Sill. **Open:** Tue to Fri L 12 to 2, Tue to Sat D 7 to 9. **Closed:** Sun, Mon. **Meals:** alc D (main courses £18 to £27). Set L £14.95 (2 courses) to £17.95. **Service:** not inc. **Details:** Cards accepted. 24 seats. Separate bar. No mobile phones. Music. Children allowed. Car parking.

Goldsborough
Fox and Hounds
Excellent food with a stunning backdrop
Goldsborough, YO21 3RX
Tel no: (01947) 893372
Modern European | £37
Cooking score: 5

One glimpse of the country views from the small windows of this perennially cosy pub and it becomes clear why chef/proprietor Jason Davies left London's the Ivy behind. Instead of feeding the beau monde in the bustling capital, Davies and family now run this tiny gastropub in a pretty hamlet on the North Yorkshire coast. The menu, which is best described as short but sweet, is unsurprisingly dominated by fish, though a winter Sunday lunch menu offered salt-beef and partridge as two of the four mains. It changes daily, and is predominantly organic. Food is delightfully simple, with sophistication present in the lightest touches: sage butter adding extra depth to an already wonderful starter of butternut squash ravioli; lemon oil turning a seared chunk of halibut with crushed potatoes and spinach from ordinary into extraordinary. The wine list, which starts at £12 for house, is extensive despite being a wall-mounted chalkboard like the menu. Sadly there are no local beers on tap yet, but the charming, unpretentious service and authentic family feel of this pub more than make up for that.

Chef/s: Jason Davies. **Open:** Wed to Sun 12 to 1, 6.30 to 8. **Closed:** bank hols, Christmas. **Meals:** alc (main courses £9 to £18). **Details:** Cards accepted. 28 seats. 16 seats outside. Wheelchair access. Music. Children's portions. Car parking.

Grange Moor

Kaye Arms

Brasserie meets pub grub
29 Wakefield Road, Grange Moor, WF4 4BG
Tel no: (01924) 848385
www.thekayearms.com
Modern British | £25
New Chef

More of an out-of-town brasserie than a country pub these days, the Kaye Arms inhabits an isolated patch of moorland beside the Huddersfield to Wakefield road. The location is clearly no deterrent, because the place gets jam-packed – especially at weekends. Plates of food now take preference over pints of beer, and eager crowds get full satisfaction from up-to-the-minute favourites such as smoked haddock and coriander risotto, twice-baked cheese soufflé and roast Barbary duck breast with poached pear and rocket salad. The kitchen also assuages pub die-hards with prawn cocktail, grilled gammon steak and a dusted-off version of scampi and chips served with pea purée and tomato fondue, while desserts don't stray much further than bread-and-butter pudding with Yorkshire custard and fresh apricots. Simple light lunches are available during the week, and there are plenty of decent wines by-the-glass on the affordable global list; bottle prices start at £14.50.

Chef/s: Simon Dyson. **Open:** Mon to Fri L 12 to 2.30, D 7 to 9.30, Sat and Sun 12 to 9.30. **Closed:** 25 Dec. **Meals:** alc (main courses £12 to £25). Light L menu

available. **Service:** not inc. **Details:** Cards accepted. 85 seats. Separate bar. Wheelchair access. Music. Children's portions. Car parking.

Harome

Star Inn

A star in every sense
High Street, Harome, YO62 5JE
Tel no: (01439) 770397
www.thestaratharome.co.uk
Modern British | £40
Cooking score: 6

With an expanding 'Pernshire' empire that takes in a corner shop, a butcher/deli, a range of Star Inn sauces and a self-published book, you might worry that Andrew Pern was spreading himself too thin. Not a bit of it. Recent visits to the heart of North Yorkshire confirm that the Star kitchen is on brilliant form, as good, if not better than ever. A spring starter of risotto of home-grown wild garlic served with wafers of Northumbrian Doddington cheese tasted as fresh and green as a spring garden, though the reporter might have relished a more assertive hand with the Périgord black truffles. Another starter of foie gras sandwiched between slices of home-made black pudding and served with caramelised apple and Pickering watercress is the Star turn in every sense, a sensational dish that defines Pern's genius for injecting the best of the local produce with de luxe extras. Roast leg of local suckling pig with Ampleforth apple compote or saddle of Duncombe Park roe deer with a little venison cottage pie, black trumpet mushrooms, York ham lardons and juniper juices, affirm his priceless ability to maximise the potential of the best regional fish, meat and game. With Highland cattle and saddleback pigs grazing in the field behind the pub, Pern's commitment to 'cuisine terroir' is hardly in question. His wine list too is superb. Not surprisingly, securing a table takes some persistence. At the time of going to press an additional dining room and outdoor dining terrace was under construction, which should ease the pressure. The no-booking cosy bar is always an option, though it is often very busy and some tables fearfully small.

Chef/s: Andrew Pern. **Open:** all week L 11.30 to 2, D 6.15 to 9.30. **Closed:** 25 Dec. **Meals:** alc L (main courses £14.50 to £17.50). Set D £48.75. **Service:** 10% (optional) at D. **Details:** Cards accepted. 100 seats. 60 seats outside. Separate bar. Wheelchair access. Music. Children's portions. Car parking.

Harrogate
Hotel du Vin & Bistro
Dedicated to first-class food
Prospect Place, Harrogate, HG1 1LB
Tel no: (01423) 856800
www.hotelduvin.com
Modern European | £32
New Chef

Tom Van Zeller was previously head chef at Malmaison Leeds, and though it would be a little unfair to say he's stepped out of the darkness and into the light, it is applicable in more than one sense. Firstly, where Malmaison was snug and low-lit, Hotel du Vin's restaurant is expansive, bright and airy. Secondly, while Van Zeller's food at the Leeds hotel was good, he seems to have been given more room to express himself here in Harrogate. Hence choices like sautéed snails with capers, garlic, mizuna salad and pancetta crisps or Texel-cross lamb loin from the very local Bank Farm in Huby, with red pepper purée, courgette, samphire and lentils. Van Zeller likes to display a humbler side too, as the fabulous Voakes pork pie and pea starter shows (a small copper pot of mint sauce the only embellishment), while locally sourced and perfectly roasted free-range chicken also makes a virtue of simplicity. Given the name, it almost goes without saying that the wine list is very good indeed, with some straightforward groupings to make decisions easier for the novice.

Chef/s: Tom Van Zeller. **Open:** all week 12 to 2 (12.30 to 2.30 Sun), 7 to 10 (6.30 to 10.30 Fri and Sat). **Meals:** alc (main courses £13.50 to £24). Set D

£15.50 (2 courses) to £17.50. **Service:** 10% optional. **Details:** Cards accepted. 98 seats. No music. Wheelchair access.

★NEW ENTRY★
Orchid Restaurant
Innovative and exciting pan-Asian cooking
Studley Hotel, 28 Swan Road, Harrogate, HG1 2SE
Tel no: (01423) 560425
www.orchidrestaurant.co.uk
Fusion/Pan-Asian | £25
Cooking score: 2

The pan-Asian kitchen team in the basement of the Studley Hotel take us on a stimulating tour of China, Japan, Vietnam, Thailand and the Philippines with a menu of some 50 dishes that is by turns innovative and exciting. Elegant pared-down dishes like crispy wasabi tiger prawns with a soy dipping sauce or light-as-a-feather fried aubergine parcels filled with beef and water chestnuts topped with Szechuan pepper are significantly a cut above mainstream Chinese. A spring special of duck breast in a tamarind and honey sauce on pak choi, finished with crushed walnuts was a delight. Even that dodgy old faithful sweet-and-sour pork from the lunchtime fast-track menu was reinvigorated with crisply battered pork, crunchy vegetables and a sauce of restrained sweetness. The Sunday brunch buffet showcases a range of Orchid dishes, or choose a combination of smaller plates. Décor is smart oriental and the wine list cleverly includes a range of Trimbach Estate Alsace wines that complement these superior oriental tastes.

Chef/s: Kenneth Poon. **Open:** all week L 12 to 2, D 6 to 10. **Closed:** 25 and 26 Dec. **Meals:** Set L £9.95 (2 courses) to £12.95, Set D £21.95. **Service:** 10%. **Details:** Cards accepted. 70 seats. 8 seats outside. Air-con. Separate bar. Wheelchair access. Music. Children allowed.

Oxford Street Brasserie

Talked-about Harrogate all-rounder
34 Oxford Street, Harrogate, HG1 1PP
Tel no: (01423) 505300
www.oxford streetbrasserie.com
Modern European | £28
Cooking score: 4

Handily placed a quick stroll from Harrogate Theatre and the International Centre, David Robson's smart young kid on the block has made a real impact since opening its doors. Readers have been quick to extol its virtues, singling out its fair prices, child-friendly attitude and the fact that you can watch the action in the kitchen. There is plenty going on here, judging by the cosmopolitan tone of the menu. David Robson once cooked with Jeff Baker at the sadly-missed Pool Court in Leeds and it shows in his mix of populist contemporary ideas, simple touches and classically rooted technique. Well-tried starters such as duck liver parfait with red onion chutney or smoked haddock and chive risotto give way to main courses of seared salmon with tarragon ravioli and lemon butter, lamb hotpot or butter-roast, corn-fed chicken with a bacon and leek 'pie'. As for desserts, think Valrhona hot chocolate soufflé or pear and apple frangipane. The wine list follows suit with a friendly mix of classic and modern names from £12.50 (£3.30 a glass).
Chef/s: David Robson. **Open:** Tue to Sat L 12 to 2.30, D 5.30 to 9.30. **Closed:** Sun, Mon, 25 and 26 Dec. **Meals:** alc (main courses £13 to £19). Set D 5.30 to 6.45 Tue to Fri £12.50 (2 courses) to £14.50. **Service:** not inc. **Details:** Cards accepted. 42 seats. Air-con. No mobile phones. Music. Children's portions.

Readers recommend

A 'readers recommend' review is a genuine quote from a report sent in by one of our readers. We intend to follow up these suggestions throughout the year to come.

Sasso

High quality Italian enoteca
8-10 Princes Square, Harrogate, HG1 1LX
Tel no: (01423) 508838
www.sassorestaurant.co.uk
Italian | £35
Cooking score: 5

The ever-enthusiastic Stefano Lancellotti's unassuming basement enoteca retains a friendly neighbourhood atmosphere with simple polished wood tables alongside a front-of-house operation as crisp as the starched napkins. His menu changes seasonally, but antipasti might include sautéed fillet steak with rocket and Parmesan or a potato and broad bean soup served with a little crostini of prosciutto. Mains might be chicken breast stuffed with roasted red pepper and wrapped in vegetable ribbons, served with a spinach and chicken mousse, while specials include a superb traditional Neopolitan dish of turbot layered with mozzarella and basil. But always make room for a mid-course of exemplary fresh egg pasta: fusilli with bacon, asparagus, egg yolk and pecorino, and spaghetti with octopus, garlic, olive oil and chilli perhaps, or, more indulgently, ravioli filled with fresh lobster, courgettes, shallots and tarragon, served in a lobster bisque. Desserts are elegant versions of Italian favourites: pannacotta, tiramisù and lemon tart with limoncello sorbet. The wine list is comprehensively deep in Italian varietals, beginning with a Garganega Chardonnay at £12.95 and peaking with a 2003 Tuscan Sassicaia Tenuta San Guido at £190 and a rare 2000 Amarone at £450. A recent addition to the Lancellotti stable is Caffè Marconi, another basement just a few doors down, serving top quality sandwiches, pastries and coffee in a smart, contemporary setting.
Chef/s: Stefano Lancellotti. **Open:** Mon to Sat 12 to 2, D 6.30 to 10 (Fri and Sat 6 to 10.30). **Closed:** bank hols, 25 and 26 Dec, 1 Jan. **Meals:** Set L £7.95 (2 courses). **Service:** not inc. **Details:** Cards accepted. 80 seats. 20 seats outside. Music. Children's portions.

▌Haworth

Weavers

Out on the wiley, windy moors
13-17 West Lane, Haworth, BD22 8DU
Tel no: (01535) 643822
www.weaverssmallhotel.co.uk
Modern British | £24
Cooking score: 3

With quirky décor and warm lighting, the three knocked-together weavers' cottages in the shadow of the Brontë Parsonage Museum ooze period charm. Colin and Jane Rushworth have a down-to-earth approach to running a restaurant − the bar area is reminiscent of a pub − and the food is copious, with much of it sourced locally. Without being too ambitious the kitchen deals in characterful modern British cooking: carpaccio of Dales beef fillet with watercress and root vegetable salad and horseradish cream sits happily beside a homespun lamb bubble and squeak with smoked Lancashire rarebit and brown sauce among starters. Main courses could bring Weavers 'meat and p'tato' pie made with Pennine-reared beef and shortcrust pastry and served with white onion relish and a jug of gravy, or excellent fillets of sea bass atop celeriac and potato rösti with chilli-glazed turnip and spicy tomato and shellfish sauce. End on a high note with suitably indulgent caramelised apple cake with custard, or sticky toffee pudding. Our questionnaire was not returned, so some of the information below may have changed.
Chef/s: Tim, Jane and Colin Rushworth. **Open:** Wed to Fri and Sun L 12 to 2, Tue to Sat D 6 to 9. **Closed:** 10 days from 25 Dec. **Meals:** alc (main courses £12.95 to £17.95). **Service:** not inc. **Details:** Cards accepted. 65 seats. Air-con. No mobile phones. Music. Children's portions.

▌Helmsley

Feversham Arms Hotel

Style-driven country hotel
High Street, Helmsley, YO62 5AG
Tel no: (01439) 770766
www.fevershamarmshotel.com
Modern Anglo-French | £33
Cooking score: 4

⇥ V

Within easy reach of York and the region's heritage hot-spots, the Feversham Arms is a style-driven country house with a contemporary outlook. Designer improvements continue apace, with a new spa promised during 2008 plus a second private dining room and expansive refurbishment of the conservatory-style restaurant. The kitchen remains firmly on course amid all of this, playing out its Anglo-French themes with skill and confidence. Whitby crab salad with orange segments and hazelnuts sits cheek-by-jowl on the menu with langoustine and spiced pork belly with butternut squash and parsley oil, while main courses also display liberal doses of 'entente cordiale': pan-roast fillet of Yorkshire beef with Anna potatoes and bourguignon garnish, for example. Wild sea bass with chorizo, fennel and basil mash drifts out into the Mediterranean, while desserts maintain the Yorkshire-meets-Europe tone: prune and cherry flapjack with pistachio mousse, warm parkin alongside poached pear with aniseed ice cream. The extensive 100-bin wine list has a goodly selection of half-bottles; prices start at £18.50.
Chef/s: Simon Kelly. **Open:** all week L 12 to 2, D 7 to 9.30. **Meals:** alc (main courses L £14.50 to £22, D £19 to £24). Set D £33. **Service:** not inc.
Details: Cards accepted. 70 seats. 30 seats outside. Separate bar. No mobile phones. Wheelchair access. Music. Children's portions. Car parking.

▌Hessle

Artisan

Humberside treasure

22 The Weir, Hessle, HU13 0RU
Tel no: (01482) 644906
www.artisanrestaurant.com
Modern British | £35
Cooking score: 4

'A super little eatery that keeps going from strength to strength,' is one typically effusive verdict on Richard and Lindsey Johns' 'unique and original' restaurant in the shadow of the Humber Bridge. Small is clearly very effective here: Lindsey does a fantastic job running the 18-cover dining room, while Richard works alone in the kitchen. There is no posturing or frippery, just good humour and serious food cooked with disarming acumen. Supper menus change every few days and the choice is kept sensibly brief, with just two options for each course. Start with new season's English asparagus 'two ways' or Cornish mackerel fillet with avocado cream, tomato vinaigrette and savoury sweetcorn sorbet. After that, expect seasonality in the shape of rump of local lamb with slow-cooked shoulder, 'hotpot' potatoes and spring vegetables or wild turbot with basil crushed potatoes, wild rocket and basil oil. Desserts favour simplicity, as in pannacotta with strawberries or milk chocolate pot with chocolate sauce and Amaretto ice cream. The new 'Taste of Everything' menu has been an instant hit with regulars, who relish the prospect of sampling six ample courses at prices which are 'frankly a steal.' The 32-bin wine list offers high quality without painful mark-ups; prices start at £18.50.
Chef/s: Richard Johns. **Open:** Tue to Sat D only from 7.15. **Closed:** Sun, Mon. **Meals:** Set D £30 (2 courses) to to £45 (6 courses). **Service:** not inc.
Details: Cards accepted. 18 seats. Air-con. No mobile phones. Wheelchair access. Music. Children's portions. Car parking.

▌Hetton

The Angel Inn

Culinary delights in Dales restro-pub

Hetton, BD23 6LT
Tel no: (01756) 730263
www.angelhetton.co.uk
Modern British | £29
Cooking score: 3

£5 OFF ▯ ⊨ V £30

The Angel is a Dales dining destination, the (in parts) 500-year-old building drawing visitors from miles around for its rural setting, character and food. That quintessential country-pub character is foremost in the bar/brasserie, courtesy of flagged floors, blazing open fires (one in an old-fashioned range), oak beams and polished wood. In the two interconnecting rooms that make up the restaurant it's a more formal setting of drapes, wallpaper and white linen-clad tables. The bar/brasserie and restaurant have separate menus – with a little crossover – but both areas celebrate seasonal produce and fresh fish, which is an Angel speciality. In the restaurant, pan-seared wild halibut fillet served with fondant potato, English asparagus, king scallops and lobster butter sauce is matched by Dales-bred lamb (maybe featuring a duo of Bolton Abbey mutton teamed with garden peas and medley of vegetables with minted mash and rosemary sauce) plus beef and seasonal game. The global wine list leans towards France, with house tipples from £15.50 and a good selection by-the-glass.
Chef/s: Mark Taft. **Open:** Restaurant D Mon to Sat 6 to 9.30, Sun L 12 to 2; Brasserie Mon to Sun L 12 to 2.15, D 6 to 9. **Closed:** 25 Dec. **Meals:** alc exc Sat D and Sun L (main courses £11.25 to £16.95). Set L Sun £24, Set D Sat £35. **Service:** optional. **Details:** Cards accepted. 60 seats. 40 seats outside. Air-con. Separate bar. No music. Wheelchair access. Children's portions. Car parking.

■ Holdsworth

Holdsworth House

Country-house splendour on the moors
Holdsworth, HX2 9TG
Tel no: (01422) 240024
www.holdsworthhouse.co.uk
Modern European | £32
Cooking score: 3

≒ V

A handsome, greystone Jacobean manor house set in the moorland just north of Halifax, Holdsworth is a country-house hotel with all the trappings, and then some. The Beatles came here on John Lennon's birthday back in the era when the world had only just heard of them. Culinary modes have moved on since that day, of course, and Gary Saunders now presides over an eclectic menu that draws influences from near and far. Meals might begin with a serving of seared king scallops with chorizo, potato and puréed cauliflower, before proceeding to a honey-glazed shoulder of lamb with dauphinoise, or a seafood dish that teams black bream with Cromer crab in basil vinaigrette. A vegetarian main option may be a tartlet of leek, onion and thyme with a soft-poached egg and hollandaise. The fine selection of painstakingly described English cheeses is an alternative to desserts such as baked chocolate and orange terrine with vanilla mascarpone. A stylistically arranged wine list has a decent range of halves, with full bottles starting at £14.25.
Chef/s: Gary Saunders. **Open:** Mon to Fri L 12 to 2, all week D 6 to 9.30. **Meals:** alc (main courses £14.95 to £22). Set L £25. **Service:** not inc.
Details: Cards accepted. 45 seats. Separate bar. Wheelchair access. Music. Children's portions. Car parking.

■ Honley

Mustard and Punch

Industrious local favourite
6 Westgate, Honley, HD9 6AA
Tel no: (01484) 662066
www.mustardandpunch.co.uk
Modern European | £26
Cooking score: 3

Deep in *Last of the Summer Wine* country, this relaxed venue is a godsend for locals and tourists alike. Richard Dunn has been doing good business behind this unassuming converted shop front for more than a decade and he runs a tireless kitchen, producing everything from breads to ice creams and preserves. He is happy to send out pot-roast chicken or Yorkshire rib-eye steak with green peppercorn sauce, but his menus also show a sense of adventure. Duck cannelloni with roast butternut squash, thyme and almond jus is a teasing starter, while mains could embrace anything from medallions of monkfish with tempura boudin noir, creamed white beans and bordelaise sauce to calf's liver with spinach and beetroot jus. To conclude, consider peach tarte Tatin or roast fig parfait with star anise ice cream and orange curd. Thirty well-spread wines offer keenly priced drinking from £13.95 (£3.50 a glass).
Chef/s: Richard Dunn and Wayne Roddis. **Open:** Mon to Sat D only 6 to 9.30. **Closed:** Sun and bank hol Mon. **Meals:** alc (main courses £14.50 to £21). Set D £19.95 (3 courses inc wine). **Service:** not inc.
Details: Cards accepted. 55 seats. Air-con. Separate bar. Music. Children's portions.

▌Huddersfield
Bradley's
Crowd-pleasing bistro food
84 Fitzwilliam Street, Huddersfield, HD1 5BB
Tel no: (01484) 516773
Modern European | £40
Cooking score: 2

V

A bastion of the Huddersfield scene for the last fifteen years, this animated town-centre brasserie is a cheery as ever, thanks to owner Andrew Bradley's boundless enthusiasm and energy. Pale wood, cane chairs and bold colours define the split-level dining room, where a crowd-pleasing menu (plus blackboard specials) keeps the punters interested. The kitchen can deliver starters of creamy prawn risotto or a warm salad of Toulouse sausage and mushrooms, ahead of salmon fillet with noodles and fennel cream or confit of duck with braised red cabbage, black pudding and apple sauce. Finish with ginger sponge and custard or passion fruit tart with coconut and lime sorbet. 'Prime time' fixed-price menus offer an excellent deal and prices on the good-value wine list start at £13.50 (with a decent choice by-the-glass). Andrew Bradley recently opened a second restaurant at 46-50 Highgate, Heaton, Bradford BD9 4BE, tel: (01274) 499890.
Chef/s: Eric Paxman. **Open:** Mon to Fri L 12 to 2, Mon to Sat D 6 to 10 (5.30 to 10 Sat). **Closed:** Sun, bank hols. **Meals:** Set L £6.95 (2 courses) to £9.50, Set D £18.95 (3 courses inc wine). **Service:** not inc. **Details:** Cards accepted. 120 seats. Air-con. Separate bar. No mobile phones. Wheelchair access. Music. Children's portions. Car parking.

Dining Rooms @ Strawberry Fair
Shoppers' salvation
14-18 Westgate, Huddersfield, HD1 1NN
Tel no: (01484) 513103
Modern European | £18
Cooking score: 1

£30

On the first floor of a long-established crockery and kitchenware shop, the Dining Rooms does a great service to Huddersfield's shoppers, tourists and business people. Lunch is the main event, and the kitchen delivers the goods in a stylishly-lit setting of cream walls and high-backed leather chairs. Chicken liver parfait with Cumberland sauce or deep-fried Brie with mango and chilli salsa could precede chicken burgers with red cabbage and fennel slaw, a daily risotto or organic Shetland sea trout fillet with new potatoes and Little Gem lettuce. Open sandwiches, salads, kids' meals and great-value two-course specials also bring in the crowds, and there's crème brûlée or sticky ginger sponge for afters. Breakfast and afternoon teas do the trick at either end of the day. Chilean house wine is £10.90 (£2.20 a glass).
Chef/s: Rachel Miller. **Open:** Mon to Sat L 11.30 to 3. Breakfast and afternoon tea available. **Closed:** Sun, bank hols (exc Good Fri), 25 Dec. **Meals:** alc (main courses £7 to £10). Set L £10.75 (2 courses).
Service: not inc. **Details:** Cards accepted. 46 seats. Air-con. No mobile phones. Wheelchair access. Music. Children's portions.

Hull

Boars Nest

North Country trencherman's feast
22 Princes Avenue, Hull, HU5 3QA
Tel no: (01482) 445577
www.theboarsnesthull.com
British | £23
Cooking score: 2

The quirky porcine moniker is spot-on, given that this admirable restaurant occupies an Edwardian butcher's shop. Some of the original details still remain (take a look at the ceramic tiled walls and the meat rails high on the ceiling), although leather seats and chandeliers have been added to the mix; there's also a new outdoor area this year. The kitchen keeps faith with the local vernacular, offering trencherman platefuls with a thick North Country drawl. Wild boar brawn with home-made piccalilli is a cracking way to start, or you might prefer a dish of potted Whitby crab. Main courses up the tempo with roast Goosnargh goose liver, mash and buttered chanterelles or turbot with ham hock, cockles, amande clams and King Edward new potatoes, while Black Forest gâteau figures among the line-up of desserts. The concise wine list makes a special feature of Burgundies from Louis Jadot; elsewhere, prices start at £14.95 (£3.75 a glass).
Chef/s: Simon Rogers. **Open:** all week 12 to 2, 6.30 to 10. **Closed:** 26 Dec, 1 Jan. **Meals:** alc (main courses £12.75 to £18.50). Set L £8 (2 courses) to £10. Set D £20 (3 courses). **Service:** 10%.
Details: Cards accepted. 62 seats. 16 seats outside. Separate bar. No mobile phones. Wheelchair access. Music. Children's portions.

Ilkley

Box Tree

Contemporary French food
35-37 Church Street, Ilkley, LS29 9DR
Tel no: (01943) 608484
www.theboxtree.co.uk
Anglo-French | £50
Cooking score: 6

The Box Tree is an Ilkley institution with 40 years under its belt. After a period in the doldrums it has been given a new lease of life by Simon Gueller who 'really seems at home here'. In Gueller's hands the restaurant has a welcoming feel and his 'immaculate food' has found a willing audience. The principle focus is contemporary, cosmopolitan cooking based on a foundation of well-sourced materials. The style is appealing without being flamboyant, with well-thought-out combinations ranging from a 'fabulous' amuse-bouche of chilled pea velouté with ham foam that impressed one reporter, via roast squab pigeon with broad beans, button onions, peas, lettuce and lardons, to dessert of lemon tartlet with citrus garnish and blood orange sorbet. The prix-fixe dinner menu has been well reported this year. It runs to some three options per course: warm salad of Morteau sausage with new potatoes and poached hen's egg, followed perhaps by sirloin of beef with a fricassee of tomatoes and leeks, pomme fondant and madeira sauce, with pudding of hot raspberry soufflé with raspberry sauce. The 'traditional but good quality' Sunday lunch has impressed, too. Service is on the ball. We weren't sent the wine list, but reports suggest the choice by-the-glass is good, with bottle prices starting at £22.
Chef/s: Simon Gueller. **Open:** Fri to Sun L 12 to 2, Tue to Sat D 7 to 9.30. **Meals:** alc (mains £27 to £32). Set L £20 to £28. Set D £30. **Service:** not inc.
Details: Cards accepted. 60 seats. Air-con. No music. Wheelchair access. Music.

Farsyde

Great-value town brasserie
1-3 New Brook Street, Ilkley, LS29 8DQ
Tel no: (01943) 602030
www.thefarsyde.co.uk
Modern British | £25
Cooking score: 4

Confident brasserie cooking matches the easy-going style of Gavin Beedham's busy, bustling venue opposite Ilkley parish church. Bare boards, peachy tones and polished tables set the scene, and the kitchen stays true to its trusted formula: influences come from far and wide, ingredients are sound and the value-for-money is never in doubt. At lunchtime, local shoppers and the office crowd pack in for excellent-value wraps, bagels and light dishes that move upwards from antipasti and salads to marinated black bean pork with vegetable stir-fry and chilli jam. Dinner brings elaboration in the shape of lamb shank timbale on parsnip purée with thyme and truffle oil sauce followed by Gressingham duck breast with duck confit rösti and apple won ton. Seafood specials are also worth checking out (perhaps sea bass on a smoked salmon and sun-blushed tomato risotto with coriander oil), while satisfying desserts have featured warm pear and frangipane tart as well as jam roly-poly with custard. Prices on the short wine list start at £10.50 and just about everything is below £20.
Chef/s: Gavin Beedham. **Open:** Tue to Sat 11.30 to 2, D 6 to 10. **Closed:** Sun, Mon, 25 and 26 Dec, 1 Jan and bank hols. **Meals:** alc (main courses L £5 to £9, D £12.50 to £17.50). Set D 6 to 7.30 £13.95 (2 courses). **Service:** not inc. **Details:** Cards accepted. 82 seats. Air-con. Separate bar. Wheelchair access. Music. Children's portions.

▌Kirk Deighton

Bay Horse Inn

Putting the emphasis on local produce
Main Street, Kirk Deighton, LS22 4DZ
Tel no: (01937) 580058
Gastropub | £25
Cooking score: 3

Flagstone floors and miscellaneous furniture create a convivial drinking atmosphere, but food is the main business at this revitalized village pub just minutes from the A1. There's an increasing reliance on local and organic produce, seen in dishes like carpaccio of venison (with homemade ginger and plum chutney), rump of Dales lamb (served with provençale vegetables and rosemary-scented jus), and locally made pork sausages. Seafood is a strong suit, say fishcakes of smoked haddock and pancetta, served with organic creamed leeks, and East Coast cod and chips with home-made tartare and organic tomato sauce. Alternatives might include glazed teriyaki duck breast with pak choi, chilli and soft noodles, with strawberry shortcakes and lemon zest crème brûlée to finish. House wine is £13.50.
Chef/s: Andrew Stirzaker. **Open:** Tue to Sun L 12 to 2.15, Mon to Sat D 6 to 9.15. **Meals:** alc (main courses £14.50 to £16.50). Set menu £13.75 (2 courses). **Service:** not inc. **Details:** Cards accepted. 55 seats. 20 seats outside. Separate bar. Wheelchair access. Children's portions. Car parking.

▌Leeds

Anthony's at Flannels

Anthony Flinn does urban cool
68-78 Vicar Lane, Leeds, LS1 7JH
Tel no: (0113) 2428732
www.anthonysatflannels.co.uk
Modern European | £18
Cooking score: 4

A window table under the beams on the spacious top floor of Flannels clothing store is one of the best seats in town for brunch, lunch, or afternoon tea. White walls, starched linen and changing exhibitions of contemporary art underline the classy feel. It's a satellite of Anthony's flagship restaurant in Boar Lane and smart as you like, but don't expect foams and air, or unnecessary graces. The watchword is a simpler style of modernism, almost minimalism with some dishes. A crisply executed three-course lunch featured pistachio duck terrine served with pickled beetroot and a garlic croûton, followed by a fillet of sea bream, crushed potatoes and fennel, all tied up by a more substantial and near-perfect bread-and-butter pudding. Wines start at £3.99 a glass, £13.85 for a bottle of Chilean Santa Rita and climb to £45.95 for Puligny Montrachet. An enterprising beer list too.

Chef/s: Mark Brankin. **Open:** Tue to Sun 10 to 6, Fri to Sat D 6 to 11. **Closed:** Mon, 25 Dec. **Meals:** Set L £18.25. **Service:** 10%. **Details:** Cards accepted. 60 seats. Air-con. Separate bar. Wheelchair access. Music. Children's portions.

Anthony's Restaurant

Avant-garde excellence
19 Boar Lane, Leeds, LS1 6EA
Tel no: (0113) 2455922
www.anthonysrestaurant.co.uk
Modern European | £42
Cooking score: 7

The Anthony Flinn revolution continues apace at this, the original address and still the flagship of what has become a little empire, along with Anthony's at Flannels (see entry above) and now a patisserie serving what are cutely referred to as 'light luncheons'. While some have bemoaned the neutral décor at Boar Lane, others have hailed it as film-set glamorous, the sophisticated monochrome offset by the odd flash of colour from fresh flowers. Clearly the idea is not to distract attention from the cooking, which is stunningly original. A stint at El Bulli in Catalonia, Mission Central for the molecular gastronomy movement, has inspired Anthony Flinn to think outside the culinary box,

creating a signature cuisine all his own. The menu keeps it short, though hardly simple, with four choices at each stage. Flavour contrasts collide productively, helped together with new gentle cooking techniques, as in a first course of poached quail with pea sorbet, cocoa and morels, or another that underscores the richness of tuna, a seared chunk and wafer-thin carpaccio, with ox tongue and horseradish. There is more to the juxtapositions than just surrealism, though, as tastes and textures counterpoint each other, entering into fascinating dialogues. Roast sea bass makes friends with pig trotter in the form of a biscuit, with coconut to ratify the alliance, while red mullet might appear with a crab sandwich and pineapple and tarragon jelly. Odd bits of creatures turn up – lamb belly, cod cheeks – and desserts introduce a cavalcade of vegetables, just when you thought you had eaten up all your greens. A cucumber granita accompanies apple crème brûlée, while a liquorice chiboust arrives with beetroot sorbet and carrot caramel. Presentations are as singular as the food demands, with a place for everything on the plate and everything in its place, surrounded with splops and streaks of sauces and dressings. It's an experience. The shortish but excellent wine list is arranged by flavour profile (much the best recourse under the circumstances). Dampt Chablis, Viña Salceda Rioja, McRae Wood Shiraz from Australia: growers are top-quality, but undoubtedly come at a price. House champagne is Veuve Clicquot, but why more wines aren't available by-the-glass remains a mystery. Bottle prices start at £14.10 for Santa Rita Sauvignon from Chile.

Chef/s: Anthony James Flinn. **Open:** Tue to Sat L 12 to 2, D 7 to 9.30. **Closed:** Sun, Mon, Christmas to New Year. **Meals:** Set L £23.95 to £60, Set D £42 to £60. **Service:** not inc. **Details:** Cards accepted. 40 seats. Air-con. Separate bar. Wheelchair access. Music. Children allowed.

Brasserie Forty Four
If it ain't broke...
44 The Calls, Leeds, LS2 7EW
Tel no: (0113) 2343232
www.brasserie44.com
Modern European | £30
Cooking score: 3

🍾 🛏️

'It's business as usual at Brasserie Forty Four' notes a reporter, 'which might constitute a fault were the place not so good at what it does'. Just as a brasserie should be, it is speedy and uncomplicated without being rushed and dull, with Serrano ham with a pea and mint mousse a prime example of what this place excels at – a simple dish that works because it's been given just enough of a twist to stop it looking too plain, but not so much that it ties up the kitchen. Good ingredients play a big part too. Bigger dishes like seared venison with buttered spinach are put together well, and deliver straightforward flavours. In the words of one regular 'they don't try to be anything they're not'. Add in a wine list that starts at £12.25 and features a big choice of bubbly, and you've got a solid offering.
Chef/s: Antoine Quentin. **Open:** Mon to Fri L 12 to 2 (1 to 3 Sat), Mon to Sat D 6 to 10 (10.30 Fri and Sat). **Closed:** bank hols. **Meals:** alc (main courses £9.50 to £16.50). **Service:** 10% optional. **Details:** Cards accepted. 96 seats. 24 seats outside. Air-con. Separate bar. Wheelchair access. Music. Children's portions.

Fourth Floor Café and Bar
Leeds' best-kept secret
Harvey Nichols, 107-111 Briggate, Leeds, LS1 6AZ
Tel no: (0113) 2048000
www.harveynichols.com
Modern British | £34
Cooking score: 4

🍾

Despite being one of the city's best and most reliable restaurants, the fact that this light, elegant and thoroughly inviting space is at the top of a shop means it is often overlooked. Given the quality of Richard Walton-Allen's food, this is something of a crime. Look over the counter and you may notice Walton-Allen seems to be found in the kitchen a little less these days (he's now executive chef), but keep your eye on your plate and you won't think anything's changed – even when he's not at the helm his team do an impressive job of maintaining impeccable standards. Dishes continue to find a way of being locally sourced and sensible, as well as suitably innovative and clever – this is Harvey Nichols after all – so you'll find classics with style like a very high quality Lishman's rib-eye steak, chargrilled with baby leeks, alongside colourful exotica such as spicy scallops with Thai greens and a blood orange dressing. The wine list, starting at £16, is not the city's longest, but comes close to being its best – particularly if you take into account the choice in the wine shop, which you can sometimes bring into the restaurant.
Chef/s: Richard Walton-Allen. **Open:** Mon to Wed L 10 to 6, Thu to Sat D 10 to 10. **Closed:** 25 and 26 Dec, 1 Jan Easter Sun. **Meals:** alc (main courses £11.50 to £20). Set L £15 (2 course) to £18, Set D £16.50 (2 courses) to £19.50. Bar menu available Mon to Sat. **Service:** 10%. **Details:** Cards accepted. 80 seats. 15 seats outside. Air-con. Separate bar. No mobile phones. Wheelchair access. Music. Children's portions.

No. 3 York Place
Still one of the city's best
3 York Place, Leeds, LS1 2DR
Tel no: (0113) 2459922
www.no3yorkplace.co.uk
Modern European | £25
Cooking score: 4

V

Last year was all about whether or not No. 3 York Place would survive the change from high-end fine dining to a more accessible brasserie style. Thankfully, the brilliant combination of chef Martel Smith and front-of-house manager Denis Lefrancq ensured it did. The heavy table linen, amuse-bouche and handmade petits fours were shown the door and the wine list was carefully pruned but, crucially, the standard of the food remained as high as ever. Service actually improved, becoming far warmer. Add a substantial price drop, and it was a great result for Leeds. This year, though little appears immediately different, an even bigger change has taken place as Smith has moved on to the Dawnay Arms (see entry), though he remains part-owner, and his protégé Simon Silver has taken over. The style of the food is uncannily unchanged, and bold but sophisticated dishes like a ham hock and pea risotto show great ability. There are some wobbly areas though – ill-conceived accompaniments, too much sauce at times – so it may take some time for Silver to reach Smith's impressive consistency. House wine is £14.

Chef/s: Simon Silver. **Open:** Mon to Fri L 12 to 2, Mon to Sat D 6.30 to 10. **Closed:** 25 Dec to 3 Jan, bank hols. **Meals:** alc (main courses £11 to £18). Set L and early D Mon to Fri £14.50 (2 courses) to £18.50. **Service:** 10% optional. **Details:** Cards accepted. 46 seats. Air-con. Separate bar. Wheelchair access. Music. Children's portions.

Salvo's
A crowd-pulling Leeds institution
115 Otley Road, Headingley, Leeds, LS6 3PX
Tel no: (0113) 2755017
www.salvos.co.uk
Italian | £24
Cooking score: 2
£5 OFF **V** £30

Headingley, a vibrant village just outside Leeds city centre, is best known for its cricket ground, but its real character lies in its melting pot of students and friendly locals. They all know Salvo's and this 30-year-old Italian restaurant sits at the heart of the community. Waiting times can be over two hours and it speaks volumes that people will still hang out in the bar while nearby restaurants remain half empty. And it's more than just pizzas – although you would never call it just 'pizza' after eating one. Mixed shellfish grill, wild mushroom risotto and slow-roast lamb appear on the menu alongside specials such as chargrilled polenta with Gorgonzola, and

confit of duck leg with roast Sicilian fennel sausage and borlotti beans. Though the main restaurant is the breadwinner, sister venue La Salumeria, a deli-café just a few doors down (107 Otley Road), shows more daring and passion on its fixed menus than the staples of its sibling (perhaps because it gets the personal attention of Gip and John Dammone, who run this family business). This place is one to watch: reports please.

Chef/s: Jamie Raby. **Open:** Mon to Sat L 12 to 2, Mon to Thu D 6 to 10.30, Fri to Sat D 5.30 to 11. **Closed:** Sun. **Meals:** alc (main courses £11.95 to £17.95). Set L £8.95 (2 courses), early bird D (to 7pm) £14.50. **Service:** not inc. **Details:** Cards accepted. 65 seats. 20 seats outside. Air-con. Separate bar. Wheelchair access. Music. Children's portions.

Sous le Nez en Ville
Subterranean jewel
The Basement, Quebec House, Quebec Street, Leeds, LS1 2HA
Tel no: (0113) 2440108
www.souslenez.com
Modern European | £28
Cooking score: 4
£5 OFF £30

The subterreanean location in the centre of Leeds explains the name. Clever use of lighting softens the impression created by dark wood, and white walls and well-chosen pictures do the rest. It's an enjoyable setting in which to drink some seriously good wines and, for those with an appetite, to eat some highly proficient and straightforward food. Menus draw on the global kitchen and manage to encompass tempura-battered pollack, Thai salmon fishcake, côte de boeuf with béarnaise, strawberry and blueberry pannacotta, and treacle tart with clotted cream, all without missing a beat. Main courses in particular bring out the urge for showmanship, perhaps matching herb-crusted halibut with pancetta, peas, baby Gem and lemon butter, or chargrilling a venison steak to a perfect contrast of black on the outside and pink within, and setting it alongside a potato galette, red onion marmalade and a sauce of lavender and elderflower. The cheeses, both French and English, are treated with respect, while desserts are a dairy-lover's treat, with a traditional crème brûlée being the mainstream alternative to roast peaches with white chocolate ice cream and praline crisps. The wine list is one of the glories of Leeds. It combs the world thoroughly for the most exciting growers and, by and large, prices do not break free of sensible restraint. Italy is strong, Australia and New Zealand are well-served, and the Burgundy and Rhône selections should make grown men weep at the agony of choosing. House selections start from £13.95 for French vins de table.

Chef/s: Andy Carter. **Open:** Mon to Sat L 12 to 2.30 (Sat 2), D 6 to 10 (Sat 10.30). **Meals:** alc (main courses £10.50 to £26.50). Set L Sat £22.95, Set D Mon to Sat 6 to 7.30 (Sat 7) £22.95 (inc wine). **Service:** not inc. **Details:** Cards accepted. 80 seats. Air-con. Separate bar. No mobile phones. Music.

ALSO RECOMMENDED

▲ Hansa's

72-74 North Street, Leeds, LS2 7PN
Tel no: (0113) 2444408
www.hansasrestaurant.com
Vegetarian/Gujurati

Hansa's continues to lead the way in Leeds, not just as a proponent of the city's thriving ethnic populous, but as trailblazers who have proven time and time again that vegetarian food doesn't have to be 'just for vegetarians'. Hansa Dabhi, still frequently to be found in the kitchen, produces Indian food typical of the Gujarati region, making this a profoundly more interesting experience than eating in any of the city's more predictable curry houses. Options include whole Kenyan aubergines, stuffed with their own spicy masala and coarsely ground peanuts (£6.50) or a rice pancake filled with spiced veg, served with sambhar sauce and coconut chutney (£5.50). Flavours are always enhanced by spicing rather than drowned in heat, and as pulses feature prominently, even hard-headed carnivores should leave feeling sated.

▲ Olive Tree

Oaklands, 55 Rodley Lane, Rodley or 74-76 Otley Rd, Headingley or 188 Harrogate Rd, Chapel Allerton, Leeds, LS13 1NG
Tel no: (0113) 2569283
www.olivetreegreekrestaurant.co.uk
Greek/Cypriot

'Very Greek, it's like going back on holiday', notes a reporter, and there's no denying the personable, friendly atmosphere of George Psarias's mini chain of restaurants – in Rodley, Headingley and Chapel Allerton – or the helpfulness of the staff. Meze is well reported, from a refreshing tsatsiki to tyropitakia (little cheese pies), while the wide selection of main courses include a good lamb moussaka or kleftico (lamb cooked slowly in the oven with oregano and garlic) and spanakopitta (spinach, feta cheese and spring onion in layers of filo pastry). Prices are reasonable, with lunch sets starting at £7.95 (2 courses) and three course early bird dinners for £13.95. House wine is £13.45. Open all week.

▲ Room

Bond House, The Bourse Courtyard, Boar Lane, Leeds, LS1 5DE
Tel no: (0113) 2426161
www.roomrestaurants.com
Modern British

Room has seen too many changes of head chef recently, but Greg Lewis, who took over in May 2008, has worked under the deservedly acclaimed Jeff Baker at Leeds' much-missed Pool Court and the signs are that the restaurant will settle down to a much-needed period of stability. Key characteristics remain unchanged – menu items sound kitsch or even naff, but are in fact cleverly reinterpreted, so a 'scotch egg' might be a stack of haggis and black pudding topped by a deep-fried egg yolk or 'Black Forest gâteau' may become a fine chocolate torte with a cherry sorbet to the side. The wine list is short but full of surprises.

Restaurant bugbears

All too often, a visit to a restaurant is memorable for all the wrong reasons. Here's our list of some of our readers' most common bugbears this year.

Out of season

The age of locally sourced produce has seen many restaurateurs turn biographers of what's on your plate. Whilst few doubt the worthiness of their cause, some have found restaurants to over-insist their ingredients' credentials; having a waiter recount your salmon's family tree when you're trying to eat it can be off-putting.

Three's-a-crowd

A restaurant can hardly be held accountable for the behaviour of your fellow customers - be they mobile phone orators or screaming children - but having tables bunched together can leave you having had the wrong sort of intimate evening.

Lost in translation

Although many relish an authentically French dining experience, few customers hope to be confronted by a menu that doubles as a translation exercise.

Delayed dishes

Whilst delays in the kitchen are an inevitable part of any operation, few things can kill a meal like watching your dining companions tucking into their desserts when you've barely begun your starter. A good restaurant should be capable of synchronising their service.

Stealth charges

Many restaurants offer bread, bruschetta or similar nibbles as soon as you are seated, often without asking their customers. Although this gesture of hospitality is often genuine, many restaurants add these items to your bill, so remember to ask first.

Tip of the iceberg?

Like it or not, it's customary to add a 12.5% service charge to your bill, but many restaurants practise the cheeky tactic of suggesting a second tip. Although generally shared between the service staff, it's not unheard of for tips to find their way into the management's pockets, so don't be afraid to specify who you want the tip to go to.

Well-seasoned

Some readers can't abide the modish practice of open salt and pepper bowls on the table. Who knows whose fingers have been there?

At ease

We regularly get complaints about uncomfortable seating in restaurants. This is often a ploy to ensure that you vacate your table all the sooner.

▲ Sukhothai

8 Regent Street, Chapel Allerton, Leeds, LS7 4PE
Tel no: (0113) 2370141
www.thaifood4u.co.uk
Thai

Expansion continues for this much-loved Thai restaurant. Once just a tiny café down a side street, it's now the pride of Chapel Allerton, a suitably trendy village just a few miles from Leeds city centre. Adjoining businesses were bought up to make space for more diners, but it's clear an increase in quantity has not lead to a decrease in quality, with reports attesting to consistently excellent service and food. No doubt the friendly atmosphere counts for a lot, but it's the food that rules. There are savvy set menus for the beginners, while the copious à la carte gives the adventurous plenty of unusual dishes to enjoy too, like chicken and duck liver, fried with garlic, black pepper, lime leaves, oyster sauce, lemongrass, onion and fresh chilli (a bargain at £8.50). Closed Mon L.

■ Leyburn

Sandpiper Inn

Stylishly rustic Yorkshire local
Market Place, Leyburn, DL8 5AT
Tel no: (01969) 622206
www.sandpiperinn.co.uk
Gastropub | £26
Cooking score: 3

£30

A fixture of Leyburn's market place for more than three centuries, the Sandpiper Inn morphed into its present form some 30 years ago and is now a serious local contender in the gastropub food stakes. The original bar still has a homespun Yorkshire feel with its cosy alcoves and blazing fire, while the green-walled dining room exudes more than a touch of stylish rusticity. Eat where you like from a short daily menu that takes its cue from carefully sourced North Country produce, although Jonathan Harrison also looks to Europe and beyond for ideas: smoked salmon and crab salad is spiked with mango salsa,

Whitby pollock is wrapped in Parma ham, while pressed shoulder of Wensleydale lamb might be served with dauphinoise potatoes and ratatouille. Sandwiches, fish and chips and 'pub grub' standards are also offered most lunchtimes. Around 40 wines provide a pleasant match for the food; prices start at £13.50.
Chef/s: Jonathan Harrison. **Open:** Tue to Sun L 12 to 2.30, D 6.30 to 9 (7 to 9 Sun). **Closed:** Mon. **Meals:** alc (main courses £10 to £17). **Service:** not inc. **Details:** Cards accepted. 40 seats. 24 seats outside. Separate bar. Music. Children's portions.

■ Lund

Wellington Inn

Top-drawer local gastropub
19 The Green, Lund, YO25 9TE
Tel no: (01377) 217294
Gastropub | £30
Cooking score: 3
â

Hard by the green and the war memorial in an out-of-the-way Wolds village, the Wellington Inn has carved out a formidable local reputation, thanks to the efforts of Russell and Sarah Jeffrey. Their candlelit restaurant is only open for dinner five nights a week, but this is a quality set up: there's nothing too outlandish about the food, and Sarah is a dab hand at refashioning well-tried classic ideas. A warm goats' cheese and chilli cheesecake is partnered by red pepper coulis and balsamic syrup, while deep-fried fish goujons are perked up with potato and caper salad and chive oil. To follow, slow-braised daube of Gloucester Old Spot pork is paired with 'devils on horseback', Caesar salad accompanies rib-eye steak, and confit shoulder of lamb is dressed with lentil jus. Desserts keep it simple with the likes of citrus posset, rum-baked bananas or lemon and hazelnut sponge pudding. Pub dishes and real ales are served in the original beamed and flagstoned bar. The enterprising wine list is a smart selection of personally-chosen bottles with some particularly good stuff from South Africa. House vins de pays are £13.75 (£3.50 a glass).

Chef/s: Sarah Jeffrey. **Open:** Tue to Sat D 7 to 9. **Closed:** Sun, Mon. **Meals:** alc (main courses £15 to £20). Bar menu available. **Service:** not inc. **Details:** Cards accepted. 40 seats. Separate bar. No mobile phones. Music. Children allowed. Car parking.

▌Marsden

Olive Branch

Ambitious pub with rooms
Manchester Road, Marsden, HD7 6LU
Tel no: (01484) 844487
www.olivebranch.uk.com
Modern British | £30
Cooking score: 4

Set in a sheltered valley on the edge of Marsden Moor Estate to the west of Huddersfield, the Olive Branch has come along way since it served as a pit-stop and refreshment point for local hikers. These days it's a fully grown 'restaurant and rooms' delivering imaginative food that aims to satisfy all palates and preferences. Lengthy menus are dotted around the place, and visitors can eat in the bar or in the modern restaurant extension at the back; either way, expect a generous mix of North Country pub staples and more ambitious ideas with some clever touches. Starters might find baked Whitby crab with mustard and Reblochon cheese gratin alongside Parma ham with caramelised shallots and champagne dressing, while main courses cover everything from steak and ale pie with a suet crust to line-caught cod with curried mussels and tomato concasse or organic salmon fillet with lobster mash, red wine and veal jus. Desserts range from tarts and cheesecake to melting chocolate pot with Kahlua ice cream and strawberries. The wine list is a serious slate with a broad sweep of grape varieties and styles; house selections start at £13.95 (£3.50 a glass).
Chef/s: Paul Kewley. **Open:** Wed to Fri L 12 to 1.45, Mon to Sat D 6.30 to 9.30, Sun 1 to 8.30. **Closed:** 26 Dec, first 2 weeks Jan. **Meals:** alc (main courses £14 to £20). Set L £11.95. Set D £15.95 (2 courses) to

£18.95. **Service:** not inc. **Details:** Cards accepted. 65 seats. 12 seats outside. Separate bar. Wheelchair access. Music. Children's portions. Car parking.

▌Marton

Appletree

Ever-evolving moorland inn
Marton, YO62 6RD
Tel no: (01751) 431457
www.appletreeinn.co.uk
Modern British | £27
Cooking score: 3

Melanie and TJ Drew have been hosting proceedings at this stone inn close to the fringes of the North York Moors since 2001, and are forever making improvements to the place: their latest project is a wine shop and bespoke deli attached to the pub. TJ now works solo in the kitchen, sending out a mix of posh pub classics and contemporary restaurant dishes based on North Country produce. Braised brisket of Marton beef might be seen in company with steamed fillet of hake, Avruga caviar, crushed potatoes and creamed spinach, while seasonal add-ons could extend to – say – roast loin of hare with sloe gin sauce. Kick off with smoked Ribblesdale goats' cheese soufflé, and wind down with Yorkshire treacle tart or Marton's 'black and blue' take on Eton mess, involving lavender meringue, blackberries and blueberries. To drink, there are real ales on tap, plus a well-considered assortment of global wines from £13 (£4 a glass).
Chef/s: T.J. Drew. **Open:** Wed to Sun L 12 to 2, D 6 to 9.30 (6.30 to 9 Sun). **Closed:** Mon, Tue, 25 Dec and 2 weeks Jan. **Meals:** alc (main courses £11.50 to £19).

Average price

The average price listed in main-entry reviews denotes the price of a three-course meal, without wine.

Service: not inc. **Details:** Cards accepted. 26 seats. 6 seats outside. Separate bar. Wheelchair access. Music. Children's portions. Car parking.

Masham

Swinton Park, Samuel's

Fine dining in a stunning country manor
Masham, HG4 4JH
Tel no: (01765) 680900
www.swintonpark.com
Modern British | £42
New Chef

£5 OFF ⊨ V

Swinton Park is a fine example of Yorkshire grandeur, with extensive grounds supplying seasonal game, while a walled garden produces vegetables and herbs – at four acres it's the largest hotel kitchen garden in the country. Within, it's almost absurdly grand: a pre-dinner lounge has ceilings that are higher than the length of the room. But despite all this, the staff create a welcoming atmosphere that's anything but 'uptight'. Sensibly, Simon Crannage makes good use of what's closest to hand, so his menu follows the seasons with starters such as a sphere of pork and barley with turnip fondant, or a celery velouté with Yorkshire Blue won ton, showing creative use of traditional ingredients. That theme is followed through to main courses, perhaps a well reported roast chump of local lamb served with its kidney alongside sage, pancetta, corn purée, winter greens and a devilled lamb sauce. Indulgent and showy desserts include a sharp lemon mousse with sherbet and liquorice ice cream. The large wine list starts at £19.

Chef/s: Simon Crannage. **Open:** all week L 12.30 to 2, D 7 to 10. **Meals:** Set menus £42 and £52. **Service:** not inc. **Details:** Cards accepted. 60 seats. Separate bar. Wheelchair access. Music. Car parking.

Vennell's Restaurant

Highly polished modern British
7 Silver Street, Masham, HG4 4DX
Tel no: (01765) 689000
www.vennellsrestaurant.co.uk
Modern British | £27
Cooking score: 5

 £5 OFF £30

Look for the aubergine-hued frontage near Masham's market square. The interior is muted and beige, and the layout appeals for the generous amount of space between tables. The consensus is firmly that Jon Vennell's cooking is worth the trip, a deceptively simple, modern British style, but with a high degree of polish, from both culinary technique and fine ingredients. A slice of ham shank terrine comes with 'eggy brioche' and onion chutney, or lobster might appear in ravioli with lardons, pine nuts and a lobster velouté. Those in the market for fish at main could well enjoy home-smoked haddock in the modern classic fashion, with spinach, crushed potato and a poached egg, while meatier appetites will gravitate to a pork dish combining the roasted belly and sautéed tongue with apple, braised shallots, mash, and mustard sauce. A serving of five Yorkshire cheeses, from Braffords goat to Buffalo Blue, is the savoury alternative to comforting desserts such as passion-fruit posset with stewed cherries or chocolate bread-and-butter pudding with white chocolate sorbet. Pick a grape variety or well-known blend, and look it up on the helpfully-arranged and annotated wine list. Growers are sound, especially in the New World. House wines start at £13.75.

Chef/s: Jon Vennell. **Open:** Sun L 12 to 2, Tue to Sat D 7.15 to 9.30. **Closed:** bank hols. **Meals:** Set D £15 (Tue to Thu winter only) to £26.50. **Service:** not inc. **Details:** Cards accepted. 30 seats. Separate bar. No mobile phones. Music.

Newton on Ouse

★NEW ENTRY★

Dawnay Arms
High-class pub food in riverside location
Newton on Ouse, YO30 2BR
Tel no: (01347) 848345
www.thedawnayatnewton.co.uk
Gastropub | £25
Cooking score: 4

After a career of smart, high-end restaurant cooking (No. 3 York Place, see entry), Martel Smith has switched to high-end pub grub in a cream-washed hostelry in a quiet riverside village north of York. Dishes like sausage and mash and steak and kidney pie set a deceptively simple baseline. Stepping up, a starter of prawn and saffron risotto is topped with perfectly timed queen scallops, and a beautifully crisp, spicy crab fishcake comes with an exquisitely balanced sweet and sour sauce. Mains of salmon with a parsley risotto and halibut on the smoothest of mash prove equally rewarding. Desserts are a familiar line-up from the school of crème brûlée and bread-and-butter pudding, but beautifully done. The bar is semi-traditional, with clunky raw wood tables paired with old pews, big mirrors and a log fire. By contrast the dining room is sunny and contemporary with big-window views to the river. The wine list starts at £14.50 for Chilean Merlot and Sauvignon Blanc, rising to £38.50 for New Zealand Chardonnay.
Chef/s: Martel Smith. **Open:** Tue to Sat L 12 to 2.30, D 6 to 9.30, Sun L 12 to 6. **Closed:** 1 to 10 Jan. **Meals:** alc (main courses £9.95 to £15.95). Set D £12 (2 courses) to £15. **Service:** not inc. **Details:** Cards accepted. 55 seats. 40 seats outside. Separate bar. Wheelchair access. Music. Children's portions. Car parking.

Osmotherley

Golden Lion
Honest food and traditional virtues
6 West End, Osmotherley, DL6 3AA
Tel no: (01609) 883526
www.goldenlionosmotherley.co.uk
European | £21
Cooking score: 3

Sincere Yorkshire hospitality and traditional virtues set the tone in the Wright family's unpretentious pub-with-rooms on the fringes of the North York Moors National Park. The owners are constantly improving the place, which essentially comprises an open-plan beamed room with whitewashed walls, a peat fire and dark wood pews.
Blackboards advertise the day's specials and the regular menu is a mix of honest, unaffected dishes based on shrewdly sourced local produce. For openers, you might be offered grilled sardines in olive oil or goats' cheese and red pepper terrine, while main courses might feature anything from cod and chips or home-made lamb burgers with mint jelly to salmon with basil cream sauce and calf's liver with mash and garlic cabbage. To finish, there are tried-and-tested favourites such as bread-and-butter pudding or poached pear with chocolate sauce. Three dozen international wines offer sound drinking from £14.95.
Chef/s: Chris Wright, Judy Wright and Sam Hind. **Open:** Wed to Sun L 12 to 2, all week D 6 to 9. **Closed:** 25 Dec. **Meals:** alc (main courses £8 to £14.50). **Service:** not inc. **Details:** Cards accepted. 95 seats. 44 seats outside. Wheelchair access. Music. Children's portions.

▌Ramsgill

Yorke Arms

Unaffected Yorkshire class
Ramsgill, HG3 5RL
Tel no: (01423) 755243
www.yorke-arms.co.uk
Modern British | £40
Cooking score: 6

£5 OFF 🍷 🛏

Visitors adore the 'picture perfect' setting and relaxed mood that pervades this creeper-clad coaching inn and shooting lodge overlooking Ramsgill village green. Frances and Gerald Atkins have imbued the place with class and an air of civilised charm: log fires blaze in the bar and lovely antique furnishings fill the dining room. The kitchen looks to its locality for inspiration, and Frances Atkins' style is a confident blend of classic thinking with sure technique and a feel for ingredients. The results, according to one correspondent, are 'always original.' Local lamb is a star turn (this is Nidderdale, after all), and Frances might celebrate it with a combo of herb-crusted loin, pastry and kidney pointed up with rosemary and madeira. The moors also provide hare and venison (perhaps served with black pudding, juniper, wild mushrooms and leek velouté), while Dales mutton could appear in company with beans, cavolo nero and baked onion skins. Elsewhere, fish from the coast makes an impact, whether it's ravioli of langoustine with chervil root, Whitby crab and Parma ham or truffled North Sea turbot with scallops and artichokes. There are homespun North Country ideas, too (Yorkshire potted beef and ham hock terrine, for example), while desserts aim for worldly sophistication in the shape of pear feuilleté with cardamom brûlée and camomile ice cream or orange and paw-paw terrine with pistachio and fennel biscotti. The wine list has its heart in France, although it provides an auspicious choice from around the globe. Beyond the vintage Bordeaux and Burgundies there are ample treasures from Australia and South Africa, plus a decent choice of half-bottles. Prices start at £14 (£3.75 a glass).

Chef/s: Frances Atkins. **Open:** all week L 12 to 2, Mon to Sat D 7 to 9. **Meals:** alc (main courses £17.50 to £26). Set L £25 to £32. Set D £65 (6 courses). **Service:** not inc. **Details:** Cards accepted. 50 seats. 20 seats outside. Separate bar. Music. Car parking.

▌Richmond

ALSO RECOMMENDED
▲ Charles Bathurst Inn

Arkengarthdale, Richmond, DL11 6EN
Tel no: (01748) 884567
www.cbinn.co.uk
Gastropub

Known locally as the 'CB', this stone hostelry has gradually evolved from eighteenth-century Dales watering hole to a sprawling destination inn complete with a modern wing of bedrooms. The day's menu (written on an imposing mirror) pleases hikers as well as foodies with its local loyalties and global outlook. Typical dishes might include home-made black pudding with tomato fondue and seared queen scallops (£6.25), Swaledale lamb shank with mixed beans (£12) and pear frangipane with lemon and honey crème fraîche ice cream (£5.25). House wine is £12.95 (£3.25 a glass). Open all week.

▌Ripley

The Boar's Head Hotel

Antiquity and culinary flair
Ripley, HG3 3AY
Tel no: (01423) 771888
www.boarsheadripley.co.uk
British | £37
Cooking score: 3

🍷 🛏

Ripley, as with most villages north of Harrogate, is an idyllic place that somehow creates the impression you've travelled back to the sixteenth century. The Boar's Head, set within the grounds of the beautiful 700-year-old Ripley Castle, does nothing to dispel this.

Even inside, the effect continues, with charmingly wonky floors, antiques and ancient oil paintings hanging on dark red walls in the restaurant. Comforting as this is, the menu is welcome proof that tradition does not hold sway in the kitchen. Duck, for example, comes as a series of immaculate 'delicacies' (smoked breast, pâté, a dark terrine), roast saddle of lamb consists of pink cuts atop a roll of belly-like meat, buttery cabbage and wild mushrooms, while rhubarb is a perfect soufflé with crème fraîche ice cream. Ripley Castle's Lady Ingilby is famous for 'interfering' in menu development – long may that continue. Lord Ingilby contents himself with putting together the extensive and pleasantly surprising wine list with equally good results.

Chef/s: Marc Guibert. **Open:** all week 12 to 2, 7 to 9 (9.30 Fri and Sat). **Meals:** Bistro: alc (main courses £9.95 to £36). Restaurant: Set D £35 to £39.50. **Details:** Cards accepted. 60 seats. Separate bar. Wheelchair access. Music. Children's portions. Car parking.

Ripon

Old Deanery

Inventive food in a gorgeous setting
Minster Road, Ripon, HG4 1QS
Tel no: (01765) 600003
www.theolddeanery.co.uk
Modern British | £38
Cooking score: 2

 £5 OFF 🍴 V

The 'most perfect setting', hard by Ripon Cathedral, is one reason why visitors are full of praise for this ever-so-comfortable, relaxed and calming restaurant. The lovely listed Georgian building has been restored and redesigned in sleek contemporary style, with polished floorboards, chandeliers and high-backed leather chairs blending seamlessly with well-preserved original features. True to form, the food follows suit. Up-to-the-minute flavours and vivid ideas point up much of the menu: rabbit and truffle terrine is accompanied by pickled wild mushrooms, pan-fried sea bass comes with lobster risotto

and desserts offer anything from rice pudding to hazelnut parfait with mandarin sorbet. Lunch brings heartier stuff in the shape of fish soup with rouille, ox liver and mash or chicken Caesar salad, while daytime snacks are served in the bar (which has been moved to the front of the building). There's also a fabulous garden at the back for al fresco imbibing. Wine prices start at £14.50 (£3.25 a glass).

Chef/s: Barrie Higginbotham. **Open:** all week L 12 to 2 (3 Sun), Mon to Sat D 6.30 to 9.30. **Closed:** 25 Dec. **Meals:** Set L £12.50 (2 courses) to £18.75, Set D £22.50 (2 courses) to £26.50. **Service:** not inc. **Details:** Cards accepted. 60 seats. 30 seats outside. Separate bar. Wheelchair access. Music. Children's portions. Car parking.

Ripponden

★NEW ENTRY★

El Gato Negro Tapas

Proper tapas in the lush Calder Valley
1 Oldham Road, Ripponden, HX6 4DN
Tel no: (01422) 823070
www.elgatonegrotapas.com
Spanish | £18
Cooking score: 5

V

There's a very cheery vibe in this funky restaurant on the main road through Ripponden. You might think the lush Calder Valley an incongruous setting for proper tapas made by a Yorkshireman and fronted by a Welshman, but chef Simon Shaw and Chris Williams have transformed this old boozer into a buzzing, sophisticated eaterie. Regular jaunts to Barcelona ensure quality, and enthusiasm for the food is unanimous – 'better than I have eaten in cities like Barcelona and Madrid' observes more than one contributor. Spinach and mushroom croquetas are soft and flavoursome, Syrian lentils fragrant and punchy with paprika, while meatballs are gamey and smooth, the accompanying frittata sauce slurped up nicely with the hoppy, sour dough bread studded with caraway. Two dishes, though, stand out: jamón Iberico, and baby roast chicken with lemon, garlic and

paprika. Puddings are a more local affair – well, you can't get more Yorkshire than sticky toffee pudding with Timothy Taylor Landlord ice cream. A reasonably priced selection of wines, carefully matched to the food, start at £11.50, with six by-the-glass from £3.
Chef/s: Simon Shaw. **Open:** Sat L 12 to 2, Wed to Sat D 6 to 10, Sun 12.30 to 6.30. **Closed:** Mon, tue, Christmas. **Meals:** Set menu for two with wine £35. **Service:** not inc. **Details:** Cards accepted. 35 seats. Music. Children's portions.

▋Scarborough

Lanterna
Proud to be North Italian
33 Queen Street, Scarborough, YO11 1HQ
Tel no: (01723) 363616
www.lanterna-ristorante.co.uk
Italian | £35
Cooking score: 3

V

The prized white truffle of Piedmont holds a place of honour in Giorgio and Rachel Alessio's reassuringly familiar fixture of the Scarborough scene. Here is a kitchen that fully respects ingredients, and the owners import much from their native region, as well as plundering Yorkshire's generous larder. Fish might include roast sea trout with herbs and warm horseradish sauce and there is always home-made pasta on offer (perhaps spaghetti with velvet crab) plus regional ideas such as sanguinaccio (black pudding with polenta and caramelised onions) or fillet steak with a roasted pepper and Gorgonzola cheese sauce. Crema di ortiche (nettle cream) is Giorgio's signature dessert and he often comes out of his kitchen to whisk up zabaglione 'a la lampada'. The wine list is a connoisseur's tour through the Italian regions, with special attention paid to bottles imported from Piedmont (including Barolo dating back to 1990). House wine is £12.50.
Chef/s: Giorgio Alessio. **Open:** Mon to Sat D only 7 to 9.30. **Closed:** Sun, 24 and 25 Dec, 2 weeks end Oct, 2 weeks Jan. **Meals:** alc (main courses £16 to £45). **Service:** not inc. **Details:** Cards accepted. 30 seats. Air-con. No music. No mobile phones. Wheelchair access. Music. Children's portions.

▋Sheffield

Artisan and Catch
Terrific-value Sheffield double-header
32-34 Sandygate Road, Crosspool, Sheffield, S10 5RY
Tel no: (0114) 266 6096
www.artisancatch.com
Modern European/Seafood | £25
Cooking score: 5

The Sheffield veteran formerly known as Thyme is now two very different, voguish metropolitan venues under one roof, thanks to local trailblazer Richard Smith. Artisan is the animated 'bistrot de luxe' on the ground floor, which wins friends thanks to its 'terrific ingredients and amazing value.' The kitchen makes much of its hand-crafted tag, fashioning all-manner of worldy-wise dishes from top-drawer raw materials. Salmon is cured with soy and served with coriander crème fraîche and Asian pear, while a 'plate of pig' brings together belly, black pudding and ham hock with crackling, apple purée and cider reduction. Pasta and risottos loom large, alongside big-hearted dishes such as spiced venison loin or braised lamb shoulder with chargrilled cutlet, Scotch broth and brown butter mash. Finally, the tempo cools a shade when it comes to familiar desserts such as dark chocolate brownie or sticky Yorkshire parkin. Above Artisan is Catch, a populist seafood café dealing in crab cakes, 'luxury' fish pie and showy offerings like tempura of nori-wrapped tuna with oriental salad, sweet potato wedges, wasabi and pickled ginger. Wines are a full-on, modern bunch with plenty of choice across the board. Prices start at £13.50 (£3.75 a glass).
Chef/s: Simon Wild. **Open:** all week L 12 to 2.30, D 6 to 10. **Closed:** 25 and 26 Dec, 1 Jan. **Meals:** alc (main courses £12 to £22). Set L £15 (3 courses). Set D £25. **Service:** not inc. **Details:** Cards accepted. 90 seats. 8 seats outside. Air-con. Separate bar. Wheelchair access. Music. Children's portions.

★NEW ENTRY★
Cricket Inn

Relaxed gastropub in idyllic countryside
Penny Lane, Totley, Sheffield, S17 3AZ
Tel no: (0114) 2365256
www.cricketinn.co.uk
British | £24
Cooking score: 2

'Dogs, kids and muddy boots welcome' is the legend over the front door of this refurbished pub on the outskirts of Sheffield and bang next to, er . . . the cricket pitch. Local restaurateurs Richard and Victoria Smith have joined forces with brewer Jim Harrison of Thornbridge Hall and Simon Webster of Henderson's Relish to create a happy, friendly, laid back pub with oak floors, tongue-and-groove walls and crackling open fires. Huge blackboards detail appealing dishes: Sheffield-style hash and dumplings with stump (mashed carrot and swede) with your personal bottle of Henderson's, naturally, or brawn with Cunningham's pickle, roast saddle of rabbit with mascarpone polenta and fennel marmalade, and a surprisingly elegant smoked haddock Welsh rarebit topped with a perfect poached egg. There's a decent wine list, too, but beer's the thing, given that it's brewed specifically for the pub (drinking suggestions are listed alongside many of the dishes).
Chef/s: Jack Baker. **Open:** Mon to Fri L 12 to 2.30, D 5 to 9. Sat 12 to 9.30, Sun 12 to 8. **Meals:** Early bird menu £12 (2 courses). **Service:** not inc.
Details: Cards accepted. 80 seats. 100 seats outside. Wheelchair access. Music. Children's portions. Car parking.

Please send us your feedback

To register your opinion about any restaurant listed in the Guide, or a new restaurant that you wish to bring to our attention, please visit the web address at the bottom of the page. Your feedback informs the content of the book and will be used to compile next year's reviews.

Greenhead House

Inventive city cooking
84 Burncross Road, Chapeltown, Sheffield, S35 1SF
Tel no: (0114) 2469004
Modern European | £37
Cooking score: 2

Reporters praise the consistency of the performance at this amicably run restaurant in an area away from the hurly-burly of the city centre. That is particular praise, given that Neil Allen is a chef who doesn't like to stand still. New ideas are being tried out all the time, and might feature a Spanish-influenced starter of Manchego cheese with salted almonds, membrillo and a salad of apple dressed in sherry vinaigrette, or another of spare rib ragù with polenta. A choice of soup, sorbet or quiche is followed by mains such as poached lemon sole fillets with salmon mousseline and a white wine cream sauce, or roast quail on a pâté of the leg meat, sauced with grapes, shallots and wine. Finish, perhaps, with a Stateside dessert like maple syrup and pecan tart with bourbon ice cream. A short, no-nonsense wine list includes house wines at £16.50.
Chef/s: Neil Allen. **Open:** Fri L 12 to 1, Wed to Sat D 7 to 8.30. **Closed:** 2 weeks in Aug, 2 weeks Easter, Christmas to New Year. **Meals:** Set D £39.50 to £43.50 (4 courses). **Service:** not inc. **Details:** Cards accepted. 32 seats. 10 seats outside. No music. Wheelchair access. Children's portions. Children allowed. Car parking.

▌Shibden, Halifax
Shibden Mill Inn

Cosy pub dining
Shibden Mill Fold, Shibden, Halifax, HX3 7UL
Tel no: (01422) 365840
www.shibdenmillinn.com
Modern British | £27
New Chef

This traditional, welcoming country inn rambles through several rooms, all of them relaxed and cosy. The bar menu offers home-made breads, antipasti, light dishes such as grilled tuna steak niçoise and starters along the lines of melon and Parma ham or smoked haddock and crab fishcakes with chilli crème fraîche. Main courses range from comfort food (traditional fish and chips; steak and kidney pudding with roasted carrot, celeriac purée and real ale gravy) to the likes of confit duck leg with Puy lentils, carrot and celeriac jus and creamed potatoes. The candle-lit first-floor restaurant provides an intimate setting for the more refined dishes from the bar menu, plus some extra choices such as seared sea bass with asparagus and hollandaise sauce. Desserts are mostly familiar favourites such as glazed lemon tart or chocolate fondant. The substantial, well-annotated wine list opens at £12.95 a bottle.

Chef/s: Ian Booth. **Open:** Mon to Fri L 12 to 2, D 6 to 9.30, Sat D 6 to 9.30, Sun 12 to 7.30. **Meals:** alc (main courses £11.50 to £17.25). **Service:** not inc. **Details:** Cards accepted. Separate bar. Music. Children's portions. Car parking.

▌ Sinnington

ALSO RECOMMENDED
▲ Fox and Hounds

Main Street, Sinnington, YO62 6SQ
Tel no: (01751) 431577
www.thefoxandhoundsinn.co.uk
Gastropub

Tucked away in a village backwater at the gateway to the North York Moors National Park, this good-looking sandstone pub is a boon for tourists and walkers alike. The kitchen shows its culinary ambition with an adventurous menu of modern pub food that puts roast breast and confit of duck with bubble and squeak, chorizo and citrus jus (£14.95) alongside beer-battered haddock and 'real chips'. Kick off with twice-baked goats' cheese soufflé accompanied by pear, honey and walnut chutney (£6.25) and conclude with dark chocolate Nemesis cake (£4.85). House wine is £12.95. Open all week.

▌ Skipton
Le Caveau
Atmospheric underground dining
86 High Street, Skipton, BD23 1JJ
Tel no: (01756) 794274
www.lecaveau.co.uk
Anglo-French | £26
Cooking score: 2

The 'felons and sheep rustlers' who were once incarcerated here surely never imagined that their dank prison would one day be a softly-lit restaurant serving classy and comfortable home-cooked food. These days, the barrel-vaulted ceiling is strung with tiny, star-like lights and the bare stone walls add to the cosy atmosphere of the sixteenth-century building. A meal might start with terrine of pork, chicken, black pudding and bacon or chargrilled hot oak-smoked salmon with asparagus on a potato rösti with poached egg and a horseradish and crème fraîche dressing, followed by half a crispy roast Gressingham duck with honey and rosemary sauce or rack of lamb with minted sweet potato mash and port wine jus. Finish with orange and passion-fruit pannacotta. The wine list kicks off with Georges Duboeuf at £12.50 then roams the world without costing the earth.

Chef/s: Richard Barker. **Open:** Tue to Fri L 12 to 2, D 7 to 9.30. Sat 5.30 to 9.45. **Closed:** Sun, Mon, bank hols. **Meals:** Set D £21, alc (main courses £11.95 to £16.95. **Service:** not inc. **Details:** Cards accepted. 26 seats. Separate bar. Music.

Symbols

🛏	Accommodation is available.
£30	Three courses for less than £30.
V	More than five vegetarian dishes.
£5 OFF	£5-off voucher scheme.
🍾	Notable wine list.

South Dalton
Pipe & Glass Inn
Country pub that's an all-round polished affair
West End, South Dalton, HU17 7PN
Tel no: (01430) 810246
www.pipeandglass.co.uk
Gastropub | £26
Cooking score: 4
V

On the site of the original gatehouse to Dalton Park, this pub-cum-restaurant is an all-round polished affair. Traditional touches prevail in the bar – real beams and huge log-burning fire – while the restaurant with its bare floorboards, leather chesterfields, chunky wooden tables and chairs has a more contemporary feel. It's a modern 'posh pub' and not at all dusty 'olde worlde', despite its centuries-old history. James Mackenzie trades in the kind of upmarket dishes you might be surprised to see in a country pub, take a little jar of potted, spiced Gloucester Old Spot pork with sticky apples and crackling salad, say, or perhaps Barnsley lamb chop with devilled kidneys, boulangère potatoes, pickled red cabbage and nettle and mint sauce. Specials are chalked up on a board, expect pub classics like 'proper' prawn cocktail or braised beef with horseradish dumplings alongside calendar-correct offerings of sea trout with wilted rock samphire and spider crab fritter. Eggnog ice cream with East Yorkshire sugar cakes is a good reason to save room for dessert. The contemporary list of wines is good value, from £13.95.

Chef/s: James Mackenzie. **Open:** Tue to Sun L 12 to 2 (4 Sun), Tue to Sat D 6.30 to 9.30. **Closed:** Mon 25 Dec, 2 weeks Jan. **Service:** not inc. **Details:** Cards accepted. 80 seats. 50 seats outside. Separate bar. Music. Children's portions.

Sowerby
Millbank
Innovative Dales gastropub
Mill Bank Road, Sowerby, HX6 3DY
Tel no: (01422) 825588
www.themillbank.com
Modern European | £27
Cooking score: 5

Set on the steep slopes of the Calderdale valley, Millbank may not be one of those pubs turned restaurants – the pubby vibe remains and there are local handpump ales on tap – but the kitchen is the real engine-house of the operation. The dining room is a low-ceilinged affair with wooden floors and plain walls hung with contemporary artwork and it has an upbeat, cosmopolitan air to match Glenn Futter's modern European cooking. With a brasserie slant, the crowd-pleasing menu is seasonally influenced, revolving around prime local produce. Witness a signature loin of Yorkshire lamb with a shepherd's pie of the shoulder, served with roast pimento, pea purée and mint oil, or halibut fillet teamed with asparagus, new potatoes and hollandaise. Simpler offerings might feature a ham hock and Yorkshire cheese pie with mash, while chocoholics will be drawn to the chocolate fondant cake (with the regulation 15-minute wait) accompanied by yoghurt ice cream to cut through the richness. The fashionable globetrotting wine list fits the bill, and comes listed by style with headings like 'aromatic and spicy whites'. It opens with house French from £11.95.

Chef/s: Glenn Futter. **Open:** Tue to Sat L 12 to 2.30, D 6 to 9.30 (10 Fri and Sat), Sun L 12.30 to 4.30, D 6 to 8. **Closed:** Mon, first week Jan, first two weeks Oct. **Meals:** alc (main course £10.95 to 18.95). Set L Tue to Sat £12.95 (2 courses), Set D Tue to Thu £12.95 (2 courses), Sun £15.95 (2 courses) to £18.95. **Service:** optional. **Details:** Cards accepted. 58 seats. 25 seats outside. Air-con. Separate bar. Wheelchair access. Music. Children's portions.

Travellers Rest

Hilltop country inn
Steep Lane, Sowerby, HX6 1PE
Tel no: (01422) 832124
www.travellersrestsowerby.co.uk
Modern British | £28
New Chef

A stone-built inn from the early Georgian era, the Travellers Rest combines a gloriously windswept hilltop location with mod cons such as a helipad for those arriving by air. Exposed stonework and a wood-burning stove strike the right kinds of interior notes, as do the outsized wine glasses. Another change of chef has meant we are unable to provide a rating once more, but the homely style of cooking continues under the new incumbent. Expect chicken breast with coq au vin sauce, or slow-braised lamb shank daubed in marmalade, sauced with port and served with a mixed mash of carrot and swede, plus a menu of fish specials. Start with smoked salmon dressed in capers and lemon, and finish with the likes of plum and almond tart with custard or blackberry and sloe gin compote with shortbread for dipping. Wines are arranged by style and start at £11.

Chef/s: Vanessa Wright. **Open:** Sat and Sun L 12 to 3, Wed to Sun D 5 to closing (Sat from 5.30). **Meals:** alc (main courses £12.50 to £22). Sun L and D £18. Bar menu available. **Service:** not inc. **Details:** Cards accepted. 100 seats. 50 seats outside. Separate bar. Wheelchair access. Music. Children's portions. Car parking.

Symbols

 Accommodation is available.

 Three courses for less than £30.

V More than five vegetarian dishes.

 £5-off voucher scheme.

 Notable wine list.

▌ Staddlebridge

McCoy's at the Tontine

Endearing but eccentric
Staddlebridge, DL6 3JB
Tel no: (01609) 882671
www.mccoysatthetontine.co.uk
Modern British | £38
Cooking score: 4

An endearingly eccentric place that has been run by the McCoy brothers for over 30 years. 'Slightly faded elegance' is their own description of the restaurant ambience, where a womb-like interior is enhanced by louvred windows, film-set chandeliers and the flickering of candles. There is also a low-ceilinged bistro and a conservatory extension, depending on what manner of dining you're in the market for. Stuart Hawkins mixes modern ideas with items from the bistro menus of yesteryear. Hence, we have smoked salmon and crab roll with scallop tartare and curry oil or a prawn cocktail, then beef fillet accompanied by rocket purée, a balsamic reduction and beurre rouge, or mustard sauce and chips. Enticing fish preparations might include sea bass with spinach, lemon, chilli and a beurre blanc, while meals might end with crème brûlée that's been spiced up, dosed with rum, and garnished with pineapple salsa, mango ice cream and a coconut tuile. The wine list is presented as though it were a vinyl record listing (Side 1, Track 4 is 'New Zealand'), but beneath the humour there are some good bottles – some very good ones indeed, for those with the resources. Prices start at £17.50.

Chef/s: Stuart Hawkins. **Open:** all week, L 12 to 2, D 6.30 to 9 (9.45 Fri and Sat). **Closed:** 25 and 26 Dec, 1 and 2 Jan. **Meals:** alc (main courses £17.60 to £25.50). Set L £16.95. Set L Sun £18.95 (Bistro). **Service:** not inc. **Details:** Cards accepted. 83 seats. Music. Children's portions. Car parking.

| Staithes

Endeavour

Famous for fish
1 High Street, Staithes, TS13 5BH
Tel no: (01947) 840825
www.endeavour-restaurant.co.uk
Seafood | £29
Cooking score: 4

On a stretch of the Yorkshire coast now famous as 'Captain Cook country', this long-running fish restaurant-with-rooms takes its name from the seafarer's celebrated ship. The setting is a 200-year-old house that shows off its history with sash windows, steep narrow staircases and old wood panelling in the cosy candlelit dining room. Regular hauls from the local boats dictate the kitchen's work and the owners recently moved over to fixed-price menus for lunch and dinner: the generous, creative style remains unchanged. Fish curing is now done on the premises and there is more emphasis on 'rod to table' dishes (home-salted pollock mousse and smoked pâté of line-caught mackerel with fennel and Pernod, for example). The kitchen also puts together cassoulets and serves gurnard fillet on lime and ginger couscous with dill and mustard vinaigrette. There's always something decent for meat fans (roast quail on savoury stuffed vine leaves), while desserts keep the sweet-toothed satisfied with, say, spiced plums with rice pudding ice cream. Organic wines (and a specially brewed organic beer) are a feature of the drinks list. House selections are £13.

Chef/s: Charlotte Willoughby and Brian Kay. **Open:** Fri and Sat L 12.30 to 2 (summer only), Tue to Sat D 7 to 11. **Closed:** Sun, Mon. **Meals:** Set L £18 (2 courses) to £21, Set D £26 (2 courses) to £29. **Service:** not inc. **Details:** Cards accepted. 16 seats. No mobile phones. Music. Children's portions. Car parking.

| Sutton-on-the-Forest

ALSO RECOMMENDED
▲ Blackwell Ox Inn

Huby Road, Sutton-on-the-Forest, YO61 1DT
Tel no: (01347) 810328
www.blackwelloxinn.co.uk
Gastropub

The original Blackwell Ox was a legendary Shorthorn Teeswater − a mighty beast of epic proportions. It is now the moniker for this 1820s drinkers' den turned affluent Yorkshire pub/restaurant-with-rooms. Drinkers still populate the bar, but main man Steven Holding concentrates his efforts on the elegant dining room. The kitchen takes its cue from the cassoulets and daubes of Southern France: fulsome, earthy flavours dominate, although ingredients are fiercely local. Steaks, chops and bangers are pure North Country, but the choice extends to seared scallops with confit pork and onion purée (£6.95) and roast duck with creamed celeriac and parsnip tarte Tatin (£15.95). Finish with baked Alaska or crème brûlée. House wine is £12.95. Closed Sun D.

| Tadcaster

Singers

Musically-themed local asset
16 Westgate, Tadcaster, LS24 9AB
Tel no: (01937) 835121
www.singersrestaurant.co.uk
Modern European | £25
Cooking score: 2

Song sheets are papered on the walls, photos of the stars look down and the tables have names like Lennon and Jagger in this musically-themed asset to the Tadcaster restaurant scene. Singers has been putting on a show for locals and visitors alike since 1994 and its food manages to keep up with the trends − without going overboard. Midweek early-evening deals are great value, but the full menu shows what the kitchen can really deliver. Starters of Mediterranean fish casserole or confit of duck with merguez sausage salad might open proceedings, before Gressingham duck breast with caramelised sweet potato mash or roast sea bass with crab, tomato and basil bisque. To close, consider something familiar such as sticky toffee pudding or apple and orange crumble. Around 40 wines open with house Duboeuf at £12.95 (£2.50 a glass).

Chef/s: Adam Hewitt and John Appleyard. **Open:** Tue to Sat D only 6 to 9.30. **Closed:** Sun, Mon, 24 Dec to 3 Jan. **Meals:** Set D £ 14.95 to £24.95. **Service:** not inc. **Details:** Cards accepted. 38 seats. Air-con. Separate bar. Wheelchair access. Music. Children allowed.

■ Todmorden

Old Hall

Historic house, contemporary cooking
Hall Street, Todmorden, OL14 7AD
Tel no: (01706) 815998
Modern British | £30
Cooking score: 2
£5 OFF **V**

The Old Hall is exactly that: a finely preserved Elizabethan manor house dressed up with an obligatory quota of mullioned windows, carved wood, huge fireplaces and weathered stonework. By contrast, the kitchen keeps its eye on current trends and makes use of as much North Country produce as it can muster. Rump of Pendle lamb comes with crispy fried leeks and redcurrant jus, medallions of Rossendale Valley pork are served with parsnip mash and crabapple sauce, while suprême of corn-fed Penrith chicken gets stuffed with Bury black pudding, pig's cheek and apple. Yorkshire and Lancashire cheeses are alternatives to desserts such as chocolate and hazelnut roulade with Fitzpatrick's raspberry 'blood tonic' coulis. The well-tuned wine list has been put together by a knowledgeable enthusiast: choice is exemplary and prices are easy on the wallet. House selections are £14.25 (£2.80 a glass).

Chef/s: Chris Roberts and Peter Windross. **Open:** Sun L 12 to 2.30, Tue to Sat D 7 to 9.30. **Closed:** Mon, 25 Dec, 1 Jan. **Meals:** alc (main courses £14 to £23.50). Set L Sun £19 (3 courses). **Service:** not inc.

Details: Cards accepted. 70 seats. 20 seats outside. Separate bar. Music. Children's portions. Car parking.

■ West Witton

★NEW ENTRY★
Wensleydale Heifer

Contemporary seafood in rural surroundings
Main Street, West Witton, DL8 4LS
Tel no: (01969) 622322
www.wensleydaleheifer.co.uk
Seafood | £25
Cooking score: 4

Chef/proprietor David Moss, last seen in the Guide at the Crab and Lobster in Ashenby (see entry), has moved down the road to this handsome, whitewashed roadhouse. It's a welcoming place (the lounge is clubby with leather sofas and tartan carpet) but those idiosyncratic touches that made the Crab and Lobster so memorable are to be admired in the gloriously eccentric Fish Bar. There's a delicious sense of humour in the fluttering flame disco lamps and plates in the form of newspapers (for your fish and chips, of course), and a retro theme nudges the menu, too, in the shape of a classic prawn cocktail made with Jack Daniels Marie Rose sauce. Elsewhere, there's punchy chilli salt squid with lime-marinated fennel and noodle salad or the well-reported Whitby cod with Black Sheep beer batter, fat chips, posh peas and home-made tartare sauce. Non-fishy dishes include local lamb with bacon bubble and squeak, and a Black Forest knickerbocker glory makes a final kitsch flourish. House wine is £14.50 a bottle.

Chef/s: David Moss. **Open:** all week 12 to 2.30, 6 to 9.30. **Meals:** alc (main courses £11.50 to £19). Set menu £13.95 (2 courses) to £16.95. **Service:** 10%. **Details:** Cards accepted. 70 seats. 35 seats outside. Separate bar. Wheelchair access. Music. Children's portions. Car parking.

Whitby

Greens
Bags of ambition
13 Bridge Street, Whitby, YO22 4BG
Tel no: (01947) 600284
www.greensofwhitby.com
Modern British | £30
Cooking score: 4

After a total refurbishment in 2007, Green's has traded some easy informality for sophistication and complexity. Admirably, in a town heavily addicted to fish and chips, Rob Green's ambition has never stood still, running an operation that stretches upstairs and downstairs from sandwiches and salads to a three-course set menu at £39.95. The smart ground floor bistro has light meals, or bulk up on beef daube, but if you like your fish fresh and largely unfussed go for the daily catch chalked up on a board – pollack-stuffed crab, or wild sea bass with fennel, all landed 200 yards away. Do not doubt the sourcing commitment: Green's name the trawler captains on the menu and sponsor the local fishing school. The dining room upstairs is where Rob Green flaunts his latest colours. Starters might be a rich shellfish bisque with red mullet, croûtons, Gruyère and rouille, followed by brill fillets with potted hot-smoked salmon, candied lemon, braised lettuce hearts and smoked horseradish velouté. There is much elaboration, a risky commitment with so much menu elsewhere on the premises, but the balancing act rarely falters. The wine list, naturally supportive of seafood, starts with a Chilean Sauvignon Blanc at £13.95 and has plenty by-the-glass.
Chef/s: Rob Green and Ryan Osborne. **Open:** Mon to Fri L 12 to 2, D 6.30 to 9.30, Sat 12 to 10, Sun 12 to 9.30. **Closed:** 25 and 26 Dec, 1 Jan. **Meals:** alc (main courses bistro £8 to £19, restaurant £16 to £22.50). Set menu restaurant £33.95 (2 courses) to £39.95. **Service:** not inc. **Details:** Cards accepted. 50 seats. Air-con. Separate bar. Wheelchair access. Music. Children's portions. Children allowed.

Magpie Café
Cheerful harbourside seafood café
14 Pier Road, Whitby, YO21 3PU
Tel no: (01947) 602058
www.magpiecafe.co.uk
Seafood | £24
Cooking score: 2
£5 OFF **V** £30

Sitting across the road from the fish market, and commanding equally appetising views of the harbour, the Magpie exerts a powerful lure. It has been in the same family since the 1950s, and is well-practised at serving daisy-fresh fish and seafood with a minimum of culinary frills. Wrapping up Whitby crab in smoked salmon as a starter is about as elaborate as it gets here. Traditional fish and chips, from lemon sole to skate, is highly praised by loyal locals, and forms a bedrock for menus that run to hot seafood pot in wine and garlic, grilled plaice with tarragon cream, and the high-rolling thermidor preparations. Vegetarian and meat listings add variety. Finish with hazelnut meringue layered with strawberry cream, or bananas in butterscotch. Staff are commended for their amiable proficiency. A short wine list begins with Chileans in all three colours at £12.95.
Chef/s: Ian Robson and Paul Gildroy. **Open:** all week 11.30 to 9. **Closed:** 8 to 27 Dec, 1 Jan. **Meals:** alc (main courses £7.95 to £19.95). **Service:** not inc. **Details:** 130 seats. Air-con. Wheelchair access. Music. Children's portions.

Yarm

Chadwick's
Easy-going continental style
104B High Street, Yarm, TS15 9AU
Tel no: (01642) 788558
Modern European | £30
Cooking score: 3
V

Billed as a continental café-cum-restaurant, Chadwick's certainly makes an impression with its striking exterior and big windows looking out onto Yarm's main street. The

interior is an uncluttered mix of mirrors, wooden furniture and yellow walls, while the flexible menu picks up influences from near and far. Informal café-style lunches provide daytime sustenance in the shape of chicken Caesar salad, Asian chicken with harissa, and smoked haddock with champ and poached egg. Evening sees a touch more elaboration added to the mix: starters of twice-baked Swiss soufflé might precede Indonesian pork satay with nasi goreng and peanut salad or seared rare tuna niçoise. Round things off with an old favourite like sticky toffee pudding or rhubarb and apple crumble with clotted cream. Late breakfasts, afternoon teas and an early-doors tapas menu are added bonuses for the local crowd. The compact wine list includes a few organics and 'discoveries'; house Duboeuf is £13.50.
Chef/s: David Brownless and Steven Conyard. **Open:** all week L 11.30 to 2.30, D 5.30 to 9.30. **Closed:** 25 and 26 Dec, bank hols. **Meals:** alc (main courses L £7.50 to £11, D £15 to £20). **Service:** not inc. **Details:** Cards accepted. 70 seats. Air-con. Separate bar. Music. Children's portions.

▌York

J. Baker's
Fine dining and fun
7 Fossgate, York, YO1 9TA
Tel no: (01904) 622688
www.jbakers.co.uk
Modern British | £28
Cooking score: 5
£5 £30
OFF

Jeff Baker came to York with a red-hot CV and in two years his Bistro Moderne has become a red-hot ticket. Perched at the top end of Fossgate, which is the city's best eating strip, his clever and vivacious cooking has left the local opposition standing. It's clever because Baker sends out exquisite plates of big bold British flavours in an atmosphere that is laid back, relaxed and fun. The fun comes on the plate with starters of beetroot trifle, or house-cured sardines with candied lemon pizza, and a high quality version of jelly and ice cream with lemon curd and buttery biscuit that he

calls 'lemon tops'. None of this takes away from the seriousness of his cooking, whether it's slow-cooked pig's cheek or quick-cooked calf's liver. As well as the à la carte, Baker has now imported the successful lunchtime grazing menu of small dishes to the evening, with seven little courses that others would dub a tasting menu. The only duff note is more than one report of a frosty front-of-house operation that's out of keeping with otherwise cheerful service. Wines are usefully listed by style, with house wine at £11.95. Upstairs is a chocolate room where you can push the boat out into decadent waters with truffles, fondue, hot chocolate or the ultimate white chocolate martini.
Chef/s: Jeff Baker. **Open:** Tue to Sat L 12 to 2.30, d 6 to 10. **Closed:** Sun and Mon. **Meals:** Set menu £25.50. **Service:** not inc. **Details:** Cards accepted. 36 seats. Separate bar. Wheelchair access. Music. Children's portions.

Melton's
Much-loved York stalwart
7 Scarcroft Road, York, YO23 1ND
Tel no: (01904) 634341
www.meltonsrestaurant.co.uk
Modern European | £30
Cooking score: 5
£5
OFF

The energy and drive of owners Michael and Lucy Hjort and head chef Annie Prescott have kept Melton's running at a consistently high standard for nearly 20 years now. Newcomers might wonder as they venture beyond the city walls to an unprepossessing suburban street and premises with a rather tired and dated décor, yet its loyal clientele vouch for pleasing yet unfussy seasonal food strong on regional sourcing, often with a refreshing global uplift. So a spring dinner might begin with a complimentary cup of gazpacho followed by cannelloni of Whitby crab in a Thai broth. A main dish of smoked haddock with sorrel pesto is served with celery, fennel and new potatoes, while local duck is agreeably surprised by five spices, soy and pak choi. Desserts revert to more established domestic comfort: bread-and-butter pudding with Yorkshire clotted cream or white chocolate parfait served with a perfectly poached rhubarb compote. A global and well-sourced wine list impresses with plenty by-the-glass, half-bottles and half-carafes. Bottles rise from £14 for a Verdicchio di Matelica to £65 for a Clos Badon-Thunevin Saint-Emilion. Bottled water and coffee are complimentary. **Chef/s:** Annie Prescott and Michael Hjort. **Open:** Tue to Sat L 12 to 2, Mon to Sat D 5.30 to 9.45. **Closed:** Sun, 2 weeks Christmas, 1 week Aug. **Meals:** alc (main courses £13.50 to £18). Set L £22.50. **Service:** not inc. **Details:** Cards accepted. 42 seats. Air-con. Music. Children's portions.

Melton's Too
Regional and seasonal flavours
25 Walmgate, York, YO1 9TX
Tel no: (01904) 629222
www.meltonstoo.co.uk
Modern European | £20
Cooking score: 2

This friendly and bustling brasserie aims at all bases with a bi-weekly changing menu of gutsy Med/British dishes that nod to the seasons and the locality. Free coffee is a nice touch with breakfast (£6.50). Lunch might be local organic root vegetable soup followed by poached salmon salad and wild garlic hollandaise. After 7pm the evening menu kicks in with mussels, Caesar salad or terrine followed by braised chicken with chorizo and fennel or Yorkshire ham with parsley sauce and cabbage. Factor in a tapas menu that runs throughout and the quantity-versus-quality equation comes into play. Warm chocolate brownie with cherries, brandy and vanilla ice cream exemplifies a selection of indulgent puddings. They keep a substantial cellar, run monthly regional produce dinners, and put on regular wine tastings and live music. House wine is £11.95.

Chef/s: Martin Hewitt. **Open:** all week 10.30 to 10.30. **Closed:** 3 days Christmas. **Meals:** alc (main courses £7.80 to £12.95). **Service:** not inc. **Details:** Cards accepted. 120 seats. Air-con. Wheelchair access. Music. Children's portions.

Middlethorpe Hall
Assured cooking in opulent surroundings
Bishopthorpe Road, York, YO23 2GB
Tel no: (01904) 641241
www.middlethorpe.com
Modern British | £41
Cooking score: 3

Stately homes don't come much more inviting than this magisterial William and Mary mansion within cantering distance of York racecourse. The whole place oozes Palladian opulence, with 20 acres of immaculate gardens and an aristocratic dining room defined by wall-to-wall panelling, portraits and antiques spanning the centuries. Nicholas Evans' cooking aims high and readers have been bowled over by his imagination and sense of humour: cod, chips and peas is a cheeky way to start, especially when it sits alongside terrine of confit Goosnargh duck with golden raisin purée, pickled kohlrabi and sherry vinegar syrup. Main courses tap into Yorkshire's seasonal larder for roast and braised mallard with curly kale, chestnuts and quince or roast fallow deer with pumpkin purée and bitter chocolate sauce, while desserts have included pistachio crème brûlée with mandarin jelly and brioche ice cream. Al fresco lunches are served on the lovely south-facing terrace. The patrician, French-biased wine list has received plaudits, with luscious pudding wines earning a special mention. Prices start at £16.50. **Chef/s:** Nicholas Evans. **Open:** all week 12.30 to 1.45, 7 to 9.30. **Meals:** Set L £17.50 (2 courses) to £23. Set D £41.50 (3 courses) to £55. **Service:** inc. **Details:** Cards accepted. 60 seats. 24 seats outside. Separate bar. No music. Wheelchair access. Children allowed. Car parking.

SCOTLAND

Borders, Dumfries & Galloway,
Lothians (inc. Edinburgh),
Strathclyde (inc. Glasgow), Central, Fife,
Tayside, Grampian, Highlands & Islands

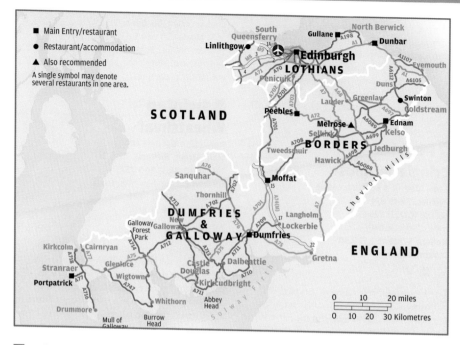

- ■ Main Entry/restaurant
- ● Restaurant/accommodation
- ▲ Also recommended

A single symbol may denote several restaurants in one area.

Ednam

Edenwater House

Personally run borderland retreat
Ednam, TD5 7QL
Tel no: (01573) 224 070
www.edenwaterhouse.co.uk
Modern European | £35
Cooking score: 4

'An oasis of calm' amid the borderlands of the Upper Tweed valley, this four-square converted manse is charmingly run by Jeff and Jacqui Kelly: he plays host and oversees the whole show, while she takes care of culinary business in the kitchen. Dinner revolves around a fixed-price, no-choice menu in true country-house style. A typically assured meal might begin with Parmesan-crusted Eyemouth scallops with cauliflower purée, tomato salsa and rouille before roast squab and breast of Coshat dove with morels. Proceedings normally conclude with something sweet (perhaps basil pannacotta

with apricots poached in Jurançon), although Jacqui sometimes moves into savoury mode and serves, say, farmhouse Gorgonzola on a brioche croûton with pickled pears and Manuka honey. Jeff knows his wines and he is blessed with an enthusiast's eye for little-known gems. House selections are £15 (£4 a glass).

Chef/s: Jacqui Kelly. **Open:** Wed to Sat D only 8pm (1 sitting). **Closed:** Dec and Jan. **Meals:** Set D £35. **Service:** not inc. **Details:** Cards accepted. 16 seats. No music. No mobile phones. Car parking.

Melrose

ALSO RECOMMENDED
▲ Burt's Hotel

Market Square, Melrose, TD6 9PL
Tel no: (01896) 822 285
British

This hotel on the Market Square has been overseen by the Henderson family for more than three decades. Set-dinner menus (£27.50/£32.75) could take in pan-fried pigeon breast with haricot bean casserole, then cod with saffron mash, confit cherry tomato and Noilly Prat foam followed by chocolate and nougatine tart with honeycomb ice cream. The owner is happy to point diners towards little-known wines on the wide-ranging list; prices start at £14.50. Open all week.

Peebles

Cringletie House
Good food in a Scottish castle
Peebles, EH45 8PL
Tel no: (01721) 725 750
www.cringletie.com
Modern Scottish | £39.50
Cooking score: 4
£5 OFF ⊨ V

The sweeping drive delivers you to this imposing turreted Scottish castle set in 28 acres of wooded grounds – 'grandeur sums it all up'. The panelled Sutherland dining room on the first floor overlooks the estate and the Trossachs in the distance and delivers food with a convincing pedigree: excellent fish and seafood, local game, fruit and vegetables from the walled kitchen garden, and a few luxuries from further afield. Craig Gibb heads a professional kitchen, producing, for example, plump scallops with onion compote and butternut velouté, and confit chicken and mushroom terrine with smoked chicken consommé jelly. Individual elements are faultless and although the presentational requirements can seem to reduce the flavour impact of some dishes, there is no doubting the excellence of, say, pork belly and fillet with caramelised apple purée, pomme maxim, anise jus and creamed Savoy cabbage. Good puddings include frozen vanilla soufflé with hazelnut shortbread and cherry ripple ice cream and the cheese selection has been well reported. 'Service is gracious and thoughtful', the wine list extensive, well annotated and starts at £19.50.

Chef/s: Craig Gibb. Open: Sun L 12 to 2, all week D 7 to 9. Meals: Set Sun L £20, set D £39.50. Service: not inc. Details: Cards accepted. 36 seats. Separate bar. Wheelchair access. Music. Children's portions. Car parking.

Swinton

Wheatsheaf
Reputable Borders inn
Main Street, Swinton, TD11 3JJ
Tel no: (01890) 860 257
www.wheatsheaf-swinton.co.uk
Modern Scottish | £29
Cooking score: 3
£5 OFF ⊨ V £30

Set in the middle of an archetypal Borders village not far from the River Tweed, the Wheatsheaf does a great service for locals, tourists and anglers alike. It combines the assets of a rock-solid inn with the attributes of an upmarket country hotel, and the emphasis is firmly on food. Lunch and dinner menus plough a similar risk-free furrow, although prices are higher in the evening. Start with smoked haddock, salmon and dill fishcake or breast of wood pigeon on black pudding with Cumberland sauce, before moving on to walnut-crusted halibut with asparagus and lemon or Scotch fillet steak with caramelised shallots and white truffle oil. For afters, try glazed lemon tart with passion fruit sorbet or have fun with warm chocolate brownie, pistachios, hot chocolate sauce and Maltester ice cream. There are special menus for vegetarians and those on gluten-free diets. The 150-bin wine list is an impressive worldwide collection, with a dozen house tipples from £11.95 (£2.95 a glass).

Chef/s: John Keir. Open: all week L 12 to 2, D 6 to 9. Closed: Christmas and New Year. Meals: alc (main courses L £9 to £16, D £11 to £21). Bar menu available. Service: not inc. Details: Cards accepted. 45 seats. Separate bar. No mobile phones. Wheelchair access. Music. Children's portions. Car parking.

Dumfries

Linen Room

Sleek setting for ambitious cooking
53 St Michael Street, Dumfries, DG1 2QB
Tel no: (01387) 255 689
www.linenroom.com
Modern European | £32
Cooking score: 3

The Linen Room is a sophisticated restaurant in a shabby street, not far from St Michael's Church where Robert Burns is buried. While simple décor – namely minimalist black (walls, leather chairs) and white (crisply ironed white tablecloths) – are as before, there's a new chef in the kitchen. Daniel Hollern delivers an ambitious menu that thrives on fresh ingredients and good combinations. A meal might kick off with a lovely pannacotta of Stilton with toasted croûtons and crisp salad leaves or a frothy white onion velouté with cep and cumin oil. Fred Ballard's Texel lamb is served with the cannon and sweetbreads, as well as purple carrots, confit garlic, spinach and eucalyptus foam, and rhubarb compote with custard tart, ginger and vanilla is a good way to finish. While the chef's ambition is evident in both composition and presentation, there were some inconsistencies at inspection and the service was haphazard although well meaning. The pedigree wine list has plenty of French classics, supplemented by an intelligent selection from around the world. House wines are £18.
Chef/s: Daniel Hollern. **Open:** Tue to Sun L 12.30 to 2.30, D 7 to 9.30. **Closed:** 2 weeks Jan, 2 weeks Oct. **Meals:** alc D (main courses £17.50 to £19). Set L £15.95, Set D £39.50. **Service:** not inc. **Details:** Cards accepted. 32 seats. No mobile phones. Wheelchair access. Music.

Moffat

Well View

All in the family
Ballplay Road, Moffat, DG10 9JU
Tel no: (01683) 220 184
www.wellview.co.uk
Franco-Scottish | £35
Cooking score: 4

While other enterprises might expand and lose their charm, Well View, a fine Victorian house in well-tended gardens, has held on to its intimate atmosphere by keeping a sense of scale and retaining a relaxed, informal mood. In 2009, the Schuckardts (Janet and daughter Lina cook, John welcomes warmly) celebrate 25 years here by continuing as before, offering a four-course, no-choice dinner (until dessert stage). Primary ingredients are generally straightforward – venison, salmon, lamb – and there is a commitment to quality Scottish produce. Meals might include Stilton and apricot tart, and roast breast of guinea fowl sauced with red wine and served with mushrooms, red peppers, courgettes and pak choi, and finish, perhaps, with chocolate heather pot or toffee parfait with butterscotch sauce. Wine is complimentary, a choice of red or white, served by the glass.
Chef/s: Janet Schuckardt and Lina Schuckardt. **Open:** all week D 7.30 (1 sitting). **Meals:** Set price D £35. **Service:** not inc. **Details:** Cards accepted. 12 seats. Car parking.

READERS RECOMMEND

The Limetree Restaurant

British
Hartfell House, Hartfell Crescent, Moffat, DG10 9HG
Tel no: (01683) 220153
www.hartfellhouse.co.uk
'New location for local favourite'

Ruth Rogers River Cafe

Why did you become a chef?
I like to eat.

At what age did you cook your first meal for other people?
When I was ten I cooked a birthday dinner for my mother.

What three ingredients could you not do without?
Olive oil, chocolate, lemon.

What's the most unusual ingredient you've cooked or eaten?
Probably veal brains.

What won't you tolerate in the kitchen?
Mediocre ingredients.

Do you always read reviews of your restaurant?
Yes.

What dish is your first food memory?
Pasta with tomato sauce.

What era of history would you most like to have eaten in?
The future.

Portpatrick

Knockinaam Lodge
Glorious isolation, splendid food
Portpatrick, DG9 9AD
Tel no: (01776) 810 471
www.knockinaamlodge.com
Modern British | £50
Cooking score: 5

£5 OFF 🍷 ⇌

Gloriously sited on its own inlet, amid wooded hills and manicured lawns leading down to a beach by the Atlantic Ocean, this grey-stone Victorian hunting lodge stands in splendid isolation. But those who have navigated the long track have reported a cheery welcome at the end, along with a comfortable lounge and bar and log fires. At its heart, Tony Pierce's kitchen operation conscientiously sources the prime Scottish ingredients on which his classically influenced cooking is based. The culinary style keeps to a country-house idiom – a four-course, fixed-price deal with no choice apart from the option of dessert or cheese – and satisfies mightily as it does so. Dinner might begin simply with grilled fillet of salted cod with a chive hollandaise, go on to cappuccino of butter bean and thyme with fresh truffle, and have as its centrepiece roast cannon of Galloway lamb (with pommes purée, haggis beignet, root vegetables and a juniper and port reduction), before finishing with pear tarte Tatin served with double vanilla bean ice cream and a ginger caramel sauce (or cheese). The Guide has not seen a copy of the wine list this year, but reporters confirm that David Ibbotson's extensive wine list is a treasure trove of quality, exerting itself in many other regions as well as France. House wines range from £20 to £24.
Chef/s: Tony Pierce. **Open:** all week L 12 to 2, D 7 to 9. **Meals:** Set L £37.50, Sun L £27.50, set D £50. **Service:** not inc. **Details:** Cards accepted. 30 seats. Separate bar. Music.

Dunbar

★NEW ENTRY★

Creel Restaurant

Simple good cooking
25, Lamer Street,The Old Harbour, Dunbar,
EH42 1HJ
Tel no: (01368) 863 279
www.creelrestaurant.co.uk
Modern British | £24
Cooking score: 3

V

This bistro in a corner building near the
harbour is as unpretentious as can be, the
cooking is straightforward and the prices a
steal. Chef/proprietor Logan Thorburn
knows a thing or two about cooking, having
worked with the likes of Rick Stein at the
Seafood Restaurant in Padstow and John
Campbell at the Vineyard at Stockcross (see
entries). As a member of the Slow Food
movement, his aims are more ethical than
commercial and he cooks without fuss and
fads, creating honest, wholesome dishes based
on locally sourced raw materials, the suppliers
of which he lists on his website. Starters might
be pastis, lemon and dill-cured organic
Shetland salmon with wholemeal bread and
butter or local moules marinière, while mains
take in seared yellow-fin tuna steak served
with laksa sauce or chargrilled ribeye of
Aberdeen Angus, cooked pink. Finish with
pannacotta with wild berries or a duo of
Scottish cheeses. The brief wine list opens at a
modest £11.95.
Chef/s: Logan Thorburn. **Open:** Thur to Mon L 12 to
2, D 6.45 to 9. **Closed:** Tues, Wed. **Meals:** alc D (main
courses £8.95 to £15.50). Set L £12.50 (two courses)
to £15.50. **Service:** not inc. **Details:** Cards accepted.
36 seats. No mobile phones. Wheelchair access.
Music. Children allowed.

Edinburgh

★NEW ENTRY★

Abstract

33-35 Castle Terrace, Edinburgh, EH1 2EL
Tel no: 0131 229 1222
www.abstractrestaurant.com
Modern European | £35
Cooking score: 4

£5
OFF

When Abstract landed on the Edinburgh
scene in early 2007 it brought an
unprecedented sense of theatre. That meant
mirror-ball pillars, faux snakeskin tables and
signature artworks; also very well executed
food that prompts a smile - or at least makes a
few people arch their eyebrows. Since launch,
the kitchen has been headed up by several
chefs, but its general professionalism has seen
it settle into a steady rhythm. The excellent
value lunch, for example, could start with
goats' cheese crème brûlée, enclosed not by a
ramekin but a tight layer of onion. That might
be followed by a salmon burger coated in
oatmeal with fennel and apple curd on the
side. To finish, many are tempted by the
caramel bavarois with space dust (and, yes, it
goes pop in your mouth). At dinner, you
could even find yourself ordering snail
bonbons just to find out what they are or
Ross-shire lamb as a main course to explore
the accompanying basil macaroni and
bolognaise sauce. The wine list is ample and
interesting, the general experience
characterised by panache and excitement.
Chef/s: Sean Kelly. **Open:** Tue to Sat L 12 to 2, D 6 to
10. **Meals:** Set L £12.95, Tasting menu £55.
Service: 12.5%. **Details:** Cards accepted. 65 seats.
Air-con. Separate bar. Wheelchair access. Music.
Children's portions.

Atrium

Contemporary, reliable cooking
10 Cambridge Street, Edinburgh, EH1 2ED
Tel no: (0131) 228 8882
www.atriumrestaurant.co.uk
Modern European | £45
Cooking score: 4

More than 15 years since launch and the Atrium keeps rolling along. The décor changed towards the end of 2007, but it was more of a wash-and-brush-up rather than a radical departure; the venue is still recognisable to anyone who has eaten there in the past (new chairs, some new colours, the same chunky wooden tables). As much could be said for the food: contemporary, competently done, reliably good. Under chef Neil Forbes, the kitchen tends to reach for high-quality Scottish ingredients and turns them into dishes like scallops with pig trotter croquette as a starter or Borders lamb with sage and Parma ham boulangère, asparagus and wild mushroom jus for a main course. Even the economical set-dinner menu could involve Inverarary venison en croûte, then leg of organic chicken from Perthshire with a mustard-and-bread crust. The Atrium also offers a decent artisan cheeseboard, well-executed desserts (apricot bavarois or tarte Tatin perhaps) and an acclaimed wine list with excellent choice by the glass. Its very longevity may sometimes see it taken for granted which is a pity - over the years this restaurant has been innovative, interesting and influential.
Chef/s: Neil Forbes. **Open:** Mon to Fri L 12 to 2, Mon to Sat D 6 to 10. **Closed:** Sun, 24 to 26 Dec, 1 and 2 Jan. **Meals:** alc (main courses £18.50 to 25.50). Set L £15.50 (2 courses £19.50, Set D £27.
Service: optional. **Details:** Cards accepted. 100 seats. Air-con. Wheelchair access. Children allowed.

Balmoral, Number One

Confident and well-established restaurant
1 Princes Street, Edinburgh, EH2 2EQ
Tel no: (0131) 556 2414
www.roccofortehotels.com
Modern European | £55
Cooking score: 6

Unlike its cousins in the south of France, the fate of the average courgette flower in Scotland is to wither away, but not at Number One. Here it will be stuffed with crab and scallop, introduced to tomato and fennel water, then served as a starter with Charentais melon. This is a flourish you might come to expect from a confident and well-established kitchen under the direction of chef Jeff Bland, the power behind the flagship dining room at Edinburgh's most iconic hotel, where golden banquettes, lacquered wall panels, white linen and the sheer sense of space simply say 'class'. If courgette flowers are not your thing, alternative starters include the likes of Anjou pigeon or sautéed foie gras with poached guinea fowl, while a typical main course might be Gressingham duck breast with plum and beetroot compote, Parmentier potatoes and chicory. Vegetarians can order off the main menu (leek tartlet then aubergine cannelloni perhaps) and the Agen prune soufflé with Armagnac ice cream is well worth the extra few minutes wait. The wine list is extensive and quality is high, but then so are the prices — by the glass from £8, and bottle £24.
Chef/s: Jeff Bland and Craig Sandle. **Open:** all week D 6 to 10. **Closed:** first 2 weeks Jan. **Meals:** Set D £55, Tasting menu £60. **Service:** 12.5% (optional). **Details:** Cards accepted. 55 seats. Air-con. No music. No mobile phones. Wheelchair access. Music. Children allowed. Car parking.

The Bonham

Contemporary Caledonian chic
35 Drumsheugh Gardens, Edinburgh, EH3 7RN
Tel no: (0131) 274 7444
www.thebonham.com
Modern European | £40
Cooking score: 4

The Bonham is a hotel a few minutes from the west end of Princes Street, part of a small chain owned by the venerable Town House Company. The exterior is classic Victorian, the interior has modern fixtures, fittings and contemporary art. Its ground-floor dining room is airy and wood panelled with décor that has been freshened up since the last edition of this Guide. The kitchen remains under the charge of Michel Bouyer whose cooking is classic French with a modern feel. Starters include the likes of monkfish and sea bream ceviche or pea and ham soup with pancetta, while main courses can be as relatively straightforward as pan-fried Aberdeen Angus with fondant potato, shallot cream and pesto crust or somewhat more adventurous, say sea trout scented with fennel pollen, rösti potato, white bean and oregano casserole. That same sense of adventure goes into desserts such as marmalade and chocolate croustillant with a mini orange soufflé. This is an estimable dinner destination, but is also economical for lunch. Wines by the glass from £4.50, and bottle £16.
Chef/s: Michel Bouyer. **Open:** all week L 12 to 2.30, D 6.30 to 10. **Meals:** alc (main courses £15 to £26.50). Set L £13.50 (2 courses) to £16.
Service: optional. **Details:** Cards accepted. 60 seats. Wheelchair access. Music. Children's portions. Car parking.

Café St Honoré

A new broom
34 NW Thistle Street Lane, Edinburgh, EH2 1EA
Tel no: (0131) 226 2211
www.cafesthonore.com
French | £35
Cooking score: 3

The Colversons, who had owned Café St Honoré since 1993, sold up and moved away in spring 2008. New owner Jim Baird intends to keep things very much the same, while management of the restaurant now falls to the highly experienced Andrew Radford and Neil Forbes of Edinburgh's Atrium. (Radford's son Ben is in the kitchen and he will oversee an evolution rather than a revolution.) The location is still beautifully romantic, set down a cobbled New Town lane, and the interior of fin de siècle French chic endures. A glance at the menu will reassure regulars. At dinner there might be a warm salad of scallops, chorizo, spring onions, tomato and pine nuts to start, then saddle of venison with pancetta, red cabbage, pear and Dijon crust, and plum crumble or orange, cinnamon and rum pudding to finish. The wine list strays far beyond the borders of France, but includes a sprinkling of premium French whites and reds for ballast; by the glass from £3.40 and bottle £14.50.
Chef/s: Neil Forbes and Ben Radford. **Open:** all week L 12 to 2.15, D 5.30 to 10 (Sat from 6). **Closed:** 24 to 26 Dec, 31 Dec, Jan 1 and 2. **Meals:** alc (main courses £15 to £20). Pre-theatre (5.30 to 6.45 – not Sat) £16 (2 courses) to £21. **Service:** not inc. **Details:** Cards accepted. 40 seats. Wheelchair access. Music. Children's portions.

Centotre

Buzzing all-day café-bar
103 George Street, Edinburgh, EH2 3ES
Tel no: (0131) 225 1550
www.centotre.com
Italian | £30
Cooking score: 2

Victor and Carina Contini are part of the celebrated Edinburgh family that runs the Valvona and Crolla empire, but in 2004 they veered off to do their own thing - a buzzing all-day caffè-bar where you can have anything from morning coffee to a three-course dinner. The premises were once a banking hall and retain a stately feel although fixtures and fittings are contemporary (for example, the bar area near the entrance has a flat screen showing Italian televison stations). In the main dining area the Continis' genuine enthusiasm for straightforward but high-quality Italian food is apparent in a simple rucola salad or antipasto that includes good prosciutto di Parma and mozzarella (delivered weekly from Campania). Mains include a great mixed seafood dish (chargrilled halibut, monkfish, scallops and fennel with lemon and parsley butter), Milanese veal (fried in egg and breadcrumbs) and a fine selection of pizza. There is a decent choice of Italian wines (by the glass from £4.25), some great ice creams, Italian cheeses and ample desserts.
Chef/s: Carina Contini. **Open:** Mon to Sat 7.30am to 11pm (summer) 10 to 10 (winter). **Closed:** 25 and 26 Dec, 1 Jan. **Meals:** Set menu £12.95. **Service:** not inc. **Details:** Cards accepted. 140 seats. 40 seats outside. No mobile phones. Wheelchair access. Music. Children's portions.

Please send us your feedback

To register your opinion about any restaurant listed in the Guide, or a new restaurant that you wish to bring to our attention, please visit the web address at the bottom of the page. Your feedback informs the content of the book and will be used to compile next year's reviews.

David Bann

56-58 St Mary's Street, Edinburgh, EH1 1SX
Tel no: (0131) 556 5888
www.davidbann.co.uk
Vegetarian | £20
Cooking score: 2

Reader feedback about this establishment is splendidly consistent: 'the best vegetarian restaurant in Scotland', notes one, 'miles ahead of the wholefood café genre' reports another. David Bann runs a slick, modern venue with dark wood and sharp lines, where starters 'can take longer to describe than to eat'. Across the entire menu, extensive and complex combinations of flavours and ingredients face off against the absence of meat or fish. An aduki bean and aubergine galette served as a main course is not just a galette, but made with organic Scottish beer crêpe, a sub-menu of spices and is accompanied by juniper-pickled cucumber and lots more besides. In similar vein, the dark-chocolate soufflé comes with vanilla ice cream, white chocolate sauce and forest fruits coulis. Wines by the glass start at £2.75 (bottles from £11.75) and with mains all under £12, this venue offers decent value for money too.
Chef/s: David Bann. **Open:** all week 11 to 10. **Closed:** 25 to 26 Dec, 1 to 2 Jan. **Meals:** Set menu £20. **Details:** Cards accepted. 80 seats. No music. Wheelchair access. Children's portions.

Forth Floor

Open-plan foodie paradise
Harvey Nichols, 30-34 St Andrews Square, Edinburgh, EH2 2AD
Tel no: (0131) 524 8350
www.harveynichols.co.uk
Modern European | £36
Cooking score: 3

The fourth floor of Harvey Nichols in Edinburgh is an open-plan foodie paradise that includes the food hall, a cocktail bar, a brasserie and the main restaurant. It also has a terrace and views of the city centre and the

Forth, hence the doubly punning name. Consequently, you can find people here buying posh sweets, sipping a mojito especial, fitting in a coffee between purchases downstairs or actually having dinner. Stuart Muir's kitchen delivers slick and modern dishes, three courses perhaps kicking off with seared tuna alongside a peanut caramel profiterole, lemon goats' cheese and ceviche sauce. Then you might try roast venison with beetroot purée, pommes Anna and sauce gibier, and kulfi parfait with saffron candy and pomegranate to finish. The wine list is extensive and truly interesting with a fair selection at under £30 with Harvey Nichols' own-brand by the glass from £4. Some vintage Bordeaux is priced to bemuse, however, well into four figures – £4,000 for a 1982 Petrus anyone?

Chef/s: Stuart Muir. **Open:** all week L 12 to 3 (3.30 Sat and Sun), Tues to Sat D 6 to 10. **Closed:** 25 Dec and 1 Jan. **Meals:** Set L £19.50 (2 courses) to £23.50. **Service:** 10%. **Details:** Cards accepted. 60 seats. 14 seats outside. Air-con. Separate bar. Wheelchair access. Music. Children's portions. Car parking.

La Garrigue

The flavour of Languedoc
31 Jeffrey Street, Edinburgh, EH1 1DH
Tel no: (0131) 557 3032
French | £30
Cooking score: 3
£5 OFF **V**

The proposition here is quite simple: an experienced chef from South West France – Jean Michel Gauffre – presenting his native Languedoc dishes in an informal environment filled with attractive wooden-sculpted furniture from the late and acclaimed craftsman Tim Stead. But this simplicity inspires more affection than virtually any other restaurant in the city – positive readers' comments could fill a page of the Guide on their own, one describing La Garrigue as 'unique, rustic, friendly and a real food lover's paradise'. As for the food, a typical three-course dinner might commence with baked sardines filled with spinach and bacon and

served with a fresh herb salad, go on to twice-cooked pork belly teamed with quince charlotte and parsley mash, and finish with bitter-chocolate mousse with confit oranges. Wines by the glass start at £4 with some great selections on the list from Languedoc including a couple of Mas de Daumas Grand Cru (1992 and 1993) at the top end. The attention to detail, authenticity, lack of pretension, relaxed environment and service are all equally well reported.

Chef/s: Jean-Michel Gauffre. **Open:** Mon to Sat L 12 to 2.30, D 6.30 to 9.30. **Closed:** Sun, 25 and 26 Dec, Hogmaney to 2 Jan. **Meals:** Set L £13 (2 courses) to £15.50, Set D £24.50 (2 courses) to £29.50. **Service:** 10%. **Details:** Cards accepted. 50 seats. Air-con. Wheelchair access. Music. Children's portions.

Haldanes

Classic Franco-Scots cuisine
13B Dundas Street, Edinburgh, EH3 6QG
Tel no: (0131) 556 8407
www.haldanesrestaurant.com
French/Scottish
Cooking score: 3
🍶

Haldane's spent around decade in Albany Street before moving here in early 2006: a New Town basement with bare stone walls, shining glassware and Jack Vettriano prints. Its reputation for classic Franco-Scots cuisine continues unabated, surely catering to a core clientele whose concept of fine dining was formed before the likes of Abstract, Forth Floor or Kitchin appeared on the local scene. This is a neighbourhood of old money and independent art galleries, however, so Haldane's has not changed its winning formula. That could see starters of haggis in filo with mustard mash and whisky sauce, while fillet of beef with roasted celeriac gratin, black-pepper sabayon and red wine sauce is a typical main course. To finish, sugar-glazed lemon tart with sorbet in a brandy basket. The wine list is a stimulating internation collection, which extends to a good selection of clarets and French regional wines. House wines from £14 to £18.

Chef/s: George Kelso. **Open:** Tue to Fri L 12 to 1.30, Tue to Sat D 6 to 9.30. **Closed:** 25 Dec, 1 Jan. **Meals:** Set D £22.25 (2 courses) to £27.75. **Service:** not inc. **Details:** Cards accepted. 50 seats. Separate bar. Wheelchair access. Music. Children's portions.

Kalpna

Champion of Indian vegetarian cooking
2-3 St Patrick Square, Edinburgh, EH8 9EZ
Tel no: (0131) 667 9890
www.kalpnarestaurant.com
Indian/Vegetarian | £20
Cooking score: 2

'Looks smarter outside, bit of a freshen-up inside,' noted a regular on the spring 2008 refurbishment of this champion of Indian vegetarian cooking. Otherwise nothing has changed. A few South Indian dishes such as masala dosa make an appearance, but the main input is from Gujerat. The menu includes traditional dishes such as paneer butter masala or dhal tarka, but it pays to check out the list of specialities: mughal kufta is cheese, onion, nuts and potato fritters served in a hot spicy sauce, while shahi sabzi is mixed vegetables, nuts and pineapple cooked in an almond saffron sauce laced with spicy spinach. The lunchtime buffet has proved disappointing and with 'sloppy curries' and pakora that had been 'sitting too long under spotlights' is best avoided 'unless you're a hungry student'. House wine is £11.75.

Chef/s: Ajay Bhartdwaj. **Open:** all week L 12 to 2, D 5.30 to 11. **Closed:** Christmas to New Year. **Meals:** alc (main courses £5.75 to £8.95). Set L £7 (2 courses). **Service:** 10%. **Details:** Cards accepted. 60 seats. Air-con. Wheelchair access. Children allowed.

Kitchin

Refined cooking in a down-to-earth atmosphere
78 Commercial Quay, Leith, Edinburgh, EH6 6LX
Tel no: (0131) 555 1755
www.thekitchin.com
Modern European | £43
Cooking score: 6

The tone is impeccably judged, from the first welcome onwards at Tom Kitchin's brilliantly understated restaurant. Largely French staff are well-informed and courteous and the low-lit ambience, with its peek-a-boo views of the kitchen and discreet window blinds, is highly relaxing. Menus are squarely in the modern European idiom and don't just represent a roll-call of standard ingredients. Deep-fried coxcomb in Madeira sauce was on offer one spring evening, as were octopus carpaccio and a main course of stuffed rabbit saddle with sautéed snails. A first-course salad of smoked eel with apple three ways (fresh, dried and jelly) that came with vivid beetroot purée and full-throttle horseradish crème fraîche was followed by a main course of Anjou pigeon served on a mixture of wild mushrooms in a red wine sauce infused with foie gras, its richness offset by puréed spinach, a cocktail stick thriftily gathering up the liver and heart of the bird, alongside pieces of bacon and onion. This was a confident, bravura performance. Desserts comprise an imaginative range, from a cheesecake variation served with Scots rhubarb, a yoghurt sorbet and chocolate sauce, to the Agen prunes speciality, in which the fruits are marinated in Armagnac for six months and then piled into a martini glass, topped with deep-flavoured prune and Armagnac ice cream. Wines are a delight. Classical French stuff is clearly the list's main sheet anchor, but there are shorter and eminently sound selections from elsewhere, and prices are not too heavy. An opening page of by-the-glass items, starting at £5.50, offers exemplary quality.

Chef/s: Tom Kitchin. **Open:** Tue to Sat 12.30 to 2.30, 7.30 to 10. **Meals:** alc (main courses £21 to £29) Set L £19.50. **Service:** not inc. **Details:** Cards accepted. 45 seats. 32 seats outside. No mobile phones. Wheelchair access. Music.

Plumed Horse

Intimate restaurant, intelligent cooking
50-54 Henderson Street, Edinburgh, EH6 6DE
Tel no: (0131) 554 5556
www.plumedhorse.co.uk
Modern European | £39
Cooking score: 5

Chef Tony Borthwick has had a couple of years to get his feet firmly under the table (or stove) since opening in Leith at the end of 2006. With comments like 'the food was superb, exquisite and surprising taste and texture combinations', Borthwick's capable cooking has certainly won over an appreciative clientele. This is a small, intimate restaurant in an unlikely location 'situated not in the best location in Leith', albeit not far from some heavyweight competitors. The art on the walls changes regularly while décor stays smart and understated. The cooking owes much to France, as evidenced by a lunch that opened with sautéed langoustine with Avruga and went on to roast fillet of John Dory with queen scallops, green beans and scallop and vermouth velouté. Dinner could bring poached and roasted fillet of free-range pork, teamed with a mousseline of foie gras, slow-braised belly, mashed potato, clapshot, Pedro Ximénez sauce and raisins, and reporters have praised 'wonderfully succulent' guinea fowl and Gressingham duck. A rhubarb crumble with clotted-cream ice cream and a pineapple tarte Tatin have found favour, too. Service has been described as 'just right'. The wine list is good and has a strong line in half bottles. House wine is £18 (from £4.50 by the glass).

Chef/s: Tony Borthwick. **Open:** Tue to Sat L 12 to 1.30, D 7 to 9. **Closed:** 25 and 26 Dec, 1 Jan. **Meals:** Set L £17.50 (2 courses) to £21, Set D £32 (2 courses) to £39. **Service:** Not inc. **Details:** Cards accepted. 38 seats. Wheelchair access. Music. Children's portions.

Prestonfield, Rhubarb

Priestfield Road, Edinburgh, EH16 5UT
Tel no: (0131) 225 1333
www.prestonfield.com
Modern European
Cooking score: 4

Time flies by. It seems not so long ago that restaurateur James Thomson added to his mini-empire of Edinburgh establishments by refurbishing the old Prestonfield House Hotel and relaunching simply as Prestonfield with Rhubarb its flagship restaurant. Five years later and the restaurant has established itself as a romantic destination diner. Prestonfield is an authentic seventeenth-century mansion, overlaid with modern fabrics and sensibilities and creating a major wow factor. Stepping into its dining room is a little like stepping into a period film set (albeit with contemporary touches). As for the food, you might start dinner with sweet garlic-crusted cod on pea purée with sauce vierge, then chicken breast on creamed Savoy cabbage with tarragon jus. If the assiette of rhubarb desserts doesn't tempt, caramelised pear and custard tart with nutmeg ice cream doubtless will. The wine list remains encyclopaedic and readers have praised the 'beautiful setting and excellent service'. Our questionnaire was not returned, so the information below may have changed.

Chef/s: John McMahon. **Open:** all week L 12 to 3, D 6 to 10.30 (11 Fri and Sat). **Meals:** alc (main courses £16 to £28). **Service:** not inc. **Details:** 100 seats. 20 seats outside. Wheelchair access. Music. Car parking.

Which? Campaigns

To find out more about Which? food and drink campaigns, please visit:
www.which.co.uk

Restaurant Martin Wishart

54 The Shore, Leith, Edinburgh, EH6 6RA
Tel no: (0131) 553 3557
www.martin-wishart.co.uk
Modern French | £50
Cooking score: 8

Martin Wishart has gone from strength to culinary strength over recent years. There is consummate attention to detail from first to last, and the acclamation of the cooking that crops up in reports – 'food as art' – indicates that customers appreciate what he is trying to do. If you're inclined to be sceptical about proliferations of canapés, this is the place to change your mind. At an inspection visit all were superb, from the Parmesan gougère to the confit duck dunked in a beetroot glaze. Prime materials are excellent, and there is generally an impeccable logic to the way flavours build in a dish, as was the case with Iberico pork loin, which came with a fondue of melting Epoisses and medjool date (an inspired touch), an array of organic vegetables and a light-brown jus infused with star-anise. Cooking treatments are notably gentle, as in the steaming of sea bass, which is accompanied by oyster ravioli and runner beans in a lemongrass cappuccino. Just occasionally, the touch might seem less sure, as was the case with the intensely vinegary, Japanese-style pickled mushrooms that came with shredded crab, blue-fin tuna sashimi and wasabi ice cream. Add a coulis of sweet red pepper, too, and the dish seemed to be pulling in too many directions. Desserts commendably aim to keep things light. Fromage frais and lemon curd in a sablé biscuit, sauced with camomile, shouldn't outface anybody, and nor does a striped terrine of yoghurt with passion fruit and apricot, served with warm pistachio mousse. Service is attentive to a tee, highly skilled, but perhaps a touch over-formal in the surroundings. The wine list has much to commend it, with a mouth-watering collection of classic French wines (including rarities such as René Muré's beefy Alsace Pinot Noir), as well as the pick of Australian growers

and good Spaniards. If there is an Achilles' heel, it lies in the surprisingly humdrum choice of wines by the glass. Bottles start at £19.50.
Chef/s: Martin Wishart. **Open:** Tue to Sat L 12 to 2, D 7 to 10. **Closed:** Christmas and New Year. **Meals:** Set D £50 to £60 (6 courses). **Service:** not inc. **Details:** Cards accepted. 54 seats. Air-con. No mobile phones. Wheelchair access. Music.

Valvona & Crolla Caffè Bar

Italian cooking with high-quality ingredients
19 Elm Row, Edinburgh, EH7 4AA
Tel no: (0131) 556 6066
www.valvonacrolla.com
Italian | £22
Cooking score: 3

Valvona and Crolla is a legendary delicatessen founded in 1934; the Caffè Bar at the rear was added in 1996. Housed in a converted stable with straightforward décor it aims to provide basic Italian cooking with high-quality ingredients, something that has won it many fans. Open throughout the day, people drop in for coffee and cake, brilliant panatella sandwiches (spicy Italian pork sausage and Modena fruit chutney, perhaps) as well as more substantial meals. If you're in the mood at lunchtime you could have bruschetta con cime di rape to start (broccoli stems sautéed with garlic and chilli on griddled sourdough bread) then great pizza, pasta or a hearty stufato di agnello (slow-cooked lamb stew with potatoes, red peppers and tomato sauce); classic lemon cake with crème fraîche for dessert. House red and white are £11 and £12 respectively, but diners can pull any bottle off the deli shelf and have it for retail price plus corkage – a great option given their selection of Italian wines. Valvona & Crolla added to their empire in 2004, opening the VinCaffè on Multrees Walk. Open in the evenings, this operates more as a restaurant, but takes a similar approach to food.

Chef/s: Pina Trano. Open: Mon to Sat 8 to 6, Sun 10.30 to 4.30. Closed: 25 and 26 Dec, 1 and 2 Jan. Meals: alc (main course £9.99 to £14.99). Service: not inc. Details: Cards accepted. 55 seats. Air-con. Music. Children's portions.

Vintners Rooms

Historic setting
The Vaults, 87 Giles Street, Leith, Edinburgh, EH6 6BZ
Tel no: (0131) 554 6767
www.thevintnersrooms.com
French | £35
Cooking score: 4

This site is home to ancient cellars that catered to Leith's wine trade with France. In the sixteenth century a single-storey warehouse was built above them, replaced by the current building in the late eighteenth century. The Vintners Rooms takes full advantage of this living history with two dining areas: a former wine sales room with impeccable stucco and a more informal space with tables by the bar. Silvio Praino (front of house) and Patrice Ginestrière (chef) make for an experienced team, offering what they describe as French-Mediterranean cooking. You might start with an unusual warm salad of smoked eel with dandelion and frisée, move on to a robust roast fillet of Buccleuch beef with Perigord truffle sauce, then finish with brioche pain perdu with rum and raisin ice cream. House wines by the glass start at £4.50, the list is strong on French and Italian examples. In early 2008, the Vintners opened its bar area all day for drinks and light dishes like oysters, asparagus omelette or beef bourguignon – a welcome move.

Chef/s: Patrice Ginestrière. Open: Tue to Sat L 12 to 2, D 7 to 10. Closed: Sun and Mon. Meals: Set L £16.50 (two courses) to £19. Details: Cards accepted. 60 seats. Separate bar. Wheelchair access. Music. Children's portions. Car parking.

Witchery by the Castle

Hubble bubble...
Castlehill, Royal Mile, Edinburgh, EH1 2NF
Tel no: (0131) 225 5613
www.thewitchery.com
Modern European | £55
Cooking score: 2

If a restaurant has a big reputation, people then have high expectations – and quite rightly so. But when it doesn't deliver? The Witchery has long been seen as a destination diner. Sitting at the top of the Royal Mile, beside Edinburgh Castle, it has a great location, enjoys many celebrity endorsements, while the candle-lit interior of red leather and wooden panelling has always been atmospheric. The enthusiastic wine list is enormous and the dinner menu offers wild rabbit terrine and Toulouse sausage with beetroot remoulade and herb salad to start, seafood platter as a main (lobster, oysters, langoustine, clams, mussels, crab and smoked salmon) and roast black figs, pain perdu and vanilla mousse for dessert. It has been around for a long time, though, and one reporter (who ate two nights running) suggests the Witchery had been 'carried away by its fame'. A bad patch for the old place then? Reports please.

Chef/s: Douglas Roberts. Open: all week L 12 to 4, D 5.30 to 11.30. Closed: 25 and 26 Dec. Meals: alc (main courses £19.95 to £50). Set L and pre-theatre £12.95 (2 courses). Service: not inc. Details: Cards accepted. 50 seats. Wheelchair access. Music.

ALSO RECOMMENDED

▲ Fishers Bistro
1 Shore, Leith, Edinburgh, EH6 6QW
Tel no: (0131) 554 5666
Seafood

Fishers Bistro has been around since 1991, sitting just where the Water of Leith flows into the docks, serving decent seafood in an informal environment. Long-standing favourites from the 'Fishers Features' menu include fish soup, half a dozen Loch Fyne oysters (£6.95) or the impressive hot shellfish platter for two (£70), although you have to order 24 hours in advance. Elsewhere, there's whole lemon sole with saffron, caper and dill butter (£17.95) and basic desserts like vanilla crème brûlée (£4.75) or roast hazelnut cake. Wines start at £11.95. Open all week. Fisher's in the City (58 Thistle Street) is the central Edinburgh branch with similar menus.

Gullane

La Potinière
Consistently outstanding
34 Main Street, Gullane, EH31 2AA
Tel no: (01620) 843 214
www.la-potiniere.co.uk
Modern British | £38
Cooking score: 6

With its pointed roofs and low ceilings, this is a singular-looking venue, and the unassuming nature of the decor, together with the disinclination to stand on ceremony, belie the fact that here is one of Scotland's premier restaurants. The reputation of La Potinière has stood it in good stead in many editions of the Guide, and under Mary Runciman and Keith Marley, the place has gone from strength to strength. Suppliers are proudly listed on the left-hand side of the menu, for everything from meats and fish to cheeses, eggs and mineral water, and there are no prizes for guessing that it's the pick of excellent Scots produce that is showcased. Menus keep things good and simple with a pair of choices at each of three stages (four at dinner when a soup such as butternut squash with a mousse of scallops and sole intervenes between starter and main). First up might be a serving of Savoy cabbage stuffed with duck confit in a truffle and wild-mushroom sauce or perhaps a scarcely less loin-girding celeriac, Brie and prune tart with a warm salad of lentils. Main course is fish or meat – either salted cod on crushed new potatoes with spring onions and a citrus sauce or poached and seared venison fillet with dauphinoise, puréed beetroot and a tangy jus containing a slosh of damson gin. Execution and timing are well-nigh flawless throughout. Desserts might be as light as a serving of rhubarb with vanilla yoghurt cream and a rhubarb and elderflower granita or as fortifying as apple and almond tart served warm with apple coulis and caramel ice cream. The compact wine list makes a commendable effort below £25, and has a good showing of halves. Five house wines come in at £16 to £18 (£3 or £4 a glass).

Chef/s: Mary Runciman. **Open:** Wed to Sun L 12.30 to 2, Wed to Sun D 7 to 8.30. **Meals:** Set menu £38. **Service:** not inc. **Details:** Cards accepted. 30 seats. No music. No mobile phones. Wheelchair access. Children's portions. Car parking.

Linlithgow

★NEW ENTRY★
Champany Inn
Aberdeen Angus steaks – and more
Philipstoun, Linlithgow, EH49 7LU
Tel no: (01506) 834 532
www.champany.com
British | £53
Cooking score: 3

The Davidsons have been running their restaurant for 25 years. Set in a collection of whitewashed, red-roofed cottages, it has a character all its own: there is a bar with beams with a wine cellar on the mezzanine floor and the dining room has exposed stone walls and a timber ceiling. This is a steak house with a win-win formula: well-hung Aberdeen Angus beef is chargrilled and they also specialise in fish from their own smokepot. A deep pocket is necessary to pay for starters such as prawn cocktail (priced at £14), or main courses such as entrecôte steak with mushrooms and mustard (a hefty £37), but the restaurant is redeemed by a 'quick lunch' menu. There is also a chop and ale house with its own kitchen team, which offers simpler, speedier and less expensive meals. House wines start at £20.50.

Chef/s: Liam Ginnane. **Open:** Mon to Fri L 12.30 to 2, Mon to Sat D 7 to 10. **Closed:** Sun. **Meals:** alc (main courses £22 to £44). Set L £19.50 (2 courses). **Service:** 10%. **Details:** Cards accepted. 50 seats. Separate bar. Car parking.

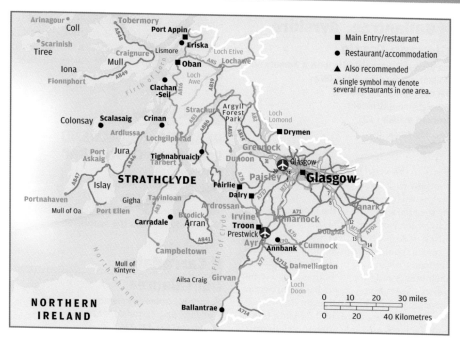

Annbank
Enterkine House

Informal Ayrshire splendour
Annbank, KA6 5AL
Tel no: (01292) 520 580
www.enterkine.com
Modern European | £45
Cooking score: 4

£5 OFF

'The informally formal country house' is how Enterkine likes to style itself, referring to the fact that, although it is furnished and decorated to five-star standards of comfort and amenity, the approach is as relaxed as one hopes to find in such a setting. In the heart of Ayrshire, it's a sparkling white edifice built in the 1930s. Paul Moffat does the place proud with a carefully considered menu of fine country-house dining. Ingredients are top-notch, whether in the soufflé of Arbroath smokie and goats' cheese, served with spinach, red peppers and wholegrain Meaux mustard or loin of red deer with red cabbage, celery root gratin, salsify and morels. Castle Douglas lamb appears as a trio of roasted loin, kidneys and caramelised sweetbreads, while Buccleuch beef is hung to maturity and then richly tricked out with foie gras, creamed celeriac, caramelised shallots and gnocchi. Technique is highly accomplished throughout, right up to desserts such as passion fruit creams with marinated pineapple and kiwi purée. Fine French cheeses from Vernier are served with quince jelly and walnut bread. The wine list does a whistle-stop tour round the main producing regions, starting at £20.50, or £5.25 a glass.

Chef/s: Paul Moffat. **Open:** all week, L 12 to 2, D 6.30 to 8.45. **Meals:** Set L £18.50, Set L Sun £25, Set D £45, Set D midweek £21.95 (2 courses) to £29.50 (4 courses). **Service:** not inc. **Details:** Cards accepted. 30 seats. Music. Children's portions. Car parking.

Ballantrae, Ayrshire

Glenapp Castle

An exclusive baronial pile with a homely air
Ballantrae, Ayrshire, KA26 0NZ
Tel no: (01465) 831 212
www.glenappcastle.com
Modern British | £55
Cooking score: 6

£5 OFF 🍽

Entry to this venerable Victorian estate is only for those with a reservation – on arrival, one is welcomed up the grand staircase to the lounge above to admire the view across the Irish Sea to the Island of Arran and Ailsa Craig. Such grandeur could be intimidating, but Fay and Graham Cowan have made Glenapp Castle their home, and they are both on hand to put guests at ease. Adam Stokes has taken over in the kitchen. Like his predecessor, Matt Weedon – now at Lords of the Manor (see entry) – he trained at Hambleton Hall (see entry). At inspection, his six-course, set-price dinner menu began with a subtle pan-fried sea bream with langoustine and minestrone consommé, and was followed by an impressively presented ballottine of foie gras with spiced pineapple and pain d'epices, then roasted sea bass with cockles, fennel and dill purée with fennel and vanilla salad. The centrepiece was choice between roast Brochneil Farm chicken served with haggis, morels, pea shoots and a thyme sauce, or roast loin of Ayrshire lamb with tortellini of lamb shoulder, broad beans, chanterelles and a rosemary jus. Scottish cheeses came next, a dozen of which were lovingly described on a separate menu. The meal ended with a choice between dark chocolate tart with orange dust and orange sorbet, and a caramel, lime and ginger soufflé with pear sorbet. A white, red and dessert wine are suggested on the menu, but cheaper options from £25 are available on the wide-ranging wine list.

Chef/s: Adam Stokes. **Open:** Daily L 12.30 to 2, D 7 to 10. **Closed:** 2 Jan to late March. **Meals:** Set L £35, set D £55. **Service:** not inc. **Details:** Cards accepted. 34 seats. No music. No mobile phones. Wheelchair access. Car parking.

Cairndow

READERS RECOMMEND
Loch Fyne Oyster Bar
Seafood
Clachan, Cairndow, PA26 8BL
Tel no: (01499) 600236
www.lochfyne.com
'Oysters direct from the suppliers'

Carradale

Dunvalanree
Hospitable home-from-home
Port Righ Bay, Carradale, PA28 6SE
Tel no: (01583) 431 226
www.dunvalanree.com
Modern Scottish | £25
Cooking score: 2

£5 OFF 🍽 V £30

The Milsteads' appealing, three-storey home-from-home stands in gardens right by the edge of Port Righ Bay (on 'Macca's' celebrated Mull of Kintyre) and they are continuing a tradition of family hospitality that stretches back more than 60 years. There's no standing on ceremony, but bags of good humour and honest intent when it comes to dinner. A typically delightful repast might begin with smoked haddock and black pudding in bacon and tomato sauce before rack of Ifferdale lamb with minted pea purée and Marsala sauce or locally caught scallops with leeks and pickled ginger. Vegetarians have a separate menu, cheeses are from Campbeltown's three artisan producers, and there might be baked lemon cheesecake with hot toddy sauce or crème brûlée with raspberries to finish. The minuscule, 10-bin wine list has bottles from £11.95 (£3.50 a glass); also explore the fine collection of malt whiskies and Arran beers.

Chef/s: Alyson Milstead. **Open:** all week D only 7.30 (1 sitting). **Closed:** Christmas. **Meals:** Set D £21 (2 courses) to £25. **Service:** not inc. **Details:** Cards accepted. 24 seats. No music. Wheelchair access. Music. Children's portions. Car parking.

Clachan-Seil

Willowburn Hotel

Tranquil waterside retreat
Clachan-Seil, PA34 4TJ
Tel no: (01852) 300 276
www.willowburn.co.uk
Modern Scottish /French | £38
Cooking score: 3

Those in search of peaceful repose (and maybe a spot of wildlife watching) should cross the Clachan Bridge over the Atlantic and head for Jan and Chris Wolfe's idyllic retreat. Their house stands in gardens running down to the waters of Clachan Sound and has been transformed into an economic set-up with self-sufficiency on its mind. The Wolfes are not only dedicated bakers, they also smoke fish and have added a polytunnel to their increasingly productive smallholding for year-round pickings. Chris translates all of this into five-course evening extravaganzas with the accent on seasonality. Ingredients from further afield often find their way into the mix, thus roast partridge might be served with Armagnac mousse, sweet potato chips and boozy red-wine sauce, while fillet of pork could be given a macadamia and herb crust with spiced apple and dried cranberries on the side. To conclude, poached rhubarb sticks in rose syrup with yogurt mousse sounds appealing, or you might prefer an indulgent trio of chocolate samosas. The ever-growing wine list reads well and prices are commendable; house selections are £14 (£3.75 a glass).
Chef/s: Chris Wolfe. **Open:** all week D only 7 (1 sitting). **Closed:** mid-Nov to mid-Mar. **Meals:** Set D £38 (5 courses). **Service:** not inc. **Details:** Cards accepted. 20 seats. Separate bar. No mobile phones. Music. Children allowed.

Colonsay, Scalasaig

The Colonsay

Get away from it all...
Scalasaigh, Isle of Colonsay, Colonsay, Scalasaig, PA61 7YP
Tel no: (01951) 200 316
www.thecolonsay.com
Modern Scottish | £25
Cooking score: 2

Colonsay is a remote, sparsely populated island rich in wildlife and archeological remains – it would be hard to get more away-from-it-all than this. So the transformation of the island's eighteenth-century inn into a boutique-style hotel with an airy, contemporary dining room and a bar serving as the island's social hub (and the place for light lunch and supper) is to be applauded. The kitchen's approach is focused on island produce with a strong line in fish from local boats and own-grown produce. It delivers simple, straightforward cooking, typified by local crab salad with brown crab dressing or Colonsay garden salad with courgette flowers stuffed with ricotta. Other dishes might include mains of poached halibut and seared monkfish with sorrel hollandaise or filet of pork stuffed with prunes and served with sage gravy. The brief wine list covers most bases and opens at £12.
Chef/s: Kevin May. **Open:** all week L 12 to 2.30, D 6 to 9. **Closed:** Nov and Feb. **Meals:** alc (main courses £9.50 to £16.95). Set menu £11.95 (2 courses) to £13.95. **Service:** not inc. **Details:** Cards accepted. 60 seats. 30 seats outside. Separate bar. Wheelchair access. Music. Children's portions. Car parking.

Readers recommend

A 'readers recommend' review is a genuine quote from a report sent in by one of our readers. We intend to follow up these suggestions throughout the year to come.

Crinan

Crinan Hotel, Westward Restaurant

Unbeatable location
Crinan, PA31 8SR
Tel no: (01546) 830 261
www.crinanhotel.com
Scottish/French | £40
Cooking score: 4

The setting on Argyll's west coast is unbeatable: Jura is just five miles across the water, while small boats pass the door as they emerge from the Crinan Canal. Nick Ryan and his wife, Frances Macdonald, have run the Crinan Hotel since the early 1970s with Scott Kennedy running the kitchen for several years now. He makes full use of local seafood (whole Loch Crinan jumbo prawns will have been landed earlier the very same day) to produce a four-course menu that inspires a sense of 'all being right with the world'. One starter might be organic chicken liver pâté, but others could feature crab, lobster or brochettes of Loch Fyne scallops. After an intermediate course of, say, gazpacho, mains may include Scotch beef and Argyll lamb or grilled halibut with dill pommes purée, green beans and red pepper pesto. Poached pear and red wine reduction with a madeleine is a typical dessert. Wines are listed by grape variety, by the glass from £4.10 and bottle £23.50.
Chef/s: Scott Kennedy. **Open:** all week L 12 to 2.30, D 6 to 8.30. **Closed:** 23 Dec to 4 Feb. **Meals:** alc (main courses £12.50 to £23.50). Set D £49.50 (4 courses). **Service:** not inc. **Details:** Cards accepted. 50 seats. 20 seats outside. Separate bar. Wheelchair access. Children's portions. Car parking.

Also recommended

An 'also recommended' entry is not a full entry, but is provisionally suggested as an alternative to main entries.

Dalry

Braidwoods

A gem of undiluted Scottishness
Drumastle Mill Cottage, Dalry, KA24 4LN
Tel no: (01294) 833 544
www.braidwoods.co.uk
Modern Scottish | £38
Cooking score: 6

Keith and Nicola Braidwood have notched up more than a dozen years in residence at their modest gem of a country restaurant in two remote whitewashed mill cottages. There's still a touch of earthy ruggedness about the place, although on-going re-decoration has given the interior a smoother, more modern look. A mood of quiet, attentive courtesy prevails and an enduring love of seasonal ingredients is at the heart of business in the kitchen. Keith cooks with natural-born sensitivity and care, bringing together incisive ideas and creating clear, clean-flavoured partnerships, whether it's hand-dived Wester Ross scallops on finely shredded Brussels sprouts with chilli and ginger or seared roast breast of quail and confit leg on a turnip and parsnip purée. The undiluted Scottishness of proceedings shines through every course, from an Arbroath smokie soup infused with saffron to a pairing of roast loin of Highland red deer and breast of squab pigeon with lemon thyme-scented Savoy cabbage. Also look out for the honey-glazed breast of duck carved on carrot purée and served with 'a wee duck cottage pie'. Beef is locally reared at nearby Auchengree Farm, cheeses are sourced from Scottish maestro Iain Mellis, and the line-up of finely tuned desserts might include caramelised lime cream on a Champagne rhubarb compote or warm Valrhona chocolate tart with maple syrup ice cream. A page of esoteric seasonal suggestions opens the wine list, which pays special attention to the French classics, but allows room for some elite bottles from New World sources. House recommendations start at £16.95 (£4 a glass) and half-bottles are plentiful.

Chef/s: Keith Braidwood. **Open:** Wed to Sun L 12 to 1.30, Tue to Sat D 7 to 9. **Closed:** Sun, 25 and 26 Dec, first 3 weeks Jan, first 2 weeks Sept. **Meals:** Set L £19 (2 courses) to £22, Set D £38 (3 courses) to £42. **Service:** not inc. **Details:** Cards accepted. 24 seats. No music. No mobile phones. Children's portions. Car parking.

▎Eriska
Isle of Eriska
Stunning island location
Ledaig, Eriska, PA37 1SD
Tel no: (01631) 720 371
www.eriska-hotel.co.uk
Scottish | £39
Cooking score: 4

This romantic hotel sits proudly on its island surrounded by the wild beauty of Scotland and the tamed beauty of a golf course. The building, known as the Big House, is a beautiful castellated creation in the Scottish baronial style, built in 1884. Inside this 'very special place' you'll find a smart and traditional country-house interior with some subtle modern additions (air-conditioning in the dining room, for example). Robert MacPherson has cooked here for more than 20 years and according to one reporter his food 'just keeps getting better'. The menus are weighted by impressive Scottish produce, from Oban-landed trout to Argyll roe deer. While the cooking is firmly rooted in the classics, it has an interesting modern edge. You could start with hand-dived Lismore scallops with confit tomato and lobster salad, Atsina cress and lime zest oil, them move on to breast of Gressingham duck with pithiviers of rillettes, olive jus and sweet onion marmalade. Round it off with anise-scented vanilla bavarois and red fruit jelly on banana sponge and sauce. A thorough, reasonably priced wine list opens at £12.50.
Chef/s: Robert MacPherson. **Open:** all week D only 7 to 9. (L residents only). **Closed:** Jan. **Meals:** Set D £39.50. **Service:** not inc. **Details:** Cards accepted. 50 seats. Air-con. Separate bar. Wheelchair access. Children's portions. Car parking.

▎Fairlie
Fins
Dedicated seafood enterprise
Fencefoot Farm, Fairlie, KA29 0EG
Tel no: (01475) 568 989
www.fencebay.co.uk
Seafood | £30
Cooking score: 2
£5 OFF

Fencebay is an admirable enterprise that originally started with a smokehouse, but now involves a farm shop and farmers' market in addition to Fins seafood restaurant. Bernard and Jill Thain have been in business here for more than two decades and they still rely heavily on the haul from Bernard's own boat. Regular lunch and dinner menus are bolstered by a blackboard full of daily specials, which vary depending on the day's catch. There is nothing too ambitious about the food, but flavours are fresh and the results are pleasing. Cullen skink, smoked fish pâté and oysters with bacon might feature among the starters, while mains could move into the realms of pepper-crusted salmon with whisky sauce or fillet of halibut with squat lobsters and langoustines in Chardonnay sauce. There are straightforward desserts to finish, plus a short list of affordable wines from £13.40 (£3.20 a glass).
Chef/s: Jane Burns. **Open:** Tue to Sun L 12 to 2.30, Tue to Sat D 7 to 9. **Closed:** Mon, 25 and 26 Dec, 1 Jan. **Meals:** alc (main courses L £10 to £18, D £14 to £20). **Service:** not inc. **Details:** Cards accepted. 50 seats. No mobile phones. Wheelchair access. Music. Children's portions. Car parking.

Glasgow

★NEW ENTRY★
An Lochan
Good-value cooking
340 Crow Road, Glasgow, G11 7HT
Tel no: (0141) 338 6606
www.anlochan.co.uk
British | £35
Cooking score: 1

The An Lochan brand started off in the mothership hotel in Cowal (see entry) and has spread over the last decade and more. It's a family business with the McKies' daughter Claire the chef at this Glasgow seafood restaurant they launched in 2004. A former café with big shopfront windows, this is a very economical establishment given the standard of cooking. Wines by the glass start at £3.95, £15.95 a bottle, and even the tasting menu is a shade under £35. This could bring half a dozen oysters and Champagne granita, then chowder, a sorbet, langoustine or whole sea bass as a main, and a dessert of gingerbread parkin. The menu generally draws on suppliers used by the Cowal hotel, which means hand-dived scallops, good venison, lamb and hot-smoked salmon, making this a restaurant well worth the relatively short trip from the city centre.
Chef/s: Claire McKie. **Open:** Tue to Sun L 12 to 2.30, Tue to Sat D 6 to 10. **Closed:** Mon, 25 Dec. **Meals:** alc (main courses £16.95 to £26.95). Set L £8.95 (2 courses), Set D £13.95 (2 courses) to £15.95. **Service:** not inc. **Details:** Cards accepted. 40 seats. 10 seats outside. No music. No mobile phones. Wheelchair access. Children's portions.

Readers recommend

A 'readers recommend' review is a genuine quote from a report sent in by one of our readers. We intend to follow up these suggestions throughout the year to come.

Brian Maule at Chardon d'Or
Classy French restaurant
176 West Regent Street, Glasgow, G2 4RL
Tel no: (0141) 248 3801
www.brianmaule.com
French | £40
Cooking score: 4
🍷

Brian Maule is Scottish, once worked as head chef at Le Gavroche, then moved to Glasgow in 2001 to set up Chardon d'Or. Based in a grand old townhouse in the city centre, it boasts an interior that is light and modern. The set-lunch menu doubles up as pre-theatre and has been praised for its value: anchovy, ham hough and parmesan salad or a competent roasted red pepper soup with pesto to start, perhaps, while the main course sampled at inspection was a perfectly fine hake fillet, although the accompanying tomato, basil and a shellfish bisque lacked the expected intensity. A selection of ice creams (caramel and strawberry) and sorbets (rhubarb and strawberry cassis) for dessert proved to be a highlight. Background music was 'hipper than expected', but overall the pre-theatre menu gave the impression of the high life glimpsed through gauze – as if you would have to come back for the full à la carte to witness the kitchen firing on all cylinders: maybe fried ox-tongue salad, followed by a roast fillet of Scotch beef with celeriac purée and truffle jus, all washed down by decent wines which start at £21.
Chef/s: Brian Maule. **Open:** Mon to Fri L 12 to 2, Mon to Sat D 6 to 10 (10.30 Fri and Sat). **Closed:** First 2 weeks Jan, 27 July to 13 Aug. **Meals:** alc (main courses £21 to £25.50). Set L and pre-theatre £16.95 (2 courses) to £19.95. **Service:** not inc. **Details:** Cards accepted. 100 seats. Music. Children's portions.

Gamba

Celebrating a decade of sound cooking
225A West George Street, Glasgow, G2 2ND
Tel no: (0141) 572 0899
www.gamba.co.uk
Seafood | £40
Cooking score: 3

Steps lure you down to Gamba's basement premises, found on the corner of West Campbell Street and West George Street. In 2008 the seafood restaurant celebrates its tenth anniversary – a decade of sound business on the part of owners Alan Tomkins and Derek Marshall, both luminaries of the local restaurant scene. The tiled floor and relatively simple furniture endure, all very tasteful with nothing to really distract from the food. Starters can be as simple as half a dozen oysters, but there might also be sea bass sashimi with wasabi, soy and pickled ginger or fish soup with crab meat, stem ginger and coriander and prawn dumplings. The Far East influence continues to resonate in a main course like hand-dived scallops with sticky rice and teriyaki sauce, less so in a simple whole roast sea bream with garlic, tomato, onion, olive oil and sweet soy. Valrhona chocolate with raspberry soufflé for dessert, perhaps, or lemon and thyme crème brûlée.
Chef/s: Derek Marshall. **Open:** Mon to Sat 12 to 2.30, D 5 to 10.30. **Closed:** Sun, Dec 25 and 26, Jan 1 and 2. **Meals:** alc (main courses £11.50 to £27.95). Set L £15.95 (2 courses) to £18.95, Pre-theatre (5 to 6.15) £15 (2 courses) to £18. **Service:** not inc. **Details:** Cards accepted. 55 seats. Separate bar. Music. Children's portions.

Michael Caines at ABode

Top-class cooking
The Arthouse, 129 Bath Street, Glasgow, G2 2SZ
Tel no: (0141) 572 6011
www.michaelcaines.com
Modern European | £40
Cooking score: 5

ABode is a joint venture on the part of hotelier Andrew Brownsword and chef Michael Caines – they now have four ABode hotels across the UK with a fifth (in Chester) scheduled for 2009. The food side of the business is branded with Michael Caines' initials, MC, which explains the name of the restaurant, although the actual chef in charge in Glasgow is Craig Dunn. The dining room is contemporary, overlaid on the Edwardian fabric of the building, while the evening à la carte gives full range to Dunn's talents. A starter of langoustine cannelloni could be difficult to pull off, but the langoustine came beautifully presented and perfectly done in its pasta wrap with braised fennel, sauce vierge and langoustine bisque. A well-reported sirloin of rare Mey beef with celeriac purée, fondant potato, baby spinach and Madeira sauce had equal aesthetic attraction. Dessert, meanwhile, was a riot: pistachio and cherry 'pain de gene' with Rivesault ice cream and wine sauce. For a restaurant of this standard the wine list feels fairly economical – lots of choice under £30 with house wine starting at £14.50, by the glass from £3.95.
Chef/s: Craig Dunn. **Open:** Tue to Sat L 12 to 2.30, D 6.30 to 10. **Closed:** Sun and Mon, 14 to 28 July. **Meals:** alc (main courses £18.50 to £23). Set L £13.50 (2 courses) to £17.50, Pre-theatre (6.30 to 7.30) £11 (2 courses). **Service:** optional. **Details:** Cards accepted. 45 seats. Air-con. Separate bar. Wheelchair access. Music. Children's portions. Car parking.

Rococo

Well-judged cooking
48 West Regent Street, Glasgow, G2 2RA
Tel no: (0141) 221 5004
www.rococoglasgow.co.uk
Modern European | £42
Cooking score: 3

It's not often that a restaurant moves premises – a few blocks across central Glasgow – but stays the same. Rococo pulled off the trick in spring 2008, its relocation to West Regent Street more a transplant than a change. The décor is still modern-swish, or fussy, depending on taste and chef Mark Tamburrini remains in charge; the venue even went from one basement to another. No radical departures on the menu either. The lunch menu doubles up with pre-theatre and could bring decent seared mackerel fillet with rocket salad and black olive dressing, while mains might feature daube of beef, monkfish or a grilled fillet of pink bream on choucroute with sauté and Roosevelt potato. Alternatively, the vegetarian option sees a very good ravioli of butternut squash, ricotta and golden raisin with incredibly intense roast ceps. Desserts might include milk chocolate torte with rum-and-raisin ice cream. Service standards are high. Wines start at £5.50 a glass, but the list has far more choice above £30 a bottle than below.
Chef/s: Mark Tamburrini. **Open:** all week L 12 to 3, D 5 to 10. **Meals:** alc (main courses £11.50 to £15.25). Set L £16 (2 courses) to £20, set D £33 (2 courses) to £42. **Service:** not inc. **Details:** Cards accepted. 40 seats. Air-con. Separate bar. Music. Children's portions.

78 St Vincent

With a turn-of-the-century French feel
78 St Vincent Street, Glasgow, G2 5UB
Tel no: (0141) 248 7878
www.78stvincent.com
Modern Scottish | £27
Cooking score: 1

Housed in a handsome building dating from 1914, 78 St Vincent has a curious mix of décor. Fixtures and fittings have a turn-of-the-century French feel (dark wood, brass rails) while one wall has a mural with human figures flying through a psychedelic sky. The economical set lunch might start with tea-smoked pigeon breast with fennel and chicory salad, followed by decent pan-seared salmon with champ mash, lime, chive and a rich plum tomato butter sauce, and a melting honeycomb parfait and poached pear for dessert. The à la carte lunch and dinner menus are a little more elaborate, the wine list is generally affordable with around three dozen bottles pitched at £25 or under, by the glass from £4.55. This venue is central, handy, the cooking has a few rough edges, but it tries hard and a Scottish reporter assured us it does the very best bread of any Glasgow restaurant. Our questionnaire was not returned, so some of the information below may have changed.
Chef/s: Robbie O'Keefe. **Open:** all week L 12 to 10 (10.30 Fri and Sat). **Meals:** alc (main courses £14.50 to £24.95). Set L and pre-theatre (served 4 to 7) £12.95 (2 courses) to £15.95. **Service:** not inc. **Details:** Cards accepted. 120 seats. No mobile phones. Wheelchair access. Music. Children's portions.

Stravaigin

A global tour

28 Gibson Street, Glasgow, G12 8NX
Tel no: (0141) 334 2665
www.stravaigin.com
Modern international | £30
Cooking score: 2

The Stravaigin empire includes this Gibson Street basement restaurant, a café-bar upstairs, and Stravaigin 2 at 8 Ruthven Lane, which operates on similar lines. In the basement restaurant, however, the corporate credo of 'think global, eat local' is given serious room to breathe. You might have a decidedly Scottish starter like west coast langoustine, crab and Mull cheddar gratin – or something more Asian such as Hong Kong red-roasted pork, soy greens with toasted peanuts and a marbled quail's egg. Mains could see a simple Smitton's Farm rump steak with chips, salad and béarnaise sauce or steamed lythe pepped up by a coconut, cashew and tamarind sauce, langoustine, mussels and snake beans, with Belgian chocolate tart and milk sorbet for dessert. Wines start at £3.55 a glass, bottles from £13.95. Good atmosphere and bags of fun.
Chef/s: Daniel Blencowe. **Open:** Fri, Sat and Sun 12 to 11, Mon to Thu D 5 to 11. **Closed:** 25 Dec, 1 Jan. **Meals:** alc (main courses £13 to £22). Pre-theatre (5 to 6.30) £12.95 (2 courses) to £15.95. **Service:** not inc. **Details:** Cards accepted. 72 seats. Air-con. Separate bar. No mobile phones. Music. Children's portions.

Ubiquitous Chip

A Glaswegian institution

12 Ashton Lane, Glasgow, G12 8SJ
Tel no: (0141) 334 5007
www.ubiquitouschip.co.uk
Scottish | £40
Cooking score: 4

The Ubiquitous Chip is a maze of bars and eating spaces that has evolved since 1971. At the moment the cobbled courtyard and indoor

space that form the main restaurant are more open-plan than previously, there is a mezzanine dining area above, a brasserie, three bars and the famous murals by Alasdair Gray. The courtyard is something special, looking well-kempt these days. This is where the kitchen gives full vent to the idea of Scottish cooking: venison haggis with mashed potato, carrot crisps and turnip cream, followed perhaps by ling on clapshot with chillied, roasted red pepper and crispy seaweed or Scottish sirloin steak with beef stovies and wild mushrooms, with oatmeal ice cream and fruit compote to finish. Glasses of house wine start at £4 (bottles from £15.95) while the huge list peaks with a 1985 Petrus. The Chip is a Glaswegian institution with a loyal fanbase and, as one reader commented, 'just superb, always'. 'Brilliant' staff and a great atmosphere are big contributing factors.
Chef/s: Ian Brown. **Open:** Mon to Sat L 12 to 2.30, Sun 12.30 to 3, Mon to Sat D 5.30 to 11, Sun D 6.30 to 11. **Closed:** 25 Dec, 1 Jan. **Meals:** Set L £23.85 (2 courses) to £29.85, Set D £34.80 (2 courses) to £39.85. **Details:** Cards accepted. 185 seats. 20 seats outside. Air-con. Separate bar. No music. Wheelchair access. Children's portions.

★NEW ENTRY★

La Vallée Blanche

Accomplished cooking

360 Byres Road, Glasgow, G12 8AY
Tel no: (0141) 334 3333
www.lavalleeblanche.com
French | £30
Cooking score: 3

When étain shut its doors in 2007, Glasgow foodies mourned its passing. Fortunately, in early 2008 chef Neil Clark moved to a new venue and took some of the étain staff with him. Far from their old Conran-inspired temple of light and glass, La Vallée Blanche (found up a flight of stairs on Byres Road) looks more like a pukka French ski-resort restaurant. The walls are covered in rough wooden slats, there are red banquettes and hessian-style floor covering. In some senses, it doesn't look promising – the wine list runs to a page, while the pre-printed menu has a drawing of a rustic wine salesman in a jaunty hat. But the actual dishes? They are accomplished. You could start with some hand-dived scallops with pea, ham and herbs or half-a-dozen Loch Fyne oysters. Then a beautiful chunk of halibut with cauliflower purée, white asparagus and zingy citrus sauce or a grilled fillet of Aberdeen Angus, and finish with a shot glass of lemon posset with citrus sorbet and mandarin pannacotta on the side. House wine is £18.50.

Chef/s: Neil Clark. **Open:** Tue to Fri L 12 to 2.15, D 5.30 to 10.30, Sat 11 to 11.30, Sun 11 to 10.30. **Closed:** Mon. **Meals:** alc (main courses £12 to £48). Set L £11.95 (2 courses) to £14.95, Set D £14.50 (2 courses) to £17.50. **Service:** optional. **Details:** Cards accepted. 65 seats. Air-con. Separate bar. Music. Children allowed.

▌Isle Of Mull

READERS RECOMMEND
Café Fish

The Pier, Main St, Tobermory, Isle Of Mull, PA75 6NU
Tel no: (01688) 301253
www.thecafefish.com
'Fantastic fish fresh from the boat'

▌Oban

★ READERS' RESTAURANT OF THE YEAR ★
SCOTLAND

Ee-Usk
Straightforward seafood cookery
North Pier, Oban, PA34 5QD
Tel no: (01631) 565 666
www.eeusk.com
Seafood | £30
Cooking score: 1

£5
OFF

'Fresh and innovative food with amazing views' is how one reader sums up the appeal of Alan MacLeod's friendly, versatile seafood restaurant on the wild Argyll coast. On one side there's a café serving pizza and pasta, on the other crowds gather in the restaurant for

Lismore oysters, smoked haddock chowder or Thai fishcakes to start, before going on to one of the extensive choice of main dishes. King scallops are served with a bacon and cabbage risotto, sea bass with creamed leeks and mash or you might opt for a royally laden seafood platter. Finish with bread-and-butter pudding laced with Bailey's, or lemon cheesecake and cream. Eight wines by the glass from £3.20 head up a short, sanely priced list.

Chef/s: Wayne Keenan. **Open:** all week, L 12 to 3, D 6 to 9.30. **Closed:** Christmas and 1 Jan. **Meals:** alc (main courses £11.95 to £19.95). **Service:** not inc. **Details:** 108 seats. 24 seats outside. Air-con. Wheelchair access. Music. Children allowed. Car parking.

ALSO RECOMMENDED
▲ Waterfront
1 The Railway Pier, Oban, PA34 4LW
Tel no: (01631) 563 110
www.waterfrontoban.co.uk
Seafood

The bayside location offers great views at this reliable seafood restaurant, which also boasts a lively bar with a more urban feel than the setting suggests. Simple classic preparations are the norm, the better to emphasise the freshness and quality of the fish and shellfish. Start perhaps with half-a-dozen local oysters dressed in chilli and coriander or a bowl of seafood chowder (£7.95), before progressing to Loch Duart salmon glazed in honey and mustard (£9.50) or seared scallops in garlic butter with spinach and potato gratin (£16.50). Homely puds include Granny Smith and blueberry strudel (£4.50). Wines from £15.50. Open all week.

Readers recommend

A 'readers recommend' review is a genuine quote from a report sent in by one of our readers. We intend to follow up these suggestions throughout the year to come.

Sorn

READERS RECOMMEND
READERS RECOMMEND
The Sorn Inn
Modern European
35 Main Street, Sorn, KA5 6HU
Tel no: (01290) 551305
www.sorninn.com
'Popular gastropub serving robust food'

Tighnabruaich

★NEW ENTRY★
An Lochan
Stunning views and local produce
Tighnabruaich, PA21 2BE
Tel no: 01700 811 239
www.anlochan.co.uk
British | £35
Cooking score: 3

In 1997 the McKie family took over the old Royal Hotel in Tighnabruaich on the sleepy Cowal peninsula and created the best hotel and restaurant for miles around. They built a reputation for great locally sourced food (especially venison and shell fish), ventured to Glasgow with a predominantly seafood restaurant in 2004 (see entry), then rebranded the whole business as An Lochan in 2006. Back at the hotel, dining options include a simple bar menu (fish pie, Buccleuch sirloin) as well as a more elaborate restaurant offering for the Deck and Crustacean at the front of the premises. The former is bistro-ish, the latter more formal; both look out over the Kyle of Bute. In the evening in either, Paul Scott's menu could bring hand-dived scallops with sweet potato purée and pancetta cream froth to start, then honey-roast duck breast or roast halibut with salsify, trompet mushroom, crispy potatoes and liquorice foam, with passion fruit soufflé to finish. Wines by the glass start at £3.95, bottles £16.95.
Chef/s: Paul Scott. Open: all week L 12.30 to 2.30, D 6.30 to 9. Closed: 2 weeks Christmas. Meals: alc (main courses £16 to £35). Details: Cards accepted.

60 seats. Separate bar. No music. No mobile phones. Wheelchair access. Children's portions. Children allowed. Car parking.

Troon

MacCallums Oyster Bar
Seafood served with warmth and cheer
The Harbour, Troon, KA10 6DH
Tel no: (01292) 319 339
Seafood | £29
Cooking score: 2
£30

'MacCallum's has a lovely, friendly atmosphere, and is simply decorated. The seafood is of the highest quality, the service is excellent, and staff are always happy to discuss what's on the menu.' So spoke a reporter for whom its absence would leave an agonising hiatus in life. Familiar fish and shellfish dishes cooked with panache will always have a following. Try oysters with shallot vinegar, grilled langoustines with garlic butter or smoked haddock and leek fishcakes to start, before settling down to the more elaborate main business. That may be roast pollack wrapped in pancetta with creamed Savoy cabbage and mustard dressing or grilled turbot with braised leeks, seared scallops and lobster sauce. For afters, there's sticky toffee pudding and ice cream or perhaps roast plums with star-anise syrup. The short wine list has plenty of stylistic choice, opening with house wines at £12.95, or £3.65 a glass.
Chef/s: Ewan McAllister. Open: Tue to Sun L 12 to 2.30, D 6.30 to 9.30. Closed: Christmas to New Year. Meals: alc (main courses £10.95 to £26.50). Service: not inc. Details: Cards accepted. 43 seats. Wheelchair access. Music. Children's portions. Car parking.

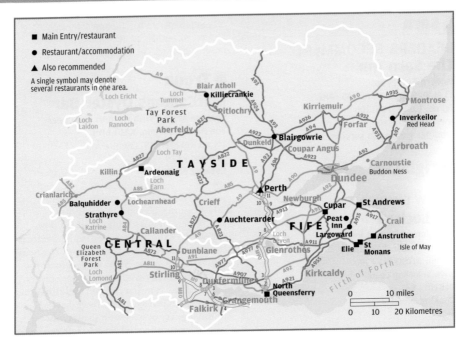

- ■ Main Entry/restaurant
- ● Restaurant/accommodation
- ▲ Also recommended

A single symbol may denote several restaurants in one area.

■ Ardeonaig

Ardeonaig Hotel

An enchanting setting
Ardeonaig, FK21 8SU
Tel no: (01567) 820 400
www.ardeonaighotel.co.uk
South African/Scottish | £26
Cooking score: 4

£5 OFF 🍾

After a bumpy trek along a single track road toward the southern shore of Loch Tay it feels like reaching the end of the world. However, we were unable to experience the thrill of visiting Ardeonaig this year as the hotel closed at the end of 2007 for total refurbishment, reopening at the end of June 2008, too late for inspection to take place. Plans include a new kitchen, a fine dining wine cellar, and a new restaurant for more casual dining for lunch and dinner. Food is the main event here and the deal is prime Scottish fare, lightly filtered through the prism of Peter Gottgen's native South Africa: local wood pigeon with apple pistachio to start, for example, then braised shoulder of local lamb with sweet potato, caramelised onions and Madeira sauce, or roast monkfish tail, wilted pak choi and soy. The wine list puts its faith 100 per cent in the cream of the South African crop, with reliable names mingling with some producers unavailable elsewhere, and some of the Cape's best pudding wines all offered by the glass. House wine is £19.50.

Chef/s: Pete Gottgens. **Open:** all week 8am to 10pm. **Meals:** alc (main courses £17.50 to £26.50). Set menu £25.50. **Service:** not inc. **Details:** Cards accepted. 75 seats. 40 seats outside. Separate bar. Wheelchair access. Music. Children allowed. Car parking.

Average price

The average price listed in main-entry reviews denotes the price of a three-course meal, without wine.

Auchterarder

Andrew Fairlie at Gleneagles

Fine French cuisine from a Scottish chef
Auchterarder, PH3 1NF
Tel no: (01764) 694 267
www.andrewfairlie.com
French | £65
Cooking score: 7

⊨ V

Although located in the hotel, the restaurant is a separate business. With no distraction except the colourful paintings of Archie Forrest (including his impressive portrait of Andrew Fairlie himself) on the dark walls, the cosseting dining room concentrates the mind on the serious business of eating and drinking. Impeccably laid tables with their Bernardaud tableware from Limoges and Spiegelau glasses add to the impression of serious intent, setting the stage for a six-act play – if you choose the no-choice dégustation menu or the menu du marché. The three-course à la carte, with five or six choices at each stage, is no less ambitious, and there is some cross-referencing between all three menus, so that one 'doesn't feel short-changed by opting for the cheaper option'. Menus are not weighed down by verbosity: each item is presented simply with the name of the main ingredient, with just a précis of accompaniments. Fairlie has perfected a culinary style that is uncompromisingly French, full of understated personal flourishes and painstaking attention to detail. Foie gras, for example, comes in three guises: sauté, parfait and cromesquis. The first comes on caramelised apples, the second on celeriac purée, and for the cromesquis the foie gras is mixed with cognac, port and Madeira, covered in batter, then deep-fried, so that the 'heavenly liquid' oozes on to the tongue. Main courses arrive in a number of presentations. Poached line-caught turbot comes with the lightest of scallop raviolis and mushrooms, roast rack of lamb is accompanied simply by fricasée of beans and creamed potatoes, while pork is represented by different parts of the pig - fillet, cheek and belly - all cooked differently to give a variety of textures and accompanied by black pudding. What impresses most is the culinary alchemist's trick of imbuing the most apparently simple of components with deep, complex flavours. This applies to desserts such as the masterful variations on an apple theme - soufflé, sorbet, crumble, parfait and tart - presented aesthetically on the plate. The wine list starts at £25 and climbs steeply thereafter to £1,650.
Chef/s: Andrew Fairlie. **Open:** Mon to Sat D only 6.30 to 10. **Closed:** 24 and 25 Dec, 3 weeks Jan. **Meals:** Set D £65 to £85. **Service:** not inc. **Details:** Cards accepted. 52 seats. Air-con. No mobile phones. Wheelchair access. Music. Car parking.

Balquhidder

Monachyle Mhor

Evolving family enterprise
Balquhidder, FK19 8PQ
Tel no: (01877) 384 622
www.mhor.net
Modern Scottish | £30
Cooking score: 5

⊨ V

The focus of a family enterprise that now incorporates a fishmongers, bakery and tearoom dotted around the Trossachs National Park, Monachyle Mhor is hidden away at the end of a tortuous six-mile track that meanders along the shores of Loch Voil. Built as a farmhouse two centuries ago, it is now a gem of a country hotel and restaurant, with local boy Tom Lewis as the driving force in the kitchen. He knows his own back yard and takes full advantage of the region's native larder, as well as gleaning produce from the hotel's organic plot for a menu that proves that this is no sleepy gastronomic backwater. An amuse bouche of Mallaig oyster with a spicy lime Tequila shot could kick-start the taste buds, before a clear-flavoured starter of white asparagus with summer truffle, Balquhidder chanterelles and hollandaise. Next, a demi-tasse of five-onion soup might precede seared fillet and slow-cooked belly of Tamworth pork with kohlrabi choucroute and wild mushrooms or pavé of Shetland salmon with spinach, fennel, tomato coulis and truffled fish velouté. Desserts are also full of clever touches; witness warm raspberry clafoutis served with fig and Marsala ice cream or a salpicon of pineapple and kiwi alongside Galliano-scented chocolate parfait. The wine list is a personal selection of fascinating bottles arranged by grape variety, plus a cluster of little-known 'oddballs'; prices start at £17 (£4 a glass).

Chef/s: Tom Lewis. **Open:** all week L 12 to 1.45, D 7 to 8.45. **Meals:** alc L (main courses £17.50). Set L Sun £31, Set D £46 (5 courses). **Service:** not inc. **Details:** Cards accepted. 40 seats. 10 seats outside. Separate bar. No mobile phones. Wheelchair access. Music. Children's portions. Car parking.

▌Strathyre

Creagan House

Dreamy views and leisurely dining
Strathyre, FK18 8ND
Tel no: (01877) 384 638
www.creaganhouse.co.uk
Modern Scottish / French | £30
Cooking score: 4

Nestling in Strathyre's 'sheltered valley' at the head of Loch Lubnaig, this converted seventeenth-century farmhouse is now a welcoming country restaurant-with-rooms. The setting is dreamy, the views are worth waking up for and the whole place is run with enthusiasm and affable good humour by Gordon and Cherry Gunn. Meals are served in the baronial dining room – complete with grand fireplace and vaulted ceiling – and a leisurely evening's pleasure is guaranteed. High points from recent dinners have included a starter of soft chicken livers with pears and macadamia nuts, and monkfish served on a 'delectable' seafood pâté, although the choice also extends to 'smokie in a pokie' and more elaborate ideas such as saddle of local lamb with crispy flank, kidney, haggis burger, garlic and rosemary gravy. Vegetables come in for special praise ('I'd be happy to eat them alone as a vegetarian option,' admitted one visitor), and the evening concludes with homemade desserts or Scottish cheeses. The well-spread, moderately priced wine list has plenty from France and elsewhere; prices start at £11.25 (£7.90 a carafe, £2.15 a glass).

Chef/s: Gordon Gunn. **Open:** Fri to Tue D only 7.30 (1 sitting). **Closed:** Wed, Thurs and Christmas. **Meals:** Set D £29.50. **Service:** not inc. **Details:** Cards accepted. 15 seats. Separate bar. No music. No mobile phones. Wheelchair access. Children's portions. Car parking.

▌**Anstruther**

Cellar

Fish of unbeatable freshness
24 East Green, Anstruther, KY10 3AA
Tel no: (01333) 310 378
Modern Seafood | £38
Cooking score: 6

One street back from the harbour, The Cellar may miss out on watery views, but is not short on character, sporting stone walls, flagstones, beams, candlelit tables and winter fires. The main draw is fish of unbeatable freshness, prepared with quiet skill and confidence by chef/proprietor Peter Jukes. His short menus are driven by the seasons, the fish always precisely cooked and beautifully and unfussily presented. Local roast langoustine with herb and garlic butter and dressed crab are star turns, but there is much more besides: a 'stunning flavoured' East Neuk smoked fish stew is a light version of Cullen skink or there could be a delicate tart of lobster and salmon. At main-course stage, caramelised scallops (diver-caught, of course) are teamed with langoustine tails, mussels and lobster, herb and garlic butter, Jersey Royals and fresh asparagus, while the perennially popular grilled fillet of halibut comes with greens, pine nuts and smoked bacon and basil mash. Individual Pavlova with home-made lemon curd ice cream, pink rhubarb and Grenadine syrup is a perfect way to finish. Susan Jukes manages the front of house with great assurance. The fish-friendly wine list opens at £18.50.

Chef/s: Peter Jukes. **Open:** Wed to Sat L at 1, Tue to Sat D 7 to 9.30. **Closed:** Sun and Mon, 4 days Christmas. **Meals:** Chef's menu £32.50, set D £33.50 (2 courses) to £38.50. **Service:** not inc. **Details:** Cards accepted. 35 seats.

▌**Cupar**

Ostlers Close

Honest and unfussy cooking
25 Bonnygate, Cupar, KY15 4BU
Tel no: (01334) 655 574
www.ostlersclose.co.uk
Modern British | £37
Cooking score: 5

After 28 years at their small cottage-restaurant, Jimmy and Amanda Graham can consider themselves old hands at the restaurant game. Yet despite their longevity they remain as enthusiastic as ever, thanks to a loyal following ('the standard of food has remained first class throughout the decades'), a well-established network of local suppliers, and a passion for foraging and gardening – supplying their own-grown herbs, soft fruits and vegetables in season. On the food front the kitchen maintains a balance between keeping customers happy with old favourites and evolving the style to avoid stagnation. The cooking is not complicated, but honest and unfussy – breast of wood pigeon with slow-cooked pork cheek on celeriac mash, for example, and roast saddle of venison with red cabbage, fondant potatoes and beetroot port sauce. Fish and seafood have been heartily endorsed: starters of Moray scallops with a stir-fry of pesto and seakale or halibut with buttered garden kale and parsley potato velouté perhaps, then mains of Pittenween seafood with winter greens and salt cod brandade with a cava sauce. Typical among desserts might be baked lemon tart with lemon posset and blackcurrant sauce. On the wine front, prices start at £14 and you can drink very well for under £25.

Chef/s: James Graham. **Open:** Sat L 12.15 to 1.30, Tue to Sat D 7 to 9.30. **Closed:** Sun and Mon, 25 and 26 Dec, Jan 1 and 2, 2 weeks in April and Oct. **Meals:** alc (main courses £18.50 to £19.95). **Service:** not inc. **Details:** Cards accepted. 26 seats. No mobile phones. Wheelchair access.

Elie

Sangster's

Well-crafted cooking
51 High Street, Elie, KY9 1BZ
Tel no: (01333) 331 001
www.sangsters.co.uk
British | £36
Cooking score: 5

Bruce Sangster paid his dues in respected hotels and by working as a private chef for an investment bank in London. In 2003 he and his wife Jacqueline moved to the sleepy village of Elie, in a touristy corner of Fife, to open their eponymous restaurant. It's a small and neat room with pleasant art on the walls and space for just 28 diners. From the outside it may not look much, but the focus here is on well-crafted cooking that takes an impeccably modern line. Venison from Glen Isla, crab from Kyle of Lochalsh, soft fruits from Tayside and pears, apples and herbs from the back garden provide the foundations for some enterprising dishes, and Sangster excels on his own terms. A spring dinner might thus proceed from scallops with chilli, ginger, galangal and coriander dressing or a never-off-the-menu twice-baked cheese soufflé, through a main course of fillet of halibut with pea purée, ham hock, mashed potato and mustard dressing, to a Scottish cheese plate starring the local Anster cheese, and finish with a celebration of oranges: pannacotta, yoghurt ice cream, caramelised syrup, orange salad, and orange sesame biscuit. A truly interesting and good-value wine list opens at £18. Booking essential.
Chef/s: Bruce Sangster. **Open:** Summer: Wed to Fri and Sun L 12.30 to 1.30, Tue to Sat D 7 to 8.30. Winter: Thu, Fri and Sun L 12 to 1.30, Wed to Sat D 7 to 8.30. **Closed:** 25 to 27 Dec, Jan. **Meals:** Set L £18.50 (2 courses) to £21, set Sun L £25, set D £30 (2 courses) to £39.50 (4 courses). **Service:** not inc. **Details:** Cards accepted. 28 seats. Wheelchair access.

Largoward

Inn at Lathones

Simple food in relaxed surroundings
Largoward, KY9 1JE
Tel no: (01334) 840 494
www.theinn.co.uk
Eastern European | £31
New Chef

🛏 V

The Inn has come of age. The past few years have seen some turmoil with changes in chefs and the upheaval of building work to increase the number of bedrooms. Owner Nick White's energy is amazing and his personality 'matches his girth'. In Paul Gibson he has found a capable, steady hand experienced in Scottish produce who can deliver: say plum tomato cake with peppered goats' cheese with a lightly dressed organic salad, sourced locally or oriental stir-fried fresh squid lightly cooked and served on a round of decidedly Scottish black pudding. Occasionally fish and shellfish are overwhelmed: scallops with toasted sesame seeds and orange also came with rounds of polenta and 'a sort of savoury custard enhanced potato and carrot rösti', more than was necessary for five beautifully fresh scallops. Service is relaxed and knowledgeable, but perhaps a little undisciplined. The oak-wood tables give a rustic feel.
Chef/s: Paul Gibson. **Open:** all week L 12.30 to 2.30, D 6 to 9.30. **Meals:** alc (main courses £13 to £19.95). **Service:** not inc. **Details:** Cards accepted. 40 seats. Separate bar. No music. Wheelchair access. Children's portions. Car parking.

Please send us your feedback

To register your opinion about any restaurant listed in the Guide, or a new restaurant that you wish to bring to our attention, please visit the web address at the bottom of the page. Your feedback informs the content of the book and will be used to compile next year's reviews.

The Good Food Guide 2009

North Queensferry

The Wee Restaurant
A gem under the Forth bridge
17 Main Street, North Queensferry, KY11 1JG
Tel no: (01383) 616 263
www.theweerestaurant.co.uk
Modern European | £27
Cooking score: 3

V

Since Craig Wood set up his aptly named Wee Restaurant, in the village of North Queensferry in 2006, it has been a massive hit. Part of the reason lies in the recent economic development of Edinburgh over the other side of the Forth. Its travel-to-work area has been spreading like an algal bloom in recent years so the audience for a decent and informal place to eat in the vicinity is bigger than ever before – Rosyth, Inverkeithing and Dunfermline are all nearby. On the supply side is Wood's experience and talent. The establishment has just 25 covers, so the kitchen should never be overburdened. Light walls, straightforward décor and a rotating show of artworks means that not much distracts from the food. At dinner three courses could bring grilled queenie scallops with garlic parsley and lemon breadcrumbs, then cod with cassoulet of cannelini beans, red peppers, chorizo sausage or roast loin of venison with mustard, celeriac cream, choucroute and sage gnocchi, and a pineapple tarte Tatin with vanilla ice cream to finish. The wine list is fairly basic, by the glass from £3.50 (£14.25 bottle).
Chef/s: Craig Wood. **Open:** Tue to Sat L 12 to 2, D 6 to 9. **Closed:** 25 and 26 Dec. **Meals:** alc (main courses £10.75 to £17.25). Set L £13.50 (2 courses) to £16.25. **Service:** not inc. **Details:** Cards accepted. 25 seats. Music. Children's portions.

Also recommended

An 'also recommended' entry is not a full entry, but is provisionally suggested as an alternative to main entries.

ALSO RECOMMENDED

▲ Dakota
Ferrymuir retail park, North Queensferry, EH30 9QZ
Tel no: 0870 423 4293
www.dakotahotels.co.uk
Modern British

Don't be put off by the massive black-glass office block, Ken McCulloch's latest venture is as one would expect, stylish and minimalist. In the kitchen there is capable cooking and the culinary aspirations are undoubtedly here. An imaginative menu reveals impeccable sourcing: Scottish asparagus, say, with a soft-boiled duck egg and tangy hollandaise (£8.50), classics such as steak tartare with thin-cut chips (£12.50) and the stunningly fresh sea-food platter (£38.00 for 2) for which the place is getting a name. Service, however, is a few steps behind the cooking. Open all week.

Peat Inn

Peat Inn
Modern cooking in a rural setting
Peat Inn, KY15 5LH
Tel no: (01334) 840 206
www.thepeatinn.co.uk
Modern British | £36
Cooking score: 5

The Smeddies took over this Fife landmark restaurant in June 2006, and visitors continue to be impressed. The white-painted, former roadside inn has an interior that is agreeable – soft colours, crisp linen – and those who stay over report back with tales of comfort and tranquility. Geoffrey Smeddie's cooking stands out from the crowd, not least because he starts with high-quality raw materials and he takes seasonality and local ingredients seriously. Dishes are frequently complex, but never fussy, and flavours are fine-tuned so that they balance rather than compete with each other: for example, in a starter of tomato consommé with tortellini of ricotta, ham and lovage. Contrasts are well handled: langoustine teamed with spiced pork belly and served with a cauliflower pannacotta, peas and morels or a main course of wild halibut with calamari provençale and globe artichokes. Desserts shine, too, in the form of hot raspberry soufflé with crème fraîche sorbet or warm apple and hazelnut financier with maple syrup ice cream. Lunch is a simpler affair, and service led by Katherine Smeddie is 'friendly, but also knowledgeable'. The wine list concentrates on quality without showiness or fanfare. France is its central passion, picked with assurance and an eye for value; shorter selections from elsewhere are no less acute. Prices start at £19.

Chef/s: Geoffrey Smeddie. **Open:** Tue to Sat L 12.30 to 2, D 7 to 9. **Closed:** Christmas, 1 to 4 Jan. **Meals:** alc (main courses £16 to £21). Set L £16, set D £32, tasting menu £48. **Service:** not inc. **Details:** Cards accepted. 45 seats. Separate bar. No music. No mobile phones. Children's portions.

Scores on the doors

As the emphasis on local and organic produce grows, the restaurant industry has come to realise that many customers value the origins of their food as much as the taste. With the 'Scores on the Doors' campaign, food hygiene finds itself brought into the age of information.

The scheme – already being successfully piloted across the UK, including in Scotland, the East Midlands and London – allows customers access to a restaurant's last inspection results (conducted by the local authority's environmental health team) for the first time. These are available by checking online or by simply glancing at the door or the window of the outlet in question.

Which? research shows that 97 per cent of customers believe they have a right to know the scores of local establishments.

You can check whether your local council participates on the Food Standard's Agency site: www.food.gov.uk/safereating/hyg/scoresonthedoors. Even if your area isn't part of the scheme, you're entitled to make a request to your local council for results under the *Freedom of Information Act.*

The FSA is currently reviewing the best way to provide this information. Following regional successes, Which? is campaigning for this scheme to be extended nationwide. For further details on the campaign, please see: www.which.co.uk.

▌St Andrews

Seafood Restaurant

Dramatic harbour setting
The Scores, Bruce Embankment, St Andrews, KY16 9AB
Tel no: (01334) 479 475
www.theseafoodrestaurant.com
Modern Seafood | £45
Cooking score: 4

This sleek glass, metal and wood construction perched on the sea wall overlooking St Andrews Bay seems to have an endless flow of eager clientele. Inside it is modern and light, the emphasis is on the celebrated 'first-class seafood', although there is confit chicken, guinea fowl and foie gras terrine and collops of beef or roasted loin of venison on the menu. The kitchen takes a fashionable view of things with starters such as smoked haddock rarebit or basil pannacotta with kiln-roasted salmon, crab, pea and shimizu cress salad showing where the heart is, while red snapper with celeriac and broad-bean ragout or cod with salt cod dumplings and tomato and chive beurre blanc are equally ambitious mains. Desserts have included cold chocolate and blueberry fondant with blueberry coulis and coconut sorbet. The wine list shows plenty of swagger in its trek across the European regions and there's a decent round-up of New World wines. House wines are £19 to £29.

Chef/s: Craig Millar and Scott Millar. **Open:** all week 12 to 2.30, 6.30 to 10. **Closed:** 25 and 26 Dec, 1 Jan. **Meals:** Set L £22 (2 courses) to £27, set D £45. **Service:** not inc. **Details:** Cards accepted. 60 seats. 30 seats outside. Air-con. No music. Wheelchair access.

█ St Monans
Seafood Restaurant

Serious seafood, dramatic seascapes
16 West End, St Monans, KY10 2BX
Tel no: (01333) 730 327
www.theseafoodrestaurant.com
Seafood | £35
Cooking score: 5

Originally a fisherman's cottage and later a pub, this top-notch seafood restaurant combines dramatic seascapes and views over the harbour to Bass Rock with food that exploits the very best of the local catch. All is relaxed, light and contemporary in the dining room, and there's a superb harbourside terrace for al fresco treats. Menus depend on the haul, the weather and the season, although some items such as home-cured gravlax with celeriac rémoulade, caper and shallot dressing are seldom absent. Sautéed langoustines with crushed mint peas and shellfish is a typically vivid starter, while main courses often show a penchant for pasta: baked cod with Pittenweem crab, basil purée and Onuga caviar tortellini or grilled halibut with shimeji mushrooms and herb pappardelle, for example. Those whose prefer their protein from the land rather than the sea might opt for pigeon breast with puy lentils followed by cassoulet of pork, lamb with confit duck. To conclude, warm chocolate tart might appear with the unexpected bonus of fennel ice cream, while steamed marmalade pudding should satisfy the traditionalists. Off-season set-lunch menus are particularly good value, and the seriously in-tune wine list features a clever mix of prestige names and in-vogue firecrackers, including classy contingents from France, Spain and Germany – all tilted towards fish-friendly whites. House selections start at £17 (£4.50 a glass).

Chef/s: Craig Millar and Roy Brown. **Open:** all week L 12 to 2.30 (Sun 12.30 to 3), D 6.30 to 9.30. **Closed:** Mon Oct to Apr, Tue Oct to May. **Meals:** Set L £14.95 (Oct to Mar) to £24. Set D £30 (2 courses) to £35. **Service:** not inc. **Details:** Cards accepted. 40 seats. 36 seats outside. Separate bar. No music. No mobile phones. Wheelchair access. Children's portions. Car parking.

Cooking score

A score of 1 is a significant achievement. The score in any review is based on several meals, incorporating feedback from both our readers and inspectors. As a rough guide, 1 denotes capable cooking with some inconsistencies, rising steadily through different levels of technical expertise, until the scores between 6 and 10 indicate exemplary skills, along with innovation, artistry and ambition. If there is a new chef, we don't score the restaurant for the first year of entry. For further details, please see the scoring section in the introduction to the Guide.

Blairgowrie
Kinloch House Hotel

Sumptuous Perthshire setting
Blairgowrie, PH10 6SG
Tel no: (01250) 884 237
www.kinlochhouse.com
Modern European | £49
Cooking score: 5

The creeper cladding of Kinloch House is so extensive that the place blends almost seamlessly into the 25 acres of rolling Perthshire countryside in which it sits. Built as a private house in the early-Victorian era, it boasts a grand oak-panelled entrance hall and a portrait gallery on the first floor. The dining-room is done in a rather lighter decorative tone than is often the way, with light-wood shades, properly dressed tables and neat arrangements of pictures on the walls. The cooking is in the grand country-house manner, offering fixed-price menus at lunch and dinner, the former three courses, the latter four. That extra course in the evening appears in the form of an intermediate soup, perhaps cauliflower served with cheese and walnut scones. Prior to that, there may have been pigeon breast with spinach, foie gras and truffle or seared scallops with herb tortellini and pesto, to awaken the appetite. Two fish and three meat form the typical main-course choice, which embraces the elaborate likes of sea bass with shellfish risotto, trompette mushrooms and asparagus, sauced with white wine and chives or roast Angus fillet with fondant potato, creamed leeks, shallots and mushrooms in red wine. Desserts are in the gently rich vein of vanilla mousse with poached plums and port syrup or blood orange soufflé with Cointreau anglaise. The wine list is a doozy, opening with wines by the glass at £6.50, and progressing through a majestic house selection (from £19.50) and on into a roll-call of Burgundy's and Bordeaux's finest, before lighting out more briefly into the New World. Choose with confidence.

Chef/s: Andrew May. **Open:** all week, L 12 to 1.30, D 7 to 8.30. **Closed:** 12 to 28 Dec. **Meals:** Set L £23.50, Set D £49. **Service:** not inc. **Details:** Cards accepted. 40 seats. Separate bar. No music. No mobile phones. Wheelchair access. Children's portions. Car parking.

Dunkeld

READERS RECOMMEND
Kinnaird

Modern British
Kinnaird Estate, Dunkeld, PH8 0LB
Tel no: (01796) 482440
www.kinnairdestate.com
'Scottish food with flair'

Inverkeilor
Gordon's

All in the family
32 Main Street, Inverkeilor, DD11 5RN
Tel no: (01241) 830 364
www.gordonsrestaurant.co.uk
Modern British | £43
Cooking score: 5

It's official – keeping it in the family pays off. Gordon's, in the village of Inverkeilor between Arbroath and Montrose, has been around for many years with the eponymous Gordon Watson in the kitchen and wife Maria front of house. Son Garry also works in the kitchen these days and the difference, for some readers, is palpable. The dining room remains a cosy affair – it seats only 24 – with wooden beams and some bare stone. This is the setting for a dinner that could start with tournedos of rabbit, foie gras parfait, white bean cassoulet and truffle jus. Then comes a twice-baked soufflé of Isle of Tobermory cheddar, with the main course comprising Scotch beef fillet with a much-admired mushroom ragout, red onion confit and tonka bean parsnip. To finish, hot chocolate fondant with basil ice cream, passion fruit and guava coulis. Diners enjoy the intensity of flavours and unfussy service. The wine list is organised by grape variety (from £13) and has useful notes so it seems a pity not to take advantage. Fortunately, Gordon's offers three bedrooms upstairs so you can make a night of it.

Chef/s: Gordon Watson and Garry Watson. **Open:** Wed to Fri and Sun L 12 to 1.45, Tue to Sat D 7 to 9. **Closed:** 2 weeks Jan. **Meals:** Set L £27, set D £43 (4 courses). **Service:** not inc. **Details:** Cards accepted. 24 seats. Wheelchair access. Car parking.

■ Killiecrankie

Killiecrankie House

Charming old stager
Killiecrankie, PH16 5LG
Tel no: (01796) 473 220
www.killiecrankiehotel.co.uk
Modern European | £31
Cooking score: 3

♦ ⊨

Killiecrankie House was built as a Victorian manse, converted to a hotel in 1939, and for many years was run by the capable Waters family, who built its excellent reputation for good wines. Henrietta Fergusson took over the reins in 2007 with a view to keeping up the good work. It sits in a beautiful part of Perthshire, best known for the 1689 battle that was part of the shenanigans in these islands following the Glorious Revolution. These days things are a little more peaceful – especially if you're walking in the hotel grounds before dinner. The cooking is a competent standard of classic Franco-Scottish, which might see starters like onion soup with gruyère crouton, or a salad of locally smoked duck breast and walnuts in an orange dressing. Mains might involve quail, oak-smoked chicken or venison with a Madeira and apricot sauce; desserts are along the lines of Pavlova or dark chocolate mousse. A lengthy wine list features a good few interesting bottles, and value is fair throughout with plenty of choice under £30. House wine is £16.90. A less formal lunch is served in the conservatory.

Chef/s: Mark Easton. **Open:** all week D 6.30 to 8.30. **Closed:** 3 Jan to 1 March. **Meals:** alc (main courses £9 to £15.50). Set D £31 to £38 (4 courses).

Service: optional. **Details:** Cards accepted. 34 seats. Separate bar. Wheelchair access. Children allowed. Car parking.

■ Perth

ALSO RECOMMENDED
▲ 63 Tay Street

63 Tay Street, Perth, PH2 8NN
Tel no: (01738) 441 451
www.63taystreet.co.uk
Modern European

'It's right up there with a fine Scotch whisky,' enthused one reader about this generously supported riverside venue in the 'restaurant wilderness of Perth'. Graeme Pallister and his team have certainly impressed the locals since their arrival, garnering plaudits for their imaginative, locally sourced food and cheery service. Fixed-price menus (£17.50 lunch, £30 dinner) offer 'exquisitely presented' dishes such as pig's head and pistachio faggot with chilled San Marzano tomatoes, organic sea trout with crab Thai noodles and aromatic courgette confit, and orange curd soufflé with cinnamon and star anise ice cream. Carefully chosen wines from £13.50 (£3.70 a glass). Open all week.

■ Stanley

READERS RECOMMEND
Apron Stage

Modern British
5 King Street, Stanley, PH1 4ND
Tel no: (01738) 828 888
'Pint-sized restaurant by the Tay'

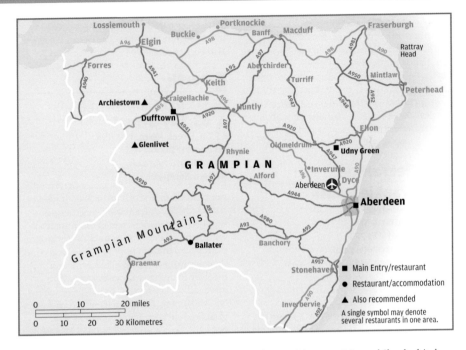

Map legend:
- ■ Main Entry/restaurant
- ● Restaurant/accommodation
- ▲ Also recommended

A single symbol may denote several restaurants in one area.

0 — 10 — 20 miles
0 — 10 — 20 — 30 Kilometres

■ Aberdeen

Silver Darling
Long-running and well-established seafood restaurant
Pocra Quay, North Pier, Aberdeen, AB11 5DQ
Tel no: (01224) 576 229
www.silverdarlingrestaurant.co.uk
Seafood | £40
Cooking score: 6

Long-running and well-established restaurants pose something of a problem for any guidebook. The Silver Darling has the same head chef as ever (Didier Dejean), it's at the same location, it still does upmarket seafood and its dining room is still in a conservatory-style space on the first floor of a solid granite building by the mouth of Aberdeen harbour. The most obvious addition in the last couple of years has been the harbour's tall and funky marine operations centre just a few metres away – whether this enhances the seaward view from the restaurant or ruins it really depends on your opinion of modern architecture. Meanwhile, the kitchen embraces modern and international influences in starters like seared Shetland king scallop in a coconut curry, or pickled seafood sashimi and oysters with rice noodle salad, sakura cress and wasabi ginger dressing or in mains such as turbot with herb and spinach risotto, samphire, smoked salmon and shimeji, plus smoked salmon froth. There has been praise, too, for well-timed steamed wild sea bass and fillet of North Sea halibut. Elaborate and well executed, this is the work of a French-schooled chef who wants to keep pushing his kitchen forward. Desserts aren't half bad either – summer berry crumble with lime and mascarpone chantilly perhaps, or raspberry shortbread mille-feuille. The wine list offers a couple of dozen whites with around half under £30. House wine is £19.50.
Chef/s: Didier Dejean. **Open:** Mon to Fri L 12 to 1.45, Mon to Sat D 7 to 9. **Closed:** Sun, 2 weeks Christmas. **Meals:** alc (main courses £19.50 to £22.50). **Service:** not inc. **Details:** Cards accepted. 45 seats. Wheelchair access. Music.

▌Archiestown

ALSO RECOMMENDED
▲ Archiestown Hotel

Archiestown, AB38 7QL
Tel no: (01340) 810 218
British

Starting proud in the centre of a sleepy village, this ivy-clad eighteenth-century stone manor house is handily placed on the dram-laden Whisky Trail. The kitchen feeds famished tourists and others from a menu that is equally proud of its Scottish heritage. Begin with venison and duck confit terrine with honey and cranberries (£8), before braised lamb shank or suprême of chicken stuffed with goat's cheese wrapped in bacon with forest mushrooms (£18.50). To finish, consider Cranachan cheesecake with raspberry compote (£5.50) or golden syrup sponge and custard. House wine is £17.50 (£5 a glass). Accommodation available. Open all week.

▌Ballater

Darroch Learg

Bastion of Scottish family hospitality
Braemar Road, Ballater, AB35 5UX
Tel no: (013397) 554 43
www.darrochlearg.co.uk
Modern Scottish | £45
Cooking score: 6

Perched on high ground in the heart of Royal Deeside, Darroch Learg (the 'oak wood on the sunny hillside') is a well-endowed Victorian mansion with a fine prospect overlooking Ballater and Craigendarroch. Inside it flaunts its Scottishness with tartan upholstery, panelling and blazing fires – although much attention is paid to events in the conservatory-style dining room. Nigel and Fiona Franks are well versed in the traditions of family hospitality and their efforts are backed up by long-serving chef David Mutter, who has been cooking here for more than a decade. He stocks his kitchen with the pick of local supplies, procuring lamb from Deeside

pastures, venison from Glen Muick estate and fish from Aberdeen market. The result is food with an emphatic seasonal accent, as in red onion tart with local wood pigeon, grapes and pigeon sauce or fillet of Aberdeen Angus beef with turnip confit, morels and béarnaise sauce. A few exotic flourishes add an extra dimension to proceedings when slow-cooked pork is served with soy and ginger dressing or panache of seafood arrives with crispy cauliflower and curry velouté. Desserts reside in the classic world of lemon tart or warm Pithivier of apples and Calvados – although vanilla pannacotta with mango jelly adds a more racy note. The wine list is a mouth-watering prospect for connoisseurs, with a sure touch when it comes to picking out Bordeaux and Burgundies and plenty of serious stuff from Italy, South Africa and elsewhere. Don't miss the 'brief encounters' selection of 'interesting, older or unlikely-to-be-repeated wines.' Bestsellers start at £22 and there are several options from £5 a glass.
Chef/s: David Mutter. **Open:** Sun L 12.30 to 2, all week D 7 to 9. **Closed:** Christmas, last 3 weeks Jan. **Meals:** Set D £45 (3 courses) to £55. **Details:** Cards accepted. 48 seats. Wheelchair access. Music. Children's portions. Car parking.

Green Inn

Going from strength to strength
9 Victoria Road, Ballater, AB35 5QQ
Tel no: (013397) 557 01
www.green-inn.com
Modern British
Cooking score: 4

Housed in a solid, stone-built building overlooking the village green, the O'Halloran's Green Inn has an agreeably lived-in feel, in that it's smart and stylish yet friendly and cheering at the same time. It seems to be going from strength to strength. In son Chris O'Halloran's finely honed modern repertoire, ingredients like foie gras, sea bass, scallops and truffle take starring roles. Terrine of fillets of roe deer, teal and pheasant, wrapped in a mousse of their livers and studded with wild mushrooms, hazelnuts and Madeira jelly is a well-reported starter, while mains eliciting plaudits this year have been organic pork tenderloin with braised cheek and wild rice, morel mushrooms and truffle cream, and local partridge teamed with foie gras and wild mushroom sausage, crepinettes and caramelised apples and pears. Desserts encompassing a variety of techniques range from slow-baked meringues with crème anglaise and bittersweet chocolate and mint oil, to poached pear in puff pastry with warm ginger butterscotch sauce, lime custard and lime sorbet. The wine list has its heart in France, but there's a sprinkling of good offerings from around the globe, a page of halves and house wines at £18.95.

Chef/s: Chris O'Halloran. **Open:** Tue to Sat D 7 to 9 (Summer from Wed). **Meals:** Set D £31.50 to £38.50. **Service:** not inc. **Details:** Cards accepted. 26 seats. Air-con. Separate bar. No mobile phones. Music.

Dufftown

La Faisanderie
French cooking with fresh Scottish ingredients
2 Balvenie Street, Dufftown, AB55 4AD
Tel no: (01340) 821 273
French | £26
Cooking score: 3

Amanda Bestwick and Eric Obry's smart little restaurant occupies a corner site on Dufftown's town square. While Eric's cooking is unmistakably French, the produce is some of the best that Scotland can offer. Expect fresh game in season – perhaps supreme of pheasant with a cabbage and pancetta choucroute and white wine sauce. Fish and seafood are also plentiful, ranging from a lunchtime starter of rainbow trout and smoked salmon mousseline with a lime and dill butter sauce to langoustine tails and sweetbread gratin with buttered leeks and Vermouth sabayon in the evening. Despite its French foundations, the food has become more adventurous lately, drawing in occasional flavours from further afield: seared breast of duck might come with haricot bean and pumpkin cassoulet and

spiced shadon beni relish, while a classic tarte tatin could be served with toffee sauce and tonka-bean ice cream. A decent list of French wines opens at £10.90 a bottle.

Chef/s: Eric Obry. **Open:** Mon L 12 to 1.30, Wed D 6 to 8.30, Thu to Sun L 12 to 2.30, Thu D 6 to 8.30, Fri to Sat D 7 to 9. **Closed:** All day Tue, Wed L. **Meals:** alc (main courses £15.70 to £18.20), Set L £13.50 (2 courses), £16.80 (3 courses), set D £26 (3 courses). **Service:** not inc. **Details:** Cards accepted. Wheelchair access. Music. Children's portions.

Elgin

READERS RECOMMEND
Restaurant 55
Modern European
55 High Street, Elgin, IV30 1EE
Tel no: (01343) 551273
'A neighbourhood restaurant with a conscience'

Glenlivet

ALSO RECOMMENDED
▲ Minmore House
Glenlivet, AB37 9DB
Tel no: (01807) 590 378
British

Set amid the Glenlivet estate, a winter wonderland at the cold end of the year, Minmore House offers a vision of grandeur at all times. There is the even the chance of spotting a ghostly calf near the fireside for those with a sixth sense. Scots baronial cooking with a modern European spin brings prawn bisque, seared West Coast scallops with champagne beurre blanc, Aberdeen Angus fillet dijonnaise with minted sugar snaps, and crêpes Suzette flamed at the table in Grand Marnier on to the lavish fixed-price menus (from £25). Afternoon tea is a speciality, but needs booking. Wines from £16.95. Open all week.

█ Udny Green

Eat on the Green

An unexpected find in an unlikely location
Udny Green, AB41 7RS
Tel no: (01651) 842 337
www.eatonthegreen.co.uk
British | £34
Cooking score: 2

Despite being a short drive from Aberdeen, the small village of Udny Green feels fairly out of the way, a couple of miles off the main road between Oldmeldrum and Ellon. But it was here that chef Craig Wilson launched Eat on the Green in 2004, in a former pub, building on sound kitchen experience gained at hotel venues like Ballathie House and Cromlix House, both in Perthshire. In the neat dining room, three-course dinner courses could start with an adventurous black pudding served with apple and cardamom patties and cider-mustard vinaigrette, then comes slow-cooked belly and juniper fillet of pork with thyme-roasted potatoes and red-onion and chorizo marmalade, and a raspberry pannacotta with a brunoise of fresh fruits to finish. This is an unexpected find in an unlikely location prompting a great deal of positive comment from readers; genuinely friendly service and the chef's willingness to chat with diners come in for particular praise.

Chef/s: Craig Wilson. **Open:** Wed to Fri and Sun L 12 to 1.45, Wed to Sun D 6.30 to 9. **Closed:** Mon and Tue, 2 weeks after New Year. **Meals:** alc (main courses £15.95 to £20.95). Set menu £37. **Service:** not inc. **Details:** Cards accepted. 60 seats. Wheelchair access. Music.

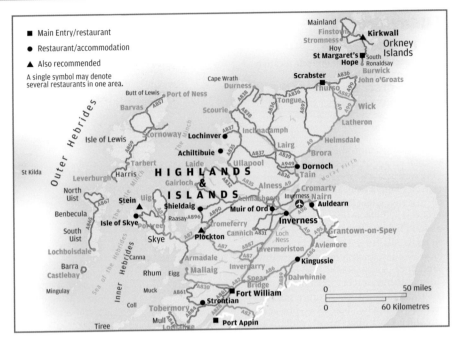

- ■ Main Entry/restaurant
- ● Restaurant/accommodation
- ▲ Also recommended

A single symbol may denote several restaurants in one area.

■ Achiltibuie

Summer Isles Hotel

Auspicious Highland refuge
Achiltibuie, IV26 2YG
Tel no: (01854) 622 282
www.summerisleshotel.co.uk
Modern European | £52
Cooking score: 5

Eye-popping sea views out to the eponymous 'summer isles' are just one reason why visitors adore this veteran Scottish hotel, which has carved out a very special niche since opening as a Highland pioneer during the 1960s. Just about everything here is either home-grown, made in-house or caught locally: the hotel's hydroponicum ensures regular pickings in this far-flung, weather-beaten outpost and the northerly waters yield a plentiful catch. The result is a daily five-course dinner menu that dazzles with its seasonal simplicity. On a typical June night, proceedings might begin with a bowl of smoked haddock and potato soup served with a home-baked seed loaf; next, carpaccio of Aberdeen Angus beef fillet with a piquant relish could lead on to a plate of local hand-dived scallops seared in Vermouth and served atop a mound of buttery champ. After that, expect the arrival of the heavily laden sweet trolley with its array of sweet delights, before fine Scottish cheeses take to the stage. Each night, guests are offered specially selected wines by the glass from the majestic 400-bin list as a complement to their food, and thorough exploration of the full tome reveals a scintillating assortment of prime pickings from the French regions, California, Italy and elsewhere. Prices start at about £20, but it pays to invest a bit more for something serious.

Chef/s: Christopher Firth-Bernard. **Open:** all week D only 8 (1 sitting). **Meals:** Set D £52 (5 courses). Bar menu available. **Service:** not inc. **Details:** Cards accepted. 28 seats. Separate bar. No music. No mobile phones. Wheelchair access. Car parking.

▌Auldearn

Boath House
Impeccable cooking
Auldearn, IV12 5TE
Tel no: (01667) 454 896
www.boath-house.com
Modern European | £55
Cooking score: 5

The Boath House is a classical Regency mansion dating to the 1820s, which opened as a small hotel in 1997, after a careful restoration. Its dining room is blessed with warm colours and fine proportions, but accommodates only 26, which makes for impeccable quality control. The cooking shows that Charlie Lockley brings not only a great deal of craft to his creations, but also true enthusiasm, although the simple descriptions do little justice to the combinations and depth of flavours in each dish – one reporter raved about details like Lockley's peasemeal oatcakes, chorizo foam and seaweed relish on a celeriac soup. Dinner is a five-course affair, which might start with another soup, say an intense pumpkin soup with seeds and oil, then go on to a seafood ravioli with cauliflower and basil, to be followed by a choice of cannon of Shetland lamb with potatoes and kale, say, or hake with haricot bean stew and pork belly. Then comes the cheese plate (Strathdon Blue, St Maure and Yarg) and there's another choice at dessert – mango custard, pineapple and sorbet or Alpaco chocolate and cocoa nib cake with milk ice cream. The wine list has a French ballast and opens at £18.50; service is attentive and friendly.
Chef/s: Charlie Lockley. **Open:** all week L 12,30 to 2, D 7 to 9. **Closed:** 24 to 26 Dec. **Meals:** Set L £19.50 (2 courses) to £26.50, set D £55 (5 courses).
Service: not inc. **Details:** Cards accepted. 26 seats. No music. No mobile phones. Wheelchair access. Children's portions. Car parking.

▌Aviemore

READERS RECOMMEND
The Mountain Café
Modern Scottish
111 Grampian Road, Aviemore, PH22 1RH
Tel no: (01479) 812473
www.mountaincafe-aviemore.co.uk
'Hearty comfort food for the weary traveller'

▌Dornoch

2 Quail
Small, but perfectly formed
Castle Street, Dornoch, IV25 3SN
Tel no: (01862) 811 811
www.2quail.com
Modern European | £38
Cooking score: 4

Comprising just 12 covers and three guest rooms, it's no wonder that Michael and Kerensa Carr's two-storey Victorian town house is billed as 'the smallest golf hotel and restaurant in Scotland'. The whole place is suffused with congenial family hospitality, although Michael's food is far from domestic in its aspirations. Dinner revolves around a concise four-course menu with Europe as its compass-point: there's no choice until desserts come around, but ideas are sharp and everything is executed with a sure touch. A typical meal might begin – appropriately – with a fricassée of quail and foie gras with grilled fresh fig and sage sauce, before supreme of halibut with sautéed endive and tarragon beurre blanc. Main courses generally feature something Scottish, perhaps roast loin of venison or beef fillet with garlic-roasted potatoes, artichokes and sherry sauce, while desserts could offer dark chocolate marquise with griottines or hot passion-fruit soufflé with coconut sauce, alongside cheeses with oatcakes. The broadly based wine list focuses much of its attention on France; prices start at £14.50.

Unusual cookbooks

Food has always inspired some of the most singular writing in history. Here are some of the weird and wonderful books available.

The Decadent Cookbook by Durian Grey

A digest of eating at the extreme. You are cordially invited to the tables of the Marquis de Sade and Edward Lear. Anything from cat food to rat may be on the menu.

The Alice B Toklas Cookbook

More an autobiography than a cookbook, this memoir by the lifelong companion of Gertrude Stein contains the famous Hashish Fudge, a mixture of fruit, nuts and cannabis resin.

De Re Coquinaria by Apicius

A survival of the late Roman period, 'On the Subject of Cooking' is often celebrated as the oldest European cookbook. If you've ever wondered about the best way of preparing flamingo, it's all here.

The Flounder by Günter Grass

One of the Nobel-winning novelist's most fully realised works, the story of a Stone Age talking fish, is packed solid with recipes from the food cultures of northern Europe.

How to Cook a Wolf by MFK Fisher

America's most spellbinding writer on food turns her attention to helping readers suffering the conditions of wartime to stretch their budgets and make do.

The Rituals of Dinner by Margaret Visser

The Canadian writer followed up her highly acclaimed 'Much Depends on Dinner' with this thoroughly off-the-wall look at the origins and development of table manners.

Les Cuisines Oubliées by Annie et Jean-Claude Molinier

'Forgotten Cuisines' gathers up old country recipes for animals we don't habitually eat any longer, from badger in pig's blood to roasted hedgehogs and magpie baked in clay. Don't try this at home!

The Romance of Food by Barbara Cartland

A prime contender for the most tasteless cookery book ever published, the doyenne of romantic fiction offers us lamb cutlets garnished with tinned apricots in honey sauce. A surefire way to tickle your fancy.

Chef/s: Michael Carr. **Open:** Tue to Sat D only 7 to 9.30 (Fri and Sat in winter). **Closed:** Sun, Mon, 1 week Christmas, 2 weeks Feb/Mar. **Meals:** Set D £38 (4 courses). **Service:** not inc. **Details:** Cards accepted. 12 seats. No mobile phones. Wheelchair access. Music.

▮ Fort William

Crannog

Town Pier, Fort William, PH33 6DB
Tel no: (01397) 705 589
www.crannog.net
Seafood | £25
Cooking score: 2

The Crannog started as an adjunct to a smokehouse business in 1989 and has been going great guns ever since. Its premises at the Town Pier – right on Loch Linnhe – have basic bistro décor, sea-themed artworks and friendly waitresses. You can start with a smoked seafood chowder, smoked salmon roulade or mussels (with onion, garlic, white wine and cream), then move on to mains like roast monkfish on pilaf rice with chilli and ginger relish, or herb crusted cod. Do check the blackboards for the catch of the day, though – whole roast sea bass perhaps – vegetarians and red meat fans also catered for. Finish off with lemon tart or sticky date pudding. One reader who praised the 'excellent fresh fish' was also taken by the 'reasonable range of white wines'. Obvious smokehouse products that crop up on the menu (hickory-roasted salmon, oak-smoked salmon) are well worth trying.
Chef/s: Robbie McDonald and Stewart MacLachlan.
Open: all week L 12 to 2.30, D 6 to 9 (to 10 summer). **Closed:** 24 Dec D, 25 Dec, 1 Jan.
Meals: alc (main courses £10.50 to £18.50).
Service: not inc. **Details:** Cards accepted. 62 seats. 38 seats outside. No mobile phones. Music. Children's portions.

Inverlochy Castle

Torlundy, Fort William, PH33 6SN
Tel no: (01397) 702177
www.inverlochycastlehotel.com
Modern European | £65
Cooking score: 6

The ruins of Inverlochy's medieval castle pale into insignificance beside Victorian grandeur of its namesake hotel nestling in the foothills of Ben Nevis. This supreme Scottish country retreat is dolled up in its finest shootin' and fishin' garb and it resonates with echoes of the past: this is the traditional country-house party taken to new heights of refined taste and personal pampering. From the moment you step into the entrance hall, two storeys high, the experience unwinds amid crystal chandeliers, portraits and antiques. Full-dress meals (jacket and tie please, gentlemen) are served in three sumptuous dining rooms festooned with silver figurines of game birds and ornate furniture presented to the hotel by the King of Norway. Since rising to head chef in 2000, Matthew Gray has honed his skills and is now achieving great things here. He is capable of turning out rigorously conceived, elaborate dishes of a high order, with Scottish produce used to telling effect. To begin, Loch Linnhe prawns might be served

with charred baby leeks, Parmesan gnocchi and caviar emulsion, before a mid-course soup (perhaps butternut squash velouté). Centrepieces increase the tempo with, perhaps, medallions of venison, hibiscus, celeriac purée and wild mushrooms or roast sea bream with a fricassee of broad beans, peas and speck foam. To conclude, toffee soufflé with toffee sauce is worth the ten-minute wait, or you might press ahead with iced maple syrup parfait, plums and sherry jelly. The wine list is a country-house heavyweight, loaded with pedigree French vintages but open-minded in its choice of serious contenders from elsewhere. House recommendations start at £30 (£6 a glass).
Chef/s: Matthew Gray and Phil Carnegie. **Open:** all week L 12.30 to 2.30, D 6 to 10. **Meals:** Set L £35. Set D £65 (4 courses). **Service:** not inc.
Details: Cards accepted. 40 seats. 12 seats outside. No music. Wheelchair access. Music. Jacket and tie required. Children's portions. Car parking.

Grantown on Spey

READERS RECOMMEND
Culdearn House Hotel
Scottish
Woodlands Terrace, Grantown on Spey, PH26 3JU
Tel no: (01749) 872 196
www.culdearn.com
'The four-course dinner menu offers thoughtful combinations'

Glass House Restaurant
Grant Road, Grantown on Spey, PH26 3LD
Tel no: (01479) 872980
www.theglasshouse-grantown.co.uk
'Small restaurant making a big noise'

Inverness

Glenmoriston Town House, Abstract Restaurant
Aspirational modern French cooking
20 Ness Bank, Inverness, IV2 4SF
Tel no: (01463) 223 777
www.abstractrestaurant.com
Modern French | £38
Cooking score: 4

Situated in a verdant quarter of Inverness overlooking the River Tay, Glenmoriston Town House Hotel is also home to Abstract – a sleek contemporary restaurant with high aspirations. Geoffrey Malmedy's cooking delves into the intricate world of modern French cuisine with all its froths, foams and quirky embellishments. He serves confit pineapple with seared scallops and braised pork cheek, conjures up pea ice cream to go with carpaccio of squat lobster, and applies a smoked meat jus to a dish of red deer with wild mushrooms, Brussels sprout fricassée and quince compote. Scottish produce is always at the heart of things, witness West Coast langoustines, an assiette of Ross-shire lamb or slow-cooked John Dory with vanilla, chervil root and pumpkin purée. Customers are advised to pre-order desserts, which says a great deal about their overt, time-consuming complexity: consider carpaccio of fig with crispy fig and frangipane, marzipan ice cream and port coulis. France makes a big impression on the swanky wine list, which majors in serious bottles with serious price tags: house selections provide light relief from £18 a go. There is a second branch of Abstract in Edinburgh (see entry).
Chef/s: Geoffrey Malmedy. **Open:** Tue to Sat D only 6 to 10. **Closed:** Sun, Mon. **Meals:** alc (main courses £14 to £19.50). Set D £50 to £75 (inc wine).
Service: not inc. **Details:** Cards accepted. 50 seats. 10 seats outside. Air-con. Separate bar. No mobile phones. Wheelchair access. Music. Children's portions. Car parking.

Rocpool

Effervescent local rendezvous
1 Ness Walk, Inverness, IV3 5NE
Tel no: (01463) 717 274
www.rocpoolrestaurant.com
Modern European | £27
Cooking score: 2

 V

A fizzy brasserie on the banks of the River Ness, Rocpool takes its name from the legendary Sydney restaurant and aims to bring some energetic pizzazz to Inverness. Locals appreciate its cool contemporary vibes, bold primary colours and family-friendly attitude, not to mention its busy modern food. Good-value lunches and early-evening deals give way to a full carte that mixes Mediterranean-inspired ideas with a fistful of eclectic 'classics': pork cutlet with seared cotechino sausage and a white-bean cassoulet could sit alongside halibut with spiced shrimp and coriander couscous, tempura prawns, minted yogurt and cucumber salad. 'Fish on Friday' specials are worth waiting for (roast fillet of wild sea bass with pea, spinach and crab risotto, for example) while desserts have featured hot lemon meringue pie and pannacotta with pink rhubarb. The global wine list promises fashionable drinking from £13.95 (£3.60 a glass).

Chef/s: Steven Devlin. **Open:** Mon to Sat L 12 to 2.30, D 5.45 to 10. Sun D 5.45 to 9.30 (Mar to Oct only). **Closed:** 25 and 26 Dec, 1 and 2 Jan. **Meals:** alc (main courses £9 to £17). Set L £9.95 (2 courses), Set D 5.45 to 6.45 £11.95 (2 courses). **Service:** not inc. **Details:** Cards accepted. 55 seats. Air-con. Wheelchair access. Music. Children's portions.

READERS RECOMMEND

The Mustard Seed

Modern European
16 Fraser Street, Inverness, IV1 1DW
Tel no: (01463) 220220
www.themustardseedrestaurant.co.uk
'Bistro dining with an enchanting view of the river Ness'

■ Isle of Skye

Three Chimneys

Enduring Highland hideaway
Colbost, Dunvegan, Isle of Skye, IV55 8ZT
Tel no: (01470) 511 258
www.threechimneys.co.uk
Modern Scottish | £45
Cooking score: 5

Shirley and Eddie Spear are now well into their third decade as hosts at this 100-year-old crofter's cottage down a single track road. Remoteness is one of the Three Chimneys' enduring virtues, and everything from the built-to-last furnishings to the smell of freshly baked bread reinforces the mood of heart-warming domesticity. But this is no sepia-tinted nostalgia trip: guests come here to sample highly polished modern food built around matchless produce from Scotland's moors, farms and waters. Fixed-price menus change each day and proceedings might open with Dunsyre Blue cheese, mustard leaf, pear and pine kernel salad or Talisker-cured organic Hebridean salmon with sweet-and-sour cucumber. Next comes a soup or a plate of Loch Harport oysters, before loin of Glen Hinnisdal lamb with its own faggot, colcannon and young neeps, poached fillet of Invernesshire Limousin beef, or roast Mallaig monkfish wrapped in Ayrshire bacon with Sconser scallops, split-pea 'purry' and black kale. Refined elaboration is the order of the day. To finish, the 'famous' hot marmalade pudding with Drambuie custard is a fixture; otherwise iced whisky and lemon parfait might fit the bill. The impressive wine list scours the classic French regions in depth before jetting off to faraway lands in search of top-quality names. House selections start at £18.50 (£4.75 a glass).

Chef/s: Michael Smith. **Open:** Mon to Sat L 12.30 to 2, all week D 6.30 to 9.30. **Closed:** L Nov to Mar. **Meals:** Set L £22.50 (2 courses) to £29.50, Set D £49.50 (3 courses) to £56. **Service:** not inc. **Details:** Cards accepted. 30 seats. 4 seats outside. Separate bar. No music. Wheelchair access. Car parking.

Kingussie

The Cross
Pure, unadorned simplicity
Tweed Mill Brae, Ardbroilach Road, Kingussie,
PH21 1LB
Tel no: (01540) 661 166
www.thecross.co.uk
Modern Scottish | £45
Cooking score: 5

Picture the scene: a converted water-powered tweed mill by a bubbling burn surrounded by enchanting riverside grounds ablaze with flowers. The Cross is a seductively bucolic Nirvana, complete with rough-stone walls, heavy beams and other original features – yet even the displays of modern art seem totally in keeping with their rustic surroundings. The eminently personable mood is matched by food that impresses with its natural, unadorned simplicity and artless craftsmanship. Everything that comes out of the kitchen is founded on the principles of treating good raw materials with the respect they deserve. What isn't strictly local is sourced from farms and producers across the length and breadth of Scotland – and that embraces everything from Shetland salmon to Ullapool oatcakes. The fixed-price dinner format couldn't be simpler: just two or three choices at each stage with the option of a couple of simpler dishes as alternatives. Seared breast of young grouse is dressed with cowberry syrup, organic Highland chicken goes into a terrine and Fraserburgh mackerel is soused. The kitchen also fashions more elaborate ideas along the way: fillet of Scrabster cod appears with tomato fondue, samphire, peas, broad beans and sea lettuce, while rack of Ayrshire Blackface lamb arrives with a croustade of kidneys, Madeira jus, curly kale and parsley root. Desserts such as pistachio and olive oil cake with baked apricots and Piedmonte ice cream look to Europe for inspiration. The seriously considered wine list is a pleasure to behold: France and Spain are front-runners, there's an increasing emphasis on organic and biodynamic production, and the excellent stock of dessert tipples is hard to beat. Prices start at about £20.
Chef/s: Becca Henderson and David Young. **Open:** Tue to Sat D only 7 to 8.45. **Closed:** Sun, Mon, Christmas and Jan. **Meals:** Set D £43 to £48. **Service:** net prices. **Details:** Cards accepted. 20 seats. Separate bar. No music. No mobile phones. Wheelchair access. Children allowed. Car parking.

Kirkwall

ALSO RECOMMENDED
▲ Dil Se
7 Bridge Street, Kirkwall, KW15 1HR
Tel no: (01856) 875 242
www.dilserestaurant.co.uk
Indian

One of the most northerly outposts of Indian cooking in the UK, this glass-fronted restaurant behind Kirkwall harbour has hit the jackpot since opening in 2005. The lengthy menu is a mix of curry-house standards ('old flames'), tandooris and a smattering of 'new-wave' specialities. Appetisers (from £3.70) range from chaats to pakoras, signature dishes include chicken chilli balti (£8.95) or you can go for a dhansak or biryani. To finish, try warm gulab jamun with a refreshing scoop of Orkney ice cream (£5.95). Unbeatable 'early-bird' menus (2 courses for £10). House wine is £11.95. Open all week 4 to 11.

Lochinver

Albannach
Chill out in Scottish style
Baddidarrach, Lochinver, IV27 4LP
Tel no: (01571) 844407
www.thealbannach.co.uk
Modern Scottish | £50
Cooking score: 6

Standing in splendid isolation among the wild moors above Lochinver, Colin Craig and Lesley Crosfield's tall white house is an alluring retreat where chilling out is the name of the game. Inside, the place remains as

snugly Scottish as ever – although there isn't a cliché in sight (apart from a stag's head). The owners make a formidable double act in the kitchen, and are totally dedicated to procuring 'all things local, free-range and wild'. Seafood is 'caught, landed and dived for by friends', local crofters are encouraged to grow organic vegetables, and meat is naturally reared in Morayshire. Dinner proceeds at a leisurely pace throughout the whole evening, as guests relax in a room of dark wood and rugs with stunning sea views. A typical five-course meal might commence with breast of guinea fowl on juniper cabbage with roast shallot and wild mushroom sauce, before a skilfully wrought lobster soufflé. As a centrepiece, there might be fillet of free-range Morayshire beef or roast Lochinver turbot served on local 'croft' greens with braised fennel, Shetland Black potatoes and red wine sauce. A brace of cheeses (say, Clava 'Scottish Brie' and Ogleshield) are taken before dessert, which might be lime torte with orange and ginger sauce and a berry fruit basket.
Albannach is now open on Mondays for B&B, and residents can order a simple three-course seafood supper on that day for half the price of dinner. Colin Craig's highly distinctive, endlessly fascinating wine list was being updated as we went to press, but expect the same catholic range as before and prices from around £14 (£4.50 a glass).
Chef/s: Colin Craig and Lesley Crosfield. **Open:** all week D only from 7 (1 sitting). **Closed:** Mon to Wed mid Nov to Dec (exc Christmas week), Jan and Feb (exc New Year week). **Meals:** Set D £50 (5 courses), seafood supper Mon £25. **Service:** not inc. **Details:** Cards accepted. 20 seats. No music. No mobile phones. Car parking.

Muir of Ord
Dower House
Cosseted domesticity
Highfield, Muir of Ord, IV6 7XN
Tel no: (01463) 870 090
www.thedowerhouse.co.uk
Modern British | £38
Cooking score: 2

Originally a thatched farmhouse on the 3,000-acre Highland Estate and later re-built as a stone 'cottage orné', the Dower House is cosseted domesticity personified – thanks to the dedicated efforts of hosts Robyn and Mena Aitchison. Their no-choice menu changes each night, everything is personally prepared by Robyn himself, and a seamlessly orchestrated, intimate dinner-party atmosphere prevails. Begin with drinks in the drawing room, then proceed to the sedate dining room (all Persian rugs, old paintings and antique mahogany tables) for, say, a starter of sautéed John Dory fillets with marinated vegetables and tomato vinaigrette, then peppered fillet of venison with piquant rowan berry sauce, plus toffee pudding to finish. The evening always draws to a close with coffee or tea and a sweet nibble (perhaps candied peel). Wines suit the occasion perfectly, and there are generally some extra 'odd bins' on offer; prices start at £18.
Chef/s: Robyn Aitchison. **Open:** all week D only 7.30 to 9.30. **Closed:** Christmas. **Meals:** Set D £38. **Service:** not inc. **Details:** Cards accepted. 12 seats. 4 seats outside. No music. No mobile phones. Wheelchair access. Children's portions. Car parking.

Plockton

ALSO RECOMMENDED
▲ Plockton Inn

Innes Street, Plockton, IV52 8TW
Tel no: (01599) 544 222
www.plocktoninn.co.uk
Gastropub

Look for the whitewashed inn by the harbour, where a wealth of good Scots produce is on offer, from West Highland beef to an array of single malts, with traditional fish and seafood the star of the show. Local prawns with garlic butter (£6.75) might start you off or there's smoked salmon, cured in-house, dressed in lemon and chives (£4.95). Mains include skate wing and black butter (£10.75) as well as a few meat dishes. Finish richly with chocolate truffle torte or more lightly with citrus sorbets (both £3.50). Australian house wines are £10.95. Accommodation. Open all week.

Port Appin

Airds Hotel

Just a lovely place
Port Appin, PA38 4DF
Tel no: (01631) 730 236
www.airds-hotel.com
Modern Scottish | £49.50
Cooking score: 5

♦★

All the ingredients are still here: chef J Paul Burns in the kitchen, the McKivragans running the hotel and the views from the dining room across the Lynn of Lorn to Lismore and beyond seducing diners. Airds is a former eighteenth-century ferry inn, small enough to feel homely, but run with light-touch professionalism and high-service standards. The kitchen is a crucial part of the show, Burns turning out a deft four courses in the evenings for residents and non-residents alike, delivering, in the words of one smitten reporter 'outstanding raw materials beautifully cooked and presented'. In the politely furnished dining room you could start with a seafood assiette (oyster, home-cured gravadlax, smoked salmon, sweet-cured herring and mussels with garlic butter), then a shellfish bisque au gratin before a choice of mains. That might be turbot, sea bass or chicken breast with seared foie gras, Puy lentils, black truffle and morels for anyone all fished out, with dark chocolate tart and orange sauce to finish. Vegetarians who book ahead get a pretty decent four courses of their own. An ample wine list starts by the glass at £4.95, with more than 30 bottles pegged at £25 or under. House white and red is £19 and £20 respectively.

Chef/s: J Paul Burns. **Open:** all week L 12 too 1.45, D 7.30 to 9. **Closed:** 2 days each week Nov to Jan. **Meals:** Set D £49.50 (4 courses). **Service:** not inc. **Details:** Cards accepted. 32 seats. No mobile phones. Music. Car parking.

Ross-shire

READERS RECOMMEND
Pool House Hotel

Modern European
Poolewe, Ross-shire, IV22 2LD
Tel no: (01445) 781272
www.poolhousehotel.com
'Fine dining with spectacular view'

St Margaret's Hope

The Creel

Front Road, St Margaret's Hope, KW17 2SL
Tel no: (01856) 831 311
www.thecreel.co.uk
Modern Scottish | £35
Cooking score: 7

The islands are a great leveller. The idea of trying to run a restaurant on South Ronaldsay, even a seasonal one, with urban wine prices would seem counter-intuitive so the list at the Creel starts at £14 a bottle and strays just twice over £30. After-dinner single malt Scotch is just £2.50 a shot and the general demeanour of the restaurant run by Alan and Joyce Craigie is accessible – from the local artwork on the walls to the general simplicity of décor. They've been doing this since 1985 and have three bedrooms upstairs for anyone who wants to stay over. Alan built the reputation of the food quite slowly, but it eventually gathered a critical mass of appreciation. Some of the regard for the Creel is certainly down to the other-worldliness of the Orkney Island group, the rest to his cooking and the ingredients he can draw upon. A mutton terrine starter comes from sheep fed on seaweed, for example, imparting a rare flavour. The menu also features seafood species that don't often find their way to domestic plates like porbeagle shark or wolf-fish, the former in a langoustine bisque, the latter steamed and served with seared scallops, basil, oven-dried tomatoes and almond pesto. Desserts are more straightforward (glazed lemon tart, or a trio of rhubarb puddings – crumble, baked custard and ice cream). Islanders grumble about the prices a little – mains are £18.50 each – but to southern eyes they don't seem so bad.

Chef/s: Alan Craigie. **Open:** Apr to Oct D only 7 to 8.45. **Closed:** Mon Apr to Oct, and Tue Apr, May, Sept and Oct. **Meals:** alc (main courses from £18.50). **Service:** not inc. **Details:** Cards accepted. 34 seats. No music. Wheelchair access. Children's portions. Car parking.

▌Scrabster

★ BEST FISH RESTAURANT ★

The Captain's Galley
Family-run restaurant by the harbour
The Harbour, Scrabster, KW14 7UJ
Tel no: (01847) 894 999
www.captainsgalley.co.uk
Seafood | £36
Cooking score: 4

£5 OFF

Jim and Mary Cowie's tiny Captain's Galley enjoys a handy location by Scrabster harbour within view of the Orkney ferry and, more significantly, the local boats that are bringing in the day's catch. It's a treat to find a small, friendly space offering such a wealth of locally sourced seafood and the fact that it's all fully sustainable is a bonus. Jim Cowie, working on his own in the kitchen, takes you on a whistle-

stop world tour, from vichyssoise with a smoked local oyster via miso-cured loin of tusk with Thai jasmine rice to 'tapas' of monkfish liver and salt fish brandade. 'In lesser hands, you'd be nervous', but in the stone-walled former ice house with the charming Mary pouring you a glass of Riesling, it feels just right. The Cowies open only for dinner, and at one price, £36.50 a head. For fish that's just hours old, caught exclusively in the seas outside the window, and Cowie's understanding of the ingredients, that's a fair price.

Chef/s: Jim Cowie. **Open:** Tue to Sat D 7 to 9. **Closed:** Sun and Mon, Christmas, 1 Jan. **Meals:** Set D £36.50. **Details:** Cards accepted. Separate bar. Wheelchair access. Music. Children's portions. Car parking.

▌Shieldaig

Tigh an Eilean Hotel
An enchanted setting
Shieldaig, IV54 8XN
Tel no: (01520) 755 251
Modern Scottish | £44
Cooking score: 3

Christopher and Cathryn Field have run this charming white-painted hotel for the past 10 years. It's setting, in a small, picturesque fishing village overlooking the waters of Loch Torridon, is nothing less than bewitching. The best-quality, locally sourced ingredients drive Christopher's daily changing fixed-price diner

Symbols

🏠	Accommodation is available.
£30	Three courses for less than £30.
V	More than five vegetarian dishes.
£5 OFF	£5-off voucher scheme.
🍾	Notable wine list.

menus, and, not unsurprisingly, there's a focus on seafood, with the daily catch from local boats delivered straight to the kitchen door, while game in season comes from the nearby Applecross estate. The cooking mixes modern ideas, say, grilled fillets of West Coast sea bream served with a provençale confit of marinated tomatoes, roasted peppers, olives and anchovies, alongside classic dishes such as fillet of Highland beef Wellington with a Madeira jus. The wine list fits the bill, a short, reasonably priced global affair with house wine from £14.50

Chef/s: Chris Field. **Open:** all week D only 7 to 8.30. **Closed:** end Oct to mid-March. **Meals:** Set D £44. **Service:** optional. **Details:** Cards accepted. 28 seats. Separate bar. No music. No mobile phones. Children's portions.

▌Stein

ALSO RECOMMENDED
▲ Loch Bay

1-2 Macleod Terrace, Stein, IV55 8GA
Tel no: (01470) 592 235
www.lochbay-seafood-restaurant.co.uk
Seafood

Simplicity is the watchword at this tiny eight-table restaurant, not 10 metres from the pier in the fishing village of Stein. Sourcing is important, with fish straight from the pier or scallops from the other side of the island. Urban favourites such as halibut and monkfish are on the menu. However, lesser-known fish such as codling or hake are also treated with a simple coating of olive oil and lemon juice, lightly grilled and served with fresh garlic butter. Main courses from £12.50. Lobster starts at £28.00. Service is knowledgeable and friendy, in keeping with the simple approach. Open from Easter to October. Closed Sun and Mon.

▌Strontian
Kilcamb Lodge

A place to treasure
Strontian, PH36 4HY
Tel no: (01967) 402 257
www.kilcamblodge.co.uk
Modern European | £48
Cooking score: 5

£5 OFF 🛏

'From the moment we entered the driveway to see this lovely Lodge overlooking Loch Sunart and the glorious hills beyond we were hooked,' reports a smitten visitor. Sally and David Ruthven-Fox's hotel, in a 'magnificent setting' of 22 acres of meadow and woodland, is a country house in the full-dress style, furnished with rich fabrics, log fires and the kind of sofas that that seemed designed to lull you off to sleep. It would be unwise to succumb to slumber, though, and miss Mark Greenaway's thoroughly accomplished, modern British cooking. There is a gentle inventive impulse at work in the conception of dishes, which might involve partnering fillet of sea bream with cucumber noodles and brown crab consommé as one starter or, at main-course stage, teaming lamb loin and rack with couscous stuffed cabbage, roasted shallots and sesame seed jus. Elsewhere, reporters have praised 'posh fish, chips and mushy peas', which turned out to be halibut with two different ways with pea and potato rösti, and 'boiled beef and carrots' – fillet steak, shredded braised oxtail and carrot in a 'tender pasta parcel'. For dessert, apple plate six ways ranges from pie, crisps, mousse, soup, sorbet to toffee sauce. The wine list, divided by grape variety, provides a concise, but wide-reaching tour of major wine-growing countries. Sensible mark-ups mean prices are fair throughout, starting at about £20.

Chef/s: Mark Greenaway. **Open:** all week L 12 to 1.30, D 3 to 11. **Closed:** Mon and Tue in Jan. **Meals:** Set L £14.75 (2 courses) to £17.50, set D £48 (4 courses). **Service:** not inc. **Details:** Cards accepted. 28 seats. Separate bar. Wheelchair access. Music. Car parking.

WALES

Glamorgan, Gwent, Mid-Wales, North-East Wales, North-West Wales, West Wales

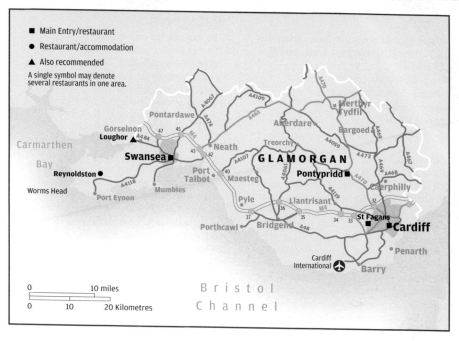

- ■ Main Entry/restaurant
- ● Restaurant/accommodation
- ▲ Also recommended

A single symbol may denote
several restaurants in one area.

▌Cardiff

Le Gallois

Entering a new era
6-10 Romilly Crescent, Canton, Cardiff, CF11 9NR
Tel no: (029) 2034 1264
www.legallois-ycymro.com
Modern European | £35
New Chef

With a new chef at the helm and part of the
ownership team departed, Le Gallois is
entering a new era. As we went to press, the
formula was largely unaltered: gently
inventive, classically based cooking served in a
stylish environment. The superb front-of-
house team seems unchanged, and there is
admirable attention to detail in everything
from home-made breads to petits fours. While
reporters remain broadly happy with the
experience, there have been rumblings that
not all the food is as 'special' as hoped. A
lunchtime starter of cauliflower soup lacked
character, but was livened by a Stilton beignet,
while a beautifully balanced main course of

pan-fried sea bream with sweet roasted fennel
and cherry tomatoes, olives, garlic and thyme
pressed all the right buttons. A dessert of
cherry clafoutis was technically perfect, but
the accompanying dark chocolate ice cream
seemed an afterthought rather than a coherent
part of the dish. Despite such niggles, Le
Gallois remains one of the best dining
experiences in the area, and we hope that as the
new kitchen team settles in, it will really hit its
stride. The wine list includes some interesting
French finds, starting at £14.50. More reports
please.
Open: Tue to Sun L 12 to 2.30 (3 Sun), Tue to Sat D
6.30 to 9.30 (10 Fri and Sat). **Closed:** Mon, 23 Dec
to 5 Jan, Easter Sun. **Meals:** alc (main courses
£13.95 to £31.50). Set L £12.95 (2 courses) to £15.95.
Service: not inc. **Details:** Cards accepted. 60 seats.
Air-con. Separate bar. Wheelchair access. Music.
Children's portions. Car parking.

Gilby's

Modern food in attractive barn conversion
Old Port Road, Culverhouse Cross, Cardiff,
CF5 6DN
Tel no: (029) 2067 0800
www.gilbysrestaurant.co.uk
Modern European | £32
Cooking score: 2

 V

A change of ownership has not drastically changed the Gilby's formula. The interior is still homely, with a large lounge giving way to a dining area in a smartly converted barn. The open kitchen turns out modern creations (perhaps pan-fried brill with saffron and chorizo risotto and deep-fried watercress) alongside classics such as home-made chicken liver and foie gras parfait with toasted brioche and home-made chutney followed by braised shank of Welsh lamb with a macédoine of vegetables, Puy lentils and a sticky honey glaze. Vegetarians now have a whole menu to themselves; Mediterranean vegetable omelette and red onion and goat's cheese tarte Tatin are typical choices. Desserts range from Kaffir lime leaf crème brûlée with a chilli-shortbread biscuit and mango sorbet to home-made sticky toffee pudding with butterscotch sauce and toffee ice cream. The wine list offers finds from around the world, starting at £13.95. Gilby's has recently spawned a Cardiff Bay offshoot, Gilby's@The Bay. Reports please.
Chef/s: Kurt Fleming. **Open:** all week L 12 to 2.15 (3.15 Sun), Mon to Sat D 6 to 9.30. **Meals:** alc D (main courses £16.95 to £21.95). Set L £14.95, Set D early eve £19.95. **Service:** not inc. **Details:** Cards accepted. 70 seats. Separate bar. Wheelchair access. Music. Children's portions. Car parking.

Scores on the Doors

To find out more about the Scores on the Doors campaign, please visit the Food Standard's Agency website: www.food.gov.uk or www.which.co.uk.

Patagonia

The Argentinian connection
11 Kings Road, Cardiff, CF11 9BZ
Tel no: (029) 2019 0265
www.patagonia-restaurant.co.uk
Modern European | £28
Cooking score: 2

Owners Joaquin and Leticia Humaran met in a hotel kitchen in Buenos Aires and moved to Europe to perfect their skills, before opening this smart little restaurant in Cardiff. While it originally doubled as a coffee house, they have recently shifted its focus to concentrate solely on fine dining. The set menu includes starters such as smoked eel with 'mi-cuit' foie gras, Granny Smith compote and sherry reduction or grilled artisan goat's cheese with baked polenta, caramelised onion and confit baby plum tomatoes. Main courses range from slow-roasted collar and crispy belly pork with Puy lentils and white cabbage braised in wheat beer to home-made butternut squash and walnut ravioli with ewe's milk cheese sauce. You might finish with chocolate pastilla and mandarin pannacotta. The owners' Argentinian links are reflected in their choice of beef (Pampas Plains grass-fed) and wines, which are priced from £11.50.
Chef/s: Joaquin Humaran. **Open:** Tue to Sat D 6.30 to 10. **Closed:** bank hols, Mon, Sun. **Meals:** Set D £23.90 (2 courses) to £27.90. **Service:** not inc. **Details:** Cards accepted. Air-con. Wheelchair access. Music. Children's portions.

Woods Brasserie

Bay views
The Pilotage Building, Stuart Street, Cardiff,
CF10 5BW
Tel no: (029) 2049 2400
www.woods-brasserie.com
Modern European | £35
New Chef

The landmark pilotage, which overlooks Cardiff Bay, is an immediately thrilling venue for a restaurant. The original stonework has been retained, while inside an open-plan kitchen creates a theatrical atmosphere and the large, modern glass extension provides a patio for summer eating. We were notified about the arrival of a new chef too late to respond with an inspection, but there are unlikely to be changes to the tried-and-tested repertoire of modern brasserie dishes. Moules marinière to start, then chargrilled rib-eye steak with sauce bordelaise or rump of lamb with Provençale vegetables, lamb jus and tapenade, are typical choices.

Chef/s: Wesley Hammond. **Open:** all week L 12 to 2, (3 Sun), D 5.30 to 10. **Closed:** Sun D Sept to June. **Meals:** Set L £16.50, pre theatre £19.95. **Service:** not inc. **Details:** Cards accepted. 90 seats. 40 seats outside. Air-con. Separate bar. Wheelchair access. Music. Children's portions. Car parking.

▌Cowbridge

READERS RECOMMEND
Huddarts

British
69 High Street, Cowbridge, CF71 7AF
Tel no: 01446 774645
www.cowbridgetown.co.uk/huddarts.htm
'Quietly confident food in cosy surroundings'

▌Loughor

ALSO RECOMMENDED
▲ Hurrens Inn on the Estuary

13 Station Road, Loughor, SA4 6TR
Tel no: (01792) 899 092
www.hurrens.co.uk
Modern European

This smart little restaurant has estuary views from its front terrace, and will soon have an upstairs bar/lounge overlooking the nearby Roman fort. Graham Hurren's increasingly interesting cooking draws on a broad range of influences, so starters could include Vrindavan mung dhal with griddled chapati (£4.95), borscht topped with organic crème fraîche and smoked duck breast with garden salad. Mains have a more classic feel – perhaps medallions of roe deer on a potato and celeriac rösti with

red wine sauce (£16.50) or canon of Welsh lamb with fondant potato and port and juniper jus. Wines from £11.95. Open all week.

▌Pontypridd
Bunch of Grapes

A fine gastropub in an unlikely spot
Ynysangharad Road, Pontypridd, CF3 4DA
Tel no: (01443) 402 934
www.bunchofgrapes.org.uk
Gastropub | £20
Cooking score: 1

Tucked down a dead-end road near a row of terraced houses, this pub looks unassuming but stands out in terms of food and drink. At the bar, you'll find real ales and ciders, while the kitchen offers an imaginative culinary romp through Wales. There is laverbread from the coast, cooked in a tart with wild mushrooms and shallots and served with a grain mustard dressing. Talgarth ham is served in a cold meat platter with venison carpaccio, smoked sausage, capers, gherkins, olives and beetroot chutney; and Welsh lamb shank is braised in Dark-O stout, baby onions, topped with a pastry lid and served with rosemary and sunflower seed mash. Vegetarians might be treated to potato, parsnip and leek pie with Welsh cider sauce and braised red cabbage. Comforting desserts include gingerbread and dark rum cheesecake and warm home-made sticky toffee pudding with butterscotch sauce and vanilla pod ice cream. Wines from £12.95. **Chef/s:** Sebastien Vanoni. **Open:** Mon to Sat L 11.30 to 3 and D 6 to 11.30. Sun D 11 to 4. **Meals:** alc (main courses £12.25 to £14.95). **Service:** not inc. **Details:** Cards accepted. Separate bar. Music. Children's portions. Car parking.

Also recommended

An 'also recommended' entry is not a full entry, but is provisionally suggested as an alternative to main entries.

▌Reynoldston

★ READERS' RESTAURANT OF THE YEAR ★
WALES

Fairyhill

Classy dining in gorgeous rural setting
Reynoldston, SA3 1BS
Tel no: (01792) 390 139
www.fairyhill.net
Modern Welsh | £40
Cooking score: 4

This lovely old country house enjoys a 'wonderful location' amid 24 acres of mature grounds. The homely interior has an air of 'understated elegance', with plenty of space for lounging over pre-dinner drinks. The atmosphere is enhanced by the front-of-house team, who create 'the feel of visiting old friends'. The menu is based around the best local ingredients, and features Welsh specialities such as laverbread and oatmeal with crispy bacon and fried bread or a fillet of Welsh Black beef with rösti, wild garlic and lemon butter. The set-price lunch menu might include salad of Welsh goat's cheese with sun-dried tomatoes and olives followed by roast cod with a Welsh rarebit crust, spinach and tomato glaze, and then mocha terrine with fresh raspberries. Typical desserts on the dinner menu are dark chocolate fondant with plum sauce and crème fraîche, and warm cider-poached pears with gin-and-lemon ice cream. Fairyhill continues to receive praise for its extensive, personally compiled wine list, which opens at £14.50. Regular wine tastings are held throughout the year.
Chef/s: Nick Jones. **Open:** all week L 12 to 2, D 7 to 9. **Closed:** 25 Dec D, 26 Dec, 1 to 24 Jan. **Meals:** alc L (main courses £14.95 to £24.50). Set L £19.95, Set D £40. **Service:** not inc. **Details:** 60 seats. 20 seats outside. Separate bar. Wheelchair access. Music. Children's portions. Car parking.

▌St Fagans

Old Post Office

The best of old and new
Greenwood Lane, St Fagans, CF5 6EL
Tel no: (029) 2056 5400
www.old-post-office.com
Modern European | £28
Cooking score: 3

Although Cardiff is just a short drive away, the village of St Fagans feels a world removed from such hustle and bustle. The Old Post Office itself is a haven of calm, decked out in surprisingly modern, minimalist style. While the original building is as old as the name suggests, it has been much extended to create a sense of space and light. Chef/proprietor Simon Kealy has succeeded in maintaining the restaurant's good reputation since he took over two years ago, and the whole experience is considered 'good value for money'. The food, like the building, is a fusion of old and new styles. An interesting choice of soups might include Sicilian fennel or roast iron bark pumpkin with a walnut dressing, while heartier starters range from fresh crab risotto to braised pig cheeks with purple sprouting broccoli and Jerusalem artichokes. Typical mains are slow-roasted belly pork with wild garlic, roasted beetroot and mash or red snapper fillet with bubble and squeak, baby leek and tomato dressing. Wine prices start at a very reasonable £10.95 a bottle.
Chef/s: Simon Kealy. **Open:** Tue to Sat L 12 to 3, Tue to Sat D 7 to 9.30. **Closed:** 25 Dec, 1 to 14 Jan. **Meals:** alc (main courses £12.95 to £16.50), Set L £11.95 (2 courses) to £14.95. **Service:** not inc. **Details:** Cards accepted. 35 seats. 30 seats outside. Air-con. Separate bar. Music. Children's portions. Car parking.

▌Swansea

Bartrams at 698

Modish Mumbles brasserie
698 Mumbles Road, Mumbles, Swansea, SA3 4EH
Tel no: (01792) 361 616
www.698.uk.com
Modern European | £28
Cooking score: 3

V

A racy addition to the Mumbles restaurant scene, this cool funky venue looks the business with its chic interior, leather seating, laid-back jazz sounds and open-to-view, glass-fronted kitchen. The kitchen casts an eye towards Europe for most of its ideas and there's a familiar ring to many of the dishes on the regularly changing carte. Starters of seared scallops with caramelised cauliflower purée, caper and sultana dressing or new season's asparagus with poached egg and hollandaise could lead on to roast loin of Welsh lamb with olive mash and tomato jus or pan-fried organic salmon with sweet potato purée and seafood sauce. To finish, try something suitably boozy such as passion fruit pyramid parfait with Pina Colada sauce or pear and blackberry crumble tart with Poire William ice cream. The carefully chosen, good-value wine list opens with South African house selections at £11.95 (£4.45 a glass).
Chef/s: Steven Bartram. **Open:** Tue to Sat L 12 to 2, D 6 to 9. **Closed:** Sun, Mon, 25 Dec. **Meals:** alc (main courses £17 to £22). Set L £13.95 (2 courses) to £16.95. Set D early-bird menu £18.95 (2 courses) to £22.95. **Service:** not inc. **Details:** Cards accepted. 42 seats. Wheelchair access. Music. Children's portions.

Didier & Stephanie

Traditional French in cosy surroundings
56 St Helens Road, Swansea, SA1 4BE
Tel no: (01792) 655 603
French | £38
Cooking score: 4

Didier Suvé and Stéphanie Danvez have a formula that works. It involves serving elegant French cooking of the traditional stamp in warmly welcoming surroundings. That may not sound desperately innovative, but there is a genuine yearning for their kind of approach in many parts of the country. A regular reporter praises the 'consistently good' results Didier achieves in menus that deal in the simple and the classic. Snail ravioli in garlic stock, or boudin noir in a mustard-dressed salad, are possible ways of beginning, and may be followed up by sea bass in saffron, or pheasant in apple and Calvados sauce. There are occasional forays towards the wilder shores, as when foie gras turns up with mango ice cream, but it may be better to stick to the familiar propositions, especially when the dessert menu brings on moelleux au chocolat with orange sauce or poached pear in red wine with cinnamon ice cream. Wines start at £11.90.
Chef/s: Didier Suvé. **Open:** Tue to Sat L 12 to 1.30, D 7 to 8.30. **Closed:** Sun, MOn, Christmas. **Meals:** alc (main courses £15 to £18). Set L £14.90. **Service:** not inc. **Details:** 25 seats. Air-con. Music. Children's portions.

Hanson at the Chelsea Restaurant

A flair for seafood
17 St Mary's Street, Swansea, SA1 3LH
Tel no: (01792) 464 068
www.hansonatthechelsearestaurant.co.uk
Modern Welsh | £28
Cooking score: 3

£5
OFF

Tucked down a side street in the heart of Swansea's wining and dining district, this smart little restaurant has a tranquil, personal feel far removed from the bustle of the city centre. Swansea Marina is just a few minutes' walk away, and chef/proprietor Andrew Hanson makes full use of this fact with his daily fish menu, which might offer chargrilled sea bass with seared scallops and deep-fried seafood parcels on three sauces, and plaice fillets in tempura batter with pea purée, hand-cut chips and tartare sauce. Meat and vegetarian options are by no means an afterthought, and might include starters of home-made beef and red wine cannelloni or crostini of apple and goats' cheese with a roast pine-nut and walnut oil-dressed salad followed by honey-roast rack of Welsh lamb with herb potato gratin and deep-fried parsnip ribbons or mixed vegetarian tortellini with tomato, basil and mascarpone sauce. Wines from £11.75.

Chef/s: Andrew Hanson. **Open:** L 12 to 2, D 6.30 to 10. **Closed:** Sun, bank hols. **Meals:** alc (main courses £9.95 to £17.95), set L £10.95 (2 courses). **Service:** not inc. **Details:** Cards accepted. Wheelchair access. Music. Children's portions.

The Restaurant @ Pilot House Wharf

Fish-centric menu
Trawler Road, Swansea, SA1 1UN
Tel no: (01792) 466 200
www.therestaurantswansea.co.uk
Modern Seafood | £27
New Chef

If you can, sit by one of the windows of this landmark turreted building in the heart of Swansea's Marina, and take in the view of fishing boats and the swish SA1 development beyond. Bare-wood tables, high-backed chairs and a brown and cream colour scheme, create a suitably relaxed atmosphere for some contemporary cooking. There's a new chef in the kitchen, but fish will continue to be a strong suit, say steamed mussels, local Gower lobster or a grilled fish platter that might offer John Dory, hake, bream and razor clams. Meat options might include herb and laverbread-crusted rump of lamb and sirloin and fillet steaks with classic garnishes. House wine is £10.95. Reports please.

Chef/s: Rob Wheatley. **Open:** Tue to Sat L 12 to 2.30, D 6.30 to 9.30. **Closed:** Sun, Mon, 25 and 26 Dec, 1 Jan, bank hols. **Meals:** alc (£14.50 to £19.95). Set L £10.95 (2 courses) to £14.95. **Service:** not inc. **Details:** Cards accepted. 45 seats. Music. Children's portions. Car parking.

★NEW ENTRY★
Slice

Smooth service and confident cooking
Eversley Road, Swansea, SA2 9DE
Tel no: (01792) 290 929
Modern British | £28
Cooking score: 3

This tiny, wedge-shaped restaurant has its kitchen downstairs, allowing passers-by on the street a full view of the action. The upstairs seating area is snug but light, with little to distract you from the food. Helen Farmer's charming front-of-house presence sets a welcoming, professional tone, while Phil Leach labours in the kitchen to produce everything from breads to petits fours. Ingredients are a roll-call of some of the best local produce, from seafood to lamb. In Phil's hands these become unpretentious modern dishes such as lobster tortellini with lobster broth or confit duck terrine with pickled wild mushrooms, followed by pan-roasted saddle of lamb on rösti potato with mint oil or roast chicken breast with warm new potato herb salad and chicken jus. Desserts such as elderflower crème brûlée with gooseberries round the meal off in style. A decent list of wines opens at £11.95 a bottle.

Chef/s: Philip Leach. **Open:** Fri to Sun L 12 to 2, Thu to Mon D 6.30 to 9. **Closed:** Tue, Wed, 25 and 26 Dec. **Meals:** Set L £15 (2 courses) to £20, Set D £38. **Service:** not inc. **Details:** Cards accepted. 18 seats. Music.

Average price

The average price listed in main-entry reviews denotes the price of a three-course meal, without wine.

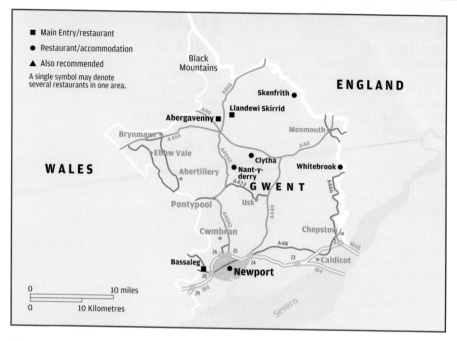

■ Abergavenny

★ BEST USE OF LOCAL PRODUCE ★

The Hardwick

Intelligent food in a welcoming setting
Old Raglan Road, Abergavenny, NP7 9AA
Tel no: (01873) 854 220
www.thehardwick.co.uk
Gastropub | £28
Cooking score: 4

 £30

When Stephen Terry set up shop in deepest Monmouthshire, his reputation went before him. A veteran of some of London's most iconic kitchens, his move to the Hardwick marked a shift to a more straightforward cooking style very much in keeping with the homely pub setting, all underpinned by the excellent ingredients available locally. However, there is a subtlety and intelligence to his cooking that ensures even the simplest-sounding dishes are deeply satisfying and full of interest. A starter of carpaccio of rare roast Herefordshire beef is served on rocket with rosemary, anchovy and garlic dressing, while main courses range from hearty slow-cooked shoulder of local lamb with mashed potato, Swiss chard, poached carrots, braised lentils, capers and parsley to the bright flavours of grilled tuna with couscous, grilled viola aubergine and chick peas with chilli, coriander, mint, natural yoghurt and rocket. A flexible lunch menu offers simple dishes (home-cooked ham with organic egg and triple-cooked chips) alongside less traditional offerings such as pan-fried pasta rotolo with roast butternut squash, spinach, Perroche goats' cheese, toasted pine nuts, pumpkin seeds, rocket and parmesan. Puddings such as treacle tart ice cream with candied pecans and golden syrup provide more reasons to linger, as does the well-balanced wine list, which opens at £13.50.

Chef/s: Stephen Terry. **Open:** Tue to Sun L 12 to 3, Tue to Sat D 6.30 to 10. **Closed:** Mon, 25 Dec and 26 Dec, 2 Jan. **Meals:** alc (main courses £9.50 to £15.95). **Service:** not inc. **Details:** Cards accepted. Separate bar. Children's portions. Car parking.

▌Bassaleg

Junction 28

Internationally inspired food
Station Approach, Bassaleg, NP10 8LD
Tel no: (01633) 891891
www.junction28.com
Modern British | £20
Cooking score: 2

This 'busy, popular' restaurant's previous life as a railway station is referenced by the interior décor, part of which mimics an old-fashioned railway carriage. Despite its lively past, this is a tranquil spot with an old parish church nearby and a rushing river below. Inside it's homely and relaxing, with a decent-sized lounge for pre-dinner drinks. The cooking gleefully combines techniques and flavours from far and wide. You could start with Chinese chicken soup with dim sum, or terrine of rabbit studded with caramelised shalotts. Cannon of Brecon lamb and mint baked en croûte with a gateau of aubergine, courgette and tomato cream cheese; and fillet of monkfish wrapped in prosciutto on sautéed pak choi with Provençal vegetable wontons and aromatic soy dressing are typical main courses. Desserts range from classic custard tart with caramelised figs to an eyebrow-raising banana and toffee mousse with vodka lime sherbet. Wines start at £13.50.
Chef/s: J.J. Payel and I. Jackson. **Open:** Mon to Sat L 12 to 2, D 5.30 to 9.30. Sun L 12 to 4. **Closed:** 26 Dec, 1 Jan. **Meals:** alc (main courses £11.95 to £18.95) Set L £11.95 (2 courses) to £13.95.
Service: not inc. **Details:** Cards accepted. Air-con. Separate bar. Wheelchair access. Music. Children's portions. Car parking.

▌Clytha

Clytha Arms

Homely pub with imaginative food
Clytha, NP7 9BW
Tel no: (01873) 840 206
www.clytha-arms.com
Modern Welsh | £30
Cooking score: 3

This pink-painted former dower house stands in its own grounds beside the old Abergavenney to Raglan road. A hearty, life-affirming authenticity runs through every aspect of the place, from the stone-floored, fire-warmed bar where visitors and locals of every age huddle round tables, prop up the bar, and fill the air with lively chatter, to the restaurant where plates groan with Andrew Canning's internationally inspired cooking. Service can sometimes be slow, but the food is worth waiting for. Typical choices include Perl Las (a Welsh cheese) and port soufflé or oysters in batter with Thai sauce followed by wild boar with Rioja and chorizo or Caribbean fruit curry. There are bar meals, too, such as lamb koftas in coriander curry or chicken and cider pie with mushy peas and chips. For a lighter bite, look to the inspired tapas list, where Penclawdd cockles rub shoulders with mini spring rolls and Basque-style chicken. The substantial wine list starts at £12.95 and includes a good selection by the glass or half bottle.
Chef/s: Andrew Canning. **Open:** Tue to Sun L 12 to 3, Tue to Sat D 6 to 12. **Closed:** 25 Dec. **Meals:** alc (main courses £13.50 to £19.50), Set D £19.50 (2 courses) to £23.80. **Service:** not inc. **Details:** Cards accepted. Separate bar. No music. Children's portions. Car parking.

Llandewi Skirrid

★NEW ENTRY★
Walnut Tree Inn
Shaun Hill's new venture
Llandewi Skirrid, NP7 8AW
Tel no: (01873) 852 797
www.thewalnuttreeinn.com
Modern British | £36
Cooking score: 5
🍷

It needed a name (and a talent) like Shaun Hill's to turn the Walnut Tree's fortunes around, and early signs are very promising. The place itself looks spick and span, from the well-tended garden to the cosy stone-floored bar and simple dining area. This is a relaxing environment; a place where the staff seem happy and the ingredients are truly themselves. The bulk of the menu is dedicated to dishes that reassure rather than challenge: perhaps local St George's mushrooms on toast, followed by rib-eye of beef with dauphinoise potatoes. With such simplicity, the delight comes from the quality of the materials, the exactness of the cooking and the clarity of the flavours. A starter of seared monkfish, for example, was lifted by the breezy freshness of a simple tomato, ginger and garlic salsa. From an excellent-value lunch menu came a warm artichoke heart with mushrooms and a perfect hollandaise, followed by a generous panache of fish (scallop, red mullet, halibut and sea bass) with tomato and butter sauce. A dessert of pear Belle Hélène was an orgy of glossy chocolate, tender pear flesh and silky ice cream, while a lemon cheesecake lacked citrusy zeal, but was likeable in a mild-mannered sort of way. Charming little extras included a memorable canapé of spinach and ricotta in won-ton batter (all crunch and curdy comfort) and (among the excellent and plentiful petits fours) a shamelessly dense and rich fudge. The wine list includes a few of Hill's favourites from his Merchant House days, plus some good-value new finds and a sprinkling of classics, priced from £16.

Chef/s: Shaun Hill and Roger Brooks. **Open:** Tue to Sat L 12 to 2.30, D 7 to 10. **Closed:** Sun, Mon, 24 to 26 Dec. **Meals:** alc (main courses £9 to £20). Set L £20. **Service:** not inc. **Details:** Cards accepted. 55 seats. 20 seats outside. Air-con. Separate bar. No music. Wheelchair access. Children's portions. Car parking.

Nant-y-derry

Foxhunter
Modern cooking in a peaceful setting
Nant-y-derry, NP7 9DN
Tel no: (01873) 881 101
www.thefoxhunter.com
Modern European | £30
Cooking score: 4
🍷🛏

The tiny village of Nant-y-derry – so small it's barely there – is home to this immaculately refurbished former pub that dates back to Victorian times. Chef Matt Tebbutt worked in some of London's top restaurants before returning to Wales, and his cooking reflects the influence of mentors such as Marco Pierre White and Sally Clarke. He also draws inspiration from closer to home, making use of the 'wonderful food resources we have in this part of Wales'. A meal might kick off with smoked eel, carrot, beetroot, local ham and shallot vinaigrette or goujons of salt cod with a Thai dip, followed by braised Longhorn beef or spring lamb rack, spiced aubergine salad and mint yoghurt. Desserts with a high-comfort rating (apple and blackberry crumble) sit alongside luxurious combinations such as roasted figs with honeycomb and mascarpone ice cream. The substantial, French-dominated wine list is nicely annotated and includes a good selection of half bottles. Prices from £14.50 a bottle.

Chef/s: Matt Tebbutt. **Open:** Tue to Sat L 12 to 2.30 D 6.30 to 9.30. Sun L 12 to 2.30. **Closed:** Mon, 25 Dec. **Meals:** alc (main courses £14.95 to £18.95). Set L £18 (2 courses). **Service:** not inc. **Details:** Cards accepted. Separate bar. Wheelchair access. Music. Children's portions. Car parking.

▌Newport

Chandlery

Classic food in a stylish former chandlery
77-78 Lower Dock Street, Newport, NP20 1EH
Tel no: (01633) 256 622
www.thechandleryrestaurant.com
Modern British | £27
Cooking score: 4

£5 £30
OFF

This lovely building, originally a ship's chandlery, has been tastefully restored to create a stylish restaurant brimming with original features. There are sofas for pre-dinner lounging, and rambling dining areas that feel spacious yet intimate. Chef Simon Newcombe is well versed in the classics, but has an eye for both comfort and invention – so starters such as seared scallop and Thai fishcakes or butternut squash and sage risotto cake might be followed by roast saddle of Middlewood Farm venison wrapped in Parma ham with creamed celeriac, braised beetroot, wild mushrooms and rösti potato. There is also a simple grill menu, which includes carefully sourced meats such as Gloucester Old Spot pork or Welsh sirloin steak. Finish with tried-and-tested desserts such as hot chocolate fondant, classic tiramisu or pecan and toffee tart with orange ice cream. At lunch, lighter options come into play, including traditional Welsh cawl, Welsh rarebit and noodle stir-fry. Set business lunches might bring deep-fried egg with warm chorizo and potato salad followed by confit of duck leg with red cabbage and mash. Wines from £12.95.
Chef/s: Simon Newcombe. **Open:** Tue to Sat L 12 to 2, D 7 to 10. Sun 12 to 2. **Closed:** Mon. **Meals:** alc (main courses £13.50 to £17.95). Set L £11.95 (2 courses). **Service:** not inc. **Details:** Cards accepted. Air-con. Separate bar. Music. Children's portions. Car parking.

★NEW ENTRY★

The Crown

Offspring of the Crown at Whitebrook
The Celtic Manor Resort, Newport, NP18 1HQ
Tel no: (01633) 413 000
www.celtic-manor.com
Modern British | £48
Cooking score: 5

🍷 ⇌

A sister restaurant to the Crown at Whitebrook (see entry), with James Sommerin as executive chef at both, the Crown provides the fine dining option at this grandiose resort hotel, in whose public areas you can find arabesque pillars and giant carved wooden dragons. In contrast, the dining room is all subtlety and restraint, with bare wooden floors and peaceful white walls adorned with fine art. In the kitchen, Tim McDougall delivers a polished and precise rendering of Sommerin's vision, though an early inspection suggested that, to begin with at least, the kitchen is playing it safe by avoiding dishes that might seem too avant-garde. There is a classic feel to the cooking, but Sommerin's trademark flair for re-designing familiar ideas is very much in evidence. A starter of cod and dill 'tart', for example, included judicious slivers of light-as-air pastry, and played up the 'filling' of beautifully fresh cod, poached quails' eggs, lentils and smoked artichoke foam. A main course of pan-fried wild sea bass came with oyster mushrooms, daintily sliced boulangère potato and confit fennel for a delightful 'bite'. A pre-dessert of vanilla pannacotta topped with orange and basil showed an equally deft handling of flavours. The wine list is full of interest, and includes some good choices by the glass. Bottles are priced from £20.
Chef/s: James Sommerin and Tim McDougall. **Open:** Tue to Sat L 12 to 2, D 7 to 10. **Closed:** Sun, Mon. **Meals:** L express menu £19.95 (2 courses) to £27.95, Set L £29.95 (2 courses) to £37.50 Set D £47.50, Tasting menu £65 (6 courses). **Service:** not inc. **Details:** Cards accepted. 52 seats. Air-con. Separate bar. Wheelchair access. Music. Children's portions.

Skenfrith

Bell at Skenfrith

Beautiful pub in a breathtaking setting
Skenfrith, NP7 8UH
Tel no: (01600) 750 235
www.skenfrith.co.uk
Gastropub | £31
Cooking score: 1

The Bell seems to have it all – a castle opposite, a river beside it and green hills all around. Extensively revamped, yet full of mature charm and real fires, there is nothing showy about the interior, yet clearly no expense has been spared in the creation of such classy rusticity. The cooking follows suit: steak and chips and game casserole are typical lunchtime offerings, with pan-roasted fillet of cod with lemon and herb bulgar wheat, wilted spinach and dill pesto bringing a lighter, modern edge to the menu. Dinner choices range from seared fillet of beef with oxtail and shallot suet pudding to chargrilled loin of tuna with brown shrimp and garden herb risotto, roasted cherry tomatoes and sauce vierge. Round it off with citrus pannacotta. Wines start at £14.

Chef/s: David Hill. **Open:** all week L 12 to 2.30, D 7 to 9.30 (9 Sun). **Closed:** Mon Nov to Easter. **Meals:** alc (main courses £14.50 to £19.50). Set L £15 (2 courses). **Service:** not inc. **Details:** Cards accepted. 80 seats. 20 seats outside. Wheelchair access. Music. Children's portions. Car parking.

Whitebrook

Crown at Whitebrook

Top-drawer romantic restaurant-with-rooms
Whitebrook, NP25 4TX
Tel no: (01600) 860 254
www.crownatwhitebrook.co.uk
Modern European | £45
Cooking score: 6

A tranquil oasis deep in a heavily wooded valley close to the River Wye sounds authentically Welsh, but there's also something of the romantic French auberge about this converted seventeenth-century inn. Meals are interspersed with all manner of fashionable extras, from exquisite canapés, amuse bouche and between-course sorbets to delightful petits fours (which are served with post-prandial coffee in the lounge). The kitchen avidly seeks out ingredients from far and wide, then allows the creative juices to flow: pan-fried red mullet might be teamed with quinoa, aubergine salsa and artichoke emulsion, while oven-roast loin of lamb could be transformed into a richly exotic star-turn with Moroccan 'ras al hanout' spices, wild rice, confit pepper and baby octopus. Elsewhere, scallops appear as 'raw and cooked' duo (carpaccio and seared), belly pork is paired with langoustines, and a dish of dourade and Cornish lobster becomes an East-West crossover with wild garlic risotto, sesame and soy sauce. Bold gestures and classically inclined ideas share the honours when it comes to desserts: dark chocolate and griottine cherry soufflé or macerated Cantaloupe melon with South African 'Groot Constantia' wine, jasmine and hibiscus, for example. The comprehensive wine list (arranged by grape variety) consists of about 250 of the most interesting tipples that the owners can lay their hands on. Half-bottles and luscious dessert wines show up well, and there are popular selections from £21 (£5.50 a glass).

Chef/s: James Sommerin. **Open:** Wed to Sun L 12 to 2, Wed to Sat D 7 to 9. **Closed:** Mon, Tue, 2 weeks Christmas. **Meals:** Set L £25 (2 courses) to £28. Set D £45. **Service:** not inc. **Details:** Cards accepted. 30 seats. 16 seats outside. No mobile phones. Wheelchair access. Music. Car parking.

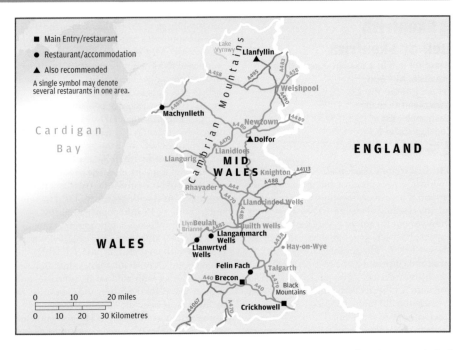

Map legend:
- ■ Main Entry/restaurant
- ● Restaurant/accommodation
- ▲ Also recommended

A single symbol may denote several restaurants in one area.

Brecon

Tipple'n'Tiffin

Informal canal-side snacking and dining
Theatr Brycheiniog, Brecon, LD3 7EW
Tel no: (01874) 611 866
Modern European | £25
Cooking score: 1

Popular for pre-threatre eats owing to its location within Brecon's Theatr Brycheiniog, this ground-floor restaurant's glass windows overlook the canal, which makes a picturesque setting for a pre-dinner stroll. Back inside, you can feast on 'tiffin' plates and bowls to share – perhaps crispy duck legs on kumara and butternut squash rösti with apple and onion compote, mussels with wine, cream and garlic or tiffin shards to dip in molten Welsh cheeses and laverbread. For a more conventional main, you could have braised oxtail in ale on mustard mash or perhaps pan-fried fillets of trout with smoked bacon and mushrooms. Lemon meringue pie and tarte au citron with blackcurrant fruit ice are typical of the home-made desserts. Wines start at £12 a bottle.

Chef/s: Richard Gardner. **Open:** Mon to Sat L 10 to 3, D 6 to 9. **Closed:** Sun, 25 Dec, 1 Jan. **Meals:** alc (sharing platters and main courses £7 to £9). **Service:** not inc. **Details:** Cards accepted. 40 seats. 20 seats outside. Wheelchair access. Music. Children's portions. Car parking.

ALSO RECOMMENDED

▲ Barn at Brynich

Brynich, Brecon, LD3 7SH
Tel no: (01874) 623 480
www.barn-restaurant.co.uk
Modern European

This magnificent converted barn feels cosy despite its great size. Snacks are served all day, but at lunch and dinner the menu becomes more serious, offering imaginative dishes made with superb local ingredients – perhaps Welsh oak-smoked duck and orange salad (£5.75) or slow-braised shank of lamb with mashed potato and sweet red cabbage (£13). A short, well-annotated wine list opens at £9.95. Closed Mon, Oct to Mar.

Crickhowell

Nantyffin Cider Mill Inn

A modern approach to local produce
Brecon Road, Crickhowell, NP8 1SG
Tel no: (01873) 810 775
www.cidermill.co.uk
British, Mediterranean | £25
New Chef

£5 OFF 🍷 £30

Set back from the road, this pink-washed building is a tranquil refuge full of historical charm. Once a drovers' inn, it retains a very traditional-looking bar, but the restaurant proper is in the old apple store. This barn-like building has been converted to form a grand yet rustic room with high stone walls and an ancient cider press at its heart. Produce comes from the surrounding area – much of it from a farm just seven miles away but inspiration for the dishes is wide ranging. Wild mushrooms in crispy beer batter or a Greek mezze plate are typical openers, while mains run from homely confit of Welsh lamb with creamed potatoes and rosemary garlic sauce to Aylesbury duck suprême with Asian-style noodle soup, pak choi and shiitake mushrooms. Finish with rhubarb fool or raspberry crème brûlée. The wine list includes a good selection from around the world, with plenty of them priced at under £20.
Chef/s: Marius Petre. **Open:** Tue to Sun 12 to 3. **Closed:** Mon except bank hols. **Meals:** alc (main courses 9.95 to £14.95). **Service:** not inc. **Details:** Cards accepted. 90 seats. 40 seats outside. Separate bar. Wheelchair access. Children's portions. Car parking.

Also recommended

An 'also recommended' entry is not a full entry, but is provisionally suggested as an alternative to main entries.

Dolfor

ALSO RECOMMENDED
▲ The Old Vicarage

Dolfor, SY16 4BN
Tel no: (01686) 629 051
www.theoldvicaragedolfor.co.uk
Modern British

Tim and Helen Withers ran the George and Dragon at Rowde (see entry, Wiltshire) for many years and are now happily ensconced in this friendly restaurant-with-rooms, rearing free-range hens and growing vegetables in their pesticide-free garden. At dinner, the limited-choice menu costs £25 for three courses. Start perhaps with Welsh Cheddar cheese soufflé with Parmesan and cream, follow with organic salmon in pastry with ginger, currants and sauce messine, and finish with meringue with cider apples, damsons and cream. Open all year. Must book L and D.

Felin Fach

Felin Fach Griffin

Beacon of hospitality
Felin Fach, LD3 0UB
Tel no: (01874) 620111
www.felinfachgriffin.co.uk
Modern British | £34
Cooking score: 3

£5 OFF 🛏 V

Once part of a working hill farm in the Welsh wilds between the Brecon Beacons and the Black Mountains, the Griffin is now emphatically in the hospitality business – hence its mantra 'Eat, Drink, Sleep'. It successfully combines the virtues of a rustic country pub and a relaxed, family-friendly restaurant dealing in locally sourced food. New set-lunch and supper menus highlight the excellent value for money, while the full carte is peppered with inviting possibilities. Try a salad of squab pigeon with beetroot and beetroot sorbet, ahead of salted cod poached in brown butter with cauliflower or saddle of local lamb with fondant potato, garden peas and mint jelly. For dessert, how about poached

rhubarb pannacotta with almond crumble? The ever-improving wine list focuses on small, independent growers with reputable names. Prices are friendly, with 'open wines' starting at £14.50 (£3.40 a glass).
Chef/s: Ricardo Van Ede. **Open:** Tue to Sun L 12.30 to 2.30, all week D 6.30 to 9.30. **Closed:** 24 and 25 Dec. **Meals:** alc (main courses L £8.50 to £12, D £16.50 to £20). Set L Tue to Sat £15.90 (2 courses) to £18.90. Set D £21 (2 courses) to £26.50.
Service: not inc. **Details:** Cards accepted. 50 seats. 20 seats outside. Separate bar. Wheelchair access. Music. Children's portions. Car parking.

Llanfyllin

ALSO RECOMMENDED
▲ Seeds
5 Penybryn Cottages, Llanfyllin, SY22 5AP
Tel no: (01691) 648 604
British

Simple bistro fare is the order of the day at this pleasant cottage restaurant. Two courses will set you back £22.75, while three courses cost £25.25. Start with home-made smoked mackerel pâté and toast, followed by roast rack of Welsh lamb with a Dijon mustard and herb crust or grilled goats' cheese on Mediterranean vegetables. Lemon posset with mixed berry sauce and treacle tart with cream are typical of the comforting desserts. A balanced, international wine list starts at £13. Open L and D Thur to Sat.

Llangammarch Wells
Lake Country House
Elegant country retreat
Llangammarch Wells, LD4 4BS
Tel no: (01591) 620 202
www.lakecountryhouse.co.uk
Modern European | £38.50
Cooking score: 2

🍷 🍽

Built in 1840 as a hunting and fishing lodge and much tinkered with over the years, this country house sports a quirky mish-mash of architectural styles, from mock-Tudor to colonial. Inside, 'a real sense of occasion' is created by antique furniture and spacious, tranquil rooms. 'Attentive and knowledgeable' service comes from a team of welcoming, unstuffy staff. You could start with a pressing of confit of lamb shoulder, globe artichokes and thyme with sweet pickled fennel, then move on to braised shin of Welsh beef with potato purée, wild mushrooms, spiced red onion jam and Madeira reduction or fillets of John Dory with Herefordshire asparagus, spiced grapes and Gewürztraminer velouté. The impressive, far-reaching wine list opens at £18.
Chef/s: Sean Cullingford. **Open:** all week L 12.30 to 2, D 7.15 to 9.15. **Meals:** Set L £15 (3 courses), Set D £38.50 (4 courses). **Service:** not inc. **Details:** Cards accepted. 40 seats. Separate bar. No music. Wheelchair access. Children's portions. Car parking.

Llanwrtyd Wells
Carlton Riverside
Classy food and service
Irfon Crescent, Llanwrtyd Wells, LD5 4RA
Tel no: (01591) 610 248
www.carltonrestaurant.co.uk
Modern British | £30
Cooking score: 6

🍷 🍽

Not so long ago Mary-Ann and Alan Gilchrist moved lock, stock and barrel from long-running Carlton House to this attractive riverside property. Their new, multi-faceted endeavour includes a jolly, welcoming locals' bar in the cellar while upstairs a refined, slightly old-fashioned ambience prevails – and very charming it is, too. Alan continues to draw praise for his 'unobtrusive service', while Mary-Ann remains on form in the kitchen. One happy diner enthuses: 'She sources the best ingredients, exercises her imagination and ingenuity, and cooks them to perfection.' If you want the full caboodle, opt for the 'menu surprise', a four-course showcase that sits alongside the regualr à la carte and table d'hôte. A main course of roast partridge, for example, comes with cabbage sautéed with bacon, punchnep (a Welsh way with turnips),

game chips and a port jus, while pan-seared fillet of line-caught cod comes with Beluga lentils, buttered leeks, sautéed potatoes and a chorizo and red wine sauce. Typical starters include a 'trio of beetroot' comprising beetroot jelly, chilled beetroot soup and a beetroot and dill rémoulade. Desserts could include crêpes Suzette or a warm chocolate brownie with pistachio ice cream. Alan's 'ample supplies of thoughtfully matched wines' mean you'd be wise to stay the night. Bottles are priced from £13.75.
Chef/s: Mary-Ann Gilchrist. **Open:** D 7 to 8.30. **Meals:** alc (main courses £12.95 to £24). Set D £17.50 (2 courses), £22.50 (3 courses). **Details:** Cards accepted. 20 seats. Separate bar. No music. No mobile phones. Wheelchair access. Children's portions. Car parking.

Lasswade Country House

Country hotel with lovely views
Station Road, Llanwrtyd Wells, LD5 4RW
Tel no: (01591) 610 515
www.lasswadehotel.co.uk
Modern British | £30
Cooking score: 2

This imposing Edwardian country house has a look of old-fashioned refinement, but Roger Stevens' cooking brings a modern edge to proceedings. Underpinning everything is a commitment to fresh, mostly organic ingredients, many of them produced in the surrounding area. Dinner is the main event and an evening could begin with drinks by the log fire in the drawing room. The menu is short and to the point, with three or four choices at each course. Start with, say, a warm salad of black pudding with lardons of pancetta or parfait of home-smoked brown trout and asparagus with citrus segments and a raspberry balsamic. Mains such as seared fillet of salmon seasoned with Chinese five spice with rice noodles and stir-fried vegetables maintain the modern tone, while more traditional tastes should be satisfied by seared

fillet of Welsh Black beef with a panache of woodland mushrooms, herb mash and a tomato hollandaise. Wines from £12.50.
Chef/s: Roger Stevens. **Open:** all week D 7.30 to 9. **Closed:** 25 Dec. **Meals:** Set D £30. **Service:** not inc. **Details:** Cards accepted. 20 seats. No music. Wheelchair access.

▌Machynlleth

Wynnstay

Eclectic food in a traditional setting
Maengwyn Street, Machynlleth, SY20 8AE
Tel no: (01654) 702 941
www.wynnstay-hotel.com
Modern Welsh | £25
Cooking score: 2

Welcoming and traditional, but not remotely fusty, this grand old coaching inn makes a relaxing environment for a meal. Chef Gareth Johns sources his ingredients with an eye to both quality and ethics, and is very active in the Slow Food movement – so expect plenty of decent Welsh produce, from meat to seafood. The cooking style is broadly traditional, with some international (especially Italian) influences. Welsh lamb might come with tomato and olive gravy; grilled Llanfair pork loin with black pudding, apple mash and sage gravy. A selection of 'small plates' could include pork and duck terrine with chef's chutney or red cabbage ravioli with rosemary butter sauce. Finish with desserts such as crème caramel, milk and chocolate pie or a selection of Welsh cheeses. The well-annotated wine list opens at £13.95 and includes some interesting finds from around the world.
Chef/s: Gareth Johns. **Open:** all week L 12 to 2, D 6.30 to 9. **Service:** not inc. **Details:** Cards accepted. 80 seats. 40 seats outside. Separate bar. No music. Children's portions. Car parking.

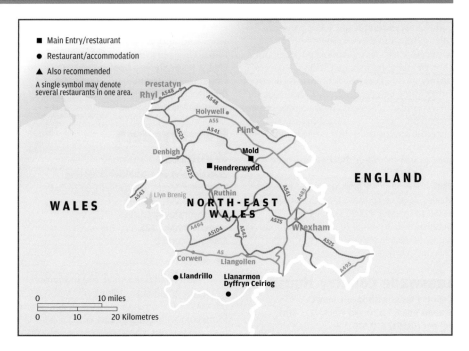

- ■ Main Entry/restaurant
- ● Restaurant/accommodation
- ▲ Also recommended

A single symbol may denote several restaurants in one area.

▌Hendrerwydd

White Horse Inn

Unpretentious food and setting
Hendrerwydd, LL16 4LL
Tel no: (01824) 790 218
www.white-horse-inn.co.uk
Gastropub | £30
Cooking score: 2

This venerable whitewashed building exudes traditional charm. The cooking is unpretentious and perfectly suited to the setting, yet leagues removed from your average pub grub. You could start with wild duck pâté with pomegranate, followed by roasted belly pork with rosemary, parsnips, red onion and pear, a white wine and sweet cider gravy and home-made crabapple cheese. Fresh fish options change daily, but a perennial offering is a half kilo of Conwy mussels served marinière-style. Side orders include home-made focaccia and hand-cut chips. Baileys bread-and-butter pudding with vanilla pod ice cream and lemon posset with grilled figs are typical desserts, but look out for the superb selection of cheeses, which typically combines excellent Welsh specialities with French finds. A shorter lunchtime menu offers two courses for £10 plus sandwiches and salads. Wines from £11.95.

Chef/s: Ruth Vintr, Chris Hurst and Pepo Havlik.
Open: Tue to Sun L 12 to 12.30, D 6 to 9.15. **Closed:** Mon, bank hols, 25 Dec, 1 Jan. **Meals:** alc (main courses £15.95 to £17.95), set L £10 (2 courses).
Service: not inc. **Details:** Cards accepted. Separate bar. Children's portions. Car parking.

Please send us your feedback

To register your opinion about any restaurant listed in the Guide, or a new restaurant that you wish to bring to our attention, please visit the web address at the bottom of the page. Your feedback informs the content of the book and will be used to compile next year's reviews.

Llanarmon Dyffryn Ceiriog

West Arms

Remote inn-with-rooms
Llanarmon Dyffryn Ceiriog, LL20 7LD
Tel no: (01691) 600 665
www.thewestarms.co.uk
Anglo-French | £33
Cooking score: 3

In a seriously remote location at the foot of the Berwyn mountains, this creeper-clad hostelry has been welcoming travellers since 1670, when it started life as a refuelling point on the old drovers' route. These days it does duty as an inn-with-rooms and still bears the hallmarks of history, from slate floors and blackened timbers to mighty inglenooks and gleaming horse brasses. The kitchen makes the most of ingredients from home and abroad for concise dinner menus with a contemporary flavour. Seared scallops on a salad of apple and herbs or a platter of cured meats with warm pear and damson chutney might precede patriotic fillet of Welsh beef glazed with Welsh rarebit or Gressingham duck breast with figs, orange and Burgundy sauce. Desserts such as coffee and walnut bavarois or blueberry and blackberry pie are alternatives to cheeses with quince jelly. France and the New World head up the international wine list, which opens with Chilean house selections at £14.95 (£3.90 a glass).
Chef/s: Grant Williams. **Open:** Sun L 12 to 2, all week D 7 to 9. **Meals:** Set D £27.95 (2 courses) to £32.90. Bar menu available. **Service:** 10%.
Details: Cards accepted. 70 seats. 42 seats outside. Separate bar. No mobile phones. Wheelchair access. Music. Children's portions. Car parking.

Shaun Hill Walnut Tree

Why did you become a chef?
I'm actually more fond of eating than cooking

Where do you eat after service?
At home - this is Wales.

What three ingredients could you not do without?
Black pepper, unsalted butter, chicken stock.

What's your guilty food pleasure?
Welsh rarebit.

What won't you tolerate in the kitchen?
Carelessness.

Do you always read reviews of your restaurant?
Yes.

What dish is your first food memory? Mashed potato with lots of butter and spring onion.

What era of history would you most like to have eaten in?
The one after next.

Llandrillo

Tyddyn Llan

Accomplished, unfussy cooking
Llandrillo, LL21 0ST
Tel no: (01490) 440 264
www.tyddynllan.co.uk
Modern British | £45
Cooking score: 7

On the fringes of Llandrillo village and in the shadow of the Berwyn mountains, this stone and slate-built Georgian house is charming in any season. In summer, you can sit out on the veranda and enjoy the immaculate garden with its lush lawns, neatly clipped hedges and ornamental fountain. In colder weather, the interior is warm and restful, with an abundance of real fires and armchairs. As always, superlatives have come in thick and fast for Susan Webb's 'excellent, attentive service' and her husband Bryan's precise and unfussy cooking. Bryan is adept at sourcing 'superb ingredients' from the surrounding area, ranging from beef to impeccably fresh fish, and he exercises an intelligent restraint when deciding what to do with them. The result is that the beauty of those ingredients shines through, unclouded by pretentious flummery. Typical of his approach is a signature dish of griddled scallops with vegetable relish and rocket, while a gutsy alternative might be deep-fried pig's trotters with tartare sauce, beetroot and relish. Among the main courses, a beautiful fillet steak of aged Welsh Black beef might be served simply 'au poivre' accompanied by gratin dauphinoise and seasonal vegetables, while breast of Gressingham duck might come with potato pancake, cider and apples. Bryan's winning combination of modern, classic and traditional British influences is exemplified by the desserts, which might include steamed ginger pudding with custard, pannacotta with blood oranges and grappa or cappuccino crème brûlée. The superb, lovingly compiled wine list is helpfully arranged by character, so you can easily locate anything from a 'light, fruity red' to a 'fruity, fragrant and aromatic'

white. There is an impressive choice of wines by the glass or half bottle, and prices start at a very reasonable £16 a bottle.
Chef/s: Bryan Webb. **Open:** Fri and Sat L 12.30 to 2, all week D 7 to 9.30. **Meals:** Set L £28 (3 courses), Set D £45 (3 courses). **Service:** not inc.
Details: Cards accepted. Wheelchair access. Children's portions. Car parking.

Mold

56 High Street

Seafood is the star
56 High Street, Mold, CH7 1BD
Tel no: (01352) 759 225
www.56highst.com
Seafood | £24
Cooking score: 3

A simple, stylish interior sets the tone here for a thoroughly modern style of cooking. Fresh fish and seafood are the stars, but landlubbers are well catered for with dishes such as 'all things pork' – loin, crispy belly, pork fillet Wellington, chorizo mash, toffee apples and port jus. Fishy signature dishes include queen scallops baked in a traditional French clay pot with Gruyère cheese, garlic and lemon butter or chargrilled monkfish wrapped in pancetta with cherry tomato and pearl barley risotto. Other highlights are mussels fresh from the Menai Strait and Pacific oysters. Praised for its 'good value, accomplished fish cooking and honest pricing', this restaurant is very popular at lunchtimes, when two courses will set you back just £8.95. The wine list is also good value, with bottles starting at £10.95, and a range of single-estate first pressings from around the world.
Chef/s: Karl Mitchell, Kirsten Robb and Martin Fawcett. **Open:** Tue to Sat L 12 to 3, D 6.30 to 9.30 (6 to 10 Fri and Sat). **Closed:** Sun and Mon. **Meals:** alc. Set L £8.95 (2 courses). **Service:** not inc.
Details: Cards accepted. Air-con. No mobile phones. Wheelchair access. Music. Children's portions.

The Good Food Guide 2009

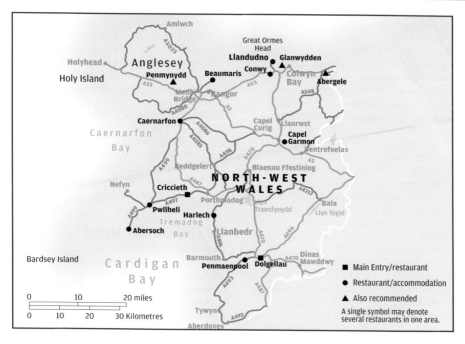

Map legend:
- ■ Main Entry/restaurant
- ● Restaurant/accommodation
- ▲ Also recommended

A single symbol may denote several restaurants in one area.

Scale:
0 10 20 miles
0 10 20 30 Kilometres

■ Abergele

ALSO RECOMMENDED
▲ The Kinmel Arms

St. George, Abergele, LL22 9BP
Tel no: (01745) 832 207
www.thekinmelarms.co.uk
Modern British

Owners Tim and Lynn Watson are forever improving their attractive restaurant-with-rooms. Lamb is now farmed in front of the building, and features on the menu throughout the year. The restaurant also has its own herb and vegetable garden. The food is imaginative, so hot-smoked salmon with brown shrimp mousse (£6.95) might be followed by pan-fried hake on curried mussel, winter vegetable and lentil broth with curly kale (£16.95). Finish with apricot and croissant bread-and-butter pudding with clotted cream. An impressive wine selection starts at £13.95, and includes 21 by the glass. Closed Sun D and Mon.

■ Abersoch

Porth Tocyn Hotel

Country house full of personal touches
Bwlchtocyn, Abersoch, LL53 7BU
Tel no: (01758) 713 303
www.porth-tocyn-hotel.co.uk
Modern European | £39
Cooking score: 4

£5 OFF

The Fletcher-Brewer family created this homely country-house hotel out of a row of former lead miners' cottages. The finished article (which continues to evolve) is the result of decades of devotion, and its distinctive, almost cottagey character makes a refreshing alternative to grander country retreats. Inside you'll find a series of interconnecting rooms filled with country-style furnishings and plenty of books and magazines. Outside are well-tended gardens, and glorious views of Cardigan Bay. Nick Fletcher-Brewer is a friendly and welcoming host, and Louise Fletcher-Brewer handles the kitchen with equal aplomb, flanked by co-chef John Bell. The cooking is technically assured, and successfully combines traditional/classical and modern/international themes. Starters, for instance, range from chicken liver parfait with red onion marmalade and toasted treacle bread to spiced aubergine won tons with crisp vegetable salad and a soy reduction. Main courses might include grilled monkfish and tempura king prawns with creamed Savoy cabbage, confit red peppers and a chive beurre blanc, pan-fried mignons of Welsh beef with fondant potato, carrot purée and a wild mushroom and brandy jus or confit duck breast over a fig tarte Tatin with truffled caramelised beans and a redcurrant jus. The lengthy, well-annotated wine list includes something for all pockets, starting at £13.95. **Chef/s:** John Bell and Louise Fletcher-Brewer. **Open:** all week L 12.15 to 2, D 7.15 to 9 (9.30 in high season). **Closed:** Early Nov to just before Easter. **Meals:** Set D £32.50 (2 courses), £39 (3 courses). **Service:** not inc. **Details:** Cards accepted. 50 seats. 30 seats outside. Separate bar. No music. No mobile phones. Children's portions. Car parking.

▍Beaumaris

Café Neptune
Seafood in a stylish setting
First Floor, 27 Castle Street, Beaumaris, LL58 8AP
Tel no: (01248) 812 990
www.cafeneptune.co.uk
Modern Seafood | £28
Cooking score: 2

As the name suggests, this restaurant majors in fish and seafood. Set above the main street in an attractive seaside town, it has striking modern décor and helpful staff. Chef Marius Cepoiu's cooking is full of international flavours, so you could start with Thai-spiced salmon and crab cake, Chinese-style duck pancakes or steamed Anglesey mussels served in an Oriental spiced sauce. Main courses are equally wide-ranging: perhaps bouillabaisse, fish and chips or pan-fried John Dory fillets with crab risotto, creamed garlic, wild mushrooms and sauce vierge. Daily specials such as fruits de mer, scallops and mussels are available when quality can be guaranteed. For diners who don't feel fishy there might be venison ragoût, fillet of Welsh beef with olive mashed potatoes, roasted vine tomatoes and royal sauce; or dolcelatte and roasted butternut squash risotto. Finish with pannacotta or white chocolate and Amaretti cheesecake. The short wine list reflects the menu's global outlook and starts at £12.95. **Chef/s:** Marius Cepoiu. **Open:** all week L 12 to 2.30, D 6 to 9.30. **Meals:** alc (main courses £10.75 to £19.75). **Service:** not inc. **Details:** Cards accepted. 48 seats. Air-con. No music.

Ye Olde Bulls Head
Anglesey aristocrat
Castle Street, Beaumaris, LL58 8AP
Tel no: (01248) 810 329
www.bullsheadinn.co.uk
Modern European | £38
Cooking score: 6

Built in 1472 and 'improved' in 1617, Ye Olde Bulls Head fully deserves its deliberately archaic name tag; it also makes the most of its location a stone's throw from majestic Beaumaris castle. Fine dining takes place in the Loft Restaurant, a heavily beamed and raftered dining room high up in the eves of the building, which has been eye-catchingly designed with circular mirrors, arty partitions and well-dressed tables. The food is also suitably lofty in style: dishes are defined by the produce of the region and meals are fashionably interspersed with lots of incidentals. Grilled pavé of locally smoked salmon is impeccably embellished with horseradish cream, parsnips chips and Avruga caviar, while fresh asparagus keeps company with poached egg and crumbled farmhouse Caerphilly. Main courses tend to be more elaborate, thus loin of Welsh lamb appears with rolled shoulder and an assemblage of thyme-scented tomatoes, crushed peas, olivette potatoes and rosemary jus. The same intent shows in fish dishes such as fillet of young halibut with Puy lentils, beetroot, pancetta and red wine reduction, while desserts are marvels of confident technique and artistry (crème brûlée with champagne rhubarb sorbet, stem ginger and Caernarfonshire butter shortbread, for example). Judiciously chosen wines from the French regions are the focus of the aristocratic list, although intriguing names from elsewhere should tempt those who want to explore. Half-bottles show up well and prices are kind: house selections come in at £18.50 (£4.80 a glass). The conservatory-style ground-floor brasserie (with its own chef) offers casual food along the lines of clam chowder, braised lamb shank and ribeye steaks.

Chef/s: Craig Yardley. **Open:** Mon to Sat D only 7 to 9.30. **Closed:** Sun, 25 and 26 Dec, 1 Jan. **Meals:** Set D £38.50 (3 courses). **Service:** not inc. **Details:** Cards accepted. 45 seats. Separate bar. No music. No mobile phones. Car parking.

▌Caernarfon

★NEW ENTRY★
Rhiwafallen
Stylish restaurant-with-rooms
Llandwrog, Caernarfon, LL54 5SW
Tel no: (01286) 830 172
www.rhiwafallen.co.uk
Modern Welsh | £29
Cooking score: 2

The immaculate interior of this Welsh farmhouse combines the best of old and new. 'It's one of the most attractive bar and restaurants we have ever visited,' reported one diner. Recent refurbishments include the addition of air-conditioning, a hardwood conservatory and new slate floors. A glance down the menu reveals plenty of comforting, traditional elements, but ultimately the approach here, too, has a stylish modern edge. Typical starters are carpaccio of spiced venison with herb salad, horseradish and roast walnut cream and king prawn and cockle linguine with courgette and lemon butter sauce, while main courses range from mustard and herb-

rolled Welsh beef with crisp-roast potatoes, garlic and shallot butter to pan-fried fillet of trout with new potato and Little Gem fondue, porcini tapenade and crisp pancetta. Depending on the time of year, you might finish with summer pudding and clotted cream or perhaps cinnamon pancakes, caramelised apples and rum and raisin ice cream. Wines from £13.95

Chef/s: Rob John. **Open:** Tue to Sat D from 7. Sun L from 12.30. **Closed:** Mon, 25 Dec. **Meals:** Set D £29.50 (3 courses), Sun L £18.50. **Service:** not inc. **Details:** Cards accepted. Air-con. Separate bar. Wheelchair access. Music. Children allowed. Car parking.

READERS RECOMMEND
Ty'n Rhos
Modern Welsh
Seion, Llanddeiniolen, Caernarfon, LL55 3AE
Tel no: 01248 670489
www.tynrhos.co.uk
'Smartly refurbished country house'

▌Capel Garmon
Tan-y-Foel Country House
Modern country-house style
Nr Betws-y-coed, Capel Garmon, LL26 0RE
Tel no: (01690) 710 507
www.tyfhotel.co.uk
Modern British | £42
Cooking score: 6

A thoroughly contemporary, relaxed take on the classic country-house hotel. Forget swags and fusty furnishings; this grand seventeenth-century stone farmhouse is light, modern and impeccably stylish inside. The wider setting is equally impressive. 'Tan-y-Foel' means 'house under the hillside', and the building enjoys sweeping views of the Conwy Valley and Snowdonia National Park. The hotel is family owned, and all aspects of the operation reflect the individuality and attention to detail that comes with truly hands-on owners. Chef/proprietor Janet Pitman is responsible for the

daily-changing, fixed-price menu, which offers two choices at each course. Expect cooking that combines imagination with technical precision. A springtime menu might open with poached cod loin with vegetable and tarragon broth or open lasagne of spinach, mushroom and parmesan with white onion cappuccino, followed by a main course of pan-seared fillet of Welsh Black beef with exotic mushrooms, Parmentier potato with black pudding, baby leaf greens, horseradish cream and rich Madeira jus; otherwise, try organic salmon with green lentil ragoût, fennel cream, vegetable lime fritter and a beetroot jus reduction. For your final course, choose between desserts or cheese. If you follow your sweet tooth, choices might include pear and ginger pudding with crème anglaise or chilled poached fig with creamed Welsh goats' cheese, lemon and blackberry Merlot syrup. Wines on the impressive 100-strong list are grouped by style, with informative notes to guide your choices. Bottles from £24. Booking essential.
Chef/s: Janet Pitman. **Open:** D 7.30 to 8. **Closed:** Dec to Jan. **Meals:** Set D £42 (3 courses).
Service: not inc. **Details:** Cards accepted. 12 seats. No music. No mobile phones. Children allowed. Car parking.

Conwy

Castle Hotel, Dawson's Cuisine
Refurbished brasserie dining-room
High Street, Conwy, LL32 8DB
Tel no: (01492) 582 800
www.castlewales.co.uk
Modern Welsh | £20
Cooking score: 2
£5 OFF 🍽 V £30

It's all change at the Castle Hotel. Major refurbishment has transformed Shakespeare's Restaurant into a modern brasserie, where the Dawson's Cuisine bar menu is now available all day. It has lost its classical elegance, although some of John Dawson Watson's paintings of scenes from Shakespeare still adorn the walls. Now it's all high banquettes,

busy wallpaper and carpet and a less harmonious décor. However, the eclectic menu and the buzzy atmosphere draw the crowds, and the chef's pedigree shines through. He names his local suppliers (or 'food heroes') on the menu, and there is a good balance between fish, meat and vegetarian dishes. Start with the Castle's home-made black pudding or a fresh organic salmon fishcake, followed by Conwy Valley lamb parcel wrapped in Carmarthen ham or roasted fillet of Irish Sea monkfish with West Coast queenies. There's sticky toffee pudding with butterscotch sauce and vanilla ice cream for dessert. The short, affordable wine list opens at £12.95.
Chef/s: Graham Tinsley. **Open:** all week 7.30am (breakfast) to 9.30pm. **Meals:** alc (main courses £10.25 to £16.95). Set L £15 (2 courses), Set D £22.50. **Service:** 10% (optional). **Details:** Cards accepted. 62 seats. 30 seats outside. Separate bar. Wheelchair access. Music. Children's portions. Car parking.

Criccieth

★NEW ENTRY★
Tir a Môr
Honest French cooking
1-3 Mona Terrace, Criccieth, LL52 0HG
Tel no: (01766) 523 084
www.tiramor.com
French | £25
Cooking score: 2
V

This modest bistro on two floors is minimalist in style, but has a warm atmosphere. New chef-proprietor, Frenchman Laurent Hebert, with his Welsh-speaking wife offering cheerful front-of-house hospitality, have brought the place back to life after a period in the doldrums. The menu is true to the restaurant's name – 'Tir a Môr' translates as 'land and sea' – and there is a good balance of fish and meat. Quickly seared scallops come with a subtle pea purée, crispy bacon, and almost an excess of salad leaves and red onion in a honey dressing. For main course choose pink and tender lamb or properly timed fillet of monkfish served with a suitably subtle curry sauce. Finish with lemon parfait with passion fruit coulis or buttermilk pannacotta with poached strawberries and shortbread biscuit. This is honest French-style country cooking with substantial portions and unpretentious presentation. The short wine list kicks off at £12.95, and doesn't exceed £35.95.

Chef/s: Laurent Hebert. **Open:** Tue to Sat D 6 to 9.30 (6.30 in winter). **Closed:** Sun and Mon, Jan. **Meals:** alc (main courses £12.50 to £19.50). **Service:** not inc. **Details:** Cards accepted. 38 seats. Wheelchair access. Music.

◼ Dolgellau

Dylanwad Da

Friendly coffee shop and restaurant
2 Ffôs-y-Felin, Dolgellau, LL40 1BS
Tel no: (01341) 422 870
www.dylanwad.co.uk
British | £25
Cooking score: 2

This smart, friendly little eatery now incorporates a daytime coffee shop offering tapas, proper coffees and home-made pastries. The restaurant menu takes over in the evenings, offering bistro-style food that combines classical and international influences. You could start with chicken and basil terrine with pesto mayonnaise or prawn and cherry tomato salad with a lime and mustard seed dressing, followed by pork, apricot and sage casserole or pan-fried hake with a cream, pea and mint sauce. Typical puddings include orange and almond steamed sponge with marmalade sauce and chocolate and ginger truffle cake. 'Dylanwad da' is Welsh for 'good influence' and a play on the name of the chef/proprietor Dylan Rowlands. His influence extends to the impressive wines, which he personally imports. These are now available day or evening, with or without food; bottles are priced from £13.

Chef/s: Dylan Rowlands. **Open:** Thu to Sat (winter) L 10 to 3, D 7 to 9. Tue to Sat (summer) L 10 to 3, D 7 to 9. **Closed:** Sun to Wed (winter), Sun and Mon (summer), Feb. **Meals:** alc (main courses £12 to £16). **Service:** not inc. **Details:** Cards accepted. Separate bar. No mobile phones. Wheelchair access. Music. Children's portions.

◼ Glanwydden

ALSO RECOMMENDED
▲ Queen's Head

Glanwydden, LL31 9JP
Tel no: (01492) 546 570
www.queensheadglanwydden.co.uk
Gastropub

This country pub gained a terrace and garden area during recent refurbishments. Food choices range from modern pub meals - perhaps Jamaican chicken curry (£9.75) or home-made lasagne – to more poised creations such as rillette of goose and ham hock terrine with a pear and sloe gin syrup (£6.50) or a duo of duck with cranberry and orange sauce (£14.75). Impressive local fish and seafood offerings include seared Anglesey scallops with pea purée and crispy pancetta and Conwy mussels marinière. Wines from £14.95. Open all week.

◼ Harlech

Castle Cottage

Family-run restaurant opposite the castle
Y Llech, Harlech, LL46 2YL
Tel no: (01766) 780 479
www.castlecottageharlech.co.uk
Modern Welsh | £34
Cooking score: 2

Regulars have praised this family-run restaurant-with-rooms for the consistently good quality of its food. It stands close to Harlech castle and despite its cottagey appearance it has a crisp, contemporary feel inside. After canapés in the bar, settle down to a meal based around excellent Welsh ingredients - a fishcake of smoked salmon from Rhydlewis, for instance, with a chive and wine sauce, followed by fillet mignon of Welsh beef grilled and served on a herb risotto with a wild mushrooms and Madeira jus or fillet of Milford Haven cod grilled and served on crushed potatoes and spinach with seared queen scallops, prawns and a shellfish sauce. Finish with rich chocolate and chestnut torte with Mount Gay rum cream or lemon tart with blackberry coulis and berry ice cream. There is a good selection of pudding wines, and the wine list proper has a truly international feel. Bottles start at £14.

Chef/s: Glyn Roberts. **Open:** all week D 7 to 9. **Closed:** 3 weeks in Nov. **Meals:** Set D (3 courses £32). **Service:** not inc. **Details:** Cards accepted. 40 seats. Separate bar. No mobile phones. Music. Children's portions. Car parking.

Maes-y-Neuadd

Food from the kitchen garden
Talsarnau, Harlech, LL47 6YA
Tel no: (01766) 780 200
www.neuadd.com
Modern Welsh | £35
Cooking score: 4

£5 OFF 🍷 🛏️

Set on a wooded hillside, this solid-looking stone mansion has spectacular views of Snowdonia. It began life in the fourteenth century and has grown over the years into a grand yet homely building full of period features. Surrounding the house are 85 acres of grounds, the highlight being the 200-year-old walled kitchen gardens – the focus of a restoration project for over a decade – that now provide the kitchen with much of its produce. In the hands of chef/patron Peter Jackson and head chef John Owen Jones these ingredients are turned into sophisticated dishes with modern, traditional and classic influences. You might start with cauliflower pannacotta with red onion marmalade and a citrus yoghurt sauce or a home-made fishcake with warm beetroot salad and a herb olive oil. Main courses centre around crowd-pleasers such as sausages with creamy mash and onion gravy or sirloin steak with grilled tomatoes,

mushrooms, gaufrette potatoes and garlic butter, but there is a touch of invention in dishes such as grilled fish of the day with niçoise salad and spicy tomato fondue. Finish with baked bara-brith-pudding or white chocolate and Cointreau mousse with a compote of berries. Wines are priced from £14.95.

Chef/s: Peter Jackson and John Owen Jones. **Open:** all week L 12 to 1.45, D 7 to 8.45. **Meals:** alc (main courses £8.95 to £14.50). **Details:** Cards accepted. 65 seats. 20 seats outside. Separate bar. No music. No mobile phones. Wheelchair access. Children's portions. Car parking.

▍Llanberis

READERS RECOMMEND
Caban
Global
Yr Hen Ysgol, Llanberis, LL55 3NR
Tel no: (01286) 685500
www.caban-cyf.org
'Organic food and stunning scenery'

▍Llandudno

Bodysgallen Hall

Civilised country house with food to match
Llandudno, LL30 1RS
Tel no: (01492) 584 466
www.bodysgallen.com
Modern British | £43
Cooking score: 5

🍷 🛏️ V

It is hard not to be drawn in by the spell Bodysgallen Hall casts. It is the ultimate country retreat set in 200 acres of parkland and 'extraordinary' gardens and 'seems to have been here since time immemorial'. Stepping inside feels like entering a bygone age; it is all supremely comfortable and easy on the eye, with dark-oak panelling, impressive oil paintings and antiques setting the scene. The two dining rooms both overlook the gardens and have an atmosphere that is relaxed and unintimidating. New chef Gareth Jones seems to have taken over seamlessly from John

Williams, and his cooking has the same hallmarks of lightness and freshness with a keen eye for seasonality. An April reporter enjoyed jellied ham and duck liver terrine with watercress mousse and Parmesan vinaigrette; next came grilled fillet of sea bass teamed with caramelised cauliflower, roast scallops, sliced truffle and red wine reduction, with an 'impressively presented' plate of tropical fruit miniature puddings with pineapple crush and passion fruit jelly for dessert. Service is sharp and obliging. An impressive wine list offers classics such as Château Lafite Rothschild 1999 for £212, but the seven house bottles start at £18.

Chef/s: Gareth Jones. **Open:** all week L 12.30 to 1.45, D 7 to 9.30. **Meals:** Set L £19 (2 courses) to £22.50, Sun L £27, Set D £43. **Service:** 10%. **Details:** Cards accepted. 60 seats. Air-con. Separate bar. No mobile phones. Wheelchair access. Car parking.

St Tudno Hotel, Terrace Restaurant
A cut above
Promenade, Llandudno, LL30 2LP
Tel no: (01492) 874 411
www.st-tudno.co.uk
Modern British | £38
Cooking score: 4
£5 OFF 🍷 ☴

This Victorian seaside resort hotel, with views of Llandudno pier, is several cuts above most others of its genre. It has been in the Bland family for more than 35 years, and this brings a degree of self-assurance to the operation. Floral wallpaper and nineteenth-century prints establish a tone of quiet elegance, as does much of the cooking - served in the Italianate dining room. Sound culinary principles and traditional cooking methods can be seen in rabbit saddle and quail terrine with sweetbread fritters or tarragon and scallop tortellini with pea shoots and langoustine dressing. These may be followed by breast of Gressingham duck with truffle hash brown and cassis glaze or more inventive steamed salmon teriyaki with a sea asparagus boudin

and vermouth cream, with a hot chocolate soufflé with chocolate truffle and raspberry compote to finish. Lunch is a simpler, set-price affair. The wine list is a well-rounded, international selection that has been put together with something like evangelical glee. House wine is £15.50.

Chef/s: Ian Watson. **Open:** all week L 12.30 to 1.45, D 7 to 9.15 (9 Sun). **Meals:** alc (main courses £14.50 to £19.50). Set L £15 (2 courses) to £18. **Service:** not inc. **Details:** Cards accepted. 55 seats. Air-con. Separate bar. No mobile phones. Children's portions. Car parking.

▮ Penmaenpool
Penmaenuchaf Hall
Classic country house
Penmaenpool, LL40 1YB
Tel no: (01341) 422 129
www.penhall.co.uk
Modern British | £40
Cooking score: 3
£5 OFF 🍷 ☴

This classic country-house hotel stands in 21 acres of wooded grounds and landscaped gardens surveying the Mawddach estuary. From the oak-panelled entrance hall to the white napery and sparkling glassware, the style is crisply classic with harmonious contemporary touches. The same could be said of the cooking. A pressing of pigeon, partridge and pheasant might be teamed with ginger chutney, while seared scallops could come with pea purée, crisp ham and star anise syrup. Typical main courses include of fillet of Welsh Black beef with parsnip purée, foie gras and port sauce, and wild seabass with braised fennel, anchovy beignets and a tomato sauce. For dessert, perhaps apple tarte Tatin with tonka bean ice cream. The Francophile wine list is expertly annotated and makes excellent pre-dinner reading. Bottles are priced from £15.50

Chef/s: Justin Pilkington. **Open:** all week L 12 to 2, D 7 to 9. **Meals:** Set L £15.95 (2 courses) to £17.95, Set D £40 (4 courses). **Details:** Cards accepted. Separate bar. Wheelchair access. Music. Children's portions. Car parking.

Penmynydd, Llanfairpwllgwyngyll

ALSO RECOMMENDED
▲ Neuadd Lwyd Country House

Penmynydd, Llanfairpwllgwyngyll, LL61 5BX
Tel no: (01248) 715 005
www.neuaddlwyd.co.uk
Modern Welsh

An elegant but stylish country-house hotel in a former rectory. The dinner menu changes daily and offers just one choice at each course, but special dietary requirements are happily catered for with advance notice. A price of £37 buys four courses – perhaps Welsh blue cheese soufflé with spiced pear and mixed leaf salad followed by slow-roasted free-range duck leg with wilted pak choi, spiced tangerine and pink fir apple cooked with garlic and thyme. A dessert of tarte Tatin might be followed by Welsh cheeses. Wines from £12.75. Open for dinner Wed to Sat.

Pwllheli

Plas Bodegroes

Superb ingredients cooked without pretence
Nefyn Road, Pwllheli, LL53 5TH
Tel no: (01758) 612 363
www.bodegroes.co.uk
Modern British | £43
Cooking score: 6

🍴 🍷

Some places find it easy to make an impact. You reach this beautiful Georgian house via a magnificent avenue of 200-year-old beech trees. For all the manorial regularity of the building's exterior, it's a homely environment that reflects the individuality of the hosts, chef Chris Chown and his wife, Gunna, who handles all things front-of-house. The panache and assuredness with which they fulfil their roles comes from more than 20 years spent here, and is generally reflected in everything from the welcome to the food itself. This year we received one grumble about poor organisation owing to an 'apparent shortage of staff', but reports remain otherwise favourable. In the restaurant, simple descriptions and understated presentation belie the sophisticated and technically assured style of cooking. Chris utilises superb Welsh ingredients and draws on classical themes, while keeping one eye to the distant horizon; so starters could include Thai green curry of monkfish and mussels, pan-fried chicken livers with black pudding and chorizo salad and spiced lentils or guinea fowl ballotine with red pepper chutney. Main courses mostly plough a more traditional furrow, with typical choices including roast loin of Welsh lamb with a pea and mint torte and rosemary jus or roast breast of Goosnargh duck with confit hash, neck sausage and quince sauce. You might finish with a cinnamon biscuit of rhubarb and apple with elderflower custard or Welsh rarebit on walnut bread with apple salad. The lengthy wine list should please all tastes and pockets, and includes an impressive selection of half bottles. Bottles from £16.
Chef/s: Christopher Chown. **Open:** Sun L 12.30 to 2, Tue to Sat D 7 to 9 (9.30 summer). **Closed:** Mon except bank hols. **Meals:** Set D £42.50, Sun L £18.50. **Service:** not inc. **Details:** Cards accepted. 40 seats. Separate bar. Wheelchair access. Car parking.

Rhoscolyn

READERS RECOMMEND
The White Eagle Inn

Modern European
Rhoscolyn, LL65 2NJ
Tel no: (01407) 860267
www.white-eagle.co.uk
'Serves the best of Anglesey produce'

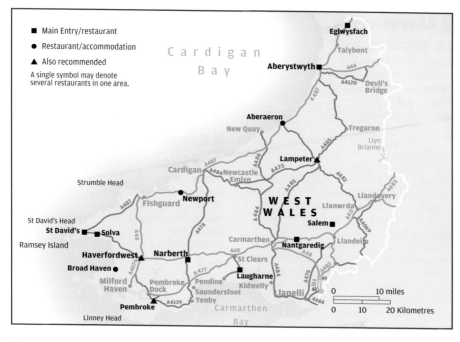

■ **Aberaeron**

Harbourmaster Hotel
Welsh zeal and local flavours
2 Pen Cei, Aberaeron, SA46 OBA
Tel no: (01545) 570 755
www.harbour-master.com
Modern Welsh | £30
Cooking score: 3

True to its name, this azure-blue Georgian residence on the quayside was once the harbourmaster's house, although it has taken on a new lease of life since the arrival of Glyn and Menna Heulyn. They have extended the interior and recently added a new warehouse bar offering drinks, brunch and a simple menu of bistro-style food. The bare-boarded restaurant echoes its location with maritime colours, paintings of seaside scenes and sturdy wooden furniture. Local ingredients show up strongly on the daily changing menus, which are written in Welsh as well as English. Seafood is a strong suit, and the kitchen might offer scallops with salsa verde, fillet of halibut with braised chicory and crème fraîche or blackened sea bream with roasted peppers and red onion. Meat eaters and vegetarians are also well served with anything from rack of Welsh lamb, roasted celeriac and caramelised shallot sauce to Pant Mayr goats' cheese and herb risotto. The wine list has a decent spread of bottles at attractive prices from £12.50 (£3.20 a glass).
Chef/s: Stephen Evans. **Open:** Tue to Sun L 12 to 2.30, all week D 6 to 9. **Meals:** alc (main courses L £10.50 to £16, D £12.50 to £21.50). Bar menu available. **Service:** not inc. **Details:** Cards accepted. 55 seats. 15 seats outside. Separate bar. Wheelchair access. Music. Children's portions. Car parking.

Average price

The average price listed in main-entry reviews denotes the price of a three-course meal, without wine.

■ Aberystwyth

Le Vignoble

Inventive French cooking
31 Eastgate Street, Aberystwyth, SY23 2AR
Tel no: (01970) 630 800
French | £27
New Chef

🍴 🍷£30

After closing for several months to regroup, Le Vignoble is once again with us, and playing a dynamic part on the west Wales culinary scene. The style of inventive, French-inflected cooking looks set to continue, as witness starters such as confit duck salad with new potatoes, French beans and a honey and mustard dressing, and mains like red mullet with truffled celeriac purée alongside a medley of seafood in saffron cream sauce or breast and leg of guinea fowl with garlic rösti, sautéed spinach and a jus of redcurrants and smoked paprika. Cheeses are mostly French, although the odd local item gets a look-in, or there may be desserts such as a tart of raspberries, almonds and pine nuts, served with mascarpone and lemon ice cream and raspberry coulis. A short wine list has helpful, succinct notes, and starts at £13.50 for house French blends. More reports, please.
Chef/s: Pawel Anusiewicz. **Open:** Fri to Sat L 12 to 2, Tue to Sat D 6 to 10. **Closed:** Sun, Mon, Christmas. **Meals:** alc (main courses £13.50 to £19.50). Set L £17.50. **Service:** not inc. **Details:** Cards accepted. 36 seats. Wheelchair access. Music. Children allowed.

ALSO RECOMMENDED
▲ Ultracomida

31 Pier Street, Aberystwyth, SY23 2LN
Tel no: (01970) 630 686
Modern European

The scent of cheese hangs heavy in the air of this beautifully laid out deli. The adjoining café bar serves a simple, vibrant selection of tapas-style dishes – perhaps yellow fin tuna with green bean, carrot and potato salad with dill mayonnaise (£3.30), Spanish omelette with aïoli or meats such as chorizo Iberico.

Cheeses can be sampled individually or as fillings for the generously proportioned bocatas and barras (£4.50). For dessert there might be dark chocolate and chestnut torte (£4) or quince and almond tart. Wines from £10.50. Open all day Mon to Sat. Closed evenings. There is a branch in Narberth (see entry).

■ Broad Haven

Druidstone

Bohemian rhapsody
Druidston Haven, Broad Haven, SA62 3NE
Tel no: (01437) 781 221
www.druidstone.co.uk
Global | £30
Cooking score: 2

🛏 V

The Bell family's imposing stone cliff-top house is one of the Guide's older entries, and certainly one of the more individual. Views are breathtaking - the land plunges away to the Atlantic below - the atmosphere relaxed and infused with a laid-back, bohemian charm; the house is lived-in, without looking scruffy. The kitchen makes the most of good (and local) ingredients, and has really made an impact with a repertoire that kicks off with a simple lemon chicken broth or monkfish with white radish and fennel. Main courses show a fondness for robust flavours, teaming chargrilled fillet of pork with a mushroom and pepper sauce or serving best-end of Welsh lamb in a honey and mustard glaze with minted mash. Satisfying desserts have included hot apple pie and bittersweet chocolate terrine. Wines start at £11.50.
Chef/s: Angus Bell, Andrew Bennett, Matthew Ash and Richard Janokovic. **Open:** all week 8.30am to 10pm. **Meals:** alc (main courses £13.50 to £19). **Service:** not inc. **Details:** Cards accepted. 35 seats. 50 seats outside. Separate bar. Wheelchair access. Music. Children's portions. Car parking.

Eglwysfach

Ynyshir Hall

Smart country-house dining
Eglwysfach, SY20 8TA
Tel no: (01654) 781 209
www.ynyshir-hall.co.uk
Modern British | £65 (5 courses)
Cooking score: 5

£5 OFF 🍷

Once owned by Queen Victoria, this tranquil country house needs no introduction as one of the leading luxury hotels in Wales. Part of the Von Essen collection since 2006, it is now managed with great charm by former owner Joan Reen. Watercolour paintings by her husband, Rob, grace the turquoise walls of the newly redecorated dining rooms. Other upgrades this year include new carpets in the drawing room, bar and hallways. Chef Shane Hughes continues to keep Ynyshir Hall on the map as a dining destination, offering an intelligent choice of menus ranging from a three-course set-price option to a full tasting menu. His cooking style can be modish and ambitious, but is underpinned by the classical training he received at the Connaught under Michel Boudin. You might start with cheese soufflé with apple, celery and hazelnuts or rabbit and scallops with ratatouille, artichoke and shellfish cappuccino. Typical main courses include Rhug Estate venison and foie gras with root vegetables, Brussels sprout leaves and juniper or, possibly, monkfish and mushroom tortellini with butternut squash, lemon and chervil. Dessert continue in a similar vein, offering Hughes' distinctive modern take on familiar classics – perhaps vanilla rice pudding with rum-roasted pineapple, coconut and a black pepper tuile or apple tarte Tatin with bay leaf ice cream and cinnamon toffee. Another recent change is the extension of the cellar and re-modelling of the wine list. This weighty leather-bound tome offers a classy selection, weighted towards France, with a good selection by the glass. Bottles are priced from £18 to £2000.

Chef/s: Shane Hughes. Open: all week L 12.30 to 1.30, D 7 to 8.45. Meals: Set L £25 (2 courses), £32 (3 courses), D £65 (5 courses), £75 (taster). Service: not inc. Details: Cards accepted. 28 seats. Separate bar. Wheelchair access. Music. Children's portions. Children allowed. Car parking.

Haverfordwest

ALSO RECOMMENDED
▲ George's

24 Market Street, Haverfordwest, SA61 1NH
Tel no: (01437) 766 683
www.thegeorges.uk.com
International

This delightfully quirky restaurant is loved for its 'decent wine', 'real ales galore' and friendly staff 'for whom nothing is too much trouble'. Under the same ownership since 1989, it has a tried-and-tested menu of imaginative home cooking, backed by interesting daily specials. Fish pie (£9.50), slow-cooked pork and apple casserole and crab crêpes (£8.50) are typical offerings. A short list of 'decent wines' starts at £12. New developments include the acquisition of a Victorian walled garden where fruit and vegetables will be grown. Open L Mon to Sat, D Sat and last Fri of each month.

Lampeter

ALSO RECOMMENDED
▲ Ty Mawr Mansion

Cilcennin, Lampeter, SA48 8DB
Tel no: (01570) 470 033
www.tymawrmansion.co.uk
Modern British

This impeccably-restored, Grade II listed building combines Georgian splendour with modern comforts. Up to 90 per cent of the ingredients used in the kitchen are produced within a 10-mile radius. Traditional Welsh cawl (soup) with a cranberry tartlet and Caerphilly cheese (£8.25) or pan-seared scallops with saffron sauce, crab ravioli and buttered leeks might be followed by fillet of Welsh Black beef with a mini cottage pie, truffled mash and baby carrots (£24.95).

Finish with a banana and toffee tart with cappuccino ice cream (£7.50). Wines from £13.90. Open for Mon to Sat D.

▌Laugharne

Cors

Authentic food in a romantic, bohemian setting
Newbridge Road, Laugharne, SA33 4SH
Tel no: (01994) 427 219
www.the-cors.co.uk
Modern British | £26
Cooking score: 3

'Cors' means 'bog' in Welsh, which probably creates the wrong image of this beautiful Victorian house set in an extraordinary fairy glade of a garden. The latter has indeed been coaxed from damp ground, the result being greener and more exotically leafy than your average patch. The rambling interior has been decorated in a spirit of magpie bohemianism. At its heart is a ruby-red grotto of a dining room, lit by candlelight, where chef-proprietor Nick Priestland delivers a sensuous, indulgent style of cooking unhampered by pretence. You might start with chargrilled halloumi with a carrot and coriander salad or smoked haddock crème brûlée. Top-notch local ingredients are name-checked, so main courses could include roasted rack of Welsh salt marsh lamb with a rosemary garlic crust and caramelised onion gravy or a fillet of organic Welsh Black beef from Pembrokeshire with green peppercorns and red wine jus. All this is backed by an international list of over 30 well-chosen wines, starting at £12.50.
Chef/s: Nick Priestland. **Open:** Thu to Sat D 7 to 12. **Closed:** Sun to Wed. **Meals:** alc (main courses £14.50 to £19.50). **Service:** not inc. **Details:** Cards accepted. 24 seats. 12 seats outside. Separate bar. Wheelchair access. Children allowed. Car parking.

Also recommended

An 'also recommended' entry is not a full entry, but is provisionally suggested as an alternative to main entries.

ALSO RECOMMENDED

▲ Stable Door Restaurant

Market Lane, Laugharne, SA33 4SB
Tel no: (01994) 427 777
www.laugharne-restaurant.co.uk
Spanish

Overlooking Laugharne's thirteenth-century castle, this eclectically styled and informally run wine and tapas bar offers an enormous sun-trap conservatory and pretty walled garden. The menu includes Spanish classics such as chorizo cooked in Rioja (£4.25), albóndigas and patatas bravas alongside halloumi kebabs and sticky chicken wings marinated with honey and BBQ sauce (£4.25). Try the home-made ice cream for dessert. Sunday lunch is a more traditional affair. Wines start at £11.95. Closed Mon to Wed.

▌Letterston

READERS RECOMMEND

Something's Cooking

Seafood
The Square, Letterston, SA62 5SB
Tel no: (01348) 840621
'Utterly charming staff serve fish and chips'

▌Nantgaredig

Y Polyn

Unpretentious country restaurant
Nantgaredig, SA32 7LH
Tel no: (01267) 290 000
www.ypolynrestaurant.co.uk
Modern British | £27
Cooking score: 3

This former toll house stands beside a quiet road in the leafy heart of Carmarthenshire, with a stream running almost underneath it. Its pretty terrace makes a tranquil spot for summer meals, while the interior is a study in understated country style. There are comfy leather sofas around the wood burner in the bar, and the main dining area is furnished with scrubbed-pine tables and reclaimed chairs. The surrounding countryside provides much fodder for the menu, from salad leaves to game, and sets an unpretentious, slightly rustic tone for the cooking. Expect classic combinations, such as a fish soup with rouille, croûtons and Gruyère cheese, or a main course of roasted Gower salt marsh lamb with onion, garlic and thyme purée. Desserts are equally comforting, and typically include treacle tart with vanilla ice cream or baked stem ginger cheesecake with rhubarb compote. A balanced list of 60-plus wines starts at £13.50.

Chef/s: Susan Manson and Maryann Wright. **Open:** Tue to Sun L 12 to 2, Tue to Sat D 7 to 9. **Closed:** Mon. **Meals:** alc L (main courses £10.50 to 13.50). Set D £27.50. **Service:** not inc. **Details:** Cards accepted. Separate bar. No mobile phones. Wheelchair access. Music. Children's portions. Car parking.

▮ Narberth

ALSO RECOMMENDED
▲ Ultracomida
Narberth, SA67 7AR
Tel no: 01834 861 491
www.ultracomida.com
Modern European

This high street delicatessen (sister to Ultracomida in Aberwyswyth, see entry) sells everything from cheese to chorizo, and the café bar at the rear makes full use of the excellent ingredients available in the shop. The interior is stylish, modern and informal – at busy times diners happily share the bare-topped wooden tables. Alongside a set-lunch menu and daily blackboard specials, mix 'n' match offerings include roasted pepper stuffed with tuna and black olives with a gratin topping (£3.50), French pork pâté on toast with cornichons, Glamorgan sausages with hot tomato pickle (£3.50) and hand-carved Serrano ham. Wines from £9.95. Open Mon to Sat.

Scores on the doors

As the emphasis on local and organic produce grows, the restaurant industry has come to realise that many customers value the origins of their food as much as the taste. With the 'Scores on the Doors' campaign, food hygiene finds itself brought into the age of information.

The scheme – already being successfully piloted across the UK, including in Scotland, the East Midlands and London – allows customers access to a restaurant's last inspection results (conducted by the local authority's environmental health team) for the first time. These are available by checking online or by simply glancing at the door or the window of the outlet in question.

Which? research shows that 97 per cent of customers believe they have a right to know the scores of local establishments.

You can check whether your local council participates on the Food Standard's Agency site: www.food.gov.uk/safereating/hyg/scoresonthedoors. Even if your area isn't part of the scheme, you're entitled to make a request to your local council for results under the *Freedom of Information Act.*

The FSA is currently reviewing the best way to provide this information. Following regional successes, Which? is campaigning for this scheme to be extended nationwide. For further details on the campaign, please see: www.which.co.uk.

Newport

Cnapan

Friendly home-from-home
East Street, Newport, SA42 0SY
Tel no: (01239) 820 575
www.cnapan.co.uk
Modern British | £28
Cooking score: 2

This friendly hotel and restaurant has been run by the same family for more than 24 years. Perhaps wearied by this fact, they have recently stopped serving lunch, although they do now open slightly earlier in the evenings. The charming pink-washed building is easily spotted on the main road into town – provided you are in Newport, Pembrokeshire, rather than the town's namesake in Gwent. The interior is peaceful, homely and resolutely traditional, and the cooking largely follows suit, although some dishes incorporate international influences. Starters range from chicken liver and smoked duck pâté with red onion marmalade and cornichons to spicy seafood chowder with mussels. Main courses reveal a similar scope, from roasted monkfish in a lemon and rosemary 'rub' with a black olive and red pepper salsa and anchovy tapenade to prime local fillet steak with a béarnaise butter. The very reasonably priced wine list starts at £12 a bottle.
Chef/s: Judith Cooper. **Open:** Wed to Mon D 6.30 to 9. **Closed:** Tue, Dec 25, Jan to mid March. **Meals:** Set D £28. **Details:** Cards accepted. 36 seats. 30 seats outside. Separate bar. Wheelchair access. Music. Children's portions.

Pembroke

ALSO RECOMMENDED
▲ Old Kings Arms

13 Main Street, Pembroke, SA71 4JS
Tel no: (01646) 683611
www.oldkingsarmshotel.co.uk
English/Continental

Local produce underpins the cooking at this traditional hotel on Pembroke's main street. The cosy, old-world dining room is a fitting backdrop for unfussy food such as duck liver pâté with hot toast (£4.75) and confit leg of duckling on juniper cabbage followed by seared Welsh lamb fillet on wilted greens with a port and redcurrant sauce (£15.95) or pork fillet flamed in brandy, served with caramelised apples. Other options include pubby light bites and fresh fish dishes such as grilled bass stuffed with herbs. The good value wine list starts at £9.50. Open all week.

Penally, Pembrokeshire

READERS RECOMMEND
Penally Abbey

Modern European
Penally, Pembrokeshire, SA70 7PY
Tel no: 01834 843033
www.penally-abbey.com
'Assured cooking with an impressive dining room'

St David's

Cwtch

Impressive local ingredients
22 High Street, St David's, SA62 6SD
Tel no: (01437) 720 491
www.cwtchrestaurant.co.uk
Modern British | £26
Cooking score: 3

This relaxed, trendy-looking restaurant on the High Street in St Davids is popular with locals and visitors alike. The simply decorated interior makes the most of the building's age-worn charm, with bare walls and pendant lamps. The irregular, many-cornered dining area befits the restaurant's name, which is Welsh for 'hug' but can also mean the 'snug' in a pub. The menu reads like a tour through the area's best produce; you could start with Pembrokeshire new potato and leek soup with Welsh rarebit or St Brides Bay potted crab with toast and tartare sauce, before local sea trout with Penclawdd cockles, marinated cucumber and sauce vierge or shoulder of Welsh lamb with port and rosemary sauce. However, mixed vegetables were served together in a side dish and the cheap selection (carrots and greens) was overcooked, which really let the excellent mains down. Desserts such as bara brith-and-butter pudding or rhubarb Pavlova with Welsh Mountain cherry liqueur round it off in modern Welsh style. The bill arrived with a little pack of Love Hearts, which sums up the cute feel at this place. A short, good-value wine list includes plenty by the glass, and starts at £13.50 a bottle.

Chef/s: Matt Cox. **Open:** Wed to Sat D from 6 (winter), all week D from 5.30 (summer). **Closed:** 25 and 26 Dec. **Meals:** Set D £22 (2 courses) to £27. **Service:** not inc. **Details:** Cards accepted. 44 seats. Wheelchair access. Children's portions.

Morgan's

20 Nun Street, St David's, SA62 6NT
Tel no: (01437) 720508
www.morgans-restaurant.co.uk
Modern British | £35
Cooking score: 2

Set in the heart of St David's, Morgan's comprises a discreet, modern dining room decked out with wood panels, flowers and candlelight. Expect dishes along modern European lines. Ingredients are drawn from the surrounding area and the back of the menu bears an impressive list of local producers. An inspection visit began with whole dressed Pembrokeshire crab with lemon and basil mayonnaise, followed by an impressive main course of sewin (Welsh sea trout) with watercress, cucumber and chive-dressed new

potatoes. An overly-dry, slow-cooked lamb ballotine was less successful, but a dessert of butterscotch and banana crumble with vanilla ice cream and fresh strawberries proved to be 'fantastic comfort food.' Local pride is evident in the list of Welsh cheeses and the presence of Welsh wine on the wine list. Elements of the operation can lack polish – notably the service and the display of cutlery in plastic trays at reception – but if you stick to the simple fish dishes, the food should satisfy. House wine starts at £13.

Chef/s: Tara Pitman. **Open:** Daily 6.30 to 11. **Closed:** Tue. **Meals:** (alc) mains £12.95 to £19.95. **Details:** Cards accepted. 38 seats. Music.

ALSO RECOMMENDED

▲ Refectory at St David's

St David's Cathedral, St David's, SA62 6RH
Tel no: (01437) 721 760
www.refectoryatstdavids.co.uk
Modern British

Wholesome home-cooked food is the mission of this modern canteen-style restaurant in St David's Cathedral. Its design showcases the building's soaring windows and time-worn walls, while the menu celebrates local produce. Choices range from tea and cake to hearty meals - perhaps home-made Welsh beef burgers served in an Italian-style bap with chilli jam, salad leaves and crisps (£7.95) or roast pepper and goats' cheese quiche with a mixed salad and rosemary roast potatoes (£6.95). Cheery young staff enhance the experience, as do drinks such as organic cider or home-made lemonade. Probably the best value eatery in St David's and a stunning location. Wines from £10.50. Open daily from 10 to 6.

Scores on the Doors

To find out more about the Scores on the Doors campaign, please visit the Food Standard's Agency website: www.food.gov.uk or www.which.co.uk.

Salem

Angel

Charming pub and restaurant
Nr Llandeilo, Salem, SA19 7LY
Tel no: (01558) 823 394
www.angelsalem.co.uk
Modern British | £26
Cooking score: 4

£5 OFF £30

This unassuming building looks like an ordinary pub on the outside, and it continues to function as one while being a much-loved dining destination. In the bar, expect comfortable sofas, real ales and excellent bar meals, which − like all the food at the Angel - are produced from scratch by chef and co-proprietor Rod Peterson and a small kitchen team. The adjoining wood-floored restaurant provides a smartly traditional backdrop for Rod's main menu, which is underpinned by expertly sourced local ingredients. You could start with a selection of home-made breads, followed by a tartlet of chorizo, spinach and mozzarella with tomato compote or perhaps Swansea Bay mussels with pesto cream sauce. Main courses provide a similar combination of classical and international influences; perhaps roast suprême of guinea fowl with leg and sage rillettes and peppered Savoy cabbage or a risotto cake of butternut squash and peperonata. For dessert, try Earl Grey and orange crème brûlée with bara brith ice cream or Baileys pannacotta with bitter chocolate sauce. The wine list, too, combines quality with affordability, starting at just £12.95 a bottle.
Chef/s: Rod Peterson. **Open:** Tues to Sun L 12 to 3, Tues to Sat D 6 to 11.30. **Closed:** Mon except bank hols. **Meals:** alc (main courses L £8 to £14, D £15 to £19). **Service:** not inc. **Details:** Cards accepted. 70 seats. Music. Children's portions. Children allowed. Car parking.

Solva

Old Pharmacy

Dispensing global flavours
5 Main Street, Solva, SA62 6UU
Tel no: (01437) 720 005
www.theoldpharmacy.co.uk
Modern European | £28
Cooking score: 2

£5 OFF **V** £30

Chef Matthew Ricketts and his wife, Becky, are now the owners of this one-time chemist's shop in the pretty harbour village of Solva. The couple are keeping things much as before, although they have introduced a flexible lunch menu tailored to families, shoppers and tourists looking for a casual bite to eat. In the evening, the kitchen makes good use of Solva crabs and lobsters, Pembrokeshire lamb and Welsh Black beef for an easy-going assortment of dishes with eclectic overtones. Seared Brecon mountain venison might appear with a caramelised red onion and Parmesan tartlet, or you might begin with a salad of Carmarthen ham and goats' cheese. Main courses could range from stomach-warming Crymych smoked sausage and belly pork casserole or bouillabaisse to Cajun-style monkfish and tiger prawn kebabs. For afters, try Tuscan orange citrus cake doused in Cointreau or one of Swansea Joe's speciality ice creams. Three dozen affordable wines, with house selections at £14.90 (£3.90 a glass).
Chef/s: Matthew Ricketts. **Open:** all week L 12 to 2.30, D 5.30 to 9.30. **Closed:** Jan. **Meals:** alc (main courses L £6 to £10, D £13 to £19). **Service:** not inc. **Details:** Cards accepted. 48 seats. 16 seats outside. No mobile phones. Wheelchair access. Music. Children's portions.

CHANNEL ISLANDS

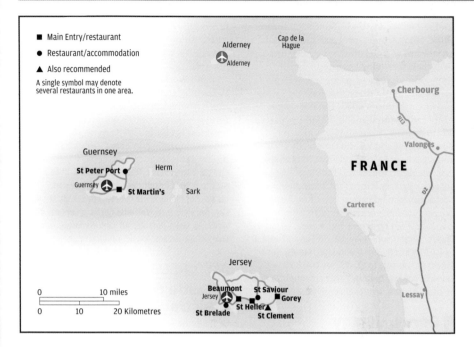

▪ Beaumont, Jersey

Bistro Soleil

Good produce and big flavours
La Route de la Haule, Beaumont, Jersey, JE3 7BA
Tel no: (01534) 720249
Modern British | £24
Cooking score: 3

A good example of the kind of sunny, seafood bistro Jersey does so well. Pine tables, sunshine yellow walls and a sprig of flowers at every table exude good cheer. The breathtaking view of the horizon is a plus, too. It fills up quickly with regulars sampling fresh local oysters and crab from the shellfish display, which communicates the day's specials just as effectively as the blackboard. At £24.50 for three courses, the slightly old-fashioned menu favours good produce and big flavours. However, a special of venison carpaccio was overwhelmed by 'too much, too-piquant horseradish', while a goats' cheese and walnut soufflé was overshadowed by a fussy salad garnish. A strong suit is the global wine list (from £13.75) with its wine of the month and around a dozen by the half-bottle.
Chef/s: Ian Jones. **Open:** all week L 12.15 to 2, Mon to Sat D 6.45 to 9.30. **Closed:** bank hols. **Meals:** Set L £10 to £14.50, set D £15 to £24.50. **Details:** Cards accepted. 55 seats. 35 seats outside. Separate bar. Wheelchair access. Music. Children's portions. Car parking.

▪ Gorey Village, Jersey

★NEW ENTRY★
Village Bistro

Simple, assured cooking in a quaint setting
Gorey Village, Jersey, JE3 9EP
Tel no: (01534) 853429
Modern European | £29
Cooking score: 3

'But for a few 'F' words emanating from a frazzled-sounding kitchen', noted a reporter, 'the atmosphere at this cute bistro in Gorey Village is entirely charming'. The interior is looking rather dowdy, but one soon forgets this as Sarah Copp emerges to greet regulars, take orders and reel off the specials – perhaps oven-baked monkfish with sun-blush tomatoes and sugarsnaps, or seared local scallops with rosemary and shallot dressing and crispy beetroot salad. The cooking is simple and assured and in the 'dinner party' idiom (a goats' cheese soufflé with wine-poached pear and walnuts, perfectly cooked and cleanly presented). A cracked crab special was just right, too, as was the chocolate-coated, sugar-encrusted thick candied peel that accompanied coffee. A set lunch and dinner plus basic wine list (with four house wines at £13) represent real value.

Chef/s: Sarah Copp. **Open:** Tue to Sun L 12 to 2, D 7 to 10.30. **Closed:** Sun D and Mon. **Meals:** Set L £13.50 (2 courses) to £15.75, set D £18.75. **Service:** not inc. **Details:** Cards accepted. 36 seats. 35 seats outside. Music. Children's portions.

▌Gorey, Jersey

Suma's

Stunning harbour views
Gorey Hill, St Martin, Gorey, Jersey, JE3 6ET
Tel no: (01534) 853291
www.sumasrestaurant.com
Modern European | £40
Cooking score: 5

£5
OFF

After over a decade of brisk business, pretty little Suma's really deserves to escape the 'little sister of Longueville Manor' tag. Which it does, although it's hard not to spot the Longueville DNA in both food and service. Chef Daniel Ward shows the same regard for top drawer ingredients and puts a modern fine dining spin on them. Meat dishes are as much a priority as fish (not always the case at Jersey's coastline bistros), with some rich, earthy dishes on offer such as pan-fried fillet of beef on braised oxtail with wild mushroom duxelles and sweetbreads or venison loin on celeriac gratin with root vegetables, braised baby leeks and glazed chestnuts. Sea bass with banana, almond and vanilla risotto and white wine foam betrays a trendy streak, while the lunch and early supper menu takes a bistro-turn with rib-eye steak with lyonnaise potatoes or wild mushroom risotto. The wine list (from £9.75) is a good round-up of New and Old World styles. Waiting staff are praised as 'friendly and helpful', with 'nothing too much trouble', though service can be overly formal – having one's napkin 'cracked' at breakfast is a bit much! Seats on the terrace offering lovely views over Gorey's harbour are highly desirable.

Chef/s: Daniel Ward. **Open:** all week L 12 to 2.30, D 6.15 to 9.30. **Closed:** Christmas to late Jan. **Meals:** Set menu £15 (2 courses) to £17.50, set Sun L £22. **Service:** 10%. **Details:** Cards accepted. 40 seats. 16 seats outside. Air-con. Separate bar. Wheelchair access. Music. Children's portions.

ALSO RECOMMENDED

▲ Castle Green Pub and Bistro

La Route de la Cote, Gorey, Jersey, JE3 6DR
Tel no: (01534) 853103
Gastropub

Jersey Pottery's loose take on the gastropub is spectacularly positioned, with unbeatable views of Mont Orgueil Castle. The menu is quirkily designed to offer 'Less' or 'More', thus some dishes such as seared tuna sashimi with Asian salad and tempura king prawns (£8.95/12.95), or Caesar salad accompanied by poached egg, grilled chicken or scallops (£5.95-12.95) comes in a choice of sizes designed for sharing or hogging. In the case of pork belly with grilled sausages (£13) or a home-made beef burger (£8.50), one size – XL – should fit all. Wine from £10.50. Closed D Sun and all Mon.

> ### Also recommended
>
> An 'also recommended' entry is not a full entry, but is provisionally suggested as an alternative to main entries.

St Brelade, Jersey

★NEW ENTRY★
Ocean Restaurant, Atlantic Hotel
Resort setting for formal fine dining
Le Mont de la Pulente, St Brelade, Jersey, JE3 8HE
Tel no: (0845) 3652395
www.theatlantichotel.com
Modern European | £45
Cooking score: 4

Shaun Rankin Bohemia

The Ocean Restaurant at the Atlantic Hotel 'transports visitors to one of those sexy Caribbean resorts most of us can't afford'. Palm trees, a Hockney-esque pool, white shutters and sea views work wonders. Inside, it's back to formal French fine dining with offerings that are a mix of classic and fanciful: Jersey chancre crab assiette; foie gras with Charentais sorbet and passion-fruit foam; or cannelloni of rabbit and sweetcorn, shredded rabbit leg and grain mustard jus. At inspection, smoked haddock and Jersey Royal pavé from the set lunch did the island's most famous export no favours. Served fridge-cold and overcooked, the sweet, nutty flavour of the potatoes was entirely lost. There was no faulting the cooking of salmon with al dente risotto and perfect asparagus, however. The combination of horseradish and Parmesan in the risotto suited the fish, although a forkful of the stuff on its own – and it was a huge portion – explained why it's not a pairing we see often. The sommelier does a terrific job, working with a list that starts at just £4 a glass, and offers around 20 half-bottles (from £8). Top marks for the classical service, some thoughtful recommendations and wine served at the correct temperature. More reports please.
Chef/s: Mark Jordan. **Open:** all week L 12 to 2.30, D 7 to 10. **Closed:** all Jan. **Meals:** Set L £19.50 (2 courses) to £22.50. Set D £45. **Service:** not inc. **Details:** Cards accepted. 60 seats. Separate bar. Wheelchair access. Music. Children's portions. Car parking.

Why did you become a chef?
I cooked with my mother at home from an early age.

What three ingredients could you not do without?
Scallops, lemon, butter.

Who would you invite to your ideal dinner party?
Tony Blair.

What's your guilty food pleasure?
Chips and béarnaise sauce.

What's your least favourite ingredient?
Celery.

Do you always read reviews of your restaurant?
Yes.

What dish is your first food memory?
Steak and kidney pie.

What era of history would you most like to have eaten in?
Late 18th and early 19th century.

What's coming up next for you?
My first book.

ALSO RECOMMENDED
▲ Wayside Cafe

Le Mont Sohier, St Brelade, Jersey, JE3 8EA
Tel no: (01534) 743915
Modern European

This popular St Brelade café starts early with a breakfast menu that covers everything from a full English to healthy fruit, yoghurt or porridge options. From noon, chef David Cameron supplements a café repertoire of panini, burgers etc with a menu of global specials that's anything but conservative. Massaman Thai curry (£12.70), feta, watermelon and mint salad (£8.50) and sea bass fillet with Spanish-style seafood rice (£13.90), give you the idea. Puddings are made for the child in all of us: Knickerberry Glory (£4.50), or home-made carrot cake with gingerbread ice cream (£4.25). Wine from £11.95. Open all week, 9am to 9.45pm (except Wed, L only).

▌St Clement, Jersey

ALSO RECOMMENDED
▲ Green Island Restaurant

Green Island, St Clement, Jersey, JE2 6LS
Tel no: (01543) 857787
www.greenislandrestaurant.com
Seafood

This seafront restaurant and terrace has become a real local favourite for its bold and beautiful seafood dishes. The menu is an effusive read, with everything 'finished', 'moistened', 'layered', even 'rubbed', and lists of ingredients as long as your arm. We can only give a précis, and say starters could be seafood cannelloni with shellfish bisque, (£8.95) or tom yam broth (£7.75); for mains, there's brill on crab linguini with vegetable ribbons (£17.95), or Parma ham-wrapped monkfish tail with tapenade (£18.30). Take it all in over a bottle of wine from the predominantly French wine list, £14.50. The restaurant's fans speak much plainer English: they love it. Closed Sun D and Mon.

▌St Helier

READERS RECOMMEND
Sirocco at The Royal Yacht Hotel

Modern European
St Helier, JE2 3NF
Tel no: (01534) 720511
www.theroyalyacht.com
'A blissful retreat for gastronomes'

▌St Helier, Jersey
Bohemia

Virtuoso cooking in a contemporary hotel
Green Street, St Helier, Jersey, JE2 4UH
Tel no: (01534) 880588
www.bohemiajersey.com
Modern European | £49
Cooking score: 7

Maybe it's performing for the crowds (four to six at a time) at the new chef's table that's got Shaun Rankin all fired-up. Whatever the reason, this hugely accomplished talent is cooking at the top of his game. A tasting menu started confidently with a big fat slab of seared foie gras on pain d'épices with cashews, mango and mint chutney and mango sorbet. What followed was less obviously fashionable, though that classic spring combo of duck egg, morels and asparagus was anything but boring, given heft by meaty local shiitakes. A taster size 'bobbin' of saffron noodles with a plump poached oyster and dollop of caviar neatly segued into red mullet with a tangle of langoustine, fennel and blood orange escabèche spiked with whole coriander seeds. Portions are on the large side. That said, a copper pan of Jersey Royals served with butter and mint was soon polished off. Flavours come bigger and bolder on the dessert menu – macerated raspberry and balsamic soufflé or peanut butter with banana and Caraïbe chocolate – 'sounded like overkill', but a pre-dessert of lavender pannacotta and passion-fruit jelly 'assured us we were in safe hands'. Balance is the watchword here. The waiting staff, smartly-clad in black, strike a fine balance between friendliness and formality, while the sommelier can recommend some suitably subtle wines (from £15.95) from a list that leans notably towards France, with champagne, always a Jersey favourite, a strong suit. It would be marvellous to be able to recommend this classy wood and leather-panelled restaurant wholeheartedly, but there is one caveat. The hotel bar next door is well-frequented by the after-work set, particularly later in the week. It gets very packed and very, very loud. Finding a quiet spot for an aperitif is not easy, nor is squeezing through crowds to get to the lavatories. On the bright side, you could come during the day when there's a super set lunch for £21.50.

Chef/s: Shaun Rankin. **Open:** Mon to Sat L 12 to 2.30, D 6.30 to 10. **Closed:** Sun, bank hols. **Meals:** Set L £21.50, alc £49, tasting menu £60. **Service:** 10%. **Details:** Cards accepted. 56 seats. Air-con. Separate bar. Wheelchair access. Music. Car parking.

▌St Martin's, Guernsey

Auberge
Accomplished cooking with sumptuous views
Jerbourg Road, St Martin's, Guernsey, GY4 6BH
Tel no: (01481) 238485
www.theauberge.gg
Modern British | £42
Cooking score: 5

Panoramic windows make the most of the view at this thrillingly-sited clifftop restaurant on Guernsey. It's satisfying to gaze out with a drink whatever the weather. But there's also a whole other level of satisfaction to be had in Daniel Green's seductive menus. The food is full of impact, both to look at and taste, and the sourcing and handling are both spot-on. Technique is drawn from around the world, so don't be surprised to find a deep-fried ham hock won ton turning up in a bowl of pea soup, or a green pea sorbet on a serving of smoked haddock risotto, alongside a dressing of sour cream fired up with horseradish. Ideas come thick and fast among the starters, while mains pursue a more obviously familiar line,

pairing roast rump of lamb with ratatouille, smoked garlic mash, olives and basil or teaming lobster and prawns as a ravioli filling, accompanied by roast cherry tomatoes and a fennel and endive salad. Steaks come with a range of textbook sauces, sides include carrots with Parmesan and the dessert list will tempt even the weight-watchers with orange and mascarpone cheesecake with orange jelly and mandarin sorbet or tiramisù with Bailey's ice cream and a poached baby pear. The brisk, brasserie-style wine list kicks off at £15.95, with by-the-glass prices from £5.25.

Chef/s: Daniel Green. **Open:** all week. L 12 to 2, D 7 to 9.30. **Closed:** Christmas. **Meals:** alc (main courses £13.50 to £25.95). Set L £18.95. **Service:** not inc. **Details:** 50 seats. 40 seats outside. Wheelchair access. Music. Children's portions. Car parking.

▌St Ouen

READERS RECOMMEND
Le Moulin de Lecq
Modern European
Le Mont de la Greve de Lecq, St Ouen, JE3 2DT
Tel no: (01534) 482818
www.moulindelecq.com
'Beautifully restored water mill serving good comfort food'

▌St Peter Port, Guernsey

La Frégate
Chic dining with sea views
Les Cotils, St Peter Port, Guernsey, GY1 1UT
Tel no: (01481) 724624
www.lafregatehotel.com
Modern European | £26
Cooking score: 4

Berthed high above the narrow streets of St Peter Port, this 'frigate' boasts magical views of the bay and the 800-year-old Castle Cornet. The original eighteenth-century manor has been sympathetically refurbished, although its oak-panelled traditionalism is now in stark contrast to the cool chic of the restaurant with its abstract paintings, bare boards and minimalist floral displays. A haul of local fish ('weather permitting') bolsters the lengthy carte, which follows a familiar modern European path. Begin with terrine of foie gras and home-smoked duck salad or scallops wrapped in pancetta with green bean and artichoke salad before roast rack of lamb carved at the table or fillet of grilled brill with pak choi, local mussels, saffron and dill sauce. To finish, desserts bring on board the likes of crêpes suzette or baked strawberry and rhubarb tart with chiboust cream and passion-fruit ice cream. The wine list offers an old-school selection of French names with a few incomers from the New World. House selections are £14.

Chef/s: Neil McGinnis. **Open:** all week L 12 to 2.30, D 7 to 10.30. **Meals:** alc (main courses £13.50 to £19). Set L £18.95. Set D £27.50. **Service:** not inc. **Details:** Cards accepted. 80 seats. 26 seats outside. Air-con. Separate bar. No music. No mobile phones. Children's portions. Car parking.

ALSO RECOMMENDED

▲ Da Nello

46 Pollet Street, St Peter Port, Guernsey, GY1 1WF
Tel no: (01481) 721552
British

Look for the mauve-coloured frontage in the heart of town. Behind it is an airy, appealing restaurant with a covered piazza at the back. The cooking is Italian/Mediterranean, with starters such as beef carpaccio dressed in olive oil, Parmesan and rocket (£7.25) or roast balsamic onions with Parma ham, mozzarella and tomato (£6.95), and mains that range from pasta and risotto dishes to specials such as veal cutlet with sage, potato rösti and roasted vine tomatoes (£18.25). Fixed-price menus are £13.25 (lunch) and £23.95 (dinner). Wine prices start at £15.25. Open all week.

▮ St Saviour, Jersey

Longueville Manor

Country-house dining from the kitchen garden
St Saviour, Jersey, JE2 7WF
Tel no: (01534) 725501
www.longuevillemanor.com
Modern European | £55
Cooking score: 5

The garden and kitchen of Longueville Manor continue to work hand-in-hand to maintain the fourteenth-century Norman manor's reputation for elegant yet contemporary country-house dining. Andrew Baird has his pick from the vast kitchen garden where apricots, figs and medlars grow in abundance, and there are herbs, leaves, soft fruit and root vegetables aplenty. This produce is paired with the finest imports such as Pyrenean lamb (in salt crust pastry with flageolet beans) or frogs' legs in a fricassée with snails. Baird's light touch is wedded to French technique, as seen in grilled John Dory with langoustine, squash, bok choy, spiced jus and beurre blanc or gratin of lobster with spinach and sauce homardine. There are two dining rooms to choose from, one a hugely atmospheric room panelled with dark wood from an old galleon, the other more classically country-house, with floral wallpaper, subtle colour palette and views into a small garden. The details – floral plates, highly polished crystal stemware, and crisp white linen – are all spot-on. The wine list numbers some 400 bins and has an impressive global reach with prices opening at £19. That said, its strengths lie in Bordeaux and Burgundy. It's just that sort of place.

Chef/s: Andrew Baird. **Open:** all week L 12 to 2, D 7 to 10. **Meals:** Set L £15 (2 courses) to £20, set D £47.50 (2 courses) to £55. **Details:** Cards accepted. 90 seats. 35 seats outside. Separate bar. Wheelchair access. Children's portions. Car parking.

NORTHERN IRELAND

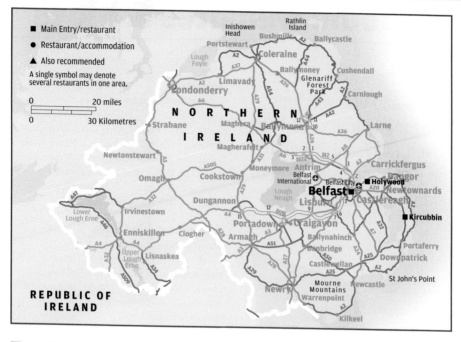

█ Belfast

Cayenne

Belfast's fusion sizzler
7 Ascot House, Shaftesbury Square, Belfast,
BT2 7DB
Tel no: (028) 90331532
www.rankingroup.co.uk
Fusion/Pan-Asian | £32
Cooking score: 4

🍷 **V**

True to its red-hot, fired-up name, Cayenne deals in live-wire funky food with a cool streetwise attitude: no wonder it's a honeypot for swarms of fun-loving young Belfast trendies. Owned by local heroes Paul and Jeanne Rankin, this dynamic cocktail of live multi-media events, hip arty interiors, high-decibel chatter and fashionable world flavours is bang on target. The menu is an eclectic back-packer's trip that hops over frontiers on its way from pumpkin risotto with pine nuts to pork pot-stickers with Asian salad. A mainline dose of East-West fusion brings on five-spice

glazed free-range pigeon with sweetcorn and scallion pancake, Chinese red-braised oxtail with shiitake mushrooms and wilted greens, and tea-smoked salmon with spiced potato salad, cucumber and avocado salsa. Desserts comfort the homesick with pear crumble or ginger and banana sticky toffee pudding, while the deeply fashion-conscious wine list cherry-picks a host of gems from around the globe. Everyday quaffing starts at £15.50 (£3.50 a glass) and there is plenty for those with a taste for finer vintages.
Chef/s: Grainne Donnelly. **Open:** Tue to Fri L 12 to 2.15, all week D 5 to 10 (6 to 11 Sat, 5 to 9 Sun). **Closed:** 25 and 26 Dec, 1 Jan. **Meals:** Set L £15.50 (3 courses). Set D £19.50 (3 courses). **Service:** 10% (optional). **Details:** Cards accepted. 150 seats. Air-con. Separate bar. Wheelchair access. Music. Children's portions.

Foodie websites & blogs

Enter the world of food blogs and you will find seasoned diners ready to give their frank opinion on just about any form of dining you can think of.

Here are some of the liveliest blog offerings that we've found online this year, as well as some of the best sources of inspiration when it comes to finding the perfect recipe, cookbook or restaurant. You'd be surprised at how easy it is to start your own website or blog these days.

deliciousdays
www.deliciousdays.com
A beautifully formed website, which was first launched in 2005 by Nicky and Oliver, a young couple based in Munich, with the heady purpose of documenting 'all things delicious'. You can read all about their latest experiments or adventures in the kitchen, or simply take in the stunning photography.

Epicurious
www.epicurious.com
Do you know your daube from your dashi? Based on the Food Lover's Companion this American site offers what must be the most exhaustive food dictionary online. You can also brush up on your cooking techniques or browse their database of recipes taken from Gourmet and bon appétit magazines.

Food and Drink in London
http://londonfood.typepad.com
Food and Drink in London is a lively and humorous blog from two London foodies, Howard and Ben. Search their catalogue of reviews and enjoy their take on the latest restaurant trends.

Opinionated About Dining
http://oad.typepad.com
Manhattan-based Steve Plotnicki's blog caters for those seriously devoted to high-end dining in the US and Europe. He also chairs a forum (strictly members only) and has set up the Opinionated About Dining Survey.

Silverbrow on Food
www.silverbrowonfood.com
Anthony Silverbrow (his 'nom de blog'), an amateur cook based in London blogs about restaurants, his recipes, cookbooks he loves and hates as well as the occasional lament on the difficulty in keeping kosher in the UK.

Word of mouth
www.blogs.guardian.co.uk/food
If you want to read the musings of restaurant critic Jay Rayner, gem up on the latest foodie issues or get some advice on a tricky recipe from Allegra McEvedy, this informative blog should be your first port of call.

The Good Food Guide 2009

James Street South

Assured big-city food
21 James Street South, Belfast, BT2 7GA
Tel no: (028) 90434310
www.jamesstreetsouth.co.uk
Modern European | £30
Cooking score: 5

Bare white walls emblazoned with displays of contemporary artwork help to invigorate the mood in this well-supported city-centre restaurant, which is bathed in natural light during the day. Chef/proprietor Niall McKenna knows all about big-city cooking, having cut his teeth with the likes of Marco Pierre White and Nico Ladenis, and there is much to applaud in his accomplished, precisely executed food. He has a modern way with fish, serving rare seared tuna with chorizo dressing and pea purée, and partnering halibut with razor clams, seared scallops and lobster bouillabaisse. Irish meat and game receive similarly expert treatment; witness sirloin of Antrim beef with bone marrow gratin and confit spring vegetables or saddle of rabbit with sweetcorn, black trompettes and pancetta crisp. To finish, explore the assiette of chocolate or venture into more challenging territory for Tokaji parfait with orange and fig roll. According to one reader, James Street South also offers the 'best set-price lunch menu in Belfast' backed by 'superb' service. The eclectic wine list promises a goodly mix of everyday tipples and rather grand classic vintages, with strong leanings towards regional varietals. House recommendations start at £18 (around £5 a glass).
Chef/s: Niall McKenna. Open: Mon to Sat L 1 to 2.35, all week D 5.45 to 10.45 (5.30 to 9 Sun). Closed: 25 and 26 Dec, 1 Jan, Easter Sun and Mon, 12 July. Meals: alc (main courses £14 to £21.50). Set L £14.50 (2 courses) to £16.50. Set D (pre theatre Mon to Thur) £16.50 (2 courses) to £19.50. Bar menu available. Service: not inc. Details: Cards accepted. 65 seats. Air-con. Separate bar. Wheelchair access. Music. Children's portions.

Nick's Warehouse

Local supplies, a global outlook and conviviality
35-39 Hill Street, Belfast, BT1 2LB
Tel no: (028) 90439690
www.nickswarehouse.co.uk
Modern European | £28
Cooking score: 3

£30

'Warehouse' is exactly right: the building started life as a bonded whiskey store belonging to Bushmills distillery, before Nick and Kathy Price came on the scene in 1989. Big-city conviviality now rules among Dublin's narrow cobbled streets. The kitchen feeds off local supplies, but there's a global outlook when it comes to putting together ideas. Expect to find fried squid with Cajun-spiced slaw rubbing shoulders with steak sandwiches and home-made piccalilli or Moroccan fish stew with lemon-scented couscous alongside asparagus and Pecorino ravioli with pesto cream. An array of no-frills 'puddings, desserts and sweets' rounds things off. Below stairs is the Anix wine bar, where crowds descend for affordable brasserie-style lunches of chicken breast with polenta and grilled trout with sweet potato chips. Wine drinkers are offered an intelligent, affordably priced global choice, with some intriguing bottles listed under the heading 'Nobody Expects – the Spanish wine list.' House wines kick off at £14.10 (£3.80 a glass).
Chef/s: Sean Craig. Open: Mon to Fri L 12 to 3, Tue to Sat D 6 to 10. Closed: Easter Mon and Tue, 12 July, 25 and 26 Dec, 1 Jan. Meals: alc (main courses £9 to £20). Set L £16.50 (2 courses) to £19.50. Service: not inc. Details: Cards accepted. 185 seats. Air-con. Separate bar. Wheelchair access. Music. Children's portions.

Also recommended

An 'also recommended' entry is not a full entry, but is provisionally suggested as an alternative to main entries.

Roscoff Brasserie

Rankin classics
7-11 Linenhall Street, Belfast, BT2 8AA
Tel no: (028) 90311150
www.rankingroup.co.uk
Modern European | £35
New Chef
£5 OFF V

Taking the original Roscoff as its blueprint, this restaurant opened in 2004 with the aim of pleasing those who missed the classic French cooking of Paul Rankin's old restaurant. With a central location behind City Hall, the airy, architect-designed building is a stylish spot for anything from business lunches to lingering evening meals. The cooking style is deceptively simple, and despite its 'classical French' foundations many of the dishes have a modern edge. The menu is sprinkled with Rankin signature dishes including his crispy confit of duck, perhaps served with roast rhubarb and Asian spices. Other starters include lobster spaghettini with basil, cherry tomatoes and olive oil, and Irish goats' cheese with beetroot carpaccio, walnut pesto and beetroot crisps. Move on to grilled quail with rosemary, mushrooms and artichokes or lamb cutlets with braised lettuce, peas and mint butter. The French accent becomes stronger for dessert, with the likes of apricot clafoutis with Amaretto ice cream or mille-feuille of fig and orange with a tangerine mousse. The wine list reflects the menu's classic/modern mix by starting in France then roaming the world. There are interesting choices for every pocket, starting from £17 a bottle. Paul Rankin's portfolio also includes Cayenne and Rain City (see main entries).
Chef/s: Paul Waterworth. Open: Mon to Fri L 12 to 2.15, Mon to Sat D 6 to late. Sun L 1 to 5. Closed: 25 Dec, 1 Jan. Meals: alc (main courses £14 to £22), Set L £19.50, D (Mon to Thu) £24.50 (3 courses). Service: not inc. Details: Cards accepted. 86 seats. Air-con. No mobile phones. Wheelchair access. Music. Children's portions.

ALSO RECOMMENDED
▲ Deanes

36-40 Howard Street, Belfast, BT1 6PF
Tel no: (028) 90331134
www.michaeldeane.co.uk
Modern European

The flagship of Michael Deane's Belfast gastro-empire, this sleek thoroughbred restaurant now comprises an urbane open-plan dining room (complete with chefs 'on show') and a bespoke bar. Up-to-the minute ideas jump out from the fiercely modern menus: John Dory in crisped couscous with pickled carrot and orange salad, nibbed cocoa and pistachio tuile (£10) could precede saddle of rabbit with macaroni gratin, roast cep, chervil root purée and verjus reduction (£19), while desserts (£8) might include wacky mango lasagne with passion-fruit marshmallow and coconut ice cream. Simpler fixed-price lunches are £17.50 to £21.50. Serious cosmopolitan wines from around £20 (£5 a glass). Closed Sun.

READERS RECOMMEND
Shu

Modern European
253 Lisburn Road, Belfast, BT9 7EN
Tel no: (028) 9038 1655
www.shu-restaurant.com
'Modern dining in trendy setting'

▮ Dundrum
READERS RECOMMEND
Mourne Seafood Bar

Seafood
10 Main Street, Dundrum, BT33 0LU
Tel no: (028) 4375 1377
www.mourneseafood.com
'Local seafood in picturesque village'

Holywood, Co Down

Bay Tree Coffee House
Simple café with a huge repertoire
118 High Street, Holywood, Co Down, BT18 9HW
Tel no: (028) 90421419
www.baytreeholywood.com
Café | £18
Cooking score: 2

Famous for its sugary, buttery cinnamon scones and domestic goddess desserts, the Bay Tree is also a haven for those with a savoury tooth. In the old days, a chatty queue that wrapped itself around the kitchen would form punctually at noon intent on appeasing appetites with a brimming bowl of steaming chowder, a crisp, precise flan of intense cheesiness, or a simple, gleaming fillet of fried fish with mash and rich green parsley butter. Things have changed – for the better. Spruced service and more room have shortened the queue, there's a great wine list, and they've brought on weekend breakfasts which might include champagne, smoked salmon and scrambled eggs. The room has been given a fresh lick of paint and some fancy furnishings; its dynamic owner and chef Sue Farmer has even published a book of Bay Tree recipes. Essentially though, the food as good as it has always been, and now daily à la carte dinners allow this brilliant, self-taught team full rein with menus such as fennel and tomato soup, scallops and orange chutney and hazelnut and treacle tart.

Chef/s: Sue Farmer. **Open:** Mon to Sat L 12 to 2.30, Sun 10 to 2.45, Mon and Wed to Sat D 6 to 9.30. **Closed:** Easter Sun, Mon and Tue, 1 May. **Meals:** alc D (£7.95 to £17.50). **Service:** not inc. **Details:** Cards accepted. 60 seats. Wheelchair access. Children's portions.

Kircubbin, Co Down

Paul Arthurs
Classy, creative cooking
66 Main Street, Kircubbin, Co Down, BT22 2SP
Tel no: (028) 42738192
www.paularthurs.com
Modern Irish | £24
Cooking score: 3

This smart restaurant occupies an unlikely spot above a chip shop, but the interior is suave and stylish, with exposed brickwork, simple furnishings and striking artwork. The straight-talking menus waste no time on flowery descriptions – and with good reason, because Paul Arthurs' classy, creative cooking speaks for itself. The seafood-dominated, internationally inspired starters could include Kicubbin Bay crab risotto with fresh herbs; seafood stew of gurnard, mussels, prawns and saffron; chunky smoked haddock chowder; and porcini mushroom tortellini with Parmesan. Main courses follow suit, but with a higher proportion of meat offerings; perhaps rack of lamb with ratatouille; grilled sirloin steak with red wine and béarnaise or sauté of Mount Stewart pheasant with 'a simple coriander curry'. For your final course, make the difficult choice between Irish cheeses with quince jelly or sweets such as fresh fruit pavlova; sticky toffee pudding or home-made ice cream. The carefully compiled and well-annotated wine list opens at £14.50.

Chef/s: Paul Arthurs. **Open:** Tue to Sat 5 to 9, Sun 12 to 2.30. **Closed:** 25 Dec, Jan. **Meals:** alc (main courses £15 to £16.95). **Service:** not inc. **Details:** Cards accepted. 45 seats. 30 seats outside. Music. Children's portions.

4

MAP 1

- ■ Main Entry/restaurant
- ● Restaurant/accommodation
- ▲ Also recommended

A single symbol may denote
several restaurants in one area.

0   10 miles

0   10   20 Kilometres

Isles of Scilly
Same scale as main map

Tresco ▲
Hugh Town   St Mary's
Isles of Scilly
(St Mary's)

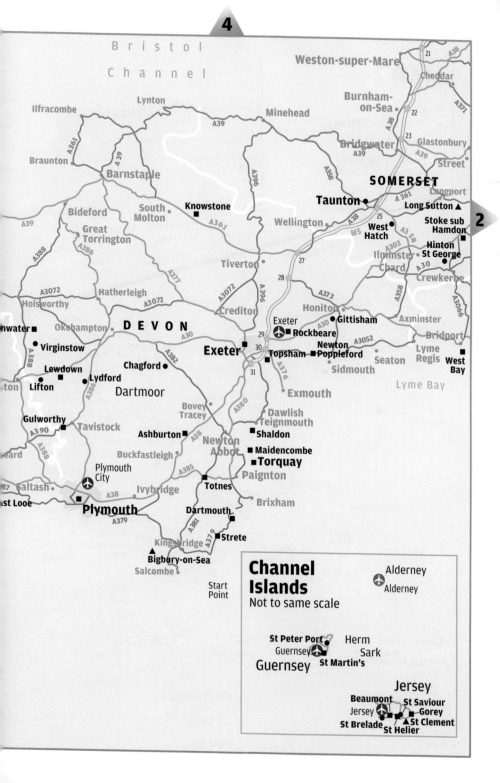

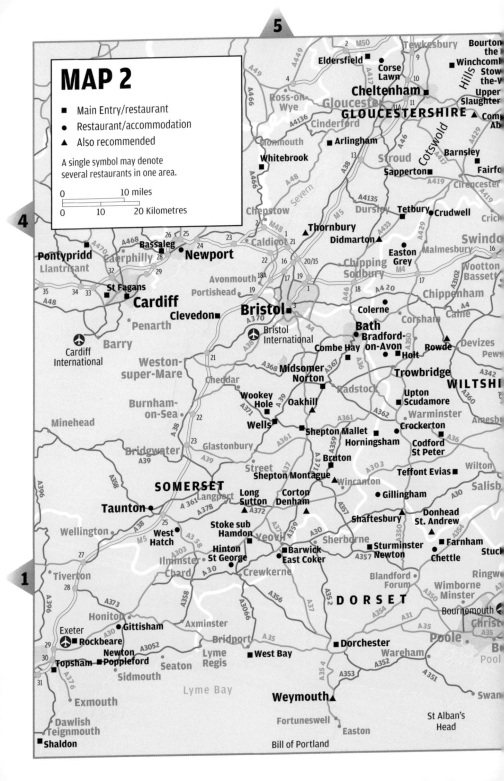

Swerford
Chipping Norton
Kidlington
Stonesfield
Woodstock
Witney
Oxford
OXFORDSHIRE
Tadpole Bridge
Fyfield
Faringdon
Wantage
Ardington
Didcot
Goring-on-Thames
Wallingford
BERKSHIRE
Chieveley
Frilsham
Marsh Benham
Newbury
Hungerford
Little Bedwyn
Highclere
Old Burghclere
Basingstoke
Andover
Longstock
Stockbridge
Winchester
Romsey
Eastleigh
Southampton
Southampton
Hythe
Brockenhurst
Beaulieu
Lymington
Barton on Sea
Yarmouth
Newport
Cowes
ISLE OF WIGHT
Isle of Wight
Sandown
Shanklin
Ventnor
Ryde
Seaview
Gosport
Portsmouth
Southsea
Fareham
Waterlooville
Havant
Emsworth
Funtington
West Stoke
Sidlesham
Selsey Bill
Chichester
Walberton
Arundel
Bognor Regis
Littlehampton
Worthing
Brighton
Lewes
Shoreham (Brighton City)
Tangmere
Lavant
Midhurst
Petersfield
Liphook
Haslemere
Horsham
Billingshurst
WEST SUSSEX
Albourne
East Chiltington
Burgess Hill
Haywards Heath
Cuckfield
East Grinstead
Crawley
London Gatwick
Godalming
Dorking
Reigate
Redhill
Abinger Hammer
Shere
Guildford
SURREY
Farnborough
Woking
Ripley
Leatherhead
Epsom
Croydon
Banstead
Limpsfield
Surbiton
Bromley
Richmond
LONDON
GREATER London
Staines
Windsor
London Heathrow
Slough
Bracknell
Wokingham
Bagshot
Camberley
Fleet
Aldershot
Farnham
Alton
HAMPSHIRE
Thatcham
Shinfield
Reading
Baughurst
Paley Street
Maidenhead
Bray
Hurley
Henley-on-Thames
Nettlebed
Stoke Row
Marlow
Cookham Dean
Wycombe
High Wycombe
Harrow
Wembley
Chiltern Hills
Amersham
Chandler's Cross
Watford
Enfield
Cheshunt
HERTFORDSHIRE
Hertford
Welwyn Garden City
Hunsdon
Datchworth
Stevenage
Hitchin
William
Luton
London Luton
Dunstable
Leighton Buzzard
Newton Longville
BUCKINGHAMSHIRE
Bicester
Aylesbury
Murcott
Kidlington
Long Crendon
Dinton
Thame
Great Milton
Chinnor
Great Missenden
Chesham
Berkhamstead
Hemel Hempstead
Bovingdon
Chipperfield Green
Frithsden
Chesham
Hemel
High
Newport

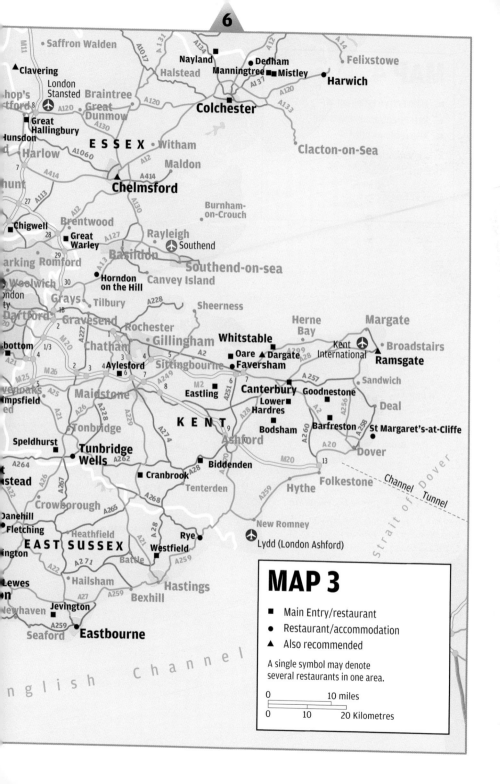

MAP 3

- ■ Main Entry/restaurant
- ● Restaurant/accommodation
- ▲ Also recommended

A single symbol may denote
several restaurants in one area.

0		10 miles
0	10	20 Kilometres

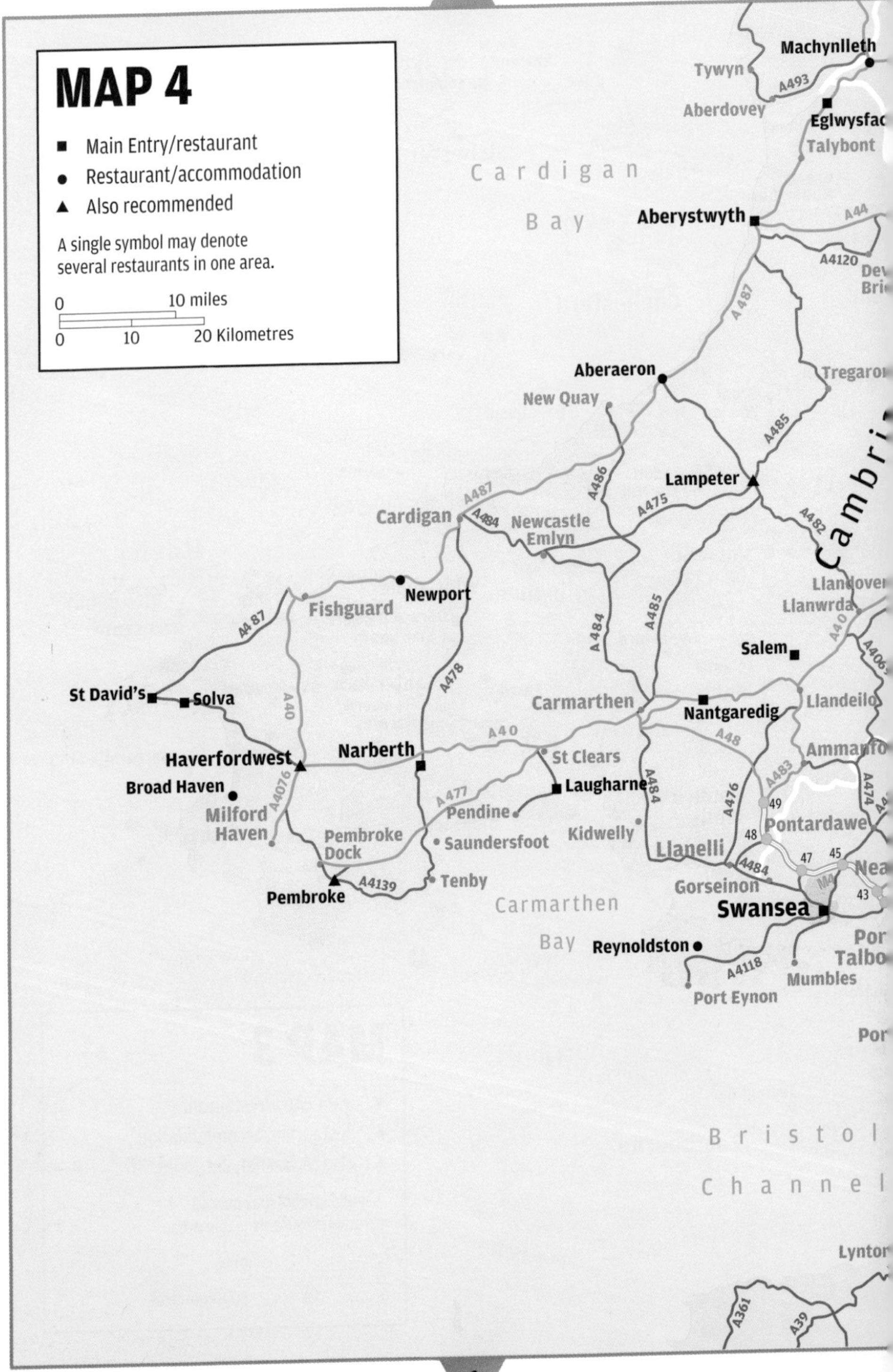

5

MAP 4

- ■ Main Entry/restaurant
- ● Restaurant/accommodation
- ▲ Also recommended

A single symbol may denote
several restaurants in one area.

0   10 miles

0   10   20 Kilometres

Machynlleth

Tywyn
A493
Aberdovey
Eglwysfac
Talybont

C a r d i g a n

B a y   Aberystwyth
A4120
Dev
Brí
A487

Aberaeron
Tregaro
New Quay
A485

Lampeter
A475

Cardigan
A487
A484
Newcastle
Emlyn
A486
A484
A485
A482

Fishguard Newport
A487
A484

Llan over
Llanwrda
Salem

St David's Solva
A40
Carmarthen Nantgaredig Llandeilo
A478
A40
A48
Ammanfo

Haverfordwest Narberth
A477
St Clears
A484
A476
A483
A474

Broad Haven
Pendine Laugharne
Milford
Haven Pembroke
Dock Saundersfoot Kidwelly Llanelli Pontardawe
49
48 47 45
A4139 Tenby A484 Nea
Pembroke Gorseinon 43
Carmarthen Swansea
Bay Reynoldston Por
Talbo
A4118 Mumbles
Port Eynon

B r i s t o l

C h a n n e l

Lynton

A361
A39

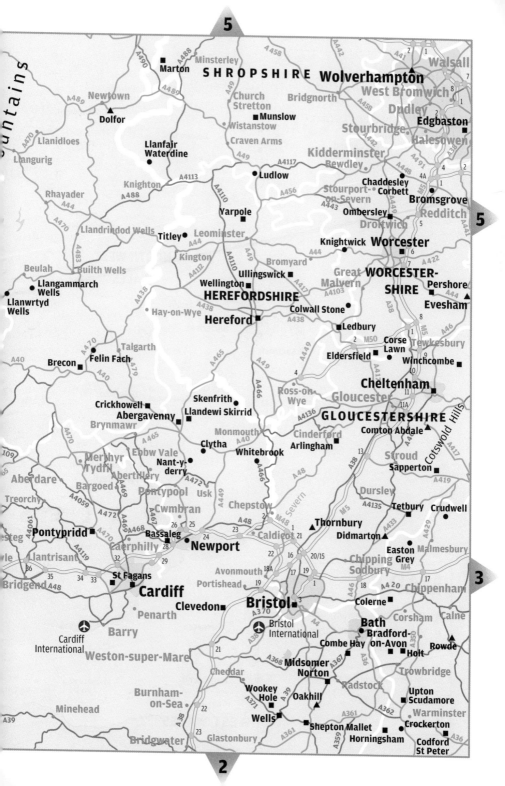

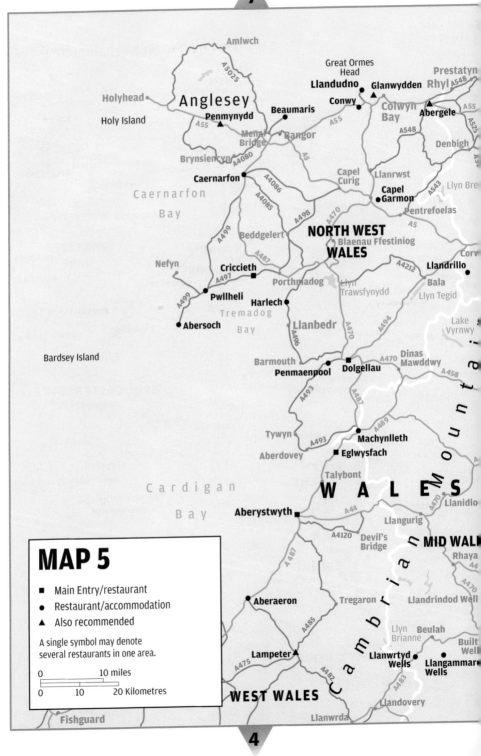

Amlwch

Great Ormes
Head

Prestatyn

Holyhead

Llandudno   Glanwydden Rhyl A548

Anglesey

Penmynydd

Beaumaris

Conwy

Colwyn
Bay

Abergele

A55

Holy Island

A55

A4080

Menai
Bridge

Bangor

A55

A548

A525

Denbigh

Brynsiencyn

A5

Caernarfon

A4086

Capel
Curig

Llanrwst

Capel
Garmon

A543

Llyn Bre

Caernarfon

A4085

A498

Pentrefoelas

Bay

A499

Beddgelert

A470

NORTH WEST
WALES

A5

Blaenau Ffestiniog

Corv

Nefyn

Criccieth

A487

Llandrillo

A4212

Porthmadog

Bala

Llyn
Trawsfynydd

Llyn Tegid

A497

Pwllheli

Harlech

A499

Tremadog

Llanbedr

Lake
Vyrnwy

Abersoch

Bay

A496

A470

A494

A458

Bardsey Island

Barmouth

Penmaenpool

Dolgellau

A470

Dinas
Mawddwy

A493

A487

A489

Tywyn

A493

Machynlleth

Aberdovey

Eglwysfach

Talybont

W   A   L   E   S

Cardigan

A44

Llanidlo

Bay

Aberystwyth

Llangurig

A4120

Devil's
Bridge

MID WAL

A487

Rhaya

A4

A470

Aberaeron

Tregaron

Llandrindod Well

A485

Llyn
Brianne

Beulah

Built
Well

Lampeter

Llanwrtyd
Wells

Llangammar
Wells

A475

A482

A483

WEST WALES

Llandovery

Fishguard

Llanwrda

MAP 5

- ■ Main Entry/restaurant
- ● Restaurant/accommodation
- ▲ Also recommended

A single symbol may denote
several restaurants in one area.

0   10 miles
0   10   20 Kilometres

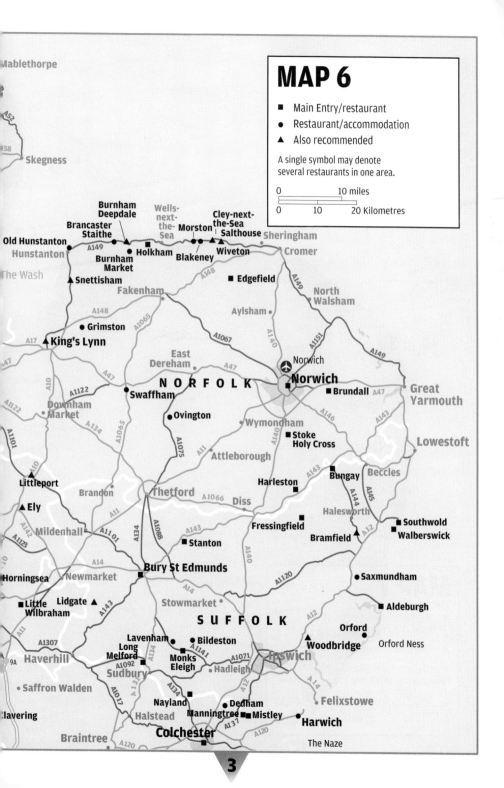

MAP 6

- ■ Main Entry/restaurant
- ● Restaurant/accommodation
- ▲ Also recommended

A single symbol may denote
several restaurants in one area.

0   10 miles
0   10   20 Kilometres

Mablethorpe

A52

A58

Skegness

The Wash

Old Hunstanton
Hunstanton

Burnham
Deepdale
Brancaster
Staithe
Burnham
Market
Holkham

Wells-
next-
the-
Sea
Morston
Blakeney
Wiveton

Cley-next-
the-Sea
Salthouse   Sheringham
Cromer

A149

Snettisham

Edgefield

Fakenham

A148

Grimston

King's Lynn

A17

A47

A1122

Downham
Market

A10

A1122

A1101

A1123

A142

Littleport

Ely

Mildenhall

Horningsea

Little
Wilbraham

Newmarket

Lidgate ▲

A143

A1307

Haverhill

9A

A11

Saffron Walden

Clavering

Braintree

A120

Colchester

Halstead

Nayland

A134

Sudbury

A1092

Long
Melford

Lavenham

Monks
Eleigh

A1141

Bildeston

A131

A1071

Hadleigh

Manningtree

Dedham

Mistley

A137

A120

Harwich

The Naze

Felixstowe

A14

Ipswich

A12

Woodbridge

Orford

Orford Ness

Aldeburgh

Saxmundham

A12

Southwold
Walberswick

Bramfield ▲

A12

Halesworth

A144

A145

Beccles

Bungay

A143

Harleston

Fressingfield

A1066

Diss

Stanton

A140

Bury St Edmunds

A14

Stowmarket

SUFFOLK

A1088

A134

Thetford

Brandon

A11

A1101

Attleborough

A1075

A11

Ovington

Swaffham

A134

A1065

Wymondham

A140

Stoke
Holy Cross

A146

Norwich

A140

East
Dereham

A47

NORFOLK

A1067

Aylsham

A140

North
Walsham

A149

A1151

A149

Great
Yarmouth

Lowestoft

A143

Brundall   A47

A148

A1065

A148

3

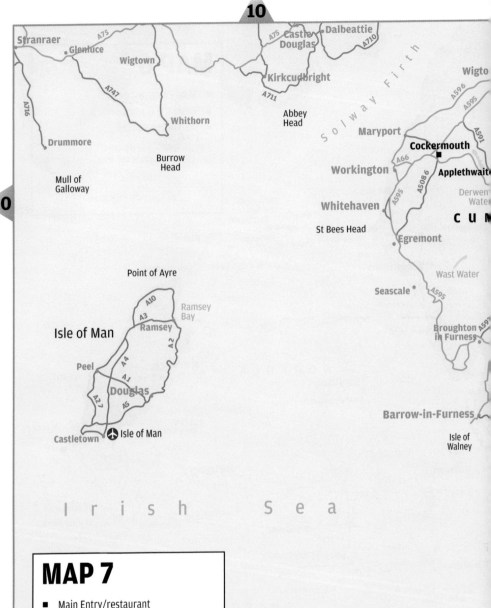

Stranraer
Glenluce
A75
Wigtown
A747
A716
Drummore
Mull of
Galloway
Burrow
Head
Whithorn

Castle
Douglas
A75
Dalbeattie
A710
Kirkcudbright
A711
Abbey
Head
Solway Firth
Maryport
Workington
A66
Cockermouth
Applethwaite
A595
A5086
Derwent
Water
C U M
Whitehaven
St Bees Head
Egremont
Wast Water
Seascale
A595
Broughton
in Furness
A595
A596
A595
A591
Wigto

Point of Ayre
Ramsey
Bay
A10
A3
Isle of Man
Ramsey
A2
Peel
A4
A1
Douglas
A2 7
A5
Castletown
Isle of Man

Barrow-in-Furness
Isle of
Walney

I r i s h   S e a

MAP 7

- ■ Main Entry/restaurant
- ● Restaurant/accommodation
- ▲ Also recommended

A single symbol may denote
several restaurants in one area.

0   10 miles
0   10   20 Kilometres

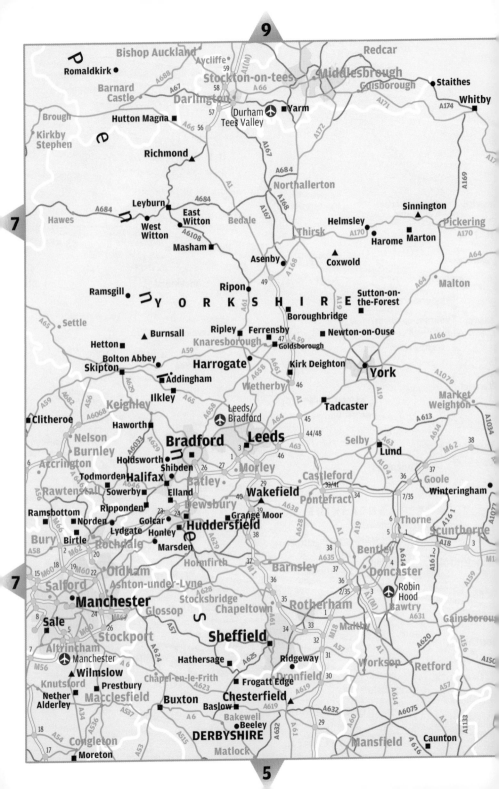

MAP 8

■ Main Entry/restaurant
● Restaurant/accommodation
▲ Also recommended

A single symbol may denote
several restaurants in one area.

0   10 miles
0   10   20 Kilometres

■ Scarborough

Filey

A165

Flamborough
Head

A614

Bridlington

Driffield A165

Bridlington
Bay

South
Malton

A1035

Hornsea

Beverley

Kingston upon Hull

Hessle

Withernsea

A1033

▲ Barton-upon-Humber

Humber

A15

A1077

Immingham

A180

Spurn Head

5

A18

Humberside

Grimsby

Cleethorpes

Brigg

A1173

A446

A18

A16

A1031

Caistor

A631

A46

Market
Rasen

Louth

Mablethorpe

A157

A153

A16

A158

A1028

A52

Lincoln

Horncastle ■

Partney

L I N C O L N S H I R E

A158

Skegness

A155

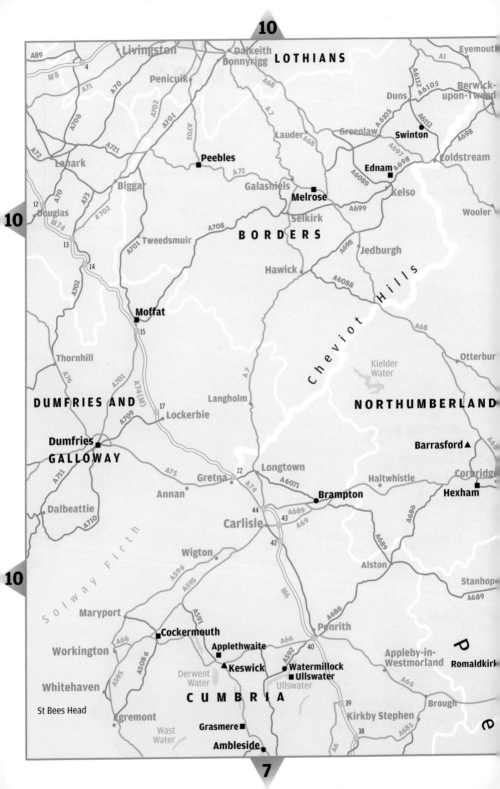

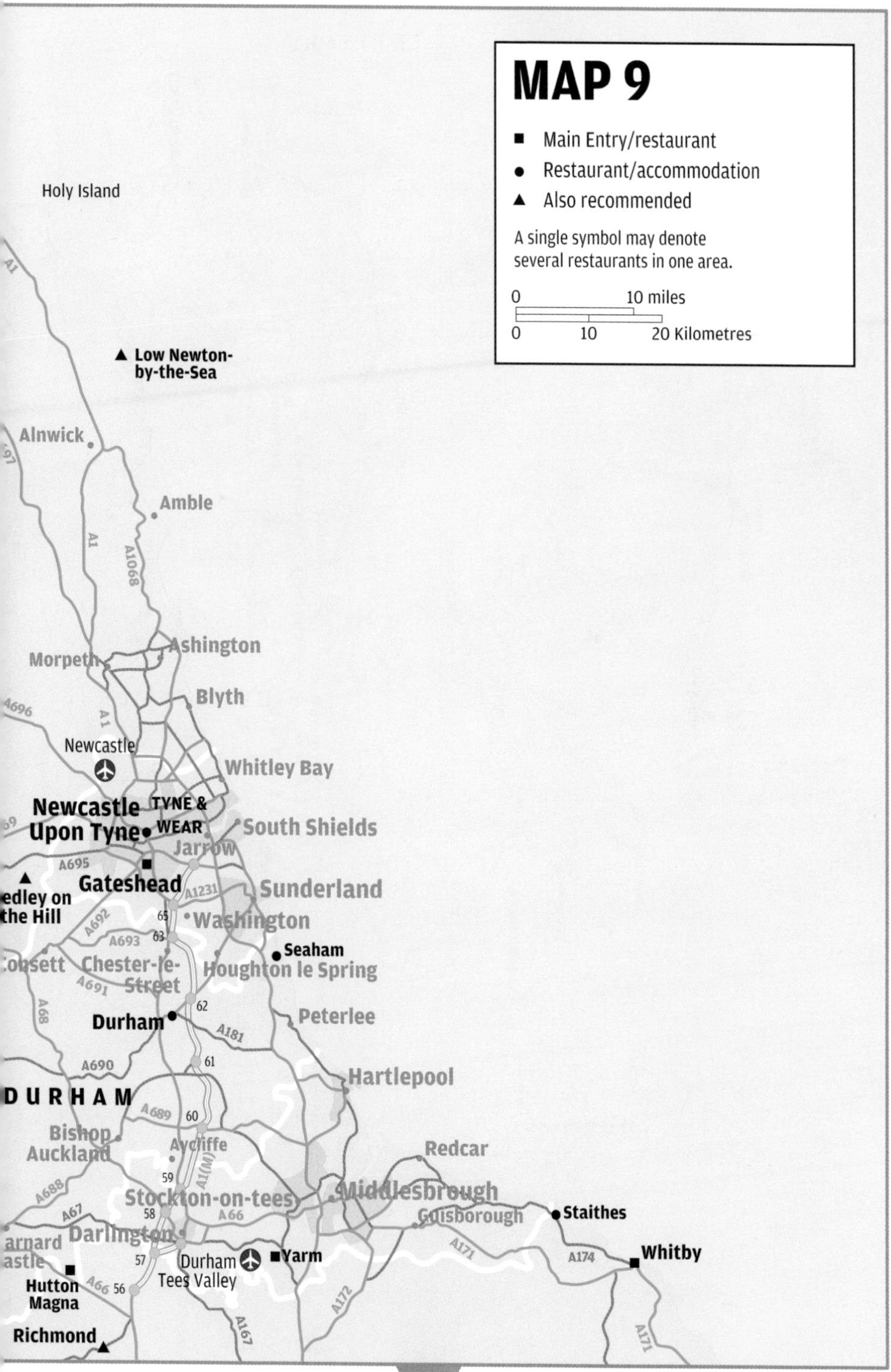

MAP 9

- ■ Main Entry/restaurant
- ● Restaurant/accommodation
- ▲ Also recommended

A single symbol may denote
several restaurants in one area.

0		10 miles	
0	10		20 Kilometres

Holy Island

▲ Low Newton-
by-the-Sea

Alnwick

Amble

Ashington

Morpeth

Blyth

Newcastle

Whitley Bay

Newcastle
Upon Tyne

TYNE &
WEAR

South Shields

Jarrow

▲
edley on
the Hill

Gateshead

Sunderland

onsett

Chester-le-
Street

65

63

Washington

Seaham

Houghton le Spring

Durham

62

Peterlee

61

Hartlepool

DURHAM

Bishop
Auckland

60

Aycliffe

Redcar

59

Stockton-on-tees

58

Middlesbrough

Guisborough

● Staithes

arnard
astle

Darlington

57

Durham
Tees Valley

■ Yarm

Whitby

Hutton
Magna

466

56

Richmond

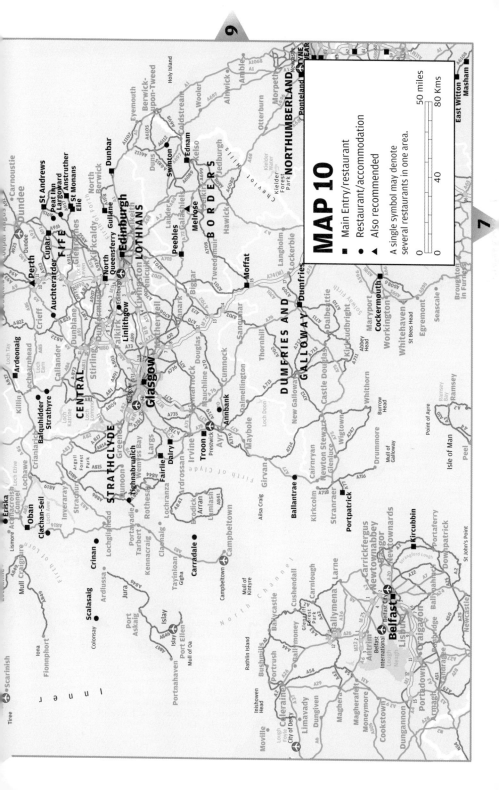

MAP 10

- ■ Main Entry/restaurant
- ● Restaurant/accommodation
- ▲ Also recommended

A single symbol may denote several restaurants in one area.

0   40   50 miles
0   80 Kms

The Good Food Guide 2009

THANK YOUS

This book couldn't happen without a cast of thousands. Our thanks are due to the following contributors:

Mrs Enid Abbott
Mr Anthony Abrahams
Mr Alasdair Adam
Mr David Adam
Mrs J Adam
Mrs Jane Adams
Mrs Linda Adams
Mrs Amanda Adams
Mr Warren Adamson
Mr Abdi Adan
Mr Richard Adler
Mrs Elizabeth Agger
Mr Sumair Ahmad
Miss Farzana Ahmed
Mr John R Aird
Mrs Lesley Aird
Mrs Catherine Alder
Mrs Minda Alexander
Mr William Alexander
Miss Jane Alexander
Mr Douglas Allan
Mr Roger Allen
Mr Martin Allen
Mrs Beverley Allen
Mr Alasdair Allward
Mr Dawan Alom
Miss Lubna Altajir
Mr Armyda Aly
Mr Steve Ambrose-Jones
Mrs Sue Amery-Behr
Mr James Anderson
Mr Jon Anderson
Mr Stewart Anderson
Miss Jana Andresikova
Mr Steve Andrew
Mr Ivan Andrew
Mr R Marshall Andrews
Mr Edward Andrews
Mr Igor Andronov
Sir Michael Angus
Mr Robert Ankcorn
Mrs Julia Ansell
Mr Robin ap Cynan
Mrs Bernadette Appert
Mr Michel Appert
Mr Paul Applegarth
Mr Dennis Archdale
Mr Jeremy Archdale
Mrs C Archer
Mrs Kathy Armes
Mr David Armitage
Mrs Lindy Armitage
Mr Chester Armstrong
Mr Jeff Arnold
Mr John Arnold
Mr Tim Arrowsmith
Mrs Jean Arrowsmith
Mr B Arthur
Ms Janie Ash
Mrs Susan Ash
Miss Fleur Ashby
Mr Mike Ashford
Mr Kenneth Ashken
Mr Ian-Paul Ashworth
Mrs Tracy Atherton
Mr Phil Atherton
Mrs Karen Atherton
Mr Junior Atkin
Miss Laura Atkinson
Ms Jenny Atkinson
Miss Delia Atkinson
Miss Aurlie Auffray
Mrs Patricia Austin
Mr David Avrell
Mrs Janet Awty
Mr Guy Ayland
Mr Roy Aylmer
Mrs Judith Babb
Mrs Gill Baggott
Mr Roger Bagnall
Mr Paul Bagwell
Mr Tristan Bailey

Mr Dave Bailey
Mrs Victoria Bailey
Miss Kim Bailey
Mr Graham Baines
Miss Louise Baines
Miss Jemma Baines
Mr Pawel Bak
Mr Richard Baker
Mr Martin Baker
Mrs Wendy Baker
Miss Alex Baker
Mr Paul Baker
Mrs Denise Baker
Mr Richard Baldock
Ms Susan Baldwin
Mrs Elisabeth Balfour
Mrs Joy Ball
Mr Alexi Balmuth
Miss Mary Ann Bamford
Mr Alfie Banes
Mr Christopher Barber
Mrs Dawn Barber
Mr John Barker
Mr John A Barker
Mr Karl Barker
Mrs Veronica Barker
Mrs Donna Barker
Mr Roger Barker
Mrs Nicky Barker
Mr Ross Barkman
Miss Eleanor Barnes
Mrs Sue Barnes
Mr William Barnes
Mr Stephen Barnett
Mrs Nicola Barnett
Mr Philip Barnett
Mr Peter Barnwell
Mrs P Baron
Mrs Paula Baron
Mr Richard Barraclough
Mrs Susie Barrett
Mrs Amanda Barrie
Mrs Mandy Barrie
Mrs Lindsey Barrow
Mr Ian Bartholomew
Mr Mervyn Bartimote
Miss Nicola Barton
Mr Richard Barton
Mr Jerry Bascombe
Mr Mark Basham
Ms Abigail Batchelor
Mr R Bateam
Mr Mike Bateman
Mr David Battiscombe
Ms Penelope Battistotti-Moore
Mrs Emma Battle
Mr Malcolm Baugh
Mrs Amanda Bayley
Mrs Pauline Bazeley
Ms Gillian Beal
Mrs Jill Beaton
Mr Howard Beattie
Mr Mark Beaumont
Mr Simon Beckett
Mrs Shanara Begum
Miss Sara Beharrell
Mr J Behrenroth
Ms Michele Beint
Mr Tony Beirne
Miss Claire Belcher
Mr Iain Bell
Mrs Diana Bell
Miss Sophie Bell
Mr John Bence
Mr Gerry Bender
Mrs Linda Benee
Mrs Hannah Bennett
Mr John R Bennett
Mr Irene Bennett
Mr Ronald Bennett
Mr Alan Bennett

Mr David Bennett
Mrs Daphne Bennett
Mr Tim Bent
Mr Jim Bentley
Mrs Christine Benzie
Mrs J M Beringer
Mr Neal Berridge
Mr W J Best
Mr Andro Beta
Mr Michael Bettell
Miss Stacey Betteridge
Mrs Bron Betteridge
Mrs Liz Bevan
Mr Ramesh Bhatt
Mrs Jacqueline Bibby
Mrs Valerie Bichener
Mrs Jill Bickley
Mr Stuart Billing
Mrs Carol Bines
Mr John Binnie OBE
Mr Julian Bion
Mrs Betty Birch
Mr Nick Birch
Mrs Rosemarie Bird
Mrs Wendy Birks
Mrs Rachel Birks
Mrs Dawn Birnie
Mr Robert Bishop
Mr Alan Bishop
Mrs E Bishop
Mrs Penny Bishopp
Mr James Black
Miss E Black
Mr Craig Blackburn
Miss Emma Blackburn
Mr Andrew Blacker
Miss Claire Blackmore
Miss Julie Blackshaw
Mr Michael Blackstaff
Mrs Judy Blagden
Mr Ricky Blair
Miss Caroline Blake
Mr Timothy Blake
Mrs Emma Blake
Mr Garry Blakeley
Mr John Blakey
Mr Malcolm Blazey
Mr Edward Blincoe
Mrs Bridget Bloom
Mrs Lucy Blythe
Mr Tony Blythe
Mrs Jo Boait
Mr Terence Boley
Mr Christopher Bolton
Mr Tony Bolton
Mrs Pauline B Bolton
Ms Michelle Bolton
Mr Ian Bond
Mr Chris Bond
Mr Neil Bonsall
Mr Alan Booker
Mr David Boor
Dr Ben Booth
Mrs Jennifer Booth
Mr Ryan Booth
Mr Peter Booth
Miss Tracy Booth
Mr Philip Borg
Mr Marc Borgia
Mrs Patricia Borthwick
Mrs Alexandrina Borthwick
Mr Andrew Borthwick-Clarke
Mr J Roderick Boswell
Mr Kenneth Bouch
Mr Roger Bousfield
Mr Christopher Bowden
Mr David Bowe
Mr Harry Bower
Miss Lydia Bowen
Mrs Ann Bowles
Mrs Jude Boyce

Mrs Shirley Boyd
Ms Sue Brace
Ms Gill Bracey
Mr Anthony Bradbury
Mr Nick Bradbury
Miss Laura Braddock
Mr Alan Bradford
Mr David Bradley
Mr Robert Bradley
Mrs Elaine Brammer
Mrs Holly Brand
Mr Nils Braun
Mr Howard Braybrook
Mrs Jill Brearley
Mr Barrie Brears
Mr Blair Breton
Ms Suzanne Brett
Mr Brewer Brewer
Mr Martin Brewer
Mr Mike Brewer
Mr T Bricout
Mrs Mia Briden
Mr James Bridges
Mr James Bridges
Mrs Amelia Bridges
Mr John Bridgewater
Mr Steve Briegel
Mr Jonathan Brierley
Mrs Jennifer Briggs
Ms Sacha Bright
Miss Jasmine Brindley
Mr David Briscoe
Mrs Helen Bristol
Mr Julian Britton
Mrs Sarah Broadbent
Mr Peter Broadbent
Mrs Katrina Brolly
Mr Ian Bronks
Mr Malcolm Brook
Mrs Lindsay Brooke
Ms Jayne Brooke
Mrs Ingrid Brooker
Miss B Brookes-Johnson
Mr Shay Brookes-Johnson
Mr Nigel Brooke-Smith
Mrs Lorna Brooks
Mrs Kathryn Broom
Miss Sarah Brown
Ms Beverley Brown
Mrs Jean Brown
Mr James Brown
Mr H Brown
Mrs Hazel Brown
Mrs Margaret Brown
Mr Peter Brown
Miss Angelica Brown
Ms Karen Brown
Mr Duncan Brown
Mr Kenneth Brown
Mr Alan Brown
Ms Jill Brown
Ms Janine Brown
Ms Jane Brown
Mrs Karen Brown
Miss Elizabeth Brown
Mr Malcolm Brown
Mr David Brown
Mr Stuart Brown
Mr Andre Brown
Mr Philip Brown
Mrs Gillian Bruce
Mr Colin Bruce
Mrs Sue Bruce
Mrs Linda Buckingham
Mr Andrew Budory
Mr Steven Buick
Mr Colin Buick
Mr John Bull
Mr John Bullough
Mr Douglas Bulmer
Miss Emily Bunce
Mrs Molly Burberry

Ms Kathryn Burford
Miss Samantha Burke
Mr Terry Burkett
Mr Clive Burkin
Mr John U B Burn
Mr Richard Burnell
Miss Kirsty Burns
Mr Stuart Burns
Mrs Barbara Burnyeat
Mrs Mary Burr
Mrs Jillian Burrell
Mr Peter Burrell
Mrs Sue Burton
Mr David Busby
Mr Mervyn Bushe
Mrs Pat Bushell
Mr Coen Bust
Mr Phillip Butler
Mrs Alison Butterworth
Mr A Buxton
Mr Peter Bye
Mr John Byrne
Mr Steve Caddy
Mrs Nichola Cadet
Mr Ian Cairns
Ms Arran Caitlin
Mr Tim Caley
Mr Jerry Caley
Mr Ian Cameron
Mrs A Cameron
Mrs Elizabeth Cameron
Miss Norma Campbell
Ms Susan Campbell
Mrs Jean Campbell
Mr George Campbell
Mrs Wendy Campbell
Mr Brian Campbell-Kearsey
Mrs Philippa Camps
Miss Joanne Canavan
Mr Jonathan Cant
Mr John Cantrill
Miss Martha Cape
Mr Brian Cardozo
Mrs Betty Carey
Mr Basil Carey
Mr Richard Carlin
Mr Richard Carman
Mr Patrick Carpenter
Mr Sam Carpenter
Mrs Karen Carr
Mr John Carr
Mrs Helen Carrick
Mr Michael Carroll
Mr John Carroll
Mr Ken Carruthers
Mrs Karen Carr
Mr John Carter
Mrs Georgina Carter
Mr Edward Carter
Mr William Casey
Mr Derek Cash
Mr Brian Cash
Mr Brian Cash
Mrs Yvonne Cash
Mrs Paula Casson
Mr Peter Castell
Mrs Allegra Castellini Baldissera
Miss Lily Castle
Ms Lyn Cecil
Ms Hilary Chadwick
Ms Felicity Chadwick-Histed
Mr Fred Chan
Mr Cyril Chan
Mr Nicholas Chant
Mrs Patricia Chaplin
Mr John Chapman
Mr Andrew Chapman
Mrs Zoe Chapman
Mr Jiri Chard

Miss Julie Charlwood
Mr Ian Chater
Mrs Katharine Chater
Mr Alanl Chattaway
Mr Stephen Cheek
Mr Andrew Chell
Mr William Chesneau
Mr William Chesters
Miss Caroline Chilton
Mr Richard Chinn
Miss Caroline Chiu
Ms Shabo Chopra
Miss Helen Chorley
Mr Nikos Christakis
Mrs Margaret Church
Mr Andrew Churchman
Mr Hakan Cihan
Mrs Jayne Clancy
Mr Roland Clare
Mrs Carolyn Claridge
Mrs Kate Clark
Mr Ian Clark
Mrs Jacqui Clark
Mrs Charlotte Clark
Mr John Clark
Mr Richard Clarke
Mr Peter Clarke
Ms Vanessa Clarkson
Mrs Samantha Clarkson
Mrs Lynne Clay
Mr John Clayton
Ms Celia Clayton
Mr James Clayton
Mr Matt Clear
Mrs Lois Clements
Mrs P J B Clements
Mrs Helen Clements
Mr Jonathan Cload
Mrs Vanessa Clouting
Miss Laura Clowes
Mr Derek Clure
Mr Tony Coates
Ms Sharon Cochrane
Mr Peter Cock
Mr Roger Cockbill
Mr Ray Coggan
Mr J Cohen
Mrs Rosalind Cohen
Miss Naomi Cohen
Mr Steven Cole
Mr David Cole
Mrs Amanda Cole
Mr Alan Cole
Mr John Coleman
Mrs K Coles
Mrs Jenny Coles
Mr Will Coles
Miss Caroline Coley
Mr Lee Collar
Mrs Janet Collett
Mrs Pauline Collie
Mr Frank Collier
Miss Pam Collins
Mr John Collins
Mrs Rosy Collis
Miss Natalia Colombani
Mr R T Combe
Ms Natalie Compton
Mrs Cathy Comrie
Mr Gary Condon
Mr Flurin Condrau
Mr Tony Connell
Mr Thomas Connor
Mr Mike Connor
Mr D H Conway
Mr Paul Cook
Mrs Vivienne Cook
Mr Melvyn Cook
Miss Aimee Cook
Mrs Jennifer Cook
Mr Charles Malcolm Cook
Mr Darren Cook
Mr Peter Cook
Mr Jason Cook
Mrs Louise Cooke
Mrs Christel Cooke
Mrs Christine Cookson

Mr Michael Cool
Mr R T Coombe
Mr Kay Coomber
Miss Natalie Coombs
Mr Paul Cooper
Mr Norman Cooper
Mrs Gainor Cooper
Mr Chris Cooper
Mr Jason Cooper
Mrs Wendy Cooper
Mr David Cooper
Mr Garth Copley
Mr John Coppenhall
Mr David Corcoran
Mr Stephen Corder
Mr Keith Cordery
Mr Andrew Cordiner
Mr Alex Coren
Miss Natalie Corfield
Mr Jonathan Cork
Mr Maxine Cormor
Mrs Sarah Corrigan
Mr Bryan Corrin
Mrs Dawn Cotton
Mr N Cottrell
Miss Holly Cottrell
Mrs Emma Cottrell
Ms Barbara Coupar
Mrs Pamela Coventry
Mr Mike Cowley
Ms Alexandra Cox
Mrs Sue Cox
Mrs Lucy Cox
Mr Nigel Cox
Mr David Cox
Ms Anna Cox
Mr Martin Coysh
Miss Jo Crabtree
Mrs Joyce Craigie
Mr Philip Crane
Mr Henry Crane
Ms Kate Crawford
Mrs Anne Critchlow
Mr Nigel Crocker
Mr Philip Croft
Mr Malcolm Croll
Mrs Sylvia Crome
Mrs Kathryn Crosby
Mrs Polly Cross
Mr George Crossley
Mr George Crossman
Mrs Susan Crowther
Mrs Rosie Cruickshank
Mr George Cruickshank
Miss Zoe Crump
Miss Polly Cubbage
Mrs Sarah Cullen
Mr Ian Culleu
Mr Graham Cummings
Mr Steve Curd
Mr Julian Curry
Mr Graham Curry
Mr William Curtis
Mrs Pauline Curtis
Mrs Rachel Curtis
Mrs Susan Curtis
Mr David Curtiss
Mr John Cusack
Mrs Paula Dadic
Mrs Elizabeth Daglish
Mrs J V Dagnall
Mr Kalvir Dahri
Mr Alexander Dale
Miss Karen Dallas
Mr Nigel Dally
Mr Simon Dallyn
Mr Michael Dalton
Mr Peter Daniels
Mr Jeremy Darby
Mr John Darkin
Mrs Jane Dashwood
Mrs Sarah Davey
Mr John Davey
Mrs Ann Davidson
Mr Hugh Davidson
Mr Alun Davies
Mr James Davies

Mr Alun Davies
Mr Duncan Davies
Mr Mark Davies
Mr Christopher Davies
Mrs M Davies
Miss Michelle Davies
Mr Chris Davies
Mrs Jill Davies
Miss Natalie Davies
Miss Melissa Davies-
Lawrence
Mrs Lin Davis
Mr Martin Davis
Mr Christopher Davis
Mr Tracey Davis
Mrs Katherine Davison
Mrs Pauline Daw
Ms Helen Dawkins
Miss Alexandra Dawson
Miss Fiona Dawson
Mr Stephen Day
Mr Sean Day-Lewis
Mrs Sandra de Ferranti
Miss Stephanie Deacon
Mr Jonathan Deans
Miss Cristina Dello Sterpaio
Mr Michael Dempsey
Ms Viveen Dennis
Mr Philip Dew
Miss Sonia Dhruve
Mr Murray Dick
Mr Paul Dicken
Mr P Dickerson
Miss Anna Dickie
Ms Jackie Dickinson
Mrs Maureen Dickson
Mr Martin Diggins
Mr Tim Dixon
Mr G M Dobb
Mr G M Dobbie
Mr Robert Dobbie
Mr Barry Dobson
Miss Diana Dobson
Mr Andy Docker
Mr Martin Dodd
Mr Kirk Dodds
Miss Sally Dodge
Mrs Ivy Doherty
Mrs Caroline Doherty
Miss Marian Doherty
Mr Jason Donavon
Miss Nicola Douglas
Mr Douglas
Mr Richard Douglas-Boyd
Mrs Lola Douthwaite
Mrs Mary Dowdle
Mr Roger Down
Mr Blair Downs
Mrs Helen Doyle
Mr Donald Doyle
Mr John Drake
Mrs Lesley Draper
Mr Robin Drummond
Mr Sarah Duce
Mr John Ducker
Mrs Elaine Duckworth
Mr Rey Duckworth
Mr John Duddridge
Mr James Duffy
Mr Terence Duffy
Mr Alayne Dugdale
Mr Neil Duncan
Mrs Rachel Duncan
Miss Jean Dunlop
Mr Martin Dunn
Mrs Hannah Dunn
Ms Karen Dunn
Mrs Wendy Durrant
Mr Clive Dutson
Mr David Dutton
Mr Andy Dyble
Mrs Alyson Dyer
Mr Nick Earle
Mrs Caroline Eason
Mr Pyers Easton
Mr James Eckford
Mr David Eddison

Mrs Christiane Eden
Mrs Adele Edgar
Mr Nick Edgar
Mr John Edwards
Mr Roy Edwards
Miss Kathryn Edwards
Mr Martin Edwards
Miss Joanne Edwards
Mrs Mary Edwards
Mr Geoffrey Edwards
Mr Ray Elderfield
Mr Desmond Eley
Mr Gary Elffett
Mrs Marian Elias
Ms Chloe Ellerton
Miss D Ellery
Mr Mike Elleston
Mr Mike Elliott
Ms Christine Elliott
Miss Nicola Elliott
Mr James Elliott
Mrs Sheila Elliott
Mrs Eileen Elston
Mr Nick Elton
Mr Christopher Elton
Mr Charles Elvin
Mrs A Elvin
Mr Jonathon Elwood
Mr George Emerson
Mrs Laura Emmerson
Mrs Rachel England
Mr James Esom
Mr A Eteve
Mrs Leigh Etienne
Ms Antonia Etim
Mr John Ette
Mr D Evans
Mr Huw Evans
Mr David Evans
Mr Gareth Evans
Mr Ramon Evans
Mr Geoffrey Evans
Mr Glyn Evans
Dr Linda Evans
Ms Jane Evans
Mr Alun Evans
Mrs Kelly Evans
Mr David Evans
Mr Bill Evans
Mr Philip Evans
Mr Kat Evans
Mrs Beryl Evans
Mrs Catherine Evans
Mrs Judith Evans
Mr Roger Everett
Ms Lynn Fairbairn
Mr Peter Fairbairn
Mr Gary Fairhurst
Mr John Fairley
Mr Ibrahim Fakhri
Mrs Jacqueline Faller
Ms Annie Fanner
Ms Michaela Farquhar
Mr Malcolm Faulk
Mr Paul Fauset
Mr Carlos Faustmann
Mr C Feather
Mr Jeff Featherstone
Mrs Sally Fennemore
Mr Alan Fensome
Mrs Margaret Fenton
Mrs Michelle Fenwick
Mr Nick Fermor
Mrs Linda Ferstendik
Mr Roy Fidmont
Mr S Field
Mr Mark Fielder
Mr Neville Filar
Mr Norman Fincham
Mr Dickon Fincham-
Jacques
Mr Antonio Fiorito
Mrs Elizabeth Firmin
Mr Adrian Firth
Mr Ewan Fisher
Mrs Susan Fisher
Mr James Fisher

Mrs Anne Marie Fisher
Mrs Suzanne Fisher
Ms Jan Fitzgerald
Mrs Sheila Fitzsimons
Mr Terence Flanagan
Mr Brendan Flanagan
Mr Terence Flanagan
Mr David Flatt
Mr Glenn Flegg
Mrs Carolynne Fleming
Ms Jean Fleming
Mr Jon Fleming
Mrs Jean Fleming
Mr Alastair Fleming
Mrs Ursula Fletcher
Mr Simon Fletcher
Mr Roger Fletcher
Miss Camilla Fletcher
Mrs Paula Fletcher
Mr Michael Fletcher
Mr Martin Fodor
Miss Suzanne Fogden
Mr Keith Folley
Mr Brian Folley
Mr Peter Ford
Mrs Marlene Ford
Mrs Deborah Ford
Mr John Fores
Mr Ian Forrest
Mr John Forrest
Mrs Beatrice Forster
Mr Simon Foster
Miss Gemma Foster
Mrs Christine Foulkes
Mr Christopher Fountain
Ms Nathalie Fournier
Mrs Sheila Fowler
Miss Karen Fowler
Mr Tom Fowler
Mr Derek Fowler
Mrs Joanna Fowles
Ms Bryony Fox
Miss Nicola Frame
Mr Adrian Francis
Ms Kathryne Fraser
Ms Sally Fraser
Miss Claire Fraser
Mr William Frazier
Mr Jason Freeman
Mrs Sam Freemantle
Mr Stephen and Margaret
Freeth
Ms Shona French
Mrs E Friend
Mrs Sue Frisby
Mr John Frost
Mrs Ann Frost
Miss Eve Frostick
Miss Rita Frumin
Miss Stella Fulton
Mrs Tina Furniss-Roe
Mr A M Furse
Mrs Karenna Galer
Miss Jane Gallagher
Mr Martin Gallagher
Miss Katie Galloway
Mrs M J Gambles
Mr R Gammon
Mr Martin Gan
Miss Leanne Gardener
Mrs Sally Gardner
Mrs Joanne Garner
Mr Christopher Garrand
Mrs Caroline Garthwaite
Mr Mark Garton
Mrs Ghislaine Garvey
Mrs Margaret Gash
Mr Martin Gates
Ms Tulay Gazler
Mr Mark Geffryes
Ms Susan Geier
Mr David George
Mr Paul George
Miss Carol George
Mr Stephen Georgiadis
Mrs Christine Gerezdi
Mr Darren Gervis

Mr Norman Gibbs
Mr Richard Gibson
Mr Simon Gibson
Mr Anthony Gilbert
Mr Martin Gilbert
Mrs Patricia Gilbert
Mr Roger Gilbraith
Mrs Jackie Gill
Mr Andrew Gill
Mr Peter Gillman
Mr David Gilmore
Mr Mark Gilpin
Miss Stephanie Gilpin
Mr Kenneth Gittoes
Mr Andy Givens
Mr David Gladwell
Mr Bryan Glastonbury
Mr John Glaze
Mrs Andrina Glen
Mr Julian Glover
Miss Alson Glover
Mr Brian Glover
Mrs Diane Goddard
Ms M Godfrey
Mrs Moira Gold
Mr Jeff Gold
Mrs Chris Goldthorp
Miss Lucy Goler
Mr Julian Golunski
Mr Jonathan Gooch
Mrs Lynn Goode
Mr Robert Goode
Mr Robin Goodfellow
Mr William Goodlad
Mrs Marjory Goodlad
Mrs Kate Gordon
Mrs E D Gordon
Mr D Gore
Mr Angus Gosman
Mr David M Gostyn
Mr Derek Gott
Ms Jenny Gottfried
Ms Veronica Gould
Mr William Robert Goymer
Mr Roger Graham
Mr David Graham
Mr Russell Graham
Mrs Erica Graham
Miss Caroline Graham
Mr J M Graham
Miss Caroline Graham
Mr Peter Graham
Mr Steve Graham
Mr David Grant
Mr Duncan Grant
Miss Holly Grant
Mr Simon Grant
Mr N K Grant
Miss Caroline Grattan
Ms Sarah-Jane Gravener
Mrs Betty Gray
Mrs Eunice Gray
Mr Alex Gray
Mr Barry Gray
Miss Fiona Greaves
Mr Michael Green
Miss Anna Green
Mr Lewis Green
Mr Michael Green
Mr Chris Green
Mr Peter & Margaret Green
Mr John Green
Mrs Nicola Green
Mrs Judith Greenburgh
Miss Kay Greenhalgh
Mrs Wendy Greenland
Mrs Zoe Greenwell
Mr Alan Greenwood
Mr J R Gregory
Mr Conal Gregory
Mr Marcus Gregson
Mr Maxwell Gregson
Mr Julian Gregson
Mr Michael Grenfell
Mrs Helen Grenville
Ms Catherine Gribble
Mr J. David Grice

Mr M Griffin
Mr Terry Griffin
Mr Sean Griffiths
Mr Robin Griffiths
Mr Harold Griffiths
Mr Brian Griffiths
Mrs Helen Griggs
Mr Peter Grigor
Mr Tony Grimes
Mrs Jean Grimes
Mr Robin Grimmett
Mrs Chrisine Grimsdell
Ms Ros Mari Grindheim
Mr Roderick Grindlay
Mr Peter Grinnall
Mrs Christine Groat
Mr Arthur Grosset
Mr Marcus Groundwater
Mr John Groundwater
Mr Stephen Groves
Miss Kelly Guest
Mr Richard Gulliver
Mr Jenevieve Gumpta
Mr Richard Gunn
Mr Ian Gunning
Mr Ian Gunning
Mrs Angela Guy
Mr Rob Gwilliam
Ms Kate Gwynfyd Sidford
Mrs Diane Hacker
Mr Faris Haddad
Miss Kate Haden
Mrs Carolyn Hadley
Mrs Patricia Hague
Mr Robin Hague
Miss Anita Hailey
Miss Jen Hall
Mr Russell Hall
Mr Jeffrey Hall
Miss Elizabeth Hall
Ms Jan Hall
Mrs Karen Hall
Miss Chloe Hall
Mr David R. Hall
Mr Ivor Hall
Mrs Romy Halliwell
Mr Colin Hamer
Mr Ian Hamilton
Mr Mark Hamilton
Mrs Rachel Hamilton-Smith
Mr Don Hammond
Mr Edward Hammond
Mrs Rona Hammond
Mrs Patti Hammond-Dinsdale
Mr Jerry Hampton
Mrs Sallyann Hampton
Mrs Sharon Handley
Mr Gordon Hands
Mrs Teresa Hands
Mr Noel Hanley
Mr Philip Hanna
Mr Haadi Hannan
Mr Clive Hanner
Ms Gabby Hansson-boe
Mr Derek C R Harden
Mr J Harding
Mrs Samantha Hardingham
Mr Grant Hardy
Miss Claire Hargan
Mr Matthew Harms
Miss Kate Harper
Mr Adrian Harper
Mr Eamonn Harrigan
Mr Jonathan Harris
Mr Lewis Harris
Mr Jocelin Harris
Mr Phil Harris
Mrs Elizabeth Harrison
Mrs Dorothy Harrison
Mr Julie Harrison
Miss Sarah Harrison
Miss Sheila Harrison
Mr Jones Harry
Mr Peter Hart
Mrs Janet Hart

Mr John Hartley
Mr James Hartley
Mr Brian Hartley
Mr John Hartley
Mrs Patricia Hartwell
Mr Peter Harvey
Mr Iain Harvey
Mr Royston Harvey
Miss Debbie Harvey
Mr Mark Harvey
Mrs Helen Harvey-Johnson
Mr S Harwin
Mr John Haslam
Miss Sherryn Haslam
Mr Stephen Haslett
Mrs Pamela Hastings
Mr Stephen Hatch
Mr Mick Hatton
Mr Tim Hawker
Mrs Shelley Hawkins
Miss Kathryn Hawkins
Mr Andrew Hawkins
Mr Denise Haworth
Mr Thomas Haworth
Mr Andy Hayler
Mrs Ann Hayward
Mr David Hayward
Mr Melody Haywood
Ms Ruth Headdon
Mr Terry Heath
Mrs Mandy Heathcote
Mrs Helen Hedger
Mr Michael Hedger
Mrs Jackie Hedges
Mr Don Heeley
Mr John Hemmings
Mrs Sarah Hemsley
Mr Paul Henderson
Mrs Carmen Henderson
Mrs Juliet Hendon
Mr Ian Henry
Mr John Henson
Mr M E Henstock
Mr Charles Hepplewhite
Mrs Janine Herron
Mr Andrew Herxheimer
Mrs Susan Hesketh
Mr Graham Hetherington
Mr John Hevey
Mr Jonathan Hewson
Mr Rob Hick
Mr John Hickman
Mrs Karen Higham
Mr Adrian Highland
Mr Robert Hill
Miss Samantha Hill
Mr James Hill
Mrs Cindy Hill
Mr Edward Hill
Mr Steve Hill
Mr Leonard Hill
Mrs Daryl Hill
Mrs Jenny Hill
Mr Philip Hill
Mrs Maddy Hill
Ms Wendy Hill
Mr Chris Hilton
Ms Florence Hindle
Mrs Lynn Hindle
Mr Jack Hines
Mr Peter Hirschmann
Mrs Ann Hirst-Smith
Miss Claire Hitch
Mr Michael Hockney
Mr Peter Hodson
Mrs Marilyn Hogg
Mr Graham Holbrook
Mrs Alison Holden
Mr Frank Holden
Mrs Jacqueline Holden
Mrs Andi Holden-Bailey
Mr Andy Holding
Mr John Holland
Mrs Jeannette Holland
Mrs Hollie Holland
Miss Suzanne Holland
Mr Adam Holliday

Mr A G R Holman
Mrs V Holman
Mrs Angela Holman
Mrs Jane Holmes
Mr Kenneth Holmes
Mr John Holroyd
Mr Colin Honey
Ms Isabel Hood
Mrs Karen Hoodless
Mr Andy Hook
Mr Mike Hookway
Mr Paul Hooper
Mr Jenny Hope
Mr Stuart Hope
Mr Ben Hopkin
Mr Oliver Hopkins
Mrs Julie Hopkins
Mr Neil Hopkins
Mr Ralph Hopton
Mr D H Hopwood
Mr David Horner
Mr Neil Hornsey
Miss Kathryn Horrey
Mrs Sharon Horsfall
Mr Ian Horsford
Mr M Horton
Mr Chris Horwood
Mrs Barbara Hosking CBE
Mr John Hostettler
Mr Mark Hotham
Mr Alice Hou
Mr Dominic Hourd
Mr Emma Howard
Mr Nick Howard
Mr Jonathan Howarth
Mrs Jeanne Howe
Mrs Nicola Howell
Mrs F M Howley
Mr Robert Hubbard
Miss Emily Hudson
Mr Steve Huetson
Mr Philip Hughes
Mr Derek Hughes
Miss Nicola Hughes
Mrs Genevieve Hughes
Miss Hanna Hughes
Mrs Diana Hughes
Ms Margaret Hughes
Mrs Penny Hull
Miss Sally Humpage
Mr Martin Hunt
Mr Giles Hunt
Ms P Hunt
Mr Martin Hunt
Ms Leigh Hunt
Mrs Louise Hunt
Mr Anthony Hunt
Mrs Philippa Hunt
Mrs Jane Hunter
Mr J Hunter
Mr Preston Hunter
Mr Peter Huntingdon
Mr Rashidul Huque
Mr S Hussain
Mr Matthew Hutchings
Mrs Mary Hutchison
Mr Gordon Hutchison
Miss Kirsty Hutchison
Miss Rebecca Hutley
Mr James Hutton
Miss Katie Hyde
Mr David Hyett
Mrs Clare Hyett
Mr Tim Bishop Ian Louden
Mr Roger Ibbetson
Mrs Lyn Imeson
Mrs Rosie Inge
Mr Peter Ingham
Mrs Fiona Irving
Mr Andrew Irwin
Mr Tony Isaacs
Mr David Ison
Mr Leslie Iversen
Miss Lotta Iverstrand
Mr Bill Ives
Mr David Izatt
Mrs Hazel Jacklin

Ms Connie Jackson
Ms Heather Jackson
Ms Catherine Jackson
Mrs Mary Jackson
Mr Daniel Jackson
Mr Eric Jackson
Miss Amanda Jackson
Mrs Shelagh Jacobs
Mr Kenneth Jacobs
Mr Paul Jacques
Mrs Claire Jaggard
Mr Chris Jagger
Mr Peter James
Miss Nicky James
Mrs Rosemary James
Mrs Partridge James
Mrs Belinda James
Mr Graham Jameson
Mr Robert Jamieson
Mrs Fiona Jane
Miss Kerry Jardine
Mr Philip Jarvis
Mr Michael Jay
Mr Michael Jeans
Mr Andrew Jedwell
Mr Chris Jefferies
Mr Lars Jeffries
Mr D F Jenkins
Mr Paul Jenkins
Mr Geraint Jenkins
Mrs Elaine Jenkins
Mr Michael Jennings
Miss Joanne Jennings
Mr David Jenvey
Mr David R W Jervois
Mr John Jesson
Ms Yvonne Jessop
Mr Hugo Jeune
Mr Barry Jewitt
Mrs Susan Jobbins
Mrs Tahera Joglu
Miss Kam Johal
Mr Daniel Johns
Mrs Joan Johnson
Mrs Jane Johnson
Mr Ronan Johnson
Mrs Michelle Johnson
Mr Brian Johnson
Mrs Rachel Johnson
Mrs Lorna Johnson
Mrs Judith Johnson
Mr Philip Johnson
Mr Jo Johnson
Ms Joan Johnston
Mr Paul Johnston
Mr Marcus Johnston
Mrs Karen Johnston
Ms Sallie Johnston
Mrs H Joiner
Mr Ian Jones
Mr Chris Jones
Mr Ian Jones
Ms Heather Jones
Mrs Rosemary Jones
Mr N J Jones
Mr David Jones
Mr John Cyrus Jones
Mr Philip Jones
Mr Norman Jones
Mr John Idris Jones
Mrs Patricia Jones
Mrs Barbara Jones
Mr Frances Jones
Miss Martha Jones
Mr Elfan Jones
Miss Caroline Jones
Mrs Laura Jones
Mr Allan Jones
Mr Alan Jones
Ms Karen Jones
Mrs Mary Jones
Miss Helen Jones
Mrs Penny Jones
Ms Rhian Jones
Mrs Diana Jones
Mr David Jones
Mrs Vivienne Jones

Miss Marion Jones
Miss Laura Jones
Mr Nick Jones
Ms Jennifer Jones
Mr Ian Jones
Mrs Juliet Jowitt
Miss Stephanie Judd
Ms Simeen Kadi
Mr Mustafa Kapasi
Mr Richard Karnehm
Mrs Dale Kay
Mr Byron Kay
Mrs Carole Kay
Mr Tom Kearney
Mr Sheamus Keehan
Ms Donna Keen
Miss Julie Kelly
Mr Allan Kelly
Mrs Sylvia Kelvedon
Ms Verity Kemp
Mr Paul Kendall
Mrs Lynn Kendell
Mr Paul Kendrick
Mr Anthony Kennaway
Mr Phil Kennedy
Mrs David Kenny
Mr Jonathan Kent
Mrs Karen Kent
Mr John Kenward
Mrs Carol Keohane
Mr Anthony Kesten
Mr Brian Key
Miss Georgina Key
Mr Nigel Keylock
Mr Khalid Khan
Mr Vimal Khosla
Mr Craig Kidd
Mr Don Kiddle
Mr Sascha Kiess
Mr Tom Kilbrandon
Mr John And Margaret Kilby
Mr John Kilby
Ms Anne Kimberley
Mr Ronald King
Mrs Harriet Kingsley
Miss Victoria Kingsley
Mrs Debra Kininmonth
Mr Roger Kinsey
Mrs Valerie Kirk
Mr Mark Kirkbride
Ms Isobel Kirkus
Mr Jonathan Kitch
Ms Gerry Kitchingman
Ms Delia Kitson
Mrs Elizabeth Klein
Miss Bernadette Knight
Mr Karl Knight
Mr R Knight
Mr Richard Knights
Mrs Silvi Knightsmith
Miss Gemma Knott
Mr Trevor Knox
Mr Alastair Knox
Mr Raymond Arno Koehler
Mrs Miranda Kraft
Miss Ali Kramer
Miss Reena Kumari
Mr Edward Kyme
Mrs Rachel Kyriazi
Mr Peter Kyte
Mr Charles Kyte
Mr Will Lacey
Mr Anthony Lacey
Mr Dizy Lacey
Miss L Lack
Mr Roger Lackner
Miss Naz Lakhi
Mr Chris Lamb
Miss Susy Lamb
Mr Roger Lambert
Miss Samantha Lambert
Mr Paul Lambert
Mrs M Lambert
Mr Fraser Lamprell
Miss Margot Landes
Mr Phillip Lane

Ms Sally Lane
Mr John Lane-Gilhespy
Mrs Leontine Langabeer
Mr Anthony Langan
Mr Gareth Langdon
Mrs Jacqueline Langley
Mrs Lorraine Langman
Mr Dave Langmead
Mr Brian Langton
Mrs Erica Larentius
Mr Daniel Larkin
Mr Nicholas Lash
Mr John Last
Mrs Wendy Latham
Ms Lesley Latimer
Mrs Patricia Latorre
Mr Martin Lau
Mr Jack Chapman Lavin MBE
Mrs Claire Lawrence
Mrs Julie Lawrence
Mrs Elizabeth Lawson
Mrs Linda Le Page
Mr David Lea
Miss Rebecca Leach
Mr John Leah
Mr Robin Leake
Miss Fiona Leavis
Mr Xavier Le-Bellego
Ms Judy Lee
Mr Stuart Lee
Mr Steven Lee
Mrs Karen Lee
Mrs Erica Lee
Mr John Legg
Mr Craig Leitch
Mr Gerrit Lemmens
Mr John Lenihan
Ms Siobhan Lennon
Ms Sandra Leonhard
Mr Leslie
Mr Robert Lester
Mr K M Letherman
Professor Kenneth Letherman
Mr Robert Lever
Mr Richard Levick
Mr Geoffrey Levy
Mrs Kate Lewin
Mr Duncan Lewis
Mr Laurence Lewis
Mr Piers Lewis
Mr Ben Lewis
Mr Jay Ley
Mrs Violet Liddington
Mr David Lindley
Miss Sarah Lindores
Mr John R Ling
Mr Mike Ling
Mr David Linnell
Miss Emma Lisk
Mr James Littell
Mr Roderick Little
Mrs Kate Littleton
Mrs Susanne Livingstone
Mr John Lloyd
Mrs G Lloyd
Miss Katy Lloyd
Mr Al Logan
Mr Barnaby Logan
Mrs Joan Lokey-Drayton
Mr Robin Lomas
Mr Chris Long
Mr Nick Longhurst
Mrs Catherine Longree
Mr Patrick Lorkin
Miss Karen Lothian
Mr David Loudoun
Ms Daisy Love
Mrs Lorraine Lovegrove-Wood
Ms Thelma Lovick
Mr Peter Lowater
Ms Carolyn Lowe
Ms Virginia Lowes
Ms Sue Lowndes
Mr Graham Lucas

Miss Cecilia Lundin
Ms F Lyon
Miss Lindsey Macare
Ms Marina MacArthur
Mr Peter Macaulay
Ms Virginia Macauley
Mr Fergus MacDermot
Mr Donald Macdonald
Mr Miles MacEacharn
Mr Fred Macey
Mrs Leigh MacFeate
Ms Ione MacGregor
Mr John Mackay
Ms Jennie Mackeith
Mr M P Mackenzie
Mrs Ann Mackinnon
Mr Hugh R Mackintosh
Mr Hugh Mackintosh CBE
Mrs Christine and Brian Mackness
Mr Colin MacLaine
Mr David Maclennan
Ms Marcia MacLeod
Mrs Gillian Macpherson
Mr Ian Macpherson
Mr Brian Macrow
Miss Margaret MacSween
Ms Jonquil Magee
Ms Ann Magee
Miss Jonquil Ros Magee
Mrs Caroline Mageean
Mr Chris Mahn
Mr Martin Maierhofer
Mr Robert Main
Mrs Rachel Maitland
Mr Richard Majoram
Mr James Malconson
Miss Tina Malhotra
Mr and Mrs Paul and Bridget Manley
Mr Paul V Manley
Mr Alexander Mann
Mr Chodury Mannan
Mr Stuart Mansbridge
Miss Kirsten Manuel
Miss Fiona Manuel
Mr J A Marchal
Mrs Angela Marchant
Mr Jeffrey Marchant
Ms Lorrie Marchington
Mr Paul Mardon
Mr Michael Margarson
Mr Richard Margree
Mr Jim Markham
Mr Janet Markus
Mr Charles Markus
Mr Gavin Markwick
Mrs Kathy Marnier
Mr David Marr
Mrs Brenda Marriott
Mr Hurenmarsh Marsh
Mrs Laura Marsh
Mr J M Marshal
Mr David Marshall
Mr Jacques Marshall
Mrs Valerie Marshall
Ms Louise Marshall
Miss Anna Marshall
Mr Tom Marshall
Mrs Maureen Marshall
Mr Paul Marshall
Mrs Mary Marshall
Mr R R Marshall-Andrews
Mr St John Marston
Mr Graham Martin
Mr Joe Martin
Mrs Karen Martin
Mrs Rosemary Martin
Mr James Martin
Mrs Rose Martin
Mr Graham Martin
Mr Martin
Mr Graham Martin
Mr John Martyn
Mr Anthony Mason
Mrs Catherine Mason
Mr Dudley Mason

Mr Malcolm Mastin
Ms Kwee Matheson
Mr David Mathewson
Mr Chris Matthews
Mr David Matthews
Mr Graham Maundrell
Miss Hanna Mawson
Mrs Jan Maxfield
Mrs Christine Maxwell
Mr Ian May
Mr Kenneth May
Miss Elizabeth May
Mr Nick May
Mr Bevan Mayall
Miss Susana Mayan Ferrer
Miss Sarah Mayhew
Mr Michael Mayo
Mr Bill Mc Allister-Lovatt
Mr Gerard McAllister
Ms Colette McAlpine
Miss Rosie McArdle
Mr Mark McArthur-Christie
Mr Derek McBride
Mr Kevin McBrien
Mr Graham McCabe
Mr Desmond McCann
Miss Anne McCart
Mrs Fiona McCarthy
Ms Kathy McConnell
Mr Liam McCormack
Mr John McCormick
Mr Andrew McCosh
Mrs Shirley McCrow
Mrs Victoria McCutcheon
Miss Rebecca McDonald
Mrs Cynthia McDowall
Miss Hazel McFadzean
Miss Helen McFarlane
Mr Colin McGhee
Mr Richard Mcgill
Miss Rachel McGregor
Mr Brian McGuirk
Mr Tony McGurk
Mr Fred McHale
Mrs Hannah Mchardy
Mrs Mary McIlhone
Miss Sally McIlhone
Mr Thomas McIntosh
Mr Kenneth McKay
Ms Ann McKenna
Mr Simon McKie
Mr Marcia McLeod
Mrs Lyn McLeod
Mrs Corinna McLeod
Mrs Sophie McLoughlin
Mr J P McMahon
Mr Andrew McManus
Mrs Fran McNicoll
Mr Kenneth McNulty
Mr Peter McQuire
Mrs Nicola McRoy
Ms Fran McSweeney
Mr Colin Mcvean
Mrs Melanie McVicker
Mr Nathan Meadows
Mr Christian Mealing
Mr Danny Meaney
Miss Lucy Medd
Mr Andrew Meddings
Mr Johnson Medhari
Mrs Jackie Melarkey
Mrs Elizabeth Meldrum
Mrs Barbara Melville
Miss Natasha Mendak
Ms Katherine Mendelsohn
Mr Tom Mercer
Mr Paul Mercieca
Mr Peter Messenger
Mr Christine Metcalf
Mr John Meyrick Thomas
Mr Kamal Miah
Mr Jalil Miah
Mr Dorothy J Michie
Mr Robin Middleton
Mr Phillip Middleton
Ms Corinne Mildiner

Mr Fred Miles
Mr Leyton Mileson
Mrs Trish Millar
Mr Adam Miller
Mrs Mary Miller
Ms Corinne Miller
Mr Andrew Miller
Mrs Pamela Miller
Mr Phil Milligan
Mrs Christine Millington
Mr Ian Millington
Mrs Victoria Millins
Mr A Mills
Ms Claire Minett
Mr Karen Minter
Mr Austen Mintern
Mr Guy Mitchell
Ms Anno Mitchell
Mrs Carol Mitchell
Miss Louise Mitchell
Mr Stuart Mitchenall
Mr Tom Mitcheson
Ms Liz Moate
Mr Kesir Mohammed
Mr Adam Moliver
Mr Adam Moliver
Mrs Charlotte Monck
Mr Wendy Montague
Mr Alan Montgomery
Mrs Linda Montgomery
Mrs Sallyann Moody
Mr George Mooney
Mrs Kathleen Mooney
Mrs Janice Moorby
Mr Barry Moorcroft
Miss Fiona Moorcroft
Mr Colin Moore
Mrs Gwen Moore
Mr David Moore
Mrs Patricia Moore
Mr Nick Moore
Mr John Moore
Mrs Alex Moorin
Mr Francis Moran
Mr C W D Morgan
Mr Terry Morgan
Mrs Lisa Morgan
Mr Duncan Morgan
Mrs Vanessa Morley
Mr Terry Morris
Mr Barry Morrison
Mr Jerome Morrow
Mr Mark Mortimer
Miss Sandra Morton
Mr Robert Moss
Mr S Moss
Mr David Mottershead
Mr Dave Moulson
Mr Paul Moynihan
Ms I G Mudd
Miss Ghaliayh Mufti
Mrs Cristina Muino
Mrs Pamela Muirhead
Mr Sandie Mulcahy
Miss Gabrielle Mulholland
Mr Chris Mulroy
Mr James Munro
Ms Deborah Murdoch
Ms Jean Murdoch
Mrs Julie Murphy
Mrs Caroline Murphy
Mr Peter Murray
Mr Jayne Murray
Mrs Patricia Murray
Mr Matthew Murray
Mrs Lynn Murray
Mr Peter Murrell
Mrs Nicola Musetti
Mr Colin Mutch
Mr Joshua Mutic
Mr Ivan Myko
Mrs Andrea Nadin
Mr David Nash
Ms Karen Nash
Ms Mal Nash
Mr Robert Nash
Mr Anthony Nathan

THANK YOUS

Mr Martin Naylor
Miss Belinda Naylor
Mrs Becky Naylor
Mr Lamine N'dour
Mr David Neale
Mr Ron Negus
Mr N Nellis
Mrs Geraldine Nelson
Mr Peter Nelson
Ms Gill Nelson
Mr John Netherwood
Mrs Joan Newberry
Mr Dominic Newbould
Mrs Heather Newbury
Mrs Colette Newcomb
Mr Fiona Newcombe
Mrs Patricia Newman
Mrs Donna Newman
Mr Brian Newman
Miss Alice Newman
Mr Garry Newton
Mrs Marijke Nibloe
Mr Peter Nibloe
Mrs J Nicholls
Mr Ralph Nichols
Mrs Penny Nicholson
Mrs Katherine Nicol
Mr Daniel Nightingale
Miss Claire Nixon
Mr Jack Nixon
Mr Sascha Noar
Mr Lawrence C Noble
Miss Annie Nolan
Mrs Jacqueline Norman
Mr Tyrone Norris
Mr Elspeth Norris
Mrs Barbara Northfield
Mrs Lesley Norton
Mr Colin Norwell
Mr David Nove
Mr Callum Nuttall
Mrs Carolyn Oakley
Mr Charles Oatwig-Thain
Mrs Mary O'Brien
Mr Mike O'Brien
Mrs Susan O'Brien
Mrs L M O'Connor
Mr Greg O'Connor
Mr Brad O'Connell
Miss Ruth O'Donovan
Ms Caroline Ogden
Mr Catherine Ogden
Mrs Angela Ogilvie
Dr David O'Halloran
Mrs Rachel O'Hara
Mr Ray O'Hara
Miss Elin Ohman
Mrs Anne O'Kane
Ms Debbie O'Keefe
Mr John Oldroyd
Miss Dana Olearnikova
Mr Tim Olivey
Mr Jan Olsen
Mr Stefan Olszowski
Mrs Jane O'Mahoney
Mr Kevin O'Mahoney
Mr Ellie O'Mahoney
Mrs Bree O'Neil
Ms Elif Onen
Mr Paul O'Reilly
Miss Denise Osborne
Miss Dawn O'Shaughnessy
Mr Kesiena Ovien
Mrs Patricia Owen
Mr Trevor Owen
Mr Charlie Owen
Mrs Sue Owens
Mrs Sarah Oxford
Mr Jerry Ozaniec
Mr Robert Packard
Miss Jane Padginton
Mr Michael Page
Mr I Page
Mr Andrew Page
Mr Manohar Pai
Mr Matthew Palmer
Ms Margaret Palmer

Mr Alan Parish
Mrs Lucinda Parish
Mr Nigel Parker
Mr Keith Parker
Mrs Lynda Parker
Mr Graeme Parker
Ms Helen Parker
Mrs Helen Parkin
Dr John Parkinson
Mrs Caroline Parkinson
Mrs Louise Parkinson
Mr Thomas Parkinson
Mrs J Parks
Mr Roger Parr
Mr Frederick Parr
Mrs Heather Parry
Mr Haneef Patel
Mrs Suzie Paton
Ms Cheryl Patrick
Mr John D Pattenden
Mr John Pattenden
Mr Chris Pattison
Mr John Paul
Mr Michael Paul
Mr Pranab Paul
Mrs Susanne Paxman
Mrs Janet Payne
Mrs Danielle Payten
Mrs Rachael Peacock
Mrs Ann Peacocke
Mr James Peak
Mr Alan Pearce
Mrs Alison Pearce
Mr Allen E Pearce
Mrs Hazel Pearce
Mr Patrick Pearce
Mrs Helen Pearce
Miss Hazel Pearce
Mr Keith Pearson
Mr F R Pearson
Mr Gary Pearson
Mr Don Pearson
Mr Matt Pearson
Mr Kenneth Peck
Ms Laura Pegg
Mrs Annie Pegler
Mr Thomas Peplinski
Miss Jenny Perkin
Ms Jane Perks
Miss Lisa Perrie
Miss Rachel Perry
Mr Brian Perryman
Ms Helen Peston
Ms Helen Peston
Mr Mike Peters
Mr Brian Pettifer
Mrs Shirley Pettit
Mr Julian Peyser
Mrs Pamela Pfeifer
Mr Ian Phair
Mr John Phillips
Mr Mark V Phillips
Mrs Janet Phillips
Mr David Phillips
Mrs Rachel Phillips
Mr Thomas Phillips
Mrs Winifred Philp
Mr Jeremy Phipps
Ms Rosemary Phizackerley
Mr Kenneth Pickles
Mr Kenneth Pickles
Ms Veronica Piekosz
Mr Stewart Piercy
Mrs Sophie Pilkington
Mr Ian Pinn
Miss Faye Pinson
Mrs K Piper
Miss Alison Pitman
Mr Steve Pitman
Mr Hugh Pitt
Mr Stephen Pitt
Mr Tim Pitt
Mr Parminder Plaha
Mr Geoff Plant
Mrs Rosemary Platt
Mr Colin Pollock
Mrs Jennifer Pollock

Miss Joanna Porter
Mr Ken Postgate
Mr William Potter
Mr Peter Pound
Mr Colin Power
Miss Kelly Pratt
Mr T D Preece
Mrs Andrea Prentice
Mr Rob Preston
Mrs Michelle Pretorius
Mr Adam Price
Mr Norman Price
Mr John Prince
Mr Andy Pringle
Mr James Prisk
Mr Julian Procter
Mr Adam Proctor
Mrs Marie Prutton
Mr Dave Pryde
Mr Rhys Pugh
Mrs Julia Pumphrey
Mr A Punter
Mr Adrian Pyatt
Mr David Pybus
Mrs Yolanda Queally
Mrs Linda Quinan
Mrs Heather Quinlan
Mrs Louise Quinn
Mr Alan Radcliffe
Mr S Rahman
Mr Ananth Raman
Mrs Jo Rammell
Mrs Bridget Ramsay
Miss Jane Ramsell
Mr James Randle
Miss Charlotte Rands
Mr John Rank
Mr Thomas A Rankin
Miss Ann Rannard
Mr Tom Ratcliffe
Ms Gill Rathbone
Mrs Sandra Raubenheimer
Miss Angela Rawson
Mrs Rosie Rayfield
Mr Tom Rayfield
Mrs Susan Rayner
Mrs Helen Raywood
Mr Simon Reade
Mrs Angela Redfern
Mrs Dorice Redmonds
Mr Bryan Reed
Mrs Valerie Rees
Mr Steve Rees
Mr David Rees
Mr Richard Rees-Jones
Mrs Sheila Reeves
Mrs Penny Reeves
Mr John Reid
Mr Alan Reid
Mrs Lesley Reilly
Ms Rosalind Renshaw
Mrs Gaynor Renwick
Mrs Carol Revill
Mr Ernie Revill
Mrs Janet Reynolds
Ms Annie Rhodes
Mr William Rhodes
Mrs Susan Riby
Mr Richard
Mr Ted Richards
Mr Nigel Richards
Ms Sheila Richards
Mrs Kate Richards
Mr Clive Richards
Mrs Geraldine Richards
Mr C John Richardson
Miss Sophie Richardson
Mr John Richardson
Ms Louise Riches
Mr Colin Richmond
Mr Gerson Riddy
Mr Malcolm Ridge
Ms Julia Ridgway
Miss Nicki Ridgway
Mr Caroline Righton
Mrs Claire Riley
Mr Bob Rishton

Mr Douglas Ritchie
Mr Graham Rix
Mrs Christine Robers
Dr Robert
Mrs Pauline Roberts
Mr Barry Roberts
Miss Jillian Roberts
Ms Lesley Roberts
Mr Trevor Roberts
Mr Robin Roberts
Mr Pete Roberts
Mr Brian Roberts
Miss Emily Roberts
Mrs Ally Roberts
Mr John Robertshaw
Mr Adam Robertson
Mr Alastair Robertson
Miss Lee Robertson
Ms Carole Robertson
Mrs Chris Robertson
Mr I Robins
Mr Tim Robins
Mrs Claire Robinson
Mrs Julie Robinson
Mrs Lianne Robinson
Miss Jan Robinson
Mr Tim Robinson
Miss Hannah Robinson
Mrs Roseanne Roblin
Mr Andy Robotham
Mr Robert Robson
Mr Margaret Robson
Mr Colin Rockall
Mr Simon Rodgers
Mr Douglas Rodgers
Ms Devra Rodriguez
Mr Peter Roe
Mrs Samantha Roger
Mrs Moira Rogers
Mrs Margaret Rogers
Miss Isobel Rogers
Mrs Miranda Rogers
Mr Chris Rollason
Mr Ian Romanis
Ms Rosemary Romero
Mrs Claudia Rosani
Mrs Sarah Roscoe
Mr Ian Rose
Miss Aimee Rose
Mr Paul Rosenfeld
Mr A H Ross
Mr Philip Ross
Mrs Buffy Ross
Mrs Rachel Ross
Mrs H Ross
Ms Elizabeth Ross
Dr Colin Roth
Dr Colin Roth
Mrs Diane Rothwell
Mrs Roberta Rounthwaite
Miss Marie Rourke
Mr Peterian Rouse
Mr John Routledge
Mr Peter Rowe
Mr Ellis Rowe
Mr Andrew Rowe
Mr Richard Rowlands
Ms Llinos Rowlands
Mr Daniel Rowlson
Mr Gavin Rowson
Miss J Roy
Ms Annette Rubery
Mrs Sewkian Rudge
Mrs Ruth Runacus
Mr John Russell
Mrs Carolyn Russell
Mrs Rosemary Russell
Mr W Ruxton
Mrs Maureen Ruxton
Mrs Thelma Ryan
Mr Aiden Ryan
Mr Terry Ryan
Mr Dominique Ryder
Mrs Patricia Ryder
Mrs Shirley Sabin
Mrs Rachel Salisbury
Mr Chris Sallnow

Mr Nick Saltmarsh
Mr Oliver Samuel
Mr Robert Samuel
Mr Graham Sanderson
Mrs Shirley Sandilands
Mrs Carolyn Sands
Ms Elaine Santin
Mr Neil Sargent
Miss Jane Sargent
Miss Jayne Saunders
Mr Steven Saunders
Mr Andrew Saunders
Mr Tom Savage
Miss Monica Sawala
Mr Brian Sawkins
Mr Derek Sawyer
Mr Phil Sayer
Mrs Sarah Saynor
Mr John Scales
Mrs Lesley Scarrott
Mr Alan Scarrott
Mr Guido Schaffhauser
Mrs Erica Schelle van Gorp
Ms Caroline Schneider
Ms Genee Schock
Mrs Glenis Schofield
Mr David Schofield
Mr Burch Schwabline
Mr Ronald Schwarz
Mr K M Scollay
Miss Jillian Scott
Ms Esme Scott
Ms Irene Scullion
Miss Natalie Seager
Mr Marin Seah
Mrs Sheila Seales
Mr Amanda Sector
Mr David Sefton
Miss Mari Segalin
Mr Dominic Seigies
Mr Paul Sellers
Mrs Julia Selwood
Mr Joanne Sewell
Mr Sidhartha Shakya
Mr David Shalit
Mr Anil Sharma
Miss Rachel Sharret
Mr John Shaw
Mr Jervis Sheil
Miss Nicole Sheinman
Mrs Diana Sheldon
Mr Chris Shemilt
Mr Brian Shepherd
Mr John Shepherd
Mrs Anne Shepherd
Mr Jeremy Sherrard-Smith
Mr Trevor Duncan Shingles
Miss Paulina Shirley
Mr Geoffrey Siddall
Mrs Marjorie Siddall
Mr Joan Siddle
Mrs Janice Sillitoe
Mr Mark Sills
Mr John Silver
Miss Sarah Simpkins
Mr John Simpson
Mr Elizabeth Simpson
Mrs S Simpson
Mr Joe Simpson
Mrs Cathryn Simpson
Mrs Uma Sims
Mr Graham Skilton
Miss Megan Skinner
Mr Dimitri Sklav
Ms Rebecca Slack
Mr John Slade
Miss Diane Slater
Mr David Sleight
Mrs Amanda Sleight
Mr David Sleight
Mr Debbie Slough
Ms Jane Sluman
Mr Richard Smail
Mr Brian Small
Ms Judith Smallwood
Ms Shilpa Smart

Mr Tom Smeaton
Mrs Christine Smeaton
Mrs Joann Smith
Mr Jonothon Smith
Mr David Smith
Miss Cora Smith
Mr S Smith
Mr Malcolm Cecil Smith
Mr Justin Smith
Miss Judy Smith
Mr David Smith
Mr Guy Smith
Mr Brian Smith
Mrs Jean Smith
Mr Roger Smith
Mr Damian Smith
Mrs Rebecca Smith
Mr Richard Smith
Miss Janis Smith
Miss Jacqueline Smith
Mrs M Smith
Mrs Sharon Smith
Mrs Claire Smith
Mr Mark Smith
Mrs Phillipa Smith
Miss Laura Smith
Miss Suzanne Smith
Mrs Polly Smith
Mrs Caroline Smith
Mrs Sarah Smith
Mrs Jan Smith
Mrs Molly Smith
Mr Brian Smith
Mrs Debbie Smyth
Mrs Jodie Smythe
Mr David Solomon
Mrs Lynsey Spall
Mr Ian Sparks
Mrs Emma Sparks
Mr Zack Spelling
Mr Torin Spence
Mrs Penny Spencer
Mrs Joanne Spencer
Mrs Meryl Spicer
Mr Matthew Spraggett
Mr A Spurr
Mr Mike Squire
Mr Brian St Clair
Mr John St Noble
Miss Natalie Stacey
Mr Peter Stahelin
Mr Kevin Staight
Mrs Darlene Stainer
Mrs Kathy Stallard
Mr John Standaloft
Mr Paul Stanger
Mrs Helen Stanwell
Mrs Ann Starkey
Ms Julia Stavordale
Ms A Steadman
Mrs Elaine Steadman
Mr Peter Steadman
Mr Robert Steadman
Ms Valerie Stebbing
Mr Joe Steel
Mr Zac Steel
Miss Rachel Steele
Mr William Steele
Mr Anthony Steen
Mr Jean-Marc Stefani
Mr John Stephens
Ms Andrea Stephenson
Mr Anthony Stern
Mrs Janette Stevens
Miss Emma Stevens
Mr J Stevenson
Mrs Louise Stevenson
Mr Andrew Stevenson
Ms Karen Stevenson
Miss Lisa Stevenson
Mrs Anne Stevenson Lucas
Miss Mairi Stewart
Capt J S Stewart OBE
Mr Ian Stickland
Mrs E Stirrat
Mr Peter Stoakley
Mrs Amanda Stobbs

Mr Hamish Stoddart
Mr Martin H Stone
Mrs Rosie Stone
Mr Tom Stones
Mr Philip Stones
Mrs Amanda Stooke
Mrs Phillippa Storar
Mr Ron Storey
Mr Michael Storm
Mr John Stott
Mr Charles Strickland
Mrs Lynda Stringer
Mr Richard Struthers
Mr Adam Strutt
Mr David Stuart
Mr Andrew Stumpf
Mr Mike Sturgess
Mr David Sturrock
Mr Brian Styles
Mr Darren Styles
Mr Abdus Subhan
Mrs Elisa Summers
Mrs Johanna Summers
Mr Tom Sutcliffe
Mrs Pamela Sutcliffe
Mr Ian Sutcliffe
Mr David Sutton
Mrs Mary Sutton
Mrs Sue Sutton
Mrs Sarah Swallow
Miss Lisa Swann
Miss Hazel Sweetman
Mr Jonathan Swift
Mrs Jen Swinbank
Mrs Sabrina Sykes
Miss Emily Sylvester
Ms Magdalena Szczesna
- Adamus
Mr Hideo Takano
Mrs Linda Talbot
Mr Douglas Talintyre
Mrs Joan Tall
Mrs Irene Tanner
Miss Andrea Taplin
Ms Anne Tate
Mr Denis Tate
Mr D Tate
Mr D W Tate
Mrs Anne Denise Tate
Miss Elizabeth Tate
Ms Fran Tattersall
Mr Tim Taylor
Miss Vivienne Taylor
Mr George E Taylor
Mr Steve Taylor
Mrs Jean Taylor
Mr Stephen Taylor
Mrs Jean Taylor
Mr Alan Taylor
Mrs Philippa Taylor
Mr Tim Taylor
Ms Janice Taylor
Mrs Judith Taylor
Mr David Taylor
Mrs Angela Taylor
Mr Alastair Taylor
Mr Peter Taylor
Mr Paul Taylor
Mr Richard Tazewell
Mrs Iris Temple
Mr Andew Temple Cox
Mr Howard Terry
Mrs Rachel Theobald
Mr Stephen Theunissen
Mr Maelgwyn Thomas
Mr Maelgwyn Thomas
Mr Richard Thomas
Mr Ben Thomas
Mr Jamie Thomas
Mr Blake Thomas
Mr Richard Thomas
Mr Sabu Thomas
Mrs Anne Thompson
Mr Michael Thompson
Mr Ian Thompson
Mrs Kim Thompson
Mrs Tina Thompson

Mr N Thornton
Mr Alex Thurlow
Mr Bob Thurlow
Mr Bob Thurlow
Mr Jim Tibbot
Mr Charles Tirner
Mr David Toal
Mr Tom Toccata
Mr A G Todd
Mr Geoffrey Todd
Mrs Rosemary Todhunter
Mr David Tolson
Mrs Eileen Tomany
Mr Peter Tomkins
Mr Peter Tomkins
Mr Roland Tomlin
Ms Penny Tompkins
Mrs Rowena Tonkin
Mr Jonathan Topping
Mr Martyn Torr
Mr Brian Towers
Mr Norman D Towers
Mr Adam Towler
Mr Adam Towler
Mr Roy Towler
Mr Ian Townsend
Mr Richard Townsend
Mr Michael Townson
Ms Sheryl Toyne
Mrs June Tozer
Mr Simon Tracey
Mr Chris Tranter
Ms Sue Travis
Mr John Travis
Mr John Tremlett
Ms Sylvia Trench
Mr John Trett
Mr Philip Tristram
Mr Roy Trowler
Mr David Tuck
Ms Aideen Tuddenham
Mr Tony Tudor
Mr Martin Tunney
Mr James Turnbull
Mr John G Turner
Mr Charles Turner
Miss Rachel Turner
Miss Sophie Turner
Mr John Turner
Mr Steven Turner
Mrs Barbara Turner
Mrs Gillian Turner Jones
Miss Zoe Twinn
Mr George Tzilivakis
Mr Asmat Ullah
Miss Una Underwood
Mr Graham Upton
Mrs Anne Ursell
Mrs Caroline Vaines
Mr Andrew Vale
Mr David Valentine
Mr Alex van Delden
Mr Nicko van Someren
Mrs Galina Varese
Mr Anil Varma
Mr Darren Varnam
Mr Michael Vaughan
Mr David Venables
Mrs Annemarie Vis
Mr Kugi Vohra
Mr Andy Voss
Mrs Veera Vuorinen
Miss Pamela Wadsworth
Mr J. Keith Wagner
Mr Michael Wake
Mr Robin Waldren
Mr Nick Walker
Mr Les Walker
Mr A Walker
Mrs Penny Walker
Mrs Margaret Walker
Mrs Sheila Walker
Mr Ed Walker
Mrs Julie Walker
Mrs Celia Walker
Mrs Joan Walklett
Mr Graham Wallis

Mrs Kerrie Wallis
Mr G Wallis
Mr Toby Wallis
Mrs Amanda Walsh
Miss Deborah Walsh
Mr Martin Walshe
Mr Roger Walton
Mr Martin Ward
Mr Chris Ward
Ms Saffron Warde-Jones
Mr Marcus Ware
Mr Richard Warner
Mr Stephen Warner
Mr Graeme Warr
Mr Charles Warren
Mr Maurice Warwick
Mrs Kirsty Warwick
Mr Jonathan Washer
Mr Tony Waterfield
Mr Lee Waterhouse
Ms Dawn Waterman
Mr Brian Wates
Mr Richard Watkins
Mrs Angela Watkins
Mrs Joy Watkins-Ellis
Ms Jane Watkinson
Mr David Watson
Mr Garry Watson
Mrs Lucie Watson
Mr John Watson
Mr Andrew Watson
Mrs Pat Watson
Miss Victoria Watson
Mrs Olivia Watson
Mrs Lesley Watts
Mrs Barbara Weaven
Mrs Margaret Webb
Mr Don Webber
Mrs Lynette Webber
Ms Marcia Webster
Miss Deborah Webster
Mrs Sarah Wehmeier
Mr Hugh Weller-Lewis
Mrs Christina Wells
Mrs Ann Wells
Mrs Samantha Welsby
Mr M West
Mr J F M West
Mrs Margaret West
Mrs Margaret West
Ms Kate West
Mr Gaza Westfall
Mrs Kath Wetherill
Miss Alison Whalley
Mr Mark Wheatley
Mr Laurie Whelan
Mrs Margaret Whellams
Mr David Whillans
Mr Richard Whitburn
Mr Alex White
Mrs Janice White
Mr Donald White
Mr Susan White
Miss Julia White
Mrs Sally White
Mr Alex White
Ms Louise White
Mrs Margaret White
Mr Daniel White
Mrs Jacqueline Whitehead
Mr Christopher Whitehouse
Mr John Whiteley
Mr Paul Whittaker
Mr Stephen Whittle
Mr Roger Whitton
Mr John Whyman
Mr Nick Whyte
Mrs Ilana Wigfield
Mr Phil Wiggett
Mr Mark Wilbourn
Mrs Joan Wilde
Miss Gill Wildman
Mr Dan Wilkes
Mr John Wilkinson
Miss Victoria Will
Mr Roger Willams
Mr John Willcock

Mr Paul Willer
Mr Price William John
Mr Anthony Williams
Ms Barbara Williams
Mrs Sally Williams
Mrs Gemma Williams
Mrs Caroline Williams
Miss Gwen Williams
Mrs Jennifer Williams
Mr Andrew Williams
Mr David Williams
Mrs Christine Williams
Mr S Williams
Mrs Sheena Williams
Mr Craig Williams
Ms Bethan Williams
Ms Eirwen Williams
Mr Graham Williams
Mr Ross Williamson
Miss Sinead Williamson
Mr Malcolm Williamson
Mrs Jackie Willis
Mr Chas Willis
Mr John Willis
Mr Nick Willson
Sir Michael Wilmot
Mr Ivor V Wilson
Ms Lorelly Wilson
Mrs Alison Wilson
Mr Gilbert Wilson
Ms Fiona Wilson
Mr Bob Wilson
Miss Joanne Wilson
Mrs Sarah Wilson
Mr Tom Wilson
Mr Christine Wilson
Mr Gilbert Wilson
Mrs Jackie Wilson
Mr William A Wiltshire
Miss Marie Windall
Mr Andrew Wingham
Miss Karen Winter
Mr Lyn Winters
Mrs Lesley Withall
Mr John Witherick
Miss Abigail Wood
Mr Stephen Wood
Mr Pam Wood
Mr Paul Woodcock
Mr Glyn Woodcraft
Ms V Woods
Mrs Suzanne Woods
Mrs Yvonne Woodward
Mr Ian Woodward
Mrs Vera Woolf
Mrs Yvonne Woozley
Mr Tim Wrigglesworth
Mr C Wright
Mr Charles Wright
Miss Cheryl Wright
Mrs Judith Wright
Mrs Cate Wright
Mrs Margaret Wright
Miss Daphne Wright
Mr Andrew Wright
Mr Lee Wyatt
Mr Douglas Wylie
Mr Graham Wymer
Mr Haigh Yaghmourian
Mrs Carol Yapp
Mr Pete Yarbrough
Mrs Sheila Yarbrough
Mr Brian Yates
Mr Robert Yates
Mrs Jill Yeardley
Mr Hugh Yendole
Miss Helen Yeo
Mr Stephen Young
Mr Iain Young
Mr Rob Youngs
Mr Jan Zelisko
Mrs Margaret Zetland
Mr Chris Zulerons

Special thank yous

We'd like to extend special thanks to the following people:

Kirstie Addis, Elizabeth Bowden, Katie Brittain, David Carter,
Martin Chapman, Peter Chapman, Claire Clarke, Paula Dadic, Claudia Dyer,
Michael Edwards, Nicola Frame, Alan Grimwade, Alex Hall and Ben Kay
at Charterhouse, Max Halliwell, Verity Hartley, Guy Haydon, Andy Hayler,
Simone Johnson, Berwyn Kinsey, Rebecca Leach, Janice Leech, Deborah Lee,
Claire Lilley, Robert Lilley, Michelle Lyttle, David Mabey, Simon Mather and
Iain Barker at AMA, Andrea McComb, Nicola McMahon, Angela Newton,
Jeffrey Ng, Henrietta Richards, John Rowlands, Louise Shepherd,
Oliver Smith, Emily Taylor, Judi Turner, Stuart Walton, Chris White,
Jenny White, Blânche Williams, Emma Wilmot and Kathryn Wilson.

Picture credits
Patrycja Cieszkowska, Rory Ferguson, Andrzej Gdula, Davide Guglielmo,
Anna Hamburg Gal, Craig Jewell, Alessandro Paiva, Cecilia Picco, Jackson
Russell, Georgios Wollbrecht, Steve Woods

Map credits
Maps designed and produced by Cosmographics,
www.cosmographics.co.uk
UK digital database © Cosmographics 2008,
Greater London map © Cosmographics 2006,
North and South London Maps © Collins Bartholomew 2007,
West, Central and East London maps © BTA (trading as VisitBritain)
2007 produced by Cosmographics and used with the kind permission
of VisitBritain.

Please send updates, queries, menus and wine lists to:
goodfoodguide@which.co.uk or write to: *The Good Food Guide*,
2 Marylebone Road, London, NW1 4DF

TERMS & CONDITIONS

This voucher can only be used in participating restaurants, highlighted by the £5 OFF symbol. It is redeemable against a pre-booked meal for a minimum of two people, provided the customer highlights the intention to use the voucher at the time of booking. Only one voucher may be used per table booked. This voucher may not be used in conjunction with any other scheme.
Offer valid from 08/09/08 to 08/09/09.
For additional terms and conditions, see below.

TERMS & CONDITIONS

This voucher can only be used in participating restaurants, highlighted by the £5 OFF symbol. It is redeemable against a pre-booked meal for a minimum of two people, provided the customer highlights the intention to use the voucher at the time of booking. Only one voucher may be used per table booked. This voucher may not be used in conjunction with any other scheme.
Offer valid from 08/09/08 to 08/09/09.
For additional terms and conditions, see below.

TERMS & CONDITIONS

This voucher can only be used in participating restaurants, highlighted by the £5 OFF symbol. It is redeemable against a pre-booked meal for a minimum of two people, provided the customer highlights the intention to use the voucher at the time of booking. Only one voucher may be used per table booked. This voucher may not be used in conjunction with any other scheme.
Offer valid from 08/09/08 to 08/09/09.
For additional terms and conditions, see below.

TERMS & CONDITIONS

This voucher can only be used in participating restaurants, highlighted by the £5 OFF symbol. It is redeemable against a pre-booked meal for a minimum of two people, provided the customer highlights the intention to use the voucher at the time of booking. Only one voucher may be used per table booked. This voucher may not be used in conjunction with any other scheme.
Offer valid from 08/09/08 to 08/09/09.
For additional terms and conditions, see below.

TERMS & CONDITIONS

This voucher can only be used in participating restaurants, highlighted by the £5 OFF symbol. It is redeemable against a pre-booked meal for a minimum of two people, provided the customer highlights the intention to use the voucher at the time of booking. Only one voucher may be used per table booked. This voucher may not be used in conjunction with any other scheme.
Offer valid from 08/09/08 to 08/09/09.
For additional terms and conditions, see below.

TERMS & CONDITIONS

This voucher can only be used in participating restaurants, highlighted by the £5 OFF symbol. It is redeemable against a pre-booked meal for a minimum of two people, provided the customer highlights the intention to use the voucher at the time of booking. Only one voucher may be used per table booked. This voucher may not be used in conjunction with any other scheme.
Offer valid from 08/09/08 to 08/09/09.
For additional terms and conditions, see below.

TERMS & CONDITIONS

This voucher can only be used in participating restaurants, highlighted by the £5 OFF symbol. It is redeemable against a pre-booked meal for a minimum of two people, provided the customer highlights the intention to use the voucher at the time of booking. Only one voucher may be used per table booked. This voucher may not be used in conjunction with any other scheme.
Offer valid from 08/09/08 to 08/09/09.
For additional terms and conditions, see below.

TERMS & CONDITIONS

This voucher can only be used in participating restaurants, highlighted by the £5 OFF symbol. It is redeemable against a pre-booked meal for a minimum of two people, provided the customer highlights the intention to use the voucher at the time of booking. Only one voucher may be used per table booked. This voucher may not be used in conjunction with any other scheme.
Offer valid from 08/09/08 to 08/09/09.
For additional terms and conditions, see below.

TERMS & CONDITIONS

This voucher can only be used in participating restaurants, highlighted by the £5 OFF symbol. It is redeemable against a pre-booked meal for a minimum of two people, provided the customer highlights the intention to use the voucher at the time of booking. Only one voucher may be used per table booked. This voucher may not be used in conjunction with any other scheme.
Offer valid from 08/09/08 to 08/09/09.
For additional terms and conditions, see below.

TERMS & CONDITIONS

This voucher can only be used in participating restaurants, highlighted by the £5 OFF symbol. It is redeemable against a pre-booked meal for a minimum of two people, provided the customer highlights the intention to use the voucher at the time of booking. Only one voucher may be used per table booked. This voucher may not be used in conjunction with any other scheme.
Offer valid from 08/09/08 to 08/09/09.
For additional terms and conditions, see below.

Vouchers are valid from 8th September 2008 to 8th September 2009. Only one £5 voucher can be used per table booked (for a minimum of 2 people). No photocopies or any other kind of reproduction of vouchers will be accepted. Some participating establishments may exclude certain times, days or menus from the scheme so long as they a) advise customers of the restrictions at the time of booking and b) accept the vouchers at a minimum of 70% of sessions when the restaurant is open. Please note that the number of participating restaurants may vary from time to time.